McDOUGAL, LITTELL

# LITERATURE
# AND LANGUAGE

ORANGE LEVEL

BLUE LEVEL

YELLOW LEVEL
*American Literature*

· **PURPLE LEVEL** ·
***English and World Literature***

# McDOUGAL, LITTELL

# LITERATURE AND LANGUAGE

## English and World Literature

### Senior Consultants

**Arthur N. Applebee**
*State University of New York at Albany*

**Andrea B. Bermudez**
*University of Houston—Clear Lake*

**Judith A. Langer**
*State University of New York at Albany*

**James Marshall**
*University of Iowa, Iowa City*

### Author

**Richard Craig Goheen**

**McDOUGAL, LITTELL & COMPANY**
Evanston, Illinois
New York   Dallas   Sacramento   Columbia, SC

## Acknowledgments

**African Universities Press:** "Telephone Conversation" by Wole Soyinka, from *Reflections: Nigerian Prose and Verse* edited by Frances Ademola. By permission of African Universities Press.

**Atlantic Monthly:** "The Secret" by Albert Moravio, from *Atlantic*, December 1958. Used by permission of the Atlantic Monthly.

**Bibliotheca Islamica, Inc.:** "The Happy Man," from *God's World* by Nagib Mahfuz, translated by Akef Abadir and Roger Allen. Copyright © 1973, 1988 by Akef Abadir and Roger Allen. Published by Bibliotheca Islamica, Box 14474, Minneapolis, MN 55414.

**Robert Bly:** "I Am Not I" by Juan Ramón Jiménez, from *Lorca and Jimenez: Selected Poems*, Beacon Press, Boston, 1973. Copyright © 1967 by Robert Bly. Reprinted with his permission.

**Rosemary Catacalos:** "Katakalos," from *Again for the First Time* by Rosemary Catacalos. Reprinted by permission of the author.

**Chinese Literature Press:** "Love Must Not Be Forgotten" by Zhang Jie, from *Seven Contemporary Chinese Women Writers*. Copyright © 1982 by Panda Books. By permission of Chinese Literature Press.

**City Lights:** "Explosion" by Delmira Agustini, from *Love Poems from Spain & Spanish America*, edited and translated by Perry Higman. Copyright © 1986 by Perry Higman. Reprinted by permission of City Lights Books.

*Continued on page 1064*

**Cover Art:** LONDON BRIDGE   1906   André Derain   Oil on canvas, 26″ × 39″   Collection, The Museum of Modern Art, New York   Gift of Mr. and Mrs. Charles Zadok.

**Frontispiece Art:** TREE OF LIFE   Lydia Bush-Brown Head   Dyed silk textile   Cooper-Hewitt Museum, New York, Smithsonian Institution   Gift of the artist.

ISBN: 0-8123-7108-9

Copyright © 1992 by McDougal, Littell & Company
Box 1667, Evanston, Illinois 60204

92 93 94 95 - DWO - 10 9 8 7 6 5 4 3 2

# Contents

## Unit One

## GLORY AND HONOR  **14**

WRITER'S WORKSHOP   Evaluation and Persuasion   66
Guided Assignment: Award Nomination

LANGUAGE FROM LITERATURE

LANGUAGE WORKSHOP   Sentence Skills   70
Avoiding Fragments and Run-ons

VOCABULARY WORKSHOP   History of English   73

## 3   IGNOBLE DEEDS                                          **131**

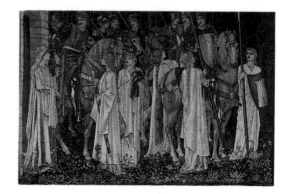

## Unit Two

## 3   PASSION FOR POWER   268

*Unit Three*

# INDIVIDUAL AND SOCIETY 378

# 3 CHALLENGING THE SYSTEM 469

## Unit Four

## 3   PERSONAL RELATIONS                                               **601**

## Unit Five

## VALUES IN QUESTION 636

## 3    CONSEQUENCES OF FATE    **730**

## Unit Six

# POWER OF THE INDIVIDUAL

## 3   PROTECTING INDIVIDUAL DIGNITY                    **888**

# *Handbook Section*

# Organization of Selections by Genre

## FICTION

## POETRY

# NONFICTION

# DRAMA

1

■ John Martin, Toronto, Canada.

# LITERATURE AND LANGUAGE AND YOU

The book you are holding is unlike any textbook you have ever used. It is based on a unique philosophy—that what you bring to this book is just as important as what the book brings to you. This means that your own experiences become the basis for your involvement with the literature and activities. The special features in **Literature and Language** promote this relationship between you and the text.

# SPECIAL FEATURES

***Great Literature.*** The selections in this book represent some of the finest examples of unadapted traditional and contemporary literature from Britain and all over the world. It contains British and world classics that have been read and enjoyed again and again, as well as exciting pieces that have never before appeared in a literature text. What you read will challenge your ways of thinking, illustrate the cultural and ethnic variety of your world, and relate to experiences in your own life. If you look at the acknowledgments in the front of the book, you will see that students like you were involved in choosing these selections.

***Important Themes.*** ***Literature and Language*** is organized both chronologically and by theme. Take a moment to preview the unit titles listed in the Table of Contents. You will find six major themes, beginning with **Glory and Honor** and ending with **Power of the Individual.** In addition to major units, you will discover subunits that sharpen the focus of the themes. For example, the unit **Values in Question** is divided into three subunits: **Reflections on War, Conflicting Loyalties,** and **Consequences of Fate.** The first few selections in each subunit are British literature, arranged chronologically. The other selections in the subunit are mostly modern pieces from all over the world that reflect on the same theme as the British pieces. You will notice similarities of ideas among all the cultures while you learn to appreciate each individual society's distinct ways of living and thinking. You will understand the major currents flowing throughout the world among the centuries, and you will see how all of the literature relates to or reflects upon important themes in modern-day America. Because authors write about such topics in various genres, or forms, you will find a mix of fiction, nonfiction, poetry, and drama within these pages.

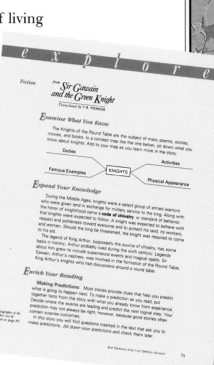

***Respect for Your Experiences.*** Your understanding of what you read is based on your previous experience with the subject. For this reason, an **Explore** page comes before each literary selection. The first section of this page will help you think about what you already know and help you recall previous experiences that may relate to the selection.

***Information and Strategies for Learning.*** The second section of the **Explore** page contains important background information about the literary selection and sometimes the culture from which it comes. At the bottom of the page you will find a third section that provides a reading or writing activity to help you better understand the literature.

***Practical Vocabulary Study.*** Most selections contain underlined vocabulary words. These are useful words to know. Making them part of your permanent vocabulary can improve your writing, reading, and communication skills. In most literature books, definitions are located in a glossary at the back. In ***Literature and Language,*** however, the vocabulary words are defined in a special box on the page where they appear. Words that are rarely used, as well as other terms and references whose meanings will enhance your understanding of the selection, are footnoted and defined separately.

*A Personal Response.*   Unlike other literature texts that ask you unimportant questions about minor details in a piece of literature, *Literature and Language* focuses on your unique personal response to what you have read. An **Explain** page provides the framework for this response. The first question on the page always asks for your immediate impression after you finish reading. The remaining questions allow you to build on your initial reactions and to explore the larger issues and themes covered in the selection. Some questions are supported by "think abouts," which will help you focus your answers. It is important to understand that there are never "right" or "wrong" answers to these questions. Any thoughtful response is acceptable as long as it can be supported by examples or evidence from the text.

*Respect for the Way You Learn.*   Each person has a "best" way of learning and of demonstrating what he or she has learned. Perhaps your strength is in reading and writing. Maybe you learn best by listening and discussing. Do you express yourself best by drawing, acting, building something, or giving an oral presentation? An **Extend** page, occurring at the end of many literature selections, will tap your unique learning and communicating styles. This page contains Options for Learning activities that offer a variety of exciting ways to show what you have learned.

*Integration of Literature and Language.*   The authors, editors, and educators who developed this textbook believe the various parts of an English program should be related to each other, or **integrated.** Therefore, literature, writing, and grammar are combined in this one book. What you read is used as a basis for related writing and language activities. Each subunit is followed by a **Writer's Workshop,** a **Language Workshop,** and a third workshop that varies in content.

   The **Writer's Workshop** presents a guided writing assignment that is linked to the ideas and themes of the literature in a particular subunit. This assignment stresses that you work with your classmates as a community of writers in developing writing ideas and revising your work.

In addition, each assignment comes with a PASSkey that provides a framework for your writing.

The **Language Workshop** is a mini-lesson that helps you revise and improve your work. Along with regular practice exercises, two special activities are often included. The exercise called Style directs you to look back at the literature to see how other writers have used the concepts taught in the workshop mini-lesson. The Analyzing and Revising Your Writing activity asks you to review your own writing based on what you have learned. The third workshop provides a mini-lesson on any of a variety of useful topics.

*A **Reading/Thinking Model.*** An important feature of this textbook is the **Strategies for Reading** lesson that follows this introduction. Built around Korean writer Hwang Sunwŏn's "The Cranes," this reading lesson lets you see what a good reader thinks about as he or she reads. You can use the same strategies to become a more effective reader and to enjoy more of what you read.

*The people who worked on this book truly believe that it offers some exciting new ways to learn about and enjoy literature and language. Since responding and communicating are important parts of our program, we invite you to share your impressions and experiences with us.*

*Strategies for*

# READING

...................................................................

What kind of reader are you? Passive readers let words slide by. Their eyes are moving, but their thoughts are often elsewhere. Active readers, on the other hand, keep their attention focused on what they are reading. They not only understand words and sentences, they also make constant mental connections, comments, and predictions about the selection.

While it is not easy to classify thoughts, the general categories in the list below show the types of connections active readers make in order to enjoy and understand what they read. To improve your own reading skills, try using these strategies. Although this kind of thinking and reacting may seem strange to you at first, it will soon become a natural part of your reading.

- **Questioning:** When a word, statement, or action is unclear, question it. It may become clear later.

- **Connecting:** Make connections with people, places, and things you know.

- **Predicting:** Try to figure out what will happen.

- **Clarifying:** Watch for answers to questions you had earlier.

- **Evaluating:** Respond to what you have read. Draw your own conclusions about characters, actions, and the whole story.

To understand how thinking and reading work together, read this story from Korea. You will see what one student was thinking as she read. Although the connections she makes with the story will be different from yours or anyone else's, they will give you an example of what it means to be an active reader.

# Cranes

HWANG SUNWŎN

The northern village lay snug beneath the high, bright autumn sky, near the border at the Thirty-eighth Parallel.

White gourds lay one against the other on the dirt floor of an empty farmhouse. Any village elders who passed by extinguished their bamboo pipes first, and the children, too, turned back some distance off. Their faces were marked with fear.

As a whole, the village showed little damage from the war, but it still did not seem like the same village Sŏngsam had known as a boy.

At the foot of a chestnut grove on the hill behind the village he stopped and climbed a chestnut tree. Somewhere far back in his mind he heard the old man with a wen[1] shout, "You bad boy, climbing up my chestnut tree again!"

The old man must have passed away, for he was not among the few village elders Sŏngsam had met. Holding on to the trunk of the tree, Sŏngsam gazed up at the blue sky for a time. Some chestnuts fell to the ground as the dry clusters opened of their own accord.

A young man stood, his hands bound, before a farmhouse that had been converted into a Public Peace Police office. He seemed to be a stranger, so Sŏngsam went up for a closer look. He was stunned: this young man was none other than his boyhood playmate, Tŏkchae.

Sŏngsam asked the police officer who had come with him from Ch'ŏnt'ae for an explanation. The prisoner was the vice-chairman of the Farmers' Communist League and had just been flushed out of hiding in his own house, Sŏngsam learned.

Sŏngsam sat down on the dirt floor and lit a cigaret.

Tŏkchae was to be escorted to Ch'ŏngdan by one of the peace police.

➤ Where is that?
*(Questioning)*

➤ Why are they scared?
*(Questioning)*

➤ What war?
*(Questioning)*

➤ He's alone. He must have come back.
*(Clarifying)*

➤ What has his friend done wrong?
*(Questioning)*

---

1. **wen:** lump on the skin.

After a time, Sŏngsam lit a new cigaret from the first
and stood up.

"I'll take him with me."

Tŏkchae averted his face and refused to look at
Sŏngsam. The two left the village.

Sŏngsam went on smoking, but the tobacco had no
flavor. He just kept drawing the smoke in and blowing it
out. Then suddenly he thought that Tŏkchae, too, must
want a puff. He thought of the days when they had
shared dried gourd leaves behind sheltering walls, hidden
from the adults' view. But today, how could he offer a
cigaret to a fellow like this?

Once, when they were small, he went with Tŏkchae to
steal some chestnuts from the old man with the wen. It
was Sŏngsam's turn to climb the tree. Suddenly the old
man began shouting. Sŏngsam slipped and fell to the
ground. He got chestnut burrs all over his bottom, but he
kept on running. Only when the two had reached a safe
place where the old man could not overtake them did
Sŏngsam turn his bottom to Tŏkchae. The burrs hurt so
much as they were plucked out that Sŏngsam could not
keep tears from welling up in his eyes. Tŏkchae produced
a fistful of chestnuts from his pocket and thrust them into
Sŏngsam's . . . Sŏngsam threw away the cigaret he had
just lit, and then made up his mind not to light another
while he was escorting Tŏkchae.

They reached the pass at the hill where he and Tŏkchae
had cut fodder for the cows until Sŏngsam had to move
to a spot near Ch'ŏnt'ae, south of the Thirty-eighth
Parallel, two years before the liberation.

Sŏngsam felt a sudden surge of anger in spite of
himself and shouted, "So how many have you killed?"

For the first time, Tŏkchae cast a quick glance at him
and then looked away.

"You! How many have you killed?" he asked again.

Tŏkchae looked at him again and glared. The glare
grew intense, and his mouth twitched.

"So you managed to kill quite a few, eh?" Sŏngsam felt
his mind becoming clear of itself, as if some obstruction
had been removed. "If you were vice-chairman of the
Communist League, why didn't you run? You must have
been lying low with a secret mission."

➤ Is he going to let his friend go?
**(Predicting)**

➤ How does he know what the guy is
like?
**(Questioning)**

➤ I'd run too!
**(Connecting)**

➤ cut fodder—what's that?
**(Questioning)**

➤ Why is he angry?
**(Questioning)**

➤ I guess Sŏngsam is taking him
because he's killed a lot of people.
**(Clarifying)**

Tŏkchae did not reply.

"Speak up. What was your mission?"

Tŏkchae kept walking. Tŏkchae was hiding something, Sŏngsam thought. He wanted to take a good look at him, but Tŏkchae kept his face averted.

Fingering the revolver at his side, Sŏngsam went on: "There's no need to make excuses. You're going to be shot anyway. Why don't you tell the truth here and now?"

"I'm not going to make any excuses. They made me vice-chairman of the League because I was a hardworking farmer, and one of the poorest. If that's a capital offense, so be it. I'm still what I used to be—the only thing I'm good at is tilling the soil." After a short pause, he added, "My old man is bedridden at home. He's been ill almost half a year." Tŏkchae's father was a widower, a poor, hardworking farmer who lived only for his son. Seven years before, his back had given out, and he had contracted a skin disease.

"Are you married?"

"Yes," Tŏkchae replied after a time.

"To whom?"

"Shorty."

"To Shorty?" How interesting! A woman so small and plump that she knew the earth's vastness, but not the sky's height. Such a cold fish! He and Tŏkchae had teased her and made her cry. And Tŏkchae had married her!

"How many kids?"

"The first is arriving this fall, she says."

Sŏngsam had difficulty swallowing a laugh that he was about to let burst forth in spite of himself. Although he had asked how many children Tŏkchae had, he could not help wanting to break out laughing at the thought of the wife sitting there with her huge stomach, one span around. But he realized that this was no time for joking.

"Anyway, it's strange you didn't run away."

"I tried to escape. They said that once the South invaded, not a man would be spared. So all of us between seventeen and forty were taken to the North. I thought of evacuating, even if I had to carry my father on my back. But Father said no. How could we farmers leave the land behind when the crops were ready for harvesting? He grew old on that farm, depending on me as the prop and

➤ Why is he laughing at his friend's wife? He's kind of rude. *(Evaluating)*

the mainstay of the family. I wanted to be with him in his last moments so I could close his eyes with my own hand. Besides, where can farmers like us go, when all we know how to do is live on the land?"

Sŏngsam had had to flee the previous June. At night he had broken the news privately to his father. But his father had said the same thing: Where could a farmer go, leaving all the chores behind? So Sŏngsam had left alone. Roaming about the strange streets and villages in the South, Sŏngsam had been haunted by thoughts of his old parents and the young children, who had been left with all the chores. Fortunately, his family had been safe then, as it was now.

They had crossed over a hill. This time Sŏngsam walked with his face averted. The autumn sun was hot on his forehead. This was an ideal day for the harvest, he thought.

When they reached the foot of the hill, Sŏngsam gradually came to a halt. In the middle of a field he espied a group of cranes that resembled men in white, all bent over. This had been the demilitarized zone along the Thirty-eighth Parallel. The cranes were still living here, as before, though the people were all gone.

Once, when Sŏngsam and Tŏkchae were about twelve, they had set a trap here, unbeknown to the adults, and caught a crane, a Tanjŏng crane. They had tied the crane up, even binding its wings, and paid it daily visits, patting its neck and riding on its back. Then one day they overheard the neighbors whispering: someone had come from Seoul with a permit from the governor-general's office to catch cranes as some kind of specimens. Then and there the two boys had dashed off to the field. That they would be found out and punished had no longer mattered; all they cared about was the fate of their crane. Without a moment's delay, still out of breath from running, they untied the crane's feet and wings, but the bird could hardly walk. It must have been weak from having been bound.

The two held the crane up. Then, suddenly, they heard a gunshot. The crane fluttered its wings once or twice and then sank back to the ground.

➤ I understand why a farmer should stay, but in a matter of life and death, I'd leave.
*(Connecting)*

➤ How did he feel about abandoning his family? Did they die?
*(Questioning)*

➤ The cranes remind me of statues I saw in Michigan.
*(Connecting)*

➤ How big is a crane if they can ride it? Cranes are birds.
*(Questioning)*

➤ I would have tried to protect the crane.
*(Connecting)*

EGRETS IN SUMMER  1945  N.C. Wyeth  Collection of the Metropolitan Life Insurance Company, New York  Photograph by Malcolm Varon.

The boys thought their crane had been shot. But the next moment, as another crane from a nearby bush fluttered its wings, the boys' crane stretched its long neck, gave out a whoop, and disappeared into the sky. For a long while the two boys could not tear their eyes away from the blue sky up into which their crane had soared.

"Hey, why don't we stop here for a crane hunt?" Sŏngsam said suddenly.

> Why would he suggest a crane hunt in the middle of taking a prisoner? *(Questioning)*

Tŏkchae was dumbfounded.

"I'll make a trap with this rope; you flush a crane over here."

Sŏngsam had untied Tŏkchae's hands and was already crawling through the weeds.

> Won't he run away? *(Predicting)*

Tŏkchae's face whitened. "You're sure to be shot anyway"—these words flashed through his mind. Any instant a bullet would come flying from Sŏngsam's direction, Tŏkchae thought.

Some paces away, Sŏngsam quickly turned toward him.

"Hey, how come you're standing there like a dummy? Go flush a crane!"

> Oh, I get it! He's releasing his friend. *(Clarifying)*
> Won't he get in trouble for that? *(Predicting)*

Only then did Tŏkchae understand. He began crawling through the weeds.

A pair of Tanjŏng cranes soared high into the clear blue autumn sky, flapping their huge wings.

> I like the ending whether he was right or wrong. I think this story could have happened. *(Evaluating)*

# GLORY AND HONOR

"*Better a thousand times to die with glory than live without honor.*"

Louis VI

ARMING AND DEPARTURE OF
THE KNIGHTS (detail) 1890 Sir
Edward Coley Burne-Jones From
the *Holy Grail Tapestry Series*
Birmingham City Council Museums
and Gallery, England.

15

# Life and Literature in Early Britain

## BRITAIN BEFORE THE ANGLO-SAXONS

For almost 300 years the Romans ruled Britain with efficiency and order. However, in A.D. 410, Rome fell, and the Roman officials and troops in Britain were called home to help defend the crumbling Roman Empire.

The departure of the Romans left undefended Britain open to continuous invasions and conquests. For 600 years neighboring tribes fought over the island nation, each leaving its mark on Britain's political system, culture, language, and literature.

## THE ANGLO-SAXON PERIOD: A.D. 449–1066

When the Romans left Britain, three Germanic tribes, the Jutes, the Angles, and the Saxons, moved in and quickly overpowered the island nation which eventually became known as "Angle-land." By A.D. 600, the **Anglo-Saxons,** as they were called, controlled most of Britain. Their crude but vigorous tribal culture dominated society and their harsh, guttural language, now called **Old English,** became the language of the people.

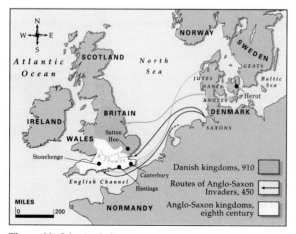

The world of the Anglo-Saxons.

## Anglo-Saxon Literature

Anglo-Saxon literature reflects the rather humorless attitude of the Germanic tribes and the harshness of their lives. Men divided their time between farming and fighting. Women, considered inferior to men, struggled to help their families survive.

Since few people read or wrote, literature was passed on orally. The Anglo-Saxons gathered in great halls where kings and nobles entertained guests and celebrated successful battles. A **scop** or professional singer would tell stories, usually in poetry form, about the adventures of tribal heroes. *Beowulf,* which was later put in written form, is an example of such a tale. The stories illustrated the values of the people: fierce loyalty to kings; obedience to tribal laws; and admiration for strength and cleverness in battle. While most of the literature reflected simple pagan beliefs involving the worship of god-heroes, some of the early poems showed a strong Christian influence.

In addition to epic poems such as *Beowulf,* the Anglo-Saxons also wrote riddles and elegaic lyrics—shorter poems in which single speakers express their thoughts on solemn subjects like death. In all Anglo-Saxon literature, a love of language and sound patterns is evident.

## Influence of Christianity

Missionaries from Europe gradually forced the Anglo-Saxons to adopt Christianity. **Monasteries,** buildings where religious men called monks lived, became important centers of social, intellectual, artistic, and literary life. Monks copied down much of the oral literature that had been related earlier, often adding the Christian themes that appear in it today.

When the Viking warriors from Denmark invaded Britain in A.D. 787, they destroyed many monasteries and the valuable literature they contained. However, in 886 King Alfred the Great defeated the Vikings and encouraged the rebirth of writing and scholarly ventures. In the constant struggle for control, the Danes reconquered England in 1016, but were again defeated in 1066 by William the Conqueror.

## THE MEDIEVAL PERIOD: 1066–1485

William the Conqueror was a Norman king from northwestern France. His conquest of Britain in 1066 finally brought stability to the island. William established **feudalism,** an economic system based on the exchange of power and land for loyalty. Kings owned all the land, but gave out large estates to those noble warriors who pledged their loyalty and their armies to the king. The nobles in turn offered protection to the common people who worked the land and served as soldiers.

This system resulted in the formation of three distinct classes. On top was the aristocracy—the kings, nobles, lords, and knights who had land and power. As the Roman Catholic Church grew in wealth and power, a second class made up of **clergy,** or churchmen, developed. The clergy were well-schooled and continued the scholarly preservation of literature, often writing in Latin, the language of the educated few. The third and largest class consisted of **serfs,** poor people with little power who farmed and fought for the nobles.

### New Forms of Literature

During the Medieval period, different classes enjoyed different literary developments.

For the aristocracy, romances became a popular literary form. **Romances** are tales of adventure about the brave deeds of noble knights who followed a **code of chivalry,** a set of rules for gentlemanly behavior. The tradition of **courtly love,** in which womanhood was highly honored, was another element common in medieval romances. The tales of King Arthur and his Knights of the Round Table are examples of popular medieval romances.

Literature developed by the clergy focused on drama—a form that was used effectively to entertain the non-reading public while presenting religious teachings. **Mystery plays** were based on Bible stories; **miracle plays** told about the lives of saints; and **morality plays** taught moral and ethical values.

The common people who could not read or write took pleasure in listening to ballads. **Ballads** were narrative songs about the adventures of ordinary people as well as legendary heroes. Popular ballad themes included love, envy, bravery, loyalty, and revenge. The tales of Robin Hood were first told in ballad form.

Along with changes in social structure and literature came changes in the spoken language. The influence of the Norman French gradually transformed Old English into what is now referred to as **Middle English.**

The most famous writer of the medieval period was Geoffrey Chaucer. His *Canterbury Tales,* written in Middle English, is a collection of stories in verse about people from all social classes. His tales illustrated the growing complexity and new ways of life of the late Medieval period.

### The Decline of Feudalism

Several factors caused the feudal system to gradually die out. In the mid-fourteenth century local woolen mills began to be built. Raw wool from the farms could now be processed locally instead of being sent overseas. Towns began to grow around the mills and a **new middle class** of merchants and craftspeople developed. The **plague** known as the Black Death in 1348 killed more than a third of the population, leaving a serious labor shortage. Many serfs, realizing their new value, left the nobles' estates and established new, more comfortable lives in towns. The **Hundred Years' War** between the English and the French also weakened the nobles' power.

# Time Line of British and World History 400–1485

**597** St. Augustine arrives in Britain as first Christian missionary

Alfred defeats **886** Vikings, ending century of violence

Alfred becomes **871** King of Britain

■ VIKING HELMET
6-8th CENTURY

BAYEUX TAPESTRY: ■
PREPARING FOR THE
NORMAN CONQUEST

**449** Germanic tribes of Angles, Saxons, and Jutes begin invading Britain

**410** German barbarians sack Rome, ending Roman rule in Britain

**787** Danes first invade Britain, beginning century of raids

**700** *Beowulf* recorded by English monks

## BRITISH HISTORY

| 400 | 500 | 600 | 700 | 800 | 900 |

## WORLD HISTORY

**476** Fall of Western Roman Empire

MOUNTED SAMURAI ■

**496** France converts to Christianity

**527** Byzantine Empire reaches height of its power under Justinian I

**542** Plague kills half of Eastern Europe population

Muhammad organizes **622** commonwealth of Islam

Ghana Empire, first **700** great black empire in Africa, flourishes

Pope crowns Charlemagne **800** Emperor of the West in Rome

Chaucer begins *The* **1385**
*Canterbury Tales*

Peasant's Revolt **1381**

Black Death plague **1347**
breaks out, killing
one-third population

Hundred Years' **1337**
War between
England and
France begins

■ LATE 15th CENTURY
PARADE SHIELD

**1295** Parliament becomes
an official part of
English government

**1215** English barons force
King John to approve
the Magna Carta

**1066** William the Conqueror
defeats the English;
Normans defeat Anglo-Saxons

| 1000 | 1100 | 1200 | 1300 | 1400 | 1485 |
|------|------|------|------|------|------|

**1000** Norsemen under Leif Ericson
land in North America

**1431** Joan of Arc
tried for
heresy in
France

**1096** First Crusade begins
for Christians to
recapture Holy Land
from Moslems

Yoritomo becomes first **1192**
shogun to rule Japan

Pope Gregory IX **1233**
establishes Inquisition

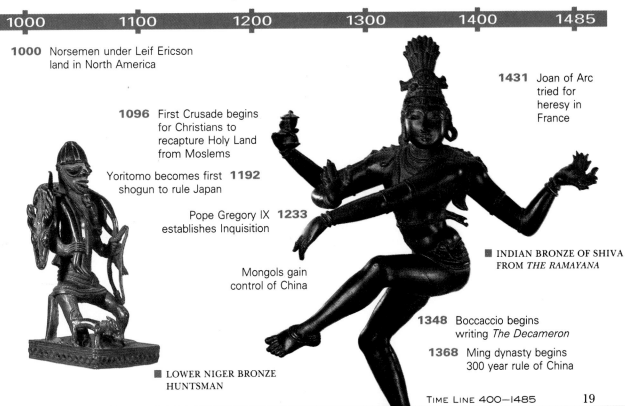

■ INDIAN BRONZE OF SHIVA
FROM *THE RAMAYANA*

Mongols gain
control of China

**1348** Boccaccio begins
writing *The Decameron*

**1368** Ming dynasty begins
300 year rule of China

■ LOWER NIGER BRONZE
HUNTSMAN

# THE MAKING OF HEROES

What does it take to make a hero? That is the question raised by the next five selections, which will challenge you to explore how and why heroes are made. Although the characters come from different times and places, you will find qualities that all have in com-

mon. You will also find differences. The characters were considered heroes in their own time and place. As you read, think about your own ideas of heroism and decide whether the characters fit your definition.

*Epic
Poetry*

*from* **Beowulf**

*Translated by* BURTON RAFFEL

## *E*xamine What You Know

*Beowulf* is a long narrative poem about a legendary hero who battles evil. Like all heroes, Beowulf represents the values admired by his society. Think about the qualities of modern heroes and the enemies they battle. Make a chart like the one below and record phrases that describe today's heroes. As you read, decide if Beowulf displays any of the qualities you listed.

| Heroic Deeds | Enemies | Powers/Abilities | Virtues |
|---|---|---|---|
| | | | |

## *E*xpand Your Knowledge

Life in the early Middle Ages (A.D. 450-800) was dominated by violence and bloody conflicts. In frequent battles, warriors were fiercely loyal to their leaders. Their only form of entertainment consisted of gatherings in mead-halls, large log structures where warriors feasted, drank mead (an alcoholic drink), and listened to **scops,** or storytellers, relate adventures of heroes.

These long tales were presented as poems, often accompanied by music. *Beowulf*, the most famous of the tales, took place in what is now Sweden and Denmark. The story was recorded by Anglo-Saxon monks around A.D. 1000, about five hundred years after it was originally told.

## *E*nrich Your Reading

**Reading Poetry**   Read *Beowulf* as you would read prose, stopping not at the end of each line, but at end punctuation that shows the end of a sentence. Practice on the following lines from the poem's opening; come to a complete stop only at the exclamation points.

> Hear me! We've heard of Danish heroes,
> Ancient kings and the glory they cut
> For themselves, swinging mighty swords!

■ *Information about the authors can be found on page 33.*

# *from* *Beowulf*

*Translated by* **BURTON RAFFEL**

*The tale of Beowulf tells about the heroes of two clans, the Danes and the Geats (gā' ats), who lived in Scandinavia. The introduction explains that Hrothgar (roth'gar), king of the Danes, built a wonderful mead-hall which he called Herot (ha' ə rot). In the passage you are about to read, Grendel, a fierce and powerful monster, invades the mead-hall.*

## Grendel

A powerful monster, living down
In the darkness, growled in pain, impatient
As day after day the music rang
Loud in that hall, the harp's rejoicing
5  Call and the poet's clear songs, sung
Of the ancient beginnings of us all, recalling
The Almighty making the earth, shaping
These beautiful plains marked off by oceans,
Then proudly setting the sun and moon
10 To glow across the land and light it;
The corners of the earth were made lovely with trees
And leaves, made quick with life, with each
Of the nations who now move on its face. And then
As now warriors sang of their pleasure:
15 So Hrothgar's men lived happy in his hall
Till the monster stirred, that demon, that fiend,
Grendel, who haunted the moors, the wild
Marshes, and made his home in a hell
Not hell but earth. He was spawned in that slime,
20 Conceived by a pair of those monsters born
Of Cain, murderous creatures banished
By God, punished forever for the crime
Of Abel's death. The Almighty drove
Those demons out, and their exile was bitter,
25 Shut away from men; they split
Into a thousand forms of evil—spirits
And fiends, goblins, monsters, giants,

**GUIDE FOR READING**

**1-14** Grendel broods in the darkness as the men of Herot fill the mead-hall with music and song. Predict how Grendel might react to such merriment.

**17 *moors:*** barren stretches of land.

**19 *spawned:*** produced.

**21 *Cain:*** a son of Adam and Eve; as told in the Bible (Genesis 4), he killed his younger brother Abel.

**19-29** *Who are Grendel's earliest ancestors? How did he come to exist?*

BEOWULF AND THE DRAGON 1932 Rockwell Kent
Rockwell Kent Legacies, Au Sable Forks, New York

A brood forever opposing the Lord's
Will, and again and again defeated. . . .

30      When darkness had dropped, Grendel
Went up to Herot, wondering what the warriors
Would do in that hall when their drinking was done.
He found them sprawled in sleep, suspecting
Nothing, their dreams undisturbed. The monster's

35    Thoughts were as quick as his greed or his claws:
He slipped through the door and there in the silence
Snatched up thirty men, smashed them
Unknowing in their beds and ran out with their bodies,
The blood dripping behind him, back

40    To his <u>lair</u>, delighted with his night's slaughter.
      At daybreak, with the sun's first light, they saw
How well he had worked, and in that gray morning
Broke their long feast with tears and <u>laments</u>
For the dead. Hrothgar, their lord, sat joyless

45    In Herot, a mighty prince mourning
The fate of his lost friends and companions,
Knowing by its tracks that some demon had torn
His followers apart. He wept, fearing
The beginning might not be the end. And that night

50    Grendel came again, so set
On murder that no crime could ever be enough,
No savage assault quench his lust
For evil. Then each warrior tried
To escape him, searched for rest in different

55    Beds, as far from Herot as they could find,
Seeing how Grendel hunted when they slept.
Distance was safety; the only survivors
Were those who fled him. Hate had triumphed.
      So Grendel ruled, fought with the righteous,

60    One against many, and won; so Herot
Stood empty, and stayed deserted for years,
Twelve winters of grief for Hrothgar, king
Of the Danes, sorrow heaped at his door
By hell-forged hands. His misery leaped

65    The seas, was told and sung in all
Men's ears: how Grendel's hatred began,
How the monster <u>relished</u> his savage war
On the Danes, keeping the bloody feud

**48-49** Hrothgar sits weeping after Grendel leaves. *What does he fear?*

**58** *In what way had hate triumphed?*

**64** *What does the phrase "hell-forged hands" suggest about Grendel?*

Alive, seeking no peace, offering
70  No truce, accepting no settlement, no price
In gold or land, and paying the living
For one crime only with another. No one
Waited for reparation from his plundering claws:
That shadow of death hunted in the darkness,
75  Stalked Hrothgar's warriors, old
And young, lying in waiting, hidden
In mist, invisibly following them from the edge
Of the marsh, always there, unseen.

Sutton Hoo drinking horn   The
Granger Collection, New York.

# Beowulf

The story of Grendel's twelve years of terror has spread throughout
the other clans. Beowulf, a young hero of the Geats, has received
permission from his king, Higlac (hig' ə lak), to sail with fourteen warriors
to offer their help to the Danes. Arriving on the Danish shore, they are
met by Hrothgar's men and escorted to Herot to greet the king.

                    "Hail, Hrothgar!
80  Higlac is my cousin and my king; the days
Of my youth have been filled with glory. Now Grendel's
Name has echoed in our land: sailors
Have brought us stories of Herot, the best
Of all mead-halls, deserted and useless when the moon
85  Hangs in skies the sun had lit,
Light and life fleeing together.
My people have said, the wisest, most knowing

**80 cousin:** a relative. Beowulf is
Higlac's nephew as well as his subject.

And best of them, that my duty was to go to the Danes'
Great king. They have seen my strength for themselves,
90  Have watched me rise from the darkness of war,
Dripping with my enemies' blood. I drove
Five great giants into chains, chased
All of that race from the earth. I swam
In the blackness of night, hunting monsters
95  Out of the ocean, and killing them one
By one; death was my errand and the fate
They had earned. Now Grendel and I are called
Together, and I've come. Grant me, then,
Lord and protector of this noble place,
100  A single request! I have come so far,
Oh shelterer of warriors and your people's loved friend,
That this one favor you should not refuse me—
That I, alone and with the help of my men,
May purge all evil from this hall. I have heard,
105  Too, that the monster's scorn of men
Is so great that he needs no weapons and fears none.
Nor will I. My lord Higlac
Might think less of me if I let my sword
Go where my feet were afraid to, if I hid
110  Behind some broad linden shield: my hands
Alone shall fight for me, struggle for life
Against the monster. God must decide
Who will be given to death's cold grip.

## The Battle with Grendel

    Out from the marsh, from the foot of misty
115  Hills and bogs, bearing God's hatred,
Grendel came, hoping to kill
Anyone he could trap on this trip to high Herot.
He moved quickly through the cloudy night,
Up from his swampland, sliding silently
120  Toward that gold-shining hall. He had visited Hrothgar's
Home before, knew the way—
But never, before nor after that night,
Found Herot defended so firmly, his reception
So harsh. He journeyed, forever joyless,

**110 *linden shield:*** a shield made from the wood of a linden tree.

**112** Beowulf insists that he fight Grendel by himself without weapons. *Why is this so important to him?*

**117** The reference to God shows the influence of Christianity. *Whose side do you think God will be on?*

---

*Words
to Know
and Use*  | **purge** (pʉrj) *v.* to cleanse or remove

125 Straight to the door, then snapped it open,
Tore its iron fasteners with a touch
And rushed angrily over the <u>threshold</u>.
He strode quickly across the inlaid
Floor, snarling and fierce: his eyes
130 Gleamed in the darkness, burned with a gruesome
Light. Then he stopped, seeing the hall
Crowded with sleeping warriors, stuffed
With rows of young soldiers resting together.
And his heart laughed, he relished the sight,
135 Intended to tear the life from those bodies
By morning: the monster's mind was hot
With the thought of food and the feasting his belly
Would soon know. But fate, that night, intended
Grendel to gnaw the broken bones
140 Of his last human supper. Human
Eyes were watching his evil steps,
Waiting to see his swift hard claws.
Grendel snatched at the first Geat
He came to, ripped him apart, cut
145 His body to bits with powerful jaws,
Drank the blood from his veins and bolted
Him down, hands and feet; death
And Grendel's great teeth came together,
Snapping life shut. Then he stepped to another
150 Still body, clutched at Beowulf with his claws,
Grasped at a strong-hearted wakeful sleeper
—And was instantly seized himself, claws
Bent back as Beowulf leaned up on one arm.
　　That shepherd of evil, guardian of crime,
155 Knew at once that nowhere on earth
Had he met a man whose hands were harder;
His mind was flooded with fear—but nothing
Could take his <u>talons</u> and himself from that tight
Hard grip. Grendel's one thought was to run
160 From Beowulf, flee back to his marsh and hide there:
This was a different Herot than the hall he had emptied.
But Higlac's follower remembered his final
Boast and, standing erect, stopped
The monster's flight, fastened those claws
165 In his fists till they cracked, clutched Grendel

*POST HEAD OF
OSEBERG* University
Museum of National
Antiquities, Oslo, Norway.

| *Words to Know and Use* | **threshold** (thresh′ ōld′, -hōld′) *n.* the wood fastened on the floor beneath a door |
|---|---|
| | **talon** (tal′ ən) *n.* a claw |

27

Replica of Sutton Hoo helmet   The British Museum, London.

Closer. The <u>infamous</u> killer fought
For his freedom, wanting no flesh but retreat,
Desiring nothing but escape, his claws
Had been caught, he was trapped. That trip to Herot
170 Was a miserable journey for the <u>writhing</u> monster!
    The high hall rang, its roof boards swayed,
And Danes shook with terror. Down
The aisles the battle swept, angry
And wild. Herot trembled, wonderfully
175 Built to withstand the blows, the struggling
Great bodies beating at its beautiful walls;
Shaped and fastened with iron, inside
And out, artfully worked, the building
Stood firm. Its benches rattled, fell
180 To the floor, gold-covered boards grating
As Grendel and Beowulf battled across them.
Hrothgar's wise men had fashioned Herot
To stand forever; only fire,
They had planned, could shatter what such skill had put

**170** Up to this point Grendel has killed
his human victims easily. *Why does he
try to run away from Beowulf?*

185 Together, swallow in hot flames such splendor
Of ivory and iron and wood. Suddenly
The sounds changed, the Danes started
In new terror, cowering in their beds as the terrible
Screams of the Almighty's enemy sang
190 In the darkness, the horrible shrieks of pain
And defeat, the tears torn out of Grendel's
Taut throat, hell's captive caught in the arms
Of him who of all the men on earth
Was the strongest. . . . That mighty protector of men
195 Meant to hold the monster till its life
Leaped out, knowing the fiend was no use
To anyone in Denmark. All of Beowulf's
Band had jumped from their beds, ancestral
Swords raised and ready, determined
200 To protect their prince if they could. Their courage
Was great but all wasted: they could hack at Grendel
From every side, trying to open
A path for his evil soul, but their points
Could not hurt him, the sharpest and hardest iron
205 Could not scratch at his skin, for that sin-stained demon
Had bewitched all men's weapons, laid spells
That blunted every mortal man's blade.
And yet his time had come, his days
Were over, his death near; down
210 To hell he would go, swept groaning and helpless
To the waiting hands of still worse fiends.
Now he discovered—once the afflictor
Of men, tormentor of their days—what it meant
To feud with Almighty God: Grendel
215 Saw that his strength was deserting him, his claws
Bound fast, Higlac's brave follower tearing at
His hands. The monster's hatred rose higher,
But his power had gone. He twisted in pain.
And the bleeding sinews deep in his shoulder
220 Snapped, muscle and bone split
And broke. The battle was over, Beowulf
Had been granted new glory: Grendel escaped,
But wounded as he was could flee to his den,
His miserable hole at the bottom of the marsh,
225 Only to die, to wait for the end

**192 _taut:_** tightly stretched.

**211** _Why can no weapons hurt Grendel?_

**222** When Grendel needs his power most, it fails him. _What causes his loss of power?_

| _Words to Know and Use_ | **ancestral** (an ses′ trəl) _adj._ inherited from ancestors |
| --- | --- |

Of all his days. And after that bloody
Combat the Danes laughed with delight.
He who had come to them from across the sea,
Bold and strong-minded, had driven affliction
230 Off, purged Herot clean. He was happy,
Now, with that night's fierce work; the Danes
Had been served as he'd boasted he'd serve them;
   Beowulf,
A prince of the Geats, had killed Grendel,
Ended the grief, the sorrow, the suffering
235 Forced on Hrothgar's helpless people
By a bloodthirsty fiend. No Dane doubted
The victory, for the proof, hanging high
From the rafters where Beowulf had hung it, was the
   monster's
Arm, claw and shoulder and all. . . .
240    And then, in the morning, crowds surrounded
Herot, warriors coming to that hall
From faraway lands, princes and leaders
Of men hurrying to behold the monster's
Great staggering tracks. They gaped with no sense
245 Of sorrow, felt no regret for his suffering,
Went tracing his bloody footprints, his beaten
And lonely flight, to the edge of the lake
Where he'd dragged his corpselike way, doomed
And already weary of his vanishing life.
250 The water was bloody, steaming and boiling
In horrible pounding waves, heat
Sucked from his magic veins; but the swirling
Surf had covered his death, hidden
Deep in murky darkness his miserable
255 End, as hell opened to receive him.
   Then old and young rejoiced, turned back
From that happy pilgrimage, mounted their hardhooved
Horses, high-spirited stallions, and rode them
Slowly toward Herot again, retelling
260 Beowulf's bravery as they jogged along.
And over and over they swore that nowhere
On earth or under the spreading sky
Or between the seas, neither south nor north,
Was there a warrior worthier to rule over men.

**239** *Why does Beowulf hang Grendel's arm from the rafters?*

*Words to Know and Use* | **pilgrimage** (pil′ grəm ij) *n.* a long journey to a holy or historical place

# explain

## Responding to Reading

### First Impressions

1. Jot down a few words or phrases that capture your clearest picture of Beowulf and Grendel. Then compare your ideas with your classmates'.

### Second Thoughts

2. How is Beowulf like or unlike the heroes described in your chart?

3. What do you think causes Grendel to attack humans?

   **Think about**
   • his relatives and ancestors
   • his actions and attitudes
   • the warriors' reactions to him

4. What feelings do the descriptions of Grendel in lines 18–28, 201–221, 243-255 give you? What is the purpose of such descriptions?

5. Why does Beowulf help a different clan in spite of the danger?

6. For what reasons do you think Beowulf is able to defeat Grendel?

7. Hrothgar's people shout about Beowulf ''. . . that nowhere . . . Was there a warrior worthier to rule over men.'' Do you agree with them?

   **Think about**
   • qualities needed for leadership in Beowulf's society
   • Beowulf's unique abilities and achievements

### Broader Connections

8. In today's society, we have our own kinds of monsters to deal with, such as bad politicians or certain diseases. Who or what do you think are today's monsters, and why are they monstrous? Who do you think are the monster-slayers of today? Why?

## Literary Concept: Epic Poetry

An epic is a long poem that narrates the adventures of a hero. Four of the major characteristics of epic poetry are the following: (1) The hero is of noble birth or high social position. (2) The hero reflects values that are important to his society. (3) The hero's actions consist of courageous, even superhuman deeds. (4) Supernatural forces are often involved.

Think about why *Beowulf* is classified as an epic poem. Find evidence in the poem of each of the characteristics described above.

## Writing Options

1. Suppose that you are a reporter assigned to do a story on either Grendel or Beowulf. Whom would you choose to write about? Make a list of five or more questions you would like to ask in an interview.

2. You have been asked by Beowulf to write a campaign speech for him, since he has decided he wants to become king. In your speech, give reasons why Beowulf would make a good king. Use examples from the poem to support your reasons.

3. Imagine that you are one of Hrothgar's warriors. Write a letter to a friend that describes what mead-hall life is like now that Grendel is making his nightly visits.

4. Think about the monsters you mentioned in **Broader Connections.** In a letter to the editor of your local newspaper, compare a modern monster to Grendel. Explain what kind of hero is needed to combat this modern monster.

## Vocabulary Practice

**Exercise** Read the sentences below and decide which word in the list best fits in the blank. Write the word on your paper next to the appropriate number. If necessary, review the meanings of the words in the **Words to Know and Use** boxes.

1. Herot was the _____ mead-hall of Hrothgar's clan.
2. Stepping across the _____ of Herot led to Grendel's doom.
3. Grendel would not _____ losing his nightly visits to Herot.
4. Each razor-sharp _____ of Grendel's claw tore his victims' flesh.
5. Piles of bones littered the floor of Grendel's _____.
6. His evil acts made Grendel _____ throughout the land.
7. Grendel was left _____ in agony on the floor after the battle.
8. When Beowulf was finally able to _____ Herot of Grendel, the clan rejoiced.
9. There was no cry or _____ for the dead Grendel.
10. Many people went on a _____ to see where Grendel had sunk into the lake.

*Words to Know and Use*

ancestral
infamous
lair
lament
pilgrimage
purge
relish
talon
threshold
writhing

## Options for Learning

**1 • Be a Storyteller**  In your own words, tell the story of Beowulf. Include a description of Grendel and give a detailed account of the battle. Convey excitement and horror in your voice. Capture your audience's interest with a dramatic storytelling style.

**2 • Create a Cartoon Strip**  Illustrate the battle between Beowulf and Grendel in comic-strip style with several panels. If you prefer, use a pad of paper and animate your battle by flipping pages so the characters seem to move. Have someone videotape your animation and show it to the class.

**3 • Build Your Own Mead-Hall**  Find a picture or a detailed description of a mead-hall in a book or encyclopedia article about the early Middle Ages. Study clues in *Beowulf*. Then build or draw a detailed model of a mead-hall.

**4 • Cut a Record**  Create song lyrics in your favorite style of music that tell the story of Beowulf's battle with Grendel. Add guitar, piano, or any other instrumental music and perform the song for the class.

**5 • Set the Style**  Design a Grendel T-shirt. Use description from the poem to draw a detailed picture of the monster. Write a clever caption for the shirt. Use fabric markers or an iron-on transfer to imprint the pictures on a plain T-shirt.

 **FACT FINDER**

*How far did Beowulf have to travel by ship to reach Herot?*

### The Authors

Nothing is known about the original authors of *Beowulf*. By studying the handwriting in the one preserved copy of the poem, historians have determined that *Beowulf* was recorded around A.D. 1000 by two unknown Anglo-Saxon monks.

Little information is available about the historical accuracy of the events described in the poem. Historians have discovered that a real King Higlac, Beowulf's king in the poem, fought another medieval clan about A.D. 520. Whether Beowulf himself actually existed is uncertain, however. Evidence from recent archaeological digs, such as the rich and well-preserved burial ship at Sutton Hoo, England, has shown that medieval clans lived in much the way life is described in *Beowulf*.

*Fiction*

### The
# Old Demon
PEARL S. BUCK

## Examine What You Know

In times of disaster and danger, ordinary people often do heroic things, saving lives and property. Why would someone suddenly act heroically? Would it be because of the situation, the person, or both? Could anyone become a hero? Talk with your classmates about why and how people become heroes. Then see if you think this story has a hero.

## Expand Your Knowledge

China is a vast country, larger than the United States, with most of its one billion people living in east coast cities or the fertile valleys of the Yellow (sometimes called Huang) and Yangtze rivers. As with much of the world,

China's rural farms and villages still use traditional farming methods, oxen-drawn plows, and old-fashioned irrigation systems. To control the seasonal flooding of the huge rivers, and to supply water to the crops, Chinese farmers use systems of dikes (earthen walls), canals, and gates.

When Japan invaded northern China (Manchuria) in 1931, most of China was unaffected. Farmers still had to farm, and villages heard little but rumor about foreign invaders. By 1937, however, the Japanese had moved south across the Great Wall, controlled Beijing, and entered the Yellow River valley. The story of "The Old Demon" takes place in the Yellow River valley in 1937.

## Write Before You Read

Imagine what would happen if your community were threatened by an invading army. In your journal or on a piece of paper, list as many different ways as you can think of that such a war would affect you, your friends and family, and your community. Consider and list the effects of war on everyday life.

■ *A biography of the author can be found on page 46.*

# The Old Demon

PEARL S. BUCK

Old Mrs. Wang knew of course that there was a war. Everybody had known for a long time that there was war going on and that Japanese were killing Chinese. But still it was not real and no more than hearsay, since none of the Wangs had been killed. The village of Three Mile Wangs on the flat banks of the Yellow River, which was old Mrs. Wang's clan village, had never even seen a Japanese. This was how they came to be talking about Japanese at all.

It was evening and early summer, and after her supper Mrs. Wang had climbed the dike[1] steps, as she did every day, to see how much the river had risen. She was much more afraid of the river than of the Japanese. She knew what the river would do. And one by one the villagers had followed her up the dike, and now they stood staring down at the malicious yellow water, curling along like a lot of snakes and biting at the high dike banks.

"I never saw it as high as this so early," Mrs. Wang said. She sat down on a little stool that her grandson, Little Pig, had brought for her and spat into the water.

"It's worse than the Japanese, this old devil of a river," Little Pig said recklessly.

"Fool!" Mrs. Wang said quickly. "The river god will hear you. Talk about something else."

So they had gone on talking about the Japanese. How, for instance, asked Wang the baker, who was old Mrs. Wang's nephew twice removed, would they know the Japanese when they saw them?

Mrs. Wang at this point said positively, "You'll know them. I once saw a foreigner. He was taller than the eaves of my house, and he had mud-colored hair and eyes the color of a fish's eyes. Anyone who does not look like us—that is a Japanese."

Everybody listened to her, since she was the oldest woman in the village and whatever she said settled something.

Then Little Pig spoke up in his disconcerting way. "You can't see them, grandmother. They hide up in the sky in airplanes."

Mrs. Wang did not answer immediately. Once she would have said positively, "I shall not believe in an airplane until I see it." But so many things had been true which she had not believed. The empress, for instance, whom she had not believed dead, was dead. The Republic[2], again, she had not believed in because she did not know what it was. She still did not know, but they said for a long time there had been one. So now she merely stared quietly about the dike where they all sat about her. It was very pleasant and cool, and she felt

---

1. **dike:** a ditch or channel for water to pass through.
2. **Republic:** In 1911, revolutionaries led by Sun Yat-sen rebelled against the Manchu dynasty, which had ruled China since the 1600's. As a result of this revolution, a republic was established, which lasted until the Communists came to power in 1949.

*Words to Know and Use*

**hearsay** (hir′ sā) *n.* information one hears but does not know to be true
**disconcerting** (dis′kən surt′ ing) *adj.* in a manner that is upsetting **disconcert** *v.*

nothing mattered if the river did not rise to flood.

"I don't believe in the Japanese," she said flatly.

## "I don't believe in the Japanese."

They laughed at her a little, but no one spoke. Someone lighted her pipe—that was Little Pig's wife, who was her favorite.

"Sing, Little Pig!" someone called.

So Little Pig began to sing an old song in a high quavering voice, and old Mrs. Wang listened and forgot the Japanese. The evening was beautiful: the sky so clear and still that the willows overhanging the dike were reflected even in the muddy water. Everything was at peace. The thirty-odd houses which made up the village straggled along beneath them. Nothing could break this peace. After all, the Japanese were only human beings.

"I doubt those airplanes," she said mildly to Little Pig when he stopped singing.

But without answering her, he went on to another song.

Year in and year out she had spent the summer evenings like this on the dike. The first time she was seventeen and a bride, and her husband had shouted to her to come out of the house and up the dike and she had come, blushing, to hide among the women while the men roared at her and made jokes about her.

All the same, they had liked her. "A pretty piece of meat in your bowl," they had said to her husband. "Feet a trifle big," he had answered deprecatingly. But she could see he

was pleased, and so gradually her shyness went away.

He, poor man, had been drowned in a flood when he was still young. And it had taken her years to get him prayed out of Buddhist purgatory.[3] Finally she had grown tired of it, what with the child and the land all on her back, and so when the priest said coaxingly, "Another ten pieces of silver and he'll be out entirely," she asked, "What's he got in there yet?"

"Only one foot," the priest said, encouraging her.

Then her patience broke. Ten dollars? It would feed them for the winter. "If it's only one foot, he can get up and walk out himself," she said firmly.

She often wondered if he had, poor silly fellow. As like as not, she had often thought gloomily, he was still lying there, waiting for her to do something about it. That was the sort of man he was. Well, someday, perhaps, when Little Pig's wife had had the first baby safely and she had a little extra, she might go back to finish him out of purgatory. There was no real hurry, though.

"Grandmother, you must go in," Little Pig's wife's soft voice said. "There is a mist rising from the river, now that the sun is gone."

"Yes, I suppose I must," old Mrs. Wang agreed.

She gazed at the river a moment. That river—it was full of good and evil together. It would water the fields when it was curbed and checked, but if an inch was allowed it, it crashed through like a roaring dragon.

---

3. **Buddhist purgatory:** a condition in which the dead are purified before they can achieve Nirvana, a state in which there is no pain, sorrow, or desire.

*Words to Know and Use* | **deprecatingly** (dep′ rə kāt′ ing lē) *adv.* in a manner that expresses disapproval

That was how he had been swept away— careless, he was, about his bit of the dike. He was always going to mend it, and then in a night the river rose and broke through. He had run out of the house, and she had climbed on the roof with the child and saved herself and it, while he was drowned.

Well, they had pushed the river back again behind its dikes, and it had stayed there this time. Every day she herself walked up and down the length of the dike for which the village was responsible and examined it.

The men laughed and said, "If anything is wrong with the dikes, Granny will tell us." It had never occurred to any of them to move the village away from the river.

Little Pig suddenly stopped singing. "The moon is coming up!" he cried. "That's not good. Airplanes come out on moonlight nights."

"Where do you learn all this about airplanes?" old Mrs. Wang exclaimed. "It is tiresome to me," she added, so severely that no one spoke.

In this silence, leaning upon the arm of Little Pig's wife, she descended slowly the earthen steps which led down into the village, using her long pipe in the other hand as a walking stick. Behind her the villagers came down, one by one, to bed.

And in her own bed at last, she fell peacefully asleep. She had lain awake a little while thinking about the Japanese and wondering why they wanted to fight.

Only very coarse persons wanted wars. In her mind she saw large, coarse persons. If they came, one must wheedle them she thought, invite them to drink tea, and explain to them, reasonably—only why should they come to a peaceful farming village?

So she was not in the least prepared for Little Pig's wife screaming at her that they were there. She sat up in bed muttering, "The tea bowls—the tea."

"Grandmother, there's no time!" Little Pig's wife screamed. "They're here!"

"Where?" old Mrs. Wang cried, now awake.

"In the sky!" Little Pig's wife wailed.

They had all run out at that into the clear early dawn and gazed up. There, like wild geese flying in autumn, were great birdlike shapes.

"But what are they?" old Mrs. Wang cried.

And then, like a silver egg dropping, something drifted straight down and fell at the far end of the village in a field. A fountain of earth flew up, and they all ran to see it. There was a hole thirty feet across, as big as a pond. They were so astonished they could not speak, and then before anyone could say anything, another and another egg began to fall and everybody was running, running . . .

Everybody, that is, but Mrs. Wang. When Little Pig's wife seized her hand to drag her along, old Mrs. Wang pulled away and sat down against the bank of the dike.

"I can't run," she remarked. "I haven't run in seventy years, since before my feet were bound. You go on. Where's Little Pig?" She looked around. Little Pig was already gone.

"Like his grandfather," she remarked—"always the first to run."

But Little Pig's wife would not leave her; not, that is, until old Mrs. Wang reminded her that it was her duty.

"If Little Pig is dead," she said, "then it is necessary that his son be born alive." And when the girl still hesitated, she struck at her gently with her pipe. "Go on—go on!" she exclaimed.

So unwillingly, because now they could scarcely hear each other speak for the roar of the dipping planes, Little Pig's wife went on with the others.

By now, the village was in ruins and the straw roofs and wooden beams were blazing. Everybody was gone. As they passed, they had shrieked at old Mrs. Wang to come on, and she had called back pleasantly, "I'm coming—I'm coming!"

But she did not go. She sat quite alone, watching what was now an extraordinary spectacle. For soon other planes came. They attacked the first ones, wheeling and darting.

When this was over, she thought she would go back into the village and see if anything were left. She was not unused to war. Once bandits had looted their village and houses had been burned then, too.

Well, now it had happened again. Burning houses one could see often, but not this darting silvery shining battle in the air. She understood none of it—not what those things were, nor how they stayed in the sky. She simply sat, growing hungry, and watching.

"I'd like to see one close," she said, aloud. And at that moment, as though in answer, one of them pointed suddenly downward, and wheeling and twisting as though it were wounded, it fell head down in a field which only yesterday Little Pig had plowed. In an

*Words to Know and Use* | **spectacle** (spek′ tə kəl) *n.* a remarkable sight instant the sky was empty again, and there was only this wounded thing on the ground and herself.

She hoisted herself carefully from the ground. At her age she need be afraid of nothing. She could, she decided, go and see what it was. So, leaning on her bamboo pipe, she made her way slowly across the fields. Behind her in the sudden stillness two or three village dogs appeared and followed, creeping close to her in their terror. When they drew near to the fallen plane, they barked furiously. Then she hit them with her pipe.

"Be quiet!" she scolded. "Hasn't there already been noise enough to split my ears?" She tapped the airplane. "Metal," she told the dogs. "Silver, doubtless." Melted, it would make them all rich.

She walked around it, examining it closely. What made it fly? It seemed dead. Nothing moved or made a sound within it. Then, coming to the side to which it tipped, she saw a young man in it, slumped into a heap in a little seat. The dogs growled, but she struck at them again and they fell back.

"Are you dead?" she inquired politely.

The young man moved a little at her voice, but did not speak. She drew nearer and peered into the hole in which he sat. His side was bleeding.

"Wounded!" she exclaimed. She took his wrist. It was warm but <u>inert</u>. She stared at him. He had black hair and a dark skin like a Chinese, and still he did not look like a Chinese.

He must be from the south, she thought. Well, the chief thing was, he was alive. "You had better come out," she remarked. "I'll put some herb plaster on your side."

The young man muttered something.

"What did you say?" she asked. But he did not say it again. "I am still quite strong," she decided after a moment. So she reached in and seized him about the waist and pulled him out slowly.

Fortunately he was a little fellow and very light. When she had him on the ground he stood shakily and clung to her, and she held him up.

"Now if you can walk to my house," she said, "I'll see if it is there."

Then he said something quite clearly. She listened but could not understand a word. She stared at him.

"What's that?" she asked.

He pointed at the dogs. They were growling, their ruffs up. Then he spoke again, and as he spoke he crumpled to the ground. The dogs fell on him, so that she had to beat them off with her hands.

"Get away!" she shouted. "Who told *you* to kill him?"

And then, when they had slunk away, she heaved him somehow onto her back, and half carrying, half pulling him, she dragged him to the ruined village and laid him in the street, while she went to find her house, taking the dogs with her.

The house was gone. She found the place easily enough. This was where it should be, opposite the water gate into the dike. She had always watched that gate herself. Miraculously, it was not injured now, nor was the dike broken.

She went back to the young man. He was lying as she had left him, propped against the dike, panting and very pale. He had opened his coat, and he had a little bag from which he was taking out strips of cloth and a bottle. Again he spoke, and again she understood nothing.

Then he made signs, and she saw it was water he wanted, so she took up a broken pot from one of the many blown about the street, and going up the dike, she filled it with river water and brought it down again and washed his wound, and she tore off the strips he made from the rolls of bandage. He knew how to put the cloth over the gaping wound, and he made signs to her, and she followed these signs. All the time he was trying to tell her something, but she could understand nothing.

"You must be from the south, sir," she said. "I have heard your language is different from ours." She laughed to put him at his ease, but he only stared at her somberly. So she said, "Now if I could find something for us to eat, it would be nice."

He did not answer. Instead, he lay back, panting heavily, and stared into space.

"You would be better with food," she went on, "and so would I," she added. She was beginning to feel unbearably hungry.

It occurred to her that in Wang the baker's shop there might be some bread. Even if it were dusty with fallen mortar, it would still be bread. She would go and see. But before she went she moved the soldier so that he lay in the edge of shadow cast by a willow tree that grew in the bank of the dike. Then she went to the baker's shop. The dogs were gone.

The baker's shop was, like everything else, in ruins. No one was there. At first she saw nothing but the mass of crumbled earthen walls. But she remembered the oven was just inside the door, and the door frame still stood erect, supporting one end of the roof. She stood in this frame, and running her hand underneath the fallen roof inside, she felt the wooden cover of the iron caldron.[4] Under this there might be steamed bread.

She worked her arm carefully in. It took a long time, but even so, clouds of lime and dust almost choked her. Nevertheless, she was right. She squeezed her hand under the cover and felt the firm smooth skin of the big steamed bread rolls, and one by one she drew out four.

"It's hard to kill an old thing like me," she remarked cheerfully to no one, and she began to eat one of the rolls as she walked back.

## "It's hard to kill an old thing like me."

It was at this moment that she heard voices. When she came in sight of the soldier, she saw surrounding him a crowd of other soldiers, who had apparently come from nowhere. They were staring at the wounded soldier, whose eyes were now closed.

"Where did you get this Japanese, old mother?" they shouted at her.

"What Japanese?" she asked.

"This one!" they shouted.

"Is he a Japanese?" she cried in the greatest astonishment. "But he looks like us. His eyes are black; his skin——"

"Japanese!" one of them shouted.

"Well," she said quietly, "he dropped out of the sky."

"Give me that bread!" another shouted.

"Take it," she said—"all except this one for him."

"A Japanese monkey eat good bread?" the soldier shouted.

"I suppose he is hungry also," old Mrs.

---

4. **caldron** (kôl′ drən): a large kettle.

*Words to Know and Use* | **somberly** (säm′ bər lē) *adv.* in a dark, gloomy, or dull way

Wang replied. She began to dislike these men. But then, she had always disliked soldiers. "I wish you would go away," she said. "What are you doing here? Our village has always been peaceful."

"It certainly looks very peaceful now," one of the men said, grinning—"as peaceful as a grave. Do you know who did that, old mother? The Japanese!"

"I suppose so," she agreed. Then she asked, "Why? That's what I don't understand."

"Why? Because they want our land, that's why!"

"Our land!" she repeated. "Why, they can't have our land."

"Never!" they shouted.

But all this time they were talking and chewing the bread they had divided among themselves, they were watching the eastern horizon.

"Why do you keep looking east?" old Mrs. Wang now asked.

"The Japanese are coming from there," the man who had taken the bread replied.

"Are you running away from them?" she asked, surprised.

"There are only a handful of us," he said apologetically. "We were left to guard a village—Pao An, in the country of——"

"I know that village," old Mrs. Wang interrupted. "I was a girl there. How is the old Pao who keeps the teashop in the main street? He's my brother."

"Everybody is dead there," the man replied. "The Japanese have taken it—a great army of men came with foreign guns and tanks, so what could we do?"

"Of course, only run," she agreed. Nevertheless, she felt sick. So he was dead, that one brother she had left! She was now the last of her father's family.

But the soldiers were straggling away again, leaving her alone. "They'll be coming, those

*A HOME TO RETURN TO* Chen Yan Ning Courtesy of Hefner Galleries, Oklahoma City, Oklahoma.

little black dwarfs," they were saying. "We'd best go on."

Nevertheless, the one who had taken the bread lingered a moment to stare down at the wounded man who lay with his eyes shut, not having moved at all.

"Is he dead?" he inquired. Then, before Mrs. Wang could answer, he pulled a short knife out of his belt. "Dead or not, I'll give him a punch or two with this."

But old Mrs. Wang pushed his arm away. "No, you won't," she said with authority. "If he is dead, then there is no use sending him into purgatory all in pieces. I am a good Buddhist myself."

The man laughed. "Oh, well, he is dead," he said, and he ran after his comrades.

A Japanese, was he? Old Mrs. Wang, left alone with this inert figure, looked at him. He was very young, she could see, now that his eyes were closed. She felt his wrist but could <u>discern</u> no pulse. She leaned over him and held to his lips the half of her roll which she had not eaten.

"Eat," she said very distinctly. "Bread!"

But there was no answer. Evidently he was dead. He must have died while she was getting the bread out of the oven.

There was nothing to do, then, but finish the bread herself. And when that was done, she wondered if she ought not to follow after Little Pig and his wife and all the villagers. The sun was mounting, and it was growing hot. If she were going, she had better go.

But first she would climb the dike and see what the direction was. They had gone west, and as far as eye could see westward was a great plain. She might even see a good-sized crowd miles away. Anyway, she could see the next village, and they might all be there.

So she climbed the dike slowly, getting very hot. There was a breeze on top of the dike, and it was good. She was shocked to see the river very near the top of the dike. Why, it had risen in the last hour!

"You old demon!" she said severely. Let the river god hear it if he liked. He was evil, that was what!

She stooped and bathed her cheeks and her wrists. The water was quite cold, as though with fresh rains somewhere. Then she stood up and gazed around her. To the west there was nothing except in the far distance the soldiers still half running, and beyond them the blur of the next village, which stood on a long rise of ground. She had better set out for that village. Doubtless Little Pig and his wife were there waiting for her.

Then, just as she was about to climb down and start out, she saw something on the eastern horizon. It was at first only an immense cloud of dust. As she stared at it, very quickly it became a lot of black dots and shining spots. Then she saw what it was. It was a lot of men—an army.

That's the Japanese, she thought. Yes, above them were the buzzing silver planes. They circled about, seeming to search for someone.

"I don't know who you're looking for," she muttered, "unless it's me and Little Pig and his wife. We're the only ones left. You've already killed my brother Pao."

She had almost forgotten that Pao was dead. Now she remembered it <u>acutely</u>. He had such a nice shop. Pao was a good man.

Besides, what about his wife and his seven children? Doubtless they were killed, too. Now they were looking for her. It occurred to her that on the dike she could easily be seen, so she clambered hastily down.

It was when she was about halfway down

*Words to Know and Use*

**discern** (di zurn´, -surn´) v. to recognize; to make out clearly
**acutely** (ə kyo͞ot´ lē) adv. clearly

that she thought of the water gate. This old river—it had been a curse to them since time began. Why should it not make up a little, now, for all the wickedness it had done? It was plotting wickedness again, trying to steal over its banks. Well, why not?

She wavered a moment. It was a pity, of course, that the dead Japanese would be swept into the flood. He was a nice-looking boy, and she had saved him from being stabbed. It was not quite the same as saving his life, of course, but still it was a little the same.

She went over to him and tugged at him until he lay near the top of the bank. Then she went down again.

She knew how to open the water gate. Any child knew how to open the sluice[5] for crops. But she knew also how to swing open the whole gate. The question was could she open it quickly enough to get out of the way?

"I'm only one old woman," she muttered. She hesitated a second more. Well, it would be a pity not to see what sort of baby Little Pig's wife would have, but one could not see everything.

She glanced again to the east. There were the Japanese coming across the plain. They were a long clear line of black dotted with thousands of glittering points. If she opened this gate the <u>impetuous</u> water would roar toward them, drowning them, maybe.

Certainly they could not keep on marching nearer and nearer to her and to Little Pig and his wife, waiting for her. Well, Little Pig and his wife—they would wonder about her, but they would never dream of this.

She turned <u>resolutely</u> to the gate. Some people fought with airplanes and some with guns, but you could fight with a river too. She wrenched out one of the huge wooden pins. A rill[6] of water burst into a strong jet. When she

wrenched one more pin the rest would give way of themselves. She pulled at it and felt it begin to slip from its hole.

I might be able to get myself out of purgatory with this, she thought, and maybe they'll let me have that old man of mine, too. What's a foot of his to all this? Then we'll—

The pin slipped away suddenly, and the gate burst flat against her and knocked her breath away. She had only time to gasp, to the river, "Come on, you old demon!"

Then she felt it seize her and lift her up to the sky. It was beneath her, around her. It rolled her joyfully hither and thither; then, holding her close and enfolded, it went rushing against the enemy. ❧

---

5. **sluice** (slo͞os): an artificial channel or passage for water, with a gate or valve at one end to control the flow.

6. **rill:** a little stream.

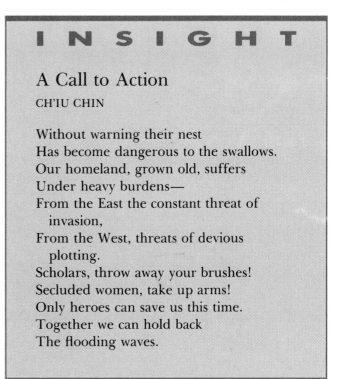

# INSIGHT

## A Call to Action

CH'IU CHIN

Without warning their nest
Has become dangerous to the swallows.
Our homeland, grown old, suffers
Under heavy burdens—
From the East the constant threat of
  invasion,
From the West, threats of devious
  plotting.
Scholars, throw away your brushes!
Secluded women, take up arms!
Only heroes can save us this time.
Together we can hold back
The flooding waves.

---

43

## Responding to Reading

### First Impressions

**1.** What was your reaction to the character of Mrs. Wang?

### Second Thoughts

**2.** At first the war is not real to Mrs. Wang, but by the end of the story she is an active participant. Why does this change occur?

**Think about**
- how the main events of the story affect Mrs. Wang
- who or what Mrs. Wang considers to be her enemies
- Mrs. Wang's attitude toward the Japanese during the story

**3.** The flood waters presumably carry Mrs. Wang to her death. What do you think were her reasons for opening the gate of the dike?

**Think about**
- how she feels about the river
- what she thinks of the soldiers
- how she feels about her own life

**4.** Explain the meaning of the title "The Old Demon." Could it refer to more than one character or object?

**5.** Do you consider Mrs. Wang a hero? Why or why not?

**6.** Do you think Mrs. Wang does the right thing? Would you have done the same? Explain.

### Broader Connections

**7.** Do you think that older people in your community are treated with respect? Compare the way Mrs. Wang is treated by her neighbors and the soldiers with how the elderly are treated in your community.

## Literary Concept: Conflict

A struggle between two forces is called **conflict.** Conflict is central to any story. The two basic kinds of conflict are external and internal. **External conflict** occurs between a character and any force outside himself, such as another person, society in general, or some force of nature. **Internal conflict** exists when a character has an inner struggle such as trying to act or make a decision.

How many different examples of conflict can you find in "The Old Demon"? Are any of them more important than the others? Which is most important?

# Writing Options

1. Suppose that you are an independent newspaper journalist writing for two different newspapers. One is conservative, such as *The Wall Street Journal*. The other is a tabloid, a sensational weekly paper, such as *The National Enquirer*. Write a headline for each newspaper that summarizes a news report based on "The Old Demon." Make each headline appropriate for the newspaper. Each headline can be one or two lines, but limit each total headline to thirty-eight letters or spaces.

2. Imagine you are Little Pig and you will speak at your grandmother's funeral. Write a eulogy, a speech of praise, for Mrs. Wang.

3. Mrs. Wang is a character with strong opinions. What opinions might she have about problems in our modern world? Choose one topic, such as pollution or the homeless, and write what you think Mrs. Wang would say.

4. Think of an elderly person you know. How is that person similar to and different from Mrs. Wang? Compare and contrast their personalities.

5. How does the poem "A Call to Action" parallel Mrs. Wang's attitude?

# Vocabulary Practice

**Exercise** Each boldfaced word below is paired with another word that may be a synonym (same meaning) or an antonym (opposite meaning) for the word. On your paper, write *Synonyms* or *Antonyms* for each pair. Then create your own sentences using the boldfaced words.

1. **hearsay**—fact
2. **inert**—motionless
3. **acutely**—keenly
4. **disconcerting**—soothing
5. **somberly**—joyfully
6. **resolutely**—unwaveringly
7. **impetuous**—well considered
8. **deprecatingly**—supportively
9. **spectacle**—extravaganza
10. **discern**—understand

> *Words to Know and Use*
>
> ---
>
> **acutely**
> **deprecatingly**
> **discern**
> **disconcerting**
> **hearsay**
> **impetuous**
> **inert**
> **resolutely**
> **somberly**
> **spectacle**

## Options for Learning

**1 • Reporting the News** With several other students, stage a news show featuring an on-the-spot interview with Chinese survivors of the Japanese attack. Have the eyewitnesses describe the flood and its effect on the Japanese soldiers as well as on the Chinese land and people. If possible, videotape the show for later viewing.

**2 • Would You Hire Her?** In the business world, job applicants are often evaluated on their ability to solve problems. Think of an appropriate job for Mrs. Wang that requires problem-solving abilities. Write a resumé for her that highlights her abilities. Show the class your resumé, and have them decide if they would hire Mrs. Wang.

**3 • Acting Is Alive** With a classmate, create an imaginary dialogue between Mrs. Wang and her husband in the afterlife. Then role-play the conversation for your class.

**4 • Engineers at Work** Build or draw a model of a dike system that shows how water can be moved through gates from the river to the crops, how it can be held in canals, and how a flood might be prevented or caused.

### FACT FINDER

*In what year did the Japanese forces withdraw from China?*

### Pearl Buck
1892–1973

No one can accuse Pearl Buck of having an easy road to success. She was only five months old when her missionary parents left Hillsboro, West Virginia, and took her to China. Life was difficult in the far interior of China, and most of her brothers and sisters died young. Yet she grew to love the Chinese people and wrote stories and articles about them. The manuscript of her first novel was destroyed when invading troops burned down her home in Nanking, China, just minutes after she and her husband had escaped. She returned to writing with great urgency when she learned that her only child was severely retarded and would require expensive care. Her next work, the novel *The Good Earth*, won both the Pulitzer and Nobel Prizes. Buck wrote over sixty-five novels and many essays and short stories, most of which were set in China. She also achieved worldwide respect for her tireless charitable work and her campaign for human rights, including rights for the handicapped. Buck donated over 7 million dollars to the Pearl Buck Foundation, a fund used for illegitimate children of American servicemen in Asia.

*Poetry*

### *from* The *Iliad*

HOMER *Translated by* ROBERT FITZGERALD

## *E*xamine What You Know

*The Iliad* (il′ ē əd) is based upon the Trojan War, a conflict between the Greeks and Trojans that probably took place around 1200 B.C. What do you know about the heroes, battles, and gods of ancient Greece? Pool your knowledge with that of your classmates.

## *E*xpand Your Knowledge

According to Homer, the Trojan War began when Paris, a prince of Troy, kidnapped Helen, the world's most beautiful woman, from her Greek home. This action naturally offended her husband, King Menelaus (men′ ə lā′ əs), who raised an army and fleet to invade Troy and bring her home.

The Greeks laid siege to the walled city of Troy, but for ten years neither side won. The Trojans finally gained the upper hand when the mighty Achilles (ə kil′ ēz′) angrily left his fellow Greeks after a dispute. Led by Paris' brother Hector, the Trojans drove the Greeks to the sea coast. During this battle, Hector killed Patroclus (pat′ rə kləs), Achilles' best friend. News about the death of Patroclus angered Achilles so much that he led a charge that forced the Trojans back into their city. As the son of a goddess, Achilles proved nearly unbeatable. Only Hector, standing alone outside the gates of Troy, would face him. It is here that this selection begins.

The gods play an active role in this battle and throughout the poem. Watch for ways they use their powers.

## *E*nrich Your Reading

**Keeping Track of Characters**   This section of *The Iliad* has seven major characters: Hector, Achilles, Zeus, Pallas Athena, Deiphobus, Patroclus, Apollo. Other names that are mentioned are not important to this part of the story. To keep the characters straight, categorize them as Greeks, Trojans, or gods. Use the notes that accompany the text to help you classify each character. Then refer to the list as you read.

■ *A biography of the author can be found on page 60.*

*HECTOR KILLED BY ACHILLES*   Peter Paul Rubens   Pau, Musée des Beaux-Arts/Giraudon/Art Resource, New York.

# from The Iliad

HOMER *Translated by* ROBERT FITZGERALD

*The Trojan warriors have just escaped the fury of Achilles by seeking safety behind the walls of Troy. The god Apollo has helped them by disguising himself as a Trojan and then leading Achilles in a wild chase away from the rest of the army. When Achilles learns he has been tricked, he runs full speed toward Troy. As Hector stands outside the gates of Troy waiting to meet his rival, his father and mother try to persuade him not to fight the strong and pitiless Achilles. They know that Achilles will not stop until he has avenged the death of his friend Patroclus.*

## From Book 22

Hector stood firm, as huge Achilles neared.
The way a serpent, fed on poisonous herbs,
coiled at his lair upon a mountainside,
with all his length of hate awaits a man
5  and eyes him evilly: so Hector, grim
and narrow-eyed, refused to yield. He leaned
his brilliant shield against a spur of wall
and in his brave heart bitterly reflected:

"Here I am badly caught. If I take cover,
10  slipping inside the gate and wall, the first
to accuse me for it will be Polydamas,
he who told me I should lead the Trojans
back to the city on that cursed night
Achilles joined the battle. No, I would not,
15  would not, wiser though it would have been.
Now troops have perished for my foolish pride,
I am ashamed to face townsmen and women.
Someone inferior to me may say:
'He kept his pride and lost his men, this Hector!'
20  So it will go. Better, when that time comes,
that I appear as he who killed Achilles

**11 Polydamas** (pə lid′ ə məs): a Trojan warrior whose earlier advice had been ignored by Hector, causing the death of many Trojan men.

**19** Hector considers the possibility of retreating behind the city walls. *How does he think he would be received?*

man to man, or else that I went down
before him honorably for the city's sake.
Suppose, though, that I lay my shield and helm
25  aside, and prop my spear against the wall,
and go to meet the noble Prince Achilles,
promising Helen, promising with her
all treasures that Alexander brought home
by ship to Troy—the first cause of our quarrel—
30  that he may give these things to the Atreidai?
Then I might add, apart from these, a portion
of all the secret wealth the city owns.
Yes, later I might take our counselors' oath
to hide no stores, but share and share alike
35  to halve all wealth our lovely city holds,
all that is here within the walls. Ah, no,
why even put the question to myself?
I must not go before him and receive
no quarter, no respect! Aye, then and there
40  he'll kill me, unprotected as I am,
my gear laid by, defenseless as a woman.
No chance, now, for charms from oak or stone
in parley with him—charms a girl and boy
might use when they enchant each other talking!
45  Better we duel, now at once, and see
to whom the Olympian awards the glory."

These were his shifts of mood. Now close at hand
Achilles like the <u>implacable</u> god of war
came on with blowing crest, hefting the dreaded
50  beam of Pelian ash on his right shoulder.
Bronze light played around him, like the glare
of a great fire or the great sun rising,
and Hector, as he watched, began to tremble.
Then he could hold his ground no more. He ran,
55  leaving the gate behind him, with Achilles
hard on his heels, sure of his own speed.
When that most lightning-like of birds, a hawk
bred on a mountain, swoops upon a dove,
the quarry dips in terror, but the hunter,
60  screaming, dips behind and gains upon it,
passionate for prey. Just so, Achilles

**28 Alexander:** a Trojan commander.

**30 Atreidai** (ə trī′ dē): Greeks.

**32** Hector thinks about offering Achilles a share of the great Trojan wealth.

**45** Why does Hector decide not to negotiate peace with Achilles?

**46 the Olympian:** Zeus, the ruler of the gods.

**50 beam of Pelian** (pē′ lē ən) **ash:** a spear made of the wood of an ash tree from Mount Pelian, originally a wedding gift to Achilles' father.

**54** Why does Hector run away from Achilles?

*Words to Know and Use*

**implacable** (im plā′ kə bəl) *adj.* inflexible; uncompromising; that cannot be soothed or comforted

50

THE DELIVERY OF BRISEIS (detail)   From a wall painting in Pompeii   Museo Nazionale, Naples, Italy/Art Resource, New York.

murderously cleft the air, as Hector
ran with flashing knees along the wall.
They passed the lookout point, the wild fig tree
65 with wind in all its leaves, then <u>veered</u> away
along the curving wagon road, and came
to where the double fountains well, the source
of eddying Scamander. One hot spring
flows out, and from the water fumes arise
70 as though from fire burning; but the other
even in summer gushes chill as hail
or snow or crystal ice frozen on water.
Near these fountains are wide washing pools
of smooth-laid stone, where Trojan wives and daughters
75 laundered their smooth linen in the days
of peace before the Achaeans came. Past these
the two men ran, pursuer and pursued,
and he who fled was noble, he behind
a greater man by far. They ran full speed,
80 and not for bull's hide or a ritual beast
or any prize that men compete for: no,
but for the life of Hector, tamer of horses.

**68 eddying Scamander** (skə man' dər): the ancient name for Menderes, a swirling river in Asia.

**76 Achaeans** (ə kē' ənz): Greeks.

51

*As Hector runs from Achilles, the gods watch the two from above. During three trips around the walls of Troy, Zeus considers helping Hector, but Athena forbids any interference in what she says is Hector's day of fate. Zeus weighs the fate of both Achilles and Hector; the scales indicate that Hector shall die, not Achilles. When Hector's fate is sealed, Apollo, the god who has helped him throughout the story, abandons him. At this point, Athena decides to assist fate and help her favorite, Achilles. She appears at Hector's side disguised as his brother Deiphobus (dē if' ə bəs). She urges him to stand and face Achilles, promising to help him in battle. After Hector is misled into believing he has assistance, he decides to stand and fight.*

And when at last the two men faced each other,
Hector was the first to speak. He said:

85  "I will no longer fear you as before,
son of Peleus, though I ran from you
round Priam's town three times and could not face you.
Now my soul would have me stand and fight,
whether I kill you or am killed. So come,
90  we'll summon gods here as our witnesses,
none higher, arbiters of a <u>pact</u>: I swear
that, terrible as you are,
I'll not insult your corpse should Zeus allow me
victory in the end, your life as prize.
95  Once I have your gear, I'll give your body
back to the Achaeans. Grant me, too, this grace."

But swift Achilles frowned at him and said:

"Hector, I'll have no talk of pacts with you,
forever unforgiven as you are.
100  As between men and lions there are none,
no concord between wolves and sheep, but all
hold one another hateful through and through,
so there can be no courtesy between us,
no sworn truce, till one of us is down

**86 *son of Peleus*** (pē′ lē əs): Achilles.

**96** Hector wants an agreement to ensure that the winner will treat the loser's corpse with respect.

**103** *What emotion is driving Achilles?*

*Words
to Know
and Use*   |   **pact** (pakt) *n.* an agreement between persons or groups

105 and glutting with his blood the war god Ares.
Summon up what skills you have. By god,
you'd better be a spearman and a fighter!
Now there is no way out. Pallas Athena
will have the upper hand of you. The weapon
110 belongs to me. You'll pay the reckoning
in full for all the pain my men have borne,
who met death by your spear."

                  He twirled and cast
his shaft with its long shadow. Splendid Hector,
keeping his eye upon the point, <u>eluded</u> it
115 by ducking at the instant of the cast,
so shaft and bronze shank passed him overhead
and punched into the earth. But unperceived
by Hector, Pallas Athena plucked it out
and gave it back to Achilles. Hector said:

120 "A clean miss. Godlike as you are,
you have not yet known doom for me from Zeus.
You thought you had, by heaven. Then you turned
into a word-thrower, hoping to make me lose
my fighting heart and head in fear of you.
125 You cannot plant your spear between my shoulders
while I am running. If you have the gift,
just put it through my chest as I come forward.
Now it's for you to dodge my own. Would god
you'd give the whole shaft lodging in your body!
130 War for the Trojans would be eased
if you were blotted out, bane that you are."

With this he twirled his long spearshaft and cast it,
hitting his enemy mid-shield, but off
and away the spear rebounded. Furious
135 that he had lost it, made his throw for nothing,
Hector stood bemused. He had no other.
Then he gave a great shout to Deiphobus
to ask for a long spear. But there was no one
near him, not a soul. Now in his heart
140 the Trojan realized the truth and said:

**105 *glutting with his blood the war god Ares*** (ā′ rēz): satisfying the god of war with his blood.

**108 *Pallas Athena*** (pal′ əs ə thē′ nə): the goddess of wisdom, who sides with the Greeks.

**119** *How does Athena give Achilles an advantage?*

**136 *bemused:*** lost in thought, confused.

**139** The brother that Hector expected to be there is gone.

| *Words to Know and Use* | **elude** (ē lo͞od′) *v.* to avoid or escape |
| --- | --- |

53

"This is the end. The gods are calling deathward.
I had thought
a good soldier, Deiphobus, was with me.
He is inside the walls. Athena tricked me.
145 Death is near, and black, not at a distance,
not to be <u>evaded</u>. Long ago
this hour must have been to Zeus's liking
and to the liking of his archer son.
They have been well disposed before, but now
150 the appointed time's upon me. Still, I would not
die without delivering a stroke,
or die ingloriously, but in some action
memorable to men in days to come."

With this he drew the whetted blade that hung
155 upon his left flank, <u>ponderous</u> and long,
collecting all his might the way an eagle
narrows himself to dive through shady cloud
and strike a lamb or <u>cowering</u> hare: so Hector
lanced ahead and swung his whetted blade.
160 Achilles with wild fury in his heart
pulled in upon his chest his beautiful shield—
his helmet with four burnished metal ridges
nodding above it, and the golden crest
Hephaestus locked there tossing in the wind.
165 <u>Conspicuous</u> as the evening star that comes,
amid the first in heaven, at fall of night,
and stands most lovely in the west, so shone
in sunlight the fine-pointed spear
Achilles poised in his right hand, with deadly
170 aim at Hector, at the skin where most
it lay exposed. But nearly all was covered
by the bronze gear he took from slain Patroclus,
showing only, where his collarbones
divided neck and shoulders, the bare throat
175 where the destruction of a life is quickest.
Here, then, as the Trojan charged, Achilles
drove his point straight through the tender neck,
but did not cut the windpipe, leaving Hector
able to speak and to respond. He fell
180 aside into the dust. And Prince Achilles
now exulted:

**154 whetted:** sharpened.

**164 Hephaestus** (hē fes' təs): god of fire and blacksmith of the gods.

**172** Hector is wearing armor that really belongs to Achilles. Achilles' friend Patroclus had worn this armor into battle. When Hector killed him, he took the armor from his body.

*Words to Know and Use*

**evade** (ē vād') *v.* to avoid or escape by cleverness or deception
**ponderous** (pän' dər əs) *adj.* very heavy
**cowering** (kou' ər iŋ) *adj.* trembling from fear **cower** *v.*
**conspicuous** (kən spik' yo͞o əs) *adj.* easy to see; noticeable; striking

"Hector, had you thought
that you could kill Patroclus and be safe?
Nothing to dread from me; I was not there.
All childishness. Though distant then, Patroclus'
185 comrade in arms was greater far than he—
and it is I who had been left behind
that day beside the deep-sea ships who now
have made your knees give way. The dogs and kites
will rip your body. His will lie in honor
190 when the Achaeans give him funeral."

Hector, barely whispering, replied:

"I beg you by your soul and by your parents,
do not let the dogs feed on me
in your encampment by the ships. Accept
195 the bronze and gold my father will provide
as gifts, my father and her ladyship
my mother. Let them have my body back,
so that our men and women may accord me
decency of fire when I am dead."

200 Achilles the great runner scowled and said:

"Beg me no beggary by soul or parents,
whining dog! Would god my passion drove me
to slaughter you and eat you raw, you've caused
such agony to me! No man exists
205 who could defend you from the carrion pack—
not if they spread for me ten times your ransom,
twenty times, and promise more as well;
aye, not if Priam, son of Dardanus,
tells them to buy you for your weight in gold!
210 You'll have no bed of death, nor will you be
laid out and mourned by her who gave you birth.
Dogs and birds will have you, every scrap."

Then at the point of death Lord Hector said:

"I see you now for what you are. No chance
215 to win you over. Iron in your breast
your heart is. Think a bit, though: this may be
a thing the gods in anger hold against you
on that day when Paris and Apollo
destroy you at the Gates, great as you are."

**190** Achilles will leave Hector's body to dogs and vultures, while he will honor the corpse of Patroclus.

**205** *carrion pack:* wild dogs that travel in groups and feed on dead flesh.

**219** *What prediction does Hector make for Achilles?*

220 Even as he spoke, the end came, and death hid him;
spirit from body fluttered to undergloom,
bewailing fate that made him leave his youth
and manhood in the world. And as he died
Achilles spoke again. He said:

225 "Die, make an end. I shall accept my own
whenever Zeus and the other gods desire."

At this he pulled his spearhead from the body,
laying it aside, and stripped
the bloodstained shield and cuirass from his shoulders.
230 Other Achaeans hastened round to see
Hector's fine body and his comely face,
and no one came who did not stab the body.
Glancing at one another they would say:

"Now Hector has turned <u>vulnerable</u>, softer
235 than when he put the torches to the ships!"

And he who said this would inflict a wound.
When the great master of pursuit, Achilles,
had the body stripped, he stood among them,
saying swiftly:

"Friends, my lords and captains
240 of Argives, now that the gods at last have let me
bring to earth this man who wrought
havoc among us—more than all the rest—
come, we'll offer battle around the city,
to learn the intentions of the Trojans now.
245 Will they give up their strong point at this loss?
Can they fight on, though Hector's dead?

But wait:
why do I ponder, why take up these questions?
Down by the ships Patroclus' body lies
unwept, unburied. I shall not forget him
250 while I can keep my feet among the living.
If in the dead world they forget the dead,
I say there, too, I shall remember him,
my friend. Men of Achaea, lift a song!

**226** Achilles knows that he too will die in battle because his mother, who is a goddess, has foretold his death.

**229** *cuirass* (kwi ras'): armored breastplate.

**232** *Why do the Greeks treat Hector's body in this manner?*

**240** *captains of Argives* (är' gīvz): Greek officers.

Down to the ships we go, and take this body,
255 our glory. We have beaten Hector down,
to whom as to a god the Trojans prayed."

Indeed, he had in mind for Hector's body
outrage and shame. Behind both feet he pierced
the tendons, heel to ankle. Rawhide cords
260 he drew through both and lashed them to his chariot,
letting the man's head trail. Stepping aboard,
bearing the great trophy of the arms,
he shook the reins, and whipped the team ahead
into a willing run. A dustcloud rose
265 above the furrowing body; the dark tresses
flowed behind, and the head so princely once
lay back in dust. Zeus gave him to his enemies
to be <u>defiled</u> in his own fatherland. . . .

*Hector's father, Priam, begs in vain for Achilles to return the body. Eventually, the gods intervene because Hector always gave them honor during his lifetime. The gods' messenger, Hermes (hʉr' mēz), leads Priam to Achilles, where he again requests Hector's body. Achilles, who is reminded of his own aging father, changes his mind and allows Priam to give Hector a proper funeral.*

ACHILLES DRAGGING THE BODY OF HECTOR  Attic hydria  Museum of Fine Arts, Boston William Francis Warden Fund.

| Words to Know and Use | **defile** (dē fīl') *v.* to make dirty; to violate the honor of |
| --- | --- |

57

# *explain*

## *Responding to Reading*

### First Impressions

1. Which character were you hoping would win the fight? Why? Jot down a few notes to explain your choice.

### Second Thoughts

2. How would you explain Hector's attitude toward fighting Achilles?

   **Think about**
   • what he believes will happen if he refuses to fight
   • his reasons for running away from Achilles
   • his decision to stand and fight

3. Why does Achilles win the battle? Is it fair that he wins? Explain.

4. How much control do Hector and Achilles have over their own lives?

5. Achilles does not honor Hector's request to return the loser's body home. What does this reveal about Achilles' attitude toward Hector?

   **Think about**
   • what Achilles says to Hector before their battle
   • how Achilles responds to Hector's last words
   • the way Hector's corpse is treated

6. Compare Hector and Achilles. In your opinion, which is more heroic? Do both characters live up to your definition of a hero? Explain.

### Broader Connections

7. Achilles and Hector fight one-on-one. Should leaders of rival nations, peoples, or gangs settle differences between themselves without involving their followers? Is it possible to settle conflicts this way?

## *Literary Concept: Epic Simile*

A **simile** is a figure of speech that compares two dissimilar things using the words *like* or *as.* "Silent as death" and "John went down like a stone" are examples of similes. Epic similes are long comparisons that often continue for a number of lines. They do not require the use of *like* or *as.*

An epic simile in lines 1–6 compares Hector to a snake. What does the simile reveal about Hector and his attitude toward Achilles? Study the similes in lines 57-62, lines 154-159, and lines 165-169. How does each simile contribute to the characterization of the heroes?

**Concept Review: Epic Poetry** Review the information on p. 31 that identifies four major elements of epic poetry. How are these elements reflected in *The Iliad?*

# *W*riting Options

1. Write an epitaph for Hector's gravestone that captures the spirit of his character.

2. Choose an epic simile from *The Iliad* that describes either Hector or Achilles. Explain what the simile is saying about the hero. Then create an epic simile of your own to describe either character.

3. As either a Greek or a Trojan general, write a commendation for Achilles or Hector that explains why you are awarding him your army's highest medal.

4. If Beowulf fought Achilles, who would win? Explain why.

# *V*ocabulary Practice

**Exercise** Write the letter of the word that is not related in meaning to the other words in the set.

1. (a) yielding (b) implacable (c) flexible (d) tolerant
2. (a) dirty (b) clean (c) defile (d) corrupt
3. (a) veer (b) avoid (c) straighten (d) turn
4. (a) conspicuous (b) striking (c) invisible (d) noticeable
5. (a) pact (b) agreement (c) contract (d) argument
6. (a) dodge (b) capture (c) elude (d) escape
7. (a) face (b) meet (c) evade (d) confront
8. (a) weak (b) vulnerable (c) strong (d) defenseless
9. (a) ponderous (b) swift (c) weighty (d) hefty
10. (a) daring (b) challenging (c) cowering (d) defying

*Words
to Know
and Use*

———

**cowering
conspicuous
defile
elude
evade
implacable
pact
ponderous
veer
vulnerable**

## Options for Learning

**1 • Saturday Night at the Fights** With a classmate, act as the play–by–play announcer and commentator for the fight between Achilles and Hector. As the announcer narrates the fight, the commentator should provide observations that make the fight more interesting for listeners. Describe the events of the battle for your classmates using Homer's information as well as modern phrases and sports clichés.

**2 • Illustrate *The Iliad*** Illustrate the fight between Hector and Achilles so that the location, armor, weapons, and methods of fighting are shown. Look in your library for pictures of the Homeric heroes and their tools of battle. If possible, find out more about Achilles' shield.

**3 • Epic Conclusion** Report on the ending of the Trojan War. Since *The Iliad* itself does not tell about the ending of the war, use an encyclopedia or another reference book to find out how it ended. Be sure to explain the strategy of the Trojan horse.

**4 • Charting the Gods** Find out more about the major gods in *The Iliad*. Then create a chart that shows which gods sided with the Trojans and which with the Greeks. Include basic information about the powers and personality of each god.

 **FACT FINDER**

*Find out what is meant by an "Achilles' heel."*

## Homer

Homer lived sometime between 800 and 600 B.C. With the possible exception of Shakespeare, no other poet in the Western world has been quoted more often than the mysterious Homer. Little is known about the author of *The Iliad* and *The Odyssey*, two equally famous epics. Most scholars now agree that there was a Homer, though some think he may not have written *The Odyssey* himself. Evidence of his life and authorship has been gathered indirectly from other writings of an-cient Greece, from historical references, and from his poems. It seems likely that he was born either in western Turkey or in the nearby Greek islands. Homer has been traditionally thought to have been blind, but the only indication of this is the fact that his name means "blind man."

Like *Beowulf*, Homer's poems trace their origin to an oral tradition. Homer probably began as a storyteller who sang his story. Unlike other storytellers, however, Homer eventually wrote down his long narratives.

*Essay*

# The Man in the Water

## ROGER ROSENBLATT

## Examine What You Know

In a disaster, such as an earthquake, a flood, or a plane crash, people react in many different ways. Talk with your class about the good and the bad things that you have seen or heard about people doing in real-life disasters. What do these behaviors suggest to you about human nature? See how your views of human nature compare to those of the author of this essay.

## Expand Your Knowledge

On January 13, 1982, a passenger jet crashed in Washington, D.C., during the evening rush hour. The jet was trying to take off in freezing rain and failed to gain enough altitude. Crashing onto the Fourteenth Street Bridge that crosses the Potomac River, the plane broke in two and fell into the icy river. Seventy-eight people died in the disaster—some of them in the plane, some in their cars, and some in the frigid waters of the Potomac.

Following the crash of Flight 90, news reports on television and in newspapers provided details of the tragedy. The essay you are about to read offers more than a news report. It presents the writer's viewpoints on the meaning of the events that took place immediately following the crash. In particular, the writer looks at how one passenger behaved in those confusing, terrifying moments and considers what his behavior says about all of us.

## Write Before You Read

Imagine that you are in the crash of Flight 90 and that you and several other passengers have been thrown from the plane into the icy river. You may drown or freeze to death any minute. A helicopter comes to the rescue, but it can pull out only one person at a time. What might you do in that situation? List your alternatives.

# The Man in the Water

## ROGER ROSENBLATT

As disasters go, this one was terrible but not unique, certainly not among the worst on the roster of U.S. air crashes. There was the unusual element of the bridge, of course, and the fact that the plane clipped it at a moment of high traffic, one routine thus intersecting another and disrupting both. Then, too, there was the location of the event. Washington, the city of form and regulations, turned chaotic, deregulated, by a blast of real winter and a single slap of metal on metal. The jets from Washington National Airport that normally swoop around the presidential monuments like famished gulls are, for the moment, emblemized by the one that fell; so there is that detail. And there was the aesthetic clash as well—blue-and-green Air Florida, the name a flying garden, sunk down among gray chunks in a black river. All that was worth noticing, to be sure. Still, there was nothing very special in any of it, except death, which, while always special, does not necessarily bring millions to tears or to attention. Why, then, the shock here?

Perhaps because the nation saw in this disaster something more than a mechanical failure. Perhaps because people saw in it no failure at all, but rather something successful about their makeup. Here, after all, were two forms of nature in collision: the elements and human character. Last Wednesday, the ele-ments, indifferent as ever, brought down Flight 90. And on that same afternoon, human nature—groping and flailing in mysteries of its own—rose to the occasion.

Of the four acknowledged heroes of the event, three are able to account for their behavior. Donald Usher and Eugene Windsor, a park police helicopter team, risked their lives every time they dipped the skids into the water to pick up survivors. On television, side by side in bright blue jumpsuits, they described their courage as all in the line of duty. Lenny Skutnik, a 28-year-old employee of the Congressional Budget Office, said: "It's something I never thought I would do"—referring to his jumping into the water to drag an injured woman to shore. Skutnik added that "somebody had to go in the water," delivering every hero's line that is no less admirable for its repetitions. In fact, nobody had to go into the water. That somebody actually did so is part of the reason this particular tragedy sticks in the mind.

But the person most responsible for the emotional impact of the disaster is the one known at first simply as "the man in the water." (Balding, probably in his 50s, an extravagant mustache.) He was seen clinging with five other survivors to the tail section of the airplane. This man was described by Usher and Windsor as appearing alert and in control. Every time they lowered a lifeline and

Actual photographs of the rescue; Lenny Skutnick (lower, right)
Photos courtesy of Sygma, New York.

flotation ring to him, he passed it on to another of the passengers. "In a mass casualty, you'll find people like him," said Windsor. "But I've never seen one with that commitment." When the helicopter came back for him, the man had gone under. His selflessness was one reason the story held national attention; his anonymity another. The fact that he went unidentified invested him with a universal character. For a while he was Everyman, and thus proof (as if one needed it) that no man is ordinary.

Still, he could never have imagined such a capacity in himself. Only minutes before his character was tested, he was sitting in the ordinary plane among the ordinary passengers, dutifully listening to the stewardess telling him to fasten his seat belt and saying something about the "no smoking sign." So our man relaxed with the others, some of whom would owe their lives to him. Perhaps he started to read, or to doze, or to regret some harsh remark made in the office that morning. Then suddenly he knew that the trip would not be ordinary. Like every other person on that flight, he was desperate to live, which makes his final act so stunning.

For at some moment in the water he must have realized that he would not live if he continued to hand over the rope and ring to others. He *had* to know it, no matter how gradual the effect of the cold. In his judgment he had no choice. When the helicopter took off with what was to be the last survivor, he watched everything in the world move away from him, and he deliberately let it happen.

Yet there was something else about the man that kept our thoughts on him and which keeps our thoughts on him still. He was *there*, in the essential, classic circumstance. Man in nature. The man in the water. For its part, nature cared nothing about the five passengers. Our man, on the other hand, cared totally. So the timeless battle commenced in the Potomac. For as long as that man could last, they went at each other, nature and man: the one making no distinctions of good and evil, acting on no principles, offering no lifelines; the other acting wholly on distinctions, principles and, one supposes, on faith.

Since it was he who lost the fight, we ought to come again to the conclusion that people are powerless in the world. In reality, we believe the reverse, and it takes the act of the man in the water to remind us of our true feelings in this matter. It is not to say that everyone would have acted as he did or as Usher, Windsor and Skutnik. Yet whatever moved these men to challenge death on behalf of their fellows is not peculiar to them. Everyone feels the possibility in himself. That is the abiding wonder of the story. That is why we would not let go of it. If the man in the water gave a lifeline to the people gasping for survival, he was likewise giving a lifeline to those who observed him.

The odd thing is that we do not even really believe that the man in the water lost his fight. "Everything in Nature contains all the powers of Nature," said Emerson. Exactly. So the man in the water had his own natural powers. He could not make ice storms or freeze the water until it froze the blood. But he could hand life over to a stranger, and that is a power of nature too. The man in the water pitted himself against an implacable, impersonal enemy; he fought it with charity; and he held it to a standoff. He was the best we can do. ☙

## Responding to Reading

### First Impressions

1. Why do you think the man in the water behaved the way he did? Jot down your reason or reasons.

### Second Thoughts

2. Why do you think the writer focused on the anonymous man in the water instead of on one of the three acknowledged heroes of the tragedy?

3. The writer says that the man in the water did not lose his fight with nature. Do you agree or disagree? Explain your reasoning.

   **Think about**
   • how the man's fight with nature is described in the last paragraph
   • the meaning of Emerson's quote about nature
   • what power humans have

4. The essay concludes with the statement, "He was the best we can do." What do you think the writer means by this statement?

5. Do you think that everyone is capable of being as heroic as the man in the water? Explain your answer.

## Literary Concept: Author's Purpose

Nonfiction writers write for one or more of the following purposes: to inform, to give an opinion, to entertain, or to persuade. Some pieces of nonfiction, such as news articles, are meant to be entirely informative and objective, that is, strictly factual without any intrusion of the author's personal opinion. Other pieces are expressive—reflecting and sometimes promoting the opinion of the writer in addition to giving facts.

What do you see as the main purpose of "The Man in the Water"? Find phrases or sentences that support your choice. In what ways does this purpose make the essay differ from a news article on the same subject?

## Writing Options

1. Choose one of the three other heroes mentioned in this essay. Decide whether you think this person or the man in the water was the more heroic of the two. Contrast the two heroes.

2. The author of this essay makes the statement that "no man is ordinary." Do you agree or disagree? Support your opinion with reasons.

# WRITER'S
## WORKSHOP

## EVALUATION AND PERSUASION

Evaluation skills are critical in today's world. People are constantly called on to make judgments, evaluate statements, or take sides on different issues. Advertisements, special offers, contracts, appeals for charity, and political candidates need to be evaluated in order to judge their worth. As a young adult, you need to be able to evaluate and make decisions about personal issues as well, such as career choices, marriage, more schooling, buying an automobile, and even where to live.

In this workshop, you will evaluate characters from this subunit and decide which one should receive an award for heroism. Then you will try to persuade a panel of judges that your choice is a good one. In this type of evaluative/persuasive writing, you will make a judgment and then justify that judgment with convincing reasons.

**Here is your PASSkey to this assignment.**

### GUIDED ASSIGNMENT: AWARD NOMINATION

An award will be given to the most heroic character in this subunit. Write a nominating application for the character you think should receive it. In your application, include at least three reasons for your choice, and support each reason with evidence from the appropriate selection.

**P**URPOSE: To evaluate and persuade

**A**UDIENCE: A panel of judges

**S**UBJECT: A heroic person

**S**TRUCTURE: Nomination application

## Prewriting

**STEP 1** **Select a character**   Before you begin, preview the nomination application on pages 68–69. Study its wording so that you become familiar with the application format. Alone or in a small group, review the traits common to heroes. Then, list the characters in the subunit "The Making of Heroes" who display those qualities. Evaluate how closely each character matches your ideas of heroism. Finally, select the one character you think is most deserving of the title "hero."

**STEP 2** **Choose heroic qualities** List all the heroic qualities the character you selected possesses. Then, choose the three that seem most important. If possible, review your list with a classmate to see if he or she agrees with your choices. These qualities will be the three main reasons on your application.

**STEP 3** **Gather evidence** Make a chart listing the three heroic qualities you chose across the top. Then, elaborate on these points by filling in the chart with examples, quotes, and phrases from the story that support your ideas. Here is part of one student's chart on Marguerite Duras, the writer of an autobiographical account titled *The War: A Memoir*.

| Puts Good of Others First | Stands by Her Principles | Acts Bravely |
|---|---|---|
| risks life to protect others from Nazis | won't save husband by turning in someone else | witness at Rabier's trial |
| gets information from Rabier | quote p. 000: ''Even if I knew . . . dare to ask me.'' | |
| [use quote from diary] | | |

◀ STUDENT MODEL

**Special Tip**

As you search through the story, you may find heroic qualities and evidence that seem stronger than those you originally selected. Feel free to change your plans during prewriting or at any other stage of the writing process.

## Drafting

**STEP 1** **Write an introduction** Your first paragraph should explain who you are nominating for the award and for what reasons. You might begin by stating your opinion of your character or by summing up his or her best qualities. You want to start off on a positive, persuasive note.

**STEP 2 Support your reasons** In the next paragraphs, restate each reason and support it with evidence from the text. If possible, use more than one example and explanation for each reason. Write a separate paragraph for each reason. Since you are trying to persuade others of your choice, you might save the best reason for last because the reader will remember that one most clearly.

## Revising and Editing

Exchange drafts with a partner and review each other's work. In the margins or on the back of your partner's application, write the answers to the following questions.

### Revision Checklist

1. Put an *R* by each reason that is clear and persuasive. Write a *?* if you do not understand the reason or explanation.
2. Underline the clearest explanation.
3. Put a check by each example from the story that shows the hero in action.
4. Underline the best piece of supporting evidence.
5. Make at least one suggestion for improving the application.

**Editing** When you have finished revising your application based on your partner's suggestions, proofread your draft for errors in spelling, punctuation, grammar, and mechanics. Then write your final nomination, with the title of the award, the date, and the names of the nominee and nominator at the top of the page, as shown in the sample application below.

Here is one student's application.

Herot Award for Heroism

**STUDENT MODEL** ▶

An annual literary award for the character who exhibits the highest degree of bravery and heroism in the face of overwhelming odds.

Date of Application: October 19, 19—
Nominee's Name: Marguerite Duras from The War: A Memoir
Nominator's Name: Juan Mendez, English 401

In the space provided below, state the nature of this person's actions and why you believe he or she should

receive the Herot Award for Heroism. Give at least three
reasons in support of your candidate's nomination.

   The actions of one woman provide the most outstanding
example of heroism in the face of overwhelming odds. The
greatest act of heroism occurs when someone willingly
puts his or her life on the line so that others may live.
My nominee, Marguerite Duras, the French writer who
worked for the Resistance in occupied Paris, repeatedly
put her own life in jeopardy to help others escape
arrest, murder, and deportation by the Nazis. For
example, she kept close track of a major Nazi
collaborator, even though she often feared that this
traitor, M. Rabier, would turn her in. As she said in her
diary, ''Rabier ought to do all he can to remove . . . the
most dangerous witness against him: a writer, the wife of
a member of the Resistance. Me. But he doesn't.'' So she
continued collecting information from him about trains
and troop movements, about the advance of the Allies, and
about impending arrests.
   Another reason for selecting Duras as the Herot Hero of
the Year is her refusal to trade her husband's life for
the location of an important Resistance member. Although
she knew her husband would probably die at Dachau, she
refused to turn in her fellow Resistance fighter.
Instead she replied simply, ''Even if I knew him it would
be disgusting of me to tell you what you ask.''

## Presenting

   Your teacher or classmates should select a panel of five to seven
judges to read the nominations. After all the nomination applications for
the candidates have been read and evaluated, the judges should decide
which candidate should receive the heroism award.

## Reflecting on Your Writing

   Write your answers to the following questions and attach them to your
paper. Put both papers in your writing portfolio.

1. What was the most difficult part of the writing process for you?
2. What part of your nomination do you think is well written? Why?
3. What part of your writing do you think you need to improve?

# LANGUAGE
## WORKSHOP

## AVOIDING FRAGMENTS AND RUN-ONS

> A **sentence** is a group of words that expresses a complete thought. It contains both a subject and a predicate. A **sentence fragment** is only part of a sentence and expresses only part of a thought. A fragment may be missing the subject, the predicate, or both.

## Sentence Fragments

Your goal as a writer is to communicate your ideas to your readers. Unless you provide the appropriate information, your readers will be confused and unable to understand your message.

One source of confusion is the sentence that contains incomplete information. From such a sentence fragment, a reader can only guess at what the writer means.

You already know that a sentence needs both a subject and a predicate. When either (or both) is missing, the result is a fragment. Fragments usually occur because the writer is in a hurry. To correct a sentence fragment, you must add the missing information.

**Fragment**    Ripped off Grendel's claws. (In this case the subject is missing, and the reader is left wondering, *Who ripped off Grendel's claws?)*

**Sentence**    Beowulf ripped off Grendel's claws.

**Fragment**    Beowulf, using only his bare hands. (Now, because the predicate is missing, the reader wonders what Beowulf did using his bare hands.)

**Sentence**    Beowulf, using only his bare hands, overpowered the mighty Grendel.

**Exercise 1**   Identify each group of words below as a *Sentence* or a *Fragment.* Then add words to make each fragment a sentence.

1. Beowulf's men unsuccessfully attacked Grendel with swords.
2. In the early Middle Ages. Only wealthy and powerful men owned swords.

3. Often handed down from generation to generation.
4. Swords were generally about two and a half feet long. With double edges.
5. The fancy decoration on the hilt, or handle, of the sword identified its owner.

# Run-on Sentences

> A **run-on sentence** is made up of two or more sentences written as though they were one sentence.

Rather than having too little information, a run-on sentence has too much. That makes it just the opposite of a sentence fragment.

Run-ons occur when two or more sentences are written incorrectly as one. You probably know someone who talks on and on without stopping, until the listener becomes tired and tunes out. A run-on sentence, going on and on without a punctuation break, can create the same problem for a reader: eventually he or she tunes out because the words stop making sense.

There are two kinds of run-ons. In the first, two or more sentences are run together without any punctuation marks to separate them. In the second, the author incorrectly separates the sentences with a comma instead of a period. This type of run-on is sometimes called a **comma splice.** To eliminate run-ons, end each complete thought with a period or other end mark and begin the next idea with a capital letter.

**PUNCTUATION**

End marks are punctuation marks that indicate the end of a sentence. The period (.), question mark (?), and exclamation point (!) are end marks.

| | |
|---|---|
| **Run-on** | *Beowulf* is an old English epic the tale was based on Norse legend and sixth-century historical events. |
| **Correct** | *Beowulf* is an old English epic. The tale was based on Norse legend and sixth-century historical events. |
| **Comma Splice** | Danish invaders brought the oral tradition of epic poetry to England, *Beowulf* was finally written down by an unknown poet around 700. |
| **Correct** | Danish invaders brought the oral tradition of epic poetry to England. *Beowulf* was finally written down by an unknown poet around 700. |

**Exercise 2**   Correct the following run-on sentences. Be sure to punctuate the revised sentences correctly.

Say It Aloud!

Sometimes you can spot run-on sentences by reading your writing aloud. Notice where you pause naturally at the end of a complete thought. Be sure you have used the correct punctuation at that point.

1. Beowulf named his sword Naegling, his sword was a source of great pride for him.
2. Less wealthy soldiers carried spears with iron tips and round wooden shields they fought bloody battles on foot.
3. Soldiers on the losing side were expected to die on the battlefield, if they won, soldiers were expected to share their new wealth.
4. Warriors led a violent life, mead-halls gave them a chance to relax.
5. The violence in the poem *Beowulf* may reflect real life in the Middle Ages, on the other hand, the writer of *Beowulf* may have known how to please an audience with great drama.

**Exercise 3**   Copy the following paragraph on a piece of paper, correcting the fragments and run-ons it contains.

Collaborative Learning

This exercise may be done in groups. One person should take notes to record the revised sentences.

Ordinary people often act as heroes, a hero acts in a moment of danger, while others merely watch. Although the watcher sees a situation and is concerned about it, he or she may not be able to move. The speed of reaction is very important, a hero reacts quickly, sometimes without thinking the watcher reacts slowly. Or sometimes not at all. The ability to think fast and to act quickly. Separates a hero and a watcher.

**Exercise 4 Style**   Fragments are often used in personal writing and in notetaking. Most writers also use fragments to make their dialogue sound natural. Some professional writers even use fragments regularly as part of their writing style.

In small groups skim through the selections you have read or through other writing, looking for fragments. Write down five fragments you find. Try turning them into sentences. Discuss the writer's possible reasons for using fragments, how their use affects the tone of the writing, and how the writing would be different if fragments were not used.

**Exercise 5 Analyzing and Revising Your Writing**

1. Review the writing you have done for this subunit.
2. Write down and correct any sentence fragments or run-on sentences that you find. Punctuate them correctly.
3. If you have written dialogue, or conversation between characters, you might allow any fragments to remain. Make sure, however, that the fragments reflect what speakers would naturally say to each other.
4. Remember to check for fragments and run-ons the next time you proof your work.

Language Handbook

For review and practice:
subjects/predicates,
    page 974
fragments,
    pages 975–76
run-on sentences,
    pages 976–77
end marks,
    pages 1035–37

# VOCABULARY
## WORKSHOP

## HISTORY OF ENGLISH

Anyone who has wrestled with the rules of English grammar has wondered why everything is so complicated. Why can't all verbs form the past tense by adding *-ed?* Why can't all nouns form the plural by adding *-s?* Why is every rule followed by at least one exception?

The answer is that English has evolved over nearly fifteen hundred years. It has been shaped and reshaped by changes in usage and contact with other languages. As a result, it is full of inconsistencies.

About fifteen hundred years ago, the Angles, Jutes, and Saxons—three tribes from what is now Germany and Denmark—invaded a small island off the coast of Europe. The Angles called their prize the "land of the Angles," which eventually became *Angle-land,* and then *England.*

The languages spoken by the Angles, Jutes, and Saxons are the ancestors of modern English. About forty-five hundred modern English words come directly from this so-called **Old English**—including words like *fire, word, drink, life,* and *house.* The great epic poem *Beowulf,* full of demons, monsters, fire-breathing dragons, and mighty warriors, was put in written form in Old English, sometime around the year 700.

Two hundred years or so after *Beowulf* was written down, England was invaded again, this time by the Vikings, fierce seafaring raiders from what is now Norway and Sweden. Although the Vikings did not remain in England, many of their words found their way into English. The last great invasion of England came in the eleventh century in the year 1066. This time the invaders, the Normans, came from what is now France, and they too left their mark on the English language.

For the next few hundred years, what is now called **Middle English** was spoken. English continued to change, however, until the 1600's. By then the language looked and sounded very much as it does now. No language is static, however, and English continues to change. New words are added, while old words die or their meanings change. Who knows what the speech of students in the year 3000 will sound like?

**Exercise**   See if you can match the following Old English words with their modern equivalents.

| **Old English** | | **Modern English** | |
|---|---|---|---|
| ceorfan | boc | home | blaze |
| blaese | faeder | night | book |
| ham | neaht | carve | father |

# A CODE OF CHIVALRY

In today's world, *chivalry* is a synonym for courtesy and good manners. In the Middle Ages, however, chivalry meant much more. It defined a strict code of behavior for knights and all those who wished to follow their example. Chivalry's high standards included bravery, honor, virtue, protection of the weak, and fair treatment of the enemy.

As you read each selection, determine whether or not the characters live up to the high expectations set forth in the code of chivalry. Also consider whether a concept of chivalry from the Middle Ages can or should be applied to people of other times and places.

*Fiction*

*from* Sir Gawain
and the Green Knight

*Translated by* Y.R. PONSOR

## Examine What You Know

The Knights of the Round Table are the subject of many poems, stories, movies, and books. In a concept map like the one below, jot down what you know about knights. Add to your map as you learn more in the story.

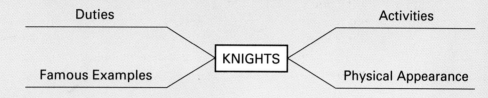

## Expand Your Knowledge

During the Middle Ages, knights were a select group of armed warriors who were given land in exchange for military service to the king. Along with the honor of knighthood came a **code of chivalry**, or standard of behavior, that knights were expected to follow. A knight was expected to behave with respect and politeness toward everyone and to protect his land, its workers, and women. Should the king be threatened, the knight was required to come to his aid.

The legend of King Arthur, supposedly the source of chivalry, has some basis in history; Arthur probably lived during the sixth century. Legends about him grew to include supernatural events and magical spells. Sir Gawain, Arthur's nephew, was involved in the formation of the Round Table, King Arthur's knights who had discussions around a round table.

## Enrich Your Reading

**Making Predictions**   Most stories provide clues that help you predict what is going to happen next. To make a prediction as you read, put together facts from the story with what you already know from experience. Decide where the events are leading and predict the next logical step. Your prediction may not always be right, however, because good stories often contain surprise outcomes.

In this story you will find questions inserted in the text that ask you to make predictions. Jot down your predictions and check them later.

■ *A biography of the author can be found on page 89.*

LA BELLE DAME SANS MERCI 1893 John William Waterhouse
Hessisches Landesmuseum, Darmstadt, Germany.

# *from* Sir Gawain and the Green Knight

*Translated by* Y. R. PONSOR

## Chapter 1

Winter lay upon the land. Cold held forest and field in its grim clutch, and in the night sky the stars glittered like gems. The wolf slid from shadow to shadow, stalking hapless prey, falling upon the unwary with death in his fangs. Deep in caverns the great trolls and other monsters mumbled in uneasy sleep, seeking warmth. Over moor and fen[1] the mists rose and fell, and strange sounds troubled the chill silence.

But on the hill, lights gleamed in the castle. In the court of Camelot were gathered all the brothers-in-arms of the Table Round and their fair highborn ladies to celebrate the Christmas season. A full fifteen days it was then, a time of merriment and mirth and rich revel. Laughter rang loud through the halls, and all the music and delight that the mind of man might devise. With merrymaking and glee the company welcomed the New Year, exchanging gifts and calling out glad Noel.

On this New Year's day, fresh and crispcold, twice the usual number of celebrants crowded the great hall; and the most noble, the fairest, and most famous was Arthur himself, the most honorable man who ever ruled a court or led an army into battle. This king was a man of the greatest good will and generosity of soul,

and it would be difficult to imagine a bolder company than that one gathered in the castle on the hill.

Among the group on the high dais[2] facing the great hall lined with tables of noble knights was Guenevere, Arthur's wife, the comeliest maid, the gracious lady of the gleaming gray eyes. Her silken garments sparkled with rich jewels, and her golden hair shone as softly as her eyes. With her sat the young Gawain, with Agravaine the Stronghand on the other side; both were the king's nephews and worthy knights who had proved their prowess many times in test and trial. At the head of the table sat the chief of all bishops in Cornwall, the saintly Bedwin, and with him, Urien's son Iwain.

But Arthur, full of his own happiness and childlike in his joy, would not sit until all were served. For most of all he loved life, its joys and its adventures, and his eager brain and young blood would not allow him to lie abed or sit around lazily. And besides, he had taken upon himself a vow that on this special day of all days, he would not eat until a rare tale of

---

1. **fen:** a marsh or swamp.
2. **dais** (dā′ is; *often* dī′-): a raised platform.

ancestors and arms and high adventure were told, or some grand marvel might be devised, or a challenge of knights to join in jeopardy, jousting life for life as fortune might favor. So he stood before the high table, speaking of trifles and laughing at the noise and fine festival of his free men as the first course was announced with the crackling of trumpets, with drums and tuneful pipers. In the corner a bard[3] awakened the lute[4] and many a heart lifted with his touch upon the strings. Then came the platters piled high with fine food, venison and other meats, and great bowls of soup, and a plenty of strong beer and fine red wine. And all drank and ate as much as they wanted.

Hardly had the first course been finished when the great hall door crashed open and in rode a terrifying knight. He must have been the hugest man on earth, so broad and thick from neck to waist, so long of leg and strong of arm that I half thought him a giant, except for his fine features of face. Everyone knows that giants are hideous to look upon, besides being fearful in size. At sight of him, all in the hall fell silent, struck dumb by this apparition. For this bold man, from toe to top, in clothes and in <u>countenance</u>, was bright green.

Believe me: all garbed in green, this man, and all his trappings. He wore a tight coat with a heavy mantle adorned with ermine,[5] the same fur lining the hood that had fallen from his head and lay upon his shoulders. Green were the stockings on his legs, and decorated with gold embroidery, and bright golden spurs on his feet, and shoes with upturned toes. His belt was set with gleaming jewels, all emerald green, and indeed they were scattered over all his <u>array</u> and that of his horse, the saddle and bridle and reins, all <u>gaudy</u> in gold and green. The trappings of the horse,

the breast-cloth and bits and bridle, even the stirrups in which he stood, all were enameled and gleamed goldenly, and the green gems glittered like the eyes of a cat. The steed itself which he straddled was a great heavy horse, hard to hold; and it was the same green as the man who rode it.

Gloriously was this man outfitted in green, and the hair of his head as green as his horse. It fanned out full and fell to his shoulders, and he had a heavy beard which reached his chest. It gleamed green upon the leather tunic.[6] Such a pair had never before been seen on earth, nor since that time! Everyone said he looked as bright as a flash of lightning, and, indeed, who could withstand his stroke! He wore neither helm[7] nor hauberk[8]—no, no coat of mail did he wear, nor want!—and he carried no weapons, neither spear nor shield to smite or to save. But in his hand he carried a bough of holly, that branch which is greenest when all others are bare; and in his other hand an ax, heavy and horrid, a cruel weapon right out of a nightmare. The head measured at least an arm's length, and was of green steel worked with gold, the bit burnished bright, the broad edge honed to shear as closely as a sharp razor. The steel of the haft[9] which he held in his hand was wrapped with iron wire to its very end, graven with green in delicate design. A thong bound it about and fastened at the head where it was tasseled and braided with bright green.

---

3. **bard:** a poet and singer.
4. **lute:** a stringed musical instrument, similar to a guitar.
5. **ermine:** the soft, white fur of certain weasels.
6. **tunic:** a loose, coatlike garment.
7. **helm:** a helmet.
8. **hauberk** (hô′ bərk): a coat of armor.
9. **haft:** a handle.

| *Words to Know and Use* | **countenance** (koun′ tə nəns) *n.* facial features <br> **array** (ə rā′) *n.* clothes <br> **gaudy** (gôd′ ē) *adj.* flashy; dazzling; showy |
| --- | --- |

 **What does the Green Knight plan to do with his ax?**

This knight moved through the great hall's silent crowd right up to the high table, and he feared no danger, greeted no one, but looked straight ahead. Then he reined in his horse and faced the room. He stared boldly at the knights, looking them up and down, and his voice thundered when he spoke.

"Where is the leader of this company? I would like to see him and to speak in courtesy with him, as the rules of chivalry require."

He waited and looked at them and considered who might among this company be the most renowned.

Everyone stared at him in wonder, marveling as to what his appearance might mean, how such a knight and such a horse might be such a strange color, green as growing grass, and glowing with enamel and gold. Everyone studied him as he sat there on his horse, and they walked cautiously around him with all the wonder in the world as to what he might do. Many strange things had they seen, but never any such as this. Possibly a phantom, or some fey[10] creature, they deemed him to be, for green is a magic color. But all of these brave knights feared to question him and, stunned at his voice, were dumbstruck. A heavy silence filled the royal chamber, and all those who had been chattering sat as if caught in a dream—some, I suppose, out of politeness, some out of uneasiness, and some in fear, but let another man decide which!

Then Arthur, standing before the dais, greeted him, and bowed courteously, for he was never rude, and said,

"Fair knight, welcome to this place. I am Arthur, the chief of this company. Alight and rest, I beg you, and whatsoever your will may be, we shall be glad to learn."

"No, God is my witness that to waste time in idle talk is not my errand," replied the knight. "But your fame, lord, is raised high, and through town and countryside you are regarded as the best and bravest ever to ride in battle gear, the noblest and the finest of the world's kind. You are all known to be valiant in dealing with all sorts of adventures, and your hall is known for courtliness.[11] Many tales of this company have reached my ears, and that is what has brought me hither at this special time.

"You may see by this branch which I bear here that I have come in peace, seeking no trouble; for had I fared forth in a frame of mind to fight, I would have brought helm and hauberk, and shield and bright-shining spear, and other weapons to wield also. But because I seek no strife, I am dressed as you see. But if you are as brave as everyone says, you will gladly grant me the game that I ask as a guest's right."

And Arthur answered, "Gentle knight, if you crave combat, you will not fail to find it here."

"No, I seek no contest, as I have told you, especially since I see on these benches only beardless children! If I were geared up for fighting and mounted on my high steed, there is no man here who could match me." And he looked upon them with scorn. "I seek in this court only a Christmas game, for it is Yule and the New Year, and the time to exchange gifts. If there should be any in this hall who considers himself brave enough in heart, hot enough in blood, or quick enough of wit that he would dare exchange stroke for stroke with me, let him come forth. I will give him as my gift this fine heavy ax—heavy enough it is to do his will!—and I shall take the first blow as bare as

---

10. **fey** (fā): strange or unusual.

11. **courtliness:** adherence to certain standards of behavior expected of members of a king's court.

here I sit. If any of these fine warriors may be so bold as to accept my challenge, let him step forth and seize this weapon. I quitclaim it forever, and he may keep it as his own, and I shall kneel before him and stand him a stroke. And then you will grant me the right to deal him an equal blow, though I will give him respite of a year and a day. Now let any man who dares speak quickly."

## Chapter 2

If the people had been astonished at first, now they all, high and low throughout the hall, sat as if turned to stone. The knight on his steed twisted in the saddle, his red eyes flashing around the room, his green hair flying with each movement of his head. Then he sat still, staring at them and stroking his beard as the silence lengthened. When no one spoke, he stood in his stirrups and, shaking his fist above his head, he shouted at them.

"What is this? Is this Arthur's court and castle, of which the whole world sings praises? Where now is your pride? Where is your fighting spirit? Where now your fierceness and game and all your fine words? Now is the reputation and glory of the Round Table overthrown by the mere words of one man, without a single blow being struck, because you are afraid to answer!"

*predict* Will any of the knights respond to this insult?

Then the blood shot for shame into Arthur's face, and he turned as angry as a stormwind, as indeed did all of them. Men muttered and surged forward in anger, half-rising from their places, white with wrath. But Arthur held up his hand and sprang to face the green man.

"Sir, by heaven! Seek no further! As you in your own folly have asked, so shall it be! No man here is afraid of your boasts. Give me your ax, and with God's help, I shall break every bone in your body. I myself accept your challenge and will meet your terms."

The Green Knight laughed aloud and leaped lightly from his horse and landed before Arthur, taller by head and shoulders than any man in the court. The king seized the ax and gripped the handle tightly and waved it about, striking this way and that to test its feel. The knight calmly removed his mantle and then his short coat, no more dismayed by the threatening blows than if some man had brought him a glass of wine.

Then Gawain, who sat by the queen, called out, "I beseech you, uncle, to grant me a kindness. Let this contest be mine. Gentle lord, give me permission to leave this table and stand in your place there. If I may without discourtesy—if my liege lady[12] will not take it amiss—I would presume to counsel you before your royal court." He stood up and spoke clearly. "I think it is not seemly that such a challenge should be raised in this high chamber, much less that you yourself should so valiantly choose to answer it while so many brave warriors remain on these benches. No better men can be found on any field of battle, nor any more skillful in arms. All men know that I am the least brave, and the feeblest of wit, and the least deserving to be of this company. In truth, it is only because I am your nephew that

---

12. **liege lady** (lēj-): a term of respect; Gawain is acknowledging his allegiance and loyalty to Lady Guenevere.

I am worthy at all; I know no bounty but your blood in my body. And since this business is so foolish and trivial, none of it should concern you at all.

"So I ask: Let it come to me, and if I fail in its performance, then the fault is in me and no blame shall fall on this court."

Arthur moved from table to table consulting with his nobles, as is the custom in such cases, and all agreed that the king should retire from the contest and give Gawain the game.

Gawain turned and bowed to the gray-eyed Guenevere and she smiled on him, and he came down from the dais and, kneeling before his king, he received the ax from Arthur's hands. And Arthur smiled affectionately upon him and raised his hand and asked God's blessing, praying that both Gawain's heart and his hand should be strong.

"Be careful, nephew," he said softly, "and set yourself for the stroke. If you direct it properly, I am sure that you will be able to bear the burden of the blow which he will later inflict." And Arthur removed himself and went and leaned against the edge of the dais and watched eagerly.

Gawain walked, ax in hand, to the Green Knight, who had been waiting patiently. He looked upon Gawain and he said, "Now, let us reaffirm our bargain before we go on. But first I would ask you, sir, what is your name?"

"I am Gawain," the young man said. "It is Gawain who gives you this blow, whatever may happen afterwards. One year from now, you may return the favor with whatever weapon you wish, asking leave of no one else."

"By God," shouted the other, "it pleases me greatly that I should receive this blow from your hands. You have rightly repeated the covenant which I made with your king—except that you must seek me, friend, where-soever you think I may be found, pledging to come alone, and return to me such wages as you deal to me today before this court."

"And where shall I look for you? Where is your home? I know neither your kingdom nor your name, kith nor kin. Tell me your realm and name and I shall certainly find you. That I swear on my honor."

"No," said the green man, "nothing more is necessary now. But I promise that when I have taken your blow, if you strike squarely, then I will tell you how to find me so that you may fulfill our bargain."

Then he laughed.

"If I do not speak, then so much the better for you; you can stay in your own land and light no wayfarer's fires. But enough! Take up your weapon and let us see how you handle an ax!"

"Sir," said Gawain, "I will," and he stroked the edge of the ax.

What will happen when Gawain chops off the Green Knight's head?   *predict*

The Green Knight knelt on the floor and bent his head and gathered his long, thick hair in one hand and drew it over the crown of his head. His bare neck shone whitely. Gawain set himself, left foot forward on the floor. He grasped the ax and lifted it aloft, and he brought it down like a lightning bolt upon the bare neck. The sharp steel sliced through the pale flesh and sundered the bones and sheared it in half, and the steel blade buried itself in the floor with a great ringing crash.

The fair head flew from the shoulders and rolled about near the tables, and some of the knights kicked at it with their feet, a grim, grisly game. Blood burst from the body, red gleaming on green. The knight did not falter or fall, but at once he sprang up on his strong legs and jumped into the crowd and snatched up his head by the hair and lifted it high for all to see. Then, striding to his horse, he caught up the reins, stepped into the stirrups and sat aloft, still holding his head high in one hand.

And they say that he sat in his saddle as though nothing whatever ailed him, headless though he was. He twisted from side to side, turning that hideous, still-bleeding body in the saddle. Those who watched in fear were even more horrified to see that he was about to speak.

He turned the grim face toward the high table, and the head lifted up its eyelids and looked at them. Then it looked at Gawain and the mouth moved and the lips spoke.

"Look to it, Gawain, that you do as you have sworn, and seek faithfully until you find me. All men know me as the knight of the Green Chapel. To the Green Chapel you must come, I charge you, to receive such a blow as you have dealt here to me today. You will find me if you try. If you fail to come, coward shall you be called by the whole world."

With a quick movement he pulled his horse around and fled through the great door, still head-in-hand, and the fire from the hooves of his flint-shod steed flashed through the hall. What native land he would return to, none there knew, any more than they knew from whence he had come. In a moment a roar of astonishment filled the hall, and Arthur and Gawain burst into laughter at the strange event. All agreed that it had been a marvel among men.

Although Arthur, ever the wise king, had a great uneasiness in his heart, he did not let a hint of it be seen, but he spoke to his queen with courtly speech.

"Dearest lady, let not today dismay you. Often such a magic and wondrous event occurs at this season, along with the music of minstrels and the laughter of lovely ladies and brave knights."

SIR GAWAIN BEHEADS THE GREEN KNIGHT, WATCHED BY KING ARTHUR AND QUEEN GUINEVERE 14th century Illuminated manuscript British Museum, London.

And he touched her hand gently and gazed into her eyes. Then he sat back, looked around the room, and cried out, "Now at last I may address myself to my dinner, for I have certainly seen a marvel, I must admit."

He smiled at Gawain with love shining on his fair face and he said, "Hang up your ax, nephew, it has done its work for today." And it was placed on the wall above the high table where all might admire and wonder at the sight and the strange adventure. Then they sat down again at the tables, each to his place, king and knights, and the servants brought double portions of all the best dishes and with all manner of good will they passed the rest of the evening.

But be sure, Sir Gawain, that fear does not cause you to fail in this test, this challenge which you yourself have taken into your own hands!

Will Gawain survive his meeting with the Green Knight in a year?

*The year passes rapidly and soon Sir Gawain sets out to find the Knight of the Green Chapel. Near Christmas he stops at a castle where the lord offers him hospitality and a chance to rest before his encounter with the Green Knight.*

*Each day the lord departs to hunt, while Gawain remains behind with the lady of the castle, who seems intent on seducing the young knight. The men have agreed to exchange what each has won during the day, and so, at the end of the first day, the lord gives Gawain a deer, and Gawain gives the lord a kiss. The second night, the lord gives Gawain a boar's, or wild pig's, head; Gawain gives him two kisses. On the third evening the lord gives Gawain a fox. Gawain gives the lord three kisses but not the magical green silk scarf that the lady has given him as protection. True to the chivalric code, Gawain has not betrayed the lord; however, he feels guilty about keeping the green scarf. He wears it as he rides out from the castle to his meeting with the Knight of the Green Chapel.*

*At a bubbling brook Gawain hears someone sharpening a scythe; the person turns out to be the Green Knight. Gawain offers himself to the knight who moves as if to deliver a fatal blow to Gawain's neck. Gawain flinches slightly, and the Green Knight reproaches him for his cowardice.*

*Gawain asks for a second chance. Again the Green Knight brings down his ax but stops before the blade hits Gawain. This time Gawain does not flinch. The Green Knight then tells Gawain to bare his throat. Gawain complies and the Green Knight nicks his neck. Gawain leaps up and prepares to defend himself, as he has now fulfilled the terms of their agreement.*

# *Chapter 11*

The Green Knight turned from him and leaned upon his ax, set the shaft to the ground and leaned upon the blade and looked at the lad who waited there. How <u>steadfast</u>, how fearless, and how bold he looked, how ready for battle! And he was pleased in his heart. He laughed with a ringing voice and spoke happily with the lad.

"Bold knight, upon this field of honor be not so fierce! No man here has used you dishonorably, nor treated you discourteously, but only as the decree at Arthur's court allowed. I owed you a stroke and you took it, so hold yourself well paid. I release you of any remnant of all other rights. If I had been more nimble, perhaps I could have wrought you a more harmful blow. First, I merely menaced you with a pretended blow and cut you with no cruel blade. That was for the agreement we made on that first night when you faithfully gave me the day's gains, as an honest man would. That second pretended blow was for the second day when you kissed my dear wife, which kisses you gave to me. And for both of those I offered you but two scant blows without scathe. For an honorable man is true to his word and he needs fear no danger.

"But on the third day you failed in that honor, and therefore you took that tap on the neck."

He looked at Gawain steadily, and Gawain at him, still as stone. And the green man continued.

"It is my garment you wear, that green silken girdle.[13] My own wife offered it to you, I know. Ah, I know all about those kisses and

---

13. **girdle:** a belt or scarf.

your character also, and the wooing of my wife! I wrought all this myself. I sent her to test you. Truly I think that you must be the most faultless man that ever walked the earth. As a pearl in purity is to white peas, so is Gawain in virtue to all famous knights. But you fell short a little there, sir; you failed in faith. But it was not for intrigue, nor for lawless lust either, but because you loved your life, and I cannot blame you for that."

Gawain still stood like one stunned, so aggrieved with embarrassment that he cried for anguish inside. All the blood of his body burned in his face and he shrank for shame as the green man talked. He took off his helm and held it in his hands. At last he spoke wrathfully.

 Gawain is ashamed. What will he do?

"Cursed be both cowardice and covetousness! In them is villainy and vice that destroys virtue!" And he caught up the pentangle[14] and tore it loose and flung it roughly down. "Lo!—there is breaking of faith. Foul be its fall! I coveted my life and cowardice led me into fault for fear of your blow, made me forsake my nature, the generosity and loyalty that are a true knight's." And he bowed his head and wept bitterly. "Now am I false indeed and from fear have I fallen into treachery and deceit. Both bring only sorrow and shame. I confess to you, sir, here on this spot, that I have indeed been false to you in my conduct. If you will but allow me to regain your good will, I shall guard against its happening again."

Then the Green Knight laughed and said amiably: "I consider it entirely acquitted, any harm that I had. You have confessed freely and are aware of your failing and you have stood the sharp penance of my sword. I hold you cleansed of that fault and made as pure as if you had never transgressed since your birth. And I give you, sir, as a gift, that very scarf, as green as my own robe." He touched the silk at Gawain's waist lightly, and laid an arm across his shoulders.

"Sir Gawain, you may think upon this particular contest as you fare forth among the great and chivalrous knights of this world. Let this be the clear token of the adventure of the Green Chapel." Then he laughed and said merrily, "Now, you shall in this New Year come back again to my dwelling and we shall revel away the remainder of this festal time. With my wife, I promise, we shall certainly reconcile you, she who you thought was your keen enemy."

Will Gawain accept the invitation to party at the Green Knight's castle?

"No," said Gawain, and he took up his helm and looked sadly at the green man. "This has been a sorrowful journey. Good fortune betide you and may He who ordains all honor grant it to you! And commend me to that gracious lady, your comely companion, and the other lady, both the honored ladies who so cunningly beguiled this knight with their tricks.

"It is no great marvel to be made a fool of or to be won to sorrow through the wiles of a woman; for so was Adam, the first man on

---

14. **pentangle:** a five-pointed star; Gawain's golden pentangle had symbolized his virtue.

---

*Words to Know and Use*

**intrigue** (in' trēg') *n.* a secret plot; scheme
**amiably** (ā' mē ə blē, ām' yə-) *adv.* in a good-natured way
**transgress** (trans gres') *v.* to do wrong; to sin
**reconcile** (rek' ən sīl') *v.* to make friends again
**beguile** (bē gīl', bi-) *v.* to trick

84

earth beguiled; and Solomon[15] by many and various women; and Samson also, Delilah[16] dealt him his wyrd![17] David was deluded by Bathsheba[18] and suffered much woe. All these men were brought to disaster by woman's wiles.

"It would be a great gain to love them and yet to believe them not. But no man can do that. For these were the noblest men of old, all blessed above other men and yet they were all beguiled by women with whom they had dealings. To find myself in that company I think must be excused." Then he shook off sad thoughts.

"But your girdle I will accept with a right good will, not for the bright gold, nor for its magic"—here Gawain blushed again—"nor for the silk or fringed sides, nay, not for worth nor worship nor noble works. But as a symbol of my transgression I shall keep it always with me, a reminder, when I ride in renown, of the fault and frailty of feeble flesh, how suscepti-ble it is to the stains of evil. And when pride of prowess inflates me, the sight of this will humble my heart.

"But one request I make, if it does not displease you: Since you are the lord of that land where I stayed with such pleasure, thanks to you, will you tell me your name? Only that and no more?"

"That I shall, certainly," replied the green man. "I am called Bercilak de Hautdesert in this land. Through the power of Morgan le Fay, who lives in my house and has the skill of magical lore, all of this has happened. Morgan, the beautiful, the mistress of Merlin— many men has she taken, for she has had love dealings with that excellent wizard who knows all the knights of your court. Morgan the goddess is also her name. There is none so high in power or pride that she cannot tame!

"She sent me in that manner to your royal court in order to test the pride of its men, to see if the reputation of the Round Table were true. She sent me in that strange way to take away your wits and to frighten the fair Guenevere, to make her die with fear at the sight of that man who spoke with his head in his hand before that Table High. She took the form of that old one in my house, the ancient lady; she is in fact your aunt, the half-sister of Arthur, daughter of the Duchess of Tintagel, that lady upon whom the mighty Uther later fathered Arthur, who is your king.

"Therefore I entreat you, dear man, to come to your aunt and rejoice in my house. My court loves you, and I do as well, indeed, as any man under heaven."

But Gawain still refused. He would not under any conditions. So they embraced in friendship and saluted each other as fine princes and parted right there in the cold. Gawain, mounted on his fine horse, hastened homeward to Arthur's court and the Green Knight wended wheresoever he would.

Gawain rode then through many wild ways in the world on Gringolet. He had been given back his life, a fine gift indeed, and many a

---

15. **Solomon:** king of Israel known for his great wisdom; according to the Bible, God punished Solomon for dabbling in the religions of his many wives.

16. **Samson and Delilah:** By taking advantage of Samson's love for her, Delilah discovered the mysterious source of Samson's legendary strength— his hair—and revealed the secret to his enemies, the Philistines.

17. **wyrd:** deathblow.

18. **David and Bathsheba:** David fell in love with Bathsheba, the wife of Uriah, an army captain. As king of Israel, David arranged for Uriah to be positioned in the midst of fierce fighting to ensure his death in battle. David and Bathsheba married after Uriah's death, but God punished David for his actions.

---

*Words to Know and Use* | **susceptible** (sə sep′ tə bəl) *adj.* easily influenced; vulnerable

thought he gave to that strange event as he traveled. Sometimes he harbored in a house and sometimes out of doors. He had many adventures in the valley and he vanquished many, but I will not take time to tell all that in this tale.

The wound in his neck healed and he wore the green belt fastened like a baldric[19] at his side, tied under his left arm, the end in a knot, as token of the fact that he was guilty of sin. And thus at last he came to the court, did Gawain the good knight.

Happiness sped through those halls when it was learned that Gawain had returned. Everyone thought it was a fine thing, indeed, and somewhat unlooked for. The king kissed the knight and the queen did also, and many knights sought him out to salute him and make inquiry of his wayfaring fortune. And he told the wondrous tale and confessed everything that had happened, the adventure at the chapel, the good will of the green man, the love of the lady, and the silk that he wore. He showed them the scar that he bore on his neck, the sign of his shameful disloyalty to the green man. He suffered when he told them and groaned with grief and mortification, and the blood burned in his face for shame when he spoke of it.

"Lo, lord," said Gawain to Arthur, as he held forth the silk, "here is the band of blame which I bear like the scar on my neck. This is the offense and the loss, the cowardice and covetousness that caught me there. This is the symbol of falsity in which I was taken. I will wear it all my life, for no one may hide his misdeed, nor may he undo it. Once guilt has touched a man, he is never free of it again."

And the king comforted the knight and all the court laughed and lovingly agreed on the spot that each man of the Table Round should henceforth wear such a baldric, the slanting ribbon of bright green, for the sake of that beloved man, and they would wear it with delight. And so it came to be accorded as the renown of the court and always afterwards anyone who wore it was especially honored.

So in Arthur's day this adventure occurred, as books of romance will witness. Many strange and curious wonders have happened in Britain since the days of Brutus,[20] whose race came from Troy.[21] But surely this tale of Gawain and his contest with the Green Knight in a trial of honor and faith is one of the most wondrous. ❧

---

19. **baldric:** a belt worn over one shoulder and across the chest to support a sword, bugle, and so on.

20. **Brutus:** according to legend, the first king of Britain, great-grandson of Aeneas, a hero of the Trojan war.

21. **Troy:** ancient city in northwest Asia Minor, a large peninsula in west Asia between the Black Sea and the Mediterranean Sea.

*Words to Know and Use* | **vanquish** (van′ kwish, van′-) *v.* to conquer; defeat

# e x p l a i n

## Responding to Reading ─────────────

### First Impressions

**1.** What was your favorite part of the story?

### Second Thoughts

**2.** Which of the predictions you made as you read were correct? What unexpected events and elements caused you to predict incorrectly?

**3.** Why does Gawain fight the Green Knight?

> **Think about**
> • the Green Knight's challenge and attitudes
> • why Gawain wants to fight
> • Arthur's response to Gawain's offer

**4.** After Gawain's test, Gawain says that he is guilty of "cowardice and covetousness." The Green Knight calls Gawain "the most faultless man . . . ever." Do you agree with either of their judgments? Explain.

**5.** Gawain says he fell into treachery and deceit because of fear. What do you think Gawain feared? Explain.

**6.** Based on this story, what is your opinion of King Arthur's code of chivalry? Did it serve any worthwhile purpose? Explain.

### Broader Connections

**7.** Gawain is faced with a difficult personal challenge. What personal challenges do you face in the future, such as graduating or getting a job? Think of the personal qualities necessary for meeting each challenge. Then develop a set of standards for a modern-day code of chivalry that could help you face these challenges.

## Literary Concept: Setting ─────────────

Some writers provide a vivid description of the **setting,** or the time and place of the story. Details that describe sights, sounds, and other aspects of the setting can help make a story come alive for you as the reader.

The first page of *Sir Gawain and the Green Knight* begins with a contrast between the bleak and cold forest outside the castle and the merry New Year's Day party inside the castle. Find phrases in both descriptions that appeal to your senses of sight and hearing. How do the descriptions and the contrast help set the mood of the party?

## *Writing Options*

1. Make a list of do's and don't's that might have been included in the knights' code of chivalry in the days of King Arthur.

2. A **symbol** is a person, place, or object that represents something beyond itself. For example, the monster Grendel in *Beowulf* might be a symbol of the evil in the world. What might Sir Gawain's green scarf symbolize? In a paragraph, explain your ideas on the meaning of the green scarf.

3. The Green Knight, Bercilak, says that he was sent by the enchantress Morgan le Fay to Arthur's court "to test the pride of its men, to see if the reputation of the Round Table were true." Write Bercilak's report to Morgan le Fay about how Arthur's knights succeeded in her test.

4. Suppose you were at a party today and a modern-day Green Knight came to make a challenge. What would he or she look like and say? Rewrite the challenge scene as it might happen today.

## *Vocabulary Practice*

**Exercise** Read each statement below. On your paper, write *Yes* if the boldfaced word is used correctly. Write *No* if the word is not used correctly, and be prepared to explain why.

1. The knights and ladies enjoyed the **revel** on New Year's Day.
2. Gawain had proven his **prowess** many times in test and trial.
3. The **countenance** of the Green Knight was covered in fur.
4. The Green Knight's fancy green-and-gold outfit was **gaudy**.
5. The Green Knight's **array** could be heard in his fearful voice.
6. It was shocking to the guests that the Green Knight would **presume** to challenge the knights in their own castle.
7. For Arthur, Gawain wanted to **reconcile** the Green Knight.
8. A knight might take it **amiss** if his wife seduced Gawain.
9. Gawain was **susceptible** to the charms of the lady of the castle.
10. Gawain looked **steadfast** as the first blow of the Green Knight made him flinch, or draw back, slightly.
11. Gawain showed **intrigue** as the Green Knight lowered the ax.
12. The ladies were able to **beguile** Gawain with their tricks.
13. As friends now, Gawain and Bercilak did not part **amiably**.
14. After the contest, Bercilak and his wife were not able to **vanquish** with Gawain.
15. Knowing that he could **transgress** showed Gawain that he was imperfect.

*Words to Know and Use*

———

amiably
amiss
array
beguile
countenance
gaudy
intrigue
presume
prowess
reconcile
revel
steadfast
susceptible
transgress
vanquish

## Options for Learning

**1** • **Heraldry** Research the subject of heraldry in the library to find information about the symbols and colors used in coats of arms. Then design a coat of arms for Sir Gawain, using the green scarf as one of his symbols. Explain why you chose each symbol and color.

**2** • **Illustrate the Classics** List the main events of the tale of *Sir Gawain and the Green Knight.* Then draw and write a comic book version that captures the adventure of the story. Check *Classics Illustrated* comics and the super-hero comics for different ways of doing this.

**3** • **Poetic License** Write a poem that tells the tale of Sir Gawain's adventure. Structure your poem in four-line stanzas, with each stanza telling a different part of the story. It may help you to refer to the poem "Robin Hood and the Three Squires" on pages 91–94. Read your poem for the class.

**4** • **Special Effects** In the library, research techniques used to create special effects in movies. Then imagine that you are the designer of special effects for the movie version of the story. Diagram and explain how you might create the effect of the Green Knight after he loses his head, continuing to move and talk. Explain your techniques to the class.

**FACT FINDER**

*The Knights of the Round Table searched for the Holy Grail. What was the Holy Grail?*

## The Gawain Poet

The original version of *Sir Gawain and the Green Knight* is a poem of more than twenty-five hundred lines. It is written in Middle English, the language of fourteenth-century medieval England. The identity of the poet has never been discovered. By studying the language as well as the customs and traditions mentioned in the poem, however, scholars have learned that the poet lived near Lancashire, England, during the second half of the fourteenth century. Since English has changed so much since that time, the original language is difficult to read and understand. Many people have translated the poem into modern English prose, as in the Y. R. Ponsor version in your text.

*Poetry*

# Robin Hood and the Three Squires

ANONYMOUS

## Examine What You Know

Because of countless books, stories, movies, and television programs about Robin Hood, many people have specific mental images of him. What do you visualize when you think of Robin Hood? his adventures? his companions? his enemies? Write down as many associations as you can. Compare notes with your classmates.

## Expand Your Knowledge

The first written ballads about Robin Hood appeared in the late fourteenth century, although his adventures were sung and told at least one hundred years earlier. Just as the Knights of the Round Table were the heroes of the upper classes, Robin Hood became the legendary champion of the commoners. He was brave, adventurous, and protected the poor, who were persecuted by powerful landowners. The legends also tell that the Sheriff of Nottingham, a cruel and corrupt government official, was Robin's most frequent enemy. There is some historical proof that Robin Hood actually existed. If he was a real person, it is likely that he lived in the Yorkshire and Nottinghamshire area of England, probably during the reigns of King Richard I and King John (1189–1216).

## Enrich Your Reading

**Using Quotation Marks in Dialogue**  This ballad contains a great deal of dialogue between Robin Hood and the people he meets. Whenever someone speaks, quotation marks ('' '') appear before and after the speaker's words. If you have trouble keeping track of who is speaking, make a chart like the one below. Fill in line numbers and the speaker's name each time you come to a set of words that begins and ends with quotation marks.

| Beginning and Ending Quotation Marks | Speaker |
|---|---|
| Lines 9–10 | Robin Hood |
| Lines 11–12 | old woman |

# Robin Hood and the Three Squires

ANONYMOUS

There are twelve months in all the year,
    As I hear many men say,
But the merriest month in all the year
    Is the merry month of May.

5  Now Robin Hood is to Nottingham gone,
    *With a link-a-down and a-day,*
And there he met a silly old woman,
    Was weeping on the way.

"What news? what news, thou silly old woman?
10    What news hast thou for me?"
Said she, "There's three squires in Nottingham town,
    Today is condemned to dee."

"O have they parishes burnt?" he said,
    "Or have they ministers slain?
15  Or have they robbed any virgin,
    Or with other men's wives have lain?"

"They have no parishes burnt, good sir,
    Nor yet have ministers slain,
Nor have they robbed any virgin,
20    Nor with other men's wives have lain."

"O what have they done?" said bold Robin Hood,
    "I pray thee tell to me."
"It's for slaying of the king's fallow deer,
    Bearing their longbows with thee."

25  "Dost thou not mind, old woman," he said,
    "Since thou made me sup and dine?
"By the truth of my body," quoth bold Robin Hood,
    "You could not tell it in better time."

**GUIDE FOR READING**

**7 silly:** poor, innocent.

**12 dee:** die.

**23 fallow:** brownish-red.

**25 mind:** remember.

Now Robin Hood is to Nottingham gone,
30    *With a link-a-down and a-day,*
And there he met with a silly old palmer,
    Was walking along the highway.

"What news? what news, thou silly old man?
    What news, I do thee pray?"
35  Said he, "Three squires in Nottingham town
    Are condemned to die this day."

"Come change thine apparel with me, old man,
    Come change thine apparel for mine.
Here is forty shillings in good silver,
40    Go drink it in beer or wine."

"O thine apparel is good," he said,
    "And mine is ragged and torn.
Wherever you go, wherever you ride,
    Laugh ne'er an old man to scorn."

45  "Come change thine apparel with me, old churl,
    Come change thine apparel with mine:
Here are twenty pieces of good broad gold,
    Go feast thy brethren with wine."

Then he put on the old man's hat,
50    It stood full high on the crown:
"The first bold bargain that I come at,
    It shall make thee come down."

Then he put on the old man's cloak,
    Was patched black, blue, and red:
55  He thought it no shame all the day long
    To wear the bags of bread.

Then he put on the old man's breeks,
    Was patched from ballup to side:
"By the truth of my body," bold Robin can say,
60    "This man loved little pride."

Then he put on the old man's hose,
    Were patched from knee to wrist:
"By the truth of my body," said bold Robin Hood,
    "I'd laugh if I had any list."

**31 *palmer:*** someone who carried a palm leaf to signify the making of a journey to the Holy Land.

**45 *churl:*** someone who is untidy and unmannerly.

**57 *breeks:*** trousers reaching to just below the knees.
**58 *ballup:*** center.
**59 *can:*** did.

**61 *hose:*** tightfitting outer garment.

**64 *list:*** wish to do so.

*SKETCH OF ROBIN HOOD* 1852
Richard Dadd   Yale Center for British
Art, New Haven, Connecticut   Paul
Mellon Collection.

65 Then he put on the old man's shoes,
    Were patched both beneath and aboon:
Then Robin Hood swore a solemn oath,
    "It's good habit that makes a man."

Now Robin Hood is to Nottingham gone,
70 *With a link-a-down and a-down,*
And there he was met with the proud sheriff,
    Was walking along the town.

"O Christ you save, O sheriff," he said,
    "O Christ you save and see:
75 And what will you give to a silly old man
    Today will your hangman be?"

"Some suits, some suits," the sheriff he said,
    "Some suits, I'll give to thee;
"Some suits, some suits, and pence thirteen,
80     Today's a hangman's fee."

**66 *aboon:*** above.

**68 *habit:*** clothing.

**73–74 *O Christ you save:*** A respectful greeting meaning "God save you" or "God be with you."

**79 *pence:*** pennies.

Then Robin he turns him round about,
    And jumps from stock to stone:
"By the truth of my body," the sheriff he said,
    "That's well jumped, thou nimble old man."

85  "I was ne'er a hangman in all my life,
    Not yet intends to trade.
But cursed be he," said bold Robin,
    "That first a hangman was made.

"I've a bag for meal, and a bag for malt,
90    And a bag for barley and corn,
A bag for bread, and a bag for beef,
    And a bag for my little small horn.

"I have a horn in my pocket:
    I got it from Robin Hood;
95 And still when I set it to my mouth,
    For thee it blows little good."

"O wind thy horn, thou proud fellow:
    Of thee I have no doubt;
I wish that thou give such a blast
100    Til both thy eyes fall out."

The first loud blast that he did blow,
    He blew both loud and shrill,
A hundred and fifty of Robin Hood's men
    Came riding over the hill.

105 The next loud blast that he did give,
    He blew both loud and amain,
And quickly sixty of Robin Hood's men
    Came shining over the plain.

"O who are those," the sheriff he said,
110    "Come tripping over the lea?"
"They're my attendants," brave Robin did say,
    "They'll pay a visit to thee."

They took the gallows from the slack,
    They set it in the glen;
115 They hanged the proud sheriff on that,
    Released their own three men.

82 *stock:* a tree stump.

97 *wind:* blow.
98 *doubt:* fear or suspicion of.

106 *amain:* with full force.

108 *shining:* riding courageously.

110 *lea:* a meadow or grassy field.

113 *slack:* a valley or hollow.

## Responding to Reading

### First Impressions

**1.** How do you feel about Robin Hood's treatment of the sheriff?

### Second Thoughts

**2.** Do you think Robin and his men are justified in hanging the sheriff on the gallows meant for Robin's men? Explain.

**3.** Poaching, the killing of the king's game, was punishable by death, even though poaching was the only way common people could get meat. Why do you think Robin wants to rescue the three squires accused of this crime?

> **Think about**
> • his conversation with the old woman
> • his personal code of chivalry

**4.** Robin treats the old woman, the palmer, and the sheriff differently. Based on this treatment, what can you say about Robin's nature?

## Literary Concept: Ballad

Narrative poems called **ballads** became popular during the medieval period because they were sung for entertainment. Since few common people at that time could read or write, the ballads were passed on orally from one generation to the next. Ballads from this time tell dramatic stories of common people, heroes, and events from legends. They often use dialogue, and the stories are usually about love, envy, bravery, loyalty, or revenge. Which of these themes can be found in "Robin Hood and the Three Squires"?

The most typical ballad form is the four-line stanza with the second and fourth lines rhyming. Repetition of words, phrases, lines, or ideas makes ballads musically appealing and easy to remember. Find three phrases and two lines that are repeated in "Robin Hood and the Three Squires."

## Writing Options

**1.** As a member of the King's imaginary press corps, write a news release about the latest terrorist attack and assassination in Nottingham by the outlaw Robin Hood.

**2.** Suppose you are a peasant in Nottingham and you have just heard about the hanging of the sheriff by Robin Hood and his men. Write a short speech to other commoners in defense of Robin Hood's action.

*Fiction*

## Two Friends

GUY DE MAUPASSANT   (gē də mō pä sän′)

### Examine What You Know

Sometimes friends talk about doing something that neither would do alone, perhaps something risky. Aside from anything illegal or truly dangerous, what risky thing have you done or planned with your friends? With your class, discuss reasons why you would not attempt this type of exploit alone. Then compare your own experiences with what you read in this story.

### Expand Your Knowledge

By the middle of the 1800's, the empire of Prussia, originally a small territory in northern Germany, had grown into two powerful states separated by several German and Austrian districts. By 1870, the Prussian armies united all of the German states under the leadership of Otto von Bismarck.

Because of this new unification, the terms *Prussian* and *German* became interchangeable.

Emperor Napoleon III of France, fearful of a unified Germany, started the Franco–Prussian War (France vs. Germany) in August 1870. In September 1870, the Germans defeated the French, captured Napoleon III, and surrounded the French capital of Paris, trying to starve the city into surrender. Without an emperor, the people of Paris established their own government, and they raised an army of nearly 600,000 men in just a few weeks. The French controlled all movement in and out of Paris, using spies and surprise escapes by balloon to harass and attack German positions everywhere for nearly four months. Still, by January 1871, the city was in danger of collapsing under the German seige. It is at this moment in history that Guy de Maupassant set his story.

### Write Before You Read

■ *A biography of the author can be found on page 105.*

Was there ever a time when you had to make a very difficult decision? In your journal or notebook, tell what this decision was and briefly explain why it was a difficult decision to make.

# Two Friends

## GUY DE MAUPASSANT

Paris was blockaded, starved, in its death agony. Sparrows were becoming scarcer and scarcer on the rooftops and the sewers were being depopulated. One ate whatever one could get.

As he was strolling sadly along the outer boulevard one bright January morning, his hands in his trousers pockets and his stomach empty, M.[1] Morissot, watchmaker by trade but local militiaman[2] for the time being, stopped short before a fellow militiaman whom he recognized as a friend. It was M. Sauvage, a riverside acquaintance.

Every Sunday, before the war, Morissot left at dawn, a bamboo pole in his hand, a tin box on his back. He would take the Argenteuil railroad, get off at Colombes and walk to Marante Island. As soon as he arrived at this ideal spot he would start to fish; he fished until nightfall.

Every Sunday he would meet a stout, jovial little man, M. Sauvage, a haberdasher in Rue Notre-Dame-de-Lorette, another ardent fisherman. Often they spent half a day side by side, line in hand and feet dangling above the current. Inevitably they had struck up a friendship.

Some days they did not speak. Sometimes they did; but they understood one another admirably without saying anything because they had similar tastes and responded to their surroundings in exactly the same way.

On a spring morning, toward ten o'clock, when the young sun was drawing up from the tranquil stream wisps of haze which floated off in the direction of the current and was pouring down its vernal[3] warmth on the backs of the two fanatical anglers, Morissot would sometimes say to his neighbor, "Nice, isn't it?" and M. Sauvage would answer, "There's nothing like it." And that was enough for them to understand and appreciate each other.

On an autumn afternoon, when the sky, reddened by the setting sun, cast reflections of its scarlet clouds on the water, made the whole river crimson, lighted up the horizon, made the two friends look as ruddy as fire, and gilded the trees which were already brown and beginning to tremble with a wintery shiver, M. Sauvage would look at Morissot with a smile and say, "Fine sight!" and Morissot, awed, would answer, "It's better than the city, isn't it?" without taking his eyes from his float.

---

1. **M.:** abbreviation for *monsieur* (mə syö'); French title which has the same meaning as *Mr.* or *Sir.*
2. **militiaman** (mə lish' ə mən): an ordinary citizen armed and prepared to fight in time of national emergency.
3. **vernal:** springlike.

*SELF-PORTRAIT* 1913 William Aiken Walker Gibbes Museum of Art, Charleston, South Carolina CAA collection.

As soon as they recognized one another they shook hands energetically, touched at meeting under such changed circumstances. M. Sauvage, with a sigh, grumbled, "What goings-on!" Morissot groaned dismally, "And what weather! This is the first fine day of the year."

The sky was, in fact, blue and brilliant.

They started to walk side by side, absent-minded and sad. Morissot went on, "And fishing! Ah! Nothing but a pleasant memory."

"When'll we get back to it?" asked M. Sauvage.

They went into a little café and had an absinthe,[4] then resumed their stroll along the sidewalks.

Morissot stopped suddenly. "How about another, eh?" M. Sauvage agreed. "If you want." And they entered another wine shop.

On leaving they felt giddy, muddled, as one does after drinking on an empty stomach. It was mild. A caressing breeze touched their faces.

The warm air completed what the absinthe had begun. M. Sauvage stopped. "Suppose we went?"

"Went where?"

"Fishing, of course."

"But where?"

"Why, on our island. The French outposts are near Colombes. I know Colonel Dumoulin; they'll let us pass without any trouble."

Morissot trembled with eagerness: "Done! I'm with you." And they went off to get their tackle.

An hour later they were walking side by side on the highway. They reached the villa[5] which the Colonel occupied. He smiled at their request and gave his consent to their <u>whim</u>. They started off again, armed with a pass.

Soon they passed the outposts, went through the abandoned village of Colombes, and reached the edge of the little vineyards which slope toward the Seine. It was about eleven.

Opposite, the village of Argenteuil seemed dead. The heights of Orgemont and Sannois dominated the whole countryside. The broad plain which stretches as far as Nanterre was empty, absolutely empty, with its bare cherry trees and its colorless fields.

---

4. **absinthe** (ab′ sin*th*′): a bitter, green, syrupy alcoholic liquor.

5. **villa**: a country house.

*Words to Know and Use* | **whim** (hwim, wim) *n.* a sudden idea; impulse

Pointing up to the heights, M. Sauvage murmured, "The Prussians are up there!" And a feeling of uneasiness paralyzed the two friends as they faced this deserted region.

"The Prussians!" They had never seen any, but for months they had felt their presence—around Paris, ruining France, pillaging, massacring, starving the country, invisible and all-powerful. And a kind of superstitious terror was superimposed on the hatred which they felt for this unknown and victorious people.

Morissot stammered, "Say, suppose we met some of them?"

His Parisian jauntiness coming to the surface in spite of everything, M. Sauvage answered, "We'll offer them some fish."

But they hesitated to venture into the country, frightened by the silence all about them.

Finally M. Sauvage pulled himself together: "Come on! On our way! But let's go carefully." And they climbed over into a vineyard, bent double, crawling, taking advantage of the vines to conceal themselves, watching, listening.

A stretch of bare ground had to be crossed to reach the edge of the river. They began to run, and when they reached the bank they plunged down among the dry reeds.

Morissot glued his ear to the ground and listened for sounds of anyone walking in the vicinity. He heard nothing. They were indeed alone, all alone.

Reassured, they started to fish.

Opposite them Marante Island, deserted, hid them from the other bank. The little building which had housed a restaurant was shut up and looked as if it had been abandoned for years.

M. Sauvage caught the first gudgeon,[6] Morissot got the second, and from then on they pulled in their lines every minute or two with a silvery little fish squirming on the end, a truly miraculous draught.

Skillfully they slipped the fish into a sack made of fine net which they had hung in the water at their feet. And happiness pervaded their whole being, the happiness which seizes upon you when you regain a cherished pleasure of which you have long been deprived.

The good sun was pouring down its warmth on their backs. They heard nothing more; they no longer thought about anything at all; they forgot about the rest of the world—they were fishing!

But suddenly a dull sound which seemed to come from under ground made the earth tremble. The cannon were beginning.

Morissot turned and saw, over the bank to the left, the great silhouette of Mount Valérien wearing a white plume on its brow, powdersmoke which it had just spit out.

And almost at once a second puff of smoke rolled from the summit, and a few seconds after the roar still another explosion was heard.

Then more followed, and time after time the mountain belched forth deathdealing breath, breathed out milky-white vapor which rose slowly in the calm sky and formed a cloud above the summit.

M. Sauvage shrugged his shoulders. "There they go again," he said.

As he sat anxiously watching his float bob up and down, Morissot was suddenly seized by the wrath which a peace-loving man will feel toward madmen who fight, and grumbled, "Folks sure are stupid to kill one another like that."

M. Sauvage answered, "They're worse than animals."

---

6. **gudgeon** (guj′ ən): a kind of small, freshwater fish.

*Words to Know and Use*

**pillaging** (pil′ ij iŋ) *v.* robbing **pillage** *v.*
**superimpose** (soo′ pər im pōz′) *v.* to put one thing on top of something else
**jauntiness** (jôn′ tē nes) *n.* liveliness
**pervade** (pər vād′) *v.* to spread throughout

99

And Morissot, who had just pulled in a bleak, went on, "And to think that it will always be like this as long as there are governments."

M. Sauvage stopped him: "The Republic[7] wouldn't have declared war—"

Morissot interrupted: "Under kings you have war abroad; under the Republic you have war at home."

And they started a leisurely discussion, unraveling great political problems with the sane reasonableness of easy-going, limited individuals, and found themselves in agreement on the point that men would never be free. And Mount Valérien thundered unceasingly, demolishing French homes with its cannon, crushing out lives, putting an end to the dreams which many had dreamt, the joys which many had been waiting for, the happiness which many had hoped for, planting in wives' hearts, in maidens' hearts, in mothers' hearts, over there, in other lands, sufferings which would never end.

"That's life for you," opined M. Sauvage.

"You'd better say 'That's death for you,'" laughed Morissot.

But they shuddered in terror when they realized that someone had just come up behind them, and looking around they saw four men standing almost at their elbows, four tall men armed and bearded, dressed like liveried[8] servants, with flat caps on their heads, pointing rifles at them.

The two fish lines dropped from their hands and floated off down stream.

In a few seconds they were seized, trussed[9] up, carried off, thrown into a rowboat and taken over to the island.

And behind the building which they had thought deserted they saw a score of German soldiers.

A kind of hairy giant who was seated astride a chair smoking a porcelain pipe asked them in excellent French: "Well, gentlemen, have you had good fishing?"

Then a soldier put down at the officer's feet a sack full of fish which he had carefully brought along. The Prussian smiled: "Aha! I see that it didn't go badly. But we have to talk about another little matter. Listen to me and don't get excited.

"As far as I am concerned, you are two spies sent to keep an eye on me. I catch you and I shoot you. You were pretending to fish in order to conceal your business. You have fallen into my hands, so much the worse for you. War is like that.

"But—since you came out past the outposts you have, of course, the password to return. Tell me that password and I will pardon you."

The two friends, side by side, pale, kept silent. A slight nervous trembling shook their hands.

The officer went on: "No one will ever know. You will go back placidly. The secret will disappear with you. If you refuse, it is immediate death. Choose."

They stood motionless, mouths shut.

The Prussian quietly went on, stretching out his hand toward the stream: "Remember that within five minutes you will be at the bottom of that river. Within five minutes! You have relatives, of course?"

---

7. **Republic:** the Second Republic of France; between the years 1848 and 1852, France had, for the first time in its history, a republic, a form of government in which the power is in the hands of all the citizens entitled to vote and is exercised by representatives elected by them.

8. **liveried:** uniformed.

9. **trussed:** tied or bound.

*Words to Know and Use* | **placidly** (plas' id lē) *adv.* calmly; quietly

LE PONT DE CHATOU   1905   Maurice Vlaminck   Private collection.

Mount Valérien kept on thundering.

The two fishermen stood silent. The German gave orders in his own language. Then he moved his chair so as not to be near the prisoners and twelve men took their places, twenty paces distant, rifles grounded.

The officer went on: "I give you one minute, not two seconds more."

Then he rose suddenly, approached the two Frenchmen, took Morissot by the arm, dragged him aside, whispered to him, "Quick, the password? Your friend won't know. I'll pretend to relent."

Morissot answered not a word.

The Prussian drew M. Sauvage aside and put the same question.

M. Sauvage did not answer.

They stood side by side again.

And the officer began to give commands. The soldiers raised their rifles.

Then Morissot's glance happened to fall on the sack full of gudgeons which was lying on the grass a few steps away.

A ray of sunshine made the little heap of still squirming fish gleam. And he almost weakened. In spite of his efforts his eyes filled with tears.

He stammered, "Farewell, Monsieur Sauvage."

M. Sauvage answered, "Farewell, Monsieur Morissot."

They shook hands, trembling from head to foot with a shudder which they could not control.

The officer shouted, "Fire!"

The twelve shots rang out together.

M. Sauvage fell straight forward, like a log. Morissot, who was taller, tottered, half turned, and fell crosswise on top of his comrade, face up, as the blood spurted from his torn shirt.

The German gave more orders.

His men scattered, then returned with rope and stones which they tied to the dead men's feet. Then they carried them to the bank.

Mount Valérien continued to roar, its summit hidden now in a mountainous cloud of smoke.

Two soldiers took Morissot by the head and the feet, two others seized M. Sauvage. They swung the bodies for a moment, then let go. They described an arc[10] and plunged into the river feet first, for the weights made them seem to be standing upright.

There was a splash, the water trembled, then grew calm, while tiny wavelets spread to both shores.

A little blood remained on the surface.

The officer, still calm, said in a low voice: "Now the fish will have their turn."

And he went back to the house.

And all at once he caught sight of the sack of gudgeons in the grass. He picked it up, looked at it, smiled, shouted, "Wilhelm!"

A soldier in a white apron ran out. And the Prussian threw him the catch of the two and said: "Fry these little animals right away while they are still alive. They will be delicious."

Then he lighted his pipe again. ❧

_____

10. **described an arc:** traced an outline of an arc, or bowlike curved line, in the air.

## *R*esponding to Reading

### First Impressions

1. "Two Friends" ends very quickly and dramatically. How do you feel about the ending of the story?

### Second Thoughts

2. Why do you think Morissot and Sauvage are willing to die?

3. The German officer offers to exchange Morissot's and Sauvage's lives for the password. Do you think the Frenchmen do the right thing by refusing?

    **Think about**
    • the German officer's promise that "No one will ever know."
    • personal honor and patriotism

4. It is possible that Morissot and Sauvage do not know the password. Would this possibility change your feelings about their actions? Explain.

5. Do you think either Morissot or Sauvage would have acted differently if he had been captured alone? Explain.

6. What do you think the author is trying to show with his use of contrast?

    **Think about**
    • the contrast on page 99 between the fishing and the cannon fire
    • the Frenchmen's and the German officer's remarks about war
    • the purpose of the Frenchmen's trip and their resulting deaths

7. In what ways are Maupassant's view of war and your view alike or different?

### Broader Connections

8. Think about incidents you have heard about in recent years concerning the treatment of prisoners, the wounded, or civilians during times of war. Which acts do you consider to be morally wrong and which ones, if any, do you think are acceptable wartime behavior?

## *L*iterary Concept: Protagonist and Antagonist

In any story, the **protagonist** is the main character who is always involved in the main action of the story. Sometimes a story has more than one protagonist. Who are the protagonists in "Two Friends"?

The force or person working against the protagonist is the **antagonist**. The antagonist can be something in nature, society, or another character, or it can be an internal force within the protagonist. Who or what is the antagonist in "Two Friends"? Briefly describe the antagonist.

## Writing Options

1. Morissot and Sauvage risked great danger to go fishing. Do you think they were right or wrong? Explain your answer.

2. If the German officer had offered to let Morissot and Sauvage write a final letter to a loved one, what might they have written? Imagine that you are Morissot or Sauvage and write such a letter to someone you love. Decide how much of your situation the officer will let you explain as well as what thoughts and feelings you want to express in your letter.

3. Rewrite the end of the story from the point at which the German soldiers raise their rifles and take aim at the Frenchmen. Consider what might have happened if either of the two men had decided to reveal the password.

4. Imagine the scene in which Morissot and Sauvage are fishing on the river. Then write a poem that creates an image of this scene. Use words and phrases that contrast the beauty and quiet of this area and the sights and sounds of the ongoing war.

## Vocabulary Practice

**Exercise** Write the letter of the word that is *not* related in meaning to the other words in the set.

1. (a) eager (b) ardent (c) passionate (d) disorderly
2. (a) inevitably (b) surely (c) harmlessly (d) certainly
3. (a) temporary (b) tranquil (c) quiet (d) serene
4. (a) fanatical (b) extreme (c) confused (d) ardent
5. (a) thought (b) conversation (c) wish (d) whim
6. (a) robbing (b) pillaging (c) misplacing (d) seizing
7. (a) superimpose (b) rotate (c) attach (d) cover
8. (a) gaiety (b) gracefulness (c) liveliness (d) jauntiness
9. (a) pervade (b) destroy (c) circulate (d) extend
10. (a) peacefully (b) calmly (c) placidly (d) flexibly

> *Words to Know and Use*
>
> ----
>
> **ardent**
> **fanatical**
> **inevitably**
> **jauntiness**
> **pervade**
> **pillaging**
> **placidly**
> **superimpose**
> **tranquil**
> **whim**

## *O*ptions for Learning

**1** • War Crimes Court  Imagine a world court being the scene of a war crimes trial of the German officer who had the Frenchmen executed. With several classmates, play the roles of judge, jury, witnesses, the German officer, and the prosecuting and defending attorneys. To prepare for the trial, the attorneys should look for evidence in the story and talk to the witnesses. They should also become familiar with the guidelines in the Geneva Convention, an international agreement about wartime treatment of prisoners, the wounded, and civilians. The rest of the class, acting as the world court, should determine the officer's guilt or innocence and pass sentence on him.

**2** • The Artist at Work  Create a visual picture of war that has a message as powerful as this story. Avoid a traditional war picture of soldiers fighting. Use paint, ink, or pencil to create an image that expresses your feelings about war.

**3** • On Stage  With classmates, write a script, including stage directions, for the scene in which Morissot and Sauvage are captured by the soldiers, questioned, and then shot. Rehearse and perform the scene for the class.

### FACT FINDER

*On a map, locate the following places named in the story: Paris, the Seine River, and Colombes.*

## *G*uy de Maupassant
### 1850–1893

Guy de Maupassant is considered by many to be one of the world's greatest short story writers. Many of his stories, like "Two Friends", deal with the Franco–Prussian War, in which he fought. Maupassant learned much of his literary technique from his friend and mentor, the famous French novelist Gustave Flaubert. Flaubert treated Maupassant like a son and advised him on his writing.

Maupassant was born in Normandy, in northern France. When he was eleven years old, his parents separated, and he was raised by his mother. The failure of his parents' marriage affected Maupassant severely, and he never married. An additional burden was the discovery that he had a debilitating disease which caused the gradual deterioration of his mental and physical health. The death of his brother by the same disease not only caused Maupassant grief but also preyed on his mind. Maupassant died in a Paris asylum one month before his forty-third birthday.

*Drama*

# The Ring of General Macías

JOSEPHINA NIGGLI

## Examine What You Know

This play portrays people on opposite sides of a revolution who struggle with their own code of chivalry as they fight for their beliefs. Make a list of things that you value enough to fight for and defend, such as family, country, love, and anything else you consider important. Then rank those items according to their importance to you. Compare your list and rankings with those of your classmates. Then compare them with the values of the characters in the play.

## Expand Your Knowledge

The Mexican Revolution was a long and bloody struggle that took place between 1910 and 1920. The Revolution began as a revolt of the peasants against the rich landowners. The Revolutionaries, led by Pancho Villa and Emiliano Zapata, wanted a new government that would redistribute land so that everyone would have a fair share. Their opponents, the Federalists, fought to protect the existing government and way of life. *The Ring of General Macías* takes place during this Revolution.

## Enrich Your Reading

**Reading Stage Directions**   The notes that tell actors and directors what to do in a play are called **stage directions.** These often appear in italics, brackets [ ], or parentheses ( ). Since a play is meant to be seen and heard by an audience, stage directions help you as a reader to visualize the setting and imagine how the actors would move and speak. In the play you are about to read, the stage directions are particularly important; if you ignore them, you will miss important actions that are key to the plot. On a chart like the one below, record five to ten important actions described in stage directions. For each action, list the actor. An example is given.

■ *A biography of the author can be found on page 122.*

| Page | Actor(s) | Action |
|---|---|---|
| 107 | Marica | finds a bottle of poison |
|  |  |  |

# The Ring of General Macías

## JOSEPHINA NIGGLI

## CHARACTERS

**Marica** (mä rē′ kä), the sister of General Macías (mä sē′ äs)

**Raquel** (rä kel′), the wife of General Macías

**Andrés de la O** (än dres′ dā lä ō), a captain in the Revolutionary Army

**Cleto** (klā′ tō), a private in the Revolutionary Army

**Basilio Flores** (bä sē′ lyō flō′ rās), a captain in the Federal Army

*Place: Just outside Mexico City*

*Time: A night in April 1912, during the Mexican Revolution*

The living room of General Macías's home is luxuriously furnished in the gold and ornate style of Louis XVI. In the Right wall are French windows leading into the patio. Flanking these windows are low bookcases. In the Back wall is, Right, a closet door; and, Center, a table holding a wine decanter[1] and glasses. The Left wall has a door Upstage, and Downstage a writing desk with a straight chair in front of it. Near the desk is an armchair. Down Right is a small sofa with a table holding a lamp at the Upstage end of it. There are pictures on the walls. The room looks rather stuffy and unlived in.

When the curtains part, the stage is in darkness save for the moonlight that comes through the French windows. Then the house door opens and a young girl in negligee enters stealthily. She is carrying a lighted candle. She stands at the door a moment listening for possible pursuit, then moves quickly across to the bookcase Down Right. She puts the candle on top of the bookcase and begins searching behind the books. She finally finds what she wants: a small bottle. While she is searching, the house door opens silently and a woman, also in negligee, enters. (These negligees are in the latest Parisian style.) She moves silently across the room to the table by the sofa, and as the girl turns with the bottle, the woman switches on the light. The girl gives a half-scream and draws back, frightened. The light reveals her to be quite young—no more than twenty—a timid, dovelike creature. The woman has a queenly air, and whether she is actually beautiful or not, people think she is. She is about thirty-two.

---

1. **decanter** (dē kant′ ər): a decorative glass bottle used for serving wine.

107

**Marica** (*trying to hide the bottle behind her*). Raquel! What are you doing here?

**Raquel.** What did you have hidden behind the books, Marica?

**Marica** (*attempting a forced laugh*). I? Nothing. Why do you think I have anything?

**Raquel** (*taking a step toward her*). Give it to me.

**Marica** (*backing away from her*). No. No, I won't.

**Raquel** (*stretching out her hand*). I demand that you give it to me.

**Marica.** You have no right to order me about. I'm a married woman. I . . . I . . . (*She begins to sob, and flings herself down on the sofa.*)

**Raquel** (*much gentler*). You shouldn't be up. The doctor told you to stay in bed. (*She bends over* Marica *and gently takes the bottle out of the girl's hand.*) It was poison, I thought so.

**Marica** (*frightened*). You won't tell the priest, will you?

**Raquel.** Suicide is a sin, Marica. A sin against God.

**Marica.** I know. I . . . (*She catches* Raquel's *hand.*) Oh, Raquel, why do we have to have wars? Why do men have to go to war and be killed?

**Raquel.** Men must fight for what they believe is right. It is an honorable thing to die for your country as a soldier.

**Marica.** How can you say that with Domingo out there fighting, too? And fighting what? Men who aren't even men. Peasants, Ranch slaves. Men who shouldn't be allowed to fight.

**Raquel.** Peasants are men, Marica. Not animals.

**Marica.** Men. It's always men. But how about the women? What becomes of us?

**Raquel.** We can pray.

**Marica** (*bitterly*). Yes, we can pray. And then comes the terrible news, and it's no use praying any more. All the reason for our praying is dead. Why should I go on living with Tomás dead?

**Raquel.** Living is a duty.

**Marica.** How can you be so cold, so hard? You are a cold and hard woman, Raquel. My brother worships you. He has never even looked at another woman since the first day he saw you. Does he know how cold and hard you are?

**Raquel.** Domingo is my—honored husband.

**Marica.** You've been married for ten years. And I've been married for three months. If Domingo is killed, it won't be the same for you. You've had ten years. (*She is crying wildly.*) I haven't anything . . . anything at all.

**Raquel.** You've had three months—three months of laughter. And now you have tears. How lucky you are. You have tears. Perhaps five months of tears. Not more. You're only twenty. And in five months Tomás will become just a lovely memory.

**Marica.** I'll remember Tomás all my life.

**Raquel.** Of course. But he'll be distant and far away. But you're young . . . and the young need laughter. The young can't live on tears. And one day in Paris, or Rome, or even Mexico City, you'll meet another man. You'll marry again. There will be children in your house. How lucky you are.

**Marica.** I'll never marry again.

**Raquel.** You're only twenty. You'll think differently when you're twenty-eight, or nine, or thirty.

**Marica.** What will you do if Domingo is killed?

**Raquel.** I shall be very proud that he died in all his courage . . . in all the greatness of a hero.

**Marica.** But you'd not weep, would you? Not you! I don't think there are any tears in you.

**Raquel.** No, I'd not weep. I'd sit here in this empty house and wait.

**Marica.** Wait for what?

**Raquel.** For the jingle of his spurs as he walks across the tiled hall. For the sound of his laughter in the patio. For the echo of his voice as he shouts to the groom to put away his horse. For the feel of his hand . . . .

**Marica** *(screams)*. Stop it!

**Raquel.** I'm sorry.

**Marica.** You do love him, don't you?

**Raquel.** I don't think even he knows how much.

**Marica.** I thought that after ten years people slid away from love. But you and Domingo—why, you're all he thinks about. When he's away from you, he talks about you all the time. I heard him say once that when you were out of his sight he was like a man without eyes or ears or hands.

**Raquel.** I know. I, too, know that feeling.

**Marica.** Then how could you let him go to war? Perhaps to be killed? How could you?

**Raquel** *(sharply)*. Marica, you are of the family Macías. Your family is a family of great warriors. A Macías man was with Ferdinand when the Moors[2] were driven out of Spain. A Macías man was with Cortés when the Aztecans[3] surrendered. Your grandfather fought in the War of Independence.[4] Your own father was executed not twenty miles from this house by the French. Shall his son be any less brave because he loves a woman?

**Marica.** But Domingo loved you enough to forget that. If you had asked him, he wouldn't have gone to war. He would have stayed here with you.

**Raquel.** No, he would not have stayed. Your brother is a man of honor, not a whining, creeping coward.

**Marica** *(beginning to cry again)*. I begged Tomás not to go. I begged him.

**Raquel.** Would you have loved him if he had stayed?

**Marica.** I don't know. I don't know.

**Raquel.** There is your answer. You'd have despised him. Loved and despised him. Now come, Marica, it's time for you to go to bed.

**Marica.** You won't tell the priest—about the poison, I mean?

**Raquel.** No. I won't tell him.

**Marica.** Thank you, Raquel. How good you are. How kind and good.

**Raquel.** A moment ago I was hard and cruel. What a baby you are. Now, off to bed with you.

**Marica.** Aren't you coming upstairs, too?

**Raquel.** No . . . I haven't been sleeping very well lately. I think I'll read for a little while.

**Marica.** Good night, Raquel. And thank you.

**Raquel.** Good night, little one.

---

2. **Moors:** Moslem people from northwest Africa whose kingdom in Spain was defeated by Ferdinand of Aragon in 1492.

3. **Aztecans** (az′ tek′ 'nz): people who lived in Mexico and had an advanced civilization before the conquest of Mexico by Cortés in 1519.

4. **War of Independence:** a revolution that took 600,000 lives from 1810 to 1821, when Mexico gained its freedom from Spain.

[Marica *goes through the house door Left, taking her candle with her.* Raquel *stares down at the bottle of poison in her hand, then puts it away in one of the small drawers of the desk. She next selects a book from the Downstage case and sits on the sofa to read it, but feeling chilly, she rises and goes to the closet, Back Right, and takes out an* afghan. *Coming back to the sofa, she makes herself comfortable, with the afghan across her knees. Suddenly she hears a noise in the patio. She listens, then convinced it is nothing, returns to her reading. But she hears the noise again. She goes to the patio door and peers out.*]

**Raquel** *(calling softly).* Who's there? Who's out there? Oh! *(She gasps and backs into the room. Two men—or rather a man and a young boy—dressed in the white pajama suits of the Mexican peasants, with their sombreros*[5] *tipped low over their faces, come into the room.* Raquel *draws herself up* regally. *Her voice is cold and commanding.)* Who are you, and what do you want here?

**Andrés.** We are hunting for the wife of General Macías.

**Raquel.** I am Raquel Rivera de Macías.

**Andrés.** Cleto, stand guard in the patio. If you hear any suspicious noise, warn me at once.

**Cleto.** Yes, my captain. *(The boy returns to the patio.)*

[*The man, hooking his thumbs in his belt, strolls around the room, looking it over. When he reaches the table at the back he sees the wine. With a small bow to* Raquel *he pours himself a glass of wine and drains it. He wipes his mouth with the back of his hand.*]

**Raquel.** How very interesting.

**Andŕes** *(startled).* What?

**Raquel.** To be able to drink wine with that hat on.

**Andrés.** The hat? Oh, forgive me, señora. *(He flicks the brim with his fingers so that it drops off his head and dangles down his back from the neck cord.)* In a military camp one forgets one's polite manners. Would you care to join me in another glass?

**Raquel** *(sitting on the sofa).* Why not? It's my wine.

**Andrés.** And very excellent wine. *(He pours two glasses and gives her one while he is talking.)* I would say Amontillado of the vintage of '87.

**Raquel.** Did you learn that in a military camp?

**Andrés.** I used to sell wines . . . among other things.

**Raquel** *(ostentatiously hiding a yawn).* I am devastated.

**Andrés** *(pulls over the armchair and makes himself comfortable in it).* You don't mind, do you?

**Raquel.** Would it make any difference if I did?

**Andrés.** No. The Federals are searching the streets for us and we have to stay somewhere. But women of your class seem to expect that senseless sort of question.

**Raquel.** Of course, I suppose I could scream.

**Andrés.** Naturally.

**Raquel.** My sister-in-law is upstairs asleep. And there are several servants in the back of the house. Mostly men servants. Very big men.

**Andrés.** Very interesting. *(He is drinking the wine in small sips with much enjoyment.)*

---

5. **sombreros** (säm brer′ ōz): broad-brimmed felt or straw hats traditionally worn by peasants in Mexico.

---

| *Words to Know and Use* | **afghan** (af′ gan′, -gən) *n.* a crocheted or knitted blanket<br>**regally** (rē′ gəl lē) *adv.* in a splendid or stately manner, as befitting a king or queen<br>**ostentatiously** (äs′ tən tā′ shəs lē) *adv.* in a showy manner<br>**devastate** (dev′ əs tāt′) *v.* to overwhelm; to make helpless |
| --- | --- |

VETERAN GUERRILLA  Jorge González Camerena  Mandeville Gallery, University of California at San Diego.

**Raquel.** What would you do if I screamed?

**Andrés** *(considering the request as though it were another glass of wine).* Nothing.

**Raquel.** I am afraid you are lying to me.

**Andrés.** Women of your class seem to expect polite little lies.

**Raquel.** Stop calling me "woman of your class."

**Andrés.** Forgive me.

**Raquel.** You are one of the fighting peasants, aren't you?

**Andrés.** I am a captain in the Revolutionary Army.

**Raquel.** This house is completely loyal to the Federal government.

**Andrés.** I know. That's why I'm here.

**Raquel.** And now that you are here, just what do you expect me to do?

**Andrés.** I expect you to offer sanctuary to myself and to Cleto.

**Raquel.** Cleto? *(She looks toward the patio and adds sarcastically.)* Oh, your army.

111

**Cleto** (*appearing in the doorway*). I'm sorry, my captain. I just heard a noise. (*Raquel stands. Andrés moves quickly to her and puts his hands on her arms from the back. Cleto has turned and is peering into the patio. Then the boy relaxes.*) We are still safe, my captain. It was only a rabbit. (*He goes back into the patio. Raquel pulls away from Andrés and goes to the desk.*)

**Raquel.** What a magnificent army you have. So clever. I'm sure you must win many victories.

**Andrés.** We do. And we will win the greatest victory, remember that.

**Raquel.** This <u>farce</u> has gone on long enough. Will you please take your army and climb over the patio wall with it?

**Andrés.** I told you that we came here so that you could give us sanctuary.

**Raquel.** My dear captain—captain without a name . . . .

**Andrés.** Andrés de la O, your servant. (*He makes a bow.*)

**Raquel** (*startled*). Andrés de la O!

**Andrés.** I am flattered. You have heard of me.

**Raquel.** Naturally. Everyone in the city has heard of you. You have a reputation for politeness—especially to women.

**Andrés.** I see that the tales about me have lost nothing in the telling.

**Raquel.** I can't say. I'm not interested in gossip about your type of soldier.

**Andrés.** Then let me give you something to heighten your interest. (*He suddenly takes her in his arms and kisses her. She stiffens for a moment, then remains perfectly still. He steps away from her.*)

**Raquel** (*rage forcing her to whisper*). Get out of here—at once!

**Andrés** (*staring at her in admiration*). I can understand why Macías loves you. I couldn't before, but now I can understand it.

**Raquel.** Get out of my house.

**Andrés** (*Sits on the sofa and pulls a small leather pouch out of his shirt. He pours its contents into his hand*). So cruel, señora, and I with a present for you? Here is a holy medal. My mother gave me this medal. She died when I was ten. She was a street beggar. She died of starvation. But I wasn't there. I was in jail. I had been sentenced to five years in prison for stealing five oranges. The judge thought it a great joke. One year for each orange. He laughed. He had a very loud laugh. (*pause*) I killed him two months ago. I hanged him to the telephone pole in front of his house. And I laughed. (*pause*) I also have a very loud laugh. (*Raquel abruptly turns her back on him.*) I told that story to a girl the other night and she thought it very funny. But of course she was a peasant girl—a girl who could neither read nor write. She hadn't been born in a great house in Tabasco. She didn't have any English governess.[6] She didn't go to school to the nuns in Paris. She didn't marry one of the richest young men in the Republic. But she thought my story very funny. Of course she could understand it. Her brother had been whipped to death because he had run away from the plantation that owned him. (*He pauses and looks at her. She does not move.*) Are you still angry with me? Even though I have brought you a present? (*He holds out his hand.*) A very nice present—from your husband.

---

6. **governess:** a woman employed in a family's home to train and teach the children.

*Words to Know and Use* | **farce** (färs) *n.* a ridiculous situation

**Raquel** *(turns and stares at him in amazement).* A present! From Domingo?

**Andrés.** I don't know him that well. I call him the General Macías.

**Raquel** *(excitedly).* Is he well? How does he look? *(with horrified comprehension)* He's a prisoner . . . your prisoner!

**Andrés.** Naturally. That's why I know so much about you. He talks about you constantly.

**Raquel.** You know nothing about him. You're lying to me.

[Cleto *comes to the window.*]

**Andrés.** I assure you, señora . . . .

**Cleto** *(interrupting).* My captain . . . .

**Andrés.** What is it, Cleto? Another rabbit?

**Cleto.** No, my captain. There are soldiers at the end of the street. They are searching all the houses. They will be here soon.

**Andrés.** Don't worry. We are quite safe here. Stay in the patio until I call you.

**Cleto.** Yes, my captain. *(He returns to the patio.)*

**Raquel.** You are not safe here. When those soldiers come, I shall turn you over to them.

**Andrés.** I think not.

**Raquel.** You can't escape from them. And they are not kind to you peasant prisoners. They have good reason not to be.

**Andrés.** Look at this ring. *(He holds his hand out, with the ring on his palm.)*

**Raquel.** Why, it's—a wedding ring.

**Andrés.** Read the inscription inside of it. *(As she hesitates, he adds sharply.)* Read it!

**Raquel** *(Slowly takes the ring. While she is reading, her voice fades to a whisper.).* "D.M.—R.R.—June 2, 1902." Where did you get this?

**Andrés.** General Macías gave it to me.

**Raquel** *(firmly and clearly).* Not this ring. He'd never give you this ring. *(with dawning horror)* He's dead. You stole it from his dead finger. He's dead.

**Andrés.** Not yet. But he will be dead if I don't return to camp safely by sunset tomorrow.

**Raquel.** I don't believe you. I don't believe you. You're lying to me.

**Andrés.** This house is famous for its loyalty to the Federal government. You will hide me until those soldiers get out of this district. When it is safe enough, Cleto and I will leave. But if you betray me to them, your husband will be shot tomorrow evening at sunset. Do you understand? *(He shakes her arm.* Raquel *looks dazedly at him.* Cleto *comes to the window.)*

**Cleto.** The soldiers are coming closer, my captain. They are at the next house.

**Andrés** *(to* Raquel*).* Where shall we hide? *(*Raquel *is still dazed. He gives her another little shake.)* Think, woman. If you love your husband at all—think!

**Raquel.** I don't know. Marica upstairs—the servants in the rest of the house—I don't know.

**Andrés.** The General has bragged to us about you. He says you are braver than most men. He says you are very clever. This is a time to be both brave and clever.

**Cleto** *(pointing to the closet).* What door is that?

**Raquel.** It's a closet . . . a storage closet.

**Andrés.** We'll hide in there.

**Raquel.** It's very small. It's not big enough for both of you.

**Andrés.** Cleto, hide yourself in there.

**Cleto.** But, my captain . . . .

**Andrés.** That's an order! Hide yourself.

**Cleto.** Yes, Sir. *(He steps inside the closet.)*

**Andrés.** And now, señora, where are you going to hide me?

**Raquel.** How did you persuade my husband to give you his ring?

**Andrés.** That's a very long story, señora, for which we have no time just now. *(He puts the ring and medal back in the pouch and thrusts it inside his shirt.)* Later I will be glad to give you all the details. But at present it is only necessary for you to remember that his life depends upon mine.

**Raquel.** Yes—yes, of course. *(She loses her dazed expression and seems to grow more queenly as she takes command of the situation.)* Give me your hat. *(Andrés shrugs and passes it over to her. She takes it to the closet and hands it to* Cleto.*)* There is a smoking jacket[7] hanging up in there. Hand it to me. *(Cleto hands her a man's velvet smoking jacket. She brings it to* Andrés.*)* Put this on.

**Andrés** *(puts it on and looks down at himself).* Such a pity my shoes are not comfortable slippers.

**Raquel.** Sit in that chair. *(She points to the armchair.)*

**Andrés.** My dear lady . . . .

**Raquel.** If I must save your life, allow me to do it in my own way. Sit down. *(Andrés sits. She picks up the afghan from the couch and throws it over his feet and legs, carefully tucking it in so that his body is covered to the waist.)* If anyone speaks to you, don't answer. Don't turn your head. As far as you are concerned, there is no one in this room—not even me. Just look straight ahead of you and . . . .

**Andrés** *(as she pauses).* And what?

**Raquel.** I started to say "and pray," but since you're a member of the Revolutionary Army I don't suppose you believe in God and prayer.

**Andrés.** My mother left me a holy medal.

**Raquel.** Oh, *yes,* I remember. A very amusing story. *(There is the sound of men's voices in the patio.)* The Federal soldiers are here. If you can pray, ask God to keep Marica upstairs. She is very young and very stupid. She'll betray you before I can shut her mouth.

**Andrés.** I'll . . . .

**Raquel.** Silence! Stare straight ahead of you and pray. *(She goes to the French window and speaks loudly to the soldiers.)* Really! What is the meaning of this uproar?

**Flores** *(off).* Do not alarm yourself, señora. *(He comes into the room. He wears the uniform of a Federal officer.)* I am Captain Basilio Flores, at your service, señora.

**Raquel.** What do you mean, invading my house and making so much noise at this hour of the night?

**Flores.** We are hunting for two spies. One of them is the notorious Andrés de la O. You may have heard of him, señora.

**Raquel** *(looking at* Andrés*).* Considering what he did to my cousin—yes, I've heard of him.

**Flores.** You're cousin, señora?

**Raquel.** *(comes to* Andrés *and puts her hand on his shoulder. He stares woodenly in front of him).* Felipe was his prisoner before the poor boy managed to escape.

**Flores.** Is it possible? *(He crosses to* Andrés.*)* Captain Basilio Flores, at your service. *(He salutes.)*

**Raquel.** Felipe doesn't hear you. He doesn't even know you are in the room.

**Flores.** Eh, it is a sad thing.

---

7. **smoking jacket:** a man's lounging jacket for wearing at home.

*Words to Know and Use* | **notorious** (nō tôr′ ē əs) *adj.* well-known for something bad; infamous

**Raquel.** Must your men make so much noise?

**Flores.** The hunt must be thorough, señora. And now if some of my men can go through here to the rest of the house . . . .

**Raquel.** Why?

**Flores.** But I told you, señora. We are hunting for two spies . . . .

**Raquel** *(speaking quickly from controlled nervousness)*. And do you think I have them hidden some place, and I the wife of General Macías?

**Flores.** General Macías! But I didn't know . . . .

**Raquel.** Now that you do know, I suggest you remove your men and their noise at once.

**Flores.** But, señora, I regret—I still have to search this house.

**Raquel.** I can assure you, captain, that I have been sitting here all evening, and no peasant spy has passed me and gone into the rest of the house.

**Flores.** Several rooms open off the patio, señora. They needn't have come through here.

**Raquel.** So . . . you do think I conceal spies in this house. Then search it by all means. Look under the sofa . . . under the table. In the drawers of the desk. And don't miss that closet, captain. Inside that closet is hidden a very fierce and wicked spy.

**Flores.** Please, señora . . . .

**Raquel** *(goes to the closet door)*. Or do you prefer me to open it for you?

**Flores.** I am only doing my duty, señora. You are making it very difficult.

**Raquel** *(relaxing against the door)*. I'm sorry. My sister-in-law is upstairs. She has just received word that her husband has been killed. They were married three months ago. She's only twenty. I didn't want . . . .

**Marica** *(calling off)*. Raquel, what is all the noise downstairs?

**Raquel** *(goes to the house door and calls)*. It is nothing. Go back to bed.

**Marica.** But I can hear men's voices in the patio.

**Raquel.** It is only some Federal soldiers hunting for two peasant spies. *(She turns and speaks rapidly to* Flores.*)* If she comes down here, she must not see my cousin. Felipe escaped, but her husband was killed. The doctor thinks the sight of my poor cousin might affect her mind. You understand?

**Flores.** Certainly, señora. What a sad thing.

**Marica** *(still off)*. Raquel, I'm afraid! *(She tries to push past* Raquel *into the room.* Raquel *and* Flores *stand between her and* Andrés.*)* Spies! In this house. Oh, Raquel!

**Raquel.** The doctor will be very angry if you don't return to bed at once.

**Marica.** But those terrible men will kill us. What is the matter with you two? Why are you standing there like that? *(She tries to see past them, but they both move so that she can't see* Andrés.*)*

**Flores.** It is better that you go back to your room, señora.

**Marica.** But why? Upstairs I am alone. Those terrible men will kill me. I know they will.

**Flores.** Don't be afraid, señora. There are no spies in this house.

**Marica.** Are you sure?

**Raquel.** Captain Flores means that no spy would dare to take refuge in the house of General Macías. Isn't that right, captain?

**Flores** *(laughing)*. Of course. All the world knows of the brave General Macías.

**Raquel.** Now go back to bed, Marica. Please, for my sake.

**Marica.** You are both acting very strangely. I think you have something hidden in this room you don't want me to see.

BAD NEWS 1895 Rodolfo Amoedo Museu Nacional de Belas-Artes, Rio De Janeiro, Brazil.

**Raquel** *(sharply).* You are quite right. Captain Flores has captured one of the spies. He is sitting in the chair behind me. He is dead. Now will you please go upstairs!

**Marica** *(gives a stifled sob).* Oh! That such a terrible thing could happen in this house. *(She runs out of the room, still sobbing.)*

**Flores** *(worried).* Was it wise to tell her such a story, señora?

**Raquel** *(tense with repressed relief).* Better that than the truth. Good night, captain, and thank you.

**Flores.** Good night, señora. And don't worry. Those spies won't bother you. If they were anywhere in this district, my men would have found them.

**Raquel.** I'm sure of it.

[*The* Captain *salutes her, looks toward* Andrés *and salutes him, then goes into the patio. He can be heard calling his men. Neither* Andrés *nor* Raquel *moves until the voices outside die away. Then*

Raquel *staggers and nearly falls, but* Andrés *catches her in time.*]

**Andrés** *(calling softly).* They've gone, Cleto. *(*Andrés *carries* Raquel *to the sofa as* Cleto *comes out of the closet.)* Bring a glass of wine. Quickly.

**Cleto** *(as he gets the wine).* What happened?

**Andrés.** It's nothing. Just a faint. *(He holds the wine to her lips.)*

**Cleto.** She's a great lady, that one. When she wanted to open the closet door my knees were trembling. I can tell you.

**Andrés.** My own bones were playing a pretty tune.

**Cleto.** Why do you think she married Macías?

**Andrés.** Love is a peculiar thing, Cleto.

**Cleto.** I don't understand it.

**Raquel** *(moans and sits up).* Are they—are they gone?

**Andrés.** Yes, they're gone. *(He kisses her hand.)* I've never known a braver lady.

**Raquel** *(pulling her hand away)*. Will you go now, please?

**Andrés.** We'll have to wait until the district is free of them—but if you'd like to write a letter to your husband while we're waiting . . . .

**Raquel** *(surprised at his kindness)*. You'd take it to him? You'd really give it to him?

**Andrés.** Of course.

**Raquel.** Thank you. *(She goes to the writing desk and sits down.)*

**Andrés** *(to* Cleto, *who has been staring steadily at* Raquel *all the while)*. You stay here with the señora. I'm going to find out how much of the district has been cleared.

**Cleto** *(still staring at* Raquel*)*. Yes, my captain.

[Andrés *leaves by the French windows.* Cleto *keeps on staring at* Raquel *as she starts to write. After a moment she turns to him.*]

**Raquel** *(irritated)*. Why do you keep staring at me?

**Cleto.** Why did you marry a man like that one, señora?

**Raquel.** You're very <u>impertinent</u>.

**Cleto** *(shyly)*. I'm sorry, señora.

**Raquel** *(after a brief pause)*. What do you mean: "a man like that one"?

**Cleto.** Well, you're very brave, señora.

**Raquel** *(lightly)*. And don't you think the general is very brave?

**Cleto.** No, señora. Not very.

**Raquel** *(staring at him with bewilderment)*. What are you trying to tell me?

**Cleto.** Nothing, señora. It is none of my affair.

**Raquel.** Come here. *(He comes slowly up to her.)* Tell me what is in your mind.

**Cleto.** I don't know, señora. I don't understand it. The captain says love is a peculiar thing, but I don't understand it.

**Raquel.** Cleto, did the general willingly give that ring to your captain?

**Cleto.** Yes, señora.

**Raquel.** Why?

**Cleto.** The general wanted to save his own life. He said he loved you and he wanted to save his life.

**Raquel.** How would giving that ring to your captain save the general's life?

**Cleto.** The general's supposed to be shot tomorrow afternoon. But he's talked about you a lot, and when my captain knew we had to come into the city, he thought perhaps we might take refuge here if the Federals got on our trail. So he went to the general and said that if he fixed it so we'd be safe here, my captain would save him from the firing squad.

**Raquel.** Was your trip here to the city very important—to your cause, I mean?

**Cleto.** Indeed yes, señora. The captain got a lot of fine information. It means we'll win the next big battle. My captain is a very clever man, señora.

**Raquel.** Did the general know about this information when he gave his ring to your captain?

**Cleto.** I don't see how he could help knowing it, señora. He heard us talking about it enough.

**Raquel.** Who knows about that bargain to save the general's life beside you and your captain?

**Cleto.** No one, señora. The captain isn't one to talk, and didn't have time to.

*Words to Know and Use* | **impertinent** (im purt′ 'n ənt) *adj.* disrespectful; insulting

117

**Raquel** *(While the boy has been talking, the life seems to have drained completely out of her)*. How old are you, Cleto?

**Cleto.** I don't know, señora. I think I'm twenty, but I don't know.

**Raquel** *(speaking more to herself than to him)*. Tomás was twenty.

**Cleto.** Who is Tomás?

**Raquel.** He was married to my sister-in-law. Cleto, you think my husband is a coward, don't you?

**Cleto** *(with embarrassment)*. Yes, señora.

**Raquel.** You don't think any woman is worth it, do you? Worth the price of a great battle, I mean?

**Cleto.** No, señora. But as the captain says, love is a very peculiar thing.

**Raquel.** If your captain loved a woman as much as the general loves me, would he have given an enemy his ring?

**Cleto.** Ah, but the captain is a great man, señora.

**Raquel.** And so is my husband a great man. He is of the family Macías. All of that family have been great men. All of them—brave and honorable men. They have always held their honor to be greater than their lives. That is a tradition of their family.

**Cleto.** Perhaps none of them loved a woman like you, señora.

**Raquel.** How strange you are. I saved you from the Federals because I want to save my husband's life. You call me brave and yet you call him a coward. There is no difference in what we have done.

**Cleto.** But you are a woman, señora.

**Raquel.** Has a woman less honor than a man, then?

**Cleto.** No, señora. Please, I don't know how to say it. The general is a soldier. He has a duty to his own cause. You are a woman. You have a duty to your husband. It is right that you should try to save him. It is not right that he should try to save himself.

**Raquel** *(dully)*. Yes, of course. It is right that I should save him. *(becoming practical again)* Your captain has been gone some time, Cleto. You'd better find out if he is still safe.

**Cleto.** Yes, señora. *(As he reaches the French windows she stops him.)*

**Raquel.** Wait, Cleto. Have you a mother—or a wife, perhaps?

**Cleto.** Oh, no, señora. I haven't anyone but the captain.

**Raquel.** But the captain is a soldier. What would you do if he should be killed?

**Cleto.** It is very simple, señora. I should be killed, too.

**Raquel.** You speak about death so calmly. Aren't you afraid of it, Cleto?

**Cleto.** No, señora. It's like the captain says . . . dying for what you believe in—that's the finest death of all.

**Raquel.** And you believe in the Revolutionary cause?

**Cleto.** Yes, señora. I am a poor peasant, that's true. But still I have a right to live like a man, with my own ground, and my own family, and my own future. *(He stops speaking abruptly.)* I'm sorry, señora. You are a fine lady. You don't understand these things. I must go and find my captain. *(He goes out.)*

**Raquel** *(rests her face against her hand)*. He's so young. But Tomás was no older. And he's not afraid. He said so. Oh, Domingo— Domingo!

[*She straightens abruptly, takes the bottle of poison from the desk drawer and stares at it. Then she crosses to the decanter and laces the wine with the poison. She hurries back to the desk and is busy writing when* Andrés *and* Cleto *return.*]

**Andrés.** You'll have to hurry that letter. The district is clear now.

**Raquel.** I'll be through in just a moment. You might as well finish the wine while you're waiting.

**Andrés.** Thank you. A most excellent idea. *(He pours himself a glass of wine. As he lifts it to his lips she speaks.)*

**Raquel.** Why don't you give some to— Cleto?

**Andrés.** This is too fine a wine to waste on that boy.

**Raquel.** He'll probably never have another chance to taste such wine.

**Andrés.** Very well. Pour yourself a glass, Cleto.

**Cleto.** Thank you. *(He pours it.)* Your health, my captain.

**Raquel** *(quickly)*. Drink it outside, Cleto. I want to speak to your captain. *(The boy looks at* Andrés, *who jerks his head toward the patio.* Cleto *nods and goes out.)* I want you to give my husband a message for me. I can't write it. You'll have to remember it. But first, give me a glass of wine, too.

**Andrés** *(pouring the wine)*. It might be easier for him if you wrote it.

**Raquel.** I think not. *(She takes the glass.)* I want you to tell him that I never knew how much I loved him until tonight.

**Andrés.** Is that all?

**Raquel.** Yes. Tell me, captain, do you think it possible to love a person too much?

**Andrés.** Yes, señora. I do.

**Raquel.** So do I. Let us drink a toast, captain—to honor. To bright and shining honor.

**Andrés** *(raises his glass)*. To honor.

[*He drains his glass. She lifts hers almost to her lips and then puts it down. From the patio comes a faint cry.*]

**Cleto** *(calling faintly in a cry that fades into silence)*. Captain. Captain.

[Andrés *sways, his hand trying to brush across his face as though trying to brush sense into his head. When he hears* Cleto, *he tries to stagger toward the window but stumbles and can't quite make it. Hanging on to the table by the sofa, he looks accusingly at her. She shrinks back against her chair.*]

**Andrés** *(his voice weak from the poison)*. Why?

**Raquel.** Because I love him. Can you understand that?

**Andrés.** We'll win. The Revolution will win. You can't stop that.

**Raquel.** Yes, you'll win. I know that now.

**Andrés.** That girl—she thought my story was funny—about the hanging. But you didn't . . . .

**Raquel.** I'm glad you hanged him. I'm glad.

[Andrés *looks at her and tries to smile. He manages to pull the pouch from his shirt and extend it to her. But it drops from his hand.*]

**Raquel** *(runs to French window and calls)*. Cleto. Cleto!

[*She buries her face in her hands for a moment, then comes back to* Andrés. *She kneels beside him and picks up the leather pouch. She opens it and, taking the ring, puts it on her finger. Then she sees the medal. She rises and, pulling out the chain from her own throat, she slides the medal on to the chain. Then she walks to the sofa and sinks down on it.*]

**Marica** *(calling off)*. Raquel! Raquel! *(*Raquel *snaps off the lamp, leaving the room in darkness.* Marica *opens the house door. She is carrying a candle which she shades with her hand. The light is too dim to reveal the dead* Andrés.*)* What are you doing down here in the dark? Why don't you come to bed?

**Raquel** *(making an effort to speak)*. I'll come in just a moment.

**Marica.** But what are you doing, Raquel?

**Raquel.** Nothing. Just listening . . . listening to an empty house. ❧

# *explain*

## *R*esponding to Reading

### First Impressions

1. What are your feelings about Raquel's actions?

### Second Thoughts

2. Why do you think Raquel poisons Andrés and Cleto, even though she knows that her husband will die if they do not return?

   **Think about**
   • Raquel's conversation with Cleto
   • General Macías's bargain and who knows about it
   • Raquel's feelings about her husband

3. What do the actions of Raquel and Andrés reveal about their personalities? Use your chart based on the stage directions to help you answer.

4. Which characters in the play meet the ideals of honor and bravery? Which are heroic? Support your opinion.

   **Think about**
   • each character's idea of honor and bravery
   • each character's actions
   • your own beliefs about honor and bravery

5. Both sides of the Mexican Revolution are represented in this play. Which side do you think the playwright favored? Which side do you think was right?

### Broader Connections

6. Is the concept of honor still important in today's world? For example, do you feel that people today would willingly die for a cause? In your discussion, consider modern attitudes toward military service, patriotism, religion, the family, and the opposite sex.

## *L*iterary Concept: Elements of Drama

Because drama is meant to be performed, it appears in a different form than fiction or poetry. As you have learned, stage directions provide instructions about the setting and action for directors and performers. The primary focus of drama, however, is the dialogue, or conversation, among characters. Most of the story is told through the dialogue.

Work with a partner and review Cleto's dialogue with Raquel on pages 116–117. List three facts from the dialogue that explain why Cleto and Andrés come to Raquel's home.

## Writing Options

1. Raquel started a letter to her husband near the end of the play. Write the letter you think she wrote.

2. Suppose an international agency is giving a Medal of Honor Award. Write a letter to the head of the agency nominating either Raquel or Andrés for the award and explain your choice.

3. Imagine that you are Andrés. Write a speech to be given to the Mexican people explaining why the peasants' cause is right.

4. Review the list that you made of things you value. Then decide how each character in the play would have ranked each item on the list. Find quotes from the play to support your decisions.

## Vocabulary Practice

**Exercise**   Decide if the boldfaced word in each sentence is used correctly. Write *Correct* or *Incorrect* on your paper for each sentence. If the word is used incorrectly, explain why.

1. Captain Flores describes Andrés as **notorious** because no one has ever heard of him.
2. An **ostentatiously** decorated home might have expensive furniture, gold sculptures, and other showy displays.
3. After Cleto and Andrés invade her home, Raquel calls the situation a **farce**, which shows respect for their actions.
4. The sensitive Marica is **devastated** by her husband's death.
5. A **sanctuary** is a place where many battles occur.
6. If Raquel had screamed and stomped her feet, she would have been acting **regally**.
7. Raquel acts **stealthily** to prevent Cleto from seeing her.
8. Andrés shows **impertinent** behavior by offering to take back a message to General Macías.
9. No one would be surprised if Raquel wore an elegant gold **afghan** on her head.
10. The Revolutionaries need a **sanctuary** to keep them safe.

> *Words to Know and Use*
> ———
> **afghan**
> **devastated**
> **farce**
> **impertinent**
> **notorious**
> **ostentatiously**
> **regally**
> **sanctuary**
> **stealthily**

## *Options for Learning*

**1** • **Set Directors** Find a book on theater or staging for ideas about how sets are made. Based on what you learn and the stage directions in this play, build or draw a model of the set for *The Ring of General Macías.*

**2** • **Speaking of History** Research the Mexican Revolution. Choose a leader of the Revolution to investigate, such as Emiliano Zapata or Pancho Villa, or a leader of the Federalists, such as General Porfirio Diaz. Share your findings in an oral presentation to your class.

**3** • **A Star Is Born** With some classmates, act out your favorite part of the play. Memorize your lines, rehearse, and perform your scene for your class.

**4** • **Scriptwriting** Write a follow-up scene to this play, such as a scene depicting what happens to General Macías when the peasants do not return, or a scene between Raquel and Marica. Have classmates help you perform your scene for the class.

### FACT FINDER

*Who won the Mexican Revolution of 1910, and what kind of government was established?*

## *Josephina Niggli*
### 1910–

Josephina Niggli was born near Hidalgo, Mexico, in 1910. The violence of the Mexican Revolution caused her family to leave Mexico and move to Texas in 1913. Her family remained in the United States, living in San Antonio, Texas, where her mother, a concert violinist, taught her daughter at home until Josephina entered high school. The aspiring young writer looked to Mexico for her subjects and inspiration. As a young adult, Niggli earned quick success; her plays were performed both on stage and on radio shows while she was in her early twenties. She eventually settled at the University of North Carolina, where she taught and continued writing plays. Niggli has written many short stories and plays about Mexican folk life.

# WRITER'S WORKSHOP

## FIRST-PERSON NARRATIVE

Although the term *chivalry* has a very specific historical definition, its modern meaning is more general and concerns conduct toward others. Basically, any action that protects or helps the weak and powerless or that shows honor and courage is considered chivalrous. All the selections in this subunit show actions that fit this definition. These stories narrate events that reflect a code of conduct that does not change, even when the danger is great.

In this workshop you will narrate an incident in which you behaved in a way that was noble or honorable. You will write an interesting, true story from your own point of view.

**Here is your PASSkey to this assignment.**

**GUIDED ASSIGNMENT:**
**AUTOBIOGRAPHICAL INCIDENT**

Write an autobiographical narrative that describes a chivalrous thing you have done. Explain the circumstances surrounding the incident, what happened, and why it was chivalrous. Tell what the incident taught you about yourself and others.

**P**URPOSE: To narrate a personal deed of chivalry

**A**UDIENCE: Your classmates

**S**UBJECT: A noble or chivalrous action of yours

**S**TRUCTURE: A multi-paragraph first-person narrative

## Prewriting

**STEP 1** **Remember and list incidents**   Make a list of incidents in your life that might be considered chivalrous. Any actions you took that you think were noble, honorable, and courageous or that helped someone in a difficult situation should be included. The list need consist only of words or phrases that remind you of each incident.

**STEP 2** **Narrow your choices**   Mark the three or four most interesting possibilities on your list. Select two of these incidents and make cluster maps of all the sights, sounds, smells, feelings, and actions that you remember about each event. Here is part of one student's cluster map.

## The Rescue of Regina

Student Model ▶

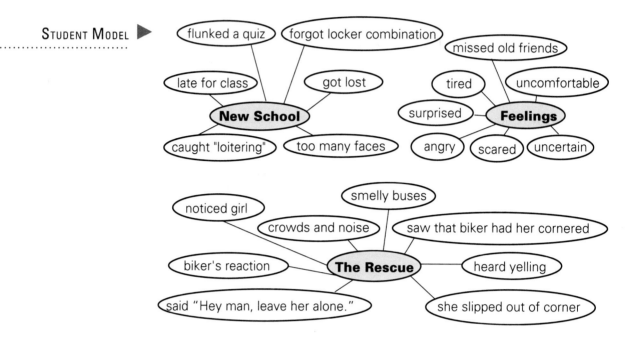

**STEP 3** **Use peer reaction** In a small group, briefly summarize both incidents for your classmates, using your cluster maps as a guide. Then ask your group which incident they think is more interesting and more chivalrous, and why. Based on their feedback and your own feelings, decide which incident will be the focus of your narrative.

**STEP 4** **Order your notes** Make a chronological list of events, actions, reactions, and any dialogue that you can specifically recall was spoken during your chosen incident. Number your list.

**STEP 5** **Add details** For each of the numbered items on your list, make a list of details that describe how you felt about each action. Limit the details to short phrases but include your feelings, fears, and reactions. Here are portions of the first and second lists from the cluster about the student's first day in a new school.

Student Model ▶

1. forgot locker combination

2. got lost on way to English

1. felt disoriented by noise, too many faces, gave up on getting book

2. nervous about being late, heard late bell, froze up

3. teacher stopped me for
   ''loitering''

3. surprised, angry,
   foolish, stammered an
   explanation

4. late for class

4. embarrassed, didn't
   have my book, heard some
   laughter

## Drafting

**STEP 1** **Write an attention-grabbing beginning**   Aim for a beginning that quickly catches your reader's attention. You might start with the moment you realized that you had to act, or with a background incident or feeling, or even near the end of the story.

Here is an example of one student's opening paragraph.

> It had to be the worst day yet for me at this new school. I'd flunked my first quiz, forgotten my locker combination, and been hassled by a teacher who thought I was loitering when I had really only gotten lost on my way to my next class. By the time the day was finally over, I was in no mood for anything else as I slammed my way out the side door and into the exhaust fumes and noise of the buses. So why didn't I ignore it when I heard this angry, shaky voice telling a biker in black leather and boots, ''Get lost—leave me alone''?

◀ STUDENT MODEL

### Special Tip

Remember that writing an autobiographical narrative is just like telling an interesting story. Try to use precise, descriptive details to help the reader "see" and "hear" and "feel" what is happening. "Show" your story instead of simply recounting a series of events.

**STEP 2** **Include your emotions**   The story will be much more exciting to your readers if you share what you felt at the time. You can describe your feelings at the end of your draft, include them in separate paragraphs within the narration of the incident, or tell them right along with the details of the events. Decide what approach to use before you begin writing, although you may find your organizational plan changing as you write.

STEP **3** **Conclude your story**   Your last paragraph should include an explanation of what you learned about yourself and, if appropriate, what you learned about others from your experience.

## Revising and Editing

In a small group, share your autobiographical incident. Use the following checklist to help you and your peers decide on the areas that need to be revised.

| **Revision Checklist** |
| --- |
| 1. What is the best part of your narrative? |
| 2. Are the events in chronological order? If not, is the order clear and easy to follow? |
| 3. Does the story need more active descriptions? |
| 4. Are there unnecessary details that could be eliminated? |
| 5. Can explanations be added to help the reader follow the story? |
| 6. Does the story involve the reader by including the writer's feelings? |

After you have reviewed the checklist with your group, ask each member to give you at least two suggestions on how to improve your writing. Use the ones that you think will help.

**Editing**   Revise your narrative. With the help of your peer group, check your revision for mechanical errors, spelling, grammar, run-on sentences or fragments, and correct first-person pronoun usage. (See the **Language Handbook** for a review of pronoun forms.)

## Presenting

Read your personal narrative to the class or have a classmate read it. Ask the class to decide which selection from this subunit describes a deed similar to yours.

## Reflecting on Your Writing

Answer the following questions. Attach your answers to your paper and put both in your writing portfolio.

1. What made this assignment easier or harder to write than others?
2. How did your group of peers help with this assignment?
3. Did making a cluster chart help you find ideas?

# LANGUAGE
### WORKSHOP

## USING THE RIGHT PRONOUNS

> A **pronoun** is a word that replaces a noun or another pronoun.

Every piece of writing has a particular point of view. An autobiographical account, for example, is written from the first-person point of view. The writer uses the pronouns *I, me, we,* and *us.*

A description of another person, on the other hand, is written from the third-person point of view. The writer uses the pronouns *he, him, she, her, they,* and *them.*

For the first two Writer's Workshops, you wrote assignments in the third person and the first person. In your writing, you should always keep your point of view consistent by using the correct pronouns throughout. The chart below lists the first- and third-person pronouns.

|  | Nominative | Objective | Possessive |
|---|---|---|---|
| **First Person** | I, we | me, us | my, mine, our, ours |
| **Third Person** | he, she, it, they | her, him, it, them | her, hers, his, its, their, theirs |

**NOTE**

The second-person pronouns are *you, your,* and *yours.* They rarely cause confusion in writing.

## Using the Nominative Form of Pronouns

As you can see from the chart, first- and third-person pronouns can also be divided into three forms. The **nominative** forms of pronouns are used as subjects of verbs and as predicate pronouns after linking verbs.

> *I* will kill you two spies immediately. (The subject of the verb *will kill* is the pronoun *I.*)
> *They* stood next to each other, terrified but proud. (The subject of the verb *stood* is the pronoun *they.*)

Even if two or more pronouns, or a noun and a pronoun, are used as the subject, you should use the nominative case.

> *He* and *I* waited for the sound of gun fire.
> Mr. Morissot and *he* studied the Prussian soldier intently.

Use the nominative form of a pronoun when a pronoun is used together with a noun as the subject of a sentence.

*We* buddies loved to spend our days fishing.

▶ Nominative forms are also used for **predicate pronouns.** Predicate pronouns are linked to the subject by a form of the verb *be.* These pronouns identify, rename, or explain the subject.

The fisherman must have been *he.*
The revolutionaries were *they.*

> **QUICK TIP**   To decide whether the subject form should be used, try reversing the subject and the predicate pronoun. The sentence should still sound correct.
>
> Raquel was *she. She* was Raquel.

## Using the Objective Form of Pronouns

The **objective** form of a pronoun is used for direct objects, indirect objects, and objects of prepositions. A direct object is the person or thing that receives the action of the verb. An indirect object tells *to whom* or *for whom* the action of the verb is done. An indirect object always comes before the direct object in a sentence. (For a review of objects see "Writing Complete Sentences" in the **Language Handbook.**)

Mr. Morissot took *me* to the cafe. (*Me* is the direct object of the verb *asked.*)
Mr. Sauvage gave *him* another drink. (*Him* is the indirect object of the verb *gave.*)

A pronoun can also be the object of a preposition.

Can you say goodbye to my family for *me?* (*Me* is the object of the preposition *for.*)

Use the objective form of a pronoun even if two or more pronouns or a noun and a pronoun are used together as the object of a preposition.

A lovely day of fishing ended in tragedy for Mr. Morissot and *him.*

**Exercise 1**   Choose the correct pronoun(s) for each sentence.

**1.** The story of *Sir Gawain and the Green Knight* was difficult but interesting reading for (I, me) and some other students.

2. My friend Marcia and (me, I) had trouble understanding Gawain's actions.
3. (Her, She) and (I, me) agreed that the idea of chivalry had changed a lot since King Arthur's time.
4. However, after reading the story, some of (we, us) seniors decided to find out more about King Arthur and his knights.
5. At first (we, us) students thought that Arthur was just a myth, but we discovered that (he, him) might really have existed.
6. (We, Us) did some further research and found out that legends about Arthur began in early Britain as folk stories.
7. Eventually, religious monks wrote (them, they) down.
8. The legends say that young Arthur proved (he, him) was the true king by pulling a sword out of a stone.
9. Many others had tried, but the sword would not move for (they, them).
10. Of course, (they, them) didn't have the help of Merlin the magician.
11. It was (he, him) who guided Arthur.
12. After a few years, (he, him) and Arthur decided it was time to choose a queen.
13. One look at the beautiful Guenevere caused Arthur to say, "That is (she, her)! (She, Her) will rule Camelot with (I, me)."
14. Merlin gave Arthur and (she, her) his blessings.
15. "(We, Us) rulers will make Camelot the most wonderful place on earth," promised Arthur.
16. (He, Him) called knights from all over the country and asked (they, them) to join him.
17. "(I, Me) and my knights will follow strict rules of honor, loyalty, and courtesy," (he, him) said.
18. So that no one would feel slighted, Arthur seated (they, them) at a round table.
19. Life was perfect for Arthur and (they, them) until the queen and Sir Lancelot fell in love.
20. (They, Them) and the evil Sir Mordred were the cause of Arthur's downfall.

## Exercise 2 Analyzing and Revising Your Writing

1. Review a piece of first-person or third-person writing you have done.
2. Are the pronouns consistent with the point of view you have chosen?
3. Correct any pronoun errors that you find.

LANGUAGE HANDBOOK
. . . . . . . . . . . . . . . . . . . . . . . . . . . . . . .
For review and practice:
nominative pronouns,
    pages 984–86
objective pronouns,
    pages 984–86

# VOCABULARY
## WORKSHOP

### WORD ORIGINS

Over the past fifteen hundred years, the English language has changed continually as new words have been added to communicate new ideas. Today, with new inventions and new discoveries being made at a faster-than-ever rate, our language is changing almost every day.

New words enter our language in several ways. One common way is simply by **borrowing** a word from another language. *Karate* is a Japanese word; *blouse* is French; *borsch* is Russian; *sauna* is Finnish.

Some new words are created by combining two existing words into a **compound word.** For example, *football, basketball, railroad, toothpick, mailbox,* and *eyelid.*

Sometimes, when two words are combined, some of the letters are dropped. The result is a new word called a **blend.** For example, the art of making movies is called *cinematography,* a blend of *cinema* and *photography.*

Other new words are created by dropping parts of a word and using the remaining part by itself. Such words are called **clipped words.** Clipped words are less formal than the original words from which they are made. For example, *phone* is less formal than *telephone. Math, burger, sax,* and *gym* are other examples of clipped words.

New words called **acronyms** can also be formed by combining the first letters of a group of words. These acronyms are often used for scientific, technical, or military terms. *Laser* is an acronym created from the first letters of *light amplification by stimulated emission of radiation.*

Whenever you need to know the origin of a word, check the dictionary. The word's history generally follows immediately after the part of speech abbreviation and is enclosed in brackets [  ].

**Exercise**  Using a dictionary, find the origin of each of the following words. Write whether the word is a **borrowed word,** a **compound,** a **blend,** a **clipped word,** or an **acronym.** If the word was borrowed, write the language from which it was taken. Otherwise, write the word or words from which it was made.

| | | | |
|---|---|---|---|
| **1.** chocolate | **5.** raincoat | **9.** cab | **13.** sonar |
| **2.** courtroom | **6.** silhouette | **10.** motorcade | **14.** memoir |
| **3.** healthcare | **7.** lab | **11.** sequin | **15.** ecosystem |
| **4.** NASA | **8.** UNICEF | **12.** stereo | |

# IGNOBLE DEEDS

The literature in the first two sections of this unit describes honorable, heroic characters who take great risks or sacrifice their lives for the good of others. Now you will read about their opposites: characters who take the low road through life, whose actions are base, deceitful, criminal, or just a little dishonest. As you read, look for attitudes and characteristics that the ignoble characters have in common. Judge whether each character completely rejects the concepts of glory and honor or simply adapts moral standards to his convenience.

*Poetry*

*from* **The Canterbury Tales**

*The Pardoner's Tale*

**GEOFFREY CHAUCER** *Translated by* **NEVILL COGHILL**

## *E*xamine What You Know

Stories are often used to teach moral lessons. For example, a preacher may tell a story to illustrate a point in a sermon; a parent may tell a story to warn of danger. Sometimes, however, the people who tell these morality tales are less than moral themselves.

In what settings have you heard stories that were intended to teach you lessons? Were these stories effective? Have you ever found out later that the storyteller did not follow his or her own advice? "The Pardoner's Tale" is an example of a morality tale told by an immoral speaker.

## *E*xpand Your Knowledge

In *The Canterbury Tales,* Chaucer vividly portrays the life of his era by creating thirty characters from various social classes. His characters include a virtuous knight, a love-struck squire, a lusty widow, a foul-mouthed miller, and a drunken cook. The characters travel together on a fifty-five mile journey from London to the holy shrine of St. Thomas à Becket in Canterbury, England. They agree to tell stories to pass the time. The most entertaining storyteller would be rewarded with a dinner.

The tale you are about to read is told by a pardoner, a preacher who has a license from the Pope to grant indulgences, that is, to forgive sins in exchange for money. Forgiveness was supposed to be given only to those who had shown great charity. In practice, however, many pardoners simply sold their pardons. To encourage business, pardoners often threatened reluctant buyers with eternal damnation. Chaucer's pardoner, a greedy and corrupt man, is one of the least likable people on the pilgrimage.

## *E*nrich Your Reading

■ *A biography of the author can be found on page 143*

**Historical Expressions**   Numerous expressions in this tale reflect medieval attitudes and beliefs. Besides references to the plague (better known as the Black Death, which killed nearly half the population of Europe in the fourteenth century), most of these are religious expressions.

# from *The Canterbury Tales*

## *The Pardoner's Tale*

GEOFFREY CHAUCER *Translated by* NEVILL COGHILL

*The Pardoner begins with a prologue, which is an introduction or preface to his tale. In his prologue he tells about his past success. He has made a fortune by preaching the same message to various audiences:* **radix malorum est cupiditas,** *Latin for "the love of money is the root of all evil." The Pardoner's own love of money, which he refers to as "avarice" and "covetousness," keeps him traveling from town to town so that he can earn enough to support his wealthy habits.*

*The following passage is an excerpt from his prologue.*

"But let me briefly make my purpose plain;
I preach for nothing but for greed of gain
And use the same old text, as bold as brass,
*Radix malorum est cupiditas.*
5 And thus I preach against the very vice
I make my living out of—<u>avarice</u>
And yet however guilty of that sin
Myself, with others I have power to win
Them from it, I can bring them to repent;
10 But that is not my principal intent.
<u>Covetousness</u> is both the root and stuff
Of all I preach. That ought to be enough."

CHAUCER  c. 1410  From the "Ellesmere Manuscript" of *The Canterbury Tales*  Culver Pictures, New York.

133

*After the Pardoner introduces the three rowdy young men who are the subject of his tale, he preaches a long sermon against their vices. He lists each of their major sins, such as drunkenness and gambling, and gives examples of famous people who were destroyed by these sins. Finally, he tells about what happened to the three "rioters." That is where the following excerpt begins.*

GUIDE FOR READING

It's of three rioters I have to tell
Who, long before the morning service bell,
15  Were sitting in a tavern for a drink.
And as they sat, they heard the hand-bell clink
Before a coffin going to the grave;
One of them called the little tavern-knave
And said "Go and find out at once—look spry!—
20  Whose corpse is in that coffin passing by;
And see you get the name correctly too."
"Sir," said the boy, "no need, I promise you;
Two hours before you came here I was told.
He was a friend of yours in days of old,
25  And suddenly, last night, the man was slain,
Upon his bench, face up, dead drunk again.
There came a privy thief, they call him Death,
Who kills us all round here, and in a breath
He speared him through the heart, he never stirred.
30  And then Death went his way without a word.
He's killed a thousand in the present plague,
And, sir, it doesn't do to be too vague
If you should meet him; you had best be wary.
Be on your guard with such an adversary,
35  Be primed to meet him everywhere you go,
That's what my mother said. It's all I know."
    The publican joined in with, "By St. Mary,
What the child says is right; you'd best be wary,
This very year he killed, in a large village
40  A mile away, man, woman, serf at tillage,
Page in the household, children—all there were.
Yes, I imagine that he lives round there.
It's well to be prepared in these alarms,
He might do you dishonour." "Huh, God's arms!"

**18 tavern-knave** (nāv): a serving boy in an inn.

**27 privy** (priv' ē): hidden or secretive.

**36** The boy's mother warned him about the plague, which brought a quick and terrible death to its victims. *Do you think she believed Death was an actual person?*

**37 publican:** an innkeeper; pub owner.

**44 God's arms:** a curse; this and the curses that follow relate to different parts of God's body.

---

*Words to Know and Use*

134

**wary** (wer' ē) *adj.* cautious; on one's guard
**adversary** (ad' vər ser' ə) *n.* enemy; opponent

THE CANTERBURY PILGRIMS
LEAVING CANTERBURY
British Museum, London.

45 The rioter said, "Is he so fierce to meet?
I'll search for him, by Jesus, street by street.
God's blessed bones! I'll register a vow!
Here, chaps! The three of us together now,
Hold up your hands, like me, and we'll be brothers
50 In this affair, and each defend the others,
And we will kill this traitor Death, I say!
Away with him as he has made away
With all our friends. God's dignity! Tonight!"
　They made their bargain, swore with appetite,
55 These three, to live and die for one another
As brother-born might swear to his born brother.
And up they started in their drunken rage
And made towards this village which the page
And publican had spoken of before.
60 Many and grisly were the oaths they swore,
Tearing Christ's blessed body to a shred;
"If we can only catch him, Death is dead!"
　When they had gone not fully half a mile,
Just as they were about to cross a stile,
65 They came upon a very poor old man
Who humbly greeted them and thus began,
"God look to you, my lords, and give you quiet!"

**60** *How might their drinking have affected their judgment?*

**64 stile:** steps used to climb a fence or wall.

To which the proudest of these men of riot
Gave back the answer, "What, old fool? Give place!
70  Why are you all wrapped up except your face?
Why live so long? Isn't it time to die?"
    The old, old fellow looked him in the eye
And said, "Because I never yet have found,
Though I have walked to India, searching round
75  Village and city on my pilgrimage,
One who would change his youth to have my age.
And so my age is mine and must be still
Upon me, for such time as God may will.
    "Not even Death, alas, will take my life;
80  So, like a wretched prisoner at strife
Within himself, I walk alone and wait
About the earth, which is my mother's gate,
Knock-knocking with my staff from night to noon
And crying, 'Mother, open to me soon!
85  Look at me, Mother, won't you let me in?
See how I wither, flesh and blood and skin!
Alas! When will these bones be laid to rest?
Mother, I would exchange—for that were best—
The wardrobe in my chamber, standing there
90  So long, for yours! Aye, for a shirt of hair
To wrap me in!' She has refused her grace,
Whence comes the <u>pallor</u> of my withered face.
    "But it dishonoured you when you began
To speak so roughly, sir, to an old man,
95  Unless he had injured you in word or deed.
It says in holy writ, as you may read,
'Thou shalt rise up before the hoary head
And honour it.' And therefore be it said
'Do no more harm to an old man than you,
100  Being now young, would have another do
When you are old'—if you should live till then.
And so may God be with you, gentlemen,
For I must go whither I have to go."
    "By God," the gambler said, "you shan't do so,
105  You don't get off so easy, by St John!
I heard you mention, just a moment gone,
A certain traitor Death who singles out
And kills the fine young fellows hereabout.
And you're his spy, by God! You wait a bit.

**80** *Why does the old man want to die?*

**90-91** *shirt of hair to wrap me in:* a sheet made of animal hair used to wrap corpses before burial.

**101** *What is the old man's complaint about their treatment of him?*

*Words to Know and Use*  |  **pallor** (pal′ ər) *n.* lack of color in the face; paleness

110 Say where he is or you shall pay for it,
By God and by the Holy Sacrament!
I say you've joined together by consent
To kill us younger folk, you thieving swine!"
"Well, sirs," he said, "if it be your design
115 To find out Death, turn up this crooked way
Towards that grove, I left him there today
Under a tree, and there you'll find him waiting.
He isn't one to hide for all your prating.
You see that oak? He won't be far to find.
120 And God protect you that redeemed mankind,
Aye, and amend you!" Thus that ancient man.
    At once the three young rioters began
To run, and reached the tree, and there they found
A pile of golden florins on the ground,
125 New-coined, eight bushels of them as they thought.
No longer was it Death those fellows sought,
For they were all so thrilled to see the sight,
The florins were so beautiful and bright,
That down they sat beside the precious pile.
130 The wickedest spoke first after a while.
"Brothers," he said, "you listen to what I say.
I'm pretty sharp although I joke away.
It's clear that Fortune has bestowed this treasure
To let us live in jollity and pleasure.
135 Light come, light go! We'll spend it as we ought.
God's precious dignity! Who would have thought
This morning was to be our lucky day?
    "If one could only get the gold away,
Back to my house, or else to yours, perhaps—
140 For as you know, the gold is ours, chaps—
We'd all be at the top of fortune, hey?
But certainly it can't be done by day.
People would call us robbers—a strong gang,
So our own property would make us hang.
145 No, we must bring this treasure back by night
Some prudent way, and keep it out of sight.
And so as a solution I propose
We draw for lots and see the way it goes;
The one who draws the longest, lucky man,
150 Shall run to town as quickly as he can
To fetch us bread and wine—but keep things dark—
While two remain in hiding here to mark
Our heap of treasure. If there's no delay,
When night comes down we'll carry it away,

**124 florins:** coins.

**133 Fortune** here means "fate." *Do you think the young men will be blessed by Fortune?*

155 All three of us, wherever we have planned."
       He gathered lots and hid them in his hand
    Bidding them draw for where the luck should fall.
    It fell upon the youngest of them all,
    And off he ran at once towards the town.

160    As soon as he had gone the first sat down
    And thus began a parley with the other:
    "You know that you can trust me as a brother;
    Now let me tell you where your profit lies;
    You know our friend has gone to get supplies

165 And here's a lot of gold that is to be
    Divided equally amongst us three.
    Nevertheless, if I could shape things thus
    So that we shared it out—the two of us—
    Wouldn't you take it as a friendly act?"

170    "But how?" the other said. "He knows the fact
    That all the gold was left with me and you;
    What can we tell him? What are we to do?"
       "Is it a bargain," said the first, "or no?
    For I can tell you in a word or so

175 What's to be done to bring the thing about."
    "Trust me," the other said, "you needn't doubt
    My word. I won't betray you, I'll be true."
       "Well," said his friend, "you see that we are two,
    And two are twice as powerful as one.

180 Now look; when he comes back, get up in fun
    To have a wrestle; then, as you attack,
    I'll up and put my dagger through his back
    While you and he are struggling, as in game;
    Then draw your dagger too and do the same.

185 Then all this money will be ours to spend,
    Divided equally of course, dear friend.
    Then we can gratify our lusts and fill
    The day with dicing at our own sweet will."
    Thus these two miscreants agreed to slay

190 The third and youngest, as you heard me say.
       The youngest, as he ran towards the town,
    Kept turning over, rolling up and down
    Within his heart the beauty of those bright
    New florins, saying, "Lord, to think I might

195 Have all that treasure to myself alone!

*THE PARDONER* Arthur Szyk The
Newberry Library, Chicago.

**186** *How do the two friends plan to kill the third?*

**189 miscreants** (mis′ krē ənts): evil persons.

*Words
to Know
and Use*  |  **parley** (pär′ lē) *n.* a talk or conference to settle differences

Could there be anyone beneath the throne
Of God so happy as I then should be?"
    And so the Fiend; our common enemy,
Was given power to put it in his thought
200  That there was always poison to be bought,
And that with poison he could kill his friends.
To men in such a state the Devil sends
Thoughts of this kind, and has a full permission
To lure them on to sorrow and perdition;
205  For this young man was utterly content
To kill them both and never to repent.
    And on he ran, he had no thought to tarry,
Came to the town, found an apothecary
And said, "Sell me some poison if you will,
210  I have a lot of rats I want to kill
And there's a polecat too about my yard
That takes my chickens and it hits me hard;
But I'll get even, as is only right,
With <u>vermin</u> that destroy a man by night."
215    The chemist answered, "I've a preparation
Which you shall have, and by my soul's salvation
If any living creature eat or drink
A mouthful, ere he has the time to think,
Though he took less than makes a grain of wheat
220  You'll see him fall down dying at your feet;
Yes, die he must, and in so short a while
You'd hardly have the time to walk a mile,
The poison is so strong, you understand."
    This cursed fellow grabbed into his hand
225  The box of poison and away he ran
Into a neighbouring street, and found a man
Who lent him three large bottles. He withdrew
And <u>deftly</u> poured the poison into two.
He kept the third one clean, as well he might,
230  For his own drink, meaning to work all night
Stacking the gold and carrying it away.
And when this rioter, this devil's clay,
Had filled his bottles up with wine, all three,
Back to rejoin his comrades <u>sauntered</u> he.
235    Why make a sermon of it? Why waste breath?
Exactly in the way they'd planned his death

198 *Fiend:* the devil, Satan.

204 *perdition:* damnation; hell. *Why does the Devil have influence over the young man?*

208 *apothecary* (ə päth′ ə ker′ ē): a druggist.

---

*Words to Know and Use*

**vermin** (vʉr′ mən) *n.* destructive or disease-carrying animals or insects
**deftly** (deft′ lē) *adv.* in a skillful, quick manner
**saunter** (sôn′ tər) *v.* to walk slowly and leisurely

They fell on him and slew him, two to one.
Then said the first of them when this was done,
"Now for a drink. Sit down and let's be merry,
240   For later on there'll be the corpse to bury."
And, as it happened, reaching for a sup,
He took a bottle full of poison up
And drank; and his companion, nothing loth,
Drank from it also, and they perished both.
245      There is, in Avicenna's long relation
Concerning poison and its operation,
Trust me, no ghastlier section to <u>transcend</u>
What these two wretches suffered at their end.
Thus these two murderers received their due,
250   So did the treacherous young poisoner too.
     One thing I should have mentioned in my tale,
Dear people. I've some relics in my bale
And pardons too, as full and fine, I hope,
As any in England, given me by the Pope.
255   If there be one among you that is willing
To have my absolution for a shilling
Devoutly given, come! and do not harden
Your hearts but kneel in humbleness for pardon;
Or else, receive my pardon as we go.
260   You can renew it every town or so
Always provided that you still renew
Each time, and in good money, what is due.
It is an honour to you to have found
A pardoner with his credentials sound
265   Who can absolve you as you ply the spur
In any accident that may occur.
For instance—we are all at Fortune's beck—
Your horse may throw you down and break your neck.
What a security it is to all
270   To have me here among you and at call
With pardon for the lowly and the great
When soul leaves body for the future state!
And I advise our Host here to begin,
The most enveloped of you all in sin.
275   Come forward, Host, you shall be the first to pay,
And kiss my holy relics right away.
Only a groat. Come on, unbuckle your purse!

**245 *Avicenna's long relation*** (av' i sen' ə): a medical text written by an Arab physician that includes descriptions of various poisons and their effects.

**249** *Why does the Pardoner say the young men "received their due"?*

**256 *absolution*** (ab' sə lo͞o sнən): forgiveness for sins committed; ***shilling:*** a coin worth a small amount.

**268** The Pardoner reminds the other pilgrims that death may come at any time. *Why does he say this?*

**277 *groat*** (grōt): a silver coin.

*Words to Know and Use* | **transcend** (tran send') *v.* to go beyond, surpass

# explain

## Responding to Reading

### First Impressions

**1.** What do you think about the way this tale ends?

### Second Thoughts

**2.** Were you surprised that the three rioters betray one another? Explain.

**3.** Why do the rioters set out to kill Death?

**Think about**
- what they learn from the boy and the tavern keeper
- their view of themselves
- other factors that may have influenced their judgment

**4.** Why do you think the old man is included in the story?

**Think about**
- the story of his life
- his views about Death
- his advice to the rioters about where to find Death

**5.** Do you think the story will make the pilgrims buy indulgences? Why or why not?

**6.** How does your knowledge of the Pardoner's life affect your understanding of his tale?

### Broader Connections

**7.** Why do so many people prefer to hear about evil characters instead of virtuous ones? What does that preference say about human nature?

## Literary Concept: Middle English

The English language is always growing. New words are added, and pronunciations and grammar rules change. *Beowulf* was written in Old English. By Chaucer's time, the language had evolved into Middle English.
The following lines from the prologue to the Pardoner's Tale are in Middle English. Which words are still recognizable? Can you figure out any other words? The last line is Latin, meaning "the love of money is the root of all evil."

> Lordinges—quod he—in chirches when I preche,
> I paine me to han an hautein speeche,
> And ringe it out as round as gooth a belle
> For can al by rote that I telle.
> My theme is alway oon, and evere was:
> *Radix malorum est cupiditas.*

# Writing Options

1. Write a contemporary version of a scene from the story. Update the setting, characters, and language to make the scene seem believable in today's world.

2. Decide whether or not the rioters found what they wanted. Then explain your opinion, using evidence from the story to support your position.

3. Write a television news report about the discovery of the three bodies. Think about how the rioters' deaths might be explained by a reporter who was not at the scene of the crimes. You may wish to include interviews with the old man and the people at the tavern.

4. Choose a person in today's world who is known for his or her moral messages. It could be an honest or a corrupt political leader, religious leader, or someone from your own life. Compare and contrast this person to the Pardoner.

# Vocabulary Practice

**Exercise** Read each sentence below. Write *true* on your paper if the statement is true. Write *false* if the statement is false, and explain why it is false.

1. If the youngest rioter had sprained his ankle, he would not have been able to **saunter** back to the meeting place.
2. People who will kill for money cannot be accused of **avarice**.
3. The shop was tastefully decorated with **vermin** and wine bottles.
4. A person who **deftly** pours liquid is likely to spill it.
5. The Pardoner shows **covetousness** by greedily asking the pilgrims for money.
6. Death is the boy's **adversary** because it is his enemy.
7. One rioter began a **parley** with his friend about his plan.
8. If the youths were **wary,** they would have been cautious.
9. The shiny gold coins possessed a definite **pallor.**
10. To **transcend** the description of the rioters' terrible death, you would describe a death that was even worse.

> *Words to Know and Use*
>
> ---
>
> adversary
> avarice
> covetousness
> deftly
> pallor
> parley
> saunter
> transcend
> vermin
> wary

# extend

## Options for Learning

**1 • Twentieth-Century Pardoner** The Pardoner makes money by stirring up guilty feelings in his audience. If he came to speak at your high school, how might he create feelings of guilt about money? Create and deliver an impromptu speech that might work on your classmates, giving specific examples of why they should feel bad. You might conclude, like the Pardoner does, by asking for money.

**2 • Illuminated Manuscript** Chaucer's stories, written before the invention of the printing press, were printed by hand. To make the manuscripts beautiful, artists embellished them with drawings and designs that explain or decorate the tales. These works are called illuminated manuscripts. Look through books about medieval art and printing to find examples of illumination. Then create your own art work for "The Pardoner's Tale."

**3 • Advertise** Develop an advertisement to "sell" the Pardoner to a larger audience. Your goal is to persuade people to come and listen to his sermon.

**4 • Dance Video** Create a dance routine in your favorite style that narrates all or some of the events of "The Pardoner's Tale." You can adapt your dance to an existing piece of music or create your own musical accompaniment. Either perform your dance for the class or show a videotape of your performance.

### FACT FINDER

*What caused the Black Death, and how was it spread?*

## Geoffrey Chaucer
### c.1343–1400

The man who is often called the father of English poetry led a life almost as interesting as his writing. Chaucer was born into London's growing middle class. His father, a wine merchant, gave his son a fine education and trained him for a life of service to kings and nobles. Chaucer gained distinction as a diplomat, a spy, a justice of the peace, and a member of Parliament. When England waged war against France, he was captured and held for ransom. As a diplomat he traveled extensively in France and Italy.

Though he was a brilliant poet, an able administrator, and a relatively wealthy man, Chaucer remains one of the most humble and likable poets of our language. He knew how to laugh at human folly without viciousness, and he knew how to laugh at himself. He even portrayed himself as one of the Canterbury pilgrims: a short, plump, slightly foolish pilgrim who commands no great respect. This plump and gentle poet gave us some of the finest poetry and most memorable characters ever created in the English language.

*Fiction*

# *The* Thief

JUNICHIRO TANIZAKI   (jo͞o nē chē rō tä nē zä kē)

## Examine What You Know

Do you think your friends know the real you, or do they see only part of the picture? List words and phrases that you have heard other people use to describe your personality. Underline those that you think are accurate. Then notice in this story the differences between the main character's view of himself and the views his friends have of him.

## Expand Your Knowledge

"The Thief" is a mystery set in a Japanese high school. Because education is crucial for success in Japan, almost all Japanese students complete high school, and many go on to universities. The most ambitious students attend private high schools or prep schools. These expensive boarding schools offer demanding courses that prepare students for entrance exams given by Japan's top universities. School success brings honor to the entire family, while failure brings disgrace.

In Japan, respect for authority, rules, and tradition is valued highly. Japanese students behave and dress more formally than American students. A Japanese prep student would never wear jeans or a T-shirt to class or talk back to a teacher. On the other hand, like Americans, Japanese students love sports, cars, and games, and they value friends.

## Enrich Your Reading

**Tracking Clues**   In a good mystery story, the writer establishes the circumstances of the crime before the action intensifies. To figure out who committed the crime, the reader must patiently keep track of the clues. As you read, fill out a copy of the following chart. See how long it takes you to positively identify the thief.

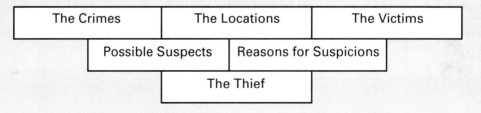

| The Crimes | The Locations | The Victims |
|---|---|---|
| Possible Suspects | Reasons for Suspicions | |
| The Thief | | |

■ *A biography of the author can be found on page 155.*

# The Thief

JUNICHIRO TANIZAKI

It was years ago, at the school where I was preparing for Tokyo Imperial University.

My dormitory roommates and I used to spend a lot of time at what we called "candlelight study" (there was very little studying to it), and one night, long after lights-out, the four of us were doing just that, huddled around a candle talking on and on.

I recall that we were having one of our confused, heated arguments about love—a problem of great concern to us in those days. Then, by a natural course of development, the conversation turned to the subject of crime: we found ourselves talking about such things as swindling, theft, and murder.

"Of all crimes, the one we're most likely to commit is murder." It was Higuchi,[1] the son of a well-known professor, who declared this. "But I don't believe I'd ever steal—I just couldn't do it. I think I could be friends with any other kind of person, but a thief seems to belong to a different species." A shadow of distaste darkened his handsome features. Somehow that frown emphasized his good looks.

"I hear there's been a rash of stealing in the dormitory lately." This time it was Hirata[2] who spoke. "Isn't that so?" he asked, turning to Nakamura,[3] our other roommate.

"Yes, and they say it's one of the students."

"How do they know?" I asked.

"Well, I haven't heard all the details—" Nakamura dropped his voice to a confidential whisper. "But it's happened so often it must be an inside job."

"Not only that," Higuchi put in, "one of the fellows in the north wing was just going into his room the other day when somebody pushed the door open from the inside, caught him with a hard slap in the face, and ran away down the hall. He chased after him, but by the time he got to the bottom of the stairs the other one was out of sight. Back in his room, he found his trunk and bookshelves in a mess, which proves it was the thief."

"Did he see his face?"

"No, it all happened too fast, but he says he looked like one of us, the way he was dressed. Apparently he ran down the hall with his coat pulled up over his head—the one thing sure is that his coat had a wisteria crest."[4]

"A wisteria crest?" said Hirata. "You can't prove anything by that." Maybe it was only my imagination, but I thought he flashed a suspicious look at me. At the same moment I felt that I instinctively made a wry face, since my own family crest is a wisteria design. It was only by chance that I wasn't wearing my crested coat that night.

---

1. **Higuchi:** (hē gōō chē)
2. **Hirata:** (hē rä tä)
3. **Nakamura:** (nä kä mōō rä)
4. **wisteria crest:** a family emblem designed in the shape of a wisteria, a flowering shrub, and made into a cloth patch that can be sewn on a coat pocket.

"If he's one of us, it won't be easy to catch him. Nobody wants to believe there's a thief among us." I was trying to get over my embarrassment because of that moment of weakness.

## "If he's one of us, it won't be easy to catch him."

"No, they'll get him in a couple of days," Higuchi said emphatically. His eyes were sparkling. "This is a secret, but they say he usually steals things in the dressing room of the bathhouse, and for two or three days now the proctors[5] have been keeping watch. They hide overhead and look down through a little hole."

"Oh? Who told you that?" Nakamura asked.

"One of the proctors. But don't go around talking about it."

"If *you* know so much, the thief probably knows it too!" said Hirata, looking disgusted.

Here I must explain that Hirata and I were not on very good terms. In fact, by that time we barely tolerated each other. I say "we," but it was Hirata who had taken a strong dislike to me. According to a friend of mine, he once remarked scornfully that I wasn't what everyone seemed to think I was, that he'd had a chance to see through me. And again: "I'm sick of him. He'll never be a friend of mine. It's only out of pity that I have anything to do with him."

He only said such things behind my back; I never heard them from him directly, though it was obvious that he loathed me. But it wasn't in my nature to demand an explanation. "If there's something wrong with me he ought to say so," I told myself. "If he doesn't have the kindness to tell me what it is, or if he thinks I'm not worth bothering with, then I won't think of *him* as a friend either." I felt a little lonely when I thought of his contempt for me, but I didn't really worry about it.

Hirata had an admirable physique and was the very type of masculinity that our school prides itself on, while I was skinny and pale and high-strung. There was something basically incompatible about us: I had to resign myself to the fact that we lived in separate worlds. Furthermore, Hirata was a judo expert of high rank and displayed his muscles as if to say: "Watch out, or I'll give you a thrashing!" Perhaps it seemed cowardly of me to take such a meek attitude toward him, and no doubt I *was* afraid of his physical strength; but fortunately I was quite indifferent to matters of trivial pride or prestige. "I don't care how contemptuous the other fellow is; as long as I can go on believing in myself, I don't need to feel bitter toward him." That was how I made up my mind, and so I was able to match Hirata's arrogance with my own cool magnanimity. I even told one of the other boys: "I can't help it if Hirata doesn't understand me, but I appreciate his good points anyway." And I actually believed it. I never considered myself a coward. I was even rather conceited, thinking I must be a person of noble character to be able to praise Hirata from the bottom of my heart.

"A wisteria crest?" That night, when Hirata cast his sudden glance at me, the malicious look in his eyes set my nerves on edge. What

---

5. **proctors:** school officials who maintain order and supervise examinations.

*Words to Know and Use*

**emphatically** (em fat′ i kəl lē) *adv.* forcefully; definitely
**loathe** (lōth) *v.* to hate
**contempt** (kən tempt′) *n.* the rejection of someone or something as worthless

Tom Curry   Illustration originally appeared in *Monkey King* by Timothy Mo.

could that look possibly mean? Did he know that my family crest was wisteria? Or did I take it that way simply because of my own private feelings? If Hirata suspected *me*, how was I to handle the situation? Perhaps I should laugh good-naturedly and say: "Then I'm under suspicion too, because I have the same crest." If the others laughed along with me, I'd be all right. But suppose one of them, say Hirata, only began looking grimmer and grimmer— what then? When I visualized that scene I couldn't very well speak out impulsively.

*Words to Know and Use*   |   **impulsively** (im pul' siv lē) *adv.* suddenly; without careful thought

It sounds foolish to worry about such a thing, but during that brief silence all sorts of thoughts raced through my mind. "In this kind of situation what difference is there, really, between an innocent man and an actual criminal?" By then I felt that I was experiencing a criminal's anxiety and isolation. Until a moment ago I had been one of their friends, one of the elite of our famous school. But now, if only in my own mind, I was an outcast. It was absurd, but I suffered from my inability to confide in them. I was uneasy about Hirata's slightest mood—Hirata who was supposed to be my equal.

"A thief seems to belong to a different species." Higuchi had probably said this casually enough, but now his words echoed ominously in my mind.

"A thief belongs to a different species. . . ." A thief! What a detestable name to be called! I suppose what makes a thief different from other men is not so much his criminal act itself as his effort to hide it at all costs, the strain of trying to put it out of his mind, the dark fears that he can never confess. And now I was becoming enshrouded by that darkness. I was trying not to believe that I was under suspicion; I was worrying about fears that I could not admit to my closest friend. Of course it must have been because Higuchi trusted me that he told us what he'd heard from the proctor. "Don't go around talking about it," he had said, and I was glad. But why should I feel glad? I thought. After all, Higuchi has never suspected me. Somehow I began to wonder about his motive for telling us.

It also struck me that if even the most virtuous person has criminal tendencies, maybe I wasn't the only one who imagined the possibility of being a thief. Maybe the others were experiencing a little of the same discomfort, the same elation. If so, then Higuchi, who had been singled out by the proctor to share his secret, must have felt very proud. Among the four of us it was he who was most trusted, he who was thought least likely to belong to that "other species." And if he won that trust because he came from a wealthy family and was the son of a famous professor, then I could hardly avoid envying him. Just as his social status improved his moral character, so my own background—I was acutely conscious of being a scholarship student, the son of a poor farmer—debased mine. For me to feel a kind of awe in his presence had nothing to do with whether or not I was a thief. We *did* belong to different species. I felt that the more he trusted me, with his frank, open attitude, the more the gulf between us deepened. The more friendly we tried to be, joking with each other in apparent intimacy, gossiping and laughing together, the more the distance between us increased. There was nothing I could do about it.

For a long time afterward I worried about whether or not I ought to wear that coat of mine with the "wisteria crest." Perhaps if I wore it around nonchalantly no one would pay any attention. But suppose they looked at me as much as to say: "Ah, he's wearing it!" Some would suspect me, or try to suppress their doubts of me, or feel sorry for me because I was under suspicion. If I became embarrassed and uneasy not only with Hirata and Higuchi but with all the students, and if I then felt obliged to put my coat away, that would seem even more sinister. What I dreaded was not the bare fact of being suspect, but all the unpleasant emotions that would be stirred up in others. If I were to cause doubt in other people's minds, I would create a barrier between myself and those who had always been my friends. Even theft itself was not as ugly as the suspicions that would be aroused by it. No one would want to think of me as a thief: as long as it hadn't been proved, they'd want to go on associating with me as freely as ever, forcing themselves to trust me. Otherwise, what would friendship mean? Thief or not, I might be guilty of a worse sin than stealing from a friend: the sin of spoiling a friendship. Sowing seeds of doubt about myself was criminal. It *was* worse than stealing. If I were a prudent, clever thief—no, I mustn't put it that way—if I were a thief with the least bit of conscience and consideration for other people, I'd try to keep my friendships untarnished, try to be open with my friends, treat them with a sincerity and warmth that I need never be ashamed of, while carrying out my thefts in secrecy. Perhaps I'd be what people call "a brazen thief," but if you look at it from the thief's point of view, it's the most honest attitude to take. "It's true that I steal, but it's equally true that I value my friends," such a man would say. "That is typical of a thief, that's why he belongs to a different species." Anyhow, when I started thinking that way, I couldn't help becoming more and more aware of the distance between me and my friends. Before I knew it I felt like a full-fledged thief.

## *Before I knew it I felt like a full-fledged thief.*

One day I mustered up my courage and wore the crested coat out on the school grounds. I happened to meet Nakamura, and we began walking along together.

"By the way," I remarked, "I hear they haven't caught the thief yet."

"That's right," Nakamura answered, looking away.

"Why not? Couldn't they trap him at the bathhouse?"

"He didn't show up there again, but you still hear about lots of things being stolen in other places. They say the proctors called Higuchi in the other day and gave him the devil for letting their plan leak out."

"Higuchi?" I felt the color drain from my face.

"Yes. . . ." He sighed painfully, and a tear rolled down his cheek. "You've got to forgive me! I've kept it from you till now, but I think you ought to know the truth. You won't like this, but you're the one the proctors suspect. I hate to talk about it—I've never suspected you for a minute. I believe in you. And because I believe in you, I just had to tell you. I hope you won't hold it against me."

"Thanks for telling me. I'm grateful to you." I was almost in tears myself, but at the same time I thought: "It's come at last!" As much as I dreaded it, I'd been expecting this day to arrive.

"Let's drop the subject," said Nakamura, to comfort me. "I feel better now that I've told you."

"But we can't put it out of our minds just because we hate to talk about it. I appreciate your kindness, but I'm not the only one who's been humiliated—I've brought shame on you too, as my friend. The mere fact that I'm under suspicion makes me unworthy of friendship. Any way you look at it, my reputation is ruined. Isn't that so? I imagine you'll turn your back on me too."

"I swear I never will—and I don't think you've brought any shame on me." Nakamura seemed alarmed by my reproachful tone. "Neither does Higuchi. They say he did his best to defend you in front of the proctors. He

---

*Words to Know and Use* | **brazen** (brā′zən) *adj.* bold; shameless
**reproachful** (ri prōch′ fəl) *adj.* expressing blame

told them he'd doubt himself before he doubted you."

"But they still suspect me, don't they? There's no use trying to spare my feelings. Tell me everything you know. I'd rather have it that way."

Then Nakamura hesitantly explained: "Well, it seems the proctors get all kinds of tips. Ever since Higuchi talked too much that night there haven't been any more thefts at the bathhouse, and that's why they suspect you."

"But I wasn't the only one who heard him!"—I didn't say this, but the thought occurred to me immediately. It made me feel even more lonely and wretched.

"But how did they know Higuchi told us? There were only the four of us that night, so if nobody else knew it, and if you and Higuchi trust me—"

"You'll have to draw your own conclusions," Nakamura said, with an imploring look. "You know who it is. He's misjudged you, but I don't want to criticize him."

A sudden chill came over me. I felt as if Hirata's eyes were glaring into mine.

"Did you talk to him about me?"

"Yes. . . . But I hope you realize that it isn't easy, since I'm his friend as well as yours. In fact, Higuchi and I had a long argument with him last night, and he says he's leaving the dormitory. So I have to lose one friend on account of another."

I took Nakamura's hand and gripped it hard. "I'm grateful for friends like you and Higuchi," I said, tears streaming from my eyes. Nakamura cried too. For the first time in my life I felt that I was really experiencing the warmth of human compassion. This was what I had been searching for while I was tormented by my sense of helpless isolation. No matter how vicious a thief I might be, I could never steal anything from Nakamura.

After a while I said: "To tell you the truth, I'm not worth the trouble I'm causing you. I can't stand by in silence and see you two lose such a good friend because of someone like me. Even though he doesn't trust me, I still respect him. He's a far better man than I am. I recognize his value as well as anyone. So why don't I move out instead, if it's come to that? Please—let *me* go, and you three can keep on living together. Even if I'm alone I'll feel better about it."

"But there's no reason for you to leave," said Nakamura, his voice charged with emotion. "I recognize his good points too, but you're the one that's being persecuted. I won't side with him when it's so unfair. If *you* leave, *we* ought to leave too. You know how stubborn he is— once he's made up his mind to go he's not apt to change it. Why not let him do as he pleases? We might as well wait for him to come to his senses and apologize. That shouldn't take very long anyway."

"But he'll never come back to apologize. He'll go on hating me forever."

Nakamura seemed to assume that I felt resentful toward Hirata. "Oh, I don't think so," he said quickly. "He'll stick to his word—that's both his strength and his weakness—but once he knows he's wrong he'll come and apologize, and make a clean breast of it. That's one of the likable things about him."

"It would be fine if he did . . . ," I said thoughtfully. "He may come back to you, but I don't believe he'll ever make friends with me again. . . . But you're right, he's really likable. I only wish he liked me too."

Nakamura put his hand on my shoulder as if to protect his poor friend, as we plodded listlessly along on the grass. It was evening and a light mist hung over the school grounds: we seemed to be on an island surrounded by endless gray seas. Now and then a few students walking the other way would glance at me and go on. They already know, I thought; they're ostracizing me. I felt an overwhelming loneliness.

That night Hirata seemed to have changed his mind; he showed no intention of moving. But he refused to speak to us—even to Higuchi and Nakamura. Yet for me to leave at this stage was impossible, I decided. Not only would I be disregarding the kindness of my friends, I would be making myself seem all the more guilty. I ought to wait a little longer.

"Don't worry," my two friends were forever telling me. "As soon as they catch him the whole business will clear up." But even after another week had gone by, the criminal was still at large and the thefts were as frequent as ever. At last even Nakamura and Higuchi lost some money and a few books.

"Well, you two finally got it, didn't you? But I have a feeling the rest of us won't be touched." I remember Hirata's taunting look as he made this sarcastic remark.

After supper Nakamura and Higuchi usually went to the library, and Hirata and I were left to confront each other. I found this so uncomfortable that I began spending my evenings away from the dormitory too, either going to the library or taking long walks. One night around nine-thirty I came back from a walk and looked into our study. Oddly enough, Hirata wasn't there, nor did the others seem to be back yet. I went to look in our bedroom, but it was empty too. Then I went back to the study and over to Hirata's desk. Quietly I opened his drawer and ferreted out the registered letter that had come to him from his home a few days ago. Inside the letter were three ten-yen money orders, one of which I leisurely removed and put in my pocket. I pushed the drawer shut again and sauntered out into the hall. Then I went down to the yard, cut across the tennis court, and headed for the dark weedy hollow where I always buried the things I stole. But at that moment someone yelled: "Thief!" and flew at me from behind, knocking me down with a blow to my head. It was Hirata.

"Come on, let's have it! Let's see what you stuck in your pocket!"

"All right, all right, you don't have to shout like that," I answered calmly, smiling at him. "I admit I stole your money order. If you ask for it, I'll give it back to you, and if you tell me to come with you I'll go anywhere you say. So we understand each other, don't we? What more do you want?"

Hirata seemed to hesitate, but soon began furiously raining blows on my face. Somehow the pain was not wholly unpleasant. I felt suddenly relieved of the staggering burden I had been carrying.

"There's no use beating me up like this, when I fell right into your trap for you. I made that mistake because you were so sure of yourself—I thought: 'Why the devil can't I steal from *him*?' But now you've found me out, so that's all there is to it. Later on we'll laugh about it together."

I tried to shake Hirata's hand good-naturedly, but he grabbed me by the collar and dragged me off toward our room. That was the only time Hirata seemed contemptible in my eyes.

"Hey, you fellows, I've caught the thief! You can't say I was taken in by him!" Hirata swaggered into our room and shoved me down in front of Nakamura and Higuchi, who were back from the library. Hearing the commotion, the other boys in the dormitory came swarming around our doorway.

"Hirata's right!" I told my two friends, picking myself up from the floor. "I'm the thief." I

*Words to Know and Use*  |  **ostracize** (äs′ trə sīz′) *v.* to refuse to associate with

151

tried to speak in my normal tone, as casually as ever, but I realized that my face had gone pale.

"I suppose you hate me," I said to them. "Or else you're ashamed of me. . . . You're both honest, but you're certainly gullible. Haven't I been telling you the truth over and over again? I even said: 'I'm not the person you think I am. Hirata's the man to trust. He'll never be taken in.' But you didn't understand. I told you: 'Even if you become friendly with Hirata again, he'll never make friends with *me*!' I went as far as to say: 'I know better than anyone what a fine fellow Hirata is!' Isn't that so? I've never lied to you, have I? You may ask why I didn't come out and tell you the whole truth. You probably think I was deceiving you after all. But try looking at it from my position. I'm sorry, but stealing is one thing I can't control. Still, I didn't like to deceive you, so I told you the truth in a roundabout way. I couldn't be any more honest than that—it's your fault for not taking my hints. Maybe you think I'm just being perverse, but I've never been more serious. You'll probably ask why I don't quit stealing, if I'm so anxious to be honest. But that's not a fair question. You see, I was born a thief. I tried to be as sincere as I could with you under the circumstances. There was nothing else I could do. Even then my conscience bothered me—didn't I ask you to let *me* move out, instead of Hirata? I wasn't trying to fool you, I really wanted to do it for your sake. It's true that I stole from you, but it's also true that I'm your friend. I appeal to your friendship: I want you to understand that even a thief has feelings."

Nakamura and Higuchi stood there in silence, blinking with astonishment.

"Well, I can see you think I've got a lot of nerve. You just don't understand me. I guess it can't be helped, since you're of a different species." I smiled to conceal my bitterness, and added: "But since I'm your friend, I'll warn you that this isn't the last time a thing like this will happen. So be on your guard! You two made friends with a thief because of your gullibility. You're likely to run into trouble when you go out in the world. Maybe you get better grades in school, but Hirata is a better man. You can't fool Hirata!"

When I singled him out for praise, Hirata made a wry face and looked away. At that moment he seemed strangely ill at ease.

Many years have passed since then. I became a professional thief and have been often behind bars; yet I cannot forget those memories—especially my memories of Hirata. Whenever I am about to commit a crime I see his face before me. I see him swaggering about as haughtily as ever, sneering at me: "Just as I suspected!" Yes, he was a man of character with great promise. But the world is mysterious. My prediction that the naïve Higuchi would "run into trouble" was wrong: partly through his father's influence, he has had a brilliant career—traveling abroad, earning a doctoral degree, and today holding a high position in the Ministry of Railways. Meanwhile nobody knows what has become of Hirata. It's no wonder we think life is unpredictable.

I assure my reader that this account is true. I have not written a single dishonest word here. And, as I hoped Nakamura and Higuchi would, I hope you will believe that delicate moral scruples can exist in the heart of a thief like me.

But perhaps you won't believe me either. Unless of course (if I may be pardoned for suggesting it) you happen to belong to my own species. &

| *Words to Know and Use* | **gullible** (gul' ə bəl) *adj.* prone to being easily cheated or tricked **gullibility** *n.*<br>**naïve** (nä ēv') *adj.* simple; childlike<br>**scruples** (skroo' pəls) *n.* concerns or doubts about what is right and wrong |
|---|---|

# *explain*

## *Responding to Reading*

### First Impressions

**1.** Did your attitude toward the main character change as you read? Explain.

### Second Thoughts

**2.** Look again at your crime detection chart. What clues helped you identify the thief, and what clues are misleading?

**3.** The narrator claims that "theft itself was not as ugly as the suspicions that would be aroused by it." Why is he so concerned about how others view him?

> **Think about**
> • his views about friendship
> • how he is affected by the opinions of others
> • the importance of reputation in Japanese culture

**4.** Why are Higuchi and Nakamura so astonished that the narrator is the thief?

**5.** Hirata makes no attempt to hide his dislike and distrust of the narrator. Why does the narrator continue to admire him?

**6.** Evaluate the narrator's judgment of himself and others.

> **Think about**
> • why he describes himself as both honorable and honest
> • his predictions for both Hirata and Higuchi
> • his opinion of Higuchi and Nakamura

### Broader Connections

**7.** Hirata chooses to turn in the thief. If you caught a friend stealing from you, what would you do? When faced with a conflict between loyalty to a friend and obedience to a law or moral principle, how do you decide?

## *Literary Concept: First-Person Point of View*

In literature, **point of view** refers to who narrates a story and how much that narrator knows. In a story told from the **first-person point of view,** the writer chooses to have a character within the story narrate it, using the first-person pronouns *I* and *me.* This method of storytelling lets the reader see and know only what that character, the narrator, sees and knows.

"The Thief" is narrated by the robber himself. What difference would it have made to the story if another character, such as Hirata, had narrated it? How would that shift have affected your view of the thief and the other characters?

## Writing Options

1. Go back through "The Thief" to find clues that you may have missed in your first reading. Add these clues to your chart and underline them so that you can tell them apart from the first clues you found. When your list is complete, discuss what you learned by rereading the story.

2. The thief says that he "didn't like to deceive" his friends, so he told "the truth in a roundabout way." Explain whether or not you think he should be considered a liar. Include specific examples from the story to back up your opinion.

3. As one of the characters in the story, write a letter home to your parents, explaining what has happened in your dormitory.

4. The narrator says that he fell into the trap that Hirata set for him. Assume that you are Hirata. Using the first-person point of view, write an article for your school newspaper in which you explain why you were suspicious and how you set your trap.

## Vocabulary Practice

**Exercise** On your paper, write the word from the list that is the best substitute for each boldfaced phrase below.

1. Everyone looked up to the **finest group**.
2. Students will **not associate with** a thief.
3. The thief strolled **without any cares**.
4. The narrator was a **shameless** thief.
5. Hirata did not **restrain** his anger.
6. The narrator felt a wave of **extreme joy**.
7. Nakamura was so **easily fooled**.
8. The two friends were **inexperienced like children**.
9. Hirata viewed the thief with **an attitude that he was worthless.**
10. Rumors about the thief rumbled **threateningly**.
11. You might expect the thief to **hate** Hirata.
12. The thief had no **moral doubts** about stealing.
13. Hirata spoke **forcefully**.
14. Some thefts were carried out **on the spur of the moment**.
15. His friend's attitude toward the thief was **expressing blame**.

*Words to Know and Use*

brazen
contempt
elation
elite
emphatically
gullible
impulsively
loathe
naïve
nonchalantly
ominously
ostracize
reproachful
scruples
suppress

## *Options for Learning*

**1** • **Peer Counseling** Sometimes a person's peers can help him or her overcome problems. Work together in small groups to evaluate the thief's problems. Create a report card in which you list major aspects of his personality, with a grade assigned for each one. Include both his negative and positive traits. At the bottom of the card, write down advice that might help him turn his life around.

**2** • **High Anxiety** Investigate the entrance exams of Japan's universities. How do high school students prepare for these tests? What happens to students who fail their exams? You might call a Japanese government or tourist office for information, or consult your local library. Then prepare an oral report describing what you found. Explain how pressures to succeed may have affected characters in the story.

**3** • **An Artist's Rendition** Draw a picture that represents how the narrator views himself. Your picture can be realistic—the image that he might see in the mirror—or symbolic. A symbolic picture might be anything from a nightmare vision to a cartoon that suggests his state of mind.

**4** • **Culture and Honor** Using what you have learned about Japan, role-play how the narrator's parents and other family members would react to the news of his crimes. Then role-play how an American family might respond to the same news about a family member. Discuss the differences and similarities between the two responses.

**FACT FINDER**

*What subjects do Japanese students study in high school?*

## *Junichiro Tanizaki*
### 1888–1965

Some critics consider Tanizaki to be the Japanese counterpart to the American Edgar Allan Poe. Like Poe, whom he read and admired, Tanizaki has been recognized as one of his own country's greatest storytellers, a writer with a fine sense of beauty and craft. However, he was also a tortured soul whose writing reflected his own fears and insecurities. Tanizaki spent his life in pursuit of beautiful and powerful women, three of whom he married. His frequently bizarre characters, like the narrator in "The Thief," are often out of control and self-destructive, victims of their own impulses. Though the subject matter of his stories and novels makes some readers uncomfortable, Tanizaki has gained respect as one of Japan's most gifted writers.

*Fiction*

# The Last Judgment

KAREL ČAPEK   (kär′ əl chä′ pek′)

## Examine What You Know

Since this story is about a man brought to trial for his crimes, it will be useful to review what you know about trials. The chart below identifies the major participants in a typical jury trial. Copy the chart and fill it in, based on your knowledge of the role each participant plays. As you read ''The Last Judgment,'' notice what is *not* typical about the participants of the trial.

| Participant | Description of Purpose |
|---|---|
| Judge | |
| Defendant | |
| Witness | |
| Jury | |
| Prosecuting lawyer | |
| Defense lawyer | |

## Expand Your Knowledge

In this story, the Czechoslovakian writer Karel Čapek (1890-1938) provides his own account of a last judgment. Many religions have versions of the Last Judgment. According to many Christians, God judges both the living and the dead at the end of the world, deciding who should be sent to heaven or hell. In the Islam faith, a person's eternal fate depends on the evidence in two books, one that records good deeds, the other with a complete account of bad deeds. Hindus believe in a process of rebirth after death called reincarnation. The soul of a good person moves to a higher form of life after death, while a bad soul takes the body of a lower animal form.

## Write Before You Read

■ *A biography of the author can be found in the Reader's Handbook.*

Many great writers have attempted to describe life after death. What are your beliefs about the existence of an afterlife? If there is an afterlife, is it the same for everyone? In your journal or notebook, describe your beliefs.

# The Last Judgment

### KAREL ČAPEK

The notorious multiple killer Kugler, pursued by several warrants and a whole army of policemen and detectives, swore that he'd never be taken. He wasn't, either—at least not alive. The last of his nine murderous deeds was shooting a policeman who tried to arrest him. The policeman indeed died, but not before putting a total of seven bullets into Kugler. Of these seven, three were fatal. Kugler's death came so quickly that he felt no pain. And so it seemed Kugler had escaped earthly justice.

When his soul left his body, it should have been surprised at the sight of the next world—a world beyond space, gray, and infinitely desolate—but it wasn't. A man who has been jailed on two continents looks upon the next life merely as new surroundings. Kugler expected to struggle through, equipped only with a bit of courage, as he had in the last world.

At length the inevitable Last Judgment got around to Kugler.

Heaven being eternally in a state of emergency, Kugler was brought before a special court of three judges and not, as his previous conduct would ordinarily merit, before a jury. The courtroom was furnished simply, almost like courtrooms on earth, with this one exception: there was no provision for swearing in witnesses. In time, however, the reason for this will become apparent.

The judges were old and worthy councillors with austere, bored faces. Kugler complied with the usual tedious formalities: Ferdinand Kugler, unemployed, born on such and such a date, died . . . at this point it was shown Kugler didn't know the date of his own death. Immediately he realized this was a damaging omission in the eyes of the judges; his spirit of helpfulness faded.

"Do you plead guilty or not guilty?" asked the presiding judge.

"Not guilty," said Kugler obdurately.

"Bring in the first witness," the judge sighed.

Opposite Kugler appeared an extraordinary gentleman, stately, bearded, and clothed in a blue robe strewn with golden stars.

At his entrance the judges arose. Even Kugler stood up, reluctant but fascinated. Only when the old gentleman took a seat did the judges again sit down.

"Witness," began the presiding judge, "Omniscient[1] God, this court has summoned You in order to hear Your testimony in the case against Kugler, Ferdinand. As You are the Supreme Truth, You need not take the oath. In the interest of the proceedings, however,

---

1. **omniscient** (äm nish' ənt): knowing all things.

BEGGAR 1938 Mirko Virius From *Naive Painters of Yugoslavia* by Nebojsa Tomasevic.

we ask You to keep to the subject at hand rather than branch out into particulars—unless they have a bearing on this case.

"And you, Kugler, don't interrupt the Witness. He knows everything, so there's no use denying anything.

"And now, Witness, if You would please begin."

That said, the presiding judge took off his spectacles and leaned comfortably on the bench before him, evidently in preparation for a long speech by the Witness. The oldest of the three judges nestled down in sleep. The recording angel opened the Book of Life.

God, the Witness, coughed lightly and began:

"Yes. Kugler, Ferdinand. Ferdinand Kugler, son of a factory worker, was a bad, unmanageable child from his earliest days. He loved his mother dearly but was unable to show it; this made him unruly and defiant. Young man, you irked everyone! Do you remember how you bit your father on the thumb when he tried to spank you? You had stolen a rose from the notary's garden."

"The rose was for Irma, the tax collector's daughter," Kugler said.

"I know," said God. "Irma was seven years old at that time. Did you ever hear what happened to her?"

"No, I didn't."

"She married Oscar, the son of the factory owner. But she died of a miscarriage. You remember Rudy Zaruba?"

"What happened to him?"

"Why, he joined the navy and died accidentally in Bombay. You two were the worst boys in the whole town. Kugler, Ferdinand, was a thief before his tenth year and an inveterate liar. He kept bad company, too: old Gribble, for instance, a drunkard and an idler, living on handouts. Nevertheless, Kugler shared many of his own meals with Gribble."

The presiding judge motioned with his hand, as if much of this was perhaps unnecessary, but Kugler himself asked hesitantly, "And . . . what happened to his daughter?"

"Mary?" asked God. "She lowered herself considerably. In her fourteenth year she married. In her twentieth year she died, remembering you in the agony of her death. By your fourteenth year you were nearly a drunkard yourself, and you often ran away from home. Your father's death came about from grief and worry; your mother's eyes faded from crying. You brought dishonor to your home, and your sister, your pretty sister Martha, never married. No young man would come calling at the home of a thief. She's still living alone and in poverty, sewing until late each night. Scrimping has exhausted her, and patronizing customers hurt her pride."

"What's she doing right now?"

"This very minute she's buying thread at Wolfe's. Do you remember that shop? Once, when you were six years old, you bought a colored glass marble there. On that very same day you lost it and never, never found it. Do you remember how you cried with rage?"

"Whatever happened to it?" Kugler asked eagerly.

"Well, it rolled into the drain and under the gutterspout. As a matter of fact, it's still there, after thirty years. Right now it's raining on earth and your marble is shivering in the gush of cold water."

Kugler bent his head, overcome by this revelation.

But the presiding judge fitted his spectacles back on his nose and said mildly, "Witness, we are obliged to get on with the case. Has the accused committed murder?"

Here the Witness nodded his head.

"He murdered nine people. The first one he killed in a brawl, and it was during his prison term for this crime that he became completely corrupted. The second victim was his unfaithful sweetheart. For that he was sentenced to death, but he escaped. The third was an old man whom he robbed. The fourth was a night watchman."

"Then he died?" Kugler asked.

"He died after three days in terrible pain," God said. "And he left six children behind him. The fifth and sixth victims were an old married couple. He killed them with an axe and found only sixteen dollars, although they had twenty thousand hidden away."

Kugler jumped up.

"Where?"

"In the straw mattress," God said. "In a linen sack inside the mattress. That's where they hid all the money they acquired from greed and penny-pinching. The seventh man he killed in America; a countryman of his, a bewildered, friendless immigrant."

"So it was in the mattress," whispered Kugler in amazement.

"Yes," continued God. "The eighth man was merely a passerby who happened to be in Kugler's way when Kugler was trying to outrun the police. At that time Kugler had periostitis[2] and was delirious from the pain. Young man, you were suffering terribly. The ninth and last was the policeman who killed Kugler exactly when Kugler shot him."

"And why did the accused commit murder?" asked the presiding judge.

"For the same reasons others have," answered God. "Out of anger or desire for money; both deliberately and accidentally—some with pleasure, others from necessity. However, he was generous and often helpful. He was kind to women, gentle with animals, and he kept his word. Am I to mention his good deeds?"

"Thank You," said the presiding judge, "but it isn't necessary. Does the accused have anything to say in his own defense?"

"No," Kugler replied with honest indifference.

"The judges of this court will now take this matter under advisement,"[3] declared the presiding judge, and the three of them withdrew.

Only God and Kugler remained in the courtroom.

"Who are they?" asked Kugler, indicating with his head the men who had just left.

"People like you," answered God. "They were judges on earth, so they're judges here as well."

Kugler nibbled his fingertips. "I expected . . . I mean, I never really thought about it. But I figured You would judge, since—"

"Since I'm God," finished the Stately Gentleman. "But that's just it, don't you see? Because I know everything, I can't possibly judge. That wouldn't do at all. By the way, do you know who turned you in this time?"

"No, I don't," said Kugler, surprised.

"Lucky, the waitress. She did it out of jealousy."

"Excuse me," Kugler ventured, "but You forgot about that good-for-nothing Teddy I shot in Chicago."

"Not at all," God said. "He recovered and is alive this very minute. I know he's an informer, but otherwise he's a very good man and terribly fond of children. You shouldn't think of any person as being completely worthless."

"But I still don't understand why You aren't the judge," Kugler said thoughtfully.

"Because my knowledge is infinite. If judges knew everything, absolutely everything, then they would also understand everything. Their hearts would ache. They couldn't sit in judgment—and neither can I. As it is, they know only about your crimes. I know all about you. The entire Kugler. And that's why I cannot judge."

"But why are they judging . . . the same people who were judges on earth?"

"Because man belongs to man. As you see, I'm only the witness. But the verdict is determined by man, even in heaven. Believe me, Kugler, this is the way it should be. Man isn't worthy of divine judgment. He deserves to be judged only by other men."

At that moment the three returned from their deliberation.

In heavy tones the presiding judge announced, "For repeated crimes of first degree murder, manslaughter, robbery, disrespect for the law, illegally carrying weapons, and for the theft of a rose: Kugler, Ferdinand, is sentenced to lifelong punishment in hell. The sentence is to begin immediately.

"Next case, please: Torrance, Frank.

"Is the accused present in court?" ❧

---

2. **periostitis** (per′ ē äs tīt′ is): a swelling of the connective tissue covering the bones.

3. **advisement** (ad vīz′ mənt): careful consideration.

## *Responding to Reading*

### First Impressions

**1.** Who is your favorite character and why?

### Second Thoughts

**2.** How does Čapek's description of the afterlife compare to your own ideas?

**3.** How would you describe the personality of God in this story?

> **Think about**
> - God's way of telling about Kugler's life
> - how the judges view God
> - God's conversation with Kugler
> - your own expectations of how God should act

**4.** Why do the judges condemn Kugler, even though God refuses to do so?

> **Think about**
> - the reasons for their decision
> - God's explanation of why he is not a judge
> - his statement that man "deserves to be judged only by other men"

## *Literary Concept: Situational Irony*

**Situational irony** occurs when a reader or character expects one thing to happen, but something entirely different happens. For example, in Čapek's trial you probably did not expect to see God on the witness stand, nor were you likely to anticipate the treatment he is given. Writers use situational irony to make their stories interesting or humorous, and sometimes to force their readers to reexamine their own thoughts and values.

Find examples of situational irony in "The Last Judgment." How does Čapek's use of irony affect your enjoyment of the story?

## *Writing Options*

**1.** If you were the judge, what would your verdict have been? Write an explanation of your verdict, giving reasons based on the story.

**2.** A defense lawyer is required by law to do everything possible to protect the rights of the defendant, even in cases when the defendant confesses to terrible crimes. As Kugler's lawyer, make a list of the points you would use to defend your client.

*Fiction*

## When
## Greek Meets Greek

### SAMUEL SELVON

## Examine What You Know

People are often judged not as individuals but by the racial, ethnic, religious, or social groups to which they belong. Groups are often stereotyped, or labeled, based on simplified and usually inaccurate ideas that people have about them. Think of inaccurate or unfair stereotypes for groups you know. Give your reasons for objecting to the stereotypes.

## Expand Your Knowledge

Samuel Selvon, the author of this story, is from the island of Trinidad in the West Indies. The West Indies are a string of islands that separate the Caribbean Sea from the Atlantic Ocean and stretch from the Bahamas, off the coast of Florida, to Trinidad, off the northern coast of Venezuela in South America. The islands were named the West Indies after Columbus mistook them for the East Indies islands of Asia. The term *Indian*, then, has come to mean any person of color from India or the West Indies, or native-born North or South American peoples.

Since Great Britain used to have colonies in both India and the West Indies, many Indians of both kinds have immigrated to London, the setting of this story, in search of a better life.

## Enrich Your Reading

**Reading Dialect**   In different areas of the world where English is spoken, particular groups of people use dialects, or different pronunciations, vocabulary, and grammatical rules. Even in the United States there are many distinct dialects of English. In this story, the dialect is Caribbean English, except when the characters speak as if they were from India. Often in the Caribbean dialect, helping verbs are dropped and the form of a verb may not follow regular usage. Notice the example below.

■ *A biography of the author can be found in the Reader's Handbook.*

"You look like a man **who looking** for a place to live," Fraser **say**.

As you read, try to hear the sounds and rhythms of this colorful dialect.

# *When Greek Meets Greek*

## SAMUEL SELVON

One morning Ramkilawansingh (after this, we calling this man Ram) was making a study of the noticeboards along Westbourne Grove what does advertise rooms to let. Every now and then he writing down an address or a telephone number, though most of the time his eyes colliding up with *No Colours, Please,* or *Sorry, No Kolors.*

"Red, white and blue, all out but you," Ram was humming a little ditty what children say when they playing whoop. Just as he get down by Bradley's Corner he met Fraser.

"You look like a man who looking for a place to live," Fraser say.

"You look like a man who could tell me the right place to go," Ram say.

"You try down by Ladbroke Grove?" Fraser ask.

"I don't want to go down in that criminal area," Ram say, "at least, not until they find the man who kill Kelso."

"Then you will never live in the Grove," Fraser say.

"You are a contact man,"[1] Ram say, "Which part you think I could get a room, boy?"

Fraser scratch his head. "I know of a landlord up the road who vow that he ain't ever taking anybody who come from the West Indies. But he don't mind taking Indians. He wouldn't know the difference when he see you

is a Indian . . . them English people so foolish they believe every Indian come from India."

"You think I stand a chance?" Ram ask.

"Sure, you stand a chance. All you have to do is put on a turban."

"I never wear a turban in my life; I am a born Trinidadian,[2] a real Creole.[3] All the same, you best hads give me the address, I will pass around there later."

So Fraser give him the address, and Ram went on reading a few more boards, but he got discourage after a while and went to see the landlord.

The first thing the landlord ask him was: "What part of the world do you come from?"

"I am an Untouchable from the heart of India," Ram say. "I am looking for a single room. I dwelt on the banks of the Ganges. Not too expensive."

"But you are not in your national garments," the landlord say.

"When you are in Rome," Ram say, making it sound like an original statement, "do as the Romans do."

---

1. **contact man:** a kind of intermediary, someone whose sources provide information that is hard to come by.
2. **Trinidadian:** someone from the West Indies island of Trinidad.
3. **Creole:** someone born in the West Indies of European parents, or a descendant of such a person.

While the landlord sizing up Ram, an Indian tenant come up the steps to go inside. This fellar was Chandrilaboodoo (after this, we calling this man Chan) and he had a big beard with a hairnet over it, and he was wearing a turban. When he see Ram, he clasp his hands with the palms touching across his chest by way of greeting.

The old Ram catch on quick and do the same thing.

"*Acha, Hindustani*," Chan say.

"*Acha, pilau, papadom, chickenvindaloo*," Ram say desperately, hoping for the best.

Chan nod his head, say good morning to the landlord and went inside.

"That was a narrow shave," Ram thought, "I have to watch out for that man."

"That was Mr. Chan," the landlord say, "he is the only other Indian tenant I have at the moment. I have a single room for two pounds. Are you a student?"

"Who is not a student?" Ram say, getting

STREET SCENE   Charles Ginner   Private collection.

into the mood of the thing. "Man is forever studying ways and means until he passes into the hands of Allah."[4]

Well, to cut a long story short, Ram get a room on the first floor, right next door to Chan, and he move in that same evening.

But as the days going by, Ram had to live like cat-and-mouse with Chan. Every time he see Chan, he have to hide in case this man start up this Hindustani talk again, or start to ask him questions about Mother India. In fact, it begin to get on Ram nerves, and he decide that he had to do something.

"This house too small for the two of we," Ram say to himself, "one will have to go."

So Ram went down in the basement to see the landlord.

"I have the powers of the occult,"[5] Ram say, "and I have come to warn you of this man Chan. He is not a good tenant. He keeps the bathroom dirty, he does not tidy up his room at all, and he is always chanting and saying his prayers loudly and disturbing the other tenants."

"I have had no complaints," the landlord say.

"But I am living next door to him," Ram say, "and if I concentrate my powers I can see through the wall. That man is a menace, and the best thing you can do is to give him notice. You have a good house here and it would be a pity to let one man spoil it for the other tenants."

"I will have a word with him about it," the landlord say.

Well, the next evening Ram was in his room when he hear a knock at the door. He run in the corner quick and stand upon his head, and say, "Come in."

The landlord come in.

"I am just practicing my yogurt," Ram say.

"I have had a word with Mr. Chan," the landlord say, "and I have reason to suspect that you have deceived me. You are not from India, you are from the West Indies."

Ram turn right-side up. "I am a citizen of the world," he say.

"You are flying false colors," the landlord say. "You do not burn incense like Mr. Chan, you do not dress like Mr. Chan, and you do not talk like Mr. Chan."

"Give me a break, old man," Ram say, falling back on the good old West Indian dialect.

"It is too late. You have already started to make trouble. You must go."

Well, the very next week find Ram out scouting again, giving the boards a perusal,[6] and who he should chance to meet but Fraser.

He start to tell Fraser how life hard, how he had to keep dodging from this Chan fellar all the time, and it was pure torture.

"Listen," Fraser say, "you don't mean a big fellar with a beard, and he always wearing a turban?"

"That sound like him," Ram say. "You know him?"

"Know him!" Fraser say. "Man, that is a fellar from Jamaica who I send to that house to get a room!" 🕭

---

4. **Allah:** the Muslim (Moslem) name for God.

5. **occult:** relating to any of the mysterious arts, such as magic or astrology.

6. **perusal:** close look.

## Responding to Reading

### First Impressions

1. Did you find the story humorous? Why or why not?

### Second Thoughts

2. How does Ram stereotype people from India?

    **Think about**
    - his treatment of Chan
    - his behavior as a tenant
    - what he says to the landlord

3. Find examples of stereotyping by every other character in the story.

4. What problems does the stereotyping in this story create?

    **Think about**
    - what happens to Ram and Chan
    - how other West Indians would be affected
    - its effect on people from India

5. The author narrates this story in Caribbean dialect. What effect does this style have on you as the reader?

6. Why do you think this story is titled "When Greek Meets Greek"?

### Broader Connections

7. What immigrants, or people from foreign countries, have settled in your area? In what ways do you think this story applies to how they are treated?

## Writing Options

1. Pretend that you are Ram and write a letter to the Bureau of Fair Housing in London complaining about the landlord's discrimination against West Indians.

2. If Ram had decided to place a want ad seeking a room to rent, he would have had to mention his needs as well as his positive points as a renter and neighbor. Using what you know about Ram from the story, write the want ad for him.

3. Rewrite the first three complete paragraphs on page 165 without the Caribbean dialect. Follow the standard rules of English grammar and usage in your writing.

# WRITER'S WORKSHOP

## EXPOSITION

Throughout history, readers have been fascinated by fictional criminals such as those in this subunit—their exploits and the punishments they earn. Stories about famous crimes capture headlines and regularly make bestseller lists.

In this workshop you will get an opportunity to find out about one or more famous criminals and create your own biographical account of his or her exploits.

Here is your PASSkey to this assignment.

### GUIDED ASSIGNMENT: BIOGRAPHICAL ARTICLE

Write a biographical article about a famous criminal or crime. Include information about the criminal's life, as well as his or her crimes. Model your article after those found in serious newsmagazines such as *Time,* or imitate the colorful style of a tabloid such as the *National Enquirer.*

**P**URPOSE: To provide information

**A**UDIENCE: Readers of popular magazines and tabloids

**S**UBJECT: A famous criminal or crime

**S**TRUCTURE: A multi-paragraph article

## Prewriting

**STEP 1** **Brainstorm with your class** Work together to create a list of criminals and their crimes. These may be criminals from the past, such as Jack the Ripper, Bonnie and Clyde, or Al Capone, or fairly recent crimes, such as England's "Great Train Robbery," the Watergate crimes, or the spy case involving U.S. Marine guards in Moscow. Choose a subject from this list that interests you, or find one of your own. If you are stuck for ideas, chat with a history teacher or a librarian.

**STEP 2** **Research your criminal or crime** Collect facts, biographical information, and perhaps some quotes by the criminal, his or her friends, victims, or the police. Look up your subject's name in the card catalog. Also, try general entries such as "crime," "law," "criminals," and "justice." If the crime is current, the *Readers' Guide to Periodical Literature* or newspaper indexes might be more useful. If you have difficulty, ask a librarian for help.

**STEP 3** **Take notes** Read the Guidelines for Research and Report Writing in the **Writer's Handbook** of this book before you begin taking notes. Then use note cards to gather information about your subject. In your own words, list one fact per card. Keep a separate card for each major idea, fact, or quotation you use. Be sure to write down the source of each quotation.

Also use your note cards to create a bibliography. Read the Guidelines for Research and Report Writing for information about bibliographies.

As you take notes, pay attention to any patterns or general topics that emerge. These patterns form the basis of a rough outline.

---

### Special Tip

To avoid plagiarism, use only your own words and phrases, never complete sentences, on your note cards. Then, when you begin your first draft you will create your own sentences from your notes. Only use the author's words when they are so vivid and descriptive that they make a point more clearly than you can. Still, use only short phrases, making sure you use quotation marks on your note cards to identify wording that is not your own.

---

**STEP 4** **Organize your notes** You might choose one of the following patterns as a way of ordering your notes and then writing.

1. Use a chronological order.
2. Begin with the crime, then move on to the criminal's life.
3. Start at the end of the criminal's life or trial, and return to his or her beginnings.
4. Open with a vivid description of the criminal or crime, and then move to the biographical information.

Whatever sequence you choose, begin with an attention-grabbing statement and end with some final idea about or event in your subject's life. Number your note cards in the order in which you plan to use them. They can then serve as a rough outline as you write.

STEP **5** **Study the competition** Decide whether your model will be a serious newsmagazine or a tabloid. Then look at several articles in that type of magazine. Notice how the articles begin. Also note the length of paragraphs and of the entire article. Analyze how the information is organized and the style of writing. Finally, pay attention to how the article ends.

## Drafting

Write a rough draft of your article, using your notes in the same order in which you arranged them. If as you write you find another organization works better, feel free to change it. You may find at a particular point that you need more information. If so, go back to the library and do more research.

Make your first paragraph snappy and captivating for your readers, something that will make them want to continue reading. Remember from your research of similar articles in magazines that your paragraphs should not be very long and that factual and biographical information should be vivid and descriptive. An occasional quote from your subject, victims, or the police is effective, but keep quotes to a minimum, and make sure you are not using another writer's words as your own.

At the end of your paper, add a bibliography. Follow the format shown in the Guidelines for Research and Report Writing.

## Revising and Editing

Share your article with a small peer group, and ask them to help you analyze your writing, using the following guidelines.

### Revision Checklist

1. What are the most interesting elements of the article?
2. How well does the opening paragraph catch the reader's attention? How might it be improved?
3. Does the information seem to be accurate?
4. Is the sequence of ideas and information easy to follow? Can anything be shifted to another place to help the flow?
5. Is there enough information to give the reader a good understanding of the crime or criminal? Where could the reader use more information?
6. Are the sources of information noted on a separate bibliography page at the end of the article?

**Editing**   After you revise your article using any helpful ideas you received from your peer group, check for errors in spelling, punctuation (particularly the use of quotation marks), capitalization, and sentence structure. Then create an intriguing title for your article.

## Presenting

Collect the articles from the class, and appoint editors, layout and design editors, proofreaders, and art editors. Work in teams to organize the articles into an actual magazine or supermarket tabloid. Select the most sensational to be the lead articles, that is, the ones that will be mentioned on the cover. Proofread, design the layout, collect and reproduce interesting artwork and photographs, and create a table of contents. Decide on a good method of distribution throughout the school and/or community.

## Reflecting on Your Writing

Answer these questions and file your responses in your writing portfolio.

1. Where did you find the best and most useful information about your subject?
2. What do you like most and least about your article? Why?
3. What part of the writing process did you find the most difficult? Why?

# LANGUAGE WORKSHOP

## STRONG INTRODUCTIONS

Just as a movie preview is meant to capture a viewer's curiosity, the introductory paragraph in your compositions should capture your reader's attention. To "hook" your reader from the very beginning, avoid weak opening sentences like the three below. These sentences lack interesting details, and in fact, they are just plain dull.

> The Homestead Act was passed by Congress in 1862.
> Aggressive behavior is a natural part of our personalities.
> Photographers have been chronicling history for many years.

The following examples show some strong ways to start introductory paragraphs.

### 1. Use a **quotation.**

> When I was a child I liked to read. I loved *Jane Eyre* especially and read it over and over. I didn't know anyone else who liked to read except my mother, and it got me in a lot of trouble because it made me into a thief and a liar. I stole books, and I stole money to buy them . . .
>
> —Jamaica Kincaid, in an interview, Aug. 19, 1990

> In 1966, at the age of 17, with no money, no connections, and no practical training, Elaine Potter Richardson left the West Indian island of Antigua, bound for New York and a job as an *au pair*. She did not return until she was 36. By then she was Jamaica Kincaid, a respected author . . .
>
> Leslie Garis

### 2. Use **intriguing questions** or **startling facts** to make your reader curious.

> When was the last time you were in a fight?
>
> Whatever you answered, you were probably wrong. It wasn't the time in the third grade when you bloodied the nose of that wise guy, and it wasn't even last week. It was this morning or a few minutes ago. You might even be in a fight right now, for all you know.
>
> David Rogers

3. Use an **anecdote,** or an interesting or amusing incident.

> On February 27, 1860, a strange-looking figure appeared at the photographic studios of Mathew Brady in New York City. The man who came to have his picture taken was a giant of a man, "half alligator, half horse," according to one of the men who met him that day. His plain black suit was of cheap broadcloth and terribly wrinkled from being packed in a suitcase on a long trip. An ordinary black ribbon, carelessly wound about his neck, served as a tie. Yet this was Abraham Lincoln of Illinois, whose reputation as a compelling speaker had brought him an invitation to speak before the New York Young Republican Party.
>
> Dorothy and Thomas Hoobler

4. Use a vivid **description** that strikes the reader's imagination.

> China! The very name is romantic. In the days of the old China trade, the name evoked spicy aromas of precious teas, visions of delicate silks, or the feel of gaily painted porcelains so moistly smooth and so resonant that nothing in the West compared to them. There were also the mouth-filling names like Houqua and Conseequa, Canton and Macao, sarcenet, nankeen, celadon, willow ware, lapsang souchong, and hyson skin.
>
> Francis Ross Carpenter

**Exercise 1**   Rewrite each introduction below to make it more interesting. Make up any details, quotes, or anecdotes you need.

1. Taking part in sports is good for you. Sports teach you about teamwork and competition. They also build self-confidence. Whether your favorite sport is basketball or diving, baseball or tennis, what you learn by playing will last all your life.

2. Watching movies is my hobby. There's something about those huge images in a dark theater that gets my imagination going. I especially like the old classics.

3. English is a difficult language. It has lots of rules and lots of exceptions to those rules. Many English words sound or look alike, too, and that can cause problems.

4. This paper is about recycling. Everyone should do it. If more people recycled, we could improve our environment, save money, and conserve natural resources.

**Exercise 2 Analyzing and Revising Your Writing**

1. Take a piece of writing from your portfolio.
2. Reread your introduction.
3. Revise your introduction so that it will capture your reader's interest.

# STUDY SKILLS
### WORKSHOP

## REFERENCE MATERIALS

You are already familiar with general reference works, such as dictionaries and encyclopedias. However, there are many other important reference sources. These are shelved in a separate room or section in the library and marked with an **R** or **REF** above the call number on the spine of the book. The descriptions below will explain what kind of information each of these resources contains.

**Almanacs and Yearbooks**   These books, published annually, are useful sources of facts, statistics, and other unusual information about countries and current events.

**Biographical References**   These books contain detailed information about the lives of well-known people. Biographical references vary greatly, so you should check the preface of each work to determine what is the best source of information for your task.

**Literary Reference Books**   These reference books provide information about literature, such as famous quotations by authors, sources for identifying and locating poems, and information about characters from literature.

**Atlases**   These books of maps often include other useful geographical information, such as statistics about the population, climate, and natural resources of various countries.

**The Vertical File**   Many libraries have current pamphlets, booklets, and clippings on a variety of subjects. These materials are often housed in file cabinets known as the vertical file.

**Periodicals**   The *Readers' Guide to Periodical Literature* is a special index for articles from magazines and other publications that appear periodically. Articles are listed alphabetically under subject and author (and titles when necessary).

**Exercise**   What type of reference from the list above would be the best source of information on the following topics or questions?

1. Nobel prize winners of the last twenty-five years
2. the climate of New Guinea
3. When did E. B. White publish his first book?
4. Who was the character Quasimodo?
5. recycling

## SPACE SAVERS

**Microforms** are very small photos of printed pages, stored on film cards or filmstrips. Microforms save space in the library; ask the librarian to demonstrate how to use the special machines for reading microfilm.

The **CD-ROM** (Compact Disc-Read Only Memory) provides a computerized method of researching magazines. A user can search the computer alphabetically for the author, title, or subject of an article and then receive a display or printout of the information.

# EXPLORING HUMAN NATURE

*he longest journey is the journey inward.*"

Dag Hammarskjöld

PHILOSOPHER IN MEDITATION
(detail)  1632  Rembrandt van Rijn
The Louvre, Paris/Giraudon/Art
Resource, New York.

175

# Life in the Renaissance

KING HENRY VIII OF ENGLAND c. 1536 after Hans Holbein The Granger Collection, New York.

## A NEW AGE IN EUROPE

A period of intense cultural excitement dawned in Italy in the 1300's, ushering Europe out of the bleakness of the Middle Ages. During this **Renaissance,** or rebirth, scholars revived an interest in classical manuscripts from ancient Greece and Rome. Under the influence of these ancient manuscripts, Europeans began to reject their former view that the world was merely a place to prepare for life after death.

Although still religious, Renaissance Europeans no longer considered the church the center of their social universe. Now they began to place a higher value on active life in this world, including political and social responsibilities. Taking a new delight in art and literature, people of the Renaissance also cultivated personal skills in such areas as athletics, music, and hunting.

## THE BIRTH OF THE BRITISH RENAISSANCE: 1485–1558

For almost two hundred years, the vibrant spirit of the Italian Renaissance barely touched England, which lay devastated by years of war. But the succession of the Tudor king Henry VII to the British throne in 1485 finally brought an end to the unrest. Now England, too, could enjoy its rebirth. During the 1500's, England provided fertile ground for Renaissance ideas to take root. As feudalism declined, English farmers swarmed into towns and cities. There they began to be exposed to exciting new ideas, many circulated in printed books.

Indeed, the spread of the Renaissance to England coincided with that country's adoption of the printing press. England's first printing press rolled out its first book in 1476. Before this revolution in printing technology, it had taken scribes a year to copy two books. Now printers could print hundreds of books in the same time. By 1530 more than half of England's population could read.

## A Renaissance Man

According to writers of the time, the ideal person developed himself in every sphere. Henry VIII, who succeeded his father in 1509, was a perfect Renaissance man. Athletic and handsome, Henry boasted formidable skill as a musician, dancer, and hunter. He could read French, Italian, and Latin. The lusty king also excelled at romance and eventually married six times.

In 1527, desperate for a male heir, Henry sought a divorce from his first wife, Catherine of Aragon. Because he could not obtain a divorce from the Roman Catholic church, in 1534 Henry simply declared himself head of a new church, the Church of England; granted his own divorce; and married Anne Boleyn.

## Religious Struggles

English noblemen and commoners alike joined their king in resenting the Roman Catholic church's abuse of wealth and power. Most supported Henry's bold move. However, some leaders, including the king's chancellor, Thomas More, opposed the king's divorce. More, the author of *Utopia,* was sentenced to death for his disloyalty.

Henry's death in 1547 left England in the fragile hands of his son, Edward, who was barely ten years old at the time of his succession. Edward's six-year reign saw an increase of Protestants—adherents of the Church of England— throughout England. Catherine of Aragon's daughter, Mary, succeeded Edward. A fiercely devout Roman Catholic, Mary attempted to reinstate Catholicism in England by burning Protestants at the stake. Her death in 1558 put an end to this bloody reign of terror. Anne Boleyn's daughter, Elizabeth I, then ascended the throne.

## THE HEIGHT OF THE RENAISSANCE: 1558–1603

If Henry VIII was a perfect Renaissance man, his daughter Elizabeth was every inch the Renaissance woman. An able scholar and accomplished poet, Elizabeth had been schooled in Latin and Greek. The young queen delighted in music, dancing, and the arts.

During her forty-five-year reign, Elizabeth led England to extraordinary achievement. After the English navy defeated the powerful Spanish Armada in 1588, England made great strides in travel and exploration. The country's most lasting achievements, however, took place in the field of literature.

### Renaissance Poetry and Song

An Italian poetic form, the fourteen-line **sonnet,** captivated the Elizabethans. Edmund Spenser, Ben Jonson, and William Shakespeare all wrote sonnets about various forms of love.

Both aristocrats and commoners delighted in popular songs. Thomas Campion published five collections of songs with lute accompaniment. These songs became available to people at every level of English society. Songs also played an important role in dramatic productions.

### The Golden Age of Drama

While miracle, mystery, and morality plays continued to be important forms of popular entertainment, new plays called Elizabethan dramas emerged. Along with devices borrowed from classical dramas, Elizabethan dramas included elements designed to entertain every member of the audience. Even serious tragedies like Shakespeare's *Macbeth* boasted scenes of low comedy and a story line guaranteed to enthrall every watcher.

As a result, people of every social class enthusiastically attended the theater. Pickpockets and thieves loved the crowded theaters, too.

## THE DECLINE OF THE RENAISSANCE: 1603–1660

By the time Queen Elizabeth died, in 1603, the influence of the **Puritans** had begun to grow in England. These strictly religious Protestants believed that the Elizabethan dramas and the rowdy crowds they attracted were highly immoral. The Puritans succeeded in closing many theaters.

While Elizabeth had pursued a moderate policy on religion, her successor, King James of Scotland, actively persecuted the Puritans. Indeed, during James's reign, many Puritans fled England to found Plymouth Colony in the New World.

Despite his persecution of the Puritans, King James rendered a service to religion and literature by commissioning a new English translation of the Bible. Completed in 1611, the King James Bible has had a lasting influence on English literature.

Shakespeare wrote his greatest tragedies, including *Macbeth*, during James's reign. Shakespeare's interest in issues of power may have been sparked by the intense conflicts between the king and **Parliament,** the lawmaking body.

The Stuart kings, James and his son Charles, both believed they had a divine right to rule, independent of Parliament. Thirteen years after Charles suspended the legislative body in 1629, England erupted in civil war. When the Puritan Revolution overthrew King Charles in 1649, the victorious Puritans finally closed all the playhouses. This act brought the final curtain down on the golden age of drama. Scholars date the end of England's Renaissance at 1660, when the country's monarchy was restored.

# Time Line of British and World History 1485—1660

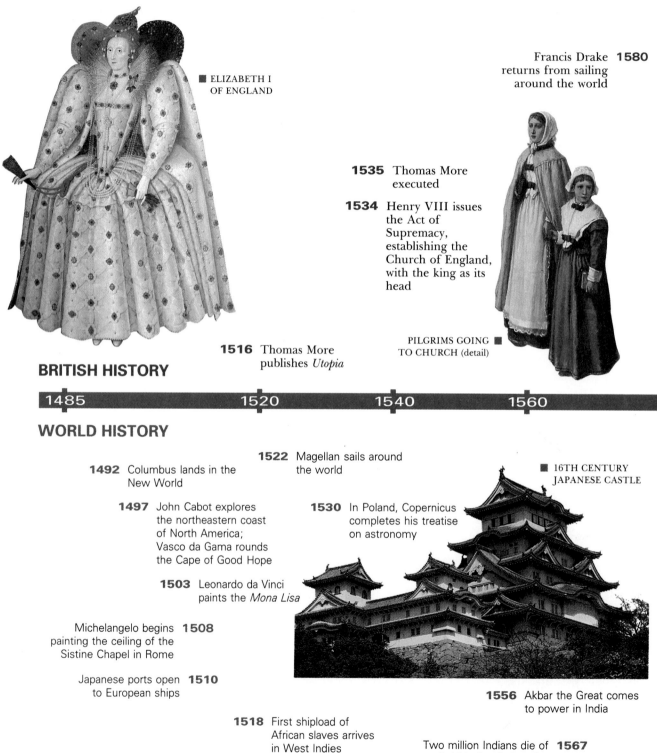

■ ELIZABETH I OF ENGLAND

Francis Drake **1580**
returns from sailing
around the world

**1535** Thomas More
executed

**1534** Henry VIII issues
the Act of
Supremacy,
establishing the
Church of England,
with the king as its
head

PILGRIMS GOING ■
TO CHURCH (detail)

**1516** Thomas More
publishes *Utopia*

## BRITISH HISTORY

**1485**     **1520**     **1540**     **1560**

## WORLD HISTORY

**1522** Magellan sails around
the world

**1492** Columbus lands in the
New World

■ 16TH CENTURY
JAPANESE CASTLE

**1497** John Cabot explores
the northeastern coast
of North America;
Vasco da Gama rounds
the Cape of Good Hope

**1530** In Poland, Copernicus
completes his treatise
on astronomy

**1503** Leonardo da Vinci
paints the *Mona Lisa*

Michelangelo begins **1508**
painting the ceiling of the
Sistine Chapel in Rome

Japanese ports open **1510**
to European ships

**1556** Akbar the Great comes
to power in India

**1518** First shipload of
African slaves arrives
in West Indies

Two million Indians die of **1567**
typhoid in South America

SIR FRANCIS
DRAKE'S SHIP
*THE GOLDEN HIND*

Monarchy restored; **1660**
theaters reopened

Puritan government **1659**
collapses

Oliver Cromwell **1653**
becomes lord
protector

Charles I beheaded **1649**

English Civil War **1642**
begins; Puritans
close theaters

**1628** William Harvey
explains blood
circulation

**1611** King James Bible
published

**1605** Shakespeare's *Macbeth*
first performed

**1599** Globe Theater opens

**1588** English navy defeats
the Spanish Armada

1580     1600     1620     1640     1660

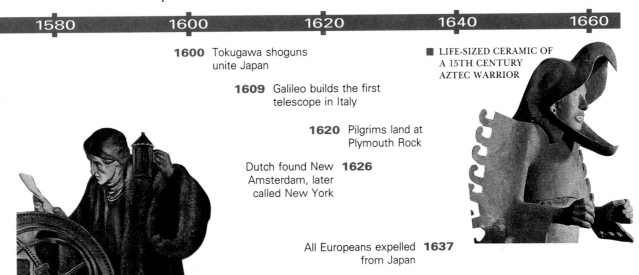

**1600** Tokugawa shoguns
unite Japan

**1609** Galileo builds the first
telescope in Italy

**1620** Pilgrims land at
Plymouth Rock

Dutch found New **1626**
Amsterdam, later
called New York

All Europeans expelled **1637**
from Japan

Ashanti tribes of Africa **1650**
unite for protection

First Dutch settlers **1652**
arrive in South Africa

■ LIFE-SIZED CERAMIC OF
A 15TH CENTURY
AZTEC WARRIOR

■ COPERNICUS STUDYING
MOVEMENT OF THE EARTH

# DEFINING RESPONSIBILITY

What is our responsibility toward other human beings? Where do we draw the line between taking care of our own needs and responding to the needs of others? Renaissance writers often asked such questions as they tried to balance Christian ideals with practical reality. For centuries, philosophers, dreamers, and social critics have sought to define responsibility in their efforts to lay the groundwork for a better society.

The first two selections in this subunit are representative of the Christian idealism of the English Renaissance. The other selections offer different perspectives on responsibility in the modern world.

*Parable*

## *from* The King James Bible
*The Parable of the Good Samaritan*

## **E**xamine What You Know

The parable of the good Samaritan is one of the most famous stories in the Bible. In small groups discuss what you may have heard about the parable and about the expression *good Samaritan*. Think of any examples you have heard that illustrate someone acting as a good Samaritan today.

## **E**xpand Your Knowledge

King James I of England commissioned a translation of the Bible in the early seventeenth century. The king appointed fifty-four distinguished scholars and clergymen to create a new translation that would be more accurate than previous English versions and more beautiful in its use of language. For over three hundred years the *King James Bible* was the main Protestant Bible in English. Even today, although many other translations are available, it still remains the most important and influential of all versions. Almost every major writer in the English language has been affected by its style and content.

The parable you are about to read is like many others that appear throughout the New Testament. Jesus frequently relied on the **parable,** a short story used to teach a moral or religious lesson, to communicate his message. In the story of the Good Samaritan, a Hebrew lawyer questions Jesus about eternal life. Jesus uses a parable about a man from Samaria to answer the lawyer. The Samaritans were hated and scorned by the Jews because their mixed ancestry and religion were considered impure. The priest and the Levite (a member of the priestly tribe), characters in this parable, would have violated Hebrew law if they had touched a dead person, a circumstance which explains their reluctance to get involved.

## **W**rite Before You Read

Who are the outcasts in today's society? Identify the types of people who are considered "unclean," that is, those people who are avoided or looked down upon by other members of society. Explain what you think are the reasons that some people are treated as outcasts.

# from *The King James Bible*

## *The Parable of the Good Samaritan*

And, behold, a certain lawyer stood up, and tempted him, saying, Master, what shall I do to inherit eternal life?

26 He said unto him, What is written in the law? how readest thou?

27 And he answering said, Thou shalt love the Lord thy God with all thy heart, and with all thy soul, and with all thy strength, and with all thy mind; and thy neighbor as thyself.

28 And he said unto him, Thou hast answered right: this do, and thou shalt live.

29 But he, willing to justify himself, said unto Jesus, And who is my neighbor?

30 And Jesus answering said, A certain man went down from Jerusalem to Jericho, and fell among thieves, which stripped him of his raiment,[1] and wounded him, and departed, leaving him half dead.

31 And by chance there came down a certain priest that way; and when he saw him, he passed by on the other side.

32 And likewise a Levite, when he was at the place, came and looked on him, and passed by on the other side.

33 But a certain Samaritan, as he journeyed, came where he was: and when he saw him, he had compassion on him.

34 And went to him, and bound up his wounds, pouring in oil and wine, and set him on his own beast, and brought him to an inn, and took care of him.

35 And on the morrow when he departed, he took out two pence and gave them to the host, and said unto him, Take care of him; and whatsoever thou spendest more, when I come again, I will repay thee.

36 Which now of these three, thinkest thou, was neighbor unto him that fell among the thieves?

37 And he said, He that showed mercy on him. Then said Jesus unto him, Go, and do thou likewise.

—Luke 10:25–37

---

1. **raiment** (rā′ mənt): clothing.

## *R*esponding to Reading

### First Impressions

**1.** What do you think of Jesus' response to the lawyer? Explain your answer.

### Second Thoughts

**2.** What might explain why the priest and Levite act the way they do? In your judgment, are they right or wrong?

> **Think about**
> - whether or not they are responsible for helping a stranger
> - the potential dangers of helping the robbery victim
> - the religious laws that influence their judgment

**3.** Why does Jesus use a Samaritan to make his point about love?

> **Think about**
> - the Hebrew lawyer's question
> - the traditional hatred of the Samaritans
> - the role of the priest and the Levite in the story

**4.** Why does Jesus use a parable to teach his lesson?

**5.** Do you think it is possible to love someone else as well as yourself?

### Broader Connections

**6.** If this parable were told today in your community, what people, or classes of people, might fit the different roles of the victim, the Samaritan, the priest, and the Levite? Review what you wrote about the outcasts of today as a starting point for discussion.

**7.** In 1964 a woman named Kitty Genovese was murdered on a street in New York City. Thirty-eight people witnessed the crime, and no one helped—or even called the police. In another case, a man stopped to help a disabled motorist and was shot for interfering. Is it smart to be a good Samaritan in today's world? How do you decide when to help others and when to protect yourself?

## *W*riting Options

**1.** List several familiar rules for living that you have heard, such as "When the going gets tough, the tough get going" or "If you can't stand the heat, get out of the kitchen." Then write a modern parable based on one of these rules. You may use humor, or you may present a serious lesson.

**2.** In a paragraph, explain why this parable is still famous and relevant almost two thousand years after it was written.

*Fiction*

### *from* *Utopia*

SIR THOMAS MORE

## Examine What You Know

What ideas does the word *utopia* bring to your mind? Pool your ideas with those of your classmates.

The word *utopia* comes from a book by Sir Thomas More. In the following excerpt from the book, More describes the jobs that he believes are essential for the well-being of society. He also refers to jobs that he considers meaningless. List jobs you consider to be the most important to society. Discuss your choices with your class and explain your reasoning.

## Expand Your Knowledge

During the Renaissance, European explorers found new lands and new ways of life in the Americas, Africa, Asia, and Australia. Travelers returned from exotic places, telling stories of unusual peoples and strange customs. Thomas More drew upon the interest in travel literature to create a description of a fictitious perfect society.

More wrote *Utopia*—a made-up word derived from two Greek words meaning "no place"—to make the English think about the problems of their own society. When More wrote this book in 1516, English society was marked by great extremes in wealth, education, and status. Though merchants, bankers, lawyers, and nobles lived very well, most citizens lived amid poverty, disease, and ignorance. *Utopia* describes an imaginary society in which all citizens live dignified, meaningful, and secure lives.

## Enrich Your Reading

**Understanding Contrast**   More uses contrast to highlight differences between the ideal Utopia and the realities of life in England. Make a chart like the one below to keep track of differences he mentions.

|  | Life in Utopia | Life in England |
|---|---|---|
| Occupations | everyone farms<br>everyone learns a craft | only some people farm<br>many people never learn a craft |
| Clothes |  |  |
|  |  |  |

■ *A biography of the author can be found on page 193.*

# from *Utopia*

SIR THOMAS MORE

*In Book One of* Utopia, *More describes how he and a friend met Raphael Hythlodaye, a sailor who has seen much of the newly discovered world. In their discussion Hythlodaye criticizes the evils of the poverty and the luxury he has seen in England. In Book Two, Hythlodaye tells about a faraway land called Utopia that does not have the inequalities or injustices of England. Here, everyone is educated and everyone has work. No one owns property in this land, and all that is produced is shared equally in a spirit of cooperation and reason. At this point, Hythlodaye talks about the various jobs men and women in Utopia have.*

## Occupations

Agriculture is the one pursuit which is common to all, both men and women, without exception. They are all instructed in it from childhood, partly by principles taught in school, partly by field trips to the farms closer to the city as if for recreation. Here they do not merely look on, but, as opportunity arises for bodily exercise, they do the actual work.

Besides agriculture (which is, as I said, common to all), each is taught one particular craft as his own. This is generally either wool-working or linen-making or masonry or metal-working or carpentry. There is no other pursuit which occupies any number worth mentioning. As for clothes, these are of one and the same pattern throughout the island and down the centuries, though there is a distinction between the sexes and between the single and married. The garments are comely to the eye, convenient for bodily movement, and fit for wear in heat and cold. Each family, I say, does its own tailoring.

Of the other crafts, one is learned by each person, and not the men only, but the women too. The latter as the weaker sex have the lighter occupations and generally work wool and flax.[1] To the men are committed the remaining more laborious crafts. For the most part, each is brought up in his father's craft, for which most have a natural inclination. But if anyone is attracted to another occupation, he is transferred by adoption to a family pursuing that craft for which he has a liking. Care is taken not only by his father but by the authorities, too, that he will be assigned to a grave and honorable householder. Moreover, if anyone after being thoroughly taught one craft desires another also, the same permission is given. Having acquired both, he practices his choice unless the city has more need of the one than of the other.

---

1. **flax:** plants with stem fibers that are spun into linen thread.

The chief and almost the only function of the syphogrants[2] is to manage and provide that no one sit idle, but that each apply himself industriously to his trade, and yet that he be not wearied like a beast of burden with constant toil from early morning till late at night. Such wretchedness is worse than the lot of slaves, and yet it is almost everywhere the life of workingmen—except for the Utopians. The latter divide the day and night into twenty-four equal hours and assign only six to work. There are three before noon, after which they go to dinner. After dinner,[3] when they have rested for two hours in the afternoon, they again give three to work and finish up with supper. Counting one o'clock as beginning at midday, they go to bed about eight o'clock, and sleep claims eight hours.

The intervals between the hours of work, sleep, and food are left to every man's discretion, not to waste in revelry or idleness, but to devote the time free from work to some other occupation according to taste. These periods are commonly devoted to intellectual pursuits. For it is their custom that public lectures are daily delivered in the hours before daybreak. Attendance is <u>compulsory</u> only for those who have been specially chosen to devote themselves to learning. A great number of all classes, however, both males and females, flock to hear the lectures, some to one and some to another, according to their natural inclination. But if anyone should prefer to devote this time to his trade, as is the case with many minds which do not reach the level for any of the higher intellectual disciplines, he is not hindered; in fact, he is even praised as useful to the commonwealth.

After supper they spend one hour in recreation, in summer in the gardens, in winter in the common halls in which they have their

meals. There they either play music or entertain themselves with conversation. Dice and that kind of foolish and ruinous game they are not acquainted with. They do play two games not unlike chess. The first is a battle of numbers in which one number plunders another. The second is a game in which the vices fight a pitched battle with the virtues. In the latter is exhibited very cleverly, to begin with, both the strife of the vices with one another and their concerted opposition to the virtues; then,

---

2. **syphogrants** (sī′ fō grants): magistrates who oversee thirty households each and represent them in the Senate.

3. Dinner was usually served between 10:00 A.M. and 11:00 A.M. in England.

*Words to Know and Use* | **compulsory** (kəm pul′ sər ē) *adj.* required; obligatory

THE EFFECTS OF GOOD GOVERNMENT ON THE CITY   Ambrogio Lorenzetti   early 14th century   Palazzo Pubblico, Siena/Scala/Art Resource, New York.

what vices are opposed to what virtues, by what forces they assail them openly, by what stratagems they attack them indirectly, by what safeguards the virtues check the power of the vices, by what arts they frustrate their designs; and, finally, by what means the one side gains the victory.

How do Utopians spend their time in a typical day?

But here, lest you be mistaken, there is one point you must examine more closely. Since they devote but six hours to work, you might

possibly think the consequence to be some scarcity of necessities. But so far is this from being the case that the aforesaid time is not only enough but more than enough for a supply of all that is requisite for either the necessity or the convenience of living. This phenomenon you too will understand if you consider how large a part of the population in other countries exists without working. First, there are almost all the women, who constitute half the whole; or, where the women are busy, there as a rule the men are snoring in their stead. Besides, how great and how lazy is the crowd of priests and so-called religious! Add to them all the rich, especially the masters of estates, who are commonly termed gentlemen

| Words to Know and Use | stratagem (strat′ ə jəm) n. any trick or scheme for achieving some purpose<br>phenomenon (fə näm′ ə nən′) n. any fact or experience that is apparent to the senses |
| --- | --- |

187

and noblemen. Reckon with them their retainers[4]—I mean, that whole rabble of good-for-nothing swashbucklers. Finally, join in the lusty and sturdy beggars who make some disease an excuse for idleness. You will certainly find far less numerous than you had supposed those whose labor produces all the articles that mortals require for daily use.

What is More's attitude toward people who do not work?

Now estimate how few of those who do work are occupied in essential trades. For, in a society where we make money the standard of everything, it is necessary to practice many crafts which are quite vain and <u>superfluous</u>, ministering only to luxury and licentiousness.[5] Suppose the host of those who now toil were distributed over only as few crafts as the few needs and conveniences demanded by nature. In the great abundance of <u>commodities</u> which must then arise, the prices set on them would be too low for the craftsmen to earn their livelihood by their work. But suppose all those fellows who are now busied with unprofitable crafts, as well as all the lazy and idle throng, any one of whom now consumes as much of the fruits of other men's labors as any two of the workingmen, were all set to work and indeed to useful work. You can easily see how small an allowance of time would be enough and to spare for the production of all that is required by necessity or comfort (or even pleasure, provided it be genuine and natural).

*After the narrator describes all the occupations of Utopia, he goes on to describe other aspects of life, including family relations, travel, politics, war, and religion. Some of his concluding comments are presented below.*

Now I have described to you, as exactly as I could, the structure of that <u>commonwealth</u> which I judge not merely the best but the only one which can rightly claim the name of a commonwealth. Outside Utopia, to be sure, men talk freely of the public welfare—but look after their private interests only. In Utopia, where nothing is private, they seriously concern themselves with public affairs. Assuredly in both cases they act reasonably. For, outside Utopia, how many are there who do not realize that, unless they make some separate provision for themselves, however <u>flourishing</u> the commonwealth, they will <u>themselves</u> starve? For this reason, necessity compels them to hold that they must take account of themselves rather than of the people, that is, of others.

Why do people outside of Utopia have to worry about themselves first?

On the other hand, in Utopia, where everything belongs to everybody, no one doubts, provided only that the public granaries are well filled, that the individual will lack nothing for his private use. The reason is that the distribution of goods is not <u>niggardly</u>.[6] In Utopia

---

4. **retainers:** servants.
5. **licentiousness** (lī sen′ shəs nes): a disregard for morals.
6. **niggardly** (nig′ərd lē): stingy.

---

*Words to Know and Use* | **superfluous** (sə pʉr′ flō̄ əs) *adj.* not needed; unnecessary; irrelevant
**commodity** (kə mäd′ ə tē) *n.* anything bought and sold; any article of commerce
**commonwealth** (käm′ ən welth′) *n.* a group of people united by common interests
**flourishing** (flʉr′ ish iŋ) *adj.* prosperous; successful

there is no poor man and no beggar. Though no man has anything, yet all are rich.

For what can be greater riches for a man than to live with a joyful and peaceful mind, free of all worries—not troubled about his

SIR THOMAS MORE   Hans Holbein the Younger   © The Frick Collection, New York.

food or harassed by the querulous demands of his wife or fearing poverty for his son or worrying about his daughter's dowry, but feeling secure about the livelihood and happiness of himself and his family: wife, sons, grandsons,

great-grandsons, great-great-grandsons, and all the long line of their descendants that gentlefolk anticipate? Then take into account the fact that there is no less provision for those who are now helpless but once worked than for those who are still working.

At this point I should like anyone to be so bold as to compare this fairness with the so-called justice prevalent in other nations, among which, upon my soul, I cannot discover the slightest trace of justice and fairness. What brand of justice is it that any nobleman whatsoever or goldsmith-banker or moneylender or, in fact, anyone else from among those who either do no work at all or whose work is of a kind not very essential to the commonwealth, should attain a life of luxury and grandeur on the basis of his idleness or his nonessential work? In the meantime, the common laborer, the carter, the carpenter, and the farmer perform work so hard and continuous that beasts of burden could scarcely endure it and work so essential that no commonwealth could last even one year without it. Yet they earn such scanty fare and lead such a miserable life that the condition of beasts of burden might seem far preferable. The latter do not have to work so incessantly nor is their food much worse (in fact, sweeter to their taste) nor do they entertain any fear for the future. The workmen, on the other hand, not only have to toil and suffer without return or profit in the present but agonize over the thought of an indigent old age. Their daily wage is too scanty to suffice even for the day: much less is there an excess and surplus that daily can be laid by for their needs in old age.

Now is not this an unjust and ungrateful commonwealth? It lavishes great rewards on so-called gentlefolk and banking goldsmiths and the rest of that kind, who are either idle or mere parasites and purveyors of empty pleasures. On the contrary, it makes no benevolent provision for farmers, colliers, common laborers, carters, and carpenters without whom there would be no commonwealth at all. After it has misused the labor of their prime and after they are weighed down with age and disease and are in utter want, it forgets all their sleepless nights and all the great benefits received at their hands and most ungratefully requites them with a most miserable death.

What is worse, the rich every day extort a part of their daily allowance from the poor not only by private fraud but by public law. Even before they did so it seemed unjust that persons deserving the best of the commonwealth should have the worst return. Now they have further distorted and debased the right and, finally, by making laws, have palmed it off as justice. Consequently, when I consider and turn over in my mind the state of all commonwealths flourishing anywhere today, so help me God, I can see nothing else than a kind of conspiracy of the rich, who are aiming at their own interests under the name and title of the commonwealth. They invent and devise all ways and means by which, first, they may keep without fear of loss all that they have amassed by evil practices and, secondly, they may then purchase as cheaply as possible and abuse the toil and labor of all the poor. These devices become law as soon as the rich have once decreed their observance in the name of the public—that is, of the poor also!

Yet when these evil men with insatiable greed have divided up among themselves all the goods which would have been enough for all the people, how far they are from the happiness of the Utopian commonwealth! In Utopia all greed for money was entirely removed with the use of money. What a mass of troubles was then cut away! What a crop of crimes was then pulled up by the roots! Who does not know that fraud, theft, rapine, quarrels, disorders, brawls, seditions, murders, treasons, poisonings, which are avenged rather than restrained by daily executions, die out with the destruction of money? Who does not know that fear, anxiety, worries, toils, and sleepless nights will also perish at the same time as money? What is more, poverty, which alone money seemed to make poor, forthwith would itself dwindle and disappear if money were entirely done away with everywhere. ❧

## *Responding to Reading*

### First Impressions

**1.** Do you think you would like to live in Utopia? Why or why not?

### Second Thoughts

**2.** How does your list of important jobs compare to the jobs that are regarded as essential in Utopia? Why might your list differ?

**3.** Most Utopians learn their father's craft, and most workers follow the same daily schedule. Is this kind of system desirable? Why or why not?

> **Think about**
> • how this system might benefit and hurt society and individuals
> • the potential conflict between society's needs and an individual's needs

**4.** What do you think of the Utopians' leisure activities?

**5.** Why do the Utopians do away with money? What do you think of this idea?

**6.** Using the chart you made contrasting Utopia and England, discuss what More finds wrong with the English social system.

**7.** How would More define responsibility? In his view, for whom is society responsible? Do you agree? Explain your opinion.

### Broader Connections

**8.** What kinds of problems might arise in a community that places the common good above the needs and desires of the individual? Should we try to turn our own society into a modern utopia? Explain.

## *Literary Concept: Identifying Tone*

In literature, **tone** describes the attitude that a writer takes toward the subject. The tone of a work is communicated by the writer's choice of words and details. A writer's tone may be sarcastic, playful, bitter, objective, serious, or any other attitude. Tone may be difficult to identify because readers have to interpret what the words suggest about the writer's attitude. Readers may disagree in their interpretation.

More's tone varies, depending on whom he is describing. His tone toward England's working poor is one of sympathy: "The common laborer, the carter, the carpenter, and the farmer perform work *so hard and continuous* that *beasts of burden* could *scarcely endure it*." The words shown in italics indicate pity yet admiration for the workers. Find descriptions of the rich in the second part of the selection, and identify the tone used.

## *W*riting Options

1. Write a letter to More that explains how you feel about his ideas for improving society.

2. Create some protest slogans that reflect More's criticisms of English society. To get people's attention, make your messages short and clever, such as "Let workers share the wealth" or "When everyone works, no one worries."

3. For his time, More was regarded as very progressive in his attitude toward women. Review the passages regarding women in Utopia, then explain your opinion of their role.

4. Write out several pieces of advice that More would give the President of the United States if he were an advisor.

## *V*ocabulary Practice

**Exercise** Some words are frequently used in discussing certain subjects. For example, the word *talons* would probably be found in a book about birds of prey. Write the vocabulary word that you would expect to find in each book below.

1. *Hard Times: A Study of the Nation's Poor*
2. *"Blackmail Betty": The Story of Her Crimes*
3. *A Directory of Caterers and Other Suppliers*
4. *Eliminating the Unnecessary*
5. *Taxes: Enough Is Enough!*
6. *The Fine Art of Generosity*
7. *Non-Stop Talkers: What Keeps Them Going?*
8. *Satisfying Teenagers' Huge Appetites*
9. *Living, Growing, and Feeling Fine*
10. *The Making of a Nation*
11. *Agricultural Products and the Stock Market*
12. *Comets, Meteors, and Other Cosmic Events*
13. *Tricks of the Trade: How to Negotiate Anything*
14. *Profiles of Whiners and Complainers*
15. *School Attendance and the Law*

*Words
to Know
and Use*

**benevolent
commodity
commonwealth
compulsory
extort
flourishing
incessantly
indigent
insatiable
phenomenon
purveyor
querulous
stratagem
suffice
superfluous**

## *O*ptions for Learning

**1** • **Design a Wardrobe** Design clothes for both men and women to wear in Utopia. Review More's description of Utopian clothing, noting the distinctions he makes. Consider how the Utopians spend their time so that you can create sensible clothing for their needs.

**2** • **Right on Schedule** Using the information on page 186 about how the days are divided, create a time schedule that shows a typical day in the life of a Utopian, hour by hour. Then draw a pie graph showing the percent of each day spent in each type of activity, such as sleeping, working, recreation, and so on. Make another pie graph that shows how your own time is typically spent and contrast your time expenditure with that of the Utopians. Which schedule would you prefer to follow?

**3** • **Renaissance Women** Find out what life was like for women during the Renaissance. Compare and contrast that life with that of Utopian women. Share your findings with the class.

**4** • **A Man for All Seasons** A modern popular play that tells the story of the relationship between Sir Thomas More and Henry VIII is *A Man for All Seasons*. Read this play and see the movie if possible. You and some classmates might present a scene from the play for your class; or you might summarize the play for your classmates.

### FACT FINDER

*What did More say just before he was beheaded?*

## *S*ir *Thomas More*
### 1477–1535

Thomas More can be described as a *Renaissance man*, someone of great learning with abilities in many different areas. More was a distinguished scholar, lawyer, statesman, musician, and businessman. He became one of the most influential writers of his age.

Though shrewdly practical, More spent his life in pursuit of ideals. At the age of twenty-two, he entered a monastery, where he lived for four years studying, praying, fasting, and sleeping only four hours a night. Later in his life, More became a friend of the young King Henry VIII. More and his wife often entertained the King at their country estate, where the men discussed current issues. By 1521, More had become such a trusted advisor to Henry VIII that he was knighted.

When More became Lord Chancellor, the highest position next to the King, Henry needed his help in a struggle with the Catholic Church, the only church in England at that time. Henry wanted to divorce his wife in order to remarry, a violation of Church rules, and he wanted to name himself as the head of the Church in England. Because More refused to cooperate with the King's plan, he was imprisoned, tried, and beheaded.

*Fiction*

# *The* Secret
### ALBERTO MORAVIA

## *E*xamine What You Know

A secret can "weigh on your conscience like a nightmare." This quote from the opening paragraph of the story you are about to read focuses on the effects of a guilty conscience. Think about a time when you had a guilty conscience and the ways in which you were affected by it. Record your thoughts in a chart like the one below. As you read, see if the main character experiences any of the effects you name in the chart.

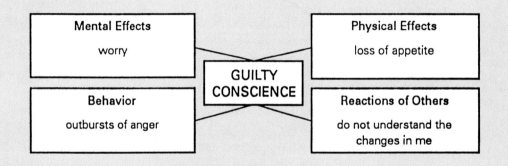

| Mental Effects | | Physical Effects |
|---|---|---|
| worry | | loss of appetite |
| | **GUILTY CONSCIENCE** | |
| Behavior | | Reactions of Others |
| outbursts of anger | | do not understand the changes in me |

## *E*xpand Your Knowledge

A hit-and-run accident is a very serious offense. A driver who leaves the scene of an accident can be charged with a misdemeanor crime. If the driver is found guilty in a court of law, the punishment is usually a fine or a short-term jail sentence. If the accident involves an injury or death, the crime is considered much more serious. A hit-and-run driver who is found guilty of causing the victim's death can be charged with a felony manslaughter crime, can lose his or her driver's license, and may face time in prison. In other countries, such as Italy, where this story takes place, the penalties are often even harsher than they are in our country.

## *W*rite Before You Read

■ *A biography of the author can be found in the Reader's Handbook.*

Based on the chart that you completed above, write your own definition of the word *conscience*. Once you have completed your definition, check it against the definition in your dictionary.

# The *Secret*

ALBERTO MORAVIA

**D**on't talk to me about secrets! I had one—and it was the kind that weighs on your conscience like a nightmare.

I am a truck driver. One beautiful spring morning, while hauling a load of lava rock from a quarry near Campagnano to Rome, I ran square into a man who was coming in the opposite direction on a motorbike. It was right at the 25 Kilometer marker on the old Cassia road. Through no fault of his, either, I had kept going on the wrong side of the road long after having passed a car, and I was speeding; he was on the right, where he belonged, and going slow. The truck hit him so hard that I barely had time to see something black fly through the blue air and then fall and lie still and black against the soft whiteness of a daisy field. The motorbike lay on the other side of the road, its wheels in the air, like a dead bug.

Lowering my head, I stepped down hard on the gas. I tore down the road to Rome and dropped my load at the yard.

The next day the papers carried the news: So-and-so, forty-three years old, a jobber by trade, leaving a wife and several children, had been run down at Kilometer 25 of the Cassia road and instantly killed. Nobody knew who had struck him. The hit-and-run driver had fled the scene of the accident like a coward. That's exactly what the paper said: *like a coward*. Except for those three little words that burned a hole in my brain, it didn't take more than four lines to report on what was, after all, only the death of a man.

During the next couple of days, I could think of nothing else. I know that I am only a truck driver, but who can claim that truck drivers have no conscience? A truck driver has a lot of time to mull over his own private business, during the long hours behind the wheel or lying in the truck's sleeping berth. And when, as in my case, that private business is not all it ought to be, thinking can get to be really pretty tough.

**O**ne thing in particular kept nagging at me. I just couldn't understand why I hadn't stopped, why I hadn't tried to help the poor guy. I lived the scene over and over again. I would be gauging the distances again before passing that car; I would feel my foot pressing down hard on the accelerator. Then the man's body would come flying up in front of my windshield . . . and at this point I would deliberately block out the picture, as you do at the movies, and I would think, "Now, jam on your brakes, jump down, run into the field, pick him up, put him in the bed of the truck and rush him to Santo Spirito Hospital. . . ."

But, you poor fool, you're just dreaming again. I had *not* stopped. I had driven straight on, with head lowered like a bull after a goring. To make a long story short, the more I thought about that split second when I had stepped on the gas instead of jamming on the brakes, the less I could make it out. Coward-ice—that was the word for it all right. But why does a man who has, or at least thinks he has guts, turn into a coward without a moment's warning? That stumped me. Yet the cold, hard facts were there: the dead man was really dead; that split second when I might have stopped had passed and was now sinking far-ther and farther away, and no one would ever be able to bring it back. I was no longer the Gino who had passed that car but another Gino who had killed a man and then had run away.

I lay awake nights over it. I grew gloomy and silent, and after a while everybody shied away from me at the yard and after work: nobody wants to pass the time with a killjoy. So I carried my secret around as if it were a hot diamond that you can't entrust to anyone or plant anywhere.

Then, after a while, I began thinking about it less and less, and I can even say that there came a time when I didn't think about it at all. But the secret was still stowed away deep down inside me, and it weighed on my conscience and kept me from enjoying life. I often thought that I would have felt better if I could have told somebody about it. I wasn't exactly looking for approval—I realized there was no pardon for what I had done—but if I could have told this secret of mine, I would have thrown off part of its dead weight onto somebody else who would have helped me carry it. But who could I tell it to? To my friends at the yard? They had other things to worry about. To my fam-ily? I had none, being a foundling. My girl-friend? She would have been the logical per-son because, as everybody knows, women are good at understanding you and giving you sympathy when you need it, but unfortu-nately, I had no girl friend.

One Sunday in May I went walking outside the Rome city gates with a girl I had met some time before when I had given her and one of her friends a lift in my truck. She had told me her name and address, and I had seen her again a couple of times. We had enjoyed each other's company, and she had made it clear that she liked me and would be willing to go out with me.

Her name was Iris. She was a lady's maid in the house of some wealthy woman who had lots of servants. I had fallen from the start for her serious little oval face and those great big sad gray eyes of hers. In short, here was just the girl for me in the present circumstances. After we had had a cup of coffee at the Expo-sition Grounds, with all those columns around us, she finally agreed in her shy, silent, and gentle way to go and sit with me in a meadow not far from St. Paul's Gate, where you get a good view of the Tiber and of the new apart-ment houses lined up on the opposite bank. She had spread out a handkerchief on the grass to keep her skirt from getting dirty and she sat quietly, her legs tucked under her, her hands in her lap, gazing across at the big white buildings on the other side of the river.

I noticed that there were lots of daisies in the grass around us; and like a flash I remem-bered the soft whiteness of those other daisies among which, just a month earlier, I had seen lying still and dead the man I had struck down. I don't know what got into me, but sud-denly I couldn't hold back the urge to tell her my secret. If I tell her, I thought, I'll get rid of the load on my chest. She wasn't one of those dizzy, empty-headed girls who, after you've told them a secret, make you feel so much worse than you did before that you could kick yourself hard for having spilled all you know. She was a nice, understanding person who had doubtless had her share of knocks in life—and they must have been pretty rough knocks if the sad little look on her face meant anything. Just to break the ice, I said to her, in an offhand way:

"What are you thinking about, Iris?"

She was just raising her hand to choke back a yawn. Perhaps she was tired. She said: "Nothing."

I didn't let that answer get me down but quickly went on. "Iris, you know that I like you a lot, don't you? That's why I feel that I shouldn't hide anything from you. You've got to know everything about me. Iris, I've got a secret."

She kept on looking at the tall buildings on the other side of the river, all the while fingering a little red lump on her chin, a tiny spring pimple.

"What secret?" she asked.

With an effort I got it out: "I've killed a man."

She didn't move but kept on poking gently at her chin. Then she shivered all over, as though she had finally understood. "You've killed a man? And you tell me about it just like that?"

"And how else do you expect me to tell you?"

She said nothing. She seemed to be looking for something on the ground. I went on. "Let's get this thing straight. I didn't mean to kill him."

Suddenly she found what she wanted: picking a long blade of grass, she put it into her mouth and began chewing on it, thoughtfully. Then, hurriedly, but without hiding anything, I told her about the accident, bringing out the part about my cowardice. I got pretty wrought up in spite of myself, but already I was beginning to feel relieved. I concluded:

"Now tell me what you think about all this."

She kept munching on her blade of grass and didn't say a word.

I insisted. "I'll bet that now you can't stand the sight of me."

I saw her shrug her shoulders, lightly. "And why shouldn't I be able to stand the sight of you?"

"Well, I don't know. After all, it was my fault that poor guy got killed."

"And it bothers you?"

"Yes. Terribly." Suddenly my throat closed tight as if over a hard knot of tears. "I feel as if I can't go on living. No man can go on living if he thinks he's a coward."

"Was it in the papers?"

"Yes. They gave it four lines. Just to say he had been killed and that nobody knew who had hit him."

Suddenly she asked, "What time is it?"

"Five-fifteen."

Another silence. "Listen, Iris, what does a man have to do to find out what's going on in that mind of yours?"

She shifted the blade of grass from one corner of her mouth to the other and said frankly, "Well, if you must know, there's nothing on my mind. I feel good and I'm not thinking about anything."

I couldn't believe my ears. I protested. "It can't be! You must have been thinking something about something. I'm sure of it."

I saw her smile, faintly. "Well, as a matter of fact, I was thinking about something. But if I tell you, you'll never believe it."

Hopefully, I asked, "Was it about me?"

"Good heavens, no! It had absolutely nothing to do with you!"

"What was it, then?"

She said slowly: "It was just one of those things that only women think about. I was looking at my shoes and seeing that they have holes in them. I was thinking that there is a big clearance sale on in Via Cola di Rienzo and that I've got to go there tomorrow and buy myself a pair of new shoes. There . . . are you satisfied?"

This time I shut up like a clam, my face dark and brooding. She noticed it and exclaimed: "Oh, dear! You're not mad, are you?"

I couldn't help blurting out: "Sure, I'm mad. Damn mad. Here I tell you the secret of my life, and it makes so little impression on you I wonder why I didn't keep it to myself!"

This bothered her a bit. "No," she said, "I'm glad you told me about it. It really did make an impression on me."

"Well, what kind of an impression?"

She thought it over and then said, scrupulously, "Well, I'm sorry that such a thing had to happen to you. It must have been awful!"

"Is that all you've got to say?"

"I also think," she added, fingering the pimple on her chin, "that it's only right it should bother you."

"Why?"

"Well, you said so yourself. You ought to have stopped to help him but you didn't."

"Then you think I am a coward?"

"A coward? Well, yes . . . and then no. After all, a thing like that could happen to anybody."

"But you just said that I ought to have stopped!"

"You should have; but you didn't . . ."

At this point I saw her glance down at something in the daisies. "Oh, look! How pretty!"

It was an insect, a green and gold beetle, resting on the white petals of a daisy. Suddenly I felt as if I were emptied out—almost as if that secret over which I had agonized so long had vanished in the spring air, carried away, lightly, like the white butterflies that were flitting around in pairs in the sunlight.

Yet with one dogged last hope, I asked: "But tell me, Iris, in your opinion, was I right or wrong not to stop?"

"You were right and you were wrong. Of course, you ought to have stopped. After all,

you had run into him. But, on the other hand, what good would it have done if you had? He was dead by that time anyway, and you would probably have got into a terrible mess. You were both right and wrong."

After these words, a thought flashed through my mind. "This is the end of Iris. I'll never take her out again. I thought she was a bright, understanding girl. Instead, she is really nothing but a halfwit. Enough is enough." I jumped to my feet.

"Come on, let's go," I said. "Otherwise, we'll be late for the movies."

Once inside the theater, in the dark, she slipped her hand into mine, forcing her fingers through mine. I didn't budge. The film was a love story, a real tear-jerker. When the lights went on at the end I saw that her big gray eyes were filled with tears and that her cheeks were wet. "I just can't help it," she said, patting her face dry with a handkerchief. "Pictures like this always make me want to cry."

Afterwards we went into a bar and ordered coffee. She pressed so close to me that our bodies touched. Just as the *espresso* machine let off a loud stream of steam, she said softly, "You know that I really like you, don't you?" staring at me with those great big beautiful eyes of hers.

I felt like answering: "Fine. You really like me, but you'll let me carry the whole weight of my secret alone!" Instead, I said nothing.

Now I understood that from her, as from everybody else, I could ask only for affection, nothing more than that.

I answered with a sigh, "I like you a lot, too."

But already she had stopped listening to me. She was peering at herself in the mirror behind the bar, absorbed and concerned as she fingered the little red lump on her chin. ❧

## Responding to Reading

### First Impressions

1. In a few words or phrases, jot down your impressions of Gino and Iris.

### Second Thoughts

2. Why do you think Gino leaves the scene of the accident?

3. Think about Gino's behavior following the hit-and-run accident. Evaluate his actions and the way he deals with his guilt.

4. What is your opinion of Iris's behavior? Explain your answer.

5. What does Gino mean at the end of the story when he says "I could ask only for affection, nothing more than that"?

   **Think about**
   • what he learns from Iris's reaction to his confession
   • what he learns about personal responsibility

6. Are Gino and Iris realistic characters? Do they remind you of people you know? Explain.

   **Think about**
   • Gino's thoughts and behavior following the accident
   • how Gino tries to lessen his feelings of guilt and self-doubt
   • what Iris says and does during and after Gino's confession

7. In what ways are Gino and Iris similar? How are they different?

### Broader Connections

8. Gino kills someone in a hit-and-run accident; he neither turns himself in to the police nor does anything to make up for his crime. What do you think should be the punishment, if any, for a person who commits these acts? Give reasons for your opinion.

## Writing Options

1. Create a new title for this story and explain how it applies. Do you like Moravia's title or yours better? Why?

2. Unloading his secret on Iris does not help Gino to relieve his feelings of guilt. Make a list of other things that Gino could do that might be more helpful to him or that might help ease the grief of the dead man's family.

*Poetry*

# Katakalos

ROSEMARY CATACALOS (kä tä' kä lōs)

## Examine What You Know

This poem tells of a man who, from youth to old age, acts with kindness and generosity toward people who are less fortunate than he. Of all the people you know, which ones stand out as being the most generous? To whom is their generosity directed, and how is it shown?

## Expand Your Knowledge

The United States has long been a nation of immigrants; most Americans' ancestors were born in other countries. For many reasons, including high unemployment in Europe, the number of immigrants rose sharply in the 1890's. In 1892 Ellis Island, in New York City's harbor, became the reception center for arriving immigrants. At Ellis Island they were given temporary shelter, food, and directions to possible job vacancies. Between 1900 and 1910 alone, nearly 9 million people passed through Ellis Island. To help more people come to America, a patron system was established that financed their travel to the United States. For example, Greek food wholesalers and shoeshine parlor owners in the United States contracted with agents to find youths in Greece to come to America to work for them.

In addition to European immigrants, many immigrants of Asian and Mexican origin have established new lives here. Rosemary Catacalos, the author of this poem, has a mixed heritage. Her grandfather was Greek and her grandmother was Mexican.

## Enrich Your Reading

**Visualizing Through Imagery**   **Imagery** refers to the use of words and phrases that appeal to the readers' senses. Poets and other writers use imagery to create characters. This poem contains several details that help the reader form mental images of the grandfather's physical appearance and experiences. For example, he is described as going to church in a plaid flannel work shirt under a fine blue suit. As you read, list words and phrases that help you form a mental picture of the Old Man.

# *K*atakalos

ROSEMARY CATACALOS

The Old Man, we always called him.
We said it with respect.
Even when he embarrassed us
by wearing his plaid flannel work shirt
5   to church under the fine blue suit
one of his up-and-coming sons,
the three prides of his life,
had bought him.
Even when he spent hours
10  straightening used nails when
we could afford to buy him new ones
so he could build the hundreds
of crooked little plant stands
that still wobble in the corners
15  of our houses.

He had come off a hard island birthplace,
a rock long ago deserted by the gods
but still sopping with the blood
of its passing from hand to hand,
20  Greek to Turk, Turk to Greek
and back again,
as if everything had not always
belonged to the sea, he said,
and to the relentless light
25  that hurt the eyes
of statues and children alike.

He was brought up on routine whippings
every Sunday, before-the-fact punishment

to fit any crime. His father, the miller,
30  followed the wisdom that parents
    can't be everywhere at once
    and in seven days any boy is bound
    to do something deserving a beating.
    Besides, by his own admission
35  he was not such a good shepherd,
    always getting sidetracked caring
    for some sick bird or dog or donkey
    that followed him everywhere ever after
    and got mixed up with the goats and sheep.

40  A draft dodger from the Turkish Army,
    he braved the maze of Ellis Island
    alone at sixteen,
    escaping with his last name intact
    and his first name changed to Sam.
45  New York fed him dog food
    those first few months
    when he couldn't read the labels
    and only knew from the pictures
    that the cans were meat and cheap.
50  He used to laugh about that.
    Said it was just as good as some of
    that Spam and stuff they sell nowadays.
    Anyway, Sam was
    the darling of immigrant flophouses,
55  giving away counsel and sometimes money,
    always finding someone who was
    a little worse off than he was.

    He hoboed all the way to Seattle
    where he pretended to be a high-flying carpenter
60  and was saved by Hagia Sophia[1] from a fall that
    would otherwise have meant certain death.
    Then he came to where they were
    burning Greeks out of Oklahoma
    and anyone who could kept moving
65  and opened a hamburger stand
    a little farther south.

GEORGE CRAIG 1980 Don Gray From *Traces* © 1980 The Bear Wallow Publishing Company, Union, Oregon.

---

1. **Hagia Sophia** (ä yē′ ä  sō fē′ ä) *Greek:* Saint Sophia, or holy wisdom.

In San Antonio he rigged up
a brightly painted horse-drawn
popcorn and ice cream wagon
70  and made the rounds on the West Side,
never quite making more than a living
since he always told poor kids
to pay him whenever they got the money.
The hamburger stands came next.
75  The cafe on Produce Row that some
old market hands still remember.
The Ideal Spot on South Presa,
where every hobo and derelict
from here to either coast
80  knew he could collect a free meal.
Good Old Sam.

But his wife was always angry.
She wanted a house of her own,
something more than glass beads.
85  She hated the way he was always
attracting winos and gypsies
and cousins from everywhere
who camped on her red velvet cushions
while he was out working hard
90  to give it all away.
She was from Lagos, Jalisco,[2]
and when they'd met
it hadn't been so much about love
as it had been simply time to get married.
95  That's what she always said.
Sam never said much about it
one way or the other,
except to smile and tell us
she'd had a hard life.

100  Still, they must have had a
little something special going.
Seeing how back then
he spoke only Greek,
a little broken English,

105  and she spoke only Spanish.
They were married through an interpreter.
Sam wore an ill-fitting suit
and carried a brown paper bag
full of sandwiches he had made
110  so as not to let the few guests go hungry.

Years later when they were old
she had never learned English
and he had never bought her a house.
He'd spent years in his by-now-perfect
115  Spanish trying to get her to see
how there was always some poor devil
who needed just a little help.
When she complained the loudest
he just listened patiently
120  and went about setting out his
sugar water in bottle caps
to feed the ants.
A smiling survivor.
A fat soft heart.
125  The Old Man.
We still say it with respect.

---

2. **Lagos, Jalisco** (lä′ gōs  hä lēs′ kō): a town and a
state in west central Mexico.

## Responding to Reading

### First Impressions

1. Picture the Old Man in your mind. Jot down several words that describe him. Compare your list to other students' in the class.

### Second Thoughts

2. What does Sam consider to be his main responsibility? How does he fulfill this responsibility?

3. Review the visual imagery you found in the poem. What qualities of Sam's personality are revealed by these images? Explain.

4. What is the attitude of Sam's wife concerning his sense of responsibility toward others? Why might she feel that way?

5. Why do you think Sam and his wife got married in the first place?

6. In spite of the fact that Sam never achieves wealth, job security, or even owning a house, do you consider him a success? Why or why not?

   **Think about**
   • the challenges Sam takes on and how he meets those challenges
   • Sam's treatment of his wife and family
   • his actions and attitudes toward other people
   • achievements that represent success to you

### Broader Connections

7. Sam gives away food, shelter, money, and advice to anyone he happens to meet who is less fortunate than himself. Today many people help the poor and needy by giving money to organized charities. Do you think that this way of giving is as helpful as Sam's way? Why or why not?

## Writing Options

1. As Sam's wife, write a letter to Dear Abby complaining about your husband's neglect of you and your family.

2. An epitaph is a short, written tribute to a dead person; it is sometimes engraved on the person's tombstone. Write an epitaph for the Old Man.

*Fiction*

# The Cabuliwallah
## (The Fruit Seller from Cabul)

RABINDRANATH TAGORE (rä bēn′ drä nät′ tə gor′)

## Examine What You Know

"The Cabuliwallah" (kä bōōl′ ē wä′ lə) focuses on the relationships between people of very different economic and religious backgrounds. Think of someone you have met who has a different background from yours. Perhaps this person is very rich or very poor, has a different religion than you, or is from another country. Obviously there are differences between you, but what are some similarities? Consider such things as values, interests, clothing, and education. In your journal or on a piece of paper, list the things you have in common with this person.

## Expand Your Knowledge

This story is set in Calcutta, India, around 1890. India has one of the most complex cultures in the world. More than seven hundred languages and dialects are spoken there, and every major religion is represented. The majority of Indians practice Hindu, one of the world's oldest religions, as do most of the characters in this story.

Since 1500 B.C., periodic invasions by foreign cultures have spread across India from nearly every corner of the globe. One result of these repeated invasions was the development of the **caste system**, a class system dictated by religious laws governing relations among the various socioeconomic classes. In 1890, caste rules were very strict. For instance, a member of a lower caste could not eat, sit, or socialize in any way with a member of a higher caste.

Other social restrictions affected non-Hindu persons and persons from other countries. Because the fruit seller in this story is a Moslem from Kabul (also spelled *Cabul*), a city in the neighboring country of Afghanistan, he would have had very limited social contact with a high-caste Hindu Indian.

## Write Before You Read

■ *A biography of the author can be found on page 214.*

What do you think are the most important responsibilities of a father toward his children? Consider the physical, social, and emotional needs of children. List what you feel a father should provide for his children.

# The Cabuliwallah
## (The Fruit Seller from Cabul)

RABINDRANATH TAGORE

Mini, my five-year-old daughter, cannot live without chattering. I really believe that in all her life she has not wasted one minute in silence. Her mother is often vexed at this and would stop her prattle, but I do not. To see Mini quiet is unnatural and I cannot bear it for long. Because of this, our conversations are always lively.

One morning, for instance, when I was in the midst of the seventeenth chapter of my new novel, Mini stole into the room and putting her hand into mine, said: "Father! Ramdayal the door keeper calls a crow a krow! He doesn't know anything, does he?"

Before I could explain the language differences in this country, she was on the trace of another subject. "What do you think, Father? Shola says there is an elephant in the clouds, blowing water out of his trunk, and that is why it rains!"

The child had seated herself at my feet near the table and was playing softly, drumming on her knees. I was hard at work on my seventeenth chapter, where Pratap Singh, the hero, had just caught Kanchanlata, the heroine, in his arms and was about to escape with her by the third-story window of the castle, when all of a sudden Mini left her play and ran to the window, crying, "A Cabuliwallah! A Cabuliwallah!" Sure enough, in the street below was a Cabuliwallah passing slowly along. He wore the loose, soiled clothing of his people and a tall turban; there was a bag on his back, and he carried boxes of grapes in his hand.

I cannot tell what my daugher's feelings were at the sight of this man, but she began to call him loudly. Ah, I thought, he will come in and my seventeenth chapter will never be finished! At this exact moment the Cabuliwallah turned and looked up at the child. When she saw this she was overcome by terror, fled to her mother's protection, and disappeared. She had a blind belief that inside the bag which the big man carried were two or three children like herself. Meanwhile, the peddler entered my doorway and greeted me with a smiling face.

So precarious was the position of my hero and my heroine that my first impulse was to stop and buy something, especially since Mini had called to the man. I made some small purchases, and a conversation began about Abdurrahman, the Russians, the English, and the Frontier Policy.[1]

As he was about to leave, he asked: "And where is the little girl, sir?"

I, thinking that Mini must get rid of her false fear, had her brought out. She stood by my chair, watching the Cabuliwallah and his bag. He offered her nuts and raisins but she would not be tempted, and only clung closer to me, with all her doubts increased. This was their first meeting.

One morning, however, not many days later, as I was leaving the house I was startled to find Mini seated on a bench near the door, laughing and talking with the great Cabuliwallah at her feet. In all her life, it appeared, my small daughter had never found so patient a listener, except for her father. Already the corner of her little sari[2] was stuffed with almonds and raisins, gifts from her visitor. "Why did you give her those?" I said, and taking out an eight-anna piece,[3] handed it to him. The man accepted the money without delay and slipped it into his pocket.

Alas, on my return an hour later, I found the unfortunate coin had made twice its own worth of trouble! The Cabuliwallah had given it to Mini, and her mother, seeing the bright, round object, had pounced on the child with: "Where did you get that eight-anna piece?"

"The Cabuliwallah gave it to me," said Mini cheerfully.

"The Cabuliwallah gave it to you!" cried her mother, much shocked. "Oh, Mini! How could you take it from him?"

Entering at this moment, I saved her from impending disaster and proceeded to make my own inquiries. I found that it was not the first or the second time the two had met. The

---

1. **Abdurrahman** (əb dōōr′ män′) . . . **Policy:** During the 1800's, Great Britain and Russia competed for control of Afghanistan. In 1880 Abdurrahman became ruler of Afghanistan when the British, reserving control of Afghanistan's foreign policy, granted him authority over his country's internal affairs.
2. **sari** (sä′ rē): a garment consisting of several yards of lightweight fabric wrapped around the body, with one end forming an ankle-length skirt and the other draped across the shoulder.
3. **eight-anna** (a′ nä) **piece:** a coin formerly used in India.

---

*Words to Know and Use* | **precarious** (prē ker′ ē əs) *adj.* uncertain
**impending** (im pend′ iŋ) *adj.* about to occur **impend** *v.*

Cabuliwallah had overcome the child's first terror by a judicious bribery of nuts and almonds, and the two were now great friends.

They had many quaint jokes which afforded them a great deal of amusement. Seated in front of him, and looking with all her tiny dignity on his gigantic frame, Mini would ripple her face with laughter and begin, "O Cabuliwallah! Cabuliwallah! what have you got in your bag?"

He would reply in the nasal accents of a mountaineer: "An elephant!" Not much cause for merriment, perhaps, but how they both enjoyed their joke! And for me, this child's talk with a grown-up man always had in it something strangely fascinating.

Then the Cabuliwallah, not to be caught behind, would take his turn with: "Well, little one, and when are you going to the father-in-law's house?"

Now most small Bengali maidens have heard long ago about the father-in-law's house, but we, being a little modern, had kept these things from our child, and at this question Mini must have been a trifle bewildered. But she would not show it, and with instant composure replied: "Are you going there?"

Among men of the Cabuliwallah's class, however, it is well known that the words "father-in-law's house" have a double meaning. It is a euphemism for jail, the place where we are well cared for at no expense. The sturdy peddler would take my daughter's question in this sense. "Ah," he would say, shaking his fist at an invisible policeman, "I will thrash my father-in-law!" Hearing this, and picturing the poor, uncomfortable relative, Mini would go into peals of laughter, joined by her formidable friend.

These were autumn mornings, the time of year when kings of old went forth to conquest; and I, never stirring from my little corner in Calcutta, would let my mind wander over the whole world. At the very name of another country, my heart would go out to it, and at the sight of a foreigner in the streets, I would fall to weaving a network of dreams: the mountains, the glens, the forests of his distant homeland with a cottage in its setting, and the free and independent life of faraway wilds. Perhaps these scenes of travel pass in my imagination all the more vividly because I lead a vegetable existence such that a call to travel would fall upon me like a thunderbolt. In the presence of this Cabuliwallah I was immediately transported to the foot of mountains, with narrow defiles twisting in and out amongst their towering, arid peaks. I could see the string of camels bearing merchandise, and the company of turbaned merchants carrying queer old firearms and some of their spears down toward the plains. I could see—but at this point Mini's mother would intervene, imploring me to "beware of that man."

Unfortunately Mini's mother is a very timid lady. Whenever she hears a noise in the street or sees people coming toward the house, she always jumps to the conclusion that they are either thieves, drunkards, snakes, tigers, malaria, cockroaches, caterpillars, or an English sailor. Even after all these years of experience, she is not able to overcome her terror. Thus she was full of doubts about the Cabuliwallah and used to beg me to keep a watchful eye on him.

I tried to gently laugh her fear away, but then she would turn on me seriously and ask solemn questions.

Were children never kidnapped?

| Words to Know and Use | **judicious** (jōō dish′ əs) *adj.* wise |
| | **composure** (kəm pō′ zhər) *n.* a calm manner |
| | **euphemism** (yōō′ fə miz′ əm) *n.* a word or phrase that is substituted for a distasteful word or phrase |
| | **formidable** (fôr′ mə də bəl) *adj.* impressive |
| | **implore** (im plôr′) *v.* to beg earnestly |

Was it, then, not true that there was slavery in Cabul?

Was it so very absurd that this big man should be able to carry off a tiny child?

I told her that, though not impossible, it was highly improbable. But this was not enough, and her dread persisted. As her suspicion was unfounded, however, it did not seem right to forbid the man to come to the house, and his familiarity went unchecked.

Once a year, in the middle of January, Rahmun[4] the Cabuliwallah was in the habit of returning to his country, and as the time approached he would be very busy going from house to house collecting his debts. This year, however, he always found time to come and see Mini. It would have seemed to an outsider that there was some conspiracy between them, for when he could not come in the morning, he would appear in the evening.

Even to me it was a little startling now and then, to suddenly surprise this tall, loose-garmented man of bags in the corner of a dark room; but when Mini would run in, smiling, with her "O Cabuliwallah! Cabuliwallah!" and the two friends so far apart in age would subside into their old laughter and their old jokes, I felt reassured.

One morning, a few days before he had made up his mind to go, I was correcting my proof sheets[5] in my study. It was chilly weather. Through the window the rays of the sun touched my feet, and the slight warmth was very welcome. It was almost eight o'clock, and the early pedestrians were returning home with their heads covered. All at once I heard an uproar in the street and, looking out, saw Rahmun bound and being led away between two policemen, followed by a crowd of curious boys. There were bloodstains on the clothes of the Cabuliwallah, and one of the

© Steve McCurry/Magnum Photos, New York.

policemen carried a knife. Hurrying out, I stopped them and inquired what it all meant. Partly from one, partly from another, I gathered that a certain neighbor had owed the peddler something for a Rampuri shawl but had falsely denied having bought it, and that in the course of the quarrel Rahmun had struck him. Now, in the heat of his excitement, the prisoner began calling his enemy all sorts of names. Suddenly, from a verandah of my house my little Mini appeared, with her usual exclamation: "O Cabuliwallah! Cabuliwallah!" Rahmun's face lighted up as he turned to her. He had no bag under his arm today, so she could not discuss the elephant with him. She at once therefore proceeded to the next question: "Are you going to the father-in-law's house?" Rahmun laughed and said: "Just where I am going, little one!" Then seeing that the reply did not amuse the child, he held up his fettered hands. "Ah," he said, "I would have thrashed that old father-in-law, but my hands are bound!"

---

4. **Rahmun** (ra män´).

5. **proof sheets:** copies on which changes or corrections are made to text that has been typeset from the author's original manuscript.

---

*Words to Know and Use* | **verandah** (və ran´ də) *n.* an open porch covered by a roof and attached along the outside of a building
**fettered** (fet´ ərd) *adj.* chained **fetter** *v.*

209

On a charge of murderous assault, Rahmun was sentenced to many years of imprisonment.

Time passed and he was forgotten. The accustomed work in the accustomed place was ours, and the thought of the once-free mountaineer spending his years in prison seldom occurred to us. Even my lighthearted Mini, I am ashamed to say, forgot her old friend. New companions filled her life. As she grew older she spent more of her time with girls, so much in fact that she came no more to her father's room. I was scarcely on speaking terms with her.

Many years passed. It was autumn once again and we had made arrangements for Mini's marriage; it was to take place during the Puja[6] holidays. With the goddess Durga returning to her seasonal home in Mount Kailas, the light of our home was also to depart, leaving our house in shadows.

The morning was bright. After the rains, there was a sense of cleanness in the air, and the rays of the sun looked like pure gold, so bright that they radiated even to the sordid brick walls of our Calcutta lanes. Since early dawn, the wedding pipes had been sounding, and at each beat my own heart throbbed. The wailing tune, Bhairavi, seemed to intensify my pain at the approaching separation. My Mini was to be married tonight.

From early morning, noise and bustle <u>pervaded</u> the house. In the courtyard the canopy had to be slung on its bamboo poles; the tinkling chandeliers should be hung in each room and verandah; there was great hurry and excitement. I was sitting in my study, looking through the accounts, when someone entered, saluting respectfully, and stood before me. It was Rahmun the Cabuliwallah, and at first I did not recognize him. He had no bag, nor the long hair, nor the same vigor that he used to have. But he smiled, and I knew him again.

"When did you come, Rahmun?" I asked him.

"Last evening," he said, "I was released from jail."

The words struck harsh upon my ears. I had never talked with anyone who had wounded his fellow man, and my heart shrank when I realized this, for I felt that the day would have been better omened if he had not turned up.

"There are ceremonies going on," I said, "and I am busy. Could you perhaps come another day?"

At once he turned to go, but as he reached the door he hesitated and said: "May I not see the little one, sir, for a moment?" It was his belief that Mini was still the same. He had pictured her running to him as she used to do, calling, "O Cabuliwallah! Cabuliwallah!" He had imagined that they would laugh and talk together, just as in the past. In fact, in memory of those former days he had brought, carefully wrapped up in paper, a few almonds and raisins and grapes, somehow obtained from a countryman—his own little fund was gone.

I said again: "There is a ceremony in the house, and you will not be able to see anyone today."

The man's face fell. He looked wistfully at me for a moment, said "Good morning," and went out.

---

6. **Puja** ($\overline{oo}'$ jä'): a day-long Hindu holiday devoted to giving special treatment to someone portraying a deity or god.

*Words to Know and Use* | **pervade** (pər vād') v. to spread throughout

I felt a little sorry and would have called him back but saw that he was returning of his own accord. He came close up to me, holding out his offerings, and said: "I brought these few things, sir, for the little one. Will you give them to her?"

I took them and was going to pay him, but he caught my hand and said: "You are very kind, sir! Keep me in your recollection; do not offer me money! You have a little girl; I too have one like her in my own home. I thought of my own and brought fruits to your child, not to make a profit for myself."

Saying this, he put his hand inside his big loose robe and brought out a small dirty piece of paper. With great care he unfolded this and smoothed it out with both hands on my table. It bore the impression of a little hand, not a photograph, not a drawing. The impression of an ink-smeared hand laid flat on the paper. This touch of his own little daughter had been always on his heart, as he had come year after year to Calcutta to sell his wares in the streets.

Tears came to my eyes. I forgot that he was a poor Cabuli fruitseller, while I was—but no, was I more than he? He was also a father.

That impression of the hand of his little Parbati in her distant mountain home reminded me of my own little Mini, and I immediately sent for her from the inner apartment. Many excuses were raised, but I would not listen. Clad in the red silk of her wedding day, with the sandal paste on her forehead, and adorned as a young bride, Mini came and stood bashfully before me.

The Cabuliwallah was staggered at the sight of her. There was no hope of reviving their old friendship. At last he smiled and said: "Little one, are you going to your father-in-law's house?"

But Mini now understood the meaning of the word "father-in-law," and she could not reply to him as in the past. She flushed at the question and stood before him with her bride's face looking down.

I remembered the day when the Cabuliwallah and my Mini first met, and I felt sad. When she had gone, Rahmun heaved a deep sigh and sat down on the floor. The idea had suddenly come to him that his daughter also must have grown up during this long time, and that he would have to make friends with her all over again. Surely he would not find her as he used to know her; besides, what might have happened to her in these eight years?

The marriage pipes sounded, and the mild autumn sun streamed around us. But Rahmun sat in the little Calcutta lane and saw before him the barren mountains of Afghanistan.

I took out a bank note and gave it to him, saying: "Go back to your own daughter, Rahmun, in your own country, and may the happiness of your meeting bring good fortune to my child!"

After giving this gift, I had to eliminate some of the festivities. I could not have the electric lights, nor the military band, and the ladies of the house were saddened. But to me the wedding feast was brighter because of the thought that in a distant land a long-lost father met again with his only child. ❧

## *Responding to Reading*

### First Impressions

1. Did your feelings about the Cabuliwallah change as you read? Explain.

### Second Thoughts

2. How would you describe the character of the Cabuliwallah?

    **Think about**
    - his friendship with Mini
    - his assault of the man who owed him money
    - his return on Mini's wedding day

3. What different views of the Cabuliwallah do the narrator, the mother, and Mini have? Whose views do you think are the most accurate, and why?

4. How would you describe the character of Mini's father?

    **Think about**
    - his helping Mini over her initial fear of the Cabuliwallah
    - his feelings and actions toward his wife and daughter
    - his treatment of the Cabuliwallah on Mini's wedding day

5. What do the two men have in common? How would you rate each as a father based on the list of responsibilities you wrote earlier?

6. What do you think is the theme of this story?

### Broader Connections

7. The Cabuliwallah is an outcast in his society, a street person selling fruit from door to door. To what type of person might you compare him today? How might such a person be received in a wealthy neighborhood?

## *Literary Concept: Characterization*

Through **characterization**, writers try to make characters believable. One method of characterization is a description of the character's physical appearance; another is the relating of the character's thoughts and feelings. A third method is through dialogue or conversation; a fourth is through the character's actions. A writer may use some or all of these methods. Which methods are used to develop the character of the Cabuliwallah? Find an example of each method you cite from the story.

**Concept Review: Point of View**   The story is narrated from the point of view of Mini's father. How would the story be different if the Cabuliwallah narrated it? Explain.

# Writing Options

1. As either Mini or the Cabuliwallah, write a farewell note to the other, to be delivered after the wedding. You might discuss what your past relationship meant to you and how you felt about seeing your friend again after eight years.

2. Reread the passage in the story about the Cabuliwallah's crime. Do you feel that the Cabuliwallah would have been punished as severely if he had been a Hindu and from a higher caste? State your opinion and support it with reasons.

3. In a paragraph, compare or contrast someone you know today with the narrator in terms of their actions toward their families and their fellow man.

4. The Cabuliwallah has not seen his daughter in many years. Imagine the reunion of the Cabuliwallah and his grown-up daughter. Write the conversation that they might have at this meeting.

# Vocabulary Practice

**Exercise** On your paper, write the word from the list that best completes each sentence.

1. To little Mini, the Cabuliwallah's size, appearance, and frightening bag made him look _____.
2. With a _____ application of food and friendship, the Cabuliwallah gained the girl's trust.
3. Mini and the Cabuliwallah used to joke about going to the "father-in-law's house," a _____ for *jail*.
4. The narrator's timid wife would _____ her husband to be more careful about Mini's friends.
5. The narrator found himself in a _____ position between his wife's fear of the Cabuliwallah and his daughter's interest in him.
6. The roofed _____ extended around several sides of the house.
7. While being arrested, the excited Cabuliwallah regained his _____ when he saw Mini come out of the house.
8. The Cabuliwallah showed Mini his _____ hands after his arrest.
9. The Cabuliwallah heard music of wedding pipes _____ the house.
10. His daughter's _____ marriage made the narrator unsure about whether to let her see the old Cabuliwallah.

> **Words to Know and Use**
>
> composure
> euphemism
> fettered
> formidable
> impending
> implore
> judicious
> pervade
> precarious
> verandah

## Options for Learning

**1** • **A Grand Affair**  Research traditional Hindu marriage customs. With a few classmates, give a creative presentation on the rituals, decorations, food, and dress at a typical Hindu wedding. You might use a narrator, photographs, costumes, role-playing, and Hindu background music, for example.

**2** • **Keep a Memory Alive**  The Cabuliwallah kept a copy of his daughter's handprint. Using ink or pencil, make a miniature portrait of the Cabuliwallah that would be a memorable keepsake for Mini. Find details in the story about the Cabuliwallah's physical appearance.

**3** • **Video Fever**  Rent the movie *Gandhi* to view on a VCR. After watching the movie, report to the class what you learned about India and Gandhi.

**4** • **Without a Word**  With some classmates, create a pantomime that represents the scene in which the Cabuliwallah is arrested. Include the characters of the two policemen, Mini's father, and Mini. Let your pantomime clearly express the actions and emotions of the characters. Perform your pantomime for the class.

### FACT FINDER

*How many miles is Kabul, Afghanistan, from Calcutta, India?*

## Rabindranath Tagore
### 1861-1941

Rabindranath Tagore was a poet, short-story writer, novelist, playwright, composer, philosopher, and painter. He came from one of the most interesting and famous families in India. His grandfather accumulated great wealth, but because of his business contacts with Moslems, he caused his Brahmin high-caste family to become outcast. This hardly stopped the growth and success of the family line—it subsequently produced some of India's most famous painters, poets, philosophers, and musicians. Tagore's family sometimes included as many as two hundred members living together on a large estate in northern Calcutta. His eleven brothers and sisters included a famous philosopher, a musician, and India's first woman novelist. Tagore's education, although very broad, was restricted mainly to private tutors on the estate until he was seventeen.

The years of sadness Tagore experienced because of the deaths of his wife, daughter, and son between the years 1902 and 1907 inspired him to write some of his best poetry. In 1913 his poetry earned him India's first Nobel Prize for literature.

Besides being a leader in the arts, Tagore became, along with his friend Mohandas Gandhi, one of India's leading activists for Indian freedom from British rule. Tagore died six years before India gained independence.

## PERSUASION

The selections in this subunit raise the timeless and universal question of how much responsibility people have for one another. Now, more than ever, we are faced with requests for time and money to help those less fortunate. We receive letters in the mail, hear pleas on television and in church, and even meet the needy face to face. Those asking for help all use persuasion techniques to convince us to give.

**Persuasion** is an attempt to convince someone else to follow a particular idea, goal, or course of action. A writer or speaker can persuade by appealing to emotion or to reason or to both. Although an appeal to reason, using logic and solid evidence, may be preferable, a combination of the two appeals is generally more effective. Notice how the following material from the Animal Rescue Fund appeals to both reason and emotions. The original material contained a series of pictures that included a snow leopard in the wild, a leopard's carcass draped over a poacher's horse, and a beautiful model wrapped in leopard fur. It also included a simple form to fill in and return with a donation.

## Animal Rescue Fund

High in the Himalayas, a snow leopard stretches lazily in the winter sun. His coat, luxurious, ashen fur has grown thick to protect him from the bitter cold. Suddenly, a shot rips through the silence---and the majestic cat falls lifeless on the ground---another victim of illegal animal poaching.

Dear Friend,

This brutal end is just the beginning of a journey that could soon become "the route to extinction" for one of the most magnificent animals on the planet.

The next stop for the snow leopard is a nearby village, where the animal's killer sells the pelt to a waiting black-market dealer. Eventually the fur finds its way to the fashion boutiques of Tokyo or Paris, where a coat made of this rare, luxurious leopard skin will bring more than $30,000.

Only with YOUR help can we begin to end the rampant, illegal trade that has put so much of our irreplaceable wildlife in danger of extinction. Please help us end the slaughter by sending a contribution today---tomorrow may be too late.

In this writing workshop you will have the opportunity to support a cause you believe in by writing your own direct-mail fund-raising letter. You will use persuasive writing to convince others to help.

**Here is your PASSkey to this assignment.**

## GUIDED ASSIGNMENT: FUND-RAISING LETTER

Write a direct-mail fund-raising letter for a charity or cause of your choice. In the letter, persuade recipients to donate money or give other assistance to your chosen cause.

**P** URPOSE: To persuade

**A** UDIENCE: The general public

**S** UBJECT: A charity or cause of your choice

**S** TRUCTURE: A fund-raising letter

## Prewriting

**STEP 1** **Examine the model** In a small group, analyze the excerpts from the sample letter. Notice how the letter starts with a vivid introduction and contains powerful descriptions throughout. It shows an immediate need for aid and attempts to get the reader involved in solving the problem. The letter also offers the reader an easy way to help.

**STEP 2** **Brainstorm** As a group, brainstorm charities or causes that exist or that you think should exist. Think of various nonprofit groups that depend on the general public funds, such as medical groups fighting specific diseases, wildlife or environmental groups, children or adults in any area of the world who face poverty, disease, famine, natural disaster, oppression, or danger from other sources. Create as long a list as possible. Then choose an organization or cause that you personally believe in. The stronger your own belief in your cause, the more convincing and effective you can make your fund-raising letter.

**STEP 3** **Analyze your audience** When writing to persuade, you need to consider your audience carefully. How much do they know about your subject? If they know little, you may need to give them background information. How closely might your audience identify with your cause? What kinds of reasoning will appeal to them? Focus on their specific concerns. To make your letter effective, keep your audience during the entire writing process.

**STEP 4** **Think of appeals** List the reasons why money is needed for your cause. Make notes to explain the problem, giving as much background information as you think is necessary. Explain why sending money will help combat the problem. For example, one student chose to write about the orphans in Romania. He listed the problems this way.

◀ STUDENT MODEL

> More than 14,000 orphans live in orphanages in Romania.
> The orphanages are in horrible condition:
>     not enough good food; kids are dying of malnutrition
>     kids have no clothes
>     no schools in orphanages; kids' minds dry up
>     kids lie in cribs all day long; no toys, no play
>     many have AIDS from blood transfusions received when
>         they were first brought to orphanages
>     no medical help for many kids with diseases and
>         handicaps
>     the government has no money to help them
>     facilities are overcrowded and in disrepair
>     very difficult for foreigners to adopt because of red
>         tape
> Money would do the following:
>     repair old buildings and build new ones
>     get medical help and supplies
>     buy food and toys and clothing
>     lobby for more government participation
>     make the path smoother for foreign adoption of orphans

Next, list the emotional appeals you can use for your audience. These are important to keep in mind as you write the introduction and conclusion of your letter. For example, if your subject is children in need, you might appeal to adults' parental instincts. If your subject is an anti-drug program or a halfway house, you might appeal to the fear of crimes caused by drug addiction. Think of phrases and images that will affect your audience.

In addition, plan to include pictures that would be most effective for your cause and audience. If none are available, sketch or make notes about what the pictures would show.

**STEP 5** **Organize your message** Plan to begin with a strong, attention-getting introduction. Then organize the logical part of your argument. Give background material early in your letter so that readers understand why you are asking for help. Emphasize that their help is needed immediately and make clear how the money will be used.

## Drafting

**STEP 1** **Write your introduction**   This is a good point at which to involve the reader emotionally in your cause. Some shocking facts coupled with visual appeals might be a strong way to start. You want recipients to read your letter, not throw it away. Create concern immediately with strong descriptions or startling statistics.

**STEP 2** **Write the body**   In this part of your letter, appeal to recipients' sense of responsibility. As you write, use strong descriptive language. For example, the writer of the Animal Rescue Fund letter used the strong phrase, "This brutal end" rather than a softer approach. Keep your paragraphs short, vivid, and focused on the main point: the reader's help is needed, immediately, for a very worthy cause.

**STEP 3** **Wind up with positive action**   Let the reader know exactly what you want from him or her. Make it easy to contribute, and explain how the money will be used.

## Revising and Editing

In a small group, share your letter with your peers. Ask them to go over the following questions with you to help create some revision ideas.

### Revision Checklist

1. Is the opening paragraph powerful? Will it capture attention?
2. Is it clear that the reader's help is needed immediately?
3. How does the letter help the reader identify with this cause?
4. Does the letter make it easy for the reader to send money?

**Editing**   After you revise your letter, correct any grammatical or mechanical errors. Copy your final letter using the modified block form found in Correct Business Letter Form in the **Writer's Handbook.**

## Presenting

Share your letter with your classmates, reading it aloud yourself or having a classmate read it. After each letter is read, have students decide if they would be willing to contribute to the charity it promotes.

# LANGUAGE
### WORKSHOP

## USING MODIFIERS CORRECTLY

Certain modifiers seem to cause particular difficulty. By studying these pages carefully, you can learn to use these problem modifiers correctly in your speech and your writing.

### Good and Well

*Good* and *well* are similar in meaning, but you cannot substitute one word for the other. *Good* is always an adjective; that is, it modifies a noun or a pronoun, never a verb.

**Incorrect**    In Utopia everyone works *good.*

**Correct**    In Utopia everyone does *good* work.

*Well* is usually an adverb, meaning "expertly" or "properly." *Well* may also mean "in good health," however; in that case, it is an adjective, used after a linking verb.

> In spite of a long prison stay, the fruit seller seemed *well.*
>    (adjective)
> Mini talked *well* for such a young child. (adverb)

Since *good* and *well* can be adjectives, they can both be used as predicate adjectives after linking verbs. To decide which word to use as a predicate adjective in a particular sentence, remember that *well* refers to health, while *good* refers to happiness, comfort, or pleasure.

> Mini stayed home from school because she didn't feel *well.*
> Mini's father felt *good* after he gave money to the
>    cabuliwallah.

### Bad and Badly

Because they are so similar, *bad* and *badly* are often used incorrectly. Remember that *bad* is an adjective; it modifies nouns and pronouns. Like any other adjective, *bad* sometimes follows a linking verb. On the other hand, *badly* is always an adverb and so should not be used with a linking verb.

**Incorrect**    The writer felt *badly* about the peddler's misfortune.

**Correct**    The writer felt *bad* about the peddler's misfortune.

## The Double Negative

Two negative words used together where only one is necessary are called a **double negative.** *No, not, never, nothing,* and *none* are the most common negative words. Remember also that the *-n't* in a contraction means "not." If you use such a contraction with another negative word, the result is a double negative.

**Incorrect**    The young girl *didn't have no* idea why the fruit seller disappeared.

**Correct**    The young girl *didn't have any* idea why the fruit seller disappeared.

**Correct**    The young girl *had no idea* why the fruit seller disappeared.

*Hardly* or *barely* used with a negative word is also incorrect.

**Incorrect**    Gino *couldn't hardly* stop thinking about the accident.

**Correct**    Gino *could hardly* stop thinking about the accident.

**Correct**    Gino *couldn't* stop thinking about the accident.

## HELP

*Kind, sort,* and *type* are usually followed by a prepositional phrase. To correct errors in sentences using these words, make sure that there is agreement among the modifier (*this, that, these,* or *those*); the word *kind, sort,* or *type;* the object of the prepositional phrase; and the verb.

*This kind* of *test* is easy. (All italicized words are singular.)

*These kinds* of *tests* are easy. (All italicized words are plural.)

## *This* and *That; These* and *Those*

*This* and *that* are adjectives that modify singular nouns. *These* and *those* are adjectives that modify plural nouns. Be especially careful when these modifiers are used with words such as *kind, sort,* and *type.*

**Incorrect**    *Those* kind of nut is expensive. (*Kind* is singular, so it should be modified by either *this* or *that.*)

**Correct**    *That* kind of nut is expensive.

**Incorrect**    *This* sorts of games enchant the little girl. (*Sorts* is plural and so requires a plural modifier.)

**Correct**    *These* sorts of games enchant the little girl.

**Exercise 1**    Correct the errors in the use of modifiers in these sentences. Some sentences may have more than one error. If a sentence is correct, write *Correct.*

1. In "The Secret," a story by Alberto Moravia, an Italian truck driver named Gino was responsible for a bad accident.
2. Gino, who usually drove good, ran into a man on a motorbike.
3. The victim was killed instantly; he had no chance to get well.
4. The cowardly truck driver couldn't barely drive away from the scene of the accident fast enough.

5. Gino felt badly about the accident; he was not used to these sort of misfortunes.

6. After the accident, Gino's conscience bothered him bad.

7. He couldn't sleep good no more.

8. When he met Iris, Gino had felt badly about his secret for so long that he wanted to tell her the truth.

9. Iris couldn't hardly stay awake during his confession.

10. She didn't have no idea why Gino was so guilt-ridden.

11. She was in a well mood and didn't want nothing to spoil her afternoon.

12. The girl seemed much more interested in daisies, shoe sales, and those sort of things.

13. Since Iris didn't have no interest in his problem, Gino couldn't barely stand to spend the rest of the evening with her.

14. Although Iris couldn't relate to Gino's real-life problem, she didn't have no trouble crying over a movie.

15. Instead of showing his anger, Gino didn't say nothing.

16. These kind of story is pessimistic about human nature.

**Exercise 2**  Work in groups to find errors in the use of modifiers in the following passage. Have one group member copy the passage on a piece of paper, substituting the correct modifiers as determined by the group. Then compare your work with that of other groups.

Thomas More, author of *Utopia*, was a man who wouldn't never go against what he thought was right. His reward for such honesty doesn't hardly seem fair; he was beheaded by King Henry VIII. As the highest judicial official in the kingdom, Thomas had always served Henry good. Then the problems began. Henry didn't want to be married to Catherine of Aragon no longer. He felt badly about getting rid of her, but he couldn't hardly contain his passion for his new love, Anne Boleyn. When Henry asked the church for a divorce, the Pope said those kind of divorces were not allowed. Henry had always been a well Catholic, but now he was furious. He decided he wouldn't let no church rule him. Instead, he set up a new church and made himself the head of it. Most people felt bad about the break, but they feared Henry too much to complain. These type of people don't really have strong principles. Thomas More, however, couldn't never give in to the idea. He resigned his position at the court and refused to sign the oath that Henry required. For this, he lost his head.

LANGUAGE HANDBOOK
........................................
problems with modifiers,
    pages 1003–05
the double negative,
    pages 1005–06

# Thinking Skills

WORKSHOP

## THE LANGUAGE OF PERSUASION

Generally, writers try to persuade by appealing to emotion or logic, and sometimes to both. **Logic** is correct reasoning. Your persuasive writing will be stronger if you follow the principles of logical thinking, avoiding **faulty arguments** and unfair uses of language such as those below.

**Loaded Language**  Loaded language appeals to the emotions; it is sometimes used instead of facts to shape opinions unfairly. Loaded language is often based on the connotations of words. The **connotation** of a word is an emotional meaning associated with it, in contrast to its dictionary definition, or **denotation.** The connotation of a word may be positive or negative. For example, you might feel differently about gathering *fans* than you would about a gathering *mob.*

**Circular Reasoning**  A statement like "We should revitalize our cities because they need new life breathed into them" is an example of circular reasoning. The writer is attempting to prove a statement simply by restating it in different words.

**Either/Or Fallacy**  An argument that presents only two alternatives, when actually there are many, is making use of the **either/or fallacy.** The statement "Either we raise taxes or we close schools" is an example. This kind of statement unfairly persuades by using false pretenses.

**Overgeneralizations**  Generalizations are statements that apply to a number of persons, places, or things. If a statement is too broad to be proven, it is called an **overgeneralization.** The statement "Today's students watch too much television" is an overgeneralization.

**Bandwagon/Snob Appeal**  Statements like "Everybody's wearing PerfectFit jeans" urge you to step in line with the crowd. **Snob appeal** is a form of bandwagon appeal; a statement like "Only an elite few will drive this car" appeals to your desire to be special.

**Exercise**  Examine the following statements. Write which kind of *faulty argument* or *faulty use of language* is used in each.

1. We should save the rain forests because they need to be preserved.
2. Vote for him? Surely you're not going to believe anything that old fuddy-duddy says.
3. The choice is clear, friends; either schools stay open all year round or our children will not learn to read.
4. Royal Lily perfume—for those who appreciate the very best.
5. Everyone who gets A's will have a successful career.

# ASPECTS OF LOVE

Love is perhaps the most complicated—and talked about—human emotion. Though it has always been a fascinating subject for writers, Renaissance authors raised the art of love to new heights. They explored love relationships of all kinds—from parental love to religious devotion, from friendship to romantic love. Long manuals were written to advise young gentlemen and gentlewomen in matters of the heart, and poets wrote candidly about their triumphs, failures, joys, sorrows, and fears in love.

In the selections that follow, you will explore love's mysteries and depths. Compare and contrast your own ideas about love with those expressed by these works.

*Poetry*

# Sonnet 30
### EDMUND SPENSER

# Sonnet 18
### WILLIAM SHAKESPEARE

## Examine What You Know

The following poems express different feelings associated with romantic love. Discuss the extremes in feelings and actions that often accompany romantic love. Are those extremes always good?

## Expand Your Knowledge

English Renaissance poets paid careful attention to poetic structure because of the value they placed on intricate and complex forms. During this period, the **sonnet** was one of the most popular poetic forms. This fourteen-line poem was used primarily for idealized expressions of love.

Spenser's Sonnet 30 is one of eighty-nine sonnets called *Amoretti*, which describes his courtship with Elizabeth Boyle, his second wife. Shakepeare's Sonnet 18 is one of a group of 154 sonnets. Some were written for a mysterious "dark lady." Others, including this one, were dedicated to W. H., perhaps a close friend.

## Enrich Your Reading

**Understanding Extended Metaphor**  A **metaphor** makes a direct comparison between two unlike things without using the words *like* or *as*. In the following poems, the poets rely on metaphors to establish their ideas. Spenser compares the woman's feelings to ice and the speaker's love to fire. Because this metaphor is continued throughout the poem, it is called an **extended metaphor.** Shakespeare's poem uses an extended metaphor that compares his love to a summer's day.

Set up comparison charts like those below to understand how these metaphors are developed. Fill out each chart with details from the poem.

■ *A biography of Spenser can be found in the Reader's Handbook and a biography of Shakespeare on page 369.*

Spenser

| Ordinary Fire | Fire of Poet's Love |
|---------------|---------------------|
| melts ice | can't melt her ice |

Shakespeare

| Ordinary Summer's Day | The Loved One |
|-----------------------|----------------|
| lovely, mild | even lovelier, milder |

# Sonnet 30

## EDMUND SPENSER

GUIDE FOR READING

My love is like to ice, and I to fire:
How comes it then that this her cold so great
is not dissolved through my so hot desire,
But harder grows the more I her entreat?

4 *entreat:* plead.

5   Or how comes it that my exceeding heat
Is not allayed by her heart-frozen cold,

6 *allayed:* lessened or relieved.

But that I burn much more in boiling sweat,
And feel my flames augmented manifold?

8 *augmented manifold:* enlarged in many ways.

What more miraculous thing may be told,
10   That fire, which all things melts, should harden ice,
And ice, which is congealed with senseless cold,

11 *congealed:* hardened; solidified.

Should kindle fire by wonderful device?
Such is the power of love in gentle mind,
That it can alter all the course of kind!

14 *kind:* nature.

## Responding to Reading

### First Impressions of "Sonnet 30"

1. Write down your reactions to Spenser's feelings about love.

### Second Thoughts on "Sonnet 30"

2. Using your comparison chart for Spenser's poem, discuss how human love is different from fire and ice.

3. Why does love seem so difficult for the poet to understand?
   **Think about**
   • the differences between nature and love
   • what the poet means in lines 13 and 14

4. What is the poet's attitude toward being in love? Is he complaining, expressing confusion, describing its wonders, or doing something else?

5. Is this poem a believable description of a love relationship? Explain your opinion.

# Sonnet 18

WILLIAM SHAKESPEARE

Shall I compare thee to a summer's day?
Thou art more lovely and more temperate:
Rough winds do shake the darling buds of May,
And summer's lease hath all too short a date:
5  Sometime too hot the eye of heaven shines,
And often is his gold complexion dimmed;
And every fair from fair sometime declines,
By chance or nature's changing course untrimmed;
But thy eternal summer shall not fade,
10  Nor lose possession of that fair thou owest;
Nor shall Death brag thou wander'st in his shade,
When in eternal lines to time thou growest:
   So long as men can breathe, or eyes can see,
   So long lives this, and this gives life to thee.

**2** *temperate:* moderate; mild.

**8** *untrimmed:* stripped of beauty.

**10** *owest:* ownest.

THE PROPOSAL 1872
Adolphe-William Bouguereau
The Metropolitan Museum of Art,
New York Gift of Mrs. Elliot L.
Kamen in memory of her father,
Bernard R. Armour, 1960.

# e x p l a i n

## Responding to Reading

### First Impressions of "Sonnet 18"

1. What difficulties did you find in reading this poem?

### Second Thoughts on "Sonnet 18"

2. Does the poet convincingly show that his loved one is superior to a summer day? Use your comparison chart and cite specific lines.

3. Poetry was viewed as a means of achieving immortality, both for the subject and the poet. How does this poem reflect that belief?

   **Think about**
   • the references to eternity and death in lines 9-11
   • the meaning of "eternal lines" in line 12
   • what "this" refers to in line 14

### Comparing the Poems

4. How are the views of love expressed in the two sonnets different?

## Literary Concepts: Sonnet/Rhyme Scheme

A **sonnet** is a fourteen-line poem that follows a precise pattern. Most English sonnets are divided into three four-line units called **quatrains** and end with two rhymed lines known as a **couplet**. The three quatrains express three different but related thoughts, while the couplet provides the conclusion. Review both sonnets to see how the quatrains show the progression of the poet's thoughts.

**Rhyme schemes** show the pattern of end rhyme in a poem by assigning a different letter of the alphabet to each rhyming sound at the end of a line. The Spenser sonnet follows an *abab bcbc cdcd ee* pattern. That means that the end of the first line, *fire,* rhymes with the end of the third line, *desire,* while the second and fourth lines rhyme, and so on. Use the letters *a* through *g* to describe the rhyme scheme of the Shakespeare sonnet. Assign an *a* to the end of the first line, *day.* Continue until you have assigned a letter to each line.

## Writing Options

1. Use an extended metaphor to create a song lyric that describes your feelings about someone. Use at least three comparisons in your lyric.

2. How would you react if you received one of these poems from a secret admirer? Write a letter to your admirer that expresses how you feel.

*Poetry*

# On My First Son
BEN JONSON

# Fear
GABRIELA MISTRAL

## Examine What You Know

Each of the following poems presents a parent's statement of love for a child. One deals with an experience of loss, the other with fears of what might be lost. What do you think are parents' greatest fears for their children? In what ways do their fears affect their children's lives?

## Expand Your Knowledge

Ben Jonson was an English poet of Shakespeare's time. Both of Jonson's children died young. His daughter Mary died in infancy, and his son Benjamin died a victim of the plague at the age of seven. "On My First Son" is his response to his son's death.

Gabriela Mistral, a Chilean poet of modern times, wrote many poems that reflected her explorations of maternal feelings, even though she herself never married and had only one child by adoption.

## Enrich Your Reading

**Approaching Difficult Poetry: "On My First Son"** Because the language in poetry is often very concentrated and subtle, it can sometimes be confusing. To understand Jonson's poem, try reading through the poem a few times to form a general impression of what it is about. Next, give the poem a closer and slower reading. Try to paraphrase or restate each line or complete sentence in your own words to clarify your understanding. Finally, try reading the poem aloud to develop understanding even further and to appreciate how sound contributes to meaning.

**Understanding Metaphors: "Fear"** As you know, a **metaphor** compares things that are basically dissimilar. Each stanza of "Fear" compares the child to a different thing or person. As you read, think about what these comparisons suggest about the child.

■ *A biography of each poet can be found in the Reader's Handbook.*

THE GRAHAM CHILDREN
(detail) William Hogarth Tate
Gallery, London/Art Resource,
New York.

# *On My First Son*

## BEN JONSON

Farewell, thou child of my right hand, and joy;
My sin was too much hope of thee, loved boy.
Seven years thou wert lent to me, and I thee pay,
Exacted by thy fate, on the just day.
5 O, could I lose all father now. For why
Will man lament the state he should envy?
To have so soon 'scaped world's, and flesh's, rage,
And if no other misery, yet age?
Rest in soft peace, and, asked, say here doth lie
10 Ben Jonson, his best piece of poetry.
For whose sake, henceforth, all his vows be such,
As what he loves may never like too much.

**1** *child of my right hand:* The Hebrew name *Benjamin* means "son of my right hand."

**4** *just:* very; same.

**5** *lose all father:* lose the feeling of being a father.

# *R*esponding to Reading

### First Impressions of "On My First Son"

**1.** Explain what kinds of feelings you experienced while reading this poem.

### Second Thoughts about "On My First Son"

**2.** What thoughts does Jonson express about the loss of his son?

> **Think about**
> • what is suggested by "My sin was too much hope of thee" in line 2
> • the meaning of "O, could I lose all father now" in line 5
> • the feelings about human life and death suggested by lines 5-8
> • the wish for "soft peace" in line 9

**3.** What does the expression "his best piece of poetry" mean?

**4.** How does Jonson propose to protect himself from grief in the future?

# *Fear*

## GABRIELA MISTRAL

I do not want them to turn
my child into a swallow;
she might fly away into the sky
and never come down again to my doormat:
5   or nest in the eaves where my hands
could not comb her hair.
I do not want them to turn
my child into a swallow.

I do not want them to make
10   my child into a princess.
In tiny golden slippers how could
she play in the field?
And when night came, no longer
would she lie by my side.
15   I do not want them to make
my child into a princess.

And I would like even less
that one day they crown her queen.
They would raise her to a throne
20   where my feet could not climb.
I could not rock her to sleep
when nighttime came.
I do not want them to make
my child into a queen.

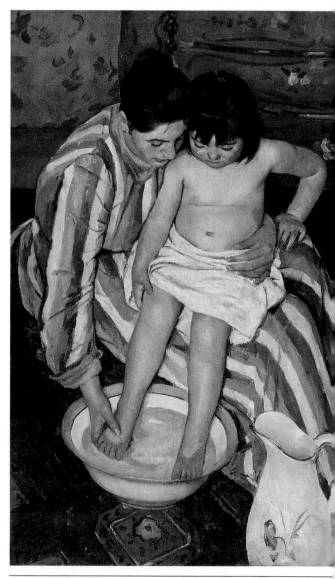

THE BATH 1891 Mary Cassatt The Art Institute of Chicago
Robert A. Waller Fund, 1910.2.

## *Responding to Reading*

### First Impressions of "Fear"

**1.** What do you think about the mother's feelings?

### Second Thoughts on "Fear"

**2.** What fears do you think each of the poem's metaphors represent?

> **Think about**
> - the changes in the daughter's life represented by each metaphor
> - what the mother is afraid of losing

### Comparing the Poems

**3.** Compare and contrast the feelings about parenthood that are presented in the Jonson and Mistral poems.

> **Think about**
> - the sense of loss expressed in the poems
> - the fears that both poems express
> - the views of the future suggested by the poems

## *Literary Concept: Speaker*

In poetry, **speaker** refers to the voice that addresses the reader. The speaker in poetry is similar to the narrator in a work of fiction. The words *speaker* and *poet* do not necessarily refer to the same thing, although sometimes a poet may choose to speak in his or her voice. Often, a poet may create a speaker with a different identity to achieve a particular effect.

In the Jonson poem, the speaker is the poet himself. Since Gabriela Mistral had no children, the speaker in her poem is someone other than the poet. What type of person is the speaker?

**Concept Review: Symbol**   In the Mistral poem, the swallow, princess, and queen stand for something beyond the words themselves. What aspects of the child's future life might these symbols represent?

## *Writing Options*

**1.** The English poet Alfred, Lord Tennyson once wrote, "'Tis better to have loved and lost/Than never to have loved at all." How do you think Jonson would respond to this view? How would the speaker in the Mistral poem respond?

**2.** Write a note to either Jonson or the speaker of the Mistral poem that offers comfort or advice.

*Fiction*

# *Long Walk to Forever*

### KURT VONNEGUT, JR.

## *E*xamine *What You Know*

You are about to read a modern love story. Think of stories you have seen on television or in movies in which an old friendship turns into romance. Why is this plot so common and popular? Think about your own friends of the opposite sex. Do you believe that men and women can truly be just friends, or is there always an element of romance in any friendship between the sexes? Explain your opinion.

## *E*xpand *Your Knowledge*

**Jargon** is the specialized vocabulary of a certain job or profession. People outside of that profession may not be familiar with those terms and phrases. In this story, one character is a soldier who uses army jargon. Some of the terms he uses are explained below.

**furlough:** a permitted absence from the army for a specified period of time.

**AWOL:** absent without leave, said of a soldier who leaves his or her post without permission and is therefore subject to punishment.

**stockade:** a military prison.

## *W*rite *Before You Read*

Have you ever not said something and later wished you had? Think about how things would have been different if you had spoken up. As you read, compare your feelings with those of the characters in the story.

■ *A biography of the author can be found in the Reader's Handbook.*

# Long Walk to Forever

KURT VONNEGUT, JR.

They had grown up next door to each other, on the fringe of a city, near fields and woods and orchards, within sight of a lovely bell tower that belonged to a school for the blind.

Now they were twenty, had not seen each other for nearly a year. There had always been playful, comfortable warmth between them, but never any talk of love.

His name was Newt. Her name was Catharine. In the early afternoon, Newt knocked on Catharine's front door.

Catharine came to the door. She was carrying a fat, glossy magazine she had been reading. The magazine was devoted entirely to brides. "Newt!" she said. She was surprised to see him.

"Could you come for a walk?" he said. He was a shy person, even with Catharine. He covered his shyness by speaking absently, as though what really concerned him were far away—as though he were a secret agent pausing briefly on a mission between beautiful, distant, and sinister points. This manner of speaking had always been Newt's style, even in matters that concerned him desperately.

"A walk?" said Catharine.

"One foot in front of the other," said Newt, "through leaves, over bridges—"

"I had no idea you were in town," she said.

"Just this minute got in," he said.

"Still in the Army, I see," she said.

"Seven months to go," he said. He was a private first class in the Artillery. His uniform was rumpled. His shoes were dusty. He needed a shave. He held out his hand for the magazine. "Let's see the pretty book," he said.

She gave it to him. "I'm getting married, Newt," she said.

"I know," he said. "Let's go for a walk."

"I'm awfully busy, Newt," she said. "The wedding is only a week away."

"If we go for a walk," he said, "it will make you rosy. It will make you a rosy bride." He turned the pages of the magazine. "A rosy bride like her—like her—like her," he said, showing her rosy brides.

Catharine turned rosy, thinking about rosy brides.

"That will be my present to Henry Stewart Chasens," said Newt. "By taking you for a walk, I'll be giving him a rosy bride."

"You know his name?" said Catharine.

"Mother wrote," he said. "From Pittsburgh?"

"Yes," she said. "You'd like him."

"Maybe," he said.

"Can—can you come to the wedding, Newt?" she said.

"That I doubt," he said.

"Your furlough isn't for long enough?" she said.

"Furlough?" said Newt. He was studying a two-page ad for flat silver. "I'm not on furlough," he said.

"Oh?" she said.

"I'm what they call A.W.O.L.," said Newt.

"Oh, Newt! You're not!" she said.

"Sure I am," he said, still looking at the magazine.

"Why, Newt?" she said.

"I had to find out what your silver pattern is," he said. He read names of silver patterns from the magazine. "Albemarle? Heather?" he said. "Legend? Rambler Rose?" He looked up, smiled. "I plan to give you and your husband a spoon," he said.

"Newt, Newt—tell me really," she said.

"I want to go for a walk," he said.

She wrung her hands in sisterly anguish. "Oh, Newt—you're fooling me about being A.W.O.L.," she said.

Newt imitated a police siren softly, raised his eyebrows.

"Where—where from?" she said.

"Fort Bragg," he said.

"North Carolina?" she said.

"That's right," he said. "Near Fayetteville—where Scarlet O'Hara went to school."

"How did you get here, Newt?" she said.

He raised his thumb, jerked it in a hitchhike gesture. "Two days," he said.

"Does your mother know?" she said.

"I didn't come to see my mother," he told her.

"Who did you come to see?" she said.

"You," he said.

"Why me?" she said.

"Because I love you," he said. "Now can we take a walk?" he said. "One foot in front of the other—through leaves, over bridges—"

They were taking the walk now, were in a woods with a brown-leaf floor.

Catharine was angry and rattled, close to tears. "Newt," she said, "this is absolutely crazy."

"How so?" said Newt.

"What a crazy time to tell me you love me," she said. "You never talked that way before." She stopped walking.

"Let's keep walking," he said.

"No," she said. "So far, no farther. I shouldn't have come out with you at all," she said.

"You did," he said.

"To get you out of the house," she said. "If somebody walked in and heard you talking to me that way, a week before the wedding—"

"What would they think?" he said.

"They'd think you were crazy," she said.

"Why?" he said.

Catharine took a deep breath, made a speech. "Let me say that I'm deeply honored by this crazy thing you've done," she said. "I can't believe you're really A.W.O.L., but maybe you are. I can't believe you really love me, but maybe you do. But—"

"I do," said Newt.

"Well, I'm deeply honored," said Catharine, "and I'm very fond of you as a friend, Newt, extremely fond—but it's just too late." She took a step away from him. "You've never even kissed me," she said, and she protected herself with her hands. "I don't mean you should do it now. I just mean this is all so unexpected. I haven't got the remotest idea of how to respond."

"Just walk some more," he said. "Have a nice time."

They started walking again.

"How did you expect me to react?" she said.

SPRING 1947 Ben Shahn Albright-Knox Art Gallery, Buffalo, New York Room of Contemporary Art Fund, 1948.

"How would I know what to expect?" he said. "I've never done anything like this before."

"Did you think I would throw myself into your arms?" she said.

"Maybe," he said.

"I'm sorry to disappoint you," she said.

"I'm not disappointed," he said. "I wasn't counting on it. This is very nice, just walking."

Catharine stopped again. "You know what happens next?" she said.

"Nope," he said.

"We shake hands," she said. "We shake hands and part friends," she said. "That's what happens next."

Newt nodded. "All right," he said. "Remember me from time to time. Remember how much I loved you."

Involuntarily, Catharine burst into tears.

She turned her back to Newt, looked into the infinite colonnade of the woods.

"What does that mean?" said Newt.

"Rage!" said Catharine. She clenched her hands. "You have no right—"

"I had to find out," he said.

"If I'd loved you," she said, "I would have let you know before now."

"You would?" he said.

"Yes," she said. She faced him, looked up at him, her face quite red. "You would have known," she said.

"How?" he said.

"You would have seen it," she said. "Women aren't very clever at hiding it."

Newt looked closely at Catharine's face now. To her consternation, she realized that what she had said was true, that a woman couldn't hide love.

Newt was seeing love now.

And he did what he had to do. He kissed her.

"You're hell to get along with!" she said when Newt let her go.

"I am?" said Newt.

"You shouldn't have done that," she said.

"You didn't like it?" he said.

## "*I*'m not sorry we kissed"

"What did you expect," she said—"wild, abandoned passion?"

"I keep telling you," he said, "I never know what's going to happen next."

"We say goodbye," she said.

He frowned slightly. "All right," he said.

She made another speech. "I'm not sorry we kissed," she said. "That was sweet. We should have kissed, we've been so close. I'll always remember you, Newt, and good luck."

"You too," he said.

"Thank you, Newt," she said.

"Thirty days," he said.

"What?" she said.

"Thirty days in the stockade," he said—"that's what one kiss will cost me."

"I—I'm sorry," she said, "but I didn't ask you to go A.W.O.L."

"I know," he said.

"You certainly don't deserve any hero's reward for doing something as foolish as that," she said.

"Must be nice to be a hero," said Newt. "Is Henry Stewart Chasens a hero?"

"He might be, if he got the chance," said Catharine. She noted uneasily that they had begun to walk again. The farewell had been forgotten.

"You really love him?" he said.

"Certainly I love him!" she said hotly. "I wouldn't marry him if I didn't love him!"

"What's good about him?" said Newt.

"Honestly!" she cried, stopping again. "Do you have any idea how offensive you're being? Many, many, many things are good about Henry! Yes," she said, "and many, many, many things are probably bad too. But that isn't any of your business. I love Henry, and I don't have to argue his merits with you!"

"Sorry," said Newt.

"Honestly!" said Catharine.

Newt kissed her again. He kissed her again because she wanted him to.

They were now in a large orchard.

"How did we get so far from home, Newt?" said Catharine.

"One foot in front of the other—through leaves, over bridges," said Newt.

"They add up—the steps," she said.

Bells rang in the tower of the school for the blind nearby.

"School for the blind," said Newt.

"School for the blind," said Catharine. She shook her head in drowsy wonder. "I've got to go back now," she said.

"Say goodbye," said Newt.

"Every time I do," said Catharine, "I seem to get kissed."

Newt sat down on the close-cropped grass under an apple tree. "Sit down," he said.

"No," she said.

"I won't touch you," he said.

"I don't believe you," she said.

She sat down under another tree, twenty feet away from him. She closed her eyes.

"Dream of Henry Stewart Chasens," he said.

"What?" she said.

"Dream of your wonderful husband-to-be," he said.

"All right, I will," she said. She closed her eyes tighter, caught glimpses of her husband-to-be.

Newt yawned.

The bees were humming in the trees, and

Catharine almost fell asleep. When she opened her eyes she saw that Newt really was asleep.

He began to snore softly.

Catharine let Newt sleep for an hour, and while he slept she adored him with all her heart.

The shadows of the apple tree grew to the east. The bells in the tower of the school for the blind rang again.

"*Chick-a-dee-dee-dee*," went a chickadee.

Somewhere far away an automobile starter nagged and failed, nagged and failed, fell still.

Catharine came out from under her tree, knelt by Newt.

"Newt?" she said.

"H'm?" he said. He opened his eyes.

"Late," she said.

"Hello, Catharine," he said.

"Hello, Newt," she said.

"I love you," he said.

"I know," she said.

"Too late," he said.

"Too late," she said.

He stood; stretched groaningly. "A very nice walk," he said.

"I thought so," she said.

"Part company here?" he said.

"Where will you go?" she said.

"Hitch into town, turn myself in," he said.

"Good luck," she said.

"You, too," he said. "Marry me, Catharine?"

"No," she said.

He smiled, stared at her hard for a moment, then walked away quickly.

Catharine watched him grow smaller in the long perspective of shadows and trees, knew that if he stopped and turned now, if he called to her, she would run to him. She would have no choice.

Newt did stop. He did turn. He did call. "Catharine," he called.

She ran to him, put her arms around him, could not speak. ❧

## *R*esponding to Reading

### First Impressions

1. Do you like the way the story ends? Why or why not?

### Second Thoughts

2. Does Catharine's final decision surprise you? Why or why not?

3. During the story, the author provides clues to suggest that Catharine is in love with Newt. Find as many clues as you can and explain how each clue suggests Catharine's love for Newt.

4. Newt goes AWOL to stop Catharine from marrying someone else. What is your opinion of his actions? Explain.

5. How would you describe Newt's character?

   **Think about**
   - what a newt is and why the author might have chosen this unusual name
   - Newt's decision to go AWOL
   - the reason he gives Catharine for coming to see her
   - his method of courting Catharine

6. Certain phrases are repeated in the story, such as "one foot in front of the other—through leaves, over bridges," "rosy bride," and "school for the blind." Why do you think the author repeats these phrases? Do you think that any of the phrases could have a hidden meaning for the story?

7. Explain the meaning of the title and how it relates to the story.

### Broader Connections

8. Do you know people who have broken their engagements at the last minute? Based on this story and the experiences of people you know, what advice would you give a person who is having second thoughts about his or her upcoming marriage?

## *W*riting Options

1. Catharine is apparently not going to marry Henry. Write a letter from Catharine to Henry explaining her decision to call off the wedding.

2. Newt is going to have to return to his army base and explain his actions to his superior officer. Write his explanation for going AWOL.

3. Imagine that Catharine announces to her parents that her wedding to Henry is off. How might her parents react? Make a list of things they might say.

Fiction

*from The* **Decameron**
*Federigo's Falcon*

GIOVANNI BOCCACCIO (jô vän′ nē bô kä′ chô)

## Examine What You Know

Boccaccio tells a familiar story about a man who sacrifices everything for the woman he loves. Share examples of sacrifices for love that you have heard of or read about. What are the most memorable sacrifices?

## Expand Your Knowledge

Boccaccio lived in the fourteenth century during the **Italian Renaissance,** a time of great achievements in art, music, and literature. His most famous work is *The Decameron,* a collection of one hundred stories told by ten people who escape the plague by leaving the city of Florence to go to the country. ''Federigo's Falcon'' is one of the stories.

Federigo (fe′ dir ē′ gô) devotes his life to a married woman, Monna Giovanna (môn′ nä jô vä′ nä). Since marriages were arranged for reasons of wealth or family reputation, men and women often looked outside the marriage for romantic attachments, which were not considered scandalous as long as the love remained idealized. Federigo also participates in sports. One sport is jousting, a contest between two knights on horseback who use a lance to try to knock each other to the ground. Another is hawking, the sport that uses trained falcons to hunt and kill small animals.

## Enrich Your Reading

■ *A biography of the author can be found on page 247.*

**Plotting Cause and Effect**   In a well-designed story, a single event often starts a chain reaction of events. Unexpected twists may complicate the chain reaction and make the plot more interesting. Keep track of the causes and effects in this story in a chart like the one below. Notice that some causes have several effects, and some effects become causes.

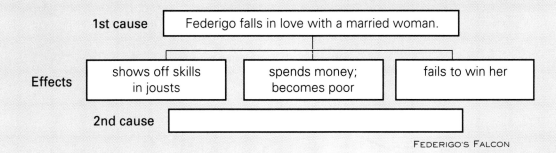

| | | |
|---|---|---|
| **1st cause** | Federigo falls in love with a married woman. | |
| **Effects** | shows off skills in jousts | spends money; becomes poor | fails to win her |
| **2nd cause** | | |

# *from* *The Decameron*

## *Federigo's Falcon*

### GIOVANNI BOCCACCIO

Filomena had already finished speaking, and when the Queen saw there was no one left to speak except for Dioneo, who was exempted because of his special privilege, she herself with a cheerful face said:

It is now my turn to tell a story and, dearest ladies, I shall do so most willingly with a tale similar in some respects to the preceding one, its purpose being not only to show you how much power your beauty has over the gentle heart, but also so that you yourselves may learn, whenever it is fitting, to be the donors of your favors instead of always leaving this act to the whim of Fortune, who, as it happens, on most occasions bestows such favors with more abundance than discretion.

You should know, then, that Coppo di Borghese Domenichi, who once lived in our city and perhaps still does, a man of great and respected authority in our times, one most illustrious and worthy of eternal fame both for his way of life and his ability much more than for the nobility of his blood, often took delight, when he was an old man, in discussing things from the past with his neighbors and with others. He knew how to do this well, for he was more logical and had a better memory and a more eloquent style of speaking than any other man. Among the many beautiful tales he told, there was one he would often tell about a young man who once lived in Florence named Federigo, the son of Messer Filippo Alberighi, renowned above all other men in Tuscany for his prowess in arms and for his courtliness.

As often happens to most men of gentle breeding, he fell in love, with a noble lady named Monna Giovanna, in her day considered to be one of the most beautiful and most charming ladies that ever there was in Florence; and in order to win her love, he participated in jousts and tournaments, organized and gave banquets, spending his money without restraint; but she, no less virtuous than beautiful, cared little for these things he did on her behalf, nor did she care for the one who did them. Now, as Federigo was spending far beyond his means and getting nowhere, as can easily happen, he lost his wealth and was reduced to poverty, and was left with nothing to his name but his little farm (from whose revenues he lived very meagerly) and one falcon, which was among the finest of its kind in the world.

More in love than ever, but knowing that he would never be able to live the way he wished to in the city, he went to live at Campi, where his farm was. There he passed his time hawking whenever he could, imposing on no one,

*Words to Know and Use*

**discretion** (di skresh′ ən) *n.* the quality of being careful about one's actions or words
**meagerly** (mē′ gər lē) *adv.* in a poor manner

and enduring his poverty patiently. Now one day, during the time that Federigo was reduced to these extremes, it happened that the husband of Monna Giovanna fell ill, and realizing death was near, he made his last will: he was very rich, and he left everything to his son, who was just growing up, and since he had also loved Monna Giovanna very much, he made her his heir should his son die without any <u>legitimate</u> children; and then he died.

## She knew that Federigo had been in love with her for some time now.

Monna Giovanna was now a widow, and every summer, as our women usually do, she would go to the country with her son to one of their estates very close to Federigo's farm. Now this young boy of hers happened to become more and more friendly with Federigo and he began to enjoy birds and dogs; and after seeing Federigo's falcon fly many times, it made him so happy that he very much wished it were his own, but he did not dare to ask for it, for he could see how precious it was to Federigo. During this time, it happened that the young boy took ill, and his mother was much grieved, for he was her only child and she loved him dearly; she would spend the entire day by his side, never ceasing to comfort him, asking him time and again if there was anything he wished, begging him to tell her what it might be, for if it was possible to obtain it, she would certainly do everything in her power to get it. After the young boy had heard her make this offer many times, he said:

PEREGRINE FALCON   Raja Serfogee of Tanjore Collection
Courtesy of the Trustees of the British Library, London.

"Mother, if you can arrange for me to have Federigo's falcon, I think I would get well quickly."

When the lady heard this, she was taken aback for a moment, and then she began thinking what she could do about it. She knew that Federigo had been in love with her for some time now, but she had never <u>deigned</u> to give him a second look; so, she said to herself:

"How can I go to him, or even send someone, and ask for this falcon of his, which is, as I have heard tell, the finest that ever flew, and furthermore, his only means of support? And how can I be so insensitive as to wish to take away from this nobleman the only pleasure which is left to him?"

And involved in these thoughts, knowing that she was certain to have the bird if she asked for it, but not knowing what to say to her son, she stood there without answering him. Finally the love she bore her son persuaded her that she should make him happy, and no matter what the consequences might be, she would not send for the bird, but rather go herself to fetch it and bring it back to him; so she answered her son:

"My son, cheer up and think only of getting well, for I promise you that first thing tomorrow morning I shall go and fetch it for you."

The child was so happy that he showed some improvement that very day. The following morning, the lady, accompanied by another woman, as if they were out for a stroll, went to Federigo's modest little house and asked for him. Since the weather for the past few days had not been right for hawking, Federigo happened to be in his orchard attending to certain tasks, and when he heard that Monna Giovanna was asking for him at the door, he was so surprised and happy that he rushed there; as she saw him coming, she rose to greet him with womanly grace, and once Federigo had welcomed her most courteously, she said:

"How do you do, Federigo?" Then she continued, "I have come to make amends for the harm you have suffered on my account by loving me more than you should have, and in token of this, I intend to have a simple meal with you and this companion of mine this very day."

To this Federigo humbly replied: "Madonna, I have no recollection of ever suffering any harm because of you; on the contrary: so much good have I received from you that if ever I was worth anything, it was because of your worth and the love I bore for you; and your generous visit is certainly so very dear to me that I would spend all over again all that I spent in the past, but you have come to a poor host."

And having said this, he humbly led her through the house and into his garden, and because he had no one there to keep her company, he said:

"My lady, since there is no one else, this good woman, who is the wife of the farmer here, will keep you company while I see to the table."

Though he was very poor, Federigo until

now had never realized to what extent he had wasted his wealth; but this morning, the fact that he had nothing in the house with which he could honor the lady for the love of whom he had in the past entertained countless people, gave him cause to reflect: in great anguish, he cursed himself and his fortune, and like someone out of his senses he started running here and there throughout the house, but unable to find either money or anything he might be able to pawn, and since it was getting late and he was still very much set on serving this noble lady some sort of meal, but unwilling to turn for help to even his own farmer (not to mention anyone else), he set his eyes upon his good falcon, which was sitting on its perch in a small room, and since he had nowhere else to turn, he took the bird, and finding it plump, he decided that it would be a worthy food for such a lady. So, without giving the matter a second thought, he wrung its neck and quickly gave it to his servant girl to pluck, prepare, and place on a spit to be roasted with care; and when he had set the table with the whitest of tablecloths (a few of which he still had left), he returned, with a cheerful face, to the lady in his garden and announced that the meal, such as he was able to prepare, was ready.

The lady and her companion rose and went to the table together with Federigo, who waited upon them with the greatest devotion, and they ate the good falcon without knowing what it was they were eating. Then, having left the table and spent some time in pleasant conversation, the lady thought it time now to say what she had come to say, and so she spoke these kind words to Federigo:

"Federigo, if you recall your former way of life and my virtue, which you perhaps mistook for harshness and cruelty, I have no doubt at all that you will be amazed by my presumption when you hear what my main reason for coming here is; but if you had children, through whom you might have experienced the power of parental love, I feel certain that you would, at least in part, forgive me. But, just as you have no child, I do have one, and I cannot escape the laws common to all mothers; the force of such laws compels me to follow them, against my own will and against good manners and duty, and to ask of you a gift which I know is most precious to you; and it is naturally so, since your extreme condition has left you no other delight, no other pleasure, no other consolation; and this gift is your falcon, which my son is so taken by that if I do not bring it to him, I fear his sickness will grow so much worse that I may lose him. And therefore I beg you, not because of the love that you bear for me, which does not oblige you in the least, but because of your own nobleness, which you have shown to be greater than that of all others in practicing courtliness, that you be pleased to give it to me, so that I may say that I have saved the life of my son by means of this gift, and because of it I have placed him in your debt forever."

When he heard what the lady requested and knew that he could not oblige her because he had given her the falcon to eat, Federigo began to weep in her presence, for he could not utter a word in reply. The lady at first thought his tears were caused more by the sorrow of having to part with the good falcon than by anything else, and she was on the verge of telling him she no longer wished it, but she held back and waited for Federigo's reply once he stopped weeping. And he said:

"My lady, ever since it pleased God for me to place my love in you, I have felt that Fortune

| Words to Know and Use | **anguish** (an′ gwish) *n.* agony |
| | **presumption** (prē zump′ shən) *n.* an attitude or act of forwardness or boldness |
| | **compel** (kəm pel′) *v.* to force to do something |
| | **oblige** (ə blīj′) *v.* to make indebted to another for a favor or service |

243

has been hostile to me in many ways, and I have complained of her, but all this is nothing compared to what she has just done to me, and I shall never be at peace with her again, when I think how you have come here to my poor home, where, when it was rich, you never deigned to come, and how you requested but a small gift, and Fortune worked to make it impossible for me to give it to you; and why this is so I shall tell you in a few words. When I heard that you, out of your kindness, wished to dine with me, I considered it only fitting and proper, taking into account your excellence and your worthiness, that I should honor you, according to my possibilities, with a more precious food than that which I usually serve to other people. So I thought of the falcon for which you have just asked me and of its value and I judged it a food worthy of you, and this very day I had it roasted and served to you as best I could. But seeing now that you desired it another way, my sorrow in not being able to serve you is so great that never shall I be able to console myself again."

After he had said this, he laid the feathers, the feet, and the beak of the bird before her as proof. When the lady heard and saw this, she first reproached him for having killed a falcon such as this to serve as a meal to a woman. But then to herself she <u>commended</u> the greatness of his spirit, which no poverty was able, or would be able, to diminish; then, having lost all hope of getting the falcon and thus, perhaps, of improving the health of her son, she thanked Federigo both for the honor paid to her and for his good intentions, and then left in grief to return to her son. To his mother's extreme sorrow, whether in disappointment in not having the falcon or because his illness inevitably led to it, the boy passed from this life only a few days later.

After the period of her mourning and her bitterness had passed, the lady was repeatedly urged by her brothers to remarry, since she was very rich and still young; and although she did not wish to do so, they became so insistent that remembering the worthiness of Federigo and his last act of generosity—that is, to have killed such a falcon to do her honor—she said to her brothers:

"I would prefer to remain a widow, if only that would be pleasing to you, but since you wish me to take a husband, you may be sure that I shall take no man other than Federigo degli Alberighi."

## "*How can you want him? He hasn't a penny to his name.*"

In answer to this, her brothers, making fun of her, replied:

"You foolish woman, what are you saying? How can you want him? He hasn't a penny to his name."

To this she replied: "My brothers, I am well aware of what you say, but I would much rather have a man who lacks money than money that lacks a man."

Her brothers, seeing that she was determined and knowing Federigo to be of noble birth, no matter how poor he was, accepted her wishes and gave her with all her riches in marriage to him; when he found himself the husband of such a great lady, whom he had loved so much and who was so wealthy besides, he managed his financial affairs with more <u>prudence</u> than in the past and lived with her happily the rest of his days. ❧

*Words to Know and Use* | **commend** (kə mend′) *v.* to praise
**prudence** (prōōd′ 'ns) *n.* careful management

## *Responding to Reading*

### First Impressions

1. Jot down your opinion of Federigo's actions.

### Second Thoughts

2. Do the actions of Federigo illustrate the nobility of love or the foolishness of love? Explain your reasoning.

   **Think about**
   - what he sacrifices for love
   - how his love affects other aspects of his life
   - why he is drawn to Monna Giovanna

3. Do you think Monna Giovanna is an admirable character? Why or why not?

4. During Boccaccio's time, Fortune, or fate, was considered one of the most powerful factors in human life. Do you think the story shows that human love is more powerful than Fortune? Explain.

   **Think about**
   - the ways in which Fortune brings Monna and Federigo together
   - the obstacles that Fortune places between them
   - whether the ending is the result mainly of Fortune or of love

5. The narrator explains that the story shows females "how much power your beauty has over the gentle heart." What other lessons does the story offer?

### Broader Connections

6. The widow Monna marries again because her brothers thought that as a young woman, it was her duty. Does our society view marriage as a duty for women? Are women under more pressure than men to marry?

## *Literary Concept: Plot*

You remember that the **plot** is the sequence of related events in a story. Most plots have several elements in common. In the **exposition**, characters are introduced, the setting is established, and the major conflict is identified. In the **rising action**, suspense builds as the conflict intensifies and complications arise. The **climax**, or **turning point**, represents the high point of the action, usually occurring when the protagonist does or does not achieve the goal or makes an important discovery or decision. After the climax, events known as the **falling action** bring the story to its logical conclusion, or **resolution**.

Use your cause and effect chart to decide which events in the story fall in each of the boldfaced categories. Discuss your decisions with your class.

## *W*riting Options

1. Monna says that she would "much rather have a man who lacks money than money that lacks a man." What do you think she means by this statement? Rewrite the statement in your own words; then write your opinion of her views.

2. Federigo probably composed love poems about Monna. Write your own version of a love poem or song that he might have written.

3. Write two diary entries for Monna. In the first, describe her attitude toward Federigo during the early part of the story; in the second, communicate her feelings about him at the story's end.

4. Compare your own views about love and marriage with those of either Federigo or Monna. Be sure to include specific examples from the story, as well as examples of your own views.

## *V*ocabulary Practice

**Exercise A** Decide whether the following pairs of words are synonyms or antonyms. On your paper, identify each pair as *Synonyms* or *Antonyms*.

1. legitimate—lawful
2. compel—force
3. meagerly—abundantly
4. deign—consent
5. discretion—recklessness
6. presumption—forwardness
7. oblige—release
8. anguish—relief
9. commend—blame
10. prudence—cautiousness

> **Words to Know and Use**
>
> anguish
> commend
> compel
> deign
> discretion
> legitimate
> meagerly
> oblige
> presumption
> prudence

**Exercise B** The following words are related in meaning to some of the Words to Know and Use: *illegitimate, compulsion, discreet, commendation, presume.* Look up these words in a dictionary. Then create a sentence for each word that illustrates your understanding of its meaning.

# *extend*

## *Options for Learning*

**1** • **Soap Opera Scenario** Many television soap operas tell stories about love overcoming great obstacles. Create a scenario, or plan, for a modernized version of "Federigo's Falcon." Select a modern setting and decide how the contemporary Federigo will try to impress his lady. Choose a new object of great value to replace the falcon. Share your scenario with your class.

**2** • **The Perfect Gift** Create the perfect wedding gift from Federigo to Monna or from Monna to Federigo. The gift should be a thoughtful expression of love, but remember that Federigo has little money. Create the gift itself or make a model or illustration of it.

**3** • **Family Forum** With classmates, improvise the complete conversation between Monna and her brothers when they convinced her to remarry. Include her words on page 244 when she said she would marry Federigo, and present their probable complete reply and final assent.

**4** • **The Sport of Love** Learn more about the ideals and practices of courtly love during the Middle Ages and the Renaissance. You might find information in an encyclopedia or in books about the time. Then report on what men did to woo their ladies and how a lady was expected to respond. Include other things Federigo might have done to win Monna.

 **FACT FINDER**

*What other sports besides jousting and hawking were popular in the 1300's?*

## *Giovanni Boccaccio*
### 1313-1375

Though he became a great poet, storyteller, and scholar, Boccaccio never had a smooth path to success. Despite an obvious talent for writing—he began writing poetry at the age of seven—his merchant father insisted that Giovanni stop writing and make a success of himself. As a young man he obeyed his father's command, spending six years as an apprentice to a banker. When he failed at banking, his father set him up to study religious law. After six more years, Boccaccio again proved a failure. He complained that because his father "strove to bend" his talent, he had not become "a distinguished poet." Eventually, of course, he did achieve distinction in both poetry and prose. Along with his friend Petrarch, Boccaccio helped to set new directions for Italian literature, and he brought renewed attention to the classical poets of ancient Rome. With the publication of *The Decameron* he became an international celebrity, though he still had to struggle with poverty and rejection in love for most of his remaining life.

*Fiction*

# Love Must Not be Forgotten

ZHANG JIE (zhan jē)

## Examine What You Know

In this story, a modern Chinese woman presents her views on love and marriage. Think of married couples you know. Based on your observations, what makes those marriages good or bad? Discuss what it takes to make a good marriage. Is love a necessary component for a successful marriage? As you read, compare your views with those of the writer.

## Expand Your Knowledge

In 1949, Mao Zedong (sometimes spelled Mao Tse-tung) and his Communist forces won control of the government of China, which for almost four thousand years had been ruled by royal families. Mao established the People's Republic of China and with his revolutionary leaders ruled the largest population in the world. After twenty years Mao felt that new blood was needed to keep the revolution alive, and in 1969 he started the Cultural Revolution. For months, groups of young students and radicals removed older established leaders either by executing them or by having them relocated in the countryside to be retrained in modern Communist thought.

In spite of the revolution, many of China's age-old customs were slow to change, including ideas about marriage. Traditionally, the family head, often the oldest male in the large, extended-family structure, made all family decisions. Until 1950, when the Communist government made women legally equal to men, most marriages were arranged by the couple's families when the two people involved were still young children. Love played no part in the families' decisions. After 1950, individuals were allowed to choose their marriage partners, but remnants of the old ways of thinking remained.

"Love Must Not Be Forgotten" is set in China ten years after the Cultural Revolution. Both main characters of the story are loyal revolutionaries who question traditional ideas about marriage.

## Write Before You Read

■ *A biography of the author can be found on page 260.*

Like everyone else, you have probably been given advice on love and marriage by your parents, siblings, relatives, or friends. List the pieces of advice you have heard on love and marriage.

# Love Must Not Be Forgotten

ZHANG JIE

I am thirty, the same age as our People's Republic. For a republic thirty is still young. But a girl of thirty is virtually on the shelf.

Actually, I have a bona fide[1] suitor. Have you seen the Greek sculptor Myron's Discobolus? Qiao Lin[2] is the image of that discus thrower. Even the padded clothes he wears in winter fail to hide his fine physique. Bronzed, with clear-cut features, a broad forehead and large eyes, his appearance alone attracts most girls to him.

But I can't make up my mind to marry him. I'm not clear what attracts me to him, or him to me.

I know people are gossiping behind my back, "Who does she think she is, to be so choosy?"

To them, I'm a nobody playing hard to get.

They take offense at such preposterous behavior.

Of course, I shouldn't be captious.[3] In a society where commercial production still exists, marriage, like most other transactions, is still a form of barter.

I have known Qiao Lin for nearly two years yet still cannot fathom whether he keeps so quiet from aversion to talking or from having nothing to say. When, by way of a small intelligence test, I demand his opinion of this or that, he says "good" or "bad" like a child in kindergarten.

Once I asked, "Qiao Lin, why do you love me?" He thought the question over seriously for what seemed an age. I could see from his normally smooth but now wrinkled forehead that the little gray cells in his handsome head were hard at work cogitating. I felt ashamed to have put him on the spot.

---

1. **bona fide** (bō′ nə fīd′): in good faith; genuine.
2. **Qiao Lin** (chē ä′ ō  lin).
3. **captious** (kap′ shəs): quick to find fault; quibbling.

249

Finally he raised his clear, childlike eyes to tell me, "Because you're good!"

Loneliness flooded my heart. "Thank you, Qiao Lin!" I couldn't help wondering, if we were to marry, whether we could discharge our duties to each other as husband and wife. Maybe, because law and morality would have bound us together. But how tragic simply to comply with law and morality! Was there no stronger bond to link us?

When such thoughts cross my mind, I have the strange sensation that instead of being a girl <u>contemplating</u> marriage I am an elderly social scientist.

Perhaps I worry too much. We can live like most married couples, bringing up children together, strictly true to each other according to the law. . . . Although living in the seventies of the twentieth century, people still consider marriage the way they did millennia ago, as a means of continuing the race, a form of barter or a business transaction in which love and marriage can be separated. As this is the common practice, why shouldn't we follow suit?

But I still can't make up my mind. As a child, I remember, I often cried all night for no rhyme or reason, unable to sleep and disturbing the whole household. My old nurse, a shrewd though uneducated woman, said an ill wind had blown through my ear. I think this judgment showed prescience,[4] because I still have that old weakness. I upset myself over things which really present no problem, upsetting other people at the same time. One's nature is hard to change.

I think of my mother too. If she were alive, what would she say about my attitude to Qiao Lin and my uncertainty about marrying him?

My thoughts constantly turn to her, not because she was such a strict mother that her ghost is still watching over me since her death. No, she was not just my mother but my closest friend. I loved her so much that the thought of her leaving me makes my heart ache.

She never lectured me, just told me quietly in her deep, unwomanly voice about her successes and failures so that I could learn from her experience. She had evidently not had many successes—her life was full of failures.

During her last days she followed me with her fine, expressive eyes, as if wondering how I would manage on my own and as if she had some important advice for me but hesitated to give it. She must have been worried by my <u>naiveté</u> and sloppy ways. She suddenly blurted out, "Shanshan, if you aren't sure what you want, don't rush into marriage—better live on your own!"

Other people might think this strange advice from a mother to her daughter, but to me it embodied her bitter experience. I don't think she underestimated me or my knowledge of life. She loved me and didn't want me to be unhappy.

"I don't want to marry, Mum!" I said, not out of bashfulness or a show of coyness. I can't think why a girl should pretend to be coy. She had long since taught me about things not generally mentioned to girls.

"If you meet the right man, then marry him. Only if he's right for you!"

"I'm afraid no such man exists!"

"That's not true. But it's hard. The world is so vast, I'm afraid you may never meet him." Whether I married or not was not what concerned her, but the quality of the marriage.

"Haven't you managed fine without a husband?"

---

4. **prescience** (presh' əns): foreknowledge; the apparent knowledge of things before they happen.

*Words to Know and Use*

**contemplate** (kän' təm plāt) v. to think about intently; consider
**naiveté** (nä ēv tā') n. a state of childlike simplicity

"Who says so?"

"I think you've done fine."

"I had no choice. . . ." She broke off, lost in thought, her face <u>wistful</u>. Her wistful, lined face reminded me of a withered flower I had pressed in a book.

"Why did you have no choice?"

"You ask too many questions," she <u>parried</u>, not ashamed to confide in me but afraid that I might reach the wrong conclusion. Besides, everyone treasures a secret to carry to the grave. Feeling a bit put out, I demanded bluntly, "Didn't you love my dad?"

"No, I never loved him."

"Did he love you?"

"No, he didn't."

"Then why get married?"

She paused, searching for the right words to explain this mystery, then answered bitterly, "When you're young, you don't always know what you're looking for, what you need, and people may talk you into getting married. As you grow older and more experienced, you find out your true needs. By then, though, you've done many foolish things for which you could kick yourself. You'd give anything to be able to make a fresh start and live more wisely. Those content with their lot will always be happy, they say, but I shall never enjoy that happiness." She added self-mockingly, "A wretched idealist, that's all I am."

Did I take after her? Did we both have genes which attracted ill winds?

"Why don't you marry again?"

"I'm afraid I'm still not sure what I really want." She was obviously unwilling to tell me the truth.

I cannot remember my father. He and Mother split up when I was very small. I just recall her telling me sheepishly that he was a fine, handsome fellow. I could see she was ashamed of having judged by appearances and made a <u>futile</u> choice. She told me, "When I can't sleep at night, I force myself to sober up by recalling all those stupid blunders I made. Of course it's so distasteful that I often hide my face in the sheet for shame, as if there were eyes watching me in the dark. But distasteful as it is, I take some pleasure in this form of atonement."

I was really sorry that she hadn't remarried. She was such a fascinating character, if she'd married a man she loved, what a happy household ours would surely have been. Though not beautiful, she had the simple charm of an ink landscape. She was a fine writer too. Another author who knew her well used to say teasingly, "Just reading your works is enough to make anyone love you!"

She would retort, "If he knew that the object of his affection was a white-haired old crone, that would frighten him away."

At her age, she must have known what she really wanted, so this was obviously an <u>evasion</u>. I say this because she had quirks which puzzled me.

For instance, whenever she left Beijing on a trip, she always took with her one of the twenty-seven volumes of Chekov's stories published between 1950 and 1955. She also warned me, "Don't touch these books. If you want to read Chekov, read that set I bought you." There was no need to caution me. Having a set of my own, why should I touch hers? Besides, she'd told me this over and over again. Still she was on her guard. She seemed bewitched by those books.

So we had two sets of Chekov's stories at home. Not just because we loved Chekov, but to parry other people like me who loved Chekov. Whenever anyone asked to borrow a volume, she would lend one of mine. Once, in

*Words to Know and Use*

**wistful** (wist′ fəl) *adj.* showing vague yearnings or longings
**parry** (par′ ē) *v.* to turn aside (a question) by a clever or evasive reply
**futile** (fyo͞ot′ 'l) *adj.* useless; hopeless; unsuccessful
**evasion** (ē vā′ zhən) *n.* the avoidance (of a question)

her absence, a close friend took a volume from her set. When she found out, she was frantic and at once took a volume of mine to exchange for it.

Ever since I can remember, those books were on her bookcase. Although I admire Chekov as a great writer, I was puzzled by the way she never tired of reading him. Why, for over twenty years, had she had to read him every single day?

Sometimes, when tired of writing, she poured herself a cup of strong tea and sat down in front of the bookcase, staring raptly at that set of books. If I went into her room, then it flustered her, and she either spilt her tea or blushed like a girl discovered with her lover.

*F or over twenty years one man had occupied her heart, but he was not for her.*

I wondered: Has she fallen in love with Chekov? She might have if he'd still been alive.

When her mind was wandering just before her death, her last words to me were: "That set. . . ." She hadn't the strength to give it its complete title. But I knew what she meant. "And my diary . . . 'Love Must Not Be Forgotten'. . . . Cremate them with me."

I carried out her last instruction regarding the works of Chekov but couldn't bring myself to destroy her diary. I thought, if it could be published, it would surely prove the most moving thing she had written. But naturally publication was out of the question.

At first I imagined the entries were raw material she had jotted down. They read neither like stories, essays, a diary or letters. But after reading the whole I formed a hazy impression, helped out by my imperfect memory. Thinking it over, I finally realized that this was no lifeless manuscript I was holding, but an anguished, loving heart. For over twenty years one man had occupied her heart, but he was not for her. She used these diaries as a substitute for him, a means of pouring out her feelings to him, day after day, year after year.

No wonder she had never considered any eligible proposals, had turned a deaf ear to idle talk, whether well-meant or <u>malicious</u>. Her heart was already full, to the exclusion of anybody else. "No lake can compare with the ocean, no cloud with those on Mount Wu." Remembering those lines I often reflected sadly that few people in real life could love like this. No one would love me like this.

I learned that toward the end of the thirties, when this man was doing underground work for the Party in Shanghai, an old worker had given his life to cover him, leaving behind a helpless wife and daughter. Out of a sense of duty, of gratitude to the dead and deep class feeling, he had unhesitatingly married the girl. When he saw the endless troubles caused by "love" of couples who had married for "love," he may have thought, "Thank Heaven, though I didn't marry for love, we get on well, able to help each other." For years, as man and wife they lived through hard times.

He must have been my mother's <u>colleague</u>. Had I ever met him? He couldn't have visited our home. Who was he?

In the spring of 1962, Mother took me to a concert. We went on foot, the theater being quite near.

*Words to Know and Use*

**malicious** (mə lish′ əs) *adj.* spiteful; intentionally harmful
**colleague** (käl′ ēg′) *n.* a fellow worker in the same profession

A black limousine pulled up silently by the pavement. Out stepped an elderly man with white hair in a black serge tunic-suit. What a striking shock of white hair! Strict, scrupulous, distinguished, transparently honest—that was my impression of him. The cold glint of his flashing eyes reminded me of lightning or swordplay. Only ardent love for a woman really deserving his love could fill cold eyes like those with tenderness.

He walked up to Mother and said, "How are you, Comrade Zhong Yu?[5] It's been a long time."

"How are you!" Mother's hand holding mine suddenly turned icy cold and trembled a little.

They stood face to face without looking at each other, each appearing upset, even stern. Mother fixed her eyes on the trees by the roadside, not yet in leaf. He looked at me. "Such a big girl already. Good, fine—you take after your mother."

Instead of shaking hands with Mother he shook hands with me. His hand was as icy as hers and trembling a little. As if transmitting an electric current, I felt a sudden shock. Snatching my hand away, I cried, "There's nothing good about that!"

"Why not?" he asked with the surprised expression grown-ups always have when children speak out frankly.

I glanced at Mother's face. I did take after her, to my disappointment. "Because she's not beautiful!"

He laughed, then said teasingly, "Too bad that there should be a child who doesn't find her own mother beautiful. Do you remember in '53, when your mum was transferred to Beijing, she came to our ministry to report for duty? She left you outside on the verandah, but like a monkey you climbed all the stairs, peeped through the cracks in doors, and caught your finger in the door of my office. You sobbed so bitterly that I carried you off to find her."

"I don't remember that." I was annoyed at his harking back to a time when I was still in open-seat pants.

"Ah, we old people have better memories." He turned abruptly and remarked to Mother, "I've read that last story of yours. Frankly speaking, there's something not quite right about it. You shouldn't have condemned the heroine. . . . There's nothing wrong with falling in love, as long as you don't spoil someone else's life. . . . In fact, the hero might have loved her too. Only for the sake of a third person's happiness, they had to <u>renounce</u> their love. . . ."

A policeman came over to where the car was parked and ordered the driver to move on. When the driver made some excuse, the old man looked round. After a hasty "Goodbye" he strode to the car and told the policeman, "Sorry. It's not his fault, it's mine. . . ."

I found it amusing watching this old cadre listening respectfully to the policeman's strictures. When I turned to Mother with a mischievous smile, she looked as upset as a first-form primary schoolchild standing forlornly in front of the stern headmistress. Anyone would have thought she was the one being lectured by the policeman.

The car drove off, leaving a puff of smoke. Very soon even this smoke vanished with the wind, as if nothing at all had happened. But the incident stuck in my mind.

---

5. **Zhong Yu** (zhôn yū).

VIGIL 1974–75 Will Barnet Private collection

nalyzing it now, he must have been the man whose strength of character won Mother's heart. That strength came from his firm political convictions, his narrow escapes from death in the revolution, his active brain, his drive at work, his well-cultivated mind. Besides, strange to say, he and Mother both liked the oboe. Yes, she must have worshipped him. She once told me that unless she worshipped a man, she couldn't love him even for one day.

But I could not tell whether he loved her or not. If not, why was there this entry in her diary?

"This is far too fine a present. But how did you know that Chekov's my favorite writer?"

"You said so."

"I don't remember that."

"I remember. I heard you mention it when you were chatting with someone."

So he was the one who had given her the *Selected Stories of Chekov*. For her that was tantamount[6] to a love letter.

Maybe this man, who didn't believe in love, realized by the time his hair was white that in his heart was something which could be called

---

6. **tantamount** (tan′ tə mount′): having equal force.

made him break off, she wondered anxiously why no one persuaded him to give up smoking. She was afraid he would get bronchitis again. Why was he so near yet so far?

He, to catch a glimpse of her, looked out of the car window every day, straining his eyes to watch the streams of cyclists, afraid that she might have an accident. On the rare evenings on which he had no meetings, he would walk by a roundabout way to our neighborhood, to pass our compound gate. However busy, he would always make time to look in papers and journals for her work.

His duty had always been clear to him, even in the most difficult times. But now confronted by this love he became a weakling, quite helpless. At his age it was laughable. Why should life play this trick on him?

Yet when they happened to meet at work, each tried to avoid the other, hurrying off with a nod. Even so, this would make Mother blind and deaf to everything around her. If she met a colleague named Wang, she would call him Guo and mutter something unintelligible.

It was a cruel ordeal for her. She wrote:

> We agreed to forget each other. But I deceived you; I have never forgotten. I don't think you've forgotten either. We're just deceiving each other, hiding our misery. I haven't deceived you deliberately, though; I did my best to carry out our agreement. I often stay far away from Beijing, hoping time and distance will help me to forget you. But on my return, as the train pulls into the station, my head reels. I stand on the platform looking round intently, as if someone were waiting for me. Of course there is no one. I realize then that I have forgotten nothing. Everything is unchanged. My love is like a tree, the roots of which strike deeper year after year—I have no way to uproot it.

love. By the time he no longer had the right to love, he made the tragic discovery of this love for which he would have given his life. Or did it go deeper than that?

This is all I remember about him.

How wretched Mother must have been, deprived of the man to whom she was devoted! To catch a glimpse of his car or the back of his head through its rear window, she carefully figured out which roads he would take to work and back. Whenever he made a speech, she sat at the back of the hall watching his face rendered hazy by cigarette smoke and poor lighting. Her eyes would brim with tears, but she swallowed them back. If a fit of coughing

Yes, Mother never let me go to the station to meet her when she came back from a trip, preferring to stand alone on the platform and imagine that he had met her. Poor mother with her graying hair was as infatuated as a girl. . . .

In spirit they were together day and night, like a devoted married couple. In fact, they spent no more than twenty-four hours together in all. Yet in that time they experienced deeper happiness than some people in a whole lifetime. Shakespeare makes Juliet say, "I cannot sum up half my sum of wealth." And probably that is how Mother felt.

He must have been killed in the Cultural Revolution. Perhaps because of the conditions then, that section of the diary is ambiguous and obscure. . . . It was clear from the tear-stained pages of Mother's diary that he had been harshly denounced; but the steadfast old man never knuckled under to the authorities. His last words were, "When I go to meet Marx, I shall go on fighting my case!"

That must have been in the winter of 1969, because that was when Mother's hair turned white overnight, though she was not yet fifty. And she put on a black armband. Her position then was extremely difficult. She was criticized for wearing this old-style mourning and ordered to say for whom she was in mourning.

"For whom are you wearing that, Mum?" I asked anxiously.

"For my lover." Not to frighten me she explained, "Someone you never knew."

Her eyes were as dry as if she had no more tears to shed. I longed to comfort her or do something to please her. But she said, "Off you go."

I felt an inexplicable dread, as if dear Mother had already half left me. I blurted out, "Mum!"

Quick to sense my desolation, she said gently, "Don't be afraid. Off you go. Leave me alone for a little."

I was right. She wrote:

You have gone. Half my soul seems to have taken flight with you.

I had no means of knowing what had become of you, much less of seeing you for the last time. I had no right to ask either, not being your wife or friend. . . . So we are torn apart. If only I could have borne that inhuman treatment for you so that you could have lived on! You should have lived to see your name cleared and take up your work again, for the sake of those who loved you. I knew you could not be a counter-revolutionary. You were one of the finest men killed. That's why I love you—I am not afraid now to avow it.

I used to walk alone along that small asphalt road, the only place where we once walked together, hearing my footsteps in the silent night. . . . I always paced to and fro and lingered there, but never as wretchedly as now. Then, though you were not beside me, I knew you were still in this world and felt that you were keeping me company. Now I can hardly believe that you have gone.

At the end of the road I would retrace my steps, then walk along it again.

Rounding the fence I always looked back, as if you were still standing there waving goodbye. We smiled faintly, like casual acquaintances, to conceal our undying love.

| Words to Know and Use | **infatuated** (in fach′ oo āt′ id) *adj.* overwhelmed by foolish or shallow love or affection<br>**ambiguous** (am big′ yoo əs) *adj.* not clear; uncertain; vague<br>**inexplicable** (in eks′ pli kə bəl) *adj.* that cannot be explained, understood, or accounted for<br>**desolation** (des′ ə lā′ shən) *n.* lonely grief; misery; loneliness |
| --- | --- |

*We were afraid we might lose control of ourselves and burst out with 'I love you' . . .*

That ordinary evening in early spring, a chilly wind was blowing as we walked silently away from each other. You were wheezing a little because of your chronic bronchitis. That upset me. I wanted to beg you to slow down, but somehow I couldn't. We both walked very fast, as if some important business were waiting for us. How we prized that single stroll we had together, but we were afraid we might lose control of ourselves and burst out with "I love you"— those three words which had tormented us for years.

Probably no one else could believe that we never once even clasped hands!

No, Mother, I believe it. I am the only one able to see into your locked heart. . . .

She went on pouring out her heart to him in her diary as she had when he was alive. Right up to the day when the pen slipped from her fingers. Her last message was:

I am a materialist, yet I wish there were a Heaven. For then, I know, I would find you there waiting for me. I am going there to join you, to be together for eternity. We need never be parted again or keep at a distance for fear of spoiling someone else's life. Wait for me, dearest, I am coming—

I do not know how Mother, on her deathbed, could still love so ardently with all her heart. To me it seemed not love but a form of madness, a passion stronger than death. If undying love really exists, she reached its extreme. She obviously died happy, because she had known true love. She had no regrets.

Now these old people's ashes have mingled with the elements. But I know that, no matter what form they may take, they still love each other. Though not bound together by earthly laws or mortality, though they never once clasped hands, each possessed the other completely. Nothing could part them. Centuries to come, if one white cloud trails another, two grasses grow side by side, one wave splashes another, a breeze follows another . . . believe me, that will be they.

Each time I read that diary "Love Must Not Be Forgotten" I cannot hold back my tears. I often weep bitterly, as if I myself experienced their ill-fated love. If not a tragedy, it was too laughable. No matter how beautiful or moving I find it, I have no wish to follow suit!

Thomas Hardy wrote that "the call seldom produces the comer, the man to love rarely coincides with the hour for loving." I cannot censure them from conventional moral standards. What I deplore is that they did not wait for a "missing counterpart" to call them.

If everyone could wait, instead of rushing into marriage, how many tragedies could be averted! . . .

Let us wait patiently for our counterparts. Even waiting in vain is better than willy-nilly marriage. To live single is not such a fearful disaster. I believe it may be a sign of a step forward in culture, education and the quality of life. ❧

# *explain*

## *Responding to Reading*

### First Impressions

1. Write down your impression of the mother. Share your thoughts with your classmates.

### Second Thoughts

2. Do you think the mother's love affair brings her happiness, unhappiness, or both? Explain your answer.

3. How did the mother's marriage affect her life and her opinions?

4. Compare and contrast the mother's views about love and marriage with those of the man she loves.

5. In what ways does her mother's advice affect the narrator?

   **Think about**
   • the narrator's feelings about her relationship with Qiao Lin
   • the narrator's views on love and marriage
   • how the narrator is viewed by her society

6. The theme of this story is found in the mother's advice that it is better to live on one's own than to rush into marriage. What is your opinion of this advice? Consider your discussion about what makes a good marriage.

7. Predict the narrator's future. Will she marry, and if so, will she be happy? Are her views of marriage so idealized that she will never find a mate, or is there a Mr. Right waiting for her? Explain your predictions.

### Broader Connections

8. At age thirty, the narrator of this story feels pressure to hurry up and get married while she has a chance. How does her society's attitude toward her age and marital status compare to that of our society?

## *Literary Concept: Theme*

You know that the **theme** of a work of literature is the message about life that the writer wants to convey. In most fiction the theme is not stated, and the reader has to figure it out. In this story, however, the theme is directly stated and illustrated, making the story seem as if it were nonfiction. Find places where the theme is stated; then explain how other elements, including plot and characters, are used to illustrate the theme.

**Concept Review: Conflict**   The story opens with the conflict that the narrator faces. How is her mother's story interwoven with this conflict? Is one story more important to the narrator than the other? Explain.

# Writing Options

1. Look back at the advice on love and marriage that you listed earlier. Compare and contrast this list with the advice that the mother gives her daughter. Which advice do you think is better? State your opinion and support it with strong reasons.

2. Find clues in the story about the personality and life of the man the mother loved. List words and phrases that describe the man.

3. Write a love letter that the mother might have written to the man she loved or one that he might have written to her.

4. In the United States, many people try to find the ideal mate by placing personal ads in newspapers and magazines. Imagine that you are the narrator. Write your own advertisement for an ideal mate. Include your good points, interests, and a description of the type of person you are looking for.

5. Imagine and write a conversation between the narrator and Catharine from "Long Walk to Forever." What advice might each character give the other?

# Vocabulary Practice

**Exercise** Write the word from the list that best completes each sentence below.

1. The idea of a Chinese woman choosing her own husband used to be considered laughable, absurd, and _____.
2. The _____ diary did not explain exactly what happened.
3. Lovers forced to live apart might feel _____ and depression.
4. Short answers and long silences might indicate an _____ to talking.
5. _____ gossip is cruel and helps no one.
6. Thoughtful people _____ marriage before rushing into it.
7. A certain simplicity or _____ is expected in children because of their lack of life experience.
8. A marriage that offers no hope for happiness is _____.
9. The mother would _____ questions with tricky answers.
10. The narrator was used to her mother's _____ of questions she did not want to answer.
11. The mystery man was a co-worker, or _____, of the mother.
12. The mother looked _____ when she thought about her beloved.
13. The mystery of the man's death was _____; no one ever explained it.
14. The mother was _____ and dazzled by someone she hardly knew.
15. To avoid hurting others, the couple had to _____ their love.

*Words to Know and Use*

ambiguous
aversion
colleague
contemplate
desolation
evasion
futile
inexplicable
infatuated
malicious
naiveté
parry
preposterous
renounce
wistful

## Options for Learning

**1 • Breaking Up Is Hard to Do** With a classmate, act out an imaginary phone conversation between the narrator and her boyfriend, Qiao Lin, in which the narrator explains her feelings about marriage. In this conversation, the narrator should either break up with Qiao Lin or put off the marriage. Make sure the narrator gives a clear explanation of the reasons behind her decision.

**2 • A Marriage Recipe** Using advice you have heard, ideas from the story, and your own beliefs, create a recipe for a successful marriage. First list the necessary ingredients, such as love, affection, and friendship, and then tell what should be done with each ingredient in step-by-step directions.

**3 • Revolutionary Ideas** Research the Chinese Cultural Revolution. Use current books about China or current encyclopedias to find out what happened, how long it lasted, and how or whether it was concluded. Organize your findings in a time line and give an oral presentation to the class.

**4 • Tape Mate** Using video equipment, create a computer dating service videotape for either the narrator or Qiao Lin. Play the role of the character yourself. Present yourself in the most complimentary way that you can, describing yourself and the kind of person you would like to meet. Show your videotape to your class and have them evaluate your presentation.

### FACT FINDER

*The narrator compares Qiao Lin to Myron's Discobolus. Find a picture of the statue. Based on the statue, is Qiao Lin handsome?*

## Zhang Jie
### 1937–

Zhang Jie is not afraid to break away from old, established ideas. Her progressive attitude shows up in "Love Must Not Be Forgotten," in which she questions attitudes toward marriage in modern China. She is a member of the Chinese Writers' Association and has created many short stories that focus on relationships between individuals and the problems of modernization. Her story "The Music of the Forests," written in 1978, won an award for being one of the best short stories of that year. Zhang Jie's skillfulness as a writer is also evidenced by the different types of writing she has done. In addition to writing short stories, she has written two successful screenplays, *The Search* and *We Are Still Young*, for China's movie industry.

# WRITER'S
WORKSHOP

## NARRATION

Switch on the television, turn on the radio, or skim a newspaper advice column. More likely than not, you'll find someone talking or singing about love. We worry about finding love, losing it, getting enough of it, defining it, and wondering how it works. Our endless fascination with the subject makes it a perfect focus for this workshop: the writing of an oral history.

An oral history is the recording of someone's oral account of actual events in his or her life. The source of research is real people rather than books. The keys to writing a successful oral history are

- deciding on a workable topic
- finding the right person(s) to interview
- asking good questions
- using excerpts from the interviews effectively in your writing

In order to write an oral history, you will need to become an interviewer. You'll create a list of questions, conduct interviews, and write up the results.

Here is your PASSkey to this assignment.

**GUIDED ASSIGNMENT: ORAL HISTORY**

Interview one or more persons about one aspect of love. Write an oral history based on your interviews.

**P**URPOSE: To narrate an oral history

**A**UDIENCE: Teenagers

**S**UBJECT: An aspect of love

**S**TRUCTURE: Narrative essay

## Prewriting

STEP **1** **Choose a focus** Decide what your focus will be. With your classmates, set up the categories of love you might deal with: romantic, parental, platonic, sibling, and so on. Then brainstorm possible topics within each category. For instance, under romantic love, here is a partial list one class created:

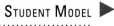

experiences with puppy love   dating long ago
first dates                    tales of a broken heart
long-lasting marriages         divorce

**STEP 2** **List questions and interviewees**   After defining your subject and your topic within that subject, decide whom to interview. For example, if you are planning to write about long-term marriages, you will need to speak to someone who has been married for many years to the same person. You might choose to interview both partners in a relationship. List several names in case some people refuse to be interviewed or turn out to be disappointing. Ask teachers, parents, and friends to suggest names of people they know.

Next, formulate a list of questions to use for your interview. Jot down as many questions as you can think of and list them so that one question leads to another. Your questions will help focus the interview and keep it on target. Be prepared to be very flexible, however; you have no way of knowing what direction the actual interview will take. Sometimes a story will naturally lead to questions that you have not written on your list.

**STEP 3** **Set up and conduct your interview**   Ask your potential interviewees for permission to interview them. Explain what your project is about, and arrange a time to meet. Since love is a very personal topic, do not be surprised if some refuse your request.

You will probably be more successful if you interview one person at a time. Begin your interview with factual questions to help relax your interviewee and make both of you comfortable with the interviewing process. As the interview progresses, phrase your questions so that your interviewee is forced to give more than one-word answers. Remember that you want to hear stories about his or her experiences. Listen carefully to the answers and be ready to respond to them. Use your questions as a guide, but pick up on hints of new directions to turn in based on what your interviewee says. (For more information about interviewing techniques, see the workshop on page 267.)

Occasionally, you may have an unsatisfactory interview, either because of the person's experiences or because of his or her reluctance to talk. In this case, you may need to interview someone else.

**STEP 4** **Draw a conclusion**   Use the results of your interviews to come to a conclusion or generalization about what you have learned. Your interviews are your base of data. You might draw a conclusion from patterns of experiences people had. You might summarize what you learned from the interviews. If you see no patterns or similarities among experiences, you might use that as a basis for your conclusion.

Two students came up with the following topic sentences for their concluding paragraphs.

> Those couples whose marriages have lasted many years seem to have a healthy respect for one another as well as a good sense of humor.

> Although the people interviewed described their first dates as embarrassing and painful experiences, all remember them fondly.

◀ STUDENT MODEL

**STEP 5** **Decide on a format**   After conducting your interviews, decide on the format you'll use to write them up. You might combine the results of your interviews by topic, giving responses to the same question, or you might write about each interview individually. Your decision may depend on the types of answers you received.

## Drafting

**STEP 1** **Write the introduction**   Your paper should begin like an essay. The first paragraph should introduce your subject and present the generalization your paper will support.

**STEP 2** **Include excerpts in the body**   The body of your oral history should contain excerpts from your interviews, ranging from several paragraphs to a few words long. You will need to introduce each excerpt and make connections between them. At this point you will become an editor as well as a writer, choosing what parts of the interview to excerpt. While you will use only the relevant parts, you might occasionally want to include details of anecdotes that capture the charm of a particular interviewee. Make the oral history interesting for the reader. Sometimes anecdotes are more interesting than answers to the questions. Here's how one student began a paragraph on dating.

> Dates were different in the old days, and parents worried about different things than they do today. Mr. Brown used to take his date to an ice cream parlor called the Pink Shop. Although it was popular with teens, the shop didn't last long. The Pink Shop's basement had a jukebox and plenty of room for dancing. Mr. Brown's mother, along with many others, was outraged that teens were be-bopping to ''wild'' music far away from the watchful eyes of parents. Once these parents decided to take action, the Pink Shop's days were numbered.

◀ STUDENT MODEL

**STEP 3** **Write a conclusion**  Wind up your narrative with the conclusion you reached in Step 4 of Prewriting. You might summarize your feelings about the interviews and the interviewees.

## Revising and Editing

Use the following checklist to help you revise your oral history. Make revisions based on the answers to the questions.

**Revision Checklist**
. . . . . . . . . . . . . . . . . . . . . . . . . . . . . . . . . . . . . . . . . . . . . . . . . . . . . . . . .

1. Is the topic of your paper clear?
2. Are the interviewees identified and their opinions obvious?
3. Have you provided material to introduce your excerpts?
4. Have you made strong logical transitions between excerpts?
5. Have you eliminated irrelevant excerpts?
6. Do the excerpts read smoothly? Are they interesting?
7. Have you drawn a conclusion and stated it for your readers?

## Presenting

Have a classmate help you present your paper. Read the material that you wrote yourself, and have your classmate read the interviewees' words. You might coach your partner on how the voices should sound.

## Reflecting on Your Writing

1. How did you like the experience of editing as well as writing?
2. Is it harder to get information from people than from books? Why?
3. How might you have improved the actual interviews?

# LANGUAGE
**WORKSHOP**

## PUNCTUATING DIALOGUE AND CONVERSATION

> **Dialogue** is a conversation between two or more people.

### 1. Use quotation marks to enclose direct quotations.

A **direct quotation** is a speaker's exact words. Use quotation marks to show where this speech begins and ends.

> "I want to go for a walk," Newt said.

When a direct quotation is interrupted by explanatory words, enclose each part of the quotation in quotation marks.

> "I'm awfully busy, Newt," she said. "The wedding is only a week away."

Begin the second part of a divided quotation with a small letter unless it is a new sentence or begins with a proper noun or the pronoun *I*.

> "Newt," Catharine said, "this is absolutely crazy."
> "How so?" said Newt. "I love you."
> "I'm getting married." Catharine replied. "The wedding is in one week!"

REMINDER
...........................................
Quotation marks are not used with indirect quotations. The word *that* often signals an indirect quotation. *Newt said* ***that*** *he just wanted to take a walk.*

### 2. Place commas and periods inside quotation marks.

> Catharine said, "I'm sorry to disappoint you."
> "I'm genuinely sorry to disappoint you," said Catharine.
> "I can't be in love with you," she continued, "because I'm marrying someone else next week."

### 3. Place exclamation points and question marks inside quotation marks if these end marks are part of the quotation itself. Place quotation marks in front of the exclamation points and question marks if these end marks are not part of the quotation.

> "Do you love this guy?" asked Newt.
> "Of course I do!" said Catharine.
> What a shock it was to hear Catharine say, "The wedding is next week"!

## 4. Begin a new paragraph every time the speaker changes.

"How did you expect me to react?" she said.

"How would I know what to expect?" he said. "I've never done anything like this before."

"Did you think I would throw myself into your arms?" she said.

**Exercise 1**   Rewrite the following sentences. Punctuate them correctly with quotation marks, end marks, and commas.

1. I love romantic stories said Laura, at the beginning of a class discussion but only if they have happy endings.
2. I agree answered Sylvia the ending of the story I just read is great!
3. Do you think asked Hank that the story is realistic?
4. Of course I do! Laura said but then, I'm a real romantic!
5. Do you know asked Sandy another definition of the word *romantic.*

**Exercise 2**   Work in groups to punctuate the following dialogue. Have one person copy the passage, beginning new paragraphs and inserting quotation marks, end marks, and commas as determined by the group.

Reading Zhang Jie's story has made me curious about China said Sharon, as she walked home with a group of friends. The story seems so modern for such an ancient country. I agree said Dennis The story might have been set in Paris or Rome or even Hollywood. I would love to visit China said Cynthia. Do you know that the People's Republic has thirty-one cities with estimated populations of over one million? That's more than any other country in the world. I'm not so interested in statistics said Sharon. I'm interested in China's history and culture. It *would* be a fascinating place to visit.

**Exercise 3   Style**   In small groups skim the selections you have read, looking for dialogue. Discuss how each story would be different if dialogue were not used.

Language Handbook

For review and practice:
quotation marks,
    pages 1044–46
commas,
    pages 1037–41
end marks,
    pages 1035–37

**Exercise 4   Analyzing and Revising Your Writing**

1. Review the papers in your portfolio, looking for a passage that could be written as dialogue.
2. Rewrite the passage as dialogue, using correct punctuation.
3. Compare the two passages. Which do you prefer? Why?
4. Consider using dialogue the next time you revise your writing.

# SPEAKING AND LISTENING
### WORKSHOP

## INTERVIEWING TECHNIQUES

To write an effective article or report, you need information, preferably from a variety of sources. In some cases, the best source of information will be a personal **interview** with someone who has first-hand knowledge about your topic. The following guidelines will help you make your interviews more productive—and more enjoyable—both for you and for the person you interview.

1. **Define your purpose.** Decide beforehand what you hope to learn from your subject. Exactly what is the purpose of the interview?
2. **Plan your questions.** Keeping your purpose in mind, write out a list of clear, direct questions.
   - Avoid questions you can answer without the interview.
   - Avoid vague questions like "Is career planning a good idea?"
3. **Be on time and be prepared.** Be sure to arrive on time with your list of questions, paper and pencil, and whatever other materials you need.
4. **Listen carefully and take brief notes.** If there's something you don't understand, ask for clarification. If you want to quote a statement directly, ask to have it repeated so you can be sure you have written it down accurately.
5. **Review and expand your notes.** *Immediately* after the interview, fill in any gaps in your notes. If you wait too long, your memory will grow hazy.
6. **Find the main ideas and the supporting details.** Review your notes and identify the most important details and the best quotes. If an important point is still unclear, telephone the person you interviewed to make sure you have your facts right.

**Exercise**   Using the steps in this workshop, interview a family member, a teacher, or a classmate on a controversial topic like "Should students be able to participate in sports if they receive a failing grade?" Follow the steps in this workshop to prepare your questions, conduct the interview, and expand your notes right after the interview.

### TO TAPE OR NOT TO TAPE

**Advantages:**
- You don't have to take notes. You can concentrate on the interview.
- Your record of the interview will be accurate. You won't forget the details.

**Disadvantages**
- Many people are uncomfortable being taped.
- It takes a great deal of time afterwards playing the tape over and over to find the pertinent information.

P.S. *Never* tape-record an interview without the consent of the person being interviewed.

# $\mathcal{P}$ASSION FOR POWER

Did you ever hear about a gruesome crime and wonder what went through the criminal's mind? Why do some people cross the boundary of evil and commit dark deeds that others imagine but never do?

The play you are about to read is one of literature's most famous explorations of the dark side of humanity. Macbeth is a gifted leader, a fierce warrior, an imaginative, sensitive soul. But he wants to be king, even if his ambition requires murder. His wife, Lady Macbeth, has an even stronger passion for power, and she pushes him relentlessly toward both glory and tragedy. In *Macbeth* you will learn about the consequences of ambition that careens out of control and about the dark forces that lurk in the shadows of our humanity.

**Drama**

# Macbeth

### WILLIAM SHAKESPEARE

## Examine What You Know

Witches, battles, murders, ghosts, and bloody nights fill Shakespeare's *Macbeth*, a terror-rich tragedy about the consequences of one man's desire for power. Think of modern examples of people who have destroyed their lives or the lives of others because of excessive ambition. What politicians, business executives, or religious leaders have abused their power and suffered a downfall? Share your knowledge with the class and discuss what happens when people allow ambition to dominate their lives, regardless of the cost.

## Expand Your Knowledge

**Elizabethan Theater**  When Shakespeare was born, in 1564, there were no public theaters in England, though the English had enjoyed plays in one form or another for centuries. Troupes of actors would perform wherever they could find an audience. They could set up their portable stage at any inn or tavern that had an enclosed yard, though they might also be asked to perform in the large houses of the nobility. Audiences at public inns stood around the stage, eating and drinking, or watched from the windows of the inn. If they disapproved of certain characters or lines, they would let the actors know by yelling, jeering, or throwing food. Large crowds often gathered, which attracted pickpockets, prostitutes, and other ne'er-do-wells, creating troubles for authorities.

The rowdy and quarrelsome behavior of audiences caused many towns and cities to list actors as vagrants, lumping them together with rogues, vagabonds, and other ''undesirables.'' Because the actors themselves were often fined and punished by the authorities whenever any rowdiness occurred, acting troupes sought the protection of wealthy patrons. Due to the scandalous nature of the theatrical profession, women were not allowed to participate, which meant that young boys had to play all female characters, from aging matrons to young lovers. Actors, who were well trained, had to be able to sing and dance, wrestle and fence, clown and weep. They also had to be able to convey subtle messages with a simple gesture or minor voice change.

Playwrights depended on the imagination of their audience. Locations and times were indicated by the words of the play and by simple props. For example, Act Two of *Macbeth* opens with "How goes the night, boy?" Though performances were in the afternoon, the audience would know immediately that it was night. The simplicity of the scenery meant the play could move quickly from scene to scene, with changes in location announced in the dialogue. In Shakespeare's *As You Like It,* for example, Rosalind comes on stage at one point and simply announces, "Well, this is the Forest of Arden."

**The Globe Theater**   The first public theater was opened in the suburbs of London in 1576. By 1600 London had more playhouses than any other European capital; its theaters included the Rose, the Swan, the Red Bull, and the Globe. Because the Globe was home to the Lord Chamberlain's Men, the acting company that employed Shakespeare, it has become the most famous of the public theaters.

The Globe was a three-story wooden structure, probably with sixteen sides, which, in Shakespeare's words, gave it the appearance of a "wooden O." Plays were performed in the open air on a platform stage, which jutted out into a courtyard where the poorer patrons, the "groundlings," stood to watch the performance. Wealthier patrons sat in the covered galleries, protected from the elements. The wealthiest or most important sat on chairs set on the edge of the stage. According to theater receipts, the Globe could hold as many as three thousand people. Crowds flocked there whenever the playhouse flag was hoisted, a signal of an upcoming performance. In an age where plague epidemics were common, the large crowds in such limited space were a constant worry for public officials, who sometimes closed down all theaters as a protection against disease.

Though Elizabethan theaters could not offer the sophisticated stagings that audiences expect today, spectators demanded a good show. A trapdoor in the stage led to a "Hell" below, from which ghosts or witches could emerge. Above the stage and its small curtained balcony was a painted ceiling with similar trapdoors for the appearance of angels and spirits from the "Heavens." The Heavens, an enclosed tower, could also be used for sound effects, such as thunder, drums, and cannons. In fact, a spark from a cannon shot started the fire that destroyed the Globe in 1613.

**The Play**  In 1603 James I became England's first Scottish king, a result of the union between England and Scotland, and Shakespeare's company earned the patronage of the King himself, who renamed it the King's Men. In honor of James I, the King's Men staged Shakespeare's Scottish play, *Macbeth,* in 1606. Shakespeare adapted his plot from Holinshed's *Chronicles of England, Scotland, and Ireland,* which includes an account of Macbeth, King of Scotland from 1040 to 1057. Shakespeare changed the story significantly, even borrowing details from other parts of Holinshed's work to heighten the drama. Shakespeare's Macbeth is much different from the man who was described by Holinshed as a good king with a legitimate claim to the throne.

In many respects *Macbeth* can be seen as a tribute to James I. The noble Banquo portrayed by Shakespeare was the King's ancestor and the founder of his family line. Even the inclusion of witches complimented the King, who prided himself on his expert knowledge of witch lore. Though James and other educated people did not actually believe in witches, most among Shakespeare's audience took them seriously. Various women of the time were tried as witches, and James himself had even interviewed women who claimed to be witches.

## *Enrich Your Reading: Reading Shakespeare*

Most people find Shakespeare's plays challenging to read. In part, the difficulty is caused by his poetic use of language. Virtually all of *Macbeth* is written in **blank verse,** a form of unrhymed poetry with ten syllables in each line, five of which are accented. Blank verse follows a predictable rhythm in which an unaccented syllable is followed by an accented one. A famous line of Lady Macbeth's illustrates this pattern; the accented syllables are marked by ╱, the unaccented ones by ◡.

⠀⠀⠀◡ ╱ ◡ ╱ ◡ ╱ ◡ ╱ ◡ ╱
But screw your courage to the sticking place

For fun, try reading Shakespeare's lines as if they were rap song lyrics, which may help you better appreciate his rhythmic sound patterns and better understand his meaning. Keep in mind that Shakespeare belongs to everyone. Don't let his difficult vocabulary or poetic techniques intimidate you or keep you from enjoying the play. Realize that the more you read, the easier it gets.

Take comfort in the knowledge that you don't have to understand every word and every expression to make sense of Shakespeare. Read for general meaning and use the notes in the **Guide for Reading** in the right margin of the text. Read the lines as if they were prose sentences, looking for punctuation to guide your search for meaning. Try any technique, from reading aloud to listening to recordings, that will help you understand the play.

# *Macbeth*

---

## WILLIAM SHAKESPEARE

## CHARACTERS

**Duncan,** King of Scotland

**Malcolm** ⎫
            ⎬ his sons
**Donalbain** ⎭

**Macbeth** ⎫
            ⎬ Generals of the Scottish Army
**Banquo** ⎭

**Macduff**

**Lennox**

**Ross**

**Menteith** (men tēth′) ⎫
                        ⎬ Noblemen of Scotland
**Angus**

**Caithness** (kāth′ nis) ⎭

**Fleance** (flā′ äns), son of Banquo

**Siward** (sē′ wʉrd), Earl of Northumberland, General of the English forces

**Young Siward,** his son

**Seyton** (sā′ tən), an Officer attending on Macbeth

**Boy,** son of Macduff

**A Captain**

**An English Doctor**

**A Scottish Doctor**

**A Porter**

**An Old Man**

**Lady Macbeth**

**Lady Macduff**

**A Gentlewoman** attending on Lady Macbeth

**Hecate** (hek′ ət), goddess of witchcraft

**Three Witches**

**The Ghost of Banquo**

**Apparitions**

**Lords, Gentlemen, Officers, Soldiers, Murderers, Messengers, Attendants**

*The Time: The eleventh century*

*The Place: Scotland and England*

*Macbeth* photographs from the 1971 film version, directed by Roman Polanski and starring Jon Finch, Francesca Annis, and Martin Shaw.

## ACT ONE

### *Scene 1*  *An open place in Scotland.*

*The play opens in a wild and lonely place in medieval Scotland. Three witches enter and speak of what they know will happen this day: The civil war will end, and they will meet Macbeth, one of the generals. Their meeting ends when their demon companions, in the form of a toad and a cat, call them away.*

| | |
|---|---|
| *[Thunder and lightning. Enter three* Witches.*]* | **GUIDE FOR READING** |
| **First Witch.** When shall we three meet again<br>In thunder, lightning, or in rain? | |
| **Second Witch.** When the hurlyburly's done,<br>When the battle's lost and won. | **3 hurlyburly:** turmoil; uproar. |
| 5  **Third Witch.** That will be ere the set of sun. | |
| **First Witch.** Where the place? | |

**Second Witch.**                    Upon the heath.

**Third Witch.** There to meet with Macbeth.

**First Witch.** I come, Graymalkin!

10  **Second Witch.** Paddock calls.

**Third Witch.**                    Anon!

**All.** Fair is foul, and foul is fair.
    Hover through the fog and filthy air.

*[Exeunt.]*

**9–10 *Graymalkin...Paddock:*** two demon helpers in the form of a cat and a toad.

**11 *Anon:*** immediately.

**12 *Fair...fair:*** The witches delight in the confusion of good and bad, beauty and ugliness.

***Exeunt*** *(Latin)*: Everyone leaves the stage.

## Scene 2  *King Duncan's camp near the battlefield.*

*Duncan, the king of Scotland, waits in his camp for news of the battle. He learns that one of his generals, Macbeth, has been victorious in several battles. Not only has Macbeth defeated the rebellious Macdonwald, but he has also conquered the armies of the king of Norway and the Scottish traitor, the thane of Cawdor. Duncan orders the thane of Cawdor's execution and announces that Macbeth will receive the traitor's title.*

*[Alarum within. Enter* Duncan, Malcolm, Donalbain, Lennox, *with* Attendants, *meeting a bleeding* Captain.*]*

**Duncan.** What bloody man is that? He can report,
    As seemeth by his plight, of the revolt
    The newest state.

**Malcolm.**                This is the sergeant
5    Who like a good and hardy soldier fought
    'Gainst my captivity. Hail, brave friend!
    Say to the King the knowledge of the broil
    As thou didst leave it.

**Captain.**                Doubtful it stood,
10    As two spent swimmers that do cling together
    And choke their art. The merciless Macdonwald
    (Worthy to be a rebel, for to that
    The multiplying villainies of nature
    Do swarm upon him) from the Western Isles
15    Of kerns and gallowglasses is supplied;
    And Fortune, on his damned quarrel smiling,
    Showed like a rebel's whore. But all's too weak;
    For brave Macbeth (well he deserves that name),

**Alarum within:** the sound of a trumpet offstage, a signal that soldiers should arm themselves.

**1–3** Because of the confusion of battle, Duncan does not know who is winning. To find out, he calls on a bloody soldier, whose condition (**plight**) shows recent fighting.

**6 'Gainst my captivity:** to save me from capture.

**7 broil:** battle.

**9–11 Doubtful...art:** The two armies are compared to two exhausted swimmers who cling to each other and thus cannot swim.

**11–17** The officer hates Macdonwald, a rebel whose evils (**multiplying villainies**) swarm like insects around him. His army consists of soldiers (**kerns and gallowglasses**) from the Hebrides, islands off the west coast of Scotland. Fortune, traditionally depicted as a fickle woman, has smiled upon him, giving him temporary success.

Disdaining Fortune, with his brandished steel,
20  Which smoked with bloody execution
    (Like valor's minion), carved out his passage
    Till he faced the slave;
    Which ne'er shook hands nor bade farewell to him
    Till he unseamed him from the nave to the chops
25  And fixed his head upon our battlements.

**Duncan.** O valiant cousin! worthy gentleman!

**Captain.** As whence the sun 'gins his reflection
    Shipwracking storms and direful thunders break,
    So from that spring whence comfort seemed to come
30  Discomfort swells. Mark, King of Scotland, mark.
    No sooner justice had, with valor armed,
    Compelled these skipping kerns to trust their heels
    But the Norweyan lord, surveying vantage,
    With furbished arms and new supplies of men,
35  Began a fresh assault.

**Duncan.**                Dismayed not this
    Our captains, Macbeth and Banquo?

**Captain.**                      Yes,
    As sparrows eagles, or the hare the lion.
40  If I say sooth, I must report they were
    As cannons overcharged with double cracks, so they
    Doubly redoubled strokes upon the foe.
    Except they meant to bathe in reeking wounds,
    Or memorize another Golgotha,
45  I cannot tell—
    But I am faint; my gashes cry for help.

**Duncan.** So well thy words become thee as thy wounds
    They smack of honor both. Go get him surgeons.

*[Exit Captain, attended.]*

*[Enter Ross and Angus.]*
    Who comes here?

50  **Malcolm.**            The worthy Thane of Ross.

**Lennox.** What a haste looks through his eyes! So
        should he look
    That seems to speak things strange.

**Ross.**                      God save the King!

55  **Duncan.** Whence cam'st thou, worthy thane?

---

**21 *valor's minion:*** the favorite of valor, meaning the bravest of all.

**24 *unseamed him...chops:*** split him open from the navel to the jaw. *What does this act suggest about Macbeth?*

**26 *cousin:*** Duncan and Macbeth are first cousins.

**27–30 *As whence...discomfort swells:*** As the rising sun is sometimes followed by storms, a new assault on Macbeth began.

**32 *to trust their heels:*** to retreat quickly.

**33–35 *the Norweyan...assault:*** The King of Norway took an opportunity to attack.

**40 *sooth:*** the truth.

**41 *double cracks:*** a double load of ammunition.

**43–44 *Except...memorize another Golgotha:*** The officer's admiration leads to exaggeration. He claims he cannot decide whether (*except*) Macbeth and Banquo wanted to bathe in blood or make the battlefield as famous as Golgotha, the site of Christ's crucifixion.

**50 *Thane:*** a Scottish noble, similar in rank to an English earl.

**Ross.**                                          From Fife, great King,
    Where the Norweyan banners flout the sky
    And fan our people cold. Norway himself,
    With terrible numbers,
60    Assisted by that most disloyal traitor
    The Thane of Cawdor, began a dismal conflict,
    Till that Bellona's bridegroom, lapped in proof,
    Confronted him with self-comparisons,
    Point against point, rebellious arm 'gainst arm,
65    Curbing his lavish spirit; and to conclude,
    The victory fell on us.

**Duncan.**                          Great happiness!

**Ross.**                                            That now
    Sweno, the Norways' king, craves composition;
70    Nor would we deign him burial of his men
    Till he disbursed, at Saint Colme's Inch,
    Ten thousand dollars to our general use.

**Duncan.** No more that Thane of Cawdor shall deceive
    Our bosom interest. Go pronounce his present death
75    And with his former title greet Macbeth.

**Ross.** I'll see it done.

**Duncan.** What he hath lost noble Macbeth hath won.

*[Exeunt.]*

---

**56–66** Ross has arrived from Fife, where Norway's troops had invaded and frightened the people. There the King of Norway, along with the Scottish traitor the Thane of Cawdor, met Macbeth (described as the husband of ***Bellona,*** the goddess of war). Macbeth, in heavy armor (***proof***), challenged the enemy, matched his strength, and achieved victory.

**69 *craves composition:*** wants a treaty.

**70 *deign;*** allow.

**71 *disbursed, at Saint Colme's Inch:*** paid at Saint Colme's Inch, an island in the North Sea between Norway and Scotland.

**73–74 *deceive / our bosom interest:*** betray our affections or friendship; ***present death:*** immediate execution.

**75** *What reward has the king decided to give to Macbeth?*

---

# *R*esponding to Reading

1. If you were the director of the play, how would you set up the first two scenes?

   **Think about**
   • how characters would enter and leave the stage
   • costumes and makeup
   • how you would create thunder, lightning, and other special effects

2. Up to this point, who do you consider "foul"? Who is "fair"? Explain.

3. Describe the qualities and abilities that make Macbeth stand out from the crowd. Cite examples from the play.

4. Do you admire Macbeth? Why or why not?

5. Fortune smiled only briefly on Macdonwald before he was killed. Do you think Fortune will be kinder to Macbeth?

***Scene 3*** *A bleak place near the battlefield.*

*While leaving the battlefield, Macbeth and Banquo meet the witches, who are gleefully discussing the trouble they have caused. The witches hail Macbeth by a title he already holds, thane of Glamis. Then they prophesy that he will become both thane of Cawdor and king. When Banquo asks about his future, they speak in riddles, saying that he will be the father of kings but not a king himself.*

*After the witches vanish, Ross and Angus arrive to announce that Macbeth has been named thane of Cawdor. The first part of the witches' prophecy has come true, and Macbeth is stunned. He immediately begins to consider the possibility of murdering King Duncan to fulfill the rest of the witches' prophecy to him. Shaken, he turns his thoughts away from this "horrid image."*

*[Thunder. Enter the three* Witches.*]*

**First Witch.** Where hast thou been, sister?

**Second Witch.** Killing swine.

**Third Witch.** Sister, where thou?

**First Witch.** A sailor's wife had chestnuts in her lap
5    And mounched and mounched and mounched. "Give
      me," quoth I.
    "Aroint thee, witch!" the rump-fed ronyon cries.
    Her husband's to Aleppo gone, master o' the
      "Tiger";
10    But in a sieve I'll thither sail
    And, like a rat without a tail,
    I'll do, I'll do, and I'll do.

**Second Witch.** I'll give thee a wind.

**First Witch.** Th' art kind.

15 **Third Witch.** And I another.

**First Witch.** I myself have all the other,
    And the very ports they blow,
    All the quarters that they know
    I' the shipman's card.
20    I'll drain him dry as hay.
    Sleep shall neither night nor day
    Hang upon his penthouse lid.
    He shall live a man forbid.
    Weary sev'nights, nine times nine,
25    Shall he dwindle, peak, and pine.

**2 *Killing swine:*** Witches were often accused of killing people's pigs.

**5 *mounched:*** munched.

**7 "*Aroint thee, witch!*"...*ronyon cries:*** "Go away, witch!" the fat-bottomed (***rump-fed***), ugly creature (***ronyon***) cries.

**8–10** The woman's husband, the master of a merchant ship (***the "Tiger"***), has sailed to Aleppo, a famous trading center in the Middle East. The witch will pursue him. Witches, who could change shape at will, were thought to sail on strainers (***sieve***).

**16–25** The witch is going to torture the woman's husband. She has control of the winds and all the places where they blow, covering all points of a compass (***shipman's card***). She will make him sleepless, keeping his eyelids (***penthouse lid***) from closing. Thus, he will lead an accursed (***forbid***) life for weeks (***sev'nights***) and weeks, wasting away with fatigue.

MACBETH AND THE WITCHES (detail)   Henry Fuseli   The National Trust, Petworth House/Art Resource, New York.

> Though his bark cannot be lost,
> Yet it shall be tempest-tost.
> Look what I have.
>
> **Second Witch.** Show me! show me!
>
> 30 **First Witch.** Here I have a pilot's thumb,
> Wracked as homeward he did come.
>
> *[Drum within.]*
>
> **Third Witch.** A drum, a drum!
> Macbeth doth come.

**26–31** Though she lacks the power to sink his ship (***bark***), she'll toss it in the wind. Finally, she brags about having a bone (***pilot's thumb***) to aid her magic.

**All.** The Weird Sisters, hand in hand,
35  Posters of the sea and land,
    Thus do go about, about,
    Thrice to thine, and thrice to mine,
    And thrice again, to make up nine.
    Peace! The charm's wound up.

*[Enter* Macbeth *and* Banquo.*]*

40  **Macbeth.** So foul and fair a day I have not seen.

**Banquo.** How far is't called to Forres? What are these,
    So withered, and so wild in their attire,
    That look not like the inhabitants o' the earth,
    And yet are on't? Live you? or are you aught
45  That man may question? You seem to understand
        me,
    By each at once her choppy finger laying
    Upon her skinny lips. You should be women,
    And yet your beards forbid me to interpret
50  That you are so.

**Macbeth.**              Speak, if you can. What are you?

**First Witch.** All hail, Macbeth! Hail to thee, Thane of
        Glamis!

**Second Witch.** All hail, Macbeth! Hail to thee, Thane
55      of Cawdor!

**Third Witch.** All hail, Macbeth, that shalt be King
        hereafter!

**Banquo.** Good sir, why do you start and seem to fear
    Things that do sound so fair? I' the name of truth,
60  Are ye fantastical, or that indeed
    Which outwardly ye show? My noble partner
    You greet with present grace and great prediction
    Of noble having and of royal hope,
    That he seems rapt withal. To me you speak not.
65  If you can look into the seeds of time
    And say which grain will grow and which will not,
    Speak then to me, who neither beg nor fear
    Your favors nor your hate.

**First Witch.** Hail!

70  **Second Witch.** Hail!

**Third Witch.** Hail!

---

**35 *posters:*** quick riders.

**38** Nine was considered a magical number by superstitious people.

**44–50 *aught:*** anything; ***choppy:*** chapped; ***your beards:*** Beards on women identified them as witches. Banquo vividly describes the witches. *What does he notice about them?*

**52–57** *What is surprising about the three titles the witches use to greet Macbeth?*

**60 *Are ye fantastical:*** Are you (the witches) imaginary?

**61–64 *My noble partner...rapt withal:*** The witches' prophecies of noble possessions (***having***)—the lands and wealth of Cawdor—and kingship (***royal hopes***) have left Macbeth dazed (***rapt withal***). Look for evidence that shows what Macbeth thinks of the prophecies.

**First Witch.** Lesser than Macbeth, and greater.

**Second Witch.** Not so happy, yet much happier.

**Third Witch.** Thou shalt get kings, though thou be
75      none.
      So all hail, Macbeth and Banquo!

**First Witch.** Banquo and Macbeth, all hail!

**Macbeth.** Stay, you imperfect speakers, tell me more!
      By Sinel's death I know I am Thane of Glamis,
80      But how of Cawdor? The Thane of Cawdor lives,
      A prosperous gentleman; and to be King
      Stands not within the prospect of belief,
      No more than to be Cawdor. Say from whence
      You owe this strange intelligence, or why
85      Upon this blasted heath you stop our way
      With such prophetic greeting. Speak, I charge you.

*[Witches* vanish.*]*

**Banquo.** The earth hath bubbles, as the water has,
      And these are of them. Whither are they vanished?

**Macbeth.** Into the air, and what seemed corporal
90      melted
      As breath into the wind. Would they had stayed!

**Banquo.** Were such things here as we do speak
      about?
      Or have we eaten on the insane root
95      That takes the reason prisoner?

**Macbeth.** Your children shall be kings.

**Banquo.**                      You shall be King.

**Macbeth.** And Thane of Cawdor too. Went it not so?

**Banquo.** To the selfsame tune and words. Who's here?

*[Enter* Ross *and* Angus.*]*

100 **Ross.** The King hath happily received, Macbeth,
      The news of thy success; and when he reads
      Thy personal venture in the rebels' fight,
      His wonders and his praises do contend
      Which should be thine or his. Silenced with that,
105      In viewing o'er the rest o' the selfsame day,
      He finds thee in the stout Norweyan ranks,

**72–75** The witches speak in riddles. Though Banquo will be less fortunate (*happy*) than Macbeth, he will be father to (*get*) future kings. *What do the witches predict for Banquo? What do you think their predictions mean?*

**78–82** Macbeth knows he is Thane of Glamis, since the title passed to him when his father, **Sinel,** died. Thus, the witches' first "prediction" is true. He questions the other two titles. However, since he does not know that he has been named Thane of Cawdor by the King and as he says, the idea of being king himself is beyond belief.

**83–84** *whence:* where. Macbeth wants to know where the witches received their knowledge (**strange intelligence**).

**88** *whither:* where.

**89** *corporal:* physical, real.

**94** *insane root:* A number of plants were believed to cause insanity when eaten.

**103–104** *His wonders...Silenced with that:* King Duncan hesitates between awe (**wonders**) and gratitude (**praise**), and is, as a result, speechless.

Nothing afeard of what thyself didst make,
Strange images of death. As thick as hail
Came post with post, and every one did bear
110  Thy praises in his kingdom's great defense
And poured them down before him.

**Angus.**                              We are sent
To give thee from our royal master thanks;
Only to herald thee into his sight,
115  Not pay thee.

**Ross.** And for an earnest of a greater honor,
He bade me, from him, call thee Thane of Cawdor;
In which addition, hail, most worthy Thane!
For it is thine.

120  **Banquo.**          What, can the devil speak true?

**Macbeth.** The Thane of Cawdor lives. Why do you dress me
In borrowed robes?

**Angus.**                    Who was the Thane lives yet,
125  But under heavy judgment bears that life
Which he deserves to lose. Whether he was combined
With those of Norway, or did line the rebel
With hidden help and vantage, or that with both
130  He labored in his country's wrack, I know not;
But treasons capital, confessed and proved,
Have overthrown him.

**Macbeth.** *[Aside]* Glamis, and Thane of Cawdor!
The greatest is behind.—*[To* Ross *and* Angus*]* Thanks
135     for your pains.
*[Aside to* Banquo*]* Do you not hope your children shall
     be kings,
When those that gave the Thane of Cawdor to me
Promised no less to them?

140  **Banquo.** *[Aside to* Macbeth*]* That, trusted home,
Might yet enkindle you unto the crown,
Besides the Thane of Cawdor. But 'tis strange!
And oftentimes, to win us to our harm,
The instruments of darkness tell us truths,
145  Win us with honest trifles, to betray's
In deepest consequence.—
Cousins, a word, I pray you.

**107–108 *Nothing afeard...didst make:*** Although Macbeth left many dead (***Strange images of death***), he obviously did not fear death himself.

**109 *post with post:*** messenger after messenger.

**114 *herald thee:*** They will act as heralds, ushering him in to Duncan.

**116 *earnest:*** partial payment.

**118 *addition:*** title.

**120–123** Notice the contrast between the reactions of Macbeth and Banquo to the news of Macbeth's new title. Their differences will become more apparent later.

**126–132 *Whether he was...overthrown him:*** The former Thane of Cawdor may have been secretly allied (***combined***) with the King of Norway, or he may have supported the traitor Macdonwald (***did line the rebel***). But he is clearly guilty of treasons that deserve the death penalty (***capital treasons***), having aimed at the country's ruin (***wrack***).

**133 *Aside:*** a stage direction that means Macbeth is speaking to himself, beyond the hearing of others.

**134 *behind:*** to follow; next in line. *What is Macbeth referring to in this aside?*

**140 *home:*** fully; completely.

**141 *enkindle you unto:*** set on fire your hopes for; inflame your ambitions.

**143–146 *to win us...consequence:*** Banquo warns that evil powers often offer little truths to tempt people. The witches may be lying about what matters most (***in deepest consequence***).

**Macbeth.** [Aside] Two truths are told,
As happy prologues to the swelling act

150 Of the imperial theme.—I thank you, gentlemen.—
[Aside] This supernatural soliciting
Cannot be ill; cannot be good. If ill,
Why hath it given me earnest of success,
Commencing in a truth? I am Thane of Cawdor.

155 If good, why do I yield to that suggestion
Whose horrid image doth unfix my hair
And make my seated heart knock at my ribs
Against the use of nature? Present fears
Are less than horrible imaginings.

160 My thought, whose murder yet is but fantastical,
Shakes so my single state of man that function
Is smothered in surmise and nothing is
But what is not.

**Banquo.**          Look how our partner's rapt.

165 **Macbeth.** [Aside] If chance will have me King, why,
chance may crown me,
Without my stir.

**Banquo.**          New honors come upon him,
Like our strange garments, cleave not to their mold

170 But with the aid of use.

**Macbeth.**          [Aside] Come what come may,
Time and the hour runs through the roughest day.

**Banquo.** Worthy Macbeth, we stay upon your leisure.

**Macbeth.** Give me your favor. My dull brain was
wrought

175 With things forgotten. Kind gentlemen, your pains
Are registered where every day I turn
The leaf to read them. Let us toward the King.
[Aside to Banquo] Think upon what hath chanced, and,

180 at more time,
The interim having weighed it, let us speak
Our free hearts each to other.

**Banquo.** [Aside to Macbeth] Very gladly.

**Macbeth.** [Aside to Banquo] Till then, enough.—Come,
friends.

[Exeunt.]

---

**148–150 Two truths...imperial theme:** The first two "prophecies" only set the stage for the more important act of becoming king.

**151–163** Macbeth separates himself from the others, his head spinning. Are the witches' predictions good or evil (**ill**)? If they are evil, why have two of them already proved true? If they are good, why is he suddenly filled with the terrible thought (**suggestion**) of killing King Duncan to make the third prediction come true? This idea (**horrible imaginings**) is more frightful than any fears justified by reality (**present fears**). Macbeth is so overwhelmed that his mind and body together (**single state of man**) are overcome by speculation (**surmise**) about the future. Nothing seems real but his imaginings (**what is not**).

**167 my stir:** my doing anything.

**169–170** Banquo excuses Macbeth's odd behavior by comparing his new honors to new (**strange**) clothes that only become comfortable with wear.

**171–172 Come what...roughest day:** the future will arrive no matter what.

**173 stay:** wait.

**176–178 your pains...read them:** I will always remember your efforts. The metaphor refers to keeping a diary and reading it regularly.

**180–182 at more time...other:** Macbeth wants to discuss the prophecies later, after he and Banquo have had time to think about them.

## *Responding to Reading*

1. What do you learn about the witches in this scene?

   **Think about**
   - their discussion in the opening
   - what Banquo says about them
   - what Macbeth says about them

2. Is there anything that Macbeth does or says in this scene that changes your opinion of him to this point? Explain.

3. How is Banquo different from Macbeth? Use examples from Scenes 2 and 3 to indicate their differences.

4. How do you think Macbeth and Banquo will act, now that they know the witches were correct in greeting Macbeth as the Thane of Cawdor?

*Scene 4*   *A room in the king's palace at Forres.*

*King Duncan receives news of the execution of the former thane of Cawdor. As the king is admitting his bad judgment concerning the traitor, Macbeth enters with Banquo, Ross, and Angus. Duncan expresses his gratitude to them and then, in a most unusual action, officially names his own son Malcolm as heir to the throne. To honor Macbeth, Duncan decides to visit Macbeth's castle at Inverness. Macbeth, his thoughts full of dark ambition, leaves to prepare for the king's visit.*

*[Flourish. Enter* Duncan, Lennox, Malcolm, Donalbain, *and* Attendants.*]*

**Duncan.** Is execution done on Cawdor? Are not
  Those in commission yet returned?

**Malcolm.**                                   My liege,
  They are not yet come back. But I have spoke
5 With one that saw him die; who did report
  That very frankly he confessed his treasons,
  Implored your Highness' pardon, and set forth
  A deep repentance. Nothing in his life
  Became him like the leaving it. He died
10 As one that had been studied in his death
  To throw away the dearest thing he owed
  As 'twere a careless trifle.

**2 Those in commission:** those who have the responsibility for Cawdor's execution.

**7 set forth:** showed.

**9–12 He died as...trifle:** He died as if he had rehearsed (**studied**) the moment. Though losing his life (**the dearest thing he owed**), he behaved with calm dignity.

**Duncan.**                    There's no art
    To find the mind's construction in the face.
15  He was a gentleman on whom I built
    An absolute trust.

*[Enter Macbeth, Banquo, Ross, and* Angus.*]*

                          O worthiest cousin,
    The sin of my ingratitude even now
    Was heavy on me! Thou art so far before
20  That swiftest wing of recompense is slow
    To overtake thee. Would thou hadst less deserved,
    That the proportion both of thanks and payment
    Might have been mine! Only I have left to say,
    More is thy due than more than all can pay.

25  **Macbeth.** The service and the loyalty I owe,
    In doing it pays itself. Your Highness' part
    Is to receive our duties; and our duties
    Are to your throne and state children and servants,
    Which do but what they should by doing everything
30  Safe toward your love and honor.

    **Duncan.**                          Welcome hither.
    I have begun to plant thee and will labor
    To make thee full of growing. Noble Banquo,
    That hast no less deserved, nor must be known
35  No less to have done so, let me infold thee
    And hold thee to my heart.

    **Banquo.**                          There if I grow,
    The harvest is your own.

    **Duncan.**                          My plenteous joys,
40  Wanton in fullness, seek to hide themselves
    In drops of sorrow. Sons, kinsmen, thanes,
    And you whose places are the nearest, know
    We will establish our estate upon
    Our eldest, Malcolm, whom we name hereafter
45  The Prince of Cumberland; which honor must
    Not unaccompanied invest him only,
    But signs of nobleness, like stars, shall shine
    On all deservers. From hence to Inverness,
    And bind us further to you.

50  **Macbeth.** The rest is labor, which is not used for you.
    I'll be myself the harbinger, and make joyful
    The hearing of my wife with your approach;
    So, humbly take my leave.

**17–24 O worthiest...pay:** The King feels that he cannot repay (**recompense**) Macbeth enough. Macbeth's qualities and accomplishments are of greater value than any thanks or payment Duncan can give.

**25–30** *How does Macbeth respond to the King? Do you think his words match his thoughts? Why or why not?*

**32–33 I have...growing:** The King plans to give more honors to Macbeth. *What might Macbeth be thinking now?*

**39–41 My plenteous...sorrow:** The King is crying tears of joy.

**45 Prince of Cumberland:** the title given to the heir to the Scottish throne. Now that Malcolm is heir, Macbeth's chances of becoming king seem reduced. *How might Macbeth react to this unexpected twist?*

**47 signs of nobleness:** titles and honors.

**48 Inverness:** site of Macbeth's castle, where the King has just invited himself, giving another honor to Macbeth.

**51 harbinger:** a representative sent before a royal party to make proper arrangements for its arrival.

**Duncan.**                    My worthy Cawdor!

55  **Macbeth.** *[Aside]* The Prince of Cumberland! That is a
        step
    On which I must fall down, or else o'erleap,
    For in my way it lies. Stars, hide your fires!
    Let not light see my black and deep desires.
60  The eye wink at the hand; yet let that be,
    Which the eye fears, when it is done, to see. *[Exit.]*

    **Duncan.** True, worthy Banquo: he is full so valiant,
        And in his commendations I am fed;
        It is a banquet to me. Let's after him,
65      Whose care is gone before to bid us welcome.
        It is a peerless kinsman.

    *[Flourish. Exeunt.]*

**58–59 *Stars...desires:*** Macbeth wants to hide his murderous thoughts.

**60–61 *The eye...to see:*** Macbeth hopes for the King's murder, although he does not want to see it.

**62–66** Duncan continues an earlier conversation with Banquo about Macbeth's merits.

## *R*esponding to Reading

1. Without Macbeth's help, Duncan might have lost his entire kingdom. Do you think he gives Macbeth enough of a reward? Why or why not?

2. When Macbeth offers to act as messenger, is he acting out of gratitude and respect for the King, or might he have other motives for arriving at Inverness before Duncan?

### Scene 5   *Macbeth's castle at Inverness.*

*Lady Macbeth reads a letter from her husband that tells her of the witches' prophecies, one of which has already come true. She is determined that Macbeth will be king. However, she fears that he lacks the courage to kill Duncan. After a messenger tells her the king is coming, she calls on the powers of evil to help her do what must be done. When Macbeth arrives, she tells him that the king must die that night but reminds him that he must appear to be a good and loyal host.*

*[Enter Lady Macbeth alone, with a letter.]*

**Lady Macbeth.** *[Reads]* "They met me in the day of
    success; and I have learned by the perfect'st report they
    have more in them than mortal knowledge. When I
    burned in desire to question them further, they made
5   themselves air, into which they vanished. Whiles I stood
    rapt in the wonder of it, came missives from the King,
    who all-hailed me Thane of Cawdor, by which title,

**1–13** Lady Macbeth is reading a letter from her husband that recounts his meeting with the witches.

before, these Weird Sisters saluted me, and referred me
to the coming on of time with 'Hail, King that shalt
10  be!' This have I thought good to deliver thee, my
dearest partner of greatness, that thou mightst not lose
the dues of rejoicing by being ignorant of what
greatness is promised thee. Lay it to thy heart, and
farewell."

15      Glamis thou art, and Cawdor, and shalt be
What thou art promised. Yet do I fear thy nature.
It is too full o' the milk of human kindness
To catch the nearest way. Thou wouldst be great;
Art not without ambition, but without
20  The illness should attend it. What thou wouldst highly,
That wouldst thou holily; wouldst not play false,
And yet wouldst wrongly win. Thou'ldst have, great
      Glamis,
That which cries "Thus thou must do," if thou have it;
25  And that which rather thou dost fear to do
Than wishest should be undone. Hie thee hither,
That I may pour my spirits in thine ear
And chastise with the valor of my tongue
All that impedes thee from the golden round
30  Which fate and metaphysical aid doth seem
To have thee crowned withal.

*[Enter Messenger.]*

                              What is your tidings?

**Messenger.** The King comes here tonight.

**Lady Macbeth.**                    Thou'rt mad to say it!
35  Is not thy master with him? who, were't so,
Would have informed for preparation.

**Messenger.** So please you, it is true. Our Thane is
      coming.
One of my fellows had the speed of him,
40  Who, almost dead for breath, had scarcely more
Than would make up his message.

**Lady Macbeth.**                    Give him tending;
He brings great news.

*[Exit Messenger.]*

                        The raven himself is hoarse
45  That croaks the fatal entrance of Duncan
Under my battlements. Come, you spirits

**16–31 Yet do...withal:** Lady Macbeth fears her husband is too good (**too full o' the milk of human kindness**) to seize the throne by murder (**the nearest way**). Lacking the necessary wickedness (**illness**), he wants to gain power virtuously (**holily**). But she is convinced he would like to be king, even if becoming king requires murder (**that which rather thou dost fear to do**). She wishes him home (**Hie thee hither**) so that she can drive out (**chastise**) his fears and anything else that stands in the way of the crown (**golden round**). Fate and the supernatural (**metaphysical aid**) seem on his side. *Do you think Lady Macbeth is right about her husband?*

**39 had the speed of him:** rode faster than he.

**44 raven:** The harsh cry of the raven, a bird symbolizing evil and misfortune, was supposed to indicate an approaching death.

That tend on mortal thoughts, unsex me here,
And fill me, from the crown to the toe, top-full
Of direst cruelty! Make thick my blood;
50 Stop up the access and passage to remorse,
That no compunctious visitings of nature
Shake my fell purpose nor keep peace between
The effect and it! Come to my woman's breasts
And take my milk for gall, you murd'ring ministers,
55 Wherever in your sightless substances
You wait on nature's mischief! Come, thick night,
And pall thee in the dunnest smoke of hell,
That my keen knife see not the wound it makes,
Nor heaven peep through the blanket of the dark
60 To cry "Hold, hold!"

[Enter Macbeth.]

                              Great Glamis! worthy Cawdor!
Greater than both, by the all-hail hereafter!
Thy letters have transported me beyond
This ignorant present, and I feel now
65 The future in the instant.

**Macbeth.**                    My dearest love,
Duncan comes here tonight.

**Lady Macbeth.**                    And when goes hence?

**Macbeth.** Tomorrow, as he purposes.

70 **Lady Macbeth.**                    O, never
Shall sun that morrow see!
Your face, my Thane, is as a book where men
May read strange matters. To beguile the time,
Look like the time; bear welcome in your eye,
75 Your hand, your tongue; look like the innocent
    flower,
But be the serpent under't. He that's coming
Must be provided for; and you shall put
This night's great business into my dispatch,
80 Which shall to all our nights and days to come
Give solely sovereign sway and masterdom.

**Macbeth.** We will speak further.

**Lady Macbeth.**                    Only look up clear.
To alter favor ever is to fear.
85 Leave all the rest to me.

[Exeunt.]

**46–60** Lady Macbeth calls on the spirits of evil to rid her of feminine weakness (***unsex me***) and to block out guilt. She wants no normal pangs of conscience (***compunctious visitings of nature***) to get in the way of her murderous plan. She asks that her mother's milk be turned to bile (***gall***) by the unseen evil forces (***murd'ring ministers, sightless substances***) that exist in nature. Furthermore, she asks that the night wrap (***pall***) itself in darkness as black as hell so that no one may see or stop the crime. *Do you think Lady Macbeth could actually kill Duncan?*

**61–62** Lady Macbeth greets her husband, echoing the witches' prophecies.

**65 *in the instant:*** at this moment.

**70–71 *O, never...see:*** She either wishes that darkness continue to hide her deeds or wishes that Duncan not live through the night.

**73–77 *To beguile...under't:*** To fool (***beguile***) everyone, act as expected at such a time, that is, as a good host. *Who is more like a serpent, Lady Macbeth or her husband?*

**79 *my dispatch:*** my management.

**81 *solely sovereign sway:*** bring absolute royal power.

**84 *To alter...fear:*** To change your expression (***favor***) is a sign of fear.

# *R*esponding to Reading

1. What is your opinion of Lady Macbeth? Use examples from this scene to support your opinion.

2. Who do you think is more interesting or memorable, Lady Macbeth or her husband? Why?

3. What does Lady Macbeth think of her husband? Do you agree with her evaluation of his character?

4. Do you think the Macbeths' plan to get the crown will work? What problems might they encounter in acting out their desires?

## Scene 6    *In front of Macbeth's castle.*

*King Duncan and his party arrive, and Lady Macbeth welcomes them. Duncan is generous in his praise of his hosts and eagerly awaits the arrival of Macbeth.*

*[Hautboys and torches. Enter* Duncan, Malcolm, Donalbain, Banquo, Lennox, Macduff, Ross, Angus, *and* Attendants.*]*

**Duncan.** This castle hath a pleasant seat. The air
Nimbly and sweetly recommends itself
Unto our gentle senses.

**Banquo.**            This guest of summer,
5   The temple-haunting martlet, does approve
By his loved mansionry that the heaven's breath
Smells wooingly here. No jutty, frieze,
Buttress, nor coign of vantage, but this bird
Hath made his pendent bed and procreant cradle.
10   Where they most breed and haunt, I have observed
The air is delicate.

*[Enter* Lady Macbeth.*]*

**Duncan.**          See, see, our honored hostess!
The love that follows us sometime is our trouble,
Which still we thank as love. Herein I teach you
15   How you shall bid God 'ield us for your pains
And thank us for your trouble.

**Lady Macbeth.**           All our service
In every point twice done, and then done double,
Were poor and single business to contend
20   Against those honors deep and broad wherewith

**Hautboys:** oboes.

**1 *seat:*** location.

**4–11 *This guest...delicate:*** The martin (**martlet**) usually built its nest on a church (**temple**), where every projection (**jutty**), sculptured decoration (**frieze**), support (**buttress**), and convenient corner (**coign of vantage**) offered a good nesting site. Banquo sees the presence of the martin's hanging (**pendent**) nest, a breeding (**procreant**) place, as a sign of healthy air.

**13–16 *The love...your trouble:*** Even though love can be troublesome, we should be thankful for it. Duncan, knowing that his visit is a great inconvenience, tells Lady Macbeth that it is a sign of love for which she should be thankful.

**19 *single business:*** weak service. Lady Macbeth claims that nothing she or her husband can do will match Duncan's generosity.

Your Majesty loads our house. For those of old,
And the late dignities heaped up to them,
We rest your hermits.

**Duncan.**                    Where's the Thane of Cawdor?
25 We coursed him at the heels and had a purpose
To be his purveyor; but he rides well,
And his great love, sharp as his spur, hath holp him
To his home before us. Fair and noble hostess,
We are your guest tonight.

30 **Lady Macbeth.**            Your servants ever
Have theirs, themselves, and what is theirs, in compt,
To make their audit at your Highness' pleasure,
Still to return your own.

**Duncan.**                    Give me your hand;
35 Conduct me to mine host. We love him highly
And shall continue our graces towards him.
By your leave, hostess.

*[Exeunt.]*

---

*Scene 7*    *A room in Macbeth's castle.*

*Macbeth has left Duncan in the middle of dinner. Alone, he begins to have second
thoughts about his murderous plan. Lady Macbeth enters and discovers that he has
changed his mind. She scornfully accuses him of cowardice and tells him that a true
man would never back out of a commitment. She reassures him of success and
explains her plan. She will make sure that the king's attendants drink too much.
When they are fast asleep, Macbeth will stab the king with the servants' weapons.*

*[Hautboys. Torches. Enter a* Sewer, *and divers* Servants *with
dishes and service over the stage. Then enter* Macbeth.*]*

**Macbeth.** If it were done when 'tis done, then 'twere
    well
It were done quickly. If the assassination
Could trammel up the consequence, and catch,
5 With his surcease, success, that but this blow
Might be the be-all and the end-all here,
But here, upon this bank and shoal of time,
We'd jump the life to come. But in these cases
We still have judgment here, that we but teach
10 Bloody instructions, which, being taught, return

**23 We rest your hermits:** We can only repay you with prayers. The wealthy used to hire hermits to pray for the dead.

**25 coursed him at the heels:** followed him closely.

**26 purveyor:** like a harbinger, one who makes advance arrangements for a royal visit. Duncan says that he wanted to prepare the way for Macbeth.

**27 holp:** helped.

**30–33** Legally, Duncan owned everything in his kingdom. Lady Macbeth politely says that they hold his property in trust (**compt**), ready to return it (**make their audit**) whenever he wants. *Why do you think Lady Macbeth is being especially gracious to Duncan?*

**Sewer:** the steward, the servant in charge of arranging the banquet and tasting the King's food; **divers:** different.

**1–11** Again, Macbeth argues with himself about murdering the King. If it could be done without causing problems later, then it would be good to do it soon. If Duncan's murder would have no negative consequences and be successfully completed with his death (**surcease**), then Macbeth would risk eternal damnation. He knows, however, that terrible deeds (**Bloody instructions**) often backfire.

To plague the inventor. This even-handed justice
Commends the ingredience of our poisoned chalice
To our own lips. He's here in double trust:
First, as I am his kinsman and his subject,
15 Strong both against the deed; then, as his host,
Who should against his murderer shut the door,
Not bear the knife myself. Besides, this Duncan
Hath borne his faculties so meek, hath been
So clear in his great office, that his virtues
20 Will plead like angels, trumpet-tongued, against
The deep damnation of his taking-off;
And pity, like a naked new-born babe,
Striding the blast, or heaven's cherubin, horsed
Upon the sightless couriers of the air,
25 Shall blow the horrid deed in every eye,
That tears shall drown the wind. I have no spur
To prick the sides of my intent, but only
Vaulting ambition, which o'erleaps itself
And falls on the other—

*[Enter Lady Macbeth.]*

30                                  How now? What news?

**Lady Macbeth.** He has almost supped. Why have you
    left the chamber?

**Macbeth.** Hath he asked for me?

**Lady Macbeth.**                    Know you not he has?

35 **Macbeth.** We will proceed no further in this business.
    He hath honored me of late, and I have bought
    Golden opinions from all sorts of people,
    Which would be worn now in their newest gloss,
    Not cast aside so soon.

40 **Lady Macbeth.**              Was the hope drunk
    Wherein you dressed yourself? Hath it slept since?
    And wakes it now to look so green and pale
    At what it did so freely? From this time
    Such I account thy love. Art thou afeard
45 To be the same in thine own act and valor
    As thou art in desire? Wouldst thou have that
    Which thou esteem'st the ornament of life,
    And live a coward in thine own esteem,
    Letting "I dare not" wait upon "I would,"
50 Like the poor cat i' the adage?

**12–29** Macbeth reminds himself that he is Duncan's relative, subject, and host and that the King has never abused his royal powers (**faculties**). In fact, Duncan is such a good person that there is no possible reason for his murder except Macbeth's own driving ambition.

**36–39 I have...so soon:** The praises that Macbeth has received are, like new clothes, to be worn, not quickly thrown away. *What has Macbeth decided?*

**40–43 Was the hope drunk...freely:** Lady Macbeth sarcastically describes Macbeth's ambition to be king (**hope**) in drinking terms. His ambition must have been drunk, because it now seems to have a hangover (**to look so green and pale**).

**44–50 Such I...adage:** Lady Macbeth criticizes Macbeth's weakened resolve to secure the crown (**ornament of life**) and calls him a coward. She compares him to a cat in a proverb (**adage**) who wouldn't catch fish because it feared wet feet.

ELLEN TERRY AS
LADY MACBETH
1889 John Singer
Sargent National
Portrait Gallery,
London.

**Macbeth.** Prithee peace!
I dare do all that may become a man.
Who dares do more is none.

**Lady Macbeth.** What beast was't then
55 That made you break this enterprise to me?
When you durst do it, then you were a man;
And to be more than what you were, you would
Be so much more the man. Nor time nor place
Did then adhere, and yet you would make both.
60 They have made themselves, and that their fitness
now
Does unmake you. I have given suck, and know
How tender 'tis to love the babe that milks me.
I would, while it was smiling in my face,
65 Have plucked my nipple from his boneless gums
And dashed the brains out, had I so sworn as you
Have done to this.

**51 *Prithee:*** a short form of "pray
thee," meaning "please."

**55 *enterprise:*** promise.
**56 *durst:*** dared.

**58–62 *Nor time...unmake you:*** You
talked bravely when the time was not
right to act. Now that we have the
opportunity (***fitness***), you are afraid.

**62 *I have given suck:*** I have nursed a
baby.

**Macbeth.**     If we should fail?

**Lady Macbeth.**     We fail?

70 But screw your courage to the sticking place,
And we'll not fail. When Duncan is asleep
(Whereto the rather shall his day's hard journey
Soundly invite him), his two chamberlains
Will I with wine and wassail so convince

75 That memory, the warder of the brain,
Shall be a fume, and the receipt of reason
A limbeck only. When in swinish sleep
Their drenched natures lie as in a death,
What cannot you and I perform upon

80 The unguarded Duncan? what not put upon
His spongy officers, who shall bear the guilt
Of our great quell?

**Macbeth.**     Bring forth men-children only,
For thy undaunted mettle should compose

85 Nothing but males. Will it not be received,
When we have marked with blood those sleepy two
Of his own chamber and used their very daggers,
That they have done't?

**Lady Macbeth.**     Who dares receive it other,

90 As we shall make our griefs and clamor roar
Upon his death?

**Macbeth.**     I am settled and bend up
Each corporal agent to this terrible feat.
Away, and mock the time with fairest show;

95 False face must hide what the false heart doth know.

*[Exeunt.]*

**70 But...place:** When each string of a guitar or lute is tightened to the peg (***sticking place***), the instrument is ready to be played.

**73 chamberlains:** servants; attendants.

**74 wassail:** carousing; partying.

**75–77 That memory...A limbeck only:** Memory was thought to be at the base of the brain, where it guarded against harmful vapors rising from the body. Lady Macbeth will get the guards so drunk that their memories will become confused and their reason will become like a still (***limbeck***) producing confused thoughts.

**81 spongy:** drunken.

**82 quell:** murder.

**83–85 Bring forth...males:** Your bold spirit (***undaunted mettle***) is better suited to raising males than females. *Do you think Macbeth's words express admiration?*

**85 received:** believed.

**92–95 I am settled...know:** Now that Macbeth has made up his mind, every part of his body (***each corporal agent***) is tightened like a bow. He and Lady Macbeth will return to the banquet and deceive everyone (***mock the time***), hiding their evil intent with gracious faces.

# *R*esponding to Reading

1. What do you think will happen if Macbeth kills Duncan?

2. What arguments does Macbeth's wife use to convince him to go ahead with the plan? How do you feel about her comments and his reaction?

   **Think about**
   • his fears and how she reassures him
   • whether her arguments are logical or emotional

3. Do you think Macbeth acts like a man in this scene? Why or why not?

4. Exactly what is Lady Macbeth's plan?

# e x p l a i n

## Responding to Reading

### First Impressions

**1.** Which characters do you respect the most? Which do you respect the least? Explain your opinions.

### Second Thoughts

**2.** Do you think Macbeth has passed the point of no return in his assassination plan? Why or why not?

**3.** Discuss the different attitudes that Banquo, Lady Macbeth, and Duncan have toward Macbeth. What might explain their differences? Give evidence from the play to support your ideas.

**4.** Do the witches control Macbeth's future, or does he control his own fate?

   **Think about**
   - the witches' prophecies, already partially fulfilled
   - Banquo's fears that the witches are "instruments of darkness"
   - how Macbeth and his wife view the prophecies
   - the "vaulting ambition" of the Macbeths

**5.** Compare and contrast the personalities of Lady Macbeth and her husband. Which is the more powerful character? Why?

   **Think about**
   - their ambitions and fears
   - their views on Duncan
   - their attitudes toward murder

**6.** What do you think will happen in Act Two?

## Literary Concept: Foreshadowing and Aside

**Foreshadowing** is a writer's use of hints or clues to indicate events that will occur later in the plot. For example, the witches foreshadow future events by their prophecies, as well as by their opening statement that "fair is foul, and foul is fair." Sometimes an author gives contradictory hints, that is, hints that suggest opposite outcomes. When Macbeth reflects about the consequences of Duncan's murder, some thoughts lead him away from murder, while others support murder. Reread his speech at the opening of Scene 7. Based on the speech, what do you think Macbeth will do? Find other examples of foreshadowing that support your prediction.

In drama an **aside** is a remark that is spoken in an undertone by one character either to the audience or to another character, which the other characters on stage do not hear. The aside expresses the speaker's candid feelings. What do the asides in Act One, Scene 3 reveal about Macbeth?

## Writing Options

1. Make a chart with two columns, one listing the factors driving Macbeth to murder, the other listing reasons that hold him back.

2. In small groups list the ways in which Banquo and Macbeth are similar. Do the same for their differences. Then develop a paragraph that summarizes their major similarities and differences.

3. In Scene 6 Lady Macbeth makes two speeches to the King welcoming him to their castle. Describe her real thoughts at this time, using a first-person point of view.

4. Write a letter from Banquo to his wife explaining the prophecies, his reaction, and his view of Macbeth's response.

*e x t e n d*

## Options for Learning

1. • **Director's Job** In a small group choose a contemporary actor or actress for each major role. Consider relevant factors such as age, physical appearance, and dramatic ability. Present your choices and explain your reasoning to the rest of the class.

2. • **Designer's Job** Create a drawing or painting that shows the set for one of the scenes in the first act. Choose set pieces and colors that reflect the time and the mood. Design your set so that it allows the actors room to move and gives the audience good views of the action.

3. • **Costumer's Job** Design and draw the costumes and makeup for the Weird Sisters. Consider the effects you want to create for the audience and for the other characters.

4. • **Technical Director's Job** Build a model of the stage of the Globe Theater. You can find pictures and dimensions of the Globe in books at the library. Include all the levels from Hell up to Heaven and the balcony.

## ACT TWO

***Scene 1***     *The court of Macbeth's castle.*

*It is past midnight, and Banquo and his son Fleance cannot sleep. When Macbeth appears, Banquo tells of his uneasy dreams about the witches. Macbeth promises that they will discuss the prophecies later, and Banquo goes to bed. Once alone, Macbeth imagines a dagger leading him toward the king's chamber. When he hears a bell, the signal from Lady Macbeth, he knows it is time to go to Duncan's room.*

*[Enter* Banquo, *and* Fleance *with a torch before him.]*

**Banquo.** How goes the night, boy?

**Fleance.** The moon is down; I have not heard the clock.

**Banquo.** And she goes down at twelve.

**Fleance.**            I take't, 'tis later,
   sir.

5   **Banquo.** Hold, take my sword. There's husbandry in
       heaven;
      Their candles are all out. Take thee that too.
      A heavy summons lies like lead upon me,
      And yet I would not sleep. Merciful powers,
10     Restrain in me the cursed thoughts that nature
      Gives way to in repose!

*[Enter* Macbeth, *and a* Servant *with a torch.]*

                  Give me my sword.
      Who's there?

**Macbeth.** A friend.

15   **Banquo.** What, sir, not yet at rest? The King's abed.
      He hath been in unusual pleasure and
      Sent forth great largess to your offices.
      This diamond he greets your wife withal
      By the name of most kind hostess, and shut up
20     In measureless content.

**Macbeth.**            Being unprepared,
      Our will became the servant to defect,
      Which else should free have wrought.

**Banquo.**             All's well.
25   I dreamt last night of the three Weird Sisters.
      To you they have showed some truth.

**5–7 husbandry...candles are all out:** The heavens show economy (**husbandry**) by keeping the lights (**candles**) out—it is a starless night.

**7 that:** perhaps his sword belt or dagger.

**8 heavy summons:** desire for sleep.

**9–11 Merciful powers...repose:** Banquo prays to angels (**merciful powers**) to help him combat bad dreams (**cursed thoughts**).

**17 largess to your offices:** gifts to the servants' quarters.

**18 withal:** with.

**19 shut up:** went to bed.

**21–23 Being . . . wrought:** Because we were unprepared, we could not entertain the King as we would have liked. *Do you believe in Macbeth's sincerity here?*

**Macbeth.**                              I think not of them.
Yet when we can entreat an hour to serve,
We would spend it in some words upon that business,
30  If you would grant the time.

**Banquo.**                              At your kind'st leisure.

**Macbeth.** If you shall cleave to my consent, when 'tis,
It shall make honor for you.

**Banquo.**                              So I lose none
35  In seeking to augment it but still keep
My bosom franchised and allegiance clear,
I shall be counseled.

**Macbeth.**                      Good repose the while!

**Banquo.** Thanks, sir. The like to you!

*[Exeunt* Banquo *and* Fleance.*]*

40  **Macbeth.** Go bid thy mistress, when my drink is ready,
She strike upon the bell. Get thee to bed.

*[Exit* Servant.*]*

Is this a dagger which I see before me,
The handle toward my hand? Come, let me clutch thee!
I have thee not, and yet I see thee still.
45  Art thou not, fatal vision, sensible
To feeling as to sight? or art thou but
A dagger of the mind, a false creation,
Proceeding from the heat-oppressed brain?
I see thee yet, in form as palpable
50  As this which now I draw.
Thou marshal'st me the way that I was going,
And such an instrument I was to use.
Mine eyes are made the fools o' the other senses,
Or else worth all the rest. I see thee still;
55  And on thy blade and dudgeon gouts of blood,
Which was not so before. There's no such thing.
It is the bloody business which informs
Thus to mine eyes. Now o'er the one half-world
Nature seems dead, and wicked dreams abuse
60  The curtained sleep. Witchcraft celebrates
Pale Hecate's offerings; and withered murder,
Alarumed by his sentinel, the wolf,
Whose howl's his watch, thus with his stealthy pace,
With Tarquin's ravishing strides, towards his design

**28 can entreat an hour:** both have the time.

**32–37 If you...be counseled:** Macbeth asks Banquo for his support (**cleave to my consent**), promising honors in return. Banquo is willing to increase (**augment**) his honor provided he can keep a clear conscience and remain loyal to the King (**keep / My bosom...clear**). *How do you think Macbeth feels about Banquo's virtuous stand?*

**42–52 Is this a dagger...to use:** Macbeth sees a dagger hanging in midair before him and questions whether it is real (**palpable**) or the illusion of a disturbed (**heat-oppressed**) mind. The floating, imaginary dagger, which leads (**marshal'st**) him to Duncan's room, prompts him to draw his own dagger. *Is Macbeth losing his mind?*

**53–54 Mine eyes...the rest:** Either his eyes are mistaken (**fools**) or his other senses are.

**55 on thy blade...blood:** drops of blood on the blade and handle.

**60–65 Witchcraft...ghost:** The acts of witches and other evil creatures please Hecate, goddess of the night and witchcraft. Macbeth compares murder to a ghost who steals through the night like Tarquin, an ancient Roman who attacked a sleeping maiden.

*"I go, and it is done."*

---

65  Moves like a ghost. Thou sure and firm-set earth,
Hear not my steps which way they walk, for fear
Thy very stones prate of my whereabout
And take the present horror from the time,
Which now suits with it. Whiles I threat, he lives;
70  Words to the heat of deeds too cold breath gives.

[A bell rings.]

I go, and it is done. The bell invites me.
Hear it not, Duncan, for it is a knell
That summons thee to heaven, or to hell.

[Exit.]

**67 prate of:** talk of or reveal.

**69–70 Whiles I...gives:** Talk (**threat**) delays action (**deeds**).

**72 knell:** funeral bell.

## *R*esponding to Reading

1. What do you learn about Banquo in this scene?

2. Why is Macbeth so concerned about getting Banquo's support? In what way might Banquo pose a threat to him?

3. What does Macbeth's vision of the hanging dagger reveal about his state of mind?

4. Should a director of this play show the dagger that Macbeth sees? Why or why not?

## *Scene 2*  *Macbeth's castle.*

*As Lady Macbeth waits for her husband, she explains how she drugged Duncan's servants. Suddenly a dazed and terrified Macbeth enters, carrying the bloody daggers that he used to murder Duncan. He imagines a voice that warns, "Macbeth shall sleep no more" and is too afraid to return to the scene of the crime. Lady Macbeth takes the bloody daggers back so that the servants will be blamed. Startled by a knocking at the gate, she hurries back and tells Macbeth to wash off the blood and change into his nightclothes.*

[*Enter* Lady Macbeth.]

**Lady Macbeth.** That which hath made them drunk hath
    made me bold;
  What hath quenched them hath given me fire. Hark!
    Peace!
5  It was the owl that shrieked, the fatal bellman
  Which gives the stern'st good-night. He is about it.
  The doors are open, and the surfeited grooms
  Do mock their charge with snores. I have drugged their
    possets,
10  That death and nature do contend about them
  Whether they live or die.

**Macbeth.** [*Within*] Who's there? What, ho?

**Lady Macbeth.** Alack, I am afraid they have awaked,
  And 'tis not done! The attempt, and not the deed,
15  Confounds us. Hark! I laid their daggers ready;
  He could not miss 'em. Had he not resembled
  My father as he slept, I had done't.

**5** *fatal bellman:* town crier.

**7** *surfeited grooms:* drunken servants.

**9** *possets:* drinks.

**13–14** *Why does the sound of Macbeth's voice make his wife so afraid?*

**15** *confounds:* destroys. If Duncan survives, they will be killed (as his attempted murderers).

*[Enter Macbeth.]*

My husband!

**Macbeth.** I have done the deed. Didst thou not hear a
20      noise?

**Lady Macbeth.** I heard the owl scream and the crickets
        cry.
        Did not you speak?

**Macbeth.**                When?

25 **Lady Macbeth.**                Now.

**Macbeth.**                As I descended?

**Lady Macbeth.** Ay.

**Macbeth.** Hark!
        Who lies i' the second chamber?

30 **Lady Macbeth.**                Donalbain.

**Macbeth.** This is a sorry sight.

**Lady Macbeth.** A foolish thought, to say a sorry sight.

**Macbeth.** There's one did laugh in's sleep, and one cried
        "Murder!"
35      That they did wake each other. I stood and heard
        them.
        But they did say their prayers and addressed them
        Again to sleep.

**Lady Macbeth.** There are two lodged together.

40 **Macbeth.** One cried "God bless us!" and "Amen!" the
        other,
        As they had seen me with these hangman's hands,
        List'ning their fear. I could not say "Amen!"
        When they did say "God bless us!"

45 **Lady Macbeth.** Consider it not so deeply.

**Macbeth.** But wherefore could not I pronounce "Amen"?
        I had most need of blessing, and "Amen"
        Stuck in my throat.

**Lady Macbeth.**        These deeds must not be thought
50      After these ways. So, it will make us mad.

**Macbeth.** Methought I heard a voice cry "Sleep no more!
        Macbeth does murder sleep"—the innocent sleep,
        Sleep that knits up the raveled sleave of care,

**33** A troubled Macbeth begins his descriptions of the voices he heard in the castle.

**42–43** ***As they...fear:*** He imagines that the sleepers could see him listening to their exclamations of fear, with his hands bloody like those of an executioner.

**43–48** *Why is Macbeth so troubled by the fact that he cannot say "Amen"?*

**52–56** ***the innocent sleep...life's feast:*** Sleep eases worries (***knits up***

The death of each day's life, sore labor's bath,
55   Balm of hurt minds, great nature's second course,
Chief nourisher in life's feast.

**Lady Macbeth.**                    What do you mean?

**Macbeth.** Still it cried "Sleep no more!" to all the house;
"Glamis hath murdered sleep, and therefore Cawdor
60   Shall sleep no more! Macbeth shall sleep no more!"

**Lady Macbeth.** Who was it that thus cried? Why, worthy
   Thane,
You do unbend your noble strength to think
So brainsickly of things. Go get some water
65   And wash this filthy witness from your hand.
Why did you bring these daggers from the place?
They must lie there. Go carry them and smear
The sleepy grooms with blood.

**Macbeth.**                    I'll go no more.
70   I am afraid to think what I have done;
Look on't again I dare not.

**Lady Macbeth.**                    Infirm of purpose!
Give me the daggers. The sleeping and the dead
Are but as pictures. 'Tis the eye of childhood
75   That fears a painted devil. If he do bleed,
I'll gild the faces of the grooms withal,
For it must seem their guilt. *[Exit. Knocking within.]*

**Macbeth.**                    Whence is that knocking?
How is't with me when every noise appals me?
80   What hands are here? Ha! they pluck out mine eyes!
Will all great Neptune's ocean wash this blood
Clean from my hand? No. This my hand will rather
The multitudinous seas incarnadine,
Making the green one red.

*[Enter* Lady Macbeth.*]*

85   **Lady Macbeth.** My hands are of your color, but I shame
To wear a heart so white. *[Knock.]* I hear a knocking
At the south entry. Retire we to our chamber.
A little water clears us of this deed.
How easy is it then! Your constancy
90   Hath left you unattended. *(Knock.)* Hark! more
   knocking.

---

*the raveled sleave of care*), relieves the aches of physical work (**sore labor's bath**), soothes the anxious (**hurt minds**), and nourishes like food. *Why is Macbeth so concerned about sleep?*

**65 *this filthy witness:*** the evidence, that is, the blood.

**72 *Infirm of purpose:*** weak-willed.

**74–75 *'Tis...a painted devil:*** She compares his fears to those that children have of a devil's picture (**painted devil**).

**76–77 *I'll gild...guilt:*** She'll cover (**gild**) the servants with blood, blaming them for the murder. *How is her attitude toward blood different from her husband's?*

**80 *they pluck out mine eyes:*** In the Bible, Jesus tells his followers that if their eyes cause them to do evil, they should pluck them out.

**82–84 *This my hand...one red:*** The blood on my hand will redden (**incarnadine**) the seas.

**89–90 *Your constancy...unattended:*** Your courage has left you.

*"Will all great Neptune's ocean wash this blood/Clean from my hand? No."*

Get on your nightgown, lest occasion call us
And show us to be watchers. Be not lost
So poorly in your thoughts.

95 **Macbeth.** To know my deed, 'twere best not know myself.

[Knock.]

Wake Duncan with thy knocking! I would thou couldst!

[Exeunt.]

**92–93 *lest...watchers:*** in case we are called for and found awake (***watchers***), which would look suspicious.

**95 *To know...myself:*** To come to terms with what I have done, I must forget about my conscience.

# *R*esponding to Reading ———————————————————————

1. What strengths and weaknesses of Lady Macbeth are revealed in this scene?

   **Think about**
   - her role in the murder and its coverup
   - her jittery response to the sound of her husband's voice
   - why she did not murder Duncan herself
   - how she deals with her husband's fears

2. What is Macbeth afraid of now that he has killed the King?

   **Think about**
   - the voice that tells him, "Macbeth does murder sleep"
   - his comments about the blood on his hands
   - his inability to say "amen"

3. Lady Macbeth claims that "a little water clears us of this deed." Do you think she and her husband will be able to wash away all guilt and regrets? Explain.

4. Do you think the play would be more interesting if Shakespeare had included a scene that showed Duncan's murder? Why or why not?

## Scene 3    *Within Macbeth's castle, near the gate.*

*The drunken porter staggers across the courtyard to answer the knocking. After Lennox and Macduff are let in, Macbeth arrives to lead them to the king's quarters. Macduff enters Duncan's room and discovers his murder. Lennox and Macbeth then go to the scene, and Macbeth, pretending to be enraged, kills the two servants. Amid all the commotion, Lady Macbeth faints. Duncan's sons, Malcolm and Donalbain, fearing for their lives, quietly leave, hoping to escape the country.*

[*Enter a* Porter. *Knocking within.*]

**Porter.** Here's a knocking indeed! If a man were porter of hell gate, he should have old turning the key. [*Knock.*] Knock, knock, knock! Who's there, i' the name of Belzebub? Here's a farmer that hanged himself on
5    the expectation of plenty. Come in time! Have napkins enow about you; here you'll sweat for't. (*Knock.*) Knock, knock! Who's there, in the other devil's name? Faith, here's an equivocator, that could swear in both the scales against either scale; who committed treason

**2 old turning the key:** plenty of key turning. Hell's porter would be busy because so many people are ending up in hell these days.

**4 Belzebub:** a devil.

**4–19** The porter pretends he is welcoming a farmer who killed himself

10 enough for God's sake, yet could not equivocate to
heaven. O, come in, equivocator! *(Knock.)* Knock,
knock, knock! Who's there? Faith, here's an English
tailor come hither for stealing out of a French hose.
Come in, tailor. Here you may roast your goose.
15 *[Knock.]* Knock, knock! Never at quiet! What are you?
But this place is too cold for hell. I'll devilporter it no
further. I had thought to have let in some of all
professions that go the primrose way to the everlasting
bonfire. *[Knock.]* Anon, anon! *[Opens the gate.]* I pray
20 you remember the porter.

*[Enter* Macduff *and* Lennox.*]*

**Macduff.** Was it so late, friend, ere you went to bed,
That you do lie so late?

**Porter.** Faith, sir, we were carousing till the second cock;
and drink, sir, is a great provoker of three things.

25 **Macduff.** What three things does drink especially
provoke?

**Porter.** Marry, sir, nose-painting, sleep, and urine.
Lechery, sir, it provokes, and unprovokes: it provokes
the desire, but it takes away the performance.
30 Therefore much drink may be said to be an
equivocator with lechery: it makes him, and it mars
him; it sets him on, and it takes him off; it persuades
him, and disheartens him; makes him stand to, and not
stand to; in conclusion, equivocates him in a sleep, and,
35 giving him the lie, leaves him.

**Macduff.** I believe drink gave thee the lie last night.

**Porter.** That it did, sir, i' the very throat on me; but I
requited him for his lie; and, I think, being too strong
for him, though he took up my legs sometime, yet I
40 made a shift to cast him.

**Macduff.** Is thy master stirring?

*[Enter* Macbeth.*]*

Our knocking has awaked him; here he comes.

**Lennox.** Good morrow, noble sir.

**Macbeth.**                              Good morrow, both.

45 **Macduff.** Is the King stirring, worthy Thane?

**Macbeth.**                              Not yet.

after his schemes to get rich
(***expectation of plenty***) failed, a double
talker (***equivocator***) who perjured
himself yet couldn't talk his way into
heaven, and a tailor who cheated his
customers by skimping on material
(***stealing out of a French hose***). The
tailor will now get plenty of heat for his
iron (***roast your goose***). Tradition holds
that hell is populated with people who
took the easy way (***primrose way***) in
life.

**19 Anon:** soon.

**19–20 I pray...the porter:** He wants a
tip.

**23 second cock:** early morning,
announced by the crow of a rooster.

**27 nose-painting:** the reddening of the
nose from heavy drinking.

**28–35** The porter jokes that alcohol
stimulates lust (***Lechery***) but makes the
lover a failure. When drunk, the lover
cannot stand up to (***stand to***) the
demands of love and instead falls
asleep.

**36–40** More jokes about alcohol, this
time described as a wrestler finally
thrown off (***cast***) by the porter, who
thus paid him back (***requited him***) for
disappointment in love. *Cast* also
means "to vomit" or "to urinate," two
other ways of dealing with alcohol.

**Macduff.** He did command me to call timely on him;
I have almost slipped the hour.

**Macbeth.**                  I'll bring you to him.

50 **Macduff.** I know this is a joyful trouble to you;
But yet 'tis one.

**Macbeth.** The labor we delight in physics pain.
This is the door.

**Macduff.**         I'll make so bold to call,
55 For 'tis my limited service. *[Exit.]*

**Lennox.** Goes the King hence today?

**Macbeth.**               He does; he did appoint so.

**Lennox.** The night has been unruly. Where we lay,
Our chimneys were blown down, and, as they say,
60 Lamentings heard i' the air, strange screams of death,
And prophesying, with accents terrible,
Of dire combustion and confused events
New hatched to the woeful time. The obscure bird
Clamored the livelong night. Some say the earth
65 Was feverous and did shake.

**Macbeth.**             'Twas a rough night.

**Lennox.** My young remembrance cannot parallel
A fellow to it.

*[Enter Macduff.]*

**Macduff.** O horror, horror, horror! Tongue nor heart
70 Cannot conceive nor name thee!

**Macbeth and Lennox.**         What's the matter?

**Macduff.** Confusion now hath made his masterpiece!
Most sacrilegious murder hath broke ope
The Lord's anointed temple and stole thence
75 The life o' the building!

**Macbeth.**          What is't you say? the life?

**Lennox.** Mean you his majesty?

**Macduff.** Approach the chamber, and destroy your sight
With a new Gorgon. Do not bid me speak.
80 See, and then speak yourselves.

*[Exeunt Macbeth and Lennox.]*

---

**47 timely:** early.

**48 slipped the hour:** missed the time.

**52 physics:** cures.

**55 limited service:** appointed duty.

**58–65** Lennox discusses the strange events of the night, from fierce winds to the continuous shrieking (**strange screams of death**) of an owl (**obscure bird**). The owl's scream, a sign of death, bodes more (**New hatched**) uproar (**combustion**) and confusion.

**67–68** I cannot remember another night as bad as this.

**72–75** Macduff mourns Duncan's death as the destruction (**Confusion**) of order and as (**sacrilegious**), violating all that is holy. In Shakespeare's time the king was believed to be God's sacred representative on earth.

**79 new Gorgon:** Macduff compares the shocking sight of the corpse to a Gorgon, a monster of Greek mythology with snakes for hair. Anyone who saw a Gorgon turned to stone.

Awake, awake!
Ring the alarum bell. Murder and treason!
Banquo and Donalbain! Malcolm! awake!
Shake off this downy sleep, death's counterfeit,
85　And look on death itself! Up, up, and see
The great doom's image! Malcolm! Banquo!
As from your graves rise up and walk like sprites
To countenance this horror! Ring the bell!

*[Bell rings.]*

*[Enter Lady Macbeth.]*

**Lady Macbeth.** What's the business,
90　That such a hideous trumpet calls to parley
The sleepers of the house? Speak, speak!

**Macduff.**　　　　　　　　　　　　O gentle lady,
'Tis not for you to hear what I can speak!
The repetition in a woman's ear
95　Would murder as it fell.

*[Enter Banquo.]*

　　　　　　　　　　　O Banquo, Banquo,
Our royal master's murdered!

**Lady Macbeth.**　　　　　　　Woe, alas!
What, in our house?

100　**Banquo.**　　　　　　　Too cruel anywhere.
Dear Duff, I prithee contradict thyself
And say it is not so.

*[Enter Macbeth, Lennox, and Ross.]*

**Macbeth.** Had I but died an hour before this chance,
I had lived a blessed time; for from this instant
105　There's nothing serious in mortality;
All is but toys; renown and grace is dead;
The wine of life is drawn, and the mere lees
Is left this vault to brag of.

*[Enter Malcolm and Donalbain.]*

**Donalbain.** What is amiss?

110　**Macbeth.**　　　　　　　You are, and do not know't.
The spring, the head, the fountain of your blood
Is stopped, the very source of it is stopped.

**84 *counterfeit:*** imitation.

**86 *great doom's image:*** a picture like the Last Judgment, the end of the world.

**87 *sprites:*** spirits. The spirits of the dead were supposed to rise on Judgment Day.

**90 *trumpet calls to parley:*** She compares the clanging bell to a trumpet used to call two sides of a battle to negotiation.

**104–108 *for from...brag of:*** From now on, nothing matters (***There's nothing serious***) in human life (***mortality***); even fame and grace have been made meaningless. The good wine of life has been removed (***drawn***), leaving only the dregs (***lees***). *Is Macbeth being completely insincere, or does he regret his crime?*

**Macduff.** Your royal father's murdered.

**Malcolm.**                                            O, by whom?

115 **Lennox.** Those of his chamber, as it seemed, had done't.
Their hands and faces were all badged with blood;
So were their daggers, which unwiped we found
Upon their pillows.
They stared and were distracted. No man's life
120 Was to be trusted with them.

**Macbeth.** O, yet I do repent me of my fury
That I did kill them.

**Macduff.**                          Wherefore did you so?

**Macbeth.** Who can be wise, amazed, temp'rate, and
125      furious,
Loyal and neutral, in a moment? No man.
The expedition of my violent love
Outrun the pauser, reason. Here lay Duncan,
His silver skin laced with his golden blood,
130 And his gashed stabs looked like a breach in nature
For ruin's wasteful entrance; there, the murderers,
Steeped in the colors of their trade, their daggers
Unmannerly breeched with gore. Who could refrain
That had a heart to love and in that heart
135 Courage to make's love known?

**Lady Macbeth.**                          Help me hence, ho!

**Macduff.** Look to the lady.

**Malcolm.** [Aside to Donalbain] Why do we hold our
      tongues,
140 That most may claim this argument for ours?

**Donalbain.** [Aside to Malcolm] What should be spoken
      here,
Where our fate, hid in an auger hole,
May rush and seize us? Let's away,
145 Our tears are not yet brewed.

**Malcolm.** [Aside to Donalbain] Nor our strong sorrow
Upon the foot of motion.

**Banquo.**                          Look to the lady.

[Lady Macbeth is carried out.]

And when we have our naked frailties hid,
150 That suffer in exposure, let us meet
And question this most bloody piece of work,

**116 badged:** marked.

**127–128 The...reason:** He claims his emotions overpowered his reason, which would have made him pause to think before he killed Duncan's servants.

**130 breach:** a military term to describe a break in defenses, such as a hole in a castle wall.

**132–133 their daggers...gore:** their knives shamefully clothed in blood.

**136** Lady Macbeth faints. *Is she only pretending?*

**138–140 Why do...ours:** Malcolm wonders why he and Donalbain are silent since they have the most right to discuss the topic (*argument*) of their father's death.

**141–145** Donalbain fears that a treacherous fate may await them at Macbeth's castle; destruction may lurk anywhere, as if concealed in a small hole.

**146–147** Our deep sorrow has not yet moved us to action.

**149–152** Banquo suggests that they all meet to discuss the murder after they have dressed (*our naked frailties hid*), since people are shivering in their nightclothes (*suffer in exposure*).

To know it further. Fears and scruples shake us.
In the great hand of God I stand, and thence
Against the undivulged pretense I fight
155     Of treasonous malice.

**Macduff.**              And so do I.

**All.**                  So all.

**Macbeth.** Let's briefly put on manly readiness
And meet i' the hall together.

160 **All.**              Well contented.

*[Exeunt all but* Malcolm *and* Donalbain.*]*

**Malcolm.** What will you do? Let's not consort with them.
To show an unfelt sorrow is an office
Which the false man does easy. I'll to England.

**Donalbain.** To Ireland I. Our separated fortune
165     Shall keep us both the safer. Where we are,
There's daggers in men's smiles; the near in blood,
The nearer bloody.

**Malcolm.**           This murderous shaft that's shot
Hath not yet lighted, and our safest way
170     Is to avoid the aim. Therefore to horse!
And let us not be dainty of leave-taking
But shift away. There's warrant in that theft
Which steals itself when there's no mercy left.

*[Exeunt.]*

**152–155** Though shaken by fears and doubts (*scruples*), he will fight against the secret plans (*undivulged pretense*) of the traitor. *Do you think Banquo suspects Macbeth?*

**161–163** Malcolm does not want to join (*consort with*) the others because one of them may have plotted the murder.

**166–167** *the near...bloody:* Being Duncan's sons, they are in greatest danger of more bloodshed.

**168–170** *This...avoid the aim:* Malcolm uses an archery metaphor to express his fear of assassination. The arrow (*shaft*) has not yet hit its target.

**172–173** *There's...left:* There's good reason (*warrant*) to steal away from a situation that promises no mercy.

# Responding to Reading

1. The porter comes onstage just after the murder of Duncan. What does his role add to the play?

   **Think about**
   • how the audience would respond to his lines
   • in what ways the castle is like the hell the porter describes
   • what Macbeth is doing while the porter is speaking

2. In what ways does Macbeth's murder of the two servants help him? How might it hurt him?

3. How convincing are the reactions of Lady Macbeth and Macbeth when the murder is discovered? Explain.

4. How do you think the other characters will respond to the sudden departure of Malcolm and Donalbain?

### Scene 4  Outside Macbeth's castle.

*Ross and an old man discuss recent unnatural events, including the strange darkness of the day and news that the king's horses have eaten each other. Macduff enters and tells them that Duncan's sons, who have fled, are accused of plotting his murder. Macbeth has been named king and will soon be crowned. Ross plans to attend the ceremony, but Macduff, uneasy with what has occurred, decides to return home.*

*[Enter Ross with an Old Man.]*

**Old Man.** Threescore and ten I can remember well;
Within the volume of which time I have seen
Hours dreadful and things strange; but this sore night
Hath trifled former knowings.

5 **Ross.**                              Ah, good father,
Thou seest the heavens, as troubled with man's act,
Threaten his bloody stage. By the clock 'tis day,
And yet dark night strangles the traveling lamp.
Is't night's predominance, or the day's shame,
10 That darkness does the face of earth entomb
When living light should kiss it?

**Old Man.**                              'Tis unnatural,
Even like the deed that's done. On Tuesday last
A falcon, tow'ring in her pride of place,
15 Was by a mousing owl hawked at and killed.

**Ross.** And Duncan's horses (a thing most strange and
      certain),
Beauteous and swift, the minions of their race,
Turned wild in nature, broke their stalls, flung out,
20 Contending 'gainst obedience, as they would make
War with mankind.

**Old Man.**          'Tis said they eat each other.

**Ross.** They did so, to the amazement of mine eyes
That looked upon't.

*[Enter Macduff.]*

25                              Here comes the good Macduff.
How goes the world, sir, now?

**Macduff.**                    Why, see you not?

---

**1–4** Nothing the old man has seen in seventy years (**Threescore and ten**) has been as strange and terrible (**sore**) as this night. It has made other times seem trivial (**hath trifled**) by comparision.

**6 as:** as if.

**7 stage:** world.

**8–11 And yet...kiss it:** Though daytime, an unnatural darkness blots out the sun (**strangles the traveling lamp**).

**14–15 A falcon...and killed:** The owl would never be expected to attack a highflying (**tow'ring**) falcon, much less defeat one. Such an act is a sure sign of nature's disruption.

**18 minions:** best or favorites.

**20 Contending 'gainst obedience:** The well-trained horses rebelliously fought against all contraints.

---

**Ross.** Is't known who did this more than bloody deed?

**Macduff.** Those that Macbeth hath slain.

30  **Ross.**                              Alas, the day!
  What good could they pretend?

  **Macduff.**                              They were suborned.
  Malcolm and Donalbain, the King's two sons,
  Are stol'n away and fled, which puts upon them
35  Suspicion of the deed.

  **Ross.**                              'Gainst nature still!
  Thriftless ambition, that will raven up
  Thine own live's means! Then 'tis most like
  The sovereignty will fall upon Macbeth.

40  **Macduff.** He is already named, and gone to Scone
  To be invested.

  **Ross.**              Where is Duncan's body?

  **Macduff.** Carried to Colmekill,
  The sacred storehouse of his predecessors
45  And guardian of their bones.

  **Ross.**                              Will you to Scone?

  **Macduff.** No, cousin, I'll to Fife.

  **Ross.**                              Well, I will thither.

  **Macduff.** Well, may you see things well done there.
50      Adieu,
  Lest our old robes sit easier than our new!

  **Ross.** Farewell, father.

  **Old Man.** God's benison go with you, and with those
  That would make good of bad, and friends of foes!

*[Exeunt omnes.]*

**31** He wonders what the servants could have hoped to achieve (**pretend**) by killing.

**32 suborned:** hired or bribed.

**36–38** He is horrified by the thought that the sons could act contrary to nature (**'Gainst nature still**) because of wasteful (**Thriftless**) ambition and greedily destroy (**raven up**) their father, the source of their own life (**Thine own live's means**).

**40–41 to Scone...invested:** Macbeth went to the traditional site (**Scone**) where Scotland's kings were crowned.

**51 Lest our...new:** He fears that life under Macbeth's rule might be harsher than under Duncan (**our old robes**).

**53–54** The old man gives his blessing (**benison**) to Macduff and all those who would restore good and bring peace to the troubled land.

# Responding to Reading

1. How does the description of the strange events in nature contribute to the mood of the play?

2. Why does Macduff choose not to attend Macbeth's coronation? What does he fear?

## Responding to Reading

### First Impressions

1. What is the most memorable mental picture you formed while reading this act? Jot down a few vivid words and phrases to describe that picture.

### Second Thoughts

2. How has Macbeth changed as a result of the events in this act? Find lines that illustrate these changes.

   **Think about**
   • what happens before and after he kills Duncan
   • his state of mind and fears for the future
   • whether you feel sympathy for him

3. The porter humorously comments on the types of people who wind up at the gates of hell. How is Macbeth like or unlike the sinners described by the porter?

4. Predict the psychological effects that the murder will have on Macbeth and his wife. Give hints from the act to support your predictions.

5. Compare and contrast *Macbeth* with frightening movies you have seen. What techniques do they share for building suspense and creating a dark, fearful atmosphere? How is *Macbeth* different from the movies?

   **Think about**
   • what happens in each scene both onstage and offstage
   • how the dialogue contributes to the overall effect
   • the effects of the setting

6. What do you think will happen next? Why?

## Literary Concept: Comic Relief

**Comic relief** is a humorous scene, incident, or speech that occurs in the midst of a serious or tragic literary work. Authors intentionally use comic relief to break tension while preparing for greater tension to follow. Shakespeare's scene with the drunken porter, one of the most famous examples of this technique in all of literature, takes place while Macbeth is washing Duncan's blood off his hands, just before the discovery of the murder. The scene does more than provide relief; it also deals with issues—such as sin, hell, deceit, and ambition—that are central to the play. Working in small groups, choose one of these issues and discuss how the scene adds to our understanding of the issue as presented in *Macbeth*.

**Concept Review: Metaphor** Find at least three metaphors in this act that help the reader better understand the character who uses the metaphor. Explain how each metaphor contributes to our knowledge of the character.

## Writing Options

1. Write a television news account of Duncan's murder and the night's strange events. Be sure to describe the major events and include comments from the key participants.

2. Create a list of phrases that are used to describe Duncan's murder, both before and after the fact. Then explain why the murder of the King was regarded as such a serious offense.

3. If *Macbeth* were turned into a movie today, the director might very well show Duncan's murder or Lady Macbeth smearing blood on Duncan's servants. Write a description of either of these scenes as it might be captured on film.

4. As a detective, write out a list of questions you would ask each of the people who were involved in the events surrounding Duncan's murder.

## extend

## Options for Learning

**1** • **Dastardly Dagger** Figure out a way of creating and hanging a prop dagger in midair (no real knives, please) to make it look like a figment of Macbeth's imagination. To test your rigging, enlist the help of someone else and stage the floating dagger scene before your classmates.

**2** • **Murder's Mystery** Role-play a detective's investigation of the murder, with students playing the parts of major and minor characters. The detective should try to establish the whereabouts of each person as well as possible motives. Remember that a detective sometimes makes even the innocent uncomfortable with relentless questioning.

**3** • **The Artist's View** Select an episode from Act Two and draw, sketch, or paint your vision of it, trying to capture its action and atmosphere. You may choose either a realistic or an abstract style of illustration.

**4** • **Masters at Work** Working in small groups, find recordings of at least three different *Macbeth* performances. Select a scene from the first or second act, then listen carefully to each recording of that scene, paying close attention to the emotions conveyed by the actors. On a chart, compare and contrast the recordings.

## ACT THREE

### Scene 1  *Macbeth's palace at Forres.*

*Banquo voices his suspicions of Macbeth but still hopes that the prophecy about his own children will prove true. Macbeth, as king, enters to request Banquo's presence at a state banquet. Banquo explains that he will be away during the day with his son Fleance but that they will return in time for the banquet. Alone, Macbeth expresses his fear of Banquo, because of the witches' promise that Banquo's sons will be kings. He persuades two murderers to kill Banquo and his son before the banquet.*

*[Enter Banquo.]*

**Banquo.** Thou hast it now—King, Cawdor, Glamis, all,
    As the Weird Women promised; and I fear
    Thou play'dst most foully for't. Yet it was said
    It should not stand in thy posterity,
5    But that myself should be the root and father
    Of many kings. If there come truth from them
    (As upon thee, Macbeth, their speeches shine),
    Why, by the verities on thee made good,
    May they not be my oracles as well
10    And set me up in hope? But, hush, no more!

*[Sennet sounded. Enter Macbeth, as King; Lady Macbeth, as Queen; Lennox, Ross, Lords, and Attendants.]*

**Macbeth.** Here's our chief guest.

**Lady Macbeth.**               If he had been forgotten,
    It had been as a gap in our great feast,
    And all-thing unbecoming.

15 **Macbeth.** Tonight we hold a solemn supper, sir,
    And I'll request your presence.

**Banquo.**               Let your Highness
    Command upon me, to the which my duties
    Are with a most indissoluble tie
20    For ever knit.

**Macbeth.**      Ride you this afternoon?

**Banquo.** Ay, my good lord.

**3–4 *it was said . . . posterity:*** It was predicted that the kingship would not remain in your family.

**6–10 *If . . . in hope:*** Despite Banquo's suspicions of foul play, he is impressed by the truth (**verities**) of the prophecies, which make Macbeth **shine** with good fortune. He hopes the witches' prediction for him will come true too (**be my oracles as well**).

**(*Sennet sounded*):** A trumpet is sounded.

**15–16** When a king speaks, he usually uses the royal pronoun *we*. Notice how Macbeth switches to *I*, keeping a personal tone with Banquo.

**17–20** Banquo says he is duty-bound to serve the king. *Do you think his tone is cold or warm here?*

**Macbeth.** We should have else desired your good advice
  (Which still hath been both grave and prosperous)
25  In this day's council; but we'll take tomorrow.
  Is't far you ride?

**Banquo.** As far, my lord, as will fill up the time
  'Twixt this and supper. Go not my horse the better,
  I must become a borrower of the night
30  For a dark hour or twain.

**Macbeth.**                    Fail not our feast.

**Banquo.** My lord, I will not.

**Macbeth.** We hear our bloody cousins are bestowed
  In England and in Ireland, not confessing
35  Their cruel parricide, filling their hearers
  With strange invention. But of that tomorrow,
  When therewithal we shall have cause of state
  Craving us jointly. Hie you to horse. Adieu,
  Till you return at night. Goes Fleance with you?

40  **Banquo.** Ay, my good lord. Our time does call upon's.

**Macbeth.** I wish your horses swift and sure of foot,
  And so I do commend you to their backs.
  Farewell.

*[Exit Banquo.]*

  Let every man be master of his time
45  Till seven at night. To make society
  The sweeter welcome, we will keep ourself
  Till supper time alone. While then, God be with you!

*[Exeunt all but* Macbeth *and a* Servant*].*

  Sirrah, a word with you. Attend those men
  Our pleasure?

50  **Servant.** They are, my lord, without the palace gate.

**Macbeth.** Bring them before us.

*[Exit Servant.]*

**Macbeth.**                    To be thus is nothing,
  But to be safely thus. Our fears in Banquo
  Stick deep, and in his royalty of nature
55  Reigns that which would be feared. 'Tis much he dares,

---

**24 grave and prosperous:** thoughtful and profitable.

**28–30 Go not . . . twain:** If his horse goes no faster than usual, he'll be back an hour or two (**twain**) after dark.

**33 bloody cousins:** murderous relatives (Malcolm and Donalbain); **bestowed:** settled.

**35 parricide:** murder of one's father.

**36 strange invention:** lies; stories they have invented. *What kinds of stories might they be telling?*

**37–38** *When . . . jointly:* when matters of state will require the attention of us both.

**44 be master of his time:** do what he wants.

**47 While:** until.

**48–49 Sirrah:** a term of address to an inferior; **Attend . . . pleasure:** Are they waiting for me?

**52–76 To be thus . . . safely thus:** To be king is worthless unless my position as king is safe. Macbeth speaks to himself about his fears of Banquo, whose kingly qualities make him a threat.

And to that dauntless temper of his mind
He hath a wisdom that doth guide his valor
To act in safety. There is none but he
Whose being I do fear; and under him
60 My genius is rebuked, as it is said
Mark Antony's was by Caesar. He chid the Sisters
When first they put the name of King upon me,
And bade them speak to him. Then, prophet-like,
They hailed him father to a line of kings.
65 Upon my head they placed a fruitless crown
And put a barren scepter in my gripe,
Thence to be wrenched with an unlineal hand,
No son of mine succeeding. If't be so,
For Banquo's issue have I filed my mind;
70 For them the gracious Duncan have I murdered;
Put rancors in the vessel of my peace
Only for them, and mine eternal jewel
Given to the common enemy of man
To make them kings, the seed of Banquo kings!
75 Rather than so, come, Fate, into the list,
And champion me to the utterance! Who's there?

*[Enter* Servant *and two* Murderers.*]*

Now go to the door and stay there till we call.

*[Exit* Servant.*]*

Was it not yesterday we spoke together?

**Murderers.** It was, so please your Highness.

80 **Macbeth.**                                          Well then, now
Have you considered of my speeches? Know
That it was he, in the times past, which held you
So under fortune, which you thought had been
Our innocent self. This I made good to you
85 In our last conference, passed in probation with you
How you were borne in hand, how crossed; the
          instruments;
Who wrought with them; and all things else that might
To half a soul and to a notion crazed
90 Say "Thus did Banquo."

**First Murderer.**                    You made it known to us.

**Macbeth.** I did so; and went further, which is now
Our point of second meeting. Do you find

56 *dauntless temper:* fearless temperament.

60–61 *My . . . Caesar:* Banquo's mere presence seems to force back (*rebuke*) Macbeth's ruling spirit (*genius*). In ancient Rome, Octavius Caesar, who became emperor, had the same effect on his rival, Mark Antony.

61 *chid:* scolded; *Sisters:* the witches.

65–74 They gave me a childless (*fruitless, barren*) crown and scepter, which will be taken away by someone outside my family (*unlineal*). It appears that I have committed murder, poisoned (*filed*) my mind, and destroyed my soul (*eternal jewel*) all for the benefit of Banquo's heirs.

75–76 *Rather . . . utterance:* Rather than allowing Banquo's heirs to become kings, he calls upon Fate itself to enter the combat arena (*list*) so that he can fight it to the death (*utterance*). *Why does he feel that he needs to fight Fate?*

81–90 Macbeth reminds the men of a past conversation in which he argued that Banquo had kept them from good fortune, not he. He supposedly proved (*passed in probation*) Banquo's role, his deception (*How you were borne in hand*), his methods, and his allies. Even a half-wit (*half a soul*) or a crazed person would agree that Banquo caused their trouble.

Your patience so predominant in your nature
95 That you can let this go? Are you so gospeled
To pray for this good man and for his issue,
Whose heavy hand hath bowed you to the grave
And beggared yours for ever?

**First Murderer.** We are men, my liege.

100 **Macbeth.** Ay, in the catalogue ye go for men,
As hounds and greyhounds, mongrels, spaniels, curs,
Shoughs, water-rugs, and demi-wolves are clept
All by the name of dogs. The valued file
Distinguishes the swift, the slow, the subtle,
105 The housekeeper, the hunter, every one
According to the gift which bounteous nature
Hath in him closed; whereby he does receive
Particular addition, from the bill
That writes them all alike; and so of men.

*"Ay, in the catalogue ye go for men..."*

110 Now, if you have a station in the file,
Not i' the worst rank of manhood, say't;
And I will put that business in your bosoms
Whose execution takes your enemy off,
Grapples you to the heart and love of us,
115 Who wear our health but sickly in his life,
Which in his death were perfect.

**Second Murderer.**                    I am one, my liege,
Whom the vile blows and buffets of the world
Have so incensed that I am reckless what
120 I do to spite the world.

**First Murderer.**            And I another,
So weary with disasters, tugged with fortune,
That I would set my life on any chance,
To mend it or be rid on't.

125 **Macbeth.**                    Both of you
Know Banquo was your enemy.

**Murderers.**                         True, my lord.

**Macbeth.** So is he mine, and in such bloody distance
That every minute of his being thrusts
130 Against my near'st of life; and though I could
With barefaced power sweep him from my sight
And bid my will avouch it, yet I must not,
For certain friends that are both his and mine,
Whose loves I may not drop, but wail his fall
135 Who I myself struck down. And thence it is
That I to your assistance do make love,
Masking the business from the common eye
For sundry weighty reasons.

**Second Murderer.**            We shall, my lord,
140 Perform what you command us.

**First Murderer.**                    Though our lives—

**Macbeth.** Your spirits shine through you. Within this
    hour at most
I will advise you where to plant yourselves,
145 Acquaint you with the perfect spy o' the time,
The moment on't; for't must be done tonight,
And something from the palace (always thought
That I require a clearness), and with him,
To leave no rubs nor botches in the work,
150 Fleance his son, that keeps him company,

---

**110–116** The men can show their high rank (**station**) only by agreeing to Macbeth's plan. He will give them a secret job (**business in your bosoms**) that will earn his loyalty (**Grapples you to the heart**) and love. Banquo's death will make this sick king healthy.

**119** *incensed:* angered.

**122** *tugged with:* knocked about by.

**128–130** Banquo is near enough to draw blood, and like a menacing swordsman, his mere presence threatens (**thrusts against**) Macbeth's existence.

**132** *bid my will avouch it:* justify it as my will.

**134** *wail his fall:* I must mourn (**wail**) his death.

**136** *do make love:* appeal.

**137** *common eye:* public view.

**138** *sundry:* various.

**142** *Your spirits shine through you:* Your courage is evident.

**147–148** *And something . . . clearness:* The murder must be done away from the palace so that I remain blameless (**I require a clearness**).

Whose absence is no less material to me
Than is his father's, must embrace the fate
Of that dark hour. Resolve yourselves apart;
I'll come to you anon.

155 **Murderers.**                    We are resolved, my lord.

**Macbeth.** I'll call upon you straight. Abide within.

*[Exeunt Murderers.]*

It is concluded. Banquo, thy soul's flight,
If it find heaven, must find it out tonight.

*[Exit.]*

151 ***absence:*** death. *Why is the death of Fleance so important?*

153 ***Resolve yourselves apart:*** Decide in private.

156 ***straight:*** soon.

# *R*esponding to Reading

1. Now that Macbeth is king, do you think he is better off? Explain.

   **Think about**
   • changes in his external and internal life
   • his speech to himself in this scene
   • his conversation with the murderers

2. Discuss the ways in which Banquo poses a threat to Macbeth. If you were in Macbeth's position, how would you deal with Banquo?

3. Discuss the strategies that Macbeth uses to persuade the two men to murder Banquo. How does he appeal to their ambition? How does he appeal to their resentment and sense of inferiority?

*Scene 2*   *Macbeth's palace at Forres.*

*Lady Macbeth and her husband discuss the troubled thoughts and bad dreams they have had since Duncan's murder. However, they agree to hide their dark emotions at the night's banquet. Lady Macbeth tries to comfort the tormented Macbeth, but her words do no good. Instead, Macbeth hints at some terrible event that will occur that night.*

*[Enter Lady Macbeth and a Servant.]*

**Lady Macbeth.** Is Banquo gone from court?

**Servant.** Ay, madam, but returns again tonight.

**Lady Macbeth.** Say to the King I would attend his leisure
    For a few words.

5 **Servant.**                Madam, I will.

*[Exit.]*

**Lady Macbeth.**                Naught's had, all's spent,
   Where our desire is got without content.
   'Tis safer to be that which we destroy
   Than by destruction dwell in doubtful joy.

*[Enter Macbeth.]*

10   How now, my lord? Why do you keep alone,
   Of sorriest fancies your companions making,
   Using those thoughts which should indeed have died
   With them they think on? Things without all remedy
   Should be without regard. What's done is done.

15 **Macbeth.** We have scotched the snake, not killed it.
   She'll close and be herself, whilst our poor malice
   Remains in danger of her former tooth.
   But let the frame of things disjoint, both the worlds
      suffer,
20   Ere we will eat our meal in fear and sleep
   In the affliction of these terrible dreams
   That shake us nightly. Better be with the dead,
   Whom we, to gain our peace, have sent to peace,
   Than on the torture of the mind to lie
25   In restless ecstasy. Duncan is in his grave;
   After life's fitful fever he sleeps well.
   Treason has done his worst: nor steel nor poison,
   Malice domestic, foreign levy, nothing,
   Can touch him further.

30 **Lady Macbeth.**                Come on.
   Gentle my lord, sleek o'er your rugged looks;
   Be bright and jovial among your guests tonight.

**Macbeth.** So shall I, love; and so, I pray, be you.
   Let your remembrance apply to Banquo;
35   Present him eminence both with eye and tongue:
   Unsafe the while, that we
   Must lave our honors in these flattering streams
   And make our faces vizards to our hearts,
   Disguising what they are.

40 **Lady Macbeth.**                You must leave this.

**Macbeth.** O, full of scorpions is my mind, dear wife!
   Thou know'st that Banquo, and his Fleance, lives.

**6–9** Nothing (**Naught**) has been gained; everything has been wasted (**spent**). It would be better to be dead like Duncan than to live in uncertain joy.

**10–14** *Does Lady Macbeth follow her own advice about forgetting Duncan's murder?*

**18–25** He would rather have the world fall apart (**the frame of things disjoint**) than be afflicted with such fears and nightmares. Death is preferable to life on the torture rack of mental anguish (**restless ecstasy**).

**31 *sleek:*** smooth.

**35 *Present him eminence:*** Pay special attention to him.

**37 *lave . . . streams:*** wash (**lave**) our honor in streams of flattery, that is, falsify our feelings.

**38 *vizards:*** masks.

**Lady Macbeth.** But in them Nature's copy's not eterne.

**Macbeth.** There's comfort yet; they are assailable.

45     Then be thou jocund. Ere the bat hath flown
    His cloistered flight, ere to black Hecate's summons
    The shard-borne beetle with his drowsy hums
    Hath rung night's yawning peal, there shall be done
    A deed of dreadful note.

50 **Lady Macbeth.**             What's to be done?

**Macbeth.** Be innocent of the knowledge, dearest chuck,
    Till thou applaud the deed. Come, seeling night,
    Scarf up the tender eye of pitiful day,
    And with thy bloody and invisible hand
55     Cancel and tear to pieces that great bond
    Which keeps me pale! Light thickens, and the crow
    Makes wing to the rooky wood.
    Good things of day begin to droop and drowse,
    Whiles night's black agents to their preys do rouse.
60     Thou marvell'st at my words; but hold thee still:
    Things bad begun make strong themselves by ill.
    So prithee go with me.

*[Exeunt.]*

---

## Scene 3   *A park near the palace.*

*The two murderers, joined by a third, ambush Banquo and Fleance, killing Banquo.
Fleance manages to escape in the darkness.*

*[Enter three* Murderers.*]*

**First Murderer.** But who did bid thee join with us?

**Third Murderer.**                 Macbeth.

**Second Murderer.** He needs not our mistrust, since he
    delivers
5     Our offices, and what we have to do,
    To the direction just.

**First Murderer.**         Then stand with us.
    The west yet glimmers with some streaks of day.
    Now spurs the lated traveler apace
10     To gain the timely inn, and near approaches
    The subject of our watch.

**43 *in them . . . not eterne:*** Nature did not give them immortality.

**45–49 *jocund:*** cheerful; merry; ***Ere the bat . . . note:*** Before nightfall, when the bats and beetles fly, something dreadful will happen.

**51 *chuck:*** chick, a term of affection.
**52 *seeling:*** blinding.

**55 *great bond:*** Banquo's life.
**56 *thickens:*** darkens.
**57 *rooky:*** gloomy; also, filled with crows (rooks).

**61** Things brought about through evil need additional evil to make them strong.

**3–6 *He needs . . . just:*** Macbeth should not be distrustful, since he gave us the orders (***offices***) and we plan to follow his directions exactly.

**9 *lated:*** tardy; late.

**10 *To gain . . . inn:*** to reach the inn before dark.

**Third Murderer.**                    Hark! I hear horses.

**Banquo.** *[Within]* Give us a light there, ho!

**Second Murderer.**                    Then 'tis he! The rest
15    That are within the note of expectation
       Already are i' the court.

**First Murderer.**                    His horses go about.

**Third Murderer.** Almost a mile; but he does usually,
       So all men do, from hence to the palace gate
20    Make it their walk.

*[Enter* Banquo, *and* Fleance *with a torch.]*

**Second Murderer.**                    A light, a light!

**Third Murderer.**                    'Tis he.

**First Murderer.** Stand to't.

**Banquo.** It will be rain tonight.

25  **First Murderer.**                    Let it come down!

*[They set upon* Banquo.*]*

**Banquo.** O, treachery! Fly, good Fleance, fly, fly, fly!
       Thou mayst revenge. O slave!

*[Dies.* Fleance *escapes.]*

**Third Murderer.** Who did strike out the light?

**First Murderer.**                    Was't not the way?

30  **Third Murderer.** There's but one down; the son is fled.

**Second Murderer.**                    We have lost
       Best half of our affair.

**First Murderer.** Well, let's away, and say how much is
       done.

*[Exeunt.]*

13 *Give us a light:* Banquo, nearing the palace, calls for servants to bring a light.

14–16 *Then 'tis . . . court:* It must be Banquo, since all the other expected guests are already in the palace.

17 *His horses go about:* Servants have taken his horses to the stable.

23 *Stand to't:* Be prepared.

27 *Thou mayest revenge:* You might live to avenge my death.

29 *Was't not the way:* Isn't that what we were supposed to do? Apparently, one of the murderers struck out the light, thus allowing Fleance to escape.

## *R*esponding to Reading

1.  Why are Macbeth and Lady Macbeth unhappy as king and queen?

2.  Why doesn't Macbeth tell his wife of his plans to murder Banquo and Fleance? Does his decision show a change in his relationship with her?

3.  Why do you think Macbeth sent a third murderer to join the other two?

4.  What effect might Fleance's escape have on Macbeth?

***Scene 4***   *The hall in the palace.*

*As the banquet begins, one of the murderers reports on Banquo's death and Fleance's escape. Macbeth is disturbed by the news and even more shaken when he returns to the banquet table and sees the bloody ghost of Banquo. Only Macbeth sees the ghost, and his terrified reaction startles the guests. Lady Macbeth explains her husband's strange behavior as an illness from childhood that will soon pass. Once the ghost disappears, Macbeth calls for a toast to Banquo, whose ghost immediately reappears. Because Macbeth begins to rant and rave, Lady Macbeth dismisses the guests, fearful that her husband will reveal too much. Macbeth, alone with his wife, tells of his suspicions of Macduff, absent from the banquet. He also says he will visit the witches again and hints at bloody deeds yet to happen.*

*[Banquet prepared. Enter* Macbeth, Lady
Macbeth, Ross, Lennox, Lords, *and* Attendants.*]*

**Macbeth.** You know your own degrees, sit down. At first
   And last the hearty welcome.

> **1 *your own degrees:*** where your rank entitles you to sit.

**Lords.**                              Thanks to your Majesty.

**Macbeth.** Ourself will mingle with society
5   And play the humble host.
   Our hostess keeps her state, but in best time
   We will require her welcome.

> **6 *keeps her state:*** sits on her throne rather than at the banquet table.

**Lady Macbeth.** Pronounce it for me, sir, to all our
      friends,
10   For my heart speaks they are welcome.

*[Enter* First Murderer *to the door.]*

**Macbeth.** See, they encounter thee with their hearts'
      thanks.
   Both sides are even: here I'll sit i' the midst.
   Be large in mirth; anon we'll drink a measure
15   The table round. *[Moves toward* Murderer *at door.]*
   There's blood upon thy face.

> **11–16 *measure:*** toast. Macbeth keeps talking to his wife and guests as he casually edges toward the door to speak privately with the murderer.

**Murderer.** 'Tis Banquo's then.

**Macbeth.** 'Tis better thee without than he within.
   Is he dispatched?

> **19 *dispatched:*** killed.

20 **Murderer.** My lord, his throat is cut. That I did for him.

**Macbeth.** Thou art the best o' the cutthroats! Yet he's
      good
   That did the like for Fleance. If thou didst it,
   Thou art the nonpareil.

> **24 *nonpareil:*** best.

**Murderer.**                    Most royal sir,

Fleance is scaped.

**Macbeth.** *[Aside]* Then comes my fit again. I had else
    been perfect;
Whole as the marble, founded as the rock,
As broad and general as the casing air.
But now I am cabined, cribbed, confined, bound in
To saucy doubts and fears.—But Banquo's safe?

**Murderer.** Ay, my good lord. Safe in a ditch he bides,
With twenty trenched gashes on his head,
The least a death to nature.

**Macbeth.**                      Thanks for that!
There the grown serpent lies; the worm that's fled
Hath nature that in time will venom breed,
No teeth for the present. Get thee gone. Tomorrow
We'll hear ourselves again.

*[Exit Murderer.]*

**Lady Macbeth.**             My royal lord,
You do not give the cheer. The feast is sold
That is not often vouched, while 'tis a-making,
'Tis given with welcome. To feed were best at home.
From thence, the sauce to meat is ceremony;
Meeting were bare without it.

*[Enter the* Ghost of Banquo, *and sits in*
Macbeth's *place.]*

**Macbeth.**                 Sweet remembrancer!
Now good digestion wait on appetite,
And health on both!

**Lennox.**              May't please your Highness sit.

**Macbeth.** Here had we now our country's honor, roofed,
Were the graced person of our Banquo present;
Who may I rather challenge for unkindness
Than pity for mischance!

**Ross.**                 His absence, sir,
Lays blame upon his promise. Please't your Highness
To grace us with your royal company?

**Macbeth.** The table's full.

**Lennox.**             Here is a place reserved, sir.

**Macbeth.** Where?

Line numbers: 25, 30, 35, 40, 45, 50, 55, 60

**27** *fit:* fever of fear.

**30** *casing:* surrounding.

**35** *The least . . . nature:* even the smallest wound being enough to cause death.

**37** *worm:* little serpent, that is, Fleance.

**39** *No teeth for the present:* too young to cause harm right now. Contrast this comment with his privately expressed fears.

**40** *hear ourselves:* talk together.

**41–46** Macbeth must not forget his duties as host. A feast will be no different from a meal that one pays for unless the host gives his guests courteous attention (**ceremony**), the best part of any meal.

**47** *Sweet remembrancer:* a term of affection for his wife, who has reminded him of his duty.

**51–54** The best people of Scotland would all be under Macbeth's roof if Banquo were present too. He hopes Banquo's absence is due to rudeness rather than to some accident (**mischance**).

**58** Macbeth finally notices that Banquo's ghost is present and sitting in the King's chair. As you read about this encounter, consider how Macbeth's reaction affects his guests.

**Lennox.** Here, my good lord. What is't that moves your
Highness?

**Macbeth.** Which of you have done this?

**Lords.**                                    What, my good lord?

65 **Macbeth.** Thou canst not say I did it. Never shake
Thy gory locks at me.

**Ross.** Gentlemen, rise. His Highness is not well.

**Lady Macbeth.** Sit, worthy friends. My lord is often thus,
And hath been from his youth. Pray you keep seat.
70 The fit is momentary; upon a thought
He will again be well. If much you note him,
You shall offend him and extend his passion.
Feed, and regard him not.—Are you a man?

**Macbeth.** Ay, and a bold one, that dare look on that
75 Which might appal the devil.

**Lady Macbeth.**                    O proper stuff!
This is the very painting of your fear.
This is the air-drawn dagger which you said
Led you to Duncan. O, these flaws and starts
80 (Impostors to true fear) would well become
A woman's story at a winter's fire,
Authorized by her grandam. Shame itself!
Why do you make such faces? When all's done,
You look but on a stool.

85 **Macbeth.** Prithee see there! behold! look! lo! How say
you?
Why, what care I? If thou canst nod, speak too.
If charnel houses and our graves must send
Those that we bury back, our monuments
90 Shall be the maws of kites.

*[Exit Ghost.]*

**Lady Macbeth.**                    What, quite unmanned in folly?

**Macbeth.** If I stand here, I saw him.

**Lady Macbeth.**                         Fie, for shame!

**Macbeth.** Blood hath been shed ere now, i' the olden
95 time,
Ere humane statute purged the gentle weal;
Ay, and since too, murders have been performed
Too terrible for the ear. The time has been

**66 gory:** ghostly.

**68–73 Sit . . . not:** Macbeth, confused and frantic, has seemed to be talking to thin air. Nervously, Lady Macbeth tries to calm the guests by claiming her husband often has such fits. She says the attack will pass quickly (**upon a thought**) and that looking at him will only make him worse (**extend his passion**). *Why does Lady Macbeth make up a story to tell the guests?*

**76–84** She dismisses his hallucination as utter nonsense (**proper stuff**). His outbursts (**flaws and starts**) are the product of imaginary fears (**imposters to true fear**) and are unmanly, the kind of behavior described in a woman's story. *Do you think her appeal to his manhood will work this time?*

**87 canst nod:** The ghost has been shaking his head in accusation.

**88–90** If burial vaults (**charnel houses**) give back the dead, then we may as well throw our bodies to the birds (**kites**), whose stomachs (**maws**) will become our tombs (**monuments**).

**94–98** Macbeth desperately tries to justify his murder of Banquo. Murder has been common from ancient times to the present, though laws (**humane statute**) have tried to rid civilized society (**gentle weal**) of violence.

That, when the brains were out, the man would die,
100 And there an end! But now they rise again,
With twenty mortal murders on their crowns,
And push us from our stools. This is more strange
Than such a murder is.

**Lady Macbeth.** My worthy lord,
105 Your noble friends do lack you.

**Macbeth.** I do forget.
Do not muse at me, my most worthy friends.
I have a strange infirmity, which is nothing
To those that know me. Come, love and health to all!
110 Then I'll sit down. Give me some wine, fill full.

**98–100** In the old days, people at least stayed dead when you killed them.

**107** *muse:* wonder.

**108** *infirmity:* sickness.

*"I drink to the general joy o' the whole table,/And to our dear friend Banquo..."*

[*Enter* Ghost.]

I drink to the general joy o' the whole table,
And to our dear friend Banquo, whom we miss.
Would he were here! To all, and him, we thirst,
And all to all.

115 **Lords.** Our duties, and the pledge.

**113–114** *To all . . . to all:* Macbeth toasts everyone, including Banquo.

**115** *Our . . . pledge:* We toast our duties and loyalty to you.

**Macbeth.** Avaunt, and quit my sight! Let the earth hide
  thee!
  Thy bones are marrowless, thy blood is cold;
  Thou hast no speculation in those eyes
120  Which thou dost glare with!

**Lady Macbeth.**                    Think of this, good peers,
  But as a thing of custom. 'Tis no other.
  Only it spoils the pleasure of the time.

**Macbeth.** What man dare, I dare.
125  Approach thou like the rugged Russian bear,
  The armed rhinoceros, or the Hyrcan tiger;
  Take any shape but that, and my firm nerves
  Shall never tremble. Or be alive again
  And dare me to the desert with thy sword.
130  If trembling I inhabit then, protest me
  The baby of a girl. Hence, horrible shadow!
  Unreal mock'ry, hence!

*[Exit Ghost.]*

                    Why, so! Being gone,
  I am a man again. Pray you sit still.

135  **Lady Macbeth.** You have displaced the mirth, broke the
    good meeting
  With most admired disorder.

**Macbeth.**                    Can such things be,
  And overcome us like a summer's cloud
140  Without our special wonder? You make me strange
  Even to the disposition that I owe,
  When now I think you can behold such sights
  And keep the natural ruby of your cheeks
  When mine is blanched with fear.

145  **Ross.**                    What sights, my lord?

**Lady Macbeth.** I pray you speak not. He grows worse and
    worse;
  Question enrages him. At once, good night.
  Stand not upon the order of your going,
150  But go at once.

**Lennox.**          Good night, and better health
  Attend his Majesty!

**Lady Macbeth.**        A kind good night to all!

*[Exeunt Lords and Attendants.]*

---

**116–120 Avaunt:** go away. Macbeth sees Banquo again. He tells Banquo that he is only a ghost, with unreal bones, cold blood, and no consciousness (**speculation**).

**122 thing of custom:** a normal event.

**124–132** Macbeth would be willing to face Banquo in any other form, even his living self. **If trembling . . . girl:** If I still tremble, call me a girl's doll.

**137 admired:** astonishing.

**138–144** Macbeth is bewildered by his wife's calm after such an event. Her reaction makes him seem a stranger to himself (**strange / Even to the disposition that I owe**): she seems to be the one with all the courage, since he is white (**blanched**) with fear.

**145** Everyone can hear Macbeth, which makes Lady Macbeth afraid that her husband will reveal too much.

**149 Stand . . . going:** Don't worry about the proper formalities of leaving.

**Macbeth.** It will have blood, they say: blood will have
155    blood.
    Stones have been known to move and trees to speak;
    Augures and understood relations have
    By maggot-pies and choughs and rooks brought forth
    The secret'st man of blood. What is the night?

160  **Lady Macbeth.** Almost at odds with morning, which is
    which.

**Macbeth.** How say'st thou that Macduff denies his person
    At our great bidding?

**Lady Macbeth.**            Did you send to him, sir?

165  **Macbeth.** I hear it by the way; but I will send.
    There's not a one of them but in his house
    I keep a servant feed. I will tomorrow
    (And betimes I will) to the Weird Sisters.
    More shall they speak; for now I am bent to know
170  By the worst means the worst. For mine own good
    All causes shall give way. I am in blood
    Stepped in so far that, should I wade no more,
    Returning were as tedious as go o'er.
    Strange things I have in head, that will to hand,
175    Which must be acted ere they may be scanned.

**Lady Macbeth.** You lack the season of all natures, sleep.

**Macbeth.** Come, we'll to sleep. My strange and self-abuse
    Is the initiate fear that wants hard use.
    We are yet but young in deed.

    *[Exeunt.]*

**154–159** Macbeth fears that Banquo's murder (*It*) will be revenged by his own murder. Stones, trees, or talking birds (***maggot-pies and choughs and rooks***) may reveal the hidden knowledge (***Augures***) of his guilt.

**162–163** *How say'st . . . bidding:* What do you think of Macduff's refusal to come? *Why do you think Macbeth is suddenly so concerned about Macduff?*

**166–167** *There's . . . feed:* Macbeth has paid (***feed***) household servants to spy on every noble, including Macduff.

**168** *betimes:* early.

**169** *bent:* determined.

**170–175** *For mine . . . scanned:* Macbeth will do anything to protect himself. He has stepped so far into a river of blood that it would make no sense to turn back. He will act upon his unnatural (***strange***) thoughts without having examined (***scanned***) them.

**176** *season:* preservative.

**177–179** His vision of the ghost (***strange and self-abuse***) is only the result of a beginner's fear (***initiate fear***), to be cured with practice (***hard use***).

# Responding to Reading

1. Soon after he cooly masterminds Banquo's murder, Macbeth sees a ghost. What does this turn of events reveal about his personality?

   **Think about**
   • his inner conflicts
   • what he is afraid of
   • his previous vision of the dagger and his hearing of voices

2. Why is Macbeth preoccupied with blood? What does blood symbolize?

3. How do you think the guests have been affected by Macbeth's "fit"?

4. What does Macbeth hope to gain by visiting the witches?

## Scene 5 *A heath.*

*The goddess of witchcraft, Hecate, scolds the three witches for dealing independently with Macbeth. She outlines their next meeting with him, planning to cause his downfall by making him overconfident. (Experts believe this scene was not written by Shakespeare but rather was added later.)*

[*Thunder. Enter the three* Witches, *meeting* Hecate.]

**First Witch.** Why, how now, Hecate? You look angerly.

**Hecate.** Have I not reason, beldams as you are,
    Saucy and overbold? How did you dare
    To trade and traffic with Macbeth
5    In riddles and affairs of death;
    And I, the mistress of your charms,
    The close contriver of all harms,
    Was never called to bear my part
    Or show the glory of our art?
10    And, which is worse, all you have done
    Hath been but for a wayward son,
    Spiteful and wrathful, who, as others do,
    Loves for his own ends, not for you.
    But make amends now. Get you gone
15    And at the pit of Acheron
    Meet me i' the morning. Thither he
    Will come to know his destiny.
    Your vessels and your spells provide,
    Your charms and everything beside.
20    I am for the air. This night I'll spend
    Unto a dismal and a fatal end.
    Great business must be wrought ere noon.
    Upon the corner of the moon
    There hangs a vap'rous drop profound.
25    I'll catch it ere it come to ground;
    And that, distilled by magic sleights,
    Shall raise such artificial sprites
    As by the strength of their illusion
    Shall draw him on to his confusion.
30    He shall spurn fate, scorn death, and bear
    His hopes 'bove wisdom, grace, and fear;
    And you all know security
    Is mortals' chiefest enemy.

**2 beldams:** hags.

**7 close contriver:** secret inventor.

**13 Loves . . . you:** cares only about his own goals, not about you.

**15 Acheron:** a river in hell, according to Greek mythology. Hecate plans to hold their meeting in a hellish place.

**20–21 This . . . end:** Tonight I'm working for a disastrous (*dismal*) and fatal end for Macbeth.

**24–29** Hecate will obtain a magical drop from the moon, treat it with secret art, and so create spirits (*artificial sprites*) that will lead Macbeth to his destruction (*confusion*).

**30–33** She predicts that he will become overconfident, convinced of his own security.

*[Music and a song within. "Come away, come away," etc.]*

Hark! I am called. My little spirit, see,

35 Sits in a foggy cloud and stays for me.

*[Exit.]*

**First Witch.** Come, let's make haste. She'll soon be back
again.

*[Exeunt.]*

## Scene 6 *The palace at Forres.*

*Lennox and another Scottish lord review the events surrounding the murders of Duncan and Banquo, indirectly suggesting that Macbeth is both a murderer and a tyrant. It is reported that Macduff has gone to England, where Duncan's son Malcolm is staying with King Edward and raising an army to regain the Scottish throne. Macbeth, angered by Macduff's refusal to see him, is also preparing for war.*

*[Enter Lennox and another Lord.]*

**Lennox.** My former speeches have but hit your thoughts,
Which can interpret farther. Only I say
Things have been strangely borne. The gracious
Duncan

5 Was pitied of Macbeth. Marry, he was dead!
And the right valiant Banquo walked too late;
Whom, you may say (if't please you) Fleance killed,
For Fleance fled. Men must not walk too late.
Who cannot want the thought how monstrous

10 It was for Malcolm and for Donalbain
To kill their gracious father? Damned fact!
How it did grieve Macbeth! Did he not straight,
In pious rage, the two delinquents tear,
That were the slaves of drink and thralls of sleep?

15 Was not that nobly done? Ay, and wisely too!
For 'twould have angered any heart alive
To hear the men deny't. So that I say
He has borne all things well; and I do think
That, had he Duncan's sons under his key

20 (As, an't please heaven, he shall not), they should find
What 'twere to kill a father. So should Fleance.
But peace! for from broad words, and 'cause he failed
His presence at the tyrant's feast, I hear
Macduff lives in disgrace. Sir, can you tell

25 Where he bestows himself?

**34–35** Like the other witches, Hecate has a demon helper (***my little spirit***). At the end of her speech, she is raised by pulley to the "Heavens" of the stage.

**1–3 *My former . . . borne:*** Lennox and the other lord had shared suspicions of Macbeth. Recent events carry their suspicions farther.

**5 *Marry:*** a mild oath. Lennox ironically suggests that Macbeth's affections lead to murder.

**7–8 *Whom . . . Fleance fled:*** Lennox is being ironic when he says that fleeing the scene of the crime must make Fleance guilty of his father's death.

**9–11 *Who . . . father:*** He says that everyone can agree on the horror of Duncan's being murdered by his sons. But Lennox has been consistently ironic, claiming to believe in what is obviously false. His words indirectly blame Macbeth.

**13 *pious:*** holy.

**16–17 *For 'twould . . . deny't:*** Again, he is being ironic. If the servants had lived, Macbeth might have been discovered.

**22 *from broad words:*** because of his frank talk.

**25 *bestows himself:*** is staying.

**Lord.**                                    The son of Duncan,
From whom this tyrant holds the due of birth,
Lives in the English court, and is received
Of the most pious Edward with such grace
30  That the malevolence of fortune nothing
Takes from his high respect. Thither Macduff
Is gone to pray the holy King upon his aid
To wake Northumberland and warlike Siward;
That by the help of these (with Him above
35  To ratify the work) we may again
Give to our tables meat, sleep to our nights,
Free from our feasts and banquets bloody knives,
Do faithful homage and receive free honors—
All which we pine for now. And this report
40  Hath so exasperate the King that he
Prepares for some attempt of war.

**Lennox.**                                   Sent he to Macduff?

**Lord.** He did; and with an absolute "Sir, not I!"
The cloudy messenger turns me his back
45  And hums, as who should say, "You'll rue the time
That clogs me with this answer."

**Lennox.**                                 And that well might
Advise him to a caution t' hold what distance
His wisdom can provide. Some holy angel
50  Fly to the court of England and unfold
His message ere he come, that a swift blessing
May soon return to this our suffering country
Under a hand accursed!

**Lord.**                              I'll send my prayers with him.

*[Exeunt.]*

---

**27 From . . . birth:** Macbeth keeps Malcolm from his birthright. As the eldest son of Duncan, Malcolm should be king.

**29 Edward:** Edward the Confessor, king of England from 1042 to 1066, a man known for his virtue and religion.

**30–31 That . . . respect:** Though Malcolm suffers from bad fortune (the loss of the throne), he is respectfully treated by Edward.

**31–39 Thither . . . for now:** Macduff wants the King to persuade the people of Northumberland (an English county near Scotland) and their earl, Siward, to join Malcolm's cause. With their help Malcolm may be able to restore order and peace in Scotland.

**39–41 And . . . war:** Macbeth is so angry (**exasperate**) at these reports from England that he prepares for war.

**43–46** The messenger, fearing Macbeth's anger, was unhappy (**cloudy**) with Macduff's refusal to cooperate. Because Macduff burdens (**clogs**) him with bad news, he will not hurry back.

**49–54 Some . . . accursed:** Lennox wants news of Macduff's appeal for military aid to arrive in England before Macduff himself, so that blessings may swiftly return to Scotland.

---

## *R*esponding to Reading

1. Why do you think the scene with Hecate was added to the play? If you were a director, would you include it in your production? Explain your reasons.

2. Summarize what Scene 6 contributes to the plot. Consider what is learned about Macbeth, his subjects, Malcolm, and Macduff.

3. Contrast Macbeth's reign with the hopes that Lennox has for the reign of Malcolm. Do you think Lennox will have his wish fulfilled?

## *Responding to Reading*

### First Impressions

1. What is your impression of Macbeth's state of mind by the end of this act?

### Second Thoughts

2. So far Macbeth has seen a bloody ghost and a floating dagger and has heard voices. What does his active imagination reveal about his inner conflicts?

3. Compare and contrast the murders of Banquo and Duncan. How does the murder of Banquo illustrate the changes that Macbeth has undergone?

   **Think about**
   - the method used in each killing
   - Macbeth's attitude before each action
   - Macbeth's reaction after each event
   - the role played by Lady Macbeth

4. How does the relationship between Macbeth and his wife change after the death of Duncan? Explain your answer with examples from Act Three.

   **Think about**
   - Macbeth's refusal to reveal his plans regarding Banquo
   - his "fit" at the banquet and her reaction
   - their feelings about Duncan's murder and its effects

5. What are your predictions about the events of the next act?

## *Literary Concept: Tragedy and the Tragic Hero*

A **tragedy** is a play, novel, or other narrative in which the main character comes to an unhappy end. The protagonist, or **tragic hero,** usually is an important person, often gifted with extraordinary abilities. The hero's downfall is usually caused by a **tragic flaw**—an error in judgment or defect in character— that leads to his or her destruction, though the downfall may be caused by outside forces. According to the Greek philosopher Aristotle, a tragedy arouses pity and fear in the audience—pity for the hero and fear for all humans, who are prone to the same defects as the hero. What qualities make Macbeth a tragic hero? What is his tragic flaw? Does Shakespeare succeed in creating a character for whom an audience can feel pity?

**Concept Review: Climax** In a five-act drama, the climax, or turning point, usually occurs in the third act. What do you think is the climax of this play? Why?

## Writing Options

1. Make two lists to describe Macbeth's view of the future. The first should include all his fears of what might happen. The second should note his hopes and wishes.

2. Write a letter to an advice columnist from Lady Macbeth, complaining about her husband's unmanly fears. Then answer the letter. As an alternative, write a letter from Macbeth complaining about his wife.

3. Write a gossip column about the strange sights and sounds at King Macbeth's latest party. Include quotes from various people who were there. Don't forget to make a few snide comments along the way.

4. Make a list of possible further victims of Macbeth's fear. Beside each name, write how you think each would die.

## Options for Learning

1 • **Mental Health Week** Working in small groups, create a psychological profile of Macbeth. First decide what categories you will use to evaluate his mental and emotional health. Then rate him in each category, using either a letter grade or a number from 1 to 10. Finally, make recommendations about how he can improve his well-being. Distribute your evaluation to the class.

2 • **Marriage on the Rocks** Role-play a marriage counseling session with Lady Macbeth, her husband, and the counselor. The counselor should try to get at the bottom of their problems, while the husband and wife should keep in character. Be sure to discuss Macbeth's manliness and Lady Macbeth's lack of sympathy.

3 • **The Mind's Images** Create a painting or drawing that shows the inside of Macbeth's mind. You might illustrate his mental image of Banquo's ghost or convey his deep-seated inner conflicts and fears. Then share your illustration with the class, explaining what you intended to convey.

4 • **Court Astrologers** Imagine that Macbeth has called in the best astrologers in the kingdom to predict his future. Stage a panel discussion in which the astrologers share their predictions, explaining in detail what Macbeth can expect. All predictions should be based on what has already happened in the play.

# ACT FOUR

***Scene 1*** *A cave. In the middle, a boiling cauldron.*

*The three witches prepare a potion in a boiling kettle. When Macbeth arrives, demanding to know his future, the witches raise three apparitions. The first, an armed head, tells him to beware of Macduff. Next, a bloody child assures Macbeth that he will never be harmed by anyone born of woman. The third apparition tells him that he will never be defeated until the trees of Birnam Wood move toward his castle at Dunsinane. Macbeth, now confident of his future, asks about Banquo's son. His confidence fades when the witches show him a line of kings who all resemble Banquo, suggesting that Banquo's sons will indeed be kings. Macbeth curses the witches as they disappear.*

*Lennox enters the cave and tells Macbeth that Macduff has gone to the English court. Hearing this, Macbeth swears to kill Macduff's family.*

[*Thunder. Enter the three* Witches.]

**First Witch.** Thrice the brinded cat hath mewed.

**Second Witch.** Thrice, and once the hedge-pig whined.

**Third Witch.** Harpier cries; 'tis time, 'tis time.

**First Witch.** Round about the cauldron go;
5     In the poisoned entrails throw.
    Toad, that under cold stone
    Days and nights has thirty-one
    Swelt'red venom sleeping got,
    Boil thou first i' the charmed pot.

10 **All.** Double, double, toil and trouble;
    Fire burn, and cauldron bubble.

**Second Witch.** Fillet of a fenny snake,
    In the cauldron boil and bake;
    Eye of newt, and toe of frog,
15     Wool of bat, and tongue of dog,
    Adder's fork, and blindworm's sting,
    Lizard's leg, and howlet's wing;
    For a charm of pow'rful trouble
    Like a hell-broth boil and bubble.

20 **All.** Double, double, toil and trouble;
    Fire burn, and cauldron bubble.

**Third Witch.** Scale of dragon, tooth of wolf,
    Witch's mummy, maw and gulf
    Of the ravined salt-sea shark,
25     Root of hemlock, digged i' the dark;

**GUIDE FOR READING**

**1–3** Magical signals and the call of the third witch's attending demon (**Harpier**) tell the witches to begin.

**4–34** The witches are stirring up a magical stew to bring trouble to humanity. Their recipe includes intestines (**entrails, chaudron**), a slice (**Fillet**) of snake, eye of salamander (**newt**), snake tongue (**Adder's fork**), a lizard (**blindworm**), a baby owl's (**howlet's**) wing, a shark's stomach and gullet (**maw and gulf**), the finger of a baby strangled by a prostitute (**drab**), and other gruesome ingredients. They stir their brew until thick and slimy (**slab**).

Liver of blaspheming Jew,
Gall of goat, and slips of yew
Slivered in the moon's eclipse;
Nose of Turk and Tartar's lips;

30   Finger of birth-strangled babe
Ditch-delivered by a drab:
Make the gruel thick and slab.
Add thereto a tiger's chaudron
For the ingredience of our cauldron.

35   **All.** Double, double, toil and trouble;
Fire burn, and cauldron bubble.

**Second Witch.** Cool it with a baboon's blood,
Then the charm is firm and good.

*[Enter* Hecate *and the other three* Witches.*]*

**Hecate.** O, well done! I commend your pains,

40   And every one shall share i' the gains.
And now about the cauldron sing
Like elves and fairies in a ring,
Enchanting all that you put in.

*[Music and a song, "Black spirit," etc.]*

**Second Witch.** By the pricking of my thumbs,

45   Something wicked this way comes.
                  Open locks,
                  Whoever knocks!

Most experts believe that the entrance
of Hecate and three more witches was
not written by Shakespeare. The
characters were probably added later to
expand the role of the witches who
were favorites of the audience.

*[Enter Macbeth.]*

**Macbeth.** How now, you secret, black, and midnight hags?
    What is't you do?

50 **All.**                A deed without a name.

**Macbeth.** I conjure you by that which you profess
    (Howe'er you come to know it), answer me.
    Though you untie the winds and let them fight
    Against the churches; though the yesty waves
55   Confound and swallow navigation up;
    Though bladed corn be lodged and trees blown down;
    Though castles topple on their warders' heads;
    Though palaces and pyramids do slope
    Their heads to their foundations; though the treasure
60   Of nature's germens tumble all together,
    Even till destruction sicken—answer me
    To what I ask you.

**First Witch.**             Speak.

**Second Witch.**           Demand.

65 **Third Witch.**            We'll answer.

**First Witch.** Say, if th' hadst rather hear it from our
    mouths
    Or from our masters.

**Macbeth.**           Call 'em! Let me see 'em.

70 **First Witch.** Pour in sow's blood, that hath eaten
    Her nine farrow; grease that's sweaten
    From the murderer's gibbet throw
    Into the flame.

**All.**          Come, high or low;
75   Thyself and office deftly show!

*[Thunder. First Apparition, an Armed Head.]*

**Macbeth.** Tell me, thou unknown power—

**First Witch.**            He knows thy thought.
    Hear his speech, but say thou naught.

**First Apparition.** Macbeth! Macbeth! Macbeth! Beware
80   Macduff;
    Beware the Thane of Fife. Dismiss me. Enough.

*[He descends.]*

**51-62** Macbeth calls upon (***conjure***) the witches in the name of their dark magic (***that which you profess***). Though they unleash winds to topple churches and make foaming (***yesty***) waves to destroy (***Confound***) ships, though they flatten wheat (***corn***) fields, destroy buildings, and reduce nature's order to chaos by mixing all seeds (***germens***) together, he demands an answer to his question. *How has Macbeth's attitude toward the witches changed from his earlier meetings?*

**68 masters:** the demons whom the witches serve.

**71 farrow:** newborn pigs; ***grease...gibbet:*** grease from a gallows where a murderer was hung.

**75 office:** function.

Each of the three apparitions holds a clue to Macbeth's future. *What do you think is suggested by the armed head?*

**Macbeth.** Whate'er thou art, for thy good caution thanks!
Thou hast harped my fear aright. But one word
more—

85 **First Witch.** He will not be commanded. Here's another,
More potent than the first.

*[Thunder. Second Apparition, a Bloody Child.]*

**Second Apparition.** Macbeth! Macbeth! Macbeth!

**Macbeth.** Had I three ears, I'd hear thee.

**Second Apparition.** Be bloody, bold, and resolute; laugh
90  to scorn
The pow'r of man, for none of woman born
Shall harm Macbeth.

*[Descends.]*

**Macbeth.** Then live, Macduff. What need I fear of thee?
But yet I'll make assurance double sure
95 And take a bond of fate. Thou shalt not live!
That I may tell pale-hearted fear it lies
And sleep in spite of thunder.

*[Thunder. Third Apparition, a Child Crowned, with a tree
in his hand.]*

What is this
That rises like the issue of a king
100 And wears upon his baby-brow the round
And top of sovereignty?

**All.**                              Listen, but speak not to't.

**Third Apparition.** Be lion-mettled, proud, and take no
care
105 Who chafes, who frets, or where conspirers are.
Macbeth shall never vanquished be until
Great Birnam Wood to high Dunsinane Hill
Shall come against him.                              *[Descends.]*

**Macbeth.**                      That will never be.
110 Who can impress the forest, bid the tree
Unfix his earth-bound root? Sweet-bodements, good!
Rebellious dead rise never till the Wood
Of Birnam rise, and our high-placed Macbeth
Shall live the lease of nature, pay his breath
115 To time and mortal custom. Yet my heart
Throbs to know one thing. Tell me, if your art

**83 *harped:*** guessed. The apparition has confirmed Macbeth's fears of Macduff.

*Who or what might the bloody child represent?*

**89–92** *How do you think this prophecy will affect Macbeth?*

**94–95** Despite the prophecy's apparent promise of safety, Macbeth decides to seek double insurance. The murder of Macduff will give Macbeth a guarantee (***bond***) of his fate and put his fears to rest.
*Who or what might the child crowned represent?*

**99 *issue:*** children.

**100–101 *the round / And top:*** the crown.

**103–108** The third apparition tells Macbeth to take courage. He cannot be defeated unless Birnam Wood travels the twelve-mile distance to Dunsinane Hill where his castle is located.

**110 *impress:*** force into service.

**111 *bodements:*** prophecies.

**112–115 *Rebellious...custom:*** Macbeth boasts that he will never again be troubled by ghosts (***Rebellious dead***) and that he will live out his expected lifespan (***lease of nature***). He believes he will die (***pay his breath***) by natural causes (***mortal custom***).

Can tell so much—shall Banquo's issue ever
Reign in this kingdom?

**All.**                          Seek to know no more.

120 **Macbeth.** I will be satisfied. Deny me this,
And an eternal curse fall on you! Let me know.
Why sinks that cauldron? and what noise is this?

                                        *[Hautboys.]*

**First Witch.** Show!

**Second Witch.** Show!

125 **Third Witch.** Show!

**All.** Show his eyes, and grieve his heart!
Come like shadows, so depart!

*[A show of eight Kings, the eighth with a glass in his hand, and
Banquo last.]*

**Macbeth.** Thou art too like the spirit of Banquo. Down!
Thy crown does sear mine eyeballs. And thy hair,
130 Thou other gold-bound brow, is like the first.
A third is like the former. Filthy hags!
Why do you show me this? A fourth? Start, eyes!
What, will the line stretch out to the crack of doom?
Another yet? A seventh? I'll see no more.
135 And yet the eighth appears, who bears a glass
Which shows me many more; and some I see
That twofold balls and treble scepters carry.
Horrible sight! Now I see 'tis true;
For the blood-boltered Banquo smiles upon me
140 And points at them for his. *[Apparitions descend.]* What?
Is this so?

**First Witch.** Ay, sir, all this is so. But why
Stands Macbeth thus amazedly?
Come, sisters, cheer we up his sprites
145 And show the best of our delights.
I'll charm the air to give a sound
While you perform your antic round,
That this great king may kindly say
Our duties did his welcome pay.

*[Music. The Witches dance, and vanish.]*

150 **Macbeth.** Where are they? Gone? Let this pernicious hour
Stand aye accursed in the calendar!
Come in, without there!

**122 Why...this:** The cauldron is sinking from sight to make room for the next apparition.
Macbeth next sees a procession (**show**) of eight kings, the last carrying a mirror (**glass**). According to legend, Fleance escaped to England, where he founded the Stuart family. James I of England, the king when this play was first performed, was the eighth Stuart king, the first to rule over both England and Scotland.

**128–141** Macbeth is outraged that all eight kings in the procession look like Banquo. The mirror held by the last one shows a future with many more Banquo look-alikes as kings. The **twofold balls and treble scepters** pictured in the mirror foretell the union of Scotland and England in 1603, the year that James became king of both realms. Banquo, his hair matted (**boltered**) with blood, claims all the kings as his descendants. *What do you think is going through Macbeth's mind?*

**142–149** Macbeth stands silent with amazement (**amazedly**). To cheer his spirits (**sprites**), the witches perform a weird circle dance (**antic round**).

**150–152 pernicious:** deadly, destructive. **aye:** always. After the witches vanish, Macbeth hears noises outside the cave and calls out.

*[Enter Lennox.]*

**Lennox.**                    What's your Grace's will?

**Macbeth.** Saw you the Weird Sisters?

155  **Lennox.**                    No, my lord.

**Macbeth.** Came they not by you?

**Lennox.**                    No indeed, my lord.

**Macbeth.** Infected be the air whereon they ride,
     And damned all those that trust them! I did hear
160  The galloping of horse. Who was't came by?

**Lennox.** 'Tis two or three, my lord, that bring you word
     Macduff is fled to England.

**Macbeth.**                    Fled to England?

**Lennox.** Ay, my good lord.

165  **Macbeth.** *[Aside]* Time, thou anticipat'st my dread
          exploits.
     The flighty purpose never is o'ertook
     Unless the deed go with it. From this moment
     The very firstlings of my heart shall be
170  The firstlings of my hand. And even now,
     To crown my thoughts with acts, be it thought and
          done!
     The castle of Macduff I will surprise,
     Seize upon Fife, give to the edge o' the sword
175  His wife, his babes, and all unfortunate souls
     That trace him in his line. No boasting like a fool!
     This deed I'll do before this purpose cool.
     But no more sights!—Where are these gentlemen?
     Come, bring me where they are.

**165–179** Frustrated in his desire to kill Macduff, Macbeth blames his own hesitation, which gave his enemy time to flee. He concludes that one's plans (**flighty purpose**) are never achieved (**o'ertook**) unless carried out at once. From now on, Macbeth promises, he will act immediately on his impulses (**firstlings of my heart**) and complete (**crown**) his thoughts with acts. He will surprise Macduff's castle at Fife and kill his wife and children. *Why does Macbeth decide to kill Macduff's family?*

# Responding to Reading

1. Summarize Macbeth's interpretation of each of the four prophecies. Discuss whether the prophecies have hidden meanings.

   **Think about**
   • what or who is suggested by the human forms of the apparitions
   • how each prophecy might be fulfilled

2. Has Macbeth finally conquered his fears by the end of the scene? Explain.

3. Compare Macbeth's plan to kill Macduff's family with his other murderous acts.

## Scene 2 *Macduff's castle at Fife.*

*Ross visits Lady Macduff to assure her of her husband's wisdom and courage. Lady Macduff cannot be comforted, believing that he left out of fear. After Ross leaves she tells her son, who is still loyal to his father, that Macduff was a traitor and is now dead. A messenger warns them to flee but is too late. Murderers sent by Macbeth burst in, killing both wife and son.*

*[Enter* Lady Macduff, *her* Son, *and* Ross.]

**Lady Macduff.** What had he done to make him fly the land?

**Ross.** You must have patience, madam.

**Lady Macduff.**                              He had none.
5     His flight was madness. When our actions do not,
      Our fears do make us traitors.

**Ross.**                              You know not
      Whether it was his wisdom or his fear.

**Lady Macduff.** Wisdom? To leave his wife, to leave his
10        babes,
      His mansion, and his titles, in a place
      From whence himself does fly? He loves us not,
      He wants the natural touch. For the poor wren,
      (The most diminutive of birds) will fight,
15    Her young ones in her nest, against the owl.
      All is the fear, and nothing is the love,
      As little is the wisdom, where the flight
      So runs against all reason.

**Ross.**                              My dearest coz,
20    I pray you school yourself. But for your husband,
      He is noble, wise, judicious, and best knows
      The fits o' the season. I dare not speak much further;
      But cruel are the times, when we are traitors
      And do not know ourselves; when we hold rumor
25    From what we fear, yet know not what we fear,
      But float upon a wild and violent sea
      Each way and move—I take my leave of you.
      Shall not be long but I'll be here again.
      Things at the worst will cease, or else climb upward
30    To what they were before.—My pretty cousin,
      Blessing upon you!

5–6 *When our...traitors:* Macduff's wife is worried that others will think her husband a traitor because his fears made him flee the country (*Our fears do make us traitors*), though he was guilty of no wrongdoing.

13 *wants the natural touch:* lacks the instinct to protect his family.

16–19 *All...reason:* Lady Macduff believes her husband is motivated entirely by fear, not by love of his family. His hasty flight is contrary to reason.

19–20 *coz:* cousin, a term used for any close relation. *school:* control; *for:* as for.

22 *fits o' the season:* disorders of the present time.

23–30 *But...were before:* Ross laments the cruelty of the times that made Macduff flee. In such times, people are treated like traitors for no reason. Their fears make them believe (*hold*) rumors, though they do not know what to fear and drift aimlessly like ships tossed by a tempest. Ross promises Lady Macduff he will return and assures her that the bad times will either end or improve (*climb upward*). He concludes by blessing Macduff's son.

**Lady Macduff.** Fathered he is, and yet he's fatherless.

**Ross.** I am so much a fool, should I stay longer,
It would be my disgrace and your discomfort.
35     I take my leave at once.            *[Exit.]*

**Lady Macduff.**        Sirrah, your father's dead;
And what will you do now? How will you live?

**Son.** As birds do, mother.

**Lady Macduff.**       What, with worms and flies?

40  **Son.** With what I get, I mean; and so do they.

**Lady Macduff.** Poor bird! thou'dst never fear the net nor
lime,
The pitfall nor the gin.

**Son.** Why should I, mother? Poor birds they are not set
45     for.
My father is not dead, for all your saying.

**Lady Macduff.** Yes, he is dead. How wilt thou do for a
father?

**Son.** Nay, how will you do for a husband?

50  **Lady Macduff.** Why, I can buy me twenty at any market.

**Son.** Then you'll buy 'em to sell again.

**Lady Macduff.** Thou speak'st with all thy wit; and yet, i'
faith,
With wit enough for thee.

55  **Son.** Was my father a traitor, mother?

**Lady Macduff.** Ay, that he was!

**Son.** What is a traitor?

**Lady Macduff.** Why, one that swears, and lies.

**Son.** And be all traitors that do so?

60  **Lady Macduff.** Every one that does so is a traitor and
must be hanged.

**Son.** And must they all be hanged that swear and lie?

**Lady Macduff.** Every one.

**Son.** Who must hang them?

65  **Lady Macduff.** Why, the honest men.

**33–35** Moved by pity for Macduff's family, Ross is near tears (**my disgrace**). He will leave before he embarrasses himself.

**36–37** *Why does Lady Macduff tell her son that his father is dead, though the boy heard her discussion with Ross?*

**38–45** The spirited son refuses to be defeated by their bleak situation. He will live as birds do, taking whatever comes his way. His mother responds in kind, calling attention to devices used to catch birds: nets, sticky birdlime (**lime**), snares (**pitfall**), and traps (**gin**). The boy playfully answers that he has nothing to fear because no one sets a trap for a worthless bird.

**50–54** Lady Macduff and her son affectionately joke about her ability to find a new husband. She expresses admiration for his intelligence (**With wit enough**).

**55–65** Continuing his banter, the son asks if his father is a traitor. Lady Macduff, understandably hurt and confused by her husband's unexplained departure, answers yes.

**Son.** Then the liars and swearers are fools; for there are
liars and swearers enow to beat the honest men and
hang up them.

**Lady Macduff.** Now God help thee, poor monkey!
70    But how wilt thou do for a father?

**Son.** If he were dead, you'd weep for him. If you would
not, it were a good sign that I should quickly have a
new father.

**Lady Macduff.** Poor prattler, how thou talk'st!

*[Enter a Messenger.]*

75  **Messenger.** Bless you, fair dame! I am not to you known,
Though in your state of honor I am perfect.
I doubt some danger does approach you nearly.
If you will take a homely man's advice,
Be not found here. Hence with your little ones!
80    To fright you thus methinks I am too savage;
To do worse to you were fell cruelty,
Which is too nigh your person. Heaven preserve you!
I dare abide no longer.                            *[Exit.]*

**Lady Macduff.**                 Whither should I fly?
85    I have done no harm. But I remember now
I am in this earthly world, where to do harm
Is often laudable, to do good sometime
Accounted dangerous folly. Why then, alas,
Do I put up that womanly defense
90    To say I have done no harm?—What are these faces?

*[Enter Murderers.]*

**Murderer.** Where is your husband?

**Lady Macduff.** I hope, in no place so unsanctified
Where such as thou mayst find him.

**Murderer.**                             He's a traitor.

95  **Son.** Thou liest, thou shag-eared villain!

**Murderer.**                             What, you egg!

*[Stabbing him.]*

    Young fry of treachery!

**Son.**                 He has killed me, mother.
    Run away, I pray you!                          *[Dies.]*

*[Exit Lady Macduff, crying "Murder!" followed by Murderers.]*

---

**66–74** Her son points out that traitors far outnumber honest men in this troubled time. The mother's terms of affection, **monkey** and **prattler** (childish talker), suggest that his playfulness has won her over.

**75–83** The messenger, who knows Lady Macduff is an honorable person (**in your state of honor I am perfect**), delivers a polite but desperate warning, urging her to flee immediately. While he apologizes for scaring her, he warns that she faces a deadly (**fell**) cruelty, one dangerously close (**too nigh**).

**87 laudable:** praiseworthy.

**92 unsanctified:** unholy.

**95 shag-eared:** long-haired. Note how quickly the son reacts to the word traitor. *How do you think he feels about his father?*

**97 Young fry:** small fish.

# *Responding to Reading*

1. Lady Macduff thinks her husband's flight to England is treasonous, while Ross defends it as wise. With whom do you agree? Why?

    **Think about**
    - the dangers that Macduff and his family face
    - what Macduff hopes to achieve in England

2. What kind of relationship do Lady Macduff and her son have?

3. Up to this point in the play, four people have been murdered. Whose murder affects you the most strongly? Why?

## Scene 3 *England. Before King Edward's palace.*

*Macduff urges Malcolm to join him in an invasion of Scotland, where the people suffer under Macbeth's harsh rule. Since Malcolm is uncertain of Macduff's motives, he tests him to see what kind of king Macduff would support. Once convinced of Macduff's honesty, Malcolm tells him that he has ten thousand soldiers ready to launch an attack. Ross arrives to tell them that some revolts against Macbeth have already begun. Reluctantly, Ross tells Macduff about the murder of his family. Wild with grief, Macduff vows to confront Macbeth and avenge the murders.*

*[Enter Malcolm and Macduff.]*

**Malcolm.** Let us seek out some desolate shade, and there
    Weep our sad bosoms empty.

**Macduff.**                  Let us rather
    Hold fast the mortal sword and, like good men,
5    Bestride our downfall'n birthdom. Each new morn
    New widows howl, new orphans cry, new sorrows
    Strike heaven on the face, that it resounds
    As if it felt with Scotland and yelled out
    Like syllable of dolor.

10 **Malcolm.**              What I believe, I'll wail;
    What know, believe; and what I can redress,
    As I shall find the time to friend, I will.
    What you have spoke, it may be so perchance.
    This tyrant, whose sole name blisters our tongues,
15    Was once thought honest; you have loved him well;
    He hath not touched you yet. I am young; but something
    You may discern of him through me, and wisdom

**1–9** In response to Malcolm's depression about Scotland, Macduff advises that they grab a deadly (***mortal***) sword and defend their homeland (***birthdom***), as a soldier might stand over a fallen (***downfall'n***) comrade to protect him. The anguished cries of Macbeth's victims strike heaven and make the skies echo with cries of sorrow (***syllable of dolor***).

**10–18** Malcolm's response shows his skeptical caution. He will grieve only for what he knows to be true; he will strike back only if the time is right (***As I shall find the time to friend***). Macduff may be honorable (***honest***), but he may be deceiving Malcolm to gain a reward from Macbeth (***something / You may discern of him through me***).

To offer up a weak, poor, innocent lamb
20  T' appease an angry god.

**Macduff.** I am not treacherous.

**Malcolm.**                    But Macbeth is.
A good and virtuous nature may recoil
In an imperial charge. But I shall crave your pardon.
25  That which you are, my thoughts cannot transpose.
Angels are bright still, though the brightest fell.
Though all things foul would wear the brows of grace,
Yet grace must still look so.

**Macduff.**                    I have lost my hopes.

30  **Malcolm.** Perchance even there where I did find my
        doubts.
Why in that rawness left you wife and child,
Those precious motives, those strong knots of love,
Without leave-taking? I pray you,
35  Let not my jealousies be your dishonors,
But mine own safeties. You may be rightly just,
Whatever I shall think.

**Macduff.**                    Bleed, bleed, poor country!
Great tyranny, lay thou thy basis sure,
40  For goodness dare not check thee! Wear thou thy
        wrongs;
The title is affeered! Fare thee well, lord.
I would not be the villain that thou think'st
For the whole space that's in the tyrant's grasp
45  And the rich East to boot.

**Malcolm.**                    Be not offended.
I speak not as in absolute fear of you.
I think our country sinks beneath the yoke;
It weeps, it bleeds, and each new day a gash
50  Is added to her wounds. I think withal
There would be hands uplifted in my right;
And here from gracious England have I offer
Of goodly thousands. But, for all this,
When I shall tread upon the tyrant's head
55  Or wear it on my sword, yet my poor country
Shall have more vices than it had before,
More suffer and more sundry ways than ever,
By him that shall succeed.

**Macduff.**                    What should he be?

**19–20** Macduff may betray the weak Malcolm, offering him as a sacrifice to please an (**angry god**), Macbeth.

**22–28** Malcolm further explains the reasons for his suspicions. Even a good person may fall (**recoil**) into wickedness because of a king's command (**imperial charge**). If Macduff is innocent, he will not be harmed by these suspicions, which cannot change (**transpose**) his nature (**That which you are**). Virtue cannot be damaged even by those who fall into evil, like Lucifer (the **brightest** angel), and disguise themselves as virtuous (**wear the brows of grace**). In contrast to evil, virtue lives up to appearance.

**30–37** Malcolm cannot understand how Macduff could leave his family, a source of inspiration (**motives**) and love, in an unprotected state (**rawness**). He asks him not to be insulted by his suspicions (**jealousies**); Malcolm is guarding his own safety.

**38–45** Losing heart because of Malcolm's comments, Macduff fears the worst for his country. Macbeth's tyranny can lay a solid foundation (**basis**) because goodness, in the person of Malcolm, will not stand against him. Macbeth can enjoy ill-gotten gains now that his right to the crown is confirmed (**affeered**), Macduff insists that nothing could turn him into a villain.

**47 I speak...of you:** I am not certain that I need to fear you.

**50–53 I think...thousands:** Malcolm says that many people (**hands**) would join his cause and that the English have already offered thousands of men.

**55–58 yet my...succeed:** To test Macduff's honor and loyalty, Malcolm begins a lengthy description of his own fictitious vices. He suggests that Scotland may suffer more under his rule than under Macbeth's.

**Malcolm.** It is myself I mean; in whom I know
60
All the particulars of vice so grafted
That, when they shall be opened, black Macbeth
Will seem as pure as snow, and the poor state
Esteem him as a lamb, being compared
65
With my confineless harms.

**Macduff.** Not in the legions
Of horrid hell can come a devil more damned
In evils to top Macbeth.

**Malcolm.** I grant him bloody,
70
Luxurious, avaricious, false, deceitful,
Sudden, malicious, smacking of every sin
That has a name. But there's no bottom, none,
In my voluptuousness. Your wives, your daughters,
Your matrons, and your maids could not fill up
75
The cistern of my lust; and my desire
All continent impediments would o'erbear
That did oppose my will. Better Macbeth
Than such an one to reign.

**Macduff.** Boundless intemperance
80
In nature is a tyranny. It hath been
The untimely emptying of the happy throne
And fall of many kings. But fear not yet
To take upon you what is yours. You may
Convey your pleasures in a spacious plenty,
85
And yet seem cold—the time you may so hoodwink.
We have willing dames enough. There cannot be
That vulture in you to devour so many
As will to greatness dedicate themselves,
Finding it so inclined.

**Malcolm.** With this there grows
90
In my most ill-composed affection such
A stanchless avarice that, were I King,
I should cut off the nobles for their lands,
Desire his jewels, and this other's house,
95
And my more-having would be as a sauce
To make me hunger more, that I should forge
Quarrels unjust against the good and loyal,
Destroying them for wealth.

**Macduff.** This avarice
100
Sticks deeper, grows with more pernicious root
Than summer-seeming lust; and it hath been

**60–65** Malcolm says that his own vices are so plentiful and deeply planted (**grafted**) that Macbeth will seem innocent by comparison.

**70 Luxurious:** lustful.

**71 Sudden:** violent; **smacking:** tasting.

**73 voluptuousness:** lust.

**75 cistern:** large storage tank.

**75–78** His lust is so great that it would overpower (**o'erbear**) all restraining obstacles (**continent impediments**).

**79–89** Macduff offers an analysis of how Malcolm's lust may be controlled after he becomes king. Macduff describes uncontrolled desire (**Boundless intemperance**) as a tyrant of human nature that has caused the early (**untimely**) downfall of many kings. When Malcolm is king, however, he can still have his pleasures in abundance and fool everyone (**the time you may so hoodwink**) into believing that he is pure (**cold**). His lustful appetite (**vulture in you**) cannot be so great that it would not be satisfied by the many women willing to give themselves (**dedicate**) to a king. *Do you think Macduff's prediction is accurate?*

**90–98** Malcolm adds insatiable greed (**stanchless avarice**) to the list of evils in his disposition (**affection**). If king, he would steal from his nobles, and his acquisitions (**more-having**) would only spur his desire for more. He would even invent excuses for destroying good nobles in order to seize their wealth.

**99–105** Macduff recognizes that greed is a deeper-rooted problem than lust, which passes as quickly as the summer

The sword of our slain kings. Yet do not fear.
Scotland hath foisons to fill up your will
Of your mere own. All these are portable,
105   With other graces weighed.

**Malcolm.** But I have none. The king-becoming graces,
As justice, verity, temp'rance, stableness,
Bounty, perseverance, mercy, lowliness,
Devotion, patience, courage, fortitude,
110   I have no relish of them, but abound
In the division of each several crime,
Acting it many ways. Nay, had I pow'r, I should
Pour the sweet milk of concord into hell,
Uproar the universal peace, confound
115   All unity on earth.

**Macduff.**              O Scotland, Scotland!

**Malcolm.** If such a one be fit to govern, speak.
I am as I have spoken.

**Macduff.**                Fit to govern?
120   No, not to live. O nation miserable,
With an untitled tyrant bloody-scept'red,
When shalt thou see thy wholesome days again,
Since that the truest issue of thy throne
By his own interdiction stands accursed
125   And does blaspheme his breed? Thy royal father
Was a most sainted king; the queen that bore thee,
Oft'ner upon her knees than on her feet,
Died every day she lived. Fare thee well!
These evils thou repeat'st upon thyself
130   Have banished me from Scotland. O my breast,
Thy hope ends here!

**Malcolm.**                Macduff, this noble passion,
Child of integrity, hath from my soul
Wiped the black scruples, reconciled my thoughts
135   To thy good truth and honor. Devilish Macbeth
By many of these trains hath sought to win me
Into his power; and modest wisdom plucks me
From over-credulous haste; but God above
Deal between thee and me! for even now
140   I put myself to thy direction and
Unspeak mine own detraction, here abjure
The taints and blames I laid upon myself
For strangers to my nature. I am yet

(**summer-seeming**). Many kings have been killed for their greed. But the King's property alone (**Of your mere own**) offers plenty (**foisons**) to satisfy his desire. Malcolm's vices can be tolerated (**are portable**) when balanced against his virtues. *Do you think Macduff's position is sensible?*

**106–115** Malcolm claims that he lacks all the virtues appropriate to a king (**king-becoming graces**). His list of missing virtues includes truthfulness (**verity**), consistency (**stableness**), generosity (**Bounty**), humility (**lowliness**), and religious devotion. In contrast, his crimes are abundant and varied. He would shatter the world's peace and destroy all harmony (**concord**) if he could.

**119–131** Macduff despairs at news of the apparent depth of Malcolm's evil. He can see no prospect of relief for Scotland's suffering under a tyrant who has no right to the throne (**untitled**). The rightful heir (**truest issue**), Malcolm, bans himself from the throne (**By his own interdiction**) because of his evil. Malcolm's vices slander his parents (**blaspheme his breed**)—his saintly father and his mother who renounced the world (**Died every day**) for the sake of her religion. Since Macduff will not help an evil man to become king, he will not be able to return to Scotland.

**132–143** Macduff has finally convinced Malcolm of his honesty, removing all suspicions (**scruples**). Malcolm explains that his caution (**modest wisdom**) resulted from his fear of Macbeth's tricks. He takes back his accusations against himself (**Unspeak mine own detraction**) and renounces (**abjure**) the evils he previously claimed.

Unknown to woman, never was forsworn,
145 Scarcely have coveted what was mine own,
At no time broke my faith, would not betray
The devil to his fellow, and delight
No less in truth than life. My first false speaking
Was this upon myself. What I am truly,
150 Is thine and my poor country's to command;
Whither indeed, before thy here-approach,
Old Siward with ten thousand warlike men
Already at a point was setting forth.
Now we'll together; and the chance of goodness
155 Be like our warranted quarrel! Why are you silent?

**Macduff.** Such welcome and unwelcome things at once
'Tis hard to reconcile.

[Enter a Doctor.]

**Malcolm.** Well, more anon. Comes the King forth, I pray
you?

160 **Doctor.** Ay, sir. There are a crew of wretched souls
That stay his cure. Their malady convinces
The great assay of art; but at his touch,
Such sanctity hath heaven given his hand,
They presently amend.

165 **Malcolm.**                    I thank you, doctor.

[Exit Doctor.]

**Macduff.** What's the disease he means?

**Malcolm.**                              'Tis called the evil:
A most miraculous work in this good king,
Which often since my here-remain in England
170 I have seen him do. How he solicits heaven
Himself best knows; but strangely-visited people,
All swol'n and ulcerous, pitiful to the eye,
The mere despair of surgery, he cures,
Hanging a golden stamp about their necks,
175 Put on with holy prayers; and 'tis spoken,
To the succeeding royalty he leaves
The healing benediction. With this strange virtue,
He hath a heavenly gift of prophecy,
And sundry blessings hang about his throne
180 That speak him full of grace.

[Enter Ross.]

**144–155** In fact, he is pure, sincere, and honest—a true servant of his country. He already has an army, ten thousand troops belonging to old Siward, the Earl of Northumberland. Now that Macduff is an ally, he hopes the battle's result will match the justice of their cause (**warranted quarrel**).
*Why is Macduff left speechless by Malcolm's revelation?*

**160–180** Edward the Confessor, King of England, could reportedly heal the disease of scrofula (**the evil**) by his saintly touch. The doctor describes people who cannot be helped by medicine's best efforts (**The great assay of art**) waiting for the touch of the King's hand. Edward has cured many victims of this disease. Each time, he hangs a gold coin around their necks and offers prayers, a healing ritual that he will teach to his royal descendants (**succeeding royalty**).

**Macduff.**                    See who comes here.

**Malcolm.** My countryman; but yet I know him not.

**Macduff.** My ever gentle cousin, welcome hither.

**Malcolm.** I know him now. Good God betimes remove
185     The means that makes us strangers!

**Ross.**                    Sir, amen.

**Macduff.** Stands Scotland where it did?

**Ross.**                    Alas, poor country,
         Almost afraid to know itself! It cannot
190     Be called our mother, but our grave; where nothing,
         But who knows nothing, is once seen to smile;
         Where sighs and groans, and shrieks that rent the air,
         Are made, not marked; where violent sorrow seems
         A modern ecstasy. The dead man's knell
195     Is there scarce asked for who; and good men's lives
         Expire before the flowers in their caps,
         Dying or ere they sicken.

**Macduff.**                    O, relation
         Too nice, and yet too true!

200  **Malcolm.**                    What's the newest grief?

**Ross.** That of an hour's age doth hiss the speaker;
         Each minute teems a new one.

**Macduff.**                    How does my wife?

**Ross.** Why, well.

205  **Macduff.**         And all my children?

**Ross.**                    Well too.

**Macduff.** The tyrant has not battered at their peace?

**Ross.** No, they were well at peace when I did leave 'em.

**Macduff.** Be not a niggard of your speech. How goes't?

210  **Ross.** When I came hither to transport the tidings
         Which I have heavily borne, there ran a rumor
         Of many worthy fellows that were out;
         Which was to my belief witnessed the rather
         For that I saw the tyrant's power afoot.
215     Now is the time of help. Your eye in Scotland
         Would create soldiers, make our women fight
         To doff their dire distresses.

**184–185 Good God...strangers:** May God remove Macbeth, who is the cause (**means**) of our being strangers.

**188–197** Ross describes Scotland's terrible condition. In a land where screams have become so common that they go unnoticed (**Are made, not marked**), violent sorrow becomes a commonplace emotion (**modern ecstasy**). So many have died that people no longer ask for their names, and good men die before their time.

**198–199 relation / Too nice:** news that is too accurate.

**201–202** If the news is more than an hour old, listeners hiss at the speaker for being outdated; every minute gives birth to a new grief.

**208 well at peace:** Ross knows about the murder of Macduff's wife and son, but the news is too terrible to report.

**211–217** Notice how Ross avoids the subject of Macduff's family. He mentions the rumors of nobles who are rebelling (**out**) against Macbeth. Ross believes the rumors because he saw Macbeth's troops on the march (**tyrant's power afoot**). The presence (**eye**) of Malcolm and Macduff in Scotland would help raise soldiers and remove (**doff**) Macbeth's evil (**dire distresses**).

**Malcolm.** Be't their comfort
We are coming thither. Gracious England hath
220 Lent us good Siward and ten thousand men.
An older and a better soldier none
That Christendom gives out.

**Ross.** Would I could answer
This comfort with the like! But I have words
225 That would be howled out in the desert air,
Where hearing should not latch them.

**Macduff.** What concern they?
The general cause? or is it a fee-grief
Due to some single breast?

230 **Ross.** No mind that's honest
But in it shares some woe, though the main part
Pertains to you alone.

**Macduff.** If it be mine,
Keep it not from me, quickly let me have it.

235 **Ross.** Let not your ears despise my tongue for ever,
Which shall possess them with the heaviest sound
That ever yet they heard.

**Macduff.** Humh! I guess at it.

**Ross.** Your castle is surprised; your wife and babes
240 Savagely slaughtered. To relate the manner
Were, on the quarry of these murdered deer,
To add the death of you.

**Malcolm.** Merciful heaven!
What, man! Ne'er pull your hat upon your brows.
245 Give sorrow words. The grief that does not speak
Whispers the o'erfraught heart and bids it break.

**Macduff.** My children too?

**Ross.** Wife, children, servants, all
That could be found.

250 **Macduff.** And I must be from thence?
My wife killed too?

**Ross.** I have said.

**Malcolm.** Be comforted.
Let's make us med'cines of our great revenge
255 To cure this deadly grief.

---

**221–222 An older...gives out:** There is no soldier with a better reputation or more experience than Siward.

**225 would:** should.

**226 latch:** catch.

**228 fee-grief:** private sorrow.

**230–231 No mind...woe:** Every honorable (**honest**) person shares in this sorrow.

**240–242 To relate...of you:** Ross won't add to Macduff's sorrow by telling him how his family was killed. He compares Macduff's dear ones to the piled bodies of killed deer (**quarry**).

**245–246 The grief...break:** Silence will only push an overburdened heart to the breaking point.

**250** Macduff laments his absence from the castle.

**Macduff.** He has no children. All my pretty ones?
Did you say all? O hell-kite! All?
What, all my pretty chickens and their dam
At one fell swoop?

260  **Malcolm.** Dispute it like a man.

**Macduff.**                          I shall do so;
But I must also feel it as a man.
I cannot but remember such things were
That were most precious to me. Did heaven look on
265  And would not take their part? Sinful Macduff,
They were all struck for thee! Naught that I am,
Not for their own demerits, but for mine,
Fell slaughter on their souls. Heaven rest them now!

**Malcolm.** Be this the whetstone of your sword. Let grief
270  Convert to anger; blunt not the heart, enrage it.

**Macduff.** O, I could play the woman with mine eyes
And braggart with my tongue! But, gentle heavens,
Cut short all intermission. Front to front
Bring thou this fiend of Scotland and myself.
275  Within my sword's length set him. If he scape,
Heaven forgive him too!

**Malcolm.**                          This tune goes manly.
Come, go we to the King. Our power is ready;
Our lack is nothing but our leave. Macbeth
280  Is ripe for shaking, and the pow'rs above
Put on their instruments. Receive what cheer you may.
The night is long that never finds the day.

*[Exeunt.]*

**256–259** *He has no children:* possibly a reference to Macbeth, who has no children to be killed for revenge. Macduff compares Macbeth to a bird of prey (*hell-kite*) who kills defenseless chickens and their mother.

**266** *Naught:* nothing.

**269** *whetstone:* grindstone used for sharpening.

**271–276** *I could play...him too:* Macduff won't act like a woman by crying or like a braggart by boasting. He wants no delay (*intermission*) to keep him from face-to-face combat with Macbeth. Macduff ironically swears that, if Macbeth escapes, he deserves heaven's mercy.

**277–282** Our troops are ready to attack, needing only the King's permission (*Our lack is nothing but our leave*). Like a ripe fruit, Macbeth is ready to fall, and heavenly powers are preparing to assist us. The long night of Macbeth's evil will be broken.

*R*esponding *to Reading* ——————————————————

1. Explain Malcolm's motives for testing Macduff the way that he does. Do you think his test was sensible and fair? Why or why not?

   **Think about**
   • Malcolm's fears for Scotland and himself
   • what Malcolm learned from his father's experience with traitors
   • Macduff's past friendship with Macbeth

2. Who do you think is the more admirable character in this scene, Macduff or Malcolm? Explain your choice, using examples from the scene.

## Responding to Reading

### First Impressions

1. Do you have any sympathy left for Macbeth? Why or why not?

### Second Thoughts

2. What do you think will happen when Malcolm and Macduff finally confront Macbeth? Give the basis of your prediction.

   **Think about**
   - the prophecies about Macbeth's future revealed in Scene 1 of this act
   - Macduff's pledge to battle Macbeth face to face
   - what motivates each of the characters

3. Do you think Malcolm would make a good king? Why or why not?

   **Think about**
   - his testing of Macduff
   - whether he has the necessary strength and virtues
   - the similarities and differences between him and Duncan

4. Some directors eliminate Malcolm's lengthy test of Macduff from their production of the play. If you were a director, would you include the scene or not? Explain what you would gain or lose by your decision.

5. Which character is the most admirable one in the play so far? Explain your choice.

## Literary Concepts: Motif and Mood

A recurring word, phrase, image, object, or action in a work of literature is called a **motif**. Motifs help to unify a work and contribute to its themes. The motif of blood appears throughout *Macbeth*. In Act One, Scene 2, King Duncan encounters a "bloody man" who tells him about the battle with the traitorous Macdonwald. In Act Two, Scene 1, Macbeth sees a bloody dagger. After the murder, he fears that he will not be able to wash his bloody "incarnadine" hands. Discuss how the references to blood contribute to your understanding of the play. Then find at least four references to blood in Act Four. How do these references contribute to your understanding of Macbeth and the effects of his actions?

**Mood** describes the dominant feeling that a literary work creates for a reader. For example, the opening scene with the witches in *Macbeth* creates an eerie and suspenseful mood. With a classmate review Scene 2 of Act Four and discuss the mood. How does Shakespeare create this mood?

## Writing Options

1. Choose one of the following motifs in the play: sleep, night, or ill-fitting clothes. Work in groups of four to find as many appearances of your motif as possible, with one person responsible for each act. Create a list of references, with act, scene, and line numbers.

2. Write out your predictions for the meaning of each of the four prophecies that Macbeth receives in Act Four, Scene 1.

3. Write a *TV Guide*-style summary of each scene in Act Four, as if they were episodes in a weekly television show.

4. Compare and contrast the leadership qualities of Macbeth and Malcolm, listing their similarities and differences in a chart.

## Options for Learning

**1** • **Witch Lore**  Working in small groups, investigate what people believed about witches during Shakespeare's time. You may find information in books about witches or Shakespeare or in introductions to *Macbeth* texts. Give an oral report of your findings.

**2** • **Double Toil and Trouble**  Imagine what might happen if a contemporary leader sought out the three Weird Sisters for predictions about current events. Choose a leader who is faced with a difficult problem, then role-play his or her meeting with the witches.

**3** • **Today's Political Stage**  Cast the parts of Duncan, Malcolm, Macduff, and Macbeth, assigning each role to a political leader, either past or present, who best fits the part. For example, you might choose a good but too trusting person for the role of Duncan or a person with a grudge for the role of Macduff. Explain your choices to the class.

**4** • **Apparitions**  Draw, sketch, or paint one or more of the apparitions that Macbeth sees, based on the descriptions given by Macbeth and in the stage directions.

**5** • **Actors' Art**  Stage one of the scenes, or part of a scene, for the class. You may want to rewrite the scene into a modern setting, using modern language, or you may prefer to perform it as Shakespeare wrote it.

# ACT FIVE

## *Scene 1*  *Macbeth's castle at Dunsinane.*

*A sleepwalking Lady Macbeth is observed by a concerned attendant, or gentlewoman, and a doctor. Lady Macbeth appears to be washing imagined blood from her hands. Her actions and confused speech greatly concern the doctor, and he warns the attendant to keep an eye on Lady Macbeth, fearing that she will harm herself.*

*[Enter a* Doctor of Physic *and a* Waiting Gentlewoman.*]*

**Doctor.** I have two nights watched with you, but can perceive no truth in your report. When was it she last walked?

**Gentlewoman.** Since his Majesty went into the field I have
5  seen her rise from her bed, throw her nightgown upon her, unlock her closet, take forth paper, fold it, write upon't, read it, afterwards seal it, and again return to bed; yet all this while in a most fast sleep.

**Doctor.** A great perturbation in nature, to receive at once
10  the benefit of sleep and do the effects of watching! In this slumb'ry agitation, besides her walking and other actual performances, what (at any time) have you heard her say?

**Gentlewoman.** That, sir, which I will not report after her.

15  **Doctor.** You may to me, and 'tis most meet you should.

**Gentlewoman.** Neither to you nor any one, having no witness to confirm my speech.

*[Enter* Lady Macbeth, *with a taper.]*

Lo you, here she comes! This is her very guise, and, upon my life, fast asleep! Observe her; stand close.

20  **Doctor.** How came she by that light?

**Gentlewoman.** Why, it stood by her. She has light by her continually. 'Tis her command.

**Doctor.** You see her eyes are open.

**Gentlewoman.** Ay, but their sense is shut.

25  **Doctor.** What is it she does now? Look how she rubs her hands.

**4 went into the field:** went to battle the rebels.

**9–10 A great . . . of watching:** To behave as though awake (**watching**) while sleeping is a sign of a greatly troubled nature.

**15 meet:** appropriate.

**16–17** The attendant won't repeat what Lady Macbeth has said because there are no other witnesses to confirm her report. *What is she worried about?*

**18–19 guise:** usual manner; **stand close:** Hide yourself.

**20 that light:** her candle.

**21–22** *Why might Lady Macbeth want a light by her at all times?*

*"Out, damned spot!*
*out, I say!"*

**Gentlewoman.** It is an accustomed action with her, to seem thus washing her hands. I have known her continue in this a quarter of an hour.

30 **Lady Macbeth.** Yet here's a spot.

**Doctor.** Hark, she speaks! I will set down what comes from her, to satisfy my remembrance the more strongly.

**Lady Macbeth.** Out, damned spot! out, I say! One; two.
35 Why then 'tis time to do't. Hell is murky. Fie, my lord, fie! a soldier, and afeard? What need we fear who knows it, when none can call our pow'r to accompt? Yet who would have thought the old man to have had so much blood in him?

40 **Doctor.** Do you mark that?

**Lady Macbeth.** The Thane of Fife had a wife. Where is she now? What, will these hands ne'er be clean? No more o' that, my lord, no more o' that! You mar all with this starting.

**34–39** Lady Macbeth's mind wanders as she repeats the motions of washing her hands. She refers to hell's darkness, then she relives how she persuaded her husband to murder Duncan; she had believed that their power would keep them from being held accountable (***accompt***). Finally, she envisions herself covered with Duncan's blood.

**41–44** Lady Macbeth shows guilt about Macduff's wife. Then she addresses her husband, as if he were having another ghostly fit (***starting***).

**Doctor.** Go to, go to! You have known what you should not.

**Gentlewoman.** She has spoke what she should not, I am sure of that. Heaven knows what she has known.

**Lady Macbeth.** Here's the smell of the blood still. All the perfumes of Arabia will not sweeten this little hand. Oh, oh, oh!

**Doctor.** What a sigh is there! The heart is sorely charged.

**Gentlewoman.** I would not have such a heart in my bosom for the dignity of the whole body.

**Doctor.** Well, well, well.

**Gentlewoman.** Pray God it be, sir.

**Doctor.** This disease is beyond my practice. Yet I have known those which have walked in their sleep who have died holily in their beds.

**Lady Macbeth.** Wash your hands, put on your nightgown, look not so pale! I tell you yet again, Banquo's buried. He cannot come out on's grave.

**Doctor.** Even so?

**Lady Macbeth.** To bed, to bed! There's knocking at the gate. Come, come, come, come, give me your hand! What's done cannot be undone. To bed, to bed, to bed!

*[Exit.]*

**Doctor.** Will she go now to bed?

**Gentlewoman.** Directly.

**Doctor.** Foul whisp'rings are abroad. Unnatural deeds
Do breed unnatural troubles. Infected minds
To their deaf pillows will discharge their secrets.
More needs she the divine than the physician.
God, God forgive us all! Look after her;
Remove from her the means of all annoyance,
And still keep eyes upon her. So good night.
My mind she has mated, and amazed my sight.
I think, but dare not speak.

**Gentlewoman.** Good night, good doctor.

*[Exeunt.]*

**52 *sorely charged:*** heavily burdened.

**53–54** The gentlewoman says that she would not want Lady Macbeth's heavy heart in exchange for being queen.

**57 *practice:*** skill.

**62 *on's:*** of his.

**63** *What has the doctor learned so far from Lady Macbeth's ramblings?*

**69 *Foul whisp'rings are abroad:*** Rumors of evil deeds are circulating.

**72** She needs a priest more than a doctor.

**74 *annoyance:*** injury. The doctor may be worried about the possibility of Lady Macbeth's committing suicide.

**76 *mated:*** astonished.

## Responding to Reading

1. What might be the causes of Lady's Macbeth's sleepwalking?

   **Think about**
   - why she is afraid of blood and darkness
   - her role in the three murders that are indirectly mentioned
   - what the doctor says about her need for a priest

2. Compare and contrast Lady Macbeth's previous attitudes and actions and her current condition.

   **Think about**
   - her comment that a "little water clears us of this deed," in Act Two, Scene 2
   - the significance of washing her hands of blood
   - her earlier comments about Macbeth's fears and visions

3. Why does the doctor "dare not speak" about what he has heard?

4. What do you think will happen to Lady Macbeth?

---

**Scene 2**   *The country near Dunsinane.*

*The Scottish rebels, led by Menteith, Caithness, Angus, and Lennox, have come to Birnam Wood to join Malcolm and his English army. They know that Dunsinane has been fortified by a furious and brave Macbeth. They also know that his men neither love nor respect him.*

[*Drum and Colors. Enter* Menteith, Caithness, Angus, Lennox, Soldiers.]

**Menteith.** The English pow'r is near, led on by Malcolm,
His uncle Siward, and the good Macduff.
Revenges burn in them; for their dear causes
Would to the bleeding and the grim alarm
5     Excite the mortified man.

**Angus.**                Near Birnam Wood
Shall we well meet them; that way are they coming.

**Caithness.** Who knows if Donalbain be with his brother?

**Lennox.** For certain, sir, he is not. I have a file
10     Of all the gentry. There is Siward's son
And many unrough youths that even now
Protest their first of manhood.

**Menteith.**              What does the tyrant?

**3–5 for their dear . . . man:** The cause of Malcolm and Macduff is so deeply felt that a dead (***mortified***) man would respond to their call to arms (***alarm***).

**11–12 many . . . manhood:** many soldiers who are too young to grow beards (***unrough***), that is, who have hardly reached manhood.

**Caithness.** Great Dunsinane he strongly fortifies.
15      Some say he's mad; others, that lesser hate him,
        Do call it valiant fury; but for certain
        He cannot buckle his distempered cause
        Within the belt of rule.

**Angus.**                              Now does he feel
20      His secret murders sticking on his hands.
        Now minutely revolts upbraid his faith-breach.
        Those he commands move only in command,
        Nothing in love. Now does he feel his title
        Hang loose about him, like a giant's robe
25      Upon a dwarfish thief.

**Menteith.**                          Who then shall blame
        His pestered senses to recoil and start,
        When all that is within him does condemn
        Itself for being there?

30 **Caithness.**                       Well, march we on
        To give obedience where 'tis truly owed.
        Meet we the med'cine of the sickly weal;
        And with him pour we in our country's purge
        Each drop of us.

35 **Lennox.**              Or so much as it needs
        To dew the sovereign flower and drown the weeds.
        Make we our march towards Birnam.

*[Exeunt, marching.]*

**17–18** Like a man so swollen with disease (***distempered***) that he cannot buckle his belt, Macbeth cannot keep his evil actions under control.

**21** Every minute, the revolts against Macbeth shame him for his treachery (***faith-breach***).

**26–29** Macbeth's troubled nerves (***pestered senses***)—the product of his guilty conscience—have made him jumpy.

**30–34** Caithness and the others will give their loyalty to the only help (***med'cine***) for the sick country (***weal***). They are willing to sacrifice their last drop of blood to cleanse (***purge***) Scotland.

**35–37** Lennox compares Malcolm to a flower that needs the blood of patriots to water (***dew***) it and drown out weeds like Macbeth.

## *Scene 3*   *Dunsinane. A room in the castle.*

*Macbeth awaits battle, confident of victory because of what he learned from the witches. After hearing that a huge army is ready to march upon his castle, he expresses bitter regrets about his life. While Macbeth prepares for battle, the doctor reports that he cannot cure Lady Macbeth, whose illness is mental, not physical.*

*[Enter Macbeth, Doctor, and Attendants.]*

**Macbeth.** Bring me no more reports. Let them fly all!
        Till Birnam Wood remove to Dunsinane,
        I cannot taint with fear. What's the boy Malcolm?
        Was he not born of woman? The spirits that know
5       All mortal consequences have pronounced me thus:

**1–5** Macbeth wants no more news of thanes who have gone to Malcolm's side.

"Fear not, Macbeth. No man that's born of woman
Shall e'er have power upon thee." Then fly, false thanes,
And mingle with the English epicures.
10 The mind I sway by and the heart I bear
Shall never sag with doubt nor shake with fear.

[*Enter* Servant.]

The devil damn thee black, thou cream-faced loon!
Where got'st thou that goose look?

**Servant.** There is ten thousand—

15 **Macbeth.**                             Geese, villain?

**Servant.**                                                Soldiers, sir.

**Macbeth.** Go prick thy face and over-red thy fear,
Thou lily-livered boy. What soldiers, patch?
Death of thy soul! Those linen cheeks of thine
20 Are counselors to fear. What soldiers, whey-face?

**Servant.** The English force, so please you.

**Macbeth.** Take thy face hence.

[*Exit* Servant.]

                              Seyton!—I am sick at heart,
When I behold—Seyton, I say!—This push
25 Will cheer me ever, or disseat me now.
I have lived long enough. My way of life
Is fallen into the sere, the yellow leaf;
And that which should accompany old age,
As honor, love, obedience, troops of friends,
30 I must not look to have; but, in their stead,
Curses not loud but deep, mouth-honor, breath,
Which the poor heart would fain deny, and dare not.
Seyton!

[*Enter* Seyton.]

**Seyton.** What's your gracious pleasure?

35 **Macbeth.**                                     What news more?

**Seyton.** All is confirmed, my lord, which was reported.

**Macbeth.** I'll fight, till from my bones my flesh be hacked.
Give me my armor.

**Seyton.**                        'Tis not needed yet.

40 **Macbeth.** I'll put it on.
Send out mo horses, skirr the country round;

**6–11** Macbeth will not be infected (*taint*) with fear, because the witches (*spirits*), who know all human events (*mortal consequences*), have convinced him that he is invincible. He mocks the self-indulgent English (*English epicures*), then swears that he will never lack confidence.

**12–13** *loon:* stupid rascal; *goose look:* a look of fear.

**17–20** Macbeth suggests that the servant cut his face so that blood will hide his cowardice. He repeatedly insults the servant, calling him a coward (*lily-livered*) and a clown (*patch*), and making fun of his white complexion (*linen cheeks, whey-face*).

**24–32** *This push . . . dare not:* The upcoming battle will either make Macbeth secure (*cheer me ever*) or dethrone (*disseat*) him. He bitterly compares his life to a withered (*sere*) leaf. He cannot look forward to old age with its friends and honor, but only to curses and empty flattery (*mouth-honor, breath*) from those too timid (*the poor heart*) to tell the truth.

**41** *mo:* more; *skirr:* scour.

Hang those that talk of fear. Give me mine armor.
How does your patient, doctor?

**Doctor.**                                   Not so sick, my lord,
45    As she is troubled with thick-coming fancies
That keep her from her rest.

**Macbeth.**                           Cure her of that!
Canst thou not minister to a mind diseased,
Pluck from the memory a rooted sorrow,
50    Raze out the written troubles of the brain,
And with some sweet oblivious antidote
Cleanse the stuffed bosom of that perilous stuff
Which weighs upon the heart?

**Doctor.**                               Therein the patient
55    Must minister to himself.

**Macbeth.** Throw physic to the dogs, I'll none of it!—
Come, put mine armor on. Give me my staff.
Seyton, send out.—Doctor, the thanes fly from me.—
Come, sir, dispatch.—If thou couldst, doctor, cast
60    The water of my land, find her disease,
And purge it to a sound and pristine health,
I would applaud thee to the very echo,
That should applaud again.—Pull't off, I say.—
What rhubarb, senna, or what purgative drug,
65    Would scour these English hence? Hear'st thou of
them?

**Doctor.** Ay, my good lord. Your royal preparation
Makes us hear something.

**Macbeth.**                           Bring it after me!
70    I will not be afraid of death and bane
Till Birnam Forest come to Dunsinane.

**Doctor.** *[Aside]* Were I from Dunsinane away and clear,
Profit again should hardly draw me here.

*[Exeunt.]*

**47–53** Macbeth asks the doctor to remove the sorrow from Lady Macbeth's memory, to erase (***Raze out***) the troubles imprinted on her mind, and to relieve her overburdened heart (***stuffed bosom***) of its guilt (***perilous stuff***). *Do you think Macbeth shares his wife's feelings of guilt?*

**56–66** Macbeth has lost his faith in the ability of medicine (***physic***) to help his wife. As he struggles into his armor, he says that if the doctor could successfully search the kingdom (***cast . . . land***) to find a cure for Lady Macbeth's disease, Macbeth would never stop praising him. *What kind of mood is Macbeth in?*

**69–71** Macbeth leaves for battle, telling Seyton to bring the armour. He declares his fearlessness before death and destruction (***bane***).

# Responding to Reading

1. What do you think will happen now that other Scottish noblemen are joining Malcolm, Macduff, and Siward?

2. What is Macbeth's state of mind in scene 3? Cite quotations to support your opinion.

***Scene 4***   *The country near Birnam Wood.*

*The rebels and English forces have met in Birnam Wood. Malcolm orders each soldier to cut tree branches to camouflage himself. In this way Birnam Wood will march upon Dunsinane.*

[*Drum and Colors. Enter* Malcolm, Siward, Macduff, Siward's Son, Menteith, Caithness, Angus, Lennox, Ross, *and* Soldiers, *marching.*]

**Malcolm.** Cousins, I hope the days are near at hand
    That chambers will be safe.

**Menteith.**　　　　　　　　　　　We doubt it nothing.

**Siward.** What wood is this before us?

5　**Menteith.**　　　　　　　　　　　The wood of Birnam.

**Malcolm.** Let every soldier hew him down a bough
    And bear't before him. Thereby shall we shadow
    The numbers of our host and make discovery
    Err in report of us.

10　**Soldiers.**　　　　　　　　It shall be done.

**Siward.** We learn no other but the confident tyrant
    Keeps still in Dunsinane and will endure
    Our setting down before't.

**Malcolm.**　　　　　　　　　　　'Tis his main hope;
15　For where there is advantage to be given,
    Both more and less have given him the revolt;
    And none serve with him but constrained things,
    Whose hearts are absent too.

**Macduff.**　　　　　　　　　　　Let our just censures
20　Attend the true event, and put we on
    Industrious soldiership.

**Siward.**　　　　　　　　　　　The time approaches
    That will with due decision make us know
    What we shall say we have, and what we owe.
25　Thoughts speculative their unsure hopes relate,
    But certain issue strokes must arbitrate;
    Towards which advance the war.

[*Exeunt, marching.*]

**6–9** Malcolm orders his men to cut down tree branches to camouflage themselves. This will conceal (**shadow**) the size of their army and confuse Macbeth's scouts. Consider the prophecy about Birnam Wood. *What do you now think the prophecy means?*

**13 *setting down:*** siege.

**14–18** Malcolm says that men of all ranks (**Both more and less**) have abandoned Macbeth. Only weak men who have been forced into service remain with him.

**19–21** Macduff warns against overconfidence and advises that they attend to the business of fighting.

**22–27** Siward says that the approaching battle will decide whether their claims will match what they actually possess (**owe**). Right now, their hopes and expectations are the product of guesswork (**thoughts speculative**); only fighting (**strokes**) can settle (**arbitrate**) the issue.

**Scene 5** *Dunsinane. Within the castle.*

*Convinced of his powers, Macbeth mocks the enemy; his slaughters have left him fearless. News of Lady Macbeth's death stirs little emotion, only a comment on the emptiness of life. However, when a messenger reports that Birnam Wood seems to be moving toward the castle, Macbeth grows agitated. Fearing that the prophecies have deceived him, he decides to leave the castle to fight and die on the battlefield.*

*[Enter Macbeth, Seyton, and Soldiers, with Drum and Colors.]*

**Macbeth.** Hang out our banners on the outward walls.
The cry is still, "They come!" Our castle's strength
Will laugh a siege to scorn. Here let them lie
Till famine and the ague eat them up.
5  Were they not forced with those that should be ours,
We might have met them dareful, beard to beard,
And beat them backward home.

*[A cry within of women.]*

What is that noise?

**Seyton.** It is the cry of women, my good lord. *[Exit.]*

10  **Macbeth.** I have almost forgot the taste of fears.
The time has been, my senses would have cooled
To hear a night-shriek, and my fell of hair
Would at a dismal treatise rouse and stir
As life were in't. I have supped full with horrors.
15  Direness, familiar to my slaughterous thoughts,
Cannot once start me.

*[Enter Seyton.]*

Wherefore was that cry?

**Seyton.** The Queen, my lord, is dead.

**Macbeth.** She should have died hereafter;
20  There would have been a time for such a word.
Tomorrow, and tomorrow, and tomorrow
Creeps in this petty pace from day to day
To the last syllable of recorded time;
And all our yesterdays have lighted fools
25  The way to dusty death. Out, out, brief candle!

**4** *ague:* fever.

**5–7** Macbeth complains that the attackers have been reinforced (**forced**) by deserters (**those that should be ours**), which has forced him to wait at Dunsinane instead of seeking victory on the battlefield.

**10-16** There was a time when a scream in the night would have frozen Macbeth in fear and a terrifying tale (**dismal treatise**) would have made his hair (**fell**) stand on end. But since he has fed on horror (**direness**), it cannot stir (**start**) him anymore.

**19–25** Macbeth wishes that his wife had died later (**hereafter**), when he would have had time to mourn her. He is moved to express despair about his own meaningless life: the future promises monotonous repetition (**Tomorrow, and tomorrow, and tomorrow**), and the past merely illustrates death's power. He wishes his life could be snuffed out like a candle.

Life's but a walking shadow, a poor player,
That struts and frets his hour upon the stage
And then is heard no more. It is a tale
Told by an idiot, full of sound and fury,
30    Signifying nothing.

[Enter a Messenger.]

Thou com'st to use thy tongue. Thy story quickly!

**Messenger.** Gracious my lord,
I should report that which I say I saw,
But know not how to do't.

35 **Macbeth.**                    Well, say, sir!

**Messenger.** As I did stand my watch upon the hill,
I looked toward Birnam, and anon methought
The wood began to move.

**Macbeth.**                    Liar and slave!

40 **Messenger.** Let me endure your wrath if't be not so.
Within this three mile may you see it coming;
I say, a moving grove.

**Macbeth.**                    If thou speak'st false,
Upon the next tree shalt thou hang alive,
45    Till famine cling thee. If thy speech be sooth,
I care not if thou dost for me as much.
I pull in resolution, and begin
To doubt the equivocation of the fiend,
That lies like truth. "Fear not, till Birnam Wood
50    Do come to Dunsinane!" and now a wood
Comes toward Dunsinane. Arm, arm, and out!
If this which he avouches does appear,
There is nor flying hence nor tarrying here.
I'gin to be aweary of the sun,
55    And wish the estate o' the world were now undone.
Ring the alarum bell! Blow wind, come wrack,
At least we'll die with harness on our back!

[Exeunt.]

**26–30** Macbeth compares life to an actor who only briefly plays a part. Life is senseless, like a tale told by a raving idiot. *Do you feel sorry for Macbeth here?*

**37 anon:** at once.

**43–57** The messenger's news has dampened Macbeth's determination (**resolution**); Macbeth begins to fear that the witches have tricked him (**To doubt the equivocation of the fiend**). His fear that the messenger tells the truth (**avouches**) makes him decide to confront the enemy instead of staying in his castle. Weary of life, he nevertheless decides to face death and ruin (**wrack**) with his armor (**harness**) on.

## *R*esponding to Reading —————————————————————————

1. Contrast Malcolm's attitude toward the upcoming battle with the views of Macduff and Siward. Who do you think is more reasonable? Why?

2. Discuss how you feel about Macbeth at the end of Scene 5.

   **Think about**
   - his reaction to the news of Lady Macbeth's death
   - the expression of despair in his "Tomorrow, and tomorrow" speech
   - his response to the news about Birnham Wood marching on Dunsinane

3. Do you think Macbeth deeply feels the death of his wife? Explain why or why not, using examples from the text to support your opinion.

**Scene 6** *Dunsinane. Before the castle.*

*Malcolm and the combined forces reach the castle, throw away their camouflage, and prepare for battle.*

*[Drum and Colors. Enter* Malcolm, Siward, Macduff, *and their* Army, *with boughs.]*

**Malcolm.** Now near enough. Your leavy screens throw
   down
   And show like those you are. You, worthy uncle,
   Shall with my cousin, your right noble son,
5   Lead our first battle. Worthy Macduff and we
   Shall take upon's what else remains to do,
   According to our order.

**1–7** Malcolm commands the troops to put down their branches (***leavy screens***) and gives the battle instructions.

**Siward.**                Fare you well.
   Do we but find the tyrant's power tonight,
10   Let us be beaten if we cannot fight.

**9 *power:*** forces.

**Macduff.** Make all our trumpets speak, give them all
   breath,
   Those clamorous harbingers of blood and death.

**13 *harbingers:*** announcers.

*[Exeunt. Alarums continued.]*

**Scene 7**  *Another part of the battlefield.*

*Macbeth kills young Siward, which restores his belief that he cannot be killed by any man born of a woman. Meanwhile, Macduff searches for the hated king. Young Siward's father reports that Macbeth's soldiers have surrendered and that many have even joined their attackers.*

*[Enter Macbeth.]*

**Macbeth.** They have tied me to a stake. I cannot fly,
But bearlike I must fight the course. What's he
That was not born of woman? Such a one
Am I to fear, or none.

*[Enter Young Siward.]*

5  **Young Siward.** What is thy name?

**Macbeth.**                     Thou'lt be afraid to hear it.

**Young Siward.** No; though thou call'st thyself a hotter
     name
Than any is in hell.

10  **Macbeth.**          My name's Macbeth.

**Young Siward.** The devil himself could not pronounce a
     title
More hateful to mine ear.

**Macbeth.**                No, nor more fearful.

15  **Young Siward.** Thou liest, abhorred tyrant! With my
     sword
I'll prove the lie thou speak'st.

*[Fight, and Young Siward slain.]*

**Macbeth.**                Thou wast born of woman.
But swords I smile at, weapons laugh to scorn,
20  Brandished by man that's of a woman born. *[Exit.]*

*[Alarums. Enter Macduff.]*

**Macduff.** That way the noise is. Tyrant, show thy face!
If thou beest slain and with no stroke of mine,
My wife and children's ghosts will haunt me still.
I cannot strike at wretched kerns, whose arms
25  Are hired to bear their staves. Either thou, Macbeth,
Or else my sword with an unbattered edge

**1–4** Macbeth compares himself to a bear tied to a post, a reference to the sport of bearbaiting, in which a bear was tied to a stake and attacked by dogs.

**18–20** *Do you think Macbeth is justified in his confidence?*

**21–27** Macduff enters alone. He wants to avenge the murders of his wife and children and hopes to find Macbeth before someone else has the chance to kill him. Macduff does not want to fight the miserable hired soldiers (**kerns**), who are armed only with spears (**staves**). If he can't fight Macbeth, Macduff will leave his sword unused (***undeeded***).

I sheathe again undeeded. There thou shouldst be.
By this great clatter one of greatest note
Seems bruited. Let me find him, Fortune!
30    And more I beg not.

*[Exit. Alarums.]*

*[Enter Malcolm and Siward.]*

**Siward.** This way, my lord. The castle's gently rendered:
    The tyrant's people on both sides do fight;
    The noble thanes do bravely in the war;
    The day almost itself professes yours,
35    And little is to do.

**Malcolm.**                We have met with foes
    That strike beside us.

**Siward.**                Enter, sir, the castle.

*[Exeunt. Alarum.]*

**27–30** After hearing sounds suggesting that a person of great distinction (**note**) is nearby, Macduff exits in pursuit of Macbeth.

**31 *gently rendered*:** surrendered without a fight.

**34** You have almost won the day.

**36–37** During the battle many of Macbeth's men deserted to Malcolm's army.

## Scene 8    *Another part of the battlefield.*

*Macduff finally hunts down Macbeth, who is reluctant to fight because he has already killed too many Macduffs. The still-proud Macbeth tells his enemy that no man born of a woman can defeat him, only to learn that Macduff was ripped from his mother's womb, thus not born naturally. Rather than face humiliation, Macbeth decides to fight to the death. After their fight takes them elsewhere, the Scottish lords, now in charge of Macbeth's castle, discuss young Siward's noble death. Macduff returns carrying Macbeth's bloody head, proclaiming final victory and declaring Malcolm king of Scotland. The new king thanks his supporters and promises rewards, while asking for God's help to restore order and harmony.*

*[Enter Macbeth.]*

**Macbeth.** Why should I play the Roman fool and die
    On mine own sword? Whiles I see lives, the gashes
    Do better upon them.

*[Enter Macduff.]*

**Macduff.**                Turn, hellhound, turn!

5    **Macbeth.** Of all men else I have avoided thee.
    But get thee back! My soul is too much charged
    With blood of thine already.

**Macduff.**                I have no words;
    My voice is in my sword, thou bloodier villain
10    Than terms can give thee out!

**1–3** Macbeth vows to continue fighting, refusing to commit suicide in the style of a defeated Roman general.

**5–7** Macbeth does not want to fight Macduff, having already killed so many members of Macduff's family. *Do you think Macbeth regrets his past actions?*

*[Fight. Alarum.]*

**Macbeth.**                                        Thou losest labor.
    As easy mayst thou the intrenchant air
    With thy keen sword impress as make me bleed.
    Let fall thy blade on vulnerable crests.
15   I bear a charmed life, which must not yield
    To one of woman born.

**Macduff.**                                        Despair thy charm!
    And let the angel whom thou still hast served
    Tell thee, Macduff was from his mother's womb
20   Untimely ripped.

**Macbeth.** Accursed be that tongue that tells me so,
    For it hath cowed my better part of man!
    And be these juggling fiends no more believed,
    That palter with us in a double sense,
25   That keep the word of promise to our ear
    And break it to our hope! I'll not fight with thee!

**Macduff.** Then yield thee, coward,
    And live to be the show and gaze o' the time!
    We'll have thee, as our rarer monsters are,
30   Painted upon a pole, and underwrit
    "Here may you see the tyrant."

**Macbeth.**                                        I will not yield,
    To kiss the ground before young Malcolm's feet
    And to be baited with the rabble's curse.
35   Though Birnam Wood be come to Dunsinane,
    And thou opposed, being of no woman born,
    Yet I will try the last. Before my body
    I throw my warlike shield. Lay on, Macduff,
    And damned be him that first cries "Hold, enough!"

*[Exeunt fighting. Alarums.]*

*[Retreat and flourish. Enter, with Drum and
Colors, Malcolm, Siward, Ross, Thanes, and
Soldiers.]*

40  **Malcolm.** I would the friends we miss were safe arrived.

**Siward.** Some must go off; and yet, by these I see,
    So great a day as this is cheaply bought.

**Malcolm.** Macduff is missing, and your noble son.

**Ross.** Your son, my lord, has paid a soldier's debt.
45   He only lived but till he was a man,

**11–16** Macbeth says that Macduff is wasting his effort. Trying to wound Macbeth is as useless as trying to wound the invulnerable (***intrenchant***) air. Macduff should attack other, more easily injured foes, described in terms of helmets (***crests***).

**19–20** *Macduff . . . untimely ripped:* Macduff was a premature baby delivered by Caesarean section, an operation that removes the child directly from the mother's womb.

**22** *cowed my better part of man:* made my spirit, or soul, fearful.

**23–26** The cheating witches (***juggling fiends***) have tricked him (***palter with us***) with words that have double meanings.

**27–31** Macduff scornfully tells Macbeth to surrender so that he can become a public spectacle (***the show and gaze o' the time***). Macbeth's picture will be hung on a pole (***Painted upon a pole***) as if he were part of a circus sideshow.

**32–39** Macbeth cannot face the shame of surrender and public ridicule. He prefers to fight to the death (***try the last***) against Macduff, even though he knows all hope is gone. *What is your opinion of Macbeth's attitude?*

The first trumpet call (***Retreat***) signals the battle's end. The next one (***flourish***) announces Malcolm's entrance.

**41–42** Though some must die (***go off***) in battle, Siward can see that their side does not have many casualties.

*"Lay on, Macduff,/And damned be him that first cries 'Hold, enough!'"*

The which no sooner had his prowess confirmed
In the unshrinking station where he fought
But like a man he died.

**Siward.**                     Then he is dead?

50  **Ross.** Ay, and brought off the field. Your cause of sorrow
Must not be measured by his worth, for then
It hath no end.

**Siward.**          Had he his hurts before?

**Ross.** Ay, on the front.

55  **Siward.**                    Why then, God's soldier be he!
Had I as many sons as I have hairs,
I would not wish them to a fairer death.
And so his knell is knolled.

**Malcolm.**                          He's worth more sorrow,
60      And that I'll spend for him.

**50–52** Ross tells old Siward that if he mourns his son according to the boy's value, his sorrow will never end.

**53 *hurts before:*** wounds before his battle with Macbeth, which would give further evidence of his courage.

**58 *knell is knolled:*** Young Siward's death bell has already rung, meaning there is no need to mourn him further. *What do you think of old Siward's refusal to grieve for his son?*

**Siward.**                              He's worth no more.
They say he parted well and paid his score,
And so, God be with him! Here comes newer comfort.

*[Enter* Macduff, *with* Macbeth's *head.]*

**Macduff.** Hail, King! for so thou art. Behold where stands

65   The usurper's cursed head. The time is free.
I see thee compassed with thy kingdom's pearl,
That speak my salutation in their minds;
Whose voices I desire aloud with mine—
Hail, King of Scotland!

70   **All.**                              Hail, King of Scotland! *[Flourish.]*

**Malcolm.** We shall not spend a large expense of time
Before we reckon with your several loves
And make us even with you. My Thanes and kinsmen,
Henceforth be Earls, the first that ever Scotland
75   In such an honor named. What's more to do
Which would be planted newly with the time—
As calling home our exiled friends abroad
That fled the snares of watchful tyranny,
Producing forth the cruel ministers
80   Of this dead butcher and his fiendlike queen,
Who (as 'tis thought) by self and violent hands
Took off her life—this, and what needful else
That calls upon us, by the grace of Grace
We will perform in measure, time, and place.
85   So thanks to all at once and to each one,
Whom we invite to see us crowned at Scone.

*[Flourish. Exeunt omnes.]*

Macduff is probably carrying Macbeth's head on a pole.

**65–66** *The time . . . pearl:* Macduff declares that the age (*time*) is now freed from tyranny. He sees Malcolm surrounded by Scotland's noblest men (*thy kingdom's pearl*).

**71–86** Malcolm promises that he will quickly reward his nobles according to the devotion (*several loves*) they have shown. He gives the thanes new titles (*Henceforth be Earls*) and declares his intention, as a sign of the new age (*planted newly with the time*), to welcome back the exiles who fled Macbeth's tyranny and his cruel agents (*ministers*). Now that Scotland is free of the butcher Macbeth and his queen, who is reported to have killed herself, Malcolm asks for God's help to restore order and harmony. He concludes by inviting all present to his coronation.

# Responding to Reading

1. What does the final confrontation between Macbeth and Macduff reveal about Macbeth's character?

   **Think about**
   • Macbeth's initial reluctance to fight Macduff
   • whether Macbeth shows guilt about his murder of Macduff's family
   • Macbeth's resolve to fight after he learns about Macduff's birth

2. Were you surprised by the manner of Lady Macbeth's death? Why or why not?

3. Do you think that Malcolm will be a successful leader as king? Why or why not?

# explain

## Responding to Reading

### First Impressions

1. Were you satisfied by the way the play ended? Why or why not?

### Second Thoughts

2. What is your judgment of Macbeth's character by the end of the play? Do you think that he showed dignity in defeat? Cite evidence from the play to support your judgment.

3. Is Macbeth's downfall a result of fate or his own actions? Use examples from the play to defend your opinion.

   **Think about**
   • to what extent the witches control his future
   • the depth of his ambition to be king
   • his evil actions

4. Compare and contrast the final days of Lady Macbeth and Macbeth. How are both characters affected by the knowledge of their evil deeds? Whom do you find more sympathetic at the end?

5. Evaluate Duncan, Banquo, Macduff, Malcolm, and Macbeth in terms of their leadership ability. Who would have made the best king?

6. What positive and negative effects of ambition does the play illustrate? Cite different characters in the play as examples of these effects.

## Literary Concepts: Soliloquy and Catastrophe

A **soliloquy** is a speech given by a character while he or she is either alone on stage or among characters who are ignored temporarily. Soliloquies reveal a character's private thoughts. Macbeth's "Tomorrow, and tomorrow" speech in Act Five, Scene 5, is a famous soliloquy. What does this speech reveal about Macbeth's state of mind? Find another soliloquy in the play and analyze what it reveals about the speaker.

**Catastrophe** refers to the resolution of a tragedy. It is the final stage in the plot and often involves the death of the hero. What characters are most affected by the catastrophe of *Macbeth*?

**Concept Review: Theme**   Great works of literature often have more than one theme, or underlying message about life. What are some of the themes of *Macbeth?* What are the play's messages about guilt, violence, and ambition? What lessons do you think *Macbeth* offers to today's leaders?

# *W*riting Options

1. Write an obituary for Macbeth. Describe his accomplishments, his strengths and failings, and the manner of his death. Include comments from people who knew him, both friends and enemies.

2. Write a review of the play, keeping in mind that a review is not the same as a plot summary. Identify and explain the play's strengths and possible weaknesses. Discuss topics such as characterization, plot, artistic value, and entertainment value.

3. With a partner write a newspaper account of the final battle. Be sure to answer the reporter's usual questions — who, what, where, when, why, and how. Look in newspapers for interesting lead paragraphs that you might imitate. Don't forget to create a catchy headline.

4. Work in groups of four to create an identification test that requires matching quotes to their speakers. Find short quotations by each major character that capture the speaker's personality. After you have finished writing your test, administer it to your classmates.

## *e x t e n d*

## *O*ptions *for Learning*

1 • **Modern Ambition** Research a modern leader in politics, business, or religion who has fallen because of unbridled ambition. Analyze the factors that contributed to his or her downfall, and draw relevant comparisons to Macbeth. Report on your investigation to your class.

2 • **Wheel of Fortune** Stage a *Macbeth* word game based on the popular television show in which contestants guess the letters in a saying or name. Use quotations and characters' names from the play. One student can play the role of host, one can be the "letter turner," and three can be contestants.

3 • A *Macbeth* Gazette With several classmates prepare a newspaper based on the events of the play. Include the standard features, such as news articles, editorials, a society or fashion section, comics, and want ads; you might even include a sports section. Feel free to make up details that will give your paper sparkle.

4 • **The Comic News** Working in small groups, draw and write a comic-book version of *The Tragedy of Macbeth*. Focus on the major events and characters of the play. You may follow the style of a contemporary superhero comic book or that of *Classics Illustrated*.

# William Shakespeare
## 1564-1616

Though Shakespeare is widely acclaimed as the world's greatest writer, many people have been disappointed by the unremarkable course of his life. Some even insist that a man of such humble origin and limited education could not have written such powerful and important plays. They have invented elaborate theories to support their claim that the playwright was not Shakespeare at all but a more distinguished and learned man.

Shakespeare was born in 1564, the son of a prominent merchant in Stratford-upon-Avon, England. Though he was neither one of the nobility nor educated at a university—two marks of a "literary gentleman"—he did receive a fine education at the Stratford Grammar School, where he learned Latin and studied the Bible and the classics of ancient Greece and Rome. He married Anne Hathaway, eight years his elder, in 1582 and fathered two daughters and a son. He probably moved to London in the late 1580's and began a career as an actor and playwright for the Lord Chamberlain's Men, London's leading theater company. England's most famous tragic actor, Richard Burbage, and its most beloved clown, Will Kempe, were fellow actors in this company, which became the King's Men in 1603 under the sponsorship of King James I.

Shakespeare quickly became one of London's most prominent and successful playwrights. His plays, which combined fascinating plots, strong characters, and beautiful poetry, appealed to both the refined aristocrats and the rowdy groundlings who were interested in sword fights and bawdy humor. No playwright of the age could match Shakespeare's range: his imaginative world is populated with tragic kings, drunken soldiers, lusty adolescents, prudish servants, witty tavern keepers, lovesick aristocrats, treasonous advisors, and a host of other interesting characters from all segments of society.

Typically, Shakespeare's plays are classified as comedies (for example, *As You Like It*, *Twelfth Night*, and *The Taming of the Shrew*), histories (such as *Henry IV, Parts 1 and 2*, *Henry V*, and *Richard III*), and tragedies (including *King Lear*, *Hamlet*, and *Othello*), though many of them defy easy classification. Shakespeare wrote more than thirty-five plays, most of which are still performed today, and more than 150 poems. His works command worldwide respect and have been translated into virtually every major language.

Shakespeare's success made him a wealthy and important citizen. He was one of the seven shareholders who financed the construction of the Globe Theater in 1599, and his plays were performed at the palace before Queen Elizabeth and King James. He was a welcome visitor to some of the finest houses in London, a respected figure in the literary establishment, a loyal friend to fellow actors, and apparently a shrewd investor who was able to live in comfortable retirement after he left the theater in 1613. Upon Shakespeare's death, Ben Jonson, a rival poet and playwright, predicted that Shakespeare would be "not of an age, but for all time." His prediction has been proved accurate.

## CREATIVE EXPRESSION

In schools across the country, whenever an English teacher announces that the class will read a Shakespearean play, some student inevitably says, "I can't understand Shakespeare. Why don't his characters speak English?" Now the characters will get a chance to "speak English" as you remove the language barrier to *Macbeth* in this opportunity for creative expression.

You are going to take a scene from *Macbeth* and modernize it by rewriting it in contemporary English, or take the characters from the play and put them in a modern context. Either way, you will bring Shakespeare's characters to life in our world.

The keys to completing this assignment successfully are deciding on the modern treatment you want to use and understanding the scene and characters you choose to explore.

> Here is your PASSkey to this assignment.

### GUIDED ASSIGNMENT: UPDATING *MACBETH*

Provide insight into the theme or characters of *Macbeth* by rewriting a scene using modern English or showing the characters in a modern context.

**P**URPOSE: To modernize *Macbeth*

**A**UDIENCE: Your classmates

**S**UBJECT: *Macbeth*

**S**TRUCTURE: Drama

## Prewriting

 **STEP 1** **Decide on the modern treatment** There are two main approaches you can take. Both are fun, and both demand creativity.

**Option 1** Take a short scene or part of a longer scene from *Macbeth* and rewrite it using modern English. Use simple, everyday speech. This approach may be easier if you try to capture a distinctive way of speaking. For instance, how would Macbeth's "Tomorrow, and tomorrow, and tomorrow" speech sound in current teen slang? Can you

see Lady Macbeth as a "valley girl" when she tries to talk Macbeth into killing Duncan? How would the witches come across if they spoke in a "rap" style in the play's first scene? Consider this excerpt from a student piece.

```
Witch 1: When shall we get together girls?
         When shall we three shake our curls?
Witch 2: In wind and rain and storms and stuff,
         When the boys decide to stop acting rough.
```

Be true to the scene. You should have a modern "translation" for every exchange in the original scene. Before you write your version, summarize each exchange in a sentence or two, explaining what is being said. Then it will be an easy next step to put that statement into new language.

**Option 2**    A second approach would be to take the characters from the play and put them in a modern context. Television is a fertile area of ideas for this option. For instance, the witches could present their recipe on *The Frugal Gourmet*. Macbeth and Macduff might appear on *Nightline*. Lady Macbeth could do a soap commercial. The porter and the doctor might reveal all on a talk show. Using this option, you can provide plenty of character-revealing dialogue, just as in Option 1.

You could also script a portion of the play as if it were a movie. Consider this partial list from one class.

```
1. Dinner ghost scene as a horror film
2. Final battle scenes as a Bruce Lee martial arts film
3. Witches tell Macbeth the future in a rock musical
4. Macbeth planning Banquo's murder as a gangster film
```

The only limit is your imagination. You might have Macbeth visit a psychiatrist to discuss his problem of seeing ghosts. You could also write a series of letters to an advice columnist from a variety of characters and provide her answers. You might have the local police chief interrogate a number of characters about Duncan's murder.

### Special Tip

Brainstorming in small groups or as a class can aid creative expression. Try to generate as many ideas as possible. The success of an assignment like this depends on finding an idea that inspires you. You should have a lot of fun with this assignment. If you're not having fun, rethink your approach.

**STEP 2** **Understand your scene and your characters** Your writing will be insightful, moving, or funny only if you stay true to the play. Macbeth should act like Macbeth even if he is on *The Tonight Show.* Of course, he will be somewhat different because of the context, but your readers should recognize the character who was in the play. Create a list of traits for each character who will appear in your paper, and refer to the list as you write your piece.

## Drafting

**STEP 1** **Set the scene** If you are using Option 1, putting a scene into modern English, it's important that you establish the setting at the beginning. In Shakespearean plays, scene setting consists of a brief mention of location before a scene begins. Go further than that, though. In at least one paragraph, describe the surroundings. For instance, if your setting is a mall, describe the mall in general as well as the shops your characters are standing in front of or wandering through. You might also include a brief description of your characters' clothing. Make the location come alive through your details.

Follow these same guidelines if you are putting the characters into a television show or a movie. In a paragraph, describe what viewers will see when the tape or film begins.

**STEP 2** **Write the dialogue** Write your scene in script form, as in the original version.

> **Macbeth:** I have done the deed. Didst thou not hear a noise?
> **Lady Macbeth:** I heard the owl scream and the crickets cry. Did not you speak?

Note that colons introduce each bit of dialogue and that quotation marks are not used.

Shakespeare didn't use stage directions, but you may want to. These are statements describing what the characters are doing when they say their words. Stage directions are enclosed in parentheses. Consider this example from a student piece describing the moment when the witches, as three homeless women, greet Macbeth and Banquo.

STUDENT MODEL ▶ Homeless Woman Three: Hello, Macbeth. Hello, Kingy Dear.
Macbeth (starts looking around as if he were expecting the
     police): Kingy?
Banquo (high fives Macbeth): Cool . . . like KING . . . like
     KING KONG, man . . . Like . . . like . . . cool.

**STEP 3** **Conclude your scene** If you chose Option 1, putting a scene into modern English, you'll end your piece when the scene ends. If you chose Option 2, you will have to devise an ending. Don't bite off more than you can chew; you don't have to script an entire half hour television show.

---

### Special Tip
............................................................................

Make sure your characters are true to the characters Shakespeare provides. Physical details or actions can help you. Lady Macbeth wrings her hands. Macbeth jumps at sudden noises. Most important, make central character traits, such as Macduff's anger or Banquo's goodness, apparent.

---

## Revising and Editing

Use the following as a checklist for your revision. Make appropriate revisions based on your answers.

---

### Revision Checklist
............................................................................

1. Is it clear where and when the scene starts? Does the beginning set the stage clearly?
2. Do the characters resemble the characters in the play?
3. Are stage directions provided, where appropriate?
4. Does the piece end at an appropriate point?

---

**Editing** Reread your scene. Check for errors in punctuation, spelling, capitalization, and grammar.

## Presenting

Your creative script is perfect for presentation. Team up with a small group to act out the scene in front of the class. Memorize the dialogue or use scripts. If you can dress for the part, all the better.

# LANGUAGE WORKSHOP

## CONFUSING VERB PAIRS

The English language has more than 790,000 words—more than any other language in the world. Not surprisingly, some of these words have similar meanings or look somewhat similar. This workshop focuses on several pairs of verbs that often cause confusion. By studying the workshop carefully, you can learn to use these verbs correctly.

### *Bring/Take, Teach/Learn,* and *Let/Leave*

|  | Present | Past | Past Participle |
|---|---|---|---|
| **Bring** and **Take** | bring | brought | (have) brought |
|  | take | took | (have) taken |
| **Learn** and **Teach** | learn | learned | (have) learned |
|  | teach | taught | (have) taught |
| **Let** and **Leave** | let | let | (have) let |
|  | leave | left | (have) left |

*Bring* indicates action directed toward the speaker. *Take* involves action directed away from the speaker.

> *Bring* that map to me, please.
> *Take* these awful costumes away!

*Teach* means "to help someone learn." *Learn* means "to gain knowledge or skill."

> Ms. Simon *taught* those poems to us last semester.
> I *have learned* my lines for our production of *Macbeth*.

*Let* means "to allow or to permit." *Leave* means "to go away from" or "to allow to remain in a specific condition."

> Our school drama coach *will let* us perform next month.
> We were so excited, we *left* the auditorium without our scripts.
> We *left* our scripts on the stage.

# Lie/Lay, Rise/Raise, and Sit/Set

|  | **Present** | **Past** | **Past Participle** |
|---|---|---|---|
| **Lie and Lay** | lie | lay | (have) lain |
|  | lay | laid | (have) laid |
| **Rise and Raise** | rise | rose | (have) risen |
|  | raise | raised | (have) raised |
| **Sit and Set** | sit | sat | (have) sat |
|  | set | set | (have) set |

*Lie* means "to rest in a flat position" or "to be in a certain place." *Lie* never has a direct object. *Lay* means "to place." *Lay* always has a direct object unless the verb is in the passive voice.

> A pile of props *was lying* on the stage floor.
> The actors *will lay* their costumes on the shelf. (*Costumes* is the direct object.)
> The props *were laid* on the floor. (passive voice)

*Rise* means "to go upward." *Rise* does not take a direct object. *Raise* means "to lift" or "to make something go upward." *Raise* always has a direct object unless the verb is in the passive voice.

> Steam from the witches' brew *rises* above the stage.
> The stagehands *raise* the curtain at the beginning of each act. (*Curtain* is the direct object.)
> The curtain *is raised* at the beginning of each act. (passive voice)

*Sit* means "to occupy a seat." *Sit* never takes a direct object. *Set* means "to place." *Set* always has a direct object unless the verb is in the passive voice.

> Our drama coach *sits* in the back of the auditorium.
> He *set* a megaphone on a nearby seat. (*Megaphone* is the direct object.)
> A megaphone *was set* on a nearby seat. (passive voice)

**Exercise 1**  Many of the following sentences have errors in the use of verbs. Rewrite these sentences, correcting the errors. If a sentence has no error, write *Correct.*

1. In English class Mr. McBride learned us about Shakespeare's plays.
2. Before we read *Macbeth* we learned about the historical background of the play.

## ACTIVE OR PASSIVE?

A verb is in the **active voice** when the subject *performs* the action.

> Carl changed the tire.

When the subject *receives* the action, the verb is in the **passive voice.**

> The tire was changed by Carl.

3. On a table in the front of our class, Mr. McBride sat a large map of ancient Scotland. On it he set miniature figures to represent the various characters in the play.

4. When a character exited or died, one of us would remove the figure and lie it on a chair.

5. "Leave me read one of the witches," begged Anita.

6. "Fine," said Mr. McBride, "but don't rise your book in front of your face. We want to hear every word."

7. The excitement raised as Macbeth and his wife prepared to murder the king.

8. "Bring your books home tonight to read ahead," our teacher said.

9. "Why won't Macbeth leave things happen naturally?" asked Lin.

10. "He's too power hungry to set around waiting," answered Chris.

**COLLABORATIVE LEARNING**

As your group works together, have one person take notes. Read your revision to the class.

**LANGUAGE HANDBOOK**

For review and practice: commonly confused verbs,
pages 1016–17

**Exercise 2**   Work in groups to revise the following passage.

Close your eyes and leave your imagination take over. You are setting in an Elizabethan theater waiting for the play to begin. The main stage is a large platform rised above the ground. There are no curtains to be rised and almost no scenery or props. The groundlings are whistling and stomping their feet. Some have had too much to eat and drink and are setting or laying on the ground. Obviously, no one has learned them any manners. Some have taken rotten vegetables with them to throw at any actor who doesn't perform well. Even the rudeness of the groundlings, however, can't bring away the excitement of seeing the very first performance of *Macbeth.* Leave the show begin!

# SPEAKING AND LISTENING

## ORAL INTERPRETATION

Oral interpretation of literature is reading a work aloud in a way that expresses your understanding of the piece. Whenever you are asked to read aloud, keep two goals in mind. First, read to express your ideas about the work. Second, read to entertain your audience.

**1. Think About the Selection.**   If possible, review the material silently before you read. If you are giving a performance, you will have plenty of time to rehearse the material aloud. If you are reading in class, you may be seeing the material for the first time. In this case, listen carefully to the person who reads before you. Draw conclusions about the ideas and characters in the literature. Think about how your ideas could be communicated with your voice.

**2. Use Your Voice.**   How much can you express with a shout, a whisper, or a laugh? What meaning can you convey by reading slower or faster or by pausing? Can you make a character sound old, young, angry? Does the character have a dialect you can imitate? Remember, changing the way you say just one word can tell a lot about a character.

**3. Listen to Other Readers.**   If you are reading a play, be ready with your lines. If the class is taking turns reading a prose selection, pay attention to previous readers so that when your turn comes, you will have a good understanding of the characters and the plot.

**4. Project.**   Make sure you can be heard by everyone. Don't shout. Instead, push your voice up and out from the bottom of your rib cage.

**5. Use good posture and gestures.**   Sit or stand up straight and keep your book or script low so that it doesn't muffle your voice. Use gestures or facial expressions to give emphasis to your reading.

**6. Entertain.**   Always remember, when you read in front of others, even if it's only in class, you have an audience. One of your goals should be to keep that audience interested and entertained.

### Exercises

1. Read the following sentence eight times, emphasizing a different word each time. Explain how the meaning changes with each reading.

   Are you going to the dance with me?

2. Choose a poem you like. Interpret it orally for the class.

# INDIVIDUAL AND SOCIETY

· · · · · · · · · · · · · · · · · · · · · · · · · · · · · · · · · · · · ·

"*Do not belong so wholly to others that you do not belong to yourself.*"

Baltasar Gracián

TAX COLLECTORS AND
VILLAGE ELDERS early 19th
century Ghulam 'Ali Khan' Arthur
M. Sackler Museum, Harvard
University, Cambridge,
Massachusetts.

379

# Life in the Restoration and Enlightenment

## AN ENLIGHTENED AGE

The period including the late 1600's and the 1700's is called the Enlightenment or the Age of Reason because it was then that people began to use scientific reasoning to understand the world. Earlier, most people had regarded natural events such as comets and eclipses as warnings from God. The new, scientific way of understanding the world suggested that by applying reason, people could know the natural causes of such events and even predict the events.

### The Scientific Method

Sir Isaac Newton set the tone for the era in his major work, *Mathematical Principles of Natural Philosophy,* published in 1687. Describing the laws of motion and gravity, Newton outlined the method by which he had arrived at his conclusions. Newton's scientific method, still employed today, consists of analyzing the facts about an event or phenomenon, developing a possible explanation, stating the explanation in mathematical terms, and then testing it by experiment.

A new organization, the Royal Society, emerged to assist English scientists in their attempts to determine the laws of the natural world. Chartered by King Charles II in 1662, the society collected and spread information on science and its applications. The organization helped propel England into a position of industrial and agricultural superiority during the eighteenth century.

### Political Theories of Enlightenment

During the Enlightenment many writers attempted to apply scientific reasoning to political and economic problems. Believing that reasonable people could create a perfect society, authors such as John Locke encouraged people to use their intelligence to rid themselves of unjust authorities. This Enlightenment emphasis on rights and freedom inspired America's Declaration of Independence, written in 1776, and became the philosophy behind the French Revolution as well.

England itself did not experience a similar revolution leading to popular democratic rule. By 1800, however, the English kings and queens had lost many of their historic powers. Historians often divide the period from 1660 to 1800 into three eras: the Restoration, the Augustan Age, and the Age of Johnson.

## THE RESTORATION: 1660–1700

In 1660 the Puritan government fell, and England restored a king, Charles II, to the throne. The reestablishment of the monarchy in England also restored the Church of England to power and ended twenty years of religious strife.

### Restoration Politics

Charles II enjoyed a twenty-five-year reign. He was succeeded by his brother, James. A Roman Catholic, James tried to revive Catholicism, but England was by then firmly Protestant. Many English people even believed that Roman Catholics had been responsible for setting the fire that had devastated London in 1666.

In 1688 Parliamentary leaders forced James to leave the country in what became known as the Glorious, or Bloodless, Revolution. When James's daughter Mary and her Protestant husband, William of Orange, accepted Parliament's invitation to reign, Parliament's power over the monarchy was established.

The triumphant Parliament outlined its rights and powers in the Revolutionary Settlement, which also extended greater freedom of religion to the public and provided specific directions for Protestant kings and queens to succeed the throne. The Glorious Revolution marked an end to the bloody battles that had ravaged England for years.

A FRENCH
FRIGATE TOWING
AN ENGLISH MAN
O'WAR INTO PORT
Thomas Rowlandson
Huntington Library,
San Marino,
California

## Restoration Literature

England's theaters, closed down under Puritan rule, reopened during the Restoration. Restoration dramatists wrote comedies of manners that poked fun at the glamorous but artificial society of the royal court. These plays had clever plots and sparkled with witty dialogue. Audiences, mostly composed of the wealthy, also enjoyed watching exciting heroic dramas, tragedies, and tragicomedies.

A wider public read the works of John Bunyan, who wrote *The Pilgrim's Progress* in 1678. This book praised the Christian virtues of faith, hope, and charity and denounced vices by personifying them in such characters as Mr. Liveloose and Mr. Hate-light.

## THE AUGUSTAN AGE: 1700–1750

The political and social calm that followed the Restoration reminded English writers of Rome under Caesar Augustus. The Augustan Age got its name from these writers, who consciously imitated Latin writing. The Romans had written epics, elegies, tragedies, and satires, and the English Augustans determined to compose works in exactly the same form.

## Augustan Satire

Satiric prose and poetry allowed the Augustans to expose the hypocrisy they saw in English society. In witty rhymed couplets, Alexander Pope made fun of high society and also explored important social issues. Joseph Addison and Richard Steele wrote gentle, satiric essays in their periodicals, commenting on current issues and attempting to improve the tastes of the reading public.

Jonathan Swift's biting satires exposed the mean and sordid side of Augustan England. Challenging the system, this brilliant writer directed his bitterest scorn at rulers and aristocrats.

## New Audience for Literature

Many of the Augustan writers found their primary audience in England's mushrooming middle class. Now that merchants, traders, shopkeepers, and government workers had more money to spend on books, they began to replace writers' wealthy patrons of the past. This new audience preferred novels about ordinary people to traditional heroic tragedies.

Published in 1719, Daniel Defoe's *Robinson Crusoe* is considered the first English novel. Novelists who followed Defoe extended the form to explore character and reveal the protagonist's developing sense of self.

## THE AGE OF JOHNSON: 1750–1800

Although Samuel Johnson died in 1784, his influence dominated the entire last half of the eighteenth century. This exceptional nonconformist was a poet, critic, essayist, journalist, and lexicographer, or writer of dictionaries. His *Dictionary of the English Language,* completed in 1755, helped standardize English spelling and still stands as a landmark in English literature.

A brilliant scholar and conversationalist, Johnson set the literary standards for his time. He criticized his fellow writers for their growing interest in simple, traditional folk literature. Nevertheless, by the late 1700's the lyrical poetry of Robert Burns and William Blake heralded the beginning of a new, more romantic era in English literature.

# Time Line of British and World History 1660—1800

■ THE GREAT FIRE OF LONDON 1666

**1690** John Locke publishes *Essay Concerning Human Understanding*

**1689** Bill of Rights becomes law

**1688** Glorious Revolution

**1687** Isaac Newton publishes *Mathematical Principles of Natural Philosophy*

Jonathan Swift publishes **1726** *Gulliver's Travels*

Daniel Defoe **1719** publishes *Robinson Crusoe*

**1666** Great Fire of London

**1663** Drury Lane Theater opens

**1662** Royal Society chartered

**1707** Great Britain created by the Act of Union

**1702** First daily newspaper begins publication

## BRITISH HISTORY

| 1660 | 1680 | 1700 | 1720 |

## WORLD HISTORY

**1700** Kabuki Theater opens in Japan

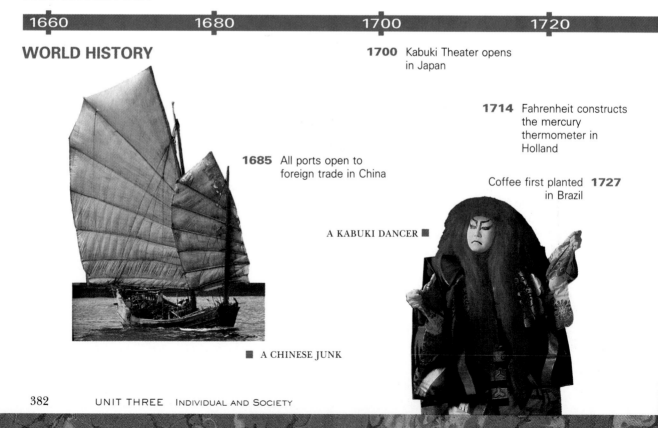

**1714** Fahrenheit constructs the mercury thermometer in Holland

**1685** All ports open to foreign trade in China

Coffee first planted **1727** in Brazil

A KABUKI DANCER ■

■ A CHINESE JUNK

■ JAMES WATT'S 1788 STEAM ENGINE

James Boswell publishes **1791**
*The Life of Samuel Johnson*

**1786** Robert Burns
publishes *Poems
Chiefly in Scottish
Dialect*

**1765** Britain imposes the
Stamp Act on the
American colonies

**1755** Samuel Johnson
publishes *Dictionary
of the English
Language*

| 1740 | 1760 | 1780 | 1800 |
|------|------|------|------|

SPIRIT OF '76 ■

**1773** American patriots pour
tea into Boston Harbor
in the Boston Tea Party

**1775** American Revolution begins

**1780** Rebellion against Spanish
rule erupts in Peru

**1784** First school for
the blind established
in France

**1749** Sign language invented
in Portugal

French Revolution begins with **1789**
the storming of the Bastille

Mungo Park explores the **1795**
Niger River in Africa

**1752** Benjamin Franklin
invents the lightning
rod in colonial America

Napoleon becomes head of the **1799**
revolutionary government in France

■ THE GUILLOTINE, A SYMBOL
OF THE FRENCH REVOLUTION

# $\mathcal{P}$ORTRAITS OF NONCONFORMISTS

The term *nonconformist* was originally used to describe religious rebels who refused to join the Church of England. The first nonconformists were stubborn and spirited; they had their own views and did not want the established powers to tell them what to do. Before long, *nonconformist* was applied to anyone who refused to go along with the crowd.

Nonconformists are people who act and think by their own sets of rules. Whether they are admired or scorned by others, they stand alone. Samuel Johnson, whom you will read about, is one of the most famous nonconformists in English history: a cantankerous, blunt, and kind-hearted man who became a celebrity of his era. The other nonconformists you will encounter are much different but no less interesting than Johnson.

**Biography**

## *from The* Life of Samuel Johnson

### JAMES BOSWELL

## Examine What You Know

It is easy to find things out about the lives of the rich and famous simply by picking up a magazine at a grocery store or newsstand. Think of a current celebrity in whom you are interested. List the kinds of information you could easily find out about this person. Compare your list with the kinds of things you read about Samuel Johnson.

## Expand Your Knowledge

*The Life of Samuel Johnson* was different from earlier biographies, which centered exclusively on great acts of famous people. This biography tells the whole story, both good and bad, about its subject, Samuel Johnson. Though Johnson came from a poor English background, he became well-known and respected as a poet, essayist, journalist, and one of the outstanding intellectuals of the eighteenth century. He compiled one of the first dictionaries of the English language.

Boswell, on the other hand, was a university-trained lawyer from a wealthy Scottish family. When the two men met, Boswell was twenty-two years old and Johnson was fifty-three. An admirer of Johnson's writings, Boswell wanted to know more about him. Eager to get the "inside scoop" on Johnson, Boswell visited Johnson's London home and recorded their conversations in a diary. Boswell's irritating personal questions caused Johnson to occasionally strike Boswell and throw him out of his home. But as time went on, Johnson became charmed by Boswell's enthusiasm. After Johnson's death in 1784, Boswell spent seven years writing the biography.

## Enrich Your Reading

**Reading for the Main Idea**   Eighteenth-century prose contains outdated expressions and vocabulary. However, you can understand the main idea by using the context. For example, Boswell mentions Johnson's essay against "gulosity," a word that is now out-of-date, in the passage about eating. From the context you can figure out that *gulosity* has something to do with eating. Use the heading of each part to get the main idea of the passage.

# from *The Life of Samuel Johnson*

JAMES BOSWELL

## *On Eating*

[1763] At supper this night he talked of good eating with uncommon satisfaction. "Some people (said he) have a foolish way of not minding, or pretending not to mind, what they eat. For my part, I mind my belly very studiously, and very carefully; for I look upon it that he who does not mind his belly will hardly mind anything else."

He now appeared to me *Jean Bull philosophe*,[1] and he was, for the moment, not only serious but <u>vehement.</u> Yet I have heard him, upon other occasions, talk with great contempt of people who were anxious to gratify their palates; and the 206th number of his *Rambler* is a masterly essay against gulosity. His practice, indeed, I must acknowledge, may be considered as casting the balance of his different opinions upon this subject, for I never knew any man who relished good eating more than he did. When at table, he was totally absorbed in the business of the moment; his looks seemed riveted to his plate; nor would he, unless when in very high company, say one word, or even pay the least attention to what was said by others, till he had satisfied his appetite, which was so fierce, and indulged with such intenseness, that while in the act of eating, the veins of his forehead swelled, and generally a strong perspiration was visible. To those whose sensations were delicate, this could not but be disgusting; and it was doubtless not very suitable to the character of a philosopher, who should be distinguished by self-command. But it must be owned that Johnson, though he could be rigidly *abstemious*, was not a *temperate* man either in eating or drinking. He could refrain, but he could not use moderately. He told me that he had fasted two days without inconvenience, and that he had never been hungry but once. They who beheld with wonder how much he ate upon all occasions when his dinner was to his taste could not easily conceive what he must have meant by hunger, and not only was he remarkable for the extraordinary quantity which he ate, but he was, or affected to be, a man of very nice discernment in the science of cookery. He used to descant[2] critically on the dishes which had been at table where he had dined or supped, and to recollect minutely what he had liked. . . .

When invited to dine, even with an intimate friend, he was not pleased if something better

---

1. **Jean Bull philosophe** (zhän bo͝ol fēl ô ′zôf): a French phrase referring to John Bull, a farmer noted for being jolly, honest, and hot-tempered, who represented typical Englishmen.
2. **descant** (des′ kant′): to discuss at length.

| *Words to Know and Use* | **vehement** (vē′ ə mənt) *adj.* having intense feeling or strong passion <br> **temperate** (tem′ pər it) *adj.* moderate in indulging the appetites; not self-indulgent; self-restrained |
| --- | --- |

than a plain dinner was not prepared for him. I have heard him say on such an occasion, "This was a good dinner enough, to be sure; but it was not a dinner to *ask* a man to." On the other hand, he was wont³ to express, with great glee, his satisfaction when he had been entertained quite to his mind.

## On Equality of the Sexes

[1778] Mrs. Knowles affected to complain that men had much more liberty allowed them than women.

JOHNSON. "Why, Madam, women have all the liberty they should wish to have. We have all the labor and the danger, and the women all the advantage. We go to sea, we build houses, we do everything, in short, to pay our court to the women."

MRS. KNOWLES. "The Doctor reasons very wittily, but not convincingly. Now, take the instance of building; the mason's wife, if she is ever seen in liquor, is ruined; the mason may get himself drunk as often as he pleases, with little loss of character; nay, may let his wife and children starve."

JOHNSON. "Madam, you must consider, if the mason does get himself drunk, and let his wife and children starve, the parish will oblige him to find security for their maintenance. We have different modes of restraining evil. Stocks for the men, a ducking-stool for women, and a pound for beasts. If we require more perfection from women than from ourselves, it is doing them honor. And women have not the same temptations that we have: they may always live in virtuous company; men must mix in the world indiscriminately. If a woman has no inclination to do what is wrong, being secured from it is no restraint to

OLIVER GOLDSMITH, JAMES BOSWELL, AND SAMUEL JOHNSON AT THE MITRE TAVERN   Engraving
The Granger Collection, New York.

her. I am at liberty to walk into the Thames; but if I were to try it, my friends would restrain me in Bedlam,⁴ and I should be obliged to them."

MRS. KNOWLES. "Still, Doctor, I cannot help thinking it a hardship that more indulgence is allowed to men than to women. It gives a superiority to men, to which I do not see how they are entitled."

JOHNSON. "It is plain, Madam, one or other must have the superiority. As Shakespeare says, 'If two men ride on a horse, one must ride behind.'"

DILLY. "I suppose, Sir, Mrs. Knowles would have them to ride in panniers,⁵ one on each side."

___

3. **wont** (wänt): in the habit; accustomed.
4. **Bedlam:** an old English insane asylum.
5. **panniers** (pan' yərz): a pair of baskets hung across the back of a horse for carrying produce.

387

JOHNSON. "Then, Sir, the horse would throw them both."

MRS. KNOWLES. "Well, I hope that in another world the sexes will be equal."

BOSWELL. "That is being too ambitious, Madam. *We* might as well desire to be equal with the angels. We shall all, I hope, be happy in a future state, but we must not expect to be all happy in the same degree. It is enough if we be happy according to our several capacities. A worthy carman[6] will get to heaven as well as Sir Isaac Newton. Yet, though equally good, they will not have the same degrees of happiness."

JOHNSON. "Probably not."

## The Fear of Death

[1769] I mentioned to him that I had seen the execution of several convicts at Tyburn,[7] two days before, and that none of them seemed to be under any concern.

JOHNSON. "Most of them, Sir, have never thought at all."

BOSWELL. "But is not the fear of death natural to man?"

JOHNSON. "So much so, Sir, that the whole of life is but keeping away the thoughts of it." He then, in a low and earnest tone, talked of his meditating upon the awful[8] hour of his own dissolution, and in what manner he should conduct himself upon that occasion: "I know not (said he) whether I should wish to have a friend by me, or have it all between God and myself. . . ."

When we were alone, I introduced the subject of death and endeavored to maintain that the fear of it might be got over. I told him that David Hume[9] said to me, he was no more uneasy to think he should *not be* after this life, than that he *had not been* before he began to exist.

JOHNSON. "Sir, if he really thinks so, his perceptions are disturbed; he is mad: if he does not think so, he lies. He may tell you, he holds his finger in the flame of a candle without feeling pain; would you believe him? When he dies, he at least gives up all he has."

BOSWELL. "Foote,[10] Sir, told me that when he was very ill he was not afraid to die."

JOHNSON. "It is not true, Sir. Hold a pistol to Foote's breast, or to Hume's breast, and threaten to kill them, and you'll see how they behave."

BOSWELL. "But may we not fortify our minds for the approach of death?" Here I am sensible[11] I was in the wrong, to bring before his view what he ever looked upon with horror; for although when in a celestial frame, in his "Vanity of Human Wishes,"[12] he has supposed death to be "kind Nature's signal for retreat" from this state of being to "a happier seat," his thoughts upon this awful change were in general full of dismal apprehensions. His mind resembled the vast amphitheater, the Colosseum at Rome.[13] In the center stood his judgment, which, like a mighty gladiator, combated those apprehensions that, like the wild beasts of the arena, were all around in cells, ready to be let out upon him. After a conflict, he drove them back into their dens;

---

6. **carman:** a driver of a carriage.

7. **Tyburn:** a place in London where criminals were hanged in public.

8. **awful:** awe-inspiring.

9. **David Hume:** a Scottish philosopher and historian (1711–1776).

10. **Foote:** Samuel Foote, actor and dramatist (1720–1777).

11. **sensible:** aware.

12. **"Vanity of Human Wishes":** a poem published in 1749.

13. **Colosseum at Rome:** a large outdoor theater of ancient Rome that was used for public entertainment such as combat between gladiators.

but not killing them, they were still assailing him. To my question whether we might not fortify our minds for the approach of death, he answered, in a passion, "No, Sir, let it alone. It matters not how a man dies, but how he lives. The act of dying is not of importance, it lasts so short a time." He added (with an earnest look), "A man knows it must be so, and submits. It will do him no good to whine."

I attempted to continue the conversation. He was so provoked that he said, "Give us no more of this"; and was thrown into such a state of agitation that he expressed himself in a way that alarmed and distressed me; showed an impatience that I should leave him, and when I was going away, called to me sternly, "Don't let us meet tomorrow."

## Johnson's Physical Courage

[1775] No man was ever more remarkable for personal courage. He had, indeed, an awful dread of death, or rather, "of something after death"; and what rational man, who seriously thinks of quitting all that he has ever known, and going into a new and unknown state of being, can be without that dread? But his fear was from reflection; his courage natural. His fear, in that one instance, was the result of philosophical and religious consideration. He feared death, but he feared nothing else, not even what might occasion death. Many instances of his resolution may be mentioned. One day, at Mr. Beauclerk's house in the country, when two large dogs were fighting, he went up to them, and beat them till they separated; and at another time, when told of the danger there was that a gun might burst if charged with many balls, he put in six or seven, and fired it off against a wall. Mr. Langton told me that when they were swimming together near Oxford, he cautioned Dr. Johnson against a pool which was reckoned particularly dangerous; upon which Johnson directly swam into it. He told me himself that one night he was attacked in the street by four men, to whom he would not yield, but kept them all at bay, till the watch came up, and carried both him and them to the round-house.[14] In the playhouse at Lichfield, as Mr. Garrick informed me, Johnson having for a moment quitted a chair which was placed for him between the side-scenes, a gentleman took possession of it, and when Johnson on his return civilly demanded his seat, rudely refused to give it up; upon which Johnson laid hold of it, and tossed him and the chair into the pit. Foote, who so successfully revived the old comedy, by exhibiting living characters, had resolved to imitate Johnson on the stage, expecting great profits from his ridicule of so celebrated a man. Johnson being informed of his intention, and being at dinner at Mr. Thomas Davies's the bookseller, from whom I had the story, he asked Mr. Davies what was the common price of an oak stick; and being answered sixpence, "Why then, Sir," said he, "give me leave to send your servant to purchase me a shilling one. I'll have a double quantity; for I am told Foote means to *take me off*,[15] as he calls it, and I am determined the fellow shall not do it with impunity."[16] Davies took care to acquaint Foote of this, which effectually checked the wantonness[17] of the mimic. Mr. Macpherson's menaces made Johnson provide himself with the same implement of defense; and had he been attacked, I have no doubt that, old as he was, he would have made his corporal prowess be felt as much as his intellectual. ❧

---

14. **watch . . . roundhouse:** patrol officers took Johnson and his four attackers to jail.

15. **take me off:** Foote intends to make a mockery of Johnson.

16. **impunity:** freedom from punishment.

17. **checked the wantonness:** controlled the playfulness.

## *R*esponding to Reading

### First Impressions

1. Which section of the biography did you find most interesting? Explain your feelings.

### Second Thoughts

2. Why do you think Boswell discusses Johnson's eating habits?

3. What is your reaction to Johnson's beliefs about equality of the sexes?

4. Do you agree with Johnson when he says that men who claim to have no fear of death are either mad or liars? Explain.

5. Why do you think Johnson risks his life if he fears death so much?

6. In your opinion, what kind of a man was Samuel Johnson?

## *L*iterary Concept: Biography

A good biography shows both the strengths and weaknesses of its subject and is objective, presenting facts rather than the author's personal feelings. Boswell includes minor details, conversations, and stories that are more accurate than flattering, even though he respects and admires Johnson. Do you think Boswell gives a balanced portrayal of Johnson? How objective is the biography? Support your opinion with evidence.

## *W*riting Options

1. Choose one of Johnson's beliefs with which you agree or disagree. Write an argument for or against this belief.

2. List questions that you would ask Johnson if you were to interview him.

## *V*ocabulary Practice

**Exercise** On your paper, write the word that is not related in meaning to the other words in each of the following sets

1. (a) fondness   (b) indentation   (c) inclination   (d) tendency
2. (a) selectively   (b) indiscriminately   (c) uncritically   (d) randomly
3. (a) privilege   (b) favor   (c) indulgence   (d) goal
4. (a) temperate   (b) excessive   (c) drastic   (d) extreme
5. (a) intense   (b) vehement   (c) passionate   (d) forgiving

*Words to Know and Use*

inclination
indiscriminately
indulgence
temperate
vehement

# *explore*

**Fiction**

## *Cross Over, Sawyer!*

JESUS DEL CORRAL   (he soos' del kô räl')

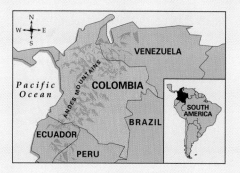

### *Examine What You Know*

Many stories and movies feature a likable rogue. Such characters may lie, cheat, rob, or commit other misdeeds, yet their charming personalities help them avoid real trouble and keep the audience on their side. Think of examples of charming scoundrels that you have encountered, perhaps even people you know. What do they have in common, and why are people so interested in their adventures? As you read, decide whether the main character in this story fits your idea of a likable rogue.

### *Expand Your Knowledge*

"Cross Over, Sawyer!" takes place in the Andes mountains of Colombia, a large country in South America. The mountains, where coffee is grown and natural resources such as minerals and forests are plentiful, have played an important role in Colombia's history and development.

The main character, Simón Perez (sē môn' pe res'), tells of his desertion from the army during a civil war in 1885. From the 1860's to the early part of this century, several long and bloody civil wars were fought in Colombia. Since men were forced by law to serve in the military, many chose to desert rather than to continue in the endless fighting.

At the time of this story, Colombia had a rigid class structure, with a few wealthy landowners at the top and Indians and laborers (called peons) at the bottom. A sawyer—a person who cuts wood for a living—was usually near the bottom of the social scale.

### *Enrich Your Reading*

**Appreciating Humor**   Look for two types of humor as you read this story. The first type, **humor of situation,** is derived from the action. Like the hero of a comic movie, the sawyer often finds himself entangled in seemingly hopeless situations, most of which he creates for himself. The second type, **humor of language,** includes exaggeration, sarcasm, irony, and double meanings. For example, the sawyer calls himself a "master craftsman" even though he has never sawed wood in his life.

■ *A biography of the author can be found on page 400.*

# Cross Over, Sawyer!

JESUS DEL CORRAL

I was opening up a plantation on the banks of the river Cauca, between Antioquia and Sopetrán. As superintendent I took along Simón Perez, a prince of a fellow, now thirty years old, twenty of which he had lived in a constant and <u>relentless</u> fight with nature, without ever suffering any real defeat.

For him obstacles just didn't exist, and whenever I proposed that he do something tough he had never tried before, his regular answer was the cheerful statement, "Sure, I'll tend to it."

One Saturday evening after we'd paid off the ranch hands, Simón and I lingered around chatting on the veranda and discussing plans for next week's undertakings. I remarked that we should need twenty boards to set up gutters in the drainage ditch but that we didn't have any sawyers on the job. Whereupon he replied, "Oh, I can saw those up for you one of these days."

"What?" was my answer. "Are you an expert at sawing lumber?"

"First class. I'm what you might call a sawyer with a diploma, and perhaps the highest paid lumberman who ever pulled a saw. Where did I learn? I'll tell you the story; it's quite funny."

And he told me the following tale, which I consider truly amusing.

In the civil war of '85, I was drafted and stationed on the coast. Soon I decided to desert along with an Indian. One night when we were on duty as sentinels,[1] we beat it, following a brook, and without bothering to leave our regards for the General.

By the following day we were deep in the mountains ten leagues[2] away from our <u>illustrious</u> ex-commander. For four days we kept on hoofing it in the forests, without food and our feet pretty well torn by the thorns, since we were really making our way through wild territory, breaking a trail like a pair of strayed cows.

I had heard about a mining outfit operated by Count de Nadal on the Nus River, and I resolved to head for that direction, groping our way and following along one side of a ravine which opened out on that river, according to reports I'd heard. And indeed, on the morning of our seventh day, the Indian and I finally emerged from our gully into the clear.

---

1. **sentinels:** guards.
2. **leagues:** one league is approximately three miles long.

---

392

MEZTIZO FARMERS OF ANIS, OCANA PROVINCE, COLOMBIA
Carmelo Fernandez 1850–59 Biblioteca Nacional de Colombia.

We were overjoyed when we spied a workman, because we were almost dead of hunger and it was a sure thing that he would give us something to eat.

"Hey, friend," I shouted to him, "what's the name of this place? Is the Nus mine far from here?"

"This is it. I'm in charge of the rope bridge, but my orders are not to send the basket over for any passengers because the mine doesn't need workers. The only labor we're accepting now is lumbermen and sawyers."

I didn't hesitate a moment with my reply.

"That's what I'd heard and that's why I've come. I'm a lumberjack. Send the basket over this way."

"How about the other man?" he asked, pointing to my companion.

The big chump didn't hesitate either with his quick reply. "I don't know anything about that job. I'm just a worker."

He didn't give me a chance to prompt him, to tell him that the essential thing for us was to get some food at all costs, even if on the following day they kicked us out like stray dogs, or even to point out the danger of dying if he had to keep on tramping along and depending on chance, as settlements were widely scattered in these regions. There was also the risk, even if he did manage to strike some town before the end of a month, of being beaten up as a deserter. It was no use. He didn't give me the time to wink an eye at him, for he repeated his statement even though he wasn't asked a second time.

There wasn't a thing I could do. The man in charge of the rope bridge sent the basket to our side of the river after shouting, "Cross over, sawyer!"

I took leave of the poor Indian and was pulled over.

Ten minutes later I was in the presence of the Count, with whom I had this conversation:

"What do you ask for your work?"

"What's the scale of pay around here?"

"I had two first-class lumberjacks, but two weeks ago one of them died. I paid them eight reals[3] a day."

"Well, Count, I can't work for less than twelve reals. That's what I've been getting at all the companies where I've been. Besides, the climate here is bad; here even the quinine[4] gets the fever."

---

3. **reals** (rā älz′): a former unit of Colombian money.

4. **quinine** (kwī′ nīn): medicine used to treat malaria.

"That's fair enough, if you're a master sawyer. Besides we need you badly, and a monkey will eat prickly pears if he has nothing else. So we'll take you on and we'll pay you your price. You had better report to the peon quarters and get something to eat. Monday, you start on the job."

God be praised! They were really going to give me something to eat! It was Saturday, and next day also I was going to get free grub, I, who could hardly speak without holding on to the wall. I was practically walking backwards through weakness from starvation.

I went into the kitchen and even gobbled up the peels of the bananas. The kitchen dog watched me in amazement, presumably saying to himself, "To the devil with this master craftsman; if he stays a week in this place, the cat and I will be dead of hunger!"

At seven o'clock that night I walked over to the Count's house, where he lived with his wife and two children.

A peon gave me some tobacco and lent me a guitar. I got busy puffing and singing a popular mountain ballad. The poor lady of the Count, who had been living there more bored than a monkey, was considerably cheered by my song, and she begged me to stay on the veranda that evening and entertain her and the children.

"Here's your chance, Simón," I softly whispered to myself. "We might as well win these nice people over to my side in case this business of sawing wood turns out badly."

So I sang to them all the ballads I knew. The fact was, I'll admit, I didn't know a thing about a lumberman's job, but when it came to popular songs, I was an old hand at it.

The upshot of it was that the lady of the manor was delighted and invited me to come over in the morning to entertain the children, for she was at her wit's end to keep them interested on Sundays. And she gave me lots of crackers with ham and guava jelly![5]

The boys spent the next day with the <u>renowned</u> master sawyer. We went bathing in the river, ate prunes and drank red wines of the best European brands.

Monday came and the boys wouldn't let the sawman report for his work, because he had promised to take them to a guava tree grove to catch orioles with snares. And the Count laughingly permitted his new lumberjack to earn his twelve reals in that most agreeable occupation.

Finally on Tuesday, I really began to tackle my job. I was introduced to the other sawyer so that we might plan our work together. I made up my mind to be high-handed with him from the start.

In the hearing of the Count, who was standing nearby, I said to him, "Friend, I like to do things in their proper order. First let's settle on what's needed most urgently—boards, planks or posts?"

"Well, we need five thousand laurel-wood boards for the irrigation ditches, three thousand planks for building jobs and about ten thousand posts."

I nearly fell over: here was work enough to last two years . . . and paid at twelve reals a day . . . and with good board and lodging . . . and no danger of being arrested as a deserter because the mine was considered "private territory" outside military <u>jurisdiction</u>.

"Very well, then, let's proceed according to some plan. The first thing we have to do is to concentrate on marking the laurel trees on the mountain that are fine and straight and thick enough to furnish us with plenty of boards. In

---

5. **guava jelly** (gwä′və): a tropical fruit jelly.

*Words to Know and Use*

renowned (ri nound′) *adj.* famous; well-known
jurisdiction (joor′ is dik′ shən) *n.* the territory which falls within the authority of a legal or military body

that way we won't waste any time. After that we'll fell them, and last of all, we'll start sawing them up. Everything according to plan, yes siree; if we don't do things in order, they won't come out right."

"That's the way I like it too," said the Count. "I can see you are a practical man. You go ahead and arrange the work as you think best."

That's how I became the master planner. The other fellow, a poor simple-minded chap, realized he would have to play second fiddle to this strutting, <u>improvised</u> lumberjack. And soon afterward we sallied out in the mountain to mark our trees. Just as we were about to enter into the timber tract, I said to my companion, "Let's not waste any time by walking along together. You work your way toward the top while I select trees down below in the ravine. Then in the afternoon we can meet here. But be very careful not to mark any crooked trees."

And so I dropped down into the ravine in search of the river. There, on its bank, I spent the whole day, smoking and washing the clothing that I had brought from the General's barracks.

In the afternoon, in the appointed place, I found my fellow lumberman and asked him, "Let's see now. How many trees did you mark?"

"Just two hundred and twenty, but they're good ones."

"You practically wasted your day; I marked three hundred and fifty, all first-class."

I had to keep the upper hand on him.

That night the Count's lady sent for me and requested that I bring the guitar, as they had a meal all set out. The boys were most eager to have me tell them the tale of Sebastian de las Gracias, and then the one about Uncle Rabbit

and Friend Armadillo, also the one about John the Fearless, which is so exciting. This program was carried out exactly. Funny stories and songs, appropriate jokes, dinner on salmon because it was the eve of a fast day,[6] cigars with a golden band on them, and a nip of brandy for the poor Count's jack who had worked so hard all that day and needed something comforting to keep up his energy. Ah, and I also put in some winks at a good-looking servant girl who brought his chocolate to the master sawyer and who was <u>enraptured</u> when she heard him singing, "Like a lovesick turtledove whose plaintive coo is heard in the mountain . . ."

Boy, did I saw wood that evening! I even sawed the Count into little pieces, I was that good. And all this clowning was intermingled for me with the fear that the lumber business wouldn't turn out too well. I told the Count that I had noticed certain <u>extravagances</u> in the kitchen of the peons' quarters and quite a lot of confusion in the storeroom service. I mentioned to him a famous remedy for lameness (thought up by me, to be sure) and I promised to gather for him in the mountain a certain medicinal herb that worked wonders in curing disorders of the stomach. (I can still remember the gorgeous-like name I gave it: Life-Restorer!)

Yes, all of them, the man and his whole family, were enchanted with the master craftsman Simón. I spent the week in the mountains marking trees with my fellow workman, or to be more accurate, not with but far away from him since I always sent him off in a different direction from the one I chose for myself. But I must confess to you that since I didn't know

---

6. **fast day:** a traditional day for fasting, which is the practice of abstaining from all or some foods for religious reasons.

what a laurel tree looked like, I had to first walk around and examine the trees that the real lumberjack had marked.

When we had selected about a thousand, we started to fell them with the aid of five laborers. On this job in which I played the role of supervisor, we spent more than two weeks.

And every evening I went to the Count's house and ate divinely. On Sundays I lunched and dined there because the boys had to be entertained—and the servant girl also.

WORKERS ON THE RAILWAY AT CHIGUACAN 1907 Jose Grijalva Museo de Arte Moderno, Casa de la Cultura Ecuatoriana.

I became the mainspring of the mine. My advice was the deciding factor, and nothing was done without consulting me.

Everything was sailing along fine when the fearful day finally dawned on which the saw-buck was to be put in place. The platform for it was all set up. To be sure, when we constructed it, there were difficulties, because my fellow craftsman asked me, "At what height do we set it up?"

"What's the usual practice around here?"

"Three meters."

"Give it three twenty, which is the generally accepted height among good sawyers." (If it works at three meters, what difference would twenty centimeters more make?)

Everything was now ready: the log athwart the platform and the markings on it made by my companion (for all I did was to give orders)—all was in place as the nuptial song relates:

"The lamp lit and the bridal veil at the altar."

The solemn moment came, and one morning we sallied forth on our way to the trestle, our long sawing blades on our shoulders. This was the first time I had ever looked right into the face of one of those wood devourers.

At the foot of the platform, the sawyer asked me "Are you operating below or above?"

To settle such a serious matter I bent down, pretending to scratch an itch in my leg and quickly thought, "If I take the upper part, it is probable this fellow will send me flying into the air with that saw blade of his." So that when I straightened up, I answered, "I'll stay below; you go on up."

He climbed upon the platform, set the blade on the traced marking and . . . we began to saw wood.

Well, sir, the queerest thing was happening. A regular jet of sawdust kept spurting all over me, and I twisted from side to side without being able to get out of the way. It was getting into my nostrils, my ears, my eyes, running down inside my shirt . . . Holy Mother! And I who had had a notion that pulling a gang-saw was a simple matter.

"Friend," my companion shouted to me, "the saw is not cutting true on the line."

*Words to Know and Use* | **nuptial** (nup' shǝl) *adj.* having to do with marriage or a wedding

"Why, devil take it, man! That's why you're up there. Steady now and watch it as you should!"

The poor fellow couldn't keep us from sawing awry. How could he prevent a deflection when I was flopping all over the place like a fish caught on a hook!

I was suffocating in the midst of all those clouds of sawdust, and I shouted to my companion, "You come down, and I'll get up there to control the direction of the saw."

We swapped places. I took my post at the edge of the scaffold, seized the saw and cried out, "Up she goes: one . . . two . . ."

The man pulled the blade down to get set for the upstroke just when I was about to say "three," and I was pulled off my feet and landed right on top of my companion. We were both bowled over, he with his nose banged up and I with some teeth knocked out and one bruised eye looking like an eggplant.

The surprise of the lumberjack was far greater than the shock of the blow I gave him. He looked as stunned as if a meteorite had fallen at his feet.

"Why, master!" he exclaimed, "why, master!"

"Master craftsman my eye! Do you want to know the truth? This is the first time in my life that I have held the horn of one of those gangsaws in my hand. And you pulled down with such force! See what you've done to me"—(and I showed him my injured eye).

"And see what a fix I'm in"—(and he showed me his banged-up nose).

Then followed the inevitable explanations, in relating which I pulled a real Victor Hugo[7] stunt. I told him my story and I almost made him weep when I described the pangs I suffered in the mountain when I deserted. I finally ended up with this speech.

"Don't you say a word of what's happened because I'll have you fired from the mine. So keep a watch on your tongue and show me how to handle a saw. In return I promise to give you every day for three months two reals out of the twelve I earn. Light up this little cigar (I offered him one) and explain to me how to manage this mastodon[8] of a saw."

As money talks, and he knew of my pull at our employers' house, he accepted my proposition and the sawing lessons started. You were supposed to take such a position when you were above, and like this when you were below; and to avoid the annoyance of the sawdust, you covered your nose with a handkerchief . . . a few insignificant hints which I learned in half an hour.

And I kept on for a whole year working in that mine as head sawyer, at twelve reals daily, when the peons got barely four. The house I now own in Sopetrán I bought with money I earned up there. And the fifteen oxen I have here all branded with a saw mark, they too came out of my money earned as a sawyer. . . . And that young son of mine, who is already helping me with the mule driving, is also the son of that servant girl of the Count and godson of the Countess. . . .

When Simón ended his tale, he blew out a mouthful of smoke, looked up at the ceiling, and then added, "And that poor Indian died of hunger . . . just because he didn't know enough to become a sawyer!" ❧

---

7. **Victor Hugo:** French novelist (1802–1885) known for writing long, sad stories of the weak, poor, and powerless.

8. **mastodon** (mas′ tə dän′): an extinct elephantlike animal.

*Words to Know and Use*
**awry** (ə rī′) *adv.* not straight; with a twist to the side; wrong
**deflection** (dē flek′ shən) *n.* a turning aside or bending

## *R*esponding to Reading

### First Impressions

1. Did you find the story enjoyable? Jot down what you liked or did not like about the story.

### Second Thoughts

2. Does the writer succeed in being humorous? Support your opinion with examples of the incidents and language that you noted while reading.

3. Review the plantation owner's description of Simón in the first few paragraphs of the story. Why does the owner find Simón such a useful employee? Explain whether or not you agree with him.

4. How does Simón justify his lies? In your judgment, is he a likable rogue or an immoral user of other people?

   **Think about**
   • why he lies about being a sawyer in the first place
   • the various demands he makes of his employer
   • his treatment of the other sawyer

5. Reread the last two paragraphs. Decide whether Simón deserved everything he got or whether he got everything he deserved.

### Broader Connections

6. If you were an employer, how would you respond to an employee who, like the sawyer, did a fine job but lied to get the job? What would you do if you found out that one of your best workers had lied on his job application or resumé?

## *L*iterary Concept: The Frame Story

The frame story is a story that takes place within another story. Sometimes the first story is never completed and only serves as a means of introducing the second story. "Cross Over, Sawyer!" opens with the plantation owner's expressing his admiration for his foreman, Simón Perez, using first-person narration. Then Simón's story is presented in Simón's own words, which makes it the story inside the frame.

How does the owner's attitude toward Simón affect your first impression of the sawyer? Would your attitude toward the sawyer be the same if you had only Simón's story, without the plantation owner's introduction?

**Concept Review: Climax** What incident marks the climax, or turning point, of the story?

# Writing Options

1. Write a list of guidelines for a successful life that Simón might have written. Your guidelines should reflect his unique ways of getting ahead.

2. Choose a character from the story, such as the other sawyer or the Count's wife. Write a character sketch of Simón from this character's point of view.

3. Imagine that Simón Perez is a student in your class and has not completed a homework assignment. Write his explanation to the teacher about why he has not done the work.

# Vocabulary Practice

**Exercise** On your paper, write the letter of the answer that best completes each sentence below.

1. A log that is cut **awry** is (a) cut crookedly (b) cut straight and true (c) cut into exactly five pieces.
2. To **enrapture** his audience, the sawyer must make them (a) bored (b) angry (c) filled with delight.
3. A **renowned** sawyer is (a) unknown (b) famous (c) not very talented.
4. The Count's kitchen was characterized by **extravagance,** or (a) wastefulness (b) moderation (c) economy.
5. The sawyer's **improvised** action had been (a) planned long in advance (b) made up quickly (c) practiced to perfection.
6. An **illustrious** general is (a) known for his talent (b) not given recognition (c) forgotten quickly.
7. The sawyer refers to a **nuptial** song that would be sung at (a) a birthday party (b) a wedding (c) graduation.
8. A **relentless** fighter (a) quits easily (b) never gives up (c) is very frightened.
9. A saw's **deflection** could be caused by (a) something in its path (b) too many people watching (c) too much noise.
10. If an area is in military **jurisdiction,** the army (a) has authority over it (b) cannot enter the area (c) should ignore it.

*Words to Know and Use*

awry
deflection
enrapture
extravagance
illustrious
improvised
jurisdiction
nuptial
relentless
renowned

## *Options for Learning*

**1 • Improvisational Theater** In small groups, act out a situation in which one student portrays a charming, Simón-like character who pretends to have expert knowledge. The situation may be anything from a job interview at an auto repair shop to a sound system problem at a rock concert. The main character should try to persuade the others that he or she can do the job. Other students might play roles such as Sceptic, Easily Impressed, and Dull-but-Honest. After all groups perform, the class can decide which group came closest to the spirit of "Cross Over, Sawyer!"

**2 • The Balladeer** Use your knowledge of ballad form (see page 95) to create your own ballad that tells of the exploits and adventures of Simón the Sawyer. Enhance your ballad with simple, traditional music, either from a recording or a live performance by another student. If you prefer, set your story to a more contemporary musical style. After rehearsing, present your ballad to your class.

**3 • Scene Painting** Draw or paint a scene from the story that captures either Simón's personality or his comic predicament. Possible scenes to consider include his arrival at the rope bridge, his first attempts at using a sawbuck, or his entertainment of the Count's family.

**4 • Timber-r-r!** Many environmentalists fear that we are cutting down trees faster than new ones can grow. Report to the class on the status of the world's timber supply. You might also wish to suggest ways to conserve this resource.

### FACT FINDER

*How much will the sawyer make at a salary of twelve reals a day, six days a week, for two years?*

## *Jesus del Corral*
### 1871-1931

Many authors have come from Colombia, where it is jokingly said that there are "two hundred writers for every hundred people." Jesus del Corral was a humanitarian and successful public servant who occasionally found time to write, though he did not publish extensively. As Colombia's Minister of Agriculture, he helped the United States Rockefeller Commission combat tropical diseases, such as malaria and yellow fever, in the jungles of Colombia. Through his political and financial support of people attempting to settle and farm the jungle, the agricultural growth of Colombia spread into the mountains and valleys of the Andes and the northwest Amazon highlands.

*Drama*

# Madman
# on the Roof

KIKUCHI KAN (kē kōō′ chē kän)

## Examine What You Know

What is your attitude toward people who suffer from insanity? Discuss the attitudes that exist in our society regarding the insane and how these individuals should be treated. Then compare present-day attitudes with the attitudes toward the insane revealed in the play.

## Expand Your Knowledge

In 1916, when this play was written, Shinto was the official state religion of Japan. Shintoists worship many gods, called *kami*, who are the basic forces in nature. Since Japan is an island, one of the more important gods is Kompira, the god of the sea and protector of sailors. Kompira has a popular shrine along the coast of the Inland Sea, which is the setting of this play.

The teachings of Buddha have had an influence on Shinto. Shintoists identify Buddhist gods as kami, and shrines throughout Japan contain statues of Buddha. Most of Japan's population practice a combination of both religions.

In the past, many Japanese thought the insane were possessed by evil demons. Others believed that a person suffering from madness was inspired by gods. A conflict of attitudes about madness as well as the age-old conflict between persons of different generations play important parts in this play.

## Enrich Your Reading

**Identifying Characters**   In the cast of characters for this play, the family name is listed first, followed by the character's first name. This name order is customary in Japan. In the play itself, however, characters are identified by first names and nicknames. If the names become confusing to you, make a chart like the one below to help you keep track of who's who.

| Yoshitaro | madman |
|-----------|--------|
| Suejiro | brother |
| Gisuke | |

■ *A biography of the author can be found on page 412.*

# Madman on the Roof

KIKUCHI KAN

## CHARACTERS

**Katsushima** (kät soo′ shē mä) **Yoshitaro** (yō′ shē tä′ rō), the madman, twenty-four years of age

**Katsushima Suejiro** (soo e′ jē rō), his brother, a seventeen-year-old high school student

**Katsushima Gisuke** ( jē′ soo ke), their father

**Katsushima Oyoshi** (ō yō′ shē), their mother

**Tosaku** (tō sä′ koo), a neighbor

**Kichiji** (kē chē′ jē), a manservant, twenty years of age

**A Priestess,** about fifty years of age

*Place: A small island in the Inland Sea*

*Time: 1900*

*The stage setting represents the back yard of the Katsushimas, who are the richest family on the island. A bamboo fence prevents one from seeing more of the house than the high roof, which stands out sharply against the rich, greenish sky of the southern island summer. At the left of the stage one can catch a glimpse of the sea shining in the sunlight.*

*Yoshitaro, the elder son of the family, is sitting astride the ridge of the roof and is looking out over the sea.*

**Gisuke** *(speaking from within the house).* Yoshi is sitting on the roof again. He'll get a sunstroke—the sun's so terribly hot. *(coming out)* Kichiji!—Where is Kichiji?

**Kichiji** *(appearing from the right).* Yes! What do you want?

**Gisuke.** Bring Yoshitaro down. He has no hat on, up there in the hot sun. He'll get a sunstroke. How did he get up there, anyway? From the barn? Didn't you put wires around the barn roof as I told you to the other day?

**Kichiji.** Yes, I did exactly as you told me.

**Gisuke** *(coming through the gate to the center of the stage and looking up to the roof).* I don't see how he can stand it, sitting on that hot slate roof. *(He calls.)* Yoshitaro! You'd better come down. If you stay up there you'll get a sunstroke and maybe die.

JAPANESE FIREWORKS   J. A. Christensen   Paper-cut from *Cut-Art: An Introduction to Chung-hua and Kiri-e*, Watson Guptill Publications, New York.

**Kichiji.** Young master! Come on down. You'll get sick if you stay there.

**Gisuke.** Yoshi! Come down quick! What are you doing up there, anyway? Come down, I say! *(He calls loudly.)* Yoshi!

**Yoshitaro** *(indifferently).* Wha-a-at?

**Gisuke.** No "whats"! Come down right away. If you don't come down, I'll get after you with a stick.

**Yoshitaro** *(protesting like a spoiled child).* No, I don't want to. There's something wonderful. The priest of the god Kompira is dancing in the clouds. Dancing with an angel in pink robes. They're calling to me to come. *(crying out ecstatically)* Wait! I'm coming!

**Gisuke.** If you talk like that, you'll fall just as you did once before. You're already crippled and insane—what will you do next to worry your parents? Come down, you fool!

**Kichiji.** Master, don't get so angry. The young master will not obey you. You should get some fried bean cake; when he sees it, he will come down, because he likes it.

**Gisuke.** No, you had better get the stick after him. Don't be afraid to give him a good shaking up.

**Kichiji.** That's too cruel. The young master doesn't understand anything. He's under the influence of evil spirits.

**Gisuke.** We may have to put bamboo guards on the roof to keep him down from there.

**Kichiji.** Whatever you do won't keep him down. Why, he climbed the roof of the Honzen Temple without even a ladder; a low roof like this one is the easiest thing in the world for him. I tell you, it's the evil spirits that make him climb. Nothing can stop him.

**Gisuke.** You may be right, but he worries me to death. If we could only keep him in the house, it wouldn't be so bad, even though he is crazy; but he's always climbing up to high places. Suejiro says that everybody as far as Takamatsu knows about Yoshitaro the Madman.

**Kichiji.** People on the island all say he's under the influence of a fox spirit, but I don't believe that. I never heard of a fox climbing trees.

**Gisuke.** You're right. I think I know the real reason. About the time Yoshitaro was born, I bought a very expensive imported rifle, and I shot every monkey on the island. I believe a monkey spirit is now working in him.

**Kichiji.** That's just what I think. Otherwise, how could he climb trees so well? He can climb anything without a ladder. Even Saku, who's a professional climber, admits that he's no match for Yoshitaro.

**Gisuke** *(with a bitter laugh).* Don't joke about it! It's no laughing matter, having a son who is always climbing on the roof. *(calling again)* Yoshitaro, come down! Yoshitaro! —When he's up there on the roof, he doesn't hear me at all—he's so engrossed. I cut down all the trees around the house so he couldn't climb them, but there's nothing I can do about the roof.

**Kichiji.** When I was a boy, I remember there was a gingko tree in front of the gate.

**Gisuke.** Yes, that was one of the biggest trees on the island. One day Yoshitaro climbed clear to the top. He sat out on a branch, at least ninety feet above the ground, dreaming away as usual. My wife and I never expected him to get down alive, but after a while, down he slid. We were all too astonished to speak.

---

*Words to Know and Use*

**ecstatically** (ek stat′ i kəl lē) *adv.* in a joyful manner
**engross** (en grōs′) *v.* to take one's entire attention

404

**Kichiji.** That was certainly a miracle.

**Gisuke.** That's why I say it's a monkey spirit that's working in him. *(He calls again.)* Yoshi! Come down! *(dropping his voice)* Kichiji, you'd better go up and fetch him.

**Kichiji.** But when anyone else climbs up there, the young master gets angry.

**Gisuke.** Never mind his getting angry. Pull him down.

**Kichiji.** Yes, master.

*(Kichiji goes out after the ladder. Tosaku, the neighbor, enters.)*

**Tosaku.** Good day, sir.

**Gisuke.** Good day. Fine weather. Catch anything with the nets you put out yesterday?

**Tosaku.** No, not much. The season's over.

**Gisuke.** Maybe it *is* too late now.

**Tosaku** *(looking up at* Yoshitaro*)*. Your son's on the roof again.

**Gisuke.** Yes, as usual. I don't like it, but when I keep him locked in a room, he's like a fish out of water. Then, when I take pity on him and let him out, back he goes up on the roof.

**Tosaku.** But after all, he doesn't bother anybody.

**Gisuke.** He bothers us. We feel so ashamed when he climbs up there and shouts.

**Tosaku.** But your younger son, Suejiro, has a fine record at school. That must be some <u>consolation</u> for you.

**Gisuke.** Yes, he's a good student, and that is a consolation to me. If both of them were crazy, I don't know how I could go on living.

**Tosaku.** By the way, a Priestess has just come to the island. How would you like to have her pray for your son? —That's really what I came to see you about.

**Gisuke.** We've tried prayers before, but it's never done any good.

**Tosaku.** This Priestess believes in the god Kompira. She works all kinds of miracles. People say the god inspires her, and that's why her prayers have more effect than those of ordinary priests. Why don't you try her once?

**Gisuke.** Well, we might. How much does she charge?

**Tosaku.** She won't take any money unless the patient is cured. If he is cured, you pay her whatever you feel like.

**Gisuke.** Suejiro says he doesn't believe in prayers. . . . But there's no harm in letting her try.

*(Kichiji enters carrying the ladder and disappears behind the fence.)*

**Tosaku.** I'll go and bring her here. In the meantime you get your son down off the roof.

**Gisuke.** Thanks for your trouble. *(After seeing that* Tosaku *has gone, he calls again.)* Yoshi! Be a good boy and come down.

**Kichiji** *(who is up on the roof by this time).* Now then, young master, come down with me. If you stay up here any longer, you'll have a fever tonight.

**Yoshitaro** *(drawing away from* Kichiji *as a Buddhist[1] might from a heathen)*. Don't touch me! The angels are beckoning to me. You're not supposed to come here. What do you want?

**Kichiji.** Don't talk nonsense! Please come down.

---

1. **Buddhist:** believer of the religion that follows Buddha, the religious philosopher and teacher Siddhartha Gautama who lived in India around 563–483 B.C.

**Yoshitaro.** If you touch me, the demons will tear you apart. (Kichiji *hurriedly catches Yoshitaro by the shoulder and pulls him to the ladder. Yoshitaro suddenly becomes <u>submissive</u>.*)

**Kichiji.** Don't make any trouble now. If you do, you'll fall and hurt yourself.

**Gisuke.** Be careful!

(*Yoshitaro comes down to the center of the stage, followed by* Kichiji. Yoshitaro *is lame in his right leg.*)

**Gisuke** (*calling*). Oyoshi! Come out here a minute.

**Oyoshi** (*from within*). What is it?

**Gisuke.** I've sent for a Priestess.

**Oyoshi** (*coming out*). That may help. You never can tell what will.

**Gisuke.** Yoshitaro says he talks with the god Kompira. Well, this Priestess is a follower of Kompira, so she ought to be able to help him.

**Yoshitaro** (*looking uneasy*). Father! Why did you bring me down? There was a beautiful cloud of five colors rolling down to fetch me.

**Gisuke.** Idiot! Once before you said there was a five-colored cloud, and you jumped off the roof. That's the way you became a cripple. A Priestess of the god Kompira is coming here today to drive the evil spirit out of you, so don't you go back up on the roof.

(*Tosaku enters, leading the* Priestess. *She has a crafty face.*)

**Tosaku.** This is the Priestess I spoke to you about.

**Gisuke.** Ah, good afternoon. I'm glad you've come—this boy is really a disgrace to the whole family.

**Priestess** (*casually*). You needn't worry any more about him. I'll cure him at once with the god's help. (*Looking at* Yoshitaro.) This is the one?

**Gisuke.** Yes. He's twenty-four years old, and the only thing he can do is climb up to high places.

**Priestess.** How long has he been this way?

**Gisuke.** Ever since he was born. Even when he was a baby, he wanted to be climbing. When he was four or five years old, he climbed onto the low shrine, then onto the high shrine of Buddha, and finally onto a very high shelf. When he was seven, he began climbing trees. At fifteen he climbed to the tops of mountains and stayed there all day long. He says he talks with demons and with the gods. What do you think is the matter with him?

**Priestess.** There's no doubt but that it's a fox spirit. I will pray for him. (*looking at* Yoshitaro) Listen now! I am the messenger of the god Kompira. All that I say comes from the god.

**Yoshitaro** (*uneasily*). You say the god Kompira? Have you ever seen him?

**Priestess** (*staring at him*). Don't say such <u>sacrilegious</u> things! The god cannot be seen.

**Yoshitaro** (*exultantly*). I have seen him many times! He's an old man with white robes and a golden crown. He's my best friend.

**Priestess** (*taken aback at this <u>assertion</u>, and speaking to* Gisuke). This is a fox spirit, all right, and a very extreme case. I will address the god.

(*She chants a prayer in a weird manner.* Yoshitaro, *held fast by* Kichiji, *watches the* Priestess *blankly. She works herself into a <u>frenzy</u> and falls to the ground in a faint. Pres-*

*ently she rises to her feet and looks about her strangely.)*

**Priestess** *(in a changed voice).* I am the god Kompira!

*(All except* Yoshitaro *fall to their knees with exclamations of reverence.)*

**Priestess** *(with affected dignity).* The elder son of this family is under the influence of a fox spirit. Hang him up on the branch of a tree and purify him with the smoke of green pine needles. If you fail to do what I say, you will all be punished!

*(She faints again. There are more exclamations of astonishment.)*

**Priestess** *(rising and looking about her as though unconscious of what has taken place).* What has happened? Did the god speak?

**Gisuke.** It was a miracle.

**Priestess.** You must do at once whatever the god told you, or you'll be punished. I warn you for your own sake.

**Gisuke** *(hesitating somewhat).* Kichiji, go and get some green pine needles.

**Oyoshi.** No! It's too cruel, even if it is the god's command.

**Priestess.** He will not suffer, only the fox spirit within him. The boy himself will not suffer at all. Hurry! *(Looking fixedly at* Yoshitaro.*)* Did you hear the god's command? He told the spirit to leave your body before it hurt.

**Yoshitaro.** That was not Kompira's voice. He wouldn't talk to a priestess like you.

**Priestess** *(insulted).* I'll get even with you. Just wait! Don't talk back to the god like that, you horrid fox!

*(Kichiji enters with an armful of green pine boughs.* Oyoshi *is frightened.)*

**Priestess.** Respect the god or be punished!

*(Gisuke and* Kichiji *reluctantly set fire to the pine needles, then bring* Yoshitaro *to the fire. He struggles against being held in the smoke.)*

**Yoshitaro.** Father! What are you doing to me? I don't like it! I don't like it!

**Priestess.** That's not his own voice speaking. It's the fox within him. Only the fox is suffering.

**Oyoshi.** But it's cruel!

*(Gisuke and* Kichiji *attempt to press* Yoshitaro's *face into the smoke. Suddenly* Suejiro's *voice is heard calling within the house, and presently he appears. He stands amazed at the scene before him.)*

**Suejiro.** What's happening here? What's the smoke for?

**Yoshitaro** *(coughing from the smoke and looking at his brother as at a savior).* Father and Kichiji are putting me in the smoke.

**Suejiro** *(angrily).* Father! What foolish thing are you doing now? Haven't I told you time and time again about this sort of business?

**Gisuke.** But the god inspired the miraculous Priestess . . .

**Suejiro** *(interrupting).* What nonsense is that? You do these insane things merely because he is so helpless.

*(With a contemptuous look at the* Priestess *he stamps the fire out.)*

**Priestess.** Wait! That fire was made at the command of the god! *(Suejiro sneeringly puts out the last spark.)*

**Gisuke** *(more courageously).* Suejiro, I have no education, and you have, so I am always willing to listen to you. But this fire was

JAPANESE WOMAN J. A. Christensen Paper-cut from *Cut-Art: An Introduction to Chung-hua and Kiri-e,* Watson Guptill Publications, New York.

made at the god's command, and you shouldn't have stamped on it.

**Suejiro.** Smoke won't cure him. People will laugh at you if they hear you've been trying to drive out a fox. All the gods in the country together couldn't even cure a cold. This Priestess is a fraud. All she wants is the money.

**Gisuke.** But the doctors can't cure him.

**Suejiro.** If the doctors can't, nobody can. I've told you before that he doesn't suffer. If he did, we'd have to do something for him. But as long as he can climb up on the roof, he is happy. Nobody in the whole country is as happy as he is—perhaps nobody in the world. Besides, if you cure him now, what

can he do? He's twenty-four years old and he knows nothing, not even the alphabet. He's had no practical experience. If he were cured, he would be conscious of being crippled, and he'd be the most miserable man alive. Is that what you want to see? It's all because you want to make him normal. But wouldn't it be foolish to become normal merely to suffer? *(looking sidewise at the Priestess)* Tosaku, if you brought her here, you had better take her away.

**Priestess** *(angry and insulted).* You disbelieve the <u>oracle</u> of the god. You will be punished! *(She starts her chant as before. She faints, rises, and speaks in a changed voice.)* I am the great god Kompira! What the brother of the patient says springs from his own selfishness. He knows if his sick brother is cured, he'll get the family estate. Doubt not this oracle!

**Suejiro** (*excitedly knocking the* Priestess *down*). That's a damned lie, you old fool.

(*He kicks her.*)

**Priestess** (*getting to her feet and resuming her ordinary voice*). You've hurt me! You savage!

**Suejiro.** You fraud! You swindler!

**Tosaku** (*coming between them*). Wait, young man! Don't get in such a frenzy.

**Suejiro** (*still excited*). You liar! A woman like you can't understand brotherly love!

**Tosaku.** We'll leave now. It was my mistake to have brought her.

**Gisuke** (*giving* Tosaku *some money*). I hope you'll excuse him. He's young and has such a temper.

**Priestess.** You kicked me when I was inspired by the god. You'll be lucky to survive until tonight.

**Suejiro.** Liar!

**Oyoshi** (*soothing* Suejiro). Be still now. (*To the* Priestess). I'm sorry this has happened.

**Priestess** (*leaving with* Tosaku). The foot you kicked me with will rot off!

(*The* Priestess *and* Tosaku *go out.*)

**Gisuke** (*to* Suejiro). Aren't you afraid of being punished for what you've done?

**Suejiro.** A god never inspires a woman like that old swindler. She lies about everything.

**Oyoshi.** I suspected her from the very first. She wouldn't do such cruel things if a real god inspired her.

**Gisuke** (*without any insistence*). Maybe so. But, Suejiro, your brother will be a burden to you all your life.

**Suejiro.** It will be no burden at all. When I become successful, I'll build a tower for him on top of a mountain.

**Gisuke** (*suddenly*). But where's Yoshitaro gone?

**Kichiji** (*pointing at the roof*). He's up there.

**Gisuke** (*having to smile*). As usual.

(*During the preceding excitement, Yoshitaro has slipped away and climbed back up on the roof. The four persons below look at each other and smile.*)

**Suejiro.** A normal person would be angry with you for having put him in the smoke, but you see, he's forgotten everything. (*He calls.*) Yoshitaro!

**Yoshitaro.** (*For all his madness there is affection for his brother.*) Suejiro! I asked Kompira, and he says he doesn't know her!

**Suejiro** (*smiling*). You're right. The god will inspire you, not a priestess like her.

(*Through a rift in the clouds, the golden light of the sunset strikes the roof.*)

**Suejiro** (*exclaiming*). What a beautiful sunset!

**Yoshitaro** (*his face lighted by the sun's reflection*). Suejiro, look! Can't you see a golden palace in that cloud over there? There! Can't you see? Just look! How beautiful!

**Suejiro** (*as he feels the sorrow of sanity*). Yes, I see. I see it, too. Wonderful.

**Yoshitaro** (*filled with joy*). There! I hear music coming from the palace. Flutes, what I love best of all. Isn't it beautiful?

(*The parents have gone into the house. The mad brother on the roof and the sane brother on the ground remain looking at the golden sunset.*) ❧

## Responding to Reading

### First Impressions

1. How did you react to Yoshitaro and Gisuke?

### Second Thoughts

2. Which character, Yoshitaro or Gisuke, did you find the most interesting? Why?

3. How does Yoshitaro's madness make Gisuke feel? Explain.

   **Think about**
   • what Gisuke says to his servant and his neighbor
   • what he says to each of his sons
   • his treatment of Yoshitaro
   • what others say to him about his son

4. Compare and contrast the personalities of Gisuke and Suejiro.

   **Think about**
   • what Gisuke and Suejiro say to each other
   • their conversations with the other characters
   • their treatment of Yoshitaro and the priestess

5. Turn back to page 408 and reread Suejiro's defense of Yoshitaro. Do you agree with his position? Why or why not?

6. The stage direction for Suejiro's last lines says that "he feels the sorrow of sanity." What do you think the writer means by this statement?

7. What do you think is the writer's attitude toward insanity? Explain.

### Broader Connections

8. Like Yoshitaro's father, many people want to keep the mentally ill hidden from view. Why do you think people are still afraid to deal openly with mental illness?

## Literary Concept: One-Act Play

Because a one-act play is short, the plot usually centers on a single conflict that builds quickly to a climax. The conflict is resolved by the end of the play. What is the conflict in *The Madman on the Roof* and how is it resolved? The one-act play usually has a small cast of characters that includes only a few rounded, or well-developed, characters whose personalities are clearly revealed through their words and actions. The other characters are flat and stereotyped in order to present a certain point of view quickly. In this play, which characters are well developed? Which characters simply represent a single viewpoint?

## Writing Options

1. An independent thinker is a person whose thoughts and actions are not influenced by others. Identify the character whom you think is the most independent person in this play. Give evidence to support your view.

2. Suppose you are Suejiro and you have decided to have Yoshitaro examined by a psychiatrist. Write out a description of Yoshitaro's behavior, attitude, and mental ability for the psychiatrist's medical records.

3. What if you had a mentally handicapped brother or sister? How would you feel? How would you treat the person? What difficulties might this person create for you? Answer as truthfully as you can.

4. Do you think Gisuke's attitude toward Yoshitaro will change because of this incident? Write a prediction about Gisuke's treatment of Yoshitaro in the days that follow.

## Vocabulary Practice

**Exercise** On your paper, write the word that best completes each sentence.

1. Yoshitaro was so _____ in his visions that he didn't hear or see anyone around him.
2. Gisuke found some _____ in Suejiro's success, but he thought that Yoshitaro's madness brought shame on his family.
3. Not everybody believed that the priestess was an _____ of the god Kompira.
4. Yoshitaro made an _____ that he had seen and spoken with Kompira.
5. The priestess behaved wildly and worked herself into a _____.
6. To convince her audience that she was Kompira, the priestess showed an _____ dignity as she spoke.
7. Instead of being _____, Yoshitaro struggled against being held in the smoke.
8. Since he believed the priestess to be a fraud, Suejiro was _____ of her.
9. The priestess thought Suejiro's disrespect for her holy work was _____.
10. Filled with joy, Yoshitaro responded _____ to the music he heard coming from the clouds.

> **Words to Know and Use**
>
> affected
> assertion
> consolation
> contemptuous
> ecstatically
> engross
> frenzy
> oracle
> sacrilegious
> submissive

## Options for Learning

**1** • **Design the Set**   Study the stage directions on page 402 and create a model or drawing of the set for the play. Find a book about staging and locate ideas on how sets are made. Based on what you learn, explain how each part of the set, including the yard, fence, roof, and the distant sea, could be made.

**2** • **Opening Night**   Choose your favorite scene from the play, cast the scene with members of your class, and rehearse the lines. Perhaps you would like to act out the scene between the priestess and the other characters. Perform the scene for your class.

**3** • **What's Your Attitude?**   Design a questionnaire and survey students, teachers, and neighbors to find out what they know about mental illness and what they think should be done to care for the mentally ill. Graph your findings as a way of sharing your information with the class.

**4** • **Theater of the Ages**   Japan's dramatic tradition is centuries old. Research the traditions of *Noh* and *Kabuki* theater. Find out what kinds of stories were performed, what costumes and makeup were like, and how actors were trained. Gather pictures of the two kinds of theater and share your information with the class.

### 📖 FACT FINDER

*What percentage of the population of the United States is being treated for some form of mental illness today?*

---

## Kikuchi Kan
### 1888–1948

The fame that Kikuchi achieved in Japan is, unfortunately, not the kind that he sought. Although he became the founder of one of Japan's premier publishing houses, he was more interested in becoming an important writer. He wrote many plays and novels but found that most of his work was not considered original enough. His artistic reputation faded as other writers, using ideas and attitudes from the West, became celebrated in literary circles. However, Kikuchi's literary magazine, *Literary Annals*, was influential in publishing many contemporary Japanese plays, and today he is best remembered as the man responsible for finding and publishing many new writers. In addition, the magazine was the forerunner of a large publishing house that provides the two most important literary prizes in Japan for new writers.

# WRITER'S WORKSHOP

## EXPOSITION

Do you know of any nerds or jocks in your school? How would you define the slang terms *nerd* and *jock?* You might give examples of each kind of person or describe the kind of behavior you'd expect from a nerd or a jock. Read the following part of a conversation, which uses examples and description to informally define the slang term *Piltdown.*

> That Jim sure is a real Piltdown. He acts like a primitive, and he's phony as they come. He always wears strange clothes. He listens to really bogus music, like that old group Scar Tissue. No one will sit with him at lunch—he eats like a caveman!

In the dictionary, a Piltdown man is defined as a species of prehistoric man whose bones were supposedly discovered in Piltdown, England in 1911; but the discovery later turned out to be a hoax. Both the **informal definition** and the **formal definition** of *Piltdown* are examples of **exposition,** an essential kind of writing that explains or informs.

In this assignment, you will define the word *nonconformist,* using your personal beliefs and feelings as well as meanings you've gleaned from the readings in this subunit. Your definition will be informal, or more personal and subjective than those found in a dictionary, an encyclopedia, or a science or social studies textbook.

> **Here is your PASSkey to this assignment.**

### GUIDED ASSIGNMENT: DEFINING A NONCONFORMIST

Write an informal definition of the word *nonconformist,* explaining the qualities and characteristics you think a nonconformist possesses.

**P**URPOSE: To write a definition

**A**UDIENCE: Other students

**S**UBJECT: A nonconformist

**S**TRUCTURE: Informal definition paper

## Prewriting

**STEP 1** **Explore the word**  With a small group of classmates, explore the meaning of the word *nonconformist,* using one or more of these ideas:

**Option 1**   Write *nonconformist* on one side of a 3 by 5 index card. Then pass the card and have each person in the group list related words on the blank side.

**Option 2**   Have each member in your group answer one of these questions about nonconformists: Who? What? Where? When? Why? and How? List the different responses to the questions.

**Option 3**   Analyze the word *nonconformist* by breaking it into parts, determining what each word part means, and then deciding the meaning of the combination of the parts.

**Option 4**   Make a word web or a tree diagram for one of the subunit characters who was a nonconformist (Samuel Johnson, Simón Perez, Yoshitaro) as in the example below.

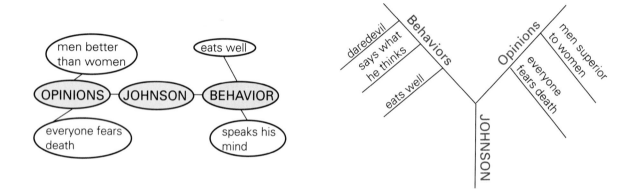

STEP **2**   **Use cubing**   After you generate ideas about nonconformists with your group, analyze your own specific feelings and opinions about the word. Use **cubing,** a technique in which you imagine a cube with six sides, each bearing one of these instructions:

- Describe it.
- Compare it.
- Associate it with other thoughts.
- Analyze it.
- Explain how it works.
- Argue for or against it.

Spend a few minutes on each side of the cube before moving onto the next side. In this way you look at your subject from different angles. One perspective may interest you and give you ideas for approaching your definition paper.

**STEP 3** **Establish an order** Organize the prewriting ideas you have gathered about nonconformists. Try using either order of importance, beginning with the least important point and ending with the most important point, or comparison and contrast, examining similarities and differences between conformists and nonconformists.

## Drafting

**STEP 1** **Writing a thesis statement** Begin your definition paper with an effective thesis statement. Write either a one-sentence definition or a general statement to explain what the word *nonconformist* means to you. Read the following thesis statement a student made for the word *paranoid*.

A paranoid is a person who, because of terrible insecurities, assumes that everyone is out to get him or her.

◀ Student Model
......................................

**STEP 2** **Write an introduction** Develop your thesis statement further in your introduction. Introduce your audience to the basic direction you plan to take in discussing nonconformists. Consider the development of the thesis in this student's introduction to a paper that informally defines the word *paranoid*.

We all know people who tend to blame others for everything that happens to them. Some of these people act as if they are above the rest of us mortals and that we in our jealousy are trying to pull them down. They are paranoids, and their most obvious quality is suspicion of everyone around them. Yet although they act as if they are special, deep down they are very insecure about themselves.

◀ Student Model
......................................

**STEP 3** **Describe characteristics** In the body paragraphs of your definition paper, explain your personal response to the word *nonconformist*. Look back at your notes from cubing in Step 2 of Prewriting. You might begin each paragraph with a topic sentence that incorporates one heading. One paragraph could describe a nonconformist, another could contrast a nonconformist with a conformist, another could argue for or against nonconformism, and so on. You do not have to write a paragraph about each topic mentioned.

Use facts, examples, descriptions, and comparisons to elaborate your definition. You might further illustrate your viewpoint by providing interesting quotations or sayings.

**STEP 4** **Conclude the paper** In a concluding paragraph, summarize your feelings about nonconformists, restating your main points in a strong way. You might end with a worthwhile quotation or with your own generalization about how you will react toward nonconformists in the future.

## Revising and Editing

Review your definition paper. Have a classmate respond to your draft, using the following checklist as a guide.

---

### Revision Checklist
...........................................................................

1. Does this definition paper fully explore the meaning of *nonconformist?*
2. Is the definition paper organized by order of importance or by comparison and contrast?
3. Is the definition of *nonconformist* supported by examples, facts, descriptions, comparisons, or analogies?
4. Does the paper include personal feelings about nonconformists?
5. Will younger students understand this definition paper?

---

**Editing** After you have finished revising your definition paper, have a peer editor proofread it for spelling, punctuation, and usage errors.

## Presenting

Obtain permission to read your definition paper to a class of younger students. After your presentation, ask the students which parts confused them and which parts they enjoyed. Have them suggest historical figures, fictional characters, or people they know who fit your definition of a nonconformist.

## Reflecting on Your Writing

Answer the following questions. Place your answers along with your essay in your writing portfolio.

1. What was the most difficult task in writing a definition paper?
2. How did writing this paper affect your opinions and ideas about nonconformists?
3. How would you change your definition paper for an audience of adults in your community?

# LANGUAGE WORKSHOP

## SUBJECT-VERB AGREEMENT

A verb must agree with its subject in number.

This is really a simple rule. If you use a singular subject, you must use a singular verb. If you use a plural subject, you must use a plural verb. Doing otherwise—using a singular subject with a plural verb, for example—is like putting a left shoe on your right foot. It just won't fit properly.

> The writer (singular) stands (singular) at the front of the classroom.
> The writers (plural) stand (plural) at the front of the classroom.

Remember that the *s* at the end of a verb, as in *stands* or *sits,* shows that the verb is singular. Most verbs drop the *s* to form the plural.

You can usually tell by ear when the subject and verb of a sentence agree in number. A sentence like "The child ask the question" is incorrect, and it sounds incorrect. Sometimes, however, you may be unsure whether to use a singular or a plural verb with a particular subject. You can avoid errors in subject-verb agreement by studying those situations in which problems commonly occur.

## Phrases Between Subjects and Verbs

One situation that sometimes causes problems is when a prepositional phrase appears between the subject and the verb. In such a situation, ignore the phrase and look for the subject outside it.

> The older *brother* in the family *sits* on the roof. (The subject is *brother.*)
> The *people* in the household *are* nervous. (The subject is *people.*)

Phrases beginning with the words *with, together with, including, as well as,* or *in addition to* are not part of the subject.

> *Yoshitaro,* together with his parents, *was spending* the evening at home. (The subject is *Yoshitaro.*)
> His *father,* in addition to other people, *wants* Yoshitaro to come down. (The subject is *father.*)

**REMINDER**

A prepositional phrase consists of a preposition, such as *to, from, at, on, around,* or *under,* and a noun or a pronoun: *from her, on the moon.*

**HINT**

Say the sentence to yourself without the phrase. This will help you to identify the true subject.

**Exercise 1**   Write the verb that agrees with the subject.

1. This drama about two brothers (take, takes) place on a Japanese island.
2. The members of this wealthy family (is, are) in turmoil.
3. The younger son, Suejiro, along with the other family members, (argue, argues) about Yoshitaro's behavior.
4. Yoshitaro, the "madman," (sit, sits) on the roof of the family home.
5. In spite of his father's pleas, Yoshitaro (refuses, refuse) to come down.
6. The main character in this drama (are, is) "mad," but happy.
7. His brother, Suejiro, (understands, understand) Yoshitaro's madness.
8. Because his older brother doesn't suffer, Suejiro (believes, believe) that Yoshitaro is happy.
9. The students in our class (discuss, discusses) this play and (decides, decide) to act it out.
10. My teacher, in addition to my classmates, (are, is) responsible for assembling all the props used by the priestess.

## Verbs with Compound Subjects

A **compound subject** consists of two or more subjects joined together and used with the same verb. Compound subjects that contain the word *and* are plural and take a plural verb.

> Simón Perez and the other workers *need* jobs.

When the parts of a compound subject are connected by *or* or *nor,* the verb agrees with the subject nearer to the verb.

> Neither Perez nor the other lumberjacks *want* to be fired. (The verb *want* agrees with *lumberjacks,* the subject nearest to the verb.)
> Neither the other lumberjacks nor Perez *wants* to be fired. (The verb *wants* agrees with *Perez,* the subject nearest to the verb.)

**Exercise 2**   Some of the following sentences contain errors in subject-verb agreement. Rewrite these sentences, correcting the errors. If a sentence has no error, write *Correct.*

1. Simón Perez and his fellow workers lives in Colombia.
2. His tale about lumberjacking begin during the Civil War of '85.
3. Neither Perez nor the other men has work.
4. Arriving at a mining outfit, Perez claim he is a lumberjack.

5. The two children of the manager love to listen to Perez's songs.
6. Perez and his assistant spends hours marking trees.
7. When Perez is supposed to be finding lumber, thoughts and daydreams constantly swims in his mind.
8. When Perez is finally forced to saw the lumber, he admit that he are far from being a master craftsman.
9. Neither Perez nor the other men gives away Perez's secret.
10. His pleasant personality and persuasive language saves Perez's job.

**Exercise 3**   The following passage contains errors in subject-verb agreement. Copy the passage and correct any errors you find.

Every day Dr. Johnson labors for hours over the dictionary he is writing. His publisher and his creditors wants to have the dictionary completed soon. Neither the publisher nor the creditors is likely to have any satisfaction on this matter. Dr. Johnson is a great scholar. He wants his dictionary to be perfect. Both the meanings and the histories of the words has to be carefully researched. Neither I nor Dr. Johnson's other friends is able to influence him to work less strenuously. Either the long hours or his own demanding nature are likely to kill him.

**Exercise 4   Style**   Find three examples of sentences with compound subjects in this book. Write the sentences on a sheet of paper and underline the subjects once and the verb twice. Then, rewrite each sentence as two different sentences, each with a single subject. Notice how the one-sentence version, with a compound subject, is much more economical than two separate sentences with single subjects. Writing sentences with compound subjects allows writers to cut down on repetition.

**Exercise 5   Analyzing and Revising Your Writing**

1. Take a paper from your writing portfolio.
2. Reread the paper, looking for errors in subject-verb agreement. Study each sentence. Ask yourself, What is the subject and what is the verb? Make sure that they agree. Be particularly careful about agreement in sentences with compound subjects or sentences with phrases between subjects and verbs.
3. Revise any errors in subject-verb agreement that you find.
4. Remember to check for errors in subject-verb agreement the next time you proofread a piece of your own writing.

LANGUAGE HANDBOOK
......................................
For review and practice:
subject-verb agreement,
pages 1018–20, 1022

# STUDY SKILLS
WORKSHOP

## READING RATES

### How to Scan

To learn to scan, try this method.

1. Choose a familiar textbook.

2. Place a folded paper or a 3″ × 5″ card over the first line of a page and move the paper quickly down the page.

3. Look for key words or phrases that indicate you are near the information you need.

4. When you locate such a clue, stop scanning and begin to read slowly.

When reading you need to vary your speed to suit the task at hand.

To locate specific information, you can **scan** a reading selection, running your eyes quickly across each page until you spot what you are looking for.

To get an overview of a piece or to find its main idea, you can **skim,** reading only the title, headlines, highlighted words or phrases, topic sentences, and any introduction, conclusion, or summary.

When studying, you'll need to read material more slowly and thoroughly. First, skim the piece to get an overview. Next, slow down and carefully read the material, looking for main ideas and supporting details. Notice all the key words, dates, and facts. As you read, take careful notes.

**Exercise** Follow these directions step by step. Do not read through all the directions at once.

**Step 1** Skim the following passage. Note the topic sentence. Write one sentence summarizing the main idea of the passage.

**Step 2** Scan the passage to identify the year in which Boswell first met Samuel Johnson. Write your answer.

**Step 3** Read the passage in depth. Write at least three details that support the main idea of the passage.

> Johnson's character, which so greatly impressed his contemporaries, has been immortalized by the extraordinary zeal and ability of the greatest of all biographers, James Boswell, whose *Life of Johnson* (1791) is one of the classics of the century. From the time when he first met Johnson in 1763, Boswell followed the great man's doings and sayings with unwearied attention. In his effort to draw Johnson out and to make him expressive, he was deterred by no rebuffs, and he was not ashamed to offer himself as the butt of his master's wit. After an acquaintance of twenty years, during which Boswell was frequently in Johnson's company studying him, making notes, and keeping a journal, he was prepared, with the same cheerful sacrifice of his own dignity, to write the biography which still keeps Johnson in the place which he won, that of the most salient figure of his epoch. Of no man in the past is our perception so extraordinarily keen and first-hand.
>
> —*A History of English Literature*

# DEVELOPING A SENSE OF SELF

Scientists of the Enlightenment studied such mysteries as the solar system and the laws of physics, while philosophers, poets, and novelists contemplated the mysteries of individuality. They asked, What makes a person unique?

Enlightenment writers often wrote about people in search of their true identities. One

of the most popular works of the period was *Robinson Crusoe*, a novel in which a shipwrecked man learns some basic lessons about himself. Crusoe's story is excerpted in this subunit. The other readings will take you to different cultures and ages, introducing you to characters who must also find their identities.

Fiction

*from* **Robinson Crusoe**

DANIEL DEFOE

## *E*xamine What You Know

Share with your class what you know about Robinson Crusoe, one of the most famous shipwreck survivors in literature. Then predict what kinds of problems a castaway like Crusoe, alone on an island, might face. Based on other stories you have heard of survivors, how might those problems be solved? Put your problems and solutions into a chart form and see how closely your predictions match what you read.

## *E*xpand Your Knowledge

In 1709, a sailor named Alexander Selkirk was rescued from a Pacific island that had been his home for five years. The ship's captain had left Selkirk on the uninhabited island, near Chile, following a quarrel between the two men. Upon returning to England, Selkirk became an instant celebrity. People were fascinated by the exotic story of his lonely life in a strange and primitive land.

Defoe capitalized on the interest in Selkirk's story and based his novel *Robinson Crusoe* on the castaway's experience. Defoe's use of a journal format, exact details, and a precise chronology made his novel so realistic that many early readers believed Crusoe to be an actual person.

## *E*nrich Your Reading

**Making Sense of Long Sentences**   In 1719, when *Robinson Crusoe* was written, it was the style to use long, complicated sentences. You can untangle these sentences by using the following strategies.

- Skim a section quickly to get a general idea of what it is about; then go back and read more carefully.
- Look for subjects and predicates in each sentence to help you focus on the main idea. (For a quick review of subjects and predicates, see the Language Handbook.)
- Pay attention to semicolons and commas, which break sentences into smaller units.
- Visualize the scenes as you read; imagine yourself in Crusoe's shoes.

■ *A biography of the author can be found on page 437.*

# *from* Robinson Crusoe

DANIEL DEFOE

*In this excerpt from the novel, Crusoe recalls the day that he arrived on his deserted island. His ship has been run aground on a reef during a terrible storm, and he is the only survivor. Note that this section is in the form of a diary entry, which is how Crusoe records the day-to-day events of his island life. In later sections, the diary form is dropped.*

*September 30, 1659.*—I, poor miserable Robinson Crusoe, being shipwrecked, during a dreadful storm, in the offing, came on shore on this dismal unfortunate island, which I called the Island of Despair, all the rest of the ship's company being drowned, and myself almost dead.

All the rest of that day I spent in <u>afflicting</u> myself at the dismal circumstances I was brought to, viz.,[1] I had neither food, house, clothes, weapon, nor place to fly to; and in despair of any relief, saw nothing but death before me; either that I should be devoured by wild beasts, murdered by savages, or starved to death for want of food. At the approach of night, I slept in a tree for fear of wild creatures, but slept soundly, though it rained all night.

*Oct. 1.*—In the morning I saw, to my great surprise, the ship had floated with the high tide, and was driven on shore again much nearer the island; which, as it was some comfort on one hand, for seeing her sit upright, and not broken to pieces, I hoped, if the wind <u>abated</u>, I might get on board, and get some food and necessaries out of her for my relief; so, on the other hand, it renewed my grief at the loss of my comrades, who, I imagined, if we had all stayed on board, might have saved the ship, or at least that they would not have been all drowned as they were; and that had the men been saved, we might perhaps have built us a boat out of the ruins of the ship, to have carried us to some other part of the world. I spent great part of this day in perplexing[2] myself on these things; but at length seeing the ship almost dry, I went upon the sand as near as I could, and then swam on

---

1. **viz.** (viz): namely; that is.
2. **perplexing:** troubling.

423

ROBINSON CRUSOE   1920   N. C. Wyeth   The Granger Collection, New York.

board; this day also it continued raining, though with no wind at all.

*From the 1st of October to the 24th.*—All these days entirely spent in many several voyages to get all I could out of the ship, which I brought on shore, every tide of flood, upon rafts. Much rain also in these days, though with some intervals of fair weather; but, it seems, this was the rainy season.

*Oct. 20.*—I overset my raft, and all the goods I had got upon it; but being in shoal[3] water, and the things being chiefly heavy, I recovered many of them when the tide was out.

*Oct. 25.*—It rained all night and all day, with some gusts of wind, during which time the ship broke in pieces, the wind blowing a little harder than before, and was no more to be seen, except the wreck of her, and that only at low water. I spent this day in covering and securing the goods which I had saved, that the rain might not spoil them.

*Oct. 26.*—I walked about the shore almost all day to find out a place to fix my habitation, greatly concerned to secure myself from an attack in the night, either from wild beasts or men. Towards night I fixed upon a proper place under a rock, and marked out a semicircle for my encampment, which I resolved to strengthen with a work, wall, or <u>fortification</u> made of double piles, lined within with cables, and without with turf.

From the 26th to the 30th I worked very hard in carrying all my goods to my new habitation, though some part of the time it rained exceeding hard.

The 31st, in the morning, I went out into the island with my gun to seek for some food, and discover the country; when I killed a she-goat, and her kid followed me home, which I afterwards killed also, because it would not feed.

*Nov. 1.*—I set up my tent under a rock, and lay there the first night, making it as large as I could, with stakes driven in to swing my hammock upon.

*Nov. 2.*—I set up all my chests and boards, and the pieces of timber which made my rafts, and with them formed a fence round me, a little within the place I had marked out for my fortification.

*Nov. 3.*—I went out with my gun, and killed two fowls like ducks, which were very good food. In the afternoon went to work to make me a table.

*Nov. 4.*—This morning I began to order my times of work, of going out with my gun, time of sleep, and time of diversion, viz., every morning I walked out with my gun for two or three hours, if it did not rain; then employed myself to work till about eleven o'clock; then eat what I had to live on; and from twelve to two I lay down to sleep, the weather being excessive hot; and then in the evening to work again. The working part of this day and of the next were wholly employed in making my table; for I was yet but a very sorry workman, though time and necessity made me a complete natural mechanic soon after, as I believe it would do anyone else.

*Nov. 5.*—This day went abroad with my gun and my dog, and killed a wild cat; her skin pretty soft, but her flesh good for nothing. Every creature I killed, I took off the skins and preserved them. Coming back by the seashore, I saw many sorts of seafowls, which I did not understand; but was surprised, and almost frightened, with two or three seals, which, while I was gazing at, not well knowing what they were, got into the sea, and escaped me for that time.

---

3. **shoal** (shōl): shallow.

*Words to Know and Use* | **fortification** (fôrt′ ə fi kā′ shən) *n.* a fort or defensive wall; earthwork

*Nov. 6.*—After my morning walk I went to work with my table again, and finished it, though not to my liking; nor was it long before I learned to mend it.

*Nov. 7.*—Now it began to be settled fair weather. The 7th, 8th, 9th, 10th, and part of the 12th (for the 11th was Sunday) I took wholly up to make me a chair, and with much ado, brought it to a tolerable shape, but never to please me; and even in the making, I pulled it in pieces several times. Note I soon neglected my keeping Sundays; for, omitting my mark for them on my post, I forgot which was which.

*Nov. 13.*—This day it rained, which refreshed me exceedingly, and cooled the earth; but it was accompanied with terrible thunder and lightning, which frightened me dreadfully, for fear of my powder.[4] As soon as it was over, I resolved to separate my stock of powder into as many little parcels as possible, that it might not be in danger.

*Nov. 14, 15, 16.*—These three days I spent in making little square chests or boxes, which might hold about a pound, or two pound at most, of powder; and so putting the powder in, I stowed it in places as secure and remote from one another as possible. On one of these three days I killed a large bird that was good to eat, but I know not what to call it.

*Nov. 17.*—This day I began to dig behind my tent into the rock, to make room for my farther convenience. Note, three things I wanted exceedingly for this work, viz., a pickaxe, a shovel, and a wheelbarrow or basket; so I desisted from my work, and began to consider how to supply that want, and make me some tools. As for a pickaxe, I made use of the iron crows,[5] which were proper enough, though heavy; but the next thing was a shovel or spade. This was so absolutely necessary,

that indeed I could do nothing effectually without it; but what kind of one to make, I knew not.

*Nov. 18.*—The next day, in searching the woods, I found a tree of that wood, or like it, which in the Brazils they call the iron tree, for its exceeding hardness; of this, with great labor, and almost spoiling my axe, I cut a piece, and brought it home, too, with difficulty enough, for it was exceeding heavy.

The excessive hardness of the wood, and having no other way, made me a long while upon this machine, for I worked it effectually, by little and little, into the form of a shovel or spade, the handle exactly shaped like ours in England, only that the broad part having no iron shod upon it at bottom, it would not last me so long. However, it served well enough for the uses which I had occasion to put it to; but never was a shovel, I believe, made after that fashion, or so long a-making.

I was still <u>deficient</u>, for I wanted a basket or a wheelbarrow. A basket I could not make by any means, having no such things as twigs that would bend to make wickerware, at least none yet found out. And as to a wheelbarrow, I fancied I could make all but the wheel, but that I had no notion of, neither did I know how to go about it; besides, I had no possible way to make the iron gudgeons[6] for the spindle or axis of the wheel to run in, so I gave it over; and so for carrying away the earth which I dug out of the cave, I made me a thing like a hod which the laborers carry mortar in, when they serve the bricklayers.

This was not so difficult to me as the making

---

4. **powder:** gun powder.
5. **iron crows:** crowbars; pry bars used as levers.
6. **gudgeons:** metal pins at the ends of axles, on which wheels turn.

*Words to Know and Use* | **deficient** (dē fish′ ənt) *adj.* lacking in some essential

of the shovel; and yet this, and the shovel, and the attempt which I made in vain to make a wheelbarrow, took me up no less than four days; I mean always, excepting my morning walk with my gun, which I seldom failed, and very seldom failed also bringing home something fit to eat.

*Nov. 23.*—My other work having now stood still because of my making these tools, when they were finished I went on, and working every day, as my strength and time allowed, I spent eighteen days entirely in widening and deepening my cave, that it might hold my goods commodiously.[7]

*Note.*—During all this time I worked to make this room or cave spacious enough to accommodate me as a warehouse or magazine, a kitchen, a diningroom, and a cellar; as for my lodging, I kept to the tent, except that sometimes in the wet season of the year it rained so hard, that I could not keep myself dry, which caused me afterwards to cover all my place within my pale[8] with long poles, in the form of rafters, leaning against the rock, and load them with flags and large leaves of trees, like a thatch.

*Dec. 10.*—I began now to think my cave or vault finished, when on a sudden (it seems I had made it too large) a great quantity of earth fell down from the top and one side, so much, that, in short, it frightened me, and not without reason too; for if I had been under it, I had never wanted a gravedigger. Upon this disaster I had a great deal of work to do over again; for I had the loose earth to carry out; and, which was of more importance, I had the ceiling to prop up, so that I might be sure no more would come down.

*Dec. 11.*—This day I went to work with it accordingly, and got two shores or posts pitched upright to the top, with two pieces of boards across over each post. This I finished the next day; and setting more posts up with boards, in about a week more I had the roof secure; and the posts standing in rows, served me for partitions to part of my house.

*Dec. 17.*—From this day to the twentieth I placed shelves, and knocked up nails on the posts to hang everything up that could be hung up; and now I began to be in some order within doors.

*Dec. 20.*—Now I carried everything into the cave, and began to furnish my house, and set up some pieces of boards, like a dresser, to order my victuals upon; but boards began to be very scarce with me; also I made another table.

*After a period of living alone, Crusoe decides to evaluate his position and weigh its good and bad aspects.*

I now began to consider seriously my condition, and the circumstance I was reduced to; and I drew up the state of my affairs in writing; not so much to leave them to any that were to come after me, for I was like to have but few heirs, as to deliver my thoughts from daily poring upon them, and afflicting my mind. And as my reason began now to master my despondency, I began to comfort myself as well as I could, and to set the good against the evil, that I might have something to distinguish my case from worse; and I stated it very impartially, like debtor and creditor, the comforts I enjoyed against the miseries I suffered, thus:

---

7. **commodiously** (kə mō′ dē əs lē): with plenty of room.

8. **pale:** enclosure

*Words
to Know
and Use*  |  **impartially** (im pär′ shəl lē) *adv.* in a manner that does not favor one side over another; fairly; justly

|                                                                                          |                                                                                                          |
| ---------------------------------------------------------------------------------------- | -------------------------------------------------------------------------------------------------------- |
| *Evil*                                                                                   | *Good*                                                                                                   |
| I am cast upon a horrible desolate island, void of all hope of recovery.                 | But I am alive, and not drowned, as all my ship's company was.                                           |
| I am singled out and separated, as it were, from all the world to be miserable.          | But I am singled out, too, from all the ship's crew to be spared from death; and He that miraculously saved me from death, can deliver me from this condition. |
| I am divided from mankind, a solitaire, one banished from human society.                 | But I am not starved and perishing on a barren place, affording no <u>sustenance.</u>                    |
| I have no clothes to cover me.                                                           | But I am in a hot climate, where if I had clothes I could hardly wear them.                              |
| I am without any defence or means to resist any violence of man or beast.                | But I am cast on an island, where I see no wild beasts to hurt me, as I saw on the coast of Africa; and what if I had been shipwrecked there? |
| I have no soul to speak to, or relieve me.                                               | But God wonderfully sent the ship in near enough to the shore, that I have gotten out so many necessary things as will either supply my wants, or enable me to supply myself even as long as I live. |

Upon the whole, here was an undoubted testimony, that there was scarce any condition in the world so miserable, but there was something negative or something positive to be thankful for in it; and let this stand as a direction from the experience of the most miserable of all conditions in this world, that we may always find in it something to comfort ourselves from, and to set in the description of good and evil on the credit side of the account.

*Crusoe describes how he encountered the mysterious footprint of another human being after fifteen years of living completely alone.*

It happened one day, about noon, going towards my boat, I was exceedingly surprised with the print of a man's naked foot on the shore, which was very plain to be seen in the sand. I stood like one thunderstruck, or as if I had seen an <u>apparition.</u> I listened, I looked round me, I could hear nothing, nor see anything. I went up to a rising ground, to look farther. I went up the shore, and down the shore, but it was all one; I could see no other impression but that one.

I went to it again to see if there were any more, and to observe if it might not be my fancy; but there was no room for that, for there was exactly the very print of a foot—

| *Words to Know and Use* | **sustenance** (sus′ tə nəns) *n.* nourishment; food <br> **apparition** (ap′ ə ris/h′ ən) *n.* a ghost-like figure that appears suddenly |
| --- | --- |

toes, heel, and every part of a foot. How it came thither I knew not, nor could in the least imagine. But after innumerable fluttering thoughts, like a man perfectly confused and out of myself, I came home to my fortification, not feeling, as we say, the ground I went on, but terrified to the last degree, looking behind me at every two or three steps, mistaking every bush and tree, and fancying every stump at a distance to be a man; nor is it possible to describe how many various shapes affrighted imagination represented things to me in, how many wild ideas were found every moment in my fancy, and what strange, unaccountable whimsies came into my thoughts by the way.

When I came to my castle, for so I think I called it ever after this, I fled into it like one pursued. Whether I went over by the ladder, as first contrived, or went in at the hole in the rock, which I called a door, I cannot remember; no, nor could I remember the next morning, for never frightened hare fled to cover, or fox to earth, with more terror of mind than I to this retreat.

I slept none that night. The farther I was from the occasion of my fright, the greater my apprehensions were; which is something contrary to the nature of such things, and especially to the usual practice of all creatures in fear. But I was so embarrassed with my own frightful ideas of the thing, that I formed nothing but dismal imaginations to myself, even though I was now a great way off it. Sometimes I fancied it must be the devil, and reason joined in with me upon this supposition; for how should any other thing in human shape come into the place? Where was the vessel that brought them? What marks were there of any other footsteps? And how was it possible a man should come there? But then to think that Satan should take human shape upon him in such a place, where there could be no manner of occasion for it, but to leave the print of his foot behind him, and that even for no purpose too, for he could not be sure I should see it; this was an amusement the other way. I considered that the devil might have found out abundance of other ways to have terrified me than this of the single print of a foot; that as I lived quite on the other side of the island, he would never have been so simple to leave a mark in a place where it was ten thousand to one whether I should ever see it or not, and in the sand too, which the first surge of the sea, upon a high wind, would have defaced entirely. All this seemed inconsistent with the thing itself, and with all the notions we usually entertain of the subtlety of the devil.

Abundance of such things as these assisted to argue me out of all apprehensions of its being the devil; and I presently concluded then, that it must be some more dangerous creature, viz., that it must be some of the savages of the mainland over against me, who had wandered out to sea in their canoes, and, either driven by the currents or by contrary winds, had made the island, and had been on shore, but were gone away again to sea, being as loath, perhaps, to have stayed in this desolate island as I would have been to have had them.

While these reflections were rolling upon my mind, I was very thankful in my thoughts that I was so happy as not to be thereabouts at that time, or that they did not see my boat, by which they would have concluded that some inhabitants had been in the place, and perhaps searched farther for me. Then terrible thoughts racked my imagination about their having found my boat, and that there were

429

ROBINSON CRUSOE 1920 N. C. Wyeth The Granger Collection, New York.

hitherto could not preserve, by His power, the provision which He had made for me by His goodness. I reproached myself with my easiness, that would not sow any more corn one year than would just serve me till the next season, as if no accident could intervene to prevent my enjoying the crop that was upon the ground. And this I thought so just a reproof, that I resolved for the future to have two or three years' corn beforehand, so that, whatever might come, I might not perish for want of bread.

How strange a checker-work of Providence[9] is the life of man! and by what secret differing springs are the affections hurried about as differing circumstances present! Today we love what tomorrow we hate; today we seek what tomorrow we shun; today we desire what tomorrow we fear; nay, even tremble at the apprehensions of. This was exemplified in me, at this time, in the most lively manner imaginable; for I, whose only affliction was that I seemed banished from human society, that I was alone, circumscribed by the boundless ocean, cut off from mankind, and condemned to what I called silent life; that I was as one whom Heaven thought not worthy to be numbered among the living, or to appear among the rest of His creatures; that to have seen one of my own species would have seemed to me a raising me from death to life, and the greatest blessing that Heaven itself, next to the supreme blessing of salvation, could bestow; I say, that I should now tremble at the very apprehensions of seeing a man, and was ready to sink into the ground at but the shadow or silent appearance of a man's having set his foot in the island!

---

9. **checker-work of Providence:** varied and different expressions of God's work.

people here; and that if so, I should certainly have them come again in greater numbers, and devour me; and if it should happen so that they should not find me, yet they would find my enclosure, destroy all my corn, carry away all my flock of tame goats, and I should perish at last for mere want.

Thus my fear banished all my religious hope. All that former confidence in God, which was founded upon such wonderful experience as I had had of His goodness, now vanished, as if He that had fed me by miracle

*Words to Know and Use*

**exemplify** (eg zem′ plə fi′) *v.* to show by example

*After sighting the footprint, Crusoe eventually discovered that cannibals were visiting the island, where they brought their prisoners, killed them, and feasted upon their flesh. For nine years Crusoe has kept his distance from the cannibals. He arms himself every time he sees them in an effort to avoid becoming their main course.*

I was surprised, one morning early, with seeing no less than five canoes all on shore together on my side of the island, and the people who belonged to them all landed, and out of my sight. The number of them broke all my measures; for seeing so many, and knowing that they always came four, or six, or sometimes more, in a boat, I could not tell what to think of it, or how to take my measures to attack twenty or thirty men single-handed; so I lay still in my castle, perplexed and discomforted. However, I put myself into all the same postures for an attack that I had formerly provided, and was just ready for action if anything had presented. Having waited a good while, listening to hear if they made any noise, at length, being very impatient, I set my guns at the foot of my ladder, and clambered up to the top of the hill, by my two stages, as usual; standing so, however, that my head did not appear above the hill, so that they could not perceive me by any means. Here I observed, by the help of my perspective-glass, that they were no less than thirty in number, that they had a fire kindled, that they had had meat dressed. How they had cooked it, that I knew not, or what it was; but they were all dancing, in I know not how many barbarous gestures and figures, their own way, round the fire.

While I was thus looking on them, I perceived by my perspective two miserable wretches dragged from the boats, where, it seems, they were laid by, and were now brought out for the slaughter. I perceived one of them immediately fell, being knocked down, I suppose, with a club or wooden sword, for that was their way, and two or three others were at work immediately, cutting him open for their cookery, while the other victim was left standing by himself, till they should be ready for him. In that very moment this poor wretch seeing himself a little at liberty, Nature inspired him with hopes of life, and he started away from them, and ran with incredible swiftness along the sands directly towards me, I mean towards that part of the coast where my habitation was.

*H*ow they cooked it, that I knew not, or what it was.

I was dreadfully frightened (that I must acknowledge) when I perceived him to run my way, and especially when, as I thought, I saw him pursued by the whole body; and now I expected that part of my dream was coming to pass, and that he would certainly take shelter in my grove; but I could not depend, by any means, upon my dream for the rest of it, viz., that the other savages would not pursue him thither, and find him there. However, I kept my station, and my spirits began to recover when I found there was not above three men that followed him; and still more was I encouraged when I found that he outstripped them exceedingly in running, and gained ground of them; so that if he could but hold it for half an hour, I saw easily he would fairly get away from them all.

There was between them and my castle the creek, which I mentioned often at the first part of my story, when I landed my cargoes out of the ship; and this I saw plainly he must necessarily swim over, or the poor wretch would be taken there. But when the savage escaping came thither he made nothing of it, though the tide was then up; but plunging in, swam through in about thirty strokes or thereabouts, landed, and ran on with exceeding strength and swiftness. When the three persons came to the creek, I found that two of them could swim, but the third could not, and that, standing on the other side, he looked at the other, but went no farther, and soon after went softly back, which, as it happened, was very well for him in the main.

I observed, that the two who swam were yet more than twice as long swimming over the creek as the fellow was that fled from them. It came now very warmly upon my thoughts, and indeed irresistibly, that now was my time to get me a servant, and perhaps a companion or assistant, and that I was called plainly by Providence to save this poor creature's life. I immediately ran down the ladders with all possible expedition, fetched my two guns, for they were both but at the foot of the ladders, as I observed above, and getting up again, with the same haste, to the top of the hill, I crossed toward the sea, and having a very short cut, and all down hill, clapped myself in the way between the pursuers and the pursued, hallooing aloud to him that fled, who, looking back, was at first perhaps as much frightened at me as at them; and I beckoned with my hand to him to come back; and, in the meantime, I slowly advanced towards the two that followed; then rushing at once upon the foremost, I knocked him down with the stock of my piece. I was loath to fire, because I would not have the rest hear; though, at that distance, it would not have been easily heard, and being out of sight of the smoke too, they would not have easily known what to make of it. Having knocked this fellow down, the other who pursued with him stopped, as if he had

been frightened, and I advanced apace towards him; but as I came nearer, I perceived presently he had a bow and arrow, and was fitting it to shoot at me; so I was then necessitated to shoot at him first, which I did, and killed him at the first shot.

The poor savage who fled, but had stopped, though he saw both his enemies fallen and killed, as he thought, yet was so frightened with the fire and noise of my piece, that he stood stock-still, and neither came forward nor went backward, though he seemed rather inclined to fly still, than to come on.

I hallooed again to him, and made signs to come forward, which he easily understood, and came a little way, then stopped again, and then a little farther, and stopped again; and I could then perceive that he stood trembling, as if he had been taken prisoner, and had just been to be killed, as his two enemies were. I beckoned him again to come to me, and gave him all the signs of encouragement that I could think of; and he came nearer and nearer, kneeling down every ten or twelve steps, in token of acknowledgment for my saving his life. I smiled at him, and looked pleasantly, and beckoned to him to come still nearer. At length he came close to me, and then he kneeled down again, kissed the ground, and laid his head upon the ground, and taking me by the foot, set my foot upon his head. This, it seems, was in token of swearing to be my slave forever. I took him up, and made much of him, and encouraged him all I could. But there was more work to do yet; for I perceived the savage whom I knocked down was not killed, but stunned with the blow, and began to come to himself; so I pointed to him, and showing him the savage, that he was not dead, upon this he spoke some words to me; and though I could not understand them, yet I thought they were pleasant to hear; for they were the first sound of a man's voice that I had heard, my own excepted, for above twenty-five years. But there was no time for reflections now. The savage who was knocked down recovered himself so far as to sit up upon the ground and I perceived that my savage began to be afraid; but when I saw that, I presented my other piece at the man, as if I would shoot him. Upon this my savage, for so I call him now, made a motion to me to lend him my sword, which hung naked in a belt by my side; so I did. He no sooner had it but he runs to his enemy, and, at one blow, cut off his head as cleverly, no executioner in Germany could have done it sooner or better; which I thought very strange for one who, I had reason to believe, never saw a sword in his life before, except their own wooden swords. However, it seems, as I learned afterwards, they make their wooden swords so sharp, so heavy, and the wood is so hard, that they will cut off heads even with them, ay, and arms, and that at one blow too. When he had done this, he came laughing to me in sign of triumph, and brought me the sword again, and with abundance of gestures, which I did not understand, laid it down, with the head of the savage that he had killed, just before me.

ROBINSON CRUSOE   Noel Poecock   From *The Life and Strange Surprising Adventures of Robinson Crusoe* by Daniel DeFoe, Garden City Publishing.

> ## "They were the first sound of a man's voice that I had heard, . . . for above twenty-five years."

But that which astonished him most was to know how I had killed the other Indian so far off; so pointing to him, he made signs to me to let him go to him; so I bade him go, as well as I could. When he came to him, he stood like one amazed, looking at him, turned him first on one side, then on t'other, looked at the wound the bullet had made, which, it seems, was just in his breast, where it had made a hole, and no great quantity of blood had followed; but he had bled inwardly, for he was quite dead. He took up his bow and arrows, and came back; so I turned to go away, and beckoned to him to follow me making signs to him that more might come after them.

Upon this he signed to me that he should bury them with sand, that they might not be seen by the rest if they followed; and so I made signs again to him to do so. He fell to work, and in an instant he had scraped a hole in the sand with his hands big enough to bury the first in, and then dragged him into it, and covered him, and did so also by the other. I believe he had buried them both in a quarter of an hour. Then calling him away, I carried him, not to my castle, but quite away to my cave, on the farther part of the island; so I did not let my dream come to pass in that part, viz., that he came into my grove for shelter.

Here I gave him bread and a bunch of raisins to eat, and a draught of water, which I found he was indeed in great distress for, by his running; and having refreshed him, I made signs for him to go lie down and sleep, pointing to a place where I had laid a great parcel of rice straw, and a blanket upon it, which I used to sleep upon myself sometimes; so the poor creature lay down, and went to sleep. ❧

# I N S I G H T

## Alexander Selkirk

RICHARD STEELE

*This selection is part of an essay that Richard Steele wrote two years after Alexander Selkirk's rescue from the uninhabited Pacific island. In addition to describing Selkirk's life on the island and his return to civilization, Steele draws a conclusion about the meaning of Selkirk's experiences for us all.*

This manner of life grew so exquisitely pleasant that he never had a moment heavy upon his hands; his nights were untroubled and his days joyous from the practice of temperance and exercise. It was his manner to use stated hours and places for exercises of devotion, which he performed aloud, in order to keep up the faculties of speech, and to utter himself with greater energy.

When I first saw him, I thought, if I had not been let into his character and story, I could have discerned that he had been much separated from company from his aspect and gesture; there was a strong but cheerful seriousness in his look, and a certain disregard to the ordinary things about him, as if he had been sunk in thought. When the ship which brought him off the island came in, he received them with the greatest indifference, with relation to the prospect of going off with them, but with great satisfaction in an opportunity to refresh and help them. The man frequently bewailed his return to the world, which could not, he said, with all its enjoyments, restore him to the tranquillity of his solitude. Though I had frequently conversed with him, after a few months' absence he met me in the street, and though he spoke to me, I could not recollect that I had seen him; familiar converse in this town had taken off the loneliness of his aspect, and quite altered the air of his face.

This plain man's story is a memorable example, that he is happiest who confines his wants to natural necessities; and he that goes further in his desires increases his wants in proportion to his acquisitions; or to use his own expression, *I am now worth eight hundred pounds, but shall never be so happy as when I was not worth a farthing.*

# explain

## Responding to Reading

### First Impressions

1. What part of Crusoe's adventures did you find most interesting? Jot down notes to describe your favorite part and explain why you liked it.

### Second Thoughts

2. Which of the problems Crusoe faces did you predict earlier? Which do you consider his most serious problem? Why?

3. What do you learn about Crusoe's personality through the different incidents he reports?

   **Think about**
   - his first reactions to being shipwrecked
   - his listing of good and bad aspects of his situation
   - his response to the sight of the footprint
   - his rescue of Friday (the prisoner) and reasons for doing it

4. If you were shipwrecked on an island, would you want Crusoe with you? Why or why not?

5. How does Crusoe change as a result of his experience? Cite evidence from the text to support your answer.

### Broader Connections

6. Eventually Crusoe learned to enjoy his island existence. Would that type of life appeal to you? Why or why not?

## Literary Concept: Realism

In literature and in art, **realism** refers to any attempt to imitate actual life. Realistic fiction contains believable characters, dialogue that reflects the speech patterns of everyday life, and accurate descriptions of a particular setting. Plots in realistic fiction often deal with complex, real-life problems that must be solved through human skill and strength, not by magical or supernatural means.

Based on these factors, why is *Robinson Crusoe* classified as realism? Use examples from the selection to support your answer.

**Concept Review: Protagonist**  A protagonist is the main character in fiction, drama, or narrative poetry. Compare and contrast Crusoe with at least two other protagonists in this book.

# *W*riting Options

1. Imagine you are stranded on an island, like Crusoe. Write your own version of a list telling what is "good" and what is "evil." Be sure to balance "the comforts . . . enjoyed" against the "miseries . . . suffered."

2. Write an advertising message to be placed on the book jacket of *Robinson Crusoe.* Try to persuade potential buyers that this is one book worth owning. Include basic information about the story that will make customers want to read more.

3. Imagine you are Crusoe and write a diary entry to describe the day after Friday's rescue. Explain how you and Friday communicate and describe the day's activities. Consider Crusoe's attitude toward Friday, his views on slavery, and his fear of revealing his castle's location.

4. Write a short position paper that explains whether or not Crusoe is a believable human being. Consider whether you think someone could do all the things Crusoe accomplished. Use specific examples from the story.

# *V*ocabulary Practice

**Exercise** Choose the word from the list that could be a substitute for the boldfaced word or phrase in each sentence below.

1. Worries and fears would be **distressing** you if you were stranded on an island without food, shelter, or weapons.
2. Crusoe needed the winds to **die down** so he could swim to the ship.
3. The home that he built also served as a defensive **stronghold.**
4. At the sight of the footprint, Crusoe acted as if he'd seen a **ghost.**
5. Crusoe reflected upon his situation in a balanced way and **fairly** examined both its positive and negative aspects.
6. Without **nourishment,** a castaway could not survive.
7. Fortunately, Crusoe's supply of food was never **inadequate.**
8. When the cannibals heard gunfire for the first time, they probably felt **fear.**
9. Crusoe believes in the **craftiness** and deceit of the devil.
10. The rescue of Friday can be said to **serve as an example of** Crusoe's courage.

*Words to Know and Use*

---

abate
afflicting
apparition
apprehension
deficient
exemplify
fortification
impartially
subtlety
sustenance

# extend

## Options for Learning

**1 • A Survival Pack** In small groups, decide what five items you would want to have with you if you were stranded on an uninhabited island. Assemble the five most important items into a survival pack, or list the items if they are not readily available. Present your group's pack or list to the class with your reasons for choosing these items. The class can choose the pack that seems most useful for survival.

**2 • Cannibal Customs** Crusoe's human enemies were cannibals. Use an encyclopedia to research the practice of cannibalism and the various reasons that cannibals ate other humans. Also find out if cannibals actually lived in the area of Crusoe's island. Report your findings to the class.

**3 • Homemade Tools** Review Crusoe's explanations of how he made his tools. Sketch or make one of his tools.

**4 • A Fortress by Design** Read the sections of *Robinson Crusoe* for November 23 through December 20, where Crusoe describes how he built his fortress into the side of a hill. Draw an illustration or build a model of Crusoe's castle fortress.

### FACT FINDER

*On a map of South America, find the mouth of the Orinoco River, near the area of Crusoe's island.*

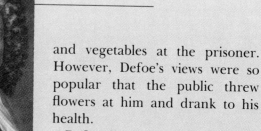

## Daniel Defoe
### 1660–1731

"No man has tasted differing fortunes more, and thirteen times I have been rich and poor." This self-description of Defoe shows the variety of ups and downs he had during his life. He alternately experienced great wealth and bankruptcy due to his talent for both making and losing money. Defoe was also active in politics and journalism, writing many pamphlets about the most controversial topics of his age. One of his pamphlets landed him in Newgate prison for six months. His punishment included time in the pillory, where onlookers usually threw rotten fruits and vegetables at the prisoner. However, Defoe's views were so popular that the public threw flowers at him and drank to his health.

Defoe did not start writing novels until he was in his late fifties. Because *Robinson Crusoe* became one of the most popular books of the century, the company that published it became one of the richest and most important publishing houses in England. Besides *Robinson Crusoe*, Defoe's other famous work is *Moll Flanders*, the story of a tough and crafty woman who married five times and was a thief.

Fiction

## The Bet

ANTON CHEKHOV (che′ kôf′)

## Examine What You Know

The debate about the death penalty versus life imprisonment has gone on for many years. What do you know about each form of punishment? Make a Venn diagram like the one below and write words or phrases that describe life imprisonment in the left circle, those that describe the death penalty in the right circle, and those that apply to both penalties in the overlapping area of the two circles.

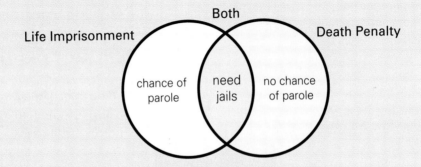

Both

Life Imprisonment     Death Penalty

chance of parole | need jails | no chance of parole

## Expand Your Knowledge

In the latter part of the nineteenth century, Russia went through a period of tremendous change. Millions of Russian peasants were freed from serfdom, a form of slavery in which peasant farmers were owned by their landlords. Though the country was still ruled by a czar who possessed absolute power, many different groups struggled to bring about changes in the political and social order. Aristocrats and members of the growing middle class, such as lawyers, doctors, writers, and business people, debated the issues of the age, sometimes risking imprisonment or exile to make their views public. Russian literature reflects those debates about what is essential for a meaningful and happy life.

## Write Before You Read

What would you be willing to bet for two million dollars? Would you be willing to give up your education, your family, or even several years of your life for the chance to win that much money? Consider the most that you would be willing to sacrifice and write out your wager.

■ A biography of the author can be found on page 446.

# The Bet

## ANTON CHEKHOV

It was a dark autumn night. The old banker was pacing from corner to corner of his study, recalling to his mind the party he gave in the autumn fifteen years ago. There were many clever people at the party and much interesting conversation. They talked among other things of capital punishment. The guests, among them not a few scholars and journalists, for the most part disapproved of capital punishment. They found it <u>obsolete</u> as a means of punishment, unfitted to a Christian State and immoral. Some of them thought that capital punishment should be replaced universally by life-imprisonment.

"I don't agree with you," said the host. "I myself have experienced neither capital punishment nor life-imprisonment, but if one may judge *a priori*,[1] then in my opinion capital punishment is more moral and more humane than imprisonment. Execution kills instantly; life-imprisonment kills by degrees. Who is the more humane executioner, one who kills you in a few seconds or one who draws the life out of you incessantly, for years?"

"They're both equally immoral," remarked one of the guests, "because their purpose is the same, to take away life. The State is not God. It has no right to take away that which it cannot give back, if it should so desire."

Among the company was a lawyer, a young man of about twenty-five. On being asked his opinion, he said:

"Capital punishment and life-imprisonment are equally immoral; but if I were offered the choice between them, I would certainly choose the second. It's better to live somehow than not to live at all."

There ensued a lively discussion. The banker who was then younger and more nervous suddenly lost his temper, banged his fist on the table, and turning to the young lawyer, cried out:

"It's a lie. I bet you two millions you wouldn't stick in a cell even for five years."

"If you're serious," replied the lawyer, "then I bet I'll stay not five but fifteen."

"Fifteen! Done!" cried the banker. "Gentlemen, I stake two millions."

"Agreed. You stake two millions, I my freedom," said the lawyer.

So this wild, ridiculous bet came to pass. The banker, who at that time had too many millions to count, spoiled and capricious, was beside himself with rapture. During supper he said to the lawyer jokingly:

"Come to your senses, young man, before it's too late. Two millions are nothing to me, but you stand to lose three or four of the best years of your life. I say three or four, because you'll never stick it out any longer. Don't forget either, you unhappy man, that voluntary is much heavier than enforced imprisonment.

---

1. **a priori** (ā′ prī ôr′ ī): based on logic instead of on experience.

The idea that you have the right to free yourself at any moment will poison the whole of your life in the cell. I pity you."

And now the banker, pacing from corner to corner, recalled all this and asked himself:

"Why did I make this bet? What's the good? The lawyer loses fifteen years of his life and I throw away two millions. Will it convince people that capital punishment is worse or better than imprisonment for life? No, No! all stuff and rubbish. On my part, it was the caprice of a well-fed man; on the lawyer's, pure greed of gold."

He recollected further what happened after the evening party. It was decided that the lawyer must undergo his imprisonment under the strictest observation, in a garden-wing of the banker's house. It was agreed that during the period he would be deprived of the right to cross the threshold, to see living people, to hear human voices, and to receive letters and newspapers. He was permitted to have a musical instrument, to read books, to write letters, to drink wine and smoke tobacco. By the agreement he could communicate, but only in silence, with the outside world through a little window specially constructed for this purpose. Everything necessary, books, music, wine, he could receive in any quantity by sending a note through the window. The agreement provided for all the minutest details, which made the confinement strictly solitary, and it obliged the lawyer to remain exactly fifteen years from twelve o'clock of November 14th, 1870, to twelve o'clock of November 14th, 1885. The least attempt on his part to violate the conditions, to escape if only for two minutes before the time freed the banker from the obligation to pay him the two millions.

During the first year of imprisonment, the lawyer, as far as it was possible to judge from his short notes, suffered terribly from loneliness and boredom. From his wing day and night came the sound of the piano. He rejected wine and tobacco. "Wine," he wrote, "excites desires, and desires are the chief foes of a prisoner; besides, nothing is more boring than to drink good wine alone," and tobacco spoiled the air in his room. During the first

PORTRAIT OF VICTOR CHOCQUET 1876–77 Paul Cézanne.

year the lawyer was sent books of a light character; novels with a complicated love interest, stories of crime and fantasy, comedies, and so on.

In the second year the piano was heard no longer and the lawyer asked only for classics. In the fifth year, music was heard again, and the prisoner asked for wine. Those who watched him said that during the whole of that year he was only eating, drinking, and lying on his bed. He yawned often and talked angrily to himself. Books he did not read. Sometimes at nights he would sit down to write. He would write for a long time and tear it all up in the morning. More than once he was heard to weep.

In the second half of the sixth year, the prisoner began zealously to study languages, philosophy, and history. He fell on these subjects so hungrily that the banker hardly had time to get books enough for him. In the space of four years about six hundred volumes were bought at his request. It was while that passion lasted that the banker received the following letter from the prisoner: "My dear jailer, I am writing these lines in six languages. Show them to experts. Let them read them. If they do not find one single mistake, I beg you to give orders to have a gun fired off in the garden. By the noise I shall know that my efforts have not been in vain. The geniuses of all ages and countries speak in different languages; but in them all burns the same flame. Oh, if you knew my heavenly happiness now that I can understand them!" The prisoner's desire was fulfilled. Two shots were fired in the garden by the banker's order.

Later on, after the tenth year, the lawyer sat immovable before his table and read only the New Testament. The banker found it strange that a man who in four years had mastered six hundred erudite[2] volumes, should have spent nearly a year in reading one book, easy to understand and by no means thick. The New Testament was then replaced by the history of religions and theology.

During the last two years of his confinement the prisoner read an extraordinary amount, quite haphazardly. Now he would apply himself to the natural sciences, then would read Byron or Shakespeare. Notes used to come from him in which he asked to be sent at the same time a book on chemistry, a textbook of medicine, a novel, and some treatise on philosophy or theology. He read as though he were swimming in the sea among broken pieces of wreckage, and in his desire to save his life was eagerly grasping one piece after another.

The banker recalled all this, and thought:

"Tomorrow at twelve o'clock he receives his freedom. Under the agreement, I shall have to pay him two millions. If I pay, it's all over with me. I am ruined for ever . . ."

Fifteen years before he had too many millions to count, but now he was afraid to ask himself which he had more of, money or debts. Gambling on the Stock Exchange, risky speculation, and the recklessness of which he could not rid himself even in old age, had gradually brought his business to decay; and the fearless, self-confident, proud man of business had become an ordinary banker, trembling at every rise and fall in the market.

"That cursed bet," murmured the old man clutching his head in despair . . . "Why didn't the man die? He's only forty years old. He will take away my last penny, marry, enjoy life, gamble on the Exchange, and I will look on like an envious beggar and hear the same

---

2. **erudite** (er′ yoo dīt′): scholarly.

**Words to Know and Use** | **zealously** (zel′ əs lē) *adv.* in an enthusiastic manner
**haphazardly** (hap′ haz′ ərd lē) *adv.* without an aim or purpose; randomly

441

words from him every day: 'I'm obliged to you for the happiness of my life. Let me help you.' No, it's too much! The only escape from bankruptcy and disgrace—is that the man should die."

The clock had just struck three. The banker was listening. In the house everyone was asleep, and one could hear only the frozen trees whining outside the windows. Trying to make no sound, he took out of his safe the key of the door which had not been opened for fifteen years, put on his overcoat, and went out of the house. The garden was dark and cold. It was raining. A keen damp wind hovered howling over all the garden and gave the trees no rest. Though he strained his eyes, the banker could see neither the ground, nor the white statues, nor the garden wing, nor the trees. Approaching the place where the garden wing stood, he called the watchman twice. There was no answer. Evidently the watchman had taken shelter from the bad weather and was now asleep somewhere in the kitchen or the greenhouse.

"If I have the courage to fulfil my intention," thought the old man, "the suspicion will fall on the watchman first of all."

In the darkness he groped for the stairs and the door and entered the hall of the garden wing, then poked his way into a narrow passage and struck a match. Not a soul was there. Someone's bed, with no bedclothes on it, stood there, and an iron stove was dark in the corner. The seals on the door that led into the prisoner's room were unbroken.

When the match went out, the old man, trembling from agitation, peeped into the little window.

In the prisoner's room a candle was burning dim. The prisoner himself sat by the table. Only his back, the hair on his head and his hands were visible. On the table, the two chairs, and on the carpet by the table, open books were strewn.

Five minutes passed and the prisoner never once stirred. Fifteen years' confinement had taught him to sit motionless. The banker tapped on the window with his finger, but the prisoner gave no movement in reply. Then the banker cautiously tore the seals from the door and put the key into the lock. The rusty lock gave a hoarse groan and the door creaked. The banker expected instantly to hear a cry of surprise and the sound of steps. Three minutes passed and it was as quiet behind the door as it had been before. He made up his mind to enter.

Before the table sat a man, unlike an ordinary human being. It was a skeleton, with tight-drawn skin, with a woman's long curly hair, and a shaggy beard. The color of his face was yellow, of an earthy shade; the cheeks were sunken, the back long and narrow, and the hand upon which he leaned his hairy head was so lean and skinny that it was painful to look upon. His hair was already silvering with gray, and no one who glanced at the senile emaciation[3] of the face would have believed that he was only forty years old. On the table, before his bended head, lay a sheet of paper on which something was written in a tiny hand.

"Poor devil," thought the banker, "he's asleep and probably seeing millions in his dreams. I have only to take and throw this half-dead thing on the bed, smother him a moment with the pillow, and the most careful examination will find no trace of unnatural death. But, first, let us read what he has written here."

The banker took the sheet from the table and read:

"Tomorrow at twelve o'clock midnight, I shall obtain my freedom and the right to mix with people. But before I leave this room and see the sun I think it necessary to say a few

---

3. **emaciation:** abnormal leanness.

words to you. On my own clear conscience and before God who sees me I declare to you that I despise freedom, life, health, and all that your books call the blessings of the world.

"For fifteen years I have diligently studied earthly life. True, I saw neither the earth nor the people, but in your books I drank fragrant wine, sang songs, hunted deer and wild boar in the forests, loved women . . . And beautiful women, like clouds ethereal,[4] created by the magic of your poets' genius, visited me by night and whispered to me wonderful tales, which made my head drunken. In your books I climbed the summits of Elbruz and Mont Blanc and saw from there how the sun rose in the morning, and in the evening overflowed the sky, the ocean and the mountain ridges with a purple gold. From there I saw how above me lightnings glimmered, cleaving the clouds; I saw green forests, fields, rivers, lakes, cities; I heard sirens[5] singing, and the playing of the pipes of Pan;[6] I touched the wings of beautiful devils who came flying to me to speak of God . . . In your books I cast myself into bottomless abysses,[7] worked miracles, burned cities to the ground, preached new religions, conquered whole countries . . .

"Your books gave me wisdom. All that unwearying human thought created in the centuries is compressed to a little lump in my skull. I know that I am more clever than you all.

"And I despise your books, despise all worldly blessings and wisdom. Everything is void, frail, visionary and delusive as a mirage. Though you be proud and wise and beautiful, yet will death wipe you from the face of the earth like the mice underground; and your posterity, your history, and the immortality of your men of genius will be as frozen slag, burnt down together with the terrestrial globe.

"You are mad, and gone the wrong way. You take lie for truth and ugliness for beauty. You would marvel if by certain conditions frogs and lizards should suddenly grow on apple and orange trees, instead of fruit, and if roses should begin to breathe the odor of a sweating horse. So do I marvel at you, who have bartered heaven for earth. I do not want to understand you.

"That I may show you in deed my contempt for that by which you live, I waive the two millions of which I once dreamed as of paradise, and which I now despise. That I may deprive myself of my right to them, I shall come out from here five minutes before the stipulated term, and thus shall violate the agreement."

When he had read, the banker put the sheet on the table, kissed the head of the strange man, and began to weep. He went out of the wing. Never at any other time, not even after his terrible losses on the Exchange, had he felt such contempt for himself as now. Coming home, he lay down on his bed, but agitation and tears kept him long from sleep . . .

The next morning the poor watchman came running to him and told him that they had seen the man who lived in the wing climbing through the window into the garden. He had gone to the gate and disappeared. With his servants the banker went instantly to the wing and established the escape of his prisoner. To avoid unnecessary rumors he took the paper with the <u>renunciation</u> from the table and, on his return, locked it in his safe. ⋗

---

4. **ethereal:** airy, delicate.

5. **sirens:** sea goddesses from Greek and Roman mythology whose singing lured sailors to their death on rocky coasts.

6. **pipes of Pan:** Pan was a Greek god of the fields and forests who played a type of flute instrument.

7. **abysses:** deep gulfs or chasms in the earth.

*Words to Know and Use*

**posterity** (päs ter′ ə tē) *n.* the next generations
**renunciation** (ri nun′ sē ā′ s/hən) *n.* a giving up of a right or claim to something

443

## Responding to Reading

### First Impressions

1. What is your reaction to the actions of the banker and the lawyer at the end of the story? Discuss your thoughts with your classmates.

### Second Thoughts

2. Why does the lawyer walk away from the money? What is your opinion of his reasons?

3. Reread paragraphs 3 and 4 on page 443. Why do you think the lawyer reaches these conclusions?

   **Think about**
   • the effects of all his reading and learning
   • how fifteen years of isolation have changed him

4. If the lawyer were given the chance to go back to the evening of the party, do you think that he would agree to the banker's bet? Explain.

5. Have the banker's values changed by the end of the story? Explain.

6. What do you think the lives of the banker and the lawyer will be like in the future? Give evidence from the story to support your predictions.

7. What are some possible themes for this story?

### Broader Connections

8. Many state governments are still debating the morality of capital punishment. How do you think that persons who commit multiple murders should be punished? Explain your answer.

## Literary Concept: Flashback

In a **flashback,** a writer stops the story and moves back to a time before the story began. "The Bet" begins when the banker is an old man, the night before the bet is due to be over. Then the story flashes back to the party (beginning in the middle of paragraph 1 on page 439). The story comes back to the present again in paragraph 1 on page 440. Then it contains a second flashback (beginning with paragraph 4 on page 440 and continuing on for most of page 441). What purpose does each of the flashbacks serve? Why do you think Chekhov chose to use this technique?

**Concept Review: Climax** You know that the climax is the most dramatic moment in a story, the point at which an important event, decision, or discovery takes place. What do you think is the climax of "The Bet"?

## Writing Options

1. Putting yourself in the role of the lawyer, write three diary entries—the first during your first year of imprisonment, the second during the middle years, and the third near the end of your imprisonment. Include in each entry your thoughts, how you spent the day, and what you learned. Have your entries show changes in your personality and thinking.

2. Write at least three pieces of graffiti that the lawyer might have written on the walls of his room.

3. Make a chart that compares and contrasts the banker and the lawyer. Consider such factors as their ages and personalities as well as their views toward punishment and money. Include any changes in either character and show likenesses and differences at both the beginning and end of the story.

4. Imagine that you have wagered fifteen years of solitary confinement against two million dollars. Explain how you will spend those years and what you will do to cope with your loneliness.

## Vocabulary Practice

**Exercise** On your paper, write the word from the list that is most clearly related to each situation described below.

1. Some guests voiced the opinion that capital punishment is an old-fashioned and inhumane way of dealing with criminals.
2. The lawyer studied languages, history, and philosophy so enthusiastically that the banker could hardly keep up with his requests for books.
3. In later years, the lawyer randomly switched his reading from one subject to another.
4. The lawyer wrote that death will wipe out the present, the past, and the future generations of mankind.
5. In his letter, the lawyer implied that he was now opposed to everything that had once seemed important to him.

> *Words to Know and Use*
>
> ---
>
> **haphazardly**
> **obsolete**
> **posterity**
> **renunciation**
> **zealously**

## Options for Learning

**1 • The Artist's Brush** Use the banker's description of the lawyer in paragraph 7 on page 442 to draw or paint a portrait of the lawyer after his fifteen years of prison.

**2 • Musical Background** Prepare a three-part musical interpretation of the lawyer's experiences during his years of isolation. Choose three pieces of music that capture his mood at the beginning, middle, and end of his imprisonment. You and some classmates might create a dance for each piece that reflects that section of the story. After each part of the performance, ask the audience to interpret what they heard and/or saw.

**3 • A Prisoner's Cell** Use details in the story to create a diagram or drawing of the room where the lawyer was imprisoned.

**4 • Prison Librarian** Suppose that you had to supply books to the lawyer for the first three years of his confinement. Next to each year, list the types of books you would provide. For example, you might include romance, crime novels, and fantasy. Also, for each year give three specific titles with their library call numbers.

### FACT FINDER

*If the lawyer had received two million dollars for his fifteen years, how much would he have earned per hour?*

## Anton Chekhov
### 1860–1904

Chekhov was born into a peasant family, and his early years were harsh and demanding. His father required hard work and discipline from the entire family. In Chekhov's story "Three Children," he may have described his own family: "I remember that Father began to teach me, or (to put it more simply) to beat me, before I was five years old. We weren't allowed to play any games." Nevertheless, the family remained close, and in later years Chekhov supported the rest of his family.

Chekhov was trained as a doctor, but he stopped practicing medicine and became a writer. His writing career began with comic advertisements, like the following, which were very popular: "Coffins of every type in the store. Discount for those dying wholesale. Gentlemen in the process of dying are warned to beware of imitations." Eventually, Chekhov became known for his tragicomic dramas, which blend tragic and comic elements. These dramas contributed to a new school of acting and are still performed today. His short stories also continue to be popular throughout the world.

In his later years, Chekhov became politically sensitive. His recommendations led to the prison reforms of 1892. Chekhov died of tuberculosis at the age of forty-four.

*Poetry*

# I Am Not I

JUAN RAMÓN JIMÉNEZ
(hwän rä mōn′ hē me′ nes)

# The Enemy

PABLO NERUDA
(päb′ lô   ne r̄ōo′ dä)

## Examine What You Know

What does the expression "inner self" mean to you? With your class, discuss what this expression means. Then jot down words and phrases that describe aspects of your personality that you keep hidden. For example, you might seem self-confident but feel very insecure inside, or you might appear outgoing but are basically shy. As you read, compare your view of your "inner self" with the poets' views of themselves.

## Expand Your Knowledge

Jiménez (1881–1958) and Neruda (1904–1973) are two of the most famous poets of the century; both were awarded the Nobel Prize in literature. Jiménez, a Spaniard, was an intensely private man who used poetry to explore his innermost feelings. By comparison, Neruda, from Chile, led a more active public life. Like Jiménez, he used poetry as a means of self-discovery, but he also used poetry to comment on the important social and political issues of his age. In the following poems, you will share in the poets' explorations of the hidden territories of the self.

## Enrich Your Reading

**Understanding Contrast in "I Am Not I"**   This poem deals with two different sides of the poet, his two different "I's." Because the two sides are discussed as if they were two different people, the poem is sometimes hard to follow. Create a chart with two columns. In one column list words and phrases that describe the "I" who is the speaker of the poem. In the other column list words or phrases that describe his other self. Note that the other self is referred to as "who" or "whom" throughout the poem.

**Making Sense of Images in "The Enemy"**   Neruda presents the character of the enemy through images that appeal to the senses. Some of these images may create a clear impression in your mind; others may prove confusing. As you read, jot down your impressions of the enemy. Develop a mental picture of him and form your own judgment of his character.

■ *A biography of each poet can be found in the Reader's Handbook.*

# I Am Not I

## JUAN RAMÓN JIMÉNEZ

I am not I.
　　　　　I am this one
walking beside me whom I do not see,
whom at times I manage to visit,
5　and whom at other times I forget;
who remains calm and silent while I talk,
and forgives, gently, when I hate,
who walks where I am not,
who will remain standing when I die.

NOT TO BE REPRODUCED  1937  René Magritte
Museum Boymans van Beuningen, Rotterdam, The
Netherlands.

## *R*esponding to Reading

### First Impressions of "I Am Not I"

**1.** After reading this poem, what questions do you have about the speaker?

### Second Thoughts on "I Am Not I"

**2.** What does the first line of the poem mean?

**3.** Using your chart, discuss the differences between the poet's two selves.

**Think about**

- why the speaker cannot see his other self
- how he sometimes visits the other self and sometimes forgets it
- the meaning of "who will remain standing when I die"

**4.** How does the speaker evaluate the two sides of himself? Why do you think he can only occasionally bring the two sides together?

# The Enemy

## PABLO NERUDA

My old enemy came to visit
today: a man hermetically sealed
in his truth, like a castle
or strong-box,
5   with his own style of breathing
and a singular sword-play
sedulously stropped to draw blood.

I saw the years in his face:
the eyes of tired water,
10  the lines of his loneliness
that had lifted his temples
little by little to consummate self-love.

We chatted a while in
broad mid-day, in windy
15  explosions that scattered
the sun on all sides and struck at the sky.
But the man showed me only
his new set of keys, his one
way to all doors. Inside him,
20  I think he was silent,
indivisibly silent:
the flint of his soul
stayed impenetrable.

I thought of that stingy integrity
25  hopelessly buried, with power
to harm only himself;
and within me I knew
my own crude truths shamed.

So we talked—each of us
30  honing his steely convictions,
each tempered by time:
two blind men defending
their individual darknesses.

**2 hermetically sealed** (hər met′ ik kə lē): completely sealed; airtight. This suggests that the man is unwilling to consider other points of view.

**6 sword-play:** Literally, sword-play refers to the act of fighting with a sword. It also suggests verbal or intellectual battle.

**7 sedulously stropped** (sej′ ᴏᴏ ləs lē sträpt): constantly sharpened.

**12 consummate** (kən sum′ it) *adj.* perfect; complete. The verb form of consummate (kan′ sə māt′), which means to bring to completion, also applies here. Though lonely and worn, the enemy loves himself completely.

**18 his new set of keys:** The keys, "his one way to all doors," are probably not actual items. This expression may be the poet's way to describe the enemy's latest ideas and his belief that he alone possesses the truth.

**23 impenetrable** (im pen′ i trə bəl) *adj.* unenterable; mysterious. The speaker cannot enter or understand his enemy's soul.

**24 integrity** (in teg′ rə tē) *n.* honesty and sincerity. Though the enemy is true to himself and his beliefs, his integrity only harms him.

**30 honing his steely convictions** (hōn′ iŋ): sharpening his strong beliefs, as one would sharpen a sword or knife. This suggests that the two men fought each other's ideas rather than engaging in physical fights.

## *R*esponding *to Reading*

### First Impressions of "The Enemy"

1. Jot down words or phrases that best describe your reaction to the poem.

### Second Thoughts on "The Enemy"

2. How would you describe the enemy? Refer to the list you made.

3. Explain how specific images help express the meaning of the poem.

    **Think about**
    - "a man hermetically sealed . . ." in lines 2-4
    - "singular sword-play . . ." in lines 6-7
    - "new set of keys . . ." in lines 18-19
    - "stingy integrity/hopelessly buried . . ." in lines 24-26

4. What are the speaker's feelings about his enemy and how do they change?

5. In what ways are the speaker and his enemy blind?

6. What does the speaker learn about himself in the poem?

### Comparing the Poems

7. Compare the two poems in terms of each speaker's attitude toward himself. Which speaker knows himself better? Which likes himself better?

## *L*iterary *Concept: Alliteration*

**Alliteration** is the repetition of initial consonant sounds, as in "sweet spring." Alliteration can be used to emphasize certain words, unify a passage, contribute to the tone, reinforce meaning, or establish musical effects. In Neruda's poem, the speaker refers to the enemy's "singular sword-play sedulously stropped." Read this expression aloud. How do these sounds affect you? What do they add to your impression of the enemy? Find other examples of alliteration in the poem and discuss what the sounds contribute to the poem.

## *W*riting *Options*

1. Which speaker would you rather know? Explain why, using specific examples from the two poems.

2. Create a list of visual images to describe your inner self. Develop a separate image for each aspect of yourself. For example, if you are really shy, you might write "a face afraid of the crowd." Let your imagination run loose.

*Autobiography*

# Beauty: When the Other Dancer Is the Self

## ALICE WALKER

## Examine What You Know

In what ways does a person's physical appearance affect his or her self-image? How does that positive or negative self-image then affect a person's life? Consider how feeling good-looking or ugly might affect a person in his or her personal relationships, school experiences, and career. Discuss your thoughts with your classmates. Then find out how Alice Walker reacts to an injury that changes her appearance.

## Expand Your Knowledge

Alice Walker was born in the small town of Eatonton, Georgia, in 1944. She grew up experiencing the difficulties of a rural African-American family in the segregated South. Central Georgia is farm country, and during the 1940's and 1950's many of the poor were tenant farmers. They lived on and worked farms that belonged to others, sharing what they made with the absentee owners. Living in the country meant doing without services and conveniences. Getting to hospitals, jobs, and stores was difficult because of long distances and lack of money and transportation. These hardships plus the problems of living in a segregated society are part of Alice Walker's background. In this autobiographical selection, Walker describes both the obstacles and the love she has encountered in her life.

## Write Before You Read

Think of a time when something happened that changed your physical appearance. How did you feel about the change, and what caused you to react the way you did? Were you affected by what others said to you? Jot down your thoughts in your journal or on a piece of paper.

■ *A biography of the author can be found on page 460.*

# Beauty: When the Other Dancer Is the Self

## ALICE WALKER

It is a bright summer day in 1947. My father, a fat, funny man with beautiful eyes and a subversive wit, is trying to decide which of his eight children he will take with him to the county fair. My mother, of course, will not go. She is knocked out from getting most of us ready: I hold my neck stiff against the pressure of her knuckles as she hastily completes the braiding and then beribboning of my hair.

My father is the driver for the rich, old white lady up the road. Her name is Miss Mey. She owns all the land for miles around, as well as the house in which we live. All I remember about her is that she once offered to pay my mother thirty-five cents for cleaning her house, raking up piles of her magnolia leaves, and washing her family's clothes, and that my mother—she of no money, eight children, and a chronic earache—refused it. But I do not think of this in 1947. I am two and a half years old. I want to go everywhere my daddy goes. I am excited at the prospect of riding in a car. Someone has told me fairs are fun. That there is room in the car for only three of us doesn't faze me at all. Whirling happily in my starchy frock, showing off my biscuit-polished[1] patent-leather shoes and lavender socks, tossing my head in a way that makes my ribbons bounce, I stand, hands on hips, before my father. "Take me, Daddy," I say with assurance; "I'm the prettiest!"

Later, it does not surprise me to find myself in Miss Mey's shiny black car, sharing the back seat with the other lucky ones. Does not surprise me that I thoroughly enjoy the fair. At home that night I tell the unlucky ones all I can remember about the merry-go-round, the man who eats live chickens, and the teddy bears, until they say: that's enough, baby Alice. Shut up now, and go to sleep.

It is Easter Sunday, 1950. I am dressed in a green, flocked, scalloped-hem dress (hand-made by my adoring sister, Ruth) that has its own smooth satin petticoat and tiny hot-pink roses tucked into each scallop. My shoes, new T-strap patent leather, again highly biscuit-polished. I am six years old and have learned one of the longest Easter speeches to be heard that day, totally unlike the speech I said when I was two: "Easter lilies / pure and white / blossom in / the morning light." When I rise to give my speech, I do so on a great wave of love

---

1. **biscuit-polished:** a method producing a high shine on patent leather.

*Words to Know and Use*

**subversive** (səb vur′ siv) *adj.* tending or seeking to overthrow, destroy, or undermine
**assurance** (ə shoor′ əns) *n.* self-confidence; certainty

452

ALICE WALKER  Brian Lanker  From *I Dream a World: Portraits of Black Women Who Changed America*, Stewart, Tabori & Chang.

and pride and expectation. People in the church stop rustling their new crinolines.[2] They seem to hold their breath. I can tell they admire my dress, but it is my spirit, bordering on sassiness (womanishness), they secretly applaud.

"That girl's a little *mess*," they whisper to each other, pleased.

Naturally I say my speech without stammer or pause, unlike those who stutter, stammer, or, worst of all, forget. This is before the word "beautiful" exists in people's vocabulary, but "Oh, isn't she the *cutest* thing!" frequently floats my way. "And got so much sense!" they gratefully add . . . for which thoughtful addition I thank them to this day.

*It was great fun being cute. But then, one day, it ended.*

I am eight years old and a tomboy. I have a cowboy hat, cowboy boots, checkered shirt and pants, all red. My playmates are my brothers, two and four years older than I. Their colors are black and green, the only difference in the way we are dressed. On Saturday nights we all go to the picture show, even my mother; Westerns are her favorite kind of movie. Back home, "on the ranch," we pretend we are Tom Mix, Hopalong Cassidy, Lash LaRue[3] (we've even named one of our dogs Lash LaRue); we chase each other for hours rustling cattle, being outlaws, delivering damsels from distress. Then my parents decide to buy my brothers guns. These are not "real" guns. They shoot "BBs," copper pellets my brothers say will kill birds. Because I am a girl, I do not get a gun. Instantly I am <u>relegated</u> to the position of Indian. Now there appears a great distance

---

2. **crinolines** (krin′ ə linz′): petticoats of a stiff, heavy cloth worn under skirts to make them puff out.

3. **Tom Mix, Hopalong Cassidy, Lash La Rue:** popular movie cowboys of the 1940's and 1950's.

---

*Words to Know and Use* | **relegate** (rel′ ə gāt′) *v.* to assign to an inferior position

453

between us. They shoot and shoot at every-thing with their new guns. I try to keep up with my bow and arrows.

One day while I am standing on top of our makeshift "garage"—pieces of tin nailed across some poles—holding my bow and ar-row and looking out toward the fields, I feel an incredible blow in my right eye. I look down just in time to see my brother lower his gun.

Both brothers rush to my side. My eye stings, and I cover it with my hand. "If you tell," they say, "we will get a whipping. You don't want that to happen, do you?" I do not. "Here is a piece of wire," says the older brother, picking it up from the roof; "say you stepped on one end of it and the other flew up and hit you." The pain is beginning to start. "Yes," I say. "Yes, I will say that is what hap-pened." If I do not say this is what happened, I know my brothers will find ways to make me wish I had. But now I will say anything that gets me to my mother.

Confronted by our parents, we stick to the lie agreed upon. They place me on a bench on the porch, and I close my left eye while they examine the right. There is a tree growing from underneath the porch that climbs past the railing to the roof. It is the last thing my right eye sees. I watch as its trunk, its branches, and then its leaves are blotted out by the rising blood.

I am in shock. First there is intense fever, which my father tries to break using lily leaves bound around my head. Then there are chills: my mother tries to get me to eat soup. Even-tually, I do not know how, my parents learn what has happened. A week after the "acci-dent" they take me to see a doctor. "Why did you wait so long to come?" he asks, looking into my eye and shaking his head. "Eyes are

sympathetic," he says. "If one is blind, the other will likely become blind too."

This comment of the doctor's terrifies me. But it is really how I look that bothers me most. Where the BB pellet struck there is a glob of whitish scar tissue, a hideous cataract,[4] on my eye. Now when I stare at people—a favorite pastime, up to now—they will stare back. Not at the "cute" little girl, but at her scar. For six years I do not stare at anyone because I do not raise my head.

Years later, in the throes of a mid-life crisis, I ask my mother and sister whether I changed after the "acci-dent." "No," they say, puzzled. "What do you mean?"

*What do I mean?*

I am eight, and, for the first time, doing poorly in school, where I have been something of a whiz since I was four. We have just moved to the place where the "accident" occurred. We do not know any of the people around us because this is a different county. The only time I see the friends I knew is when we go back to our old church. The new school is the former state penitentiary. It is a large stone building, cold and drafty, crammed to over-flowing with boisterous, ill-disciplined chil-dren. On the third floor there is a huge, cir-cular imprint of some partition that has been torn out.

"What used to be here?" I ask a sullen girl next to me on our way past it to lunch.

"The electric chair," says she.

At night I have nightmares about the elec-tric chair and about all the people reputedly

---

4. **cataract:** a white spot on the lens of the eye causing partial or total blindness.

*Words to Know and Use* | **boisterous** (bȯis′ tər əs) *adj.* noisy and unruly; rowdy
**reputedly** (ri pyo͞ot′ id lē) *adv.* thought to be; supposedly

"fried" in it. I am afraid of the school, where all the students seem to be budding criminals.

"What's the matter with your eye?" they ask, critically.

When I don't answer (I cannot decide whether it was an "accident" or not), they shove me, insist on a fight.

My brother, the one who created the story about the wire, comes to my rescue. But then brags so much about "protecting" me I become sick.

After months of torture at the school, my parents decide to send me back to our old community, to my old school. I live with my grandparents and the teacher they board. But there is no room for Phoebe, my cat. By the time my grandparents decide there *is* room, and I ask for my cat, she cannot be found. Miss Yarborough, the boarding teacher, takes me under her wing and begins to teach me to play the piano. But soon she marries an African—a "prince," she says—and is whisked away to his continent.

At my old school there is at least one teacher who loves me. She is the teacher who "knew me before I was born" and bought my first baby clothes. It is she who makes life bearable. It is her presence that finally helps me turn on the one child at the school who continually calls me "one-eye." One day I simply grab him by his coat and beat him until I am satisfied. It is my teacher who tells me my mother is ill.

My mother is lying in bed in the middle of the day, something I have never seen. She is in too much pain to speak. She has an abscess[5] in her ear. I stand looking down on her, knowing that if she dies, I cannot live. She is being treated with warm oils and hot bricks held against her cheek. Finally a doctor comes. But I must go back to my grandparents' house.

The weeks pass but I am hardly aware of it. All I know is that my mother might die, my father is not so jolly, my brothers still have their guns, and I am the one sent away from home.

"You did not change," they say.

*Did I imagine the anguish of never looking up?*

I am twelve. When relatives come to visit, I hide in my room. My cousin Brenda, just my age, whose father works in the post office and whose mother is a nurse, comes to find me. "Hello," she says. And then she asks, looking at my recent school picture, which I did not want taken, and on which the "glob," as I think of it, is clearly visible, "You still can't see out of that eye?"

"No," I say, and flop back on the bed over my book.

That night, as I do almost every night, I abuse my eye. I rant and rave at it in front of the mirror. I plead with it to clear up before morning. I tell it I hate and despise it. I do not pray for sight. I pray for beauty.

"You did not change," they say.

I am fourteen and baby-sitting for my brother Bill, who lives in Boston. He is my favorite brother and there is a strong bond between us. Understanding my feelings of shame and ugliness, he and his wife take me to a local hospital, where the "glob" is removed by a doctor named O. Henry. There is still a small bluish crater where the scar tissue was, but the ugly white stuff is gone. Almost immediately I become a different person from the girl who does not raise her head. Or so I think. Now that I've raised my head, I win the boyfriend of my dreams. Now that I've raised my head, I have plenty of friends. Now that I've raised my head, classwork comes from my lips as faultlessly as Easter speeches did, and I leave high school as valedictorian, most popular stu-

---

5. **abscess:** a swollen, inflamed area in which pus gathers.

dent, and *queen*, hardly believing my luck. Ironically, the girl who was voted most beautiful in our class (and was) was later shot twice through the chest by a male companion, using a "real" gun, while she was pregnant. But that's another story in itself. Or is it?

"You did not change," they say.

It is now thirty years since the "accident." A beautiful journalist comes to visit and to interview me. She is going to write a cover story for her magazine that focuses on my latest book. "Decide how you want to look on the cover," she says. "Glamorous, or whatever."

Never mind "glamorous," it is the "whatever" that I hear. Suddenly all I can think of is whether I will get enough sleep the night before the photography session: if I don't, my eye will be tired and wander, as blind eyes will.

At night I think up reasons why I should not appear on the cover of a magazine. "My meanest critics will say I've sold out," I say. "My family will now realize I write scandalous books."

"But what's the real reason you don't want to do this?" [my friend] asks.

"Because in all probability," I say in a rush, "my eye won't be straight."

"It will be straight enough," he says. Then, "Besides, I thought you'd made your peace with that."

And I suddenly remember that I have.

*I remember.*

I am talking to my brother Jimmy, asking if he remembers anything unusual about the day I was shot. He does not know I consider that day the last time my father, with his sweet home remedy of cool lily leaves, chose me, and that I suffered and raged inside because of this. "Well," he says, "all I remember is standing by the side of the highway with Daddy, trying to flag down a car. A white man stopped, but when Daddy said he needed somebody to take his little girl to the doctor, he drove off."

*I remember:*

I am in the desert for the first time. I fall totally in love with it. I am so overwhelmed by its beauty, I confront for the first time, consciously, the meaning of the doctor's words years ago: "Eyes are sympathetic. If one is blind, the other will likely become blind too." I realize I have dashed about the world madly, looking at this, looking at that, storing up images against the fading of the light. *But I might have missed seeing the desert!* The shock of that possibility—and gratitude for over twenty-five years of sight—sends me literally to my knees. Poem after poem comes—which is perhaps how poets pray.

## ON SIGHT

I am so thankful I have seen
The Desert
And the creatures in the desert
And the desert Itself.

The desert has its own moon
Which I have seen
With my own eye.

There is no flag on it.
Trees of the desert have arms
All of which are always up
That is because the moon is up
The sun is up
Also the sky
The stars
Clouds
None with flags.

If there *were* flags, I doubt
the trees would point.
Would you?

*But mostly, I remember this:*

I am twenty-seven, and my baby daughter is almost three. Since her birth, I have worried about her discovery that her mother's eyes are different from other people's. Will she be embarrassed? I think. What will she say? Every day she watches a television program called "Big Blue Marble." It begins with a picture of the earth as it appears from the moon. It is bluish, a little battered-looking, but full of light, with whitish clouds swirling around it. Every time I see it I weep with love, as if it is a picture of Grandma's house. One day when I am putting Rebecca down for her nap, she suddenly focuses on my eye. Something inside me cringes, gets ready to try to protect myself. All children are cruel about physical differences, I know from experience, and that they don't always mean to be is another matter. I assume Rebecca will be the same.

But no-o-o-o. She studies my face intently as we stand, her inside and me outside her crib. She even holds my face maternally between her dimpled little hands. Then, looking every bit as serious and lawyerlike as her father, she says, as if it may just possibly have slipped my attention: "Mommy, there's a *world* in your eye." (As in, "Don't be alarmed, or do anything crazy.") And then, gently, but with great interest: "Mommy, where did you *get* that world in your eye?"

For the most part, the pain left then. (So what, if my brothers grew up to buy even more powerful pellet guns for their sons and to carry real guns themselves. So what, if a young "Morehouse man" once nearly fell off the steps of Trevor Arnett Library because he thought my eyes were blue.) Crying and laughing I ran to the bathroom, while Rebecca mumbled and sang herself off to sleep. Yes indeed, I realized, looking into the mirror. There *was* a world in my eye. And I saw that it was possible to love it: that in fact, for all it had taught me of shame and anger and inner vision, I *did* love it. Even to see it drifting out of orbit in boredom, or rolling up out of fatigue, not to mention floating back at atten-

tion in excitement (bearing witness, a friend has called it), deeply suitable to my personality, and even characteristic of me.

That night I dream I am dancing to Stevie Wonder's song "Always" (the name of the song is really "As," but I hear it as "Always"). As I dance, whirling and joyous, happier than I've ever been in my life, another bright-faced dancer joins me. We dance and kiss each other and hold each other through the night. The other dancer has obviously come through all right, as I have done. She is beautiful, whole, and free. And she is also me. ❧

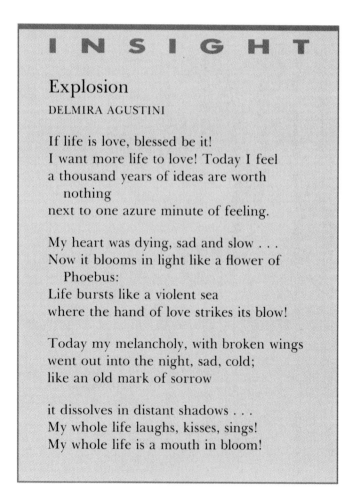

# INSIGHT

## Explosion

DELMIRA AGUSTINI

If life is love, blessed be it!
I want more life to love! Today I feel
a thousand years of ideas are worth
    nothing
next to one azure minute of feeling.

My heart was dying, sad and slow . . .
Now it blooms in light like a flower of
    Phoebus:
Life bursts like a violent sea
where the hand of love strikes its blow!

Today my melancholy, with broken wings
went out into the night, sad, cold;
like an old mark of sorrow

it dissolves in distant shadows . . .
My whole life laughs, kisses, sings!
My whole life is a mouth in bloom!

## Responding to Reading

### First Impressions

1. In what parts of the essay, if any, did you identify with the author? Explain.

### Second Thoughts

2. How important is appearance to Walker as a child? Use examples from the text to explain your answer.

3. What kinds of changes does Walker go through in the years immediately following the accident?

4. When Walker is fourteen, the scar tissue on her eye is removed. What effect does this have on her? Explain.

5. While others say they saw no change after the accident, Walker insists that there was a dramatic change. How do you explain this contrast?

6. In your opinion, who helped Walker deal with the effects of her accident the most? Use evidence from the selection to defend your choice.

7. What is the meaning of the last paragraph of the essay?

   **Think about**
   • why Walker is so happy
   • who the other dancer is
   • what change has occurred

### Broader Connections

8. Many people's views of how they should look are based on the ideas communicated by society. How does our society define beauty? What are the effects of television and magazine advertising on how people regard themselves and others? Are these effects good, or are they bad? Explain.

## Literary Concept: Autobiographical Essay

An **autobiographical essay** is a factual account of the writer's own life experiences. It is usually written in first-person point of view to give the reader insight into the writer's character, feelings, and attitudes. The autobiographical essay highlights significant events in the writer's life and reflects on how those events affected him or her. For this reason it is sometimes called a **reflective essay.** List the significant events from Walker's life that her essay covers. Why do you think she chose those events?

**Concept Review: Style**   Describe Walker's writing style. Consider such things as verb tense, repetition, and how she covers passage of time.

# *W*riting Options

1. Select one of Walker's memories that involves another person. Rewrite that part of the story from the other person's point of view.

2. Walker makes numerous references to guns throughout the essay. Find these and use them to write a summary of her attitude toward guns.

3. Explain in a paragraph how the main idea of the poem "Explosion" relates to Walker's essay. Use quotes from both pieces in your explanation.

4. Create a poem that reflects the message of Walker's essay. The form, length, rhythm, rhymes, and word images you choose should help the reader understand the meaning of the poem.

# *V*ocabulary Practice

**Exercise** On your paper, write the letter of the situation that best demonstrates the meaning of each boldfaced word.

> *Words to Know and Use*
>
> ---
>
> **assurance**
> **boisterous**
> **relegate**
> **reputedly**
> **subversive**

1. **subversive**
   a. a coach sending a new player into the game
   b. a stranger asking for directions
   c. a terrorist planning a bombing

2. **assurance**
   a. a child speaking confidently about her completed assignment
   b. a friend revealing self-doubt to you privately
   c. a suspect sweating under police questioning

3. **relegate**
   a. a government agency creating new rules for business
   b. the last child picked for the team being assigned the worst position
   c. a politician running for a second term in office

4. **boisterous**
   a. a playground full of children playing at recess
   b. several new teachers listening during their staff meeting
   c. a mother fixing a large dinner for guests

5. **reputedly**
   a. a medical student studying for a test
   b. a family watching slides of their last vacation
   c. a neighbor listening to gossip about the man next door

## *Options for Learning*

**1 • Checking the Emotions** Design an L-shaped graph that shows the changes in Walker's image of herself as revealed in her essay. Decide how to label the emotional side of the graph, such as strong, medium, and weak feelings or positive, neutral, and negative. Plot this against the events of the essay.

**2 • Art Design** Create a collage that represents the events and memories of Walker's essay. You may use pictures, cut-out words, photos, or drawings. Your collage should reflect your understanding of Walker's experiences.

**3 • The Eye Surgeon** Research the causes and prevention of sympathetic blindness. Were Walker's fears of acquiring this condition justified? Report your findings to the class.

**4 • Poster Art** Design a poster that shows Walker's point of view about guns. Use quotes and images from the essay.

**5 • The Music Critic** Hand out to your classmates copies of the lyrics to Stevie Wonder's ''As,'' the song that Walker mentions at the end of her essay. Play the recording for the class. Then either explain what you think the song means to Walker or lead a class discussion on this subject.

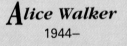 **FACT FINDER**

*What is the population of Eatonton, Georgia, Walker's birthplace?*

### *A lice Walker*
#### 1944–

Recognized as both an accomplished poet and novelist, Walker is perhaps best known as the author of *The Color Purple*. This Pulitzer Prize-winning novel, a story about growing up in the South, was later made into a very successful movie.

During Walker's college years, she was active in the struggle against the segregation of African Americans. After graduating from Sarah Lawrence College, Walker lived in Mississippi and participated in the civil rights movement. During this time she married a civil rights lawyer. They later divorced.

Through her essays, poems, and novels, Walker reflects her concerns—poverty, family, women's rights, and civil rights. "Family relationships are sacred," Walker says. "No amount of outside pressure and injustice must make us lose sight of that fact."

# WRITER'S WORKSHOP

## DESCRIPTION

Form a mental picture of yourself. What characteristics do you see? What kind of expression do you have? annoyed? amused? serious? What different personality traits do you perceive? As you visualize yourself, think about how you would convey this image to a reader.

When you want to bring people, places, objects, or events to life, you use **description.** Your aim in using description is to make a reader see something or someone in his or her mind's eye. Instead of using a brush and canvas or a camera and film, you use words to create a vivid picture. One important technique is the use of **sensory details**—words that describe sight, sound, smell, touch, or taste. This example from "The Bet" appeals to the sense of sight:

> The color of his face was yellow, of an earthy shade, the cheeks were sunken, the back long and narrow, and the hand upon which he leaned his hairy head was so lean and skinny that it was painful to look upon.

An example from "Beauty: When the Other Dancer Is the Self" appeals to the sense of touch: "She is being treated with warm oils and hot bricks held against her cheek."

**Comparisons** also help you create a memorable description. Use either a simile, which compares two things using the word *like* or *as,* or a metaphor, which compares two things without using the word *like* or *as.* For example, Pablo Neruda uses both the simile "a man hermetically sealed / in his truth, like a castle" and the metaphor "eyes of tired water" in "The Enemy."

Another way to make your description come alive is to use **descriptive language,** or specific nouns, verbs, adjectives, and adverbs. *Chestnut* is more descriptive than *dark brown; staggered* is more lively than *walked awkwardly.* Call on your powers of observation to help you choose accurate, precise words. As you write your "Who Am I?" essay for the following assignment, use a variety of sensory details, comparisons, and descriptive language to create a one-of-a-kind portrait for your classmates.

## GUIDED ASSIGNMENT: "WHO AM I?" ESSAY

Write an essay about yourself in which you answer the question "Who am I?" by describing your appearance, personality, behavior, or experiences.

**Here is your PASSkey to this assignment.**

**P**URPOSE: To describe

**A**UDIENCE: Your classmates

**S**UBJECT: Yourself

**S**TRUCTURE: Essay

## Prewriting

**STEP 1** **Brainstorm general categories** To gather details for your Who Am I? essay, work with a partner or a group of classmates to brainstorm a list of categories you might explore. Here's a sample list:

STUDENT MODEL ▶

| | | | | |
|---|---|---|---|---|
| appearance | attitudes | beliefs | activities | behavior |
| interests | ethnic heritage | goals | dreams | family |

**STEP 2** **Narrow the categories** Now work together to break down your brainstorming list further into more specific ideas. Develop several lists you can use easily for gathering specific details about yourself. For instance, hair, eyes, height, weight, clothes, posture, and walk further describe appearance.

**STEP 3** **Gather details** Your brainstorming list is the key to unlocking specific details. Pinpoint details by freewriting, making a word web, or making a list. Using the brainstorming categories, supply information that describes you. Consider one student's partial word web.

STUDENT MODEL ▶

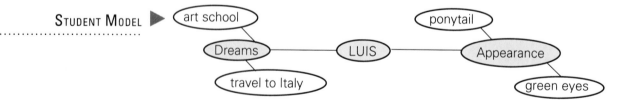

**STEP 4** **Choose effective details** Look over your prewriting carefully. Which details are most striking? Which details help others really see you? Choose details that you think will create a memorable self-portrait. Your Who Am I? essay will focus on personality, behavior, experiences, or appearance; group the best details accordingly.

**STEP 5** **Organize your details**   Once you have chosen details for
your essay, present them clearly for your classmates.
Organize details by using spatial order (top to bottom) for physical
description, order of importance (least to most important) for description
of behavior or personality, or chronological order (time order of events)
for description of experiences.

## Drafting

**STEP 1** **Draft an introduction**   Interest your classmates in finding
out your answer to "Who am I?" by drafting a compelling
introductory paragraph. Write a thesis statement that introduces the
essay topic and draft sentences that develop the thesis statement.
Create drama by hinting at what is to come later in the essay or by
drawing the reader's attention to some interesting detail or image that
captures the spirit of your essay.

**STEP 2** **Draft the body**   Now that you've captured your classmates'
attention, write the body paragraphs. In each paragraph, focus
on one aspect or one kind of detail until you've answered Who am I?
Don't just state the obvious; probe hidden qualities that make you
unique. Use your prewriting to help you see how details might be
arranged in different paragraphs, linking the paragraphs with transitional
words and phrases such as *in addition, most important, next.* Include
sensory details, comparisons, and descriptive language.

**Option 1**   Use the first-person point of view (I, me myself) consistently
in your essay to make your description more personal.
**Option 2**   Use the third-person point of view (he, she; him, her;
himself, herself) consistently for a more detached perspective.

**STEP 3** **Draft the conclusion**   Bring your description to a conclusion
in a final paragraph, using a quotation or a sharp image to end
your essay. See the conclusion of "Beauty: When the Other Dancer Is
the Self" for a good example of this technique.

# Revising and Editing

Have a peer reviewer use this checklist to help you revise your essay. Think about whether a reader can actually form a mental picture of you.

> ### Revision Checklist
> ................................................................................................
>
> 1. Does the essay fully answer the question Who am I? about the writer?
> 2. Does the essay include sensory details that create a clear portrait?
> 3. Does the essay contain vivid nouns, verbs, and modifiers?
> 4. Does the essay have a strong introduction and conclusion?
> 5. Do the body paragraphs present details in an understandable order?

**Editing**  Proofread your essay for spelling, punctuation, usage, and grammar errors. Have a peer editor check the final copy of your essay.

# Presenting

**Option 1**  Make a class oral history. Use a tape recorder to make recordings of your Who Am I? essays, or videotape your presentations.
**Option 2**  Use your Who Am I? essays as the basis for a quiz show. After your teacher reads each essay aloud without naming the writer, have a panel of three "contestants" guess who is being described.

# Reflecting on Your Writing

Answer the following questions. Place the answers along with your essay in your writing portfolio.

1. What did you learn about yourself by writing this essay?
2. Which technique best brought your description to life: sensory details, comparisons, or descriptive language? Why?
3. What was the most striking image in your essay? the least?

# SENTENCE COMBINING I

The dancer looked in the mirror. She checked her costume. She also checked her makeup. Then she closed her eyes. She imagined herself on stage. Then the curtain rose.

This example sounds childish and repetitious because the author has strung together one short, simple sentence after another. To avoid this in your own writing, combine short, related sentences. Doing so will give you a smoother, more mature writing style.

## Joining Sentence Parts

Sometimes two sentences express such closely related ideas that they actually use many of the same words. Often you can combine such sentences by eliminating repeated or unnecessary words and joining the important sentence parts with a conjunction.

To join similar sentence parts, use *and.* (Notice below that in joining sentences, the italicized words are eliminated.)

> The shipwrecked Crusoe had no food. *He also had* no clothes.
> The shipwrecked Crusoe had no food **and** no clothes.

To join contrasting sentence parts, use *but.*

> At night he worried about wild beasts. *He* slept soundly anyway.
> At night he worried about wild beasts **but** slept soundly anyway.

To join sentence parts that present a choice, use *or.*

> Crusoe hoped he would be rescued by a passing trade ship. *Another possibility he hoped for was that he would be rescued by an* exploratory vessel.
> Crusoe hoped he would be rescued by a passing trade ship **or** exploratory vessel.

**REMINDER**

The words *and, or, nor, for, but, so,* and *yet* are called **coordinating conjunctions.** You can use coordinating conjunctions to combine sentences and sentence parts.

**Exercise 1**  Combine each pair of sentences. Use the combining word given in parentheses and eliminate the word or words in italics.

1. After the shipwreck Crusoe clung to life. *He* came ashore on a dismal island. **(and)**

2. At first Crusoe despaired at his dismal circumstances. *He believed that he would surely die.* **(and)**

3. He slept his first night in a tree. *He woke up refreshed the next day.* **(but)**

4. Would Robinson Crusoe survive his terrifying ordeal? *Would he succumb to nature's cruel forces?* **(or)**

5. The next day he reached the wounded ship. *He carried off many supplies.* **(and)**

6. For the next three weeks, Crusoe found goods on the ship. *He used a raft to float the supplies to shore.* **(and)**

7. Then, during the days, he hunted for food. *Sometimes he worked to build his new home.* **(or)**

8. By December Crusoe had carried all his things into his cave. *He had begun to furnish his new home.* **(and)**

9. Crusoe had been cast upon a desolate island. *He was nevertheless alive and well.* **(but)**

10. He knew that his circumstances were miserable. *However, he continued the struggle for survival.* **(but)**

## Adding Words to Sentences

Sometimes you can combine sentences by taking a word or two from one sentence and adding it to another, related sentence. When you add words to another sentence in this way, place them close to the person, thing, or action they describe.

> The banker was delighted by the bet. *The banker was* spoiled.
> The **spoiled** banker was delighted by the bet.

Sometimes you can combine more than two sentences when one sentence contains the main idea and the others add only details. In such cases, you may have to separate the added words with a comma or the word *and.*

> "The Bet" took place one night. *The night was* cold. *It was* dark.
> "The Bet" took place one **cold, dark** night.

Sometimes you may need to change the form of a word when you combine sentences. This usually means adding an ending such as *-y, -ed, -ing,* or *-ly.*

> The young lawyer bet fifteen years of his life. *His action was* brash.
> The young lawyer **brashly** bet fifteen years of his life.

**Exercise 2**   Combine each pair of sentences by adding one or more words to one of the sentences. Eliminate the words in italics. Remember that you may need to change the form of a word.

1. Alice Walker writes about her childhood. *She writes* sensitively.
2. The story about her eye injury seems so realistic. *The story seems* poignant. *Her eye injury must have been* frightening.
3. I can imagine Alice at eight years old, dressed in cowboy gear from head to foot. *The gear would have been* red.
4. Her brother hit her with a BB from his gun. *The brother's action was* accidental.
5. From that day on, the glob of whitish scar tissue changed Walker's sense of herself. *The glob was* hideous.
6. Nineteen years later, Walker's daughter made a comment about her mother's eye; that comment allowed Walker to feel whole again. *The daughter was* young. *Her comment was* loving.

**Exercise 3**   Work in a small group to rewrite the following passage. Combine the sentences within each pair of parentheses, eliminating the words in italics. Add words or word endings as necessary.

(Some of my favorite characters in literature have developed their senses of self in spite of great odds. *The literature was* classical.)
(For example, Anne Shirley, in *Anne of Green Gables,* was an orphan who hated her hair. *Her hair was a* shocking red *color.*) (Sent to Green Gables by mistake, Anne managed, with support from her adoptive family, to grow into a loving young woman. *The young Anne was* spunky. *She was also* intelligent.)
(Another character who overcame great odds was Jim Hawkins, the young boy who learned about the treasure in *Treasure Island. The treasure was* buried.) (Hawkins, with the rest of the crew, helped to thwart a mutiny. *He* learned about life at the same time.)

**Exercise 4   Analyzing and Revising Your Writing**

1. Take a paper from your portfolio. Choose a passage to analyze.
2. Rewrite the passage using the sentence-building skills you have learned in this workshop. Remember that not all sentences need to be combined; your goal should be to vary the length of your sentences.
3. Check for correct punctuation.
4. Compare your revision to the original passage. Which do you prefer?
5. Remember to check for related sentences that might be combined the next time you proofread your work.

LANGUAGE HANDBOOK
combining sentences,
   pages 977–78
compound sentences,
   pages 1024–25

# LIFE SKILLS
**WORKSHOP**

## FILLING OUT APPLICATIONS

Whether you're applying for a driver's license, a job, or admission to a college or vocational school, the first step is generally to fill out an application. When filling out an application, keep these guidelines in mind:

1. Before you write anything, read all the directions carefully. Collect all the information you need, such as your social security number, your parents' birthdates, or information about your previous employers.

2. Be neat. Use a good pen or a typewriter. Do not use a pencil unless you are specifically told to do so.

3. Fill out the application line by line. Read the directions for each line before filling it in. Plan ahead to make your response fit the space available. If you make a mistake, carefully draw a single neat line through the error and write the correct information above the line.

4. Be prepared to answer some basic questions. For example, you will often be asked to list two or three references—people who know you well and who are willing to discuss your abilities. Teachers, coaches, and former employers make fine references. Be sure to ask permission in advance from people you want to use as references. Also ask for their daytime telephone numbers and complete addresses, including ZIP Codes.

5. Complete every line, if possible. If an item does not apply to you, write "Does not apply" or the abbreviation *na* (for "not applicable"). When you finish, check the application for accuracy, spelling, and completeness.

**Exercise** As a homework assignment, find a blank employment application and bring it to class. Exchange applications with a partner and fill out your partner's application. Then, discuss any problems you encountered. Report your findings to the class.

# CHALLENGING THE SYSTEM

The Enlightenment was an age of new and bold ideas about society. The questions raised about nearly every social issue led to new concepts about government, the economy, individual rights, religion, and the legal system. In such a turbulent age, literature became an effective means of social criticism. Writers mocked the reigning powers, unmasked the follies of the powerful, and challenged the social system.

Jonathan Swift's stinging and inventive attacks on society made even his friends uncomfortable. In this subunit you will read an excerpt from his most famous work, as well as more up-to-date forms of protest, ranging from the unhappy memories of an Indian school girl to the quiet victory of a Canadian baseball fan. These selections will challenge you to think about social problems great and small and the solutions that individuals may offer.

**Fiction**

## *from* Gulliver's Travels
### *A Voyage to Lilliput*
JONATHAN SWIFT

## Examine What You Know

*Gulliver's Travels* has been one of the most widely read books of the last three centuries. It was written for adults but has been loved by children for its adventure and for the illustrations that have been made to accompany it. As a class, discuss what you know about the travels of Gulliver and the reasons for the continued popularity of the story.

## Expand Your Knowledge

*Gulliver's Travels* tells about the four fantastic voyages of Lemuel Gulliver, an ordinary man who found himself in extraordinary lands. His first and most famous voyage took him to Lilliput, where the six-inch tall citizens took him captive. His other voyages led him to a land of towering giants, one of foolish philosophers, and one of rational horses with human slaves.

Like Thomas More in *Utopia,* Swift uses the context of an imaginary voyage to comment on the follies and problems of England and other European countries. In various ways, Swift attacks the lords and leaders of England, using humor to highlight the flaws of human institutions and of human nature.

## Enrich Your Reading

**Appreciating Satire**   Swift is most famous for his **satire,** which relies on mockery and a sense of the ridiculous to expose foolishness or wrongdoing in people or institutions. For example, Swift mocks the ambitions of politicians by having the ministers of Lilliput dance on a rope to please the king and gain advancement. Through a meaningless rope dance, Swift makes the satirical point that some politicians will do anything to get ahead.

As you read the selection, think about what Swift is satirizing. The questions and quotes inserted in the text will help you to identify his comic targets. You will learn more about satire on page 478.

■ *A biography of the author can be found on page 480.*

# *from* Gulliver's Travels

## A Voyage to Lilliput

JONATHAN SWIFT

*In "The Voyage to Lilliput," Lemuel Gulliver is shipwrecked after a storm and cast upon the shore. When he awakens, Gulliver finds himself tied up, head to foot, and secured to the ground. He discovers that some ten thousand very little people, only six inches tall, have captured him. Once he realizes that force will not work, Gulliver decides to cooperate with his captors, planning to charm his way to freedom. At this point in the story, his legs are still chained, though he has some mobility.*

My gentleness and good behavior had gained so far on the Emperor and his court, and indeed upon the army and people in general, that I began to conceive hopes of getting my liberty in a short time. I took all possible methods to cultivate this favorable disposition.[1] The natives came by degrees to be less <u>apprehensive</u> of any danger from me. I would sometimes lie down and let five or six of them dance on my hand. And at last the boys and girls would venture to come and play at hide and seek in my hair. I had now made a good progress in understanding and speaking their language. The Emperor had a mind one day to entertain me with several of the country shows, wherein they exceed all nations I have known, both for <u>dexterity</u> and magnificence. I was <u>diverted</u> with none so much as that of the rope dancers, performed upon a slender white thread, extended about two foot, and

twelve inches from the ground. Upon which I shall desire liberty, with the reader's patience, to enlarge a little.

This diversion is only practiced by those persons who are candidates for great employments, and high favor, at court. They are trained in this art from their youth and are not always of noble birth or liberal education.[2] When a great office is vacant either by death or disgrace (which often happens), five or six of those candidates petition the Emperor to entertain his Majesty and the court with a dance on the rope, and whoever jumps the highest without falling succeeds in the office. Very often the chief ministers themselves are commanded to show their skill and to convince the Emperor that they have not lost their

---

1. **disposition** (dis′ pə zish′ ən): frame of mind.
2. **liberal education:** a broad education about many subjects rather than specialized training.

---

471

faculty. Flimnap,[3] the Treasurer, is allowed to cut a caper[4] on the strait rope, at least an inch higher than any other lord in the whole empire. I have seen him do the summerset[5] several times together upon a trencher[6] fixed on the rope, which is no thicker than a common packthread in England. My friend Reldresal, Principal Secretary for Private Affairs, is, in my opinion, if I am not partial, the second after the Treasurer; the rest of the great officers are much upon a par.[7]

**What do the rope-dancing contests reveal about the court and its way of governing?**

These diversions are often attended with fatal accidents, whereof great numbers are on record. I myself have seen two or three candidates break a limb. But the danger is much greater when the ministers themselves are commanded to show their dexterity; for by contending[8] to excel themselves and their fellows, they strain so far that there is hardly one of them who hath not received a fall, and some of them two or three. I was assured that, a year or two before my arrival, Flimnap would have infallibly[9] broke his neck, if one of the King's cushions, that accidentally lay on the ground, had not weakened the force of his fall.

There is likewise another diversion, which is only shown before the Emperor and Empress, and first minister, upon particular occasions. The Emperor lays on a table three fine silken threads of six inches long. One is blue, the other red, and the third green.[10] These threads are proposed as prizes for those persons whom the Emperor hath a mind to distinguish by a peculiar mark of his favor. The ceremony is performed in his Majesty's great chamber of state, where the candidates are to undergo a trial of dexterity very different from the former, and such as I have not observed the least resemblance of in any other country of the old or the new world. The Emperor holds a stick in his hands, both ends parallel to the horizon, while the candidates, advancing one by one, sometimes leap over the stick, sometimes creep under it backwards and forwards several times, according as the stick is advanced or depressed. Sometimes the Emperor holds one end of the stick, and his first minister the other; sometimes the minister has it entirely to himself. Whoever performs his part with most agility, and holds out the longest in leaping and creeping, is rewarded with the blue-colored silk; the red is given to the next, and the green to the third, which they all wear girt[11] twice round about the middle; and you see few great persons about this court who are not adorned with one of these girdles.

The horses of the army, and those of the royal stables, having been daily led before me, were no longer shy, but would come up to my very feet without starting. The riders would leap them over my hand as I held it on the ground, and one of the Emperor's huntsmen, upon a large courser,[12] took my foot, shoe and

---

3. **Flimnap:** a reference to the British politician Robert Walpole, one of Swift's political enemies.

4. **cut a caper:** to jump and leap playfully.

5. **summerset:** somersault.

6. **trencher:** a wooden board.

7. **much upon a par:** almost equal to each other.

8. **contending:** striving; fighting.

9. **infallibly** (in fal′ lə blē): without fail; surely.

10. **three fine silken threads:** the three colors represent England's orders of the Garter, the Bath, and the Thistle. The king granted membership in these orders as a sign of his favor.

11. **girt:** fastened like a belt.

12. **courser:** a war horse; a charger.

---

*Words to Know and Use* | **faculty** (fak′ əl tē) *n.* power or ability to do some particular thing; special aptitude or skill

"I lay all this while, as the reader may believe, in great uneasiness." Culver Pictures, New York.

all; which was indeed a prodigious leap. I had the good fortune to divert the Emperor one day after a very extraordinary manner. I desired he would order several sticks of two foot high, and the thickness of an ordinary cane, to be brought me; whereupon his Majesty commanded the master of his woods to give directions accordingly, and the next morning six woodmen arrived with as many carriages, drawn by eight horses to each. I took nine of these sticks, and fixing them firmly in the ground in a quadrangular[13] figure, two foot and a half square, I took four other sticks, and tied them parallel at each corner, about two foot from the ground; then I fastened my handkerchief to the nine sticks that stood erect, and extended it on all sides till it was as tight as the top of a drum; and the four parallel sticks, rising about five inches higher than the handkerchief, served as ledges on each side. When I had finished my work, I desired the Emperor to let a troop of his best horse, twenty-four in number, come and exercise upon this plain. His Majesty approved of the proposal, and I took them up one by one in my hands, ready mounted and armed, with the proper officers to exercise them. As soon

_____

13. **quadrangular** (kwä′ draŋ′ gyōō lər): in a shape with four angles and four sides.

as they got into order, they divided into two parties, performed mock skirmishes, discharged blunt arrows, drew their swords, fled and pursued, attacked and retired, and in short discovered the best military discipline I ever beheld. The parallel sticks secured them and their horses from falling over the stage; and the Emperor was so much delighted that he ordered this entertainment to be repeated several days, and once was pleased to be lifted up and give the word of command; and, with great difficulty, persuaded even the Empress herself to let me hold her in her close chair within two yards of the stage, from whence she was able to take a full view of the whole performance. It was my good fortune that no ill accident happened in these entertainments, only once a fiery horse that belonged to one of the captains pawing with his hoof struck a hole in my handkerchief, and his foot slipping, he overthrew his rider and himself; but I immediately relieved them both, for covering the hole with one hand, I set down the troop with the other, in the same manner as I took them up. The horse that fell was strained in the left shoulder, but the rider got no hurt, and I repaired my handkerchief as well as I could; however, I would not trust to the strength of it any more in such dangerous enterprises.

*clarify*

What does the image of a mock cavalry battle upon a handkerchief suggest about Swift's view of the military?

About two or three days before I was set at liberty, as I was entertaining the court with these kinds of feats, there arrived an express[14] to inform his Majesty that some of his subjects, riding near the place where I was first taken up, had seen a great black substance lying on the ground, very oddly shaped, extending its edges round as wide as his Majesty's bedchamber, and rising up in the middle as high as a man; that it was no living creature, as they at first apprehended, for it lay on the grass without motion, and some of them had walked round it several times; that by mounting upon each others' shoulders, they had got to the top, which was flat and even, and stamping upon it they found it was hollow within; that they humbly <u>conceived</u> it might be something belonging to the Man-Mountain, and if his Majesty pleased, they would undertake to bring it with only five horses. I presently knew what they meant, and was glad at heart to receive this intelligence. It seems upon my first reaching the shore after our shipwreck, I was in such confusion that before I came to the place where I went to sleep, my hat, which I had fastened with a string to my head while I was rowing, and had stuck on all the time I was swimming, fell off after I came to land; the string, as I <u>conjecture</u>, breaking by some accident which I never observed, but thought my hat had been lost at sea. I entreated his Imperial Majesty to give orders it might be brought to me as soon as possible, describing to him the use and the nature of it; and the next day the wagoners arrived with it, but not in a very good condition; they had bored two holes in the brim, within an inch and half of the edge, and fastened two hooks in the holes; these hooks were tied by a long cord to the harness, and thus my hat was dragged along for above half an English mile: but the ground in that country being extremely smooth and level, it received less damage than I expected.

Two days after this adventure, the Emperor having ordered that part of his army which

---

14. **express:** an urgent official message.

quarters in and about his metropolis to be in a readiness, took a fancy of diverting himself in a very singular manner. He desired I would stand like a colossus,[15] with my legs as far asunder[16] as I conveniently could. He then commanded his general (who was an old experienced leader, and a great patron of mine) to draw up the troops in close order, and march them under me, the foot by twenty-four in a breast, and the horse by sixteen, with drums beating, colors flying, and pikes advanced. This body consisted of three thousand foot and a thousand horse. His Majesty gave orders, upon pain of death, that every soldier in his march should observe the strictest decency with regard to my person; which, however, could not prevent some of the younger officers from turning up their eyes as they passed under me. And, to confess the truth, my breeches were at that time in so ill a condition that they afforded some opportunities for laughter and admiration.

I had sent so many memorials[17] and petitions for my liberty that his Majesty at length mentioned the matter, first in the cabinet, and then in a full council; where it was opposed by none, except Skyresh Bolgolam, who was pleased, without any <u>provocation</u>, to be my mortal enemy. But it was carried against him by the whole board, and confirmed by the Emperor. That minister was *Galbet*, or Admiral of the Realm, very much in his master's confidence, and a person well versed in affairs, but of a morose and sour complexion.[18] However, he was at length persuaded to <u>comply</u>; but prevailed that the articles and conditions upon which I should be set free, and to which I must swear, should be drawn up by himself. These articles were brought to me by Skyresh Bolgolam in person, attended by two under-secretaries, and several persons

Historical Pictures Service, Chicago.

15. **colossus** (kə läs′ əs): a gigantic statue; a reference to the Colossus of Rhodes, a huge statue of Apollo whose legs spanned the harbor entrance of Rhodes, an ancient city.

16. **asunder** (ə sun′ dər): apart or separate in direction or position.

17. **memorials:** statements of facts, often with petitions that something be done.

18. **complexion:** personality.

475

of distinction. After they were read, I was demanded to swear to the performance of them; first in the manner of my own country, and afterwards in the method prescribed by their laws; which was to hold my right foot in my left hand, to place the middle finger of my right hand on the crown of my head, and my thumb on the tip of my right ear. But because the reader may perhaps be curious to have some idea of the style and manner of expression peculiar to that people as well as to know the articles upon which I recovered my liberty, I have made a translation of the whole instrument word for word, as near as I was able, which I here offer to the public.

GOLBASTO MOMAREN EVLAME GURDILO SHEFIN MULLY ULLY GUE, most mighty Emperor of Lilliput, delight and terror of the universe, whose dominions extend five thousand blustrugs (about twelve miles in circumference) to the extremities of the globe; monarch of all monarchs, taller than the sons of men; whose feet press down to the center, and whose head strikes against the sun; at whose nod the princes of the earth shake their knees; pleasant as the spring, comfortable as the summer, fruitful as autumn, dreadful as winter. His most sublime Majesty proposeth to the Man-Mountain, lately arrived at our celestial dominions,[19] the following articles, which by a solemn oath he shall be obliged to perform.

First, The Man-Mountain shall not depart from our dominions, without our license under our great seal.

Secondly, He shall not presume to come into our metropolis, without our express order; at which time the inhabitants shall have two hours warning to keep within their doors.

Thirdly, The said Man-Mountain shall confine his walks to our principal high roads, and not offer to walk or lie down in a meadow or field of corn.

*He shall take the utmost care not to trample upon the bodies of any of our loving subjects.*

Fourthly, As he walks the said roads, he shall take the utmost care not to trample upon the bodies of any of our loving subjects, their horses, or carriages, nor take any of our said subjects into his hands, without their own consent.

Fifthly, If an express require extraordinary dispatch, the Man-Mountain shall be obliged to carry in his pocket the messenger and horse a six days' journey once in every moon, and return the said messenger back (if so required) safe to our Imperial Presence.

Sixthly, He shall be our ally against our enemies in the island of Blefuscu,[20] and do his utmost to destroy their fleet, which is now preparing to invade us.

Seventhly, That the said Man-Mountain shall, at his times of leisure, be aiding and assisting to our workmen, in helping to raise certain great stones, toward covering the wall of the principal park, and other of our royal buildings.

---

19. **celestial dominions** (sə les′ chəl də min′ yənz): heavenly, divine, or God-given territory or country.
20. **Blefuscu** (blə fyo͞o′ kyo͞o): a reference to France, the country most frequently at war with England.

Eighthly, That the said Man-Mountain shall, in two moons' time, deliver in an exact survey of the circumference of our dominions by a computation of his own paces round the coast.

Lastly, That upon his solemn oath to observe all the above articles, the said Man-Mountain shall have a daily allowance of meat and drink sufficient for the support of 1,728 of our subjects, with free access to our Royal Person, and other marks of our favor. Given at our palace at Belfaborac the twelfth day of the ninety-first moon of our reign.

I swore and subscribed to these articles with great cheerfulness and content, although some of them were not so honorable as I could have wished; which proceeded wholly from the malice of Skyresh Bolgolam the High Admiral; whereupon my chains were immediately unlocked, and I was at full liberty; the Emperor himself in person did me the honor to be by at the whole ceremony. I made my acknowledgments by prostrating[21] myself at his Majesty's feet: but he commanded me to rise; and after many gracious expressions, which, to avoid the censure of vanity,[22] I shall not repeat, he added that he hoped I should prove a useful servant and well deserve all the favors he had already conferred upon me, or might do for the future.

The reader may please to observe, that in the last article for the recovery of my liberty, the Emperor stipulates to allow me a quantity of meat and drink sufficient for the support of 1,728 Lilliputians. Some time after, asking a friend at court how they came to fix on that determinate number, he told me that his Majesty's mathematicians, having taken the height of my body by the help of a quadrant, and finding it to exceed theirs in the proportion of twelve to one, they concluded from the similarity of their bodies, that mine must contain at least 1,728 of theirs, and consequently would require as much food as was necessary to support that number of Lilliputians. By which the reader may conceive an idea of the ingenuity of that people, as well as the prudent and exact economy of so great a prince. ❧

---

21. **prostrating** (präs trāt′ iŋ): throwing oneself face down, flat on the ground.

22. **censure of vanity** (sen′ shər): strong disapproval of excessive pride.

*Words to Know and Use*

**stipulate** (stip′ yōō lāt′) *v.* to demand something specific in an agreement
**ingenuity** (in′ jə nōō′ ə tē) *n.* skill or cleverness

477

## Responding to Reading

### First Impressions

**1.** What do you think is the most interesting part of the story? Explain why.

### Second Thoughts

**2.** What skills and abilities must the ministers of Lilliput possess to get ahead? What does this suggest about Swift's view of government leaders?

> **Think about**
> • how people are chosen for government positions and honors
> • the role of the Emperor in the decision-making process

**3.** How does Swift poke fun at the military? Compare his views about the military with your own.

**4.** What kind of person and leader is the Emperor?

> **Think about**
> • what people do to gain his favor
> • his relations with Gulliver
> • his views of himself as expressed in the treaty with Gulliver

**5.** Decide whether the treaty Gulliver signs is a fair and sensible one. What point might Swift be making about treaties in general?

**6.** Consider the different ways in which the Lilliputians may be viewed as small. How does their smallness contribute to the theme of the selection?

### Broader Connections

**7.** If Swift were writing today, what authority figures would he be likely to attack? Which of their actions would be worthy targets of his satire?

## Literary Concept: Satire

**Satire** is a literary technique that mixes criticism with humor. Satirists, who include newspaper columnists, screenwriters, songwriters, and many comedians, try to amuse their audiences while making them think about the faults and frailties of their world. Through ridicule and mockery, the satirist tries to bring about changes in individuals or institutions.

Satirists reflect different attitudes toward their subjects. Some satires are playfully amusing and provoke gentle laughter. Others are outrageous or bitter and provoke a darker kind of laughter. What do you think Swift's attitude is toward the Lilliputians? Cite examples from the story to support your answer. Why do you think he chose this method to put forth his views?

**Concept Review: Characterization** Swift tried to create a believable main character. Find details that reveal aspects of Gulliver's personality.

## Writing Options

1. Select a well-known person to receive the Swift Silken Thread Award for Meaningless Achievement. Explain why this person deserves an award for impressing people with deeds that really have no value or importance.

2. Imagine you are a Lilliputian who has an opportunity to observe the giant Gulliver closely. In a letter to a fellow citizen, describe this "Man-Mountain" and your reactions to him.

3. Paraphrase the treaty that Gulliver signed. Your paraphrase should restate the introduction and state each point in clear, simple English.

4. Follow Swift's lead and write a satirical description of how people get ahead in school, work, or an activity of your choice. Use a ridiculous, fantastic situation—like Swift's use of the rope dance or stick jump—to illustrate your point

## Vocabulary Practice

**Exercise** Write the word from the list that best completes the meaning of the sentence.

1. Gulliver became _____ when he found he was a prisoner.
2. He hoped his various entertainments might _____ his captors and win their favor.
3. In Lilliput, physical _____ was a more important qualification than intelligence or administrative ability for obtaining government jobs.
4. A minister's _____ for governing was tested by rope dancing.
5. Only a writer with a bold imagination could _____ of such a name as Skyresh Bolgolam.
6. A person with mathematical interests might _____ about the amount of food that a Man-Mountain would require.
7. Gulliver agrees to _____ with the treaty to gain liberty.
8. One of the ministers, without any _____ from Gulliver, took an immediate dislike to the giant.
9. It took cleverness and scientific _____ on the Lilliputians' part to figure out how much food Gulliver required each day.
10. Treaties usually do not _____ that one party shall not "trample upon the bodies" of the other party.

*Words
to Know
and Use*

**apprehensive
comply
conceive
conjecture
dexterity
divert
faculty
ingenuity
provocation
stipulate**

## Options for Learning

**1 • The Journalist** With a classmate, stage an interview with one of the ministers at the rope dance. Find out what motivates the minister and how he copes with the potential embarrassment of his situation. Your interview can be in the style of "hard-nosed" journalism, such as television's *Sixty Minutes* show, or of "soft" human interest stories, such as those found in *People* magazine.

**2 • The Armchair General** Following Gulliver's instructions, construct the handkerchief field to scale. Find some six-inch high toy soldiers and demonstrate the cavalry's maneuvers on your model.

**3 • In the Emperor's Court** With other students, re-create the signing of the treaty, impersonating the main and minor characters present. Include a public reading of the agreement. Try to capture the formality of the occasion.

**4 • Swift's Illustrator** Choose one or more scenes described in this selection and illustrate them.

### FACT FINDER

*Explain how the Lilliputians arrived at the sum of 1,728 for Gulliver's food needs.*

## *J*onathan Swift
**1667–1745**

Although his biographers agree that Swift is the greatest English satirist, they disagree about how to judge his life. Some believe he led a dark and bitter life, while others view him as charming, sociable, and idealistic.

Swift was born in Ireland, the son of English parents. His father died before he was born, and he was separated from his mother for nearly four years. Though poor, he was given a superior education by wealthy relatives. As a young man he worked as a secretary to Sir William Temple, a position that allowed him to meet London's most important politicians and writers. To support himself, he later became a priest in the Anglican church.

Swift's satires attacked major political parties, religions, and philosophies of his age. At one point, the government offered a reward to anyone who would lead them to the author of a piece that Swift had published under an assumed name.

Swift's personal life remains shrouded in mystery. He had a long, unusual romance with one woman, which was complicated by his relationship with another. Biographers used to claim that Swift suffered insanity in his last years. However, experts now believe he suffered from a rare ear disease that left him deaf and often disoriented but never insane.

*Autobiography*

# By Any Other Name

SANTHA RAMA RAU (sän´ tha rä´ mä rou)

## Examine What You Know

Think of a time when you were made to feel uncomfortable because you were different from others. Perhaps you were the new student in a school, a foreigner in a strange land, or an outsider in some similar situation. Discuss what it felt like to not be accepted.

## Expand Your Knowledge

Santha Rama Rau grew up in a well-to-do Indian household during the time of British rule. The British, who first came to India in the 1600's, had controlled the country for about two hundred years. Because the British dominated nearly all aspects of Indian life—the economy, the military, education, and the government—Indians often had to adapt to British ways and attitudes in order to succeed. They faced the difficulty of choosing between their own native customs, which went back thousands of years, and those of their foreign "masters."

This selection from Rau's book *Gifts of Passage* is a true story about her first experience in a British school.

## Enrich Your Reading

**Understanding Motivation**   In literature, as in real life, it is often difficult to understand the motives behind an action. Readers have to "read between the lines" to figure out why characters act the way they do. For example, in the opening scene of this selection, the headmistress, or principal, of the school changes the names of the Indian children. She says that she cannot pronounce them. However, if you think about her reasoning, you will realize that she does not want to learn how to pronounce Indian names, probably because she thinks that English names—and English customs—are superior to Indian ones.

As you read about the actions in this story, consider the possible motives behind them. Keep in mind that people do not always provide an honest account of their behavior. Look at all the evidence, both stated and implied, surrounding their actions.

■ *A biography of the author can be found on page 490.*

# By Any Other Name

SANTHA RAMA RAU

At the Anglo-Indian day school in Zorinabad to which my sister and I were sent when she was eight and I was five and a half, they changed our names. On the first day of school, a hot, windless morning of a north Indian September, we stood in the headmistress's study and she said, "Now you're the *new* girls. What are your names?"

My sister answered for us. "I am Premila, and she"—nodding in my direction—"is Santha."

The headmistress had been in India, I suppose, fifteen years or so, but she still smiled her helpless inability to cope with Indian names. Her rimless half-glasses glittered, and the precarious bun on the top of her head trembled as she shook her head. "Oh, my dears, those are much too hard for me. Suppose we give you pretty English names. Wouldn't that be more jolly? Let's see, now— Pamela for you, I think." She shrugged in a baffled way at my sister. "That's as close as I can get. And for *you*," she said to me, "how about Cynthia? Isn't that nice?"

My sister was always less easily <u>intimidated</u> than I was, and while she kept a stubborn silence, I said, "Thank you," in a very tiny voice.

We had been sent to that school because my father, among his responsibilities as an officer of the civil service, had a tour of duty to perform in the villages around that steamy little provincial town, where he had his headquarters at that time. He used to make his shorter inspection tours on horseback, and a week before, in the stale heat of a typically postmonsoon[1] day, we had waved goodbye to him and a little procession—an assistant, a secretary, two bearers, and the man to look after the bedding rolls and luggage. They rode away through our large garden, still bright green from the rains, and we turned back into the twilight of the house and the sound of fans whispering in every room.

Up to then, my mother had refused to send Premila to school in the British-run establishments of that time, because, she used to say, "you can bury a dog's tail for seven years and it still comes out curly, and you can take a Britisher away from his home for a lifetime and he still remains insular."[2] The examinations and degrees from entirely Indian schools were not, in those days, considered valid. In my

---

1. **postmonsoon:** after a rainy season.
2. **insular** (in′ sə lər): characteristic of an isolated people; having a narrow-minded viewpoint.

*Words to Know and Use* | **intimidate** (in tim′ ə dāt′) *v.* to make afraid; to threaten with violence

case, the question had never come up, and probably never would have come up if Mother's extraordinary good health had not broken down. For the first time in my life, she was not able to continue the lessons she had been giving us every morning. So our Hindi[3] books were put away, the stories of the Lord Krishna[4] as a little boy were left in mid-air, and we were sent to the Anglo-Indian school.

That first day at school is still, when I think of it, a remarkable one. At that age, if one's name is changed, one develops a curious form of dual personality. I remember having a certain detached and disbelieving concern in the actions of "Cynthia," but certainly no responsibility. Accordingly, I followed the thin, erect back of the headmistress down the veranda to my classroom feeling, at most, a passing interest in what was going to happen to me in this strange, new atmosphere of School.

The building was Indian in design, with wide verandas opening onto a central courtyard, but Indian verandas are usually whitewashed, with stone floors. These, in the tradition of British schools, were painted dark brown and had matting on the floors. It gave a feeling of extra intensity to the heat.

I suppose there were about a dozen Indian children in the school—which contained perhaps forty children in all—and four of them

---

3. **Hindi** (hin′ dē): the main language of India.
4. **Lord Krishna** (krish′ nə): one of the most important gods of Hinduism, the major religion of India.

were in my class. They were all sitting at the back of the room, and I went to join them. I sat next to a small, solemn girl who didn't smile at me. She had long, glossy-black braids and wore a cotton dress, but she still kept on her Indian jewelry—a gold chain around her neck, thin gold bracelets, and tiny ruby studs in her ears. Like most Indian children, she had a rim of black kohl[5] around her eyes. The cotton dress should have looked strange, but all I could think of was that I should ask my mother if I couldn't wear a dress to school, too, instead of my Indian clothes.

I can't remember too much about the proceedings in class that day, except for the beginning. The teacher pointed to me and asked me to stand up. "Now, dear, tell the class your name."

I said nothing.

"Come along," she said, frowning slightly. "What's your name, dear?"

"I don't know," I said, finally.

The English children in the front of the class—there were about eight or ten of them—giggled and twisted around in their chairs to look at me. I sat down quickly and opened my eyes very wide, hoping in that way to dry them off. The little girl with the braids put out her hand and very lightly touched my arm. She still didn't smile.

Most of that morning I was rather bored. I looked briefly at the children's drawings pinned to the wall and then concentrated on a lizard clinging to the ledge of the high, barred window behind the teacher's head. Occasionally it would shoot out its long yellow tongue for a fly, and then it would rest, with its eyes closed and its belly palpitating, as though it were swallowing several times quickly. The lessons were mostly concerned with reading and writing and simple numbers—things that

my mother had already taught me—and I paid very little attention. The teacher wrote on the easel blackboard words like *bat* and *cat*, which seemed babyish to me; only *apple* was new and incomprehensible.

When it was time for the lunch recess, I followed the girl with braids out onto the veranda. There the children from the other classes were assembled. I saw Premila at once and ran over to her, as she had charge of our lunch box. The children were all opening packages and sitting down to eat sandwiches. Premila and I were the only ones who had Indian food—thin wheat chapatties,[6] some vegetable curry,[7] and a bottle of buttermilk. Premila thrust half of it into my hand and whispered fiercely that I should go and sit with my class, because that was what the others seemed to be doing.

The enormous black eyes of the little Indian girl from my class looked at my food longingly, so I offered her some. But she only shook her head and plowed her way solemnly through her sandwiches.

I was very sleepy after lunch, because at home we always took a siesta. It was usually a pleasant time of day, with the bedroom darkened against the harsh afternoon sun, the drifting off into sleep with the sound of Mother's voice reading a story in one's mind, and, finally, the shrill, fussy voice of the ayah[8] waking one for tea.

---

5. **kohl** (kōl): a cosmetic preparation used in some Eastern countries for eye makeup.

6. **chapatties** (chə pät′ ēz): flat, thin pieces of bread baked in a hot, dry skillet.

7. **curry** (kʉr′ ē): a stew made with curry powder, a combination of various spices used frequently in Indian cooking.

8. **ayah** (ä′ yə): a native nursemaid or lady's maid in India.

*Words to Know and Use* | **incomprehensible** (in′ käm′ prē hen′ sə bəl) *adj.* beyond understanding; not intelligible

At school, we rested for a short time on low, folding cots on the veranda, and then we were expected to play games. During the hot part of the afternoon, we played indoors, and after the shadows had begun to lengthen and the slight breeze of the evening had come up, we moved outside to the wide courtyard.

I had never really grasped the system of competitive games. At home, whenever we played tag or guessing games, I was always allowed to "win"—"because," Mother used to tell Premila, "she is the youngest, and we have to allow for that." I had often heard her say it, and it seemed quite reasonable to me, but the result was that I had no clear idea of what "winning" meant.

When we played twos-and-threes that afternoon at school, in accordance with my training, I let one of the small English boys catch me, but was naturally rather puzzled when the other children did not return the courtesy. I ran about for what seemed like hours without ever catching anyone, until it was time for school to close. Much later I learned that my attitude was called "not being a good sport," and I stopped allowing myself to be caught, but it was not for years that I really learned the spirit of the thing.

When I saw our car come up to the school gate, I broke away from my classmates and rushed toward it yelling, "Ayah! Ayah!" It seemed like an eternity since I had seen her that morning—a wizened,[9] affectionate figure in her white cotton sari, giving me dozens of urgent and useless instructions on how to be a good girl at school. Premila followed more sedately, and she told me on the way home never to do that again in front of the other children.

When we got home we went straight to Mother's high white room to have tea with her, and I immediately climbed onto the bed and bounced gently up and down on the springs. Mother asked how we had liked our first day in school. I was so pleased to be home and to have left that peculiar Cynthia behind that I had nothing whatever to say about school, except to ask what *apple* meant. But Premila told Mother about the classes, and added that in her class they had weekly tests to see if they had learned their lessons well.

I asked, "What's a test?"

Premila said, "You're too small to have them. You won't have them in your class for donkey's years." She had learned the expression that day and was using it for the first time. We all laughed enormously at her wit. She also told Mother, in an aside, that we should take sandwiches to school the next day. Not, she said, that *she* minded. But they would be simpler for me to handle.

That whole lovely evening I didn't think about school at all. I sprinted barefoot across the lawns with my favorite playmate, the cook's son, to the stream at the end of the garden. We quarreled in our usual way, waded in the tepid water under the lime trees, and waited for the night to bring out the smell of the jasmine. I listened with fascination to his stories of ghosts and demons, until I was too frightened to cross the garden alone in the semidarkness. The ayah found me, shouted at the cook's son, scolded me, hurried me in to supper—it was an entirely usual, wonderful evening.

It was a week later, the day of Premila's first test, that our lives changed rather abruptly. I was sitting at the back of my class, in my usual inattentive way, only half listening to the teacher. I had started a rather guarded

---

9. **wizened** (wiz′ ənd): dried up; shriveled.

| Words to Know and Use | **sedately** (si dāt′ lē) *adv.* calmly; quietly; steadily<br>**tepid** (tep′ id) *adj.* moderately warm<br>**inattentive** (in′ ə ten′ tiv) *adj.* not paying attention; absent-minded |
| --- | --- |

485

© Suzanne Murphy/TSW/Click Chicago.

friendship with the girl with the braids, whose name turned out to be Nalini (Nancy, in school). The three other Indian children were already fast friends. Even at that age it was apparent to all of us that friendship with the English or Anglo-Indian children was out of the question. Occasionally, during the class, my new friend and I would draw pictures and show them to each other secretly.

The door opened sharply and Premila marched in. At first, the teacher smiled at her in a kindly and encouraging way and said, "Now, you're little Cynthia's sister?"

Premila didn't even look at her. She stood with her feet planted firmly apart and her shoulders rigid, and addressed herself directly to me. "Get up," she said. "We're going home."

I didn't know what had happened, but I was aware that it was a crisis of some sort. I rose obediently and started to walk toward my sister.

"Bring your pencils and your notebook," she said.

I went back for them, and together we left the room. The teacher started to say something just as Premila closed the door, but we didn't wait to hear what it was.

In complete silence we left the school grounds and started to walk home. Then I asked Premila what the matter was. All she would say was "We're going home for good."

It was a very tiring walk for a child of five and a half, and I dragged along behind Premila with my pencils growing sticky in my hand. I can still remember looking at the dusty hedges and the tangles of thorns in the ditches by the side of the road, smelling the faint fragrance from the eucalyptus trees and wondering whether we would ever reach home. Occasionally, a horse-drawn tonga[10] passed us, and the women, in their pink or green silks, stared at Premila and me trudging along on the side of the road. A few coolies[11] and a line of women carrying baskets of vegetables on their heads smiled at us. But it was nearing the hottest time of day, and the road was almost deserted. I walked more and more slowly and shouted to Premila from time to time, "Wait for me!" with increasing peevishness.[12] She spoke to me only once, and that was to tell me to carry my notebook on my head, because of the sun.

---

10. **tonga** (täŋ gə): a two-wheeled carriage of India.

11. **coolies:** unskilled native laborers, especially in India or China.

12. **peevishness** (pē′ vish nis): state of being irritable or hard to please.

When we got to our house, the ayah was just taking a tray of lunch into Mother's room. She immediately started a long, worried questioning about what are you children doing back here at this hour of the day.

Mother looked very startled and very concerned, and asked Premila what had happened.

Premila said, "We had our test today, and she made me and the other Indians sit at the back of the room, with a desk between each one."

Mother said, "Why was that, darling?"

"She said it was because Indians cheat," Premila added. "So I don't think we should go back to that school."

Mother looked very distant and was silent a long time. At last she said, "Of course not, darling." She sounded displeased.

We all shared the curry she was having for lunch and afterward I was sent off to the beautifully familiar bedroom for my siesta. I could hear Mother and Premila talking through the open door.

Mother said, "Do you suppose she understood all that?"

Premila said, "I shouldn't think so. She's a baby."

Mother said, "Well, I hope it won't bother her."

Of course, they were both wrong. I understood it perfectly, and I remember it all very clearly. But I put it happily away because it had all happened to a girl called Cynthia, and I never was really particularly interested in her. ❧

---

# INSIGHT

## My Name
### *Nomgqibelo Ncamisile Mnqhibisa*

MAGOLENG WA SELEPE

Look what they have done to my name . . .
the wonderful name of my great-great-
    grandmothers
*Nomgqibelo Ncamisile Mnqhibisa*

The burly bureaucrat was surprised.
What he heard was music to his ears
"Wat is daai, sê nou weer?"
"I am from Chief Daluxolo Velayigodle of
    emaMpodweni
And my name is Nomgqibelo Ncamisile
    Mnqhibisa."

Messia, help me!
My name is so simple
and yet so meaningful,
but to this man it is trash . . .

He gives me a name
Convenient enough to answer his whim:
I end up being

Maria . . .
I . . .
*Nomgqibelo Ncamisile Mnqhibisa.*

## *R*esponding to Reading

### First Impressions

1. In what ways, if any, does the story remind you of your own experiences?

### Second Thoughts

2. Discuss the motives of Premila's teacher in separating the Indians during the test. Why are her remarks insulting?

3. Do you think that Premila does the right thing by walking out in the middle of school? Why or why not? Should she have done something different to protest her treatment and to challenge the British-dominated system?

4. Why does Santha and Premila's mother agree that the children should not go back to the British school?

   **Think about**
   • what the mother has said about the British
   • what she is displeased about
   • the family's position in society and their view of themselves

5. How are the Indian children affected by the British treatment of them?

   **Think about**
   • Santha's two personalities as "Santha" and "Cynthia"
   • how Premila responds to school
   • what motivates other children to adapt to British ways
   • how the teachers view the Indians

6. Why does Rau tell her story from the point of view of a five-year-old?

### Broader Connections

7. Premila's sense of pride and self-worth enable her to walk out of school rather than face continued humiliation. Discuss examples you have seen of people who have stood up to injustice or unfair treatment. Do you think that an individual's self-esteem affects how other people treat him or her?

## *L*iterary Concept: Minor Character

Even when an author describes an actual incident, he or she chooses what to focus on and how much to reveal. Although Santha and her sister encounter many different people at school, the author chooses to describe only a few in detail: the headmistress, two teachers, Santha's Indian friend, and her other

Indian classmates. These **minor characters** provide important contrasts to Santha and her sister and show both British and Indian attitudes and behavior. Discuss how each of the minor characters affects the actions and attitudes of the two sisters.

**Concept Review: Autobiography**   An autobiography usually focuses on experiences that shaped the writer's life. How do you think Santha's early experience with the British might have affected her later?

# Writing Options

1. Choose one of the following characters and analyze her motives: the headmistress, Premila's teacher, or Santha and Premila's mother.

2. The title of this selection comes from Juliet's lines in *Romeo and Juliet*: "What's in a name? That which we call a rose / By any other name would smell as sweet." Explain how the quote applies to this selection.

3. Explain what you think the mother means on page 482 when she compares the British to a "dog's tail" that will never lose its curl.

4. Create a conversation among the girls' teachers and the headmistress in which they discuss the sisters' walkout. Considering their views of Indians, how will they explain the event?

# Vocabulary Practice

**Exercise** Write the letter of the word or phrase that best completes each sentence below.

1. **Sedately** describes how Premila (a) angrily told her story (b) walked (c) hurried out of school.
2. If a word were **incomprehensible,** Santha would (a) know how to spell it (b) use it often (c) not understand it.
3. A teacher might **intimidate** a child and make her feel (a) nervous and shy (b) proud (c) unaware of what is happening.
4. If she were **inattentive,** Santha might (a) not remember what she heard (b) memorize what she heard (c) challenge the speaker.
5. **Tepid** water is (a) scalding (b) lukewarm (c) cool.

> *Words to Know and Use*
>
> ---
>
> **inattentive**
> **incomprehensible**
> **intimidate**
> **sedately**
> **tepid**

# *extend*

## *Options for Learning*

**1** • **Stories Close to Home** Interview people in your neighborhood to discover how they have resisted unfair treatment because of their culture, race, social class, or other reasons. Ask your subjects what they believe are the most effective methods of fighting injustice. Compare what you learn with what your classmates learn and decide as a group which methods are most effective.

**2** • **A Taste of India** Santha Rama Rau once wrote an Indian cookbook as a way of helping Westerners appreciate Eastern food. Work in a small group to plan an Indian menu. If possible, prepare the food and serve it to your class. Add other Indian touches, such as clothing or music, to make your meal more authentic.

**3** • **Photo Essay** Look through books or magazine articles about India to find pictures that could relate to the story. For example, you might choose pictures of young Indians in traditional dress. Then compile your pictures, or photocopies of them, into a photo essay to accompany the story.

**4** • **Birth of a Nation** With a small group, research the history of India's independence movement. Explain the movement's major figures and the strategies used by the Indians. Present your findings to the rest of the class.

 **FACT FINDER**

*When did India achieve independence from British rule?*

---

### *Santha Rama Rau*
#### 1923–

Although she was raised to be a traditional Indian wife who would tend to the needs of her family and household, Rau sought and found a life of adventure. Shortly after her first school experience, her father was transferred to England, where Rau attended a private school and traveled widely. Her travels took her throughout England and to India,

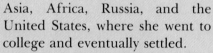

Asia, Africa, Russia, and the United States, where she went to college and eventually settled.

Rau has published eleven books, ranging from fiction and autobiography to cookbooks and travelogues. She began her writing career when a famous Indian poet, Madame Sarojini Naidu, encouraged her to write about her travels and experiences. Much of Rau's writing helps readers to appreciate other cultures and lands.

*Nonfiction*

# Crackling Day

### PETER ABRAHAMS

## Examine What You Know

Jot down words, phrases, or names that come to mind when South Africa is mentioned. In small groups, share what you know about the racial problems of South Africa and the people who are trying to solve those problems.

## Expand Your Knowledge

The country at the southern tip of Africa, settled by Dutch and British colonists, is known for its bitter racial conflicts. Though whites make up only 15 percent of the population, they control the government and the economy. Blacks, Asians, and Coloureds (people of mixed ancestry) have long been denied basic rights of citizenship. The government tells the nonwhites where they can live, limits their choice of jobs and their access to education,

and denies their right to vote. A system of forced racial separation, called *apartheid* (ə pär′ tāt), has been in place since 1948. In recent years, many South Africans have fought against this system. The world community has joined together to protest apartheid and press for change.

This selection from the autobiography of Peter Abrahams, an internationally known writer, shares one of his memories of growing up in South Africa in the 1920's. He describes events that occurred soon after he moved from the slums of the capital, Johannesburg, to live with his aunt and uncle on a small farm.

## Write Before You Read

■ *A biography of the author can be found on page 501.*

Think back to a time when you or someone you know was treated unfairly because of race, religion, sex, economic status, or even a style of clothing. Describe what happened and tell how you felt during and after the incident.

# Crackling Day

PETER ABRAHAMS

Wednesday was crackling day. On that day the children of the location made the long trek to Elsburg siding[1] for the squares of pig's rind that passed for our daily meat. We collected a double lot of cow dung the day before; a double lot of *moeroga*.[2]

I finished my breakfast and washed up. Aunt Liza was at her washtub in the yard. A misty, sickly sun was just showing. And on the open veld[3] the frost lay thick and white on the grass.

"Ready?" Aunt Liza called.

I went out to her. She shook the soapsuds off her swollen hands and wiped them on her apron. She lifted the apron and put her hand through the slits of the many thin cotton dresses she wore. The dress nearest the skin was the one with the pocket. From this she pulled a sixpenny piece. She tied it in a knot on the corner of a bit of colored cloth and handed it to me.

"Take care of that. . . . Take the smaller piece of bread in the bin, but don't eat it till you start back. You can have a small piece of crackling with it. Only a small piece, understand?"

"Yes, Aunt Liza."

"All right."

I got the bread and tucked it into the little canvas bag in which I would carry the crackling.

" 'Bye, Aunt Liza." I trotted off, one hand in my pocket, feeling the cloth where the money was. I paused at Andries's home.

"Andries!" I danced up and down while I waited. The cold was not so terrible on bare feet if one did not keep still.

Andries came trotting out of his yard. His mother's voice followed, desperate and plaintive:

"I'll skin you if you lose the money!"

"Women!" Andries said bitterly.

I glimpsed the dark, skinny woman at her washtub as we trotted across the veld. Behind and in front of us, other children trotted in twos and threes.

There was a sharp bite to the morning air I sucked in; it stung my nose so that tears came to my eyes; it went down my throat like an icy draft; my nose ran. I tried breathing through my mouth, but this was worse. The cold went through my shirt and shorts; my skin went pimply and chilled; my fingers went numb and began to ache; my feet felt like frozen lumps that did not belong to me, yet jarred and hurt each time I put them down. I began to feel sick and desperate.

"Jesus God in heaven!" Andries cried suddenly.

---

1. **siding:** a short railroad track connected to a main track and used for unloading or bypassing.
2. **moeroga** (mo͞o og′ ä): dried cow manure used for cooking fires.
3. **veld** (velt): open, grassy country in southern Africa.

*Words to Know and Use* | **plaintive** (plān′ tiv) *adj.* mournful; sad

I looked at him. His eyes were rimmed in red. Tears ran down his cheeks. His face was drawn and purple, a sick look on it.

"Faster," I said.

"Think it'll help?"

# *It was a half-human monster with evil thoughts, evil intentions, bent on destroying us.*

I nodded. We went faster. We passed two children, sobbing and moaning as they ran. We were all in the same desperate situation. We were creatures haunted and hounded by the cold. It was a cruel enemy who gave no quarter. And our means of fighting it were pitifully inadequate. In all the mornings and evenings of the winter months, young and old, big and small, were helpless victims of the bitter cold. Only toward noon and in the early afternoon, when the sun sat high in the sky, was there a brief respite. For us children, the cold, especially the morning cold, assumed an awful and malevolent personality. We talked of "it." "It" was a half-human monster with evil thoughts, evil intentions, bent on destroying us. "It" was happiest when we were most miserable. Andries had told me how "it" had, last winter, caught and killed a boy.

Hunger was an enemy too, but one with whom we could come to terms, who had many virtues and values. Hunger gave our pap, *moeroga*, and crackling a feastlike quality. When it was not with us, we could think and talk kindly about it. Its memory could even give moments of laughter. But the cold of winter was with us

all the time. "It" never really eased up. There were only more bearable degrees of "it" at high noon and on mild days. "It" was the real enemy. And on this Wednesday morning, as we ran across the veld, winter was more bitterly, bitingly, freezingly real than ever.

The sun climbed. The frozen earth thawed, leaving the short grass looking wet and weary. Painfully our feet and legs came alive. The aching numbness slowly left our fingers. We ran more slowly in the more bearable cold.

In climbing, the sun lost some of its damp look and seemed a real, if cold, sun. When it was right overhead, we struck the sandy road, which meant we were nearing the siding. None of the others were in sight. Andries and I were alone on the sandy road on the open veld. We slowed down to a brisk walk. We were sufficiently thawed to want to talk.

"How far?" I said.

"A few minutes," he said.

"I've got a piece of bread," I said.

"Me too," he said. "Let's eat it now."

"On the way back," I said. "With a bit of crackling."

"Good idea. . . . Race to the fork."

"All right."

"Go!" he said.

We shot off together, legs working like pistons. He soon pulled away from me. He reached the fork in the road some fifty yards ahead.

"I win!" he shouted gleefully, though his teeth still chattered.

We pitched stones down the road, each trying to pitch farther than the other. I won and wanted to go on doing it. But Andries soon grew weary with pitching. We raced again. Again he won. He wanted another race, but I refused. I wanted pitching, but he refused. So, sulking with each other, we reached the pig farm.

| *Words to Know and Use* | **respite** (res′ pit) *n.* a temporary relief or rest<br>**malevolent** (mə lev′ ə lənt) *adj.* having or showing spite or hatred |
| --- | --- |

We followed a fenced-off pathway round sprawling white buildings. Everywhere about us was the grunt of pigs. As we passed an open doorway, a huge dog came bounding out, snarling and barking at us. In our terror we forgot it was fenced in, and we streaked away. Surprised, I found myself a good distance ahead of Andries. We looked back and saw a young white woman call the dog to heel.

"Damn Boer[4] dog," Andries said.

"Matter with it?" I asked.

"They teach them to go for us. Never get caught by one. My old man's got a hole in his bottom where a Boer dog got him."

I remembered I had outstripped him.

"I won!" I said.

"Only because you were frightened," he said.

"I still won."

"Scare arse," he jeered.

"Scare arse, yourself!"

"I'll knock you!"

"I'll knock you back!"

A couple of white men came down the path and ended our possible fight. We hurried past them to the distant shed where a queue[5] had already formed. There were grown-ups and children. All the grown-ups and some of the children were from places other than our location.

The line moved slowly. The young white man who served us did it in leisurely fashion, with long pauses for a smoke. Occasionally he turned his back.

At last, after what seemed hours, my turn came. Andries was behind me. I took the sixpenny piece from the square of cloth and offered it to the man.

"Well?" he said.

"Sixpence crackling, please."

Andries nudged me in the back. The man's stare suddenly became cold and hard. Andries whispered into my ear.

"Well?" the man repeated coldly.

"Please, *baas*[6]," I said.

"What d'you want?"

"Sixpence crackling, please."

"What?"

Andries dug me in the ribs.

"Sixpence crackling, please, *baas*."

"What?"

"Sixpence crackling, please, *baas*."

"You new here?"

"Yes, *baas*." I looked at his feet while he stared at me.

At last he took the sixpenny piece from me. I held my bag open while he filled it with crackling from a huge pile on a large canvas sheet on the ground. Turning away, I stole a fleeting glance at his face. His eyes met mine, and there was amused, challenging mockery in them. I waited for Andries at the back of the queue, out of the reach of the white man's mocking eyes.

The cold day was at its mildest as we walked home along the sandy road. I took out my piece of bread and, with a small piece of greasy crackling, still warm, on it, I munched as we went along. We had not yet made our peace, so Andries munched his bread and crackling on the other side of the road.

"Dumb fool!" he mocked at me for not knowing how to address the white man.

"Scare arse!" I shouted back.

Thus, hurling curses at each other, we reached the fork. Andries saw them first and moved over to my side of the road.

"White boys," he said.

There were three of them, two of about our own size and one slightly bigger. They had school bags and were coming toward us up the road from the siding.

---

4. **Boer** (b$\overline{oo}$r): a white South African whose ancestors were Dutch. The whites in South Africa are mainly of British and Dutch descent.

5. **queue** (ky$\overline{oo}$): a line of people waiting to be served.

6. **baas** (bäs): master, sir; a South African term of address for a white man.

ON THE PLAINS   1971   Paul Collins   From *Black Portrait of an African Journey* by Paul Collins.

"Better run for it," Andries said.

"Why?"

"No, that'll draw them. Let's just walk along, but quickly."

"Why?" I repeated.

"Shut up," he said.

Some of his anxiety touched me. Our own scrap was forgotten. We marched side by side as fast as we could. The white boys saw us and hurried up the road. We passed the fork. Perhaps they would take the turning away from us. We dared not look back.

"Hear them?" Andries asked.

"No." I looked over my shoulder. "They're coming," I said.

"Walk faster," Andries said. "If they come closer, run."

"Hey, *klipkop*!"[7]

"Don't look back," Andries said.

"Hottentot!"[8]

We walked as fast as we could.

"Bloody kaffir!"[9]

Ahead was a bend in the road. Behind the bend were bushes. Once there, we could run without their knowing it till it was too late.

"Faster," Andries said.

They began pelting us with stones.

"Run when we get to the bushes," Andries said.

The bend and the bushes were near. We would soon be there.

---

7. **klipkop:** "rock head," a term of contempt.

8. **Hottentot** (hät' 'n tät'): a member of a nomadic, peaceful people of southwestern Africa; used as an insult here.

9. **kaffir** (kaf' ər): a black African in South Africa; a term of contempt.

A clear young voice carried to us: "Your fathers are dirty black baboons!"

"Run!" Andries called.

A violent, unreasoning anger suddenly possessed me. I stopped and turned.

"You're a liar!" I screamed it.

The foremost boy pointed at me. "An ugly black baboon!"

In a fog of rage I went toward him.

"Liar!" I shouted. "My father was better than your father!"

*A violent, unreasoning anger suddenly possessed me. I stopped and turned.*

I neared them. The bigger boy stepped between me and the one I was after.

"My father was better than your father! Liar!"

The big boy struck me a mighty clout on the side of the face. I staggered, righted myself, and leaped at the boy who had insulted my father. I struck him on the face, hard. A heavy blow on the back of my head nearly stunned me. I grabbed at the boy in front of me. We went down together.

"Liar!" I said through clenched teeth, hitting him with all my might.

Blows rained on me—on my head, my neck, the side of my face, my mouth—but my enemy was under me and I pounded him fiercely, all the time repeating:

"Liar! Liar! Liar!"

Suddenly stars exploded in my head. Then there was darkness.

I emerged from the darkness to find Andries kneeling beside me.

"God, man! I thought they'd killed you."

I sat up. The white boys were nowhere to be seen. Like Andries, they'd probably thought me dead and run off in panic. The inside of my mouth felt sore and swollen. My nose was tender to the touch. The back of my head ached. A trickle of blood dripped from my nose. I stemmed it with the square of colored cloth. The greatest damage was to my shirt. It was ripped in many places. I remembered the crackling. I looked anxiously about. It was safe, a little off the road on the grass. I relaxed. I got up and brushed my clothes. I picked up the crackling.

"God, you're dumb!" Andries said. "You're going to get it! Dumb idiot!"

I was too depressed to retort. Besides, I knew he was right. I was dumb. I should have run when he told me to.

"Come on," I said.

One of many small groups of children, each child carrying his little bag of crackling, we trod the long road home in the cold winter afternoon.

There was tension in the house that night. When I got back, Aunt Liza had listened to the story in silence. The beating or scolding I expected did not come. But Aunt Liza changed while she listened, became remote and withdrawn. When Uncle Sam came home she told him what had happened. He, too, just looked at me and became more remote and withdrawn than usual. They were waiting for something; their tension reached out to me, and I waited with them, anxious, apprehensive.

The thing we waited for came while we were having our supper. We heard a trap[10] pull up outside.

---

10. **trap:** a light, two-wheeled carriage.

*Words to Know and Use* | **retort** (ri tôrt′) *v.* to answer a challenge or insult
**withdrawn** (with drôn′) *adj.* isolated; shy; reserved

"Here it is," Uncle Sam said, and got up.

Aunt Liza leaned back from the table and put her hands in her lap, fingers intertwined, a cold, unseeing look in her eyes.

Before Uncle Sam reached the door, it burst open. A tall, broad, white man strode in. Behind him came the three boys. The one I had attacked had swollen lips and a puffy left eye.

"Evening, *baas*," Uncle Sam murmured.

"That's him," the bigger boy said, pointing at me.

The white man stared till I lowered my eyes.

"Well?" he said.

"He's sorry, *baas*," Uncle Sam said quickly. "I've given him a hiding he won't forget soon. You know how it is, *baas*. He's new here, the child of a relative in Johannesburg, and they don't know how to behave there. You know how it is in the big towns, *baas*." The plea in Uncle Sam's voice had grown more pronounced as he went on. He turned to me. "Tell the *baas* and young *basies* how sorry you are, Lee."[11]

I looked at Aunt Liza and something in her lifelessness made me stubborn in spite of my fear.

"He insulted my father," I said.

The white man smiled.

"See, Sam, your hiding couldn't have been good."

There was a flicker of life in Aunt Liza's eyes. For a brief moment she saw me, looked at me, warmly, lovingly; then her eyes went dead again.

"He's only a child, *baas*," Uncle Sam murmured.

"You stubborn too, Sam?"

"No, *baas*."

"Good. Then teach him, Sam. If you and he are to live here, you must teach him. Well—?"

"Yes, *baas*."

Uncle Sam went into the other room and returned with a thick leather thong. He wound it once round his hand and advanced on me. The man and the boys leaned against the door, watching. I looked at Aunt Liza's face. Though there was no sign of life or feeling on it, I knew suddenly, instinctively, that she wanted me not to cry.

Bitterly, Uncle Sam said: "You must never lift your hand to a white person. No matter what happens, you must never lift your hand to a white person. . . ."

He lifted the strap and brought it down on my back. I clenched my teeth and stared at Aunt Liza. I did not cry with the first three strokes. Then, suddenly, Aunt Liza went limp. Tears showed in her eyes. The thong came down on my back again and again. I screamed and begged for mercy. I groveled[12] at Uncle Sam's feet, begging him to stop, promising never to lift my hand to any white person. . . .

> *B*itterly, Uncle Sam said: "You must never lift your hand to a white person."

At last the white man's voice said: "All right, Sam."

Uncle Sam stopped. I lay whimpering on the floor. Aunt Liza sat like one in a trance.

"Is he still stubborn, Sam?"

"Tell the *baas* and *basies* you are sorry."

"I'm sorry," I said.

"Bet his father is one of those who believe in equality."

"His father is dead," Aunt Liza said.

---

11. **Lee:** boyhood nickname of author Peter Abrahams.

12. **groveled** (gruv′ əld): crawled on the ground without self-respect.

"Good night, Sam."

"Good night, *baas*. Sorry about this."

"All right, Sam." He opened the door. The boys went out first, then he followed. "Good night, Liza."

Aunt Liza did not answer. The door shut behind the white folk, and soon we heard their trap moving away. Uncle Sam flung the thong viciously against the door, slumped down on the bench, folded his arms on the table, and buried his head on his arms. Aunt Liza moved away from him, sat down on the floor beside me, and lifted me into her large lap. She sat rocking my body. Uncle Sam began to sob softly. After some time he raised his head and looked at us.

"Explain to the child, Liza," he said.

"You explain," Aunt Liza said bitterly. "You are the man. You did the beating. You are the head of the family. This is a man's world. You do the explaining."

"Please, Liza."

"You should be happy. The whites are satisfied. We can go on now."

With me in her arms, Aunt Liza got up. She carried me into the other room. The food on the table remained half eaten. She laid me on the bed on my stomach, smeared fat on my back, then covered me with the blankets. She undressed and got into bed beside me. She cuddled me close, warmed me with her own body. With her big hand on my cheek, she rocked me, first to silence, then to sleep.

For the only time during my stay there, I slept on a bed in Elsburg.

When I woke next morning, Uncle Sam had gone. Aunt Liza only once referred to the beating he had given me. It was in the late afternoon, when I returned with the day's cow dung.

"It hurt him," she said. "You'll understand one day."

That night Uncle Sam brought me an orange, a bag of boiled sweets, and a dirty old picture book. He smiled as he gave them to me, rather anxiously. When I smiled back at him, he seemed to relax. He put his hand on my head, started to say something, then changed his mind and took his seat by the fire.

Aunt Liza looked up from the floor, when she dished out the food.

"It's all right, old man," she murmured.

"One day . . ." Uncle Sam said.

"It's all right," Aunt Liza repeated insistently. 🔊

GORÉE 1971 Paul Collins
From *Black Portrait of an African Journey* by Paul Collins.

# explain

## Responding to Reading

### First Impressions

**1.** Jot down some words that describe the feelings you have after reading this account of Abrahams's experience. What produced those feelings?

### Second Thoughts

**2.** For which characters do you have the most sympathy? For which do you have the least sympathy? Explain your opinions.

**3.** Why does the white man demand that Sam beat his nephew?

**4.** Why does Sam react the way he does to the questions and orders from the white man? Explain whether or not you believe he does the right thing.

> **Think about**
> - the harshness of the beating and Sam's words to his nephew
> - Sam's actions after the white man leaves
> - what might have happened if he had refused to cooperate

**5.** How does this selection show the effects of discrimination?

> **Think about**
> - the boys' journey to get crackling
> - the contrast between Peter and Andries
> - the effects of the beating on Liza, Sam, and Peter

### Broader Connections

**6.** What kinds of effects does racial discrimination have on individuals and societies? In your opinion, what is the worst effect?

## Literary Concept: Mood

The **mood** is the atmosphere or feeling that the writer creates for the reader. Mood is produced by the writer's choice of words, by the events described, and by the setting. For example, a story about an ax murderer about to commit a crime in a dark alley may evoke a mood of terror. How would you describe the mood of "Crackling Day"? What feelings did you experience as you read the account? Look back through the selection to find evidence of how Abrahams created mood.

**Concept Review: Tone**   Tone, the writer's attitude toward the subject, is similar to mood, but the two are not necessarily the same. For example, in the description of the beating, the reader's mood may be one of outrage, but the author's tone is detached, as if he is a neutral observer. Review other events in the selection and decide whether the tone differs from the mood.

## Writing Options

1. Imagine that you are Aunt Liza or Uncle Sam. Describe what was going through your mind from the time the white man entered your house until after he left.

2. Think about how other characters in Unit 3 would have responded to the white man's demand for a beating. Select a character in another selection, such as Alice Walker or Samuel Johnson. As the character, write a letter to Sam, giving him advice on how he should handle the situation.

3. Describe what lesson Peter probably learned as a result of his fight and beating. Explain how these events may influence his behavior and attitudes.

4. Write an editorial for the Elsburg daily newspaper that expresses your opinion about the crackling day incidents and your views about what should be done about such situations in the future.

## Vocabulary Practice

**Exercise** Write the letter of the situation that best demonstrates the meaning of the boldfaced word.

1. **respite**
   a. A young boy fears older youths.
   b. Sheep huddle to find relief from the cold.
   c. A man is so angry that he humiliates his nephew.
2. **withdrawn**
   a. A solitary woman refuses to deal with others.
   b. A boy spends his money on a special treat.
   c. Prejudice creates problems in a teenager's life.
3. **retort**
   a. A boy chooses to run rather than fight.
   b. A beaten child tells his parents what happened.
   c. A girl screams insults in reply to vicious comments.
4. **malevolent**
   a. A gang of boys humiliates a child who is different.
   b. A child finds courage to defend himself.
   c. Words of comfort fail to soothe a child in pain.
5. **plaintive**
   a. Someone fights the effects of prejudice in court.
   b. A song expresses a sadness felt by many.
   c. People assume that skin color makes them superior.

> *Words to Know and Use*
>
> ---
>
> **malevolent**
> **plaintive**
> **respite**
> **retort**
> **withdrawn**

# *extend*

## *Options for Learning*

**1** • **South Africa Today**  With a group of students, research recent magazines and newspapers in your library to find out the political and economic situation of the different peoples in South Africa. Find out whether conditions have changed since Abrahams's story was published in 1954. Then present your findings to the class.

**2** • **Debate the Issues**  With a classmate, research the political issues surrounding control of the government in South Africa. One of you should focus on the views held by the whites; the other should focus on the different views of Blacks, Asians, and Coloureds. For purposes of debate, choose an extreme view and prepare to defend it, even though you may not agree with it. Then stage a debate, with each of you representing an extreme position. After your debate, the entire class should come up with ideas for compromise.

**3** • **Mood Collage**  Write a word that describes the mood of the story. Surround that word with photographs and pictures from magazines that convey its meaning. Your collage should include pictures of current events.

**4** • **Tracking Emotions**  In a small group, create a line graph to chart the intensity of emotion throughout the selection. Graph the major events from beginning to end, noting where the reader's emotions rise and where they fall.

**FACT FINDER**

*On a map of South Africa, locate Johannesburg and Elsburg. How many miles apart are they?*

## *Peter Abrahams*
### 1919–

Abrahams grew up in the Coloured slums of Johannesburg amid poverty and illiteracy. Economic necessity forced him to find work as a tinsmith's helper at the age of nine instead of attending school. Fortunately, a typist where he worked entertained him with tales from Shakespeare, sparking an interest in education. With a gritty determination, Abrahams found a way to attend school, though the need for employment frequently interrupted his progress. He held jobs such as kitchen helper, porter, clerk, and dishwasher.

Abrahams left South Africa in his late teens to find better employment. He settled in England, where he held various writing jobs and published his stories, novels, and autobiography, *Tell Freedom: Memories of Africa.* Throughout his career, he has defended African rights and promoted unity among African cultures. Abrahams settled permanently in Jamaica in 1956.

*Fiction*

## The Thrill of the Grass

### W. P. KINSELLA

## Examine What You Know

Baseball is called America's national pastime. Why do you think the public loves the game so much? Are you a baseball fan? Discuss what you like and don't like about the game—as a spectator or as a participant. Then find out what the narrator in this story does in response to his feelings about baseball.

## Expand Your Knowledge

In the mid-1960's, when the city of Houston built its Astrodome—the first indoor baseball stadium—a new product called Astroturf was used to cover the floor. This nylon, grasslike carpet, which is padded and covers a concrete surface, can be used indoors or outdoors. Over the past several years, the owners of baseball parks in numerous cities have switched to synthetic coverings for their stadiums. The advantages and disadvantages of Astroturf over real grass are still being argued. Since it holds up well in any weather, artificial turf requires less maintenence. It is also a faster surface for running and turning. Those who oppose it cite the types of injuries produced on artificial turf, its hardness, and the fact that it does not have the smell or appearance of real grass.

Kinsella's story, which deals with the issue of artificial turf, is set during the baseball strike of 1981, when the players refused to play until they had a new contract. The strike went on for forty-nine days. That summer without baseball was upsetting to many loyal fans, particularly those who think of the game as something that ties them to their youth when the game was free and played on real grass.

## Write Before You Read

Think of people that you know who have challenged the system, either in large or small ways. What personality traits do these people have in common? Do you think that you are the type of person who could challenge the system? Describe your feelings.

■ *A biography of the author can be found on page 512.*

# The *Thrill* of the *Grass*

W. P. KINSELLA

1981: the summer the baseball players went on strike. The dull weeks drag by, the summer deepens, the strike is nearly a month old. Outside the city the corn rustles and ripens in the sun. Summer without baseball: a disruption to the psyche.[1] An unexplainable aimlessness engulfs me. I stay later and later each evening in the small office at the rear of my shop. Now, driving home after work, the worst of the rush-hour traffic over, it is the time of evening I would normally be heading for the stadium.

I enjoy arriving an hour early, parking in a far corner of the lot, walking slowly toward the stadium, rays of sun dropping softly over my shoulders like tangerine ropes, my shadow gliding with me, black as an umbrella. I like to watch young families beside their campers, the mothers in shorts, grilling hamburgers, their men drinking beer. I enjoy seeing little boys dressed in the home-team uniform, barely toddling, clutching hotdogs in upraised hands.

I am a failed shortstop. As a young man, I saw myself diving to my left, graceful as a toppling tree, fielding high grounders like a cat leaping for butterflies, bracing my right foot and tossing to first, the throw true as if a steel ribbon connected my hand and the first baseman's glove. I dreamed of leading the American League in hitting—being inducted into the Hall of Fame. I batted .217 in my senior year of high school and averaged 1.3 errors per nine innings.

I know the stadium will be deserted; nevertheless I wheel my car down off the freeway, park, and walk across the silent lot, my footsteps rasping and mournful. Strangle-grass and creeping charlie are already inching up through the gravel, surreptitious, surprised at their own ease. Faded bottle caps, rusted bits of chrome, an occasional paper clip, recede into the earth. I circle a ticket booth, sunfaded, empty, the door closed by an oversized padlock. I walk beside the tall, machinery-green, board fence. A half mile away a few cars hiss along the freeway; overhead a single-engine plane fizzes lazily. The whole place is silent as an empty classroom, like a house suddenly without children.

It is then that I spot the door shape. I have to check twice to be sure it is there: a door cut in the deep-green boards of the fence, more the promise of a door than the real thing, the kind of door, as children, we cut in the sides of

---

1. **psyche** (sī′ kē): the human soul.

503

WORLD SERIES   Arnold Friedman   The Phillips Collection, Washington, D.C.

cardboard boxes with our mother's paring knives. As I move closer, a golden circle of lock, like an acrimonious[2] eye, establishes its certainty.

I stand, my nose so close to the door I can smell the faint odor of paint, the golden eye of a lock inches from my own eyes. My desire to be inside the ballpark is so great that for the first time in my life I commit a criminal act. I have been a locksmith for over forty years. I take the small tools from the pocket of my jacket, and in less time than it would take a speedy runner to circle the bases I am inside the stadium. Though the ballpark is open-air,

it smells of abandonment; the walkways and seating areas are cold as basements. I breathe the odors of rancid popcorn and wilted cardboard.

The maintenance staff was laid off when the strike began. Synthetic grass does not need to be cut or watered. I stare down at the ball diamond, where just to the right of the pitcher's mound, a single weed, perhaps two inches high, stands defiant in the rain-pocked dirt.

---

2. **acrimonious** (ak′ ri mō′ nē əs): bitter and harsh in temper and manner.

The field sits breathless in the orangy glow of the evening sun. I stare at the potato-colored earth of the infield, that wide, dun arc, surrounded by plastic grass. As I <u>contemplate</u> the prickly turf, which scorches the <u>thighs</u> and buttocks of a sliding player as if he were being <u>seared</u> by hot steel, it stares back in its uniform ugliness. The seams that send routinely hit ground balls veering at tortuous[3] angles, are vivid, gray as scars.

I remember the ballfields of my childhood, the outfields full of soft hummocks[4] and brown-eyed gopher holes.

I stride down from the stands and walk out to the middle of the field. I touch the stubble that is called grass, take off my shoes, but find it is like walking on a row of toothbrushes. It was an evil day when they stripped the sod from this ballpark, cut it into yard-wide swathes,[5] rolled it, memories and all, into great green-and-black cinnamon-roll shapes, trucked it away. Nature temporarily defeated. But Nature is patient.

Over the next few days an idea forms within me, ripening, swelling, pushing everything else into a corner. It is like knowing a new, wonderful joke and not being able to share. I need an accomplice.

I go to see a man I don't know personally, though I have seen his face peering at me from the financial pages of the local newspaper and the *Wall Street Journal*, and I have been watching his profile at the baseball stadium, two boxes to the right of me, for several years. He is a fan. Really a fan. When the weather is intemperate, or the game not close, the people around us disappear like flowers closing at sunset, but we are always there until the last pitch. I know he is a man who attends because of the beauty and mystery of the game, a man who can sit during the last of the ninth with the game decided innings ago and draw joy from watching the first baseman adjust the angle of his glove as the pitcher goes into his windup.

He, like me, is a first-base-side fan. I've always watched baseball from behind first base. The positions fans choose at sporting events are like politics, religion, or philosophy: a view of the world, a way of seeing the universe. They make no sense to anyone, have no basis in anything but stubbornness.

I brought up my daughters to watch baseball from the first-base side. One lives in Japan and sends me box scores from Japanese newspapers and Japanese baseball magazines with pictures of superstars politely bowing to one another. She has a season ticket in Yokohama; on the first-base side.

"Tell him a baseball fan is here to see him," is all I will say to his secretary. His office is in a skyscraper, from which he can look out over the city to where the prairie rolls green as mountain water to the limits of the eye. I wait all afternoon in the artificially cool, glassy reception area with its yellow and mauve chairs, chrome and glass coffee tables. Finally, in the late afternoon, my message is passed along.

"I've seen you at the baseball stadium," I say, not introducing myself.

"Yes," he says. "I recognize you. Three rows back, about eight seats to my left. You have a red scorebook and you often bring your daughter . . ."

"Granddaughter. Yes, she goes to sleep in my lap in the late innings, but she knows how

---

3. **tortuous:** full of twists and turns.

4. **hummocks:** low, rounded hills.

5. **swathes** (swa*th*s): the spaces or widths covered with one cut of a mowing device.

*Words to Know and Use*

**contemplate** (kän′ təm plāt′) *v.* to look at intently; to gaze at
**sear** (sir) *v.* to scorch or burn the surface of

505

to calculate an ERA[6] and she's only in Grade 2."

"One of my greatest regrets," says this tall man, whose moustache and carefully styled hair are polar-bear white, "is that my grandchildren all live over a thousand miles away. You're very lucky. Now, what can I do for you?"

"I have an idea," I say. "One that's been creeping toward me like a first baseman when the bunt sign is on. What do you think about artificial turf?"

"Hmmmf," he snorts, "that's what the strike should be about. Baseball is meant to be played on summer evenings and Sunday afternoons, on grass just cut by a horse-drawn mower," and we smile as our eyes meet.

"I've discovered the ballpark is open, to me anyway," I go on. "There's no one there while the strike is on. The wind blows through the high top of the grandstand, whining until the pigeons in the rafters flutter. It's lonely as a ghost town."

"And what is it you do there, alone with the pigeons?"

"I dream."

"And where do I come in?"

"You've always struck me as a man who dreams. I think we have things in common. I think you might like to come with me. I could show you what I dream, paint you pictures, suggest what might happen . . ."

He studies me carefully for a moment, like a pitcher trying to decide if he can trust the sign his catcher has just given him.

"Tonight?" he says. "Would tonight be too soon?"

"Park in the northwest corner of the lot about 1:00 A.M. There is a door about fifty yards to the right of the main gate. I'll open it when I hear you."

He nods.

I turn and leave.

The night is clear and cotton warm when he arrives. "Oh, my," he says, staring at the stadium turned chrome blue by a full moon. "Oh, my," he says again, breathing in the faint odors of baseball, the reminder of fans and players not long gone.

"Let's go down to the field," I say. I am carrying a cardboard pizza box, holding it on the upturned palms of my hands, like an offering.

When we reach the field, he first stands on the mound, makes an awkward attempt at a windup, then does a little sprint from first to about halfway to second. "I think I know what you've brought," he says, gesturing toward the box, "but let me see anyway."

I open the box in which rests a square foot of sod, the grass smooth and pure, cool as a swatch of satin, fragile as baby's hair.

"Ohhh," the man says, reaching out a finger to test the moistness of it. "Oh, I see."

We walk across the field, the harsh, prickly turf making the bottoms of my feet tingle, to the left-field corner where, in the angle formed by the foul line and the warning track, I lay down the square foot of sod. "That's beautiful," my friend says, kneeling beside me, placing his hand, fingers spread wide, on the verdant[7] square, leaving a print faint as a veronica.[8]

I take from my belt a sickle-shaped blade, the kind used for cutting carpet. I measure along the edge of the sod, dig the point in and pull carefully toward me. There is a ripping

---

6. **ERA:** earned run average for a baseball pitcher; the average number of runs a pitcher allows every nine innings.

7. **verdant:** green; covered with green vegetation.

8. **faint as a veronica:** a simile referring to the image of Jesus' face supposedly left in the handkerchief of Veronica after she wiped his bleeding face.

sound, like tearing an old bed sheet. I hold up the square of artificial turf like something freshly killed, while all the time digging the sharp point into the packed earth I have exposed. I replace the sod lovingly, covering the newly bared surface.

"A protest," I say.

"But it could be more," the man replies.

"I hoped you'd say that. It could be. If you'd like to come back . . ."

"Tomorrow night?"

"Tomorrow night would be fine. But there will be an admission charge . . ."

"A square of sod?"

"A square of sod two inches thick . . ."

"Of the same grass?"

"Of the same grass. But there's more."

"I suspected as much."

"You must have a friend . . ."

"Who would join us?"

"Yes."

"I have two. Would that be all right?"

"I trust your judgment."

"My father. He's over eighty," my friend says. "You might have seen him with me once or twice. He lives over fifty miles from here, but if I call him he'll come. And my friend . . ."

"If they pay their admission they'll be welcome . . ."

"And *they* may have friends . . ."

"Indeed they may. But what will we do with this?" I say, holding up the sticky-backed square of turf, which smells of glue and fabric.

"We could mail them anonymously to baseball executives, politicians, clergymen."

"Gentle reminders not to tamper with Nature."

We dance toward the exit, rampant with excitement.

"You will come back? You'll bring the others?"

"Count on it," says my friend.

They do come, those trusted friends, and friends of friends, each making a live, green deposit. At first, a tiny row of sod squares begins to inch along toward left-center field. The next night even more people arrive, the following night more again, and the night after there is positively a crowd. Those who come once seem always to return accompanied by friends, occasionally a son or young brother, but mostly men my age or older, for we are the ones who remember the grass.

Night after night the pilgrimage continues. The first night I stand inside the deep-green door, listening. I hear a vehicle stop; hear a car door close with a snug thud. I open the door when the sound of soft-soled shoes on gravel tells me it is time. The door swings silent as a snake. We nod curt greetings to each other. Two men pass me, each carrying a grasshopper-legged sprinkler. Later, each sprinkler will sizzle like frying onions as it wheels, a silver sparkler in the moonlight.

During the nights that follow, I stand sentinel-like at the top of the grandstand, watching as my cohorts arrive. Old men walking across a parking lot in a row, in the dark, carrying coiled hoses, looking like the many wheels of a locomotive, old men who have slipped away from their homes, skulked down their sturdy sidewalks, breathing the cool, grassy, after-midnight air. They have left behind their sleeping, gray-haired women, their immaculate bungalows, their manicured lawns. They continue to walk across the parking lot, while occasionally a soft wheeze, a nibbling, breathy sound like an old horse might make, divulges

JIM RICE AT BAT 1983 Alex Powers By permission of the artist.

their humanity. They move methodically toward the baseball stadium which hulks against the moon-blue sky like a small mountain. Beneath the tint of starlight, the tall light standards which rise above the fences and grandstand glow purple, necks bent forward, like sunflowers heavy with seed.

My other daughter lives in this city, is married to a fan, but one who watches baseball from behind third base. And like marrying outside the faith, she has been converted to the third-base side. They have their own season tickets, twelve rows up just to the outfield side of third base. I love her, but I don't trust her enough to let her in on my secret.

I could trust my granddaughter, but she is too young. At her age she shouldn't have to face such responsibility. I remember my own daughter, the one who lives in Japan, remember her at nine, all knees, elbows and missing teeth—remember peering in her room, seeing her asleep, a shower of well-thumbed baseball cards scattered over her chest and pillow.

I haven't been able to tell my wife—it is like my <u>compatriots</u> and I are involved in a ritual for true believers only. Maggie, who knew me when I still dreamed of playing professionally myself—Maggie, after over half a lifetime together, comes and sits in my lap in the com-

fortable easy chair which has adjusted through the years to my thickening shape, just as she has. I love to hold the lightness of her, her tongue exploring my mouth, gently as a baby's finger.

"Where do you go?" she asks sleepily when I crawl into bed at dawn.

I mumble a reply. I know she doesn't sleep well when I'm gone. I can feel her body rhythms change as I slip out of bed after midnight.

"Aren't you too old to be having a change of life," she says, placing her toast-warm hand on my cold thigh.

I am not the only one with this problem.

"I'm developing a reputation," whispers an <u>affable</u> man at the ballpark. "I imagine any number of private investigators following any number of cars across the city. I imagine them creeping about the parking lot, shining penlights on license plates, trying to guess what we're up to. Think of the reports they must prepare. I wonder if our wives are disappointed that we're not discoing with frizzy-haired teenagers?"

Night after night, virtually no words are spoken. Each man seems to know his assignment. Not all bring sod. Some carry rakes, some hoes, some hoses, which, when joined together, snake across the infield and outfield, dispensing the blessing of water. Others cradle in their arms bags of earth for building up the infield to meet the thick, living sod.

I often remain high in the stadium, looking down on the men moving over the earth, dark as ants, each sodding, cutting, watering, shaping. Occasionally the moon finds a knife blade as it trims the sod or slices away a chunk of artificial turf and tosses the reflection skyward like a bright ball. My body tingles. There should be symphony music playing. Everyone should be humming America The Beautiful.

Toward dawn, I watch the men walking away in groups, like small patrols of soldiers, carrying, instead of arms, the tools and utensils which breathe life back into the arid ballfield.

Row by row, night by night, we lay the little squares of sod, moist as chocolate cake with green icing. Where did all the sod come from? I picture many men, in many parts of the city, surreptitiously cutting chunks out of their own lawns in the leafy midnight darkness, listening to the uncomprehending protests of their wives the next day—pretending to know nothing of it—pretending to have called the police to investigate.

When the strike is over, I know we will all be here to watch the workouts, to hear the recalcitrant joints crackling like twigs after the forced inactivity. We will sit in our regular seats, scattered like popcorn throughout the stadium, and we'll nod as we pass on the way to the exits, exchange secret smiles, proud as new fathers.

For me, the best part of all will be the surprise. I feel like a magician who has gestured hypnotically and produced an elephant from thin air. I know I am not alone in my wonder. I know that rockets shoot off in half-a-hundred chests; the excitement of birthday mornings, Christmas eves, and hometown doubleheaders boils within each of my conspirators. Our secret rites have been performed with love, like delivering a valentine to a sweetheart's door in that blue-steel span of morning just before dawn.

Players and management are meeting round the clock. A settlement is <u>imminent</u>. I have watched the stadium covered square foot by square foot until it looks like green graph paper. I have stood and felt the cool odors of the grass rise up and touch my face. I have studied the lines between each small square, watched those lines fade until they were visible to my eyes alone, then not even to them.

What will the players think, as they straggle into the stadium and find the miracle we have created? The old-timers will raise their heads like ponies, as far away as the parking lot, when the thrill of the grass reaches their nostrils. And, as they dress, they'll recall sprawling in the lush outfields of childhood, the grass as cool as a mother's hand on a forehead.

"Goodbye, goodbye," we say at the gate, the smell of water, of sod, of sweat, small perfumes in the air. Our secrets are safe with each other. We go our separate ways.

Alone in the stadium in the last, chill darkness before dawn, I drop to my hands and knees in the center of the outfield. My palms are sodden. Water touches the skin between my spread fingers. I lower my face to the silvered grass, which, wonder of wonders, already has the ephemeral[9] odors of baseball about it. 🐦

---

9. **ephemeral** (e fem′ ər əl): short-lived; passing quickly.

509

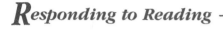

## *R*esponding to Reading

### First Impressions

1. Do you approve or disapprove of the actions of the narrator and his friends? Explain.

### Second Thoughts

2. Why do you think the narrator chooses to spend so much time and energy replacing the artificial turf with real grass?

3. When the narrator chooses his accomplice, how does he know this man will share his dream?

   **Think about**
   - what he recognizes in the character of this man
   - what it means to be a "true believer"

4. What might happen when the strike is over and others discover what has been done in the stadium?

   **Think about**
   - the different ways the owners, players, and fans might react
   - what could happen among and to the "true believers"

5. Why do you think Kinsella wrote this story in the first-person present tense?

6. Do you think this story could really happen? Explain your position.

### Broader Connections

7. Why are spectator sports so popular? Consider the needs and desires that spectator sports may fulfill in people. What is your own attitude toward spectator sports?

## *L*iterary Concept: Imagery

Writers often use words and phrases that create mental pictures, or **imagery**, for their readers. Imagery appeals to one or more of the five senses and makes objects and experiences seem real for the reader. In "The Thrill of the Grass," the author describes his square foot of grass as being "cool as a swatch of satin." To what sense does this description appeal? Find five other examples of imagery that appeal to the senses of sight, hearing, smell, taste, or touch.

**Concept Review: Simile** The author uses a simile when he describes the square of sod as being "cool as a swatch of satin." Find five other similes in the story.

# Writing Options

1. As a sportswriter, write a newspaper account of the first game back at the ballpark when the real grass is discovered. Include the reactions of the fans, umpires, managers, and players. Perhaps you might quote a few individuals.

2. As the narrator, send a telegram to your daughter in Japan reporting what you did at the ballpark and what happened at the first post-strike game. As in a real telegram, use twenty-five words or less, phrases instead of complete sentences, and the word *stop* instead of periods.

3. Imagine what might have happened if the narrator's wife had insisted on an explanation from her husband on his late night exploits. Write the conversation the two might have had.

4. List other methods of protest the narrator could have tried to get the turf replaced. Briefly explain which method would have worked best and why.

# Vocabulary Practice

**Exercise** On your paper, write the letter of the word that is not related in meaning to the others in the set.

1. (a) secretive (b) open (c) surreptitious (d) sneaky
2. (a) immaculate (b) unsoiled (c) unreal (d) spotless
3. (a) whack (b) hit (c) strike (d) sear
4. (a) sociable (b) humorous (c) affable (d) friendly
5. (a) divulge (b) swell (c) expand (d) increase
6. (a) creep (b) sneak (c) skulk (d) pout
7. (a) delayed (b) likely (c) probable (d) imminent
8. (a) compatriot (b) associate (c) ally (d) officer
9. (a) ignore (b) neglect (c) contemplate (d) omit
10. (a) uncontrollable (b) wild (c) weak (d) rampant

> *Words to Know and Use*
>
> **affable**
> **compatriot**
> **contemplate**
> **divulge**
> **immaculate**
> **imminent**
> **rampant**
> **sear**
> **skulk**
> **surreptitious**

## Options for Learning

**1** • **The Scales of Justice**   Conduct a trial for the lawbreakers. Assign roles of prosecutor, defense attorney, judge, jury, and defendants. Decide what charges will be brought against the defendants and prepare both sides of the case. If the defendants are found guilty, the judge should pass an appropriate sentence.

**2** • **Why America's Pastime?**   Create a survey that asks how people feel about baseball. In your survey, include questions about the different aspects of baseball and experiences that people might have had with the game. Use the results of your survey to report to the class on the differences between a fan and a nonfan.

**3** • **Thanks for the Memories**   In a small group, brainstorm ways that the narrator could thank his compatriots for their help. Some ideas could involve using the electronic scoreboard or composing a cheer. Compare your group's ideas with those of another group.

**4** • *Field of Dreams*   Kinsella also wrote the book, *Shoeless Joe,* that was made into the popular movie *Field of Dreams.* Rent the movie and watch it. Report to the class on the similarities and differences between the movie and "The Thrill of the Grass." Focus on subject matter, tone, mood, and theme.

 **FACT FINDER**

*How many major league baseball parks use artificial turf and how many use real grass?*

## W. P. Kinsella
### 1935–

Kinsella, a Canadian, showed his sense of humor when he said about himself, "I have been a part-time Viking for many years, but there is not much work in that field." Kinsella certainly found opportunities for work in the field of writing. Even though he didn't publish his first collection of stories until age forty-two, he now makes his living as a writer. The two major subjects of Kinsella's writing have been North American Indians and baseball. His Indian stories often show the modern world through the eyes of Native Americans. His baseball stories are entertaining and nostalgic glimpses of summertime and dreams. Kinsella believes that a writer's duty is "to make people laugh and cry."

# WRITER'S WORKSHOP

## EXPOSITION

Recall how you have learned about important news stories, such as the Chinese student protests in Tiananmen Square or the destruction of the Berlin Wall between East and West Germany. You probably listened to a television news report or read an article about the event. If you wanted to understand the event in depth, you might have gained insight through a news **analysis.** Commentators on television programs such as *Nightline* or *Meet the Press,* for example, analyze an event by breaking it down into its separate parts and by presenting related facts and evidence.

In a similar way, a **literary analysis** provides insight into a complex work of literature. The purpose of a literary analysis, as in other kinds of exposition, is to explain or inform.

In the assignment that follows, you will explain your ideas about the **theme,** or central underlying meaning, of a selection in this subunit. The theme is just one element you can isolate and analyze in order to appreciate and understand literature better.

> **Here is your PASSkey to this assignment.**

**GUIDED ASSIGNMENT:**
**LITERARY ANALYSIS**

Write a literary analysis of the theme of "By Any Other Name," "Crackling Day," or "The Thrill of the Grass."

**P**URPOSE: To explain or inform

**A**UDIENCE: Your classmates

**S**UBJECT: The theme of a selection

**S**TRUCTURE: A literary analysis

## Prewriting

**STEP 1** **Choose a selection** Choose one of the three selections listed above. Be sure to select literature that you especially enjoyed. On your own, review the selection carefully, paying particular attention to details and clues that point to a possible theme. Then form a group with other classmates who chose the same selection and discuss your ideas about the theme.

**STEP 2 Determine the theme** Keep in mind the general theme of the subunit, "Challenging the System." Ask yourself what system is being challenged, who controls the system, and what is good and bad about the system. Then think about the challenger—why and how does he or she challenge the system? What does he or she accomplish? Does the challenge change anything, or is the fight itself worthwhile enough? Think also about the author's purpose in writing. What is his or her point? Your answers to all these questions should point you to the central theme of the story.

Try writing a one-sentence summary of the selection. This summary may help you pinpoint the underlying meaning, or central idea, of the selection. Read one student's summary of "Beauty: When the Other Dancer Is the Self," a selection from the previous subunit.

STUDENT MODEL ▶

> The selection traces a woman's development as she moves from hating a childhood facial wound to accepting and finally even loving the unique effects of the scar on her appearance and personality.

**STEP 3 Draft a thesis statement** Once you have determined the theme, write a thesis statement. Concisely state your interpretation of the meaning of the selection. This will be the focus of your paper, and you will use evidence from the literature to support it.

Here are sample thesis statements some students came up with in trying to identify a theme.

STUDENT MODEL ▶

> • A school that treats one group of people as less important than others is not truly educating students.
> • Standing up for your rights is more important than anything else you do.
> • Injustice hurts everyone—both those who cause it and those who receive it.
> • One person alone can make a change.

**STEP 4 Find evidence to support your thesis statement** One way to support your thesis is to compare and contrast characters and what happens to them. For example, in "Crackling Day" you might compare and contrast the attitudes of the boy, his Uncle Sam, and the white man to explain your thesis. Another way is to examine the plot. Show how the conflict and its resolution support your thesis statement. You might organize your thinking in terms of cause and effect. For example, one student formed this chart as a way of looking at "The Thrill of the Grass" in terms of cause and effect.

STUDENT MODEL ▶

> Thesis statement: One man can change the system.

```
Cause:  unhappiness over artificial turf
Effect: wants to revert to old days of real grass
Cause:  baseball strike
Effect: baseball field is empty until strike is settled
Cause:  one man has idea and excites another with it
Effect: idea spreads until many take up the cause
```

You can also use other elements of literature, such as style, mood, and point of view, to support your point.

As you think about how you will logically arrange your points, find and jot down details, examples, and quotes from the selection that support each idea.

**STEP 5** **Organize your ideas**  A literary analysis consists of several parts: an introduction, several body paragraphs, and a conclusion. In the introduction you name the title and author of the selection and give your thesis statement. In the body paragraphs you explain your theory, elaborate on it, and support it with examples and quotes from the story. In the conclusion you restate the thesis statement in a different way and sum up your position.

Arrange or number your notes so that you have them in logical order. Remember that you are making a statement, explaining and proving it, and then summing it up.

## Drafting

**STEP 1** **Write your introductory paragraph**  In this paragraph, you set the tone and state the purpose of your paper. Identify the title and author of the selection and make your thesis statement. Avoid sounding tentative or uncertain; make your statement sound strong and confident.

**STEP 2** **Write the body**  Following the organization you planned, discuss only one point in each paragraph. Elaborate or explain that point and include quotations or summaries of events in the selection that support it. Use transitional words and phrases to make relationships between ideas clear.

### Special Tip
. . . . . . . . . . . . . . . . . . . . . . . . . . . . . . . . . . . . . . . . . . . . . . . . . . . . . . . . . . . . . . . . . . .
Use only those quotations from the selection that support or illustrate your interpretation of the theme. Don't overuse quotations; one good quotation is better than three weak ones.

STEP **3** **Conclude the paper**  Restate your thesis statement in your concluding paragraph. Leave a definite impression on the reader by ending with a strong quotation, a vivid image, or an invitation to draw his or her own conclusions about the theme after reading the selection.

## Revising and Editing

Exchange your literary analysis paper with that of a classmate, and use the following checklist as a guide for revision suggestions.

### Revision Checklist

1. Does the essay fully analyze the theme of one of the selections?
2. Is the thesis statement clearly stated in the introduction?
3. Is the organization of ideas apparent? Can you follow the logic of the writer?
4. Are quotes and examples included that support the main points?
5. Does the conclusion restate the thesis and bring a successful end to the essay?

**Editing**  Proofread your literary analysis paper for spelling, punctuation, and usage errors. Then make a clean copy to distribute to other students who wrote about the same selection.

## Presenting

Read aloud your analysis to a group of classmates who wrote about the same selection. With the group, discuss each writer's conclusions and compare the similarities and differences.

## Reflecting on Your Writing

Answer the following questions. Then put your answers together with your literary analysis in your writing portfolio.

1. What was the most challenging task in writing a literary analysis paper?
2. How did your opinion of the selection you wrote about change as you drafted your paper?
3. Do you think that literary analysis is useful? Why or why not?

## USING EFFECTIVE TRANSITIONS

A transition is a word or a phrase that is used to show the relationship between two ideas. Consider this example:

> The Lilliputians were much smaller than Gulliver. *Therefore,* they were afraid of him.

The word *therefore* is a transition. It shows that the second statement is a conclusion based on the first statement. By using transitions, you can show your readers how your ideas are related.

Here are some words commonly used in transitions.

---

**Transitions That Show Time**

> after, before, during, finally, first, second, third, sometimes, often, when, whenever, immediately, at first, in the beginning

**Transitions That Show Relationships in Space**

> at the top, at the bottom, in the middle, in the foreground, behind, above, around, near, beside, toward, beneath, there

**Transitions That Show Order of Importance**

> more important, most important, mainly, primarily

**Transitions That Show Cause and Effect**

> as a result, because, therefore, so, for that reason, consequently

**Transitions That Show Comparison or Contrast**

> on the other hand, yet, but, however, in contrast, in comparison, as, than, similarly, likewise

**Transitions That Indicate an Example**

> for example, for instance, one example, one type, one kind

**Transitions That Indicate a Conclusion**

> in summary, consequently, therefore, so, as a result, in conclusion, finally

---

**Exercise 1**   Read the following passage. Write the correct transition from the two in parentheses.

For Santha and Premila, life changed rather abruptly the day of Premila's first test. Santha was sitting at the back of her classroom, listening inattentively, as usual. **1.** (To sum up, Suddenly) the door opened sharply and Premila marched in. **2.** (On the contrary, Then) Premila walked directly up to her younger sister's desk and announced, "Get up. We're going home." **3.** (In contrast, Immediately) they left the room and started the long walk home. **4.** (After a while, On the other hand) Santha started to drag behind her older sister, but Premila kept walking, nevertheless. **5.** (As soon as, Also) the two girls arrived home, they went directly to their mother's room. Their mother looked quite startled. **6.** (As a result, Also) Premila spoke at once, explaining in detail about the test and her teacher's comments about Indians. **7.** (When, Moreover,) Premila was finished speaking, her mother seemed silent and distant. **8.** (Earlier, Afterwards) they all shared their mother's lunch, and **9.** (then, now) Santha was sent off for her siesta. **10.** (After that day, Until that day) the two girls never returned to that school.

**Exercise 2**   Read the following paragraphs. Work in a small group to rewrite the following paragraphs, adding transitional words or phrases to connect the ideas. Compare your work with that done by the other groups to see the variety of transitions used in good writing.

Julio stared across the playground. The sound of children playing, laughing, and shouting filled the air. Julio felt very much alone. He missed his friends and his home. He wished Papa had never brought the family to this new country.

A hard shove sent him sprawling to the ground. He looked up into the grinning face of a tall blond boy he recognized from his classroom.

"Why don't you go back where you belong?" the boy sneered.

Julio didn't understand the words. He did understand the meaning. He rose to his feet. He turned away. He heard the boy laughing at his back. Julio knew that if he walked away from this first threat, he would never feel safe in this place.

**Exercise 3   Analyzing and Revising Your Writing**

1. Choose a piece of writing from your portfolio.
2. Revise the paper, adding transitions where appropriate.
3. Compare your revision to the original piece. Which one communicates your ideas more clearly?

# STUDY SKILLS

### WORKSHOP

## TAKING STANDARDIZED TESTS

Standardized tests measure skills and knowledge accumulated over a long time, so it's not practical to cram for such a test at the last minute. During the test use the following strategies:

1. Budget your time. Don't get bogged down on one question.
2. Read directions carefully. Be sure you know what is being asked.
3. Answer the questions you know first. If you're having trouble with a question, move on; you can always come back to it later.
4. Find out beforehand whether it pays for you to guess on questions that you cannot answer. This differs from test to test.
5. Mark the answer sheet carefully. From time to time check that the number on your answer sheet matches the number of the question.

**Exercise** After you have answered the questions below, work in a small group to make up three of each type of question. Then share your questions with other students in your class.

1. **Antonym Question.** Write the letter of the word that is most nearly opposite in meaning to the given word.
   TRIVIAL:   (A) irritating   (B) unique   (C) important
   (D) insignificant   (E) pleasant

2. **Sentence Completion.** Write the letter of the pair of words that best completes the sentence.

   The senator did not _____ compromise, but he _____ it.
   (A) enjoy . . . accepted   (B) desire . . . hated
   (C) welcome . . . rejected   (D) favor . . . wanted
   (E) try . . . loved

3. **Sentence Correction.** Write the answer that best replaces the italicized words.

   *After eating, having caught its prey* the hawk flew away.
   (A) After eating, having caught prey
   (B) As a result of catching and eating its prey,
   (C) After catching its prey, and eating,
   (D) After catching its prey and eating it
   (E) Because it caught its prey, and ate,

You'll do better on a test if you are relaxed and if you approach the test in a positive frame of mind. Get a good night's sleep and eat a good breakfast before the test. Approach the test with confidence in your own ability to do well on it. During the test, work quickly but don't rush yourself.

# SEARCHING FOR ANSWERS

" *The life which is*

*unexamined is*

*not worth*

*living.* "

Plato

# Life in the Romantic and Victorian Periods

## THE ROMANTIC PERIOD: 1800–1832

The passion for freedom and equality that inspired the French Revolution in 1789 ushered in an age of gradually increasing democracy in England. Shortly after it began, the democratic revolution in France had been overtaken by a bloody Reign of Terror. England's ruling class feared that agitation for increased rights in England might lead to a similar breakdown of order.

To avert a popular revolution, the ruling classes passed the Reform Bill of 1832, extending the right to vote to most middle-class males. This bill paved the way for other reforms. Indeed the passage of the Reform Bill of 1832 is considered to have begun the Victorian Era even though Victoria did not take the throne until 1837.

During the Age of Reason, the classics of ancient Greece and Rome provided models for writers. Inspired by the romance of the French Revolution, intellectuals now turned instead to medieval English ballads and to the works of John Milton and Shakespeare. The interest in common experience and politics gave way to the Romantics' concern with individual emotion and the inspiring power of the natural world.

To the Romantics, emotion became more important than reason. In their new forms of lyrical poetry, Romantic poets sang of love, truth, death, and of the timeless beauties of nature. Several of the Romantic poets—John Keats, Percy Bysshe Shelley, and George Gordon, Lord Byron—lived passion-filled lives, cut tragically short. They seemed to write as they lived, with an overflow of feelings intensified by a heightened awareness of death.

Romantic literature reached its height in the poetry of Keats, Shelley, Byron, Blake, and Wordsworth. However, the Romantic Period also produced some great novelists. Jane Austen, Sir Walter Scott, and the Brontë Sisters, Charlotte and Emily, all wrote novels during the early 1800s that are still enjoyed by modern readers.

## THE VICTORIAN ERA: 1832–1900

Queen Victoria, whose lengthy reign extended from 1837 to 1901, presided over a prosperous England at peace with the rest of Europe. With England's far-flung collection of colonies spread all over the globe, it could be truly said that "the sun never sets over the British Empire." By 1900 Victoria was Queen-Empress over more than two million people outside Great Britain, and England was the wealthiest and most powerful nation in the world.

### The Industrial Revolution

The prosperity for England's empire building stemmed from the Industrial Revolution that transformed England into the first modern industrial state. By 1850 England boasted 18,000 cotton mills and produced half the pig iron in the world. Five thousand miles of railroad tracks transported raw materials to factories and then carried manufactured products to seaports.

The Industrial Revolution also created vast new wealth for England's rapidly growing middle class. These self-made men and women endorsed the values of hard work, discipline, a strong home life, righteousness, and religion that seemed embodied in the person of their sturdy monarch, Victoria.

In the midst of rising prosperity for the middle and upper classes, however, conditions for the poor grew ever more intolerable. As home manufacture gave way to factory production, poor people deserted their small farms to try to find work and housing in filthy, overcrowded cities.

Wages were so low that for many families, the only way to survive was to send their young children to work. In nineteenth century England, children as young as five toiled at dangerous, exhausting jobs. Like donkeys, little boys pulled carts of coal out of mines. Many others slaved for sixteen-hour days in dark factories, seeing sunlight only on Sundays.

WORK   1852-3   Ford Madox Brown   The Granger Collection, New York.

In the early 1840s, unemployment soared in England, leaving many families without a breadwinner. The potato blight and famine that devastated Ireland in 1845 forced two million starving people to emigrate. Many crowded into England's already squalid slums.

Working class agitation led to the formation of labor unions and the passage of laws that regulated some of the worst working conditions. For example, in 1833, a law was passed to protect children working in factories. Another law reduced the usual working day to ten hours and established a half-day holiday on Saturday.

In 1867 the Second Reform Bill gave some male workers the vote. By the end of the century, almost all men could vote, though women would not be able to do so until 1928, eight years after women won suffrage in America.

## Victorian Literature

During the Victorian Era, book publishing became a thriving business. Members of the newly-thriving middle class, Victorian prose writers brought to attention the plight of England's poor.

Novelists Charles Dickens and Mary Ann Evans, who published under the name George Eliot, wrote brilliant novels. Their books, filled with social concern, found an enthusiastic audience in a middle class that had the money to buy books and the leisure to read. These huge Victorian novels made great family entertainment when they were read aloud.

During the late 1800s people also sought to understand the history of the earth and its creatures. After years of careful observation, Charles Darwin formulated the theory of evolution in his book, *On The Origin of Species,* published in 1859.

With the new popularity of science, poetry lost some of its previous appeal. The Romantic concentration on the glories of nature now gave way to a more rational approach that included detailed descriptions.

## The End of the Victorian Era

At the end of the nineteenth century, England found its leadership position in the world under increasing challenge. The United States had recently emerged as a bold, new world power. Other European countries had grown eager to compete with England for the rich resources of Africa and China. International tensions contributed to an expensive arms race which would soon culminate in World War I. As the calm, peaceful world of the Victorian Era drew to a close, new writers began to question whether the Victorian values of decency and integrity could prevail in a cruel, modern world.

# Time Line of British and World History
## 1800—1900

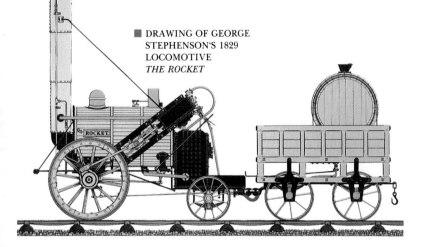

■ DRAWING OF GEORGE
STEPHENSON'S 1829
LOCOMOTIVE
*THE ROCKET*

First Public Health Act **1848**

Charlotte Brontë **1847**
publishes *Jane Eyre*

Irish potato **1845**
famine begins

William Wordsworth **1843**
becomes poet laureate

**1837** Victoria becomes queen;
Charles Dickens writes
*Oliver Twist* in serial form

**1833** Slavery abolished in
British empire

**1832** First Reform Act
extends voting rights

**1813** Jane Austen publishes
*Pride and Prejudice*

**1801** Act of Union creates
United Kingdom of
Great Britain and Ireland

**1824** First labor unions
permitted

## BRITISH HISTORY

| 1800 | 1820 | 1840 |
|---|---|---|

## WORLD HISTORY

Samuel F. B. Morse patents the **1844**
telegraph in the United States

In Belgium, Marx and Engels **1848**
publish *Communist Manifesto*

**1802** Toussaint L'Ouverture
leads rebellion against
French rule in Haiti

**1803** United States
purchases Louisiana
Territory from France

**1804** Napoleon crowns
himself Emperor in
France

■ NAPOLEON AT THE
BATTLE OF JENA
OCTOBER 14, 1806
(detail)

WEST AFRICAN ■
MASK MADE BY
THE DAN PEOPLE

**1810** Simón Bolívar leads rebellions against
Spanish rule in South America

**1813** Mexico declares independence

**1815** Napoleon defeated at Waterloo, Belgium

**1818** First steamship crosses Atlantic

**1823** In the United States, the Monroe Doctrine closes
the Americas to future European colonization

■ PARLIAMENT
IN LONDON

Queen Victoria dies **1901**

**1887**  First Sherlock Holmes
tale published

**1869**  Debtors' prisons
abolished

**1859**  Charles Darwin publishes
*On the Origin of Species*

■ QUEEN VICTORIA
OF ENGLAND

**1850**  Elizabeth Barrett Browning
publishes *Sonnets from the Portuguese*

**1860**　　　　　　　　　　**1880**　　　　　　　　　　**1900**

**1854**  Japan reopens trade
with the West

Sino-Japanese War  **1894**
begins in Asia

**1861**  Civil War begins in the
United States

First modern Olympics  **1896**
held in Greece

**1869**  Suez Canal completed
in Egypt

Pierre and Marie Curie  **1898**
discover radium in France

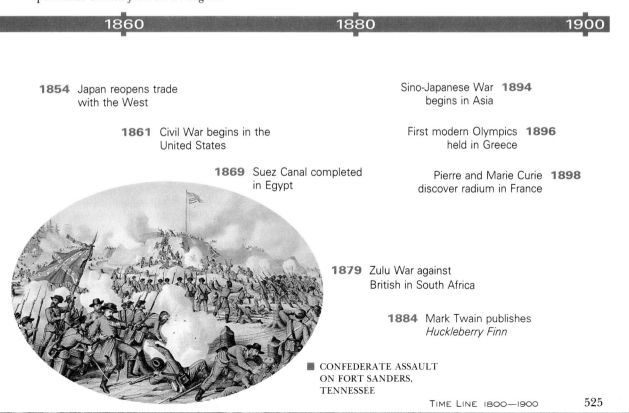

**1879**  Zulu War against
British in South Africa

**1884**  Mark Twain publishes
*Huckleberry Finn*

■ CONFEDERATE ASSAULT
ON FORT SANDERS,
TENNESSEE

Many of us today believe that individuals must find their own truth, whether it be in religion, in nature, in personal relationships, or deep within the inner self. That belief shows our debt to the Romantics and Victorians, who emphasized the search of the individual for answers to life's meaning. The nineteenth-century writers asked fundamental questions we are still trying to answer today.

You will be reading about different quests for truth by celebrated English poets, a great Russian writer, and a famous Native American. Though these authors are long gone, their thoughts and dreams have influenced generations. Their searches challenge you to define your own values and beliefs.

Poetry

## The *Tables Turned*
### WILLIAM WORDSWORTH

## *Flower in the Crannied Wall*
### ALFRED, LORD TENNYSON

## *E*xamine *What You Know*

Every year millions of Americans travel to pursue the beauties of nature, visiting national parks or camping in the wilderness; others appreciate natural wonders closer to home. Why do you think so many people feel a need to experience nature? What do people gain from these experiences?

## *E*xpand *Your Knowledge*

Wordsworth's vigorous walks in the green, mountainous splendor of northern England inspired some of his greatest poetry. Nature was to Wordsworth what a monastery is to a monk: a place to reflect on the mysteries of human existence and to live as a pilgrim in search of truth. Unlike most English poets before him, who celebrated city life as the height of civilization, Wordsworth advised his readers to return to nature.

As you will see, nature also played an important role in Tennyson's poetry. Tennyson followed in the footsteps of the **Romantic movement** that Wordsworth had helped to establish, a movement that called for poets to study nature in order to understand life. The Romantics valued imagination more than reason and emotions more than abstract ideas. They believed that individuals must search within themselves for answers to life.

## *E*nrich *Your Reading*

### Identifying the Argument of a Poem: "The Tables Turned"

"The Tables Turned" is a response to another Wordsworth poem called "Expostulation and Reply." That poem presents a conversation between two friends, William and Matthew. Matthew accuses William of wasting his time by trying to find wisdom in nature instead of in books, and William defends himself. In "The Tables Turned," William turns the argument around and tries to turn his friend away from book learning. Each stanza of the poem makes a separate point in his argument. As you read, summarize the point that the speaker is making in each stanza.

### Visualizing Imagery: "Flower in the Crannied Wall"   In
Tennyson's poem the poet has created a simple image to convey a deep meaning. As you read, visualize the picture he has created.

■ *Biographies of the authors can be found on page 531.*

# The Tables Turned

## WILLIAM WORDSWORTH

Up! up! my friend, and quit your books,
Or surely you'll grow double;
Up! up! my friend, and clear your looks;
Why all this toil and trouble?

5  The sun, above the mountain's head,
A freshening luster mellow[1]
Through all the long green fields has spread,
His first sweet evening yellow.

Books! 'tis a dull and endless strife:
10  Come, hear the woodland linnet,[2]
How sweet his music! on my life,
There's more of wisdom in it.

And hark! how blithe the throstle[3] sings!
He, too, is no mean preacher;
15  Come forth into the light of things,
Let Nature be your teacher.

She has a world of ready wealth,
Our minds and hearts to bless—
Spontaneous wisdom breathed by health,
20  Truth breathed by cheerfulness.

One impulse from a vernal[4] wood
May teach you more of man,
Of moral evil and of good,
Than all the sages can.

25  Sweet is the lore[5] which Nature brings;
Our meddling intellect
Misshapes the beauteous forms of things—
We murder to dissect.

Enough of Science and of Art;
30  Close up those barren leaves;
Come forth, and bring with you a heart
That watches and receives.

---

1. **a freshening luster mellow:** the sun no longer has the harsh brightness it has at midday; its luster, or brightness, is mellow, or soft.
2. **linnet:** a small European finch; a songbird.
3. **blithe:** cheerful, carefree; **throstle** (thräs′ əl): a songbird found mostly in Europe and Asia.
4. **vernal:** springlike; fresh, warm, mild.
5. **lore:** teaching; instruction.

## *R*esponding to Reading

### First Impressions of "The Tables Turned"

**1.** Does Wordsworth's argument make sense to you? Why or why not?

### Second Thoughts on "The Tables Turned"

**2.** What is the speaker's advice to his friend? Evaluate his arguments.

**3.** Why does the speaker present such a negative view of book learning? Use evidence from the poem to support your opinion.

**4.** Do you agree with the speaker's position? Why or why not?

# *Flower in the Cranied Wall*

ALFRED, LORD TENNYSON

Flower in the crannied wall,
I pluck you out of the crannies,
I hold you here, root and all, in my hand,
Little flower—but *if* I could understand
5    What you are, root and all, and all in all,
I should know what God and man is.

FLOWERING HEATH AND ROUND
STONES, NEAR FLAAJOKULL,
ICELAND 1972 Eliot Porter By
permission of the Eliot Porter Studio.

## *R*esponding to Reading

### First Impressions of "Flower in the Crannied Wall"

1. Do you agree with the speaker that one can learn about God and man from a single flower? Why or why not?

### Second Thoughts on "Flower in the Crannied Wall"

2. Why do you think the speaker is so fascinated by this flower?

3. What can a flower have in common with a person? How might that flower provide answers to the mysteries of human life and nature?

### Comparing the Poems

4. Which of the speakers seems more sure of his own ability to find the answers nature provides? In your answer be sure to address the meaning of *if* in line 4 of the Tennyson poem.

## *L*iterary Concept: Personification

Writers use **personification,** a form of figurative language, to describe an object, place, animal, or idea as if it were human. For example, Wordsworth refers to nature as "your teacher," giving nature the qualities of a good and caring teacher. Find other places in the poem where objects or animals seem to have human qualities. What are the effects of this personification?

## *W*riting Options

1. Write an argument in dialogue form between the speaker of "The Tables Turned" and a schoolteacher about whether homework is worth doing.

2. Create a script for a television commercial that emphasizes our need to protect the environment. Include lines from one or both poems in your ad.

## William Wordsworth
### 1770–1850

Though Wordsworth supported the French Revolution, fathered an illegitimate child, and changed the direction of English poetry, he led a quiet life, which he described as "unusually barren of events."

Wordsworth grew up in northern England. Orphaned by the age of thirteen, he was put in the care of his uncles, who educated him at the best schools in England, including Cambridge University. However, he was a confused, uncertain young man. A walking tour of the Alps and a few years in France in the midst of its bloody revolution helped shape his thinking and pushed him toward becoming a poet. At the age of twenty-eight, he published *Lyrical Ballads*, collaborating with his friend Samuel Taylor Coleridge to produce a most influential collection of poems.

Wordsworth felt that to be effective, poetry had to reflect deep truths about humanity and nature and be written about ordinary events and people in ordinary language. He viewed poets as moral teachers who must strive to make their readers "wiser, better, and happier."

By 1807 most of his greatest poetry had been written, though he wrote until his death. He lived most of his life with his sister, Dorothy; his wife, Mary; and his five children.

## Alfred, Lord Tennyson
### 1809–1892

Tennyson was one of the best loved and most hated of English poets. At the height of his power, he confidently spoke for the entire nation. Ministers, statesmen, young poets—all sought his advice. He thrilled audiences with public readings of his poetry and eventually made a fortune—and earned a title—writing it.

Such success did not come easily. Early in life Tennyson had to struggle with poverty; the death of his best friend, Arthur Hallam; family problems; poor health; and bad reviews. He had to wait twelve years to marry the woman he loved, because her father did not approve of him and his finances were too uncertain. His prospects were not improved by a ten-year period in which he published nothing.

Tennyson's stature was secured with *In Memoriam*, a long, philosophic poem in which he came to terms with the death of Hallam and the problems of Victorian life. Other famous works include "The Lady of Shallott"; "Idylls of the King"; and "Ulysses." However, even before his death, younger poets ridiculed Tennyson's achievements. For decades many poets and critics mocked his work, probably because it represented an outdated era and attitude toward life. Today, Tennyson's reputation is once more secure.

Poetry     The *Lamb*
WILLIAM BLAKE

The *Tyger*
WILLIAM BLAKE

## *E*xamine *What You Know*

As you will see, Blake uses the symbols of the lamb and the tiger to represent two very different visions of life. What images and associations come to mind when you think of a lamb? What comes to mind when you think of a tiger? Discuss how these animals might symbolize opposite ways of looking at life.

## *E*xpand *Your Knowledge*

In 1794 Blake wrote two groups of poems, *Songs of Innocence,* which includes "The Lamb," and *Songs of Experience,* which includes "The Tyger." These poems have a simple, childlike rhythm and owe much to the street ballads sung by London's children. However, the poems also reflect the complex and original mind of their creator.

"Two Contrary States of the Human Soul," Blake's subtitle for the combined cycles of poems, announces what he intended to show. The poems in *Songs of Innocence* are often about happy children and depict gentle, innocent love. By contrast, *Songs of Experience* presents a darker side of life, brimming with deceit, violence, and sorrow.

## *E*nrich *Your Reading*

**Comparing Poems** Both of these poems deal with the same basic situation. A speaker seeks an answer to the question of origins, asking, "Who made thee?" As you read, look for similarities and differences in how each speaker's question is handled or dealt with. Consider whether the maker of the lamb and the maker of the tiger are one and the same.

■ *A biography of the author can be found in the Reader's Handbook.*

# The Lamb

WILLIAM BLAKE

Little Lamb, who made thee?
  Dost thou know who made thee?
Gave thee life, and bid thee feed,
By the stream and o'er the mead;
5  Gave thee clothing of delight,
Softest clothing, woolly, bright;
Gave thee such a tender voice,
Making all the vales rejoice?
  Little Lamb, who made thee?
10  Dost thou know who made thee?

  Little Lamb, I'll tell thee,
  Little Lamb, I'll tell thee:
He is callèd by thy name,
For He calls Himself a Lamb.
15  He is meek, and He is mild;
He became a little child.
I a child, and thou a lamb,
We are callèd by His name.
  Little Lamb, God bless thee!
20  Little Lamb, God bless thee!

**4 mead** (mēd): meadow.

**8 vales:** valleys

---

# Responding to Reading

## First Impressions of "The Lamb"

**1.** What went through your mind as you were reading this poem?

## Second Thoughts on "The Lamb"

**2.** Cite examples from the poem that reveal the speaker's feelings toward the lamb. Explain your opinion of the speaker's feelings.

**3.** In the Bible, Jesus describes himself as the "Lamb of God." How does that expression explain the speaker's beliefs in the second stanza?

**4.** How do the attitudes and beliefs expressed in the poem reflect the young age and innocence of the "child" speaker?

# The *Tyger*

**WILLIAM BLAKE**

TIGER FIRE  1973  David Shepherd  Courtesy of
Rolls-Royce Motor Cars Limited, Crewe, England.

Tyger! Tyger! burning bright
In the forests of the night,
What immortal hand or eye
Could frame thy fearful symmetry?

5 In what distant deeps or skies
Burnt the fire of thine eyes?
On what wings dare he aspire?
What the hand dare seize the fire?

And what shoulder, and what art,
10 Could twist the sinews of thy heart?
And when thy heart began to beat,
What dread hand? and what dread feet?

What the hammer? what the chain?
In what furnace was thy brain?
15 What the anvil? what dread grasp?
Dare its deadly terrors clasp?

When the stars threw down their spears,
And water'd heaven with their tears,
Did he smile his work to see?
20 Did he who made the Lamb make thee?

Tyger! Tyger! burning bright
In the forests of the night,
What immortal hand or eye
Dare frame thy fearful symmetry?

**4 symmetry** (sim′ ə trē): balance of
form.

**7–8 he** refers to the tiger's creator;
**aspire:** to soar or ascend; to seek
after. The lines suggest that the creator
has acted boldly.

**9–12 sinews:** muscle tendons. The
"shoulder," "art," "dread hand," and
"dread feet" belong to the tiger's
creator. What do these terms suggest
about the creator?

**13–15** Note the images of
metalworking used to describe the
creation of the tiger, as if it were
created in a blacksmith's shop.

**17–18 stars:** the angels who wept
after being tossed out of heaven for
rebelling.

## *R*esponding to Reading

### First Impressions of "The Tyger"

1. Compare your thoughts and feelings while reading "The Tyger" to those you had while reading "The Lamb."

### Second Thoughts on "The Tyger"

2. Why do you think the tiger is described in such unusual ways? Your answer should include an explanation of the unusual spelling *tyger.*

3. Each stanza expresses wonder about the tiger's creator. What qualities and abilities does the speaker think were needed to create such an animal?

4. What do you think is the answer to the question "Did he who made the Lamb make thee?" What difference does it make whether the answer is yes or no?

### Comparing the Poems

5. What are major differences between the "innocence" of the lamb and the "experience" of the tiger? Which poem comes closest to your views of life?

## *L*iterary Concept: Repetition

**Repetition** is a frequently used literary technique in which sounds, words, phrases, or lines are repeated for the purpose of emphasis or unity. In "The Lamb" Blake repeats key words and sentences to reinforce the speaker's youth and the innocence of the speaker and his simple views. Find examples of repetition in "The Tyger" and discuss their effects.

**Concept Review: Alliteration**   Find examples of **alliteration,** repetition of consonant sounds, in both poems. How does alliteration contribute to meaning?

## *W*riting Options

1. Select a different animal to symbolize your understanding of our place in the universe. Either explain how that animal is symbolic to you or write a poem that expresses your feelings about that animal symbol.

2. Find photos that illustrate the innocence expressed by "The Lamb." Arrange them in a montage, a composite picture formed with different photos or parts of photos. Caption your montage with a quote from the poem. Make a similar montage for "The Tyger" that expresses experience.

*Fiction*

# *What Men Live By*

### LEO TOLSTOY

## *Examine What You Know*

There are countless needy and homeless people in cities all over the world. Think about a time when you or someone you know encountered a stranger in need. How did you or that other person react to the stranger? Read to find out how a nineteenth-century Russian peasant reacts in a similar situation and what happens as a result of the encounter.

## *Expand Your Knowledge*

During the nineteenth century, the peasants of Russia were poor and struggling. Russia was still a Christian nation then, and it was ruled by emperors called czars. Although the peasants were freed from a form of slavery called serfdom during the 1800's, there was still a distinct difference in living standards between the wealthy landowners and the poor peasant class.

Tolstoy was a wealthy landowner of the aristocracy, but despite his wealth he became a leader in the fight to change his society and educate the peasant class. Toward the end of his writing career, he began recording folk tales told by peasants that included messages about the meaning of life. He believed these messages revealed truths that could improve the quality of life for all. "What Men Live By" is Tolstoy's version of one of those tales. Since this story is long, you will find questions inserted throughout that focus on interesting and important ideas.

## *Write Before You Read*

The Bible says that man does not live by bread alone. What principles or values do you think men—and women—live by? Which is most important? Write your thoughts in your journal or on a piece of paper.

■ *A biography of the author can be found on page 553.*

# *What Men Live By*

### LEO TOLSTOY

## *I*

A shoemaker named Simon, who had neither house nor land of his own, lived with his wife and children in a peasant's hut and earned his living by his work. Work was cheap but bread was dear, and what he earned he spent for food. The man and his wife had but one sheepskin coat between them for winter wear, and even that was worn to tatters, and this was the second year he had been wanting to buy sheepskins for a new coat. Before winter Simon saved up a little money: a three-ruble note lay hidden in his wife's box, and five rubles and twenty kopeks[1] were owed him by customers in the village.

So one morning he prepared to go to the village to buy the sheepskins. He put on over his shirt his wife's wadded nankeen[2] jacket, and over that he put his own cloth coat. He took the three-ruble note in his pocket, cut himself a stick to serve as a staff, and started off after breakfast. "I'll collect the five rubles that are due to me," thought he, "add the three I have got, and that will be enough to buy sheepskins for the winter coat."

He came to the village and called at a peasant's hut, but the man was not at home. The peasant's wife promised that the money should be paid next week, but she would not pay it herself. Then Simon called on another peasant, but this one swore he had no money, and would only pay twenty kopeks which he owed for a pair of boots Simon had mended.

Simon then tried to buy the sheepskins on credit, but the dealer would not trust him.

"Bring your money," said he, "then you may have your pick of the skins. We know what debt collecting is like."

So all the business the shoemaker did was to get the twenty kopeks for boots he had mended and to take a pair of felt boots a peasant gave him to sole with leather.

Simon felt downhearted. He spent the twenty kopeks on vodka and started homewards without having bought any skins. In the morning he had felt the frost; but now, after drinking the vodka, he felt warm even without a sheepskin coat. He trudged along, striking his stick on the frozen earth with one hand, swinging the felt boots with the other, and talking to himself.

"I'm quite warm," said he, "though I have no sheepskin coat. I've had a drop and it runs through my veins. I need no sheepskins. I go along and don't worry about anything. That's the sort of man I am! What do I care? I can live without sheepskins. I don't need them. My wife will fret, to be sure. And, true enough, it *is* a shame; one works all day long and then does not get paid. Stop a bit! If you don't bring

---

1. **kopeks** (kō′ peks): Russian coins worth one hundredth of a ruble, the basic money unit of Russia.
2. **nankeen:** buff colored, durable cotton cloth.

that money along, sure enough I'll skin you, blessed if I don't. How's that? He pays twenty kopeks at a time! What can I do with twenty kopeks? Drink it—that's all one can do! Hard up, he says he is! So he may be—but what about me? You have house, and cattle, and everything; I've only what I stand up in! You have corn of your own growing, I have to buy every grain. Do what I will, I must spend three rubles every week for bread alone. I come home and find the bread all used up and I have to work out another ruble and a half. So just you pay up what you owe, and no nonsense about it!"

By this time he had nearly reached the shrine at the bend of the road. Looking up, he saw something whitish behind the shrine. The daylight was fading, and the shoemaker peered at the thing without being able to make out what it was. "There was no white stone here before. Can it be an ox? It's not like an ox. It has a head like a man, but it's too white; and what could a man be doing there?"

He came closer, so that it was clearly visible. To his surprise it really was a man, alive or dead, sitting naked, leaning motionless against the shrine. Terror seized the shoemaker, and he thought, "Someone has killed him, stripped him, and left him here. If I meddle I shall surely get into trouble."

So the shoemaker went on. He passed in front of the shrine so that he could not see the man. When he had gone some way he looked back, and saw that the man was no longer leaning against the shrine but was moving as if looking toward him. The shoemaker felt more frightened than before, and thought, "Shall I go back to him or shall I go on? If I go near him something dreadful may happen. Who knows who the fellow is? He has not come here for any good. If I go near him he may jump up and throttle me, and there will be no getting away. Or if not, he'd still be a burden on one's hands. What could I do with a naked

man? I couldn't give him my last clothes. Heaven only help me to get away!"

So the shoemaker hurried on, leaving the shrine behind him—when suddenly his conscience smote[3] him and he stopped in the road.

"What are you doing, Simon?" said he to himself. "The man may be dying of want, and you slip past afraid. Have you grown so rich as to be afraid of robbers? Ah, Simon, shame on you!"

So he turned back and went up to the man.

## II

Simon approached the stranger, looked at him and saw that he was a young man, fit, with no bruises on his body, but evidently freezing and frightened, and he sat there leaning back without looking up at Simon, as if too faint to lift his eyes. Simon went close to him and then the man seemed to wake up. Turning his head, he opened his eyes and looked into Simon's face. That one look was enough to make Simon fond of the man. He threw the felt boots on the ground, undid his sash, laid it on the boots, and took off his cloth coat.

"It's not a time for talking," said he. "Come, put this coat on at once!" And Simon took the man by the elbows and helped him to rise. As he stood there, Simon saw that his body was clean and in good condition, his hands and feet shapely, and his face good and kind. He threw his coat over the man's shoulders, but the latter could not find the sleeves. Simon guided his arms into them, and drawing the coat on well, wrapped it closely about him, tying the sash round the man's waist.

_____

3. **smote:** dealt a mental blow to.

Simon even took off his cap to put it on the man's head, but then his own head felt cold and he thought: "I'm quite bald, while he has long curly hair." So he put his cap on his own head again. "It will be better to give him something for his feet," thought he; and he made the man sit down and helped him to put on the felt boots, saying, "There, friend, now move about and warm yourself. Other matters can be settled later on. Can you walk?"

The man stood up and looked kindly at Simon but could not say a word.

"Why don't you speak?" said Simon. "It's too cold to stay here, we must be getting home. There now, take my stick, and if you're feeling weak lean on that. Now step out!"

The man started walking and moved easily, not lagging behind.

As they went along, Simon asked him, "And where do you belong to?"

"I'm not from these parts."

"I thought as much. I know the folks hereabouts. But how did you come to be there by the shrine?"

"I cannot tell."

"Has someone been ill-treating you?"

"No one has ill-treated me. God has punished me."

"Of course God rules all. Still, you'll have to find food and shelter somewhere. Where do you want to go to?"

"It is all the same to me."

Simon was amazed. The man did not look like a rogue, and he spoke gently, but yet he gave no account of himself. Still Simon thought, "Who knows what may have happened?" And he said to the stranger: "Well then, come home with me and at least warm yourself awhile."

So Simon walked toward his home, and the stranger kept up with him, walking at his side. The wind had risen and Simon felt it cold under his shirt. He was getting over his tipsiness by now and began to feel the frost. He went along sniffling and wrapping his wife's coat round him, and he thought to himself: "There now—talk about sheepskins! I went out for sheepskins and come home without even a coat to my back, and what is more, I'm bringing a naked man along with me. Matrëna won't be pleased!" And when he thought of his wife he felt sad, but when he looked at the stranger and remembered how he had looked up at him at the shrine, his heart was glad.

## III

Simon's wife had everything ready early that day. She had cut wood, brought water, fed the children, eaten her own meal, and now she sat thinking. She wondered when she ought to make bread: now or tomorrow? There was still a large piece left.

"If Simon has had some dinner in town," thought she, "and does not eat much for supper, the bread will last out another day."

She weighed the piece of bread in her hand again and again and thought: "I won't make any more today. We have only enough flour left to bake one batch. We can manage to make this last out till Friday."

So Matrëna put away the bread and sat down at the table to patch her husband's shirt. While she worked she thought how her husband was buying skins for a winter coat.

"If only the dealer does not cheat him. My good man is much too simple; he cheats nobody, but any child can take him in. Eight rubles is a lot of money—he should get a good coat at that price. Not tanned skins, but still a proper winter coat. How difficult it was last winter to get on without a warm coat. I could neither get down to the river nor go out anywhere. When he went out he put on all we

OLD WOMAN AT THE STOVE 1974 Ivan Generalić From *The Magic World of Ivan Generalić* by Nebojsa Tomasević.

had, and there was nothing left for me. He did not start very early today, but still it's time he was back. I only hope he has not gone on the spree!"

Hardly had Matrëna thought this than steps were heard on the threshold and someone entered. Matrëna stuck her needle into her work and went out into the passage. There she saw two men: Simon, and with him a man without a hat and wearing felt boots.

Matrëna noticed at once that her husband smelt of spirits. "There now, he has been drinking," thought she. And when she saw that he was coatless, had only her jacket on, brought no parcel, stood there silent, and seemed ashamed, her heart was ready to break with disappointment. "He has drunk the money," thought she, "and has been on

the spree with some good-for-nothing fellow whom he has brought home with him."

Matrëna let them pass into the hut, followed them in, and saw that the stranger was a young, slight man, wearing her husband's coat. There was no shirt to be seen under it, and he had no hat. Having entered, he stood neither moving nor raising his eyes, and Matrëna thought: "He must be a bad man—he's afraid."

Matrëna frowned, and stood beside the stove looking to see what they would do.

Simon took off his cap and sat down on the bench as if things were all right.

"Come, Matrëna; if supper is ready, let us have some."

Matrëna muttered something to herself and did not move but stayed where she was, by the stove. She looked first at the one and then at the other of them and only shook her head. Simon saw that his wife was annoyed, but tried to pass it off. Pretending not to notice anything, he took the stranger by the arm.

"Sit down, friend," said he, "and let us have some supper."

The stranger sat down on the bench.

"Haven't you cooked anything for us?" said Simon.

Matrëna's anger boiled over. "I've cooked, but not for you. It seems to me you have drunk your wits away. You went to buy a sheepskin coat but come home without so much as the coat you had on and bring a naked vagabond home with you. I have no supper for drunkards like you."

"That's enough, Matrëna. Don't wag your tongue without reason! You had better ask what sort of man—"

"And you tell me what you've done with the money?"

Simon found the pocket of the jacket, drew out the three-ruble note, and unfolded it.

"Here is the money. Trifonov did not pay, but promises to pay soon."

Matrëna got still more angry; he had bought no sheepskins but had put his only coat on some naked fellow and had even brought him to their house.

She snatched up the note from the table, took it to put away in safety, and said: "I have no supper for you. We can't feed all the naked drunkards in the world."

"There now, Matrëna, hold your tongue a bit. First hear what a man has to say—!"

"Much wisdom I shall hear from a drunken fool. I was right in not wanting to marry you—a drunkard. The linen my mother gave me you drank; and now you've been to buy a coat—and have drunk it too!"

Simon tried to explain to his wife that he had only spent twenty kopeks; tried to tell how he had found the man—but Matrëna would not let him get a word in. She talked nineteen

to the dozen[4] and dragged in things that had happened ten years before.

Matrëna talked and talked, and at last she flew at Simon and seized him by the sleeve.

"Give me my jacket. It is the only one I have, and you must needs take it from me and wear it yourself. Give it here, you mangy dog, and may the devil take you."

"As I came to the shrine I saw him sitting all naked and frozen."

Simon began to pull off the jacket, and turned a sleeve of it inside out; Matrëna seized the jacket and it burst its seams. She snatched it up, threw it over her head, and went to the door. She meant to go out, but stopped undecided—she wanted to work off her anger, but she also wanted to learn what sort of a man the stranger was.

## IV

Matrëna stopped and said: "If he were a good man he would not be naked. Why, he hasn't even a shirt on him. If he were all right, you would say where you came across the fellow."

"That's just what I am trying to tell you," said Simon. "As I came to the shrine I saw him sitting all naked and frozen. It isn't quite the weather to sit about naked! God sent me to him or he would have perished. What was I to do? How do we know what may have happened to him? So I took him, clothed him, and

---

4. **nineteen to the dozen:** a great deal; Matrëna speaks nineteen words for every twelve words Simon hears.

brought him along. Don't be so angry, Matrëna. It is a sin. Remember, we must all die one day."

Angry words rose to Matrëna's lips, but she looked at the stranger and was silent. He sat on the edge of the bench, motionless, his hands folded on his knees, his head drooping on his breast, his eyes closed, and his brows knit as if in pain. Matrëna was silent, and Simon said: "Matrëna, have you no love of God?"

Matrëna heard these words, and as she looked at the stranger, suddenly her heart softened toward him. She came back from the door, and going to the stove she got out the supper. Setting a cup on the table, she poured out some kvas.[5] Then she brought out the last piece of bread and set out a knife and spoons.

"Eat, if you want to," said she.

Simon drew the stranger to the table.

"Take your place, young man," said he.

Simon cut the bread, crumbled it into the broth, and they began to eat. Matrëna sat at the corner of the table, resting her head on her hand and looking at the stranger.

And Matrëna was touched with pity for the stranger and began to feel fond of him. And at once the stranger's face lit up; his brows were no longer bent, he raised his eyes and smiled at Matrëna.

*infer*  **How has Matrëna's attitude toward the stranger changed?**

When they had finished supper, the woman cleared away the things and began questioning the stranger. "Where are you from?" said she.

"I am not from these parts."

"But how did you come to be on the road?"

"I may not tell."

"Did someone rob you?"

"God punished me."

"And you were lying there naked?"

"Yes, naked and freezing. Simon saw me and had pity on me. He took off his coat, put it on me, and brought me here. And you have fed me, given me drink, and shown pity on me. God will reward you!"

Matrëna rose, took from the window Simon's old shirt she had been patching, and gave it to the stranger. She also brought out a pair of trousers for him.

"There," said she, "I see you have no shirt. Put this on, and lie down where you please, in the loft or on the stove."[6]

The stranger took off the coat, put on the shirt, and lay down in the loft. Matrëna put out the candle, took the coat, and climbed to where her husband lay on the stove.

Matrëna drew the skirts of the coat over her and lay down but could not sleep; she could not get the stranger out of her mind.

When she remembered that he had eaten their last piece of bread and that there was none for tomorrow and thought of the shirt and trousers she had given away, she felt grieved; but when she remembered how he had smiled, her heart was glad.

Long did Matrëna lie awake, and she noticed that Simon also was awake—he drew the coat toward him.

"Simon!"

"Well?"

"You have had the last of the bread and I have not put any to rise. I don't know what we shall do tomorrow. Perhaps I can borrow some of neighbor Martha."

"If we're alive we shall find something to eat."

---

5. **kvas** (k väs′): a Russian drink made from fermented grains and often flavored.

6. **stove:** the large stoves and ovens in peasant homes often had tops large enough to sleep on for extra warmth.

The woman lay still awhile, and then said, "He seems a good man, but why does he not tell us who he is?"

"I suppose he has his reasons."

"Simon!"

"Well?"

"We give; but why does nobody give us anything?"

Simon did not know what to say; so he only said, "Let us stop talking" and turned over and went to sleep.

## V

In the morning Simon awoke. The children were still asleep; his wife had gone to the neighbor's to borrow some bread. The stranger alone was sitting on the bench, dressed in the old shirt and trousers, and looking upwards. His face was brighter than it had been the day before.

Simon said to him, "Well, friend; the belly wants bread and the naked body clothes. One has to work for a living. What work do you know?"

"I do not know any."

This surprised Simon, but he said, "Men who want to learn can learn anything."

"Men work and I will work also."

"What is your name?"

"Michael."

"Well, Michael, if you don't wish to talk about yourself, that is your own affair; but you'll have to earn a living for yourself. If you will work as I tell you, I will give you food and shelter."

"May God reward you! I will learn. Show me what to do."

Simon took yarn, put it round his thumb and began to twist it.

"It is easy enough—see!"

Michael watched him, put some yarn round his own thumb in the same way, caught the knack, and twisted the yarn also.

Then Simon showed him how to wax the thread. This also Michael mastered. Next Simon showed him how to twist the bristle in, and how to sew, and this, too, Michael learned at once.

Whatever Simon showed him he understood at once, and after three days he worked as if he had sewn boots all his life. He worked without stopping and ate little. When work was over he sat silently, looking upwards. He hardly went into the street, spoke only when necessary, and neither joked nor laughed. They never saw him smile, except that first evening when Matrëna gave him supper.

## VI

Day by day and week by week the year went round. Michael lived and worked with Simon. His fame spread till people said that no one sewed boots so neatly and strongly as Simon's workman, Michael; from all the district round people came to Simon for their boots, and he began to be well off.

One winter day, as Simon and Michael sat working, a carriage on sledge runners, with three horses and with bells, drove up to the hut. They looked out of the window; the carriage stopped at their door; a fine servant jumped down from the box and opened the door. A gentleman in a fur coat got out and walked up to Simon's hut. Up jumped Matrëna and opened the door wide. The gentleman stooped to enter the hut, and when he drew himself up again his head nearly reached the ceiling and he seemed quite to fill his end of the room.

Simon rose, bowed, and looked at the gentleman with astonishment. He had never seen anyone like him. Simon himself was lean, Michael was thin, and Matrëna was dry as a bone, but this man was like someone from another world: red faced, burly, with a neck like a bull's, and looking altogether as if he were cast in iron.

The gentlemen puffed, threw off his fur coat, sat down on the bench, and said, "Which of you is the master bootmaker?"

"I am, your Excellency," said Simon, coming forward.

Then the gentleman shouted to his lad, "Hey, Fédka, bring the leather!"

The servant ran in, bringing a parcel. The gentleman took the parcel and put it on the table.

"Untie it," said he. The lad untied it.

The gentleman pointed to the leather.

"Look here, shoemaker," said he, "do you see this leather!"

"Yes, your honor."

"But do you know what sort of leather it is?"

Simon felt the leather and said, "It is good leather."

"Good, indeed! Why, you fool, you never saw such leather before in your life. It's German and cost twenty rubles."

Simon was frightened and said, "Where should I ever see leather like that?"

"Just so! Now, can you make it into boots for me?"

"Yes, your Excellency, I can."

Then the gentleman shouted at him: "You *can*, can you? Well, remember whom you are to make them for, and what the leather is. You must make me boots that will wear for a year, neither losing shape nor coming unsewn. If you can do it, take the leather and cut it up; but if you can't, say so. I warn you now, if your boots come unsewn or lose shape within a year I will have you put in prison. If they don't burst or lose shape for a year, I will pay you ten rubles for your work."

Simon was frightened and did not know what to say. He glanced at Michael and nudging him with his elbow, whispered: "Shall I take the work?"

Michael nodded his head as if to say, "Yes, take it."

Simon did as Michael advised and undertook to make boots that would not lose shape or split for a whole year.

Calling his servant, the gentleman told him to pull the boot off his left leg, which he stretched out.

"Take my measure!" said he.

Simon stitched a paper measure seventeen inches long, smoothed it out, knelt down, wiped his hands well on his apron so as not to soil the gentleman's sock, and began to measure. He measured the sole, and round the instep, and began to measure the calf of the leg, but the paper was too short. The calf of the leg was as thick as a beam.

"Mind you don't make it too tight in the leg."

Simon stitched on another strip of paper. The gentleman twitched his toes about in his sock looking round at those in the hut, and as he did so he noticed Michael.

"Whom have you there?" asked he.

"That is my workman. He will sew the boots."

"Mind," said the gentleman to Michael, "remember to make them so that they will last me a year."

Simon also looked at Michael and saw that Michael was not looking at the gentleman, but was gazing into the corner behind the gentleman, as if he saw someone there. Michael looked and looked, and suddenly he smiled, and his face became brighter.

"What are you grinning at, you fool?" thundered the gentleman. "You had better look to it that the boots are ready in time."

"They shall be ready in good time," said Michael.

"Mind it is so," said the gentleman, and he put on his boots and his fur coat, wrapped the latter round him, and went to the door. But he forgot to stoop, and struck his head against the lintel.[7]

He swore and rubbed his head. Then he took his seat in the carriage and drove away.

When he had gone, Simon said: "There's a figure of a man for you! You could not kill him with a mallet. He almost knocked out the lintel, but little harm it did him."

And Matrëna said: "Living as he does, how should he not have grown strong? Death itself can't touch such a rock as that."

## VII

Then Simon said to Michael: "Well, we have taken the work, but we must see we don't get into trouble over it. The leather is dear, and the gentleman hot-tempered. We must make no mistakes. Come, your eye is truer and your hands have become nimbler than mine, so you take this measure and cut out the boots. I will finish off the sewing of the vamps."[8]

Michael did as he was told. He took the leather, spread it out on the table, folded it in two, took a knife and began to cut out.

Matrëna came and watched him cutting and was surprised to see how he was doing it. Matrëna was accustomed to seeing boots made, and she looked and saw that Michael was not cutting the leather for boots, but was cutting it round.

She wished to say something, but she thought to herself: "Perhaps I do not understand how gentlemen's boots should be made. I suppose Michael knows more about it—and I won't interfere."

When Michael had cut up the leather he took a thread and began to sew not with two ends, as boots are sewn, but with a single end, as for soft slippers.

Again Matrëna wondered, but again she did not interfere. Michael sewed on steadily till

noon. Then Simon rose for dinner, looked around, and saw that Michael had made slippers out of the gentleman's leather.

"Ah!" groaned Simon, and he thought, "How is it that Michael, who has been with me a whole year and never made a mistake before, should do such a dreadful thing? The gentleman ordered high boots, welted, with whole fronts, and Michael has made soft slippers with single soles and has wasted the leather. What am I to say to the gentleman? I can never replace leather such as this."

And he said to Michael, "What are you doing, friend? You have ruined me! You know the gentleman ordered high boots, but see what you have made!"

Hardly had he begun to rebuke Michael, when 'rat-tat' went the iron ring hung at the door. Someone was knocking. They looked out of the window; a man had come on horseback and was fastening his horse. They opened the door, and the servant who had been with the gentleman came in.

"Good day," said he.

"Good day," replied Simon. "What can we do for you?"

"My mistress has sent me about the boots."

"What about the boots?"

"Why, my master no longer needs them. He is dead."

"Is it possible?"

"He did not live to get home after leaving you but died in the carriage. When we reached home and the servants came to help him alight, he rolled over like a sack. He was dead already, and so stiff that he could hardly be got out of the carriage. My mistress sent me here, saying: 'Tell the bootmaker that the gentleman who ordered the boots of him and left the leather for them no longer needs the

---

7. **lintel:** the horizontal cross piece above a door.

8. **vamps:** in shoes or boots, the parts covering the instep or the instep and toes.

boots, but that he must quickly make soft slippers for the corpse. Wait till they are ready and bring them back with you.' That is why I have come."

Michael gathered up the remnants of the leather; rolled them up, took the soft slippers he had made, slapped them together, wiped them down with his apron, and handed them and the roll of leather to the servant, who took them and said: "Good-bye, masters, and good day to you!"

 *infer*    How do you think Michael knew that he should make slippers?

## VIII

Another year passed, and another, and Michael was now living his sixth year with Simon.

WINTER 1944 Ivan Generalić From *The Magic World of Ivan Generalić* by Nebojsa Tamasević.

He lived as before. He went nowhere, only spoke when necessary, and had only smiled twice in all those years—once when Matrëna gave him food, and a second time when the gentleman was in their hut. Simon was more than pleased with his workman. He never now asked him where he came from and only feared lest Michael should go away.

They were all at home one day. Matrëna was putting iron pots in the oven; the children were running along the benches and looking out of the window; Simon was sewing at one window and Michael was fastening on a heel at the other.

One of the boys ran along the bench to Michael, leant on his shoulder, and looked out of the window.

"Look, Uncle Michael! There is a lady with little girls! She seems to be coming here. And one of the girls is lame."

When the boy said that, Michael dropped his work, turned to the window, and looked out into the street.

Simon was surprised. Michael never used to look out into the street, but now he pressed against the window, staring at something. Simon also looked out and saw that a well-dressed woman was really coming to his hut, leading by the hand two little girls in fur coats and woolen shawls. The girls could hardly be told one from the other, except that one of them was crippled in her left leg and walked with a limp.

The woman stepped into the porch and entered the passage. Feeling about for the entrance she found the latch, which she lifted and opened the door. She let the two girls go in first, and followed them into the hut.

"Good day, good folk!"

"Pray come in," said Simon. "What can we do for you?"

## IX

The woman sat down by the table. The two little girls pressed close to her knees, afraid of the people in the hut.

"I want leather shoes made for these two little girls, for spring."

"We can do that. We never have made such small shoes, but we can make them; either welted or turnover shoes, linen lined. My man, Michael, is a master at the work."

Simon glanced at Michael and saw that he had left his work and was sitting with his eyes fixed on the little girls. Simon was surprised. It was true the girls were pretty, with black eyes, plump, and rosy cheeked, and they wore nice kerchiefs and fur coats, but still Simon could not understand why Michael should look at them like that—just as if he had known them before. He was puzzled but went on talking with the woman and arranging the price. Having fixed it, he prepared the measure. The woman lifted the lame girl onto her lap and said: "Take two measures from this little girl. Make one shoe for the lame foot and three for the sound one. They both have the same-sized feet. They are twins."

Simon took the measure and, speaking of the lame girl, said: "How did it happen to her? She is such a pretty girl. Was she born so?"

"No, her mother crushed her leg."

Then Matrëna joined in. She wondered who this woman was and whose the children were, so she said: "Are not you their mother, then?"

"No, my good woman; I am neither their mother nor any relation to them. They were quite strangers to me, but I adopted them."

"They are not your children and yet you are so fond of them?"

"How can I help being fond of them? I fed them both at my own breasts. I had a child of my own, but God took him. I was not so fond of him as I now am of these."

"Then whose children are they?"

The woman, having begun talking, told them the whole story.

"It is about six years since their parents died, both in one week: their father was buried on the Tuesday, and their mother died on the Friday. These orphans were born three days after their father's death, and their mother did not live another day. My husband and I were then living as peasants in the village. We were neighbors of theirs, our yard being next to theirs. Their father was a lonely man, a woodcutter in the forest. When felling trees one day, they let one fall on him. It fell across his body and crushed his bowels out. They hardly got him home before his soul went to God; and that same week his wife gave birth to twins—these little girls. She was poor and alone; she had no one, young or old, with her. Alone she gave them birth, and alone she met her death.

"The next morning I went to see her, but when I entered the hut, she, poor thing, was already stark and cold. In dying she had rolled onto this child and crushed her leg. The village folk came to the hut, washed the body, laid her out, made a coffin, and buried her. They were good folk. The babies were left alone. What was to be done with them? I was the only woman there who had a baby at the time. I was nursing my firstborn—eight weeks old. So I took them for a time. The peasants came together, and thought and thought what to do with them; and at last they said to me: 'For the present, Mary, you had better keep the girls, and later on we will arrange what to do for them.' So I nursed the sound one at my breast, but at first I did not feed this crippled one. I did not suppose she would live. But then I thought to myself, why should the poor innocent suffer? I pitied her and began to feed her. And so I fed my own boy and these two—the three of them—at my own breast. I was young and strong and had good food, and God gave me so much milk that at times it even overflowed. I used sometimes to feed two at a time, while the third was waiting. When one had had enough I nursed the third. And God so ordered it that these grew up, while my own was buried before he was two years old. And I had no more children, though we prospered. Now my husband is working for the corn merchant at the mill. The pay is good and we are well off. But I have no children of my own, and how lonely I should be without these little girls! How can I help loving them! They are the joy of my life!"

She pressed the lame little girl to her with one hand, while with the other she wiped the tears from her cheeks.

 **clarify**   How were the twins able to survive after their mother's death?

And Matrëna sighed, and said: "The proverb is true that says, 'One may live without father or mother, but one cannot live without God.' "

So they talked together, when suddenly the whole hut was lighted up as though by summer lightning from the corner where Michael sat. They all looked toward him and saw him sitting, his hands folded on his knees, gazing upwards and smiling.

## X

The woman went away with the girls. Michael rose from the bench, put down his work, and took off his apron. Then, bowing low to Simon and his wife, he said: "Farewell, masters. God has forgiven me. I ask your forgiveness, too, for anything done amiss."

And they saw that a light shone from Michael. And Simon rose, bowed down to Michael, and said: "I see, Michael, that you are no common man, and I can neither keep you

nor question you. Only tell me this: how is it that when I found you and brought you home, you were gloomy, and when my wife gave you food you smiled at her and became brighter? Then when the gentleman came to order the boots, you smiled again and became brighter still? And now, when this woman brought the little girls, you smiled a third time and have become as bright as day? Tell me, Michael, why does your face shine so, and why did you smile those three times?"

*S*uddenly the whole hut was lighted up as though by summer lightning.

And Michael answered: "Light shines from me because I have been punished, but now God has pardoned me. And I smiled three times, because God sent me to learn three truths, and I have learnt them. One I learnt when your wife pitied me, and that is why I smiled the first time. The second I learnt when the rich man ordered the boots, and then I smiled again. And now, when I saw those little girls, I learnt the third and last, and I smiled the third time."

And Simon said, "Tell me, Michael, what did God punish you for? and what were the three truths? that I, too, may know them."

And Michael answered: "God punished me for disobeying him. I was an angel in heaven and disobeyed God. God sent me to fetch a woman's soul. I flew to earth and saw a sick woman lying alone who had just given birth to twin girls. They moved feebly at their mother's side but she could not lift them to her breast. When she saw me, she understood that God had sent me for her soul, and she wept and said: 'Angel of God! My husband has just been buried, killed by a falling tree. I have neither sister, nor aunt, nor mother: no one to care for my orphans. Do not take my soul! Let me nurse my babes, feed them, and set them on their feet before I die. Children cannot live without father or mother.' And I hearkened to her. I placed one child at her breast and gave the other into her arms, and returned to the Lord in heaven. I flew to the Lord, and said: 'I could not take the soul of the mother. Her husband was killed by a tree; the woman has twins and prays that her soul may not be taken. She says: "Let me nurse and feed my children, and set them on their feet. Children cannot live without father or mother." I have not taken her soul.' And God said: 'Go—take the mother's soul, and learn three truths: Learn *What dwells in man, What is not given to man,* and *What men live by.* When thou hast learnt these things, thou shalt return to heaven.' So I flew again to earth and took the mother's soul. The babes dropped from her breasts. Her body rolled over on the bed and crushed one babe, twisting its leg. I rose above the village, wishing to take her soul to God, but a wind seized me and my wings drooped and dropped off. Her soul rose alone to God, while I fell to earth by the roadside."

For what was Michael punished? What was his punishment?

## XI

And Simon and Matrëna understood who it was that had lived with them and whom they had clothed and fed. And they wept with awe and with joy. And the angel said: "I was alone in the field, naked. I had never known human needs, cold and hunger, till I became a man. I was famished, frozen, and did not know what to do. I saw, near the field I was in, a shrine built for God, and I went to it hoping to find shelter. But the shrine was locked and I could not enter. So I sat down behind the shrine to shelter myself at least from the wind. Evening drew on, I was hungry, frozen, and in pain. Suddenly I heard a man coming along the road. He carried a pair of boots and was talking to himself. For the first time since I became a man I saw the mortal face of a man, and his face seemed terrible to me and I turned from it. And I heard the man talking to himself of how to cover his body from the cold in winter, and how to feed wife and children. And I thought: 'I am perishing of cold and hunger and here is a man thinking only of how to clothe himself and his wife, and how to get bread for themselves. He cannot help me.' When the man saw me he frowned and became still more terrible and passed me by on the other side. I despaired; but suddenly I heard him coming back. I looked up and did not recognize the same man: before, I had seen death in his face; but now he was alive and I recognized in him the presence of God. He came up to me, clothed me, took me with him, and brought me to his home. I entered the house; a woman came to meet us and began to speak. The woman was still more terrible than the man had been; the spirit of death came from her mouth; I could not breathe for the stench of death that spread around her. She wished to drive me out into the cold, and I knew that if she did so she would die. Suddenly her husband spoke to her of God, and the woman changed at once. And when she brought me food and looked at me, I glanced at her and saw that death no longer dwelt in her; she had become alive, and in her too I saw God.

"Then I remembered the first lesson God had set me: '*Learn what dwells in man.*' And I understood that in man dwells Love! I was glad that God had already begun to show me what He had promised, and I smiled for the first time. But I had not yet learnt all. I did not yet know *What is not given to man*, and *What men live by*.

"I lived with you and a year passed. A man came to order boots that should wear for a year without losing shape or cracking. I looked at him, and suddenly, behind his shoulder, I saw my comrade—the angel of death. None but me saw that angel; but I knew him, and knew that before the sun set he would take the rich man's soul. And I thought to myself, 'The man is making preparation for a year and does not know that he will die before evening.' And I remembered God's second saying, *'Learn what is not given to man.'*

"What dwells in man I already knew. Now I learnt what is not given him. It is not given to man to know his own needs. And I smiled for the second time. I was glad to have seen my comrade angel—glad also that God had revealed to me the second saying.

"But I still did not know all. I did not know *What men live by*. And I lived on, waiting till God should reveal to me the last lesson. In the sixth year came the girl twins with the woman; and I recognized the girls and heard how they had been kept alive. Having heard the story, I thought, 'Their mother besought me for the children's sake, and I believed her when she said that children cannot live without father or mother; but a stranger has nursed them and has brought them up.' And when the woman showed her love for the children that were not her own and wept over them, I saw in her the living God, and understood *What men live by*. And I knew that God had revealed to me the last lesson and had forgiven my sin. And then I smiled for the third time."

# XII

And the angel's body was bared, and he was clothed in light so that eye could not look on him; and his voice grew louder, as though it came not from him but from heaven above. And the angel said: "I have learnt that all men live not by care for themselves, but by love.

"It was not given to the mother to know what her children needed for their life. Nor was it given to the rich man to know what he himself needed. Nor is it given to any man to know whether, when evening comes, he will need boots for his body or slippers for his corpse.

"I remained alive when I was a man, not by care of myself but because love was present in a passer-by and because he and his wife pitied and loved me. The orphans remained alive not because of their mother's care, but because there was love in the heart of a woman, a stranger to them, who pitied and loved them. And all men live not by the thought they spend on their own welfare, but because love exists in man.

"I knew before that God gave life to men and desires that they should live; now I understood more than that.

"I understood that God does not wish men to live apart, and therefore he does not reveal to them what each one needs for himself; but he wishes them to live united, and therefore reveals to each of them what is necessary for all.

"I have now understood that though it seems to men that they live by care for themselves, in truth it is love alone by which they live. He who has love, is in God, and God is in him, for God is love."

And the angel sang praise to God, so that the hut trembled at his voice. The roof opened, and a column of fire rose from earth to heaven. Simon and his wife and children fell to the ground. Wings appeared upon the angel's shoulders and he rose into the heavens.

And when Simon came to himself the hut stood as before, and there was no one in it but his own family. ❧

# explain

## Responding to Reading

### First Impressions

1. What is your reaction to Michael's explanation of what men live by? How does his explanation compare to yours?

### Second Thoughts

2. Remember your earlier discussion about encountering needy strangers. Compare your reactions to Simon's when he encounters Michael. Is Simon's reaction typical of most people's? Explain.

3. How are Simon and Matrëna similar? How are they different?

   **Think about**
   - their initial reactions to Michael and the changes in their attitudes
   - how each of them copes with poverty
   - the role of God in each of their lives

4. Do you think Michael deserved to be punished by God? Explain your opinion.

5. Were you able to figure out ahead of time that Michael was an angel? If so, how?

6. Explain how Michael learns each of the three lessons about life. Is any one of the lessons more important than the others?

   **Think about**
   - why Matrëna's behavior changes from bitter and selfish to kind and giving
   - why Michael knows that he should make slippers for the rich man
   - why the twins were able to survive without their natural mother

7. Summarize in one sentence what you think the theme of this story is. Do you think the theme is valid as a principle for living today? Explain.

8. According to this story, what is "The Source of Truth"?

### Broader Connections

9. What do you think would happen if Michael appeared in your neighborhood as a stranger in need of food, clothing, and shelter? Would it be possible for him to learn the same lessons? If not, what would he learn about what men live by today?

## *Literary Concept: Folk Tale*

Many stories told in different parts of the world come from oral tradition, that is, they have been passed by word of mouth from generation to generation. One kind of story that comes from oral tradition is the folk tale. A **folk tale** is a simple story set in the past that has animal, human, or superhuman characters. It usually has supernatural events and presents a theme. Often in folk tales, things happen in threes. What characters and events in this story characterize it as a folk tale?

**Concept Review: Plot** The numbered headings in this story can be used to divide the story into four main parts (I-V, VI-VII, VIII-IX, X-XII). Summarize the plot of the story by creating an appropriate subtitle for each of the four parts.

## *Writing Options*

1. Imagine that you saw Michael on the street and were undecided about whether to approach him. Create a chart that lists your arguments both for and against getting involved.

2. Michael learned three truths by which men and women live. Write your own three maxims for living that would help people develop more meaningful and rewarding lives. Feel free to include ideas that are very different from Tolstoy's.

3. As a reporter for the local paper, write a news story on Michael's mysterious ascent to heaven. Include eyewitness accounts from Simon and Matrëna, as well as information from the neighbors and local residents.

4. Write an episode from the lives of Simon and Matrëna that occurs after Michael has left them. Write your episode in the same style as the story and show how Michael affected the couple's lives.

# *e x t e n d*

## *O*ptions for Learning

**1 • Russian Peasant Clothing** The clothing of nineteenth century Russian peasants was practical and distinctive in its style. After doing some research on this style, design and illustrate costumes for Simon and Matrëna that reflect their peasant heritage.

**2 • Religious Art** Create a painting or drawing of Michael in one of the scenes from the story. If you choose to show Michael's ascent to heaven, consult books on Russian religious art for ideas on style.

**3 • A Day in the Life** If Michael were sent to your school, what truths to live by would he see in action? Create a typical school scene in which Michael, as an angel in human form, learns the principles that guide the lives of teenagers today. You might include a narrator. Read or act out your scene for the class.

**4 • The Movie** Design and draw a storyboard for one of the four main parts of this story. A storyboard is a series of sketches that shows the sequence of scenes or camera shots that will make up a film. Each sketch shows the set and the placement and actions of the actors. Include as much detail as you need in order to show your plan for the film. Present your storyboard to the class as if you were a director trying to sell your idea to a producer.

**FACT FINDER**

*When were the Russian peasants freed from serfdom?*

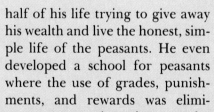

## *L*eo *Tolstoy*
### 1828–1910

The most famous of Russian writers, Leo Tolstoy wrote over ninety volumes of novels, stories, plays, diaries, and essays. Tolstoy's *War and Peace*, set during Napoleon's invasion of Russia in 1812, is considered one of the greatest novels ever written.

Tolstoy wrote about himself, "I am ugly, awkward, uncleanly, irritable, a bore to others, not modest, intolerant, and . . . am almost an ignoramus. . . . There is a thing I love more than goodness, and that is fame." A man of great contradictions, Tolstoy spent the second half of his life trying to give away his wealth and live the honest, simple life of the peasants. He even developed a school for peasants where the use of grades, punishments, and rewards was eliminated. He was a progressive educator who believed that teaching should be adapted to the needs of each student.

After numerous arguments with his wife over money matters, Tolstoy finally signed his entire estate over to her. He eventually fled one night, at the age of eighty-two, with one of his daughters and his doctor, only to die in a train station.

Speech

# Our People Are Ebbing Away

### CHIEF SEATTLE

## Examine What You Know

As white European settlers spread west across America, they encountered a culture much different from their own. Based on what you already know, compare and contrast the white settlers' culture with that of the American Indians. Consider religious beliefs, government, arts and crafts, and methods of providing food and shelter. Record your thoughts in a chart like the one below. Then look for differences that Chief Seattle mentions in his speech.

|  | White European Culture | Native American Culture |
|---|---|---|
| Religious Beliefs |  |  |

## Expand Your Knowledge

Each of the four hundred major Indian tribes in North America had its own customs and beliefs. The environment in which a tribe lived—mountains, plains, woodland, or desert—determined its economic system. These systems varied from basic hunting and gathering societies to more settled agricultural communities. Despite these differences, some generalizations can be made about the Native American culture. The idea of afterlife was tied closely to the land, which Native Americans believed was inhabited by the spirits of nature and the ancestors of the tribe. Since the land both gave life and received the dead, it was considered sacred. Even though Indians defended their tribal lands, actual ownership and alteration of lands were concepts unknown to them. Contracts and written treaties were ideas introduced by white settlers. Chief Seattle discusses some of these attitudes in his speech to Isaac Stevens, governor of the Washington Territory, in 1855.

## Write Before You Read

■ *A biography of the author can be found in the Reader's Handbook.*

The title of this speech is a quotation from the speech. Find the sentence that contains the quotation on page 556. Read the sentence and reflect on its meaning. Then jot down your predictions about the contents of the rest of the speech.

# Our People Are Ebbing Away

## CHIEF SEATTLE

Yonder sky that has wept tears of compassion upon my people for centuries untold and which to us appears changeless and eternal, may change. Today is fair. Tomorrow it may be overcast with clouds. My words are like the stars that never change. Whatever Seattle says, the great chief at Washington can rely upon with as much certainty as he can upon the return of the sun or the seasons. The White Chief says that Big Chief at Washington sends us greetings of friendship and good will. This is kind of him, for we know he has little need of our friendship in return. His people are many. They are like the grass that covers vast prairies. My people are few. They resemble the scattering trees of a storm-swept plain. The Great and—I presume—good White Chief sends us word that he wishes to buy our land but is willing to allow us enough to live comfortably. This indeed appears just, even generous, for the Red Man no longer has rights that he need respect, and the offer may be wise also, as we are no longer in need of an extensive country.

There was a time when our people covered the land as the waves of a wind-ruffled sea cover its shell-paved floor, but that time long since passed away with the greatness of tribes that are now but a mournful memory. I will not dwell on, nor mourn over, our untimely decay, nor reproach my paleface brothers with hastening it, as we too may have been somewhat to blame.

Youth is impulsive. When our young men grow angry at some real or imaginary wrong and disfigure their faces with black paint, it denotes that their hearts are black—and then they are often cruel and relentless, and our old men and old women are unable to restrain them. Thus it has ever been. Thus it was when the white man first began to push our forefathers westward. But let us hope that the hostilities between us may never return. We would have everything to lose and nothing to gain. Revenge by young braves is considered gain, even at the cost of their own lives, but old men who stay at home in times of war, and mothers who have sons to lose, know better.

Our good father at Washington—for I presume he is now our father as well as yours, since King George[1] has moved his boundaries farther north—our great and good father, I say, sends us word that if we do as he desires he will protect us. His brave warriors will be to us a bristling wall of strength, and his wonderful ships of war will fill our harbors so that our ancient enemies far to the northward—the

---

1. **King George:** 1762-1830; George IV of England. In 1846 the Oregon Treaty moved the boundary between Canada and the United States north of Puget Sound, along the 49th Parallel. Queen Victoria ruled England by this time.

Hidas and Timpsions[2] will cease to frighten our women, children and old men. Then in reality will he be our father and we his children. But can that ever be? Your God is not our God! Your God loves your people and hates mine. He folds his strong protecting arms lovingly about the paleface and leads him by the hand as a father leads his infant son—but He has forsaken His red children— if they are really His. Our God, the Great Spirit, seems also to have forsaken us. Your God makes your people wax[3] strong every day. Soon they will fill all the land. Our people are ebbing away like a rapidly receding tide that will never return. The white man's God can not love our people, or He would protect them. They seem to be orphans who can look nowhere for help. How then can we be brothers? How can your God become our God and renew our prosperity and awaken in us dreams of returning greatness? If we have a common Heavenly Father, He must be partial—for He came to His paleface children. We never saw Him. He gave you laws but had no word for His red children, whose teeming multitudes once filled this vast continent as stars fill the firmament.[4] No. We are two distinct races with separate origins and separate destinies. There is little in common between us.

To us the ashes of our ancestors are sacred, and their resting place is hallowed[5] ground. You wander far from the graves of your ancestors and seemingly without regret. Your religion was written on tables of stone by the iron finger of your God so that you could not forget. The Red Man could never comprehend nor remember it. Our religion is the traditions of our ancestors—the dreams of our old men, given them in the solemn hours of night by the Great Spirit, and the visions of our sachems[6]—and is written in the hearts of our people.

Your dead cease to love you and the land of their nativity[7] as soon as they pass the portals of the tomb and wander away beyond the stars. They are soon forgotten and never return. Our dead never forget the beautiful world that gave them being. They still love its verdant valleys, its murmuring rivers, its magnificent mountains, sequestered vales and verdant-lined lakes and bays, and ever yearn in tender, fond affection over the lonely-hearted living, and often return from the Happy Hunting Ground[8] to visit, guide, console and comfort them.

Day and night can not dwell together. The Red Man has ever fled the approach of the White Man as the morning mist flees before the rising sun.

However, your proposition seems fair, and I think that my folks will accept it and will retire to the reservation you offer them. Then we will dwell apart in peace, for the words of the Great White Chief seem to be the voice of Nature speaking to my people out of dense darkness.

It matters little where we pass the remnant of our days. They will not be many. The Indian's night promises to be dark. Not a single star of hope hovers above his horizon. Sad-voiced winds moan in the distance. Grim Nemesis[9] seems to be on the Red Man's trail,

---

2. **Hidas and Timpsions:** also spelled *Haidas* and *Tsimshians*; Indian tribes of British Columbia, north of Puget Sound and traditional enemies of the Puget Sound tribes.

3. **wax:** grow gradually stronger and more numerous.

4. **firmament:** the sky.

5. **hallowed** (hal′ ōd): holy or sacred.

6. **sachems** (sa′ chəmz): chiefs.

7. **nativity** (nə tiv′ ə tē): birth.

8. **Happy Hunting Ground:** according to Indian tradition, the place where the dead reside.

9. **Grim Nemesis** (nem′ ə sis): the cruel force that finally defeats everyone and everything; fate.

THE MIST BETWEEN THE DAY AND NIGHT   1985   Earl Biss   Courtesy of Paul Zueger, Gallery One, Denver, Colorado.

and wherever he goes he will hear the approaching footsteps of his fell destroyer and prepare to stolidly meet his doom, as does the wounded doe that hears the approaching footsteps of the hunter.

A few more moons. A few more winters—and not one of the descendants of the mighty hosts that once moved over this broad land or lived in happy homes, protected by the Great Spirit, will remain to mourn over the graves of a people once more powerful and hopeful than yours. But why should I mourn at the untimely fate of my people? Tribe follows tribe, and nation follows nation, like the waves of the sea. It is the order of nature, and regret is useless. Your time of decay may be distant—but it will surely come, for even the White Man whose God walked and talked with him as friend with friend can not be exempt from the common destiny. We may be brothers after all. We will see.

We will ponder your proposition, and when we decide we will let you know. But should we accept it, I here and now make this condition—that we will not be denied the privilege without molestation of visiting at any time the tombs of our ancestors, friends and children. Every part of this soil is sacred, in the estimation of my people. Every hillside, every valley, every plain and grove has been hallowed by some sad or happy event in days long vanished. Even the rocks, which seem to be dumb and dead as they swelter in the sun along the silent shore, thrill with memories of stirring events connected with the lives of my people, and the very dust upon which you now stand responds more lovingly to their footsteps than to yours, because it is rich with the dust of our ancestors, and our bare feet are conscious of the sympathetic touch. Our departed braves; fond mothers; glad, happy-hearted maidens;

and even the little children who lived here and rejoiced here for a brief season still love these somber solitudes, and at eventide they grow shadowy of returning spirits. And when the last Red Man shall have perished, and the memory of my tribe shall have become a myth among the white man, these shores will swarm with the invisible dead of my tribe, and when your children's children think themselves alone in the field, the store, the shop, upon the highway or in the silence of the pathless woods, they will not be alone. In all the earth there is no place dedicated to solitude. At night when the streets of your cities and villages are silent and you think them deserted, they will throng with the returning hosts that once filled them and still love this beautiful land. The White Man will never be alone.

Let him be just and deal kindly with my people, for the dead are not powerless. Dead—I say? There is no death. Only a change of worlds. ❧

# explain

## Responding to Reading

### First Impressions

**1.** What thoughts did you have after reading Chief Seattle's speech?

### Second Thoughts

**2.** What is Seattle's position on the treaty?

   **Think about**
   - his evaluation of the dwindling tribe's needs
   - his feelings about young men's revenge
   - the condition he makes at the end of his speech

**3.** Seattle believes that Native Americans and whites must live separately. On what does he base this idea? Do you agree with his reasoning? Explain.

**4.** What is Seattle's attitude about the future of man? Do you share his feelings? Explain your opinion.

**5.** What does Chief Seattle have in common with Tennyson and Wordsworth?

## Literary Concept: Figurative Language

Language that communicates ideas beyond the ordinary, literal meanings of words is called **figurative language.** A writer can make comparisons using similes, assign human qualities to an object, or create word pictures to describe ordinary things in unusual ways. Chief Seattle uses many comparisons and draws pictures with his words. For example, he says his people "resemble the scattering trees of a storm-swept plain." Point out five other examples of figurative language in the speech, including at least one simile. What mental picture do you get from each example?

## Writing Options

**1.** Compare Chief Seattle's speech with another piece in this subunit. What does each author say is the source of truth? What religious beliefs does each have? How does each feel about his fellow humans?

**2.** Using examples of figurative language from the speech, create a poem that expresses Chief Seattle's attitude toward the plight of his people.

**3.** Consider Seattle's words about the President in the fourth paragraph. Then write a letter, either serious or humorous, that Seattle might write the President to express these views.

# Writer's

## WORKSHOP

## PERSONAL NARRATIVE

How does a person learn what is true and what is not? One way is shown in Tolstoy's story "What Men Live By." In this story an angel learns three truths through personal experience. Personal experience teaches us a good deal of what we know. In fact, many people believe that "experience is the greatest teacher."

You have probably had many experiences that taught you important lessons. You can share these lessons by writing **reflective essays.** There are many kinds of reflective essays, but the most common kind starts with a story, or **narrative,** from your life. Then, you **reflect** on, or think about, this story on paper to tell its meaning or significance. That is, you tell what lesson, or truth, the experience taught you.

If you think about it, you use this format all the time when talking to friends. You tell about something that happened to you. Then you tell how you felt, what consequences the experience had for you, what you learned, and so on. You've probably been speaking reflective essays for years!

In a reflective essay you don't have to come up with a grand truth that will hold for all people in all times. In fact, an essay is a good place for considering an experience and what it might mean. The word *essay* comes from a French word that means "an attempt"—as opposed to a finished work. The French writer Michel de Montaigne first used the word this way to describe short pieces of nonfiction writing in which he thought on paper, without necessarily coming to lasting conclusions.

> Here is your PASSkey to this assignment.

### GUIDED ASSIGNMENT:
### REFLECTIVE ESSAY

Choose a personal experience through which you found a truth. Write a reflective essay in which you narrate the experience and explain what you learned.

**P**URPOSE: To narrate and reflect

**A**UDIENCE: Your classmates

**S**UBJECT: A personal experience

**S**TRUCTURE: A multi-paragraph essay

# Prewriting

**STEP 1** **Explore ideas**   You don't have to come up with a dramatic event in order to write an interesting, important essay. You don't have to have canoed down the Amazon or climbed Mount Everest. The most ordinary events can be filled with meaning and can teach important truths. For example, imagine a student who is hurrying from one class to another and accidentally knocks into another student, sending books flying and causing both to be late. Such a minor experience might lead to many reflections: Is it a good idea for people to hurry so much? What are the consequences of the fast-paced lives we lead? Should schools be as regimented as they are, with bells and back-to-back classes? Is that the best atmosphere for learning? Important, interesting questions like these can grow out of a simple event.

Think about experiences you have had recently and what they've taught you. Maybe something occurred that gave you an insight into life after high school or an idea for the future or that taught you something about love, or family, or growing up, or responsibility, or breaking away.

Also think about events from your past: What were the turning points in your life? When you think of yourself at particular ages, what do you remember clearly? What experiences left the deepest, most lasting impressions?

**STEP 2** **Select the best idea**   Choose two events and begin freewriting about them. When you use **freewriting,** you write about a general topic for several minutes without worrying whether your writing makes sense or is grammatically correct. You are basically thinking on paper.

After you use freewriting to describe both events, decide which event seems more vivid or meaningful. This is the one you will explore.

**STEP 3** **Gather information about the event**   Once you've settled on an event to write about, jot down any memories that were not covered in your freewriting, then reflect on the memories. Following are some ways you might do this:

- **Interview people who shared the experience with you.** Ask them for their impressions of the event. Take notes on what they say.
- **Reflect on the experience.** Close your eyes and think about the event. Try to keep your mind focused on the event itself. Remember details. How did things look, smell, sound, feel, and

taste? What were your emotions during the experience? How were things different afterward? After reflecting, write down your recollections.

- **Write a dialogue about the event.** One great way to explore ideas is to write dialogues. Try writing a dialogue about the event between two sides of your own personality or between two people who were involved. This will help you to see the experience from different perspectives.
- **Draw pictures or write descriptions of where the event happened.** Concentrate on details that will appeal to your readers' senses. Remember that sensory descriptions make writing come alive.

## Drafting

**STEP 1** **Choose a method of introduction** One way to write an introduction for a reflective narrative is simply to tell about the first thing that happened. Another way is to raise a question that your story, and your reflection about it, will answer. Yet another way is to begin with a general statement about the experience that you are going to tell about.

Notice how one student began his reflective essay about worrying.

STUDENT MODEL ▶

> Before I fell asleep last night, I began to tally up all the little things I'm worried about: the paper I have to write for English, the argument I had with Mom about whether or not I could play football, the girl I want to ask to the pep rally dance. When I woke up, the sheets were wrinkled from my tossing around, and my cheek had a red streak where the wrinkled pillow had pressed.

**STEP 2** **Tell your story, step-by-step, using vivid details** Tell the events of your story in the order in which they happened, from first to last. This method of organization is called **chronological order,** or **time order.** Make your reader feel that he or she is right inside your story. You can do this by elaborating your sentences with words that appeal to the reader's senses of smell, touch, taste, hearing, and sight. Don't write, "I was nervous." Instead, write, "My palms were damp and my shoulders ached with tension as I sat in the hard chair waiting for the teacher to return the papers." Another way to make an experience come alive is to use dialogue. Don't write, "She was funny." Instead, write something such as this student wrote:

Susan looked deep into my eyes and said somberly,
''Fee, fi, fo, fum.''

"What?" I asked, in amazement.

"I smell the blood of a freshMUN." She laughed as we
walked together to our first tenth-grade class.

◀ STUDENT MODEL

**STEP 3** **Conclude with a paragraph that tells the meaning of your story** Reflect on your experience and tell what meaning it had for you. For example, you might tell what lesson you learned or what general truth the experience taught you.

Here is the final paragraph from one student's reflective essay:

◀ STUDENT MODEL

Then I thought about a story by Lewis Carroll that I
read when I was a kid. In the story there was a character
called the White Queen. She would worry and cry for days
because she knew that eventually she was going to prick
her finger with a needle. Then when she did finally hurt
her finger, she wouldn't have to cry. That's what
worrying is like. It's a ritual to ward off danger, but it
doesn't really work. You end up suffering longer than you
would if you just faced the difficulty when it occurred.

## Revising and Editing

Use the following checklist to evaluate and revise your work, or ask a
classmate to review your work according to this checklist.

### Revision Checklist

**1.** Are the events presented in order, from first to last?

**2.** Does the reader have the sense of actually being there? Has the
writer used vivid details and/or dialogue?

**3.** Does the last paragraph explain the meaning of the experience?
Do the conclusions connect clearly with the experience?

**Editing** When you have finished revising, exchange drafts with a
classmate and proofread each other's papers.

## Presenting

In a small group, read your narrative aloud. The group should think of
each narrative as a fable, a story that has a moral or a lesson to teach.
After each narrative is read, together write a one-line moral for it. Then
combine the stories and their morals in a book of fables.

# UNDERSTANDING CLAUSES

> A **clause** is a group of words that contains both a subject and a predicate. An **independent clause** (or **main clause**) can stand on its own as a sentence. A **subordinate clause** (or **dependent clause**) cannot stand on its own as a sentence.

## Independent Clauses

An independent clause, like an independent person, can stand alone, without anything added to it. Each of these sentences has two independent, or main, clauses:

> Poetry class <u>ended</u> and gym class <u>began</u>.
>
> After a while the <u>bell</u> <u>rang</u>, and the excited <u>students</u> <u>rushed</u> into the halls.

In these sentences, the subject of each clause has been underlined once; the verb has been underlined twice.

The clauses in the sample sentences above can themselves stand alone as sentences. Because they can stand alone, they are called independent clauses.

> Poetry class ended. Gym class began.
>
> The bell rang. Students rushed into the halls.

## Subordinate Clauses

A subordinate clause cannot stand alone. A dependent, or subordinate, clause needs to be attached to an independent clause. Here are two examples of subordinate clauses. In each clause the subject is underlined once and the verb twice.

> when the <u>audience</u> <u>applauded</u>        that <u>I</u> <u>like</u> best

To form a sentence with a subordinate clause, add an independent clause.

When the audience applauded, the poet bowed her head.
That is the poem that I like best.

Remember, if a clause can stand alone as a sentence, it is independent. If it cannot stand alone, it is subordinate.

**Exercise 1**   Some of the following sentences contain two independent clauses. Some contain an independent clause and a subordinate clause. Write the sentences on a sheet of paper. Draw brackets around each clause and label each one *IC* for *Independent Clause* or *SC* for *Subordinate Clause*. Then, underline the subject of each clause once and the verb twice.

## Example
                              SC                                      IC
[Before Napoleon made himself emperor,] [Blake considered him a hero.]

1. William Blake lived during the Romantic Era, and William Wordsworth did, too.
2. The Romantic Era began when the French Revolution occurred.
3. The French Revolutionaries championed individual rights, and they overthrew the nobles.
4. The nobles deserved defeat because they mistreated the poor.
5. Poets like Blake and Wordsworth welcomed the revolution, since they also believed in freedom for common people.

## Essential and Nonessential Clauses

> Use commas to set off a nonessential clause from the rest of the sentence. Do not use commas to set off an essential clause from the rest of the sentence.

Some clauses modify nouns. Consider the following example.

This is the poem *that we read in class*.

The clause *that we read in class* modifies the noun *poem*. In other words, it provides additional information about the poem.

When a clause modifies a noun, you need to tell whether it is essential or nonessential. An **essential clause** limits, or restricts, the range of the noun that it modifies. In other words, it answers the question Which one? about the noun. In the example above, the clause *that we read in class* limits, or restricts, the meaning of the noun *poem*. When you read the clause, you realize that *poem* doesn't refer to any poem; it refers to

REMINDER
····································
Subordinate clauses are introduced by relative pronouns or by subordinating conjunctions.

**Relative Pronouns**

who, whom, whose, which, that

**Subordinating Conjunctions**

**Time:** after, as, as long as, as soon as, before, since, until, when, whenever, while

**Manner:** as, as if

**Place:** where, wherever

**Cause or reason:** because, since

**Comparison:** as, as much as, than

**Condition:** although, as long as, even if, even though, if, provided that, though, unless, while

**Purpose:** in order that, so that, that

PUNCTUATION
····································
When a dependent, or subordinate, clause comes at the beginning of a sentence, place a comma after it.
*After the principal finished her talk*, the students left for home.

the one *that we read in class*. Here are some more sentences with essential clauses in them:

> That was the last poem *that <u>Blake</u> <u>wrote</u>*. (The clause *that Blake wrote* tells Which one? about the noun *poem*.)
> The French Revolution was the most important event *that <u>occurred</u> during the eighteenth century*. (The clause *that occurred during the eighteenth century* tells Which one? about the noun *event*.)

A **nonessential clause** modifies a noun in a way that simply adds extra information to the sentence. It doesn't limit, or restrict, the range of the noun that it modifies. Consider these examples:

> We read a poem by William Blake, *<u>who</u> <u>is</u> my favorite poet*. (The clause *who is my favorite poet* does not answer Which one? about *William Blake*.)

> "The Tyger," *<u>which</u> <u>is</u> one of Blake's most famous poems*, sounds great when read aloud. (The clause *which is one of Blake's most famous poems* does not answer Which one? about "The Tyger." There is only one poem named "The Tyger.")

Notice that a nonessential clause like *who is my favorite poet* is separated from the rest of the sentence by one or more commas. An essential clause is not separated by commas.

**Exercise 2**  Complete each of the following sentences by adding either an essential or a nonessential clause that expresses the idea given in parentheses. Be sure to add commas if necessary. (Do not separate the added clause with commas if the clause answers Which one? about the noun that it modifies. Remember: the clause modifies the noun closest to it.)

1. William Blake was an English poet _____. (He lived in the second half of the eighteenth century.)
2. Blake _____ painted watercolors, made engravings, and wrote poetry. (He was quite talented artistically.)
3. Often Blake illustrated his own poetry _____. (His poetry was known for its powerful, emotional qualities.)
4. From early boyhood, Blake had visions _____. (He wrote about these visions in his poems.)
5. His engravings _____ illustrated the books of poems that he produced. (His engravings were highly detailed.)

**LANGUAGE HANDBOOK**
For review and practice: using clauses, pages 1025–26

# VOCABULARY
## WORKSHOP

## ANALOGIES

An analogy question asks you to identify the relationship between two words and then to recognize a similar relationship in another word pair. A typical analogy question looks like this:

> Choose the lettered pair of words that best expresses a relationship similar to that of the original words.
>
> _____ SPARROW : BIRD :: (a) flower : pot (b) eagle : hawk
> (c) book : library (d) beagle : dog (e) state : country

An analogy can be expressed in this way: "A <u>sparrow</u> is to a <u>bird</u> as a _____ is to a _____."

> To answer an analogy question, follow these steps:
>
> **1.** First form a sentence that shows the relationship between the first pair of words: "A <u>sparrow</u> is a type of <u>bird</u>."
> **2.** Remove the two words: "A _____ is a type of _____."
> **3.** Place the possible answers in the blanks to see which pair makes sense.
> "A <u>flower</u> is a type of <u>pot</u>." (This doesn't make sense and isn't the correct answer.)
> "A <u>beagle</u> is a type of <u>dog</u>." (This makes sense and is correct.)

**CRITICAL THINKING:**
**TYPES OF ANALOGIES**

Here are some common types of relationships used in analogies.

**Part to whole:** piece : pie

**Whole to part:** wheel : spoke

**Object to purpose:** pen : write

**Action to object:** fly : kite

**Item to category:** pear : fruit

**Young to old:** foal : horse

**Word to synonym:** curt : abrupt

**Word to antonym:** versatile : unadaptable

**Worker to tool:** dentist : drill

Can you think of examples in each category?

**Exercise** Answer these analogy questions.

**1.** _____ READ : BOOK :: (a) write : pen (b) fade : flower (c) kick : soccer ball (d) eat : recipe

**2.** _____ TIMID : MEEK :: (a) haughty : arrogant (b) cold : hot (c) big : bigger (d) silly : sad

**3.** _____ FINGER : HAND :: (a) pencil : paper (b) ice : water (c) song : voice (d) chapter : book

**4.** _____ TALL : SHORT :: (a) happy : sweet (b) honest : truthful (c) daring : cautious (d) busy : smart

**5.** _____ PHOTOGRAPHER : CAMERA :: (a) artist : sculpture (b) carpenter : hammer (c) chef : cook (d) root : leaves

# FACING DEATH

Many nineteenth-century writers were obsessed with death. Poets routinely wrote about their darkest fears, novelists turned the death scene into a staple of their art, and nearly everyone wrote about death's meaning for the living. Elaborate rituals evolved to help people face death, including expensive funerals, lengthy periods of mourning during which loved ones wore only black, and superstitious behaviors to protect the living.

Audiences have always been fascinated by this dark subject, for everyone has suffered from death's consequences, however indirectly. As you read the selections, try to understand the concerns of the authors and characters. Put yourself in their situations.

*Poetry*

# When I Have Fears That I May Cease to Be

JOHN KEATS

# Ozymandias

PERCY BYSSHE SHELLEY

## Examine What You Know

Both of the following poems represent attempts to understand the meaning of death. Keats's poem describes the fears produced by the thought of his own death. Shelley's poem deals with death in a more impersonal and philosophic way. What kinds of fears do you have about death? What lessons, if any, does death offer to the living?

## Expand Your Knowledge

Keats wrote this poem as a young man at the beginning of his career. Ironically, his fears of an early death were realized. Three years after writing this poem, he died of tuberculosis, the disease that killed his mother and his brother Tom, who died just months after the poem was published.

Shelley's "Ozymandias" reflects the English fascination with ancient Egyptian ruins, many of which were discovered and studied in Shelley's lifetime. Ozymandias is the Greek name for Ramses II, the most famous of all pharaohs. Ramses, known for his military successes, built many monumental buildings and temples, as well as large statues of himself. Some statues included inscriptions that boasted about his power and accomplishments. He called himself "king of kings" and dared other kings to match his achievements. Shelley's poem is about a once majestic statue that is now broken and crumbling.

## Write Before You Read

Make a list of the characteristics that people are most likely to remember about you—for example, personality traits, talents, or achievements. Choose the three characteristics that mean the most to you.

■ *Biographies of the authors can be found on page 573.*

# When I Have Fears That I May Cease to Be

JOHN KEATS

When I have fears that I may cease to be
   Before my pen has gleaned my teeming brain,
Before high-pilèd books, in charactery,
   Hold like rich garners the full-ripened grain;
5 When I behold, upon the night's starred face,
   Huge cloudy symbols of a high romance,
And think that I may never live to trace
   Their shadows, with the magic hand of chance;
And when I feel, fair creature of an hour,
10    That I shall never look upon thee more,
Never have relish in the fairy power
   Of unreflecting love—then on the shore
Of the wide world I stand alone, and think
Till love and fame to nothingness do sink.

**2-4** The speaker uses the language of farming to discuss his fear that death will prevent him from harvesting his ideas for writing. He compares writing to *gleaning,* or gathering grain. Further he compares books, filled with *charactery*—that is, alphabet letters—to *garners,* or granaries.

**6 romance:** an imaginary story of heroic adventure; also, love.

**8 chance:** fortune or fate. The speaker fears that he will be denied a life guided by the "magic hand of chance" or fate.

**11 relish:** pleasure.
*fairy:* romantic and imaginative.

**12** Consider the possible meanings of *unreflecting.*

## Responding to Reading

### First Impressions of "When I Have Fears . . ."

**1.** Do you feel that you understand what the speaker fears? Explain.

### Second Thoughts on "When I Have Fears . . ."

**2.** Describe what the speaker thinks he will miss if he dies young. Tell also how he feels about the prospect of those losses.

**Think about**

- the importance of writing ("my pen") in his life
- what it might mean to "trace [the] shadows" of "romance"
- his relationship with the "fair creature"

**3.** What conclusion does the speaker draw in the last lines of the poem?

# *Ozymandias*

## PERCY BYSSHE SHELLEY

I met a traveler from an antique land
Who said: Two vast and trunkless legs of stone
Stand in the desert . . . Near them, on the sand,
Half sunk, a shattered visage lies, whose frown,
5  And wrinkled lip, and sneer of cold command,
Tell that its sculptor well those passions read
Which yet survive, stamped on these lifeless things,
The hand that mocked them, and the heart that fed:
And on the pedestal these words appear:
10  "My name is Ozymandias, king of kings:
Look on my works, ye Mighty, and despair!"
Nothing beside remains. Round the decay
Of that colossal wreck, boundless and bare
The lone and level sands stretch far away.

**2 *trunkless legs:*** legs separated from the rest of a body.

**4 *visage:*** face.

**6 *those passions:*** Ozymandias' passions.

**7 *lifeless things:*** the stone materials of the statue.

**8** This line may be paraphrased as "The sculptor's hand mocked the passions of the king; the king's heart fed those passions."

**14** *What image do the last three lines suggest?*

THE QUESTIONER OF THE SPHINX  Elihu Vedder  The Museum of Fine Arts, Boston  Bequest of Mrs. Martin Brimmer.

## Responding to Reading

### First Impressions of "Ozymandias"

1. Describe your mental picture of the broken statue and its setting.

### Second Thoughts on "Ozymandias"

2. What does the poem suggest about the personality of Ozymandias? Consider the statue's expression, the sculptor's attitude, and the inscription.

3. Why does Ozymandias tell the "Mighty" to "look on my works . . . and despair"? Would the "Mighty" despair if they saw the statue now?

4. How do the final three lines affect your opinion of Ozymandias and his power? What point about death and decay is Shelley making?

### Comparing the Poems

5. Compare the endings of the two poems in terms of their attitudes toward death. Which ending do you think is the most effective? Explain.

## Literary Concept: Meter

**Meter** refers to the regular sound patterns in poetry that are established by stressed and unstressed syllables. In the first two lines of his poem, Keats alternates unstressed and stressed syllables (marked by ∪ and ╱):

> ∪ ╱ ∪ ╱ ∪ ╱ ∪ ╱ ∪ ╱
> When I have fears that I may cease to be
> ∪ ╱ ∪ ╱ ∪ ╱ ∪ ╱ ∪ ╱
> Before my pen has gleaned my teeming brain,

Poets use meter as musicians use beat. Meter creates a predictable rhythm to enhance the meaning and beauty of the words and to make poems memorable.

Keats used **iambic pentameter,** the most common sound pattern in English poetry. An **iamb,** or **foot,** is a basic unit of sound consisting of an unstressed syllable followed by a stressed one, as in the word *be-fore.* **Pentameter** is verse having five ("penta") iambs, or feet, in each line. On a sheet of paper, copy the rest of "When I Have Fears . . ." and mark the meter.

## Writing Options

1. Write an inscription for a statue honoring your life and accomplishments.

2. Review the information on pages 224 and 227 and explain why Keats's poem can be considered a sonnet.

## John Keats
### 1795–1821

Keats led a short and difficult life. His father died when he was a boy, and he was separated from his alcoholic mother, who later died of tuberculosis. A few years after her death, his brother also contracted the disease, from which he eventually died. While Keats was caring for his brother, he fell passionately in love with Fanny Brawne. Their sometimes troubled love is immortalized in their letters. Unfortunately, his poverty and failing health kept them from marrying.

Keats was educated to be a pharmacist and a surgeon, but he abandoned medicine at the age of twenty to pursue the less certain path of writing poetry. When he made his decision, he had not yet proved his talent. Despite savage reviews, ill health, and a lack of money, he honed his skills and became one of the most important poets in the English language. Keats wrote some of his finest work while suffering from the tuberculosis which led to his death at age twenty-five.

## Percy Bysshe Shelley
### 1792–1822

Shelley's life might easily be the subject of a soap opera. At age nineteen, Shelley scandalized his wealthy family by mailing an essay defending atheism, the doctrine that denies God's existence, to civic and church leaders. This action resulted in his dismissal from Oxford University and his separation from his family. The same year, in a chivalrous gesture, he eloped with sixteen-year-old Harriet Westbrook to save her from an abusive father. A few years later, however, Shelley abandoned his wife and moved to France with his new love, Mary Godwin. His wife refused his invitation to join the new couple in France and eventually killed herself. He then married Mary Godwin, who later—as Mary Shelley—became famous as the author of *Frankenstein*.

Ironically, Shelley never tried to be scandalous. He was simply a young man whose passions and ideals often led him to ignore practical consequences. He was a dreamer, a radical, a defender of freedom in both love and politics—and perhaps the most dedicated poet of the last two centuries. The man whom another poet, Lord Byron, called "the best and least selfish man I ever knew" drowned in a boating accident in Italy at the age of twenty-nine. When his body was cremated, his heart did not burn; Mary Shelley carried it with her, wrapped in a silken shroud, for the rest of her life.

*Fiction*

# *Godfather Death*

JAKOB AND WILHELM GRIMM

## *Examine What You Know*

In both oral and written tradition, writers and storytellers have personified death. What do you think death would look like if it were a person? Draw or describe your mental picture of Death. Think about how you would expect Death to act. Then as you read compare your image with the portrayal in this story.

## *Expand Your Knowledge*

Every culture has its **folk tales,** simple stories set in the past that were handed down orally from one generation to the next. If it were not for the Grimm brothers of Germany, many of the folk tales from Germany, Switzerland, and Austria would be lost to us. Called *Hausmarchen,* literally "household tales," the Grimm collection was actually gathered by these brothers directly from the peasants they interviewed during their travels through Europe in the early nineteenth century. The brothers made a serious effort to record the tales as they heard them, in the style and language of the common people. The Grimm collection had a wide distribution in Germany and eventually all over the world. There are now translations of the collection in seventy languages.

You may be familiar with some of the Grimm tales from your childhood, such as "The Shoemaker and the Elves," "Hansel and Gretel," "Sleeping Beauty," and "Snow White and the Seven Dwarfs." "Godfather Death," although it blends fantasy and reality, is not a story for children.

## *Write Before You Read*

Think about the title of this story and imagine how Death could be a godfather. In addition, recall what you know about folk tales. Then write three predictions that tell what you think will happen in this story.

# Godfather Death

## JAKOB AND WILHELM GRIMM

A poor man had twelve children and worked night and day just to get enough bread for them to eat. Now when the thirteenth came into the world, he did not know what to do and in his misery ran out onto the great highway to ask the first person he met to be godfather. The first to come along was God, and he already knew what it was that weighed on the man's mind and said, "Poor man, I pity you. I will hold your child at the font and I will look after it and make it happy upon earth." "Who are you?" asked the man. "I am God." "Then I don't want you for a godfather," the man said. "You give to the rich and let the poor go hungry." That was how the man talked because he did not understand how wisely God shares out wealth and poverty, and thus he turned from the Lord and walked on. Next came the Devil and said, "What is it you want? If you let me be godfather to your child, I will give him gold as much as he can use, and all the pleasures of the world besides." "Who are you?" asked the man. "I am the Devil." "Then I don't want you for a godfather," said the man. "You deceive and mislead mankind." He walked on and along came spindle-legged Death striding toward him and said, "Take me as godfather." The man asked, "Who are you?" "I am Death who makes all men equal." Said the man, "Then you're the one for me; you take rich and poor without distinction. You shall be godfather." Answered Death, "I will make your child rich and famous, because the one who has me for a friend shall want for nothing." The man said, "Next Sunday is the baptism. Be there in good time." Death appeared as he had promised and made a perfectly fine godfather.

When the boy was of age, the godfather walked in one day, told him to come along, and led him out into the woods. He showed him an herb which grew there and said, "This is your christening gift. I shall make you into a famous doctor. When you are called to a patient's bedside I will appear and if I stand at the sick man's head you can boldly say that you will cure him and if you give him some of this herb he will recover. But if I stand at the sick man's feet, then he is mine, and you must say there is no help for him and no doctor on this earth could save him. But take care not to use the herb against my will or it could be the worse for you."

It wasn't long before the young man had become the most famous doctor in the whole world. "He looks at a patient and right away he knows how things stand, whether he will get better or if he's going to die." That is what they said about him, and from near and far the people came, took him to see the sick, and gave him so much money he became a rich man. Now it happened that the king fell ill. The doctor was summoned to say if he was going to get well. When he came to the bed, there stood Death at the feet of the sick man, so that no herb on earth could have done him any good. If I could only just this once outwit Death! thought the doctor. He'll be annoyed, I know, but I am his godchild and he's sure to turn a blind eye. I'll take my chance. And so he lifted the sick man and laid him the other way around so that Death was standing at his head. Then he gave him some of the herb and the king began to feel better and was soon in perfect health. But Death came toward the doctor, his face dark and angry, threatened him with raised forefinger, and said, "You have tricked me. This time I will let it pass because you are my godchild, but if you ever dare do such a thing again, you put your own head in the noose and it is you I shall carry away with me."

Soon after that, the king's daughter lapsed into a deep illness. She was his only child, he wept day and night until his eyes failed him and he let it be known that whoever saved the princess from death should become her husband and inherit the crown. When the doctor came to the sick

DEATH AND THE MISER (detail) 1485–90 Hieronymus Bosch National Gallery of Art, Washington Samuel H. Kress Collection.

girl's bed, he saw Death at her feet. He ought to have remembered his godfather's warning, but the great beauty of the princess and the happiness of becoming her husband so bedazzled him that he threw caution to the winds, nor did he see Death's angry glances and how he lifted his hand in the air and threatened him with his bony fist. He picked the sick girl up and laid her head where her feet had lain, then he gave her some of the herb and at once her cheeks reddened and life stirred anew.

When Death saw himself cheated of his property the second time, he strode toward the doctor on his long legs and said, "It is all up with you, and now it is your turn," grasped him harshly with his ice-cold hand so that the doctor could not resist, and led him to an underground cave, and here he saw thousands upon thousands of lights burning in rows without end, some big, some middle-sized, others small. Every moment some went out and others lit up so that the little flames seemed to be jumping here and there in perpetual exchange. "Look," said Death, "these are the life lights of mankind. The big ones belong to children, the middle-sized ones to married couples in their best years, the little ones belong to very old people. Yet children and the young often have only little lights." "Show me my life light," said the doctor, imagining that it must be one of the big ones. Death pointed to a little stub threatening to go out and said, "Here it is." "Ah, dear godfather," said the terrified doctor, "light me a new one, do it, for my sake, so that I may enjoy my life and become king and marry the beautiful princess." "I cannot," answered Death. "A light must go out before a new one lights up." "Then set the old on top of a new one so it can go on burning when the first is finished," begged the doctor. Death made as if to grant his wish, reached for a tall new taper, but because he wanted revenge he purposely fumbled and the little stub fell over and went out. Thereupon the doctor sank to the ground and had himself fallen into the hands of death. ❧

## *Responding to Reading*

### First Impressions

**1.** Did this tale end the way you expected? Explain.

### Second Thoughts

**2.** Do you agree with the father's reasons for choosing Death as the godfather instead of God or the Devil? Why or why not?

**3.** What were the doctor's reasons for tricking Death? Do you think he got what he deserved? Explain.

**4.** What qualities does the character of Death have in this story? Which of those qualities do you personally associate with the concept of death?

## *Literary Concept: External and Internal Conflicts*

The plots of most stories center around a **conflict,** or a struggle between opposing forces. A conflict can be internal or external. **External conflict** is a struggle between a character and a force outside of himself. **Internal conflict** is a struggle within a character's mind. Does this story have external conflict, internal conflict, or both? Support your answer with evidence from the story.

**Concept Review: Elements of Folk Tales**  What events or people come in threes in this folk tale? What supernatural elements are involved? What other elements of a folk tale (see page 552) does the story contain?

## *Writing Options*

**1.** Explain how this story fits into the theme of this section, "Facing Death."

**2.** Write a folk tale that tells what might have happened to the son if either God or the Devil had become the godfather. Center your tale around the poor father's beliefs about the roles of God and the Devil in the lives of the peasants.

**Nonfiction**

*from*
# Phaedo
## The Death of Socrates
### PLATO

## Examine What You Know

You are about to read one of history's most famous death scenes. It is the philosopher Plato's account of the death of Socrates, his teacher and role model. Think about people who know they are about to die. From what you have read or from your own experience, what attitudes do such people take? What role does religion play in their acceptance or rejection of the inevitable? Discuss these questions with your classmates.

## Expand Your Knowledge

Socrates was an ancient Greek philosopher who left no written records of his thoughts. After his death his student Plato drew on the teachings of Socrates to compose dialogues, which featured Socrates discussing his ideas with a variety of people. In *Phaedo* (fē′ dō), Plato recreates Socrates' last day. Phaedo, a student of Socrates who was present at his death, tells Echecrates (e ke′ krə tēz), who was not there, what happened, sometimes addressing him by name.

Socrates was put on trial in 399 B.C., charged with corrupting the young and failing to honor the gods. The charges were probably made up as a way of punishing him for a lifetime of making people in authority uncomfortable. Though deeply religious, Socrates challenged traditional ways of thinking. This angered many important people, as did his refusal to compromise his beliefs. This short, squat, stub-nosed teacher lived his life seeking moral truths through a rigorous questioning process that required independent thought and self-reflection.

## Write Before You Read

How have you been affected by someone's death? Did you feel anger and sorrow? Maybe you felt indifference or even some happiness. Were the manner of death and the age and personality of the person factors in your reaction? Write your thoughts.

■ *A biography of the author can be found in the Reader's Handbook.*

# *from* ***Phaedo***

## *The Death of Socrates*

PLATO

*This excerpt from* Phaedo *follows a long discussion in which Socrates argues that his soul is immortal and that his death will lead him to a new and happier form of life. According to his sentence, Socrates has to drink a potion made from the poisonous hemlock flower before the end of the day. With that knowledge, he has spent his last day in pleasant conversation about the meaning of death. His friends and students, who earlier offered to help him escape, are much more upset by the prospect of his death than he is.*

Socrates said, "It is about time that I took my bath. I prefer to have a bath before drinking the poison rather than give the women the trouble of washing me when I am dead."

When he had finished speaking, Crito[1] said, "Very well, Socrates. But have you no directions for the others or myself about your children or anything else? What can we do to please you best?"

"Nothing new, Crito," said Socrates; "just what I am always telling you. If you look after yourselves, whatever you do will please me and mine and you too, even if you don't agree with me now. On the other hand, if you neglect yourselves and fail to follow the line of life as I have laid it down both now and in the past, however <u>fervently</u> you agree with me now, it will do no good at all."

"We shall try our best to do as you say," said Crito. "But how shall we bury you?"

"Any way you like," replied Socrates, "that is, if you can catch me and I don't slip through your fingers."[2] He laughed gently as he spoke, and turning to us went on: "I can't persuade Crito that I am this Socrates here who is talking to you now and <u>marshaling</u> all the arguments; he thinks that I am the one whom he will see presently lying dead; and he asks how he is to bury me! As for my long and <u>elaborate</u> explanation that when I have drunk the poison I shall remain with you no longer, but depart to a state of heavenly happiness, this attempt to console both you and myself seems to be wasted on him. You must give an assurance to Crito for me—the opposite of the one

---

1. **Crito** (krē′ tō): a young student of Socrates.
2. Socrates jokes that he cannot be buried because his soul—his "real self"—cannot be caught.

| *Words to Know and Use* | **fervently** (fur′ vənt lē) *adv.* intensely, passionately<br>**marshal** (mar′ shəl) *v.* to arrange ideas or things in order<br>**elaborate** (e lab′ ə rit) *adj.* complicated; developed in great detail |
|---|---|

which he gave to the court which tried me. He undertook that I should stay; but you must assure him that when I am dead I shall not stay; but depart and be gone. That will help Crito to bear it more easily and keep him from being distressed on my account when he sees my body being burned or buried, as if something dreadful were happening to me; or from saying at the funeral that it is Socrates whom he is laying out or carrying to the grave or burying. Believe me, my dear friend Crito: misstatements are not merely jarring in their immediate context; they also have a bad effect upon the soul. No, you must keep up your spirits and say that it is only my body that you are burying; and you can bury it as you please, in whatever way you think is most proper."[3]

With these words he got up and went into another room to bathe; and Crito went after him, but told us to wait. So we waited, discussing and reviewing what had been said or else dwelling upon the greatness of the calamity which had befallen us; for we felt just as though we were losing a father and should be orphans for the rest of our lives. Meanwhile, when Socrates had taken his bath, his children were brought to see him—he had two little sons and one big boy—and the women of his household—you know—arrived.[4] He talked to them in Crito's presence and gave them directions about carrying out his wishes, then he told the women and children to go away and came back himself to join us.

It was now nearly sunset, because he had spent a long time inside. He came and sat down, fresh from the bath; and he had only been talking for a few minutes when the prison officer came in and walked up to him. "Socrates," he said, "at any rate I shall not have to find fault with you, as I do with others, for getting angry with me and cursing when I tell them to drink the poison—carrying out Government orders. I have come to know during this time that you are the noblest and the gentlest and the bravest of all the men that have ever come here, and now especially I am sure that you are not angry with me, but with them; because you know who are responsible. So now—you know what I have come to say—goodbye, and try to bear what must be as easily as you can." As he spoke he burst into tears, and turning round, went away.

Socrates looked up at him and said, "Goodbye to you, too; we will do as you say." Then addressing us, he went on, "What a charming person! All the time I have been here he has visited me and sometimes had discussions with me and shown me the greatest kindness; and how generous of him now to shed tears for me at parting! But come, Crito, let us do as he says. Someone had better bring in the poison, if it is ready prepared; if not, tell the man to prepare it."

"But surely, Socrates," said Crito, "the sun is still upon the mountains; it has not gone down yet. Besides, I know that in other cases people have dinner and enjoy their wine, and sometimes the company of those whom they love, long after they receive the warning; and only drink the poison quite late at night. No need to hurry; there is still plenty of time."

"It is natural that these people whom you speak of should act in that way, Crito," said Socrates, "because they think that they gain by it. And it is also natural that I should not; because I believe that I should gain nothing by

---

3. Crito had tried to convince Socrates' judges that they should allow him freedom until the day of his execution because he could be trusted not to run away. Now, Socrates reminds Crito that his soul will depart from his body at the moment of death.
4. Earlier, Socrates said his last farewell to his wife.

*Words to Know and Use*  |  **jar** (jar) v. to affect harshly; disturb

580

THE DEATH OF SOCRATES 1787 Jacques Louis David The Metropolitan Museum of Art, New York Wolfe Fund, 1931, Catherine Lorillard Wolfe Collection.

drinking the poison a little later—I should only make myself ridiculous in my own eyes if I clung to life and hugged it when it has no more to offer. Come, do as I say and don't make difficulties."

At this Crito made a sign to his servant, who was standing nearby. The servant went out and after spending a considerable time, returned with the man who was to administer the poison; he was carrying it ready prepared in a cup. When Socrates saw him he said,

"Well, my good fellow, you understand these things; what ought I to do?"

"Just drink it," he said, "and then walk about until you feel a weight in your legs, and then lie down. Then it will act of its own accord."

As he spoke, he handed the cup to Socrates, who received it quite cheerfully, Echecrates, without a <u>tremor</u>, without any change of color or expression, and said, looking up under his brows with his usual steady gaze, "What do you say about pouring a libation[5] from this drink? Is it permitted, or not?"

"We only prepare what we regard as the normal dose, Socrates," he replied.

"I see," said Socrates. "But I suppose I am allowed, or rather bound, to pray the gods that my removal from this world to the other may be prosperous. This is my prayer, then; and I hope that it may be granted." With these words, quite calmly and with no sign of distaste, he drained the cup in one breath.

Up till this time most of us had been fairly successful in keeping back our tears; but when we saw that he was drinking, that he had actually drunk it, we could do so no longer; in spite of myself the tears came pouring out so that I covered my face and wept brokenheartedly—not for him, but for my own calamity in losing such a friend. Crito had given up even before me and had gone out when he could not restrain his tears. But Apollodorus, who had never stopped crying even before, now broke out into such a storm of passionate weeping that he made everyone in the room break down, except Socrates himself, who said:

"Really, my friends, what a way to behave! Why, that was my main reason for sending away the women, to prevent this sort of disturbance; because I am told that one should make one's end in a tranquil frame of mind. Calm yourselves and try to be brave."

This made us feel ashamed, and we controlled our tears. Socrates walked about, and presently, saying that his legs were heavy, lay down on his back—that was what the man recommended. The man (he was the same one who had administered the poison) kept his hand upon Socrates and after a little while examined his feet and legs; then pinched his foot hard and asked if he felt it. Socrates said no. Then he did the same to his legs; and moving gradually upward in this way, let us see that he was getting cold and numb. Presently he felt him again and said that when it reached the heart, Socrates would be gone.

The coldness was spreading about as far as his waist when Socrates uncovered his face—for he had covered it up—and said (they were his last words): "Crito, we ought to offer a cock to Asclepius.[6] See to it, and don't forget."

"No, it shall be done," said Crito. "Are you sure that there is nothing else?"

Socrates made no reply to this question, but after a little while he stirred; and when the man uncovered him, his eyes were fixed. When Crito saw this, he closed the mouth and eyes.

Such, Echecrates, was the end of our comrade, who was, we may fairly say, of all those whom we knew in our time, the bravest and also the wisest and most upright man. ❧

---

5. **libation:** a way of honoring the gods by pouring liquid out as an offering to them.

6. **a cock to Asclepius** (as kle′ pē əs): Asclepius was the god of medicine and healing. People made animal sacrifices to him in thanks for a cure. Socrates' joking comment shows that he views death as a "cure" for the pains of life.

## *R*esponding to Reading

### First Impressions

1. What were your thoughts as Socrates drank the cup of hemlock?

### Second Thoughts

2. What is your opinion of Socrates' attitude toward death?

3. What do the actions and words of Socrates reveal about his character?

   **Think about**
   • the way he treats his friends and jailers
   • how he chooses to spend his time on his last day
   • the manner in which he faces death

4. How does Socrates show that he is still a teacher even while facing death?

5. How do you think Plato feels about Socrates? Cite evidence from the selection to support your opinion. Do you agree with Plato's judgment?

## *W*riting Options

1. Socrates had the chance to escape. If he had taken this opportunity, would his friends have felt the same way about him? Write your thoughts.

2. What would you have said to Socrates before he drank the poison? Write as if you were talking to him.

## *V*ocabulary Practice

**Exercise** Write the word that is most clearly related to the boldfaced word in each sentence.

1. A philosopher like Socrates must **organize** ideas logically.
2. Other poisons might have caused a **trembling** in Socrates.
3. Socrates knows that if his students have forgotten his lessons about the soul, his death will greatly **disturb** them.
4. The philosopher offers a **complex** explanation of immortality.
5. Socrates' students believed **wholeheartedly** in his virtue.

> *Words to Know and Use*
> ───────
> elaborate
> fervently
> jar
> marshal
> tremor

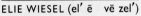

*Autobiography*

### *from* Night

ELIE WIESEL (el´ē  vē zel´)

## *E*xamine What You Know

This is a true account from Elie Wiesel's book *Night*, which tells of his experiences in a German concentration camp when he was a boy. Discuss what you know about the Holocaust—that is, the slaughter of Jews in Europe during World War II—and how you learned what you know.

## *E*xpand Your Knowledge

When Adolf Hitler became chancellor of Germany in 1933, he planned to make Germany a world empire. As the leader of the Nazis, the political party in control of Germany, he carried out a policy of military aggression and expansion. In order to seize control of other countries in Europe, he built up Germany's armed forces and set up his private army, known as the SS. Hitler permitted no opposition to Nazism and created an atmosphere of terror in his country. He organized a secret police force, called the Gestapo, that hunted down his suspected enemies.

Under Hitler's leadership, Germany's invasion of Poland in 1939 started World War II. About this time Hitler began a campaign to eliminate the European Jews, whom he claimed were responsible for all the evils in the world. Jews were forced into concentration camps, where thousands were killed in gas chambers or shot by firing squads. Thousands of others died through torture, starvation, and disease. The dead were cremated in huge ovens.

Auschwitz-Birkenau, in Poland, was one of the largest of these death camps. It covered fifteen square miles and was under the direction of Rudolf Hess, who later testified that 2½ million people had been executed and 500,000 more had been starved to death at Auschwitz. Josef Mengele was the Nazi camp doctor at Auschwitz who became infamous for his medical experiments on the inmates. In total, about 6 million Jews died in concentration camps. It was Elie Wiesel who first used the term **Holocaust** in reference to this mass slaughter.

## *W*rite Before You Read

List words and phrases you think would describe the thoughts and feelings of a person living in a concentration camp. As you read this selection, compare your notes with Wiesel's thoughts and feelings.

■ *A biography of the author can be found on page 592.*

# *from* *Night*

## ELIE WIESEL

The SS gave us a fine New Year's gift.

We had just come back from work. As soon as we had passed through the door of the camp, we sensed something different in the air. Roll call did not take so long as usual. The evening soup was given out with great speed and swallowed down at once in anguish.

## *And soon a terrible word was circulating—selection.*

I was no longer in the same block as my father. I had been transferred to another unit, the building one, where, twelve hours a day, I had to drag heavy blocks of stone about. The head of my new block was a German Jew, small of <u>stature</u>, with piercing eyes. He told us that evening that no one would be allowed to go out after the evening soup. And soon a terrible word was circulating—selection.

We knew what that meant. An SS man would examine us. Whenever he found a weak one, a *musulman*, as we called them, he would write his number down: good for the <u>crematory</u>.

After soup, we gathered together between the beds. The veterans said:

"You're lucky to have been brought here so late. This camp is paradise today, compared with what it was like two years ago. Buna was a real hell then. There was no water, no blankets, less soup and bread. At night we slept almost naked, and it was below thirty degrees. The corpses were collected in hundreds every day. The work was hard. Today, this is a little paradise. The Kapos[1] had orders to kill a certain number of prisoners every day. And every week—selection. A merciless selection. . . . Yes, you're lucky."

"Stop it! Be quiet!" I begged. "You can tell your stories tomorrow or on some other day."

They burst out laughing. They were not veterans for nothing.

"Are you scared? So were we scared. And there was plenty to be scared of in those days."

The old men stayed in their corner, dumb, motionless, haunted. Some were praying.

An hour's delay. In an hour, we should know the verdict—death or a <u>reprieve</u>.

And my father? Suddenly I remembered him. How would he pass the selection? He had aged so much. . . .

---

1. **Kapos** (käp′ ōz): the prisoners who served as foremen, or heads, of each building or cell block.

---

*Words to Know and Use* | **stature** (stac/h′ ər) *n.* the height of a person
**crematory** (krē′ mə tôr′ ē) *n.* a furnace for cremating dead bodies; also **crematorium**
**reprieve** (ri prēv′) *n.* a postponement of a penalty, especially death

585

The head of our block had never been outside concentration camps since 1933. He had already been through all the slaughterhouses, all the factories of death. At about nine o'clock, he took up his position in our midst:

"*Achtung!*"

There was instant silence.

"Listen carefully to what I am going to say." (For the first time, I heard his voice quiver.) "In a few moments the selection will begin. You must get completely undressed. Then one by one you go before the SS doctors. I hope you will all succeed in getting through. But you must help your own chances. Before you go into the next room, move about in some way so that you give yourselves a little color. Don't walk slowly, run! Run as if the devil were after you! Don't look at the SS. Run, straight in front of you!"

He broke off for a moment, then added:

"And, the essential thing, don't be afraid!"

Here was a piece of advice we should have liked very much to be able to follow.

I got undressed, leaving my clothes on the bed. There was no danger of anyone stealing them this evening.

Tibi and Yossi, who had changed their unit at the same time as I had, came up to me and said:

"Let's keep together. We shall be stronger."

Yossi was murmuring something between his teeth. He must have been praying. I had never realized that Yossi was a believer. I had even always thought the reverse. Tibi was silent, very pale. All the prisoners in the block stood naked between the beds. This must be how one stands at the last judgment.

"They're coming!"

There were three SS officers standing round the notorious Dr. Mengele, who had received us at Birkenau. The head of the block, with an attempt at a smile, asked us:

"Ready?"

Yes, we were ready. So were the SS doctors. Dr. Mengele was holding a list in his hand: our numbers. He made a sign to the head of the block: "We can begin!" As if this were a game!

# You're too thin, you're weak, . . . you're good for the furnace.

The first to go by were the "officials" of the block: *Stubenaelteste*,[2] Kapos, foremen, all in perfect physical condition, of course! Then came the ordinary prisoners' turn. Dr. Mengele took stock of them from head to foot. Every now and then, he wrote a number down. One single thought filled my mind: not to let my number be taken; not to show my left arm.

There were only Tibi and Yossi in front of me. They passed. I had time to notice that Mengele had not written their numbers down. Someone pushed me. It was my turn. I ran without looking back. My head was spinning: you're too thin, you're weak, you're too thin, you're good for the furnace. . . . The race seemed <u>interminable</u>. I thought I had been running for years. . . . You're too thin, you're too weak. . . . At last I had arrived exhausted. When I regained my breath, I questioned Yossi and Tibi:

"Was I written down?"

---

2. **Stubenaelteste** (s/htoo′ bin ôl tes tə): literally, "the elders of the rooms"; the Kapos.

*Words to Know and Use* | **interminable** (in tʉr′ mi nə bəl) *adj.* lasting, or seeming to last, forever; endless

"No," said Yossi. He added, smiling: "In any case, he couldn't have written you down, you were running too fast. . . ."

I began to laugh. I was glad. I would have liked to kiss him. At that moment, what did the others matter! I hadn't been written down.

Those whose numbers had been noted stood apart, abandoned by the whole world. Some were weeping in silence.

The SS officers went away. The head of the block appeared, his face reflecting the general weariness.

"Everything went off all right. Don't worry. Nothing is going to happen to anyone. To anyone."

Again he tried to smile. A poor, <u>emaciated</u>, dried-up Jew questioned him avidly in a trembling voice:

"But . . . but, *Blockaelteste*,[3] they did write me down!"

The head of the block let his anger break out. What! Did someone refuse to believe him!

"What's the matter now? Am I telling lies then? I tell you once and for all, nothing's going to happen to you! To anyone! You're wallowing in your own despair, you fool!"

The bell rang, a signal that the selection had been completed throughout the camp.

With all my might I began to run to Block 36. I met my father on the way. He came up to me:

"Well? So you passed?"

"Yes. And you?"

"Me too."

How we breathed again, now! My father had brought me a present—half a ration of bread obtained in exchange for a piece of rubber, found at the warehouse, which would do to sole a shoe.

BUCHENWALD 1945   Margaret Bourke-White   *Life* Magazine © Time-Warner, Inc.

The bell. Already we must separate, go to bed. Everything was regulated by the bell. It gave me orders, and I automatically obeyed them. I hated it. Whenever I dreamed of a better world, I could only imagine a universe with no bells.

Several days had elapsed. We no longer thought about the selection. We went to work as usual, loading heavy stones into railway wagons. Rations had become more meager: this was the only change.

We had risen before dawn, as on every day. We had received the black coffee, the ration of bread. We were about to set out for the yard as usual. The head of the block arrived, running.

"Silence for a moment. I have a list of numbers here. I'm going to read them to you.

---

3. **Blockaelteste** (blôk′ ôl tes tə): literally, "the elders of the building", the Kapos.

587

Those whose numbers I call won't be going to work this morning; they'll stay behind in the camp."

And, in a soft voice, he read out about ten numbers. We had understood. These were numbers chosen at the selection. Dr. Mengele had not forgotten.

The head of the block went toward his room. Ten prisoners surrounded him, hanging onto his clothes:

"Save us! You promised . . . ! We want to go to the yard. We're strong enough to work. We're good workers. We can . . . we will. . . ."

He tried to calm them, to reassure them about their fate, to explain to them that the fact that they were staying behind in the camp did not mean much, had no tragic significance.

"After all, I stay here myself every day," he added.

It was a somewhat feeble argument. He realized it, and without another word went and shut himself up in his room.

The bell had just rung.

"Form up!"

It scarcely mattered now that the work was hard. The essential thing was to be as far away as possible from the block, from the crucible of death, from the center of hell.

I saw my father running toward me. I became frightened all of a sudden.

"What's the matter?"

Out of breath, he could hardly open his mouth.

"Me, too . . . me, too . . . ! They told me to stay behind in the camp."

They had written down his number without his being aware of it.

"What will happen?" I asked in anguish.

But it was he who tried to reassure me.

"It isn't certain yet. There's still a chance of escape. They're going to do another selection today . . . a decisive selection."

I was silent.

He felt that his time was short. He spoke quickly. He would have liked to say so many things. His speech grew confused; his voice choked. He knew that I would have to go in a few moments. He would have to stay behind alone, so very alone.

"Look, take this knife," he said to me. "I don't need it any longer. It might be useful to you. And take this spoon as well. Don't sell them. Quickly! Go on. Take what I'm giving you!"

The inheritance.

"Don't talk like that, Father." (I felt that I would break into sobs.) "I don't want you to say that. Keep the spoon and knife. You need them as much as I do. We shall see each other again this evening, after work."

He looked at me with his tired eyes, veiled with despair. He went on:

"I'm asking this of you. . . . Take them. Do as I ask, my son. We have no time. . . . Do as your father asks."

Our Kapo yelled that we should start.

The unit set out toward the camp gate. Left, right! I bit my lips. My father had stayed by the block, leaning against the wall. Then he began to run, to catch up with us. Perhaps he had forgotten something he wanted to say to me. . . . But we were marching too quickly. . . . Left, right!

We were already at the gate. They counted us, to the din of military music. We were outside.

The whole day, I wandered about as if sleepwalking. Now and then Tibi and Yossi would throw me a brotherly word. The Kapo, too, tried to reassure me. He had given me easier work today. I felt sick at heart. How well they were treating me! Like an orphan! I thought: even now, my father is still helping me.

I did not know myself what I wanted—for the day to pass quickly or not. I was afraid of finding myself alone that night. How good it would be to die here!

At last we began the return journey. How I longed for orders to run!

The military march. The gate. The camp.

I ran to Block 36.

Were there still miracles on this earth? He was alive. He had escaped the second selection. He had been able to prove that he was still useful. . . . I gave him back his knife and spoon. 🐦

# INSIGHT

## *from* The Nobel Prize Acceptance Speech
ELIE WIESEL

It is with a profound sense of humility that I accept the honor you have chosen to bestow upon me. I know: your choice transcends me. This both frightens and pleases me.

It frightens me because I wonder: do I have the right to represent the multitudes who have perished? Do I have the right to accept this great honor on their behalf? I do not. That would be presumptuous. No one may speak for the dead; no one may interpret their mutilated dreams and visions.

It pleases me because I may say that this honor belongs to all the survivors and their children and, through us, to the Jewish people with whose destiny I have always identified.

I remember: it happened yesterday or eternities ago. A young Jewish boy discovered the kingdom of night. I remember his bewilderment; I remember his anguish. It all happened so fast. The ghetto. The deportation. The sealed cattle car. The fiery altar upon which the history of our people and the future of mankind were meant to be sacrificed.

I remember: he asked his father, "Can this be true? This is the twentieth century, not the Middle Ages. Who would allow such crimes to be committed? How could the world remain silent?"

And now the boy is turning to me: "Tell me," he asks. "What have you done with my future? What have you done with your life?"

And I tell him that I have tried. That I have tried to keep memory alive, that I have tried to fight those who would forget. Because if we forget, we are guilty, we are accomplices.

And then I explained to him how naive we were, that the world did know and remained silent. And that is why I swore never to be silent whenever and wherever human beings endure suffering and humiliation. We must always take sides. Neutrality helps the oppressor, never the victim. Silence encourages the tormentor, never the tormented.

## Responding to Reading

### First Impressions

1. To which part of the story did you react most strongly? Explain.

### Second Thoughts

2. What do you consider the worst thing about this part of Wiesel's experience in the concentration camp? Explain your answer.

3. Based on Wiesel's account, what psychological effects do you conclude prisoners in a death camp suffer?

4. In your opinion, are any of the prisoners' actions admirable or heroic?

5. Why did Wiesel call his book *Night?*

   **Think about**
   • what he says in his speech
   • what night might symbolize
   • what happened to the Jews

6. According to his Nobel Prize acceptance speech, why has Wiesel continued to speak and write about the Holocaust?

### Broader Connections

7. Do you think something like the Holocaust could happen again anywhere today, to any specific race, religion, or other group? Why or why not?

## Literary Concept: Journalistic Style

**Journalistic style** is the distinctive way in which writers of newspaper and magazine articles express their ideas. The journalist's writing is characterized by factual information, quotations, and short sentences. Even though the writing is supposed to be objective, the words and details the journalist chooses create a certain emotional response in the reader. Why do you think Wiesel chose a journalistic style of writing in *Night?* What is the effect on the reader?

**Concept Review: Author's Tone**   What words describe the tone of this piece (that is, Wiesel's attitude toward his subject)? Cite examples that support your opinion. Why do you think he uses that tone rather than another?

# Writing Options

1. In his speech Wiesel says, "I swore never to be silent whenever and wherever human beings endure suffering and humiliation. We must always take sides." Do you agree with him? Explain.

2. Imagine you are the judge at Mengele's trial after the war. Write out your sentence for the so-called Butcher of Auschwitz and explain why it is fitting.

3. Wiesel often speaks in public about his experiences in the death camp. Write a list of questions you would ask Wiesel if you had the chance to meet him.

4. Imagine that you are one of the American soldiers who helped to liberate Auschwitz. Write a letter home explaining what you saw there and how you felt after meeting some of the prisoners and guards.

# Vocabulary Practice

**Exercise** Choose the word from the list that would be the best substitute for each boldfaced word or phrase.

1. Lack of food and the presence of disease resulted in the prisoners' looking **close to starvation.**
2. The governor issued a **stay of execution** for the criminal.
3. Rather than be buried in a grave, some people plan to have their bodies burned in a **furnace** after they die.
4. Her child's operation seemed **endless** to the frightened parent.
5. Many men of short **height** are extremely strong and solidly built.

> *Words to Know and Use*
>
> ---
>
> **crematory**
> **emaciated**
> **interminable**
> **reprieve**
> **stature**

# e x t e n d

## Options for Learning

**1** • **Color of Fear**  Create an abstract painting or drawing that expresses the extreme emotions Wiesel felt during this part of his experience. Use shapes and color to convey his fear, dread, relief, or other feelings. Then present your work to the class and have your classmates guess what part of the story it illustrates.

**2** • **Crime and Punishment**  Investigate the Nuremberg trials of Nazi war criminals. In your library's card catalog, look up information under Nuremberg, War Criminals, Josef Mengele, Rudolph Hess, and World War II. Find out who was captured, tried, and convicted and what sentences were passed. Report your findings to the class.

**3** • **Night**  Read the whole book to find out more about Wiesel's experiences during and after Auschwitz. Present a summary in an oral report.

**4** • **The Hunt**  Not all the Nazi leaders were captured at the end of the war. Find out about the people who hunted down the escapees, how the manhunts were carried out, and how successful they were. Summarize your findings and present them orally to the class.

### FACT FINDER

*Find out the names of other Nazi concentration camps and locate the camps on a map of Europe.*

### Elie Wiesel
1928–

In 1944 the SS deported all 15,000 Jews from Wiesel's hometown in Romania. Wiesel was fifteen years old when he, his parents, and his three sisters were sent to Auschwitz.

When Wiesel was freed from Auschwitz in 1945, he swore a ten-year vow of silence, during which he wrote nothing about the Holocaust even though he worked as a journalist and writer. "I didn't want to use the wrong words," he said. "I was afraid that words might betray it. I waited."

Wiesel's first attempt at writing about the Holocaust was *Night*, but his 800-page manuscript could not be sold. After cutting it to 127 pages, he found a publisher in France in 1958. He has since written numerous histories, articles, stories, and novels about the Holocaust. He has also worked and spoken in support of oppressed people everywhere, including South Africa's black population, the Southeast Asian boat people, and the native Miskito Indians of Nicaragua. As the leading writer about the Nazi concentration camp experience, Wiesel received the Nobel Peace Prize in 1986.

# WRITER'S WORKSHOP

## EXPOSITION: COMPARISON-CONTRAST

Leaf through a telephone directory in any large American city and you will see an astonishing variety of names: Akmajian, Bhattacherya, Chin, Cohen, Domblewski, Jimenez, Klemperer, Kurasawa, MacMahon, O'Neill, Saussure, Tkaczyk, and so on. Why are there so many different names representing so many different places? Because the United States has been a nation of immigrants from its beginnings. People came for many different reasons, bringing with them their own traditions, beliefs, and ceremonies. The nation became what one U.S. senator has called ''a great stew'' of cultural differences.

In this lesson you will be asked to do a **research report.** You will study two or three cultures' customs regarding some important event in life in order to see how their approaches are alike and different. You might deal with different cultures' approach to death, in keeping with the theme of this subunit. Or, if you prefer, you could deal with some other event common to all cultures, such as birth, initiation into adulthood, marriage, or a particular holiday celebration. In your report, you will compare and contrast the cultures with respect to the event that interests you.

> Here is your PASSkey to this assignment.

### GUIDED ASSIGNMENT: RESEARCH REPORT

Choose an important event in life and study how customs regarding this event differ from one culture to another. Write a research report in which you compare and contrast the approaches of these cultures.

**P** URPOSE: To compare and contrast

**A** UDIENCE: Your classmates

**S** UBJECT: The customs of different cultures

**S** TRUCTURE: A research report

## Prewriting

STEP **1** **Explore ideas** One way to come up with a topic for this paper is to start with what you know. Think of rituals and customs from your own culture that are interesting. For example, if you are from a Catholic family, you might begin by thinking about how Catholics deal with birth, baptism, christening, confirmation, marriage, death, and holidays such as New Year's Day or Christmas. Then you might choose to compare one of these events to a similar event in one or two other cultures. For example, you might compare the Catholic confirmation (in which the child is recognized as an adult) with the Jewish bar or bat mitzvah (which also marks the passage into adulthood).

Another way to find a topic is to go to the library and read about other cultures until you find a custom or tradition that interests you. Browse through encyclopedias, books on other peoples, and magazines like *National Geographic* and *Smithsonian.* Travel guides are also excellent sources of information on other cultures. You might want to start by choosing two races, ethnic groups, religious groups, or nationalities that interest you and then reading about them. You might find it particularly interesting to look into a more primitive culture such as that of the Australian aborigines, the Masai tribe of Tanzania and Kenya, the Bushmen of the Kalahari Desert, or the rain forest Indians of Brazil.

**STEP 2** **Once you have a topic, write a statement of purpose** A statement of purpose is a one-sentence summary of what your paper will explain. Your purpose statement will help you focus your research and writing and stay on target. Here are some examples written by other students:

STUDENT MODEL ▶

1. To compare and contrast Independence Day celebrations in the United States and Mexico (the Fourth of July and the Cinco de Mayo).
2. To compare and contrast Eastern Orthodox and Roman Catholic marriage ceremonies.
3. To compare and contrast the ways in which ancient Egyptians and modern Americans bury their leaders.
4. To compare and contrast the training of warriors by the modern U.S. Army and by the ancient Hopi Indians.

**STEP 3** **Gather information about the event** After you select a topic, gather information by reading in the library and, if appropriate, by interviewing knowledgeable people. Take notes on note cards. Follow the procedures for notetaking, quoting sources, and creating a bibliography in the Guidelines for Research and Report Writing in the Writer's Handbook.

**STEP 4** **Organize your ideas and make a rough outline** Make a rough outline to help you organize information and show areas where more research is needed.

You can choose either of two simple ways to organize your material. One method is to deal first with one culture and then with the other. A rough outline for this method might look like this:

The Ostyaks of Siberia
    What happens to soul after death
    What happens at funeral
The Nambikwara Indians of Brazil
    What happens to soul after death
    What happens at funeral

Another format for organization is point by point, like this:

What happens to soul after death
    The Ostyaks of Siberia
    The Nambikwara Indians of Brazil
What happens at funeral
    The Ostyaks of Siberia
    The Nambikwara Indians of Brazil

## Drafting

**STEP 1** **Write the body first, following your outline**   Write the body in your own words, occasionally including quotations from your sources. Begin each paragraph with a topic sentence that states a main point from your outline. Then complete the paragraph by elaborating on the main idea and incorporating the subpoints in your outline. Start a new paragraph for your next main point.

When you quote someone or restate his or her ideas, credit your source. That is, include parentheses containing the source's last name and the page number or numbers if the source is a written one. Put quotation marks around all quoted material. Notice how one student credited his sources.

◀ STUDENT MODEL

    People from different cultures have very different ideas about what happens to the soul after death. The Nambikwara Indians of the Brazilian jungle believe that ''after death, the souls of men are embodied in jaguars; but those of women and children are carried up into the air where they vanish forever'' (Levi-Strauss 325). In contrast, the Ostyak people of northern Siberia believe that the dead go to one of three different lands near the Arctic Ocean. One land is for people who died violent deaths. Another is for sinners. And yet another is for people who had ordinary lives (van Gennep 150-151).

**STEP 2** **Write your introduction and conclusion**   After the body of your paper is finished, write the introduction and conclusion. The introduction should raise the question that your paper will explore. The conclusion should summarize your findings.

**STEP 3** **Write your final bibliography**   After your whole paper is finished, make a final bibliography.

## Revising and Editing

Use the following checklist to evaluate and revise your work, or ask a classmate to review your work according to this checklist.

---

### Revision Checklist
· · · · · · · · · · · · · · · · · · · · · · · · · · · · · · · · · · · · · · · · · · · · · · · · · · · · · · · · · · · · · · · · · · ·

**1.** Is the organization of the paper clear?

**2.** Are enough details given to make the description of each culture's practices interesting?

**3.** Does the paper have a clear introduction, body, and conclusion?

**4.** Have sources been credited properly?

---

**Editing**   When you have finished revising, proofread your papers for spelling, clarity, organization, and mechanics.

## Presenting

In books and magazines find pictures of the cultures that you wrote about. In class give an oral report on the findings in your paper using the pictures as illustrations. After reports have been given, create a class collage for a bulletin board on cultures and customs around the world.

## Reflecting on Your Writing

Answer the following questions about this assignment. Place your answers along with your essay in your writing portfolio.

**1.** Would you do your research differently the next time? Explain.

**2.** Were you able to state most ideas in your own words?

**3.** Are there some steps in this workshop that you think should be skipped or deleted? Explain.

# SENTENCE COMBINING II

You have already learned that combining sentences can make your writing smoother and less repetitive. You have learned how to combine sentences in two ways: (1) by using the conjunctions *and, or,* and *but;* and (2) by inserting a key word or phrase from one sentence into another. The following are some other useful sentence-combining techniques.

## Inserting Word Groups

> Use the word *who* to add information about a person or a group of persons. Use the word *that* or *which* to add information about a place, idea, or thing.

Percy Shelley was a British poet. He wrote the poem "Ozymandias."

Percy Shelley, who wrote the poem "Ozymandias," was a British poet.

Notice that there are commas around the *who* clause in the combined sentence above. The clause supplies additional information, but it is not absolutely necessary to complete the writer's thought. If the clause is dropped, the sentence will still make sense. Now look at a slightly different combination:

Percy Shelley was *the* British poet. He wrote the poem "Ozymandias."

Percy Shelley was *the* British poet *who* wrote the poem "Ozymandias."

Notice that no commas are needed around the clause beginning with *who* in this combined sentence. This is because the clause is essential to the meaning of the sentence. Without the clause, the reader might ask, "The British poet who did what?"

*That* or *which* can also be used to combine word groups. In a clause that is not essential to the meaning of the sentence, you would use *which.* In a clause that is essential to the meaning of the sentence, you should use *that.*

REMINDER

The words that introduce clauses that show relationships are **subordinating conjunctions**. For a complete list of these conjunctions, see the margin notes in the Language Workshop **Understanding Clauses**, pp. 564-566.

Remember that a clause beginning with *which* always requires a comma. A clause beginning with *that* never does.

> A sculpture attracted the traveler. A sculpture was in ruins.
> A sculpture, *which* was in ruins, attracted the traveler.

The added information is not necessary to the sentence; therefore, *which* is used and the clause is set off by commas.

> The sculpture attracted the traveler. The sculpture was in ruins.
> The sculpture *that* was in ruins attracted the traveler.

In the second combination, the added information defines *sculpture* in a way that is necessary to complete the writer's thought. Therefore, the writer used *that*. Notice that you as the writer decide what information is essential to your meaning and what information is not. Then you choose *that* or *which* according to your decision.

**Exercise 1**   Combine each pair of sentences by eliminating the word in italics. Remember to use correct punctuation.

1. Socrates is considered one of the world's greatest teachers. *Socrates* was a Greek philosopher. (Use *who* and commas.)
2. His teachings gave his enemies reasons to arrest him. *His teachings* were unorthodox. (Use *which* and commas.)
3. Socrates accepted the court's condemnation of his teachings. *Socrates* believed in the judicial rights of the courts. (Use *who* and commas.)
4. The man was one of Socrates' finest pupils. *The man* wrote about the death of Socrates. (Use *who* and no commas.)
5. The poison was hemlock. Socrates drank *the poison*. (Use *that* and no commas.)

## Showing Relationships

> When the ideas in two sentences are related, you can often combine the sentences by using a combining word that shows *when, why*, and *under what conditions* something occurs.

You can use words such as *when, after*, or *before* to show when something happened. You can use the word *because* to show why something happened. You can use words like *although* and *if* to explain under what conditions something occurred. In the following examples, notice how the combining word shows the connection between the two ideas.

> Socrates took a bath. He drank the poison.
> Socrates took a bath *before* he drank the poison.

> Socrates was put on trial. His enemies believed he corrupted the youth of Athens.
> Socrates was put on trial *because* his enemies believed he corrupted the youth of Athens.

> Socrates was a religious man. He raised questions about the gods.
> Socrates was a religious man *although* he raised questions about the gods.

Word groups that are used to explain *when, why*, and *under what conditions* are called **subordinate clauses**. Sometimes the subordinate clause may occur at the beginning of the sentence, followed by a comma.

> Although he raised questions about the gods, Socrates was a religious man.

Here are some words that can express relationships of *time, cause*, and *condition*.

| Time | Cause | Condition |
|---|---|---|
| after | because | if |
| until | since | whether |
| while | | unless |

**Exercise 2**   Work in a small group to rewrite the following passage. Combine each pair of sentences, using the word enclosed in parentheses. Eliminate any boldfaced words. Remember to use commas when necessary.

1. Elie Wiesel is a prominent writer. **He** was born in Romania in 1928. (who) 2. His parents and a sister were killed in Nazi concentration camps. Wiesel survived two of the **Nazi concentration** camps. (although) 3. His writings are about the events of the Holocaust. **His writings** have won many awards. (which) 4. Wiesel's books make a demand. **They demand** that we confront the evil side of human nature. (that) 5. Wiesel may have written his books **for a special reason**. He wanted to pay tribute to his family. (because) 6. You read Wiesel's books. You will know why we should not forget the Holocaust. (when)

LANGUAGE HANDBOOK
...............................
For review and practice:
complex sentences,
   pages 1025–27
compound-complex
   sentences,
   page 1027

# EFFECTIVE NOTE TAKING

These guidelines will help you to take notes when preparing a report.

**1.** Each time you find a relevant fact or idea in your reading, write it down on a 4" x 6" note card:

**GUIDELINE**

This tells what the note is about.

**SOURCE NUMBER**

This is the number of the bibliography card for the source.

**NOTE**

The note can be quoted, paraphrased, or summarized.

A **quotation** gives the exact words of the source and should be placed in quotation marks.

A **paraphrase** gives the ideas of the source in different words.

A **summary** gives the main ideas of the source in different and fewer words.

**PAGE REFERENCE**

Make sure you record this correctly.

> **John Keats's student days**  3
>   "One of his notebooks has survived from this period [the period when Keats was in medical school]. . . . Keats was not altogether a good note taker."
> **p.51**

**2.** Use a separate card for each note. Limit the amount of information you put on each card. Do not put information from more than one source on the same card.

**3.** Put quotation marks around any material that you copy from a source word for word. Do not put quotation marks around material that you paraphrase or summarize in your own words.

**4.** Copy a direct quotation exactly, rechecking it when you are finished to make sure that everything is precisely as in the original.

**5.** Remember that you can cut out nonessential information from a quotation. Use ellipsis points (. . . or . . . .) to show that you have left out material that was in the original. Use ellipses only within a quotation, not at the beginning or end of it.

**6.** If you wish to add your own explanatory material to a quotation, put this material in brackets [ ].

**7.** In the bottom left-hand corner, write the page number(s) of your source.

**8.** On a separate card, write a bibliography entry for your source. Record the author, title, place of publication, publisher, and date of publication. Number the bibliography card and put the number of the bibliography card in the upper right-hand corner of your note card.

```
                              3
Gittings, Robert.
John Keats. Boston:
Little, Brown & Co.,
1968.
```
**Bibliography Card**

**Exercise**   Research one of the following topics: Romantic poetry, Percy Bysshe Shelley, Plato, or the Holocaust. Go to the library and find two sources. Make up two note cards, one from each source. On one, paraphrase your source. On the other, quote your source directly.

# PERSONAL RELATIONS

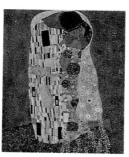

Personal relationships involving love, marriage, and friendship became especially important for the Romantics and Victorians. Such ties of affection were idealized from the pulpit, celebrated by poets, and defended by public figures. The home became a refuge that offered comfort and love in an uncertain and often brutal world.

Not all relationships, of course, offer comfort. Some become laughable, despite best intentions; others turn dark and even criminal. As you will see in the following selections, relationships can bring one a little closer to heaven . . . or to despair.

*Poetry*

# *Porphyria's Lover* (pôr fir' ē əz)

## ROBERT BROWNING

## *E*xamine What You Know

Simply by listening to the news, you can tell that many crimes are committed in the heat of passion. How can love lead to crime? Discuss with your class what causes a positive personal relationship to turn into a tragedy.

## *E*xpand Your Knowledge

"Porphyria's Lover" first appeared with another Browning poem under the title "Madhouse Cells," a title that showed the author's fascination with abnormal states of mind. Though Browning himself was a respectable, well-balanced, and happy person, the characters in his poems include murderous dukes, devilish savages, corrupt bishops, failed artists, and other strange characters.

Originally a playwright, Browning became known for his mastery of the technique of the **dramatic monologue** in his poetry. This technique features a speaker talking to a silent listener about a dramatic event or experience. "Porphyria's Lover" is one of Browning's earliest monologues.

## *E*nrich Your Reading

**Making Inferences**  You make inferences to figure out what is unstated in a piece of literature. To make an inference, you take clues provided by the writer and add them to your own knowledge. In order to understand this poem, you will need to make inferences about the speaker's changing moods. Look for clues in what he says about Porphyria and in his behavior. Use a chart like the one below to keep track of your inferences.

| Speaker's Mood | Clues | Line Numbers |
|---|---|---|
| depressed | rain, wind, heart fit to break | 1–5 |
|  |  |  |

■ *A biography of the author can be found in the Reader's Handbook.*

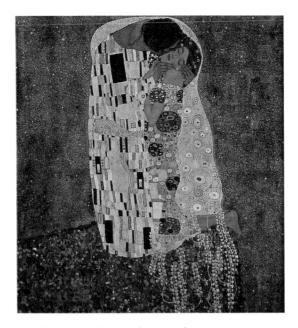

# Porphyria's Lover

### ROBERT BROWNING

The rain set early in tonight,
   The sullen wind was soon awake,
It tore the elm-tops down for spite,
   And did its worst to vex the lake:
5    I listened with heart fit to break.
When glided in Porphyria; straight
   She shut the cold out and the storm,
And kneeled and made the cheerless grate
   Blaze up, and all the cottage warm;
10    Which done, she rose, and from her form
Withdrew the dripping cloak and shawl,
   And laid her soiled gloves by, untied
Her hat and let the damp hair fall,
   And, last, she sat down by my side
15    And called me. When no voice replied,
She put my arm about her waist,
   And made her smooth white shoulder bare,
And all her yellow hair displaced,
   And, stooping, made my cheek lie there,
20    And spread, o'er all, her yellow hair,
Murmuring how she loved me—she
   Too weak, for all her heart's endeavor,
To set its struggling passion free
   From pride, and vainer ties dissever,
25    And give herself to me forever.
But passion sometimes would prevail,
   Nor could tonight's gay feast restrain
A sudden thought of one so pale
   For love of her, and all in vain:
30    So, she was come through wind and rain.

Be sure I looked up at her eyes
   Happy and proud; at last I knew
Porphyria worshiped me: surprise
   Made my heart swell, and still it grew
35    While I debated what to do.
That moment she was mine, mine, fair,
   Perfectly pure and good: I found
A thing to do, and all her hair
   In one long yellow string I wound
40    Three times her little throat around,
And strangled her. No pain felt she;
   I am quite sure she felt no pain.
As a shut bud that holds a bee,
   I warily oped her lids: again
45    Laughed the blue eyes without a stain.
And I untightened next the tress
   About her neck; her cheek once more
Blushed bright beneath my burning kiss:
   I propped her head up as before,
50    Only, this time my shoulder bore
Her head, which droops upon it still:
   The smiling rosy little head,
So glad it has its utmost will,
   That all it scorned at once is fled,
55    And I, its love, am gained instead!
Porphyria's love: she guessed not how
   Her darling one wish would be heard.
And thus we sit together now,
   And all night long we have not stirred,
60    And yet God has not said a word!

## *Responding to Reading*

### First Impressions

1. What is your reaction to the speaker and his actions? Explain.

### Second Thoughts

2. Why do you think the speaker kills Porphyria?

    **Think about**

    • the speaker's view of what a relationship should be
    • his opinion of Porphyria and her love
    • what he hopes to achieve by his action

3. How can the changes in the speaker's mood help you explain his action? Use the evidence you gathered for your chart to guide your response.

4. How do the last three lines show the speaker's judgment of his own actions? What is your opinion of his reasoning and state of mind?

5. What do you think might happen next?

## *Literary Concept: Dramatic Monologue*

In a **dramatic monologue,** the speaker expresses his or her innermost thoughts and feelings about a critical moment in his or her life. A listener, though present, remains silent, allowing the speaker to proceed without interruption or argument. This technique allows the poet to explore very different types of characters, from criminals to saints, and different ways of thinking. In a sense, the poet brings the reader inside the mind of the speaker.

Why do you think a poet would create a character like Porphyria's lover? How does the use of a dramatic monologue affect your reading experience and your judgment of the speaker? Compare this dramatic monologue to that of Macbeth on page 296 or to another you have read.

## *Writing Options*

1. Assume the identity of the speaker and write the defense you would use at your trial to explain the events that led up to the murder.

2. Give your judgment of what would be a just punishment for the speaker.

*Poetry/Letter*

# Sonnet 43

ELIZABETH BARRETT BROWNING

# A Warning Against Passion

CHARLOTTE BRONTË (brän tē)

## Examine What You Know

The two selections you are about to read express very different attitudes about romantic relationships. How would you describe your approach to romance? Below are four scales on which you can judge yourself. For each set of opposite qualities, decide approximately at which end of the line you think your romantic personality falls.

| Idealistic | Adventurous | Emotional | Open |
|---|---|---|---|
| | | | |
| Practical | Cautious | Rational | Reserved |

## Expand Your Knowledge

Elizabeth Barrett and Robert Browning were two of England's most famous lovers. When they met, Elizabeth, an invalid, was already famous, while Robert was just beginning his career. Elizabeth's overprotective father strongly opposed Robert's attentions. The two lovers eventually eloped to Italy, where Elizabeth's health improved and their careers flourished. Elizabeth secretly wrote forty-four poems, including this sonnet, during their courtship, but she did not show them to Robert until after they married. The poems were titled *Sonnets from the Portuguese* to hide the identity of the two lovers.

Charlotte Brontë, the author of the famous novel *Jane Eyre,* offers a different perspective on love. Her personal letter to her close friend Ellen Nussey, or Nell, responds to Nussey's request for advice in handling the attentions of a Mr. Vincent. Nussey, a quiet, reserved young woman, feared a marriage proposal from him, since the idea of an intimate relationship with someone she hardly knew frightened her. Although Mr. Vincent never proposed, Brontë's letter has become classic advice.

## Enrich Your Reading

■ *Biographies of the authors can be found in the Reader's Handbook.*

**Evaluating the Author's Attitude**  As you read, rate each author on the scales above. Since the Brontë selection is somewhat difficult, use the footnotes if you need help. Evaluate the authors' attitudes toward love and compare them to your own.

# Sonnet 43

ELIZABETH BARRETT BROWNING

How do I love thee? Let me count the ways.
I love thee to the depth and breadth and height
My soul can reach, when feeling out of sight
For the ends of Being and ideal Grace.
5  I love thee to the level of every day's
Most quiet need, by sun and candlelight.
I love thee freely, as men strive for Right;
I love thee purely, as they turn from Praise.
I love thee with the passion put to use
10  In my old griefs, and with my childhood's faith.
I love thee with a love I seemed to lose
With my lost saints—I love thee with the breath,
Smiles, tears, of all my life!—and, if God choose,
I shall but love thee better after death.

YOUNG GIRL WRITING A LOVE LETTER  c.
1755  Pietro Antonio Rotari  The Norton Simon
Foundation, Pasadena, California.

## *R*esponding *to Reading*

### First Impressions of "Sonnet 43"

1. Discuss whether you like the poem and the feelings it expresses.

### Second Thoughts on "Sonnet 43"

2. Evaluate the different ways of loving that Browning "counts." Which ways make sense to you, and which ways seem impractical or unrealistic?

3. In several places the speaker describes her love in religious terms. What does this convey about her attitudes toward love and religion?

4. Do you think it is desirable to love or be loved in these ways? Explain.

# A Warning Against Passion

## CHARLOTTE BRONTË

*November 20th, 1840.*

My Dearest Nell,
That last letter of thine treated of matters so high and important I cannot delay answering it for a day. Now I am about to write thee a discourse,[1] and a piece of advice which thou must take as if it came from thy grandmother.

But in the first place, before I begin with thee, I have a word to whisper in the ear of Mr. Vincent, and I wish it could reach him. In the name of St. Chrysostom, St. Simon, and St. Jude,[2] why does not that amiable young gentleman come forward like a man and say all that he has to say personally, instead of trifling with kinsmen and kinswomen. "Mr. Vincent," I say, "go personally, and say: 'Miss ———, I want to speak to you.'[3] Miss ——— will of course civilly answer: 'I am at your service, Mr. Vincent.' And then, when the room is cleared of all but yourself and herself, just take a chair nearer. Insist upon her laying down that silly . . . work, and listening to you. Then begin, in a clear, distinct, deferential, but determined voice: 'Miss ———, I have a question to put to you—a very important question: "Will you take me as your husband, for better, for worse. I am not a rich man, but I have sufficient to support us. I am not a

great man, but I love you honestly and truly. Miss ———, if you knew the world better you would see that this is an offer not to be despised—a kind attached heart and a moderate competency.'" Do this, Mr. Vincent, and you may succeed. Go on writing sentimental and love-sick letters to ———, and I would not give sixpence for your suit." So much for Mr. Vincent.

Now Miss ———'s turn comes to swallow the black bolus,[4] called a friend's advice. Say to her: "Is the man a fool? Is he a knave? A humbug, a hypocrite, a ninny, a noodle? If he is

---

1. **discourse:** communication of ideas by conversation or writing.

2. **St. Chrysostom, St. Simon, and St. Jude:** saints known for their honesty, sincerity, and courage. The reference suggests that Brontë has a low opinion of Mr. Vincent's tactics.

3. Brontë writes as if she is addressing Mr. Vincent. She advises him to speak directly to Nell rather than write to her relatives, as he had been doing. "Miss———," an example of a standard Victorian technique for discussing people without using their names, refers to Nell.

4. **bolus** (bō′ ləs): a small, round lump or mass, as of chewed food. At this point Brontë begins her advice to Nell. Brontë pretends, perhaps in an effort to save her shy friend from embarrassment, that Nell will be relaying Brontë's advice to Miss ———.

---

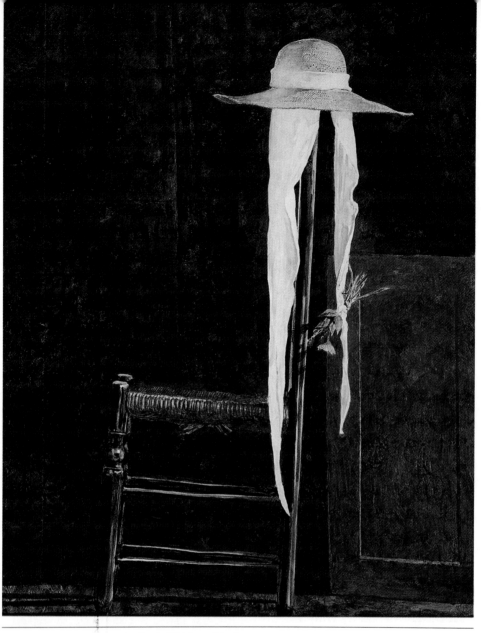

WOLFBANE 1984 James Wyeth © 1984 James Wyeth.

any or all of these, of course there is no sense in trifling with him. Cut him short at once—blast his hopes with lightning rapidity and keenness. Is he something better than this? Has he at least common sense, a good disposition, a manageable temper? Then consider the matter." Say further: "You feel a disgust toward him now—an utter <u>repugnance</u>. Very likely, but be so good as to remember you don't know him; you have only had three or four days' acquaintance with him. Longer and closer intimacy might reconcile you to a wonderful extent. And now I'll tell you a word of truth, at which you may be offended or not as you like." Say to her: "From what I know of your character, and I think I know it pretty

*Words to Know and Use* | **repugnance** (ri pug′ nəns) *n.* extreme dislike or distaste

well, I should say you will never love before marriage. After that ceremony is over, and after you have had some months to settle down, and to get accustomed to the creature you have taken for your worse half, you will probably make a most affectionate and happy wife; even if the individual should not prove all you could wish, you will be indulgent toward his little follies and foibles,[5] and will not feel much annoyance at them. This will especially be the case if he should have sense sufficient to allow you to guide him in important matters." Say also: "I hope you will not have the romantic folly to wait for what the French call 'une grande passion.' My good girl, 'une grande passion' is 'une grande folie.'[6] Mediocrity in all things is wisdom; mediocrity in the sensations is superlative wisdom." Say to her: "When you are as old as I am (I am sixty at least, being your grandmother), you will find that the majority of those worldly precepts,[7] whose seeming coldness shocks and repels us in youth, are founded in wisdom."

No girl should fall in love till the offer is actually made. This maxim is just. I will even extend and confirm it: No young lady should fall in love till the offer has been made, accepted, the marriage ceremony performed, and the first half year of wedded life has passed away. A woman may then begin to love, but with great precaution, very coolly, very moderately, very rationally. If she ever loves so much that a harsh word or a cold look cuts her to the heart she is a fool. If she ever loves so much that her husband's will is her

law, and that she has got into a habit of watching his looks in order that she may anticipate his wishes, she will soon be a neglected fool.

Did I not once tell you of an instance of a relative of mine who cared for a young lady till he began to suspect that she cared more for him and then instantly conceived a sort of contempt for her?[8] You know to what I allude—never as you value your ears mention the circumstance—but I have two studies.[9] You are my study for the success, the credit, and the respectability of a quiet, tranquil character; Mary is my study for the contempt, the remorse, the misconstruction which follow the development of feelings in themselves noble, warm, generous, devoted, and profound, but which, being too freely revealed, too frankly bestowed, are not estimated at their real value. I never hope to see in this world a character more truly noble. She would die willingly for one she loved. Her intellect and her attainments are of the very highest standard. Yet I doubt whether Mary will every marry. . . . ❧

---

5. **foibles** (foi′ bəlz): small weaknesses or frailties of character.

6. **'une grande passion'** is **'une grande folie':** a great passion is a great foolishness. The phrases are French.

7. **precepts:** commandments or directions meant as rules of conduct.

8. Brontë refers to a failed romance between her other friend Mary Taylor and her brother, Branwell.

9. Brontë contrasts her two friends, the sensible Nell and the more romantic and passionate Mary Taylor. Ironically, Brontë's personality resembled Mary's much more than Nell's.

| *Words to Know and Use* | **indulgent** (in dul′ jənt) *adj.* kind or lenient, often to excess<br>**mediocrity** (mē′ dē ăk′ rə tē) *n.* the quality or state of being ordinary, neither very good nor very bad |
| --- | --- |

# *explain*

## *R*esponding to Reading

### First Impressions of "A Warning Against Passion"

**1.** Do you think you would like Brontë? Why or why not?

### Second Thoughts on "A Warning Against Passion"

**2.** Summarize Brontë's advice about love and marriage in your own words. Which aspects of her advice do you agree with? Which do you disagree with? Explain your opinions.

**3.** How do you think Brontë views men? Use evidence from the letter to support your opinion.

**4.** Compare Brontë's views about love and marriage to those of most people today. Would young people be better off if they adopted her views?

### Comparing the Selections

**5.** Which of the two authors do you think would make a better wife? Why?

**6.** Discuss how you rated each author on the Romantic Attitudes Scale. Use your evaluation to contrast Brontë and Browning.

## *W*riting Options

**1.** Write a parody, or humorous imitation, of "Sonnet 43" describing a less-than-ideal relationship, such as "How Do I Hate Thee?"

**2.** Write a note of advice about love from Brontë to Browning or vice versa.

## *V*ocabulary Practice

**Exercise: Analogies** Write the letter of the word pair that expresses a relationship closest to that of the original pair.

**1.** MEDIOCRITY : EXCELLENCE :: (a) dullness : boredom
(b) eyes : sight (c) company : insurance (d) dimness : brightness
**2.** DEFERENTIAL: DISRESPECTFUL :: (a) annoying : soothing
(b) tall : taller (c) gloomy : depressing (d) literary : poetic
**3.** REPUGNANCE : DISGUST :: (a) swimming : backstroke
(b) airplanes : wings (c) worship : adoration (d) fin : fish
**4.** PARENT: INDULGENT :: (a) giant : small (b) criminal : honest
c) athlete : strong (d) baby : old
**5.** COMPETENCY : SKILL :: (a) education : learning (b) lies : truth
(c) money : checkbook (d) memory : mind

> *Words to Know and Use*
>
> ---
>
> **competency**
> **deferential**
> **indulgent**
> **mediocrity**
> **repugnance**

## Like
the Sun

R. K. NARAYAN (nu rī yən)

### Examine What You Know

In small groups role-play a situation like the following: Your friend has just bought a new outfit, gotten a radical new haircut, or has a new romance. Your friend, who is very proud of and pleased with the new look or relationship, asks your opinion. You really think that the outfit or haircut or romantic interest is terrible. What will you say to your friend? Act out the parts of the two friends.

### Expand Your Knowledge

This story takes place in a village in India. The Indian school is based on the British school system, in which students enter secondary school at age eleven. For the next seven years they progress through forms, the British equivalent of grades. In this story the teacher's students are in the third form, comparable to ninth grade in our country. The principal of their school is called the headmaster.

The crucial episode of the story revolves around the singing and playing of Indian music. This music sounds unusual to Western ears because it is based on a different musical scale and does not rely on harmonies. In this story the vocalist sings well-known traditional songs that reflect India's centuries-old musical heritage.

### Write Before You Read

Most people tell white lies occasionally. Recall the last one you told. Why did you tell it? Was the result harmless, damaging, or helpful? Write about the incident in your journal or on a sheet of paper.

■ *A biography of the author can be found on page 617.*

# *Like the Sun*

## R.K. NARAYAN

MAN IN WINDOW 1980 Rufino Tamayo Courtesy of B. Lewin Galleries, Palm Springs, California.

Truth, Sekhar reflected, is like the sun. I suppose no human being can ever look it straight in the face without blinking or being dazed. He realized that, morning till night, the essence of human relationships consisted in tempering truth so that it might not shock. This day he set apart as a unique day—at least one day in the year we must give and take absolute Truth whatever may happen. Otherwise life is not worth living. The day ahead seemed to him full of possibilities. He told no one of his experiment. It was a quiet resolve, a secret pact between him and eternity.

The very first test came while his wife served him his morning meal. He showed hesitation over a tidbit, which she had thought was her culinary masterpiece. She asked, "Why, isn't it good?" At other times he would have said, considering her feelings in the matter, "I feel full up; that's all." But today he said, "It isn't good. I'm unable to swallow it." He saw her wince and said to himself, Can't be helped. Truth is like the sun.

His next trial was in the common room when one of his colleagues came up and said,

"Did you hear of the death of so and so? Don't you think it a pity?" "No," Sekhar answered. "He was such a fine man—" the other began. But Sekhar cut him short with: "Far from it. He always struck me as a mean and selfish brute."

During the last period, when he was teaching geography for Third Form A, Sekhar received a note from the headmaster: "Please see me before you go home." Sekhar said to himself: It must be about these horrible test papers. A hundred papers in the boys' scrawls; he had shirked this work for weeks, feeling all the time as if a sword were hanging over his head.

The bell rang and the boys burst out of the class.

Sekhar paused for a moment outside the headmaster's room to button up his coat; that

612

was another subject the headmaster always sermonized about.

He stepped in with a very polite "Good evening, sir."

The headmaster looked up at him in a very friendly manner and asked, "Are you free this evening?"

Sekhar replied, "Just some outing which I have promised the children at home—"

"Well, you can take them out another day. Come home with me now."

"Oh . . . yes, sir, certainly . . . " And then he added timidly, "Anything special, sir?"

"Yes," replied the headmaster, smiling to himself . . . "You didn't know my weakness for music?"

"Oh, yes, sir . . . "

"I've been learning and practicing secretly, and now I want you to hear me this evening. I've engaged a drummer and a violinist to accompany me—this is the first time I'm doing it full dress[1] and I want your opinion. I know it will be valuable."

Sekhar's taste in music was well known. He was one of the most dreaded music critics in the town. But he never anticipated his musical inclinations would lead him to this trial. . . . "Rather a surprise for you, isn't it?" asked the headmaster. "I've spent a fortune on it behind closed doors. . . ." They started for the headmaster's house. "God hasn't given me a child, but at least let him not deny me the consolation of music," the headmaster said, pathetically, as they walked. He incessantly chattered about music: how he began one day out of sheer boredom; how his teacher at first laughed at him and then gave him hope; how his ambition in life was to forget himself in music.

At home the headmaster proved very <u>ingratiating</u>. He sat Sekhar on a red silk carpet, set

before him several dishes of delicacies, and fussed over him as if he were a son-in-law of the house. He even said, "Well, you must listen with a free mind. Don't worry about these test papers." He added half humorously, "I will give you a week's time."

"Make it ten days, sir," Sekhar pleaded.

"All right, granted," the headmaster said generously. Sekhar felt really relieved now— he would attack them at the rate of ten a day and get rid of the nuisance.

The headmaster lighted incense sticks. "Just to create the right atmosphere," he explained. A drummer and a violinist, already seated on a Rangoon mat, were waiting for him. The headmaster sat down between them like a professional at a concert, cleared his throat, and began an alapana,[2] and paused to ask, "Isn't it good Kalyani?"[3] Sekhar pretended not to have heard the question. The headmaster went on to sing a full song composed by Thyagaraja[4] and followed it with two more. All the time the headmaster was singing, Sekhar went on commenting within himself. He croaks like a dozen frogs. He is bellowing like a buffalo. Now he sounds like loose window shutters in a storm.

The incense sticks burnt low. Sekhar's head throbbed with the medley of sounds that had <u>assailed</u> his eardrums for a couple of hours now. He felt half stupefied. The headmaster had gone nearly hoarse, when he paused to ask, "Shall I go on?" Sekhar replied, "Please don't, sir, I think this will do. . . ." The headmaster looked stunned. His face was beaded

---

1. **full dress:** in rehearsal of an entire performance, with costumes included.

2. **alapana** (ā läp′ än ə): improvisational Indian music done in a classical manner.

3. **Kalyani:** traditional folk songs from the state of Mysore, India.

4. **Thyagaraja:** 1756–1847; famous Indian composer.

---

*Words to Know and Use* | **ingratiating** (in grā′ shē āt′ iŋ) *adj.* gaining favor or acceptance by deliberate effort
**assail** (ə sāl′) *v.* to attack violently

with perspiration. Sekhar felt the greatest pity for him. But he felt he could not help it. No judge delivering a sentence felt more pained and helpless. Sekhar noticed that the headmaster's wife peeped in from the kitchen, with eager curiosity. The drummer and the violinist put away their burdens with an air of relief. The headmaster removed his spectacles, mopped his brow, and asked, "Now, come out with your opinion."

"Can't I give it tomorrow, sir?" Sekhar asked tentatively.

"No. I want it immediately—your frank opinion. Was it good?"

"No, sir . . . ," Sekhar replied.

"Oh! . . . Is there any use continuing my lessons?"

"Absolutely none, sir . . . ," Sekhar said with his voice trembling. He felt very unhappy that he could not speak more soothingly. Truth, he reflected, required as much strength to give as to receive.

All the way home he felt worried. He felt that his official life was not going to be smooth sailing hereafter. There were questions of increment and confirmation and so on, all depending upon the headmaster's goodwill. All kinds of worries seemed to be in store for him. . . . Did not Harischandra[5] lose his throne, wife, child, because he would speak nothing less than the absolute Truth, whatever happened?

At home his wife served him with a sullen face. He knew she was still angry with him for his remark of the morning. Two casualties for today, Sekhar said to himself. If I practice it for a week, I don't think I shall have a single friend left.

He received a call from the headmaster in his classroom next day. He went up apprehensively.

"Your suggestion was useful. I have paid off the music master. No one would tell me the truth about my music all these days. Why such antics at my age! Thank you. By the way, what about those test papers?"

"You gave me ten days, sir, for correcting them."

"Oh, I've reconsidered it. I must positively have them here tomorrow. . . ." A hundred papers in a day! That meant all night's sitting up! "Give me a couple of days, sir . . ."

"No. I must have them tomorrow morning. And remember, every paper must be thoroughly scrutinized."

"Yes, sir," Sekhar said, feeling that sitting up all night with a hundred test papers was a small price to pay for the luxury of practicing Truth. 🙢

---

5. **Harischandra:** the ancient ruler of the state of Mysore in what is now India.

## INSIGHT

### The Wayfarer

STEPHEN CRANE

The wayfarer
Perceiving the pathway to truth
Was struck with astonishment.
It was thickly grown with weeds.
"Ha," he said.
"I see that none has passed here
In a long time."
Later he saw that each weed
Was a singular knife.
"Well," he mumbled at last,
"Doubtless there are other roads."

---

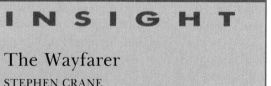

*Words to Know and Use*

**tentatively** (ten′ tə tiv′ lē) *adv.* timidly; hesitantly
**sullen** (sul′ ən) *adj.* gloomy; ill humored; resentfully silent
**scrutinize** (skroot′ ′n īz′) *v.* to examine closely

## Responding to Reading

### First Impressions

**1.** What is your first impression of the teacher Sekhar? In your journal or on a piece of paper, write words and phrases to describe him.

### Second Thoughts

**2.** What kind of person is Sekhar?

**Think about**

- his reasons for telling the truth
- his relationships with other people
- his attitude toward his work
- his reputation as a music critic

**3.** Sekhar says that if you don't tell the truth, life isn't worth living. Why does he only tell the truth one day a year?

**4.** Sekhar's truth experiments have some unexpected results. Explain the reactions of his wife and the headmaster. Are their reactions natural?

**5.** Reread the last sentence of the story. Despite the problems, does Sekhar really feel that it was all worthwhile? Will he add more truthful days to his year?

### Broader Connections

**6.** Sometimes you are asked to judge other students' work in peer groups. How truthful do you try to be? Do you temper the truth, or are you totally honest? What kinds of remarks prove most helpful?

## Literary Concept: Third-Person Point of View

When planning a story, an author usually chooses between **first-person point of view,** in which the narrator is a character, and **third-person point of view,** in which the narrator is not a story participant.

Third-person narrators can be classified as omniscient or limited, depending on how much they know. In the **omniscient** point of view, the narrator is all-knowing and so can describe every character's thoughts. By contrast, a narrator in a third-person **limited** point of view possesses limited knowledge, often confined to one or two characters. "Like the Sun" is an example of third-person limited narration because the narrator only knows the thoughts of Sekhar. How would this story be different if told by a first-person narrator, perhaps the headmaster, or by an omniscient narrator, who reports everyone's thoughts?

**Concept Review: Theme**   What do you think the author is trying to say about truth and personal relationships?

# Writing Options

1. Write out what you believe the headmaster is thinking during the scene where he thanks Sekhar for his honesty but demands the graded papers.

2. Rewrite Sekhar's comments to his wife, the other teacher, and his headmaster in a way that communicates truth without hurting their feelings.

3. This story begins with a proverb about the truth being like the sun. Write your own proverb about truth.

4. Using an omniscient point of view, describe an incident in which Sekhar is told an unpleasant truth about himself by another character. Show how Sekhar responds to such honesty.

# Vocabulary Practice

**Exercise** Decide whether the boldfaced words are used correctly in the sentences below. Identify each usage as *Correct* or *Incorrect.* If the answer is *Incorrect,* write a sentence explaining why.

1. Few critics are known for **tempering** their criticisms with words of encouragement and support.
2. A person who seeks truth with **resolve** lacks willpower and a sense of purpose.
3. A critic who predicts that a musician will **assail** his listeners' ears is being complimentary.
4. Teachers who **shirk** their duties are probably very effective.
5. If a husband sees his wife **wince,** he knows she is happy.
6. Sekhar's **ingratiating** insults please his headmaster.
7. A student who explores the **essence** of human relationships wants only superficial information.
8. To **scrutinize** a paper, the teacher must study it carefully.
9. For a husband, dining with a **sullen** wife can be unpleasant.
10. When Sekhar responds **tentatively** to the headmaster, he shows that he is not timid or uncertain.

*Words to Know and Use*

assail
essence
ingratiating
resolve
scrutinize
shirk
sullen
tempering
tentatively
wince

## *Options for Learning*

**1 • Truth in Advertising** With a small group collect printed ads that stretch the truth to sell a product. Decide how each ad distorts the truth. For example, does it use exaggeration? half-truths? misleading claims? Choose one advertisement and create a completely honest revision of it. Compare your version with the original and discuss why advertisers stretch the truth.

**2 • The Music of India** Choose a type of Indian music—classical, folk, or popular—that you would like to research. Your local library or music store may offer to help you in finding recordings and information. Play some of the recordings you find for the class. If possible, provide illustrations of the instruments and explain how they are played.

**3 • Grading the Teacher** Create a report card for Sekhar that grades him as his headmaster might. Include categories such as "Work Habits," "Sensitivity," and "Honesty." Explain your evaluation to the class.

**4 • Know the Truth** See how many proverbs about truth you can find. Check references such as *Bartlett's Familiar Quotations* and the *Dictionary of Quotations,* as well as asking family and friends.

### 📖 FACT FINDER

*If Sekhar corrects 100 papers in 24 hours and spends the same amount of time on each, how many minutes will he spend on each one?*

### R. K. Narayan
1906–

Narayan is one of India's greatest writers. Ironically, he turned to writing after he proved a failure at teaching, having held two different jobs for a grand total of two days. As the son of a prominent headmaster, Narayan grew up in a household where education was highly valued, and he was pushed toward an educational career. Though educated at fine private schools, he confesses, he hated school because he did not like having other people tell him what to do. Eventually, Narayan gained fame as a novelist and short story writer. Most of his stories are set in the imaginary village of Malgudi, South India, where characters of all types must learn to deal with hardship. Although struggles for existence are central to Narayan's work, he usually treats his characters with a comic, sympathetic touch.

Narayan writes his fiction in English, though he was raised in India and still resides in Mysore, the city of his birth. Because India was once a colony of Great Britain, the English language continues to play an important role in India's culture. Narayan has said about his second language, "I was never aware that I was using a different, a foreign language. . . . English is a very adaptable language."

*Poetry*

# Eve to Her Daughters

## JUDITH WRIGHT

## Examine What You Know

Are there differences between the ways men and women think and act? With your classmates discuss what those differences might be and why they exist. Consider the effects of cultural expectations, family and school expectations, and biological differences on both sexes.

## Expand Your Knowledge

Over the centuries the biblical story of Adam and Eve has been retold in many ways. Poets, storytellers, cartoonists, and even advertisers have adapted this story for different audiences and for different purposes. Wright's poem is a dramatic monologue in which Eve is speaking to her daughters long after she and Adam were banished from the Garden of Eden. In expressing her thoughts and concerns about their situation, Eve focuses on her life with Adam and on her observations about his character. As you read the poem, think about the speaker's feelings concerning the differences between man and woman.

## Enrich Your Reading

**Reading Critically**   Poets are so economical with words that their lines often hold more meaning than a literal reading suggests. To get the most meaning from a poem, you need to think carefully about individual lines. In this poem, questions in the margin will help you consider Wright's meaning. In your journal or reading log, use a chart like the one below to record answers to the questions. Apply the same kind of critical thinking to other poems you read.

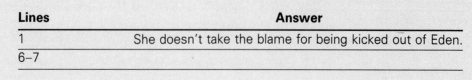

| Lines | Answer |
|-------|--------|
| 1 | She doesn't take the blame for being kicked out of Eden. |
| 6–7 | |

■ *A biography of the author can be found in the Reader's Handbook.*

# Eve to Her Daughters

JUDITH WRIGHT

It was not I who began it.
Turned out into draughty caves,
hungry so often, having to work for our bread,
hearing the children whining,
5  I was nevertheless not unhappy.
Where Adam went I was fairly contented to go.
I adapted myself to the punishment: it was my life.

But Adam, you know . . . !
He kept on brooding over the insult,
10  over the trick They had played on us, over the scolding.
He had discovered a flaw in himself
and he had to make up for it.
Outside Eden the earth was imperfect,
the seasons changed, the game was fleet-footed,
15  he had to work for our living, and he didn't like it.
He even complained of my cooking
(it was hard to compete with Heaven).

So, he set to work.
The earth must be made a new Eden
20  with central heating, domesticated animals,
mechanical harvesters, combustion engines,
escalators, refrigerators,
and modern means of communication
and multiplied opportunities for safe investment
25  and higher education for Abel and Cain
and the rest of the family.
You can see how his pride has been hurt.

**1** *How does Eve's version of the story differ from the traditional Bible interpretation?*

**6–7** *In the beginning, what was Eve's attitude toward male-female roles?*

**10** *Who are "They"?*
**11–12** *What flaw did Adam think he had?*

**19–26** *What is the purpose of all our modern conveniences?*

THE GARDEN OF EDEN  Alvar  Edmund Newman Galleries, Swampscott, Massachusetts.

In the process he had to unravel everything,
because he believed that mechanism
30   was the whole secret—he was always mechanical-minded.
He got to the very inside of the whole machine
exclaiming as he went, So this is how it works!
And now that I know how it works, why, I must have
    invented it.
35   As for God and the Other, they cannot be demonstrated,
and what cannot be demonstrated
doesn't exist.
You see, he had always been jealous.

**30** *What secret was Adam trying to find out?*

**35–37** *What is Adam's logic?*

**38** *Of what is Adam jealous?*

Yes, he got to the center
40  where nothing at all can be demonstrated.
And clearly he doesn't exist; but he refuses
to accept the conclusion.
You see, he was always an egotist.

It was warmer than this in the cave;
45  there was none of this fallout.
I would suggest, for the sake of the children,
that it's time you took over.

But you are my daughers, you inherit my own faults
   of character;
50  you are submissive, following Adam
even beyond existence.
Faults of character have their own logic
and it always works out.
I observed this with Abel and Cain.

55  Perhaps the whole elaborate fable
right from the beginning
is meant to demonstrate this; perhaps it's the whole secret.
Perhaps nothing exists but our faults?

But it's useless to make
60  such a suggestion to Adam.
He has turned himself into God,
who is faultless, and doesn't exist.

**46–47** *What is Eve's suggestion?*

**48–51** *In light of those faults, is she withdrawing her suggestion?*

**52–54** *Cain killed Abel. What feelings about her sons does Eve show in this passage?*

**55** *Why does she call it a fable?*

**61–62** *What attitude toward Adam does Eve show in this passage?*

## Responding to Reading

### First Impressions

1. Jot down words or phrases that describe your impressions of Eve.

### Second Thoughts

2. Is Adam typical of all men, and is Eve typical of all women? Explain your views in terms of your own ideas about men and women.

3. According to Eve, what are Adam's faults? Do you agree that these are faults? Explain your opinion.

4. Does Eve love Adam? Cite evidence from the poem to support your answer.

5. Specifically, what is Eve's message to her daughters?

6. In broader terms what is the author's message to today's society?

   **Think about**
   - the modern attitudes that Adam might represent
   - the modern "daughters of Eve" and their situation in the world
   - relationships between men and women today

## Literary Concept: Free Verse

A poem that has no regular rhythm, rhyme, or line length is called **free verse.** In free verse the stanzas may be of varying lengths depending on the ideas that are being developed. Writers of free verse have more options than writers of traditional poetic forms, since there is no given form they must follow. Compare "Eve to Her Daughters" with Shakespeare's "Sonnet 18," on page 226 or Wordsworth's "The Tables Turned," on page 528. What do you notice about the differences in the occurrence or pattern of rhythm, rhyme, and line length? Which poem gives more emphasis to ideas than to sound and structure?

**Concept Review: Tone**   In what ways does the author's tone, or attitude, change in the poem? Refer to specific line numbers in your answer.

## Writing Options

1. In a free verse poem, have Adam explain to his sons his version of what happened.

2. Make two lists that show what you think are the strengths and weaknesses of the opposite sex. Check the items with which Eve might agree.

*Fiction*

# Three Letters... and a Footnote

### HORACIO QUIROGA (hə rä′ shō kir ō′ gə)

## Examine What You Know

What do you do when you want to get the attention of someone of the opposite sex to whom you are attracted? Discuss with the class the subtle and not-so-subtle ways that people flirt. Distinguish between flirting habits that are more typical of men and those that are more typical of women.

## Expand Your Knowledge

Although Quiroga, who was from the South American country of Uruguay, wrote most of his stories more than sixty years ago, they are still popular today. Their appeal comes from a simple style that focuses on situations, attitudes, and feelings common to all of us. Quiroga uses an ancient storytelling device, the exchange of letters between two people, to present a young woman's reactions to the flirtatious behavior of men. Notice how he uses language of warfare, such as *maneuver, defense,* and *conquest,* to suggest his humorous attitude toward the "battle between the sexes."

## Enrich Your Reading

**Recognizing Generalizations**   A conclusion stated about a whole group of people or things is called a **generalization.** An example is "Most men are taller than their mothers." While some generalizations are true, some are untrue because they are too broad, as with "All men are taller than their mothers." Some generalizations are untrue because there is no evidence to back them up.

Some of the humor of this story comes from the generalizations that a character makes about the opposite sex. As you read, watch for these generalizations and decide whether you consider each to be true or false.

■ *A biography of the author can be found in the Reader's Handbook.*

# Three Letters... and a Footnote

## HORACIO QUIROGA

Sir:

I am taking the liberty of sending you these lines, hoping you will be good enough to publish them under your own name. I make this request of you because I am informed that no newspaper would accept these pages if I sign them myself. If you think it wiser, you may alter my impressions by giving them a few masculine touches, which indeed may improve them.

My work makes it necessary for me to take the streetcar twice a day, and for five years I have been making the same trip. Sometimes, on the return ride, I travel in the company of some of my girlfriends, but on the way to work I always go alone. I am twenty years old, tall, and not too thin. My mouth is somewhat large but not pale. My impression is that my eyes are not small. These outward features which I've estimated modestly, as you have observed, are nevertheless all I need to help me form an opinion of many men, in fact so many that I'm tempted to say all men.

You know also that you men have the habit before you board a streetcar of looking rapidly at its occupants through the windows. In that way you examine all the faces (of the women, of course, since they are the only ones that have any interest for you). After that little ceremony you enter and sit down.

Very well then; as soon as a man leaves the sidewalks, walks over to the car and looks inside, I know perfectly what sort of fellow he is, and I never make a mistake. I know if he is serious, or if he merely intends to invest the ten cents of his fare in finding an easy pickup. I quickly distinguish between those who like to ride at their ease and those who prefer less room at the side of some girl.

When the place beside me is unoccupied, I recognize accurately, according to the glance through the window, which men are <u>indifferent</u> and will sit down anywhere; which are only half-interested and will turn their heads in order to give us the once-over slowly, after they have sat down; and finally, which are the <u>enterprising</u> fellows who will pass by seven empty places so as to perch uncomfortably at my side, way back in the rear of the vehicle.

Presumably, these fellows are the most interesting. Quite contrary to the regular habit of girls who travel alone, instead of getting up and offering the inside place to the newcomer, I simply move over toward the window to leave plenty of room for the enterprising arrival.

Plenty of room! That's a meaningless phrase. Never will the three-quarters of a bench abandoned by a girl to her neighbor be

ON THE R & R 1985 Jerome Witkin NYNEX, White Plains, New York Courtesy of Sherry French Gallery, New York.

That's the way such men are: one could swear that they're thinking about the moon. However, all this time, the right foot (or the left) continues slipping delicately down the aforementioned plane.

I'll admit that while this is going on, I'm very far from being bored. With a mere glance as I shift toward the window, I have taken the measure of my gallant. I know whether he is a spirited fellow who yields to his first impulse or whether he is really someone brazen enough to give me cause for a little worry. I know whether he is a courteous young man or just a vulgar one, whether a hardened criminal or a tenderfoot pickpocket, whether he is really a seductive Beau Brummel (the *séduisant* and not the *séducteur* of the Frenchy) or a mere petty masher.[1]

At first view it might seem that only one kind of man would perform the act of letting his foot slip slyly over while his face wears a hypocritical mask, namely the thief. However, that is not so, and there isn't a girl that hasn't made this observation. For each different type she must have ready a special defense. But very often, especially if the man is quite young or poorly dressed, he is likely to be a pickpocket.

The tactics followed by the man never vary. First of all the sudden rigidity and the air of thinking about the moon. The next step is a fleeting glimpse at our person which seems to linger slightly over our face, but whose sole purpose is to estimate the distance that intervenes between his foot and ours. This information acquired, now the conquest begins.

sufficient. After moving and shifting at will, he seems suddenly overcome by a surprising motionlessness, to the point where he seems paralyzed. But that is mere appearance, for if anyone watches with suspicion this lack of movement, he will note that the body of the gentleman, imperceptibly and with a slyness that does honor to his absent-minded look, is slipping little by little down an imaginary inclined plane toward the window, where the girl happens to be, although he isn't looking at her and apparently has no interest in her at all.

---

1. **Beau Brummel . . . séduisant . . . petty masher:** terms to describe different types of men who flirt— the fancy dresser, the charming flirt, and the common, crude flirt.

---

*Words to Know and Use*

**imperceptibly** (im′ pər sep′ tə blē) *adj.* in a manner that is not plain to the senses or mind; gradually or subtly
**hypocritical** (hip′ ə krit′ i kəl) *adj.* pretending to be more pious, honest, or virtuous than one really is

625

I think there are few things funnier than that maneuver you men execute, when you move your foot along in gradual shifts of toe and heel alternately. Obviously you men can't see the joke; but this pretty cat and mouse game, played with a size eleven shoe at one end and at the other, up above, near the roof, a simpering idiotic face (doubtless because of emotion), bears no comparison so far as absurdity is concerned with anything else you men do.

I said before that I was not bored with these performances. And my entertainment is based upon the following fact: from the moment the charmer has calculated with perfect precision the distance he has to cover with his foot, he rarely lets his gaze wander down again. He is certain of his measurement and he has no desire to put us on our guard by repeated glances. You will clearly realize that the attraction for him lies in making contact, and not in merely looking.

Very well then: when this amiable neighbor has gone about halfway, I start the same maneuver that he is executing, and I do it with equal slyness and the same semblance of absent-minded <u>preoccupation</u> with, let us say, my doll. Only, the movement of my foot is away from his. Not much; a few inches are enough.

It's a treat to behold, presently, my neighbor's surprise when, upon arriving finally at the calculated spot, he contacts absolutely nothing. Nothing! His size eleven shoe is entirely alone. This is too much for him; first he takes a look at the floor, and then at my face. My thought is still wandering a thousand leagues away, playing with my doll; but the fellow begins to understand.

Fifteen out of seventeen times (I mention these figures after long experience), the an-noying gentleman gives up the enterprise. In the two remaining cases I am forced to resort to a warning look. It isn't necessary for this look to indicate by its expression a feeling of insult, or contempt, or anger: it is enough to make a movement of the head in his direction, toward him but without looking straight at him. In these cases it is better always to avoid crossing glances with a man who by chance has been really and deeply attracted to us. There may be in any pickpocket the makings of a dangerous thief. This fact is well known to the cashiers who guard large amounts of money and also to young women, not thin, with mouths not little and eyes not small, as in the case with yours truly,

M.R.

Dear Miss:

Deeply grateful for your kindness. I'll sign my name with much pleasure to the article on your impressions, as you request. Nevertheless, it would interest me very much, and purely as your collaborator, to know your answer to the following question. Aside from the seventeen concrete cases you mention, haven't you ever felt the slightest attraction toward some neighbor, tall or short, blond or dark, stout or lean? Haven't you ever felt the vaguest temptation to yield, ever so vague, which made the withdrawing of your own foot disagreeable and troublesome?

H.Q.

Sir:

To be frank, yes, once, once in my life, I felt that temptation to yield to someone, or more accurately, that lack of energy in my foot to which you refer. That person was *you*. But you didn't have sense to take advantage of it.

M.R.

626

*Words to Know and Use*

**preoccupation** (prē ăk′ yə pā′ s/hən) *n.* the state or condition of being absorbed in one's thoughts

# e x p l a i n

## Responding to Reading

### First Impressions

1. Did you find the letters humorous? Why or why not?

### Second Thoughts

2. Why does M. R. write to the newspaperman?

   **Think about**
   • the reasons she gives in the beginning
   • what she says in her second letter

3. How does the woman, M. R., feel about the way men act toward women? Do you think she resents their actions, or does she treat each encounter as a game? Explain your opinion.

4. M. R. makes several generalizations about men and their motives. Do you agree or disagree with her? Why?

5. What is ironic, or opposite of what you might have expected, about the way the story ends?

6. What do you think is the meaning of the term *footnote* in the title?

## Writing Options

1. Write H. Q.'s letter of reply to the second letter from M. R.

2. Write a "footnote" that describes some method of flirtation. Use language of warfare to show the tactics, moves, and results of an encounter between two interested strangers.

## Vocabulary Practice

**Exercise** Write the letter of the word that is not related in meaning to the other words in each set.

1. (a) precise (b) indifferent (c) careful (d) cautious
2. (a) ambitious (b) eager (c) enterprising (d) easygoing
3. (a) imperceptibly (b) openly (c) gradually (d) barely
4. (a) sickly (b) insincere (c) dishonest (d) hypocritical
5. (a) preoccupation (b) prediction (c) forecast (d) prophecy

*Words to Know and Use*

---

enterprising
imperceptibly
preoccupation
hypocritical
indifferent

# WRITER'S WORKSHOP

## EXPOSITION

Many people believe that the best accompaniment to good food is pleasant conversation. In fact, some hosts spend more time planning guest lists than they do arranging menus. To ensure that a social event is festive and entertaining, hosts will often go to great lengths to combine people of varied backgrounds, experience, and attitudes—people who will find one another interesting. In this assignment, you'll have the opportunity to create and explain your own guest list for a stimulating dinner party. Your guests will be characters from selections in this book.

> Here is your PASSkey to this assignment.

### GUIDED ASSIGNMENT:
### DINNER FOR EIGHT

Imagine that you are giving a dinner party for eight literary characters. Write a composition in which you explain why you chose these particular pairs of characters and how you think they might react to each other.

**P**URPOSE: To explain

**A**UDIENCE: Your classmates

**S**UBJECT: A dinner party of literary characters

**S**TRUCTURE: A multi-paragraph composition

## Prewriting

**STEP 1** **Choose your guests** At least two of your guests must come from this subunit. Your remaining guests can be from any other selections in the book.

To begin, list the characters from all the selections in this subunit. Do not cross out any names yet—someone might make an interesting combination with a character from another subunit. Then look at the table of contents. Jot down names of memorable characters from other selections you have read. Now start pairing. You may make any combination of gender and age. Try combining one character with different partners until you find the most interesting combination. Remember that people don't necessarily need to have had similar experiences in order to be good dinner companions; disagreement can provoke interesting exchanges.

**STEP 2** **Chart characteristics**   Once you have selected your four pairs, explore possible conversational topics by making a chart of their personality characteristics, interests, and attitudes on various subjects. Here is a chart one student made about her first pair, Charlotte Brontë from "A Warning Against Passion" and Zhang Jie's mother from "Love Must Not Be Forgotten."

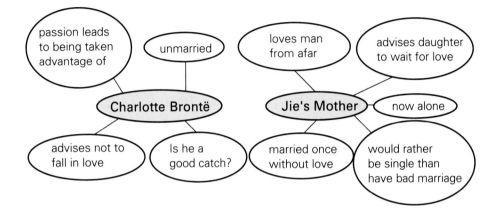

In addition, describe each individual character with four carefully chosen adjectives. Keep this list of adjectives for later use.

**STEP 3** **Organize your ideas**   Beside each pair of characters, jot down your reasons for pairing them, and list a conversational topic or two. For example, the student who put Brontë and Jie's mother together thought they would make an interesting pair because the advice they gave to others was opposite. She noted, however, that the women also had something in common—both gave advice about love although neither had been particularly successful herself. The student thought they might exchange personal experiences and end up becoming friends even though they disagreed about love.

## Drafting

**STEP 1** **Draft an introductory paragraph**   The unusual nature of this assignment requires you to think of a clever way to introduce your paper. You need to capture your readers' interest and explain what your paper is about. One student who chose to invite only pairs with opposing beliefs wrote the following introduction.

> A hostess who wants a calm evening of boring conversation and good manners should invite people whose lives and goals are almost identical. On the other hand,

◀ STUDENT MODEL

for an exciting and unpredictable evening, the guests should have firm beliefs based on totally different experiences and be willing to speak out for those beliefs. A dinner party of outspoken literary characters from a variety of works should result in a lively evening of excellent conversation, both for the guests and the hostess.

**STEP 2** **Draft the body paragraphs** Draft a separate paragraph for each pair of dinner partners. In each paragraph be sure to explain why you paired the characters, what direction you think the conversation will take, and how you think the characters will react to each other.

Make sure the characters' reactions are true to their personalities as portrayed in the selections. Use your list of adjectives that describe each character in Step 2 of Prewriting to keep focused on the character's personality and outlook.

---

### Special Tip

Choose any order in which to present your characters. You might begin with the pair that has the most in common and progress to the pair with the least in common. You might start with the pair who would be most in conflict and end with the pair who would be most compatible. You might save your best, most exciting combination for last.

---

**STEP 3** **Draft your conclusion** The conclusion of your paper could be a brief summary of how you think the characters will feel at the end of the party. Which partners will end up as friends? as enemies? Who will learn something? Will anyone change his or her mind about an issue?

## Revising and Editing

Before exchanging papers with a peer editor for suggested revisions, try these methods of revising your own paper.

- Check transitions from one paragraph to the next. Although each paragraph discusses a different pair of characters, include words to help your reader follow your thinking. An example is "To the right of Charlotte Brontë and Jie's mother will sit . . ."

- Check pronouns and their antecedents. Is it clear about whom you are talking at all times? Too many *she*'s and *he*'s may confuse the reader.
- Add an adverb to both your introduction and your conclusion to make a verb in each more specific.

Once you have completed your own revisions, exchange papers with a classmate and review each other's work. Use the following questions as a guide.

## Revision Checklist

1. Does the introduction explain the subject of the paper?
2. Does each paragraph explain why a particular pair of guests was chosen?
3. Does the writer explore ways the pair might interact and what their conversation will be about?
4. Are characters' reactions and points of view consistent with what you know from the selection?
5. Does the conclusion speculate about the party and its results?

**Editing** When you have finished revising your essay, proofread for spelling, clarity, and mechanics. Then make a clean, final copy.

## Presenting

In a small group, read your essay aloud. Discuss the similarities and differences in the ways different students paired characters. As a group, choose favorite pairs of characters, make up dialogue, and act out dinner party conversations in front of the class.

## Reflecting on Your Writing

Briefly answer the following questions about your writing. Place your answers with your paper in your writing portfolio.

1. Was it difficult to imagine characters from different selections interacting with each other?
2. Did the assignment stimulate your imagination?
3. Did you find the introduction and conclusion easier or harder to write than the body paragraphs? Why?
4. Did you learn anything new about the characters?

# LANGUAGE

### WORKSHOP

## PARALLELISM

> The word *and* is used to join similar sentence parts. These similar sentence parts should be in the same form. When they are in the same form, they are **parallel.**

Consider the following sentence:

**Faulty**     During their conversation Nell asked Charlotte for *her opinion* and *to give advice.*

The parts *her opinion* and *to give advice* serve the same function in the sentence. They tell what Nell asked Charlotte for. Therefore, the two parts should be in the same form. The sentence is improved when the parts are parallel.

**Parallel**     During their conversation Nell asked Charlotte for her opinion and advice. (Both *opinion* and *advice* are nouns.)

Many sentences with faulty parallelism can be corrected in more than one way, although one change will probably sound the most natural. Compare these examples:

**Faulty**     A successful marriage requires self-confidence, independence, and you have to be cautious.

**Parallel**     A successful marriage requires you to be self-confident, independent, and cautious.

**Parallel**     A successful marriage requires self-confidence, independence, and caution.

**Faulty**     Elizabeth Browning was a poet of great ability and who was a good wife to Robert.

**Parallel**     Elizabeth Browning was a poet of great ability and a good wife to Robert.

**Parallel**     Elizabeth Browning was a poet who had great ability and who was a good wife to Robert.

Parallelism can be a very powerful technique in the hands of a good writer. Sometimes, a writer will use a series of parallelisms to create emphasis or drama. Look at this excerpt from President John F. Kennedy's Inaugural Address:

> Let every nation know, whether it wishes us well or ill, that we shall *pay any price, bear any burden, meet any hardship, support any friend, oppose any foe*, in order to assure the survival and the success of liberty.

Note the series of parallel phrases, each consisting of three words, each beginning with a verb, each ending with a noun, and each repeating the word *any*. Notice how this parallel structure captures your attention and pulls you along to the end of the sentence.

**Exercise 1**   For each of the following word groups, come up with one other word group that has the same form.

**Example**     in the evening

**Possible Answer**   *after the party*

1. a good poet
2. to write a letter
3. who lives in India
4. for a long time
5. brilliantly conceived

**Exercise 2**   Revise the following sentences to make the italicized parts of each sentence parallel.

1. Elizabeth Barrett grew up surrounded by *natural beauty* and *her family was loving*.
2. At the age of fifteen she fell from a horse; the accident *injured her spine* and *leaving her an invalid*.
3. Other tragedies also marred her childhood, including *the financial troubles of her father* and *her mother died*.
4. *She moved to London at the age of eighteen*, and *at twenty her first book of poetry was published*.
5. Her brother's death shortly thereafter contributed to making Elizabeth even more *fragile* and *she was sickly*.
6. Then, in the mid-1840's Elizabeth *met Robert Browning, had a tempestuous courtship*, and *marrying him*.
7. Robert Browning was *young, handsome, talented, scholarly*, and *his was a fiery personality*.
8. Elizabeth wrote many poems about *love* and *to show her feelings*.

**H**INT
. . . . . . . . . . . . . . . . . . . . . . . . . . .
Many different parts of speech and grammatical forms can be used in parallel constructions.

**Nouns:** the city, the state, and the nation.

**Verbs:** sing and dance

**Adjectives:** small, cute, and cuddly

**Adverbs:** softly and slowly

**Prepositional phrases:** of the people, by the people, for the people

**Infinitives:** to die, to sleep, perchance to dream

**Gerunds:** swimming and sailing

**9.** The Brownings *left England* and *settling in Italy*.

**10.** *Marrying Robert* and *the move to Italy* improved her health and her outlook on life considerably.

**Exercise 3**   Work in groups to revise the following passage. Study how the conjunction *and* is used incorrectly and then change the sentence construction to achieve parallelism.

Close your eyes, be sitting someplace comfortable, and try to imagine this scene: Sekhar's truth experiment is tried for one day, by everyone, and it's tried throughout the world. How might our lives, our work, and the friendships we have change? What would happen in that one day?

In Sekhar's one day of truth, he offended his wife and was making his boss angry. What would happen if millions of people, from many cultures and who spoke many languages, tried the same experiment? Would the world be a better place after this one day of truth? Seeing is to believe. Maybe we should try it and see.

**Exercise 4   Style**   Look through the selections in this text for an example of parallel construction, such as the lines from President Kennedy's Inaugural Address. Write out the example and underline the parallel parts. Then share the example you've found with other students.

**Exercise 5   Analyzing and Revising Your Writing**

**1.** Take a piece of writing from your writing portfolio.

**2.** Reread it, looking for either examples of faulty parallelism or places where adding a parallel construction could add impact to your writing.

**3.** Rewrite one or two paragraphs in which you can correct errors in parallel construction or create parallel construction.

**4.** Check to see that you have punctuated your new sentences correctly.

**5.** Compare your revised sentences with the original ones. Which sentences do you prefer? Remember to check for faulty parallelism the next time you proofread your writing.

# STUDY SKILLS
## WORKSHOP

## SPECIALIZED DICTIONARIES

If you look up the word *sonnet* in an ordinary dictionary, you'll get a brief definition, such as "a fourteen-line, rhymed lyric poem." If you want a more detailed definition, with examples, you'll need to look in a specialized dictionary like Hohman's *Handbook of Literary Terms* or Deutsch's *Poetry Handbook: A Dictionary of Terms*. There are many specialized dictionaries available in libraries, including the following:

**Subject-Area Dictionaries**   There are specialized dictionaries for almost every field of human activity. There are dictionaries of art, of literature, of religion, of filmmaking, of philosophy, of music, of science, of law, and of medicine. There are dictionaries of specific sciences such as psychology or geology. There are dictionaries devoted to specific areas of technology such as computers or automotives. There are dictionaries about particular areas of literature such as poetry or drama. All these dictionaries provide in-depth information about the subject.

**Specialized Language Dictionaries**   Some special types of language cannot be found in an ordinary dictionary. For this reason, people create dictionaries that deal with special varieties of language such as dialects, jargon, and slang. Other special language dictionaries deal with word origins, clichés, rhymes, synonyms and antonyms, and problems in usage.

**Foreign Language Dictionaries**   Of course, dictionaries exist for many different languages. Particularly useful to students are bilingual dictionaries, such as ones that give English equivalents of Spanish words and Spanish equivalents of English words.

**Exercise**   Working with another student, follow the directions below. You will need to work in a library.

1. Look up the word *sonnet* in a dictionary of literary terms or a dictionary of poetry. Find out the difference between an Elizabethan sonnet and a Petrarchan sonnet.

2. Look up the word *tawdry* in an etymological dictionary, or dictionary of word origins. Tell what the word means today and how it came to have that meaning.

3. Using a Latin/English dictionary, look up the individual words in the phrase *Ars longa vita brevis*. Explain what the phrase means.

4. Look up the phrase *sotto voce* in a music dictionary. What does this phrase mean?

# VALUES IN QUESTION

"*ruth resides in every human heart, and one has to search for it there.*"

Mohandas K. Gandhi

ITALIAN LANDSCAPE II: EUROPA
1944  Ben Shahn  By permission of the
estate of Ben Shahn.

637

# Life in the Early Twentieth Century (1900–1939)

## BRITAIN BEFORE WORLD WAR I

Queen Victoria's eldest son, Edward VII, succeeded to the throne in 1901. The first decade of the twentieth century was named for the new king, who ruled until 1910. During the Edwardian Era, England's upper classes flaunted their wealth and expressed a self-satisfied pride at their country's prominence in the world.

At the same time, powerful labor unions agitated to improve conditions for working people. New measures to protect workers and their families included health and unemployment insurance, improved housing, and benefits for occupational injuries. Common people also won new political power in 1911 when a Parliamentary act further restricted the power of the House of Lords.

Before World War I, the countries of Europe had banded together in mutually-protective alliances in an attempt to prevent armed conflict. However, a feverish sense of nationalism led England and other nations to stockpile arms and issue increasingly violent threats to their enemies. Tensions rose until a major crisis became inevitable.

## WORLD WAR I: 1914–1918

Since earlier wars had been small-scale conflicts, a generation of patriotic young British men eagerly enlisted to fight Germany when war finally broke out in 1914. These young men felt that defending their nation would be a glorious experience. The reality of World War I turned out to be a shocking surprise.

Employing modern weapons such as submarines, machine guns, tanks, hand grenades, and poison gas, the opposing nations involved in the war each sacrificed millions of soldiers for no apparent gain. In northern France, for example, hundreds of men dug into and remained in muddy trenches where they fought over and over again for the same piece of territory. These trenches crawled with rats and lice and stunk with the corpses of dead soldiers. During a single battle, the Battle of Ypres, 300,000 young men were killed or wounded.

OVER THE TOP   John Nash   The Granger Collection, New York.

By the time World War I ended in 1918, England had lost almost an entire generation. Almost one million British men died and twice as many suffered wounds or were disabled.

### War Literature

Before the war, many British poets composed lyrical and romantic poems, often glorifying their native England. Rupert Brooke expressed this traditional patriotism in the gentle poems he wrote at the beginning of the war.

However, the senseless slaughter during the war soon stimulated a darker literary mood. Now poets such as Thomas Hardy and William Butler Yeats expressed the irony and bitterness the horrible war had produced.

## The Empire Begins to Crumble

After defeating Germany, Britain expanded its empire by adding several former German colonies. However, British administrators in Africa and Asia were finding their territories more and more difficult to rule. Homegrown nationalist movements began to stir popular feeling for independence in India, Palestine, and Egypt.

Self-governing states such as Canada, South Africa, Australia, and New Zealand also sought increased freedom. In 1926, Britain declared these countries to be independent communities within a British Commonwealth. The sun was finally beginning to set on the once mighty British empire.

## A Divided Ireland

Ireland, too, experienced a new surge of nationalism at the turn of the century. During the war, Irish soldiers fought with conflicting loyalties to defend an Empire they detested.

Irish Republicans felt no such loyalty and openly sought German support in an unsuccessful attempt to overthrow British rule in the Easter Rebellion of 1916. Continued skirmishes erupted into full-scale warfare in November, 1919. By 1921, the British and their Irish opponents agreed on an uneasy truce. Ireland was divided into a northern portion that still remains today under British rule and a southern part that eventually gained its independence.

## POST-WAR BRITAIN

After the war, England struggled to regain its former position of strength in the world. Burdened with huge war debts, the country faced tough competition from thriving industries in Japan and the United States. As unemployment rose, working class people pressured their government for change. During the post-war years, the Labor party became a force in British government for the first time. The Labor Party supported democratic socialism, a system in which the government rather than private individuals controls and distributes wealth for the community.

## New Trends in Literature

In post-war Britain, Victorian novels with happy endings gave way to a body of literature which emphasized the unpredictable consequences of fate. The authors James Joyce, Virginia Woolf, and Katherine Mansfield began to experiment with new, highly personal forms of expression. Novels and stories became grimmer and more cynical during the post-war years as a "lost generation" felt a new sense of anxiety and disillusionment.

## The Threat of a New War

The crash of the American stock market in October, 1929, thrust the entire world into a severe economic depression. Britain's weakened economy grew even more troubled as a million workers lost their jobs.

The worldwide depression contributed to the rise of dictatorships in Italy, Germany, and Russia. By the late 1930's, a heavily armed German army under Adolf Hitler had begun to march through Europe, occupying the Rhineland and Austria. Eager to preserve "peace in our time," British Prime Minister Neville Chamberlain agreed to Hitler's takeover of part of Czechoslovakia in 1938.

However, England was determined to defend her ally, Poland. England's pledge to defend Poland came due in September, 1939, when Hitler's forces invaded that country. Soon the entire world was plunged back into a war whose horrors would exceed those of the First World War.

# Time Line of British and World History 1900—1940

Lady Astor becomes first **1919**
female member of Parliament

Women over 30 achieve right to vote; **1918**
Rupert Brooke's *Collected Poems* published

Easter Rebellion **1916**
in Ireland

Britain enters **1914**
World War I

**1910** South Africa gains
independence from
Britain

■ WORLD WAR I FRENCH
PLANE, NIEUPORT 17C

WORLD WAR I ■
BRITISH SOLDIER

**1904** Saki publishes his first stories

**1901** Edward VII becomes king

## BRITISH HISTORY

1900                    1910

## WORLD HISTORY

**1903** In the United States, Orville and Wilbur
Wright build first successful airplane

**1905** In Germany, Albert Einstein
proposes the theory of relativity

SINKING OF THE TITANIC, ■
APRIL 14, 1912

**1909** Explorers reach the North Pole

**1911** Explorers reach the South Pole

**1913** Stravinsky's revolutionary ballet,
"The Rite of Spring," causes a riot
at its Paris premiere

**1914** Panama Canal opens

Russian Revolution **1917**

World War I ends **1918**
with 8 million dead

■ MATTHEW ALEXANDER HENSON

1926 ROLLS-ROYCE ■

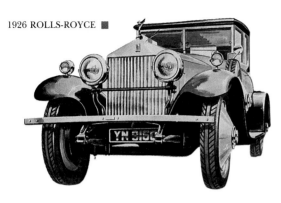

Britain enters **1939**
World War II

First BBC television **1936**
broadcast

Radar developed by **1935**
British physicists

BBC MICROPHONE ■

**1925** John L. Baird transmits
first television pictures

**1921** Irish Free State formed

**1920** Katherine Mansfield publishes
*Bliss and Other Stories*

**1920** ┼ **1930** ┼ **1940**

**1920** Gandhi leads nonviolent
protests against British
rule in India

**1927** Charles Lindbergh makes
first solo transatlantic flight

**1922** Mussolini forms fascist
government in Italy

**1929** Beginning of
worldwide depression

**1924** In Soviet Union, Lenin dies

**1932** Famine kills 5 million
people in Soviet Union

**1936** Civil War in Spain

**1937** Pablo Picasso
creates "Guernica"
mural

Germany's Hitler **1938**
annexes Austria

German forces invade **1939**
Poland, beginning
World War II

■ MOHANDAS GANDHI

ROARING 20'S DANCERS, ■
DRAWN BY JOHN HELD, JR.

# $\mathcal{R}$EFLECTIONS ON WAR

The first half of the twentieth century was one of the most bloody and violent times in human history. Two world wars and countless revolutions and civil wars brought millions to an early grave. Warfare achieved new and horrifying levels of destructiveness: bombs destroyed children as well as soldiers, schools as well as arms depots and whole populations suffered.

Many writers of this century have wrestled with questions about the purpose and value of war. The following selections will challenge you to define your own views and beliefs. You will read about war's participants and victims, its idealists and cynics, and share in the experience of its consequences.

*Poetry*

# The Man He Killed

### THOMAS HARDY

# An Irish Airman Foresees His Death

### WILLIAM BUTLER YEATS

# The Soldier

### RUPERT BROOKE

## Examine What You Know

If the United States were suddenly at war with another country, would you volunteer for military service? Would you serve your country in some other way? Consider and discuss whether or not your decision would depend on the cause of the war, its location, or the identity of the enemy.

## Expand Your Knowledge

Before World War I, most people believed that the world had finally outgrown the need for major international conflict. At the beginning of the twentieth century, it seemed that long, drawn-out wars were no longer even possible. People were optimistic.

During the nineteenth century, however, **nationalism**, or loyalty to one's own nation, did in fact cause conflicts between countries with differing goals. The growth of nationalism in turn encouraged popular support for the buildup of military power and the use of force to achieve a country's goals. Then in 1914, an assassination ignited a war that drew in the major powers in Europe. The war that people believed was impossible consumed lives and resources as it spread across Europe to the Middle East, Africa, Asia, and the Pacific. Four years later, after 8 1/2 million deaths, the world no longer looked the same. Differing views of the war and the enemy are reflected in much British poetry that was published during and after World War I.

## Enrich Your Reading

**Determining Attitudes**  The World War I British military men in these poems express different attitudes about the war and the enemy. In a chart like the one below, write words and phrases that describe each speaker's attitudes.

■ *Biographies of the authors can be found in the Reader's Handbook.*

|  | War | The Enemy |
|---|---|---|
| The Man He Killed |  |  |
| An Irish Airman... |  |  |
| The Soldier |  |  |

# The Man He Killed

### THOMAS HARDY

"Had he and I but met
By some old ancient inn,
We should have sat us down to wet
Right many a nipperkin![1]

5 "But ranged as infantry,
And staring face to face,
I shot at him as he at me,
And killed him in his place.

"I shot him dead because—
10 Because he was my foe,
just so: my foe of course he was;
That's clear enough; although

"He thought he'd 'list,[2] perhaps,
Offhand like—just as I—
15 Was out of work—had sold his traps—
No other reason why.

"Yes; quaint and curious war is!
You shoot a fellow down
You'd treat if met where any bar is,
20 Or help to half-a-crown."[3]

---

1. **nipperkin:** about half a pint of ale or beer.
2. **'list:** enlist in the military.
3. **half-a-crown:** old British coin.

## *R*esponding to Reading

### First Impressions of "The Man He Killed"

**1.** Does the speaker react to killing his enemy in a way that you expected? Explain.

### Second Thoughts on "The Man He Killed"

**2.** Why does the speaker kill his enemy? Does he seem satisfied with his reason? Consider the third stanza in your explanation.

**3.** Why did the speaker become a soldier?

**4.** What is the speaker's attitude toward his enemy?

# An Irish Airman Foresees His Death

WILLIAM BUTLER YEATS

I know that I shall meet my fate
Somewhere among the clouds above;
Those that I fight I do not hate,
Those that I guard I do not love;[1]
5  My country is Kiltartan Cross,
My countrymen Kiltartan's poor,
No likely end could bring them loss
Or leave them happier than before.
Nor law, nor duty bade[2] me fight,
10  Nor public men, nor cheering crowds,
A lonely impulse of delight
Drove to this tumult in the clouds;
I balanced all, brought all to mind,
The years to come seemed waste of breath,
15  A waste of breath the years behind
In balance with this life, this death.

THE BOMBING OF EL AFULEH (detail)   Imperial War Museum, London.

---

1. **Those. . .love:** The Irish hated their English rulers even though they fought beside them against the Germans.

2. **bade:** past tense of bid; commanded.

## Responding to Reading

### First Impressions of "An Irish Airman. . . "

**1.** What would you say to the speaker if you met him?

### Second Thoughts on "An Irish Airman. . . "

**2.** How do you think the speaker feels each time he gets into his plane?

**3.** Why has the speaker gone to war?

**4.** What does the speaker believe is his fate? How does he feel about it?

# The *Soldier*

RUPERT BROOKE

If I should die, think only this of me:
    That there's some corner of a foreign field
That is forever England. There shall be
    In that rich earth a richer dust concealed;
5  A dust whom England bore, shaped, made aware;
    Gave, once, her flowers to love, her ways to roam,
A body of England's breathing English air,
    Washed by the rivers, blest by suns of home.

And think, this heart, all evil shed away,
10    A pulse in the eternal mind, no less
      Gives somewhere back the thoughts by England given;
Her sights and sounds; dreams happy as her day;
    And laughter, learnt of friends; and gentleness,
      In hearts at peace, under an English heaven.

HIGHLANDERS
RESTING 1918 John
Singer Sargent © The
Fitzwilliam Museum,
Cambridge, England.

## Responding to Reading ─────────────────────────

### First Impressions of "The Soldier"

**1.** Does the soldier remind you of anyone you know or have heard about? Explain.

### Second Thoughts on "The Soldier"

**2.** What does the speaker mean when he says that his burial site in a foreign land will be "forever England"?

> **Think about**
> • how his death represents England in a foreign country
> • the meaning of the "richer dust concealed"

**3.** What does the speaker believe his single death will mean to England?

**4.** What is the speaker's attitude toward England? How does his attitude compare with your attitude toward your country?

### Comparing the Poems

**5.** Using the words and phrases from your chart, contrast the attitudes of the speakers toward the war and their enemies.

### Broader Connections

**6.** When these poems were written, only men were part of the regular army. Today, women fill many important roles in the service and are often sent to combat zones as support personnel. How do you feel about women in the army? Should they be allowed to fight on the front lines alongside men? Why or why not?

## Writing Option ────────────────────────────

Which of the three speakers would make the best soldier? Explain your opinion.

*Fiction*

## The Sniper

### LIAM O'FLAHERTY

## Examine What You Know

This story is set in Ireland during the Irish Civil War of the early 1920's. In small groups, discuss the differences between a civil war and a war fought between nations, perhaps using examples from United States history. Then develop a chart to show the contrasts between these two kinds of wars, creating separate categories for major differences. Compare your chart with charts from other groups.

## Expand Your Knowledge

England dominated Ireland for centuries, often denying the Irish people basic rights of citizenship such as the freedom to worship, to own property, and to vote. The Irish periodically rebelled against English rule, finally winning partial freedom in 1921 with a treaty that created an Irish Free State. The treaty, however, did not include the northern counties of Ireland, and it called for a loyalty oath to the British king. This caused a bitter split between Free Staters, who supported the treaty, and Republicans, who wanted total independence and a united Ireland. Civil war began in 1922 when terrorism, arson, bombings, and street warfare erupted between the sides.

At the time of this story, the Irish Republican Army (the IRA) had taken control of the government buildings of Dublin known as Four Courts. Free Staters encircled the area and fought building to building with their enemies, eventually defeating them. In 1948, after numerous setbacks, Ireland—the southern counties—finally achieved complete independence; however, Northern Ireland remained separate, a part of the British Commonwealth.

## Write Before You Read

Write your own definition of *sniper*. Then create a list of words and phrases that come to mind when you think of a sniper. Compare your list with those of others and discuss the different connotations suggested by the word.

■ *A biography of the author can be found in the Reader's Handbook.*

# The *Sniper*

LIAM O'FLAHERTY

The long June twilight faded into night. Dublin lay enveloped in darkness but for the dim light of the moon that shone through fleecy clouds, casting a pale light as of approaching dawn over the streets and the dark waters of the Liffey.[1] Around the beleaguered Four Courts the heavy guns roared. Here and there through the city, machine guns and rifles broke the silence of the night, spasmodically, like dogs barking on lone farms. Republicans and Free Staters were waging civil war.

On a rooftop near O'Connell Bridge, a Republican sniper lay watching. Beside him lay his rifle, and over his shoulders was slung a pair of field glasses. His face was the face of a student, thin and ascetic, but his eyes had the cold gleam of the fanatic. They were deep and thoughtful, the eyes of a man who is used to looking at death.

He was eating a sandwich hungrily. He had eaten nothing since morning. He had been too excited to eat. He finished the sandwich, and taking a flask of whiskey from his pocket, he took a short draught. Then he returned the flask to his pocket. He paused for a moment, considering whether he should risk a smoke. It was dangerous. The flash might be seen in the darkness, and there were enemies watching. He decided to take the risk. Placing a cigarette between his lips, he struck a match, inhaled the smoke hurriedly and put out the light. Almost immediately, a bullet flattened itself against the parapet of the roof. The sniper took another whiff and put out the cigarette. Then he swore softly and crawled away to the left.

Cautiously he raised himself and peered over the parapet.[2] There was a flash, and a bullet whizzed over his head. He dropped immediately. He had seen the flash. It came from the opposite side of the street.

He rolled over the roof to a chimney stack in the rear and slowly drew himself up behind it until his eyes were level with the top of the parapet. There was nothing to be seen—just the dim outline of the opposite housetop against the blue sky. His enemy was under cover.

Just then an armored car came across the bridge and advanced slowly up the street. It stopped on the opposite side of the street fifty yards ahead. The sniper could hear the dull panting of the motor. His heart beat faster. It was an enemy car. He wanted to fire, but he knew it was useless. His bullets would never pierce the steel that covered the gray monster.

Then round the corner of a side street came an old woman, her head covered by a tattered shawl. She began to talk to the man in the turret of the car. She was pointing to the roof where the sniper lay. An informer.

The turret opened. A man's head and shoulders appeared, looking toward the

---

1. **Liffey** (lif′ ē): the river flowing through Dublin, the capital of Ireland.

2. **parapet** (par′ ə pet′): a low wall or railing, as along a balcony or roof.

KALISHNIKOF  1987  Julio Larraz  Nohra Haime Gallery, New York.

sniper. The sniper raised his rifle and fired. The head fell heavily on the turret wall. The woman darted toward the side street. The sniper fired again. The woman whirled round and fell with a shriek into the gutter.

Suddenly from the opposite roof a shot rang out, and the sniper dropped his rifle with a curse. The rifle clattered to the roof. The sniper thought the noise would wake the dead. He stopped to pick the rifle up. He couldn't lift it. His forearm was dead. "Christ," he muttered, "I'm hit."

Dropping flat on to the roof, he crawled back to the parapet. With his left hand he felt the injured right forearm. The blood was oozing through the sleeve of his coat. There was no pain—just a deadened sensation, as if the arm had been cut off.

Quickly he drew his knife from his pocket, opened it on the breastwork of the parapet and ripped open the sleeve. There was a small hole where the bullet had entered. On the other side there was no hole. The bullet had lodged in the bone. It must have fractured it. He bent the arm below the wound. The arm bent back easily. He ground his teeth to overcome the pain.

Then, taking out his field dressing, he ripped open the packet with his knife. He broke the neck of the iodine bottle and let the bitter fluid drip into the wound. A paroxysm[3] of pain swept through him. He placed the cotton wadding over the wound and wrapped the dressing over it. He tied the end with his teeth.

Then he lay still against the parapet, and closing his eyes, he made an effort of will to overcome the pain.

In the street beneath all was still. The armored car had retired speedily over the bridge, with the machine gunner's head hanging lifeless over the turret. The woman's corpse lay still in the gutter.

The sniper lay for a long time nursing his wounded arm and planning escape. Morning must not find him wounded on the roof. The enemy on the opposite roof covered his escape. He must kill that enemy, and he could not use his rifle. He had only a revolver to do it. Then he thought of a plan.

Taking off his cap, he placed it over the muzzle of his rifle. Then he pushed the rifle slowly upward over the parapet until the cap was visible from the opposite side of the street. Almost immediately there was a report, and a

---

3. **paroxysm** (par′ əks iz′əm): a sudden convulsion, spasm, or outburst.

bullet pierced the center of the cap. The sniper slanted the rifle forward. The cap slipped down into the street. Then, catching the rifle in the middle, the sniper dropped his left hand over the roof and let it hang, lifelessly. After a few moments he let the rifle drop to the street. Then he sank to the roof, dragging his hand with him.

Crawling quickly to the left, he peered up at the corner of the roof. His ruse[4] had succeeded. The other sniper, seeing the cap and rifle fall, thought that he had killed his man. He was now standing before a row of chimney pots, looking across, with his head clearly silhouetted against the western sky.

The Republican sniper smiled and lifted his revolver above the edge of the parapet. The distance was about fifty yards—a hard shot in the dim light, and his right arm was paining him like a thousand devils. He took a steady aim. His hand trembled with eagerness. Pressing his lips together, he took a deep breath through his nostrils and fired. He was almost deafened with the report, and his arm shook with the recoil.

Then, when the smoke cleared, he peered across and uttered a cry of joy. His enemy had been hit. He was reeling over the parapet in his death agony. He struggled to keep his feet, but he was slowly falling forward, as if in a dream. The rifle fell from his grasp, hit the parapet, fell over, bounded off the pole of a barber's shop beneath and then clattered on to the pavement.

Then the dying man on the roof crumpled up and fell forward. The body turned over and over in space and hit the ground with a dull thud. Then it lay still.

The sniper looked at his enemy falling, and he shuddered. The lust of battle died in him. He became bitten by remorse. The sweat stood out in beads on his forehead. Weakened by his wound and the long summer day of fasting and watching on the roof, he revolted from the sight of the shattered mass of his dead enemy. His teeth chattered. He began to gibber to himself, cursing the war, cursing himself, cursing everybody.

He looked at the smoking revolver in his hand, and with an oath he hurled it to the roof at his feet. The revolver went off with the concussion, and the bullet whizzed past the sniper's head. He was frightened back to his senses by the shock. His nerves steadied. The cloud of fear scattered from his mind, and he laughed.

Taking the whiskey flask from his pocket, he emptied it at a draught. He felt reckless under the influence of the spirits. He decided to leave the roof and look for his company commander to report. Everywhere around was quiet. There was not much danger in going through the streets. He picked up his revolver and put it in his pocket. Then he crawled down through the skylight to the house underneath.

When the sniper reached the laneway on the street level, he felt a sudden curiosity as to the identity of the enemy sniper whom he had killed. He decided that he was a good shot whoever he was. He wondered if he knew him. Perhaps he had been in his own company before the split in the army. He decided to risk going over to have a look at him. He peered around the corner into O'Connell Street. In the upper part of the street there was heavy firing, but around here all was quiet.

The sniper darted across the street. A machine gun tore up the ground around him with a hail of bullets, but he escaped. He threw himself face downward beside the corpse. The machine gun stopped.

Then the sniper turned over the dead body and looked into his brother's face. ❧

---

4. **ruse** (r$\overline{oo}$z): a trick; hoax.

## *Responding to Reading*

### First Impressions

1. How did the last line of the story affect you?

### Second Thoughts

2. Is the main character the type of person you would expect a sniper to be? Why or why not?

3. Why does the sniper become "bitten by remorse" after shooting his rooftop enemy even though he showed no regrets about his first two victims?

4. Do you think the sniper was right or wrong in killing each of his victims?

   **Think about**
   - the cause for which he was fighting
   - the possibility of his death when the old woman revealed his position
   - which is more important, the enemy's life or the sniper's cause

5. Do you think the sniper will continue to fight in the civil war? Why or why not?

6. What is the writer's attitude toward the war? Explain your reasoning.

## *Literary Concept: Irony*

**Irony** results when there is a difference between what appears to be happening and what is actually happening. For example, when a character or reader expects or assumes one thing and the opposite is true, the writer has created irony. In "The Sniper," what is ironic about the two shooters? How important is irony in the story?

**Concept Review: Point of View**   Review the three points of view explained on page 615. Which one does O'Flaherty use, and why?

## *Writing Options*

1. Compare the story with "The Man He Killed" on page 644. Consider the main incidents and their ironies as well as the writers' attitudes toward war.

2. Reread the last eight paragraphs of the story. Add an additional paragraph to the ending that shows what might happen next.

*Diary*

*from* Hiroshima Diary

MICHIHIKO HACHIYA (mē chē hē kō hä chē yä)

## Examine What You Know

You are about to read a diary entry written by a man who experienced the horrors of an atomic bomb attack. Make a word web like the one below to list words and phrases that you associate with the atomic bomb.

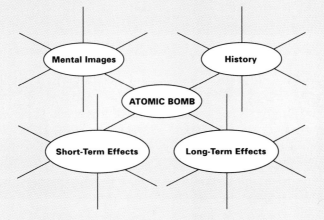

## Expand Your Knowledge

Near the end of World War II, on the morning of August 6, 1945, the United States dropped an atomic bomb—the first in history—on Hiroshima, Japan. The dropping of the bomb was a decision reached when the military powers in the United States feared that over one million American lives might be lost if the Allied forces carried out their planned invasion of the mainland of Japan. Over 67 percent of the city of Hiroshima was destroyed by a single bomb equal to twenty thousand tons of TNT. Four square miles in the center of the city were instantly leveled, and between 70,000 and 100,000 people died as a direct result of the bombing. Three days later, the Allied forces dropped a larger atomic bomb on Nagasaki, Japan. Japan's official surrender on September 2, 1945, ended the war. This diary entry is written by a Japanese doctor who survived the bombing of Hiroshima.

## Write Before You Read

■ *A biography of the author can be found on page 662.*

Do you worry about the threat of nuclear war? Write your thoughts and feelings about this subject in your journal or on a sheet of paper.

# *from* *Hiroshima Diary*

MICHIHIKO HACHIYA

August 6, 1945.

The hour was early; the morning still, warm, and beautiful. Shimmering leaves, reflecting sunlight from a cloudless sky, made a pleasant contrast with shadows in my garden as I gazed absently through wide-flung doors opening to the south.

Clad in drawers and undershirt, I was sprawled on the living room floor exhausted because I had just spent a sleepless night on duty as an air warden in my hospital.

Suddenly, a strong flash of light startled me—and then another. So well does one recall little things that I remember vividly how a stone lantern in the garden became brilliantly lit, and I debated whether this light was caused by a magnesium flare[1] or sparks from a passing trolley.

Garden shadows disappeared. The view where a moment before all had been so bright and sunny was now dark and hazy. Through swirling dust I could barely discern a wooden column that had supported one corner of my house. It was leaning crazily, and the roof sagged dangerously.

Moving instinctively, I tried to escape, but rubble and fallen timbers barred the way. By picking my way cautiously, I managed to reach the rōka[2] and stepped down into my garden. A profound weakness overcame me, so I stopped to regain my strength. To my surprise I discovered that I was completely naked. How odd! Where were my drawers and undershirt?

What had happened?

All over the right side of my body I was cut and bleeding. A large splinter was protruding from a mangled wound in my thigh, and something warm trickled into my mouth. My cheek was torn, I discovered as I felt it gingerly, with the lower lip laid wide open. Embedded in my neck was a sizable fragment of glass, which I matter-of-factly dislodged, and with the detachment of one stunned and shocked, I studied it and my bloodstained hand.

Where was my wife?

Suddenly thoroughly alarmed, I began to yell for her: "Yecko-san![3] Yecko-san! Where are you?"

Blood began to spurt. Had my carotid artery[4] been cut? Would I bleed to death? Frightened and irrational, I called out again:

---

1. **magnesium flare:** a type of fire bomb that produces a tremendous white light.
2. **rōka** (rō kə): hallway.
3. **Yecko-san:** *—san* is a title of respect added to Japanese names.
4. **carotid** (kə rät′ id) **artery:** one of the two principal arteries in the neck, which carry blood from the aorta to the head.

*Words to Know and Use*

**protrude** (prō trōōd′) *v.* to thrust or jut out; project
**detachment** (dē tach′ mənt) *n.* the state of being disinterested, impartial, or aloof
**irrational** (ir rash′ ə nəl) *adj.* contrary to reason; senseless; unreasonable; absurd

UNTITLED #20
1968 Eikoh Hosoe
Sheldon Memorial
Art Gallery, University of
Nebraska, Lincoln.

"It's a five-hundred-ton bomb! Yecko-san, where are you? A five-hundred-ton bomb has fallen!"

Yecko-san, pale and frightened, her clothes torn and bloodstained, emerged from the ruins of our house holding her elbow. Seeing her, I was reassured. My own panic assuaged, I tried to reassure her.

"We'll be all right," I exclaimed. "Only let's get out of here as fast as we can."

She nodded, and I motioned for her to follow me.

The shortest path to the street lay through the house next door, so through the house we went—running, stumbling, falling, and then running again until in headlong flight we tripped over something and fell sprawling into the street. Getting to my feet, I discovered that I had tripped over a man's head.

"Excuse me! Excuse me, please!" I cried hysterically.

There was no answer. The man was dead. The head had belonged to a young officer whose body was crushed beneath a massive gate.

We stood in the street, uncertain and afraid, until a house across from us began to sway and then with a rending motion[5] fell almost at our feet. Our own house began to sway, and in a minute it, too, collapsed in a cloud of dust. Other buildings caved in or toppled. Fires sprang up and, whipped by a vicious wind, began to spread.

It finally dawned on us that we could not stay there in the street, so we turned our steps toward the hospital [a few hundred yards away]. Our home was gone; we were wounded and needed treatments, and after all, it was my duty to be with my staff. This latter was an irrational thought—what good could I be to anyone, hurt as I was.

We started out, but after twenty or thirty steps I had to stop. My breath became short, my heart pounded, and my legs gave way under me. An overpowering thirst seized me, and I begged Yecko-san to find me some water. But there was no water to be found. After a little my strength somewhat returned, and we were able to go on.

5. **rending motion:** a violent tearing, ripping, or pulling movement.

I was still naked, and although I did not feel the least bit of shame, I was disturbed to realize that modesty had deserted me. On rounding a corner we came upon a soldier standing idly in the street. He had a towel draped across his shoulder, and I asked if he would give it to me to cover my nakedness. The soldier surrendered the towel quite willingly but said not a word. A little later I lost the towel, and Yecko-san took off her apron and tied it around my loins.

Our progress toward the hospital was interminably slow, until finally my legs, stiff from drying blood, refused to carry me farther. The strength, even the will, to go on deserted me, so I told my wife, who was almost as badly hurt as I, to go on alone. This she objected to, but there was no choice. She had to go ahead and try to find someone to come back for me.

Yecko-san looked into my face for a moment and then, without saying a word, turned away and began running toward the hospital. Once, she looked back and waved, and in a moment she was swallowed up in the gloom. It was quite dark now, and with my wife gone, a feeling of dreadful loneliness overcame me.

I must have gone out of my head, lying there in the road, because the thing I recall was discovering that the clot on my thigh had been dislodged and blood was again spurting from the wound. I pressed my hand to the bleeding area, and after a while the bleeding stopped and I felt better.

Could I go on?

I tried. It was all a nightmare—my wounds, the darkness, the road ahead. My movements were ever so slow; only my mind was running at top speed.

In time I came to an open space where the houses had been removed to make a fire lane. Through the dim light I could make out ahead of me the hazy outlines of the Communications Bureau's big concrete building, and beyond it the hospital. My spirits rose because I knew that now someone would find me; and if I should die, at least my body would be found.

I paused to rest. Gradually things around me came into focus. There were the shadowy forms of people, some of whom looked like walking ghosts. Others moved as though in pain, like scarecrows, their arms held out from their bodies with forearms and hands dangling. These people puzzled me until I suddenly realized that they had been burned and were holding their arms out to prevent the painful friction of raw surfaces rubbing together. A naked woman carrying a naked baby came into view. I <u>averted</u> my gaze. Perhaps they had been in the bath. But then I saw a naked man, and it occurred to me that, like myself, some strange thing had deprived them of their clothes. An old woman lay near me with an expression of suffering on her face; but she made no sound. Indeed, one thing was common to everyone I saw—complete silence.

All who could were moving in the direction of the hospital. I joined in the dismal parade when my strength was somewhat recovered, and at last reached the gates of the Communications Bureau.

Familiar surroundings, familiar faces. There was Mr. Iguchi and Mr. Yoshihiro and my old friend Mr. Sera, the head of the business office. They hastened to give me a hand, their expressions of pleasure changing to alarm when they saw that I was hurt. I was too happy to see them to share their concern.

No time was lost over greetings. They eased me onto a stretcher and carried me into the Communications Building, ignoring my protests that I could walk. Later, I learned that

*Words to Know and Use* | **avert** (ə vurt′) *v.* to turn away one's glance

the hospital was so overrun that the Communications Bureau had to be used as an emergency hospital. The rooms and corridors were crowded with people, many of whom I recognized as neighbors. To me it seemed that the whole community was there.

My friends passed me through an open window into a janitor's room recently converted to an emergency first-aid station. The room was a shambles; fallen plaster, broken furniture, and debris littered the floor; the walls were cracked; and a heavy steel window casement was twisted and almost wrenched from its seating. What a place to dress the wounds of the injured.

To my great surprise, who should appear but my private nurse, Miss Kado, and Mr. Mizoguchi and old Mrs. Saeki. Miss Kado set about examining my wounds without speaking a word. No one spoke. I asked for a shirt and pajamas. They got them for me, but still no one spoke. Why was everyone so quiet?

Miss Kado finished the examination, and in a moment it felt as if my chest was on fire. She had begun to paint my wounds with iodine, and no amount of entreaty[6] would make her stop. With no alternative but to endure the iodine, I tried to divert myself by looking out the window.

The hospital lay directly opposite, with part of the roof and the third-floor sunroom in plain view, and as I looked up, I witnessed a sight which made me forget my smarting wounds. Smoke was pouring out of the sunroom windows. The hospital was afire!

"Fire!" I shouted. "Fire! Fire! The hospital is on fire!"

My friends looked up. It was true. The hospital *was* on fire.

The alarm was given, and from all sides people took up the cry. The high-pitched voice of Mr. Sera, the business officer, rose above the others, and it seemed as if his was the first voice I had heard that day. The uncanny stillness was broken. Our little world was now in pandemonium.

I remember that Dr. Sasada, chief of the Pediatric Service, came in and tried to reassure me, but I could scarcely hear him above the din. I heard Dr. Hinoi's voice and then Dr. Koyama's. Both were shouting orders to evacuate the hospital, and with such vigor that it sounded as though the sheer strength of their voices could hasten those who were slow to obey.

The sky became bright, as flames from the hospital mounted. Soon the Bureau was threatened, and Mr. Sera gave the order to evacuate. My stretcher was moved into a rear garden and placed beneath an old cherry tree. Other patients limped into the garden or were carried, until soon the entire area became so crowded that only the very ill had room to lie down. No one talked, and the ominous silence was relieved only by a subdued rustle among so many people, restless, in pain, anxious, and afraid, waiting for something else to happen.

The sky filled with black smoke and glowing sparks. Flames rose and the heat set currents of air in motion. Updrafts became so violent that sheets of zinc roofing were hurled aloft and released, humming and twirling, in erratic flight. Pieces of flaming wood soared and fell like fiery swallows. While I was trying to beat out the flames, a hot ember seared my ankle. It was all I could do to keep from being burned alive.

The Bureau started to burn, and window after window became a square of flame, until the whole structure was converted into a crackling, hissing inferno.

---

6. **entreaty:** an earnest request or prayer.

| Words to Know and Use | **uncanny** (un kan′ ē) *adj.* mysterious or unfamiliar in a frightening, eerie way<br>**pandemonium** (pan′ də mō′ nē əm) *n.* any scene of wild disorder or confusion<br>**evacuate** (ē vak′ yo͞o āt′) *v.* to remove inhabitants from an area for safety<br>**erratic** (er rat′ ik) *adj.* having no fixed course or direction; irregular; random |
|---|---|

Scorching winds howled around us, whipping dust and ashes into our eyes and up our noses. Our mouths became dry, our throats raw and sore from the biting smoke pulled into our lungs. Coughing was uncontrollable. We would have moved back, but a group of wooden barracks behind us caught fire and began to burn like tinder.

The heat finally became too intense to endure, and we were left no choice but to abandon the garden. Those who could, fled; those who could not, perished. Had it not been for my devoted friends, I would have died, but again, they came to the rescue and carried my stretcher to the main gate on the other side of the Bureau.

Here, a small group of people were already clustered, and here I found my wife. Dr. Sasada and Miss Kado joined us.

Fires sprang up on every side as violent winds fanned flames from one building to another. Soon, we were surrounded. The ground we held in front of the Communications Bureau became an oasis in a desert of fire. As the flames came closer, the heat became more intense, and if someone in our group had not had the presence of mind to drench us with water from a fire hose, I doubt if anyone could have survived.

Hot as it was, I began to shiver. The drenching was too much. My heart pounded; things began to whirl until all before me blurred.

*"Kurushii,"* I murmured weakly. "I am done."

The sound of voices reached my ears as though from a great distance and finally became louder as if close at hand. I opened my eyes; Dr. Sasada was feeling my pulse. What had happened? Miss Kado gave me an injection. My strength gradually returned. I must have fainted.

Huge raindrops began to fall. Some thought a thunderstorm was beginning and would extinguish the fires. But these drops were capricious. A few fell and then a few more, and that was all the rain we saw.

The first floor of the Bureau was now ablaze, and flames were spreading rapidly toward our little oasis by the gate. I could hardly understand the situation, much less do anything about it.

An iron window frame, loosened by fire, crashed to the ground behind us. A ball of fire whizzed by me, setting my clothes ablaze. They drenched me with water again. From then on I am confused as to what happened.

I do remember Dr. Hinoi because of the pain, the pain I felt when he jerked me to my feet. I remember being moved, or rather dragged, and my whole spirit rebelling against the torment I was made to endure.

My next memory is of an open area. The fires must have <u>receded</u>. I was alive. My friends had somehow managed to rescue me again. . . . The entire northern side of the city was completely burned. The sky was still dark, but whether it was evening or midday I could not tell. It might even have been the next day. Time had no meaning. What I had experienced might have been crowded into a moment or been endured through the monotony of eternity. . . .

The streets were deserted except for the dead. Some looked as if they had been frozen by death while in the full action of flight; others lay sprawled as though some giant had flung them to their death from a great height.

Hiroshima was no longer a city but a burnt-over prairie. To the east and to the west everything was flattened. The distant mountains seemed nearer than I could ever remember.

*Words to Know and Use* | **recede** (ri sēd′) *v.* to become less; diminish

The hills of Ushita and the woods of Nigitsu loomed out of the haze and smoke like the nose and eyes on a face. How small Hiroshima was with its houses gone.

The wind changed, and the sky again darkened with smoke.

Suddenly, I heard someone shout: "Planes! Enemy planes!"

Could that be possible after what had already happened? What was there left to bomb? My thoughts were interrupted by the [coming of Dr. Katsube, the hospital's head surgeon, and being carried to an operating room.] . . . The distance was only a hundred meters, but it was enough to cause my heart to pound and make me sink and faint.

I recall the hard table and the pain when my face and lip were sutured[7], but I have no recollection of the forty or more other wounds Dr. Katsube closed before night.

They removed me to an adjoining room, and I remember feeling relaxed and sleepy. The sun had gone down, leaving a dark red sky. The red flames of the burning city had scorched the heavens. I gazed at the sky until sleep overtook me. ❧

---

7. **sutured** (sōō′ chərd): joined together with stitches.

# I N S I G H T

## The Mokusatsu Tragedy

ROY A. GALLANT

On July 26, 1945—after Germany had been defeated in World War II—the governments of the United States, Great Britain, and China sent a radio message to Japan, calling on her to surrender. On July 27 the Japanese cabinet met and considered this message. The majority of the cabinet were in favor of peace, but they felt they needed time to do two things before they agreed to surrender. They had to persuade the stubborn generals to quit fighting, and they wanted to prepare the Japanese people for news of defeat. So the head of the Japanese government announced that an offer of peace had been received, but he said the cabinet was not yet ready to comment on it. When he made this statement, he used the word *mokusatsu*,[1] which means *withhold comment*. Unfortunately it also means *ignore*.

Most Japanese who saw *mokusatsu* in the newspapers could guess which meaning the government intended to give the word, but one Japanese guessed wrong. He was the man who prepared an English language radio broadcast of the news story. He said—in English—that the Japanese cabinet had decided to *ignore* the peace offer.

On July 28 American newspapers printed stories saying that Japan had *ignored* the chance to make peace.

On August 6 President Truman announced that the Japanese had rejected peace terms and that he had ordered an atom bomb dropped on Hiroshima. This bomb killed more than sixty-six thousand men, women, and children and injured tens of thousands more with radiation.

Some experts say that the atom bomb never would have been dropped if the Japanese translator had said *without comment* instead of *ignore*. A more careful choice of words might possibly have saved large numbers of innocent people from disaster.

---

1. **Mokusatsu:** mō kōō sät′ sōō

## Responding to Reading

### First Impressions

1. Describe the mental picture that stands out most clearly for you from this account of the Hiroshima tragedy.

### Second Thoughts

2. What do you think was the most difficult part of the narrator's experience? Cite parts of the diary to support your answer.

3. Were you surprised by the behavior of the victims during the crisis? Was their behavior typical of most disaster victims? Explain.

   **Think about**
   • the narrator's thoughts when the bomb first fell
   • the silence of the crowds at the hospital
   • the people's actions toward each other

4. If an American city were destroyed as Hiroshima was, do you think the American victims would react like the Japanese victims? Explain.

5. Summarize the main idea of "The Mokusatsu Tragedy." How might history have changed based on another interpretation of a word?

### Broader Connections

6. In what ways has the existence of the bomb and the fact that so many nations have it changed the way we live and think today?

## Literary Concept: Diary

A **diary** is a personal day-to-day account of a writer's own experiences and impressions. Most diaries are kept private because their writers often include very personal thoughts not intended to be shared. Some diaries, however, are published because they are well written and provide insights into historical events or time periods. Why might people want to read this diary?

In order to have an accurate record of a day's happenings, writers of diaries usually record their thoughts promptly. How might Hachiya's entry be different if it had been written at a much later time?

**Concept Review: Imagery** In this diary entry, find five examples of imagery that create a clear picture of the Hiroshima tragedy.

## Writing Options

1. As the narrator Hachiya, write a later diary entry that describes your thoughts and feelings about the dropping of the bomb.

2. The President of the United States had to decide whether or not to drop the bomb on Japan. Write an internal dialogue he might have had that reflects the difficulty of this decision.

3. As a radio news reporter in Hiroshima, write your report on the events of August 6, 1945.

4. Write a newspaper editorial that explains your opinion about the way the United States ended the war.

## Vocabulary Practice

**Exercise** Write the word that best completes the meaning of each sentence.

1. The bomb blast interrupted the calmness of the day and caused great _____ to break out.
2. The people who did not _____ their gaze from the flash of the blast were blinded.
3. Hachiya was _____ and said things that didn't make sense.
4. Only with his own fears partially _____ could Hachiya try to comfort someone else.
5. As Hachiya discovered, very serious wounds or shock can produce a quiet, curious _____.
6. He saw pieces of wood, glass, and metal _____ from the bodies of victims.
7. The _____ outbreak of fires all over the city caused panic everywhere. No one knew where or when the next one might occur.
8. The _____ calmness during this time of crisis made Hachiya feel uneasy.
9. Survivors had to _____ the burning buildings.
10. Later, the winds and fires finally began to _____.

*Words to Know and Use*

assuaged
avert
detachment
erratic
evacuate
irrational
pandemonium
protrude
recede
uncanny

## *Options for Learning*

**1 • The Decision** With several classmates, conduct a panel discussion on the issue of whether dropping the atomic bomb was right or wrong. In preparation for the debate, research the issues involved at the time the decision was made. Find out the reasons for the choice of Hiroshima as the site of the bombing and for the uncertainty of the scientists over the effects of the bomb blast.

**2 • The Growth of an Industry** The development of the atomic, hydrogen, and neutron bombs; the expansion of delivery systems; and the increased accuracy and power of these weapons has continued ever since the bombing of Hiroshima. Research the different areas of growth in the nuclear weapons industry. Then, using diagrams, pictures, and statistics, present a report to the class.

**3 • A Child's View** The children of Hiroshima who survived the bombing have, over the years, created a great deal of art work and writing about their experiences. Research their works and present examples to the class.

**4 • An Artist's Eye** Create your own work of art about the Hiroshima experience in any medium or style that visually captures the narrator's experience.

**5 • An American View** Shortly after the bombing of Hiroshima, American novelist John Hersey visited the city and observed the effects of the bombing on the survivors. His book *Hiroshima* includes personal survival stories of the Japanese victims. Read the book and present an oral report to the class.

 **FACT FINDER**

*What was the population of Hiroshima at the time the atomic bomb was dropped?*

## *Michibiko Hachiya*
### 1903–

Hachiya was a quiet, middle-aged doctor in Hiroshima at the time the bomb was dropped. Born and educated in Okayama, Japan, he served as the director of the Hiroshima Communications Hospital during the war. Although Hiroshima was a military center, this hospital served local government employees. Ironically, Dr. Hachiya was one of the first patients to be treated in the nearly destroyed hospital where he worked. As he was recovering, he began writing his journal on any burned scraps of paper he could find. Although many people wrote about their experiences at the time the bomb was dropped, Hachiya's diary remains one of the most powerful eyewitness accounts of the effects of a nuclear explosion.

*Essay*

# It All Started with Stones and Clubs

### RICHARD ARMOUR

## Examine What You Know

When someone mentions the Stone Age and primitive people, what humorous images come to your mind? Share your thoughts with the class and discuss where you got these ideas of our ancient ancestors. Then list ways in which cartoonists, comedians, and writers have used Stone Age topics and characters to make comments on modern times.

## Expand Your Knowledge

Writers often use humor to make important statements about human beings and their behavior. One type of humor, **parody**, involves imitating a serious or scholarly style of writing in order to make fun of a subject. In this parody, Armour makes fun of mankind's love of warfare. He presents explanations, such as the following, that show the absurdity of human behavior:

> The earliest armed conflicts were probably between two men. Casualties were heavy, usually about 50 percent.

## Enrich Your Reading

**Wordplay**   Besides using parody to create humor, Armour also uses a writing technique called wordplay. **Wordplay** is the use of a word or phrase in a way that creates a humorous contrast between two or more meanings of the word or phrase. A good example of wordplay can be found in the first sentence of the second paragraph and in the accompanying footnote. One meaning of "above" refers to Stone Age people's physical position in relation to most animals. The other meaning refers to humans' level of intelligence in comparison to that of the animals. As you read this selection, list other examples of wordplay that create humorous images and ideas. Be prepared to explain the double meanings.

# It All Started with Stones and Clubs

RICHARD ARMOUR

Back in the Stone Age, man was too uncivilized and unimaginative to wage war. All he did was eat and sleep and try to keep warm. He also reproduced, though he did not know this was what he was doing when he did it.

Stone Age man was very little above the animal.[1] Fortunately for his status, animals did not wage war either, so man did not develop an inferiority complex. Unlike man, animals never progressed to the point of making war. This is one reason why animals have remained animals and, over the centuries, have lagged so far behind man.

Not only was man too uncivilized to wage war during the Stone Age, but he had no reason to do so.

He had no desire to take territory away from other men, since he had more territory (and more stones) than he could possibly use.

He had no desire to take *anything* away from anybody else, because every man had roughly the same things: a rough, cold cave, a rough, cold wife, and an empty stomach.

He did not declare war when someone came bounding over his boundary, because there were no boundaries. There were not even any walls or barbed wire or border guards or customs officials.

He did not declare war out of dislike for someone else's ideology, because everyone had the same ideology, which was: Try to Stay Alive If You Can.

He did not wage war to save national honor, because there were no nations and there was no honor. Nor did he wage war to save face, face at that time being only the front part of the head and in no danger of being lost unless the whole head was.

He was not stimulated to declare war by reading books or newspapers or hearing over the radio or TV about what people on the other side were planning to do to him if he didn't do it to them first.

In fact there was no other side. This shows how primitive primitive man was.

Had man remained in this unhappy condition, there would have been no fortunes made through the manufacture of munitions, no memoirs ghostwritten for generals, no heroes, no medals, no war orphans, no national cemeteries. There would be no veterans' benefits, no veterans' hospitals. There would be no victory monuments, and pigeons would have to find some other place.

The situation was intolerable.

Fortunately, man took things into his own hands.

The first thing he took into his own hands

---

1. In fact, when animals were in trees, he was below the animal, which made him uneasy.

SHAM BATTLE   Richard Wilt   Butler Institute of Fine Arts, Youngstown, Ohio.

was either a club or a stone.[2] He may even have had a club in one hand and a stone in the other, an early instance of overkill.

The club and the stone were the first offensive weapons. The first defensive weapon was the skull, rapidly followed by the defensive club and the defensive stone. These were approximately the same size and shape as the offensive club and the offensive stone.

An important factor in early warfare was the cave. The person in the cave had the advantage over anyone entering the cave because his eyes were accustomed to the darkness. Once dark glasses were invented, this advantage no longer existed. But primitive man had no dark glasses. In fact he had no glasses of any kind, and this deprived him, if he had bad eyesight, of the opportunity of having his vision corrected to the standard that made him eligible for killing other people. When on the defensive, it also cost him the delay gained while saying, "Wait till I take my glasses off," during which time his opponent might get out of the notion.

The earliest armed conflicts were probably between two men. Casualties were heavy, usually about 50 percent. Women, children, and old people who stood around watching were called noncombatants and were in no danger whatsoever.

However, there was not as yet any such thing as war, war being armed conflict between nations. When one man kills another

2. Teddy Roosevelt was not, as some think, the first to use the slogan "Carry a big stick."

man it is murder, which is very different. Who ever heard of murder rallies, murder songs, murder bonds? Primitive man was too dimwitted to realize that if enough people could kill enough people it would no longer be murder, it would be war. Then, instead of being frowned upon, it would bring cheers and speeches.[3]

Another difference between murder and war is when and where they take place. Murder takes place in dark alleys and behind closed doors and when nobody is looking. War takes place on battlefields, out in the open, with newspaper reporters and photographers and even television cameras to record it. Obviously there is something sneaky about murder, as contrasted with war.

Primitive man, unaware of the moral and social advantages of war, nonetheless made some progress. Though he continued to kill in the old-fashioned way, one person at a time, he made important advances in weaponry.

With the discovery of copper, iron, and other metals, he was able to construct weapons with sharp points and keen edges that had obvious advantages over the stone and the club. It was now possible to get rid of an opponent by thrusting a piece of metal through him. This was far easier and less time-consuming than beating him over the head. Even if the old method of beating over the head was resorted to, a piece of metal was not likely to break or splinter as a club sometimes did, to the embarrassment of everyone.

Invention of the wheel brought mobility. Instead of walking all the way to get within striking distance of his enemy, and being tired out on arrival, a man could ride there. Or, if he decided not to fight, he could get away faster than by running. Also, not getting out of breath, he could yell fiercely and even chant war songs, thereby contributing to the literary and musical arts.

Discovery of fire made it possible to go after one's enemy with a lighted torch and to burn the hair off his chest unless, of course, he was fleeing. It also made it possible to fight after dark, utilizing time that had previously been wasted in sleep.

Despite these encouraging developments, man was in a pretty sad state, warwise, for thousands of years. ❧

3. It is a matter of taste, but there are those who prefer a long war to a long speech.

# explain

## Responding to Reading

### First Impressions

1. Did you find this parody funny? Why or why not?

### Second Thoughts

2. According to Armour, why didn't primitive people wage war? How does his explanation ridicule modern people?

3. What distinctions does Armour make between war and murder? Are these real distinctions, or is there some other meaning behind his words? Explain.

4. Do you think Armour's purpose is to make a serious statement or simply to entertain? Explain.

   **Think about**
   • whether the wordplays make a serious point
   • Armour's attitude toward his subject
   • how well his parody works

## Literary Concept: Sarcasm

**Sarcasm** is verbal irony that mocks or ridicules its subject. The meaning of a sarcastic remark seems complimentary, but it is actually critical. This selection contains a number of sarcastic remarks, such as the first sentence: "Back in the Stone Age, man was too uncivilized and unimaginative to wage war." In this remark Armour suggests that warfare is a civilized way of settling disputes. Knowing the nature of warfare, however, the reader realizes that Armour actually means the opposite—that by engaging in warfare, modern man is behaving in an uncivilized manner.

Find other examples of sarcasm in the selection. What is the actual meaning of each example?

## Writing Options

1. Write a sarcastic headline supporting war as a solution to an imaginary crisis.

2. Draw a Stone Age cartoon and include a caption that suggests one of the ideas presented in the selection.

3. Use parody to write about a problem, situation, or event in your school.

## EXPOSITION: CAUSE AND EFFECT

A conflict is a clash between opposing forces. The selections in this subunit all deal with the ultimate conflict—war. Not all conflicts, however, are life-threatening, although they may be of great importance to the participants. Local resistance to a rise in property taxes, the national struggle with the budget deficit, a city's fight to prevent the building of a waste dump—all are conflicts that, like war, are the results of a series of actions or conditions. They are usually caused by a number of events. To fully understand any conflict, you have to explore its causes.

In this assignment, you will have the opportunity to play the role of a television newscaster. You will present a local or national conflict and explain its causes.

> Here is your PASSkey to this assignment.

### GUIDED ASSIGNMENT:
### CURRENT AFFAIRS NEWS REPORT

Informally research a current local or national conflict. Then write a news report for your school in which you explain the causes of the situation.

**P**URPOSE: To explain cause and effect

**A**UDIENCE: Students of your school

**S**UBJECT: A current local or national conflict

**S**TRUCTURE: A news report

## Prewriting

**STEP 1** **Brainstorm possible topics**  Working with a small group of classmates, brainstorm a list of general categories in which conflicts might exist. Think of events currently in the news. Consider such categories as crises around the world, local events, the environment, the economy, the government, crime, medicine, science and technology, sports, entertainment, and education. Add as many other subject groupings as you can.

Then, working with the same small group, select one or two of the categories that interest you and your classmates. For each category, make a web to explore possible areas of conflict that might be used as topics. One group made this web.

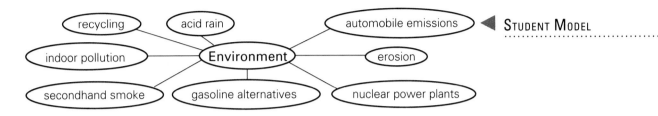

◀ STUDENT MODEL

**STEP 2** **Select a specific topic**   On your own, select a topic that was mentioned in the group or choose another that interests you. Narrow the focus of the topic. Remember that you are writing a brief news account, not a lengthy, complex report. Erosion is much too broad a topic to cover in a news broadcast, for example, but the conflict that farmers who practice soil management are experiencing with state agriculture boards would be a manageable focus for this assignment. Be sure that your topic is complex enough to have several causes.

**STEP 3** **Explore your topic**   Even if you already know a great deal about your topic, you will need to do some research. Examine newspapers and magazines, and watch television news shows. Remember that you are looking for the causes of a troublesome situation. Do not look for a single cause—events are rarely caused by one simple event. You may need to research further back in time to find the roots of the situation. For example, one student chose to research a controversial Supreme Court decision. She found that in order to understand the controversy, she had to research related Supreme Court rulings of the past.

Try to use at least three sources, including interviews and books if they are available and appropriate. Keep track of the complete bibliographic information about your sources. Although this is not a research paper, you will need to list your sources at the end of your news report.

**STEP 4** **Gather and organize information**   As you read about your topic, take notes as if you were a journalist. You might record your information in a chart like the one on the next page.

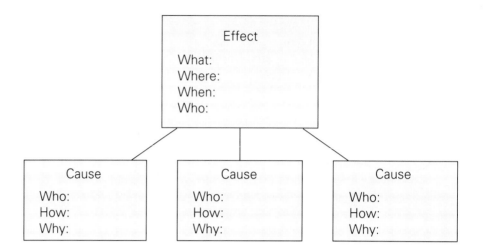

Once you have gathered the information and have some understanding of the causes of the conflict, write a **thesis statement.** This will be the focus of your report. In the statement, summarize the conflict, which is the effect. Then summarize the causes or choose the most outstanding one. Your news report will explain your thesis to readers and listeners.

## Drafting

STEP **1** **Write an introductory paragraph** Keep in mind that your job is to present the conflict (the effect) and to explain or speculate about its causes. Because of the limited time devoted to each story in a news broadcast, your introductory paragraph is especially important. You need to get to the point quickly. Describe the information in your Effect box to identify the conflict for viewers.

You can use any of a variety of techniques to capture attention in your introductory paragraph, such as a startling statistic, an authoritative quotation, an upsetting question, or an intriguing anecdote. The student who wrote the following example chose to shock his audience with statistics.

STUDENT MODEL ▶

Last year, 39 million people vacationed in southern Florida. Their sunny paradise, however, may quickly be approaching collapse. Although water seems to be everywhere, it is saltwater—not the two hundred gallons of fresh water that each person uses daily. In order to meet the enormous demand for fresh water, Florida has been more thoroughly drained, diked, and developed than almost any other area of the United States. Due to shocking mismanagement and uncontrolled demand, Florida may soon become a wasteland.

**STEP 2** **Draft the body paragraphs** You have outlined the conflict, or the effect, in your introduction. The body paragraphs should explain the causes of the problem. Each paragraph should explain one cause, using the information from your chart.

Aim for straightforward and precise language as you write. Because a news broadcast must be short, make every word count. Use active verbs and concrete nouns. Interpretations based on facts can be used, but avoid opinions based on personal experience or feeling.

**STEP 3** **Draft a conclusion** Your concluding paragraph should emphasize the importance of the problem. You can suggest solutions or name specific groups that are trying to settle the conflict. You might introduce a final quotation or a set of statistics.

On a separate sheet of paper at the end of your news report, write a bibliography of your sources, using the format provided on pages 968–69.

## Revising and Editing

Before revising in terms of organization and ideas, think specifically about your sentences. In order to keep your report short and still effective, read your draft and look for ways to do the following:

1. Combine two sentences into one by incorporating phrases from one into the other and getting rid of words that do not add information.
2. Look for and eliminate repetition.
3. Make sure your conclusion does not merely repeat information in the body of your paper; it should be concise and offer something new, whether it is a suggestion or more information about the problem.
4. Remember your audience and the news format. Use crisp, clear language and make sure all sentences stick to the point.

**Editing** When you are satisfied with your revision, proofread your essay for spelling, clarity, and errors in mechanics.

## Presenting

With classmates, discuss some of the characteristics a successful television news reporter needs, such as clear pronunciation and an expressive voice. Practice reading your news reports aloud. Then deliver your news reports as news broadcasts in your class or in another class.

# LANGUAGE
## WORKSHOP

## ACTIVE AND PASSIVE VERBS

Suppose that a package was delivered to your home yesterday. If you know who delivered it, you could say, "The mail carrier delivered a package yesterday." However, if you don't know who delivered the package, you might say, "A package was delivered yesterday."

In the first sentence, the subject, *mail carrier,* tells who performed the action. If the subject performs the action, the verb is **active,** and the sentence is in the **active voice.**

In the second sentence, the subject, *package,* tells what was acted upon. If the subject names what was acted upon or what receives the action, the verb is **passive,** and the sentence is in the **passive voice.**

## Forming the Passive

▶ Usually, the **subject** of a sentence does the action. The **direct object** receives the action or is acted upon. To change a sentence from the passive to the active voice, you make the direct object the subject, the subject the object of a preposition, and change the verb. Sometimes you can drop the subject altogether.

**Active Voice** The sniper fired a shot. (The subject is *sniper.* The direct object is *shot.*)

**Passive Voice** A shot was fired by the sniper. (The direct object has become the subject, the subject is the object of a preposition, and the verb has been changed.)

**Passive Voice** A shot was fired. (The doer of the action has been dropped altogether.)

Sentences in the passive voice are wordier and often duller than those in the active voice. For these reasons, try to avoid passive verbs. When revising your writing, look for passive verbs and make them active.

**Passive** Dublin's Abbey Theatre was founded by William Butler Yeats in 1904. Many young Irish playwrights were encouraged by this theater. In fact, one might say that an Irish Renaissance was made possible by the Abbey Theatre.

**Active** William Butler Yeats founded Dublin's Abbey Theatre in 1904. This theater encouraged many young Irish playwrights. In fact, one might say that the Abbey Theatre made possible an Irish Renaissance.

## GRAMMAR

In the passive voice, the direct object becomes the new subject of the sentence. The passive voice verb is made from a form of the verb *to be* and the past participle.

**Active:**

Jim ate the banana. (*Jim* is the subject; *banana* is the direct object.)

**Passive:**

The banana was eaten by Jim. (The direct object, *banana,* of the active sentence has become the subject of the passive sentence. The verb has been changed to a past tense form of *to be, was,* plus the past participle of *to eat, eaten*.)

On rare occasions you may choose the passive voice. You might write a passive sentence to emphasize the receiver of an action.

**Passive**   The sniper was surprised by the identity of the victim.

**Active**    The identity of the victim surprised the sniper.

The sentence in the active voice is forceful but draws more attention to the identity than to the sniper. To place emphasis on the sniper, you need the passive voice.

You can also use the passive voice to express an action performed by an unknown person.

> The war had been fought for months. (The persons performing the action are not known.)

The active voice is usually best. Use the passive only when it meets a specific need. Avoid mixing passive and active in the same sentence.

**Exercise 1**   Rewrite each sentence, changing all active verbs to passive and all passive verbs to active. Add or change words as needed.

1. War has been described by many writers throughout history.
2. War has often been viewed by poets in symbolic terms.
3. Life-and-death struggles have been written about by many authors.
4. Liam O'Flaherty wrote a classic story about civil war.
5. In "The Sniper," gunshot sounds broke the silence of the night.
6. A lone man with a gun ate a sandwich on a rooftop near a bridge.
7. A loaded rifle and a pair of field glasses were carried by the sniper.
8. A lone enemy was seen by the sniper on a nearby roof.
9. The sniper killed the solitary gunman with a single shot.
10. Shockingly, his own brother had been killed by the sniper.

**Exercise 2**   Work with other students in a small group to revise the following paragraph, correcting unnecessary passives.

> William Butler Yeats is considered by many people one of the greatest poets of the twentieth century. Three major themes that run throughout his writing are noticed by his readers. Art, Irish nationalism and folklore, and the occult are themes that are woven by Yeats into much of his drama and poetry. Painting was studied by Yeats when he was a young man. However, the focus of his talent was soon turned by this gifted artist to poetry.

**LANGUAGE HANDBOOK**

For review and practice:
active and passive
voice, pages 1015–16

# STUDY SKILLS
## WORKSHOP

# TAKING ESSAY TESTS

## ESSAY CLUES

Many students go off track when answering essay questions because they fail to do what the question actually asks. These key words will tell you what the question is aiming at and how to structure your answer.

**Analyze:** This means that you should break something down into its parts and explain each part or how the parts are related.

**Compare and contrast:** Point out similarities and differences.

**Discuss:** Make a general statement, then support it with pertinent facts and details.

**Explain:** Make a process, problem, relationship, or term understandable.

**Define:** Place the thing into a group or class and tell how it differs from other members of that class by describing its specific qualities.

**Interpret:** Explain in your own words what something means.

**Summarize:** Give a condensed version of something.

Let's assume that you've studied hard for a test. You know the important facts, and you've thought carefully about the main issues covered in the material. You open the test and there they are: essay questions. What can you do to ensure the best possible results?

**Plan your overall strategy.** Skim all the questions. Note the key words that tell you what to do—words like *analyze, contrast*, or *summarize*. Decide on the difficulty of each question. Finally, set a rough time limit for each question, based on how much each question is worth; if a question is worth 20 percent of your total score, don't spend 50 percent of your time on it.

**Plan each answer.** Whether you start with the easiest question, the hardest question, or simply the first question, take time to plan your answer. Read the question carefully, paying special attention to those key words you noted. Look for the parts into which your answer should be organized. If possible, make a brief rough outline before answering. Jot down the main ideas and specific facts to include in your answer.

▶ **Answer the question.** Start with a strong thesis statement—a clear statement of your essay's main idea. For example, suppose you are asked to discuss the view of war expressed in Liam O'Flaherty's "The Sniper" and Thomas Hardy's "The Man He Killed." Your answer might begin, "For Liam O'Flaherty and Thomas Hardy, the special cruelty of war is that the 'enemies' we kill are people much like us."

After writing your introduction, including your thesis statement, write a separate paragraph for each of your main ideas. Support each main idea with specific facts. The teacher wants to know what you know, so provide as much information as you can. Use transitions to connect ideas.

When you've made all your key points, write a brief conclusion that either recaps your main ideas or states a general answer to the essay question, based on the information provided in the rest of your essay. Quickly go back over your essay and check for content, spelling, and grammar errors. Then move on to the next question. Remember to check the clock!

**Exercise** Write a thesis statement and rough outline for this question:

> Discuss the following statement, pro and con: Women should be allowed to serve in all positions in the armed forces, including those involving combat duty.

# CONFLICTING LOYALTIES

The early twentieth century was a time of profound and unsettling change in Great Britain and around the world. New attitudes and philosophies evolved, challenging the comforts and certainties of the past. Lower classes openly questioned the rights of the privileged, women demanded a new order, revolutionaries dreamed of a new world, and the down-trodden were no longer content to stay uncomplainingly in their place. As a result, many individuals had to make difficult choices between conflicting political, social, or family loyalties.

The following selections are about people whose loyalties are divided. As you read, think about how you would handle the problems they face.

*Drama*

## The Rising of the Moon

### LADY ISABELLA AUGUSTA GREGORY

## Examine What You Know

This play focuses on a moral dilemma: a man must choose between opposing sides, each of which seems to be right. Think of a time when you had to make a hard choice between two "right" sides. In small groups, discuss your experience and how you made your decision.

## Expand Your Knowledge

When this play was first performed, in 1907, the Irish were struggling to gain independence from Great Britain. Some patriots worked for gradual change using peaceful means; others wanted immediate separation and sometimes used violence. This play is about an Irish rebel in the late 1800's, a member of a group that plotted to overthrow the British.

Two popular revolutionary folk songs are important to the play. "The Rising of the Moon" celebrates a famous Irish rebellion of 1798. The song tells about rebels who gathered at moonrise, armed and ready to fight. It ends by thanking God that there are still men "who would follow in their footsteps at the rising of the moon." The other song, "Granuaile" (gran ū āl'), describes Ireland as a maiden who has been brutalized by the English, "a ruffian band." At one time, the English had passed laws forbidding the name of Ireland to be spoken. To keep the name alive, substitutions were made, and *Granuaile* was one often used.

## Enrich Your Reading

**Appreciating Dialect** The Irish speak different dialects of English, which vary from county to county. This play reflects the dialect spoken in Galway County in western Ireland. Longer vowel sounds and differences in grammar, sentence structure, and pronunciation, such as *me* for *my,* give a musical quality to the language. An example from the play illustrates these differences: "till I see will some sailor buy a ballad off me that would give me my supper." The American equivalent is "until I see if some sailor will buy a ballad from me to pay for my supper." Read some of the play's passages aloud to see if you can hear the differences in the language.

■ *A biography of the author can be found on page 686.*

# The *Rising of the Moon*

### LADY ISABELLA AUGUSTA GREGORY

Scene: *Side of a quay*[1] *in a seaport town. Some posts and chains. A large barrel. Enter three policemen. Moonlight.*

Sergeant, *who is older than the others, crosses the stage to right and looks down steps. The others put down a pastepot and unroll a bundle of placards.*[2]

**Policeman B.** I think this would be a good place to put up a notice. *(He points to barrel.)*

**Policeman X.** Better ask him. *(calls to* Sergeant*)* Will this be a good place for a placard? *(no answer)*

**Policeman B.** Will we put up a notice here on the barrel? *(no answer)*

**Sergeant.** There's a flight of steps here that leads to the water. This is a place that should be minded well. If he got down here, his friends might have a boat to meet him; they might send it in here from outside.

**Policeman B.** Would the barrel be a good place to put a notice up?

**Sergeant.** It might; you can put it there. *(They paste the notice up.)*

**Sergeant** *(reading it).* Dark hair—dark eyes, smooth face, height five feet five—there's not much to take hold of in that—It's a pity I had no chance of seeing him before he broke out of jail. They say he's a wonder, that it's he makes all the plans for the whole organization. There isn't another man in Ireland would have broken jail the way he did. He must have some friends among the jailers.

**Policeman B.** A hundred pounds[3] is little enough for the Government to offer for him. You may be sure any man in the force that takes him will get a promotion.

**Sergeant.** I'll mind this place myself. I wouldn't wonder at all if he came this way. He might come slipping along there *(points to side of quay)*, and his friends might be waiting for him there *(points down steps)*, and once he got away it's little chance we'd have of finding him; it's maybe under a load of kelp[4] he'd be in a fishing boat, and not one to help a married man that wants it to the reward.

**Policeman X.** And if we get him itself, nothing but abuse on our heads for it from the people, and maybe from our own relations.

**Sergeant.** Well, we have to do our duty in the force. Haven't we the whole country depending on us to keep law and order? It's

---

1. **quay** (kē): a wharf, or landing place, for loading and unloading ships.

2. **placards:** posters.

3. **hundred pounds:** English money; at that time worth about $280, a large sum for a working man.

4. **kelp:** seaweed, used for keeping caught fish fresh.

those that are down would be up and those that are up would be down, if it wasn't for us. Well, hurry on, you have plenty of other places to placard yet, and come back here then to me. You can take the lantern. Don't be too long now. It's very lonesome here with nothing but the moon.

**Policeman B.** It's a pity we can't stop with you. The Government should have brought more police into the town, with *him* in jail, and at assize[5] time too. Well, good luck to your watch. *(They go out.)*

**Sergeant** *(walks up and down once or twice and looks at placard).* A hundred pounds and promotion sure. There must be a great deal of spending in a hundred pounds. It's a pity some honest man not to be the better of that. *(A ragged man appears at left and tries to slip past.* Sergeant *suddenly turns.)*

**Sergeant.** Where are you going?

**Man.** I'm a poor ballad singer, your honor. I thought to sell some of these *(holds out bundle of ballads)* to the sailors. *(He goes on.)*

**Sergeant.** Stop! Didn't I tell you to stop? You can't go on there.

**Man.** Oh, very well. It's a hard thing to be poor. All the world's against the poor!

**Sergeant.** Who are you?

**Man.** You'd be as wise as myself if I told you, but I don't mind. I'm one Jimmy Walsh, a ballad singer.

**Sergeant.** Jimmy Walsh? I don't know that name.

**Man.** Ah, sure, they know it well enough in Ennis. Were you ever in Ennis, Sergeant?

**Sergeant.** What brought you here?

**Man.** Sure, it's to the assizes I came, thinking I might make a few shillings[6] here or there. It's in the one train with the judges I came.

**Sergeant.** Well, if you came so far, you may as well go farther, for you'll walk out of this.

**Man.** I will, I will; I'll just go on where I was going. *(goes toward steps)*

**Sergeant.** Come back from those steps; no one has leave to pass down them tonight.

**Man.** I'll just sit on the top of the steps till I see will some sailor buy a ballad off me that would give me my supper. They do be late going back to the ship. It's often I saw them in Cork carried down the quay in a hand-cart.

---

5. **assize** (ə sīz): a court session held periodically in the country.

6. **shillings:** coins worth one twentieth of a pound.

**Sergeant.** Move on, I tell you. I won't have anyone lingering about the quay tonight.

**Man.** Well, I'll go. It's the poor have the hard life! Maybe yourself might like one, Sergeant. Here's a good sheet now. *(turns one over)* "Content and a Pipe"—that's not much. "The Peeler and the Goat"—you wouldn't like that. "Johnny Hart"—that's a lovely song.

**Sergeant.** Move on.

**Man.** Ah, wait till you hear it. *(sings)*
> There was a rich farmer's daugh-
>    ter lived near the town of Ross;
> She courted a Highland soldier,[7]
>    his name was Johnny Hart;
> Says the mother to her daughter,
>    "I'll go distracted mad
> If you marry that Highland sol-
>    dier dressed up in Highland
>    plaid."

**Sergeant.** Stop that noise. *(Man wraps up his ballads and shuffles toward the steps.)*

**Sergeant.** Where are you going?

**Man.** Sure you told me to be going, and I am going.

**Sergeant.** Don't be a fool. I didn't tell you to go that way; I told you to go back to the town.

**Man.** Back to the town, is it?

**Sergeant** *(taking him by the shoulder and shoving him before him)*. Here, I'll show you the way. Be off with you. What are you stopping for?

**Man** *(who has been keeping his eye on the notice, points to it)*. I think I know what you're waiting for, Sergeant.

**Sergeant.** What's that to you?

**Man.** And I know well the man you're waiting for—I know him well—I'll be going. *(He shuffles on.)*

**Sergeant.** You know him? Come back here. What sort is he?

**Man.** Come back is it, Sergeant? Do you want to have me killed?

**Sergeant.** Why do you say that?

**Man.** Never mind. I'm going. I wouldn't be in your shoes if the reward was ten times as much. *(goes on off stage to left)* Not if it was ten times as much.

**Sergeant** *(rushing after him)*. Come back here, come back. *(drags him back)* What sort is he? Where did you see him?

**Man.** I saw him in my own place, in the County Clare. I tell you you wouldn't like to be looking at him. You'd be afraid to be in the one place with him. There isn't a weapon he doesn't know the use of, and as to strength, his muscles are as hard as that board. *(slaps barrel)*

**Sergeant.** Is he as bad as that?

**Man.** He is then.

**Sergeant.** Do you tell me so?

**Man.** There was a poor man in our place, a sergeant from Ballyvaughan—It was with a lump of stone he did it.

**Sergeant.** I never heard of that.

**Man.** And you wouldn't, Sergeant. It's not everything that happens gets into the papers. And there was a policeman in plain clothes, too. . . . It is in Limerick he was. . . . It was after the time of the attack on the police barrack at Kilmallock. . . . Moonlight . . . just like this . . . waterside. . . . Nothing was known for certain.

**Sergeant.** Do you say so? It's a terrible county to belong to.

**Man.** That's so, indeed! You might be standing there, looking out that way, thinking you saw him coming up this side of the quay *(points)*, and he might be coming up this other side *(points)*, and he'd be on you before you knew where you were.

---

7. **Highland soldier:** a Scottish soldier, hated by the Irish because of Scotland's ties to England.

**Sergeant.** It's a whole troop of police they ought to put here to stop a man like that.

**Man.** But if you'd like me to stop with you, I could be looking down this side. I could be sitting up here on this barrel.

**Sergeant.** And you know him well, too?

**Man.** I'd know him a mile off, Sergeant.

**Sergeant.** But you wouldn't want to share the reward?

**Man.** Is it a poor man like me, that has to be going the roads and singing in fairs, to have the name on him that he took a reward? But you don't want me. I'll be safer in the town.

**Sergeant.** Well, you can stop.

**Man** (getting up on barrel). All right, Sergeant. I wonder, now, you're not tired out, Sergeant, walking up and down the way you are.

**Sergeant.** If I'm tired I'm used to it.

**Man.** You might have hard work before you tonight yet. Take it easy while you can. There's plenty of room up here on the barrel, and you see farther when you're higher up.

**Sergeant.** Maybe so. (Gets up beside him on barrel, facing right. They sit back to back, looking different ways.) You made me feel a bit queer with the way you talked.

**Man.** Give me a match, Sergeant (he gives it and Man lights pipe); take a draw yourself? It'll quiet you. Wait now till I give you a light, but you needn't turn round. Don't take your eye off the quay for the life of you.

**Sergeant.** Never fear, I won't. (Lights pipe. They both smoke.) Indeed it's a hard thing to be in the force, out at night and no thanks for it, for all the danger we're in. And it's little we get but abuse from the people, and no choice but to obey our orders, and never asked when a man is sent into danger, if you are a married man with a family.

**Man** (sings).

As through the hills I walked to
  view the hills and shamrock
  plain,
I stood awhile where nature
  smiles to view the rocks and
  streams,
On a matron fair I fixed my eyes
  beneath a fertile vale,
As she sang her song it was on the
  wrong of poor old Granuaile.

**Sergeant.** Stop that; that's no song to be singing in these times.

**Man.** Ah, Sergeant, I was only singing to keep my heart up. It sinks when I think of him. To think of us two sitting here, and he creeping up the quay, maybe, to get to us.

**Sergeant.** Are you keeping a good lookout?

**Man.** I am; and for no reward too. Amn't I the foolish man? But when I saw a man in trouble, I never could help trying to get him out of it. What's that? Did something hit me? (rubs his heart)

**Sergeant** (patting him on the shoulder). You will get your reward in heaven.

**Man.** I know that, I know that, Sergeant, but life is precious.

**Sergeant.** Well, you can sing if it gives you more courage.

**Man** (sings).

Her head was bare, her hands
  and feet with iron bands were
  bound,
Her pensive strain and plaintive
  wail mingles with the evening
  gale,
And the song she sang with
  mournful air, I am old Granuaile.
Her lips so sweet that monarchs
  kissed . . .

**Sergeant.** That's not it. . . . "Her gown she wore was stained with gore." . . . That's it— you missed that.

**Man.** You're right, Sergeant, so it is; I missed it. *(repeats line)* But to think of a man like you knowing a song like that.[8]

**Sergeant.** There's many a thing a man might know and might not have any wish for.

**Man.** Now, I daresay, Sergeant, in your youth, you used to be sitting up on a wall, the way you are sitting up on this barrel now, and the other lads beside you, and you singing "Granuaile"?. . .

**Sergeant.** I did then.

**Man.** And the "Shan Bhean Bhocht"?[9] . . .

**Sergeant.** I did then.

**Man.** And the "Green on the Cape"?

**Sergeant.** That was one of them.

**Man.** And maybe the man you are watching for tonight used to be sitting on the wall, when he was young, and singing those same songs. . . . It's a queer world.

**Sergeant.** Whisht! . . . I think I see something coming. . . . It's only a dog.

**Man.** And isn't it a queer world?. . . Maybe it's one of the boys you used to be singing with that time you will be arresting today or tomorrow, and sending into the dock.

**Sergeant.** That's true indeed.

**Man.** And maybe one night, after you had been singing, if the other boys had told you some plan they had, some plan to free the country, you might have joined with them . . . and maybe it is you might be in trouble now.

**Sergeant.** Well, who knows but I might? I had a great spirit in those days.

**Man.** It's a queer world, Sergeant, and it's little any mother knows when she sees her child creeping on the floor what might happen to it before it has gone through its life, or who will be who in the end.

**Sergeant.** That's a queer thought now, and a true thought. Wait now till I think it out. . . . If it wasn't for the sense I have, and for my wife and family, and for me joining the force the time I did, it might be myself now would be after breaking jail and hiding in the dark, and it might be him that's hiding in the dark and that got out of jail would be sitting up where I am on this barrel. . . . And it might be myself would be creeping up trying to make my escape from himself, and it might be himself would be keeping the law, and myself would be breaking it, and myself would be trying maybe to put a bullet in his head, or to take up a lump of a stone the way you said he did . . . no, that myself did. . . . Oh! *(Gasps. After a pause.)* What's that? *(grasps* Man's *arm)*

**Man** *(jumps off barrel and listens, looking out over water).* It's nothing, Sergeant.

**Sergeant.** I thought it might be a boat. I had a notion there might be friends of his coming about the quays with a boat.

**Man.** Sergeant, I am thinking it was with the people you were, and not with the law you were, when you were a young man.

**Sergeant.** Well, if I was foolish then, that time's gone.

**Man.** Maybe, Sergeant, it comes into your head sometimes, in spite of your belt and your tunic, that it might have been as well for you to have followed Granuaile.

**Sergeant.** It's no business of yours what I think.

**Man.** Maybe, Sergeant, you'll be on the side of the country yet.

---

8. **a song like that:** as a police officer, the Sergeant is paid to uphold British laws. One would not expect him to know the words to "Granuaile," an anti-British revolutionary anthem.

9. **"Shan Bhean Bhocht"** (shôn ben bōkt): a revolutionary song about Ireland's troubles. Like "Granuaile," this song title refers to Ireland; literally, the phrase means "the poor old woman."

CAPTAIN NED BISHOP WITH OFFICERS ON THE BRIDGE OF THE S. S. EAGLE  David
Blackwood   Collection of Memorial University, St. John's, Newfoundland.

**Sergeant** *(gets off barrel)*. Don't talk to me like that. I have my duties and I know them. *(looks round)* That was a boat; I hear the oars. *(goes to the steps and looks down)*

**Man** *(sings)*.

> O, then, tell me, Shawn O'Farrell,
> > Where the gathering is to be.
> In the old spot by the river
> > Right well known to you and
> > > me!

**Sergeant.** Stop that! Stop that, I tell you!

**Man** *(sings louder)*.

> One word more, for signal token,
> > Whistle up the marching tune,
> With your pike upon your shoul-
> > > der,
> At the Rising of the Moon.

**Sergeant.** If you don't stop that, I'll arrest you.

*(A whistle from below answers, repeating the air.)*

**Sergeant.** That's a signal. *(stands between him and steps)* You must not pass this way. . . .

Step farther back. . . . Who are you? You are no ballad singer.

**Man.** You needn't ask who I am; that placard will tell you. *(points to placard)*

**Sergeant.** You are the man I am looking for.

**Man** *(Takes off hat and wig. Sergeant seizes them.)*. I am. There's a hundred pounds on my head. There is a friend of mine below in a boat. He knows a safe place to bring me to.

**Sergeant** *(looking still at hat and wig)*. It's a pity! It's a pity. You deceived me. You deceived me well.

**Man.** I am a friend of Granuaile. There is a hundred pounds on my head.

**Sergeant.** It's a pity, it's a pity!

**Man.** Will you let me pass, or must I make you let me?

**Sergeant.** I am in the force. I will not let you pass.

**Man.** I thought to do it with my tongue. *(puts hand in breast)* What is that?

*(voice of* Policeman X *outside)* Here, this is where we left him.

**Sergeant.** It's my comrades coming.

**Man.** You won't betray me . . . the friend of Granuaile. *(slips behind barrel)*

*(voice of* Policeman B*)* That was the last of the placards.

**Policeman X** *(as they come in)*. If he makes his escape it won't be unknown he'll make it. *(*Sergeant *puts hat and wig behind his back.)*

**Policeman B.** Did anyone come this way?

**Sergeant** *(after a pause)*. No one.

**Policeman B.** No one at all?

**Sergeant.** No one at all.

**Policeman B.** We had no orders to go back to the station; we can stop along with you.

**Sergeant.** I don't want you. There is nothing for you to do here.

**Policeman B.** You bade us to come back here and keep watch with you.

**Sergeant.** I'd sooner be alone. Would any man come this way and you making all that talk? It is better the place to be quiet.

**Policeman B.** Well, we'll leave you the lantern anyhow. *(hands it to him)*

**Sergeant.** I don't want it. Bring it with you.

**Policeman B.** You might want it. There are clouds coming up and you have the darkness of the night before you yet. I'll leave it over here on the barrel. *(goes to barrel)*

**Sergeant.** Bring it with you I tell you. No more talk.

**Policeman B.** Well, I thought it might be a comfort to you. I often think when I have it in my hand and can be flashing it about into every dark corner *(doing so)* that it's the same as being beside the fire at home, and the bits of bogwood blazing up now and again. *(flashes it about, now on the barrel, now on* Sergeant*)*

**Sergeant** *(furious)*. Be off the two of you, yourselves and your lantern!

*(They go out.* Man *comes from behind barrel. He and* Sergeant *stand looking at one another.)*

**Sergeant.** What are you waiting for?

**Man.** For my hat, of course, and my wig. You wouldn't wish me to get my death of cold?

*(*Sergeant *gives them.)*

**Man** *(going toward steps)*. Well, good night, comrade, and thank you. You did me a good turn tonight, and I'm obliged to you. Maybe I'll be able to do as much for you when the small rise up and the big fall down . . . when we all change places at the Rising *(waves his hand and disappears)* of the Moon.

**Sergeant** *(turning his back to audience and reading placard)*. A hundred pounds reward! A hundred pounds! *(turns toward audience)* I wonder, now, am I as great a fool as I think I am? ❧

Curtain

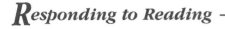

## *R*esponding to Reading

### First Impressions

1. Write words and phrases that describe your thoughts about the sergeant.

### Second Thoughts

2. Do you think the sergeant does the right thing in allowing the man to escape? What would you have done in the sergeant's position?

    **Think about**
    - how other people, in the words of Policeman X, might give him "nothing but abuse" if he turns in the revolutionary
    - what the reward might do for the sergeant's family
    - the sergeant's reasons for letting him go

3. Discuss the different strategies the man uses to persuade the sergeant to let him go. Which do you think works best?

    **Think about**
    - how the songs affect the sergeant
    - the stories about the powers of the escaped revolutionary
    - how the man compares the sergeant to himself

4. Will the sergeant later regret his decision? Consider how he might balance his views about the reward money with his patriotism.

5. Compare and contrast the sergeant's views of duty and rebellion with those of the revolutionary.

6. Which of the two main characters do you admire more? Explain why.

### Broader Connections

7. The sergeant obviously broke the law by letting the man escape. When, if ever, is it permissible to break a law for the sake of a cause? Explain your reasoning by using examples.

## *L*iterary Concept: Suspense

**Suspense** is created when an author purposely leaves readers uncertain or apprehensive about what will happen. Writers rely on suspense to entertain and to hold the interest of their audiences. Lady Gregory uses several suspense-building techniques, such as the sounds the sergeant hears in the dark and the man's hiding behind the barrel. What else in the play adds to the suspense?

**Concept Review: Setting**   How do the elements of setting—the physical location and time—contribute to the suspense and mood of the play?

## *Writing Options*

1. Write a complete version of the placard describing the man. Include the reasons why he is regarded as a dangerous criminal.

2. Create a chart that shows both sides of the sergeant's conflicting loyalties. One side should list the reasons for turning in the revolutionary, the other side the reasons for letting him escape.

3. Write a scene in which the sergeant tells his wife the story of the man's escape. Decide if he will tell her the truth about his role or change the story. Try to capture his concerns for his family as well as for the revolutionary cause.

4. Write the lyrics to an original ballad that tells the story of the sergeant and the rebel.

5. Create two columns that show the differences between standard English and the dialect of the play. In one column, list at least five examples of dialect. In the other column, "translate" each expression into standard English.

6. Explain how this play fits into the theme "Conflicting Loyalties."

## *Options for Learning*

**1** • **The Irish Balladeer** Research the traditional Irish ballad and find out more about its characteristics. Present your findings to your classmates, along with a few recordings of ballads. Some of the more popular singers of Irish ballads are the Clancy Brothers, Michael O'Donnaill, and a group called De Dannaan.

**2** • **"Rising" Revival** With some classmates, stage your interpretation of the play. You might do a dramatic reading using a different person for each part, or a full-scale production, including rehearsals, costumes, music, sound effects, and even Irish accents.

**3** • **Opening Night** This play opened in 1907 at the famous Abbey Theatre in Dublin, the national theater of Ireland. Create an advertising poster for the play. Draw an appropriate picture and write an attention-getting caption.

**4** • **Behind the Barrel** With a small group, rewrite the play's ending so that Policeman B discovers the man's disguise and hiding place. Show how everyone reacts to his discovery. Present your scene to the class.

### FACT FINDER

*When was the Republic of Ireland founded?*

## *Lady Isabella Augusta Gregory* 1852-1932

Lady Gregory, a late bloomer, did not take an active interest in literature until after the death of her husband in 1892. When her young son Robert told her that he wanted to learn to speak with the people who lived on their estate, she began the study of Gaelic (gāl' ik), the original language of the Irish. She became fascinated with Gaelic myths, legends, and folk tales, eventually collecting and translating them. Her interest in Irish traditions led her to a close friendship with William Butler Yeats, Ireland's foremost poet. The two were leading figures in the Irish Revival, which sought to preserve and renew cultural traditions. Together, they helped found the Abbey Theatre in Dublin, which became world famous.

Gregory, a friend and patron to countless writers, wrote her first play at the age of fifty-two and went on to write or translate forty more plays. Yeats said of her, "She has been to me a mother, friend, sister, and brother. I cannot realize the world without her."

*Fiction*

## A *Cup of Tea*
### KATHERINE MANSFIELD

## *E*xamine *What You Know*

Why do rich people help poor people? Create two lists, one showing noble motives for charity and the other showing self-serving ones. Then, as you read this story, see if you can figure out why the rich woman chooses to help the young beggar woman.

## *E*xpand *Your Knowledge*

Class structure in England is more rigid than in the United States. Wealthy English have traditionally attended the best schools, lived in the best neighborhoods, shopped in separate stores on exclusive streets, and rarely associated with the lower class. In fact, the name of the street where one lived or shopped indicated his or her social class. The upper-class wife never worked in or outside her home and spent her days shopping, visiting, and entertaining. It was considered improper for her to associate with the lower classes unless they were serving her in some way.

## *W*rite *Before You Read*

Make a copy of the chart below. Read the two dictionary definitions given for the word *patronize*. On the two middle lines, illustrate each definition with an example of your own. Then, as you read the story, find a behavior of Rosemary's that illustrates each definition and write it on the lowest lines.

**PATRONIZE**

**Dictionary Definitions**

**1.** to be kind or helpful to, but in a snobbish way
**2.** to be a regular customer of a store or merchant

**Example for Each Definition**

**1.** _____
**2.** _____

**How Each Definition Applies to Rosemary**

**1.** _____
**2.** _____

■ *A biography of the author can be found on page 697.*

# A Cup of Tea

Rosemary Fell was not exactly beautiful. No, you couldn't have called her beautiful. Pretty? Well, if you took her to pieces . . . But why be so cruel as to take anyone to pieces? She was young, brilliant, extremely modern, exquisitely well dressed, amazingly well read in the newest of the new books, and her parties were the most delicious mixture of the really important people and . . . artists—quaint creatures, discoveries of hers, some of them too terrifying for words, but others quite presentable and amusing.

Rosemary had been married two years. She had a duck of a boy. No, not Peter—Michael. And her husband absolutely adored her. They were rich, really rich, not just comfortably well off, which is odious and stuffy and sounds like one's grandparents. But if Rosemary wanted to shop she would go to Paris as you and I would go to Bond Street. If she wanted to buy flowers, the car pulled up at that perfect shop in Regent Street, and Rosemary inside the shop just gazed in her dazzled,[1] rather exotic way, and said: "I want those and those and those. Give me four bunches of those. And that jar of roses. Yes, I'll have all the roses in the jar. No, no lilac. I hate lilac. It's got no shape." The attendant bowed and put the lilac out of sight, as though this was only too true; lilac was dreadfully shapeless. "Give me those stumpy little tulips. Those red and white

ones." And she was followed to the car by a thin shopgirl staggering under an immense white paper armful that looked like a baby in long clothes. . . .

One winter afternoon she had been buying something in a little antique shop in Curzon Street. It was a shop she liked. For one thing, one usually had it to oneself. And then the man who kept it was ridiculously fond of serving her. He beamed whenever she came in. He clasped his hands; he was so gratified he could scarcely speak. Flattery, of course. All the same, there was something. . . .

"You see, madam," he would explain in his low respectful tones, "I love my things. I would rather not part with them than sell them to someone who does not appreciate them, who has not that fine feeling which is so rare. . . ." And, breathing deeply, he unrolled a tiny square of blue velvet and pressed it on the glass counter with his pale fingertips.

Today it was a little box. He had been keeping it for her. He had shown it to nobody as yet. An exquisite little enamel box with a glaze so fine it looked as though it had been baked in cream. On the lid a minute creature stood under a flowery tree, and a more minute creature still had her arms around his neck. Her hat, really no bigger than a geranium petal, hung from a branch; it had green ribbons.

---

1. **dazzled:** surprised, awed, or confused.

*Words to Know and Use*

**exquisitely** (eks′ kwi zit lē) *adv.* in a very beautiful or lovely manner
**quaint** (kwānt) *adj.* unusual; odd
**odious** (o′ dē əs) *adj.* arousing or deserving hatred; disgusting; offensive
**exotic** (eg zät′ ik) *adj.* strange or different in a striking or fascinating way

THE BREAKFAST  1911  William McGregor Paxton  Collection of Dr. and Mrs. John J. McDonough.

And there was pink cloud like a watchful cherub[2] floating above their heads. Rosemary took her hands out of her long gloves. She always took off her gloves to examine such things. Yes, she liked it very much. She loved it; it was a great duck. She must have it. And, turning the creamy box, opening and shutting it, she couldn't help noticing how charming her hands were against the blue velvet. The shopman, in some dim cavern of his mind, may have dared to think so too. For he took a pencil, leaned over the counter, and his pale bloodless fingers crept timidly toward those rosy, flashing ones, as he murmured gently: "If I may venture to point out to madam, the flowers on the little lady's bodice."[3]

"Charming!" Rosemary admired the flowers. But what was the price? For a moment the shopman did not seem to hear. Then a murmur reached her. "Twenty-eight guineas,[4] madam."

"Twenty-eight guineas." Rosemary gave no sign. She laid the little box down; she buttoned her gloves again. Twenty-eight guineas. Even if one is rich . . . She looked vague. She stared at a plump teakettle like a plump hen above the shopman's head, and her voice was

2. **cherub:** a chubby, rosy-faced child with wings.
3. **bodice** (bäd′ is): the upper part of a woman's dress.
4. **guineas:** gold coins of England used only for pricing luxury items.

dreamy as she answered: "Well, keep it for me—will you? I'll . . ."

But the shopman had already bowed as though keeping it for her was all any human being could ask. He would be willing, of course, to keep it for her forever.

# She saw a little battered creature with enormous eyes.

The discreet door shut with a click. She was outside on the step, gazing at the winter afternoon. Rain was falling, and with the rain it seemed the dark came too, spinning down like ashes. There was a cold bitter taste in the air, and the new-lighted lamps looked sad. Sad were the lights in the houses opposite. Dimly they burned as if regretting something. And people hurried by, hidden under their hateful umbrellas. Rosemary felt a strange pang. She pressed her muff to her breast; she wished she had the little box, too, to cling to. Of course, the car was there. She'd only to cross the pavement. But still she waited. There are moments, horrible moments in life, when one emerges from shelter and looks out, and it's awful. One oughtn't to give way to them. One ought to go home and have an extra-special tea. But at the very instant of thinking that, a young girl, thin, dark, shadowy—where had she come from?—was standing at Rosemary's elbow and a voice like a sigh, almost like a sob, breathed: "Madam, may I speak to you a moment?"

"Speak to me?" Rosemary turned. She saw a little battered creature with enormous eyes, someone quite young, no older than herself,

who clutched at her coat collar with reddened hands and shivered as though she had just come out of the water.

"M-madam," stammered the voice, "would you let me have the price of a cup of tea?"

"A cup of tea?" There was something simple, sincere in that voice; it wasn't in the least the voice of a beggar. "Then have you no money at all?" asked Rosemary.

"None, madam," came the answer.

"How extraordinary!" Rosemary peered through the dusk, and the girl gazed back at her. How more than extraordinary! And suddenly it seemed to Rosemary such an adventure. It was like something out of a novel by Dostoevski,[5] this meeting in the dusk. Supposing she took the girl home? Supposing she did do one of those things she was always reading about or seeing on the stage, what would happen? It would be thrilling. And she heard herself saying afterward to the amazement of her friends: "I simply took her home with me," as she stepped forward and said to that dim person beside her: "Come home to tea with me."

The girl drew back startled. She even stopped shivering for a moment. Rosemary put out a hand and touched her arm. "I mean it," she said, smiling. And she felt how simple and kind her smile was. "Why won't you? Do. Come home with me now in my car and have tea."

"You—you don't mean it, madam," said the girl, and there was pain in her voice.

"But I do," cried Rosemary. "I want you to. To please me. Come along."

The girl put her fingers to her lips and her eyes devoured Rosemary. "You're—you're

---

5. **Dostoevski** (dŏs' tō yef' skē): 1821-1881; a famous Russian writer of novels about the poor and the underprivileged.

*Words to Know and Use* | **discreet** (di skrēt') *adj.* careful about what one says or does

not taking me to the police station?" she stammered.

"The police station!" Rosemary laughed out. "Why should I be so cruel? No, I only want to make you warm and to hear—anything you care to tell me."

Hungry people are easily led. The footman held the door of the car open, and a moment later they were skimming through the dusk.

"There!" said Rosemary. She had a feeling of triumph as she slipped her hand through the velvet strap. She could have said, "Now I've got you," as she gazed at the little captive she had netted. But of course she meant it kindly. Oh, more than kindly. She was going to prove to this girl that—wonderful things did happen in life, that—fairy godmothers were real, that—rich people had hearts, and that women *were* sisters. She turned impulsively, saying: "Don't be frightened. After all, why shouldn't you come back with me? We're both women. If I'm the more fortunate, you ought to expect . . ."

But happily at that moment, for she didn't know how the sentence was going to end, the car stopped. The bell was rung, the door opened, and with a charming, protecting, almost embracing movement, Rosemary drew the other into the hall. Warmth, softness, light, a sweet scent, all those things so familiar to her she never even thought about them, she watched the other receive. It was fascinating. She was like the little rich girl in her nursery with all the cupboards to open, all the boxes to unpack.

"Come, come upstairs," said Rosemary, longing to begin to be generous. "Come up to my room." And, besides, she wanted to spare this poor little thing from being stared at by the servants; she decided as they mounted the stairs she would not even ring for Jeanne, but take off her things by herself. The great thing was to be natural!

And "There!" cried Rosemary again, as they reached her beautiful big bedroom with the curtains drawn, the fire leaping on her wonderful lacquer furniture, her gold cushions and the primrose and blue rugs.

The girl stood just inside the door; she seemed dazed. But Rosemary didn't mind that.

"Come and sit down," she cried, dragging her big chair up to the fire, "in this comfy chair. Come and get warm. You look so dreadfully cold."

"I daren't, madam," said the girl, and she edged backward.

"Oh, please"—Rosemary ran forward—"you mustn't be frightened, you mustn't, really. Sit down, and when I've taken off my things we shall go into the next room and have tea and be cozy. Why are you afraid?" And gently she half pushed the thin figure into its deep cradle.

But there was no answer. The girl stayed just as she had been put, with her hands by her sides and her mouth slightly open. To be quite sincere, she looked rather stupid. But Rosemary wouldn't acknowledge it. She leaned over her, saying: "Won't you take off your hat? Your pretty hair is all wet. And one is so much more comfortable without a hat, isn't one?"

There was a whisper that sounded like "Very good, madam" and the crushed hat was taken off.

"Let me help you off with your coat, too," said Rosemary.

The girl stood up. But she held on to the chair with one hand and let Rosemary pull. It was quite an effort. The other scarcely helped her at all. She seemed to stagger like a child, and the thought came and went through Rosemary's mind that if people wanted helping they must respond a little, just a little, otherwise it became very difficult indeed. And

THE MIRROR 1890 Dennis
Miller Bunker Daniel J. Terra
Collection Terra Museum of
American Art, Chicago.

what was she to do with the coat now? She left
it on the floor, and the hat too. She was just
going to take a cigarette off the mantelpiece
when the girl said quickly, but so lightly and
strangely: "I'm very sorry, madam, but I'm
going to faint. I shall go off, madam, if I don't
have something."

"Good heavens, how thoughtless I am!"
Rosemary rushed to the bell.

"Tea! Tea at once! And some brandy immediately!"

The maid was gone again, but the girl
almost cried out. "No. I don't want no brandy.
I never drink brandy. It's a cup of tea I want,
madam." And she burst into tears.

It was a terrible and fascinating moment.
Rosemary knelt beside her chair.

"Don't cry, poor little thing," she said.
"Don't cry." And she gave the other her lace
handkerchief. She really was touched beyond
words. She put her arm round those thin,
birdlike shoulders.

Now at last the other forgot to be shy, forgot
everything except that they were both women,
and gasped out: "I can't go on no longer like
this. I can't bear it. I shall do away with myself.
I can't bear no more."

"You shan't have to. I'll look after you.
Don't cry any more. Don't you see what a good
thing it was that you met me? We'll have tea
and you'll tell me everything. And I shall
arrange something. I promise. *Do* stop crying.
It's so exhausting. Please!"

The other did stop just in time for Rosemary to get up before the tea came. She had the table placed between them. She plied the poor little creature with everything, all the sandwiches, all the bread and butter, and every time her cup was empty she filled it with tea, cream and sugar. People always said sugar was so nourishing. As for herself she didn't eat; she smoked and looked away tactfully so that the other should not be shy.

And really the effect of that slight meal was marvelous. When the tea table was carried away a new being, a light, frail creature with tangled hair, dark lips, deep, lighted eyes, lay back in the big chair in a kind of sweet languor, looking at the blaze. Rosemary lit a fresh cigarette; it was time to begin.

"And when did you have your last meal?" she asked softly.

But at that moment the door handle turned.

"Rosemary, may I come in?" It was Philip.

"Of course."

He came in. "Oh, I'm so sorry," he said, and stopped and stared.

"It's quite all right," said Rosemary smiling. "This is my friend, Miss—"

"Smith, madam," said the languid figure, who was strangely still and unafraid.

"Smith," said Rosemary. "We are going to have a little talk."

"Oh, yes," said Philip. "Quite," and his eye caught sight of the coat and hat on the floor. He came over to the fire and turned his back to it. "It's a beastly afternoon," he said curiously, still looking at that listless figure, looking at its hands and boots, and then at Rosemary again.

"Yes, isn't it?" said Rosemary enthusiastically. "Vile."

Philip smiled his charming smile. "As a matter of fact," said he, "I wanted you to come into the library for a moment. Would you? Will Miss Smith excuse us?"

The big eyes were raised to him, but Rosemary answered for her. "Of course she will." And they went out of the room together.

"I say," said Philip, when they were alone. "Explain. Who is she? What does it all mean?"

## "My darling girl," said Philip, "You're quite mad, you know."

Rosemary, laughing, leaned against the door and said: "I picked her up in Curzon Street. Really. She's a real pickup. She asked me for the price of a cup of tea, and I brought her home with me."

"But what on earth are you going to do with her?" cried Philip.

"Be nice to her," said Rosemary quickly. "Be frightfully nice to her. Look after her. I don't know how. We haven't talked yet. But show her—treat her—make her feel—"

"My darling girl," said Philip, "You're quite mad, you know. It simply can't be done."

"I knew you'd say that," retorted Rosemary. "Why not? I want to. Isn't that a reason? And besides, one's always reading about these things. I decided—"

"But," said Philip slowly, and he cut the end of a cigar, "she's so astonishingly pretty."

"Pretty?" Rosemary was so surprised that

she blushed. "Do you think so? I—I hadn't thought about it."

"Good Lord!" Philip struck a match. "She's absolutely lovely. Look again, my child. I was bowled over when I came into your room just now. However . . . I think you're making a ghastly mistake. Sorry, darling, if I'm crude and all that. But let me know if Miss Smith is going to dine with us in time for me to look up *The Milliner's Gazette*."[6]

"You absurd creature!" said Rosemary, and she went out of the library, but not back to her bedroom. She went to her writing room and sat down at her desk. Pretty! Absolutely lovely! Bowled over! Her heart beat like a heavy bell. Pretty! Lovely! She drew her checkbook toward her. But no, checks would be no use, of course. She opened a drawer and took out five pound notes, looked at them, put two back, and holding the three squeezed in her hand, she went back to her bedroom.

Half an hour later Philip was still in the library, when Rosemary came in.

"I only wanted to tell you," said she, and she leaned against the door again and looked at him with her dazzled exotic gaze, "Miss Smith won't dine with us tonight."

Philip put down the paper. "Oh, what's happened? Previous engagement?"

Rosemary came over and sat down on his knee. "She insisted on going," said she, "so I gave the poor little thing a present of money. I couldn't keep her against her will, could I?" she added softly.

Rosemary had just done her hair, darkened her eyes a little, and put on her pearls. She put up her hands and touched Philip's cheeks.

"Do you like me?" said she, and her tone, sweet, husky, troubled him.

"I like you awfully," he said, and he held her tighter. "Kiss me."

There was a pause.

Then Rosemary said dreamily, "I saw a fascinating little box today. It cost twenty-eight guineas. May I have it?"

Philip jumped her on his knee. "You may, little wasteful one," said he.

But that was not really what Rosemary wanted to say.

"Philip," she whispered, and she pressed his head against her bosom, "am I *pretty?*" 🙡

---

6. ***The Milliner's Gazette:*** a trade newspaper about dressmaking for working-class people.

# INSIGHT

## A Cup of Tea

ANONYMOUS

Nan-in, a Japanese master during the Meiji era (1868–1912), received a university professor who came to inquire about Zen.

Nan-in served tea. He poured his visitor's cup full and then kept on pouring.

The professor watched the overflow until he no longer could restrain himself. "It is overfull. No more will go in!"

"Like this cup," Nan-in said, "you are full of your own opinions and speculations. How can I show you Zen unless you first empty your cup?"

# explain

## Responding to Reading

### First Impressions

1. Jot down words or phrases that describe your thoughts about Rosemary.

### Second Thoughts

2. What is Rosemary's motivation for inviting Miss Smith to her home?

   **Think about**
   - Rosemary's experiences before meeting Miss Smith
   - her thoughts when Miss Smith asks her for money
   - the reasons she gives to Miss Smith and to Philip

3. What do Rosemary's words and actions reveal about her personality?

   **Think about**
   - how she spends her time
   - how she treats Miss Smith
   - her relationship with her husband

4. Why does Rosemary send Miss Smith on her way? Is this behavior consistent with her personality?

5. What is Mansfield's attitude toward Rosemary and those whom she represents? Cite evidence from the story to support your answer.

### Broader Connections

6. In our society, what do shopping habits reveal about a person's status, personality, and background? Cite specific examples in your discussion.

## Literary Concept: Tone

**Tone** refers to the attitude a writer has toward his or her subject. Mansfield chooses words and details that express her feelings toward Rosemary, the main character in this story. These details describe Rosemary's appearance, actions, and thoughts. For example, as Miss Smith is crying, Rosemary responds, "*Do* stop crying. It's so exhausting. Please!" By choosing words that show Rosemary's self-centeredness, Mansfield reveals her critical attitude toward Rosemary. Find other details that contribute to the critical tone of this story.

**Concept Review: Minor Characters**   How do the words and actions of the shopkeeper, Miss Smith, and Philip help you understand Rosemary's personality?

# Writing Options

1. Using Mansfield's style of writing and Philip's manner of speaking, write Philip's response to Rosemary's final question.

2. Mansfield does not include the scene in which Rosemary sends Miss Smith away. Write that scene and include a conversation between the two characters that is consistent with what you know about them.

3. As a gossip columnist for a local newspaper in London, write an article in which you detail Rosemary's "good deed." Since Rosemary and Philip have a high social status, your column should probably be flattering.

4. Rewrite the scene with the shopkeeper, adding what he is thinking as he waits on Rosemary.

# Vocabulary Practice

**Exercise** On your paper, answer each question below and explain your answer.

1. Would a **discreet** person go on an extravagant shopping spree?
2. Can **vile** weather make a person feel depressed?
3. What would you expect to buy in a **quaint** gift shop?
4. Is an **exotic** gift usually practical?
5. Would a beggar woman be dressed **exquisitely?**
6. Might a **listless** person need help cleaning the house?
7. Can you **ply** and ignore a person at the same time?
8. Would a good meal help a starving man recover his **languor?**
9. Might a caring person be described as **odious?**
10. Would words spoken **tactfully** be offensive?

> **Words to Know and Use**
>
> discreet
> exotic
> exquisitely
> languor
> listless
> odious
> ply
> quaint
> tactfully
> vile

## Options for Learning

**1** • **The Modern Playwright** In play form, write a modern version of the scene in which Rosemary meets Miss Smith and takes her home. Use modern characters and a setting with which you are familiar, perhaps your school or neighborhood. Present this updated interpretation of the scene to the class.

**2** • **Rich Lady, Poor Lady** As Miss Smith, tell the story of your unusual encounter with the rich lady as if you were speaking to a friend. Include those things that made the strongest impression on you. Also focus on the differences you saw and felt between your world and Rosemary's.

**3** • **Dinner Guest** Decide what would have happened if Rosemary had invited Miss Smith to dine with herself and Philip. Rewrite the end of the story to include the dinner scene. Act out the scene with a few classmates.

**4** • **Craftsperson at Work** Draw, paint, or build the enamel box and lid as described in the story.

**FACT FINDER**

*What are three English pounds worth in U.S. dollars today?*

# Katherine Mansfield
## 1888-1923

Although Mansfield was born in New Zealand, she received her college education in London, England. On her return to New Zealand, she was so unhappy with her life there that her father sent her back to London. In 1909 she married George Bowden, but she left him after a few days and began a writing career. After the death of her soldier brother in 1915, Mansfield began writing stories based on memories of her life in New Zealand. These stories brought her fame as a writer. During the next two years, she reached the height of her writing career. She found her greatest joy in writing stories about real people in real-life situations. Mansfield became ill with tuberculosis in 1917 and died in 1923. Despite her short writing career, she is considered to have made a major contribution to the form and style of the modern short story.

*Fiction*

# As the Night the Day

ABIOSEH NICOL (ä′ bē ō′ sə ni kōl′)

## Examine What You Know

This story is about blame and punishment. Recall times when you have seen someone blamed for something he or she did not do. Discuss with your class why innocent people sometimes get blamed. Decide if the same people are accused often, and if so, why. What is the effect of unfair accusations on innocent people?

## Expand Your Knowledge

"As the Night the Day" is set in a Christian boys' school in Sierra Leone (sē er′ə lē ōn′), a small nation on the west coast of Africa. The population of Sierra Leone, a former colony of Great Britain, includes many different African ethnic groups as well as Arab and Indian traders and shopkeepers in the cities. Half the people adhere to tribal religions, one-third are Islam, and the rest are Christian. Because of poverty and a lack of educational resources, only a small minority of teenagers are able to attend school, usually the children of the wealthy. Like schools in the United States, the schools of Sierra Leone sometimes reflect the ethnic tensions of the larger society.

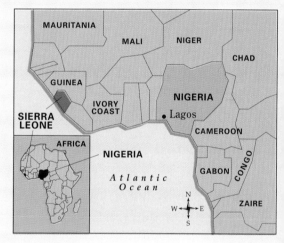

## Write Before You Read

What would you do if you accidentally broke or damaged school property and there were no witnesses? Would you report the damage immediately or not? Write an explanation of what you would do and why.

■ *A biography of the author can be found on page 712.*

# As the Night the Day

ABIOSEH NICOL

Kojo[1] and Bandele[2] walked slowly across the hot, green lawn, holding their science manuals with moist fingers. In the distance they could hear the junior school collecting in the hall of the main school building, for singing practice. Nearer, but still far enough, their classmates were strolling toward them. The two reached the science block and entered it. It was a low building set apart from the rest of the high school, which sprawled on the hillside of the African savanna.[3] The laboratory was a longish room, and at one end they saw Basu,[4] another boy, looking out of the window, his back turned to them. Mr. Abu,[5] the ferocious laboratory attendant, was not about. The rows of multicolored bottles looked inviting. A Bunsen burner soughed[6] loudly in the heavy, weary heat. Where the tip of the light-blue triangle of flame ended, a shimmering plastic transparency started. One could see the restless hot air moving in the minute tornado. The two African boys watched it, interestedly, holding hands.

"They say it is hotter inside the flame than on its surface," Kojo said, doubtfully. "I wonder how they know."

"I think you mean the opposite; let's try it ourselves," Bandele answered.

"How?"

"Let's take the temperature inside."

"All right, here is a thermometer. You do it."

"It says ninety degrees now. I shall take the temperature of the outer flame first, then you can take the inner yellow one."

Bandele held the thermometer gently forward to the flame, and Kojo craned to see. The thin thread of quicksilver[7] shot upward within the stem of the instrument with swift malevolence, and there was a slight crack. The stem had broken. On the bench the small, bulbous drops of mercury which had spilled from it shivered with glinting, playful <u>malice</u> and shuddered down to the cement floor, dashing themselves into a thousand shining pieces, some of which <u>coalesced</u> again and shook gaily, as if with silent laughter.

"Oh my God!" whispered Kojo hoarsely.

---

1. **Kojo:** (kō′ jō).
2. **Bandele:** (ban del′ ə).
3. **African savanna:** a treeless plain or grassland.
4. **Basu:** (bä sōō′).
5. **Abu:** (ä bōō′).
6. **soughed** (sɷud): made a soft, low, murmuring sound.
7. **quicksilver:** mercury, a liquid metal.

"Shut up!" Bandele said, <u>imperiously</u>, in a low voice.

# "See no evil, hear no evil, speak no evil," he whispered to Kojo.

Bandele swept the few drops on the bench into his cupped hand and threw the blob of mercury down the sink. He swept those on the floor under an adjoining cupboard with his bare feet. Then, picking up the broken halves of the thermometer, he tiptoed to the waste bin and dropped them in. He tiptoed back to Kojo, who was standing petrified by the blackboard.

"See no evil, hear no evil, speak no evil," he whispered to Kojo.

It all took place in a few seconds. Then the rest of the class started pouring in, chattering and pushing each other. Basu, who had been at the end of the room with his back turned to them all the time, now turned round and limped laboriously across to join the class, his eyes screwed up as they always were.

The class ranged itself loosely in a semicircle around the demonstration platform. They were dressed in the school uniform of white shirt and khaki shorts. Their official age was around sixteen, although, in fact, it ranged from Kojo's fifteen years to one or two boys of twenty-one.

Mr. Abu, the laboratory attendant, came in from the adjoining store and briskly cleaned the blackboard. He was a retired African sergeant from the Army Medical Corps and was feared by the boys. If he caught any of them in any petty thieving, he offered them the choice of a hard smack on the bottom or of being reported to the science masters. Most boys chose the former, as they knew the matter would end there, with no <u>protracted</u> interviews, moral recrimination,[8] or entry in the conduct book.

The science master stepped in and stood on his small platform. A tall, thin, dignified Negro, with graying hair and silver-rimmed spectacles badly fitting on his broad nose and always slipping down, making him look avuncular.[9] "Vernier"[10] was his nickname, as he insisted on exact measurement and exact speech "as fine as a vernier scale," he would say, which measured, of course, things in thousandths of a millimeter. Vernier set the experiments for the day and demonstrated them, then retired behind the *Church Times*, which he read seriously in between walking quickly down the aisles of lab benches, advising boys. It was a simple heat experiment to show that a dark surface gave out more heat by radiation than a bright surface.

During the class, Vernier was called away to the telephone and Abu was not about, having retired to the lavatory for a smoke. As soon as a posted sentinel announced that he was out of sight, minor pandemonium broke out. Some of the boys raided the store. The wealthier ones swiped rubber tubing to make catapults and to repair bicycles and helped themselves to chemicals for developing photographic films. The poorer boys were in deadlier earnest and took only things of strict commercial interest which could be sold easily in the market. They emptied stuff into bottles in

---

8. **recrimination:** an accusation given in return; a countercharge.
9. **avuncular** (ə vuŋ′ kyo͞o lər): like an uncle.
10. **Vernier:** (vʉr′ nē ər).

*Words to Know and Use* | **imperiously** (im pir′ ē əs lē) *adv.* in an overbearing, arrogant manner
**protracted** (prō trakt′ id) *adj.* long and drawn out

EX. 4-TRINITY'S TRINE 1964 Jess (Jess Collins) Oil on canvas over wood, 45 7/8″ × 48 1/8″
Collection, The Museum of Modern Art, New York  Purchased with the aid of funds from the National Endowment for the Arts and an anonymous donor.

their pockets. Soda for making soap, magnesium sulphate for opening medicine, salt for cooking, liquid paraffin for women's hairdressing, and fine yellow iodoform powder much in demand for sprinkling on sores. Kojo protested mildly against all this. "Oh, shut up!" a few boys said. Sorie,[11] a huge boy who always wore a fez[12] indoors and who, rumor said, had already fathered a child, commanded respect and some leadership in the class. He was sipping his favorite mixture of diluted alcohol and bicarbonate—which he called "gin and fizz"—from a beaker. 'Look here, Kojo, you are getting out of hand. What do you think our parents pay taxes and school fees for? For us to enjoy—or to buy a new car every year for Simpson?" The other boys laughed. Simpson was the European headmaster, feared by the small boys, adored by the boys in the middle school, and liked, in a critical fashion, with reservations, by some of the senior boys and African masters. He had a passion for new motorcars, buying one yearly.

"Come to think of it," Sorie continued to Kojo, "you must take something yourself, then we'll know we are safe." "Yes, you must," the other boys insisted. Kojo gave in and, unwillingly, took a little nitrate for some gunpowder experiments which he was carrying out at home.

"Someone!" the lookout called.

The boys <u>dispersed</u> in a moment. Sorie swilled out his mouth at the sink with some

---

11. **Sorie:** (sôr′ ē).

12. **fez:** a man's brimless hat, shaped like a cone with a flat top and black tassels.

701

water. Mr. Abu, the lab attendant, entered and observed the innocent collective expression of the class. He glared round suspiciously and sniffed the air. It was a physics experiment, but the place smelled chemical. However, Vernier came in then. After asking if anyone was in difficulty and finding that no one could momentarily think up anything, he retired to his chair and settled down to an article on Christian reunion, adjusting his spectacles and thoughtfully sucking an empty tooth-socket.

Toward the end of the period, the class collected around Vernier and gave in their results, which were then discussed. One of the more political boys asked Vernier: if dark surfaces gave out more heat, was that why they all had black faces in West Africa? A few boys giggled. Basu looked down and tapped his clubfoot embarrassedly on the floor. Vernier was used to questions of this sort from the senior boys. He never committed himself, as he was getting near retirement and his pension and became more guarded each year. He sometimes even feared that Simpson had spies among the boys.

"That may be so, although the opposite might be more convenient."

Everything in science had a loophole, the boys thought, and said so to Vernier.

"Ah! that is what is called research," he replied, enigmatically.

Sorie asked a question. Last time, they had been shown that an electric spark with hydrogen and oxygen atoms formed water. Why was that method not used to provide water in town at the height of the dry season, when there was an acute water shortage?

"It would be too expensive," Vernier replied, shortly. He disliked Sorie, not because of his different religion, but because he thought that Sorie was a bad influence and also asked ridiculous questions.

Sorie persisted. There was plenty of water during the rainy season. It could be split by lightning to hydrogen and oxygen in October and the gases compressed and stored, then changed back to water in March during the shortage. There was a faint ripple of applause from Sorie's admirers.

"It is an impracticable idea," Vernier snapped.

The class dispersed and started walking back across the hot grass. Kojo and Bandele heaved sighs of relief and joined Sorie's crowd, which was always the largest.

# Kojo kept walking on in a blind panic.

"Science is a bit of a swindle," Sorie was saying. "I do not for a moment think that Vernier believes any of it himself," he continued. "Because, if he does, why is he always reading religious books?"

"Come back, all of you, come back!" Mr. Abu's stentorian[13] voice rang out, across to them.

They wavered and stopped. Kojo kept walking on in a blind panic.

"Stop," Bandele hissed across. "You fool." He stopped, turned, and joined the returning crowd, closely followed by Bandele. Abu joined Vernier on the platform. The loose semicircle of boys faced them.

"Mr. Abu just found this in the waste bin," Vernier announced, gray with anger. He held

---

13. **stentorian** (sten tôr′ ē ən): very loud.

*Words to Know and Use* | **enigmatically** (en′ ig mat′ ik lē) *adv.* in a perplexing or obscure manner; mysteriously

up the two broken halves of the thermometer. "It must be due to someone from this class, as the number of thermometers was checked before being put out."

A little wind gusted in through the window and blew the silence heavily this way and that.

"Who?"

No one answered. Vernier looked round and waited.

"Since no one has owned up, I am afraid I shall have to detain you for an hour after school as punishment," said Vernier.

There was a murmur of dismay and anger. An important soccer house-match was scheduled for that afternoon. Some boys put their hands up and said that they had to play in the match.

"I don't care," Vernier shouted. He felt, in any case, that too much time was devoted to games and not enough to work.

He left Mr. Abu in charge and went off to fetch his things from the main building.

"We shall play 'Bible and Key,'" Abu announced as soon as Vernier had left. Kojo had been afraid of this, and new beads of perspiration sprang from his troubled brow. All the boys knew the details. It was a method of finding out a culprit by divination.[14] A large door-key was placed between the leaves of a Bible at the New Testament passage where Ananias and Sapphira were struck dead before the Apostles for lying, and the Bible suspended by two bits of string tied to both ends of the key. The combination was held up by someone, and the names of all present were called out in turn. When that of the sinner was called, the Bible was expected to turn round and round violently and fall.

Now Abu asked for a Bible. Someone produced a copy. He opened the first page and then shook his head and handed it back. "This won't do," he said. "It's a Revised Version; only the genuine Word of God will give us the answer."

An Authorized King James Version was then produced, and he was satisfied. Soon he had the contraption fixed up. He looked round the semicircle, from Sorie at one end, through the others, to Bandele, Basu, and Kojo at the other, near the door.

"You seem to have an honest face," he said to Kojo. "Come and hold it." Kojo took the ends of the string gingerly with both hands, trembling slightly.

Abu moved over to the low window and stood at attention, his sharp profile outlined against the red hibiscus flowers, the green trees, and the molten sky. The boys watched anxiously. A black-bodied lizard scurried up a wall and started nodding its pink head with grave impartiality.

Abu fixed his ageing, bloodshot eyes on the suspended Bible. He spoke hoarsely and slowly:

"Oh, Bible, Bible, on a key,
Kindly tell it unto me,
By swinging slowly round and true,
To whom this sinful act is due. . . ."

He turned to the boys and barked out their names in a parade-ground voice, beginning with Sorie and working his way round, looking at the Bible after each name.

To Kojo, trembling and shivering as if ice-cold water had been thrown over him, it seemed as if he had lost all power and that some gigantic being stood behind him holding up his tired, aching elbows. It seemed to him as if the key and Bible had taken on a life of their own, and he watched with fascination the whole combination moving slowly, jerkily, and rhythmically in short arcs as if it had acquired a heartbeat.

"Ayo Sogbenri, Sonnir Kargbo, Oji Ndebu." Abu was coming to the end now. "Tommy Longe, Ajayi Cole, Bandele Fagb . . ."

---

14. **divination:** the act of trying to foretell the future or explore the unknown by supernatural means.

Kojo dropped the Bible. "I am tired," he said, in a small scream. "I am tired."

"Yes, he is," Abu agreed, "but we are almost finished; only Bandele and Basu are left."

"Pick up that book, Kojo, and hold it up again." Bandele's voice whipped through the air with cold fury. It sobered Kojo, and he picked it up.

"Will you continue, please, with my name, Mr. Abu?" Bandele asked, turning to the window.

"Go back to your place quickly, Kojo," Abu said. "Vernier is coming. He might be vexed. He is a strongly religious man and so does not believe in the Bible-and-Key ceremony."

Kojo slipped back with sick relief, just before Vernier entered.

In the distance the rest of the school was assembling for closing prayers. The class sat and stood around the blackboard and demonstration bench in attitudes of exasperation, resignation, and self-righteous indignation. Kojo's heart was beating so loudly that he was surprised no one else heard it.

> "Once to every man and nation
> Comes the moment to decide . . ."[15]

The closing hymn floated across to them, interrupting the still afternoon.

Kojo got up. He felt now that he must speak the truth, or life would be intolerable ever afterward. Bandele got up swiftly before him. In fact, several things seemed to happen all at the same time. The rest of the class stirred. Vernier looked up from a book review which he had started reading. A butterfly, with black and gold wings, flew in and sat on the edge of the blackboard, flapping its wings quietly and waiting too.

"Basu was here first before any of the class," Bandele said firmly.

Everyone turned to Basu, who cleared his throat.

"I was just going to say so myself, sir," Basu replied to Vernier's inquiring glance.

"Pity you had no thought of it before," Vernier said, dryly. "What were you doing here?"

"I missed the previous class, so I came straight to the lab and waited. I was over there by the window, trying to look at the blue sky. I did not break the thermometer, sir."

A few boys tittered. Some looked away. The others muttered. Basu's breath always smelt of onions, but although he could play no games, some boys liked him and were kind to him in a tolerant way.

"Well, if you did not, someone did. We shall continue with the detention."

Vernier noticed Abu standing by. "You need not stay, Mr. Abu," he said to him. "I shall close up. In fact, come with me now and I shall let you out through the back gate."

He went out with Abu.

When he had left, Sorie turned to Basu and asked mildly:

"You are sure you did not break it?"

"No, I didn't."

"He did it," someone shouted.

"But what about the Bible-and-Key?" Basu protested. "It did not finish. Look at him." He pointed to Bandele.

"I was quite willing for it to go on," said Bandele. "You were the only one left."

Someone threw a book at Basu and said, "Confess!"

---

15. **Once to . . . decide:** These words of the hymn are from "Present Crisis," a poem by the American poet James Russell Lowell (1819-1891). The poem is about standing up for oneself or one's country when the need arises.

| *Words to Know and Use* | **exasperation** (eg zas′ pər ā′ shən) *n.* great irritation or annoyance<br>**self-righteous** (self rī′ chəs) *adj.* convinced of one's own moral superiority; smugly virtuous<br>**indignation** (in′ dig nā′ shən) *n.* anger aroused by something unjust or mean |
| --- | --- |

Basu backed on to a wall. "To God, I shall call the police if anyone strikes me," he cried fiercely.

"He thinks he can buy the police," a voice called.

"That proves it," someone shouted from the back.

"Yes, he must have done it," the others said, and they started throwing books at Basu. Sorie waved his arm for them to stop, but they did not. Books, corks, boxes of matches rained on Basu. He bent his head and shielded his face with his bent arm.

A nger and rage against everything different seized him.

"I did not do it, I swear I did not do it. Stop it, you fellows," he moaned over and over again. A small cut had appeared on his temple, and he was bleeding. Kojo sat quietly for a while. Then a curious hum started to pass through him, and his hands began to tremble, his armpits to feel curiously wetter. He turned round and picked up a book and flung it with desperate force at Basu, and then another. He felt somehow that there was an awful swelling of guilt which he could only shed by punishing himself through hurting someone. Anger and rage against everything different seized him, because if everything and everyone had been the same, somehow he felt nothing would have been wrong and they would all have been happy. He was carried away now by a torrent which swirled and pounded. He felt that somehow Basu was in the wrong, must be in the wrong, and if he hurt him hard enough, he would convince the others and therefore himself that he had not broken the thermometer and that he had never done anything

wrong. He groped for something bulky enough to throw and picked up the Bible.

"Stop it," Vernier shouted through the open doorway. "Stop it, you hooligans, you beasts."

They all became quiet and shamefacedly put down what they were going to throw. Basu was crying quietly and hopelessly, his thin body shaking.

"Go home, all of you, go home. I am ashamed of you." His black face shone with anger. "You are an utter disgrace to your nation and to your race."

They crept away, quietly, uneasily, avoiding each other's eyes, like people caught in a secret passion.

Vernier went to the first-aid cupboard and started dressing Basu's wounds.

Kojo and Bandele came back and hid behind the door, listening. Bandele insisted that they should.

Vernier put Basu's bandaged head against his waistcoat and dried the boy's tears with his handkerchief, gently patting his shaking shoulders.

"It wouldn't have been so bad if I had done it, sir," he mumbled, snuggling his head against Vernier, "but I did not do it. I swear to God I did not."

"Hush, hush," said Vernier comfortingly.

"Now they will hate me even more," he moaned.

"Hush, hush."

"I don't mind the wounds so much, they will heal."

"Hush, hush."

"They've missed the football match and now they will never talk to me again, oh-ee, oh-ee, why have I been so punished?"

"As you grow older," Vernier advised, "you must learn that men are punished not always for what they do, but often for what people think they will do, or for what they are. Remember that and you will find it easier to forgive them. 'To thine own self be true!' "

Vernier ended with a flourish, holding up his clenched fist in a mock dramatic gesture, quoting from the Shakespeare examination set-book for the year and declaiming to the dripping taps and empty benches and still afternoon, to make Basu laugh.

Basu dried his eyes and smiled wanly and replied: " 'And it shall follow as the night the day.'[16] Hamlet, Act One, Scene Three, Polonius to Laertes."

"There's a good chap. First Class, Grade One. I shall give you a lift home."

Kojo and Bandele walked down the red laterite[17] road together, Kojo dispiritedly kicking stones into the gutter.

"The fuss they made over a silly old thermometer," Bandele began.

"I don't know, old man, I don't know," Kojo said impatiently.

They had both been shaken by the scene in the empty lab. A thin, invisible wall of hostility and mistrust was slowly rising between them.

"Basu did not do it, of course," Bandele said.

Kojo stopped dead in his tracks. "Of course he did not do it," he shouted; "we did it."

"No need to shout, old man. After all, it was your idea."

"It wasn't," Kojo said furiously. "You suggested we try it."

"Well, you started the argument. Don't be childish." They tramped on silently, raising small clouds of dust with their bare feet.

"I should not take it too much to heart," Bandele continued. "That chap Basu's father hoards foodstuff like rice and palm oil until there is a shortage and then sells them at high prices. The police are watching him."

"What has that got to do with it?" Kojo asked.

"Don't you see, Basu might quite easily have broken that thermometer. I bet he has done things before that we have all been punished for." Bandele was emphatic.

They walked on steadily down the main road of the town, past the Syrian and Lebanese shops crammed with knickknacks and rolls of cloth, past a large Indian shop with dull red carpets and brass trays displayed in its windows, carefully stepping aside in the narrow road as the British officials sped by in cars to their hill-station bungalows for lunch and siesta.

Kojo reached home at last. He washed his feet and ate his main meal for the day. He sat about heavily and restlessly for some hours. Night soon fell with its usual swiftness, at six, and he finished his homework early and went to bed.

Lying in bed he rehearsed again what he was determined to do the next day. He would go up to Vernier:

"Sir," he would begin, "I wish to speak with you privately."

"Can it wait?" Vernier would ask.

"No, sir," he would say firmly, "as a matter of fact, it is rather urgent."

Vernier would take him to an empty classroom and say, "What is troubling you, Kojo Ananse?"

"I wish to make a confession, sir. I broke the thermometer yesterday." He had decided he would not name Bandele; it was up to the latter to decide whether he would lead a pure life.

Vernier would adjust his slipping glasses up his nose and think. Then he would say:

"This is a serious matter, Kojo. You realize you should have confessed yesterday?"

"Yes, sir, I am very sorry."

"You have done great harm, but better late than never. You will, of course, apologize in

---

16. **And it shall . . . the day:** The complete quotation is "To thine own self be true, and it must follow, as the night the day, thou canst not then be false to any man." In other words, be honest with yourself and you will be honest with others.

17. **laterite:** a red soil often found in tropical forests.

CONFRONTATION 1964
Ben Shahn By permission of
the Estate of Ben Shahn.

front of the class and particularly to Basu, who has shown himself a finer chap than all of you."

"I shall do so, sir."

"Why have you come to me now to apologize? Were you hoping that I would simply forgive you?"

"I was hoping you would, sir. I was hoping you would show your forgiveness by beating me."

Vernier would pull his glasses up his nose again. He would move his tongue inside his mouth reflectively. "I think you are right. Do you feel you deserve six strokes or nine?"

"Nine, sir."

"Bend over!"

Kojo had decided he would not cry, because he was almost a man.

Whack! Whack!!

Lying in bed in the dark thinking about it all as it would happen tomorrow, he clenched his teeth and tensed his buttocks in imaginary pain.

Whack! Whack!! Whack!!!

Suddenly, in his little room, under his thin cotton sheet, he began to cry. Because he felt the sharp lancing pain already cutting into him. Because of Basu and Simpson and the thermometer. For all the things he wanted to do and be which would never happen. For all the good men they had told them about—Jesus Christ, Mohammed, and George Washington, who never told a lie. For Florence Nightingale[18] and David Livingstone.[19] For Kagawa,[20] the Japanese man, for Gandhi,[21] and for Kwegyir Aggrey,[22] the African. Oh-ee, oh-ee. Because he knew he would never be as straight and strong and true as the school song said they should be. He saw, for the first time, what this thing would be like, becoming a man. He touched the edge of an <u>inconsolable</u>

18. **Florence Nightingale:** 1820-1910; an English nurse regarded as founder of modern nursing.

19. **David Livingstone:** 1813-1873; a Scottish missionary and explorer in Africa.

20. **Kagawa** (kä′ gä wä′): 1888-1960; a Japanese pacifist, social reformer, and Christian evangelist.

21. **Gandhi** (gan′ dē): 1869-1948; an Indian leader known for nonviolent methods and spirituality.

22. **Kwegyir Aggrey** (kweg′ yir äg′ grā): 1875-1927; an African educator and writer who said "For harmony, you must play both the black and white [piano keys]."

eternal grief. Oh-ee, oh-ee; always, he felt, always I shall be a disgrace to the nation and the race.

His mother passed by his bedroom door, slowly dragging her slippered feet as she always did. He pushed his face into his wet pillow to stifle his sobs, but she had heard him. She came in and switched on the light.

"What is the matter with you, my son?"

He pushed his face farther into his pillow.

"Nothing," he said, muffled and choking.

"You have been looking like a sick fowl all afternoon," she continued.

She advanced and put the back of her moist, cool fingers against the side of his neck.

"You have got fever," she exclaimed. "I'll get something from the kitchen."

When she had gone out, Kojo dried his tears and turned the dry side of the pillow up. His mother reappeared with a thermometer in one hand and some quinine mixture in the other.

"Oh, take it away, take it away," he shouted, pointing to her right hand and shutting his eyes tightly.

"All right, all right," she said, slipping the thermometer into her bosom.

He is a queer boy, she thought, with pride and a little fear as she watched him drink the clear, bitter fluid.

She then stood by him and held his head against her broad thigh as he sat up on the low bed, and she stroked his face. She knew he had been crying but did not ask him why, because she was sure he would not tell her. She knew he was learning, first slowly and now quickly, and she would soon cease to be his mother and be only one of the womenfolk in the family. Such a short time, she thought, when they are really yours and tell you everything. She

sighed and slowly eased his sleeping head down gently.

The next day Kojo got to school early and set to things briskly. He told Bandele that he was going to confess but would not name him. He half hoped he would join him. But Bandele had said, threateningly, that he had better not mention his name, let him go and be a Boy Scout on his own. The sneer strengthened him, and he went off to the lab. He met Mr. Abu and asked for Vernier. Abu said Vernier was busy and what was the matter, anyhow.

"I broke the thermometer yesterday," Kojo said in a businesslike manner.

Abu put down the glassware he was carrying.

"Well, I never!" he said. "What do you think you will gain by this?"

"I broke it," Kojo repeated.

"Basu broke it," Abu said impatiently. "Sorie got him to confess, and Basu himself came here this morning and told the science master and myself that he knew now that he had knocked the thermometer by mistake when he came in early yesterday afternoon. He had not turned round to look, but he had definitely heard a tinkle as he walked by. Someone must have picked it up and put it in the waste bin. The whole matter is settled, the palaver[23] finished."

He tapped a barometer on the wall and, squinting, read the pressure. He turned again to Kojo.

"I should normally have expected him to say so yesterday and save you boys missing the game. But there you are," he added, shrugging and trying to look reasonable; "you cannot hope for too much from a Syrian boy." ❧

---

23. **palaver** (pə lav' ər): talk, especially idle chatter.

# The Explosion in the Parlor

BAI XIAO-YI

The host poured tea into the cup and placed it on the small table in front of his guests, who were a father and daughter, and put the lid on the cup with a clink. Apparently thinking of something, he hurried into the inner room, leaving the thermos on the table. His two guests heard a chest of drawers opening and a rustling.

They remained sitting in the parlor, the ten-year-old daughter looking at the flowers outside the window, the father just about to take his cup, when the crash came, right there in the parlor. Something was hopelessly broken.

It was the thermos, which had fallen to the floor. The girl looked over her shoulder abruptly, startled, staring. It was mysterious. Neither of them had touched it, not even a little bit. True, it hadn't stood steadily when their host placed it on the table, but it hadn't fallen then.

The crash of the thermos caused the host, with a box of sugar cubes in his hand, to rush back from the inner room. He gawked at the steaming floor and blurted out, "It doesn't matter! It doesn't matter!"

The father started to say something. Then he muttered, "Sorry, I touched it and it fell."

"It doesn't matter," the host said.

Later, when they left the house, the daughter said, "Daddy, *did* you touch it?"

"No. But it stood so close to me."

"But you *didn't* touch it. I saw your reflection in the windowpane. You were sitting perfectly still."

The father laughed. "What then would you give as the cause of its fall?'

"The thermos fell by itself. The floor is uneven. It wasn't steady when Mr. Li put it there. Daddy, *why* did you say that you . . ."

"That won't do, girl. It sounds more acceptable when I say I knocked it down. There are things which people accept less the more you defend them. The truer the story you tell, the less true it sounds."

The daughter was lost in silence for a while. Then she said, "Can you explain it only this way?"

"Only this way," her father said.

## $R$*esponding to Reading*

### First Impressions

1. Do any characters in this story make you angry? Explain.

### Second Thoughts

2. Why do the students blame Basu so quickly?

3. Why does Basu confess to a crime he did not commit? What would you have done in his position?

   **Think about**
   - how the other students view him
   - his comment on page 705: "Now they will hate me even more."
   - how Sorie might have persuaded him to confess

4. Who is most responsible for what happens to Basu? Using examples from the story, explain why. Consider the actions of all the characters, including Basu himself.

5. What motivates Kojo to act the way he does? What is your judgment of his actions?

   **Think about**
   - his silence when asked who broke the thermometer
   - his participation in the attack on Basu
   - the reasons behind his attempt to confess

6. After the thermometer incident, Kojo cries because he thinks he's a disgrace. Discuss whether you think he should feel better about himself at the end of the story.

7. What do you think is the worst act of injustice in the story? Why?

### Broader Connections

8. When the other students assault Basu, even Kojo joins them. Reread the two paragraphs that describe the assault. What does this behavior reveal about how mobs can affect an individual?

## $L$*iterary Concept: Allusion*

An **allusion** is a reference to a historical or literary figure, event, or text. Writers use allusions to tap the memories and knowledge of their readers, which makes their work more suggestive and meaningful. For example, the lines from James Lowell's poem may remind many Christian readers of the rest of the hymn, which is about the need to do right at all costs. As a result, readers may better understand Kojo's feelings of guilt. How does the allusion "to thine own self be true" from Shakespeare's *Hamlet* help readers understand Kojo's actions?

**Concept Review: Theme**   Write a sentence that captures the story's theme.

# *W*riting Options

1. Compare Basu's action with what the father does in "The Explosion in the Parlor."

2. Create a comparison/contrast chart featuring Basu, Kojo, and Bandele. Use categories such as "Personality," "Background," "Motivations," and "Action." Review the story to find details to fill each category.

3. Choose another character in this book who reminds you of Kojo, Basu, or Bandele. List ways in which the two characters are alike.

4. Write a letter to the editor of your school or local newspaper about an individual or group that is being unfairly blamed for a problem in your school or community. Describe the situation and its injustices.

# *V*ocabulary Practice

**Exercise**  On your paper, write the word from the list that best completes each sentence.

1. Troublemakers may _____ at the sight of a person in authority.
2. Basu was _____ after the attack, until Vernier's words of comfort made him feel better.
3. Feeling proudly superior, Abu discussed Basu in a _____ tone.
4. Angry and thoughtless people may _____ to form a mob.
5. Basu acted _____ by admitting to a crime that he did not commit; his action mystified Kojo.
6. Prejudice causes _____ problems which take a long time to solve.
7. If Basu had shown _____ at being wrongly accused, he might have angrily punched his attackers.
8. Mobs often act with _____ against their victims.
9. Even calm and patient school administrators may show _____ when confronting a difficult situation.
10. Although Bandele was the guilty one, he acted _____ toward Basu, whom he regarded as inferior.

*Words to Know and Use*

**coalesce**
**disperse**
**enigmatically**
**exasperation**
**imperiously**
**inconsolable**
**indignation**
**malice**
**protracted**
**self-righteous**

## Options for Learning

**1 • Wonders of Science** In small groups, find answers to the following questions: 1) How do scientists know that the inside of a flame is hotter than the outside? 2) Why isn't water broken down into hydrogen and oxygen and stored, as Sorie suggests? 3) If dark surfaces give off more heat, why are Africans dark instead of light?

**2 • Crossing Traditions** Abu's Bible-and-key strategy shows how different traditions sometimes come together, in this case tribal and Christian beliefs. Find out more about how different cultures and traditions are blended in West African countries. Report your findings to the class.

**3 • Grade the Teachers** In small groups, decide how Vernier and Abu should be evaluated as teachers. First create categories that can be used in judging. Then grade the two characters in each category, using the same grading system your school does. Compile your grades in a report card and share them with the rest of your class.

**4 • Hail to the Heroes** Choose one of the role models Kojo thinks about when he is alone in his room. Research that person's life to discover what makes him or her worthy of praise. Also look in books of familiar quotations for possible words of wisdom from that person. Share your findings with the class.

 **FACT FINDER**

*For what is the vernier scale used?*

### Abioseh Nicol
1924–

Abioseh Nicol is the pen name of Dr. Davidson Nicol who has gained international distinction in science, politics, education, and literature. Trained as a doctor and a biochemist, Nicol has taught and conducted research at medical schools in Sierra Leone, Nigeria, and England. He also has worked as a top-ranking administrator of the University of Sierra Leone. More recently, he served his country as an ambassador to the United Nations and in other diplomatic posts.

Nicol began writing because he felt that most stories about Africa "seldom gave any nobility to their African characters." His works, which have made him one of Africa's most celebrated writers, are often about middle-class Africans who struggle to come to terms with their heritage.

Fiction

# Marriage Is a Private Affair

CHINUA ACHEBE (chin′ ōō ə ə chā′ bā)

## Examine What You Know

Marriage customs are different throughout the world. In some cultures, marriages are traditionally arranged by the parents for their children, while in other cultures, the parents play little part. Discuss the various reasons why parents might object to their child's choice of a marriage partner. Are they justified in objecting for any of those reasons?

## Expand Your Knowledge

Before Nigeria was unified in 1914, this West African country was divided between the inland northern tribes and kingdoms and the southern coastal tribes. For more than a thousand years, the Ibo (ē′ bō), Yoruba (yō′ rōō bə), and Beni (bē nē) tribes of the south and the Bornu (bôr nōō) and Hausa (hou′ sə) tribes of the north built cities and created sophisticated artwork. By the time the Portuguese and British arrived in the south, and the Arabs in the north, Nigeria was already a mixture of numerous cultures, races, and religions. Britain ruled all of Nigeria from 1906 until Nigeria became independent in 1960. Since that time, Lagos, the capital city of Nigeria, has grown tremendously and is now the center of industry, business, and government for much of western Africa. (See map on page 698.)

## Write Before You Read

Imagine that your parents are going to select your marriage partner. Describe their idea of the perfect spouse for you. Consider the importance that race, religion, nationality, social class, and education would play in their choice.

■ *A biography of the author can be found on page 721.*

# Marriage Is a Private Affair

CHINUA ACHEBE

"Have you written to your dad yet?" asked Nene[1] one afternoon as she sat with Nnaemeka[2] in her room at 16 Kasanga Street, Lagos.[3]

"No. I've been thinking about it. I think it's better to tell him when I get home on leave!"

"But why? Your leave is such a long way off yet—six whole weeks. He should be let into our happiness now."

Nnaemeka was silent for a while and then began very slowly, as if he groped for his words: "I wish I were sure it would be happiness to him."

"Of course it must," replied Nene, a little surprised. "Why shouldn't it?"

"You have lived in Lagos all your life, and you know very little about people in remote parts of the country."

"That's what you always say. But I don't believe anybody will be so unlike other people that they will be unhappy when their sons are engaged to marry."

"Yes. They are most unhappy if the engagement is not arranged by them. In our case it's worse—you are not even an Ibo."

This was said so seriously and so bluntly that Nene could not find speech immediately. In the cosmopolitan atmosphere of the city, it had always seemed to her something of a joke that a person's tribe could determine whom he married.

At last she said, "You don't really mean that he will object to your marrying me simply on that account? I had always thought you Ibos were kindly disposed to other people."

"So we are. But when it comes to marriage, well, it's not quite so simple. And this," he added, "is not peculiar to the Ibos. If your father were alive and lived in the heart of Ibibio-land, he would be exactly like my father."

"I don't know. But anyway, as your father is so fond of you, I'm sure he will forgive you soon enough. Come on then, be a good boy and send him a nice, lovely letter . . ."

"It would not be wise to break the news to him by writing. A letter will bring it upon him with a shock. I'm quite sure about that."

"All right, honey, suit yourself. You know your father."

As Nnaemeka walked home that evening, he turned over in his mind different ways of

---

1. **Nene** (nē nə).
2. **Nnaemeka** ('n nä' ə mä' kə).
3. **Lagos** (lä' gäs).

*Words to Know and Use*

**cosmopolitan** (käz' mə päl' ə tən) *adj.* worldly; common to most parts of the world

714

THE VILLAGE OF GUNGU, NIGERIA 1959 Eliot Elisofon National Museum of African Art, Smithsonian Institution, Washington, D.C.

overcoming his father's opposition, especially now that he had gone and found a girl for him. He had thought of showing his letter to Nene but decided on second thought not to, at least for the moment. He read it again when he got home and couldn't help smiling to himself. He remembered Ugoye quite well, an Amazon[4] of a girl who used to beat up all the boys, himself included, on the way to the stream, a complete dunce at school.

*I have found a girl who will suit you admirably— Ugoye[5] Nweke, the eldest daughter of our neighbor, Jacob Nweke. She has a proper Christian upbring-ing. When she stopped schooling some years ago, her father (a man of sound judgement) sent her to live in the house of a pastor where she has received all the training a wife could need. Her Sunday School teacher has told me that she reads her Bible very fluently. I hope we shall begin* negotiations *when you come home in December.*

On the second evening of his return from Lagos, Nnaemeka sat with his father under a cassia tree. This was the old man's retreat, where he went to read his Bible when the parching December sun had set and a fresh, reviving wind blew on the leaves.

"Father," began Nnaemeka suddenly, "I have come to ask for forgiveness."

"Forgiveness? For what, my son?" he asked in amazement.

"It's about this marriage question."

"Which marriage question?"

"I can't—we must—I mean it is impossible for me to marry Nweke's daughter."

"Impossible? Why?" asked his father.

"I don't love her."

---

4. **Amazon:** a large, strong, masculine woman.
5. **Ugoye** (o͞o gō′ yə).

*Words to Know and Use* | **negotiations** (ni gō′ shē ā′ shənz) *n.* bargaining to reach an agreement

715

"Nobody said you did. Why should you?" he asked.

"Marriage today is different . . ."

"Look here, my son," interrupted his father, "nothing is different. What one looks for in a wife are a good character and a Christian background."

Nnaemeka saw there was no hope along the present line of argument.

"Moreover," he said, "I am engaged to marry another girl who has all of Ugoye's good qualities and who . . ."

His father did not believe his ears. "What did you say?" he asked slowly and <u>disconcertingly</u>.

"She is a good Christian," his son went on, "and a teacher in a Girls' School in Lagos."

"Teacher, did you say? If you consider that a qualification for a good wife, I should like to

## "*Marriage today is different ...*"

point out to you, Emeka, that no Christian woman should teach. St. Paul in his letter to the Corinthians says that women should keep silence." He rose slowly from his seat and paced forward and backward. This was his pet subject, and he condemned vehemently those church leaders who encouraged women to teach in their schools. After he had spent his emotion on a long homily,[6] he at last came back to his son's engagement, in a seemingly milder tone.

"Whose daughter is she, anyway?"

"She is Nene Atang."

"What!" All the mildness was gone again. "Did you say Neneataga? What does that mean?"

"Nene Atang from Calabar.[7] She is the only girl I can marry." This was a very rash reply, and Nnaemeka expected the storm to burst. But it did not. His father merely walked away into his room. This was most unexpected and perplexed Nnaemeka. His father's silence was infinitely more menacing than a flood of threatening speech. That night the old man did not eat.

When he sent for Nnaemeka a day later, he applied all possible ways of <u>dissuasion</u>. But the young man's heart was hardened, and his father eventually gave him up as lost.

"I owe it to you, my son, as a duty to show you what is right and what is wrong. Whoever put this idea into your head might as well have cut your throat. It is Satan's work." He waved his son away.

"You will change your mind, Father, when you know Nene."

"I shall never see her," was the reply. From that night the father scarcely spoke to his son. He did not, however, cease hoping that he would realize how serious was the danger he was heading for. Day and night he put him in his prayers.

Nnaemeka, for his own part, was very deeply affected by his father's grief. But he kept hoping that it would pass away. If it had occurred to him that never in the history of his people had a man married a woman who spoke a different tongue, he might have been less optimistic. "It has never been heard," was the verdict of an old man speaking a few weeks later. In that short sentence he spoke for all of his people. This man had come with others to <u>commiserate</u> with Okeke[8] when news went round about his son's behavior. By that <u>time the son had gone</u> back to Lagos.

6. **homily:** a solemn, moralizing talk.
7. **Calabar:** a large seaport in southeast Nigeria.

*Words to Know and Use* | **disconcertingly** (dis′ kən sʉrt′ iŋ lē) *adv.* in a manner that shows one's confusion
**dissuasion** (di swā′ zhən) *n.* the act of advising against an action
**commiserate** (kə miz′ ər āt′) *v.* to sympathize with

"It has never been heard," said the old man again with a sad shake of his head.

"What did Our Lord say?" asked another gentleman. "Sons shall rise against their Fathers; it is there in the Holy Book."

"It is the beginning of the end," said another.

The discussion thus tending to become theological, Madubogwu, a highly practical man, brought it down once more to the ordinary level.

"Have you thought of consulting a native doctor about your son?" he asked Nnaemeka's father.

"He isn't sick," was the reply.

"What is he then? The boy's mind is diseased, and only a good herbalist can bring him back to his right senses. The medicine he requires is *Amalile,* the same that women apply with success to recapture their husbands' straying affection."

"Madubogwu is right," said another gentleman. "This thing calls for medicine."

"I shall not call in a native doctor." Nnaemeka's father was known to be obstinately ahead of his more superstitious neighbors in these matters. "I will not be another Mrs. Ochuba.[9] If my son wants to kill himself, let him do it with his own hands. It is not for me to help him."

"But it was her fault," said Madubogwu. "She ought to have gone to an honest herbalist. She was a clever woman, nevertheless."

"She was a wicked murderess," said Jonathan, who rarely argued with his neighbors because, he often said, they were incapable of reasoning. "The medicine was prepared for her husband, it was his name they called in its preparation, and I am sure it would have been perfectly beneficial to him. It was wicked to put it into the herbalist's food and say you were only trying it out."

Six months later, Nnaemeka was showing his young wife a short letter from his father:

*It amazes me that you could be so unfeeling as to send me your wedding picture. I would have sent it back. But on further thought I decided just to cut off your wife and send it back to you because I have nothing to do with her. How I wish that I had nothing to do with you either.*

When Nene read through this letter and looked at the mutilated picture, her eyes filled with tears, and she began to sob.

"Don't cry, my darling," said her husband. "He is essentially good-natured and will one day look more kindly on our marriage." But years passed and that one day did not come.

For eight years, Okeke would have nothing to do with his son, Nnaemeka. Only three times (when Nnaemeka asked to come home and spend his leave) did he write to him.

"I can't have you in my house," he replied on one occasion. "It can be of no interest to me where or how you spend your leave—or your life, for that matter."

The prejudice against Nnaemeka's marriage was not confined to his little village. In Lagos, especially among his people who worked there, it showed itself in a different way. Their women, when they met at their village meeting, were not hostile to Nene. Rather, they paid her such excessive deference as to make her feel she was not one of them. But as time went on, Nene gradually broke through some of this prejudice and even began to make friends among them. Slowly and grudgingly they began to admit that she kept her home much better than most of them.

---

8. **Okeke** (ō kā′ kə).
9. **Ochuba** (ō chōō′ bə).

717

AFRICAN VARIATION
1984 Gregory Alexander Bankside
Gallery, London.

The story eventually got to the little village in the heart of the Ibo country that Nnaemeka and his young wife were a most happy couple. But his father was one of the few people in the village who knew nothing about this. He always displayed so much temper whenever his son's name was mentioned that everyone avoided it in his presence. By a tremendous effort of will he had succeeded in pushing his son to the back of his mind. The strain had nearly killed him, but he had <u>persevered</u>, and won.

Then one day he received a letter from Nene, and in spite of himself he began to glance through it perfunctorily[10] until all of a sudden the expression on his face changed and he began to read more carefully.

*. . . Our two sons, from the day they learnt that they have a grandfather, have insisted on being taken to him. I find it impossible to tell them that you will not see them. I implore you to allow Nnaemeka to bring them home for a short time during his leave next month. I shall remain here in Lagos . . .*

The old man at once felt the resolution he had built up over so many years falling in. He was telling himself that he must not give in. He tried to steel his heart against all emotional appeals. It was a reenactment of that other struggle. He leaned against a window and looked out. The sky was overcast with heavy black clouds, and a high wind began to blow, filling the air with dust and dry leaves. It was one of those rare occasions when even Nature takes a hand in a human fight. Very soon it began to rain, the first rain in the year. It came down in large, sharp drops and was accompanied by the lightning and thunder which mark a change of season. Okeke was trying hard not to think of his two grandsons. But he knew he was now fighting a losing battle. He tried to hum a favorite hymn, but the pattering of large raindrops on the roof broke up the tune. His mind immediately returned to the children. How could he shut his door against them? By a curious mental process he imagined them standing, sad and forsaken, under the harsh, angry weather—shut out from his house.

That night he hardly slept, from <u>remorse</u>— and a vague fear that he might die without making it up to them. ❧

---

10. **perfunctorily:** carelessly or indifferently.

*Words
to Know
and Use*

**persevere** (pŭr' s vir') *v.* to continue or persist in spite of difficulty
**remorse** (ri môrs') *n.* a deep sense of guilt over a wrong that one has committed

# explain

## Responding to Reading

### First Impressions

1. What do you think of Nnaemeka's father? Jot down your thoughts.

### Second Thoughts

2. Why does the father refuse to accept his son's marriage? Are his feelings understandable?

   **Think about**
   • his Ibo traditions
   • his Christian beliefs
   • his lack of contact with people from other parts of Nigeria

3. How are Nnaemeka and his father similar? How are they different?

4. What kinds of problems do Nnaemeka and Nene face because of their mixed marriage? How well do they handle their difficulties? Use examples from the story to support your answer.

5. Do the father's feelings toward his son's marriage change by the end of the story? Support your answer with evidence from the story.

6. Explain how the title of the story reflects the theme.

### Broader Connections

7. How does this story reflect the problems that arise when a tribal society unites into one nation? Where else in the world do similar problems exist?

## Literary Concept: Setting

**Setting** involves more than physical location. The culture and attitudes of the society at the time the story takes place are also part of the setting. For example, stories set in pioneer America reflect a vastly different culture and different conflicts than stories set in modern urban America.

How does the cultural setting of this story contribute to the conflict and the attitudes of the characters? If the story had been set thirty years later, would the villagers' attitudes have been different? Explain.

**Concept Review: Character Motivation**   Why does Nene send a letter to Nnaemeka's father? What does this action reveal about her values?

# *W*riting Options

1. Create a chart that shows the father's and son's conflicting values. When choosing what categories to include, consider traditional and modern views, family and personal needs, and city and rural attitudes.

2. List the reasons you would give Nnaemeka for or against marrying Nene.

3. Reread the section in the story about Mrs. Ochuba. Then write an explanation of what happened.

4. Write a description, using dialogue, of how the first encounter between Nnaemeka's father and his two grandsons might go. You may wish to include Nnaemeka or Nene in your description.

# *V*ocabulary Practice

**Exercise** Decide if each pair of words are synonyms or antonyms. On paper, write *S* for synonyms or *A* for antonyms.

1. cosmopolitan—worldly
2. negotiations—dealings
3. disconcertingly—calmly
4. dissuasion—acceptance
5. commiserate—sympathize
6. theological—religious
7. obstinately—stubbornly
8. deference—disrespect
9. persevere—quit
10. remorse—guilt

*Words to Know and Use*

**commiserate**
**cosmopolitan**
**deference**
**disconcertingly**
**dissuasion**
**negotiations**
**obstinately**
**persevere**
**remorse**
**theological**

## *O*ptions for Learning

**1** • **Native Medicine** Research herbal medicine in African society. Check the *Readers' Guide to Periodical Literature* and books on medicine, herbal healing, and folk healing. Report to the class on the medicines and treatments that are used by traditional native doctors in Africa.

**2** • **The Tribal Marriage Ceremony** Find out about the traditional African marriage ceremony of the Ibos or some other African tribe. With several classmates, re-create the ceremony, perhaps using traditional dress, music, and food.

**3** • **Modern Marriage Problems** Stage this story for the class, but use a modern American family and setting. Using the same basic story line, show the objections an American parent might have toward his or her child's partner, and the effects of the marriage on the relationships between family members.

**4** • **The Ibos** Research the Ibos of Nigeria. Find out about their traditional way of life, such as the roles of their men and women and their marriage and social customs. Investigate the ways in which these roles and customs are changing today. Report your findings to the class.

### FACT FINDER

*What is the population of Lagos, Nigeria?*

## *C*hinua Achebe
### 1930–

Achebe is an Ibo who was educated in Nigeria. He received his university degree in 1954. His first novel, *Things Fall Apart*, was published in 1959 and immediately became known worldwide. It reflects a common African theme about the clash of traditional and modern values. In 1960, when Nigeria became independent from British rule, Achebe wrote a novel about how a European-educated African copes with the transition of his country into a modern nation. Achebe's works continue to reflect Nigeria's problems, and his literary themes currently concern political corruption, democracy, and the disintegration of tribal economy and ecology.

# WRITER'S WORKSHOP

## ARGUMENTATION

In the selections in this subunit, characters are forced to make a choice between two sides of an issue. For example, the sergeant in "The Rising of the Moon" has to choose between his duty as a British soldier and his patriotism as an Irish citizen. Arguments can be made for and against either side. The same is true of controversial issues today. An issue is controversial when groups of people believe in different sides and can argue logically for their particular position.

For the following assignment, you will write an **argumentative essay** to persuade your classmates to accept your point of view on a controversial issue. In an argumentative essay, you present and defend your own position and show why the opposing position is weak. The issue you choose can be political or economic or one involving beliefs or ethics; it can be local, national, or international.

> **Here is your PASSkey to this assignment.**

### GUIDED ASSIGNMENT: ARGUMENTATIVE ESSAY

Write an argumentative essay in which you present and defend your position on an issue and show why the opposite position is wrong.

**P**URPOSE: To inform and persuade

**A**UDIENCE: Your classmates

**S**UBJECT: A controversial issue

**S**TRUCTURE: An argumentative essay

## Prewriting

**STEP 1** **Choose a topic**  Use brainstorming or word webbing to find controversial issues about which you have strong feelings. You might look in newspapers and magazines for ideas, listen to radio and television news reports, and talk to parents and friends. Be sure to choose a topic that has two distinct sides and one about which you have strong feelings. One student brainstormed the following topics:

STUDENT MODEL ▶

```
School: canceling fall dance        State: lowering
Community: closing town pool        driving age
World: destruction of rain          Country: providing
forests                             housing for homeless
```

**2** **State your claim**    Your **claim** is a statement that presents your position or opinion about the issue. Write your claim in one clear, direct sentence. Next, think of and list arguments that support your position. Then, list the opposing side's arguments. These will be the reasons you **refute**, or prove wrong or weak. Use a chart like the one below to clarify the arguments for and against your position.

**CLAIM**

> The rain forests of Brazil and the Amazon Basin should be protected from the cutting of trees and clearing of land.

◀ STUDENT MODEL

**Arguments for My Position:**

1. destroys plant species that may have important medical and scientific benefits not yet discovered
2. ruins habitat of tropical animals
3. could lead to extinction of some species
4. must protect earth from those who want to make money
5. native peoples will be displaced and their culture threatened
6. contributes to global warming
7. depletes world's oxygen supply

**Arguments for the Opposition:**

1. tree-cutting and land-clearing create jobs in poor countries
2. provides lumber
3. creates farmland necessary for feeding large populations
4. makes money for some
5. products and by-products to other countries can help Amazon countries pay their debts
6. We have no right to tell these countries what to do with their resources.

**STEP 3** **Gather evidence** Choose about four of your strongest arguments and collect as much evidence as possible to support them. Use current reference works, periodicals, books, and interviews with experts. Find examples, facts, and statistics to illustrate each reason.

At the same time, look for evidence that **refutes** the arguments of your opponents. When you write your argumentation paper, you will not only defend your own argument point by point, you must also present the arguments of the opposition and explain why each one is weak or false. For example, the opposition's first argument is that jobs are created by cutting trees and clearing land. You could refute this argument by pointing out that other jobs could be created, such as harvesting natural forest products, without destroying trees.

**STEP 4** **Organize your information** Plan to organize your essay in the following manner, which is typical of argumentation.

**Introduction**
1. Present your position. This is your **claim**—the position which you will defend.
2. Give the history or background of the issue, explaining how the controversy arose.

**Body**
1. Restate your claim.
2. Support your claim with evidence, reason by reason.
3. Present the opposing point of view.
4. Refute the opposing point of view. Show how the arguments are weak, incomplete, wrong, and so on.

**Conclusion**
Summarize your argument and make a final appeal to the reader to accept your opinion on the issue.

## Drafting

**STEP 1** **Draft an introduction** Begin your essay with a quotation, an anecdote, a question, or some other detail to catch your classmates' interest. Include a brief explanation of your topic, your position on the issue, and a statement explaining how you will use evidence to support your argument. Here's one student's introduction.

STUDENT MODEL ▶

In the time it takes you to read this sentence, about fifty-three acres of the world's rain forest will be destroyed. The wanton destruction of the rain forest is the most serious environmental problem today. Since the

1960's, farmers, ranchers, builders, and loggers have been clearing the tropical rain forest. This practice must stop, as the following evidence clearly shows.

**STEP 2** **Draft the body** Write each reason as a topic sentence for a paragraph. Use facts, examples, illustrations, statistics, and expert testimony to support that reason.

When you have elaborated on all the reasons that support your argument, present the arguments for the opposing side. Show why each argument is inaccurate, illogical, or unproven. Be careful to refute, not insult, the opposing position.

**STEP 3** **Draft the conclusion** In the concluding paragraph, summarize your argument and appeal to your classmates to accept your position. Here is one student's conclusion.

> The destruction of the rain forest must be stopped. Human greed is causing the loss of valuable vegetation and therefore the loss of a habitat for tropical animals. These unique animals and plants are headed for extinction. There may be devastating effects for the rest of the world as well, including erosion and global warming, which could drastically affect the climate everywhere. For the sake of our own species as well as of others, each of us should join the worldwide effort to save the tropical rain forest.

◀ STUDENT MODEL

## Revising and Editing

Exchange argumentative essays with a classmate. Acting as peer editors, use the following revision checklist to suggest revisions.

### Revision Checklist

1. Does the essay address a controversial, arguable topic?
2. Is the argument stated clearly and precisely?
3. Are logical arguments and reliable evidence used—facts, illustrations, expert opinions—to support the argument?
4. Are opposing arguments listed and refuted?
5. Does the concluding paragraph summarize the argument?

**Editing** Have a peer editor proofread your essay for errors in grammar, spelling, usage, and punctuation.

# LANGUAGE
## WORKSHOP

## VARIETY IN SENTENCE STRUCTURE

Even if you're a chocolate lover, a diet of nothing but chocolate ice cream would get boring—not to mention unhealthy—very quickly. Too much of anything is just too much, and that goes for your writing as well as your diet.

Too many long sentences can leave your reader feeling weary and perhaps confused. On the other hand, too many short sentences can result in dull, choppy writing. It's a good idea, then, to vary both the length of your sentences and the kinds of sentences you use.

In your writing, do you use mostly simple sentences or are some of your sentences more complex, with clauses and phrases smoothly woven together? Let's review the different kinds of sentence structure you can use. But first, a word about clauses.

Every sentence is made up of one or more clauses. A **clause** is a group of words containing a subject and a verb. An **independent clause** can stand alone as a sentence. A **subordinate clause** cannot stand alone as a sentence.

A **simple sentence** contains a single independent clause. The parts of the subject or the verb in this clause may be compound. Look at these examples.

| Subject | Predicate |
|---|---|
| All the students | gathered in the lab. |
| The teacher | started the lecture. |
| The teacher and his assistant | left the room. |

► A **compound sentence** consists of two or more independent clauses joined together. The parts of a compound sentence may be joined in any of the ways described in the margin.

Rosemary Fell was walking from the shop to her waiting car; a young stranger accosted her on the street.

Rosemary stopped for a moment, and the young woman spoke to her.

Rosemary could listen or she could leave.

Rosemary was a bit startled; however, she was also thrilled by the thought of an adventure.

## PUNCTUATION

To form a compound sentence, join two simple sentences in one of these ways:

1. If the two sentences are very short, use a coordinating conjunction (*and, or, nor, for, but, so,* or *yet*) by itself: *I directed and they acted.*

2. If the two sentences are longer, use a comma and a coordinating conjunction: *I directed the play, and they acted in it.*

3. Use a semicolon: *I directed the play; they acted in it.*

4. Use a semicolon, a conjunctive adverb such as *therefore* or *however,* and a comma: *I directed the play; however, they acted in it.*

A **complex sentence** contains an independent clause and a subordinate clause.

| Independent Clause | Subordinate Clause |
| --- | --- |
| The stranger seemed dazed | until she drank her tea. |

| Subordinate Clause | Independent Clause |
| --- | --- |
| Once Rosemary gave her some money, | the young woman left. |

Read the following passage, paying special attention to the variety of sentences used.

> Rosemary was thrilled with this adventure. It was a scene out of a novel. Once they arrived at her home, Rosemary brought the frail creature up to her bedroom. She half pushed the young woman into the deep cradle of the big chair near the fireplace. Rosemary tried to help the woman take off her coat, but the woman resisted her help. It was quite an effort for Rosemary. The timid young woman staggered like a child. Finally, she spoke. She needed tea; she was afraid of fainting without a cup of tea. Then she burst into tears. Rosemary knelt beside the chair and put her arm around those thin, birdlike shoulders. Rosemary was truly touched.

How many different kinds of sentences can you find in the passage? How do the sentences differ in structure? Find examples of each kind of sentence. Then think about how the sentences all work together to communicate not only a specific scene but also a feeling of suspense.

The next time you sit down to write, try to vary your sentences. Remember that a writer's skill shows in the way a variety of sentences work together to create a satisfying piece of writing.

**Exercise 1**   For each sentence, write *Simple, Compound,* or *Complex* to show what kind of structure it has.

1. "Marriage Is a Private Affair" is a good title for this story.
2. Nnaemeka and Nene were a young couple in Lagos who planned to marry.
3. Nnaemeka didn't tell his father about their plans because his father had arranged a marriage for him.
4. Nnaemeka's father loved him, but the old man would not forgive his son's disobedience.
5. Once the couple married, would his father accept their union?
6. After many years of silence, Okeke still had not accepted his son's marriage.
7. Finally, Nene wrote to the old man and described her children.

8. Okeke was hooked; he thought about his grandsons all the time.

9. When he thought of the children, he felt strong emotions.

10. The true end of this story occurred after the short story was finished.

**Exercise 2**   Work in a small group to revise the following passage. All the sentences in this passage are simple sentences. Rewrite the passage, building sentence variety by using compound and complex sentences. Change words as necessary and make up any necessary details. Share your revisions with other groups.

> Arranged marriages have a long history. Maybe we should try them in this country. Royal families always preferred arranged marriages. They preferred them for their children. Why? Sometimes the reasons were political. Sometimes the reasons were financial. Sometimes the reasons were a combination of the two. Many nonroyal families also arranged marriages. These marriages were business deals. They were practical transactions. They were like buying a new house. Even today, arranged marriages exist. In some parts of the world, love is not the main reason for marriage.
>
> Imagine arranged marriages in modern society! Dating services would go out of business. Teenagers and college students would concentrate on their studies. They would stop thinking so much about each other. Merchants could merge families. They could build bigger businesses. Neighbors could merge families. They could own larger plots of land. But what about love? Would it survive?

**Exercise 3**   **Style**   Skim the selections you have read, looking for passages with sentence variety. Find one example each of a simple sentence, a compound sentence, a complex sentence, and a compound-complex sentence. Write each sentence on your paper and underline each independent clause once and each dependent clause twice.

**Exercise 4**   **Analyzing and Revising Your Writing**

1. Take a piece of writing from your writing portfolio.

2. Reread it, looking for opportunities to vary your kinds of sentences.

3. Rewrite one or two paragraphs to improve the sentence variety.

4. Check to see that you have punctuated your new sentences correctly.

LANGUAGE HANDBOOK

For review and practice: sentence structure, pages 1024–27

5. Compare your revised sentences with the original ones. Which sentences do you prefer? Remember to work for sentence variety the next time you revise your writing.

# THINKING SKILLS
## WORKSHOP

## INDUCTION AND DEDUCTION

A logical argument can be inductive or deductive. An **inductive argument** starts with examples or facts and then draws a conclusion from these.

| | |
|---|---|
| **Specific Fact** | Twenty students took the school's new study skills course last year. |
| **Specific Fact** | Since taking the course, every student has increased his or her grade average. |
| **Conclusion** | The course makes a real difference in student achievement and should be required for everyone. |

**DANGER! FAULTY REASONING**

The most dangerous form of overgeneralization is *stereotyping*, in which conclusions, often negative, are drawn about whole groups of people. Stereotyping ignores individual differences and encourages bigotry.

The conclusion reached by inductive argument is probable but not certain. In the above example, something else could have caused the students' grades to rise, even though the conclusion seems logical.

One danger to avoid with inductive arguments is to **overgeneralize**— to draw a conclusion that is too broad. Suppose, for example, that you met two teenagers who hate rap music. You couldn't conclude that all teenagers hate rap music. That would be overgeneralizing.

In the second type of logical argument, the **deductive argument**, you start with a generalization and then come to a specific conclusion.

| | |
|---|---|
| **Generalization** | Every student in the study skills course improved his or her grades. |
| **Specific Fact** | Marcia was in the study skills course. |
| **Conclusion** | Therefore, Marcia improved her grades. |

Notice that the conclusion of a deductive argument is an inevitable result of the statements it is based on. If those statements, called **premises,** are true, the conclusion is necessarily true.

**Exercise**   Follow the directions below.

1. Working with other students, brainstorm a list of facts about various contact sports. Then, based on these facts, come up with some conclusions about contact sports in general. Are these conclusions the result of inductive or deductive reasoning? Explain.

2. Draw three conclusions from the following statement: *All cats are carnivores.* Are these conclusions the result of inductive or deductive reasoning? Explain.

# CONSEQUENCES OF FATE

Do individuals control their destiny or are they controlled by fate? Writers have been asking this question since ancient times, but the twentieth century has given it a new urgency. One philosopher even compares modern life to the roll of dice, suggesting that we are "thrown" into an existence that we cannot control.

Other writers insist that individuals can rise above the complications and confusions of the modern world to master their destiny.

In the following selections you will read about characters who confront a fate which may or may not be of their own making. Judge for yourself how well they deal with those fates.

*Fiction*

# The *Rocking Horse Winner*

### D. H. LAWRENCE

## Examine What You Know

In your opinion, how important are love, money, and luck in achieving happiness? Rank these things in the order of their importance, and explain your reasoning. Then, as you read, determine the role that each plays in the lives of the characters in this story.

## Expand Your Knowledge

Horse racing is one of the oldest sporting events in the world. In England, where this story is set, horse racing goes back at least eight hundred years. Over the centuries, the sport has expanded and evolved into a year-round calendar of events with several different kinds of races. The five great races held annually in England are called the Classics and include St. Leger and the Derby mentioned in this story. Other races mentioned in the story are the Grand National Steeplechase, the Ascot, and the Lincolnshire.

Large sums of money are bet on horse races. How much a bettor can win from betting on a race depends on the odds. The odds are expressed as a ratio, such as 3 to 1, and determined by the proportion of the total sum of money bet on the race to the total sum bet on a particular horse. The more money bet on the horse, the lower the odds and the lower the payoff. For example, the favorite horse, the one with the most money wagered, might have odds as low as 2 to 1. This means that if the favorite wins, a bettor receives two dollars for every one dollar bet. The long shot, the horse with the least money wagered, might have odds as high as 20 to 1. If the long shot wins, a bettor receives twenty dollars for every dollar bet.

A bettor wagers on a horse to *win, place,* or *show.* The owner of a win ticket collects if the horse finishes first. The owner of a place ticket collects if the horse is first or second. If the horse comes in first, second, or third, the owner of a show ticket collects, but the ticket offers the smallest payoff.

## Enrich Your Reading

■ *A biography of the author can be found on page 745.*

**Analyzing a Character**  As you read this story, watch for clues to Paul's personality and the changes he goes through. Notice and jot down descriptive details, and pay attention to how other characters affect him.

# The Rocking Horse Winner

## D. H. LAWRENCE

There was a woman who was beautiful, who started with all the advantages, yet she had no luck. She married for love, and the love turned to dust. She had bonny[1] children, yet she felt they had been thrust upon her, and she could not love them. They looked at her coldly, as if they were finding fault with her. And hurriedly she felt she must cover up some fault in herself. Yet what it was that she must cover up she never knew. Nevertheless, when her children were present, she always felt the center of her heart go hard. This troubled her, and in her manner she was all the more gentle and anxious for her children, as if she loved them very much. Only she herself knew that at the center of her heart was a hard little place that could not feel love, no, not for anybody. Everybody else said of her: "She is such a good mother. She adores her children." Only she herself, and her children themselves, knew it was not so. They read it in each other's eyes.

There were a boy and two little girls. They lived in a pleasant house with a garden, and they had discreet servants and felt themselves superior to anyone in the neighborhood.

Although they lived in style, they felt always an anxiety in the house. There was never enough money. The mother had a small income, and the father had a small income, but not nearly enough for the social position which they had to keep up. The father went into town to some office. But though he had good prospects, these prospects never materialized. There was always the grinding sense of the shortage of money, though the style was always kept up.

At last the mother said, "I will see if *I* can't make something." But she did not know where to begin. She racked her brains and tried this thing and the other but could not find anything successful. The failure made deep lines come into her face. Her children were growing up; they would have to go to school. There must be more money; there must be more money. The father, who was always very handsome and expensive in his tastes, seemed as if he never *would* be able to do anything worth doing. And the mother, who had a great belief in herself, did not succeed any better and her tastes were just as expensive.

And so the house came to be haunted by the unspoken phrase: *There must be more money! There must be more money!* The children could hear it all the time, though nobody said it aloud. They heard it at Christmas, when the expensive and splendid toys filled the nursery. Behind the shining modern rocking horse, behind the smart doll's house, a voice would start whispering: "There *must* be more money!

---

1. **bonny** *British:* handsome or pretty.

There *must* be more money!" And the children would stop playing to listen for a moment. They would look into each other's eyes to see if they had all heard. And each one saw in the eyes of the other two that they too had heard. "There *must* be more money! There *must* be more money!"

It came whispering from the springs of the still-swaying rocking horse, and even the horse, bending his wooden, champing head, heard it. The big doll, sitting so pink and smirking in her new pram,[2] could hear it quite plainly and seemed to be smirking all the more self-consciously because of it. The foolish puppy, too, that took the place of the teddy bear, he was looking so extraordinarily foolish for no other reason but that he heard the secret whisper all over the house: "There *must* be more money!"

Yet nobody ever said it aloud. The whisper was everywhere, and therefore no one spoke it. Just as no one ever says: "We are breathing!" in spite of the fact that breath is coming and going all the time.

"Mother," said the boy Paul one day, "why don't we keep a car of our own? Why do we always use Uncle's, or else a taxi?"

"Because we're the poor members of the family," said the mother.

"But why *are* we, Mother?"

"Well—I suppose," she said slowly and bitterly, "it's because your father has no luck."

The boy was silent for some time.

"Is luck money, Mother?" he asked, rather timidly.

"No, Paul. Not quite. It's what causes you to have money."

"Oh!" said Paul vaguely. "I thought when Uncle Oscar said *filthy lucker,* it meant money."

"*Filthy lucre* does mean money," said the mother. "But it's lucre, not luck."

"Oh!" said the boy. "Then what *is* luck, Mother?"

"It's what causes you to have money. If you're lucky, you have money. That's why it's better to be born lucky than rich. If you're rich, you may lose your money. But if you're lucky, you will always get more money."

"Oh! Will you? And is Father not lucky?"

"Very unlucky, I should say," she said bitterly. The boy watched her with unsure eyes.

"Why?" he asked.

"I don't know. Nobody ever knows why one person is lucky and another unlucky."

"Don't they? Nobody at all? Does *nobody* know?"

"Perhaps God. But He never tells."

"He ought to, then. And aren't you lucky either, Mother?"

"I can't be, if I married an unlucky husband."

"But by yourself, aren't you?"

"I used to think I was, before I married. Now I think I am very unlucky indeed."

"Why?"

"Well—never mind! Perhaps I'm not really," she said.

The child looked at her, to see if she meant it. But he saw, by the lines of her mouth, that she was only trying to hide something from him.

"Well, anyhow," he said stoutly, "I'm a lucky person."

"Why?" said his mother, with a sudden laugh.

He stared at her. He didn't even know why he had said it.

"God told me," he asserted, brazening it out.

"I hope He did, dear!" she said, again with a laugh, but rather bitter.

"He did, Mother!"

"Excellent!" said the mother, using one of her husband's exclamations.

---

2. **pram** *British:* from perambulator, a baby carriage.

THE SPINET 1902 Thomas Wilmer Dewing National Museum of American Art, Smithsonian Institution, Washington, D.C./Art Resource, New York.

The boy saw she did not believe him; or rather, that she paid no attention to his assertion. This angered him somewhere and made him want to compel her attention.

He went off by himself, vaguely, in a childish way, seeking for the clue to "luck." Absorbed, taking no heed of other people, he went about with a sort of stealth, seeking inwardly for luck. He wanted luck, he wanted it, he wanted it. When the two girls were playing dolls in the nursery, he would sit on his big rocking horse, charging madly into space, with a frenzy that made the little girls peer at him uneasily. Wildly the horse <u>careened</u>, the waving dark hair of the boy tossed, his eyes

had a strange glare in them. The little girls dared not speak to him.

When he had ridden to the end of his mad little journey, he climbed down and stood in front of his rocking horse, staring fixedly into its lowered face. Its red mouth was slightly open; its big eye was wide and glassy-bright.

"Now!" he would silently command the snorting steed. "Now, take me to where there is luck! Now take me!"

And he would slash the horse on the neck with the little whip he had asked Uncle Oscar for. He *knew* the horse could take him to where there was luck, if only he forced it. So he would mount again and start on his furious

*Words to Know and Use*

**careen** (kə rēn′) *v.* to move wildly from side to side

ride, hoping at last to get there. He knew he could get there.

"You'll break your horse, Paul!" said the nurse.

"He's always riding like that! I wish he'd leave off!" said his elder sister Joan.

But he only glared down on them in silence. Nurse gave him up. She could make nothing of him. Anyhow he was growing beyond her.

One day his mother and his Uncle Oscar came in when he was on one of his furious rides. He did not speak to them.

"Hallo, you young jockey! Riding a winner?" said his uncle.

"Aren't you growing too big for a rocking horse? You're not a very little boy any longer, you know," said his mother.

But Paul only gave a blue glare from his big, rather close-set eyes. He would speak to nobody when he was in full tilt. His mother watched him with an anxious expression on her face.

At last he suddenly stopped forcing his horse into the mechanical gallop and slid down.

"Well, I got there!" he announced fiercely, his blue eyes still flaring, and his sturdy long legs straddling apart.

"Where did you get to?" asked his mother.

"Where I wanted to go," he flared back at her.

"That's right, son!" said Uncle Oscar. "Don't you stop till you get there. What's the horse's name?"

"He doesn't have a name," said the boy.

"Gets on without all right?" asked the uncle.

"Well, he had different names. He was called Sansovino last week."

"Sansovino, eh? Won the Ascot. How did you know his name?"

"He always talks about horse races with Bassett," said Joan.

The uncle was delighted to find that his small nephew was posted with all the racing news. Bassett, the young gardener, who had been wounded in the left foot in the war and had got his present job through Oscar Cresswell, whose batman[3] he had been, was a perfect blade of the "turf."[4] He lived in the racing events, and the small boy lived with him.

Oscar Cresswell got it all from Bassett.

"Master Paul comes and asks me, so I can't do more than tell him, sir," said Bassett, his face terribly serious, as if he were speaking of religious matters.

"And does he ever put anything on a horse he fancies?"

"Well—I don't want to give him away—he's a young sport, a fine sport, sir. Would you mind asking him himself? He sort of takes a pleasure in it, and perhaps he'd feel I was giving him away, sir, if you don't mind."

Bassett was serious as a church.

The uncle went back to his nephew and took him off for a ride in the car.

"Say, Paul, old man, do you ever put anything on a horse?" the uncle asked.

The boy watched the handsome man closely.

"Why, do you think I oughtn't to?" he parried.

"Not a bit of it! I thought perhaps you might give me a tip for the Lincoln."

The car sped on into the country, going down to Uncle Oscar's place in Hampshire.

"Honor bright?" said the nephew.

"Honor bright, son!" said the uncle.

"Well, then, Daffodil."

"Daffodil! I doubt it, sonny. What about Mirza?"

"I only know the winner," said the boy. "That's Daffodil."

---

3. **batman:** a British army officer's aide.

4. **blade of the turf:** someone very knowledgeable about race tracks.

"Daffodil, eh?"

There was a pause. Daffodil was an <u>obscure</u> horse comparatively.

"Uncle!"

"Yes, son?"

"You won't let it go any further, will you? I promised Bassett."

"Bassett be damned, old man! What's he got to do with it?"

"We're partners. We've been partners from the first. Uncle, he lent me my first five shillings, which I lost. I promised him, honor bright, it was only between me and him; only you gave me that ten-shilling note I started winning with, so I thought you were lucky. You won't let it go any further, will you?"

The boy gazed at his uncle from those big, hot, blue eyes, set rather close together. The uncle stirred and laughed uneasily.

"Right you are, son! I'll keep your tip private. Daffodil, eh? How much are you putting on him?"

"All except twenty pounds," said the boy. "I keep that in reserve."

The uncle thought it a good joke.

"You keep twenty pounds in reserve, do you, you young romancer? What are you betting, then?"

"I'm betting three hundred," said the boy gravely. "But it's between you and me, Uncle Oscar! Honor bright?"

The uncle burst into a roar of laughter.

"It's between you and me all right, you young Nat Gould,"[5] he said, laughing. "But where's your three hundred?"

"Bassett keeps it for me. We're partners."

"You are, are you! And what is Bassett putting on Daffodil?"

"He won't go quite as high as I do, I expect. Perhaps he'll go a hundred and fifty."

"What, pennies?" laughed the uncle.

"Pounds," said the child, with a surprised look at his uncle. "Bassett keeps a bigger reserve than I do."

Between wonder and amusement Uncle Oscar was silent. He pursued the matter no further, but he determined to take his nephew with him to the Lincoln races.

"Now, son," he said, "I'm putting twenty on Mirza, and I'll put five for you on any horse you fancy. What's your pick?"

"Daffodil, Uncle."

"No, not the fiver on Daffodil!"

"I should if it was my own fiver," said the child.

"Good! Good! Right you are! A fiver for me and a fiver for you on Daffodil."

The child had never been to a race meeting before, and his eyes were blue fire. He pursed his mouth tight and watched. A Frenchman just in front had put his money on Lancelot. Wild with excitement, he flayed his arms up and down, yelling *Lancelot! Lancelot!* in his French accent.

Daffodil came in first, Lancelot second, Mirza third. The child, flushed and with eyes blazing, was curiously serene. His uncle brought him four five-pound notes, four to one.

"What am I to do with these?" he cried, waving them before the boy's eyes.

"I suppose we'll talk to Bassett," said the boy. "I expect I have fifteen hundred now; and twenty in reserve; and this twenty."

His uncle studied him for some moments.

"Look here, son!" he said. "You're not serious about Bassett and that fifteen hundred, are you?"

---

5. **Nat Gould:** a well-known British racing writer and authority.

*Words to Know and Use* | **obscure** (əb skyo͞or′) *adj.* not well-known; not famous

"Yes, I am. But it's between you and me, Uncle. Honor bright!"

"Honor bright all right, son! But I must talk to Bassett."

"If you'd like to be a partner, Uncle, with Bassett and me, we could all be partners. Only, you'd have to promise, honor bright, Uncle, not to let it go beyond us three. Bassett and I are lucky, and you must be lucky, because it was your ten shillings I started winning with. . . ."

Uncle Oscar took both Bassett and Paul into Richmond Park for an afternoon, and there they talked.

"It's like this, you see, sir," Bassett said. "Master Paul would get me talking about racing events, spinning yarns, you know, sir. And he was always keen on knowing if I'd made or if I'd lost. It's about a year since, now, that I put five shillings on Blush of Dawn for him; and we lost. Then the luck turned, with that ten shillings he had from you: that we put on Singhalese. And since that time, it's been pretty steady, all things considering. What do you say, Master Paul?"

"We're all right when we're sure," said Paul. "It's when we're not quite sure that we go down."

"Oh, but we're careful then," said Bassett.

"But when are you *sure?*" smiled Uncle Oscar.

"It's Master Paul, sir," said Bassett, in a secret, religious voice. "It's as if he had it from heaven. Like Daffodil, now, for the Lincoln. That was as sure as eggs."

"Did you put anything on Daffodil?" asked Oscar Cresswell.

"Yes, sir. I made my bit."

"And my nephew?"

Bassett was obstinately silent, looking at Paul.

"I made twelve hundred, didn't I, Bassett? I told Uncle I was putting three hundred on Daffodil."

"That's right," said Bassett, nodding.

"But where's the money?" asked the uncle.

"I keep it safe locked up, sir. Master Paul he can have it any minute he likes to ask for it."

"What, fifteen hundred pounds?"

"And twenty! And *forty,* that is, with the twenty he made on the course."

"It's amazing!" said the uncle.

"If Master Paul offers you to be partners, sir, I would, if I were you: if you'll excuse me," said Bassett.

Oscar Cresswell thought about it.

HURDLE RHYTHMS   Fay Moore
© Fay Moore, New York.

"I'll see the money," he said.

They drove home again, and, sure enough, Bassett came round to the garden house with fifteen hundred pounds in notes. The twenty pounds reserve was left with Joe Glee, in the Turf Commission deposit.[6]

"You see, it's all right, Uncle, when I'm sure! Then we go strong, for all we're worth. Don't we, Bassett?"

"We do that, Master Paul."

"And when are you sure?" said the uncle, laughing.

"Oh, well, sometimes I'm *absolutely* sure, like about Daffodil," said the boy; "and sometimes I have an idea; and sometimes I haven't even an idea, have I, Bassett? Then we're careful, because we mostly go down."

"You do, do you! And when you're sure, like about Daffodil, what makes you sure, sonny?"

"Oh, well, I don't know," said the boy uneasily. "I'm sure, you know, Uncle; that's all."

"It's as if he had it from heaven, sir," Bassett <u>reiterated</u>.

"I should say so!" said the uncle.

But he became a partner. And when the Leger was coming on, Paul was "sure" about Lively Spark, which was a quite inconsiderable horse. The boy insisted on putting a thousand on the horse, Bassett went for five hundred, and Oscar Cresswell two hundred. Lively Spark came in first, and the betting had been ten to one against him. Paul had made ten thousand.

"You see," he said, "I was absolutely sure of him."

Even Oscar Cresswell had cleared two thousand.

"Look here, son," he said, "this sort of thing makes me nervous."

"It needn't, Uncle! Perhaps I shan't be sure again for a long time."

"But what are you going to do with your money?" asked the uncle.

"Of course," said the boy, "I started it for Mother. She said she had no luck, because Father is unlucky, so I thought if *I* was lucky, it might stop whispering."

"What might stop whispering?"

"Our house. I *hate* our house for whispering."

"What does it whisper?"

"Why—why"—the boy fidgeted—"why, I don't know. But it's always short of money, you know, Uncle."

"I know it, son, I know it."

"You know people send Mother writs,[7] don't you, Uncle?"

"I'm afraid I do," said the uncle.

"And then the house whispers, like people laughing at you behind your back. It's awful, that is! I thought if I was lucky—"

"You might stop it," added the uncle.

The boy watched him with big blue eyes that had an uncanny cold fire in them, and he said never a word.

"Well, then!" said the uncle. "What are we doing?"

"I shouldn't like Mother to know I was lucky," said the boy.

"Why not, son?"

"She'd stop me."

"I don't think she would."

"Oh!"—and the boy writhed in an odd way—"I *don't* want her to know, Uncle."

"All right, son! We'll manage it without her knowing."

They managed it very easily. Paul, at the other's suggestion, handed over five thousand

---

6. **Turf Commission deposit:** bank where bettors keep their money for future bets.

7. **writs:** legal documents, used in this case to collect unpaid bills.

*Words to Know and Use* | **reiterate** (rē it′ ə rāt′) *v.* to say or do again

pounds to his uncle, who deposited it with the family lawyer, who was then to inform Paul's mother that a relative had put five thousand pounds into his hands, which sum was to be paid out a thousand pounds at a time, on the mother's birthday, for the next five years.

"So she'll have a birthday present of a thousand pounds for five successive years," said Uncle Oscar. "I hope it won't make it all the harder for her later."

Paul's mother had her birthday in November. The house had been "whispering" worse than ever lately, and, even in spite of his luck, Paul could not bear up against it. He was very anxious to see the effect of the birthday letter telling his mother about the thousand pounds.

When there were no visitors, Paul now took his meals with his parents, as he was beyond the nursery control. His mother went into town nearly every day. She had discovered that she had an odd knack of sketching furs and dress materials, so she worked secretly in the studio of a friend who was the chief "artist" for the leading drapers. She drew the figures of ladies in furs and ladies in silk and sequins for the newspaper advertisements. This young woman artist earned several thousand pounds a year, but Paul's mother only made several hundreds, and she was again dissatisfied. She so wanted to be first in something, and she did not succeed, even in making sketches for drapery advertisements.

She was down to breakfast on the morning of her birthday. Paul watched her face as she read her letters. He knew the lawyer's letter. As his mother read it, her face hardened and became more expressionless. Then a cold, determined look came on her mouth. She hid the letter under the pile of others and said not a word about it.

"Didn't you have anything nice in the post for your birthday, Mother?" said Paul.

"Quite moderately nice," she said, her voice cold and absent.

She went away to town without saying more.

But in the afternoon Uncle Oscar appeared. He said Paul's mother had had a long interview with the lawyer, asking if the whole five thousand could not be advanced at once, as she was in debt.

"What do you think, Uncle?" said the boy.

"I leave it to you, son."

"Oh, let her have it, then! We can get some more with the other," said the boy.

"A bird in the hand is worth two in the bush, laddie!" said Uncle Oscar.

"But I'm sure to *know* for the Grand National; or the Lincolnshire; or else the Derby. I'm sure to know for *one* of them," said Paul.

So Uncle Oscar signed the agreement, and Paul's mother touched the whole five thousand. Then something very curious happened. The voices in the house suddenly went mad, like a chorus of frogs on a spring evening. There were certain new furnishings, and Paul had a tutor. He was *really* going to Eton, his father's school, in the following autumn. There were flowers in the winter and a blossoming of the luxury Paul's mother had been used to. And yet the voices in the house, behind the sprays of mimosa and almond blossom, and from under the piles of iridescent cushions, simply trilled and screamed in a sort of ecstasy: "There *must* be more money! Oh-h-h; there *must* be more money. Oh, now, now-w! Now-w-w—there *must* be more money!—more than ever! More than ever!"

It frightened Paul terribly. He studied away at his Latin and Greek with his tutors. But his intense hours were spent with Bassett. The Grand National had gone by: he had not "known" and had lost a hundred pounds. Summer was at hand. He was in agony for the

Lincoln. But even for the Lincoln he didn't "know," and he lost fifty pounds. He became wild-eyed and strange, as if something were going to explode in him.

"Let it alone, son! Don't you bother about it!" urged Uncle Oscar. But it was as if the boy couldn't really hear what his uncle was saying.

"I've got to know for the Derby! I've got to know for the Derby!" the child reiterated, his big blue eyes blazing with a sort of madness.

His mother noticed how overwrought he was.

"You'd better go to the seaside. Wouldn't you like to go now to the seaside, instead of waiting? I think you'd better," she said, looking down at him anxiously, her heart curiously heavy because of him.

But the child lifted his uncanny blue eyes.

"I couldn't possibly go before the Derby, Mother!" he said. "I couldn't possibly!"

"Why not?" she said, her voice becoming heavy when she was opposed. "Why not? You can still go from the seaside to see the Derby with your uncle Oscar, if that's what you wish. No need for you to wait here. Besides, I think you care too much about these races. It's a bad sign. My family has been a gambling family, and you won't know till you grow up how much damage it has done. But it has done damage. I shall have to send Bassett away and ask Uncle Oscar not to talk racing to you, unless you promise to be reasonable about it: go away to the seaside and forget it. You're all nerves!"

"I'll do what you like, Mother, so long as you don't send me away till after the Derby," the boy said.

"Send you away from where? Just from this house?"

"Yes," he said, gazing at her.

"Why, you curious child, what makes you care about this house so much, suddenly? I never knew you loved it."

He gazed at her without speaking. He had a secret within a secret, something he had not divulged, even to Bassett or to his Uncle Oscar.

But his mother, after standing undecided and a little bit sullen for some moments, said:

"Very well then! Don't go to the seaside till after the Derby, if you don't wish it. But promise me you won't let your nerves go to pieces. Promise you won't think so much about horse racing and events, as you call them!"

"Oh, no," said the boy casually. "I won't think much about them, Mother. You needn't worry. I wouldn't worry, Mother, if I were you."

"If you were me and I were you," said his mother, "I wonder what we *should* do!"

"But you know you needn't worry. Mother, don't you?" the boy repeated.

"I should be awfully glad to know it," she said wearily.

"Oh, well, you *can*, you know. I mean, you *ought* to know you needn't worry," he insisted.

"Ought I? Then I'll see about it," she said.

Paul's secret of secrets was his wooden horse, that which had no name. Since he was emancipated from a nurse and a nursery governess, he had had his rocking horse removed to his own bedroom at the top of the house.

"Surely, you're too big for a rocking horse!" his mother had remonstrated.

"Well, you see, Mother, till I can have a *real* horse, I like to have *some* sort of animal about," had been his quaint answer.

"Do you feel he keeps you company?" she laughed.

740

*Words to Know and Use* | **overwrought** (ō' vər rôt') *adj.* very nervous or excited
**emancipate** (ē man' sə pāt') *v.* to set free from restraint or control

"Oh, yes! He's very good; he always keeps me company, when I'm there," said Paul.

So the horse, rather shabby, stood in an arrested prance in the boy's bedroom.

The Derby was drawing near, and the boy grew more and more tense. He hardly heard what was spoken to him, he was very frail, and his eyes were really uncanny. His mother had sudden strange seizures of uneasiness about him. Sometimes, for half an hour, she would feel a sudden anxiety about him that was almost anguish. She wanted to rush to him at once and know he was safe.

Two nights before the Derby, she was at a big party in town, when one of her rushes of anxiety about her boy, her firstborn, gripped her heart till she could hardly speak. She fought with the feeling, might and main, for she believed in common sense. But it was too strong. She had to leave the dance and go downstairs to telephone to the country. The children's nursery governess was terribly surprised and startled at being rung up in the night.

"Are the children all right, Miss Wilmot?"

"Oh, yes, they are quite all right."

"Master Paul? Is he all right?"

"He went to bed as right as a trivet.[8] Shall I run up and look at him?"

"No," said Paul's mother reluctantly. "No! Don't trouble. It's all right. Don't sit up. We shall be home fairly soon." She did not want her son's privacy intruded upon.

"Very good," said the governess.

It was about one o'clock when Paul's mother and father drove up to their house. All was still. Paul's mother went to her room and slipped off her white fur cloak. She had told her maid not to wait up for her. She heard her husband downstairs, mixing a whisky and soda.

And then, because of the strange anxiety at her heart, she stole upstairs to her son's room. Noiselessly she went along the upper corridor. Was there a faint noise? What was it?

She stood, with arrested muscles, outside his door, listening. There was a strange, heavy, and yet not loud noise. Her heart stood still. It was a soundless noise, yet rushing and powerful. Something huge, in violent, hushed motion. What was it? What in God's name was it? She ought to know. She felt that she knew the noise. She knew what it was.

Yet she could not place it. She couldn't say what it was. And on and on it went, like a madness.

Softly, frozen with anxiety and fear, she turned the door handle.

The room was dark. Yet in the space near the window, she heard and saw something plunging to and fro. She gazed in fear and amazement.

"*It's Malabar!*" *he screamed, in a powerful, strange voice. "It's Malabar!*"

Then suddenly she switched on the light and saw her son, in his green pajamas, madly surging on the rocking horse. The blaze of light suddenly lit him up, as he urged the wooden horse, and lit her up, as she stood, blonde, in her dress of pale green and crystal, in the doorway.

"Paul!" she cried. "Whatever are you doing?"

"It's Malabar!" he screamed, in a powerful, strange voice. "It's Malabar!"

His eyes blazed at her for one strange and senseless second, as he ceased urging his wooden horse. Then he fell with a crash to the

---

8. **right as a trivet:** a British expression meaning "without any problems." A trivet is a three-legged stand for holding pots or hot dishes.

ground, and she, all her tormented mother-hood flooding upon her, rushed to gather him up.

But he was unconscious, and unconscious he remained, with some brain fever. He talked and tossed, and his mother sat stonily by his side.

"Malabar! It's Malabar! Bassett, Bassett, I *know!* It's Malabar!"

So the child cried, trying to get up and urge the rocking horse that gave him his inspiration.

"What does he mean by Malabar?" asked the heart-frozen mother.

"I don't know," said the father stonily.

"What does he mean by Malabar?" she asked her brother Oscar.

"It's one of the horses running for the Derby," was the answer.

And, in spite of himself, Oscar Cresswell spoke to Bassett, and himself put a thousand on Malabar: at fourteen to one.

The third day of the illness was critical; they were waiting for a change. The boy, with his rather long, curly hair, was tossing ceaselessly on the pillow. He neither slept nor regained consciousness, and his eyes were like blue stones. His mother sat, feeling her heart had gone, turned actually into a stone.

In the evening, Oscar Cresswell did not come, but Bassett sent a message, saying could he come up for one moment, just one moment? Paul's mother was very angry at the intrusion, but on second thoughts she agreed. The boy was the same. Perhaps Bassett might bring him to consciousness.

The gardener, a shortish fellow with a little brown mustache, and sharp little brown eyes, tiptoed into the room, touched his imaginary cap to Paul's mother, and stole to the bedside, staring with glittering, smallish eyes at the tossing, dying child.

"Master Paul!" he whispered. "Master Paul! Malabar came in first all right, a clean win. I did as you told me. You've made over seventy thousand pounds, you have; you've got over eighty thousand. Malabar came in all right, Master Paul."

"Malabar! Malabar! Did I say Malabar, Mother? Did I say Malabar? Do you think I'm lucky, Mother? I knew Malabar, didn't I? Over eighty thousand pounds! I call that lucky, don't you, Mother? Over eighty thousand pounds! I knew, didn't I know I knew? Malabar came in all right. If I ride my horse till I'm sure, then I tell you, Bassett, you can go as high as you like. Did you go for all you were worth, Bassett?"

"I went a thousand on it, Master Paul."

"I never told you, Mother, that if I can ride my horse, and *get there,* then I'm absolutely sure—oh, absolutely! Mother, did I ever tell you? I *am* lucky!"

"No, you never did," said the mother.

But the boy died in the night.

And even as he lay dead, his mother heard her brother's voice saying to her: "My God, Hester, you're eighty-odd thousand to the good, and a poor devil of a son to the bad. But, poor devil, poor devil, he's best gone out of a life where he rides his rocking horse to find a winner." 🐎

## *Responding to Reading*

### First Impressions

**1.** In your opinion, what is the most memorable scene or image in this story? Jot down reasons for your choice.

### Second Thoughts

**2.** What causes Paul to become obsessed with racing?

> **Think about**
> • his mental and emotional health
> • the influence his mother has on him
> • the "voices" in the house

**3.** What kind of person is Paul's mother? Does she change by the end of the story? Explain your opinion.

> **Think about**
> • her view of herself and her family
> • her attitude toward social status and the importance of money
> • how she manages her money
> • how she reacts to Paul's deteriorating mental and physical condition

**4.** Discuss the relationship between Paul and his mother. What does the relationship show about each of them?

**5.** Are Bassett and Uncle Oscar a good or a bad influence on Paul? Cite evidence from the story to support your opinion.

**6.** Who or what is responsible for Paul's death? Could it have been prevented?

**7.** What is the writer's message for living revealed in this story?

### Broader Connections

**8.** How do Paul's family's values compare with the values held by many families in society today? Cite examples to support your answer.

## *Literary Concept: Fantasy*

**Fantasy** is a type of fiction that contains events, places, or other details that could not exist in the real world. The characters in a fantasy are often realistic, but they have experiences that overstep the bounds of reality. The aim of a fantasy may be purely to delight the reader, or it may be to make a serious comment on life. What events in this story make it a fantasy? How does the writer use fantasy to comment on life?

**Concept Review: Repetition**   Notice the repetition of the sentence *There must be more money.* Where in the story is it repeated? What is the effect of this repetition?

# *W*riting Options

1. Imagine and describe life in Paul's household five years after his death. Consider whether or not Paul's death has changed his mother's attitude toward money and social status.

2. Write an editorial either for or against legalized gambling. Use examples from the story to support your viewpoint.

3. As Paul's mother, write a letter to an advice columnist explaining his strange behavior and asking for advice. Then write the columnist's advice to her.

4. Write a ten-question short-answer quiz that focuses on the main events and characters of the story.

# *V*ocabulary Practice

**Exercise**  Read each phrase below and write the word from the list suggested by the phrase.

1. a slave being set free
2. a car spinning out of control on an icy road
3. a teacher repeating a set of directions
4. a mother waiting for news about her child's surgery
5. an unknown writer trying to have a work published

> *Words to Know and Use*
>
> careen
> emancipate
> obscure
> overwrought
> reiterate

# $e$ $x$ $t$ $e$ $n$ $d$

## Options for Learning

**1** • **Expressive Dancing** Select one of the scenes from the story, perhaps the last one, and choreograph a dance that describes the scene. Be sure your dance reflects the mood, choosing appropriate music to accompany it. Perform your dance for the class.

**2** • **The Artist's Eye** Draw or paint the image of Paul's furious ride on his rocking horse. Try to convey his strange facial expression as described in the story.

**3** • **Police Work** As a police investigator, write your report of your investigation into Paul's unusual death. Include statements from witnesses and the evidence on which you base your conclusions about the cause of death.

**4** • **A Radio Play** In a small group, rewrite the story as a radio dramatization. Remember that a radio dramatization primarily uses dialogue. You may wish to include descriptive passages between scenes to be read by a narrator. Also include sound effects, such as the voices of the house. Perform your dramatization for the class.

 **FACT FINDER**

*The horse Malabar won at odds of 14 to 1. Since Paul won 70,000 pounds, how much did he bet?*

## David Herbert Lawrence
### 1885-1930

D. H. Lawrence was one of the most controversial writers of the early twentieth century. Many of his novels, short stories, and books of poetry were destroyed or had their publication delayed because of objections to Lawrence's treatment of the relationships between men and women.

He not only broke literary conventions, he fought against the restricting social, political, and moral conventions of his day. He felt that "one has to be so terribly religious to be an artist . . . and it's rather an awful feeling."

Lawrence frequently traveled with his wife, Freida. He lived all over the world, trying to discover a better way to relate, live, and grow with other people. Late in his life, he wrote that "the magnificent here and now of life in the flesh is ours, and ours alone, and ours only for a time. We ought to dance with rapture that we should be alive." Today, Lawrence is studied and admired for the new thoughts, styles, and attitudes he brought to literature and living.

**Fiction**

# *The* Ant and the Grasshopper

W. SOMERSET MAUGHAM (sum′ ər set′ môm)

## Examine What You Know

"The Ant and the Grasshopper" is the title of a well-known fable. Discuss what you know about the fable and the lesson it teaches. Then, as you read, look for similarities and differences between this story and the fable.

## Expand Your Knowledge

A **fable** is a short story that teaches a moral, or lesson, about human nature. The characters in most fables are animals who act and speak like humans. Traditionally, fables have been told to children for the purpose of instructing them in wise behavior. Aesop's fables from Greece, Uncle Remus's African stories told in the American South, and La Fontaine's fables from France are all well-known fables. In fact, La Fontaine's fables are still used as part of the elementary school curriculum in several countries.

Maugham's story is not a fable, but it uses the story of the ant and the grasshopper as its starting point. It goes off in a different direction, however, poking fun at both the moral of "The Ant and the Grasshopper" and the people who live by it.

## Write Before You Read

Are you more like the ant or the grasshopper in the fable? Explain your choice.

■ *A biography of the author can be found in the Reader's Handbook.*

# The Ant and the Grasshopper

## W. SOMERSET MAUGHAM

When I was a very small boy I was made to learn by heart certain of the fables of La Fontaine, and the moral of each was carefully explained to me. Among those I learnt was *The Ant and the Grasshopper,* which is devised to bring home to the young the useful lesson that in an imperfect world industry is rewarded and giddiness[1] punished. In this admirable fable (I apologize for telling something which everyone is politely, but inexactly, supposed to know) the ant spends a laborious summer gathering its winter store, while the grasshopper sits on a blade of grass singing to the sun. Winter comes and the ant is comfortably provided for, but the grasshopper has an empty larder:[2] he goes to the ant and begs for a little food. Then the ant gives him her classic answer:

"What were you doing in the summer time?"

"Saving your presence, I sang, I sang all day, all night."

"You sang. Why, then go and dance."

I do not ascribe[3] it to perversity on my part, but rather to the inconsequence of childhood, which is deficient in moral sense, that I could never quite reconcile myself to the lesson. My sympathies were with the grasshopper and for some time I never saw an ant without putting my foot on it. In this summary (and as I have discovered since, entirely human) fashion I sought to express my disapproval of prudence and common sense.

I could not help thinking of this fable when the other day I saw George Ramsay lunching by himself in a restaurant. I never saw anyone wear an expression of such deep gloom. He was staring into space. He looked as though the burden of the whole world sat on his shoulders. I was sorry for him: I suspected at once that his unfortunate brother had been causing trouble again. I went up to him and held out my hand.

"How are you?" I asked.

"I'm not in hilarious spirits," he answered.

"Is it Tom again?"

He sighed.

"Yes, it's Tom again."

"Why don't you chuck him? You've done everything in the world for him. You must know by now that he's quite hopeless."

I suppose every family has a black sheep. Tom had been a sore trial to his for twenty

---

1. **giddiness:** a state of being playful or frivolous.
2. **larder:** a place where food is stored; pantry.
3. **ascribe:** to assign or attribute to a supposed cause.

---

*Words
to Know
and Use* | **perversity** (pər vur′ sə tē) *n.* the condition of being stubbornly against what is right

747

years. He had begun life decently enough: he went into business, married, and had two children. The Ramsays were perfectly respectable people and there was every reason to suppose that Tom Ramsay would have a useful and honorable career. But one day, without warning, he announced that he didn't like work and that he wasn't suited for marriage. He wanted to enjoy himself. He would listen to no expostulations.[4] He left his wife and his office. He had a little money and he spent two happy years in the various capitals of Europe. Rumors of his doings reached his relations from time to time and they were profoundly shocked. He certainly had a very good time. They shook their heads and asked what would happen when his money was spent. They soon found out: he borrowed. He was charming and unscrupulous. I have never met anyone to whom it was more difficult to refuse a loan. He made a steady income from his friends and he made friends easily. But he always said that the money you spent on necessities was boring; the money that was amusing to spend was the money you spent on luxuries. For this he depended on his brother George. He did not waste his charm on him. George was a serious man and insensible to such enticements.[5] George was respectable. Once or twice he fell to Tom's promises of amendment and gave him considerable sums in order that he might make a fresh start. On these Tom bought a motorcar and some very nice jewelry. But when circumstances forced George to realize that his brother would never settle down and he washed his hands of him, Tom, without a qualm, began to blackmail him. It was not very nice for a respectable lawyer to find his brother shaking cocktails behind the bar of his favorite restaurant or to see him waiting on the box seat of a taxi outside his club. Tom said that to serve in a bar or to drive a taxi was a perfectly decent occupation, but if George could oblige him with a couple of hundred pounds he didn't mind for the honor of the family giving it up. George paid.

Once Tom nearly went to prison. George was terribly upset. He went into the whole discreditable affair. Really Tom had gone too far. He had been wild, thoughtless, and selfish, but he had never before done anything dishonest, by which George meant illegal; and if he were prosecuted he would assuredly be convicted. But you cannot allow your only brother to go to jail. The man Tom had cheated, a man called Cronshaw, was vindictive. He was determined to take the matter into court; he said Tom was a scoundrel and should be punished. It cost George an infinite deal of trouble and five hundred pounds to settle the affair. I have never seen him in such a rage as when he heard that Tom and Cronshaw had gone off together to Monte Carlo the moment they cashed the check. They spent a happy month there.

For twenty years Tom raced and gambled, philandered[6] with the prettiest girls, danced, ate in the most expensive restaurants, and dressed beautifully. He always looked as if he had just stepped out of a bandbox. Though he was forty-six you would never have taken him for more than thirty-five. He was a most amusing companion and though you knew he was perfectly worthless you could not but enjoy his society. He had high spirits, an unfailing gaiety, and incredible charm. I never

---

4. **expostulations:** objections to a person's actions or intentions.

5. **enticements:** temptations that offer the hope of reward or pleasure.

6. **philandered:** engaged in passing love affairs.

---

*Words to Know and Use*

**unscrupulous** (un skrōō′ pyə ləs) *adj.* not held back by ideas of right and wrong; unprincipled
**qualm** (kwäm) *n.* a twinge of conscience or doubt
**vindictive** (vin dik′ tiv) *adj.* inclined to seek revenge

grudged the contributions he regularly levied[7] on me for the necessities of his existence. I never lent him fifty pounds without feeling that I was in his debt. Tom Ramsay knew everyone and everyone knew Tom Ramsay. You could not approve of him, but you could not help liking him.

Poor George, only a year older than his scapegrace[8] brother, looked sixty. He had never taken more than a fortnight's holiday[9] in the year for a quarter of a century. He was in his office every morning at nine-thirty and never left it till six. He was honest, industrious, and worthy. He had a good wife, to whom he had never been unfaithful even in thought, and four daughters to whom he was the best of fathers. He made a point of saving a third of his income and his plan was to retire at fifty-five to a little house in the country where he proposed to cultivate his garden and play golf. His life was blameless. He was glad that he was growing old because Tom was growing old too. He rubbed his hands and said:

"It was all very well when Tom was young and good-looking, but he's only a year younger than I am. In four years he'll be fifty. He won't find life so easy then. I shall have thirty thousand pounds by the time I'm fifty. For twenty-five years I've said that Tom would end in the gutter. And we shall see how he likes that. We shall see if it really pays best to work or be idle."

Poor George! I sympathized with him. I wondered now as I sat down beside him what infamous thing Tom had done. George was evidently very much upset.

"Do you know what's happened now?" he asked me.

I was prepared for the worst. I wondered if

Tom had got into the hands of the police at last. George could hardly bring himself to speak.

"You're not going to deny that all my life I've been hardworking, decent, respectable, and straightforward. After a life of industry and thrift I can look forward to retiring on a small income in gilt-edged securities. I've always done my duty in that state of life in which it has pleased Providence to place me."

"True."

"And you can't deny that Tom has been an idle, worthless, <u>dissolute</u>, and dishonorable rogue. If there were any justice he'd be in the workhouse."

"True."

George grew red in the face.

"A few weeks ago he became engaged to a woman old enough to be his mother. And now she's died and left him everything she had. Half a million pounds, a yacht, a house in London, and a house in the country."

George Ramsay beat his clenched fist on the table.

"It's not fair, I tell you, it's not fair. Damn it, it's not fair."

I could not help it. I burst into a shout of laughter as I looked at George's wrathful face, I rolled in my chair, I very nearly fell on the floor. George never forgave me. But Tom often asks me to excellent dinners in his charming house in Mayfair, and if he occasionally borrows a trifle from me, that is merely from force of habit. It is never more than a sovereign.[10]

---

7. **levied:** burdened; imposed.
8. **scapegrace:** an unprincipled fellow; rogue; rascal.
9. **fortnight's holiday:** a vacation of two weeks.
10. **sovereign** (säv′ rən): a British gold coin equal to one pound.

*Words to Know and Use* | **dissolute** (dis′ ə lo͞ot′) *adj.* immoral

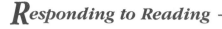

## Responding to Reading

### First Impressions

1. Did you find the story amusing? Explain your opinion.

### Second Thoughts

2. Do you feel any sympathy for George? Why or why not?

3. What makes George different from other people who give money to Tom?

   **Think about**

   • the tactics Tom uses to get money from George
   • how George views Tom's personality
   • possible reasons for George's negative feelings toward Tom

4. What is your opinion of Tom? Cite examples from the story to support your opinion.

5. What is the moral of this story?

## Writing Options

1. Many families have both "ants" and "grasshoppers" as members. How much responsibility do you think the "ants" should take for the "grasshoppers"?

2. Compare either George or Tom with someone you know or have read about. Use words and phrases from the story to describe both individuals.

## Vocabulary Practice

**Exercise** On your paper, answer each question and explain your answer.

1. Do you expect high moral standards from **unscrupulous** people like Tom?
2. Does a person of good conscience feel a **qualm** about stealing?
3. Is a **dissolute** person a good or bad influence on others?
4. If a man feels **vindictive** toward you, have you pleased or angered him?
5. Does **perversity** cause a person to do the right or the wrong thing?

> *Words*
> *to Know*
> *and Use*
> ___
> **dissolute**
> **perversity**
> **qualm**
> **unscrupulous**
> **vindictive**

**Fiction**

# *The* **Interlopers**

SAKI (H. H. MUNRO) (sä′ kē)

## Examine What You Know

The cause of the conflict in this story is a long-standing feud over a piece of land. Think about feuds between groups of people. What kinds of groups have had feuds, both in the past and in the present? What usually causes a feud to start? What are the effects of feuds?

## Expand Your Knowledge

This story takes place in the rugged Carpathian Mountains of eastern Europe. These mountains extend from northern Romania to eastern Czechoslovakia. This heavily forested, rocky region is home to a rich variety of wildlife, including deer, bears, and wolves. Landowners in this mountain range have traditionally been very protective of their rights, refusing to allow others to hunt on their land. Hunting illegally on someone else's land or hunting out of season is called **poaching** and is often severely punished. An **interloper** is someone who either trespasses or in some way interferes with the rights of a landowner. In a broader sense, an interloper is anyone who meddles in someone else's affairs. Think about both definitions as you read this story, and decide who or what are the interlopers.

## Enrich Your Reading

**Understanding Exposition**   The beginning of a short story presents the background information that readers need to understand the plot. In this part of the story, called the **exposition,** the setting and characters are introduced, the tone is established, and the conflict is revealed. In "The Interlopers," the exposition is concentrated in the first two paragraphs. Read them carefully to get a mental picture of the setting and to learn about the main characters and their conflict.

■ *A biography of the author can be found on page 759.*

# The *Interlopers*

Saki (H. H. MUNRO)

In a forest of mixed growth somewhere on the eastern spurs of the Carpathians, a man stood one winter night watching and listening, as though he waited for some beast of the woods to come within the range of his vision, and, later, of his rifle. But the game for whose presence he kept so keen an outlook was none that figured in the sportsman's calendar as lawful and proper for the chase; Ulrich von Gradwitz[1] patrolled the dark forest in quest of a human enemy.

The forest lands of Gradwitz were of wide extent and well stocked with game; the narrow strip of <u>precipitous</u> woodland that lay on its outskirt was not remarkable for the game it harbored or the shooting it afforded, but it was the most jealously guarded of all its owner's territorial possessions. A famous lawsuit, in the days of his grandfather, had wrested it from the illegal possession of a neighboring family of petty landowners; the <u>dispossessed</u> party had never <u>acquiesced</u> in the judgment of the Courts, and a long series of poaching affrays[2] and similar scandals had embittered the relationships between the families for three generations. The neighbor feud had grown into a personal one since Ulrich had come to be head of his family; if there was a man in the world whom he detested and wished ill to it was Georg Znaeym,[3] the inheritor of the quarrel and the tireless game-snatcher and raider of the disputed border forest. The feud might, perhaps, have died down or been compromised if the personal ill will of the two men had not stood in the way; as boys they had thirsted for one another's blood, as men each prayed that misfortune might fall on the other, and this wind-scourged winter night Ulrich had banded together his foresters to watch the dark forest, not in quest of four-footed quarry,[4] but to keep a lookout for the prowling thieves whom he suspected of being afoot from across the land boundary. The roebuck,[5] which usually kept in the sheltered hollows during a storm wind, were running like driven things tonight, and there was movement and unrest among the creatures that were wont[6] to sleep through the dark hours. Assuredly there was a disturbing element in the forest, and Ulrich could guess the quarter from whence it came.

What is Ulrich looking for?

He strayed away by himself from the watchers whom he had placed in ambush on the crest of the hill, and wandered far down the

---

1. **Ulrich von Gradwitz** (o͞ol′ rik fŏn gräd′ vitz).
2. **affrays:** noisy brawls or quarrels; public fights.
3. **Georg Znaeym** (gā ôrg′ z′nē′ əm).
4. **quarry:** an animal that is being hunted.
5. **roebuck:** the male of the roe deer.
6. **wont:** accustomed.

*Words to Know and Use*

**precipitous** (prē sip′ ə təs) *adj.* steep
**dispossessed** (dis′ pə zest′) *adj.* deprived of the possession of something
**acquiesce** (ak′ wē es′) *v.* to agree to without protest
**scourged** (skʉrjd) *adj.* whipped

BORDER PATROL 1948 Andrew Wyeth Private collections.

steep slopes amid the wild tangle of under-growth, peering through the tree trunks and listening through the whistling and skirling[7] of the wind and the restless beating of the branches for sight or sound of the <u>marauders</u>. If only on this wild night, in this dark, lone spot, he might come across Georg Znaeym, man to man, with none to witness—that was the wish that was uppermost in his thoughts. And as he stepped round the trunk of a huge beech he came face to face with the man he sought.

The two enemies stood glaring at one an-other for a long silent moment. Each had a rifle in his hand, each had hate in his heart and murder uppermost in his mind. The chance had come to give full play to the pas-sions of a lifetime. But a man who has been brought up under the code of a restraining civilization cannot easily nerve himself to shoot down his neighbor in cold blood and without word spoken, except for an offense against his hearth[8] and honor. And before the moment of hesitation had given way to action a deed of Nature's own violence overwhelmed them both. A fierce shriek of the storm had

---

7. **skirling:** a shrill sound.
8. **hearth:** the fireside, representing home and family life.

753

been answered by a splitting crash over their heads, and ere they could leap aside a mass of falling beech tree had thundered down on them. Ulrich von Gradwitz found himself stretched on the ground, one arm numb beneath him and the other held almost as helplessly in a tight tangle of forked branches, while both legs were pinned beneath the fallen mass. His heavy shooting-boots had saved his feet from being crushed to pieces, but if his fractures were not as serious as they might have been, at least it was evident that he could not move from his present position till someone came to release him. The descending twigs had slashed the skin of his face, and he had to wink away some drops of blood from his eyelashes before he could take in a general view of the disaster. At his side, so near that under ordinary circumstances he could almost have touched him, lay Georg Znaeym, alive and struggling, but obviously as helplessly pinioned[9] down as himself. All round them lay a thick-strewn wreckage of splintered branches and broken twigs.

*clarify* **What has happened to both Ulrich and Georg?**

Relief at being alive and exasperation at his captive plight brought a strange medley of pious thank offerings and sharp curses to Ulrich's lips. Georg, who was nearly blinded with the blood which trickled across his eyes, stopped his struggling for a moment to listen, and then gave a short, snarling laugh.

"So you're not killed, as you ought to be, but you're caught, anyway," he cried; "caught fast. Ho, what a jest, Ulrich von Gradwitz snared in his stolen forest. There's real justice for you!"

And he laughed again, mockingly and savagely.

"I'm caught in my own forest-land," retorted Ulrich. "When my men come to release us you will wish, perhaps, that you were in a better plight than caught poaching on a neighbor's land, shame on you."

Georg was silent for a moment; then he answered quietly:

"Are you sure that your men will find much to release? I have men, too, in the forest tonight, close behind me, and *they* will be here first and do the releasing. When they drag me out from under these damned branches it won't need much clumsiness on their part to roll this mass of trunk right over on the top of you. Your men will find you dead under a fallen beech tree. For form's sake I shall send my condolences to your family."

"It is a useful hint," said Ulrich fiercely. "My men had orders to follow in ten minutes' time, seven of which must have gone by already, and when they get me out—I will remember the hint. Only as you will have met your death poaching on my lands I don't think I can decently send any message of condolence to your family."

*clarify* **What threat does each make to the other?**

"Good," snarled Georg, "good. We fight this quarrel out to the death, you and I and our foresters, with no cursed interlopers to come between us. Death and damnation to you, Ulrich von Gradwitz."

"The same to you, Georg Znaeym, forest-thief, game-snatcher."

---

9. **pinioned:** disabled by the binding of the arms.

*Words to Know and Use* | **pious** (pī′ əs) *adj.* springing from actual or pretended religious feelings
**condolence** (kən dō′ ləns) *n.* an expression of sympathy for another's grief

Both men spoke with the bitterness of possible defeat before them, for each knew that it might be long before his men would seek him out or find him; it was a bare matter of chance which party would arrive first on the scene.

Both had now given up the useless struggle to free themselves from the mass of wood that held them down; Ulrich limited his <u>endeavors</u> to an effort to bring his one partially free arm near enough to his outer coat pocket to draw out his wine flask. Even when he had accomplished that operation it was long before he could manage the unscrewing of the stopper or get any of the liquid down his throat. But what a Heaven-sent draught[10] it seemed! It was an open winter, and little snow had fallen as yet, hence the captives suffered less from the cold than might have been the case at that season of the year; nevertheless, the wine was warming and reviving to the wounded man, and he looked across with something like a throb of pity to where his enemy lay, just keeping the groans of pain and weariness from crossing his lips.

"Could you reach this flask if I threw it over to you?" asked Ulrich suddenly; "there is good wine in it, and one may as well be as comfortable as one can. Let us drink, even if tonight one of us dies."

"No, I can scarcely see anything; there is so much blood caked round my eyes," said Georg, "and in any case I don't drink wine with an enemy."

Ulrich was silent for a few minutes, and lay listening to the weary screeching of the wind. An idea was slowly forming and growing in his brain, an idea that gained strength every time that he looked across at the man who was fighting so grimly against pain and exhaustion. In the pain and languor that Ulrich himself was feeling the old fierce hatred seemed to be dying down.

"Neighbor," he said presently, "do as you please if your men come first. It was a fair compact. But as for me, I've changed my mind. If my men are the first to come you shall be the first to be helped, as though you were my guest. We have quarrelled like devils all our lives over this stupid strip of forest, where the trees can't even stand upright in a breath of wind. Lying here tonight, thinking, I've come to think we've been rather fools; there are better things in life than getting the better of a boundary dispute. Neighbor, if you will help me to bury the old quarrel I—I will ask you to be my friend."

Georg Znaeym was silent for so long that Ulrich thought, perhaps, he had fainted with the pain of his injuries. Then he spoke slowly and in jerks.

"How the whole region would stare and gabble[11] if we rode into the market-square together. No one living can remember seeing a Znaeym and a von Gradwitz talking to one another in friendship. And what peace there would be among the forester folk if we ended our feud tonight. And if we choose to make peace among our people there is none other to interfere, no interlopers from outside. . . . You would come and keep the Sylvester night[12] beneath my roof, and I would come and feast on some high day at your castle. . . . I would never fire a shot on your land, save when you invited me as a guest; and you should come and shoot with me down in the marshes where the wildfowl are. In all the

---

10. **draught** (draft): the amount taken at one drink.
11. **gabble:** to talk rapidly and incoherently; chatter.
12. **Sylvester night:** December 31; a celebration of St. Sylvester.

countryside there are none that could hinder if we willed to make peace. I never thought to have wanted to do other than hate you all my life, but I think I have changed my mind about things too, this last half-hour. And you offered me your wine flask. . . . Ulrich von Gradwitz, I will be your friend."

For a space both men were silent, turning over in their minds the wonderful changes that this dramatic <u>reconciliation</u> would bring about. In the cold, gloomy forest, with the wind tearing in fitful gusts through the naked branches and whistling round the tree trunks, they lay and waited for the help that would now bring release and succor[13] to both parties. And each prayed a private prayer that his men might be the first to arrive, so that he might be the first to show honorable attention to the enemy that had become a friend.

 What change in feelings has occurred?

Presently, as the wind dropped for a moment, Ulrich broke silence.

"Let's shout for help," he said; "in this lull our voices may carry a little way."

"They won't carry far through the trees and undergrowth," said Georg, "but we can try. Together, then."

The two raised their voices in a prolonged hunting call.

"Together again," said Ulrich a few minutes later, after listening in vain for an answering halloo.

"I heard something that time, I think," said Ulrich.

"I heard nothing but the <u>pestilential</u> wind," said Georg hoarsely.

There was silence again for some minutes, and then Ulrich gave a joyful cry.

"I can see figures coming through the wood. They are following in the way I came down the hillside."

Both men raised their voices in as loud a shout as they could muster.

"They hear us! They've stopped. Now they see us. They're running down the hill toward us," cried Ulrich.

"How many of them are there?" asked Georg.

"I can't see distinctly," said Ulrich; "nine or ten."

"Then they are yours," said Georg; "I had only seven out with me."

"They are making all the speed they can, brave lads," said Ulrich gladly.

"Are they your men?" asked Georg. "Are they your men?" he repeated impatiently as Ulrich did not answer.

"No," said Ulrich with a laugh, the idiotic chattering laugh of a man unstrung with hideous fear.

"Who are they?" asked Georg quickly, straining his eyes to see what the other would gladly not have seen.

"*Wolves.*" ❧

---

13. **succor** (suk′ ər) aid; help; relief.

## Responding to Reading

### First Impressions

1. What was your reaction to the end of the story?

### Second Thoughts

2. What is ironic about the ending?

3. What causes the two men to be caught beneath the tree—fate or their own actions?

   **Think about**
   • the causes of the feud
   • why each man is in the forest that night
   • the role of nature

4. Why do the men finally become friends?

5. Who are the interlopers in the story? Explain your reasoning.

### Broader Connections

6. In addition to families, other groups, such as rival gangs and people from different countries, carry on feuds. How are these feuds similar to and different from family feuds? Consider how the feuds start, continue, and end.

## Literary Concept: Multiple Conflicts

The plot of a story usually centers on a **conflict,** or struggle, that the characters face. A character can be in conflict with another character, society, a force in nature, or himself or herself through internal conflict. This story has multiple conflicts. Find an example of three kinds of conflicts in the story.

**Concept Review: Setting**   How is the plot of this story affected by the setting?

# Writing Options

1. The story ends abruptly. Either rewrite the ending to make it more satisfying to you or add to the ending to show what happens next.

2. If both Ulrich's and Georg's men arrive after the wolves and discover what has happened, each group might react in several ways. List the different possibilities, and select the one you think would be most likely to occur. Explain your choice.

3. Imagine that you are a newspaper reporter covering the discovery of the men in the woods. Write the headline for an article about the discovery.

4. Compare and contrast the role of fate in this story with its role in another selection you have read in this book. Consider which events, if any, are beyond the characters' control.

# Vocabulary Practice

**Exercise A: Analogies** Complete the following analogies. Choose the word from the list that makes the second pair of underlined words relate in the same way as the first pair.

1. Conclusion is to completion as attempt is to _____.
2. Green is to plant as _____ is to cliff.
3. Doubt is to certainty as breakup is to _____.
4. Clapping is to appreciation as _____ is to sympathy.
5. Serpent is to snake as bandit is to _____.

**Exercise B** Write the word from the list suggested by each phrase.

1. a family being evicted from their home
2. a person kneeling at an altar in a church
3. hurricane winds breaking windows and hurling debris
4. a cruel master beating his servant
5. an employee accepting a decision without protest

> *Words to Know and Use*
>
> ---
>
> **acquiesce
> condolence
> dispossessed
> endeavor
> marauder
> pestilential
> pious
> precipitous
> reconciliation
> scourge**

## *O*ptions for Learning

**1** • **Young Actors at Work** With a classmate, act out the scene between the two men. Begin with their confrontation before the tree pins them down. Try to show the changes each man goes through before they become aware of the wolves.

**2** • **A Modern Family Feud** Write a modern version of this story with a contemporary setting and characters, but use the idea of the two feuding enemies being trapped together. Act out your story with the help of your classmates.

**3** • **A Musical Interpretation** Write a folk song, ballad, or modern rap song that tells this story. Set it to music and perform it for the class.

**4** • **Wolf Research** Using research sources in your library, find out how a pack of wolves would react if they sighted humans in a situation similar to the one in this story. Report your findings to the class.

### ◆ **FACT FINDER**

*Approximately how many years did the feud last?*

## *S*aki *(Hector Hugh Munro)*
### 1870–1916

Munro probably took his pen name from an eleventh century poem called "The Rubáiyát of Omar Khayyám." In this famous Persian poem, a wine bearer named Saki passes among his guests, filling their glasses.

Saki was born in Burma of a British military family. His mother died when Saki was two, and he was sent to England to be raised by his two unmarried aunts, who did not understand children and so were very strict with Saki and his sister. Believing that the boy was sickly, the aunts kept him inside, where he and his sister drew cartoons and developed elaborate practical jokes.

As an adult, Saki joined the Burma police but had to quit because of recurring bouts of malaria. He returned to England and wrote parodies and short stories until he became a foreign correspondent for an English newspaper and lived abroad. After six years he again returned to England and continued writing. When World War I started, Saki at age forty-four, enlisted in the army. A brave soldier, he was killed in battle.

Many of Saki's stories show the humor, cruelty, and unhappiness of childhood. His popular stories often make fun of stuffy, self-important people and show animals taking revenge on adults.

*Fiction*

## *The* *Winner*

BARBARA KIMENYE (kə men′ yā)

## *E*xamine *What You Know*

In this story, a man's life is significantly changed when he wins a large sum of money. Think of the stories you have heard about people who have suddenly acquired wealth, such as lottery winners. In what ways, including emotionally and socially, are these people affected by their winnings?

## *E*xpand *Your Knowledge*

**AFRICA**

**UGANDA**

This story is set in Uganda, a country in central Africa bordering Lake Victoria. Like many African nations, Uganda blends traditional tribal values and lifestyles with modern attitudes and experiences. Kampala, the capital, is a bustling city of nearly half a million people. Outside this industrial city, however, the inhabitants of the small villages carry on a simple, backward way of life that is hundreds of years old.

Soccer is a popular sport in Uganda as it is in other parts of the world. Part of the popularity of this sport, called football everywhere but in the United States, comes from the football pools, in which the public bets. Each week, bettors try to select the winners of all the football games played in a professional league or in a particular country that week. Since large numbers of people bet in these pools, the winners often collect vast sums of money. As you read the story, notice how the modern world clashes with the traditional ways of Uganda.

## *E*nrich *Your Reading*

**Foreign Names** Stories set in foreign countries often present difficulties for even the most experienced readers. Characters with unfamiliar and difficult-to-pronounce foreign names are sometimes hard to keep straight. As you read this story, pronounce each foreign name aloud the first time it appears. Look for the pronunciation of the name in a footnote. Pay close attention to information that reveals the character's traits, motivations, and experiences. These strategies will help you keep track of who's who and better understand what is going on in the story.

■ *A biography of the author can be found on page 771.*

# The *Winner*

BARBARA KIMENYE

When Pius Ndawula[1] won the football pools, overnight he seemed to become the most popular man in Buganda.[2] Hosts of relatives converged upon him from the four corners of the kingdom: cousins and uncles, of whose existence he had never before been aware, turned up in Kalasanda by the busload, together with crowds of individuals who, despite their downtrodden appearance, assured Pius that they, and they alone, were capable of seeing that his money was properly invested—preferably in their own particular business. Also lurking around Pius's unpretentious mud hut were newspaper reporters, slick young men weighed down with cameras and sporting loud, check caps or trilbies,[3] worn at a consciously jaunty angle, and serious young men from Radio Uganda, who were anxious to record Pius's delight at his astonishing luck for the general edification of the Uganda listening public.

The rest of Kalasanda were so taken by surprise that they could only call and briefly congratulate Pius before being elbowed out of the way by his more garrulous[4] relations. All, that is to say, except Pius's greatest friend, Salongo,[5] the custodian of the Ssabalangira's[6] tomb. He came and planted himself firmly in the house, and nobody attempted to move him. Almost blind and very lame, he had tottered out with the aid of a stout stick. Just to see him arrive had caused a minor sensation in the village, for he hadn't left the tomb for years, but recognizing at last a chance to house the Ssabalangira's remains in a state befitting his former glory made the slow, tortuous journey worthwhile to Salongo.

Nantondo hung about long enough to have her picture taken with Pius. Or rather she managed to slip beside him just as the cameras clicked, and so it was that every Uganda newspaper, on the following day, carried a front-page photograph of "Mr. Pius Ndawula and his happy wife," a caption that caused Pius to shake with rage and threaten legal proceedings, but over which Nantondo gloated as she proudly showed it to everybody she visited.

"Tell us, Mr Ndawula, what do you intend to do with all the money you have won?"

"Tell us, Mr. Ndawula, how often have you completed the pools coupon?"

"Tell us . . . Tell us . . . Tell us . . ."

---

1. **Pius Ndawula** (pī′ əs n'dä′ w$\overline{oo}$ lə).
2. **Buganda** (b$\overline{oo}$ gän′ də): the largest province of Uganda.
3. **trilbies:** soft, felt hats with narrow brims and indented crowns.
4. **garrulous:** talking too much about unimportant things.
5. **Salongo** (sä lon′ gō).
6. **Ssabalangira** (s′ sa′ bä′ lan gē′ rə).

---

*Words to Know and Use* | **unpretentious** (un′ prē ten′ sḥəs) *adj.* modest; simple
**edification** (ed′ i fi kā′ sḥən) *n.* instruction; improvement

761

Pius's head was reeling under this bombardment of questions, and he was even more confused by Salongo's constant nudging and muttered advice to "Say nothing!" Nor did the relatives make things easier. Their persistent clamoring for his attention, and the way they kept shoving their children under his nose, made it impossible for him to think, let alone talk.

It isn't at all easy, when you have lived for sixty-five years in complete obscurity, to adjust yourself in a matter of hours to the role of a celebrity, and the strain was beginning to tell.

Behind the hut—Pius had no proper kitchen—gallons of tea were being boiled, whilst several of the female cousins were employed in ruthlessly hacking down the bunches of matoke[7] from his meager plantains, to cook for everybody. One woman— she had introduced herself as Cousin Sarah— discovered Pius's hidden store of banana beer and dished it out to all and sundry as though it were her own. Pius had become very wary of Cousin Sarah. He didn't like the way in which she kept loudly remarking that he needed a woman about the place, and he was even more seriously alarmed when suddenly Salongo gave him a painful dig in the ribs and muttered, "You'll have to watch that one—she's a sticker!"

Everybody who came wanted to see the telegram that announced Pius's win. When it arrived at the Ggombolola Headquarters, Musizi had brought it personally, delighted to be the bearer of such good tidings. At Pius's request, he had gone straightaway to tell Salongo, and then back to his office to send an acknowledgement on behalf of Pius to the pools firm, leaving the old man to dream rosy dreams. An extension of his small coffee shamba,[8] a new roof on his house—or maybe an entirely new house, concrete blocks this time, with a verandah perhaps. Then there were hens. Salongo always said there was money in hens these days, now that the women ate eggs and chicken: not that either of them agreed with the practice. Say what you liked, women eating chicken and eggs were fairly asking to be infertile. That woman Welfare Officer who came snooping occasionally, tried to say it was all nonsense, that chicken meat and eggs made bigger and better babies. Well, they might look bigger and better, but nobody could deny that they were fewer, which only goes to show.

But it is surprising how news leaks out in Africa. Perhaps the newspapers have contacts in the pools offices. Anyway, before the telegram actually reached Pius, there was a small announcement in all the local papers, and Pius was still quietly lost in his dream when the first batch of visitors arrived. At first he was at a loss to understand what was happening. People he hadn't seen for years and only recognized with difficulty, fell upon him with cries of joy. "Cousin Pius, the family are delighted." "Cousin Pius, why have you not visited us all this time?"

Pius was pleased to see his nearest and dearest gathered around him. It warmed his old heart once more to find himself in the bosom of his family, and he welcomed them effusively. The second crowd to arrive were no less well received, but there was a marked coolness on the part of the forerunners.

However, as time went by, and the flood of strange faces gained momentum, Pius's

---

7. **matoke** (mə tō′ kə): fruit from plantains, or banana plants.

8. **shamba** (sḥäm′ bə): garden, farm, or plantation.

*Words to Know and Use* | **obscurity** (əb skyo͞or′ ə tē) *n.* the condition of not being well-known or famous
**effusively** (e fyo͞o′ siv lē) *adv.* in an excessively emotional manner

THE FLIGHT OF THE PINK BIRD  1970  Romare Bearden  Shorewood Publishers.

shamba began to resemble a political meeting. All to be seen from the door of the house were white kanzus and brilliant busutis,[9] and the house itself was full of people and cigarette smoke.

The precious telegram was passed from hand to hand until it was reduced to a limp fragment of paper with the lettering partly <u>obliterated</u>, not that it mattered very much, for only a few members of the company could read English.

"Now, Mr. Ndawula, we are ready to take the recording." The speaker was a slight young man wearing a check shirt. "I shall ask you a few questions, and you simply answer me in your normal voice." Pius looked at the leather box with its two revolving spools and licked his lips.

"Say nothing," came a hoarse whisper from Salongo. The young man steadfastly ignored him and went ahead in his best B.B.C. manner.

"Well, Mr. Ndawula, first of all let me congratulate you on your winning the pools. Would you like to tell our listeners what it feels like to suddenly find oneself rich?" There was an uncomfortable pause, during which Pius stared as if <u>mesmerized</u> at the racing spools and the young man tried frantically to cover

---

9. **kanzus** (kän′ zūs): men's white, long-sleeved garments; **busutis** (bu sū′ tis): long cloaks decorated with needlework.

763

the gap by asking, "I mean, have you any plans for the future?" Pius swallowed audibly, and opened his mouth to say something, but shut it again when Salongo growled, "Tell him nothing."

The young man snapped off the machine, shaking his head in exasperation. "Look here, Sir, all I want you to do is say something—I'm not asking you to make a speech! Now, I'll tell you what. I shall ask you again what it feels like to suddenly come into money, and you say something like 'It was a wonderful surprise, and naturally I feel very pleased'—and will you ask your friend not to interrupt! Got it? OK., off we go."

The machine was again switched on, and the man brightly put his question, "Now Mr. Ndawula, what does it feel like to win the pools?" Pius swallowed, then quickly chanted in a voice all off key, "It was a wonderful surprise and naturally I feel very happy and will you ask your friend not to interrupt!"

Tears came to the young man's eyes. This happened to be his first assignment as a radio interviewer, and it looked like being his last. He switched off the machine and gazed sadly into space. At that moment, Cousin Sarah caught sight of him. "Perhaps I can help you," she said. "I am Mr. Ndawula's cousin." She made this pronouncement in a manner that suggested Pius had no other. The young man brightened considerably. "Well, Madam, if you could tell me something about Mr. Ndawula's plans, I would be most grateful."

Cousin Sarah folded her arms across her imposing bosom, and when the machine again started up, she was off. Yes, Mr. Ndawula was very happy about the money. No, she didn't think he had any definite plans on how to spend it—with all these people about, he didn't have time to think. Yes, Mr. Ndawula

SOLID AS A ROCK   1970   William Pajaud   Contemporary Crafts, Los Angeles.

lived completely alone, but she was prepared to stay and look after him for as long as he needed her. (Here a significant glance passed between the other women in the room, who clicked their teeth and let out long "Eeeeeehs!" of incredulity.) Yes, she believed she was Mr. Ndawula's nearest living relative by marriage.

Pius listened to this tirade with growing horror, whilst Salongo frantically nudged him and whispered, "There! What did I tell you? That woman's a sticker!"

Words to Know and Use

incredulity (in' krə dōō' lə tē) n. unwillingness or inability to believe; doubt
tirade (tī' rād) n. a long, noisy, scolding speech

764

Around three in the afternoon, matoke and tea were served, the matoke on wide, fresh plantain leaves, since Pius only owned three plates, and the tea in anything handy—tin cans, jars, etc., because he was short of cups, too. Pius ate very little, but he was glad of the tea. He had shaken hands so much that his arm ached, and he was tired of the chatter and of the comings and goings in his house of all these strangers. Most of all he was tired of Cousin Sarah, who insisted on treating him like an idiot invalid. She kept everybody else at bay, as far as she possibly could, and when one woman plonked a sticky, fat baby on his lap, Cousin Sarah dragged the child away as though it were infectious. Naturally, a few cross words were exchanged, but by this time Pius was past caring.

Yosefu Mukasa and Kibuka called in the early evening, when some of the relatives were departing with effusive promises to come again tomorrow. They were both alarmed at the weariness they saw in Pius's face. The old man looked utterly worn out, his skin gray and sickly. Also, they were a bit taken aback by the presence of Cousin Sarah, who pressed them to take tea and behaved in every respect as though she were mistress of the house. "I believe my late husband knew you very well, Sir," she told Yosefu. "He used to be a Miruka Chief in Buyaga County. His name was Kivumbi."

"Ah, yes," Yosefu replied, "I remember Kivumbi very well indeed. We often hunted together. I was sorry to hear of his death. He was a good man." Cousin Sarah shrugged her shoulders, "Yes, he was a good man. But what the Lord giveth, the Lord taketh away." Thus was the late Kivumbi dismissed from the conversation.

Hearing all this enabled Pius to define the exact relationship between himself and Cousin Sarah, and even by Kiganda standards it was virtually nonexistent, for the late Ki-

vumbi had been the stepson of one of Pius's cousins.

"Your stroke of luck seems to have exhausted you, Pius," Kibuka remarked, when he and Yosefu were seated on the rough wooden chairs brought forth by Cousin Sarah.

Salongo glared at the world in general and snarled, "Of course he is exhausted! Who wouldn't be with all this carrion[10] collected to pick his bones?" Pius hushed him as one would a child. "No, no, Salongo. It is quite natural that my family should gather round me at a time like this. Only I fear I am perhaps a little too old for all this excitement." Salongo spat expertly through the open doorway, narrowly missing a group of guests who were on their way out, and said, "That woman doesn't think he's too old. She's out to catch him. I've seen her type elsewhere."

Yosefu's mouth quirked with amusement at the thought that "elsewhere" could only mean the Ssabalangira's tomb, which Salongo had guarded for the better part of his adult life. "Well, she's a fine woman," he remarked. "But see here, Pius, don't be offended by my proposal, but wouldn't it be better if you came and stayed with us at Mutunda for tonight? Miriamu would love to have you, and you look as though you need a good night's rest, which you wouldn't get here, because those relatives of yours outside are preparing a fire and are ready to dance the night away."

"I think that's a wonderful idea!" cried Cousin Sarah, bouncing in to remove the tea cups. "You go with Mr. Mukasa, Cousin Pius. The change will do you as much good as the rest. And don't worry about your home— I shall stay here and look after things." Pius hesitated. "Well, I think I shall be all right here—I don't like to give Miriamu any extra work . . ."

---

10. **carrion:** here, birds and other animals that feed on carrion, the decaying flesh of a dead body.

Salongo muttered, "Go to Yosefu's. You don't want to be left alone in the house with that woman—there is no knowing what she might get up to . . ."

"I'll pack a few things for you, Pius." Cousin Sarah bustled off before anything more could be said, pausing only long enough to give Salongo a look that spoke volumes.

So Pius found himself being driven away to Mutunda in Yosefu's car, enjoying the pleasant sensation of not having to bother about a thing. Salongo too had been given a lift to as near the tomb as the car could travel, and his wizened old face was contorted into an irregular smile, for Pius had promised to help him build a new house for the Ssabalangira. For him the day had been well spent, despite Cousin Sarah.

Pius spent an enjoyable evening with the Mukasas. They had a well-cooked supper, followed by a glass of cool beer, as they sat back and listened to the local news on the radio. Pius had so far relaxed as to modestly tell the Mukasas that he had been interviewed by Radio Uganda that morning, and when Radio Newsreel was announced, they waited breathlessly to hear his voice. But instead of Pius, Cousin Sarah's came booming over the air. Until that moment, the old man had completely forgotten the incident of the tape recording. In fact he had almost forgotten Cousin Sarah. Now it all came back to him with a shiver of apprehension. Salongo was right. That woman did mean business. It was a chilling thought. However, it didn't cause him to lose any sleep. He slept like a cherub that night, as if he hadn't a care in the world.

Because he looked so refreshed the following morning, Miriamu insisted on keeping him at Mutunda for another day. "I know you feel better, but after seeing you yesterday, I think a little holiday with us will do you good. Go home tomorrow, when the excitement has died down a bit," she advised.

Soon after lunch, as Pius was taking a nap in a chair on the verandah, Musizi drove up in the Landrover, with Cousin Sarah by his side. Miriamu came out to greet them, barely disguising her curiosity about the comely woman of whom she had heard so much. The two women sized each other up and decided to be friends.

Meanwhile, Musizi approached the old man. "Sit down, son." Pius waved him to a chair at his side. "Miriamu feeds me so well, it's all I can do to keep awake."

"I am glad you are having a rest, Sir," Musizi fumbled in the pocket of his jacket, "There is another telegram for you. Shall I read it?" The old man sat up expectantly and said, "If you'll be so kind."

Musizi first read the telegram in silence, then he looked at Pius and commented, "Well, Sir, I'm afraid it isn't good news."

"Not good news? Has anybody died?"

Musizi smiled. "Well, no. It isn't really as bad as that. The thing is the pools firm say they have discovered that the prize money has to be shared among three hundred other people."

Pius was stunned. Eventually he murmured, "Tell me, how much does it mean I shall get?"

"Three hundred into seventeen thousand pounds won't give you much over a thousand shillings."

To Musizi's amazement, Pius sat back and chuckled. "More than a thousand shillings!" he said. "That is a lot of money!"

"But it's not, when you expected so much more!"

Words
to Know
and Use

**contort** (kən tôrt') *v.* to twist out of its usual form; distort

"I agree. And yet, son, what would I have done with all those thousands of pounds? I am getting past the age when I need a lot."

Miriamu brought a mat on to the verandah, and she and Cousin Sarah made themselves comfortable near the men, whilst Musizi explained what had happened. "What a disappointment," cried Miriamu, but Cousin Sarah sniffed and said, "I agree with Cousin Pius. He wouldn't know what to do with seventeen thousand pounds, and the family would be hanging round his neck for ever more."

At mention of Pius's family, Musizi frowned, "I should warn you, Sir, those relatives of yours have made a terrific mess of your shamba—your plantains have been stripped—and Mrs. Kivumbi here," nodding at Sarah, "was only just in time to prevent them digging up your sweet potatoes."

"Yes, Cousin Pius," added Sarah, "it will take us some time to put that shamba back in order. They've trodden down a whole bed of young beans."

"Oh, dear," said Pius weakly. "That is dreadful news."

"Don't worry. They will soon disappear when I tell them there is no money, and then I shall send for a couple of my grandsons to come and help us do some replanting." Pius could not but help admire the way Sarah took things in her stride. Musizi rose from his chair. "I'm afraid I can't stay any longer, so I will go now and clear the crowd, and see you tomorrow to take you home." He and Sarah climbed back into the Landrover, and Sarah waved energetically until the house was out of sight.

"Your cousin is a fine woman," Miriamu told Pius before going indoors. Pius merely grunted, but for some odd reason he felt the remark to be a compliment to himself.

All was quiet at Pius's house when Musizi brought him home next day. He saw at once that his shamba was well nigh wrecked, but his drooping spirits quickly revived when Sarah placed a mug of steaming tea before him, and sat on a mat at his feet, explaining optimistically how matters could be remedied. Bit by bit he began telling her what he had planned to do with the prize money, ending with: "Of course, I shan't be able to do everything now, especially since I promised Salongo something for the tomb."

Sarah poured some more tea and said, "Well, I think the roof should have priority. I noticed last night that there are several leaks. And whilst we're about it, it would be a good idea to build another room on and a small outside kitchen. Mud and wattle is cheap enough, and then the whole place can be plastered. You can still go ahead and extend your coffee, and as for hens, well, I have six good layers at home, as well as a fine cockerel.[11] I'll bring them over."

Pius looked at her in silence for a long time. "She is a fine-looking woman," he thought, "and that blue busuti suits her. Nobody would ever take her for a grandmother—but why is she so anxious to throw herself at me?"

"You sound as if you are planning to come and live here," he said at last, trying hard to sound casual. Sarah turned to face him and replied, "Cousin Pius, I shall be very frank with you. Six months ago my youngest son got married and brought his wife to live with me. She's a very nice girl, but somehow I can't get used to having another woman in the house. My other son is in Kampala, and although I know I would be welcome there, he too has a wife, and three children, so if I went there I wouldn't be any better off. When I saw that bit

---

11. **cockerel:** a young rooster, less than a year old.

about you in the paper, I suddenly remembered—although I don't expect you do—how you were at my wedding and were so helpful to everybody. Well, I thought to myself, here is somebody who needs a good housekeeper, who needs somebody to keep the leeches off, now that he has come into money. I came along right away to take a look at you, and I can see I did the right thing. You do need me." She hesitated for a moment and then said, "Only you might prefer to stay alone. I'm so used to having my own way, I never thought about that before."

Pius cleared his throat. "You're a very impetuous woman," was all he could find to say.

A week later, Pius wandered out to the tomb and found Salongo busily polishing the Ssabalangira's weapons. "I thought you were dead," growled Salongo. "It is so long since you came here—but then, this tomb thrives on neglect. Nobody cares that one of Buganda's greatest men lies here."

"I have been rather busy," murmured Pius, "but I didn't forget my promise to you. Here! I've brought you a hundred shillings, and I only wish it could have been more. At least it will buy a few cement blocks."

Salongo took the money and looked at it as if it were crawling with lice. Grudgingly he thanked Pius and then said, "Of course, you will find life more expensive now that you are keeping a woman in the house."

"I suppose Nantondo told you?" Pius smiled sheepishly.

"Does it matter who told me? Anyway, never say I didn't warn you. Next thing she'll want will be a ring marriage."

Pius gave an uncertain laugh. "As a matter of fact, one of the reasons I came up here was to invite you to the wedding—it's next month."

Salongo carefully laid the spear he was rubbing down on a piece of clean barkcloth and stared at his friend as if he had suddenly grown another head. "What a fool you are! All this stems from your writing circles and crosses on a bit of squared paper. I knew it would bring no good. At your age you ought to have more sense. Well, all I can advise is that you run while you still have a chance."

For a moment, Pius was full of misgivings. Was he, after all, behaving like a fool? Then he thought of Sarah, and the wonders she had worked with his house and his shamba in the short time they had been together. He felt reassured. "Well, I'm getting married, and I expect you at both the church and the reception, and if you don't appear, I shall want to know why!" He secretly delighted at the note of authority in his voice, and Salongo's face was the picture of astonishment. "All right," he mumbled, "I shall try and come. Before you go, cut a bunch of bananas to take home to your good lady, and there might be a cabbage ready at the back. After all, it seems she is the winner!" ❧

# e x p l a i n

## Responding to Reading

### First Impressions

1. Would you like to be in Pius's position? Why or why not?

### Second Thoughts

2. Why do you think Pius lets everyone else in the story take charge of his actions?

3. Salongo says that Sarah is the winner. Do you agree? Explain who you think the winner is and why.

4. What do you think of Sarah? Cite examples from the story to support your opinion.

5. Salongo's advice to Pius is to "say nothing" in response to the bombardment of questions. Is this good advice?

6. Which character is most genuinely concerned with Pius's well-being? Cite evidence from the story to support your answer.

7. Do you think Pius will be happy with Sarah? Explain.

### Broader Connections

8. How do you feel about people betting on sporting events? What are good and bad effects of this? Should it be legal or not? Explain your opinion.

## Literary Concept: Motivation

**Motivation** is the reason a character acts or responds in a certain way. A writer may state the reasons for a character's behavior or may require the reader to draw his or her own conclusions about the character's motivation. What motivates most of Pius's guests to visit him? What motivates Pius to marry Sarah? Cite evidence from the story to support your reasoning.

**Concept Review: Irony** Cite examples of irony in Pius's situation.

## Writing Options

1. List all of the consequences of Pius's winning the football pool. Check those that are positive.

2. Write a wedding toast that Salongo might give at the reception. Make sure the toast reflects Salongo's attitudes and feelings toward his old friend.

3. If you were in Pius's position, explain how you would handle the situation.

4. Explain how you think one of the other characters, such as Salongo or Sarah, would have handled winning the money. Base your explanation on what you know about him or her.

5. Using examples from the story, explain how money can bring, or fail to bring, happiness.

## Vocabulary Practice

**Exercise: Antonyms** Write the letter of the word that is the most nearly opposite in meaning to the capitalized word.

1. EFFUSIVE: (a) quick (b) aloof (c) loving (d) emotional
2. UNPRETENTIOUS: (a) simple (b) cheap (c) showy (d) noble
3. CONTORT: (a) untwist (b) argue (c) admire (d) agree
4. INCREDULITY: (a) amazement (b) pleasure (c) belief (d) doubt
5. MESMERIZED: (a) fascinated (b) excited (c) unhappy (d) bored
6. OPTIMISTICALLY: (a) totally (b) hopelessly (c) partially (d) eagerly
7. EDIFICATION: (a) betterment (b) decay (c) article (d) improvement
8. TIRADE: (a) criticism (b) scolding (c) rebuke (d) praise
9. OBSCURITY: (a) fame (b) rudeness (c) unhappiness (d) solitude
10. OBLITERATED: (a) rebuilt (b) hidden (c) ruined (d) destroyed

*Words to Know and Use*

contort
edification
effusive
incredulity
mesmerized
obliterated
obscurity
optimistically
tirade
unpretentious

# extend

## Options for Learning

**1** • **Lotto Fever** Using the *Readers' Guide to Periodical Literature,* locate articles about lottery winners. Read the articles to find out how much money the winners won and how their lives were affected. Report your findings to the class.

**2** • **Pictures from Africa** Do a picture study of modern Uganda. In magazines and newspapers find photographs that show both sides of Africa today—the traditional and the modern aspects of a culture in transition. If possible, also include photographs that represent the type of village and home in which Pius lived. Share your photo essay with the class.

**3** • **Radio Uganda** In small groups, conduct a follow-up interview between Pius and the nervous reporter. Focus the interview either on Pius's reaction to the news in the second telegram or on his married life with Sarah. Perform your interview for the class.

### FACT FINDER

*What is the largest ethnic group living in Uganda?*

## Barbara Kimenye

### 1940-

Born and educated in Uganda, Kimenye has worked as a journalist, a columnist for the Kampala newspaper called *Uganda Nation,* a social worker in London, and a private secretary for the Kabaka, or constitutional ruler, of the province of Buganda. She is well known in Africa for her newspaper work, her two collections of short stories, and her children's books. She likes to put her characters into all kinds of difficult situations, some of which concern cultural clashes or clashes with authorities. Her characters are primarily good, positive people who try to cope with a negative environment.

*Fiction*

# The Meeting

JORGE LUIS BORGES (hôr′ hā  l oo ēs′  bôr′ hes)

## Examine What You Know

Discuss times when you have witnessed a fight that was started by an insult. In each situation, what kinds of behavior preceded the fight? How important was the involvement of spectators? How did the fight end? As you read this story, see if you find any patterns similar to those you have discussed.

## Expand Your Knowledge

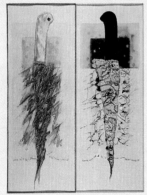

Jorge Borges, the writer of this story, is considered one of the most important writers of the twentieth century. He is known for his stories which combine realism with a dream-like quality.

"The Meeting" is set in Borges's homeland of Argentina, South America's second-largest country. Argentina's population is 85 percent European— mostly the descendants of immigrants—and about 15 percent Indian and mestizo, people of mixed Indian and European ancestry. The original Indian population was drastically reduced by disease. While Spanish is the principal language, Argentina's culture is a rich mixture of Spanish, Indian, and other European heritages.

As you may recall from reading *The Ring of General Macías,* honor has traditionally been very important to Latin-American men and women. Honor must be protected, requiring men especially to stand up for themselves and fight if necessary. In a fight of honor, no one interferes.

## Enrich Your Reading

**Determining Causes**  When the causes of a fight are studied afterward, various explanations are often discovered. Just as causes in real life are not always simple or clear-cut, the cause of the fight in this story allows for various interpretations. It is up to you to decide which explanation, based on the evidence presented, is the most reasonable one. As you read the story, jot down causes and evidence that supports each cause. Then after you finish reading, decide which explanation is the most convincing.

■ *A biography of the author can be found in the Reader's Handbook.*

# *The* *Meeting*

### JORGE LUIS BORGES

Anyone leafing his way through the morning paper does so either to escape his surroundings or to provide himself with small talk for later in the day, so it is not to be wondered at that no one any longer remembers—or else remembers as in a dream—the famous and once widely discussed case of Maneco Uriarte[1] and of Duncan. The event took place, furthermore, back around 1910, the year of the comet and the Centennial,[2] and since then we have had and have lost so many things. Both protagonists are now dead; those who witnessed the episode solemnly swore silence. I, too, raised my hand for the oath, feeling the importance of the ritual with all the romantic seriousness of my nine or ten years. I do not know whether the others noticed that I had given my word; I do not know whether they kept theirs. Anyway, here is the story, with all the inevitable variations brought about by time and by good or bad writing.

My cousin Lafinur took me to a barbecue that evening at a country house called The Laurels, which belonged to some friends of his. I cannot fix its exact location; let us take any of those suburban towns lying just north, shaded and quiet, that slope down to the river and that have nothing in common with sprawling Buenos Aires and its surrounding prairie. The journey by train lasted long enough to seem endless to me, but time for children—as is well known—flows slowly. It was already dark when we passed through the villa's main gate. Here, I felt, were all the ancient, elemental things: the smell of meat cooking golden brown, the trees, the dogs, the kindling wood, and the fire that brings men together.

The guests numbered about a dozen; all were grown-ups. The eldest, I learned later, was not yet thirty. They were also—this I was soon to find out—well versed in matters about which I am still somewhat backward: racehorses, the right tailors, motorcars, and notoriously expensive women. No one ruffled my shyness, no one paid any attention to me. The lamb, slowly and skillfully prepared by one of the hired men, kept us a long time in the big dining room. The dates of vintage were argued back and forth. There was a guitar; my cousin, if I remember correctly, sang a couple of Elías Regules' ballads about gauchos in the back country of Uruguay and some verses in dialect, in the incipient *lunfardo*[3] of those days, about a knife fight in a brothel[4] on Junín Street. Coffee and Havana cigars were brought in. Not a word about getting back. I felt (in the words of the poet Lugones) the fear of what is suddenly too late. I dared not look at the clock. In order to disguise my boyish loneliness among grown-ups, I put away—not really liking it—a glass or two of wine. Uriarte,

---

1. **Maneco Uriarte** (mä ne′ kô o͞or ē är′ tä).

2. **the Centennial:** the one-hundredth anniversary of Argentina's independence from Spain.

3. *lunfardo:* Argentine slang for gangster; in this case, the language or dialect gangsters use.

4. **brothel:** a house of prostitution.

THE BOTTLE 1963
Rafael Tufiño Museo de
Arte de Ponce, Puerto
Rico Foundation of
Louis A. Ferre
Photograph by Antonio
de Jesus.

in a loud voice, proposed to Duncan a two-handed game of poker. Someone objected that that kind of play made for a poor game and suggested a hand of four. Duncan agreed, but Uriarte, with a stubbornness that I did not understand and that I did not try to understand, insisted on the first scheme. Outside of *truco*[5]—a game whose real aim is to pass time with mischief and verses—and of the modest mazes of solitaire, I never enjoyed cards. I

slipped away without anyone's noticing. A rambling old house, unfamiliar and dark (only in the dining room was there light), means more to a boy than a new country means to a traveler. Step by step, I explored the rooms; I recall a billiard room, a long gallery with rectangular and diamond-shaped panes, a couple of rocking chairs, and a window from which

5. *truco* (tr$\overline{oo}'$ kô) *Spanish:* a trick.

you could just make out a summerhouse. In the darkness I lost my way; the owner of the house, whose name, as I recall after all these years, may have been Acevedo or Acebal, finally came across me somehow. Out of kindness or perhaps out of a collector's vanity, he led me to a display cabinet. On lighting a lamp, I saw the glint of steel. It was a collection of knives that had once been in the hands of famous fighters. He told me that he had a bit of land somewhere to the north around Pergamino,[6] and that he had been picking up these things on his travels back and forth across the province. He opened the cabinet, and, without looking at what was written on the tags, he began giving me accounts of each item; they were more or less the same except for dates and place names. I asked him whether among the weapons he might have the dagger of Juan Moreira, who was in that day the archetype[7] of the gaucho, as later Martín Fierro and Don Segundo Sombra would be. He had to confess that he hadn't but that he could show me one like it, with a U-shaped crosspiece in the hilt.[8] He was interrupted by the sound of angry voices. At once he shut the cabinet and turned to leave; I followed him.

Uriarte was shouting that his opponent had tried to cheat him. All the others stood around the two players. Duncan, I remember, was a taller man than the rest of the company, and was well built, though somewhat round shouldered; his face was expressionless, and his hair was so light it was almost white. Maneco Uriarte was nervous, dark, with perhaps a touch of Indian blood, and wore a skimpy, petulant[9] moustache. It was obvious that everybody was drunk; I do not know whether there were two or three emptied bottles on the floor or whether an excess of movies suggests this false memory to me. Uriarte's insults did not let up; at first sharp, they now grew obscene. Duncan appeared not to hear, but

finally, as though weary, he got up and threw a punch. From the floor, Uriarte snarled that he was not going to take this outrage, and he challenged Duncan to fight.

## Someone—may he be forgiven for it—remarked that weapons were not lacking.

Duncan said no and added, as though to explain, "The trouble is I'm afraid of you."
Everybody howled with laughter.
Uriarte, picking himself up, answered, "I'm going to have it out with you, and right now."
Someone—may he be forgiven for it—remarked that weapons were not lacking.
I do not know who went and opened the glass cabinet. Maneco Uriarte picked out the showiest and longest dagger, the one with the U-shaped crosspiece; Duncan, almost absent-mindedly, picked a wooden-handled knife with the stamp of a tiny tree on the blade. Someone else said it was just like Maneco to play it safe, to choose a sword. It astonished no one that his hand began shaking; what was astonishing is that the same thing happened with Duncan.
Tradition demands that men about to fight should respect the house in which they are guests and step outside. Half on a spree, half seriously, we all went out into the damp night.

6. **Pergamino:** a city in Argentina, northwest of Buenos Aires.
7. **archetype** (är′ kə tīp′): the original pattern or model.
8. **U-shaped crosspiece in the hilt:** the guard piece between the handle and blade of a sword or dagger.
9. **petulant:** irritable, indicating a quick temper.

I was not drunk—at least, not on wine—but I was reeling with adventure; I wished very hard that someone would be killed, so that later I could tell about it and always remember it. Maybe at that moment the others were no more adult than I was. I also had the feeling that an overpowering current was dragging us on and would drown us. Nobody believed the least bit in Maneco's accusation; everyone saw it as the fruit of an old rivalry, exacerbated[10] by the wine.

We pushed our way through a clump of trees, leaving behind the summerhouse. Uriarte and Duncan led the way, wary of each other. The rest of us strung ourselves out around the edge of an opening of lawn. Duncan had stopped there in the moonlight and said, with mild authority, "This looks like the right place."

The two men stood in the center, not quite knowing what to do. A voice rang out: "Let go of all that hardware and use your hands!"

But the men were already fighting. They began clumsily, almost as if they were afraid of hurting each other; they began by watching the blades, but later their eyes were on one another. Uriarte had laid aside his anger, Duncan his contempt or aloofness. Danger, in some way, had transfigured them; these were now two men fighting, not boys. I had imagined the fight as a chaos of steel; instead, I was able to follow it, or almost follow it, as though it were a game of chess. The intervening years may, of course, have exaggerated or blurred what I saw. I do not know how long it lasted; there are events that fall outside the common measure of time.

Without ponchos to act as shields, they used their forearms to block each lunge of the knife. Their sleeves, soon hanging in shreds, grew black with blood. I thought that we had gone wrong in supposing that they knew nothing about this kind of fencing. I noticed right off that they handled themselves in different ways. Their weapons were unequal. Duncan, in order to make up for his disadvantage, tried to stay in close to the other man; Uriarte kept stepping back to be able to lunge out with long, low thrusts. The same voice that had called attention to the display cabinet shouted out now: "They're killing each other! Stop them!"

But no one dared break it up. Uriarte had lost ground; Duncan charged him. They were almost body to body now. Uriarte's weapon sought Duncan's face. Suddenly the blade seemed shorter, for it was piercing the taller man's chest. Duncan lay stretched out on the grass. It was at this point that he said, his voice very low, "How strange. All this is like a dream."

He did not shut his eyes, he did not move, and I had seen a man kill another man.

Maneco Uriarte bent over the body, sobbing openly, and begged to be forgiven. The thing he had just done was beyond him. I know now that he regretted less having committed a crime than having carried out a senseless act.

I did not want to look anymore. What I had wished for so much had happened, and it left me shaken. Lafinur told me later that they had had to struggle hard to pull out the weapon. A makeshift[11] council was formed. They decided to lie as little as possible and to elevate this duel with knives to a duel with swords. Four of them volunteered as seconds, among them Acebal. In Buenos Aires anything can be fixed; someone always has a friend.

On top of the mahogany table where the men had been playing, a pack of English cards and a pile of bills lay in a jumble that nobody wanted to look at or to touch.

---

10. **exacerbated:** made worse.
11. **makeshift:** temporary.

In the years that followed, I often considered revealing the story to some friend, but always I felt that there was a greater pleasure in being the keeper of a secret than in telling it. However, around 1929, a chance conversation suddenly moved me one day to break my long silence. The retired police captain, Don José Olave, was recalling stories about men from the tough riverside neighborhood of the Retiro who had been handy with their knives; he remarked that when they were out to kill their man, scum of this kind had no use for the rules of the game, and that before all the fancy playing with daggers that you saw now on the stage, knife fights were few and far between. I said I had witnessed one, and gave him an account of what had happened nearly twenty years earlier.

He listened to me with professional attention, then said, "Are you sure Uriarte and What's-His-Name never handled a knife before? Maybe they had picked up a thing or two around their fathers' ranches."

"I don't think so," I said. "Everybody there that night knew one another pretty well, and I can tell you they were all amazed at the way the two men fought."

Olave went on in his quiet manner, as if thinking aloud. "One of the weapons had a U-shaped crosspiece in the handle. There were two daggers of that kind which became quite famous—Moriera's and Juan Almada's. Almada was from down south, in Tapalquén."

Something seemed to come awake in my memory. Olave continued. "You also mentioned a knife with a wooden handle, one with the Little Tree brand. There are thousands of them, but there was one—"

He broke off for a moment, then said, "Señor Acevedo had a big property up around Pergamino. There was another of these famous toughs from up that way—Juan Almanza was his name. This was along about the turn of the century. When he was fourteen, he killed his first man with one of these knives. From then on, for luck, he stuck to the same one. Juan Almanza and Juan Almada had it in for each other, jealous of the fact that many people confused the two. For a long time they searched high and low for one another, but they never met. Juan Almanza was killed by a stray bullet during some election brawl or other. The other man, I think, died a natural death in a hospital bed in Las Flores."

Nothing more was said. Each of us was left with his own conclusions.

Nine or ten men, none of whom is any longer living, saw what my eyes saw—that sudden stab and the body under the night sky—but perhaps what we were really seeing was the end of another story, an older story. I began to wonder whether it was Maneco Uriarte who killed Duncan or whether in some uncanny way it could have been the weapons, not the men, which fought. I still remember how Uriarte's hand shook when he first gripped his knife, and the same with Duncan, as though the knives were coming awake after a long sleep side by side in the cabinet. Even after their gauchos were dust, the knives—the knives, not their tools, the men—knew how to fight. And that night they fought well.

Things last longer than people; who knows whether these knives will meet again, who knows whether the story ends here. ❧

# *explain*

## *Responding to Reading*

### First Impressions

1. What did you find unusual or strange in this story? Explain.

### Second Thoughts

2. What do you think is the cause of the fight?

   **Think about**
   - the reason for the argument
   - the tradition of defending one's honor
   - the choice of weapons and their history
   - the fighting ability of the two men

3. What reasons do the onlookers at the fight have for keeping its causes a secret? Are they right or wrong to do this? Explain.

4. Why does the author include the police captain's story about the knives?

   **Think about**
   - how the story affects the narrator's understanding of the killing
   - the meeting referred to in the title of the story

5. How much control do you think Uriarte and Duncan have over their own fates? Cite evidence from the story to support your opinion.

### Broader Connections

6. In any society, to what degree do you think that weapons in the hands of angry people affect their behavior? Support your opinion with reasons.

## *Literary Concept: Foreshadowing*

The dropping of hints about what will occur later in a story is called **foreshadowing.** One example of foreshadowing in this story is the swearing of the witnesses to silence in the first paragraph. Find two other examples.

## *Writing Options*

1. Write a police report of this incident. Include statements from witnesses.

2. Suppose that the truth about this fight were revealed. How would you judge and sentence Maneco Uriarte? Write your judgment.

# WRITER'S WORKSHOP

## EXPOSITION

Read the following help-wanted advertisement:

> Terrific opportunity for highly motivated, independent candidate. Duties include walking town streets, calling out news, making public announcements, and announcing time of town meetings. Loud voice and strong legs a plus. Hours: dawn to dusk. Salary: negotiable.

Can you guess what kind of job this ad is describing? Maybe not. The occupation of town crier no longer exists; the invention of the printing press in the 1400's and the start of newspaper publication in the 1600's helped make the position obsolete. Technology is creating many new occupations and replacing or changing others. There are no more lamplighters, water carriers, scribes, or pony express riders; we now have electric company executives, environmental engineers, data processors, and airplane pilots.

Several characters in this subunit—Paul, Tom Ramsay, and Pius Ndawula—suddenly receive a fortune. Most people, however, must work for a living. To help you keep up with the changing world of employment, you will use this assignment to research different aspects of an occupation that interests you. You will write an **occupational profile,** or a composition that discusses significant features of a career or job of your choice. In your paper, you will explain what kind of work is involved in the job, the requirements for entry, the pay, the opportunities for advancement, and so forth.

---

**Here is your PASSkey to this assignment.**

**GUIDED ASSIGNMENT: OCCUPATIONAL PROFILE**

Write an occupational profile that explores a career you might choose to pursue.

**P**URPOSE: To inform

**A**UDIENCE: Your classmates

**S**UBJECT: A career that interests you

**S**TRUCTURE: An occupational profile

# Prewriting

**STEP 1** **Brainstorm your interests** With a small group of classmates, brainstorm your interests and discuss occupations that you might pursue. Use the following list of questions to help you in your discussion:

1. What are your most and least favorite school subjects? What are your best subjects?
2. What extracurricular activities do you enjoy?
3. What part-time jobs or volunteer positions have you held?
4. What are you good at doing? What should you avoid?
5. Do you plan to attend college or trade school, or will you work right after graduating from high school?
6. What job would you *like* to be doing five years from now?
7. How important is money in your choice of career?

**STEP 2** **Choose a specific occupation** From these fifteen occupational groups, determine the broad category or categories in which your interests fall:

- agriculture
- business
- sciences
- education
- personal services
- arts or humanities

- hospitality and recreation
- communications and media
- marketing and distribution

- transportation
- manufacturing
- construction
- health
- public service
- natural resources and environment

After you decide what general area interests you, list specific job titles under that category. To get ideas, look in the help-wanted section of the newspaper. Talk to parents and friends, asking them to name all the jobs their friends have. Talk to a job counselor or guidance counselor. Look in career reference books. Narrow your choices to one occupation that interests you.

**STEP 3** **Gather information** Copy these headings on a sheet of paper, leaving space for writing in between. The information you collect in each of these areas will be the data for your paper.

- duties, responsibilities
- skills
- pay, benefits

- hours
- education, training
- location

- environment
- job outlook
- personality traits

To gather information for each area, begin by using the most recent edition of one or more of the reference works listed below. Check your community or school library for these books or ask your teacher to help you locate them. Record information about your sources for a bibliography.

- *Occupational Outlook Handbook*
- *Occupational Outlook Quarterly*
- *What Color Is Your Parachute?*
- *Career World*
- *Dictionary of Occupational Titles*
- *Guide for Occupational Exploration*
- *Career Guide to Professional Organizations*
- *National Trade and Professional Associations of the United States and Canada and Labor Unions*
- *Real World*

Your school may have a computer program that offers information about careers. If so, use it.

Then, talk to someone who works in the occupation you are researching. If you can't talk to someone directly in the field, try contacting a representative of a professional or trade organization or a labor union.

As you find information about each phase of the job, fill in facts in the appropriate categories. Here are the notes of one student on the educational requirements for becoming an architect:

```
education, training:
. must have either a Bachelor of Architecture degree or a
  Master's degree in architecture
. must then work as an apprentice for three years in order
  to take a licensing examination
```

◀ STUDENT MODEL

# Drafting

**STEP 1** **Write an introduction**  Begin your occupational profile by naming the occupation and stating what your paper will explain about it. You might summarize your findings as you introduce it. For example, one student started with this introduction:

```
    It takes a special kind of person to be a successful
elementary school teacher. For those who love children,
it can be a wonderfully rewarding career, but it is
hardly a dream job. This paper will explore the
essentials of the job—the training needed, the job
opportunities, salary and benefits, and the positive and
negative aspects of the job.
```

◀ STUDENT MODEL

**STEP 2** **Write paragraphs from your notes** Simply turn each section of information from Step 3 in Prewriting into a paragraph. Sometimes you can combine two or three sections into one paragraph, such as hours and pay and benefits. Begin each paragraph with a topic sentence that tells the type of information in the paragraph.

**STEP 3** **Write a conclusion** You might wind up your paper with a summary of your feelings about the occupation. You might decide that it is or is not an occupation you want to pursue. Your conclusion might be a summary of your feelings about those who pursue this career.

## Revising and Editing

Review your occupational profile. Ask a classmate to read your profile, using the checklist below. Make any necessary revisions.

### Revision Checklist

1. Does the introduction clearly state the purpose of the paper?

2. Is the information about the occupation accurate and complete?

3. Are details organized in paragraphs with clear topic sentences?

4. Does the conclusion summarize the writer's feelings about the occupation or those who do the job?

**Editing** When you have finished reviewing your profile, ask a peer editor to proofread it for errors in spelling, punctuation, and usage.

## Publishing

With your classmates, create a directory of occupations. Classify your profiles by type of work, salary range, educational requirements, and so on. Arrange profiles in a binder with a table of contents. Place the binder in the school library for other students.

## Reflecting on Your Writing

Answer the following questions. Keep the answers in your portfolio.

1. What did you like best about writing an occupational profile? least?
2. Which specific resources—including people—were most helpful?
3. Was the researching and writing of the profile useful to you?

# LANGUAGE
## WORKSHOP

## MISPLACED MODIFIERS

> Place a modifier as close as possible to the word it modifies.

A **modifier** is a word or group of words that tells about another word or group of words. Adjectives, adverbs, and phrases are all types of modifiers.

A modifier should be placed close to the word or group of words that it modifies. A modifier placed so that it seems to modify the wrong word is called a **misplaced modifier**.

| | |
|---|---|
| **Misplaced** | The rocking horse was coveted by the boy *in the shop window*. (The phrase incorrectly modifies the word *boy*.) |
| **Correct** | The rocking horse *in the shop window* was coveted by the boy. (The phrase has been moved to modify *rocking horse*.) |
| **Misplaced** | *Painted in beautiful, bright colors*, the boy saw the horse sitting in a shop window. (The phrase incorrectly modifies the word *boy*.) |
| **Correct** | The boy saw the horse, *painted in beautiful, bright colors*, sitting in a shop window. (The phrase has been moved to modify the word *horse*.) |

Changing the placement of a modifier can change the meaning of a sentence. Notice how the meaning of the following sentence changes as the word *only* is moved from one place to another.

Only the boy wanted to bet on one race. (*Only* modifies *boy*.)

The boy only wanted to bet on one race. (*Only* modifies *wanted*.)

The boy wanted to bet on only one race. (*Only* modifies *one*.)

Sometimes the word that the modifier is supposed to modify is completely missing from the sentence. A modifier with nothing that it can sensibly modify is called a **dangling modifier**.

| | |
|---|---|
| **Dangling Modifier** | Rocking on the horse, Mother called out, "Supper." (What is the phrase *rocking on the horse* supposed to modify?) |
| **Correct** | Rocking on the horse, Paul heard his mother call out, "Supper." |

Read your writing out loud to check for misplaced and dangling modifiers. Listen closely; try to forget about what you intended to say and concentrate only on what is actually on the page. You'll hear misplaced modifiers and dangling modifiers that you would otherwise miss.

**Exercise 1**   Revise or rewrite the following sentences to correct the dangling and misplaced modifiers.

1. The young boy with its shiny wooden head loved the modern rocking horse.
2. Playing in the nursery with his sisters, the rocking horse would rock Paul into a frenzy.
3. Bitter about life, worries about money tortured Paul's mother.
4. Rocking on the horse, winning horses were identified.
5. Betting on his visions, Paul only thought about making money for his mother.
6. Paul placed bets so that the whispering about money would stop at his house.
7. Partying with friends, anxiety gripped his mother until she could hardly speak.
8. Racing home from the party, the boy on the horse frightened his mother.
9. Rocking until he was unconscious, the identity of the winning horse appeared to Paul.
10. To make his family rich, his life was risked and finally lost.

**Exercise 2**   Work in groups to revise the following passage. Rewrite all sentences with misplaced or dangling modifiers.

Jorge Luis Borges was born in Argentina at the end of the last century. Having an English grandmother, English was a language that he learned at an early age. Borges loved to read Robert Louis Stevenson, the author of *Treasure Island, Kidnapped,* and *Dr. Jekyll and Mr. Hyde,* as a young man in his native Buenos Aires. Later, Borges began to write stories about criminals and detectives for an Argentine newspaper. Many of his stories had elements of magic in them, which reached a wide audience. Working for many years as a librarian, the government made him director of the National Library of Buenos Aires in 1955. Despite problems with his eyesight, he continued writing his wonderful stories, which he finally lost, becoming almost completely blind.

**LANGUAGE HANDBOOK**

For review and practice: using modifiers, pages 994–97

# LIFE SKILLS
## WORKSHOP

## WRITING A RESUMÉ

When you apply for a job, you will probably have to submit a **resumé**. A resumé provides a prospective employer with essential information about your background and abilities. Following is an example of a well-prepared resumé.

---

RUTH MARIE MYERS

2941 Grove Street
Lansing, Michigan 48927
(517) 555-2549

| | |
|---|---|
| OBJECTIVE | To work as a word processor or administrative assistant. |
| EDUCATION | Valley High School, Lansing, Michigan, 1988–1992. Courses in typing, word processing, data processing, and the computerized office. |
| WORK EXPERIENCE | October 1991–present. Clerk-typist (part-time). Municipal License Bureau. Lansing, Michigan. Duties include word processing, filing, correspondence, and some customer service.<br><br>June 1990–August 1991. Sales clerk (full-time summer help). Maxine's-on-the-Mall. East Lansing, Michigan.<br><br>June 1989–August 1990. Games coordinator. Longfellow Park, Lansing Parks and Recreation. Planned and supervised a range of summer activities for children 6 to 12. |
| SKILLS | Excellent word processor (80 wpm); experienced with IBM word processing and office computers. |
| PERSONAL | Employee of the month, July, 1991, Maxine's-on-the-Mall. Varsity Soccer Team, Valley High, 1991, 1992. Valley High Chorale, 1988–1992. |
| REFERENCES | Available upon request. |

---

### THE PARTS OF A RESUMÉ

1. **Identifying information:** your name, address, and telephone number.
2. **Objective:** a statement of the position or general kind of work you are seeking.
3. **Education:** the name of your high school, its address, your expected date of graduation, and any special achievements or courses you have taken.
4. **Work experience:** titles, duties, places of employment, and periods of employment.
5. **Skills:** a list of any special job-related abilities that you have.
6. **Personal information (optional):** a list of awards, hobbies, special interests, offices held, and volunteer work.
7. **References:** names of people who will speak on your behalf, such as teachers or employers; it is acceptable to say that you will supply these names on request.

**Exercise**   Imagine that you want to apply for a job as a summer intern at a local company, organization, or business. Write a resumé that you could use as part of an application for that internship.

# POWER OF THE INDIVIDUAL

*"Do not rely completely on any other human being . . . We meet all life's greatest tests alone."*

Agnes Macphail

CONTEMPLATION (detail)  1988
Alfredo Castaneda  Courtesy of
Mary-Anne Martin/Fine Art, New
York.

# Life in the Contemporary Period (1939–Present)

## WORLD WAR II: 1939–1945

Between 1939 and the end of 1941, when the United States joined the war, Britain stood alone in battling Adolf Hitler's mighty German army. Everyone in the country took part in Britain's war effort. Civilians volunteered to spot planes, to drive ambulances, and to fight the fires set off by incendiary bombs. Others pitched in as volunteer fire fighters or police officers.

Nightly German bomb attacks on London and other large cities forced residents to huddle in the subways for shelter. Thousands of British citizens were killed and even more people lost their homes during this two-year "Battle of Britain." The bombs also turned churches, schools, shops, and libraries into rubble. In stirring words, Britain's wartime Prime Minister, Winston Churchill, urged his countrymen to keep up their courage throughout the difficult fight against the Nazi enemy.

Even after the German bombing raids ended, the British people had to survive several more years of rationing and shortages as well as a strict military government. In 1945 the war ended with the surrender of both Germany and Japan.

World War II, the bloodiest conflict in history, caused the deaths of well over twenty million people, many of them civilians. The forced labor camps and gas chambers of the Nazis killed millions of Europeans, including six million Jews.

On August 6, 1945, to force the Japanese to surrender, the United States dropped an atomic bomb that completely destroyed the Japanese city of Hiroshima. The close of the war ushered in the new atomic age along with a new sense of anxiety about the very future of civilization.

## THE POSTWAR YEARS: 1945–1960

For at least ten years after the war, Britain suffered from shortages of vital goods, continuous poverty, and a general mood of uncertainty about the future. To re-establish social order, the new Labor government took control of almost every industry, including the radio stations, the steel companies, and the railroads and bus lines. The government also socialized medical care, employment, and housing.

By the middle 1950's, England had finally made an economic recovery from the war. Food rationing ended and industries such as machinery, appliances, and automobiles were thriving.

The coronation of Queen Elizabeth II in 1953 with all its pomp and traditional ceremony seemed to recall the earlier greatness of Elizabethan England. However, Britain never has regained its earlier position as the most powerful country in the world.

## POSTWAR LITERARY TRENDS

Many of the writers who came of age during the 1920's and 1930's continued writing during the postwar decade and afterward. In their postwar work, writers such as W. H. Auden, Elizabeth Bowen, George Orwell, and Aldous Huxley explored the experience of the individual in an anxious and uncertain world.

Some writers concentrated on portraying the grim political and social realities of postwar Britain. A group of "angry young men" in the 1950's screamed out the rage of poor working class people in novels, plays, and movies.

Other authors pushed the conventions of drama to their very limits in order to demonstrate the absurdity of modern life. In the Theatre of the Absurd, playwrights such as Samuel Beckett and Harold Pinter surprised their audiences with modernistic, often plotless, plays, filled with strange characters and unexpected happenings.

## BRITAIN IN THE MODERN AGE: 1960–PRESENT

During the 1960's and 1970's, Britain experienced a student-led revolt against the "Establishment." From religion to middle class morals, from Parliament to the royal family—everything now seemed an appropriate subject for parody or ridicule. Traditional art forms gave way to brash experiments in music, art, and literature.

While pop artists splashed geometrical patterns on canvas to give the illusion of movement, beat poets praised individual freedom in poetry readings. The Beatles initiated a world-wide passion for British rock music and pop culture that spanned the decade of the 1970's.

Modern technological development—jet travel, television, medical advances, computers, and satellite communication—have thrust Britain into today's world, an inter-global net-

The psychedelic look of the 60's in Chelsea, England   Dennis Stock/c Magnum Photos, Inc., New York.

work of developed nations. Like the United States, contemporary England struggles to retain some of its cultural traditions in a new and interdependent world. And, like the United States, Britain has also recently absorbed large numbers of third-world immigrants who have sprinkled their own lively and exotic traditions into the British cultural stew.

## BRITISH LITERATURE TODAY

By the early 1960's, Britain had given up control of almost all her remaining colonies. Although most of those former colonies remain in the British Commonwealth, many have also taken their place at the United Nations as independent countries.

Writers from these Commonwealth countries have contributed immensely to modern British literature. A varied and far-flung group of British Commonwealth writers includes Doris Lessing and Nadine Gordimer from Southern Africa, V.S. Naipaul and Derek Walcott from the Caribbean, Frank O'Connor from Ireland, Wole Soyinka and Chinua Achebe from sub-Saharan Africa, Judith Wright and Evan Jones from Australia, and Margaret Atwood and Robertson Davies from Canada.

Contemporary British fiction ranges from the spy novels of John Le Carre to the science fiction of Arthur C. Clarke and Joan Aiken and from the dark humor of Martin Amis to the fanciful fairy tales of J.R.R. Tolkien.

Twentieth-century poets have reacted to the huge growth of technology by denouncing it or ignoring it. However, some contemporary poets have begun to use their verse to confront the anxieties of our nuclear age.

# Time Line of British and World History 1940—Present

**ROYAL BRITISH CROWN**

**1953** Coronation of Queen Elizabeth II; Winston Churchill knighted, wins Nobel Prize for literature

**1949** Irish Free State becomes Republic of Ireland

**1947** Coal mines nationalized

**1946** United Nations meets in London

**1945** Elizabeth Bowen writes "The Demon Lover"

**THE BEATLES**

**1962** Doris Lessing publishes *The Golden Notebook*

**1940** Winston Churchill becomes Prime Minister

## BRITISH HISTORY

1940 ——————— 1950 ——————— 1960

## WORLD HISTORY

**1941** Japan bombs Pearl Harbor and America joins World War II

**MUSHROOM CLOUD FROM AN ATOMIC BOMB EXPLOSION**

**1945** United States drops bombs on Hiroshima and Nagasaki; World War II ends

**1947** India and Pakistan gain independence from Britain

Nation of Israel is **1948** created by partitioning Palestine

Mao Tse-Tung **1949** establishes People's Republic of China

Korean War begins **1950**

**1953** Edmund Hillary climbs Mount Everest

**1955** Martin Luther King, Jr. leads black boycott of Montgomery buses

**1957** Russia launches Sputnik, first spaceship

**1959** Fidel Castro seizes power in Cuba

**1960** Berlin Wall built

**MAO TSE TUNG**

United States troops **1964** begin fighting in Vietnam

**1981** Royal wedding of Crown Prince Charles and Princess Diana

**1980** Strikes in government-run steel and mining industries

Margaret Thatcher **1979** becomes first female Prime Minister

First supersonic passenger **1976** jet leaves London

■ PRINCE CHARLES AND PRINCESS DIANA AT THEIR WEDDING

**1973** Britain and Ireland join Common Market

**1972** Britain imposes direct rule on Northern Ireland

**1986** First American football game played in England

1970      1980      1990

**1966** Indira Gandhi becomes Prime Minister of India

**1969** America lands two men on the moon

**1971** Women gain the right to vote in Switzerland

**1973** Worldwide energy crisis

■ CELEBRATION AT THE BERLIN WALL

■ A STARVING CHILD IN ETHIOPIA

Drought and warfare result in great **1985** famine in Ethiopia

Accident at Chernobyl nuclear plant in Russia **1986**

Berlin Wall comes down as Eastern **1989** European communist nations seek freedom

# $\mathscr{P}$UTTING UP A FIGHT

Wars, prison camps, ghettos, dictators, the threat of nuclear destruction—the modern world has not been an easy one in which to live. Many people have suffered extraordinary hardships caused by persecution, injustice, violence, or fate, and they have fought back with courage and with cunning. Some people have led

armies in battle, while others have employed more quiet forms of resistance.

The following selections focus on resilient and tough-minded people who stand up to various obstacles. Such readings may inspire you to fight against the obstacles in your own life.

*Speech*

## from The Speeches
# May 19, 1940
### WINSTON CHURCHILL

## Examine What You Know

Of the many leaders who gained fame during wartime, one of the most famous statesmen of all was Winston Churchill. In a chart like the one below, record words and phrases that tell what you know about this man.

| Professional Life | Achievements | Famous Quotations | Personal Life |
|---|---|---|---|
| | | | |

## Expand Your Knowledge

World War II started in Europe two years before the United States became involved. Between 1939 and the time of the speech you are about to read, Hitler's armies conquered Austria, Czechoslovakia, Denmark, Norway, and Poland. Just nine days before Churchill's speech, the German army invaded Holland and Belgium, sweeping through these countries on its way into France. By the morning of May 19, 1940, the British troops that had been fighting in western Europe were trapped against the ocean and ready to retreat to England. The German army had crossed the Maginot (mazh′ə nō′) line of defense north of Paris and appeared too strong for any resistance.

Churchill had just been elected Prime Minister and had three hours to prepare this speech to be delivered on British radio (the BBC). Although Churchill had been in politics for years, his wartime speeches made him famous and inspired the English people who were working on the home front to greater efforts. The spirit and determination of these workers, both male and female, during the darkest moments of the war are reflected in Churchill's speeches.

## Write Before You Read

Think about the most memorable speech you have ever heard. Jot down words and phrases that describe your most vivid memories of the speech. Your description may include powerful statements made by the speaker, details about the speaker's tone of voice and body language, the emotions you felt during the speech, or the reaction of the audience.

■ *A biography of the author can be found on page 799.*

# from *The* *Speeches*
## *May 19, 1940*

### WINSTON CHURCHILL

Winston Churchill broadcasting this speech, Bettmann/Hulton, New York.

I speak to you for the first time as Prime Minister in a solemn hour for the life of our country, of our Empire, of our Allies, and, above all, of the cause of Freedom. A tremendous battle is raging in France and Flanders. The Germans, by a remarkable combination of air bombing and heavily armored tanks, have broken through the French defenses north of the Maginot Line, and strong columns of their armored vehicles are ravaging the open country, which for the first day or two was without defenders. They have penetrated deeply and spread alarm and confusion in their track. Behind them there are now appearing infantry in lorries,[1] and behind them, again, the large masses are moving forward. The regroupment of the French armies to make head against, and also to strike at, this intruding wedge has been proceeding for several days, largely assisted by the magnificent efforts of the Royal Air Force.

We must not allow ourselves to be intimidated by the presence of these armored vehicles in unexpected places behind our lines. If they are behind our Front, the French are also

1. **lorries:** British term for motor trucks.

at many points fighting actively behind theirs. Both sides are therefore in an extremely dangerous position. And if the French Army, and our own Army, are well handled, as I believe they will be; if the French retain that genius for recovery and counterattack for which they have so long been famous; and if the British Army shows the dogged endurance and solid fighting power of which there have been so many examples in the past—then a sudden transformation of the scene might spring into being.

It would be foolish, however, to disguise the gravity of the hour. It would be still more foolish to lose heart and courage or to suppose that well-trained, well-equipped armies numbering three or four millions of men can be overcome in the space of a few weeks, or even months, by a scoop, or raid of mechanized vehicles, however formidable. We may look with confidence to the stabilization of the Front in France, and to the general engagement of the masses, which will enable the qualities of the French and British soldiers to be matched squarely against those of their adversaries. For myself, I have invincible confidence in the French Army and its leaders. Only a very small part of that splendid army has yet been heavily engaged; and only a very small part of France has yet been invaded. There is good evidence to show that practically the whole of the specialized and mechanized forces of the enemy have been already thrown into the battle; and we know that very heavy losses have been inflicted upon them. No officer or man, no brigade or division, which grapples at close quarters with the enemy, wherever encountered, can fail to make a worthy contribution to the general result. The Armies must cast away the idea of resisting behind concrete lines or natural obstacles, and must realize that mastery can only be regained by furious and unrelenting assault. And this spirit must not only animate the High Command, but must inspire every fighting man.

In the air—often at serious odds—often at odds hitherto thought overwhelming—we have been clawing down three or four to one of our enemies; and the relative balance of the British and German Air Forces is now considerably more favorable to us than at the beginning of the battle. In cutting down the German bombers, we are fighting our own battle as well as that of France. My confidence in our ability to fight it out to the finish with the German Air Force has been strengthened by the fierce encounters which have taken place and are taking place. At the same time, our heavy bombers are striking nightly at the taproot[2] of German mechanized power and have already inflicted serious damage upon the oil refineries on which the Nazi effort to dominate the world directly depends.

We must expect that as soon as stability is reached on the Western Front, the bulk of that hideous apparatus of aggression which gashed Holland into ruin and slavery in a few days, will be turned upon us. I am sure I speak for all when I say we are ready to face it; to endure it; and to retaliate against it—to any extent that the unwritten laws of war permit. There will be many men, and many women, in

---

2. **taproot:** a main root from which small branch roots spread out.

this island who when the ordeal comes upon them, as come it will, will feel comfort, and even a pride—that they are sharing the perils of our lads at the Front—soldiers, sailors, and airmen, God bless them—and are drawing away from them a part at least of the on-slaught they have to bear. Is not this the appointed time for all to make the utmost exertions in their power? If the battle is to be won, we must provide our men with ever-increasing quantities of the weapons and ammunition they need. We must have, and have quickly, more airplanes, more tanks, more shells, more guns. There is imperious need for these vital munitions. They increase our strength against the powerfully armed enemy. They replace the wastage of the obstinate struggle; and the knowledge that wastage will speedily be replaced enables us to draw more readily upon our reserves and throw them in now that everything counts so much.

Our task is not only to win the battle—but to win the War. After this battle in France abates its force, there will come the battle for our island—for all that Britain is, and all that Britain means. That will be the struggle. In that supreme emergency we shall not hesitate to take every step, even the most drastic, to call forth from our people the last ounce and the last inch of effort of which they are capable. The interests of property, the hours of labor, are nothing compared with the struggle for life and honor, for right and freedom, to which we have vowed ourselves.

I have received from the Chiefs of the French Republic, and in particular from its <u>indomitable</u> Prime Minister, M. Reynaud, the most sacred pledges that whatever happens they will fight to the end, be it bitter or be it glorious. Nay, if we fight to the end, it can only be glorious.

Having received His Majesty's commission, I have found an administration of men and women of every party and of almost every point of view. We have differed and quarreled in the past; but now one bond unites us all—to wage war until victory is won, and never to surrender ourselves to servitude and shame, whatever the cost and the agony may be. This is one of the most awe-striking periods in the long history of France and Britain. It is also beyond doubt the most <u>sublime</u>. Side by side, unaided except by their kith and kin[3] in the great Dominions and by the wide Empires which rest beneath their shield—side by side, the British and French peoples have advanced to rescue not only Europe but mankind from the foulest and most soul-destroying tyranny which has ever darkened and stained the pages of history. Behind them—behind us—behind the armies and fleets of Britain and France—gather a group of shattered States and bludgeoned[4] races: the Czechs, the Poles, the Norwegians, the Danes, the Dutch, the Belgians—upon all of whom the long night of barbarism will descend, unbroken even by a star of hope, unless we conquer, as conquer we must; as conquer we shall.

Today is Trinity Sunday.[5] Centuries ago words were written to be a call and a spur to the faithful servants of Truth and Justice: "Arm yourselves, and be ye men of valor, and be in readiness for the conflict; for it is better for us to perish in battle than to look upon the outrage of our nation and our altar. As the Will of God is in Heaven, even so let it be." ❧

---

3. **kith and kin:** friends, acquaintances, and relatives.
4. **bludgeoned:** bullied.
5. **Trinity Sunday:** the eighth Sunday after Easter, dedicated to the Trinity (Father, Son, and Holy Spirit).

*Words to Know and Use* | **indomitable** (in däm′ i tə bəl) *adj.* not easily discouraged or defeated
**sublime** (sə blīm′) *adj.* noble; majestic

## *Responding to Reading*

### First Impressions

**1.** If you had been living in England at the time of this speech, would Churchill's words have inspired you to help the war effort? Why or why not?

### Second Thoughts

**2.** What actions does Churchill want the English to take against the Germans?

**3.** What emotional response is Churchill trying to arouse in his audience? How does he accomplish this? Cite evidence that supports your answer.

**4.** Reread the first three paragraphs. What military problems face the English and the French?

> **Think about**
> • the weaponry of the German military forces
> • the location of the German armies
> • the kinds of resistance needed to stop the Germans

**5.** What is Churchill's attitude toward the English, French, and Germans? Cite words and phrases that suggest those attitudes.

**6.** Which parts of the speech do you think are the most effective? Support your answer with details from the speech.

### Broader Connections

**7.** If Churchill were to give his speech today, it would be televised. How might he have changed it? What visual appeals might he have used? Do you think the speech would have been more or less powerful on television? Why?

## *Literary Concept: Persuasion*

**Persuasion** is a technique used by speakers to convince an audience to adopt a particular opinion, perform an action, or both. Churchill's speech is considered one of the greatest persuasive speeches of all time, having stirred the British people to hold out against the German assault on their homeland. The speech is so effective largely because of its balancing of intellectual and emotional appeals. Churchill's arguments are logical and clearly stated. He also uses **loaded language**, that is, words and phrases loaded with strong emotional content, to gather support for his idea of defeating the enemy at all costs. These words and phrases arouse fear, pride, and patriotism. Cite examples of Churchill's use of loaded language.

## Writing Options

1. Churchill ends his speech by stating that "it is better for us to perish in battle than to look upon the outrage of our nation and our altar." Explain the meaning of this statement and why you agree or do not agree with Churchill.

2. Even though speeches do not have titles, quotations from the speeches themselves are sometimes used in referring to them. This speech has been called "Be Ye Men of Valor." Use another memorable quotation from the speech to write an alternative title for it.

3. A pacifist is totally against war for any reason. Pretend you are a pacifist and write a short persuasive speech that presents your views and arguments against entering the war.

4. In the speech, find two emotionally loaded sentences, one about the British and the other about the Germans. Rewrite the sentences to make them less extreme in emotional content.

## Vocabulary Practice

**Exercise A: Analogies**  Write the letter of the word pair that best expresses a relationship similar to that of the first pair.

1. GRAVITY : GAIETY :: (a) love : happiness  (b) speaker : speech  (c) abundance : scarcity  (d) evaluation : grade
2. STABILIZATION : STABLE :: (a) affection : caring  (b) division : divided  (c) gang : hostile  (d) artist : famous
3. GRAPPLE : WRESTLE :: (a) surrender : defeat  (b) shout : whisper  (c) fly : travel  (d) conquer : defeat
4. ANIMATE : INSPIRE :: (a) run : walk  (b) evaluate : judge  (c) dig : build  (d) race : win
5. RETALIATE : INJURE :: (a) reward : punish  (b) end : finish  (c) walk : swim  (d) forget : remember

**Exercise B**  On your paper, write the word in the group that the boldfaced word would *not* be used to describe.

1. **dogged:** (a) determination  (b) courage  (c) fighting  (d) peace
2. **indomitable:** (a) army  (b) forest  (c) salesman  (d) spirit
3. **unrelenting:** (a) coach  (b) runner  (c) picture  (d) storm
4. **invincible:** (a) warrior  (b) mountain  (c) perfume  (d) monster
5. **sublime:** (a) criminal  (b) scenery  (c) moment  (d) beauty

*Words to Know and Use*

animate
dogged
grapple
gravity
indomitable
invincible
retaliate
stabilization
sublime
unrelenting

## *Options for Learning*

**1 • In Churchill's Name** Read Churchill's speech aloud in the manner in which you think he presented it on British radio. You may wish to divide the speech into parts and present it with a few of your classmates. Use vocal expression that reflects the emotional content of the speech.

**2 • War in 1940** Create a World War II map of western Europe. Show the territories controlled by the different armies at the time of Churchill's speech. Use a historical atlas and books on World War II as informational resources. Display your map in the classroom.

**3 • After the Speech** Using a historical atlas and books on World War II, find out what happened in the six months following Churchill's speech. What was the situation in France, how much progress was made by the Germans in their conquest of western Europe, and what were conditions like on the British home front? Report your findings to the class.

**4 • The Great Speakers** Recordings have been made of many famous twentieth-century speakers, including Churchill, Franklin Roosevelt, John Kennedy, and Martin Luther King, Jr. Listen to two different speakers and give an oral report that compares their speeches, including the style and speaking quality. Using examples from the two speeches, explain which you think is the better speech and why.

 **FACT FINDER**

*During what years was Winston Churchill Prime Minister of Great Britain?*

## *Winston Churchill*
### 1874–1965

Winston Churchill received a traditional English education provided by his father, an English lord, and his mother, the daughter of an American businessman. Since his school record was not particularly distinguished, Churchill joined the military at age nineteen. Enjoying both writing and the army, he served both as a war correspondent and as an officer. He entered politics in 1900 and forty years later became a compromise Prime Minister over a split government. His public speaking ability and talent at working with opposing forces united the British people and led them to victory over the Germans. Despite his involvement in politics throughout his life (he served as Prime Minister twice), he never stopped writing. His six-volume history of World War II won the Nobel Prize for Literature in 1953.

*Poetry*

# Do Not Go Gentle into That Good Night

### DYLAN THOMAS

## Examine What You Know

Think of people you know or have heard about who fought back against serious disease, physical or mental disability, or death. Discuss the attitudes of these people toward their situations and how they resisted. What role did a positive mental attitude play in their struggles?

## Expand Your Knowledge

Personal tragedy is the focus of many great poems. Poets sometimes cope with such tragedy by finding an image or idea and then developing it into a poem that expresses their thoughts and feelings.

Dylan Thomas, a poet from South Wales, wrote this poem at the time his father, a schoolteacher, was dying. Thomas was a careful craftsman who combined words to create intense images and sounds in his poems. He has been called the most original English poet since Yeats and Eliot, and he became popular in America for his oral readings of poems. As he grew older, he dealt often with the subject of death, as well as other personal subjects. Compare and contrast his attitude toward death with that of some of the poets you read in Unit 2. Notice how Thomas uses repetition and sound to emphasize his strong feelings.

## Write Before You Read

Thomas chooses "that good night" as his image of death. Think of other popular images that suggest death. In your journal or notebook, list those you have heard about and make up some of your own. After you read this poem, look at your list and see if your images reflect the same attitude toward death that Thomas conveys with his.

■ *A biography of the author can be found in the Reader's Handbook.*

# Do Not Go Gentle into That Good Night

DYLAN THOMAS

Do not go gentle into that good night,
Old age should burn and rave at close of day;
Rage, rage against the dying of the light.

Though wise men at their end know dark is right,
5 Because their words had forked no lightning they
Do not go gentle into that good night.

Good men, the last wave by, crying how bright
Their frail deeds might have danced in a green bay,
Rage, rage against the dying of the light.

10 Wild men who caught and sang the sun in flight,
And learn, too late, they grieved it on its way,
Do not go gentle into that good night.

Grave men, near death, who see with blinding sight
Blind eyes could blaze like meteors and be gay,
15 Rage, rage against the dying of the light.

And you, my father, there on the sad height,
Curse, bless, me now with your fierce tears, I pray.
Do not go gentle into that good night.
Rage, rage against the dying of the light.

TIME AND SPACE   1945   William S. Schwartz
Collection of the Montclair Art Museum, New Jersey
Museum purchase, Blanche R. Pleasants Acquisition.

# *e x p l a i n*

## Responding to Reading

### First Impressions

**1.** Jot down two or three phrases that describe your reaction to this poem.

### Second Thoughts

**2.** What is the speaker's attitude toward death? How do the line repetitions convey this attitude?

**3.** Explain the speaker's reasoning. Why does he use the four types of men in his argument?

**4.** Do you agree or disagree with the speaker? Why?

**5.** What is the connection between this poem and the unit title, "Power of the Individual"?

**6.** How might Thomas respond to Winston Churchill's speech?

## *Literary Concepts: Assonance and Consonance*

Poets often use the sound devices of assonance and consonance in their writing. **Assonance** is the repetition of the same vowel sound within words. An example of assonance in the first stanza is the long i sound in dying and light. **Consonance** is the repetition of consonant sounds within and at the ends of words. Consonance differs from rhyme in that the vowels that precede the like consonants differ. An example of consonance in the first stanza is the t sound in not, gentle, into, that, and night. Both assonance and consonance are used to emphasize certain words, create the mood, and add a musical quality to the poem. Find other examples of assonance and consonance in the poem.

**Concept Review: Alliteration**  Thomas also uses alliteration, the repetition of initial consonant sounds, to create sound effects. Find examples of alliteration in the poem.

## *Writing Options*

**1.** In poetic, letter, or conversational form, write the father's reply to his son.

**2.** List three pieces of advice for the speaker of the poem that will help him understand and cope with his father's approaching death.

*Fiction*

# *L*amb to
the *S*laughter
ROALD DAHL

## *E*xamine *What You Know*

Crime stories are one of the most popular
forms of fiction. Think of good crime stories
you have read or seen on television. What makes these stories popular?
What causes some to be of a better quality than others? Discuss with your
class why crime shows last longer on television than some other types of
shows.

## *E*xpand *Your Knowledge*

As a writer of adult stories, mysteries, and children's tales, Roald Dahl
uses his vivid imagination, a sense of humor, twist endings, and clear,
precise writing. Some of his most popular stories, such as *Charlie and the
Chocolate Factory* and *Witches*, have been made into movies. Dahl's writing
is somewhat bizarre, rarely moralistic, and yet satisfying to his audiences
because it flaunts conventional formats.

This suspenseful short story by Dahl was adapted for television. When it
appeared in 1958 as an episode on a weekly series of psychological thrillers
called *Alfred Hitchcock Presents,* it became one of the most popular of
Hitchcock's television films. The story contains all the stylistic elements
found in Dahl's best writing.

## *W*rite *Before You Read*

Following is a list of words and phrases from "Lamb to the Slaughter."
Using these clues, create a short version of what you think will happen in
this story:

| | | |
|---|---|---|
| warm, clean home | drinks | violence |
| policeman | a shock | detectives |
| pregnant wife | leg of lamb | weapon |

■ *A biography of the
author can be
found in the
Reader's Handbook.*

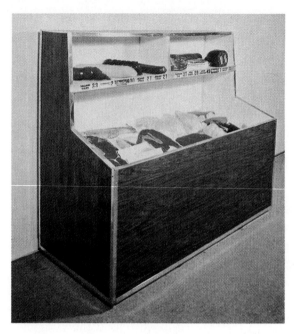

# Lamb to the Slaughter

### ROALD DAHL

The room was warm and clean, the curtains drawn, the two table lamps alight—hers and the one by the empty chair opposite. On the sideboard behind her, two tall glasses, soda water, whiskey. Fresh ice cubes in the thermos bucket.

Mary Maloney was waiting for her husband to come home from work.

Now and again she would glance up at the clock, but without anxiety, merely to please herself with the thought that each minute gone by made it nearer the time when he would come. There was a slow smiling air about her and about everything she did. The drop of the head as she bent over her sewing was curiously tranquil. Her skin—for this was her sixth month with child—had acquired a wonderful translucent quality, the mouth was soft, and the eyes, with their new placid look, seemed larger, darker than before.

When the clock said ten minutes to five, she began to listen, and a few moments later, punctually as always, she heard the tires on the gravel outside, and the car door slamming, the footsteps passing the window, the key turning in the lock. She laid aside her sewing, stood up, and went forward to kiss him as he came in.

"Hullo, darling," she said.

"Hullo," he answered.

She took his coat and hung it in the closet. Then she walked over and made the drinks, a strongish one for him, a weak one for herself; and soon she was back again in her chair with the sewing, and he in the other, opposite, holding the tall glass with both his hands, rocking it so the ice cubes tinkled against the side.

For her, this was always a blissful time of day. She knew he didn't want to speak much until the first drink was finished, and she, on her side, was content to sit quietly, enjoying his company after the long hours alone in the house. She loved to luxuriate in the presence of this man and to feel—almost as a sunbather feels the sun—that warm male glow that came out of him to her when they were alone together. She loved him for the way he sat loosely in a chair, for the way he came in a door or moved slowly across the room with long strides. She loved the intent, far look in his eyes when they rested on her, the funny shape of the mouth, and especially the way he remained silent about his tiredness, sitting still with himself until the whiskey had taken some of it away.

"Tired, darling?"

"Yes," he said. "I'm tired." And as he spoke, he did an unusual thing. He lifted his glass and drained it in one swallow although there was still half of it, at least half of it left. She wasn't really watching him, but she knew what he had done because she heard the ice cubes falling back against the bottom of the empty glass when he lowered his arm. He paused a moment, leaning forward in the chair, then he got up and went slowly over to fetch himself another.

"I'll get it!" she cried, jumping up.

"Sit down," he said.

When he came back, she noticed that the new drink was dark amber with the quantity of whiskey in it.

"Darling, shall I get your slippers?"

"No."

She watched him as he began to sip the dark yellow drink, and she could see little oily swirls in the liquid because it was so strong.

"I think it's a shame," she said, "that when a policeman gets to be as senior as you, they keep him walking about on his feet all day long."

He didn't answer, so she bent her head again and went on with her sewing; but each time he lifted the drink to his lips, she heard the ice cubes clinking against the side of the glass.

"Darling," she said. "Would you like me to get you some cheese? I haven't made any supper because it's Thursday."

"No," he said.

"If you're too tired to eat out," she went on, "it's still not too late. There's plenty of meat and stuff in the freezer, and you can have it right here and not even move out of the chair."

Her eyes waited on him for an answer, a smile, a little nod, but he made no sign.

"Anyway," she went on, "I'll get you some cheese and crackers first."

"I don't want it," he said.

She moved uneasily in her chair, the large eyes still watching his face. "But you *must* have supper. I can easily do it here. I'd like to do it. We can have lamb chops. Or pork. Anything you want. Everything's in the freezer."

"Forget it," he said.

"But darling, you *must* eat! I'll fix it anyway, and then you can have it or not, as you like."

She stood up and placed her sewing on the table by the lamp.

"Sit down," he said. "Just for a minute, sit down."

It wasn't till then that she began to get frightened.

"Go on," he said. "Sit down."

She lowered herself back slowly into the chair, watching him all the time with those large, bewildered eyes. He had finished the second drink and was staring down into the glass, frowning.

"Listen," he said. "I've got something to tell you."

"What is it, darling? What's the matter?"

He had now become absolutely motionless, and he kept his head down so that the light from the lamp beside him fell across the upper part of his face, leaving the chin and mouth in shadow. She noticed there was a little muscle moving near the corner of his left eye.

"This is going to be a bit of a shock to you, I'm afraid," he said. "But I've thought about it a good deal and I've decided the only thing to do is tell you right away. I hope you won't blame me too much."

And he told her. It didn't take long, four or five minutes at most, and she sat very still through it all, watching him with a kind of dazed horror as he went farther and farther away from her with each word.

"So, there it is," he added. "And I know it's kind of a bad time to be telling you, but there simply wasn't any other way. Of course I'll give you money and see you're looked after. But there needn't really be any fuss. I hope not anyway. It wouldn't be very good for my job."

Her first instinct was not to believe any of it, to reject it all. It occurred to her that perhaps he hadn't even spoken, that she herself had imagined the whole thing. Maybe, if she went about her business and acted as though she hadn't been listening, then later, when she sort of woke up again, she might find none of it had ever happened.

"I'll get the supper," she managed to whisper, and this time he didn't stop her.

When she walked across the room, she couldn't feel her feet touching the floor. She couldn't feel anything at all—except a slight nausea and a desire to vomit. Everything was automatic now—down the steps to the cellar, the light switch, the deep freeze, the hand inside the cabinet taking hold of the first object it met. She lifted it out and looked at it. It was wrapped in paper, so she took off the paper and looked at it again.

A leg of lamb.

All right then, they would have lamb for supper. She carried it upstairs, holding the thin bone-end of it with both her hands, and as she went through the living room, she saw him standing over by the window with his back to her, and she stopped.

"For God's sake," he said, hearing her but not turning round. "Don't make supper for me. I'm going out."

At that point, Mary Maloney simply walked up behind him, and without any pause she swung the big frozen leg of lamb high in the air and brought it down as hard as she could on the back of his head.

She might just as well have hit him with a steel club.

She stepped back a pace, waiting, and the funny thing was that he remained standing there for at least four or five seconds, gently swaying. Then he crashed to the carpet.

The violence of the crash, the noise, the small table overturning, helped bring her out of the shock. She came out slowly, feeling cold and surprised, and she stood for a while blinking at the body, still holding the ridiculous piece of meat tight with both hands.

All right, she told herself. So I've killed him.

It was extraordinary, now, how clear her mind became all of a sudden. She began thinking very fast. As the wife of a detective, she knew quite well what the penalty would be. That was fine. It made no difference to her. In fact, it would be a relief. On the other hand, what about the child? What were the laws about murderers with unborn children? Did they kill them both—mother and child? Or did they wait until the tenth month? What did they do?

Mary Maloney didn't know. And she certainly wasn't prepared to take a chance.

She carried the meat into the kitchen, placed it in a pan, turned the oven on high, and shoved it inside. Then she washed her hands and ran upstairs to the bedroom. She sat down before the mirror, tidied her hair, touched up her lips and face. She tried a smile. It came out rather peculiar. She tried again.

"Hullo, Sam," she said brightly, aloud.

The voice sounded peculiar too.

"I want some potatoes please, Sam. Yes, and I think a can of peas."

That was better. Both the smile and the voice were coming out better now. She rehearsed it several times more. Then she ran downstairs, took her coat, went out the back door, down the garden, into the street.

It wasn't six o'clock yet, and the lights were still on in the grocery shop.

"Hullo, Sam," she said brightly, smiling at the man behind the counter.

"Why, good evening, Mrs. Maloney. How're *you?*"

"I want some potatoes, please, Sam. Yes, and I think a can of peas."

The man turned and reached up behind him on the shelf for the peas.

"Patrick's decided he's tired and doesn't want to eat out tonight," she told him. "We usually go out Thursdays, you know, and now he's caught me without any vegetables in the house."

"Then how about meat, Mrs. Maloney?"

"No, I've got meat, thanks. I got a nice leg of lamb from the freezer."

"Oh."

"I don't much like cooking it frozen, Sam, but I'm taking a chance on it this time. You think it'll be all right?"

"Personally," the grocer said, "I don't believe it makes any difference. You want these Idaho potatoes?"

"Oh yes, that'll be fine. Two of those."

"Anything else?" The grocer cocked his head on one side, looking at her pleasantly. "How about afterwards? What you going to give him afterwards?"

"Well—what would you suggest, Sam?"

The man glanced around his shop. "How about a nice big slice of cheesecake? I know he likes that."

"Perfect," she said. "He loves it."

And when it was all wrapped and she had paid, she put on her brightest smile and said, "Thank you, Sam. Good night."

"Good night, Mrs. Maloney. And thank *you*."

And now, she told herself as she hurried back, all she was doing now, she was returning home to her husband, and he was waiting for his supper; and she must cook it good and make it as tasty as possible because the poor man was tired; and if, when she entered the house, she happened to find anything unusual, or tragic, or terrible, then naturally it would be a shock and she'd become frantic with grief and horror. Mind you, she wasn't *expecting* to find anything.

She was just going home with the vegetables. Mrs. Patrick Maloney going home with the vegetables on Thursday evening to cook supper for her husband.

That's the way, she told herself. Do everything right and natural. Keep things absolutely natural and there'll be no need for any acting at all.

Therefore, when she entered the kitchen by the back door, she was humming a little tune to herself and smiling.

"Patrick!" she called. "How are you, darling?"

She put the parcel down on the table and went through into the living room; and when she saw him lying there on the floor with his legs doubled up and one arm twisted back underneath his body, it really was rather a shock. All the old love and longing for him welled up inside her, and she ran over to him, knelt down beside him, and began to cry her heart out. It was easy. No acting was necessary.

A few minutes later she got up and went to the phone. She knew the number of the police station, and when the man at the other end answered, she cried to him, "Quick! Come quick! Patrick's dead!"

"Who's speaking?"

"Mrs. Maloney. Mrs. Patrick Maloney."

"You mean Patrick Maloney's dead?"

"I think so," she sobbed. "He's lying on the floor, and I think he's dead."

"Be right over," the man said.

The car came very quickly, and when she opened the front door, two policemen walked in. She knew them both—she knew nearly all the men at that precinct—and she fell right into Jack Noonan's arms, weeping hysterically. He put her gently into a chair, then went over to join the other one, who was called O'Malley, kneeling by the body.

"Is he dead?" she cried.

"I'm afraid he is. What happened?"

Briefly, she told her story about going out to the grocer and coming back to find him on the floor. While she was talking, crying and talking, Noonan discovered a small patch of congealed blood on the dead man's head. He showed it to O'Malley, who got up at once and hurried to the phone.

Soon, other men began to come into the house. First a doctor, then two detectives, one of whom she knew by name. Later, a police photographer arrived and took pictures, and a man who knew about fingerprints. There was a great deal of whispering and muttering beside the corpse, and the detectives kept asking her a lot of questions. But they always treated her kindly. She told her story again, this time right from the beginning, when Patrick had come in, and she was sewing, and he was tired, so tired he hadn't wanted to go out for supper. She told how she'd put the meat in the oven— "it's there now, cooking"—and how she'd slipped out to the grocer for vegetables, and come back to find him lying on the floor.

"Which grocer?" one of the detectives asked.

She told him, and he turned and whispered something to the other detective, who immediately went outside into the street.

In fifteen minutes he was back with a page of notes, and there was more whispering, and through her sobbing she heard a few of the whispered phrases—". . . acted quite normal . . . very cheerful . . . wanted to give him a good supper . . . peas . . . cheesecake . . . impossible that she . . ."

After a while, the photographer and the doctor departed, and two other men came in and took the corpse away on a stretcher. Then the fingerprint man went away. The two detectives remained, and so did the two policemen. They were exceptionally nice to her, and Jack Noonan asked if she wouldn't rather go somewhere else, to her sister's house perhaps, or to his own wife, who would take care of her and put her up for the night.

No, she said. She didn't feel she could move even a yard at the moment. Would they mind awfully if she stayed just where she was until she felt better? She didn't feel too good at the moment, she really didn't.

Then hadn't she better lie down on the bed? Jack Noonan asked.

No, she said. She'd like to stay right where she was, in this chair. A little later perhaps, when she felt better, she would move.

So they left her there while they went about their business, searching the house. Occasionally one of the detectives asked her another question. Sometimes Jack Noonan spoke at her gently as he passed by. Her husband, he told her, had been killed by a blow on the back of the head administered with a heavy, blunt instrument, almost certainly a large piece of metal. They were looking for the weapon. The murderer may have taken it with him, but on the other hand he may've thrown it away or hidden it somewhere on the premises.

"It's the old story," he said. "Get the weapon, and you've got the man."

Later, one of the detectives came up and sat beside her. Did she know, he asked, of anything in the house that could've been used as the weapon? Would she mind having a look around to see if anything was missing—a very big spanner,[1] for example, or a heavy metal vase.

They didn't have any heavy metal vases, she said.

"Or a big spanner?"

She didn't think they had a big spanner. But there might be some things like that in the garage.

The search went on. She knew that there were other policemen in the garden all around the house. She could hear their foot-

---

1. **spanner:** British for *wrench*.

steps on the gravel outside, and sometimes she saw the flash of a torch through a chink in the curtains. It began to get late, nearly nine, she noticed by the clock on the mantle. The four men searching the rooms seemed to be growing weary, a trifle exasperated.

"Jack," she said, the next time Sergeant Noonan went by. "Would you mind giving me a drink?"

"Sure, I'll give you a drink. You mean this whiskey?"

"Yes, please. But just a small one. It might make me feel better." He handed her the glass.

"Why don't you have one yourself," she said. "You must be awfully tired. Please do. You've been very good to me."

"Well," he answered, "it's not strictly allowed, but I might take just a drop to keep me going."

One by one the others came in and were persuaded to take a little nip of whiskey. They stood around rather awkwardly with the drinks in their hands, uncomfortable in her presence, trying to say consoling things to her. Sergeant Noonan wandered into the kitchen, came out quickly, and said, "Look, Mrs. Maloney. You know that oven of yours is still on, and the meat still inside."

"Oh *dear* me!" she cried. "So it is!"

"I better turn it off for you, hadn't I?"

"Will you do that, Jack? Thank you so much."

When the sergeant returned the second time, she looked at him with her large, dark, tearful eyes. "Jack Noonan," she said.

"Yes?"

"Would you do me a small favor—you and these others?"

"We can try, Mrs. Maloney."

"Well," she said. "Here you all are, and good friends of dear Patrick's too, and helping to catch the man who killed him. You must be terribly hungry by now because it's long past your suppertime, and I know Patrick would never forgive me, God bless his soul, if I allowed you to remain in his house without offering you decent hospitality. Why don't you eat up that lamb that's in the oven. It'll be cooked just right by now."

"Wouldn't dream of it," Sergeant Noonan said.

"Please," she begged. "Please eat it. Personally I couldn't touch a thing, certainly not what's been in the house when he was here. But it's all right for you. It'd be a favor to me if you'd eat it up. Then you can go on with your work again afterwards."

There was a good deal of hesitating among the four policemen, but they were clearly hungry, and in the end they were persuaded to go into the kitchen and help themselves. The woman stayed where she was, listening to them through the open door, and she could hear them speaking among themselves, their voices thick and sloppy because their mouths were full of meat.

"Have some more, Charlie?"

"No. Better not finish it."

"She *wants* us to finish it. She said so. Be doing her a favor."

"Okay, then. Give me some more."

"That's a hell of a big club the guy must've used to hit poor Patrick," one of them was saying. "The doc says his skull was smashed all to pieces just like from a sledgehammer."

"That's why it ought to be easy to find."

"Exactly what I say."

"Whoever done it, they're not going to be carrying a thing like that around with them longer than they need."

One of them belched.

"Personally, I think it's right here on the premises."

"Probably right under our very noses. What do you think, Jack?"

And in the other room, Mary Maloney began to giggle. ❧

## Responding to Reading

### First Impressions

1. Did you like this story? Why or why not?

### Second Thoughts

2. Do you want Mary to get away with her crime? Do you think she will? Explain your answers.

3. In what ways does Mary change in the course of the story?

   **Think about**
   • her behavior toward Patrick before and after his announcement
   • her reaction to the murder

4. Are the characters in this story believable? Cite evidence to support your opinion.

   **Think about**
   • the relationship between Mary and Patrick
   • how Mary deals with her situation
   • the words and actions of the policemen and detectives

5. Explain the irony in the title of the story.

## Literary Concepts: Dynamic and Static Characters

In a short story, the main character is usually the only one who develops and grows in the course of the story. Such a character is said to be **dynamic**. The ones who do not change are said to be **static**. Static characters are usually uninteresting as people but help advance the plot. Identify the dynamic and static characters in this story. How are your opinions of these characters affected by how much you know or do not know about them?

**Concept Review: Point of View** Is this story narrated in first-person, third-person limited, or third-person omniscient point of view? Explain.

## Writing Options

1. Write Patrick's explanation to Mary about why he is leaving.

2. As Mary, write a tongue-in-cheek, or humorously ironic, obituary for Patrick. Use words from the story, such as *lamb, policemen,* and *drink.*

*Fiction*

# *E*scape
ILYA VARSHAVSKY

## *E*xamine *What You Know*

Think about science fiction stories
you have read or seen on film. What
elements do these stories have in
common? Consider the settings,
characters, and events in the plots.

## *E*xpand *Your Knowledge*

Most science fiction stories are set in futuristic societies, some located in
the distant future and others in the not-so-distant future. In science fiction
books and films such as *2001, A Space Odyssey; Blade Runner;* and *1984,*
the settings are based on societies very similar to our own. While some
stories use the positive elements of our present space-age society, others
focus on the negative elements. For example, they show tyranny,
domination, and the political and social victims of police-controlled states.

Varshavsky's story criticizes life in the Soviet Union during the 1970's,
focusing on that society's most negative elements. All the elements in his
story have some basis in scientific reality, but they have not yet been used
in the way that Varshavsky describes.

## *E*nrich *Your Reading*

**Making Inferences**   When a writer chooses not to fill in every detail,
the reader must make logical guesses by using the evidence the writer
provides. This process of drawing conclusions based on known facts or
evidence is called **making inferences**. "Escape" is broken into separate
time sections. At the beginning of each section, you must make some
inferences about the unstated time leap between that section and the
previous one. In such an imaginative story, you must infer other details as
well. A few questions are provided throughout the story to help you make
these inferences.

■ *A biography of the
author can be
found on page 823.*

# $E$ scape

ILYA VARSHAVSKY

## 1

"One, two, three, HOIST! One, two, three, HOIST!"

A primitive device—a board and two ropes, plus some muscle—and the heavy rocks clattered into the truck.

"Come on, get going!"

It was an average load, but the little fellow in striped fatigues,[1] trying desperately to move his pile of rocks into the truck, couldn't budge them.

"Come on, come on!"

One of the prisoners tried to give him a hand. Too late: the overseer was on his way.

"What's going on here?"

"Nothing, sir."

"Then get going!"

The little fellow made another unsuccessful attempt to move his load. He broke into a fit of coughing and covered his mouth with his hand.

The overseer waited patiently for the attack to subside.

"Let's see your hand."

The outstretched palm was bloody.

"OK, knock off!"

The overseer jotted down the number stamped on the prisoner's jacket.

"Go to the infirmary!"

Another prisoner quickly filled the sick man's place.

"Excuse me, sir," pleaded the little fellow, "but can't I . . ."

"I thought I told you to go to the infirmary. Get going!"

As the stooped figure moved off, he rechecked the number in his notebook: △☐ 15/13264. Well, it was all quite clear: the triangle meant he was a deserter; the rectangle—life imprisonment. From the looks of him, this chap's sentence didn't have long to run. It was the cotton fields for him.

"One, two, three, HOIST!"

## 2

The tired, gray eyes of the doctor peered carefully through thick lenses. Here, in Meden's <u>subterranean</u> camps, human life was very valuable. And for good reason! The planet desperately needed uranium in the fierce struggle to maintain its dominant position over other planets.

"Get dressed!"

The prisoner's long, thin arms pulled his jacket quickly around his emaciated body.

"Stand over there!"

A light press on the pedal and the prisoner's number was blocked out by a large red cross. Henceforth, prisoner △☐ 15/13264 would be

---

1. **fatigues:** sturdy work clothing.

known once more as Arp Zumbi. A <u>humanitarian</u> gesture toward those condemned to labor in the cotton fields.

The cotton fields. The prisoners knew little about them except that one never returned from them. It was rumored that the intensely hot, dry climate shriveled the body into dry brushwood—excellent fuel for the crematorium's ovens.

"You are excused from any further work in this camp. Here is your certificate. You may go."

*clarify*  Why is Arp being sent to the cotton fields?

Arp Zumbi showed the barracks sentry his certificate. A familiar <u>acrid</u> smell of disinfectant stung his nostrils. With its Dutch tile and overpowering odor of disinfectant, the barracks resembled a public toilet. Its white walls were broken only by a large poster proclaiming "Death by torture for escapees."

A structure like an enormous honeycomb ran along one of the walls. These were the prisoners' quarters, cubicles separated by solid partitions to prevent communication between their occupants. Comfortable and hygienic.

Since it was forbidden to enter one's cubicle during working hours, Arp passed the time away on a bench. His thoughts turned to the cotton fields. Every two weeks a new lot of prisoners, collected from a number of camps, was transported to the fields; and two days after each shipment, a new group of prisoners would be delivered to Arp's camp. The last group had arrived five days ago, and one of the new arrivals had been placed in the cubicle next to Arp's. Some kind of nut. Yesterday at dinner he had given Arp half his bread ration.

"Here, take it," he insisted, "or you won't hold up your pants much longer." Who ever heard of giving away bread?! This guy was probably a psycho.

Arp's thoughts returned to the cotton fields. He knew it was the end of the line for him, but, for some reason, he wasn't too upset. After ten years in the mines, one grew accustomed to the idea of death. Yet he wondered what it was really like in the cotton fields.

This was the first day he had not worked during his ten years in the labor camp. No wonder time passed so slowly.

Toward evening Arp's fellow prisoners returned from the mines, and the smell of barracks disinfectant fused with the sweetish odor of decontamination[2] fluid. Those who worked with uranium had to take prophylactic[3] showers. It was one of the measures taken to extend the work life of the prisoners.

Arp took his place in line and marched off to dinner.

At meals, the guards tended to be lax about the "no talking" rule. After all, how much could one say with a mouth full of food?

Arp finished his portion in silence and waited for the command to rise.

"Here, take it!" Again that psycho offered him half his ration.

"No, thanks."

The guard bellowed the command to rise and fall in. Arp noticed that all eyes were focused on him. Probably, he thought, because of the red cross on his back. Doomed men always arouse curiosity.

"Step lively!"

---

2. **decontamination:** that which is used to get rid of a polluting or harmful substance, such as poison gas or radioactive products.

3. **prophylactic:** preventive or protective, especially against disease.

| Words to Know and Use | **humanitarian** (hyoō man′ ə ter′ ē ən) *adj.* helping humanity, especially by reducing pain and suffering<br>**acrid** (ak′ rid) *adj.* sharp, bitter, or irritating to the taste or smell |
| --- | --- |

This was directed at Arp's neighbor. His row had fallen in, but he had remained seated. Then, he and Arp rose together, and, as he walked toward his place in line, Arp barely caught the words:

"There's a way to escape."

Arp pretended not to hear; the camp was crawling with informers, and the prospect of death by torture certainly did not appeal to him. Better the cotton fields.

*infer*     Why doesn't Arp trust the man?

## 3

The voice rose and fell, alternating between screeching and barely audible whispering which compelled its captive audience to strain its ears. It poured from a loudspeaker fastened to the head of each prisoner's bed. This was the regular brainwashing session.

It was impossible to escape the voice that pounded its messages into the prisoners three times a day: before sleep, during sleep, and before reveille.[4] Like the shouting of the overseers, it could not be blocked from one's consciousness. It was an eternal reminder to all that this was a penal colony and not a health resort.

Arp lay there with his eyes closed, trying to think about the cotton fields. The brainwashing session was over, but he was disturbed by a rhythmic tapping coming from the other side of the partition. That psycho again, he thought.

"What the hell do you want!?" Arp yelled through his cupped hand pressed against the partition.

"Meet me in the latrine."

Without thinking, Arp slid off his bunk and walked toward the gurgling sound of water.

It was hot in the latrine, so damn hot that two minutes in that sweatbox was more than a man could take. Arp was dripping wet before the newcomer appeared.

"Do you want to escape?"

"Go to hell!" whispered Arp hoarsely. As a veteran of camp life, he was very familiar with the tricks of these informers.

"Don't be afraid," he tried to reassure Arp. "I'm from the Liberation Committee. Tomorrow we're going to try to move the first group out of here and get them in a safe place. You have nothing to lose. You will receive a poison capsule. In case the escape fails . . ."

"Then what?"

"You'll take the capsule. It's a lot better than death in the cotton fields. Right?"

Arp found himself nodding in agreement.

"You will receive instructions in the morning, in your bread. Be careful!"

Arp nodded again and left.

For the first time in ten years he was so deeply lost in dreams, dreams of hope and freedom, that the second and third brainwashing sessions were completely blocked out.

## 4

At breakfast Arp Zumbi stood at the end of the serving line because the idle were the last to receive their rations.

The gangling prisoner distributing bread looked carefully at Arp and, grinning faintly, tossed him a chunk of bread set apart from the rest. After gulping down his porridge, Arp crumpled the bread gently. It was there! He hid the tiny wad of paper in his cheek.

Now he must wait until the column left for work.

---

4. **reveille** (rev′ ə lē): a signal to rise or assemble sounded early in the morning.

The command to rise rang out. Bringing up the rear of the column, Arp marched from the mess hall and, reaching the gallery, turned left while the others marched straight ahead.

Here, beyond the bend, Arp was relatively safe. Since the barracks clean-up detail was still busily at work, it was too early for the sentries to take their posts.

The instructions were very brief. Arp read them three times and crumpled the note into a wad and swallowed it after he was certain that he had memorized it thoroughly.

Now that the moment had arrived for him to begin his flight to freedom he was seized by fear. He hesitated. Death in the cotton fields seemed preferable to death by torture.

"The poison!" he remembered, and the thought of it calmed his nerves. After all, what did he have to lose?

Fear gripped him once again as he handed his medical certificate to the sentry at the border zone.

"Where are you going?"

"To the doctor."

"OK, go on."

Trudging slowly along the gallery, Arp's legs felt like cotton as he sensed danger lurking behind him. Any moment he expected to hear shouts, followed by a burst of machine-gun fire. Fugitives were always shot in the legs; in that way the penalty for escaping, death by torture, could be properly executed. Prisoners must not be deprived of such an instructive spectacle.

Turn here!

AT THE BORDER VII: EXPEDITION   Robert Indermaur
Courtesy of J. Noblett Gallery, Hot Springs, California.

Arp turned the corner and rested against the wall. His heart pounded wildly, and he was covered with sweat. His teeth chattered like the drumbeat at an execution.

An eternity passed before he decided to push on. Somewhere in the vicinity he should find a recess in the ground, the site of the garbage tanks. Arp recalled the instructions and once more was assailed by doubts. Suppose it was a put-up job? The instant he crawled into one of the tanks he'd be nabbed! And he hadn't received the poison yet. Fool! Blockhead! He shouldn't have agreed until he had the stuff. Arp was ready to beat his head against the wall. Some informer had really hooked him!

Ah, ha! Here were the tanks. Someone had left paintbrushes by the left one, just as the note had said. Arp hesitated. Maybe he should turn back?

Suddenly he heard loud voices and dogs barking. Rounds! No time to think. With surprising agility he leaped onto a sawhorse and dived into a tank.

The voices came closer. He heard the yelping of a dog straining at the leash and the pounding of hobnailed boots.

"Zip! Gar!"

"Someone's in the tank."

"Probably rats. The place is full of them."

"No, Gar doesn't bark like that at rats."

"Rubbish! Let's get going. And calm your hound."

"Easy there, Gar!"

The footsteps died down.

Now Arp could inspect his refuge. The tank was one-quarter full. No point trying to get out: it was a good twelve feet to the top. Arp ran his hand along the wall and felt the two small holes described in the note. They were in the embossed sign, "Labor Camp," which circled the tank. Arp would have to breathe through these two openings when the covers were slammed shut.

When the covers were slammed shut! What a trap! How would this wild adventure end? What was this Liberation Committee? He had never heard any mention of it in camp. Perhaps it was composed of those same lads who had helped him desert from the army ten years ago? Oh, how stupid he had been! He had disobeyed them and visited his mother, where he was caught. If he hadn't been such a damn fool, how differently things would have turned out.

He heard voices again and the scraping of wheels. Arp pressed his eye against one of the holes and relaxed. Two prisoners were hauling a bucket of garbage. Probably the clean-up detail. They were taking their time. Sitting down leisurely in the cart, they took turns smoking a butt discarded by one of the guards. Arp's mouth watered as he watched the pale puffs of smoke. Lucky dogs!

They dragged all they could from the butt. The bucket crawled upward, and the cable pulling it was thrown across the pulley above Arp's head. He covered his head with his hands as the contents of the bucket slurped over him.

Only now, after the prisoners had gone, was he conscious of the foul odor in his refuge. The breathing holes were at eye level, so he had to pile garbage under his feet to raise himself.

He must be <u>vigilant</u> now. Garbage collection usually ended at ten o'clock; then the tanks were covered, raised, and hauled to the dump.

# 5

Where the rough, wide board had come from was a mystery. One end rested against the wall at the bottom of the tank; the other end lay against the tank's opposite wall, extending slightly above Arp's head. Like the sawhorse, it was evidence of someone's concern for the fate of this fugitive. Arp was especially aware of it when a sharp metal rod poked through the thick refuse and bumped against the board. If not for the board . . .

**Where did the board come from?**

The inspection of the tank seemed endless.

"Well, what'cha got there?" asked a hoarse voice.

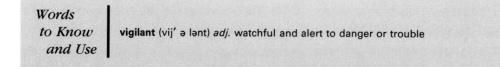

*Words to Know and Use* | **vigilant** (vij′ ə lənt) *adj.* watchful and alert to danger or trouble

"Nothing, just an old board."

"OK, slam the cover on. Now, heave!"

A light jolt, the rattle of a gate, and the tank, rocking, moved up the shaft. As it ascended it banged against the sides of the shaft, and Arp's face, pressed to the wall, felt sharp blows.

After the last and worst blow, the cover opened with a loud noise. Once more the rod poked through the rubbish, and again the life-saving board concealed the trembling man hiding beneath it.

Now the breathing holes faced a concrete enclosure, and Arp's visual world consisted of a rough, gray surface. But it was a world full of long-forgotten sounds: the whirring of automobile tires, the voices of pedestrians, and even the chirping of sparrows. How close and dear freedom seemed to him now.

Suddenly, a new sound: a rhythmic, persistent tapping on the cover of the tank. Arp froze. The tapping grew more frequent, more persistent, more terrifying. And then it dawned on him. "Of course," he laughed to himself, "it's raining."

# 6

It was a long, harrowing night for Arp. From the moment he was tossed from the tank into the rat-infested garbage dump his exhausted body found no rest. Somewhere nearby he could hear automobiles speeding along a highway. Every now and then their headlights would illuminate the mound of garbage behind which Arp was hiding. The rats would scurry into the darkness squealing, scratch his face with their sharp claws, and bite him if he tried to push them away.

Arp was sure that his escape had been discovered by now, and he tried to picture what was happening at the camp. Suppose the dogs picked up his scent leading to the garbage tanks?

Two bright beams of light struck him like a hammer blow, and he jumped up. The headlights went off, and a small light went on inside the truck. It was a military van, the kind used to transport military supplies. The driver motioned to Arp to come closer.

Arp breathed a sigh of relief. The door opened, and Arp grasped someone's outstretched hand. Once more he found himself in darkness.

The van was stuffy. Seated on the floor, Arp heard heavy breathing and felt the pressure of bodies surrounding him. Gently rocking on its springs, the van rolled silently through the dark night.

Arp was awakened by a light shining in his face. Something was wrong! The rocking motion that had lulled him to sleep had ceased.

"Take a break!" said the man with the flashlight. "You can go out for five minutes."

Arp had no desire to leave the van, but the press of bodies behind him left him no choice, and he had to jump out with the rest of them.

Everyone crowded around the cab of the truck; no one would risk wandering away from the van.

"Hey, boys!" said their rescuer, shining his flashlight on the figures in prison garb. "So far everything has gone well, but anything could happen before we deliver you to your destination. Do you know what the penalty for escaping is?"

Silence.

"Yes, I'm sure you do. Therefore, the Committee offers you poison. One capsule per person. It works instantaneously. Take it only as a last resort. Is that clear?"

Arp received a capsule wrapped in silver foil and climbed into the van.

817

The capsule clutched in his fist gave him a feeling of control over his own destiny. Now his jailors could not hurt him. With this comforting thought, he fell asleep.

Trouble! It could be sensed in everything around him: in the motionless van, in the white faces of the fugitives illuminated by a shaft of light coming through the cab's rear window, in the loud wrangling coming from the road.

Arp started to rise, but dozens of hands signaled to him to sit still.

"Military vehicles are not subject to inspection," came the voice of the driver.

"And I'm telling you that I have an order. This evening . . . "

The engine suddenly roared, and the van shot ahead in a hail of machine-gun fire. Chips flew from the roof of the van.

When Arp finally raised his head, he found himself clutching someone's tiny hand. Dark eyes looked up at him from beneath a shaven forehead. Prisoner's garb could not conceal the feminine curves of the figure beside him. On the left sleeve was a green star, symbol of the lowest caste.

Instinctively Arp unclasped his hand and rubbed it on his trousers. Contact with Meden's lowest caste was prohibited by Meden's laws.

"They won't catch us, will they?"

The trembling voice sounded so pathetic that Arp, ignoring the law, shook his head in response to reassure her.

"What's your name?"

"Arp."

"Mine's Jetta."

Arp dropped his head onto his chest and pretended to doze. He wondered how his rescuers at his final destination might react to such contact.

The van turned off the highway and bounced along a road full of potholes. Arp was hungry and began to feel ill from the jostling ride. Afraid of disturbing the others, he tried to suppress a cough, but this only made matters worse. He was doubled over and suddenly broke into a wracking, bloody cough. So exhausting was the attack that Arp was too weak to push aside the arm with the green star that was wiping his perspiring forehead.

# 7

The warm night air was filled with the fragrance of exotic flowers and the chirping of cicadas.

Their prison garb had been discarded. An ankle-length unbleached linen shirt cooled his body pleasantly. He had just come from a steam bath. Arp carefully spooned the last bits of porridge from his bowl.

At one end of the dining hall, three people stood next to a <u>dais</u> constructed of old kegs and boards: a tall man with gray hair and the sunburned face of a farmer—evidently the leader; a handsome chap in the uniform of Meden's army—the van driver; and a short woman in a white smock, with a thick red braid wound around her head.

They were waiting for the fugitives to finish their supper.

When the rattle of spoons died down, the leader leaped nimbly to the dais.

"Welcome, friends!"

In response to this unusual greeting, a joyful murmur swept through the hall.

"First of all, I must tell you that you are completely safe here. The location of our evacuation point is not known to the authorities."

The haggard, gray faces radiated happiness.

*Words to Know and Use* | **dais** (dā′ is) *n.* a raised platform on which a speaker stands

"You will spend five to ten days at the evacuation center. The exact period will be determined by the doctor, because you will have a long, difficult journey ahead of you. The place we are taking you to is, of course, no paradise. You will have to work there. We win every inch of earth for our settlements from the jungle. However, you will be free there. You can raise a family and work for your own welfare. At the beginning you will live in quarters prepared for you by those who preceded you there. That is our tradition. Now, I am ready for your questions."

During the question period Arp tried to summon up the courage to ask if one could marry a girl of lower caste in these settlements. By the time he raised his hand timidly, the tall man had already left the dais.

The woman in the white smock addressed the fugitives in a soft, melodious voice, and Arp had to strain his ears to catch her instructions.

W*hile asleep he . . . felt the cold touch of a stethoscope.*

She asked everyone to go to their quarters, to go to sleep and await their physical examinations.

Arp found his bunk with his name on it, lay down on the cool, crisp sheets, and fell asleep quickly.

While asleep he had the sensation of being turned onto his side and felt the cold touch of a stethoscope. Opening his eyes, he saw a short woman with a red braid writing something in a notebook.

"So, you woke up?" she smiled, revealing her dazzling white, even teeth.

Arp nodded.

"You are very weak. Your lungs aren't too good either. You will sleep for seven days, and when you wake up you will feel much better. We'll put you to sleep now."

She pushed several buttons on a white console near his bed, and a strange hum whirred in Arp's head.

"Sleep!" came a very distant, melodious voice, and Arp fell asleep.

# 8

Arp had an amazing dream, full of sunlight and happiness.

Only in a dream was such entrancing slow motion possible; only in a dream could one experience such weightlessness, could one soar through the air like a bird.

An enormous meadow was covered with dazzling white flowers. In the distance Arp saw a high tower, shining with all the colors of the rainbow. He was irresistibly drawn to the shining tower, from which emanated an inexplicable air of bliss.

Arp was not alone. From all directions people were streaming toward the mysterious tower. Like him, they were dressed in long, flowing white gowns. And Jetta was among them, too, with a skirtful of white blossoms.

"What is that?" she asked Arp, pointing to the tower.

"The pillar of freedom. Come, let's go to it!"

Holding hands, they floated together through the sun-filled air.

"Wait!"

Arp stopped to pick a skirtful of white blossoms, and they continued on their way.

SCENES FROM THE FUTURE: MUSEUM OF MODERN ART 1983–84 Komar & Melamid Collection of Cindy & Alan Lewin Courtesy of Ronald Feldman Fine Arts, New York.

When Arp fell asleep by the dying fire, a tiny hand was resting in his.

When the fires went out, varicolored lights circling the tower went on. Below, at ground level, a door opened, and two huge mechanical paws shoveled the cotton inside.

In a glass-enclosed cupola[6] an old man with a sunburned face looked at the arrow on the scale.

"Wow! They picked five times more than all the preceding groups," he announced, turning off the conveyer. "I'm afraid they won't last a week at such a mad pace."

"I'll bet you two bottles of vodka," the handsome chap in military dress grinned, "that they last the usual twenty days. Hypnosis is a marvelous technique! You could have died laughing, watching them devour those baked turnips as if they were shashlik. You can get them to do anything under hypnosis. Right, Doctor?"

The short woman with the thick red braid was slow to reply. She walked over to the window, turned on the floodlights, and looked down carefully at their faces, which, with their tightly drawn skins, resembled skulls.

"You are overestimating the possibilities of electrohypnosis," she smiled. "The powerful radiation of the psi-field can do more than impart a rhythm to their work. The most basic factor in their conditioning is a preliminary psychological tuning. The <u>fabricated</u> escape, the <u>contrived</u> dangers—all this created a sense of freedom won at a terrible cost. It is difficult to foresee what colossal reserves can be released in the human organism by lofty aspirations and goals." ❧

---

5. **shashlik** (shäsh′ lik): skewered and broiled meat kebabs.
6. **cupola** (kyo͞o′ pə lə): a dome-shaped structure.

At the foot of the tower they emptied their skirts, heaping the blossoms in a huge pile.

"Who can pick the most?" shouted Jetta as she flitted among the gray stalks. "Come on, friends, try and outpick us!"

Their example fired the others. Within a short time the entire base of the tower was overflowing with white blossoms.

*infer*  **What are the white blossoms? Where is Arp?**

Then bonfires were lit, and huge chunks of meat strung on long, thin skewers were roasted. The delightful smell of shashlik[5] together with the scent of burning twigs revived very old and pleasant memories.

After quenching their thirst, they lay on the ground by the fire, gazing at the stars, enormous, strange stars in an ink black sky.

*Words to Know and Use* | **fabricated** (fab′ ri kāt′ əd) *adj.* made-up; invented
**contrived** (kən trīvd′) *adj.* planned, not spontaneous or natural

## Responding to Reading

### First Impressions

**1.** Did the ending of the story surprise, confuse, disappoint, or satisfy you? Explain why.

### Second Thoughts

**2.** What is Arp really experiencing under hypnosis?

> **Think about**
> • Arp's escape
> • his dream at the evacuation center
> • at what point his hypnosis begins
> • the conversation between the doctor and the prison official at the end

**3.** What are the doctors and prison officials trying to accomplish through hypnosis?

**4.** Do you think Arp's hypnotized state has improved his life? Is his short-term happiness worth more than knowledge of the truth or a long life? Explain your answer.

**5.** Do you agree with the last sentence in the story? Besides this story, what other evidence supports your opinion?

### Broader Connections

**6.** What threats to individual liberty exist in the United States today? How should individuals respond to these threats? Explain.

## Literary Concept: Science Fiction

Science fiction has been a part of literature since the seventeenth century when Cyrano de Bergerac wrote about a trip to the moon. In the nineteenth century, Jules Verne and H. G. Wells popularized science fiction in novels still enjoyed today. **Science fiction** requires the creative imagination of the writer and a story with a central element of genuine scientific fact or possibility. Most science fiction comments on present-day society through the writer's conception of a future society. What elements make "Escape" science fiction? What comments does the story make about modern society?

**Concept Review: Suspense**   What suspense-building techniques does Varshavsky use in this story?

## Writing Options

1. The instructions that Arp receives are brief, but they give exact details about the escape. Write out these instructions based on where Arp goes and what he does.

2. Make a list of all the problems threatening individual freedoms that exist in the society depicted in the story.

3. Assume that the Liberation Committee exists and succeeds in overthrowing the government. List the criminal charges to be brought against the government for the way it has run the prison. Include all the likely criminal behaviors of the prison officials, guards, and doctors.

4. Create a motto for the Liberation Committee.

## Vocabulary Practice

**Exercise A: Analogies**  Write the letter of the word pair that best expresses a relationship similar to that expressed in the first pair.

1. INFIRMARY : DOCTOR :: (a) tree : acorn (b) mountain : valley (c) school : teacher (d) sandwich : bread
2. SUBTERRANEAN : UNDERGROUND :: (a) ancient : modern (b) evil : good (c) regretful : sorry (d) pure : polluted
3. DAIS : SPEAKER :: (a) hall : room (b) earth : moon (c) audience : auditorium (d) mound : pitcher
4. VIGILANT : WATCHMAN :: (a) educated : scholar (b) religious : author (c) nervous : policeman (d) solemn : clown
5. FABRICATED : TRUE :: (a) obese : fat (b) usual : rare (c) heroic : likable (d) fantastic : wonderful

**Exercise B**  Write the letter of the unrelated word in each group below.

1. (a) contrived (b) fabricated (c) invented (d) expected
2. (a) flow (b) empty (c) emanate (d) proceed
3. (a) watchful (b) frightening (c) distressing (d) harrowing
4. (a) tyrant (b) humanitarian (c) dictator (d) oppressor
5. (a) agreeable (b) irritating (c) bitter (d) acrid

> *Words to Know and Use*
>
> acrid
> contrived
> dais
> emanate
> fabricated
> harrowing
> humanitarian
> infirmary
> subterranean
> vigilant

## Options for Learning

**1** • **Hypnotism** Find out who invented the techniques of hypnotism. What is the history of its development, and what uses have been discovered for it? Report your findings to the class.

**2** • **Betsy Ross at Work** Design a symbol for a flag that represents the Liberation Committee. Draw, paint, or actually sew the new flag. Display it in the classroom.

**3** • **Art and Action** Illustrate a comic book version of this story. In each panel, show a change in the action. Use either word balloons or captions. Display your comic book where others can read it.

**4** • **Amnesty International** Research the countries that have high rates of human rights violations. The *Readers' Guide to Periodical Literature* may provide sources for articles and publications by Amnesty International, an organization that tracks these kinds of violations around the world. What country comes closest to the society depicted in "Escape"? Make a case for your opinion and present it to the class.

 **FACT FINDER**

*Who first used the term hypnosis?*

### *I*lya Varshavsky
**1909–1974**

Varshavsky trained and worked as a sailor for the Soviet navy most of his life. His naval education included advanced degrees in design and engineering. At age fifty-three, while still working as an engineer, he began to write. His scientific background helped to establish him as one of the most popular writers of science fiction in the Soviet Union.

Best known for his humorous and satiric views of Soviet society, Varshavsky's works focus on the misuse of science by a government trying to maintain its power. His characters include programmed robots who replace humans, evil doctors, prison camp officials, and a variety of tyrannical authority figures. The word *dystopia*, that is, the opposite of the perfect utopia, is often used to describe the fictional societies that Varshavsky created.

*Autobiography*

### ᶠʳᵒᵐ *Kaffir Boy*

MARK MATHABANE (mä tä bä′ nē)

## Examine What You Know

How has your attitude toward school changed since the beginning of your education? Think about experiences you have had with former teachers, classmates, and academic activities and how those experiences have affected your feelings toward school. On a time line like the one below, briefly record the significant changes in your attitude over the years.

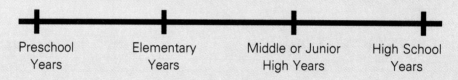

| Preschool | Elementary | Middle or Junior | High School |
| Years | Years | High Years | Years |

## Expand Your Knowledge

This story is from Mark Mathabane's autobiography, *Kaffir Boy.* In South Africa, *kaffir* (ka′ fər) is an insulting term for black Africans. Mathabane's book focuses on how, with the help and influence of a few strong and caring individuals, he escaped the poverty and violence of the South African system of apartheid. **Apartheid** is the government's policy of rigid racial segregation. This policy allows for the forced removal of blacks from their homelands, requires work and travel passes that limit opportunities for blacks, and destroys black families. The tribal school Mathabane attended actually limited what he could study, and, were it not for a few open-minded people, he would never have broken free from these limitations. Through those few people, Mathabane discovered the illegal books that showed how different the world was outside apartheid. This knowledge was the first step away from ignorance, fear, and mistaken beliefs about the value of education.

## Write Before You Read

Briefly describe your parents' or guardians' attitudes toward your education. What effect have they had on your own attitude toward education? Explain.

■ *A biography of the author can be found on page 837.*

# from *Kaffir Boy*

MARK MATHABANE

*"Education will open doors where none seem to exist."*

When my mother began dropping hints that I would soon be going to school, I vowed never to go, because school was a waste of time. She laughed and said, "We'll see. You don't know what you're talking about." My philosophy on school was that of a gang of ten-eleven- and twelve-year-olds whom I so revered that their every word seemed that of an oracle.

These boys had long left their homes and were now living in various neighborhood junkyards, making it on their own. They slept in abandoned cars, smoked glue and benzene,[1] ate pilchards[2] and brown bread, sneaked into the white world to caddy and, if unsuccessful, came back to the township to steal beer and soda bottles from shebeens,[3] or goods from the Indian traders on First Avenue. Their lifestyle was exciting, adventurous and full of surprises; and I was attracted to it. My mother told me that they were no-gooders, that they would amount to nothing, that I should not associate with them, but I paid no heed. What does she know? I used to tell myself. One thing she did not know was that the gang's way of life had <u>captivated</u> me wholly, particularly their philosophy on

school: they hated it and considered an education a waste of time.

They, like myself, had grown up in an environment where the value of an education was never emphasized, where the first thing a child learned was not how to read and write and spell, but how to fight and steal and rebel; where the money to send children to school was grossly lacking, for survival was first priority. I kept my membership in the gang, knowing that for as long as I was under its influence, I would never go to school.

One day my mother woke me up at four in the morning.

"Are they here? I didn't hear any noises," I asked in the usual way.

"No," my mother said. "I want you to get into that washtub over there."

"What!" I balked upon hearing the word *washtub.* I feared taking baths like one feared the plague. Throughout seven years of hectic living, the number of baths I had taken could be counted on one hand with several fingers

---

1. **benzene:** a clear, flammable, poisonous liquid, used as a solvent.
2. **pilchards:** sardines.
3. **shebeens** (shi bēnz′): illegal establishments where liquor is sold.

825

missing. I simply had no natural inclination for water; cleanliness was a trait I still had to acquire. Besides, we had only one bathtub in the house, and it constantly sprang a leak.

"I said get into that tub!" My mother shook a finger in my face.

Reluctantly, I obeyed, yet wondered why all of a sudden I had to take a bath. My mother, armed with a scrubbrush and a piece of Life-buoy soap, purged me of years and years of grime till I ached and bled. As I howled, feeling pain shoot through my limbs as the thistles of the brush encountered stubborn callouses, there was a loud knock at the door.

Instantly my mother leaped away from the tub and headed, on tiptoe, toward the bed-room. Fear seized me as I, too, thought of the police. I sat frozen in the bathtub, not knowing what to do.

"Open up, Mujaji [my mother's maiden name]," Granny's voice came shrilling through the door. "It's me."

My mother heaved a sigh of relief; her tense limbs relaxed. She turned and headed to the kitchen door, unlatched it, and in came Granny and Aunt Bushy.

"You scared me half to death," my mother said to Granny. "I had forgotten all about your coming."

"Are you ready?" Granny asked my mother.

"Yes—just about," my mother said, beckoning me to get out of the washtub.

She handed me a piece of cloth to dry myself. As I dried myself, questions raced through my mind: What's going on? What's Granny doing at our house this ungodly hour of the morning? And why did she ask my mother, "Are you ready?" While I stood debating, my mother went into the bedroom and came out with a stained white shirt and a pair of faded black shorts.

"Here," she said, handing me the togs,[4] "put these on."

"Why?" I asked.

"Put them on, I said!"

I put the shirt on; it was grossly loosefitting. It reached all the way down to my ankles. Then I saw the reason why: it was my father's shirt!

"But this is Papa's shirt," I complained. "It don't fit me."

"Put it on," my mother insisted. "I'll make it fit."

"The pants don't fit me either," I said. "Whose are they, anyway?"

"Put them on," my mother said. "I'll make them fit."

Moments later I had the garments on; I

---

4. **togs:** clothes.

looked ridiculous. My mother started working on the pants and shirt to make them fit. She folded the shirt in so many intricate ways and stashed it inside the pants, they too having been folded several times at the waist. She then choked the pants at the waist with a piece of sisal rope to hold them up. She then lavishly smeared my face, arms and legs with a mixture of pig's fat and vaseline. "This will insulate you from the cold," she said. My skin gleamed like the morning star, and I felt as hot as the center of the sun, and I smelled God knows like what. After embalming[5] me, she headed to the bedroom.

"Where are we going, Gran'ma?" I said, hoping that she would tell me what my mother refused to tell me. I still had no idea I was about to be taken to school.

"Didn't your mother tell you?" Granny said with a smile. "You're going to start school."

"What!" I gasped, leaping from the chair where I was sitting as if it were made of hot lead. "I am not going to school!" I blurted out and raced toward the kitchen door.

My mother had just reappeared from the bedroom, and, guessing what I was up to, she yelled, "Someone get the door!"

Aunt Bushy immediately barred the door. I turned and headed for the window. As I leaped for the windowsill, my mother lunged at me and brought me down. I tussled, "Let go of me! I don't want to go to school! Let me go!" but my mother held fast onto me.

"It's no use now," she said, grinning triumphantly as she pinned me down. Turning her head in Granny's direction, she shouted, "Granny! Get a rope quickly!"

Granny grabbed a piece of rope nearby and came to my mother's aid. I bit and clawed every hand that grabbed me, and howled protestations against going to school; however, I was no match for the two determined matriarchs. In a jiffy they had me bound, hands and feet.

"What's the matter with him?" Granny, bewildered, asked my mother. "Why did he suddenly turn into an imp when I told him you're taking him to school?"

"You shouldn't have told him that he's being taken to school," my mother said. "He doesn't want to go there. That's why I requested you come today, to help me take him there. Those boys in the streets have been a bad influence on him."

As the two matriarchs hauled me through the door, they told Aunt Bushy not to go to school but stay behind and mind the house and the children.

The sun was beginning to rise from beyond the veld when Granny and my mother dragged me to school. The streets were beginning to fill with their everyday traffic: old men and women, wizened, bent and ragged, were beginning their rambling; workless men and women were beginning to assemble in their usual coteries and head for shebeens in the backyards where they discussed how they escaped the morning pass raids and contemplated the conditions of life amidst intense beer drinking and vacant, uneasy laughter; young boys and girls, some as young as myself, were beginning their aimless wanderings along the narrow, dusty streets in search of food, carrying bawling infants piggyback.

As we went along some of the streets, boys and girls who shared the same fears about school as I were making their feelings known in a variety of ways. They were howling their protests and trying to escape. A few managed to break loose and make a mad dash for freedom, only to be recaptured in no time, admonished or whipped, or both, and ordered to march again.

As we made a turn into Sixteenth Avenue, the street leading to the tribal school I was being taken to, a short, chubby black woman

---

5. **embalming:** preserving a dead body with chemicals to prevent decay.

came along from the opposite direction. She had a scuttle[6] overflowing with coal on her *doek*-covered (cloth-covered) head. An infant, bawling deafeningly, was loosely swathed with a piece of sheepskin onto her back. Following closely behind the woman, and picking up pieces of coal as they fell from the scuttle and placing them in a small plastic bag, was a half-naked, potbellied and thumb-sucking boy of about four. The woman stopped abreast. For some reason we stopped too.

"I wish I had done the same to my oldest son," the strange woman said in a regretful voice, gazing at me. I was confounded by her stopping and offering her <u>unsolicited</u> opinion.

"I wish I had done that to my oldest son," she repeated, and suddenly burst into tears; amidst sobs, she continued, "before . . . the street claimed him . . . and . . . turned him into a *tsotsi*."[7]

Granny and my mother offered consolatory remarks to the strange woman.

"But it's too late now," the strange woman continued, tears now streaming freely down her puffy cheeks. She made no attempt to dry them. "It's too late now," she said for the second time, "he's beyond any help. I can't help him even if I wanted to. *Uswile*[8] [He is dead]."

"How did he die?" my mother asked in a sympathetic voice.

"He shunned school and, instead, grew up to live by the knife. And the same knife he lived by ended his life. That's why whenever I see a boy-child refuse to go to school, I stop and tell the story of my dear little *mbitsini*[9] [heartbreak]."

Having said that, the strange woman left as mysteriously as she had arrived.

"Did you hear what that woman said!" my mother screamed into my ears. "Do you want the same to happen to you?"

I dropped my eyes. I was confused.

"Poor woman," Granny said ruefully. "She must have truly loved her son."

Finally, we reached the school and I was ushered into the principal's office, a tiny cubicle facing a row of privies and a patch of yellowed grass.

"So this is the rascal we'd been talking about," the principal, a tall, wiry man, foppishly[10] dressed in a black pin-striped suit, said to my mother as we entered. His <u>austere</u>, shiny face, <u>inscrutable</u> and imposing, reminded me of my father. He was sitting behind a brown table upon which stood piles of dust- and cobweb-covered books and papers. In one upper pocket of his jacket was arrayed a variety of pens and pencils; in the other nestled a lily white handkerchief whose presence was more decorative than <u>utilitarian</u>. Alongside him stood a disproportionately portly black woman, fashionably dressed in a black skirt and a white blouse. She had but one pen, and this she held in her hand. The room was hot and stuffy and buzzing with flies.

"Yes, Principal," my mother answered, "this is he."

"I see he's living up to his notoriety," remarked the principal, noticing that I had been bound. "Did he give you too much trouble?"

"Trouble, Principal," my mother sighed. "He was like an imp."

"He's just like the rest of them, Principal," Granny sighed. "Once they get out into the

---

6. **scuttle:** a coal bucket with a wide lip.

7. **tsotsi** (tsôʹ tsē): a gangster.

8. **Uswile** ($\overline{oo}$ wēʹ lē).

9. **mbitsini** (mbē tsēʹ nē).

10. **foppishly:** like a vain man who pays too much attention to his clothes.

*Words to Know and Use*

**unsolicited** (un sə lisʹ i tid) *adj.* unasked for; not wanted
**austere** (ô stirʹ) *adj.* showing strict self-discipline and self-denial
**inscrutable** (in skr$\overline{oo}$tʹ ə bəl) *adj.* not easily understood; obscure or mysterious
**utilitarian** (y$\overline{oo}$ tilʹ ə terʹ ē ən) *adj.* useful more than beautiful

MIGRANT LABOUR CAMP, LANGA, CAPE TOWN 1980 Paul Konings From *South Africa: the Cordoned Heart* edited by Omar Badsha.

streets, they become wild. They take to the many vices of the streets like an infant takes to its mother milk. They begin to think that there's no other life but the one shown them by the *tsotsis*. They come to hate school and forget about the future."

"Well," the principal said. "We'll soon remedy all that. Untie him."

"He'll run away," my mother cried.

"I don't think he's that foolish to attempt that with all of us here."

"He *is* that foolish, Principal," my mother said as she and Granny began untying me. "He's tried it before. Getting him here was an ordeal in itself."

The principal rose from his seat, took two steps to the door and closed it. As the door swung closed, I spotted a row of canes of different lengths and thicknesses hanging behind it. The principal, seeing me staring at the

canes, grinned and said, in a manner suggesting that he had wanted me to see them, "As long as you behave, I won't have to use any of those on you."

Use those canes on me? I gasped. I stared at my mother—she smiled; at Granny—she smiled too. That made me abandon any <u>inkling</u> of escaping.

"So, they finally gave you the birth certificate and the papers," the principal addressed my mother as he returned to his chair.

"Yes, Principal," my mother said, "they finally did. But what a battle it was. It took me nearly a year to get all them papers together." She took out of her handbag a neatly wrapped package and handed it to the principal. "They've been running us around for so long that there were times when I thought he would never attend school, Principal," she said.

"That's pretty much standard procedure, Mrs. Mathabane," the principal said, unwrapping the package. "But you now have the papers, and that's what's important."

"As long as we have the papers," he continued, minutely perusing the contents of the package, "we won't be breaking the law in admitting your son to this school, for we'll be in full compliance with the requirements set by the authorities in Pretoria."

"Sometimes I don't understand the laws from Pitori," Granny said. "They did the same to me with my Piet and Bushy. Why, Principal, should our children not be allowed to learn because of some piece of paper?"

"The piece of paper you're referring to, Mrs. Mabaso [Granny's maiden name]," the principal said to Granny, "is as important to our children as a pass is to us adults. We all hate passes; therefore, it's only natural we should hate the regulations our children are subjected to. But as we have to live with passes, so our children have to live with the regulations, Mrs. Mabaso. I hope you understand, that is the law of the country. We would have admitted your grandson a long time ago, as you well know, had it not been for the papers. I hope you understand."

"I understand, Principal," Granny said, "but I don't understand," she added <u>paradoxically</u>.

One of the papers caught the principal's eye, and he turned to my mother and asked, "Is your husband a Shangaan,[11] Mrs. Mathabane?"

"No, he's not, Principal," my mother said. "Is there anything wrong? He's Venda[12] and I'm Shangaan."

The principal reflected for a moment or so and then said, concernedly, "No, there's nothing seriously wrong. Nothing that we can't

take care of. You see, Mrs. Mathabane, technically, the fact that your child's father is a Venda makes him ineligible to attend this tribal school because it is only for children whose parents are of the Shangaan tribe. May I ask what language the children speak at home?"

"Both languages," my mother said worriedly, "Venda and Shangaan. Is there anything wrong?"

The principal coughed, clearing his throat, then said, "I mean which language do they speak more?"

"It depends, Principal," my mother said, swallowing hard. "When their father is around, he wants them to speak only Venda. And when he's not, they speak Shangaan. And when they are out at play, they speak Zulu and Sisotho."[13]

"Well," the principal said, heaving a sigh of relief. "In that case, I think an exception can be made. The reason for such an exception is that there's currently no school for Vendas in Alexandra. And should the authorities come asking why we took in your son, we can tell them that. Anyway, your child is half-half."

Everyone broke into a nervous laugh, except me. I was bewildered by the whole thing. I looked at my mother, and she seemed greatly relieved as she watched the principal register me; a broad smile broke across her face. It was as if some enormously heavy burden had finally been lifted from her shoulders and her conscience.

---

11. **Shangaan** (shäŋ gän'): a member of a tribe in the northeastern Transvaal, South Africa.

12. **Venda:** a member of a tribe whose homeland in the northern Transvaal is recognized as an independent political region only by South Africa. This allows the government of South Africa to exclude the Venda from any benefits of its society.

13. **Zulu** (zo͞o' lo͞o) **and Sisotho:** (si so͞o' to͞o): Bantu tribal languages of Natal in eastern South Africa.

*Words to Know and Use* | **paradoxically** (par' ə däk' i kəl lē)) *adv.* in a manner expressing a seeming contradiction

"Bring him back two weeks from today," the principal said as he saw us to the door. "There're so many children registering today that classes won't begin until two weeks hence. Also, the school needs repair and cleaning up after the holidays. If he refuses to come, simply notify us, and we'll send a couple of big boys to come fetch him, and he'll be very sorry if it ever comes to that."

As we left the principal's office and headed home, my mind was still against going to school. I was thinking of running away from home and joining my friends in the junkyard.

I didn't want to go to school for three reasons: I was reluctant to surrender my freedom and independence over to what I heard every school-going child call "tyrannous discipline." I had heard many bad things about life in tribal school—from daily beatings by teachers and mistresses who worked you like a mule to long school hours—and the sight of those canes in the principal's office gave me ample <u>credence</u> to rumors that school was nothing but a torture chamber. And there was my allegiance to the gang.

But the thought of the strange woman's lamentations over her dead son presented a somewhat strong case for going to school: I didn't want to end up dead in the streets. A more compelling argument for going to school, however, was the vivid recollection of all that humiliation and pain my mother had gone through to get me the papers and the birth certificate so I could enroll in school. What should I do? I was torn between two worlds.

But later that evening something happened to force me to go to school.

I was returning home from playing soccer when a neighbor <u>accosted</u> me by the gate and told me that there had been a bloody fight at my home.

"Your mother and father have been at it again," the neighbor, a woman, said.

"And your mother left."

I was stunned.

"Was she hurt badly?"

"A little bit," the woman said. "But she'll be all right. We took her to your grandma's place."

I became hot with anger.

"Is anyone in the house?" I stammered, trying to control my rage.

"Yes, your father is. But I don't think you should go near the house. He's raving mad. He's armed with a meat cleaver. He's chased out your brother and sisters, also. And some of the neighbors who tried to intervene he's threatened to carve them to pieces. I have never seen him this mad before."

I brushed aside the woman's warnings and went. Shattered windows convinced me that there had indeed been a skirmish of some sort. Several pieces of broken bricks, evidently broken after being thrown at the door, were lying about the door. I tried opening the door; it was locked from the inside. I knocked. No one answered. I knocked again. Still no one answered, until, as I turned to leave:

"Who's out there?" my father's voice came growling from inside.

"It's me, Johannes," I said.

"Go away, you bastard!" he bellowed. "I don't want you or that mother of yours setting foot in this house. Go away before I come out there and kill you!"

"Let me in!" I cried. "Dammit, let me in! I want my things!"

"What things? Go away, you black swine!"

I went to the broken window and screamed obscenities at my father, daring him to come

831

out, hoping that if he as much as ever stuck his black face out, I would pelt him with the half-a-loaf brick in my hand. He didn't come out. He continued launching a tirade of obscenities at my mother and her mother. He was drunk, but I wondered where he had gotten the money to buy beer, because it was still the middle of the week and he was dead broke. He had lost his entire wage for the past week in dice and had had to borrow bus fare.

"I'll kill you someday for all you're doing to my mother," I threatened him, overwhelmed with rage. Several nosy neighbors were beginning to congregate by open windows and doors. Not wanting to make a spectacle of myself, which was something many of our neighbors seemed to always expect from our family, I backtracked away from the door and vanished into the dark street. I ran, without stopping, all the way to the other end of the township, where Granny lived. There I found my mother, her face swollen and bruised and her eyes puffed up to the point where she could scarcely see.

"What happened, Mama?" I asked, fighting to hold back the tears at the sight of her disfigured face.

"Nothing, child, nothing," she mumbled, almost apologetically, between swollen lips. "Your papa simply lost his temper, that's all."

"But why did he beat you up like this, Mama?" Tears came down my face. "He's never beaten you like this before."

My mother appeared reluctant to answer me. She looked searchingly at Granny, who was pounding millet with pestle and mortar and mixing it with sorghum[14] and nuts for an African delicacy. Granny said, "Tell him, child, tell him. He's got a right to know. Anyway, he's the cause of it all."

"Your father and I fought because I took you to school this morning," my mother began. "He had told me not to, and when I told

him that I had, he became very upset. He was drunk. We started arguing, and one thing led to another."

"Why doesn't he want me to go to school?"

"He says he doesn't have money to waste paying for you to get what he calls a useless white man's education," my mother replied. "But I told him that if he won't pay for your schooling, I would try and look for a job and pay, but he didn't want to hear that, also. 'There are better things for you to work for,' he said. 'Besides, I don't want you to work. How would I look to other men if you, a woman I owned, were to start working?' When I asked him why shouldn't I take you to school, seeing that you were now of age, he replied that he doesn't believe in schools. I told him that school would keep you off the streets and out of trouble, but still he was belligerent."

"Is that why he beat you up?"

"Yes, he said I disobeyed his orders."

"He's right, child," Granny interjected. "He paid *lobola* [bride price] for you. And your father ate it all up before he left me."

To which my mother replied, "But I desperately want to leave this beast of a man. But with his *lobola* gone I can't do it. That worthless thing you call your husband shouldn't have sold Jackson's scrawny cattle and left you penniless."

"Don't talk like that about your father, child," Granny said. "Despite all, he's still your father, you know. Anyway, he asked for *lobola* only because he had to get back what he spent raising you. And you know it would have been taboo for him to let you or any of your sisters go without asking for *lobola*."

"You and Papa seemed to forget that my sisters and I have minds of our own," my mother said. "We didn't need you to tell us whom to

14. **sorghum:** a syrup made from the sweet juices of the sorgo plant.

marry, and why, and how. If it hadn't been for your interference, I could have married that schoolteacher."

Granny did not reply; she knew well not to. When it came to the act of "selling" women as marriage partners, my mother was vehemently opposed to it. Not only was she opposed to this one aspect of tribal culture, but to others as well, particularly those involving relations between men and women and the upbringing of children. But my mother's sharply differing opinion was an exception rather than the rule among tribal women. Most times, many tribal women questioned her sanity in daring to question well-established mores.[15] But my mother did not seem to care; she would always scoff at her opponents and call them fools in letting their husbands enslave them completely.

Though I disliked school, largely because I knew nothing about what actually went on there, and the little I knew had painted a dreadful picture, the fact that a father would not want his son to go to school, especially a father who didn't go to school, seemed hard to understand.

"Why do you want me to go to school, Mama?" I asked, hoping that she might, somehow, clear up some of the confusion that was building in my mind.

"I want you to have a future, child," my mother said. "And, contrary to what your father says, school is the only means to a future. I don't want you growing up to be like your father."

The latter statement hit me like a bolt of lightning. It just about shattered every defense mechanism and every <u>pretext</u> I had against going to school.

"Your father didn't go to school," she con-

tinued, dabbing her puffed eyes to reduce the swelling with a piece of cloth dipped in warm water, "that's why he's doing some of the bad things he's doing. Things like drinking, gambling and neglecting his family. He didn't learn how to read and write; therefore, he can't find a decent job. Lack of any education has narrowly focused his life. He sees nothing beyond himself. He still thinks in the old, tribal way and still believes that things should be as they were back in the old days when he was growing up as a tribal boy in Louis Trichardt. Though he's my husband, and your father, he doesn't see any of that."

"Why didn't he go to school, Mama?"

"He refused to go to school because his father led him to believe that an education was a tool through which white people were going to take things away from him, like they did black people in the old days. And that a white man's education was worthless insofar as black people were concerned because it prepared them for jobs they can't have. But I know it isn't totally so, child, because times have changed somewhat. Though our lot isn't any better today, an education will get you a decent job. If you can read and write you'll be better off than those of us who can't. Take my situation: I can't find a job because I don't have papers, and I can't get papers because white people mainly want to register people who can read and write. But I want things to be different for you, child. For you and your brother and sisters. I want you to go to school, because I believe that an education is the key you need to open up a new world and a new life for yourself, a world and life different from either your father's or mine. It is the only key that can do that, and only those who

---

15. **mores** (môr′ ēz): customs that are considered necessary for the welfare of society.

seek it earnestly and perseveringly will get anywhere in the white man's world. Education will open doors where none seem to exist. It'll make people talk to you, listen to you and help you; people who otherwise wouldn't bother. It will make you soar, like a bird lifting up into the endless blue sky, and leave poverty, hunger and suffering behind. It'll teach you to learn to embrace what's good and shun what's bad and evil. Above all, it'll make you a somebody in this world. It'll make you grow up to be a good and proud person. That's why I want you to go to school, child, so that education can do all that, and more, for you."

A long, awkward silence followed, during which I reflected upon the significance of my mother's lengthy speech. I looked at my mother; she looked at me.

Finally, I asked, "How come you know so much about school, Mama? You didn't go to school, did you?"

"No, child," my mother replied. "Just like your father, I never went to school." For the second time that evening, a mere statement of fact had a thunderous impact on me. All the confusion I had about school seemed to leave my mind, like darkness giving way to light. And what had previously been a dark, yawning void in my mind was suddenly transformed into a beacon of light that began to grow larger and larger, until it had swallowed up, blotted out, all the blackness. That beacon of light seemed to reveal things and facts, which, though they must have always existed in me, I hadn't been aware of up until now.

"But unlike your father," my mother went on, "I've always wanted to go to school, but couldn't because my father, under the sway of tribal traditions, thought it unnecessary to educate females. That's why I so much want you to go, child, for if you do, I know that someday I too would come to go, old as I would be then. Promise me, therefore, that no matter what, you'll go back to school. And I, in turn, promise that I'll do everything in my power to keep you there."

With tears streaming down my cheeks and falling upon my mother's bosom, I promised her that I would go to school "forever." That night, at seven and a half years of my life, the battlelines in the family were drawn. My mother on the one side, illiterate but determined to have me drink, for better or for worse, from the well of knowledge. On the other side, my father, he too illiterate, yet determined to have me drink from the well of ignorance. Scarcely aware of the magnitude of the decision I was making or, rather, the decision which was being emotionally thrusted upon me, I chose to fight on my mother's side, and thus my destiny was forever altered. ❧

# INSIGHT

## They Have Not Been Able
ARMANDO VALLADARES

They have not been able to take away
the rain's song
not yet
not even in this cell
but perhaps they'll do it tomorrow
that's why I want to enjoy it now,
to listen to the drops
drumming against
the boarded windows.
And suddenly it comes
through I don't know what crack
through I don't know what opening
that pungent odor
of wet earth
and I inhale deeply
filling myself to the brim
because perhaps they will also
prohibit that tomorrow.

## *R*esponding to Reading

### First Impressions

1. Which incident from the selection stands out most strongly in your mind? Why?

### Second Thoughts

2. Do you think the mother is right to force her son to go to school? Why or why not?

3. How has the father been affected by apartheid? Does this justify his actions in any way? Explain.

4. How do the attitudes of the mother and grandmother differ? What has produced these differences?

5. If you were the boy, would you come to the same conclusion he does at the end of the story? Explain.

6. What injustices does Mathabane present? Which do you think is the worst? Why?

   **Think about**
   • how the lives of the blacks are controlled by the white government
   • the system that produced his parents' marriage
   • the quality of education for blacks

7. Who is the most powerful individual in the story? Why?

### Broader Connections

8. For Mathabane, education did "open doors where none seem to exist." Do you think his mother's statement is true for our society? Why or why not?

## *L*iterary Concept: Autobiography

Autobiographies are nonfiction. In *Kaffir Boy,* Mathabane presents factual information from his memory about the people and events that had a big influence on him when he was a child. His writing style, however, makes the account seem like fiction. How are the events in this account like the plot of a short story? How are the conflicts the main character faces like those that confront fictional characters? Did you find the style of writing easy or difficult to read?

**Concept Review: Dialogue** Mathabane uses dialogue to help tell the story, but he also uses it to give background about his society and to help present his theme. Find examples of each of these uses of dialogue.

## Writing Options

1. Write a comparison between a character in this story and someone you know. Focus on the personalities and attitudes of these individuals.

2. One college fund advertises that "A mind is a terrible thing to waste." Write a one-sentence public service announcement that suggests Mathabane's attitude toward education.

3. Write pieces of graffiti that reflect the gang members' views on school and education.

4. How is the speaker in "They Have Not Been Able" like Mathabane's mother? Write what you think they have in common.

5. Explain how you think another character in this unit might have reacted in Mathabane's place.

## Vocabulary Practice

**Exercise**   Answer each question below and explain your answer.

1. Would an **austere** person throw a wild party? Why or why not?
2. If someone speaks **paradoxically,** does he contradict or reinforce his own words?
3. Which is more **utilitarian,** a vase or a bucket? Why?
4. What **pretext** might a thief use for stealing?
5. Does a person who has an **inkling** have positive knowledge or only a suspicion?
6. If you put **credence** in an idea, do you accept it or reject it?
7. From whom do you personally receive **unsolicited** advice?
8. Are you pleased or unhappy when strangers **accost** you? Why?
9. Which might **captivate** you—an exciting movie or a boring one?
10. Is it easy or difficult to tell what an **inscrutable** person is thinking? Why?

> *Words to Know and Use*
>
> accost
> austere
> captivate
> credence
> inkling
> inscrutable
> paradoxically
> pretext
> unsolicited
> utilitarian

# extend

## Options for Learning

**1 • Education in South Africa** Using the *Readers' Guide to Periodical Literature* and contemporary books, research education in South Africa today. Report to the class on the present laws and situation, pointing out the changes since Mathabane was a child.

**2 • African Women** Research the changing role of women in Africa today. Find out how the economic, marital, and educational opportunities have changed and the effects of these changes. Using pictures or other visual aids, give an oral report to your class.

**3 • Dramatic Interpretation** With a few classmates, act out one of the scenes from the story. Decide on the action, movement, lines, and characterizations before you rehearse. Then perform for the class.

**4 • Two Views of School** Draw, paint, or build two different visions of the school as seen through the eyes of the mother and the gang. Your interpretations might be realistic, abstract, or symbolic. Display your art in the classroom.

**5 • *Kaffir Boy*** Read Mathabane's entire autobiography. Report to the class on other events and learning experiences in Mathabane's struggle to rise above apartheid.

 **FACT FINDER**

*What percentage of black adults in South Africa can read and write?*

## *M*ark *Mathabane*
### 1960–

As Mark Mathabane was growing up, he suffered through the worst extremes of apartheid in South Africa. His parents were of different tribes and consequently were not legally allowed to live together as husband and wife. Because Mark's grandmother worked for an open-minded white family, he was exposed to different attitudes from those of most white South Africans. Through comic books and other books, such as *Treasure Island*, he taught himself English, which tribal blacks were not permitted to speak. It was in the home of his grandmother's employers that he picked up his first tennis racket. He learned the white minority's sport so well that he got the help of anti-apartheid tennis greats Arthur Ashe and Stan Smith. Tennis allowed Mathabane to escape the poverty and violence of his homeland through a scholarship to an American college.

Mathabane says that he cannot deny the anger and bitterness that apartheid produced but that "if I can turn that anger into something positive, I am really in a very good position to go on with my life." He hopes his writings and life will inspire "other boys and girls into believing that you can still grow up to be as much of an individual as you have the capacity to be."

# WRITER'S WORKSHOP

## PERSUASION

Imagine that you are putting together a home-assembly television cart. You've followed Steps 1 through 19, from "align slot A with slot B" to "attach part YY to part ZZ." Now that you're ready to put on the finishing touches, you look at the remaining nuts and bolts. You've got enough wing nuts to secure half of China, but you don't have one lock washer to save your life. What do you do?

If you've ever felt cheated by a defective product or poor service, then here's your chance to lodge a complaint. Companies usually want to know if you have experienced a problem with their goods or services; most are interested in providing good service. For this assignment, you will write a **letter of complaint** expressing your displeasure with a particular product or service and suggesting a way to remedy the problem. Just as in this subunit Winston Churchill, Mary Maloney, Arp Zumbi, and Mark Mathabane rebel against injustice in their ways, you can put up a fight in another way!

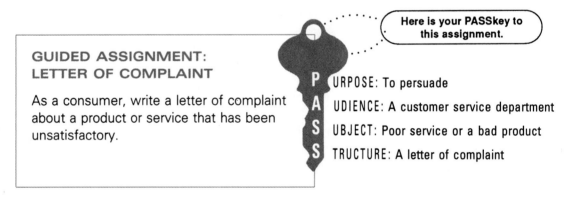

Here is your PASSkey to this assignment.

**GUIDED ASSIGNMENT: LETTER OF COMPLAINT**

As a consumer, write a letter of complaint about a product or service that has been unsatisfactory.

**P**URPOSE: To persuade
**A**UDIENCE: A customer service department
**S**UBJECT: Poor service or a bad product
**S**TRUCTURE: A letter of complaint

## Prewriting

**STEP 1** **Find a topic**  Try freewriting and looping to find a topic for your letter of complaint.

**Freewriting**  For five minutes write about as many of your experiences with poor service or defective or inferior products as you can remember. Don't lift your pen or pencil from the paper, and don't worry about the quality of your writing. Just let your mind wander on paper. After you've finished, circle the experience that annoyed you most.

**Looping** Using freewriting, write for five more minutes about the experience you circled. You should get more ideas as you write. Then find the best idea from this second freewriting and use freewriting again. Each time you write, you make a "loop" of freewriting. By the time you have two or three loops, you should have a topic for your letter of complaint as well as several details to use in your complaint.

**STEP 2** **Find a name and address** Locate the name and address of the company representative to whom you will send your letter. If you cannot get the name of a specific person, send the letter to the consumer department of the business. In this case your salutation would read "Dear Sir or Madam."

---

### Special Tip

Many products come with a toll-free phone number for consumer comments. Call to find out the name and address of the company representative to whom you should complain. If your complaint is with a local business, use the Yellow Pages to find the address.

---

## Drafting

**STEP 1** **State the purpose** In the first paragraph of your letter, state your purpose for writing. Here is an example from one student writer:

> One of the Tasti Foods products I recently tried may be dangerously contaminated.

◀ STUDENT MODEL

**STEP 2** **Describe the product or service and identify the problem** In the next paragraph of your letter, describe the product or service, giving specific information such as the date and place of purchase, model number, cost, size, color, and so on. Then identify the problem. Here's the same student's product description and complaint.

> Three weeks ago, I purchased a six-ounce can of Mama Lucia's Tomato Paste at the Food Barn Market. The tomato paste was spoiled. When I opened the can, it exploded! Not only did it ruin the sweater I was wearing, but I'm still washing tomato paste off the kitchen walls.

◀ STUDENT MODEL

**STEP 3** **Establish a proper tone** As you write your letter of complaint, think about the tone of your letter. You want to present your problem clearly and suggest a reasonable solution; you don't want to anger the person to whom you are writing. Remember that the person who receives the complaint probably is not directly responsible for the poor service or defective part, nor was the mistake intentional. Although you might feel very upset about your experience, avoid using loaded language or emotional appeal. Keep your letter polite, and it will be more effective. Read the two examples below. If you received both letters, which would you be more likely to answer?

> **Complaint 1** You yokels know nothing about your business! I paid forty dollars for a pile of junk. Have you ever tried putting together one of your television carts? Did it ever occur to you to include the lock nuts? What a bunch of idiots you are! Obviously *you* are the nuts!

> **Complaint 2** Recently I purchased your television cart at a cost of forty dollars and began to assemble it. I was disappointed to find no lock nuts anywhere in the package. As a result, I could not assemble the cart. I would appreciate your sending me a new kit that has all the parts necessary for assembly.

**STEP 4** **Suggest a resolution** Suggest a way of resolving the problem, or explain what action you'd like the responsible party to take. The student who bought the spoiled tomato paste made this suggestion.

 STUDENT MODEL ▶

> I would greatly appreciate it if Tasti Foods would send me a refund of eighty-nine cents for the tomato paste and $21.95 for the sweater I was wearing that was ruined when the can burst. It might also be a good idea to test the entire batch of tomato paste for contamination.

---

### Special Tip

Make your request reasonable and diplomatic. What kind of results do you think you'll get if you ask for a million dollars?

---

**STEP 5** **Use the proper form** Follow the correct form for a business letter as described in Correct Business Letter Form in the **Writer's Handbook.** Write your letter either in full block or modified block form.

## Revising and Editing

Before exchanging letters with a classmate for revising, use this list of suggestions to help you revise your letter.

- Circle any phrases that show anger or disgust. Replace them with less emotional language.
- Add one adjective and one adverb to make a noun and a verb more specific.
- Find two sentences that can be combined to sound smoother.
- Rewrite the sentence that tells what you expect the company or organization to do about the problem. Decide whether to keep the original sentence or the revised one.

Exchange letters with a classmate and use the following revision checklist as a guide for improvements.

---

**Revision Checklist**

1. Is the purpose of the complaint letter clearly stated?
2. Is the problem clearly described and a reasonable solution suggested?
3. Is the letter properly written in full or modified block form?
4. Does the letter have an appropriate tone?
5. If you received this letter, would you know what the writer expected? Would you want to do something about it? Explain.

---

**Editing**   Check your letter of complaint for correct grammar, spelling, usage, punctuation, and business letter form.

## Publishing

Type your letter on stationery. If your letter is about a recent and real problem, send it to the company. After three or four weeks, compare the results of your letter with those of your classmates who actually sent their letters. Analyze why some letters elicited responses and others did not. Did the businesses that did respond offer acceptable compensation?

## Reflecting on Your Writing

Answer these questions and file the answers in your writing portfolio.

1. What was the hardest part of writing a letter of complaint?
2. Did the revising techniques you used improve your letter? Explain.

# REFLEXIVE AND INTENSIVE PRONOUNS

> Reflexive and intensive pronouns are formed by adding *-self* or *-selves* to certain personal pronouns.
>
> **Singular**  myself, yourself, himself, herself, itself
>
> **Plural**  ourselves, yourselves, themselves
>
> There are no other acceptable reflexive or intensive pronouns. *Hisself* and *theirselves* are nonstandard and should be avoided.

A **reflexive pronoun** refers back to the subject of the sentence. Sometimes a reflexive pronoun acts as an **indirect object.** That is, it tells to whom or for whom the action of the verb is done.

> The couple made *themselves* snacks. (*Themselves* refers back to *couple.*)

In the sentence above, *themselves* tells for whom the snacks were made.

Sometimes writers make the mistake of using a reflexive pronoun without the noun to which it refers.

**Incorrect**  Patrick and *myself* are going home. (*Myself* does not refer to another noun in the sentence.)

**Correct**  Patrick and *I* are going home.

**Incorrect**  The cooking was divided between Mary and *myself.*

**Correct**  The cooking was divided between Mary and *me.*

An **intensive pronoun** adds emphasis to a noun in the sentence.

> Mary *herself* killed her husband. (*Herself* refers back to and emphasizes the noun *Mary.*)

Intensive pronouns can sometimes be placed in various positions in a sentence. For example, the preceding sentence could be written:

> Mary killed her husband *herself.*

Be careful when placing an intensive pronoun in some position other than next to the noun to which it refers. This can create confusion.

| **Incorrect** | The sergeant inspected the dead husband himself. (It is unclear whether *himself* refers to *the sergeant* or to *the husband.* |
|---|---|
| **Correct** | The sergeant himself inspected the dead husband. |

**Exercise 1**  Correct any errors in the use of reflexive or intensive pronouns. If a sentence contains no error, write *Correct.*

1. My friends and myself love the stories of Roald Dahl.
2. I myself particularly enjoy the ironic, surprising, diabolical plots.
3. The plots are so strange that Dahl probably scared hisself with them.
4. In one story by Dahl, detectives investigating a murder accidentally get rid of the murder weapon theirselves—by eating it!
5. Only ourselves and the murderer know that the murder weapon was a leg of lamb!
6. How strange that detectives should dispose of weapons themselves!
7. Luisa's mom told Luisa and myself that Dahl's "Lamb to the Slaughter" was made into a TV script by Alfred Hitchcock.
8. Hitchcock was attracted to Dahl's macabre stories because he was a pretty macabre fellow hisself.
9. Dahl and himself were certainly two of a kind!
10. They created many of the most horrific stories themselves.

**Exercise 2**  Revise the following dialogue, adding intensive pronouns in two places. Compare your revision to those done by your classmates. Notice that the choice of where to place the intensive pronouns is a choice about what elements in the paragraph should be emphasized.

    "Dylan Thomas's poetry is read in most schools in the English-speaking world," the teacher said. "However, Thomas had very little schooling."
    "Can a person really become a great poet without lots of formal education?" asked Marta.
    "Sure," said the teacher. "Thomas is proof of that. However, Thomas learned a lot from reading and writing on his own. He did both constantly."
    "Will I become a great poet if I read and write a lot?" Marta asked, to everyone's surprise.
    "If you want that to happen, you can make it happen," the teacher replied.

**LANGUAGE HANDBOOK**

For review and practice:
reflexive and intensive
  pronouns, pages 989–90

# VOCABULARY
## WORKSHOP

## LEVELS OF LANGUAGE

### FORMAL OR INFORMAL?

**Informal**

    Conversation

    Letters between friends

    Some writing for magazines and newspapers

**Formal**

    Formal speeches

    Professional documents

    Reports for school or work

**Standard English** is English that follows accepted grammatical rules and guidelines. Standard English can be either **formal** or **informal. Formal English,** used primarily in writing, is appropriate in any situation that is serious or ceremonial. Here is an example:

> I speak to you for the first time as Prime Minister in a solemn hour for the life of our country, of our Empire, of our Allies, and, above all, of the cause of Freedom.
> —Winston Churchill, May 19, 1940

**Informal English** is used in casual letters, in conversation, and in some magazine and newspaper articles. Consider the following example:

> We've got to stick together now, keep a stiff upper lip, and support the brave boys in the RAF.

### NOTE

In practice, language is rarely absolutely formal or absolutely informal. Instead, it usually falls somewhere between these two extremes.

|  | **Formal Language** | **Informal Language** |
|---|---|---|
| **Tone** | Serious, academic | Personal, friendly |
| **Vocabulary** | Uses difficult words and no contractions | Uses simpler words and contractions |
| **Organization** | Has longer, carefully constructed sentences | Has short, chatty sentences |

**Exercise**    The following letter was written in response to a job advertisement for a radio station. Rewrite the letter in a more appropriate style.

Hello Mr. Randolph,

    I've just seen your ad for an office assistant at KDGG. This is right up my alley! I listen to KDGG all the time. It's great! I've worked in the office at my Dad's business for the last three years. I mean, I really know about office work. Computers and I get along great, and I've spent hours in front of the copy machine! I'm really responsible, which you can tell from my grades, my being president of the Student Council, and all that stuff. So, I hope you'll give me a chance at this job. Call me soon. This is Tommy DeSoto, signing off. (Just a little DJ joke, there.)

# CONFRONTING THE UNEXPECTED

Contemporary writers often find their subjects in life's strange, amusing, bewildering, even terrifying surprises. Many stories, books, and movies take us into the minds and lives of isolated characters who are confronted with unexpected twists of fate, whether dark problems or shining victories. Sometimes the inspiration for such narratives comes from the evening news or an author's vivid memories; at other times, the plot arises from the wild and misty places of a writer's imagination.

The following selections will introduce you to characters who face mysterious, baffling, or threatening circumstances.

Fiction

# The Demon Lover

## ELIZABETH BOWEN

## Examine What You Know

What does the title of this story suggest to you about its characters, setting, and plot? Consider whether the story might be realistic or supernatural. Jot down your ideas. Then present your predictions in a class discussion.

## Expand Your Knowledge

This story is set in London, England, during World War II. During the period from August 1940 to May 1941, known as the blitz, Germany conducted nightly air-raid attacks on London in its attempt to force Britain to surrender. During these raids, Londoners sought safety in subway tunnels. Those who could afford to left the city and moved to the countryside. The main character in this story, Mrs. Drover, lived with her family in the wealthy Kensington district of London before moving to the countryside during the blitz. The story opens upon her return to her Kensington home after the blitz to reclaim some valued personal belongings. World War I also plays a part in this story in a brief flashback to Mrs. Drover's younger years and her relationship with a young soldier.

## Enrich Your Reading

**Recognizing Flashbacks**  This story is told from a limited third-person point of view. That is, the narrator is outside the story but is able to describe Mrs. Drover's thoughts and feelings. A disturbing event causes Mrs. Drover to drift back and forth in thought from present reality to past experiences. To help you recognize these time shifts, or **flashbacks,** and other important details in the story, read and think about the questions inserted throughout the text.

■ *A biography of the author can be found on page 855.*

# The Demon Lover

## ELIZABETH BOWEN

Toward the end of her day in London, Mrs. Drover went round to her shut-up house to look for several things she wanted to take away. Some belonged to herself, some to her family, who were by now used to their country life. It was late August; it had been a steamy, showery day: at the moment, the trees down the pavement glittered in an escape of humid yellow afternoon sun. Against the next batch of clouds, already piling up, ink-dark, broken chimneys and parapets stood out. In her once-familiar street, as in any unused channel, an unfamiliar queerness had silted up;[1] a cat wove itself in and out of railings, but no human eye watched Mrs. Drover's return. Shifting some parcels under her arm, she slowly forced round her latchkey in an unwilling lock, then gave the door, which had warped, a push with her knee. Dead air came out to meet her as she went in.

The staircase window having been boarded up, no light came down into the hall. But one door, she could just see, stood ajar, so she went quickly through into the room and unshuttered the big window in there. Now the prosaic woman, looking about her, was more perplexed than she knew by everything that she saw, by traces of her long former habit of life—the yellow smoke stain up the white marble mantelpiece; the ring left by a vase on the top of the escritoire;[2] the bruise in the wallpaper where, on the door being thrown open widely, the china handle had always hit the wall. The piano, having gone away to be stored, had left what looked like claw marks on its part of the parquet.[3] Though not much dust had seeped in, each object wore a film of another kind; and, the only ventilation being the chimney, the whole drawing room smelled of the cold hearth. Mrs. Drover put down her parcels on the escritoire and left the room to proceed upstairs; the things she wanted were in a bedroom chest.

She had been anxious to see how the house was—the part-time caretaker she shared with some neighbors was away this week on his holiday, known to be not yet back. At the best of times he did not look in often, and she was never sure that she trusted him. There were some cracks in the structure, left by the last

---

1. **silted up:** filled or choked up; settled uncomfortably.
2. **escritoire** (es' kri twär'): a writing desk or table.
3. **parquet** (pär kā'): a floor of inlaid woodwork in geometric forms.

847

bombing, on which she was anxious to keep an eye. Not that one could do anything—

A shaft of <u>refracted</u> daylight now lay across the hall. She stopped dead and stared at the hall table—on this lay a letter addressed to her.

*Y*ou may expect me, therefore, at the hour arranged. Until then . . .

She thought first—then the caretaker *must* be back. All the same, who, seeing the house shuttered, would have dropped a letter in at the box? It was not a circular; it was not a bill. And the post office redirected, to the address in the country, everything for her that came through the post. The caretaker (even if he *were* back) did not know she was due in London today—her call here had been planned to be a surprise—so his negligence in the manner of this letter, leaving it to wait in the dusk and the dust, annoyed her. Annoyed, she picked up the letter, which bore no stamp. But it cannot be important, or they would know . . . She took the letter rapidly upstairs with her, without a stop to look at the writing till she reached what had been her bedroom, where she let in light. The room looked over the garden and other gardens: the sun had gone in; as the clouds sharpened and lowered, the trees and rank lawns seemed already to smoke with dark. Her reluctance to look again at the letter came from the fact that she felt intruded upon—and by someone contemptuous of her ways. However, in the tenseness preceding the fall of rain she read it: it was a few lines.

INTERIOR WITH SEATED WOMAN   1908   Vilhelm Hammershoi   Aarhus Kunstmuseum, Denmark.

Dear Kathleen: You will not have forgotten that today is our anniversary, and the day we said. The years have gone by at once slowly and fast. In view of the fact that nothing has changed, I shall rely upon you to keep your promise. I was sorry to see you leave London, but was satisfied that you would be back in time. You may expect me, therefore, at the hour arranged. Until then . . .

K.

*Words to Know and Use*

**refracted** (ri frakt' id) *adj.* bent or angled, such as light waves

Who is "K"? What does this person want?

Mrs. Drover looked for the date: it was to-day's. She dropped the letter on to the bed-springs, then picked it up to see the writing again—her lips, beneath the remains of lip-stick, beginning to go white. She felt so much the change in her own face that she went to the mirror, polished a clear patch in it and looked at once urgently and stealthily in. She was confronted by a woman of forty-four, with eyes starting out under a hat brim that had been rather carelessly pulled down. She had not put on any more powder since she left the shop where she ate her solitary tea. The pearls her husband had given her on their marriage hung loose round her now rather thinner throat, slipping in the V of the pink wool jumper her sister knitted last autumn as they sat round the fire. Mrs. Drover's most normal expression was one of controlled worry, but of assent. Since the birth of the third of her little boys, attended by a quite serious illness, she had had an <u>intermittent</u> muscular flicker to the left of her mouth, but in spite of this she could always sustain a man-ner that was at once energetic and calm.

Turning from her own face as precipitately[4] as she had gone to meet it, she went to the chest where the things were, unlocked it, threw up the lid and knelt to search. But as rain began to come crashing down, she could not keep from looking over her shoulder at the stripped bed on which the letter lay. Be-hind the blanket of rain the clock of the church that still stood struck six—with rapidly heightening apprehension she counted each of the slow strokes. "The hour arranged . . . My God," she said, "*what* hour? How should I . . . ? After twenty-five years . . ."

The young girl talking to the soldier in the garden had not ever completely seen his face. It was dark; they were saying goodbye under a tree. Now and then—for it felt, from not see-ing him at this intense moment, as though she had never seen him at all—she verified his presence for these few moments longer by putting out a hand, which he each time pressed, without very much kindness, and painfully, on to one of the breast buttons of his uniform. That cut of the button on the palm of her hand was, principally, what she was to carry away. This was so near the end of a leave from France that she could only wish him already gone. It was August 1916. Being not kissed, being drawn away from and looked at, intimidated Kathleen till she imagined spec-tral[5] glitters in the place of his eyes. Turning away and looking back up the lawn, she saw, through branches of trees, the drawing room window alight; she caught a breath for the moment when she could go running back there into the safe arms of her mother and sister and cry: "What shall I do, what shall I do? He has gone."

Who are the young girl and the soldier? *clarify*

Hearing her catch her breath, her fiancé said, without feeling: "Cold?"

"You're going away such a long way."

"Not so far as you think."

"I don't understand?"

"You don't have to," he said. "You will. You know what we said."

"But that was—suppose you—I mean, sup-pose."

---

4. **precipitately:** hastily; suddenly.
5. **spectral:** phantom; ghostly.

---

*Words to Know and Use* | **intermittent** (in′ tər mit′ ′nt) *adj.* pausing from time to time

849

"I shall be with you," he said, "sooner or later. You won't forget that. You need do nothing but wait."

Only a little more than a minute later she was free to run up the silent lawn. Looking in through the window at her mother and sister, who did not for the moment perceive her, she already felt that unnatural promise drive down between her and the rest of all humankind. No other way of having given herself could have made her feel so apart, lost and forsworn. She could not have plighted a more sinister troth.[6]

Kathleen behaved well when, some months later, her fiancé was reported missing, presumed killed. Her family not only supported her but were able to praise her courage without <u>stint</u> because they could not regret, as a husband for her, the man they knew almost nothing about. They hoped she would, in a year or two, console herself—and had it been only a question of consolation, things might have gone much straighter ahead. But her trouble, behind just a little grief, was a complete dislocation from everything. She did not reject other lovers, for these failed to appear: for years she failed to attract men—and with the approach of her thirties she became natural enough to share her family's anxiousness on this score. She began to put herself out, to wonder; and at thirty-two she was very greatly relieved to find herself being courted by William Drover. She married him, and the two of them settled down in this quiet, arboreal[7] part of Kensington: in this house the years piled up, her children were born and they all lived till they were driven out by the bombs of the next war. Her movements as Mrs. Drover were circumscribed,[8] and she dismissed any idea that they were still watched.

As things were—dead or living, the letter-writer sent her only a threat. Unable, for some minutes, to go on kneeling with her back exposed to the empty room, Mrs. Drover rose from the chest to sit on an upright chair whose back was firmly against the wall. The desuetude[9] of her former bedroom, her married London home's whole air of being a cracked cup from which memory, with its reassuring power, had either evaporated or leaked away, made a crisis—and at just this crisis the letter-writer had, knowledgeably, struck. The hollowness of the house this evening cancelled years on years of voices, habits and steps. Through the shut windows she only heard rain fall on the roofs around. To rally herself, she said she was in a mood—and, for two or three seconds shutting her eyes, told herself that she had imagined the letter. But she opened them—there it lay on the bed.

On the supernatural side of the letter's entrance she was not permitting her mind to dwell. Who, in London, knew she meant to call at the house today? Evidently, however, this had been known. The caretaker, *had* he come back, had had no cause to expect her: he would have taken the letter in his pocket, to forward it, at his own time, through the post. There was no other sign that the caretaker had been in—but, if not? Letters dropped in at doors of deserted houses do not fly or walk to tables in halls. They do not sit on the dust of empty tables with the air of certainty that they will be found. There is needed some human hand—but nobody but the caretaker had a key. Under circumstances she did not care to consider, a house can be entered without a

---

6. **plighted a more sinister troth:** made a more evil promise of marriage.

7. **arboreal:** tree-lined.

8. **circumscribed:** restricted; confined; restrained.

9. **desuetude** (des′ wi tōōd′): disuse.

*Words to Know and Use* | **stint** (stint) *n.* limit or restriction

key. It was possible that she was not alone now. She might be being waited for, downstairs. Waited for—until when? Until "the hour arranged." At least that was not six o'clock: six had struck.

She rose from the chair and went over and locked the door.

The thing was, to get out. To fly? No, not that: she had to catch her train. As a woman whose utter dependability was the keystone of her family life, she was not willing to return to the country, to her husband, her little boys and her sister, without the objects she had come up to fetch. Resuming work at the chest, she set about making up a number of parcels in a rapid, fumbling-decisive way. These, with her shopping parcels, would be too much to carry; these meant a taxi—at the thought of the taxi her heart went up and her normal breathing resumed. *I will ring up the taxi now; the taxi cannot come too soon: I shall hear the taxi out there running its engine, till I walk calmly down to it through the hall. I'll ring up—But no: the telephone is cut off . . .* She tugged at a knot she had tied wrong.

*The idea of flight . . . He was never kind to me, not really. I don't remember him kind at all. Mother said he never considered me. He was set on me, that was what it was—not love. Not love, not meaning a person well. What did he do, to make me promise like that? I can't remember—*But she found that she could.

*infer*     What had she promised?

She remembered with such dreadful acuteness that the twenty-five years since then dissolved like smoke and she instinctively looked for the weal[10] left by the button on the palm of her hand. She remembered not only all that he said and did but the complete suspension of *her* existence during that August week. *I was not myself—they all told me so at the time.* She remembered—but with one white burning blank as where acid has dropped on a photograph: *under no conditions* could she remember his face.

*So, wherever he may be waiting, I shall not know him. You have no time to run from a face you do not expect.*

The thing was to get to the taxi before any clock struck what could be the hour. She would slip down the street and round the side of the square to where the square gave on the main road. She would return in the taxi, safe, to her own door and bring the solid driver into the house with her to pick up the parcels from room to room. The idea of the taxi driver made her decisive, bold: she unlocked her door, went to the top of the staircase and listened down.

She heard nothing—but while she was hearing nothing, the *passé*[11] air of the staircase was disturbed by a draft that traveled up to her face. It emanated from the basement: down there a door or window was being opened by someone who chose this moment to leave the house.

What is going on in the basement?     *infer*

The rain had stopped; the pavements steamily shone as Mrs. Drover let herself out by inches from her own front door into the empty street. The unoccupied houses opposite continued to meet her look with their damaged stare. Making toward the thoroughfare and the taxi, she tried not to keep looking behind. Indeed, the silence was so intense—one of those creeks of London silence exaggerated this summer by the damage of war—

---

10. **weal:** a mark raised on the skin.

11. *passé* (pä sā′) *French:* rather old; stale.

VIEW OF HEATH STREET BY NIGHT 1882 John Atkinson Grimshaw Tate Gallery, London/Art Resource, New York.

that no tread could have gained on hers unheard. Where her street debouched[12] on the square where people went on living, she grew conscious of, and checked, her unnatural pace. Across the open end of the square two buses impassively passed each other: women, a perambulator,[13] cyclists, a man wheeling a barrow signalized, once again, the ordinary flow of life. At the square's most populous corner should be—and was—the short taxi rank. This evening, only one taxi—but this, although it presented its blank rump, appeared already to be alertly waiting for her. Indeed, without looking round, the driver started his engine as she panted up from behind and put her hand on the door. As she did so, the clock struck seven. The taxi faced the main road; to make the trip back to her house it would have to turn—she had settled back on the seat and the taxi *had* turned before she, surprised by its knowing movement, recollected that she had

not "said where." She leaned forward to scratch at the glass panel that divided the driver's head from her own.

The driver braked to what was almost a stop, turned round and slid the glass panel back: the jolt of this flung Mrs. Drover forward till her face was almost into the glass. Through the aperture,[14] driver and passenger, not six inches between them, remained for an eternity eye to eye. Mrs. Drover's mouth hung open for some seconds before she could issue her first scream. After that she continued to scream freely and to beat with her gloved hands on the glass all round as the taxi, accelerating without mercy, made off with her into the hinterland of deserted streets. ❧

---

12. **debouched** (dē boosht′): emerged.
13. **perambulator:** a baby buggy.
14. **aperture:** an opening; hole.

*Words to Know and Use*  |  **impassively** (im pas′ iv lē) *adv.* calmly; unemotionally

# explain

## Responding to Reading

### First Impressions

**1.** Did this story end the way you thought it might? Explain.

### Second Thoughts

**2.** What do you think happens to Mrs. Drover at the end of the story? Cite evidence from the story to support your opinion.

**3.** What conclusions can the reader draw about Kathleen's soldier boyfriend?

**Think about**
- his words and actions during the 1916 farewell meeting with Kathleen
- how Kathleen reacts to him during the meeting
- how Kathleen feels about him today

**4.** What events in the story are caused by fate?

**5.** Do you think that Mrs. Drover's frightening experiences are caused by nervous hallucinations? Why or why not?

**Think about**
- her state of mind early in the story
- whether the driver is a ghost or her live ex-boyfriend

**6.** How does the author build suspense in the story?

### Broader Connections

**7.** Why do you think that stories about the supernatural are so popular with the general public? Do you like these kinds of stories? Why or why not?

## Literary Concept: Supernatural Tale

A story that goes beyond the bounds of reality is called a **supernatural tale.** Supernatural tales include beings, powers, or events that are unexplainable by known forces or laws of nature. In such tales, fate causes events to occur that are unexpected and beyond the characters' control. Characters who come face to face with supernatural forces often meet their doom. What elements make "The Demon Lover" a supernatural tale?

**Concept Review: Foreshadowing**  What clues provide hints about the outcome of the story?

THE DEMON LOVER     853

## Writing Options

1. Write a scene to follow the end of this story. Use your scene to show your interpretation of the preceding events.

2. Sensory details contribute to the mood of this story. List some of these details.

3. Write a logical, non-supernatural explanation of what happens in the story. Your explanation could be psychological, medical, or some other realistic explanation.

4. Create a method of escape from the taxi for Mrs. Drover.

## Vocabulary Practice

**Exercise** On your paper, write the word from the list that best completes each sentence.

1. The bombing of London went on night after night without _____.
2. _____ rain continued off and on throughout the day.
3. The lovely young Kathleen grew up to be a _____ middle-aged matron.
4. _____ rays of sunlight fell across the bare floor.
5. People stared _____ at the screaming woman and then went about their business.

## Options for Learning

**1** • **A Demon Love Letter** Re-create the letter found by Mrs. Drover. To give it a supernatural appearance, use old handwriting or calligraphy and old, yellowed paper, perhaps slightly stained.

**2** • **A Movie Poster** Draw or paint a poster of the taxi scene to be used as advertising for a movie version of this story. Include the actors' names as well as quotes from movie reviews.

**3** • **The Supernatural** With some classmates, research the supernatural, especially beliefs and attitudes about the existence of demons similar to the one in this story. Report your findings to the class.

**4** • **The Musical Score** With a classmate, select appropriate music and sound effects for a dramatic reading of the story. Plan a presentation for the class. One of you might read the story while the other plays the music and sound effects.

### ◆ FACT FINDER

*How many years passed between the end of World War I and England's entrance into World War II?*

## Elizabeth Bowen
### 1899–1973

Although Elizabeth Bowen spent much of her life in Ireland, she is considered by many critics to be one of the major British writers of the twentieth century. She worked with psychologically scarred, or shell-shocked victims of World War I and as a writer and air-raid warden for the government during World War II. The moral, physical, and psychic visions in her writing seem to come from a personal understanding of life. She has said that "when I write, I am re-creating what was created for me." Known primarily as a novelist, Bowen also enjoyed the short-story format because it allowed her to concentrate on mood, a single character, and the emotional atmosphere of a single scene or event. "I feel happiest . . . in the short story. . . . [It] has the dangers of perfection," she said.

*Fiction*

# *First Confession*

### FRANK O'CONNOR

## *E*xamine *What You Know*

Young children are often told fear-inspiring stories to make them behave or avoid dangerous situations. Discuss stories you remember from childhood that were meant to scare you into good behavior. How did these stories affect you? As you read, see how the young boy in this story is affected by the stories he hears about confession.

## *E*xpand *Your Knowledge*

Catholicism, as it was practiced in Ireland several generations ago, emphasized that sin without forgiveness would damn the sinner to hell. Because of this teaching, confession was an important element in the lives of all Catholics. They were expected to regularly confess their sins to a priest, who would then require the sinner to perform some kind of penance, or act of repentance. The confessional was a small, closet-sized room with just enough space for the person to kneel in and lean against a rail in prayer. The confessor and priest would speak to each other through a grille that separated them. Children going to their first confession were easily frightened by the dark setting, by the thought that they might go to hell, and by the stories they heard of "bad confessions," that is, confessions that were less than completely truthful. A bad confession was considered a mortal sin, serious enough to send them to hell.

This story takes a humorous look at the fears a child experiences leading up to his first confession. The dialogue between the characters, as well as the narrator's language, is written in the dialect of southern Ireland's County Cork. Notice the unusual word order that is occasionally used and certain expressions that reflect this particular Irish dialect. Also notice how the use of dialect helps make the characters and setting seem real.

## *W*rite *Before You Read*

Think back to your earliest recollection of a church, Sunday school, synagogue, or other religious experience. What images and feelings stand out most in your mind? Write a brief description of your experience.

■ *A biography of the author can be found on page 865.*

# First Confession

### FRANK O'CONNOR

All the trouble began when my grandfather died and my grandmother—my father's mother—came to live with us. Relations in the one house are a strain at the best of times, but, to make matters worse, my grandmother was a real old country woman and quite unsuited to the life in town. She had a fat, wrinkled old face and, to Mother's great indignation, went round the house in bare feet—the boots had her crippled, she said. For dinner she had a jug of porter[1] and a pot of potatoes with—sometimes—a bit of salt fish, and she poured out the potatoes on the table and ate them slowly, with great relish, using her fingers by way of a fork.

Now, girls are supposed to be <u>fastidious,</u> but I was the one who suffered most from this. Nora, my sister, just sucked up to the old woman for the penny she got every Friday out of the old-age pension, a thing I could not do. I was too honest, that was my trouble; and when I was playing with Bill Connell, the sergeant-major's son, and saw my grandmother steering up the path with the jug of porter sticking out from beneath her shawl, I was <u>mortified.</u> I made excuses not to let him come into the house, because I could never be sure what she would be up to when we went in.

When Mother was at work and my grandmother made the dinner, I wouldn't touch it. Nora once tried to make me, but I hid under the table from her and took the bread knife with me for protection. Nora let on to be very indignant (she wasn't, of course, but she knew Mother saw through her, so she sided with Gran) and came after me. I lashed out at her with the bread knife, and after that she left me alone. I stayed there till Mother came in from work and made my dinner, but when Father came in later, Nora said in a shocked voice: "Oh, Dadda, do you know what Jackie did at dinner time?" Then, of course, it all came out; Father gave me a flaking; Mother interfered, and for days after that he didn't speak to me, and Mother barely spoke to Nora. And all because of that old woman! God knows, I was heart scalded.

Then, to crown my misfortunes, I had to make my first Confession and Communion. It was an old woman called Ryan who prepared us for these. She was about the one age with Gran; she was well-to-do, lived in a big house on Montenotte, wore a black cloak and bonnet, and came every day to school at three o'clock, when we should have been going home, and talked to us of Hell. She may have

---

1. **porter:** a dark-brown beer.

857

mentioned the other place as well, but that could only have been by accident, for Hell had the first place in her heart.

She lit a candle, took out a new half-crown,[2] and offered it to the first boy who would hold one finger—only one finger!—in the flame for five minutes by the school clock. Being always very ambitious, I was tempted to volunteer, but I thought it might look greedy. Then she asked were we afraid of holding one finger—only one finger!—in a little candle flame for five minutes and not afraid of burning all over in roasting-hot furnaces for all eternity. "All eternity! Just think of that! A whole lifetime goes by and it's nothing, not even a drop in the ocean of your sufferings." The woman was really interesting about Hell, but my attention was all fixed on the half-crown. At the end of the lesson she put it back in her purse. It was a great disappointment; a religious woman like that, you wouldn't think she'd bother about a thing like a half-crown.

Another day she said she knew a priest who woke one night to find a fellow he didn't recognize leaning over the end of his bed. The priest was a bit frightened—naturally enough—but he asked the fellow what he wanted, and the fellow said in a deep, husky voice that he wanted to go to Confession. The priest said it was an awkward time and wouldn't it do in the morning, but the fellow said that last time he went to Confession, there was one sin he kept back, being ashamed to mention it, and now it was always on his mind. Then the priest knew it was a bad case, because the fellow was after making a bad confession and committing a mortal sin. He got up to dress, and just then the cock crew in the yard outside, and—lo and behold!—when the priest looked round there was no sign of the fellow, only a smell of burning timber, and when the priest looked at his bed, didn't he see the print of two hands burned in it? That was because the fellow had made a bad confession.

This story made a shocking impression on me.

But the worst of all was when she showed us how to examine our conscience. Did we take the name of the Lord, our God, in vain? Did we honor our father and our mother? (I asked her did this include grandmothers, and she said it did.) Did we love our neighbor as ourselves? Did we covet our neighbor's goods? (I thought of the way I felt about the penny that Nora got every Friday.) I decided that, between one thing and another, I must have broken the whole ten commandments, all on account of that old woman, and so far as I could see, so long as she remained in the house, I had no hope of ever doing anything else.

I was scared to death of Confession. The day the whole class went I let on to have a toothache, hoping my absence wouldn't be noticed; but at three o'clock, just as I was feeling safe, along comes a chap with a message from Mrs. Ryan that I was to go to Confession myself on Saturday and be at the chapel for Communion with the rest. To make it worse, Mother couldn't come with me and sent Nora instead.

Now, that girl had ways of tormenting me that Mother never knew of. She held my hand as we went down the hill, smiling sadly and saying how sorry she was for me, as if she were bringing me to the hospital for an operation.

"Oh, God help us!" she moaned. "Isn't it a terrible pity you weren't a good boy? Oh, Jackie, my heart bleeds for you! How will you ever think of all your sins? Don't forget you have to tell him about the time you kicked Gran on the shin."

"Lemme go!" I said, trying to drag myself free of her. "I don't want to go to Confession at all."

---

2. **half-crown:** a former British coin equal to about one-eighth of a pound; about twenty-five American cents.

"But sure, you'll have to go to Confession, Jackie," she replied in the same regretful tone. "Sure, if you didn't, the parish priest would be up to the house, looking for you. 'Tisn't, God knows, that I'm not sorry for you. Do you remember the time you tried to kill me with the bread knife under the table? And the language you used to me? I don't know what he'll do with you at all, Jackie. He might have to send you up to the Bishop."

I remember thinking bitterly that she didn't know the half of what I had to tell—if I told it. I knew I couldn't tell it—and understood perfectly why the fellow in Mrs. Ryan's story made a bad confession; it seemed to me a great shame that people wouldn't stop criticizing him. I remember that steep hill down to the church, and the sunlit hillsides beyond the valley of the river, which I saw in the gaps between the houses, like Adam's last glimpse of Paradise.

Then, when she had maneuvered me down the long flight of steps to the chapel yard, Nora suddenly changed her tone. She became the raging, malicious devil she really was.

"There you are!" she said with a yelp of triumph, hurling me through the church door. "And I hope he'll give you the penitential psalms,[3] you dirty little caffler."

I knew then I was lost, given up to eternal justice. The door with the colored-glass panels swung shut behind me, the sunlight went out and gave place to deep shadow, and the wind whistled outside so that the silence within seemed to crackle like ice under my feet. Nora sat in front of me by the confession box. There were a couple of old women ahead of her, and then a miserable-looking poor devil came and wedged me in at the other side, so that I couldn't escape even if I had the courage. He joined his hands and rolled his eyes in the direction of the roof, muttering aspirations in an anguished tone, and I wondered had he a grandmother too. Only a grandmother could

PAS MECHE  1882  Jules Bastien-Lepage  National Galleries of Scotland, Edinburgh.

account for a fellow behaving in that heart-broken way, but he was better off than I, for he at least could go and confess his sins; while I would make a bad confession and then die in the night and be continually coming back and burning people's furniture.

Nora's turn came, and I heard the sound of something slamming, and then her voice as if butter wouldn't melt in her mouth, and then another slam, and out she came. God, the hypocrisy of women! Her eyes were lowered, her head was bowed, and her hands were

---

3. **penitential psalms:** long repetitions of various biblical songs or holy poems.

joined very low down on her stomach, and she walked up the aisle to the side altar looking like a saint. You never saw such an exhibition of devotion; and I remembered the devilish malice with which she had tormented me all the way from our door, and wondered were all religious people like that, really. It was my turn now. With the fear of damnation in my soul I went in, and the confessional door closed of itself behind me.

It was pitch-dark, and I couldn't see priest or anything else. Then I really began to be frightened. In the darkness it was a matter between God and me, and He had all the odds. He knew what my intentions were before I even started; I had no chance. All I had ever been told about Confession got mixed up in my mind, and I knelt to one wall and said: "Bless me, father, for I have sinned; this is my first confession." I waited for a few minutes, but nothing happened, so I tried it on the other wall. Nothing happened there either. He had me spotted, all right.

It must have been then that I noticed the shelf at about one height with my head. It was really a place for grown-up people to rest their elbows, but in my distracted state I thought it was probably the place you were supposed to kneel. Of course, it was on the high side and not very deep, but I was always good at climbing and managed to get up all right. Staying up was the trouble. There was room only for my knees, and nothing you could get a grip on but a sort of wooden molding a bit above it. I held on to the molding and repeated the words a little louder, and this time something happened, all right. A slide was slammed back; a little light entered the box, and a man's voice said: "Who's there?"

" 'Tis me, father," I said for fear he mightn't see me and go away again. I couldn't see him

at all. The place the voice came from was under the molding, about level with my knees, so I took a good grip of the molding and swung myself down till I saw the astonished face of a young priest looking up at me. He had to put his head on one side to see me, and I had to put mine on one side to see him, so we were more or less talking to one another up-side-down. It struck me as a queer way of hearing confessions, but I didn't feel it my place to criticize.

"Bless me, father, for I have sinned; this is my first confession," I rattled off all in one breath and swung myself down the least shade more to make it easier for him.

"What are you doing up there?" he shouted in an angry voice, and the strain the politeness was putting on my hold of the molding, and the shock of being addressed in such an uncivil tone, were too much for me. I lost my grip, tumbled, and hit the door an unmerciful wallop before I found myself flat on my back in the middle of the aisle. The people who had been waiting stood up with their mouths open. The priest opened the door of the middle box and came out, pushing his biretta[4] back from his forehead; he looked something terrible. Then Nora came scampering down the aisle.

"Oh, you dirty little caffler!" she said. "I might have known you'd do it. I might have known you'd disgrace me. I can't leave you out of my sight for one minute."

Before I could even get to my feet to defend myself she bent down and gave me a clip across the ear. This reminded me that I was so stunned I had even forgotten to cry, so that people might think I wasn't hurt at all, when in fact I was probably maimed for life. I gave a roar out of me.

---

4. **biretta:** a hard, square ceremonial hat worn by Catholic priests.

*Words to Know and Use* | **maim** (mām) *v.* to cripple, mutilate, or disable

"What's all this about?" the priest hissed, getting angrier than ever and pushing Nora off me. "How dare you hit the child like that, you little vixen?"

"But I can't do my penance with him, father," Nora cried, cocking an outraged eye up at him.

"Well, go and do it, or I'll give you some more to do," he said, giving me a hand up. "Was it coming to Confession you were, my poor man?" he asked me.

" 'Twas, father," said I with a sob.

"Oh," he said respectfully, "a big hefty fellow like you must have terrible sins. Is this your first?"

" 'Tis, father," said I.

"Worse and worse," he said gloomily. "The crimes of a lifetime. I don't know will I get rid of you at all today. You'd better wait now till I'm finished with these old ones. You can see by the looks of them they haven't much to tell."

"I will, father," I said with something approaching joy.

## " I had it all arranged to kill my grandmother. "

The relief of it was really enormous. Nora stuck out her tongue at me from behind his back, but I couldn't even be bothered retorting. I knew from the very moment that man opened his mouth that he was intelligent above the ordinary. When I had time to think, I saw how right I was. It only stood to reason that a fellow confessing after seven years would have more to tell than people that went every week. The crimes of a lifetime, exactly as he said. It was only what he expected, and the rest was the cackle of old women and girls with their talk of Hell, the Bishop, and the penitential psalms. That was all they knew. I

started to make my examination of conscience, and, barring the one bad business of my grandmother, it didn't seem so bad.

The next time, the priest steered me into the confession box himself and left the shutter back the way I could see him get in and sit down at the farther side of the grille from me.

"Well, now," he said, "what do they call you?"

"Jackie, father," said I.

"And what's a-trouble to you, Jackie?"

"Father," I said, feeling I might as well get it over while I had him in good humor, "I had it all arranged to kill my grandmother."

He seemed a bit shaken by that, all right, because he said nothing for quite a while.

"My goodness," he said at last, "that'd be a shocking thing to do. What put that into your head?"

"Father," I said, feeling very sorry for myself, "she's an awful woman."

"Is she?" he asked. "What way is she awful?"

"She takes porter, father," I said, knowing well from the way Mother talked of it that this was a mortal sin, and hoping it would make the priest take a more favorable view of my case.

"Oh, my!" he said, and I could see he was impressed.

"And snuff, father," said I.

"That's a bad case, sure enough, Jackie," he said.

"And she goes round in her bare feet, father," I went on in a rush of self-pity, "and she knows I don't like her, and she gives pennies to Nora and none to me, and my da sides with her and flakes me, and one night I was so heart scalded I made up my mind I'd have to kill her."

"And what would you do with the body?" he asked with great interest.

"I was thinking I could chop that up and carry it away in a barrow I have," I said.

"Begor, Jackie," he said, "do you know you're a terrible child?"

"I know, father," I said, for I was just thinking the same thing myself. "I tried to kill Nora too with a bread knife under the table, only I missed her."

"Is that the little girl that was beating you just now?" he asked.

" 'Tis, father."

"Someone will go for her with a bread knife one day, and he won't miss her," he said rather cryptically. "You must have great courage. Between ourselves, there's a lot of people I'd like to do the same to, but I'd never have the nerve. Hanging is an awful death."

"Is it, father?" I asked with the deepest interest—I was always very keen on hanging. "Did you ever see a fellow hanged?"

"Dozens of them," he said solemnly. "And they all died roaring."

"Jay!" I said.

"Oh, a horrible death!" he said with great satisfaction. "Lots of the fellows I saw killed their grandmothers too, but they all said 'twas never worth it."

He had me there for a full ten minutes talking and then walked out the chapel yard with me. I was genuinely sorry to part with him, because he was the most entertaining character I'd ever met in the religious line. Outside, after the shadow of the church, the sunlight was like the roaring of waves on a beach; it dazzled me; and when the frozen silence melted and I heard the screech of trams[5] on the road, my heart soared. I knew now I wouldn't die in the night and come back, leaving marks on my mother's furniture. It would be a great worry to her, and the poor soul had enough.

Nora was sitting on the railing, waiting for me, and she put on a very sour puss when she saw the priest with me. She was mad jealous because a priest had never come out of the church with her.

"Well," she asked coldly, after he left me, "what did he give you?"

"Three Hail Marys[6]," I said.

"Three Hail Marys," she repeated incredulously. "You mustn't have told him anything."

"I told him everything," I said confidently.

"About Gran and all?"

"About Gran and all."

(All she wanted was to be able to go home and say I'd made a bad confession.)

"Did you tell him you went for me with the bread knife?" she asked with a frown.

"I did, to be sure."

"And he only gave you three Hail Marys?"

"That's all."

She slowly got down from the railing with a baffled air. Clearly, this was beyond her. As we mounted the steps back to the main road, she looked at me suspiciously.

"What are you sucking?" she asked.

"Bullseyes."[7]

"Was it the priest gave them to you?"

" 'Twas."

"Lord God," she wailed bitterly, "some people have all the luck! 'Tis no advantage to anybody trying to be good. I might just as well be a sinner like you." ❧

---

5. **trams:** streetcars.

6. **Hail Marys:** Prayers to the Virgin Mary, used in the Roman Catholic Church.

7. **Bullseyes:** hard, round candies.

*Words to Know and Use* | **cryptically** (krip′ ti kəl lē) *adv.* in the manner of having a hidden or mysterious meaning
**incredulously** (in krej′ oo ləs lē) *adv.* in a manner displaying an unwillingness or inability to believe

# explain

## Responding to Reading

### First Impressions

1. What part of the story did you enjoy the most? Why?

### Second Thoughts

2. How is Jackie affected by the stories he hears about confession?

3. What do you think Jackie learns from his first confession?

4. What kind of a person is the priest?

    **Think about**
    • how he acts toward Jackie
    • his stories of grandmother-killers
    • his reaction to Nora

5. How are the teacher's and Nora's reasons for scaring Jackie the same, and how are they different?

6. Who do you think is the most sinful character in the story? Cite evidence to support your answer.

7. How might an author of a selection in "Putting Up a Fight," such as Mark Mathabane or Dylan Thomas, react to this story?

### Broader Connections

8. Think about the methods that the teacher, Nora, and the priest each use to control Jackie's behavior. Then discuss the methods that you think are the most and least effective in getting a child to behave. Explain your reasoning.

## Literary Concept: Comedy

**Comedy** is a light and amusing type of fiction. The main character in a comedy is usually an ordinary person who is confronted by obstacles that lead to some humorous situations. The humor in these situations comes from the fact that they could actually happen even though they seem absurd. Which events in the story seem realistic and possible to you? Which do not?

**Concept Review: Dialect**   Find three examples of dialect in this story. How does dialect contribute to the story?

# Writing Options

1. Pretend that you are Nora, the grandmother, or the priest. Describe how you view Jackie.

2. Find a list of the Ten Commandments. Decide which ones Jackie might have broken and which ones he probably did not break. Write a sentence or two for each commandment, explaining why you think he did or did not break it.

3. A penance is the punishment that a priest decides for a confessor. Write an appropriate penance for Nora to do to make up for her sins.

4. Imagine that Nora has gone back to the teacher to tell her what Jackie did wrong in his first confession. Write a dialogue between Nora and the teacher that shows their reactions to Jackie's experience.

# Vocabulary Practice

**Exercise** Write the letter of the word or phrase that best completes each sentence.

1. If a friend spoke **cryptically** to you about last night, you might (a) ask her what she meant (b) feel insulted (c) call a doctor.
2. Whom would you expect to be the most **fastidious**? (a) a happy-go-lucky clown (b) a strict piano teacher (c) a beggar.
3. You might react **incredulously** if someone told you that (a) a new movie was playing at the theater (b) your teacher was planning a test (c) your best friend won a huge lottery.
4. Which of these actions could **maim** you? (a) you are careless around machinery (b) you oversleep (c) you find a quarter on the floor.
5. If your sister were to **mortify** you in a shopping mall, you would probably (a) buy a necklace for her (b) compliment her good taste (c) blush.

> **Words to Know and Use**
>
> **cryptically
> fastidious
> incredulously
> maim
> mortify**

## *O*ptions for Learning

**1** • **The Cartoonist**  Draw a cartoon that shows what happened to Jackie in the confessional box.

**2** • **The Scene After**  With one or two of your classmates, act out a scene in which Nora and Jackie's teacher discuss Jackie's confession. You might want to include Jackie in the scene to show his reaction to their conversation.

**3** • **An Outside Observer**  From the point of view of an observer in the church at the time of Jackie's confession, tell your class the story of Jackie, Nora, and the priest.

**4** • **Modern Confessions**  Using the *New Catholic Encyclopedia* and the *Readers' Guide to Periodical Literature*, research the changes that have occurred in the practice of confession in the Roman Catholic Church. Report on these changes to the class.

**FACT FINDER**

*How many people in the world today are Roman Catholic?*

## *F*rank O'Connor
### 1903–1966

Frank O'Connor, whose real name was Michael John O'Donovan, seems to have had two sides to him. He showed his political side by joining the Irish Republican Army at sixteen and fighting in the Irish Civil War. He also fought against the censorship of writers and artists. In fact, because of his political involvement, he had to change his name so that he could continue to be published.

The other side of his personality showed when he became famous as a short story writer whose simple style and sense of humor as-sured his literary importance alongside William Butler Yeats and Lady Gregory. He once said, "I was intended by God to be a painter, but I was very poor, and pencil and paper were the cheapest. Literature is the poor man's art." O'Connor was constantly changing his stories, even after they were published. He apparently enjoyed the writing process so much that he characterized it as a growing child: "As a writer I like the feeling I get when some story which I've been trying to bring up in the right way gets up and tells me to go to hell."

*Fiction*

### The
# Happy Man

NAGUIB MAHFOUZ (nu gēb′ mä fōōz′)

## *E*xamine What You Know

In this story, the main character asks if complete happiness is an impossible quest. Do you think it is possible to experience complete happiness in life? If so, what ingredients are necessary? Discuss your opinion with your classmates. Then see how the man in this story is affected by an unexpected surge of happiness.

## *E*xpand Your Knowledge

Naguib Mahfouz is a modern Egyptian writer living in Cairo, the capital of Egypt. Cairo lies on the Nile River and has a population of about 10 million people, more than in any other African city. Like many large cities, Cairo has a wide variety of people, politics, businesses, and problems. As the center of modern Egyptian life, Cairo is at the crossroads of traffic into the Arab world and Africa. Although it has a large middle class whose work and lives resemble those of many Americans, Cairo also has many of the severe problems associated with poverty, lack of education, and unemployment.

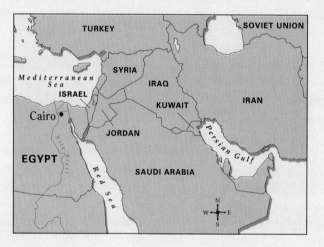

## *W*rite Before You Read

■ *A biography of the author can be found in the Reader's Handbook.*

Think about people you know who seem to be truly happy. Briefly describe their lives and what you think is the source of their happiness.

# The *Happy Man*

NAGUIB MAHFOUZ

He woke up in the morning and discovered that he was happy. "What's this?" he asked himself. He could not think of any word which described his state of mind more accurately and precisely than "happy." This was distinctly peculiar when compared with the state he was usually in when he woke up. He would be half-asleep from staying so late at the newspaper office. He would face life with a sense of strain and contemplation. Then he would get up, whetting his determination to face up to all inconveniences and withstand all difficulties.

Today he felt happy, full of happiness, as a matter of fact. There was no arguing about it. The symptoms were quite clear, and their vigor and obviousness were such as to impose themselves on his senses and mind all at once. Yes, indeed; he was happy. If this was not happiness, then what was? He felt that his limbs were well proportioned and functioning perfectly. They were working in superb harmony with each other and with the world around him. Inside him, he felt a boundless power, an imperishable energy, an ability to achieve anything with confidence, precision, and obvious success. His heart was overflowing with love for people, animals, and things, and with an all-engulfing sense of optimism and joy. It was as if he were no longer troubled or bothered by fear, anxiety, sickness, death, argument, or the question of earning a living. Even more important than that, and something he could not analyze, it was a feeling which penetrated to every cell of his body and soul; it played a tune full of delight, pleasure, serenity, and peace, and hummed in its incredible melodies the whispering sound of the world, which is denied to the unhappy.

He felt drunk with ecstasy and savored it slowly with a feeling of surprise. He asked himself where it had come from and how; the past provided no explanation, and the future could not justify it. Where did it come from, then, and how?! How long would it last? Would it stay with him till breakfast? Would it give him enough time to get to the newspaper office? Just a minute though, he thought . . . it won't last because it can't. If it did, man would be turned into an angel or something even higher. So he told himself that he should devote his attention to savoring it, living with it, and storing up its nectar before it became a mere memory with no way of proving it or even being sure that it had ever existed.

He ate his breakfast with a relish, and this time nothing distracted his attention while he was eating. He gave "Uncle" Bashir, who was waiting on him, such a beaming smile that the poor man felt rather alarmed and taken aback. Usually he would only look in his direction to give orders or ask questions, although, on most occasions, he treated him fairly well.

"Tell me, 'Uncle' Bashir," he asked the servant, "am I a happy man?"

The poor man was startled. He realized why his servant was confused; for the first time ever he was talking to him as a colleague or friend. He encouraged his servant to forget about his worries and asked him with unusual insistence to answer his question.

"Through God's grace and favor, you are happy," the servant replied.

"You mean, I should be happy. Anyone with my job, living in my house, and enjoying my health, should be happy. That's what you want to say. But do you think I'm really happy?"

The servant replied, "You work too hard, Sir"; after yet more insistence, "It's more than any man can stand. . . ."

He hesitated, but his master gestured to him to continue with what he had to say.

"You get angry a lot," he said, "and have fierce arguments with your neighbors. . . ."

He interrupted him by laughing loudly. "What about you?" he asked. "Don't you have any worries?"

"Of course, no man can be free of worry."

"You mean that complete happiness is an impossible quest?"

"That applies to life in general. . . ."

How could he have dreamed up this incredible happiness? He or any other human being? It was a strange, unique happiness, as though it were a private secret he had been given. In the meeting hall of the newspaper building, he spotted his main rival in this world sitting down thumbing through a magazine. The man heard his footsteps but did not look up from the magazine. He had undoubtedly noticed him in some way and was therefore pretending to ignore him so as to keep his own peace of mind. At some circulation meetings, they would argue so violently with each other that sparks began to fly and they would exchange bitter words. One stage more, and they would come to blows. A week ago, his rival had won in the union elections, and he

had lost. He had felt pierced by a sharp, poisoned arrow, and the world had darkened before his eyes. Now here he was approaching his rival's seat; the sight of him sitting there did not make him excited, nor did the memories of their dispute spoil his composure. He approached him with a pure and carefree heart, feeling drunk with his incredible happiness; his face showed an expression full of tolerance and forgiveness. It was as though he were approaching some other man toward whom he had never had any feelings of enmity, or perhaps he might be renewing a friendship again. "Good morning!" he said without feeling any compunction.

The man looked up in amazement. He was silent for a few moments until he recovered, and then returned the greeting curtly. It was as though he did not believe his eyes and ears.

He sat down alongside the man. "Marvelous weather today. . . ." he said.

"Okay. . . ." the other replied guardedly.

"Weather to fill your heart with happiness."

His rival looked at him closely and cautiously. "I'm glad that you're so happy. . . ." he muttered.

"Inconceivably happy. . . ." he replied with a laugh.

"I hope," the man continued in a rather hesitant tone of voice, "that I shan't spoil your happiness at the meeting of the administrative council. . . ."

"Not at all. My views are well-known, but I don't mind if the members adopt your point of view. That won't spoil my happiness!"

"You've changed a great deal overnight," the man said with a smile.

"The fact is that I'm happy, inconceivably happy."

*Words to Know and Use*

**enmity** (en' mə tē) *n.* a bitter attitude toward or hatred for an enemy; hostility
**compunction** (kəm puŋk' shən) *n.* regret
**inconceivably** (in' kən sēv' ə blē) *adv.* in a manner that cannot be understood, imagined, or believed

MAN GLOWING WITH HAPPINESS 1968 Rufino Tamayo Museo Rufino Tamayo,
Mexico City Photograph by Jesus Sanchez Uribe.

The man examined his face carefully. "I bet your dear son has changed his mind about staying in Canada?!" he asked.

"Never, never, my friend," he replied, laughing loudly. "He is still sticking to his decision. . . ."

"But that was the principal reason for your being so sad. . . ."

"Quite true. I've often begged him to come back out of pity for me in my loneliness and to serve his country. But he told me that he's going to open an engineering office with a Canadian partner; in fact, he's invited me to join him in it. Let him live where he'll be happy. I'm quite happy here—as you can see, inconceivably happy. . . ."

The man still looked a little doubtful. "Quite extraordinarily brave!" he said.

"I don't know what it is, but I'm happy in the full meaning of the word."

Yes indeed, this was full happiness; full, firm, weighty, and vital. As deep as absolute power, widespread as the wind, fierce as fire, bewitching as scent, transcending nature. It could not possibly last.

The other man warmed to his display of affection. "The truth is," he said, "that I always picture you as someone with a fierce and violent temperament which causes him a good deal of trouble and leads him to trouble other people."

"Really?"

"You don't know how to make a truce; you've no concept of intermediate solutions. You work with your nerves, with the marrow in your bones. You fight bitterly, as though any problem is a matter of life and death!"

"Yes, that's true."

He accepted the criticism without any difficulty and with an open heart. His wave expanded into a boundless ocean of happiness. He struggled to control an innocent, happy laugh, which the other man interpreted in a way far removed from its pure motives.

"So then," he asked, "you think it's necessary to be able to take a balanced view of events, do you?"

"Of course. I remember, by way of example, the argument we had the day before yesterday about racism. We both had the same views on the subject; it's something worth being zealous about, even to the point of anger. But what kind of anger? An intellectual anger, abstract to a certain extent; not the type which shatters your nerves, ruins your digestion, and gives you palpitations. Not so?"

"That's obvious; I quite understand...." He struggled to control a second laugh and succeeded. His heart refused to renounce one drop of its joy. Racism, Vietnam, Palestine,... no problem could assail that fortress of happiness which was encircling his heart. When he remembered a problem, his heart guffawed. He was happy. It was a tyrannical happiness, despising all misery and laughing at any hardship; it wanted to laugh, dance, sing, and distribute its spirit of laughter, dancing, and singing among the various problems of the world.

He could not bear to stay in his office at the newspaper; he felt no desire to work at all. He hated the very idea of thinking about his daily business and completely failed to bring his mind down from its stronghold in the kingdom of happiness. How could he possibly write about a trolley bus falling into the Nile when he was so intoxicated by this frightening happiness? Yes, it really was frightening. How could it be anything else, when there was no reason for it at all, when it was so strong that it made him exhausted and paralyzed his will; apart from the fact that it had been with him for half a day without letting up in the slightest degree?!

He left the pages of paper blank and started walking backward and forward across the room, laughing and cracking his fingers. . . .

He felt slightly worried; it did not penetrate deep enough to spoil his happiness but paused on the surface of his mind like an abstract idea. It occurred to him that he might recall the tragedies of his life so that he could test their effect on his happiness. Perhaps they would be able to bring back some idea of balance or security, at least until his happiness began to flag a little. For example, he remembered his wife's death in all its various aspects and details. What had happened? The event appeared to him as a series of movements without any meaning or effect, as though it had happened to some other woman, the wife of another man, in some distant historical age. In fact, it had a contagious effect which prompted a smile and then even provoked laughter. He could not stop himself laughing, and there he was guffawing, ha . . . ha . . . ha!

The same thing happened when he remembered the first letter his son had sent him saying that he wanted to emigrate to Canada. The sound of his guffaws as he paraded the bloody tragedies of the world before him would have attracted the attention of the newspaper workers and passersby in the street, had it not been for the thickness of the walls. He could do nothing to dislodge his happiness. Memories of unhappy times hit him like waves being thrown onto a sandy beach under the golden rays of the sun.

He excused himself from attending the administrative council and left the newspaper office without writing a word. After lunch, he lay down on his bed as usual but could not sleep. In fact, sleep seemed an impossibility to him. Nothing gave him any indication that it was coming, even slowly. He was in a place alight and gleaming, resounding with sleeplessness and joy. He had to calm down and relax, to quiet his senses and limbs, but how could he do it? He gave up trying to sleep and got up. He began to hum as he was walking around his house. If this keeps up, he told himself, I won't be able to sleep, just as I can't work or feel sad. It was almost time for him to go to the club, but he did not feel like meeting any friends. What was the point of exchanging views on public affairs and private worries?! What would they think if they found him laughing at every major problem? What would they say? How would they picture things? How would they explain it? No, he did not need anyone, nor did he want to spend the evening talking. He should be by himself and go for a long walk to get rid of some of his excess vitality and think about his situation. What had happened to him? How was it that this incredible happiness had overwhelmed him? How long would he have to carry it on his shoulders? Would it keep depriving him of work, friends, sleep, and peace of mind?! Should he resign himself to it? Should he abandon himself to the flood to play with him as the whim took it? Or should he look for a way out for himself through thought, action, or advice?

♦ ♦ ♦ ♦

When he was called into the examination room in the clinic of his friend, the specialist in internal medicine, he felt a little alarmed. The doctor looked at him with a smile. "You don't look like someone who's complaining about being ill," he said.

"I haven't come to see you because I'm ill," he told the doctor in a hesitant tone of voice, "but because I'm happy!"

The doctor looked piercingly at him with a questioning air.

"Yes," he repeated to underline what he had said, "because I'm happy!"

There was a period of silence. On one side, there was anxiety, and on the other, questioning and amazement.

"It's an incredible feeling which can't be defined in any other way, but it's very serious . . . ."

The doctor laughed. "I wish your illness were contagious," he said, prodding him jokingly.

"Don't treat it as a joke. It's very serious, as I told you. I'll describe it to you. . . ."

He told him all about his happiness from the time he had woken up in the morning till he had felt compelled to visit him.

"Haven't you been taking drugs, alcohol, or tranquilizers?"

"Absolutely nothing like that."

"Have you had some success in an important sphere of your life: work . . . love . . . money?"

"Nothing like that either. I've twice as much to worry about as I have to make me feel glad . . . ."

"Perhaps if you were patient for a while . . . ."

"I've been patient all day. I'm afraid I'll be spending the night wandering around. . . ."

The doctor gave him a precise, careful, and comprehensive examination and then shrugged his shoulders in despair. "You're a picture of health," he said.

"And so?"

"I could advise you to take a sleeping pill, but it would be better if you consulted a nerve specialist. . . ."

The examination was repeated in the nerve specialist's clinic with the selfsame precision, care, and comprehensiveness. "Your nerves are sound," the doctor told him. "They're in enviable condition!"

"Haven't you got a plausible explanation for my condition?" he asked hopefully.

"Consult a gland specialist!" the doctor replied, shaking his head.

The examination was conducted for a third time in the gland specialist's clinic with the same precision, care, and comprehensiveness. "I congratulate you!" the doctor told him. "Your glands are in good condition."

He laughed. He apologized for laughing, laughing as he did so. Laughter was his way of expressing his alarm and despair.

He left the clinic with the feeling that he was alone, alone in the hands of his tyrannical happiness, with no helper, no guide, and no friend. Suddenly, he remembered the doctor's sign he sometimes saw from the window of his office in the newspaper building. It was true that he had no confidence in psychiatrists even though he had read about the significance of psychoanalysis. Apart from that, he knew that their tentacles were very long and they kept their patients tied in a sort of long association. He laughed as he remembered the method of cure through free association and the problems which it eventually uncovers. He was laughing as his feet carried him toward the psychiatrist's clinic, and imagined the doctor listening to his incredible complaints about feeling happy, when he was used to hearing people complain about hysteria, schizophrenia[1], anxiety, and so on.

"The truth is, Doctor, that I've come to see you because I'm happy!"

He looked at the doctor to see what effect his statement had had on him but noticed that he was keeping his composure. He felt ridiculous. "I'm inconceivably happy. . . ." he said in a tone of confidence.

He began to tell the doctor his story, but the latter stopped him with a gesture of his hand. "An overwhelming, incredible, debilitating happiness?" he asked quietly.

He stared at him in amazement and was on the point of saying something, but the doctor spoke first. "A happiness which has made you stop working," he asked, "abandon your friends, and detest going to sleep. . . ?"

"You're a miracle!" he shouted.

"Every time you get involved in some misfortune," the psychiatrist continued quietly, "you dissolve into laughter . . . ?"

"Sir . . . are you familiar with the invisible?"

"No!" he said with a smile, "nothing like that. But I get a similar case in my clinic at least once a week!"

"Is it an epidemic?" he asked.

"I didn't say that, and I wouldn't claim that it's been possible to analyze one case into its primary elements as yet."

"But is it a disease?"

"All the cases are still under treatment."

"But are you satisfied without any doubt that they aren't natural cases . . . ?"

"That's a necessary assumption for the job; there's only. . . ."

"Have you noticed any of them to be deranged in . . . ?" he asked anxiously, pointing to his head.

"Absolutely not," the doctor replied convincingly. "I assure you that they're all intelligent in every sense of the word. . . ."

The doctor thought for a moment. "We should have two sessions a week, I think?" he said.

"Very well. . . ." he replied in resignation.

"There's no sense in getting alarmed or feeling sad. . . ."

Alarmed, sad? He smiled, and his smile kept on getting broader. A laugh slipped out, and before long, he was dissolving into laughter. He was determined to control himself, but his resistance collapsed completely. He started guffawing loudly. . . . ❧

---

1. **schizophrenia** (skit′ se frē′ nē ə): a severe mental disorder characterized by a distortion of reality.

*Words to Know and Use*

**debilitating** (dē bil′ ə tāt′ iŋ) *adj.* making weak or feeble
**deranged** (dē rānjd′) *adj.* insane **derange** *v.*

## Responding to Reading

### First Impressions

    **1.** Did you like this story? Why or why not?

### Second Thoughts

    **2.** How is the main character affected by his newly found happiness?

        **Think about**
- what both his servant and main rival say about how he used to be
- what he considers to be important now
- his psychological reaction to his happiness

    **3.** Why is it ironic that the man seeks medical treatment for his happiness?

    **4.** Do you think that the main character is genuinely happy, or does he really need a psychiatrist? Support your answer with evidence from the story.

    **5.** What is the writer of this story suggesting about the relationship of happiness to life in the modern world?

## Writing Options

    **1.** If you were the psychiatrist in the story, how would you attempt to "cure" the man so that he could function in society? Write your explanation.

    **2.** Can people choose to be happy, or does the source of happiness lie outside the individual? Explain your opinion.

## Vocabulary Practice

**Exercise: Analogies** On your paper, write the letter of the word pair that best expresses a relationship similar to that of the first pair.

    **1.** COMPUNCTION : REGRET :: (a) thankfulness : gratitude (b) complexity : simplicity (c) bird : nest (d) virus : cold

    **2.** ILLNESS : DEBILITATING :: (a) speech : shouting (b) exercise : strengthening (c) hunter : hunting (d) finger : pointing

    **3.** DERANGED : MIND :: (a) towering : skyscraper (b) lively : liveliness (c) old : child (d) ill : medicine

    **4.** ENEMY : ENMITY :: (a) kitten : cat (b) weapons : war (c) trail : path (d) friend : friendship

    **5.** INCONCEIVABLY : BELIEVABLY :: (a) insanely : madly (b) mightily: strongly (c) thirstily : hungrily (d) carelessly : carefully

> *Words to Know and Use*
>
> ---
>
> **compunction**
> **debilitating**
> **deranged**
> **enmity**
> **inconceivably**

Fiction

# A Vietnamese Doll

**VIGDIS STOKKELIEN**

## Examine What You Know

Discuss the different reasons people have for adopting a child. What are the rewards of adoption? What are the problems? What special problems might exist for a couple who adopt a child from a different culture or race? As you read, discover the problems faced in this story by a Norwegian couple who adopt a young Vietnamese child.

## Expand Your Knowledge

During the war in Vietnam, tens of thousands of Vietnamese children became orphans. Many saw their parents killed when their villages and cities were destroyed, while others were deserted by one or both parents. Still others were fathered by American soldiers who returned to the United States without them. Numerous organizations around the world undertook large-scale efforts to find homes for these orphaned children. Several countries, including the Scandinavian countries of Norway, Denmark, and Sweden, were leaders in these efforts to help the small victims of war.

## Write Before You Read

Sometimes we hold very high expectations for someone who ends up being a disappointment to us. Write a brief explanation of a time when you were disappointed by someone of whom you expected more. What did you expect of this person, and why? In what ways were your expectations not met?

# A Vietnamese Doll

### VIGDIS STOKKELIEN

Every morning, until she heard Esther squeaking like a rat in the bedroom, Gøril hoped that it was just a bad dream. The child hadn't arrived yet—in a while she'd go to town, choose some pretty dresses, small shoes, cuddly teddy bears, soft dolls, building bricks, eat lunch with Leif and plan everything for the new child: a musical kindergarten, trips to the zoo . . .

Esther lay on her back in the yellow crib. She stared at the ceiling; her eyes were expressionless.

The cheerful curtains with Donald Duck figures stirred in the light sea breeze. Gøril could hear the waves smack the shore. It smelled of warm earth and cherry trees.

Everything she'd bought during the long waiting period stood untouched on the long, low shelf: a white doll and a black doll, a red-painted doll house with tiny furniture, a candy-striped ball, alphabet blocks, a flute, a drum, a bucket and spade.

Each thing was chosen with care. She'd even tried to find a Vietnamese doll, but there weren't any. So she'd bought a black doll with curly hair, thinking it was more "homey" than a white one. But Esther's skin wasn't dark, it was very light. The dresses in the closet were also unused; the four-year-old could only wear baby clothes.

Lifting the child out of bed, Gøril took in her strange smell, an acridness that reminded her of bark, and for a moment she felt complete aversion. Esther's hair was thin on the crown; little drops of sweat sprang out on her forehead. The narrow brown eyes stared past her, but the child stopped squeaking.

At the airport, when she and Leif stood there together with eight other adoptive parents, she knew immediately that something was wrong. The local paper took pictures: Leif lifting the child up, Gøril giving her the black doll, the child stiff as an Oriental ivory figure.

In the evening the family came to see "the new child." Esther sat where they'd placed her, on the blue sofa, and stared straight ahead; the pile of gifts in cheerful wrappings was left untouched.

"Take her right to the hospital before you get attached to her," said her mother-in-law. "It's sad, but I've had years of experience with children, and this child isn't normal."

"Get attached to." Gøril felt only confusion when she picked up the child; feelings came over her almost too strongly—disgust, fear, compassion.

One of her friends had put it brutally: "You should have a right to a refund on a kid like that. When you're nice enough to take one, they shouldn't send an idiot."

But she was certain that the child wasn't an idiot. Inside she had the strange feeling that Esther was somehow sleeping; if she could only reach her, she would wake up.

"Maybe we should look for a child psychiatrist," Leif had said last night. He tried to talk to Esther, pointed at himself, said "Papa," pointed at the doll and said "Baby."

When he straightened up, she saw that his face was damp with perspiration, that he tried to hide his aversion.

She poured water in the bassinet, set the child in it. Unclad, Esther was a pitiful thing, with a swollen stomach and small baby limbs. She had bad balance, too; her head wobbled, her body moved in little jerks. It was like a weird dance.

Gøril was afraid to soap the small limbs, felt a disgust that crept through her whole body; her fingers twitched away when they came in contact with the tense skin.

One morning when Esther lay there unmoving in a blue towel and she was drying her, a feeling of hopelessness rose in Gøril.

She called the nurse who'd brought the children to this country, expecting to get good advice, sympathy—or maybe she'd really been wishing that the nurse would come and fetch the child, that her days with Esther would lose themselves in memory like a bad dream.

The nurse had said angrily, "I thought you were mature people. Did you believe you'd get a doll baby when you got a child from a country that's been in a war so long?" She'd called forth terrors Gøril could hardly grasp, talked about napalm[1] and death.

It was too awful to listen to.

"She doesn't even understand the language," the nurse had said. "Don't go dragging her around to specialists, give her time, have enough love . . ."

Gøril put the little boat she'd bought a few days ago down in the bath water, pushed it back and forth while she cried, "Tutututu-tut."

For a moment it was as if Esther followed the boat with her eyes—didn't she see the signs of a glimmer of joy in the slanted Asian eyes? No, she stared straight ahead, without expression.

Gøril dressed her, carried her out to the kitchen, brought out vitamins and cornflakes, boiled an egg.

Esther ate a couple of mouthfuls.

"Shall we go to the beach and swim, Esther? Swim?"

Did happiness glint in the dark eyes? Did Esther understand? How should she understand? The child hadn't uttered a sound in the three weeks that she'd been with them, not even in her own language.

To go to the beach took all Gøril's willpower. They were stared at on the road, chattered about in the gardens: "That's the Vietnamese child they took in when they couldn't have one themselves—she's the one who can't have children—and then they got an idiot. Imagine."

Esther could walk, if she wanted; she took a few steps, then sank down on her bottom. Her head wobbled back and forth, her body stiffened when Gøril pulled on her leg.

She'd bought a stroller for the four-year-old, and now Esther was sitting in it, stiff as a stick, staring straight ahead.

On the way to the beach, Gøril prattled along automatically—"See the tree—the car's driving fast—see the kitty—the dog—the flower."

Everyone they met stared at them, stared curiously at the foreign child. Gøril was ready to cry.

She'd dreamed in the months before the adoption came through how it would be, how they would run to the beach, play in the garden.

---

1. **napalm:** a jellylike substance used in flame throwers and bombs.

THE ROAD MENDER'S DAUGHTER   1973   David Shepherd.

Had thought of how the child would rejoice with happiness to come to a home like this—live in a big house with a garden, have good food, real toys, her own room.

They called her Esther after Leif's grandmother. Now it went coldly through Gøril—she couldn't even keep her real name—everything had to be alarmingly foreign.

Down at the beach she lifted Esther high in the air. A gull came toward them on wide wings; the child's fragile body shook.

"Bird—bird," said Gøril and pointed, but Esther didn't follow it with her eyes.

She set the child on a blanket, brought out the colorful buckets and shovels, built a castle, decorated it with shells and seaweed, made ramparts around it.

Far away down the beach some children laughed; they were playing with a polka-dot beach ball.

Suddenly Gøril wept.

"Mama's going swimming."

A sort of longing arose in her to swim far far out, to swim and swim until the water soothed this feeling of helplessness.

The water washed coolingly up toward her thighs. Esther sat there on the blanket, and Gøril imagined that Esther was following her with her eyes, wanting to wave.

Gøril lay in the sea, floating. The sun was hot just over the sea and the shore. In the west, dark clouds floated in over the skerries.[2]

---

2. **skerries:** isolated rocks or reefs in the sea.

On the beach Esther sat like a statue, only her hair lifting in the slight breeze.

Water sprinkled the child as Gøril went ashore, knelt on the sand, filled the colorful buckets, turned them over, saying, "Sand cakes, sand cakes."

It was like talking to a stone.

Then a little finger came as if by accident near the sand cakes; Gøril took the thin hand in hers, led it over the bucket, the sand cakes.

A trembling went through the hand.

Esther slept, and Gøril rigged up a kind of sunscreen, lay down, and peered up at the drifting clouds. As a child she'd made up fairy tales about such clouds, had seen how they took wonderful forms; elves, trolls, fairies from the stories. Now and then a complete pirate ship floated across the sky with filled sails and Captain Kidd[3] at the helm.

She herself must have slept as well, for when she looked up, the sky was dark. Esther squeaked.

"Home, shall we go home?"

Gøril felt a numb tiredness, barely managed to push the stroller over the beach.

It would be that way at home, too. She would pace back and forth, looking at Esther while her dejection grew. Dust settled on bookshelves, the dishes piled up in the sink; she threw together precooked food for dinner, no longer had morning coffee with her friends.

Lightning flashed across the sky.

Esther stirred, and suddenly Gøril's nerves crept to the fingertips of her shaking hands.

Esther got up, holding fast to the stroller frame, and stood there looking at her.

It was eerie, like a dead person waking. Gøril let go of her grip, took a step backward.

Esther just looked at her, and Gøril thought there was hate in her eyes.

Then the thunder sounded over the beach; the lightning zigzagged toward the waves.

Esther threw herself forward, and Gøril caught her in the air, falling to the sand with the child. Esther had gone crazy, was trying to bury herself.

The lightning was so near that Gøril saw it strike; the sand scorched.

And suddenly she clasped the child, covered her completely with her own body, whispered consoling words in her ear, heard herself sob.

Ashamed, Gøril brushed them off, hoped no one had seen it all.

Esther was still sobbing.

And suddenly she understood that Esther believed it was a bombing attack, that she must have dug like that in the earth before, trying to hide herself.

Gøril felt a burning tenderness, held the child close to her, kissed her hair, her cheeks, her nose, whispered meaningless words, "My Esther, no bombs here—they're gulls, not planes—it's thunder and lightning."

For a moment Esther was a tense, shrieking bundle, then she looked right at Gøril.

A little hand stroked Gøril's chin cautiously; tiny fingers caressed her.

They sat there, both of them, and sobbed aloud. 🕭

---

3. **Captain Kidd:** 1645–1701; a famous pirate who was tried and hanged for murder and piracy.

## Responding to Reading

### First Impressions

**1.** With which of the characters, if any, do you sympathize? Explain your answer.

### Second Thoughts

**2.** Why is Gøril so disappointed by Esther?

> **Think about**
> • her expectations about the adoption
> • how she is affected by others' reactions
> • her memories of her own childhood
> • Esther's unresponsiveness

**3.** Why do you think Esther behaves the way she does?

**4.** Who or what is the main source of the difficulties that exist between Esther and her adoptive parents? Cite evidence from the story to support your answer.

**5.** Did your opinion of Gøril change at the end of the story? Why or why not?

**6.** What might Gøril and Esther's relationship be like in the future? What makes you think so?

**7.** How does this story show the power of the individual in human relationships?

### Broader Connections

**8.** Some people believe that cross-cultural adoption is bad for the adoptive parents and especially bad for the child, since it deprives the child of his or her own heritage. What is your opinion about cross-cultural adoption? Why do you feel this way?

## Writing Options

**1.** List possible meanings of the title of this story.

**2.** Write a recommendation to an adoption agency that tells how they might lessen the difficulties faced by adoptive parents of war orphans.

# WORKSHOP

## CREATIVE EXPRESSION

Did you know that the Broadway musical *Les Miserables* is based on a novel by Victor Hugo? Similarly, *Cats* comes from the poems of T. S. Eliot, and *Fiddler on the Roof* is based on the stories of Sholem Aleichem Tevye. The ideas for plays come from every imaginable source, including other works of literature.

As you read "The Demon Lover," "First Confession," "The Happy Man," and "A Vietnamese Doll," you might have visualized what the characters looked like, how they spoke, how they moved, and where they lived. These vivid images in your mind's eye can be brought to others through drama.

In this assignment you will work with a group of classmates to convert fiction to drama. Using the characters, plot, and setting of a short story as the basis for a play, you will tap your creative powers to "translate" one genre to another.

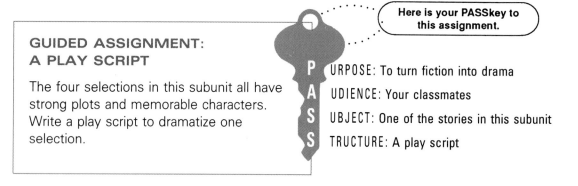

**GUIDED ASSIGNMENT:**
**A PLAY SCRIPT**

The four selections in this subunit all have strong plots and memorable characters. Write a play script to dramatize one selection.

Here is your PASSkey to this assignment.

**P** URPOSE: To turn fiction into drama

**A** UDIENCE: Your classmates

**S** UBJECT: One of the stories in this subunit

**S** TRUCTURE: A play script

## Prewriting

**STEP 1** **Review the selection** Decide which selection you will dramatize and form a group with others who chose the same one. Individually, review the selection carefully. Then, as a group, create a chart that identifies the characters and scenes of the action for your play. Have one group member record the whole group's ideas on the chart. Save planning the plot for later.

One group of students made the following chart to identify the characters and possible scenes for a dramatization of *Kaffir Boy* in the first subunit of this unit.

| Characters | Scenes (settings) |
|---|---|
| Mark: seven-year-old boy<br>Mark's mother<br>Aunt Bushy, Mark's<br>grandmother<br>Woman on street<br>Principal<br>Mark's father | Room where Mark and his<br>mother live<br>The street<br>The principal's office<br>Mark's father's home<br>Aunt Bushy's home |

**STEP 2** **Select events for the plot**  Make an outline or time line of events in the short story. From these events, select those that are key, plus any others that will have dramatic appeal in a play. As you choose events from the short story, fit them onto the basic plot structure below. You might refer to page 245 in "Federigo's Falcon" to remind yourself about the elements of a plot.

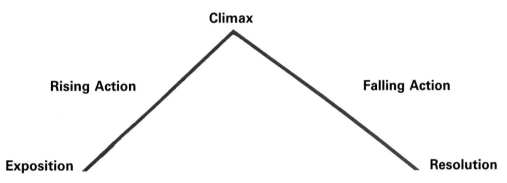

**Climax**

**Rising Action**

**Falling Action**

**Exposition**

**Resolution**

Divide your play into short scenes to indicate changes in location and time.

As scriptwriters, you can take a little creative liberty to make your story work as a play. For example, the group who selected *Kaffir Boy* decided to make the climax of their play the scene between Mark and his father. They made their plot structure as follows:

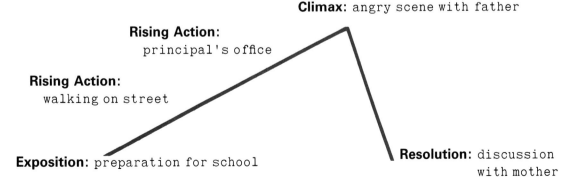

**Climax:** angry scene with father

**Rising Action:** principal's office

**Rising Action:** walking on street

**Exposition:** preparation for school

**Resolution:** discussion with mother

**STEP 3** **Study play formats**   Look carefully at the format of the plays you have read in this book. Model your play script after one of these plays. Pay particular attention to punctuation and capitalization.

**STEP 4** **Consider the effect on the audience**   Before you begin the draft of your play script, think about the tone of the short story. Will your play be a comedy, a tragedy, a farce, a mystery, a tragicomedy? Will the tone be serious, humorous, silly, suspenseful, sentimental? Think about how you want your audience to react to the play. You as writers will influence how the audience feels by what you choose to portray and how you choose to portray it.

## Drafting

**STEP 1** **Write dialogue**   Remember that the plot of a play is revealed through dialogue. Dialogue expresses what the characters feel and think. Use it to inform the audience. Some dialogue can be lifted word for word from the story, but you will need to add more dialogue to the play to present that information that is told in the story by the narrator.

To write the dialogue as a group, you might divide the story into scenes and have two or three people write each scene. In this case, be sure to check for consistency between scenes when all are put together. Or you might assign one or two recorders to write while the group works together through the whole story.

**STEP 2** **Write stage directions**   Write stage directions to indicate the actions that each character takes. Use them also to tell how an actor should deliver a line, when you have a specific manner in mind. Put the stage directions in brackets or parentheses and insert them at the point where the actors and director need to know them.

Here's one student group's dramatization of part of a paragraph from "First Confession."

STUDENT MODEL ▶ **Ryan** *(lighting a candle).* Here's a shiny half-crown, my pretties! Who'll be the first to hold his finger in the flame? Just five minutes, and this coin will be yours. *(loudly taunting)* Are you afraid then? *(slowly and deliberately)* If you're afraid to hold your finger in a little candle flame for five minutes, then shouldn't you be afraid of burning all over in the roasting hot furnaces for all eternity?

**STEP 3** **Check for props and scenery** Make sure your stage directions have identified necessary props. List the props separately. Decide how much scenery is needed to identify each scene. Keep props and scenery to a minimum.

## Revising and Editing

Exchange scripts with another group. Review each other's scripts, using the following questions as a guide for revision. You might want to do a run-through of the play to find sections that need to be revised.

---

### Revision Checklist

1. Is any important part of a scene missing? Will the audience be able to follow the plot easily?
2. Does the dialogue explain what the audience needs to know?
3. Are the directions for actors, scenery, and props described in the stage directions?
4. Is the script in proper form and easy for actors to follow?

---

**Editing** Proofread your play script for correct grammar, usage, spelling, and punctuation. Make a neat, easy to read copy of the script, and duplicate it so that every member of the group has a copy.

## Presenting

Have members of your group volunteer as actors, director, costume designer, lighting designer, choreographer, set designer, music director, and stagehands. Practice your play and then perform it for your class or other classes. You might videotape the performance and store the videotapes in the school library for others to view.

## Reflecting on Your Writing

Answer these questions. Attach your answers to your script and put both in your writing portfolio.

1. How much did your group change the story to fit the dramatic genre? Would you have preferred to change more? less?
2. Which part of the script do you think is strongest? weakest?
3. What were the advantages and disadvantages of writing as a group?
4. Do you think your selection is more or less effective as a play than as a short story? Why?

# LANGUAGE
### WORKSHOP

## UNITY AND COHERENCE

> Two essential qualities of good writing are unity and coherence. A piece of writing has **unity** when all of its ideas are related. A piece of writing has **coherence** when its ideas are linked to one another logically.

### Unity

The sentences in a paragraph and the paragraphs in a composition are like the members of a team. All must work together toward the same goal. If a sentence or paragraph is unrelated or irrelevant, it spoils the unity of the whole work and may confuse the reader. Consider the following paragraph:

> The nineteenth and twentieth centuries saw the emergence of English as a literary language around the globe. Today one finds major works of English-language fiction, drama, and poetry being produced not only in England and the United States but also in places like India and Nigeria. Nigeria has a population of over 64 million. Of all the writers in the so-called third world who are producing works in English, my favorites are India's Kamala Markayana and Nigeria's Chinua Achebe.

Notice that the sentence about the population of Nigeria is unrelated to the purpose of the paragraph, which is to introduce two people from developing countries who write in English. Correcting a problem involving unity is usually quite simple: you just delete the unrelated material. On rare occasions you may find that the unrelated material is what really interests you. If so, you may want to cut everything else and do additional research to make this "unrelated material" the primary focus.

### Coherence

You have just seen that the ideas in a piece of writing should all be related to a single major theme, topic, or purpose. In addition, each idea in a piece of writing should be clearly related to the idea that precedes it and to the one that follows it. In other words, one idea should lead logically to the next throughout the piece.

A piece of writing has coherence when there are clear links between its individual ideas. One way to ensure that your writing has coherence is to organize your ideas in a logical way. Following are some common methods of organization that you can use.

**Chronological Order**  Organization by time of occurrence (first to last or last to first)

**Spatial Order**  Organization by position in space (bottom to top, top to bottom, left to right, right to left, near to far, far to near, etc.)

**Order of Importance**  Organization by importance (least important to most important or vice versa)

**Comparison and Contrast**  Organization by similarities and differences (all the similarities and then all the differences, or vice versa; or one characteristic after another)

**General to Specific**  Organization beginning with broad idea and then giving specifics

**Specific to General**  Organization beginning with specifics and ending with broad idea

Another way to organize ideas is through **part-to-part order.** When you use part-to-part order, you have no overall organizational scheme, but you make sure that each idea is clearly linked to the ideas preceding and following it.

Whatever organizational pattern you choose, you need to link individual ideas together. One way to do this is to use **transitions** such as *next, finally, as a result, to the right, furthermore, on the other hand,* and *consequently.* You can also link ideas by repeating words, by using synonyms, or by using pronouns. Notice in the following example how the phrase "each thing" in the second paragraph refers back to the first paragraph, thus tying the two together.

> Everything she'd bought during the long waiting period stood untouched on the long, low shelf: a white doll and a black doll, a red-painted dollhouse with tiny furniture, a candy-striped ball, alphabet blocks, a flute, a drum, a bucket and spade.
>
> Each thing was chosen with care. She'd even tried to find a Vietnamese doll, but there weren't any.

TRANSITIONS
..........................................
See the Language Workshop at the end of Unit 3, Subunit 3, for a complete treatment of transitions.

**Time:** after, before, during, finally, first, meanwhile, sometimes, when, whenever, immediately

**Place:** above, around, beneath, down, here, there

**Order of importance:** first, second, mainly, most important

**Cause and effect:** as a result, because, therefore, so, for that reason, consequently

**Contrast:** on the other hand, yet, but, however, in contrast

**Comparison:** as, than, in the same way, similarly, likewise

**Exercise 1**   Working with other students in a small group, revise the following paragraph to improve its unity and coherence. Reorganize the ideas in a logical order. Add transitions to show how ideas are connected to one another. Delete any unrelated ideas.

> Make a sketch on the canvas of the object that you want to paint. Place the canvas on the easel. Paint in any large areas of background color, such as for the sky, bodies of water, grass, or foliage. Painting a house can also be enjoyable, but it's completely different, of course. Add the foreground details. Of course, you need to gather all the materials you will need, including an easel, canvas, brushes, paints, paint thinner, paint remover, towels, a palette, and a palette knife. These are the steps that you need to take to do a painting in oils.

**Exercise 2**   Suppose that you are writing each piece below. Explain what method of organization you might use for each and why.

1. a short story about a best friend who turns out, unexpectedly, to be a spy for a foreign country
2. a description of a haunted house
3. a persuasive speech to convince your town to pass a recycling ordinance

**Exercise 3   Style**   Working with other students in a group, look through the selections you have read, or skim through some new selections, and find five examples of transitions. Write the sentences containing the transitions on a sheet of paper and circle the transitions. For each transition, tell what relationship it reveals. Then, look through the selections in this book to find a paragraph organized in spatial order. Find one organized in chronological order. Can you find examples of any other organizational patterns?

**Exercise 4   Analyzing and Revising Your Writing**

1. Choose a piece of writing from your portfolio.
2. Reread the composition, looking for ways to improve its unity and coherence.
3. Revise the composition, deleting unrelated ideas, adding transitions, and improving the organization.
4. Compare your revision to the original piece. Which one communicates your ideas more clearly and effectively?
5. Remember to check for unity and coherence every time you revise your writing.

# Speaking and Listening
### WORKSHOP

## COLLEGE AND JOB INTERVIEWS

Applying for college admission or for a job usually involves an interview. The interview gives the employer or admissions counselor an opportunity to form a first-hand impression of you and of your abilities. It's also an opportunity for you to form an impression of the employer or of the school. For any interview, you need to be prepared.

**1. Do your homework.**   Find out as much as you can before the interview. Brochures, catalogs, and other written materials are a good place to start. Also, try to talk with current students or recent graduates or with current employees. The more you know, the more you'll enjoy and benefit from the interview.

Make a list of questions you think the interviewer might ask. (A school counselor can help with this.) Think carefully about your own skills and abilities as you answer each question clearly and concisely. (Remember to think about what work you *like* to do as well as about your skills. Often what you like to do is what you do best.) Then practice your responses by role-playing with a friend or family member.

Finally, prepare a few questions of your own. Remember that the interview is not just for the interviewer's benefit; it's for yours, too.

**2. Dress appropriately.**   It's better to be a bit overdressed than to appear too casual. Whatever you wear, present a neat appearance.

**3. Be on time.**   Absolutely, positively, do not be late. Find out beforehand where you're going and give yourself plenty of time for unexpected delays.

**4. Speak clearly and thoughtfully.**   An interview is not a conversation with a friend. Your language should be grammatically correct, without slang or negative remarks. Give complete answers, not just yes or no. Try to relax and to speak in a normal conversational tone, addressing the interviewer by name. Show the interviewer that you do not speak without thinking.

**5. Use good body language.**   Use your body to show you are calm and confident. Shake hands firmly, sit up straight, and make eye contact.

**6. Have confidence!**   Remember, you have lots of good qualities. An interview allows you to let those qualities shine. If they do, you'll do well.

**Exercise**   Working with a partner, list questions you might be asked in a college or job interview. Write your own answers to the questions; then take turns role-playing the interview. After each session, review the experience and discuss the effectiveness of the responses.

### QUESTIONS COMMONLY ASKED IN JOB INTERVIEWS

Why are you interested in this job?

Why do you think you can be successful in this job?

What experience do you have?

What has been your best work experience?

### QUESTIONS COMMONLY ASKED IN COLLEGE INTERVIEWS

What are your best subjects?

What subjects do you like least?

What books have you read recently?

Why do you want to attend this college?

What do you want to be doing in ten years?

# PROTECTING INDIVIDUAL DIGNITY

Contemporary history owes much to the stories of individuals and groups who have raised their voices to demand fair treatment or who have quietly defended their dignity. In countries around the world, women, minorities of all kinds, and members of neglected majorities have challenged existing rules and changed power structures to protect individual rights. People of strength, wisdom, and perseverance have proven that individuals can indeed make a difference in matters both large and small.

As you will see, writers from England to Nigeria have been concerned about the protection of individual dignity.

*Fiction*

# No Witchcraft for Sale

## DORIS LESSING

## *E*xamine What You Know

This story, which is set in Southern Rhodesia (rō dē′ zhə), a country in southern Africa now known as Zimbabwe (zim bä′ bwā), describes a conflict caused by misunderstanding between blacks and whites. Using your own experience as a starting point, discuss racial misunderstandings and the factors that contribute to them. In your opinion, how well do blacks and whites know each other?

## *E*xpand Your Knowledge

In the 1800's and early 1900's, most African countries became colonies of European powers, such as Great Britain, France, and Germany, and were dominated politically, economically, and culturally by their rulers. In 1900 Great Britain took possession of Southern Rhodesia, a land of great beauty and mineral wealth that had a large population of British settlers. The white minority dominated the country and kept blacks in inferior positions. In 1965 Southern Rhodesia declared its independence from Great Britain. After a sometimes violent struggle, the black majority gained control of the country in 1980 and renamed it Zimbabwe.

Doris Lessing grew up on a large farm in Southern Rhodesia during the time of British rule. Many of her stories and novels deal sympathetically with the problems that blacks faced in a white-controlled country. In this story she also shows her understanding of African folk medicine. The "witchcraft" of the major black character, Gideon, is derived from his knowledge of healing herbs.

## *E*nrich Your Reading

**Contrasting Attitudes** As you read the story, look for evidence of the contrast between the attitudes of blacks and whites. The questions within the story will help you to think about major cultural differences between the black and white characters.

■ *A biography of the author can be found on page 898.*

# No Witchcraft for Sale

## DORIS LESSING

The Farquars had been childless for years when little Teddy was born; and they were touched by the pleasure of their servants, who brought presents of fowls and eggs and flowers to the homestead when they came to rejoice over the baby, exclaiming with delight over his downy golden head and his blue eyes. They congratulated Mrs. Farquar as if she had achieved a very great thing, and she felt that she had—her smile for the lingering, admiring natives was warm and grateful.

Later, when Teddy had his first haircut, Gideon the cook picked up the soft gold tufts from the ground and held them reverently in his hand. Then he smiled at the little boy and said: "Little Yellow Head." That became the native name for the child. Gideon and Teddy were great friends from the first. When Gideon had finished his work, he would lift Teddy on his shoulders to the shade of a big tree and play with him there, forming curious little toys from twigs and leaves and grass or shaping animals from wetted soil. When Teddy learned to walk it was often Gideon who crouched before him, clucking encouragement, finally catching him when he fell, tossing him up in the air till they both became breathless with laughter. Mrs. Farquar was fond of the old cook because of his love for her child.

There was no second baby; and one day Gideon said: "Ah, missus, missus, the Lord above sent this one; Little Yellow Head is the most good thing we have in our house." Because of that "we" Mrs. Farquar felt a warm impulse toward her cook, and at the end of the month she raised his wages. He had been with her now for several years; he was one of the few natives who had his wife and children in the compound and never wanted to go home to his kraal,[1] which was some hundreds of miles away. Sometimes a small piccanin,[2] who had been born the same time as Teddy, could be seen peering from the edge of the bush, staring in awe at the little white boy with his miraculous fair hair and Northern blue eyes. The two little children would gaze at each other with a wide, interested gaze, and once Teddy put out his hand curiously to touch the black child's cheeks and hair.

Gideon, who was watching, shook his head wonderingly, and said: "Ah, missus, these are both children, and one will grow up to be a baas,[3] and one will be a servant"; and Mrs. Farquar smiled and said sadly, "Yes, Gideon, I was thinking the same." She sighed. "It is God's will," said Gideon, who was a mission boy. The Farquars were very religious people, and this shared feeling about God bound servant and masters even closer together.

---

1. **kraal** (kräl): a native village.
2. **piccanin:** a native child.
3. **baas** (bäs): boss.

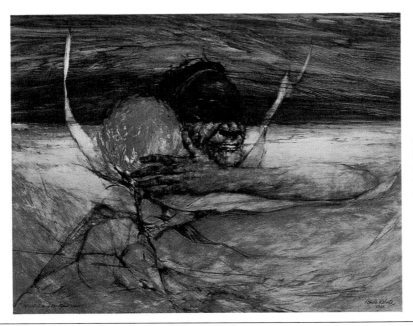

WARATAH AND THE
BLIND HUNTER 1966
Ainslie Roberts from *The
Dawn of Time: Australian
Aboriginal Myths.*

Teddy was about six years old when he was given a scooter and discovered the intoxications of speed. All day he would fly around the homestead, in and out of flowerbeds, scattering squawking chickens and irritated dogs, finishing with a wide, dizzying arc into the kitchen door. There he would cry: "Gideon, look at me!" And Gideon would laugh and say: "Very clever, Little Yellow Head." Gideon's youngest son, who was now a herdsboy, came especially up from the compound to see the scooter. He was afraid to come near it, but Teddy showed off in front of him. "Piccanin," shouted Teddy, "get out of my way!" And he raced in circles around the black child until he was frightened and fled back to the bush.

*infer*          How does Teddy view blacks?

"Why did you frighten him?" asked Gideon, gravely reproachful.

Teddy said defiantly: "He's only a black boy," and laughed. Then, when Gideon turned away from him without speaking, his face fell. Very soon he slipped into the house and found an orange and brought it to Gideon, saying: "This is for you." He could not bring himself to say he was sorry; but he could not bear to lose Gideon's affection either. Gideon took the orange unwillingly and sighed. "Soon you will be going away to school, Little Yellow Head," he said wonderingly, "and then you will be grown-up." He shook his head gently and said, "And that is how our lives go." He seemed to be putting a distance between himself and Teddy, not because of resentment, but in the way a person accepts something inevitable. The baby had lain in his arms and smiled up into his face; the tiny boy had swung from his shoulders and played with him by the hour. Now Gideon would not let his flesh touch the flesh of the white child. He was kind, but there was a grave formality in his voice that made Teddy pout and sulk away. Also, it made him into a man: With Gideon he was polite and carried himself formally, and if he came into the kitchen to ask for something, it was in the way a white man uses toward a servant, expecting to be obeyed.

But on the day that Teddy came staggering into the kitchen with his fists to his eyes, shrieking with pain, Gideon dropped the pot full of hot soup that he was holding, rushed to the child, and forced aside his fingers. "A snake!" he exclaimed. Teddy had been on his scooter and had come to a rest with his foot on the side of a big tub of plants. A tree snake, hanging by its tail from the roof, had spat full into his eyes. Mrs. Farquar came running when she heard the commotion. "He'll go blind," she sobbed, holding Teddy close against her. "Gideon, he'll go blind!" Already the eyes, with perhaps half an hour's sight left in them, were swollen up to the size of fists: Teddy's small white face was distorted by great purple oozing protuberances. Gideon said: "Wait a minute, missus, I'll get some medicine." He ran off into the bush.

Mrs. Farquar lifted the child into the house and bathed his eyes with permanganate.[4] She had scarcely heard Gideon's words; but when she saw that her remedies had no effect at all, and remembered how she had seen natives with no sight in their eyes because of the spitting of a snake, she began to look for the return of her cook, remembering what she heard of the efficacy of native herbs. She stood by the window, holding the terrified, sobbing little boy in her arms, and peered helplessly into the bush. It was not more than a few minutes before she saw Gideon come bounding back, and in his hand he held a plant.

"Do not be afraid, missus," said Gideon, "this will cure Little Yellow Head's eyes." He stripped the leaves from the plant, leaving a small white fleshy root. Without even washing it, he put the root in his mouth, chewed it vigorously, and then held the spittle there while he took the child forcibly from Mrs. Farquar. He gripped Teddy down between his knees and pressed the balls of his thumbs into the swollen eyes, so that the child screamed and Mrs. Farquar cried out in protest: "Gideon, Gideon!" But Gideon took no notice. He knelt over the writhing child, pushing back the puffy lids till chinks of eyeball showed, and then he spat hard, again and again, into first

one eye and then the other. He finally lifted Teddy gently into his mother's arms and said: "His eyes will get better." But Mrs. Farquar was weeping with terror, and she could hardly thank him: It was impossible to believe that Teddy could keep his sight. In a couple of hours the swellings were gone. The eyes were inflamed and tender, but Teddy could see. Mr. and Mrs. Farquar went to Gideon in the kitchen and thanked him over and over again. They felt helpless because of their gratitude: It seemed they could do nothing to express it. They gave Gideon presents for his wife and children, and a big increase in wages, but these things could not pay for Teddy's now completely cured eyes. Mrs. Farquar said: "Gideon, God chose you as an instrument for His goodness," and Gideon said: "Yes, missus, God is very good."

Now, when such a thing happens on a farm, it cannot be long before everyone hears of it. Mr. and Mrs. Farquar told their neighbors, and the story was discussed from one end of the district to the other. The bush is full of secrets. No one can live in Africa, or at least on the veld,[5] without learning very soon that there is an ancient wisdom of leaf and soil and season—and, too, perhaps most important of all, of the darker tracts of the human mind—which is the black man's heritage. Up and down the district people were telling anecdotes, reminding each other of things that had happened to them.

"But I saw it myself, I tell you. It was a puff adder[6] bite. The kaffir's[7] arm was swollen to

---

4. **permanganate** (pər man′ gə nāt′): a chemical compound used as a disinfectant.
5. **veld:** open, grassy country in southern Africa.
6. **puff adder:** a large, poisonous snake.
7. **kaffir** (ká fər): a term of contempt for a black African.

*Words to Know and Use*

**protuberance** (prō tōō′ bər əns) *n.* a bulge or swelling
**efficacy** (ef′ i kə sē) *n.* power to achieve results or to produce intended effects; effectiveness

the elbow, like a great shiny black bladder. He was groggy after a half a minute. He was dying. Then suddenly a kaffir walked out of the bush with his hands full of green stuff. He smeared something on the place, and next day my boy was back at work, and all you could see was two small punctures in the skin."

This was the kind of tale they told. And, as always, with a certain amount of exasperation, because while all of them knew that in the bush of Africa are waiting valuable drugs locked in bark, in simple-looking leaves, in roots, it was impossible to ever get the truth about them from the natives themselves.

The story eventually reached town; and perhaps it was a sundowner party, or some such function, that a doctor who happened to be there challenged it. "Nonsense," he said, "These things get exaggerated in the telling. We are always checking up on this kind of story, and we draw a blank every time."

 What are the different attitudes toward healing herbs?

Anyway, one morning there arrived a strange car at the homestead, and out stepped one of the workers from the laboratory in town, with cases full of test tubes and chemicals.

Mr. and Mrs. Farquar were flustered and pleased and flattered. They asked the scientist to lunch, and they told the story all over again, for the hundredth time. Little Teddy was there too, his blue eyes sparkling with health, to prove the truth of it. The scientist explained how humanity might benefit if this new drug could be offered for sale, and the Farquars were even more pleased: They were kind, simple people who liked to think of

something good coming about because of them. But when the scientist began talking of the money that might result, their manner showed discomfort. Their feelings over the miracle (that was how they thought of it) were so strong and deep and religious that it was distasteful to them to think of money. The scientist, seeing their faces, went back to his first point, which was the advancement of humanity. He was perhaps a trifle perfunctory: It was not the first time he had come salting the tail[8] of a fabulous bush secret.

Why is the scientist skeptical? *infer*

Eventually, when the meal was over, the Farquars called Gideon into their living room and explained to him that this baas here was a Big Doctor from the Big City, and he had come all that way to see Gideon. At this Gideon seemed afraid; he did not understand; and Mrs. Farquar explained quickly that it was because of the wonderful thing he had done with Teddy's eyes that the Big Baas had come.

Gideon looked from Mrs. Farquar to Mr. Farquar and then at the little boy, who was showing great importance because of the occasion. At last he said grudgingly: "The Big Baas want to know what medicine I used?" He spoke incredulously, as if he could not believe his old friends could so betray him. Mr. Farquar began explaining how a useful medicine could be made out of the root, and how it could be put on sale, and how thousands of people, black and white, up and down the continent of Africa, could be saved by the medicine when that spitting snake filled their eyes

8. **salting the tail:** trying to catch the truth.

893

with poison. Gideon listened, his eyes bent on the ground, the skin of his forehead puckering in discomfort. When Mr. Farquar had finished he did not reply. The scientist, who all this time had been leaning back in a big chair, sipping his coffee and smiling with skeptical good humor, chipped in and explained all over again, in different words, about the making of drugs and the progress of science. Also, he offered Gideon a present.

There was a silence after this further explanation, and then Gideon remarked indifferently that he could not remember the root. His face was sullen and hostile, even when he looked at the Farquars, whom he usually treated like old friends. They were beginning to feel annoyed, and this feeling <u>annulled</u> the guilt that had been sprung into life by Gideon's accusing manner. They were beginning to feel that he was unreasonable. But it was at that moment that they all realized that he would never give in. The magical drug would remain where it was, unknown and useless except for the tiny scattering of Africans who had the knowledge, natives who might be digging a ditch for the municipality in a ragged shirt and a pair of patched shorts but who were still born to healing, hereditary healers, being the nephews or sons of the old witch doctors, whose ugly masks and bits of bone and all the uncouth properties of magic were the outward signs of real power and wisdom.

How are the Farquars feeling about Gideon now?

The Farquars might tread on that plant fifty times a day as they passed from house to garden, from cow kraal to mealie[9] field, but they would never know it.

But they went on persuading and arguing, with all the force of their exasperation; and Gideon continued to say that he could not remember, or that there was no such root, or that it was the wrong season of the year, or that it wasn't the root itself, but the spit from his mouth that had cured Teddy's eyes. He said all these things one after another and seemed not to care they were contradictory. He was rude and stubborn. The Farquars could hardly recognize their gentle, lovable old servant in this ignorant, perversely obstinate African, standing there in front of them with lowered eyes, his hands twitching his cook's apron, repeating over and over whichever one of the stupid refusals first entered his head.

And suddenly he appeared to give in. He lifted his head; gave a long, blank, angry look at the circle of whites, who seemed to him like a circle of yelping dogs pressing around him; and said: "I will show you the root."

They walked single file away from the homestead down a kaffir path. It was a blazing December afternoon, with the sky full of hot rain clouds. Everything was hot: The sun was like a bronze tray whirling overhead, there was a heat shimmer over the fields, the soil was scorching underfoot, the dusty wind blew gritty and thick and warm in their faces. It was a terrible day, fit only for reclining on a veranda with iced drinks, which is where they would normally have been at that hour.

From time to time, remembering that on the day of the snake it had taken ten minutes to find the root, someone asked: "Is it much farther, Gideon?" And Gideon would answer over his shoulder, with angry politeness: "I'm looking for the root, baas." And indeed, he

_____

9. **mealie:** an African name for Indian corn.

*Words
to Know
and Use* | **annul** (ə nul') *v.* to do away with; abolish; declare invalid

would frequently bend sideways and trail his hand among the grasses with a gesture that was insulting in its perfunctoriness. He walked them through the bush along unknown paths for two hours in that melting, destroying heat, so that the sweat trickled coldly down them and their heads ached. They were all quite silent; the Farquars because they were angry, the scientist because he was being proved right again; there was no such plant. His was a tactful silence.

At last, six miles from the house, Gideon suddenly decided they had had enough; or perhaps his anger evaporated at that moment. He picked up, without an attempt at looking anything but casual, a handful of blue flowers from the grass, flowers that had been growing plentifully all down the paths they had come.

He handed them to the scientist without looking at him and marched off by himself on the way home, leaving them to follow him if they chose.

 **Has Gideon given the scientist what he wants?**

When they got back to the house, the scientist went to the kitchen to thank Gideon: he was being very polite, even though there was an amused look in his eyes. Gideon was not there. Throwing the flowers casually into the back of his car, the <u>eminent</u> visitor departed on his way back to his laboratory.

Gideon was back in his kitchen in time to prepare dinner, but he was sulking. He spoke to Mr. Farquar like an unwilling servant. It was days before they liked each other again.

The Farquars made enquiries about the root from their laborers. Sometimes they were answered with distrustful stares. Sometimes the natives said: "We do not know. We have never heard of the root." One, the cattle boy, who had been with them a long time and had grown to trust them a little, said: "Ask your boy in the kitchen. Now, there's a doctor for you. He's the son of a famous medicine man who used to be in these parts, and there's nothing he cannot cure." Then he added politely: "Of course, he's not as good as the white man's doctor, we know that, but he's good for us."

## "There's nothing he cannot cure."

After some time, when the soreness had gone from between the Farquars and Gideon, they began to joke: "When are you going to show us the snake root, Gideon?" And he would laugh and shake his head, saying, a little uncomfortably: "But I did show you, missus, have you forgotten?"

Much later, Teddy, as a schoolboy, would come into the kitchen and say: "You old rascal, Gideon! Do you remember that time you tricked us all by making us walk miles all over the veld for nothing? It was so far my father had to carry me!"

And Gideon would double up with polite laughter. After much laughing, he would suddenly straighten himself up, wipe his old eyes, and look sadly at Teddy, who was grinning mischievously at him across the kitchen: "Ah, Little Yellow Head, how you have grown! Soon you will be grown-up with a farm of your own . . ." ❧

---

## *Responding to Reading*

### First Impressions

**1.** Were you glad that Gideon did not share his knowledge of the root with the scientist? Why or why not?

### Second Thoughts

**2.** Why does Gideon refuse to share his knowledge?

> **Think about**
> - the attitude of the whites toward traditional African medicine
> - what might happen to medicine men if they shared their knowledge
> - other reasons Gideon might have for keeping the knowledge to himself

**3.** What is the scientist's attitude toward folk medicine? Is he prejudiced against African traditions or merely cautious as a scientist should be?

**4.** The Farquars believe they are people of "good will." Do you agree? Why or why not?

**5.** How does Teddy's relationship with Gideon and the black children reflect the attitudes of his parents and other whites?

**6.** Both Gideon and Mrs. Farquar say that master and servant roles are "God's will." What do you think is the author's attitude toward those roles? Do you think the story is a protest against conditions in Rhodesia? Explain.

### Broader Connections

**7.** What types of problems do you think occurred when white-controlled Rhodesia made the transition to black-controlled Zimbabwe? How would people such as Teddy, his parents, and Gideon have responded to these changes?

## *Literary Concept: Motivation*

A character's **motivation** is his or her reason or reasons for acting in a certain way. A good author supplies clues about the reasons, impulses, and circumstances that influence the character's behavior, though many times the reader must read between the lines to catch the clues. Create a chart that lists the main motives of Gideon, the scientist, the Farquars, and Teddy. Then compare your chart to those of your classmates.

**Concept Review: Conflict**   What are the major conflicts in the story? How are these conflicts affected by the motivations of the characters?

# Writing Options

1. Compare and contrast Gideon and another character in the book who acts to protect his or her dignity. Which of the two characters do you think is more admirable?

2. As the scientist, write a letter to your colleagues that describes your attempt to find the "magic herb." Make sure that the letter expresses the scientist's attitudes toward African medicine and tradition.

3. Write a dialogue between Gideon and his son in which Gideon explains why he did not give the scientist the healing root.

4. Explain what you think the title means, using examples from the story to support your ideas. Then think of another title that would fit the story.

# Vocabulary Practice

**Exercise**   Write the letter of the sentence that best demonstrates the meaning of the boldfaced word.

1. **eminent**
   a. The obituary listed the awards that the director had won.
   b. Few people knew about her criminal record.
   c. The emergency room seemed frantic after the accident.

2. **efficacy**
   a. Carbon monoxide poisoning can be fatal.
   b. Their family inherited a fortune from a long-lost uncle.
   c. The leader's commands were always obeyed exactly.

3. **protuberance**
   a. The general ordered a dawn invasion of enemy territory.
   b. The wind blew gently through the wheat fields.
   c. The boxer's lips were swollen and bulging after the fight.

4. **annul**
   a. The contractor bought several cases of tiles on sale.
   b. Only a high-ranking official can cancel this agreement.
   c. The coach hoped to build on the team's winning momentum.

5. **perfunctory**
   a. The children listlessly completed their chores.
   b. The violinist gave a spirited performance.
   c. We never expected to learn so much from the tour guide.

## *O*ptions for Learning

**1** • Zimbabwe Independence Investigate the major events that took place before and during the transition from Southern Rhodesia to Zimbabwe. What were the negative and positive effects of the changes in the country?

**2** • Pro and Contra Stage a debate between two teams. One team should argue in favor of Gideon's refusal to share his knowledge; the other should argue against his position. The rest of the class should decide which team presents the most convincing argument.

**3** • Snake Bit Work with a partner to find out how snake poison affects the human body, including the effects of poison that is sprayed in the eye. Give an oral report on your research.

**4** • Folk Pharmacies Research the folk medicine customs of either Africa or a place closer to home. Describe practices that have scientific merit, such as the use of herbal medicines. Then explain the religious or superstitious beliefs that accompany such practices.

### Fact Finder

*What country did Northern Rhodesia become?*

## *D*oris Lessing
### 1919–

Though Doris Lessing was born in Persia (now Iran), her English parents moved to Southern Rhodesia when she was five. She grew up there on a large farm, which employed many poorly paid black workers. Her family lived miles away from the nearest neighbors, and Doris divided her time between reading and long, solitary walks in the African bush. Never comfortable in school, she claimed that her education came from "the storms, the winds, the silences of the bush, the sunlit or rain-whipped mountains, fields of maize miles long." Rebelling against her parents' wishes, she left school at the age of fifteen and worked as a nursemaid, typist, and telephone operator in Salisbury, Southern Rhodesia, until she married at the age of nineteen.

After two failed marriages, Lessing moved to Great Britain in 1949, carrying her two-year-old son and the manuscript for her first novel. Her early fiction was based upon her own life and her intimate knowledge of Rhodesia, especially of the problems between blacks and whites. Because of her outspoken criticism of racism and her radical political sympathies, Lessing was banned from her homeland and South Africa. Her fiction has become increasingly more complex and ambitious, ranging from futuristic fantasies to feminist protests, assuring her reputation as one of the most important writers of the century.

*Poetry*

## The Unknown Citizen

W. H. AUDEN

### Examine What You Know

Think about the attributes of a typical citizen in our society. Fill in a chart like the one below with information that describes this person. Then read to find out how the speaker in this poem views the typical citizen.

| Job | Income | Marital Status | Number of Children | Organizational Memberships |
|-----|--------|----------------|--------------------|----------------------------|
|     |        |                |                    |                            |

### Expand Your Knowledge

With the increased use of computers, the latter part of the twentieth century has become the information age. Records and information about every citizen are kept by many agencies, organizations, and businesses. The government alone has many agencies and departments that keep files on us, such as the Internal Revenue Service, the Bureau of Vital Statistics, the FBI, and Social Security. Advertisers, marketing researchers, union rosters, and personnel departments do the same for businesses. Even schools and local communities have numbered files that track our progress as citizens.

This element of our society was a focus for W. H. Auden and is reflected in his poetry. He is known for his concerns about and criticism of the impersonal nature of our society, which often views people as little more than numbers. This attitude led Auden to create another name for our time: the age of anxiety.

### Write Before You Read

In what agencies, departments, schools, and other groups are you listed as a number? In what public places are you treated as a number? List these groups and places. Then compare your list with those of your classmates.

■ *A biography of the author can be found in the Reader's Handbook.*

# The Unknown Citizen

### W. H. AUDEN

**(To JS/07/M/378 This Marble Monument Is Erected by the State)**

He was found by the Bureau of Statistics to be
One against whom there was no official complaint,
And all the reports on his conduct agree
That, in the modern sense of an old-fashioned word, he was a saint,
5  For in everything he did he served the Greater Community.
Except for the War till the day he retired
He worked in a factory and never got fired,
But satisfied his employers, Fudge Motors Inc.
Yet he wasn't a scab[1] or odd in his views,
10  For his Union reports that he paid his dues,
(Our report on his Union shows it was sound)
And our Social Psychology workers found
That he was popular with his mates and liked a drink.
The Press are convinced that he bought a paper every day
15  And that his reactions to advertisements were normal in every way.
Policies taken out in his name prove that he was fully insured,
And his Health-card shows he was once in hospital but left it cured.
Both Producers Research and High-Grade Living declare
He was fully sensible to the advantages of the Installment Plan[2]
20  And had everything necessary to the Modern Man,
A phonograph, a radio, a car and a frigidaire.
Our researchers into Public Opinion are content
That he held the proper opinions for the time of year;
When there was peace, he was for peace; when there was war, he went.
25  He was married and added five children to the population,
Which our Eugenist[3] says was the right number for a parent of his generation,
And our teachers report that he never interfered with their education.
Was he free? Was he happy? The question is absurd:
Had anything been wrong, we should certainly have heard.

---

1. **scab:** a worker who refuses to support a union strike and crosses a picket line.
2. **Installment Plan:** a payment schedule for a loan.
3. **Eugenist** (yo͞o′ jē nist): a scientist who tries to improve the human race by controlling hereditary factors.

## Responding to Reading

### First Impressions

1. What was your reaction to the unknown citizen?

### Second Thoughts

2. Whom or what does the speaker of this poem represent?

3. What is the speaker's opinion of the unknown citizen? On what is his opinion based? Cite evidence from the poem to support your answer.

4. Do you think the unknown citizen was free and happy? Explain why or why not.

5. What is Auden's attitude toward government and its effect on the individual?

   **Think about**
   • the dedication at the beginning of the poem
   • the kinds of accomplishments cited by the speaker
   • the tone of the poem
   • the meaning of the last two lines

## Literary Concept: Irony

**Irony** is created when a writer says one thing but really means something else. The speaker in this poem says that the unknown citizen "in the modern sense of an old-fashioned word . . . was a saint." What is the meaning of this statement? Consider how the phrase "in the modern sense" affects the meaning. What other examples of irony can you find?

**Concept Review: Free Verse**   How do the irregular rhythm, rhyme, and line length help to reveal the writer's attitude toward society?

## Writing Options

1. List the ways in which you are an "unknown citizen."

2. Explain what you think this poem suggests about the importance of individual dignity and expression. Cite evidence to support your opinion.

*Drama*  # Mother's Day

J. B. PRIESTLEY

## Examine What You Know

Discuss typical complaints that parents and children have about each other. Which complaints, if any, do you think are justified? Why do you think so? As you read, see how the mother in this play, with the help of a neighbor, battles a difficult family situation.

## Expand Your Knowledge

*Mother's Day* is set in a London suburb in the 1930's. The focus of the play is a typical middle-class English family. Like other women of her class and time, the mother is a homemaker whose life centers around her family. She does all the household chores and takes care of all her family's needs. Her grown children, who still live under the same roof, do little to help around the house. Her husband spends most of his free time at his club. Priestley pokes fun at the manners and habits of these characters. A product of a middle-class upbringing himself, he often ridiculed ordinary middle-class characters in his plays and novels.

## Enrich Your Reading

**Understanding Staging** As you read this play, pay careful attention to the stage directions. Some will help you visualize the stage setting. Others will help you visualize the actions of the characters. Still others will help you "hear" how the dialogue might be spoken. Try to imagine a way of performing this play that would make it believable to an audience.

■ *A biography of the author appears on page 917.*

# Mother's Day

J. B. PRIESTLEY

## CHARACTERS

**Mrs. Annie Pearson**

**George Pearson**

**Doris Pearson**

**Cyril Pearson**

**Mrs. Fitzgerald**

The action takes place in the living room of the Pearsons' house in a London suburb.

*Time: The present*

*Scene—The living room of the Pearson family. Afternoon.*

MARY SETTING THE TABLE 1980 Frank Wright Private collection Kennedy Galleries, New York.

*It is a comfortably furnished, much lived-in room in a small suburban semidetached villa.[1] If necessary only one door need be used, but it is better with two—one up left, leading to the front door and the stairs, and the other in the right wall, leading to the kitchen and the back door. There can be a muslin-covered[2] window in the left wall and possibly one in the right wall, too. The fireplace is assumed to be in the fourth wall. There is a settee[3] up right, an armchair down left and one down right. A small table with two chairs either side of it stands center.*

*When the curtain rises it is an afternoon in early autumn, and the stage can be well lit. Mrs. Pearson, at right, and Mrs. Fitzgerald, at left, are sitting opposite each other at the small table, on which are two teacups and saucers and the cards with which Mrs. Fitzgerald has been telling Mrs. Pearson's fortune. Mrs. Pearson is a pleasant but worried-looking woman in her forties. Mrs. Fitzgerald is older,* heavier and a strong and sinister personality. She is smoking. It is very important that these two should have sharply contrasting voices—Mrs. Pearson *speaking in a light, flurried sort of tone, with a touch of suburban Cockney[4] perhaps; and* Mrs. Fitzgerald *with a deep voice, rather Irish perhaps.*

**Mrs. Fitzgerald** *(collecting up the cards)*. And that's all I can tell you, Mrs. Pearson. Could be a good fortune. Could be a bad one. All depends on yourself now. Make up your mind—and there it is.

---

**Mrs. Pearson.** Yes, thank you, Mrs. Fitzgerald. I'm much obliged, I'm sure. It's wonderful having a real fortuneteller living next door. Did you learn that out East, too?

**Mrs. Fitzgerald.** I did. Twelve years I had of it, with my old man rising to be Lieutenant Quartermaster. He learnt a lot, and I learnt a lot more. But will you make up your mind now, Mrs. Pearson dear? Put your foot down, once an' for all, an' be the mistress of your own house an' the boss of your own family.

**Mrs. Pearson** (*smiling apologetically*). That's easier said than done. Besides, I'm so fond of them even if they are so thoughtless and selfish. They don't mean to be . . .

**Mrs. Fitzgerald** (*cutting in*). Maybe not. But it'ud be better for them if they learnt to treat you properly . . .

**Mrs. Pearson.** Yes, I suppose it would, in a way.

**Mrs. Fitzgerald.** No doubt about it at all. Who's the better for being spoilt—grown man, lad or girl? Nobody. You think it does 'em good when you run after them all the time, take their orders as if you were the servant in the house, stay at home every night while they go out enjoying themselves? Never in all your life. It's the ruin of them as well as you. Husbands, sons, daughters should be taking notice of wives an' mothers, not giving 'em orders an' treating 'em like dirt. An' don't tell me you don't know what I mean, for I know more than you've told me.

**Mrs. Pearson** (*dubiously*). I—keep dropping a hint . . .

**Mrs. Fitzgerald.** Hint? It's more than hints your family needs, Mrs. Pearson.

**Mrs. Pearson** (*dubiously*). I suppose it is. But I do hate any unpleasantness. And it's so hard to know where to start. I keep making up my mind to have it out with them—but somehow I don't know how to begin. (*She glances at her watch or at a clock.*) Oh—good gracious! Look at the time. Nothing ready and they'll be home any minute—and probably all in a hurry to go out again . . .

(*As she is about to rise,* Mrs. Fitzgerald *reaches out across the table and pulls her down.*)

**Mrs. Fitzgerald.** Let 'em wait or look after themselves for once. This is where your foot goes down. Start now. (*She lights a cigarette from the one she has just finished.*)

**Mrs. Pearson** (*embarrassed*). Mrs. Fitzgerald—I know you mean well—in fact, I agree with you—but I just can't—and it's no use you trying to make me. If I promise you I'd really have it out with them, I know I wouldn't be able to keep my promise.

**Mrs. Fitzgerald.** Then let me do it.

**Mrs. Pearson** (*flustered*). Oh no—thank you very much, Mrs. Fitzgerald—but that wouldn't do at all. It couldn't possibly be somebody else—they'd resent it at once and wouldn't listen—and really I couldn't blame them. I know I ought to do it—but you see how it is? (*She looks apologetically across the table, smiling rather miserably.*)

**Mrs. Fitzgerald** (*coolly*). You haven't got the idea.

**Mrs. Pearson** (*bewildered*). Oh—I'm sorry—I thought you asked me to let you do it.

**Mrs. Fitzgerald.** I did. But not as me—as *you.*

**Mrs. Pearson.** But—I don't understand. You couldn't be me.

*Words to Know and Use* | **dubiously** (do͞o′ bē əs lē) *adv.* doubtfully; hesitatingly

**Mrs. Fitzgerald** *(coolly).* We change places. Or—really—bodies. You look like me. I look like you.

**Mrs. Pearson.** But that's impossible.

**Mrs. Fitzgerald.** How do you *know?* Ever tried it?

**Mrs. Pearson.** No, of course not . . .

**Mrs. Fitzgerald** *(coolly).* I have. Not for some time, but it still ought to work. Won't last long, but long enough for what we want to do. Learnt it out East, of course, where they're up to all these tricks. *(She holds her hand out across the table, keeping the cigarette in her mouth.)* Gimme your hands, dear.

**Mrs. Pearson** *(dubiously).* Well— I don't know—is it right?

**Mrs. Fitzgerald.** It's your only chance. Give me your hands an' keep quiet a minute. Just don't think about anything. *(taking her hands)* Now look at me.

*(They stare at each other.)*

*(muttering) Arshtatta dum—arshtatta lam—arshtatta lamdumbona . . .*

*(Mrs. Fitzgerald, now with Mrs. Pearson's personality, looks down at herself and sees that her body has changed and gives a scream of fright.)*

**Mrs. Fitzgerald** *(with Mrs. Pearson's personality).* Oh—it's happened.

**Mrs. Pearson** *(complacently).* Of course it's happened. Very neat. Didn't know I had it in me.

**Mrs. Fitzgerald** *(alarmed).* But whatever shall I do, Mrs. Fitzgerald? George and the children can't see me like this.

**Mrs. Pearson** *(grimly).* They aren't going to—

THE LETTER   Frank Wright   Private collection   Kennedy Galleries, New York.

that's the point. They'll have me to deal with—only they won't know it.

**Mrs. Fitzgerald** *(still alarmed).* But what if we can't change back? It'ud be *terrible.*

**Mrs. Pearson.** Here—steady, Mrs. Pearson— if you had to live my life it wouldn't be so bad. You'd have more fun as me than you've had as you . . .

**Mrs. Fitzgerald.** Yes—but I don't want to be anybody else . . .

**Mrs. Pearson.** Now—stop worrying. It's easier changing back—I can do it any time we want . . .

**Mrs. Fitzgerald.** Well—do it now . . .

**Mrs. Pearson.** Not likely. I've got to deal with your family first. That's the idea, isn't it? Didn't know how to begin with 'em, you said. Well. I'll show you.

**Mrs. Fitzgerald.** But what am I going to do?

**Mrs. Pearson.** Go into my house for a bit— there's nobody there—then pop back and see how we're doing. You ought to enjoy it. Better get off now before one of 'em comes.

**Mrs. Fitzgerald** *(nervously rising).* Yes—I suppose that's best. You're sure it'll be all right?

**Mrs. Pearson** *(chuckling).* It'll be *wonderful.* Now off you go, dear.

*(Mrs. Fitzgerald crosses and hurries out through the door right. Left to herself,* Mrs. Pearson *smokes away—lighting another cigarette—and begins laying out the cards for patience on the table.*

*After a few moments* Doris Pearson *comes bursting in left. She is a pretty girl in her early twenties who would be pleasant enough if she had not been spoilt.)*

**Doris** *(before she has taken anything in).* Mum—you'll have to iron my yellow silk. I must wear it tonight. *(She now sees what is happening and is astounded.)* What are you doing? *(She moves down left center.)*

*(Mrs. Pearson* now uses her ordinary voice, but her manner is not fluttering and apologetic but cool and *incisive.)*

**Mrs. Pearson** *(not even looking up).* What d'you think I'm doing—whitewashing the ceiling?

**Doris** *(still astounded).* But you're *smoking!*

**Mrs. Pearson.** That's right, dear. No law against it, is there?

**Doris.** But I thought you didn't smoke.

**Mrs. Pearson.** Then you thought wrong.

**Doris.** Are we having tea in the kitchen?

**Mrs. Pearson.** Have it where you like, dear.

**Doris** *(angrily).* Do you mean it isn't ready?

**Mrs. Pearson.** Yours isn't. I've had all I want. Might go out later and get a square meal at the Clarendon.

**Doris** *(hardly believing her ears).* Who might?

**Mrs. Pearson.** I might. Who d'you think?

**Doris** *(staring at her).* Mum—what's the matter with you?

**Mrs. Pearson.** Don't be silly.

**Doris** *(indignantly).* It's not me that's being silly—and I must say it's a bit much when I've been working hard all day and you can't even bother to get my tea ready. Did you hear what I said about my yellow silk?

**Mrs. Pearson.** No. Don't you like it now? I never did.

**Doris** *(indignantly).* Of course I like it. And I'm going to wear it tonight. So I want it ironing.

**Mrs. Pearson.** Want it ironing? What d'you think it's going to do—iron itself?

**Doris.** No, you're going to iron it for me—you always do.

**Mrs. Pearson.** Well, this time I don't. And don't talk rubbish to me about working hard, I've a good idea how much you do, Doris Pearson. I put in twice the hours you do and get no wages nor thanks for it. Why are you going to wear your yellow silk? Where are you going?

**Doris** *(sulkily).* Out with Charlie Spence.

**Mrs. Pearson.** Why?

**Doris** *(wildly).* Why? Why? What's the matter with you? Why shouldn't I go out with Charlie Spence if he asks me and I want to? Any objections? Go on—you might as well tell me . . .

**Mrs. Pearson** *(severely).* Can't you find anybody better? I wouldn't be seen dead with Charlie Spence. Buck teeth and half-witted. . . .

*Words to Know and Use*

**incisive** (in sī′ siv) *adj.* sharp; keen; penetrating
**indignantly** (in dig′ nənt lē) *adv.* in an angry or scornful manner

**Doris.** He isn't . . .

**Mrs. Pearson.** When I was your age I'd have found somebody better than Charlie Spence—or given myself up as a bad job.

**Doris** (*nearly in tears*). Oh—shut up!

(Doris *runs out left.* Mrs. Pearson *chuckles and begins putting the cards together.*

After a moment Cyril Pearson *enters left. He is the masculine counterpart of Doris.*)

**Cyril** (*briskly*). Hello—Mum. Tea ready?

**Mrs. Pearson.** No.

**Cyril** (*moving to the table; annoyed*). Why not?

**Mrs. Pearson** (*coolly*). I couldn't bother.

**Cyril.** Feeling off-color⁵ or something?

**Mrs. Pearson.** Never felt better in my life.

**Cyril** (*aggressively*). What's the idea then?

**Mrs. Pearson.** Just a change.

**Cyril** (*briskly*). Well, snap out of it, Ma—and get cracking. Haven't too much time.

(Cyril *is about to go when* Mrs. Pearson's *voice checks him.*)

**Mrs. Pearson.** *I've* plenty of time.

**Cyril.** Yes, but I haven't. Got a busy night tonight. (*moving left to the door*) Did you put my things out?

**Mrs. Pearson** (*coolly*). Can't remember. But I doubt it.

**Cyril** (*moving to the table; protesting*). Now—look. When I asked you this morning, you promised. You said you'd have to look through 'em first in case there was any mending.

**Mrs. Pearson.** Yes—well now I've decided I don't like mending.

**Cyril.** That's a nice way to talk—what would happen if we all talked like that?

**Mrs. Pearson.** You all do talk like that. If there's something at home you don't want to do, you don't do it. If it's something at your work, you get the Union to bar it. Now all that's happened is that *I've* joined the movement.

**Cyril** (*staggered*). I don't get this, Mum. What's going on?

**Mrs. Pearson** (<u>laconic</u> *and sinister*). Changes.

(Doris *enters left. She is in the process of dressing and is now wearing a wrap. She looks pale and red eyed.*)

**Mrs. Pearson.** You look terrible. I wouldn't wear that face even for Charlie Spence.

**Doris** (*moving above the table; angrily*). Oh—shut up about Charlie Spence. And anyhow I'm not ready yet—just dressing. And if I do look terrible, it's your fault—you made me cry.

**Cyril** (*curious*). Why—what did she do?

**Doris.** Never you mind.

**Mrs. Pearson** (*rising and preparing to move to the kitchen*). Have we any stout⁶ left? I can't remember.

**Cyril.** Bottle or two, I think. But you don't want stout now.

**Mrs. Pearson** (*moving left slowly*). I do.

**Cyril.** What for?

**Mrs. Pearson** (*turning at the door*). To drink—you clot!

(Mrs. Pearson *exits right. Instantly* Cyril *and* Doris *are in a huddle, close together at left center, rapidly whispering.*)

**Doris.** Has she been like that with you, too?

**Cyril.** Yes—no tea ready—couldn't care less . . .

---

5. **off-color:** slightly ill.

6. **stout:** a dark brown beer.

*Words to Know and Use*

**laconic** (lə kän′ ik) *adj.* using just a few words; concise

907

**Doris.** Well, I'm glad it's both of us. I thought I'd done something wrong.

**Cyril.** So did I. But it's her of course . . .

**Doris.** She was smoking and playing cards when I came in. I couldn't believe my eyes.

**Cyril.** I asked her if she was feeling off-color and she said she wasn't.

**Doris.** Well, she's suddenly all different. An' that's what made me cry. It wasn't what she said but the way she said it—an' the way she *looked*.

**Cyril.** Haven't noticed that. She looks just the same to me.

**Doris.** She doesn't to me. Do you think she could have hit her head or something— y'know—an' got—what is it?—y'know . . .

**Cyril** *(staggered)*. Do you mean she's barmy?[7]

**Doris.** No, you fathead. Y'know—concussion. She might have.

**Cyril.** Sounds far-fetched.

**Doris.** Well, she's far-fetched, if you ask me. *(She suddenly begins to giggle.)*

**Cyril.** Now then—what is it?

**Doris.** If she's going to be like this when Dad comes home . . . *(She giggles again.)*

**Cyril** *(beginning to guffaw)*. I'm staying in for that—two front dress circles for the first house[8] . . .

*(Mrs. Pearson enters right, carrying a bottle of stout and a half-filled glass. Cyril and Doris try to stop their guffawing and giggling, but they are not quick enough. Mrs. Pearson regards them with contempt.)*

**Mrs. Pearson** *(coldly)*. You two are always talking about being grown-up—why don't you both try for once to be your age? *(She moves to the settee and sits.)*

**Cyril.** Can't we laugh now?

**Mrs. Pearson.** Yes, if it's funny. Go on, tell me. Make me laugh. I could do with it.

**Doris.** Y'know you never understand our jokes, Mum . . .

**Mrs. Pearson.** I was yawning at your jokes before you were born, Doris.

**Doris** *(almost tearful again)*. What's making you talk like this? What have we done?

**Mrs. Pearson** *(promptly)*. Nothing but come in, ask for something, go out again, then come back when there's nowhere else to go.

**Cyril** *(aggressively)*. Look—if you won't get tea ready, then I'll find something to eat myself . . .

**Mrs. Pearson.** Why not? Help yourself. *(She takes a sip of stout.)*

**Cyril** *(turning on his way to the kitchen)*. Mind you, I think it's a bit thick.[9] I've been working all day.

**Doris.** Same here.

**Mrs. Pearson** *(calmly)*. Eight-hour day?

**Cyril.** Yes—eight-hour day—an' don't forget it.

**Mrs. Pearson.** I've done my eight hours.

**Cyril.** That's different.

**Doris.** Of course it is.

**Mrs. Pearson** *(calmly)*. It *was*. Now it isn't. Forty-hour week for all now. Just watch it at the week-end when I have my two days off.

*(Doris and Cyril exchange alarmed glances. Then they stare at Mrs. Pearson, who returns their look calmly.)*

**Cyril.** Must grab something to eat. Looks as if I'll need to keep my strength up.

*(Cyril exits to the kitchen.)*

---

7. **barmy:** British slang for crazy.

8. **two front dress circles for the first house:** seats in the lowest balcony above the stage for the first show of the night.

9. **thick:** British slang for excessive; too much to be tolerated.

**Doris** *(moving to the settee; anxiously)*. Mummie, you don't mean you're not going to do *anything* on Saturday and Sunday?

**Mrs. Pearson** *(airily)*. No, I wouldn't go that far. I might make a bed or two and do a bit of cooking *as a favor*. Which means, of course, I'll have to be asked very nicely and thanked for everything and generally made a fuss of. But any of you forty-hour-a-weekers who expect to be waited on hand and foot on Saturday and Sunday, with no thanks for it, are in for a nasty disappointment. Might go off for the week-end perhaps.

**Doris** *(aghast)*. Go off for the week-end?

**Mrs. Pearson.** Why not? I could do with a change. Stuck here day after day, week after week. If I don't need a change, who does?

**Doris.** But where would you go, who would you go with?

**Mrs. Pearson.** That's my business. You don't ask me where you should go and who you should go with, do you?

**Doris.** That's different.

**Mrs. Pearson.** The only difference is that I'm a lot older and better able to look after myself, so it's you who should do the asking.

**Doris.** Did you fall or hit yourself with something?

**Mrs. Pearson** *(coldly)*. No. But I'll hit you with something, girl, if you don't stop asking silly questions.

*(Doris stares at her open-mouthed, ready to cry.)*

**Doris.** Oh—this is awful . . . *(She begins to cry, not passionately.)*

**Mrs. Pearson** *(coldly)*. Stop blubbering. You're not a baby. If you're old enough to go out with Charlie Spence, you're old enough to behave properly. Now stop it.

*(George Pearson enters left. He is about fifty, fundamentally decent but solemn, self-important, pompous. Preferably he should be a heavy, slow-moving type. He notices Doris's tears.)*

**George.** Hello—what's this? Can't be anything to cry about.

**Doris** *(through sobs)*. You'll see.

*(Doris runs out left, with a sob or two on the way. George stares after her a moment, then looks at Mrs. Pearson.)*

**George.** Did she say 'You'll see'?

**Mrs. Pearson.** Yes.

**George.** What did she mean?

**Mrs. Pearson.** Better ask her.

*(George looks slowly again at the door, then at Mrs. Pearson. Then he notices the stout that Mrs. Pearson raises for another sip. His eyes almost bulge.)*

**George.** Stout?

**Mrs. Pearson.** Yes.

**George** *(amazed)*. What are you drinking stout for?

**Mrs. Pearson.** Because I fancied some.

**George.** At this time of day?

**Mrs. Pearson.** Yes—what's wrong with it at this time of day?

**George** *(bewildered)*. Nothing, I suppose, Annie—but I've never seen you do it before . . .

**Mrs. Pearson.** Well, you're seeing me now.

**George** *(with heavy distaste)*. Yes, an' I don't like it. It doesn't look right. I'm surprised at you.

*Words to Know and Use*  | **pompous** (päm′ pəs) *adj.* characterized by exaggerated self-importance

**Mrs. Pearson.** Well, that ought to be a nice change for you.

**George.** What do you mean?

**Mrs. Pearson.** It must be some time since you were surprised at me, George.

**George.** I don't like surprises—I'm all for a steady going on—you ought to know that by this time. By the way, I forgot to tell you this morning I wouldn't want any tea. Special snooker[10] match night at the club tonight—an' a bit of supper going. So no tea.

**Mrs. Pearson.** That's all right. There isn't any.

**George** *(astonished)*. You mean you didn't get any ready?

**Mrs. Pearson.** Yes. And a good thing, too, as it's turned out.

**George** *(aggrieved)*. That's all very well, but suppose I'd wanted some?

**Mrs. Pearson.** My goodness! Listen to the man! Annoyed because I don't get a tea for him that he doesn't even want. Ever tried that at the club?

**George.** Tried what at the club?

**Mrs. Pearson.** Going up to the bar and telling 'em you don't want a glass of beer but you're annoyed because they haven't already poured it out. Try that on them and see what you get.

**George.** I don't know what you're talking about.

**Mrs. Pearson.** They'd laugh at you even more than they do now.

**George** *(indignantly)*. Laugh at me? They don't laugh at me.

**Mrs. Pearson.** Of course they do. You ought to have found that out by this time. Anybody else would have done. You're one of their standing jokes. Famous. They call you

Pompy-ompy Pearson because they think you're so slow and pompous.

**George** *(horrified)*. Never!

**Mrs. Pearson.** It's always beaten me why you should want to spend so much time at a place where they're always laughing at you behind your back and calling you names. Leaving your wife at home, night after night. Instead of going out with her, who doesn't make you look a fool . . .

(Cyril *enters right, with a glass of milk in one hand and a thick slice of cake in the other.* George, *almost dazed, turns to him appealingly.*)

**George.** Here, Cyril, you've been with me to the club once or twice. They don't laugh at me and call me Pompy-ompy Pearson, do they?

(Cyril, *embarrassed, hesitates.*)

*(angrily)* Go on—tell me. Do they?

**Cyril** *(embarrassed)*. Well—yes, Dad. I'm afraid they do.

(George *slowly looks from one to the other, staggered.*)

**George** *(slowly)*. Well—I'll be—damned!

(George *exits left slowly, almost as if somebody had hit him over the head.* Cyril, *after watching him go, turns indignantly to* Mrs. Pearson.)

**Cyril.** Now you shouldn't have told him that, Mum. That's not fair. You've hurt his feelings. Mine, too.

**Mrs. Pearson.** Sometimes it does people good to have their feelings hurt. The truth oughtn't to hurt anybody for long. If your father didn't go to the club so often, perhaps they'd stop laughing at him.

---

10. **snooker:** a variety of pool played with fifteen red balls and six other balls.

*Words to Know and Use* | **aggrieved** (ə grēvd') *adj.* offended; wronged

**Cyril** (*gloomily*). I doubt it.

**Mrs. Pearson** (*severely*). Possibly you do, but what I doubt is whether your opinion's worth having. What do you know? Nothing. You spend too much time and good money at greyhound races and dirt tracks and ice shows . . .

**Cyril** (*sulkily*). Well, what if I do? I've got to enjoy myself somehow, haven't I?

**Mrs. Pearson.** I wouldn't mind so much if you were really enjoying yourself. But are you? And where's it getting you?

*(There is a sharp, hurried knocking heard off left.)*

**Cyril.** Might be for me. I'll see.

*(Cyril hurries out left. In a moment he re-enters, closing the door behind him.)*

It's that silly old bag from next door—Mrs. Fitzgerald. You don't want her here, do you?

**Mrs. Pearson** (*sharply*). Certainly I do. Ask her in. And don't call her a silly old bag neither. She's a very nice woman, with a lot more sense than you'll ever have.

*(Cyril exits left. Mrs. Pearson finishes her stout, smacking her lips.*

*Cyril re-enters left, ushering in Mrs. Fitzgerald, who hesitates in the doorway.)*

Come in, come in, Mrs. Fitzgerald.

**Mrs. Fitzgerald** (*moving to left center; anxiously*). I—just wondered—if everything's—all right . . .

**Cyril** (*sulkily*). No, it isn't.

**Mrs. Pearson** (*sharply*). Of course it is. You be quiet.

**Cyril** (*indignantly and loudly*). Why should I be quiet?

**Mrs. Pearson** (*shouting*). Because I tell you to—you silly, spoilt, young pie-can.[11]

**Mrs. Fitzgerald** (*protesting nervously*). Oh—no—surely . . .

**Mrs. Pearson** (*severely*). Now, Mrs. Fitzgerald, just let me manage my family in my own way—*please!*

**Mrs. Fitzgerald.** Yes—but Cyril . . .

**Cyril** (*sulky and glowering*). Mr. Cyril Pearson to you, please, Mrs. Fitzgerald.

*(Cyril stalks off into the kitchen.)*

**Mrs. Fitzgerald** (*moving to the settee; whispering*). Oh—dear—what's happening?

**Mrs. Pearson** (*calmly*). Nothing much. Just putting 'em in their places, that's all. Doing what you ought to have done long since.

**Mrs. Fitzgerald.** Is George home? (*She sits beside* Mrs. Pearson *on the settee.*)

**Mrs. Pearson.** Yes, I've been telling him what they think of him at the club.

**Mrs. Fitzgerald.** Well, they think a lot of him, don't they?

**Mrs. Pearson.** No, they don't. And now he knows it.

**Mrs. Fitzgerald** (*nervously*). Oh—dear—I wish you hadn't, Mrs. Fitzgerald . . .

**Mrs. Pearson.** Nonsense! Doing 'em all a world of good. And they'll be eating out of your hand soon—you'll see . . .

**Mrs. Fitzgerald.** I don't think I want them eating out of my hand . . .

**Mrs. Pearson** (*impatiently*). Well, whatever you want, they'll be doing it—all three of 'em. Mark my words, Mrs. Pearson.

*(George enters left, glumly. He is unpleasantly surprised when he sees the visitor. He moves to the*

_____

11. **pie-can:** slang for a fool; half-wit.

*armchair left, sits down heavily, and glumly lights his pipe. Then he looks from* Mrs. Pearson *to* Mrs. Fitzgerald, *who is regarding him anxiously.)*

**George.** Just looked in for a minute, I suppose, Mrs. Fitzgerald?

**Mrs. Fitzgerald** *(who doesn't know what she is saying)*. Well—yes—I suppose so, George.

**George** *(aghast)*. George!

**Mrs. Fitzgerald** *(nervously)*. Oh—I'm sorry . . .

**Mrs. Pearson** *(impatiently)*. What does it matter? Your name's George, isn't it? Who d'you think you are—Duke of Edinburgh?

**George** *(angrily)*. What's he got to do with it? Just tell me that. And isn't it bad enough without her calling me George? No tea. Pompy-ompy Pearson. And poor Doris has been crying her eyes out upstairs—yes, crying her eyes out.

**Mrs. Fitzgerald** *(wailing)*. Oh—dear—I ought to have known . . .

**George** *(staring at her, annoyed)*. *You* ought to have known! Why ought you to have known? Nothing to do with you, Mrs. Fitzgerald. Look—we're at sixes and sevens here just now—so perhaps you'll excuse us . . .

**Mrs. Pearson** *(before* Mrs. Fitzgerald *can reply)*. I won't excuse you, George Pearson. Next time a friend and neighbor comes to see me, just say something when you see her—"Good evening" or "How d'you do?" or something—an' don't just march in an' sit down without a word. It's bad manners . . .

**Mrs. Fitzgerald** *(nervously)*. No—it's all right . . .

**Mrs. Pearson.** No, it isn't all right. We'll have some decent manners in this house—or I'll know the reason why. *(glaring at* George) Well?

**George** *(intimidated)*. Well what?

**Mrs. Pearson** *(taunting him)*. Why don't you get off to your club? Special night tonight, isn't it? They'll be waiting for you—wanting to have a good laugh. Go on then. Don't disappoint 'em.

**George** *(bitterly)*. That's right. Make me look silly in front of her now! Go on—don't mind me. Sixes and sevens! Poor Doris been crying her eyes out! Getting the neighbors in to see the fun! *(suddenly losing his temper, glaring at* Mrs. Pearson *and shouting)* All right—let her hear it. What's the matter with you? Have you gone barmy—or what?

**Mrs. Pearson** *(jumping up; savagely)*. If you shout at me again like that, George Pearson, I'll slap your big fat silly face . . .

**Mrs. Fitzgerald** *(moaning)*. Oh—no—no—no—please, Mrs. Fitzgerald . . .

*(Mrs. Pearson sits.)*

**George** *(staring at her, bewildered)*. Either I'm off my chump or you two are. How d'you mean—"No—no, please, Mrs. Fitzgerald"? Look—*you're* Mrs. Fitzgerald. So why are you telling yourself to stop when you're not doing anything? Tell *her* to stop—then there'd be some sense in it. *(staring at* Mrs. Pearson*)* I think you must be tiddly.

**Mrs. Pearson** *(starting up; savagely)*. Say that again, George Pearson.

**George** *(intimidated)*. All right—all right—all right . . .

*(Doris enters left slowly, looking miserable. She is still wearing the wrap.* Mrs. Pearson *sits on the settee.)*

**Mrs. Fitzgerald.** Hello—Doris dear!

*Words to Know and Use* | **taunt** (tônt) *v.* to mock; ridicule

**Doris** *(miserably)*. Hello—Mrs. Fitzgerald!

**Mrs. Fitzgerald.** I thought you were going out with Charlie Spence tonight.

**Doris** *(annoyed)*. What's that to do with you?

**Mrs. Pearson** *(sharply)*. Stop that!

**Mrs. Fitzgerald** *(nervously)*. No—it's all right . . .

**Mrs. Pearson** *(severely)*. It isn't all right. I won't have a daughter of mine talking to anybody like that. Now answer Mrs. Fitzgerald properly, Doris—or go upstairs again . . .

*(Doris looks wonderingly at her father.)*

**George** *(in despair)*. Don't look at me. I give it up. I just give it up.

**Mrs. Pearson** *(fiercely)*. Well? Answer her.

**Doris** *(sulkily)*. I was going out with Charlie Spence tonight—but now I've called it off . . .

**Mrs. Fitzgerald.** Oh—what a pity, dear! Why have you?

**Doris** *(with a flash of temper)*. Because—if you must know—my mother's been going on at me—making me feel miserable—an' saying he's got buck teeth and is half-witted . . .

**Mrs. Fitzgerald** *(rather bolder; to Mrs. Pearson)*. Oh—you shouldn't have said that . . .

**Mrs. Pearson** *(sharply)*. Mrs. Fitzgerald, I'll manage my family—you manage yours.

**George** *(grimly)*. Ticking *her* off now, are you Annie?

**Mrs. Pearson** *(even more grimly)*. They're waiting for you at the club, George, don't forget. And don't you start crying again, Doris . . .

**Mrs. Fitzgerald** *(getting up; with sudden decision)*. That's enough—quite enough.

*(George and Doris stare at her, bewildered.)*

*(To George and Doris)* Now listen, you two. I want to to have a private little talk with Mrs. Fitz—*(she corrects herself hastily)* with Mrs. Pearson, so I'll be obliged if you'll leave us alone for a few minutes. I'll let you know when we've finished. Go on, please. I promise you that you won't regret it. There's something here that only I can deal with.

**George** *(rising)*. I'm glad somebody can—'cos I can't. Come on, Doris.

*(George and Doris exit left. As they go Mrs. Fitzgerald moves to left of the small table and sits. She eagerly beckons Mrs. Pearson to do the same thing.)*

**Mrs. Fitzgerald.** Mrs. Fitzgerald, we must change back now—we really must . . .

**Mrs. Pearson** *(rising)*. Why?

**Mrs. Fitzgerald.** Because this has gone far enough. I can see they're all miserable—and I can't bear it . . .

**Mrs. Pearson.** A bit more of the same would do 'em good. Making a great difference already . . . *(She moves to right of the table and sits.)*

**Mrs. Fitzgerald.** No, I can't stand any more of it—I really can't. We must change back. Hurry up, please, Mrs. Fitzgerald.

**Mrs. Pearson.** Well—if you insist . . .

**Mrs. Fitzgerald.** Yes—I do—please—*please.*

*(She stretches her hands across the table eagerly. Mrs. Pearson takes them.)*

**Mrs. Pearson.** Quiet now. Relax.

*(Mrs. Pearson and Mrs. Fitzgerald stare at each other.)* *(muttering; exactly as before)* Arshtatta dum—arshtatta lam—arshtatta lamdumbona . . .

*(They carry out the same action as before, going* <u>lax</u> *and then coming to life. But this time, of course, they become their proper personalities.)*

---

**Mrs. Fitzgerald.** Ah well—I enjoyed that.

**Mrs. Pearson.** I didn't.

**Mrs. Fitzgerald** Well, you ought to have done. Now—listen, Mrs. Pearson. Don't go soft on 'em again, else it'll all have been wasted . . .

**Mrs. Pearson.** I'll try not to, Mrs. Fitzgerald.

**Mrs. Fitzgerald.** They've not had as long as I'd like to have given 'em—another hour or two's rough treatment might have made it certain . . .

**Mrs. Pearson.** I'm sure they'll do better now—though I don't know how I'm going to explain . . .

**Mrs. Fitzgerald** (severely). Don't you start any explaining or apologizing—or you're done for.

**Mrs. Pearson** (with spirit). It's all right for you, Mrs. Fitzgerald. After all, they aren't your husband and children . . .

**Mrs. Fitzgerald** (impressively). Now you listen to me. You admitted yourself you were spoiling 'em—and they didn't appreciate you. Any apologies—any explanations—an' you'll be straight back where you were. I'm warning you, dear. Just give 'em a look—a tone of voice—now an' again, to suggest you might be tough with 'em if you wanted to be—an' it ought to work. Anyhow, we can test it.

**Mrs. Pearson.** How?

**Mrs. Fitzgerald.** Well, what is it you'd like 'em to do that they don't do? Stop at home for once?

**Mrs. Pearson.** Yes—and give me a hand with supper . . .

**Mrs. Fitzgerald.** Anything you'd like 'em to do—that you enjoy whether they do or not?

**Mrs. Pearson** (hesitating). Well—yes. I—like a nice game of rummy—but, of course, I hardly ever have one—except at Christmas . . .

**Mrs. Fitzgerald** (getting up). That'll do then. (She moves toward the door left, then turns.) But remember—keep firm—or you've had it. (She opens the door. Calling.) Hoy! You can come in now. (Coming away from the door and moving right slightly. Quietly.) But remember—remember—a firm hand.

(George, Doris, and Cyril *file in through the doorway, looking apprehensively at* Mrs. Pearson.)

I'm just off. To let you enjoy yourself.

(The family looks anxiously at Mrs. Pearson, *who smiles. Much relieved, they smile back at her.*)

**Doris** (anxiously). Yes, Mother?

**Mrs. Pearson** (smiling). Seeing that you don't want to go out, I tell you what I thought we'd do . . .

**Mrs. Fitzgerald** (giving a final warning). Remember!

**Mrs. Pearson** (nodding, then looking sharply at the family). No objections, I hope?

**George** (humbly). No, Mother—whatever you say . . .

**Mrs. Pearson** (smiling). I thought we'd have a nice family game of rummy—and then you children could get the supper ready while I have a talk with your father . . .

**George** (firmly). Suits me. (He looks challengingly at the children.) What about you two?

**Cyril** (hastily). Yes—that's all right.

**Doris** (hesitating). Well—I . . .

**Mrs. Pearson** (sharply). What? Speak up!

**Doris** (hastily). Oh—I think it would be lovely . . .

**Mrs. Pearson** (smiling). Good-bye, Mrs. Fitzgerald. Come again soon.

**Mrs. Fitzgerald.** Yes, dear. 'Night all—have a nice time.

(Mrs. Fitzgerald *exits left, and the family cluster round Mother as the curtain falls.*)

## *Responding to Reading*

### First Impressions

**1.** Do you sympathize with any characters in the play? If so, who? If not, why not?

### Second Thoughts

**2.** In what ways, if any, does Mrs. Fitzgerald help Mrs. Pearson? Use evidence from the play to support your answer.

**3.** Whose fault is it that Mrs. Pearson's children and husband treat her the way they do early in the play? Explain.

> **Think about**
> • what the family members expect of one another
> • what the sources of their expectations might be
> • which family members communicate their needs

**4.** Do you think that Mrs. Fitzgerald went too far in her involvement with the Pearsons' family problems? Explain.

**5.** How would you defend Mrs. Pearson's attitude when she is not very grateful to Mrs. Fitzgerald?

**6.** Do you think the changes in each of the Pearsons at the end of the play will be permanent or temporary? Explain your reasoning.

### Broader Connections

**7.** Is Mrs. Pearson's dilemma typical of mothers' problems today? How are her problems like or different from those of mothers you know?

## *Literary Concept: Farce*

A **farce** is a comic play that is based on an absurd plot, ridiculous situations, and humorous dialogue. The sole purpose of a farce is to keep an audience laughing most of the time. The characters are usually stereotyped, like the middle-class Pearsons, and placed in situations that may start out reasonable but soon become far-fetched and laughable. Cite examples of ridiculous situations and humorous dialogue in this play.

**Concept Review: Drama**  What special problems would the director and actors face in staging *Mother's Day?*

## *W*riting Options

1. As a drama critic, write a review of this play. Remember that a critic does not summarize, but rather focuses on what works or doesn't work in the play. Include an evaluation of the play's humor, its meaning, and its effectiveness as a whole.

2. While in Mrs. Pearson's body, Mrs. Fitzgerald says that "sometimes it does people good to have their feelings hurt. The truth oughtn't to hurt anybody for long." Explain why you think she is right or wrong.

3. List some household rules that Mrs. Fitzgerald would want Mrs. Pearson to establish for her husband and children.

4. Write the scene for later that evening in which Mrs. Pearson talks with her husband while her children fix supper. As an alternative, write a scene for the next morning that shows how the family treats the mother after a little time has passed.

## *V*ocabulary Practice

**Exercise** On your paper, write the word from the list that has roughly the same meaning as the words in each pair below.

1. frowning, glaring, _____
2. angrily, furiously, _____
3. injured, offended, _____
4. smugly, self-satisfactorily, _____
5. ridicule, tease, _____
6. doubtfully, uncertainly, _____
7. brief, concise, _____
8. sharp, piercing, _____
9. loose, slack, _____
10. conceited, pretentious, _____

*Words to Know and Use*

aggrieved
complacently
dubiously
glowering
incisive
indignantly
laconic
lax
pompous
taunt

## Options for Learning

**1 • The Play's the Thing** With several classmates, stage this play for your class or school, either in a middle-class English setting of the 1930's or updated to a 1990's American household.

**2 • More of Priestley** Priestley wrote many popular plays, such as *Dangerous Corner* and *An Inspector Calls,* that involve different kinds of character switches. Read one of these other works and report to the class on the similarities and differences between it and *Mother's Day.*

**3 • Comic Switch** With another student whose personality is very different from yours, role-play the switch of your personalities. Use what you know about each other to imitate each other's personality in a convincing way.

**4 • A New Television Series** Imagine that this play is the pilot episode for a new television situation comedy. The second show in the series might continue the conflicts established in the first show. With a few classmates, write this second episode of *Mother's Day.* You might consider having Doris's boyfriend come over for dinner or having one of George's club friends drop by unexpectedly.

 **FACT FINDER**

*In Britain, what is the difference between "tea" and "supper"?*

### J. B. Priestley
1894–1984

Priestley is known for the characters he developed in his novels and plays. These characters come from the entire range of English society, and often their personalities and actions point out some absurd social, political, or business attitude. His works criticize the upper and middle classes, and the working class is also a target for his satire and humor. An extremely popular writer, Priestley completed more than one hundred books and plays, becoming very successful and wealthy. He said, however, that he never wrote to create bestsellers. "I really don't think like that. After all, I don't know what people want—they don't know themselves—and what I am sure of is what I want to do myself."

Essay

# *Black Men and Public Space*
### BRENT STAPLES

## *E*xamine What You Know

Discuss the types of people you see on the street that make you fearful or uneasy. Why are you uncomfortable around these individuals? If you were walking down the street late at night, would others view you as a likely victim or as a possible victimizer? Explain why they would view you as they do and how this makes you feel. Then read to find out how one man is viewed by strangers, and how he is affected by their reactions.

## *E*xpand Your Knowledge

Much of the news we are exposed to on television, on the radio, and in newspapers concerns rising crime rates. Assaults, rapes, robberies, and murders seem to dominate the local evening news shows. There are numerous reasons why these crimes are increasing, including population growth, poverty, drug use, and a lack of economic and educational opportunities. People's fears of certain situations and of specific members of our society, however, have been heightened by the focus of the media. This essay describes an African-American's observations, experiences, and feelings about "being ever the suspect" in urban America.

## *E*nrich Your Reading

**Reading an Essay**   A well-written essay can be more interesting and exciting than fiction when it contains attention-getting devices, real-life experiences, and ironic twists. In this essay, there is an ironic twist in the opening paragraph. As you read this paragraph, be aware of the opinion you are forming of the narrator. Then, as you read on, see if your opinion changes. Try to figure out the effect of the opening paragraph.

■ *A biography of the author can be found in the Reader's Handbook.*

# Black Men and Public Space

### BRENT STAPLES

My first victim was a woman—white, well dressed, probably in her early twenties. I came upon her late one evening on a deserted street in Hyde Park, a relatively <u>affluent</u> neighborhood in an otherwise mean, impoverished section of Chicago. As I swung onto the avenue behind her, there seemed to be a discreet, uninflammatory[1] distance between us. Not so. She cast back a worried glance. To her, the youngish black man—a broad six feet two inches with a beard and billowing hair, both hands shoved into the pockets of a bulky military jacket—seemed menacingly close. After a few more quick glimpses, she picked up her pace and was soon running in earnest. Within seconds she disappeared into a cross street.

That was more than a decade ago. I was twenty-two years old, a graduate student newly arrived at the University of Chicago. It was in the echo of that terrified woman's footfalls that I first began to know the <u>unwieldy</u> inheritance I'd come into—the ability to alter public space in ugly ways. It was clear that she thought herself the quarry of a mugger, a rapist, or worse. Suffering a bout of insomnia, however, I was stalking sleep, not defenseless wayfarers. As a softy who is scarcely able to take a knife to a raw chicken—let alone to hold one to a person's throat—I was surprised, embarrassed, and dismayed all at once. Her flight made me feel like an accomplice in tyranny. It also made it clear that I was indistinguishable from the muggers who occasionally seeped into the area from the surrounding ghetto. That first encounter, and those that followed, signified that a vast, unnerving gulf lay between nighttime pedestrians—particularly women—and me. And I soon gathered that being perceived as dangerous is a hazard in itself. I only needed to turn a corner into a dicey[2] situation, or crowd some frightened, armed person in a foyer somewhere, or make an <u>errant</u> move after being pulled over by a policeman. Where fear and weapons meet—and they often do in urban America—there is always the possibility of death.

In that first year, my first away from my hometown, I was to become thoroughly familiar with the language of fear. At dark, shadowy intersections, I could cross in front of a car stopped at a traffic light and <u>elicit</u> the

---

1. **uninflammatory:** not likely to rouse excitement, anger, or violence.
2. **dicey:** hazardous; chancy; risky.

| *Words to Know and Use* | **affluent** (af′ lo͞o ənt) *adj.* wealthy; prosperous; rich<br>**unwieldy** (un wēl′ dē) *adj.* hard to handle or deal with; awkward<br>**errant** (er′ ənt) *adj.* erring or straying from what is right<br>**elicit** (ē lis′ it) *v.* to cause to be revealed |
|---|---|

*thunk, thunk, thunk, thunk* of the driver—black, white, male, or female—hammering down the door locks. On less traveled streets after dark, I grew accustomed to but never comfortable with people crossing to the other side of the street rather than pass me. Then there were the standard unpleasantries with policemen, doormen, bouncers, cabdrivers, and others whose business it is to screen out troublesome individuals *before* there is any nastiness.

I moved to New York nearly two years ago and I have remained an avid night walker. In central Manhattan, the near-constant crowd cover minimizes tense one-on-one street encounters. Elsewhere—in SoHo, for example, where sidewalks are narrow and tightly spaced buildings shut out the sky—things can get very taut indeed.

After dark, on the warrenlike[3] streets of Brooklyn where I live, I often see women who fear the worst from me. They seem to have set their faces on neutral, and with their purse straps strung across their chests bandolier-style,[4] they forge ahead as though bracing themselves against being tackled. I understand, of course, that the danger they perceive is not a hallucination. Women are particularly vulnerable to street violence, and young black males are drastically over-represented among the perpetrators of that violence. Yet these truths are no solace[5] against the kind of alienation that comes of being ever the suspect, a fearsome entity with whom pedestrians avoid making eye contact.

It is not altogether clear to me how I reached the ripe old age of twenty-two without being conscious of the lethality[6] nighttime pedestrians attributed to me. Perhaps it was because in Chester, Pennsylvania, the small, angry industrial town where I came of age in the 1960s, I was scarcely noticeable against a backdrop of gang warfare, street knifings, and murders. I grew up one of the good boys, had

perhaps a half-dozen fistfights. In retrospect, my shyness of combat has clear sources.

As a boy, I saw countless tough guys locked away; I have since buried several, too. They were babies, really—a teenage cousin, a brother of twenty-two, a childhood friend in his mid-twenties—all gone down in episodes of bravado[7] played out in the streets. I came to doubt the virtues of intimidation early on. I chose, perhaps unconsciously, to remain a shadow—timid, but a survivor.

The fearsomeness mistakenly attributed to me in public places often has a perilous flavor. The most frightening of these confusions occurred in the later 1970s and early 1980s, when I worked as a journalist in Chicago. One day, rushing into the office of a magazine I was writing for with a deadline story in hand, I was mistaken for a burglar. The office manager called security and, with an ad hoc posse,[8] pursued me through the labyrinthine[9] halls, nearly to my editor's door. I had no way of proving who I was. I could only move briskly toward the company of someone who knew me.

Another time I was on assignment for a local paper and killing time before an interview. I entered a jewelry store on the city's affluent Near North Side. The proprietor excused herself and returned with an enormous red Doberman pinscher straining at the end of a leash. She stood, the dog extended toward

---

3. **warrenlike:** crowded like a rabbit-breeding and -living area.

4. **bandolier-style:** over one shoulder and across the chest.

5. **solace:** comfort; consolation.

6. **lethality:** ability to cause death.

7. **bravado:** pretended courage or defiant confidence when there is really little or none.

8. **ad hoc posse:** a group of armed men picked for a single, special purpose.

9. **labyrinthine** (lab′ ə rin′ *th*in): intricate; complicated; like a labyrinth.

HOMAGE TO STERLING BROWN 1972 Charles White Private collection.

me, silent to my questions, her eyes bulging nearly out of her head. I took a cursory look around, nodded, and bade her good night.

Relatively speaking, however, I never fared as badly as another black male journalist. He went to nearby Waukegan, Illinois, a couple of summers ago to work on a story about a murderer who was born there. Mistaking the reporter for the killer, police officers hauled him from his car at gunpoint and but for his press credentials would probably have tried to book him. Such episodes are not uncommon. Black men trade tales like this all the time.

Over the years, I learned to smother the rage I felt at so often being taken for a criminal. Not to do so would surely have led to madness. I now take precautions to make myself less threatening. I move about with care, particularly late in the evening. I give a wide berth[10] to nervous people on subway platforms during the wee hours, particularly when I have exchanged business clothes for jeans. If I happen to be entering a building

behind some people who appear skittish,[11] I may walk by, letting them clear the lobby before I return, so as not to seem to be following them. I have been calm and extremely congenial on those rare occasions when I've been pulled over by the police.

And on late-evening constitutionals[12] I employ what has proved to be an excellent tension-reducing measure: I whistle melodies from Beethoven and Vivaldi and the more popular classical composers. Even steely New Yorkers hunching toward nighttime destinations seem to relax, and occasionally they even join in the tune. Virtually everybody seems to sense that a mugger wouldn't be warbling bright, sunny selections from Vivaldi's *Four Seasons*. It is my equivalent of the cowbell that hikers wear when they know they are in bear country. ❧

---

10. **wide berth:** large space or area.
11. **skittish:** easily frightened; jumpy.
12. **constitutionals:** walks taken for one's health.

921

## Responding to Reading

### First Impressions

1. Did anything in Staples's essay cause you to examine your own feelings and behaviors? Explain.

### Second Thoughts

2. How does Staples's view of himself differ from the way others view him? How does his understanding of these differences affect his behavior?

3. How does Staples's introduction of himself in the first paragraph contrast with the image he presents of himself in later paragraphs? Why do you think he begins his essay the way he does?

4. Do you think the fears of the people Staples encounters are justified? Explain.

5. Do you approve of the ways Staples chooses to deal with the fears of others? Why or why not?

6. In what ways is Staples's problem a problem for everyone? What could be done to eliminate the problem?

## Writing Options

1. Write a descriptive paragraph of Staples from the point of view of the female "victim" presented in the first paragraph of the essay. Then write another paragraph that describes Staples as he sees himself.

2. In a protest letter to a newspaper, explain how people have threatened and damaged the dignity and pride of black men and other male minorities.

## Vocabulary Practice

**Exercise**  On your paper, write *Correct* if the boldfaced word is used correctly or *Incorrect* if it is not. Be prepared to explain each of your answers.

1. Women carrying **unwieldy** purses act as if Staples wants to mug them.
2. He **elicits** defensive behaviors from strangers who fear him.
3. **Affluent** individuals are especially tense in Staples's presence.
4. Staples whistles **errant** melodies to calm nervous passersby.
5. Staples's essay is a **cursory** description of his experiences.

*Words
to Know
and Use*

**affluent**
**cursory**
**elicit**
**errant**
**unwieldy**

*Poetry*

# Telephone Conversation

WOLE SOYINKA (wō′ lā sho yin′ kə)

## Examine What You Know

Think of someone you talked to on the telephone before you met him or her. What mental picture did you form of that person? What words and tone caused that mental picture? When you met the person face to face, how was the person like or different from what you expected? Read this poem to find out the impressions two individuals form of each other through their telephone conversation.

## Expand Your Knowledge

Soyinka created a worldwide awareness of Nigerian culture and Yoruba tribal customs through his plays and poetry. As a Nigerian educated in both Nigeria and London, his understanding of the black experience in a white culture is revealed in his writings. His years as a student in London could easily have given him the experience for this poem. As you read, recall the story on page 163, "When Greek Meets Greek," also about a black man who tries to secure an apartment from a stranger in a predominately white society. Notice that underneath the humor of both pieces lies a commentary on how an individual's dignity can be assaulted in different ways.

## Write Before You Read

Suppose you were renting an apartment to someone. What would you ask a prospective renter who might call? As a landlady or landlord, list questions that you would ask someone who was interested in renting an apartment in your building.

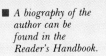

■ *A biography of the author can be found in the Reader's Handbook.*

# Telephone Conversation

### WOLE SOYINKA

TELEPHONE BOOTHS 1967 Richard Estes Thyssen-Bornemisza Collection, Lugano, Switzerland.

The price seemed reasonable, location
Indifferent. The landlady swore she lived
Off premises. Nothing remained
But self-confession. "Madam," I warned,
5 "I hate a wasted journey—I am African."
Silence. Silenced transmission of
Pressurized good breeding. Voice, when it came,
Lipstick coated, long-gold rolled
Cigarette holder pipped. Caught I was, foully.
10 "HOW DARK?" . . . I had not misheard. . . . "ARE YOU LIGHT
OR VERY DARK?" Button B. Button A. Stench
Of rancid breath of public hide-and-speak.
Red booth. Red pillar box. Red double-tiered
Omnibus squelching tar. It *was* real! Shamed
15 By ill-mannered silence, surrender
Pushed dumbfounded to beg simplification.
Considerate she was, varying the emphasis—
"ARE YOU DARK? OR VERY LIGHT?" Revelation came.
"You mean—like plain or milk chocolate?"
20 Her assent was very clinical, crushing in its light
Impersonality. Rapidly, wave-length adjusted,
I chose. "West African sepia"—and as afterthought,
"Down in my passport." Silence for spectroscopic
Flight of fancy, till truthfulness clanged her accent
25 Hard on the mouthpiece. "WHAT'S THAT?" conceding
"DON'T KNOW WHAT THAT IS." "Like brunette."
"THAT'S DARK, ISN'T IT?" "Not altogether.
Facially, I am brunette, but madam, you should see
The rest of me. Palm of my hand, soles of my feet
30 Are a peroxide blonde. Friction, caused—
Foolishly madam—by sitting down, has turned
My bottom raven black—One moment madam!"—sensing
Her receiver rearing on the thunderclap
About my ears—"Madam," I pleaded, "wouldn't you rather
35 See for yourself?"

**9** *What is the speaker's mental picture of the landlady?*

**11** ***Button B. Button A:*** buttons on a British pay phone used to connect with the party at the other end of the line or to hang up.
**13** ***Red pillar box:*** a mail collection box.
**14** ***Omnibus:*** a two-tiered bus.
**16** *How does the speaker react to the landlady's questions?*

**22** *sepia:* a dark reddish-brown color.

**32** *Why is the speaker describing the different shades of color of his body?*
**34** *What does the speaker sense that the landlady is about to do?*

## *R*esponding to Reading

### First Impressions

1. What is your impression of the landlady? What gave you that impression?

### Second Thoughts

2. Why does the speaker think that if he does not identify himself as African, his visit to the landlady's building might be a wasted journey?

3. How and why does the speaker's attitude toward the landlady change throughout the poem? Cite evidence to support your answer.

   **Think about**
   • the landlady's questions about the speaker's appearance
   • the speaker's replies to her questions
   • the landlady's nonverbal reactions to the speaker

4. What is your opinion of the landlady? Refer to your list of questions from Write Before You Read and to lines in the poem to support your opinion.

5. What does the speaker mean by his last question? Is his response justified? Why or why not?

6. Compare the ways in which the speaker of this poem and Brent Staples protect their individual dignity. Which way is more effective? Why?

## *L*iterary Concept: Satire

**Satire** is a literary technique that combines a critical attitude with wit and humor for the purpose of improving society. The attitude of the satirist can be either gentle and polite or biting and angry. What or who is being satirized in "Telephone Conversation"? What is the attitude of the satirist toward his subject?

## *W*riting Options

1. Rewrite the poem as a short telephone skit. Use dialogue from the poem and stage directions so that your skit can be performed for the class.

2. Compare and contrast this poem to "When Greek Meets Greek" on page 163.

## EVALUATION

The yearbook, the senior prom, a class trip, graduation, an embarrassing moment—what will you remember most about your four years of high school? Which experiences have enriched you most? What experiences have frustrated or annoyed you? What would you have liked to change? What person from high school has been most influential in your life?

The characters in the selections in this subunit all have to **evaluate** how to protect their individual dignity; each confronts institutional, cultural, or personal limitations. In this final Guided Assignment, you will have the opportunity to reflect on your high school years and to evaluate your school in a **critical review.**

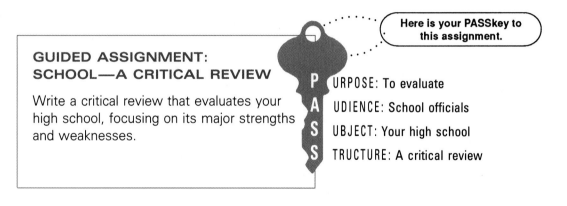

Here is your PASSkey to this assignment.

### GUIDED ASSIGNMENT: SCHOOL—A CRITICAL REVIEW

Write a critical review that evaluates your high school, focusing on its major strengths and weaknesses.

**P**URPOSE: To evaluate

**A**UDIENCE: School officials

**S**UBJECT: Your high school

**S**TRUCTURE: A critical review

## Prewriting

**STEP 1** **Identify elements to evaluate** To help you explore the topic, run through a mental videotape or diary of everything that happens within the course of a typical school day. Try to remember not only a day typical of this year, but think back to ordinary days when you were a freshman or sophomore. Then, with your classmates, brainstorm a list of specific aspects of your high school that you could evaluate. Here is part of a list brainstormed by students:

STUDENT MODEL ▶

| | | |
|---|---|---|
| required courses | school spirit | school rules |
| atmosphere | quality of teaching | athletic program |
| extracurricular activities | course electives | parent involvement |

**STEP 2** **Establish criteria**   Develop criteria with which you will judge your school. What are the qualities of a good school? Does your school possess those qualities? What are the school's strengths? Compare and contrast your school with others. Set your own standards for judging your school's success or failure.

**STEP 3** **Apply the criteria**   Decide which aspects from your list you want to discuss in your paper. Then evaluate how each aspect measures up to your standards. You might rate each aspect on a scale of 1 to 5, with 5 being the best. If you give a poor rating to one aspect, identify your reason. Consider what the administrators, teachers, or students could do to improve it. Think of both positive and negative things to say about the aspects.

**STEP 4** **Organize your information**   Organize by order of importance the points you wish to cover in your review. You might wish to make a topic or sentence outline of your critical review. Be sure to provide evidence—facts, statistics, details, and examples—to support your opinion.

## Drafting

**STEP 1** **Write an introduction**   In your introductory paragraph set the tone of your review. State the subject of your review and indicate your critical position. Use an appropriate, fair tone; don't insult, mock, or unfairly criticize. You want readers, especially the school administrators, to understand that your opinions are well thought out and serious, neither a whining tirade against the school nor gushing tribute to it. Neither "The school stinks" nor "The school is wonderful" is probably true.

**STEP 2** **Write the body**   Write your analysis of your high school, aspect by aspect. Devote a paragraph to each aspect, supporting each rating with specific details and examples. Include both positive and negative points where appropriate. When possible, show how improvements could be made.

### Special Tip
Use precise critical vocabulary in your review. You might use a thesaurus to find words that are specific. For example, "an *enthusiastic* attitude" is more specific than "a *good* attitude."

**STEP 3** **Write the conclusion** End your review by summarizing the strengths and weaknesses of your school and by giving your overall opinion of it. Leave a definite impression—one that emphatically conveys your stand on school issues to the reader.

## Revising and Editing

Use the revision checklist as a guide to help you revise your critical review. Then ask a classmate to read your paper, using the same guidelines.

---

### Revision Checklist

1. Is your critical review a fair evaluation of the school?
2. Is the tone appropriate throughout your review?
3. Are your opinions supported by specific details and examples?
4. Did you include both negative and positive points?
5. If you included a suggestion for improvement, is the suggestion practical and useable?

---

**Editing** Proofread your review for grammar, usage, spelling, punctuation, and capitalization.

## Publishing

As a class and with your teacher's help, analyze the main points presented in the class's critical reviews. Create a school report card to be given to your school principal. Also make copies of the reviews to give to the principal along with the report card.

## Reflecting on Your Writing

Answer the following questions. Turn in the answers with your review.

1. What was the most challenging aspect of reviewing your school?
2. Do you think a school administrator will benefit from reading your paper? Will he or she take it seriously? Explain.
3. Which of the problems that you named do you think could be corrected most easily?

# WRITER'S WORKSHOP

## SELF-ASSESSMENT
## YEAR-END PORTFOLIO REVIEW

Most Writer's Workshops in this book conclude with a section called Reflecting on Your Writing. The questions in these sections ask you to think about the writing you've just completed and to analyze and evaluate your work. Most writers find it very helpful to review their work, even long after the last revision has been completed, because it gives them a chance to examine their progress and to set goals for future writing.

Write a one-page essay in which you report on your achievement this year as a writer. You might wish to write your own PASSKEY for the assignment, identifying your purpose, audience, subject, and structure.

**Prewriting**   Review your writing portfolio. Take extensive notes on what you find there. Be as objective as possible. Think about the aspects of your writing that were weakest at the beginning of the year. If possible, examine a paper you wrote at the end of last year as well. Decide which papers are the best and take notes on the areas in which you improved. Consider which parts of the writing process (prewriting, drafting, revising, editing) are your strengths. Identify some features of your writing that still need work. Make a list of goals for any writing you do in the future.

**Drafting**   Using your notes and lists, write a draft of your essay. As you write, be sure to apply the various standards of good writing you've worked on this year. Keep in mind the need for the following:

- an interesting opening that tells your audience where you are going
- specific details (facts, observations, quotations, summaries) that support each main point
- thoughtful explanations and careful reasoning
- effective, logical organization

Conclude your essay with your future writing goals.

**Revising and Editing**   Design your own Revision Checklist for this assignment and use it to review your essay as honestly as you can. Write a final draft. When you have finished revising, proofread for spelling, clarity, and mechanics.

# LANGUAGE WORKSHOP

## PRONOUN PROBLEMS

**Pronouns,** those words that we use to stand for nouns or other pronouns, are among the first words that we learn as children. They are extremely simple words, but they can cause problems in usage. Fortunately, it's fairly easy to avoid common pronoun problems.

### ▶ Ambiguous Pronoun Reference

When you look at a sentence and can't tell what noun or pronoun the pronoun refers to, what you are seeing is an **ambiguous pronoun reference.**

| | |
|---|---|
| **Unclear** | Gideon found the root of the plant and chewed it. (Did Gideon chew the root or the plant? We can't tell which thing the pronoun *it* refers to. The reference of the pronoun is ambiguous.) |
| **Clear** | After Gideon found the plant, he chewed its root. (The pronoun *its* clearly refers to *plant.*) |
| **Clear** | Gideon found the root and chewed it. (The pronoun *it* clearly refers to *root.*) |

### Lack of Antecedent

▶ The **antecedent** is the word to which the pronoun should refer. Sometimes writers accidently leave out the antecedent, and the reader cannot determine the full meaning of the sentence.

| | |
|---|---|
| **Unclear** | A venomous snake in a tree had sprayed it in Teddy's eyes. (The pronoun *it* does not have a clear antecedent. What did the snake spray?) |
| **Clear** | A venomous snake in a tree had sprayed poison in Teddy's eyes. |

### Pronouns and Contractions

When you join two words and leave out one or more letters, you are making a **contraction.** In a contraction, an apostrophe (') shows where the material is left out of the sentence.

**REMINDER**

Sometimes writers say, *It says in the book.* This is an ambiguous pronoun reference. The correct way to refer to a book is to say, *The book says* or, even better, *The author says.*

**REMINDER**

The noun or pronoun that a pronoun stands for is called the antecedent. In the following sentence, *mime* is the antecedent of *his:* The mime charmed his students.

it's = it + is          they're = they + are

you're = you + are     who's = who + is

Sometimes the contractions shown above are confused with the possessive pronouns *its, your, their,* and *whose.*

**Incorrect**    Its a story that is not about witchcraft at all. (The writer used the possessive pronoun *Its* instead of the contraction *It's.*)

**Correct**      It's a story that is not about witchcraft at all.

**Incorrect**    Gideon will not give the root to the Farquars, and their angry with him. (The writer has used the possessive pronoun *their* instead of the contraction *they're.*)

**Correct**      Gideon will not give the root to the Farquars, and they're angry with him.

One way to determine which word you need is to substitute the words that the contraction stands for. If the sentence sounds right with the contraction spelled out, then the contraction is the word you need.

**Exercise 1**    Rewrite the following sentences, correcting ambiguous pronoun references, missing antecedents, and mistakes in the use of contractions.

1. The two main characters in *Mother's Day* are women with families who decide to have some fun.
2. Mrs. Fitzgerald was telling Mrs. Pearson's fortune and discussing her family problems.
3. Mrs. Pearson could see the problem because she told her all about it.
4. She spoiled her children, and they're ingratitude made her feel like a maid.
5. Mrs. Pearson's feelings were hurt because he was insensitive.

## Who and Whom

Use *who* as a subject or after a linking verb such as *is* or *was.* Use *whom* as an object of a verb or a preposition.

Who wrote that story? (*Who* is the subject of the verb *wrote.*)

The author was who? (*Who* is used after the linking verb *was.*)

Whom did she spoil? (*Whom* is the object of the verb *spoil.*)

To whom did she complain? (*Whom* is the object of the preposition *to.*)

**Exercise 2**  Write the correct pronoun from the choices given in parentheses.

1. (Who, Whom) was the unknown citizen in Auden's poem?
2. For (who, whom) did this citizen work?
3. Did the state really know (who, whom) this citizen was?
4. According to the poem, there was no complaint against (who, whom)?
5. (Who, whom) has any evidence that the unknown citizen was unhappy?

## *We* and *Us* with Nouns

Sometimes the pronouns *we* and *us* are used with nouns, as in the phrase *we novelists* or *us characters.* If you have trouble deciding which pronoun to use, drop the noun and see how the sentence sounds with the pronoun alone.

**Problem**  (We, Us) novelists like to create colorful characters.

**Analysis**  *Us like to create colorful characters* sounds incorrect. *We like to create colorful characters* sounds correct. Therefore, *we* is the correct pronoun to use.

**Problem**  Novelists create (we, us) fictional characters.

**Analysis**  *Novelists create we* sounds incorrect. *Novelists create us* sounds correct. Therefore, *us* is the correct pronoun to use.

**Exercise 3**  Write the correct pronoun from the choices given in parentheses.

1. If (your, you're) reading something by J. B. Priestley, you are probably reading a domestic comedy.
2. (We, Us) readers sometimes compare Priestley to Dickens.
3. However, (they're, their) not exactly alike, as Priestley would tell you himself if he could.
4. (It's, Its) a rare novelist who likes to be compared all the time to a writer who lived before him.
5. (Who's, Whose) going to be content to be compared to others all the time?

LANGUAGE HANDBOOK
.............................
For review and practice:
using pronouns,
pages 987–89, 992–93

# THINKING SKILLS
## WORKSHOP

## MAKING JUDGMENTS AND EVALUATING

> A **judgment** is an informed decision about something. **Evaluation** is the process by which one arrives at a judgment.

Every day you make judgments about people, institutions, products, and ideas. Some of the judgments that you make will be about small matters. Other judgments will affect your life for years to come.

When someone says that a person has good judgment, we might assume that that person was born with the ability to make evaluations, just as some people are born with brown eyes. However, this is not the case. The ability to make sound judgments is a learned skill, like the ability to write or to play basketball. You, too, can learn to make sound judgments by following a few simple guidelines.

## Guidelines for Evaluation

1. The most important step in making an evaluation is to establish **criteria,** or standards against which you will measure your subject. For example, you might use the following criteria to evaluate a car: Do cars of this make and model have a reputation for low maintenance? Will repairs be expensive? Is the car fuel-efficient? Does it have safety features such as seat belts, anti-lock brakes, and an air bag?

2. The next step is to gather information to determine whether the subject meets your criteria. In the case of evaluating a car, you might look at publications such as *Consumer Reports* or *Road and Track* to find maintenance and fuel-efficiency statistics. You might also consult experts, such as your local mechanic.

3. The final step is, of course, to draw a general conclusion about the subject based on whether it meets your specific criteria.

**Exercise** Write criteria for evaluating (1) a stereo system or CD player, (2) a professional football team, (3) a television program, (4) a part-time employer, (5) a congressperson, and (6) a short story. Share your criteria with other students in a class discussion. Combine your lists and come to a consensus, or agreement, on each set of criteria.

### USING GRAPHIC DEVICES

Some people keep track of criteria by making a **pros and cons chart**. To make one of these, you simply list all the positive information that you learn in one column, under the heading "Pros," and all the negative information that you learn in another column, under the heading "Cons." Another possibility is to rate your subject on a scale of 1 to 5, or 1 to 10, with regard to each criterion. Then you can make a bar chart that graphically shows your evaluation of the subject, as in the following example:

| | |
|---|---|
| Cost | XXX |
| Durability | XX |
| Quality | XXXX |
| | 1 2 3 4 5 |

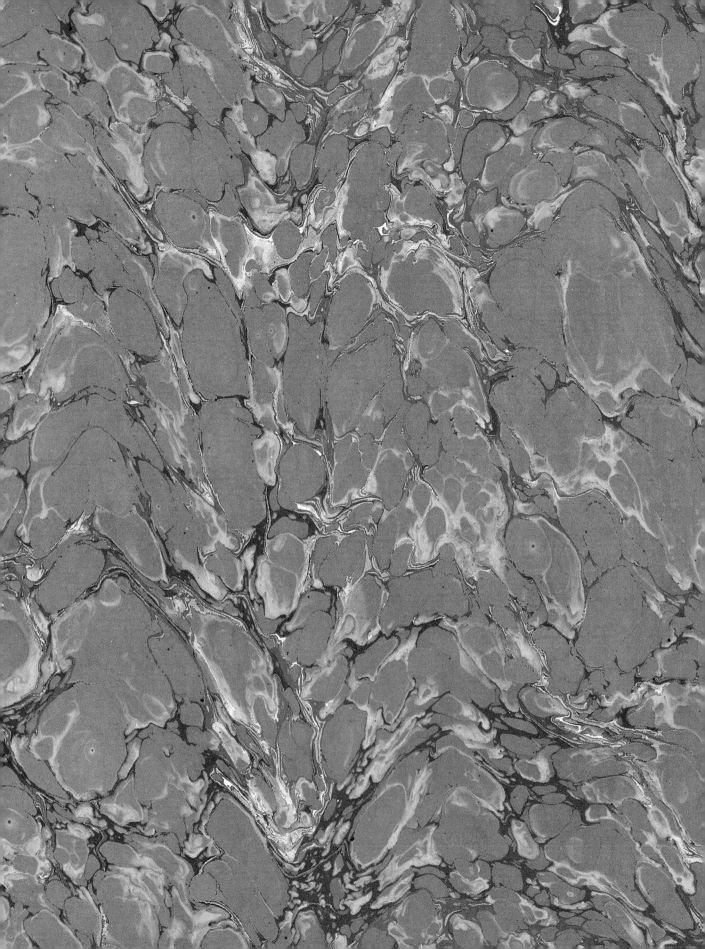

# *Handbook Contents*

## READER'S HANDBOOK

## WRITER'S HANDBOOK

## LANGUAGE HANDBOOK

## GLOSSARY

The **glossary** is an alphabetical listing of words from the selections, with meanings. The glossary gives the following information:

1. **The entry word broken into syllables.**

2. **The pronunciation of each word.** The **respelling** is shown in parentheses. The Pronunciation Key on the next page shows the symbols for the sounds of letters and key words that contain these sounds.

   A **primary accent** ′ is placed after the syllable that is stressed the most when the word is spoken. A **secondary accent** ′ is placed after a syllable that has a lighter stress.

3. **The part of speech of the word.** These abbreviations are used:

   *n.* noun    *v.* verb    *adj.* adjective    *adv.* adverb

4. **The meaning of the word.** The definitions listed in the glossary apply to selected ways a word is used in these selections.

1. entry word —
3. part of speech —
2. respelling
4. meaning

> **def er en tial** (def′ ər en′ shəl)
> *adj.* showing courteous regard
> or respect

## Pronunciation Key

| Symbol | Key Words | Symbol | Key Words | Symbol | Key Words | Symbol | Key Words |
|---|---|---|---|---|---|---|---|
| a | at, gas | o͞o | tool, crew | a in ago | | ch | chin |
| ā | ape, day | o͝o | look, pull | e in agent | | sh | she |
| ä | car, lot | yo͞o | use, cute, few | ə { i in sanity | | th | thin |
| e | elf, ten | yo͝o | cure | o in comply | | th | then |
| ē | even, me | oi | oil, coin | u in focus | | zh | leisure |
| i | is, hit | ou | out, sour | | | ŋ | ring |
| ī | bite, fire | u | up, cut | ər | perhaps, murder | ' | able (ā'b'l) |
| ō | own, go | ur | fur, bird | | | | |
| ô | law, horn | | | | | | |

|   | Foreign | à | salle | n | mon |
|---|---|---|---|---|---|
|   | Symbols | ë | coeur | ô̂ | abuelos |
|   | | ö | feu | r | gringos |
|   | | ü | rue | | |

## A

**a bate** (ə bāt') *v.* to lessen or end

**ac cost** (ə kôst') *v.* to greet first, in a pushy way

**ac qui esce** (ak' wē es') *v.* to agree to without protest

**ac rid** (ak' rid) *adj.* sharp, bitter, or irritating to the taste or smell

**a cute ly** (ə kyo͞ot' lē) *adv.* clearly

**ad ver sar y** (ad' vər ser' ē) *n.* enemy; opponent

**af fa ble** (af' ə bəl) *adj.* pleasant; easy to talk to

**af fect ed** (ə fekt' id) *adj.* behaving in an artificial way to impress people **affect** *v.*

**af flict** (ə flikt') *v.* to cause pain and suffering to

**af flu ent** (af' lo͞o ənt) *adj.* wealthy; prosperous; rich

**af ghan** (af' gan', -gən) *n.* a crocheted or knitted blanket

**ag grieved** (ə grēvd') *adj.* offended; wronged

**am big u ous** (am big' yo͞o əs) *adj.* not clear; uncertain; vague

**a mi a bly** (ā' mē ə blē, ām' yə —) *adv.* in a good-natured way

**a miss** (ə mis') *adv.* in the wrong way

**an ces tral** (an ses' trəl) *adj.* inherited from ancestors

**an guish** (aŋ' gwish) *n.* agony

**an i mate** (an' i māt') *v.* to stimulate to action; inspire

**an nul** (ə nul') *v.* to do away with; abolish; declare invalid

**ap par i tion** (ap' ə rish' ən) *n.* a ghost-like figure that appears suddenly

**ap pre hen sion** (ap' rē hen' shən) *n.* dread; fear

**ap pre hen sive** (ap' rē hen' siv) *adj.* anxious or fearful; uneasy

**ar dent** (ärd' 'nt) *adj.* intensely enthusiastic

**ar ray** (ə rā') *n.* clothes

**as sail** (ə sāl') *v.* to attack violently

**as ser tion** (ə sur' shən) *n.* positive statement; declaration

**as suaged** (ə swājd') *adj.* calmed; pacified **assuage** *v.*

**as sur ance** (ə sho͞or' əns) *n.* self-confidence; certainty

**aus tere** (ô stir') *adj.* showing strict self-discipline and self-denial

**av a rice** (av' ə ris) *n.* greed for wealth

**a ver sion** (ə vur' zhən) *n.* an intense or definite dislike

**a vert** (ə vurt') *v.* to turn away one's glance

**a wry** (ə rī') *adv.* not straight; with a twist to the side; wrong

## B

**be guile** (bē gīl', bi—) *v.* to trick

**be nev o lent** (bə nev' ə lənt) *adj.* doing good; kindly; charitable

**bois ter ous** (bois' tər əs) *adj.* noisy and unruly; rowdy

**bra zen** (brā' zən) *adj.* bold; shameless

## C

**cap ti vate** (kap′ tə vāt′) *v.* to capture the attention or affection of; fascinate

**ca reen** (kə rēn′) *v.* to move wildly from side to side

**co a lesce** (kō′ ə les′) *v.* to unite; combine

**col league** (käl′ ēg′) *n.* a fellow worker in the same profession

**com mend** (kə mend′) *v.* to praise

**com mis er ate** (kə miz′ ər āt′) *v.* to sympathize with

**com mod i ty** (kə mad′ ə tē) *n.* anything bought and sold; any article of commerce

**com mon wealth** (käm′ ən welth′) *n.* a group of people united by common interests

**com pa tri ot** (kəm pā′ trē ət) *n.* a colleague; associate

**com pel** (kəm pel′) *v.* to force to do something

**com pe ten cy** (käm′ pə tən sē) *n.* sufficient resources or money for one's needs. Also, ability, skill, capability

**com pla cent ly** (kəm plā′ sənt lē) *adv.* in a self-satisfied manner

**com ply** (kəm pli′) *v.* to act in agreement with

**com po sure** (kəm pō′ zhər) *n.* a calm manner

**com pul so ry** (kəm pul′ sə rē) *adj.* required; obligatory

**com punc tion** (kəm puŋk′ shən) *n.* regret

**con ceive** (kən sēv′) *v.* to think or imagine; to hold as one's opinion

**con do lence** (kən dō′ ləns) *n.* an expression of sympathy for another's grief

**con jec ture** (kən jek′ chər) *v.* to make a guess or prediction based on incomplete evidence

**con so la tion** (kän′ sə lā′ shən) *n.* comfort

**con spic u ous** (kən spik′ yōō əs) *adj.* easy to see; noticeable; striking

**con tem plate** (kän′ təm plāt′) *v.* to look at intently; to gaze at

**con tempt** (kən tempt′) *n.* the rejection of someone or something as worthless

**con temp tu ous** (kən temp′ chōō əs) *adj.* scornful

**con tort** (kən tôrt′) *v.* to twist out of its usual form; distort

**con trived** (kən trīvd′) *adj.* planned, not spontaneous or natural

**cos mo pol i tan** (käz′ mə päl′ ə tən) *adj.* worldly; common to most parts of the world

**coun te nance** (koun′ tə nəns) *n.* facial features

**cov et ous ness** (kuv′ ət əs nis) *n.* greed

**cowering** (kou′ ər iŋ) *adj.* trembling from fear   **cower** *v.*

**cre dence** (krēd′ ′ns) *n.* belief

**cre ma to ry** (krē′ mə tôr′ ē) *n.* a furnace for cremating dead bodies; also **crematorium**

**cryp ti cal ly** (krip′ ti kəl lē) *adv.* in the manner of having a hidden or mysterious meaning

**cur sory** (kur′ sə rē) *adj.* hasty; performed rapidly with little attention to detail

## D

**de bil i ta ting** (dē bil′ ə tāt′ iŋ) *adj.* making weak or feeble

**def er ence** (def′ ər əns) *n.* courteous respect

**def er en tial** (def′ ər en′ shəl) *adj.* very respectful

**de fi cient** (dē fish′ ənt) *adj.* lacking in some essential

**de file** (dē fīl′) *v.* to make dirty; to violate the honor of

**de flec tion** (dē flek′ shən) *n.* a turning aside or bending

**deft ly** (deft′ lē) *adv.* in a skillful, quick manner

**deign** (dān) *v.* to stoop to do something beneath one's dignity

**dep re cat ing ly** (dep′ rə kāt′ iŋ lē) *adv.* in a manner that expresses disapproval

**de ranged** (dē rānjd′) *adj.* insane

**des o la tion** (des′ ə lā′ shən) *n.* lonely grief; misery; loneliness

**de tach ment** (dē tach′ mənt) *n.* the state of being disinterested, impartial, or aloof

**dev as tate** (dev′ əs tāt′) *v.* to overwhelm; to make helpless

**dex ter i ty** (deks ter′ ə tē) *n.* skill in using one's hands or body

**dis cern** (di zurn′) *v.* to recognize; to make out clearly

**dis con cert ing** (dis′ kən surt′ iŋ) *adj.* in a manner that is upsetting   **disconcert** *v.*

**dis con cert ing ly** (dis′ kən surt′ iŋ lē) *adv.* in a manner that shows one's confusion

**dis creet** (di skrēt′) *adj.* careful about what one says or does

**dis cre tion** (di skresh′ ən) *n.* the quality of being careful about one's actions or words

**dis perse** (di spurs′) *v.* to break up and scatter; to spread widely

**dis pos sessed** (dis′ pə zest′) *adj.* deprived of the possession of something

**dis sect** (di sekt′) *v.* to cut apart into separate pieces, often for studying

**dis so lute** (dis′ ə lōōt′) *adj.* immoral

**dis sua sion** (di swā′ zhən) *n.* the act of advising against an action

**di vert** (də vurt′) *v.* to amuse; entertain

**di vulge** (də vulj′) *v.* to make known; reveal

**dog ged** (dôg′ id) *adj.* stubborn, persistent
**du bi ous ly** (doo′ bē əs lē) *adv.* doubtfully; hesitatingly

## E

**ec stat i cal ly** (ek stat′ i kəl lē) *adv.* in a joyful manner
**ed i fi ca tion** (ed′ i fi kā′ shən) *n.* instruction; improvement
**ef fi ca cy** (ef′ i kə sē) *n.* power to achieve results or to produce intended effects; effectiveness
**ef fus ive** (e fyoo′ siv) *adj.* excessively emotional
**e lab o rate** (e lab′ ə rit) *adj.* complicated; developed in great detail
**e la tion** (ē lā′ shən) *n.* extreme joy
**e lic it** (ē lis′ it) *v.* to cause to be revealed
**e lite** (ä lēt′, i lēt′) *n.* the finest or best group
**e lude** (ē lood′) *v.* to avoid or escape
**e ma ci at ed** (ē mā′ shē āt′ id) *adj.* abnormally lean or thin, as from starvation or disease
**em a nate** (em′ ə nāt′) *v.* to come forth from a source
**e man ci pate** (ē man′ sə pāt′) *v.* to set free from restraint or control
**em i nent** (em′ ə nənt) *adj.* renowned; distinguished; honored
**em phat i cal ly** (em fat′ i kəl lē) *adv.* forcefully; definitely
**en deav or** (en dev′ ər) *n.* an earnest attempt or effort
**en gross** (en grōs′) *v.* to take one's entire attention
**e nig mat i cal ly** (en′ ig mat′ ik lē) *adv.* in a perplexing or obscure manner; mysteriously
**en mi ty** (en′ mə tē) *n.* a bitter attitude toward or hatred for an enemy; hostility
**en rap ture** (en rap′ chər) *v.* to fill with great pleasure or delight; enchant
**en ter pris ing** (en′ tər prī′ ziŋ) *adj.* full of energy and initiative
**er rant** (er′ ənt) *adj.* erring or straying from what is right
**er rat ic** (er rat′ ik) *adj.* having no fixed course or direction; irregular; random
**es sence** (es′ əns) *n.* the fundamental nature or most important quality of something
**eu phe mism** (yoo′ fə miz′ əm) *n.* a word or phrase that is substituted for a distasteful word or phrase
**e vac u ate** (ē vak′ yoo āt′) *v.* to remove inhabitants from a place or area for protective purposes
**e vade** (ē vād′) *v.* to avoid or escape by cleverness or deception

**e va sion** (ē vā′ zhən) *n.* the avoidance (of a question)
**ex as per a tion** (eg zas′ pər ā′ shən) *n.* great irritation or annoyance
**ex em pli fy** (eg zem′ plə fī′) *v.* to show by example
**ex ot ic** (eg zät′ ik) *adj.* strange or different in a striking or fascinating way
**ex qui site ly** (eks′ kwi zit lē) *adv.* in a very beautiful or lovely manner
**ex tort** (eks tôrt′) *v.* to get money or goods from someone by violence, threats, or misuse of authority
**ex trav a gance** (ek strav′ ə gəns) *n.* a spending of more than is necessary or reasonable; wasteful spending

## F

**fab ri cat ed** (fab′ ri kāt id) *adj.* made-up; invented
**fac ul ty** (fak′ əl tē) *n.* power or ability to do some particular thing; special aptitude or skill
**fa nat i cal** (fə nat′ i kəl) *adj.* overly enthusiastic
**farce** (färs) *n.* a ridiculous situation
**fas tid i ous** (fas tid′ ē əs) *adj.* not easy to please; very critical
**fer vent ly** (fur′ vənt lē) *adv.* intensely, passionately
**fet tered** (fet′ ərd) *adj.* chained   **fetter** *v.*
**flour ish ing** (flur′ ish iŋ) *adj.* prosperous, successful
**for mi da ble** (fôr′ mə də bəl) *adj.* impressive
**for ti fi ca tion** (fôrt′ ə fi kā′ shən) *n.* a fort or defensive wall, earthwork
**fren zy** (fren′ zē) *n.* a wild outburst of feeling
**fu tile** (fyoot′ ′l) *adj.* useless; hopeless; unsuccessful

## G

**gaud y** (gôd′ ē) *adj.* flashy; dazzling; showy
**glow er ing** (glou′ ər iŋ) *adj.* staring with anger; scowling
**grap ple** (grap′ əl) *v.* to struggle in hand-to-hand combat
**grav i ty** (grav′ i tē) *n.* danger or threat; seriousness, as of a situation
**gul li ble** (gul′ ə bəl) *adj.* prone to being easily cheated or tricked   **gullibility** *n.*

## H

**hap haz ard ly** (hap′ haz′ ərd lē) *adv.* without an aim or purpose; randomly
**har row ing** (har′ ō iŋ) *adj.* causing mental distress; tormenting
**hear say** (hir′ sā) *n.* information one hears but does not know to be true

**hu man i tar i an** (hyo͞o man′ ə ter′ ē ən) *adj.* helping humanity, especially by reducing pain and suffering

**hyp o crit i cal** (hip′ ə krit′ i kəl) *adj.* pretending to be more pious, honest, or virtuous than one really is

**I**

**il lus tri ous** (i lus′ trē əs) *adj.* very distinguished; famous; outstanding

**im mac u late** (im mak′ yo͞o lit) *adj.* perfectly clean; without a spot or stain

**im mi nent** (im′ ə nənt) *adj.* likely to happen without delay

**im par tial ly** (im pär′ shəl lē) *adv.* in a manner that does not favor one side over another; fairly; justly

**im pas sive ly** (im pas′ iv lē) *adv.* calmly; unemotionally

**im pend ing** (im pend′ iŋ) *adj.* about to occur

**im per cep ti bly** (im′ pər sep′ tə blē) *adv.* in a manner that is not plain to the senses or mind; gradually or subtly

**im pe ri ous ly** (im pir′ ē əs lē) *adv.* in an overbearing, arrogant manner

**im per ti nent** (im pʉrt′ ′n ənt) *adj.* disrespectful; insulting

**im pet u ous** (im pech′ o͞o əs) *adj.* acting suddenly with little thought; impulsive

**im pla ca ble** (im plā′ kə bəl) *adj.* inflexible; uncompromising; that cannot be soothed or comforted

**im plore** (im plôr′) *v.* to beg earnestly

**im pro vised** (im′ prə vīzd′) *adj.* composed or made up on the spot, without preparation **improvise** *v.*

**im pul sive ly** (im pul′ siv lē) *adv.* suddenly; without careful thought

**in at ten tive** (in′ ə ten′ tiv) *adj.* not paying attention; absent-minded

**in ces sant ly** (in ses′ ənt lē) *adv.* constantly; endlessly

**in ci sive** (in sī′ siv) *adj.* sharp; keen; penetrating

**in cli na tion** (in′ klə nā′ shən) *n.* a liking or preference; tendency

**in com pre hen si ble** (in′ käm prē hen′ sə bəl) *adj.* beyond understanding; not intelligible

**in con ceiv a bly** (in′ kən sēv′ ə blē) *adv.* in a manner that cannot be understood, imagined, or believed

**in con sol a ble** (in′ kən sōl′ ə bəl) *adj.* unable to be comforted; brokenhearted

**in cre du li ty** (in′ krə do͞o′ lə tē) *n.* unwillingness or inability to believe; doubt

**in cred u lous ly** (in krej′ o͞o ləs lē) *adv.* displaying an unwillingness or inability to believe

**in dif fer ent** (in dif′ ər ənt) *adj.* having or showing no interest, concern, or feeling; uninterested

**in di gent** (in′ di jənt) *adj.* in poverty; needy; poor

**in dig nant ly** (in dig′ nənt lē) *adv.* in an angry or scornful manner

**in dig na tion** (in′ dig nā′ shən) *n.* anger aroused by something unjust or mean

**in dis crim i nate ly** (in′ di skrim′ i nit lē) *adv.* in a manner not based on careful selection; randomly

**in dom i ta ble** (in däm′ i tə bəl) *adj.* not easily discouraged or defeated

**in dul gence** (in dul′ jəns) *n.* favor; privilege; leniency

**in dul gent** (in dul′ jənt) *adj.* kind or lenient, often to excess

**in ert** (in ʉrt′) *adj.* lacking the ability to move or act

**in ev i ta bly** (in ev′ i tə blē) *adv.* unavoidably

**in ex pli ca ble** (in eks′ pli kə bəl) *adj.* that cannot be explained, understood, or accounted for

**in fa mous** (in′ fə məs) *adj.* having a very bad reputation

**in fat u at ed** (in fach′ o͞o āt′ id) *adj.* overwhelmed by foolish or shallow love or affection

**in fir mar y** (in fʉr′ mə rē) *n.* a place for the care of the sick or injured

**in ge nu i ty** (in′ jə no͞o′ ə tē) *n.* skill or cleverness

**in gra ti ating** (in grā′ shē āt′ iŋ) *adj.* gaining favor or acceptance by deliberate effort

**ink ling** (ink′ liŋ) *n.* a vague idea or notion

**in sa ti a ble** (in sā′ shə bəl) *adj.* very greedy; constantly wanting more

**in scru ta ble** (in skro͞ot′ ə bəl) *adj.* not easily understood; obscure or mysterious

**in ter mi na ble** (in tʉr′ mi nə bəl) *adj.* lasting, or seeming to last, forever; endless

**in ter mit tent** (in′ tər mit′ ′nt) *adj.* pausing from time to time

**in tim i date** (in tim′ ə dāt′) *v.* to make afraid; to threaten with violence

**in trigue** (in trēg′) *n.* a secret plot; scheme

**in vin ci ble** (in vin′ sə bəl) *adj.* unconquerable

**ir ra tion al** (ir rash′ ə nəl) *adj.* contrary to reason; senseless; unreasonable; absurd

**J K**

**jar** (jär) *v.* to affect harshly; disturb

**jaun ti ness** (jôn′ tē nes) *n.* liveliness

**ju di cious** (jōō dish′ əs) *adj.* wise

**ju ris dic tion** (jōōr′ is dik′ shən) *n.* the territory which falls within the authority of a legal or military body

## L

**la con ic** (lə kän′ ik) *adj.* using just a few words; concise

**lair** (ler) *n.* a den of a wild animal

**la ment** (lə ment′) *n.* an outward expression of grief; crying or wailing

**lan guor** (lan′ gər) *n.* a lack of vitality; weakness

**lax** (laks) *adj.* slack; limp

**le git i mate** (lə jit′ ə mət) *adj.* born of parents who are legally married to each other

**list less** (list′ lis) *adj.* having no interest in what is going on because of illness, weakness, or dejection

**loathe** (lō*th*) *v.* to hate

## M

**maim** (mām) *v.* to cripple, mutilate, or disable

**ma lev o lent** (mə lev′ ə lənt) *adj.* having or showing spite or hatred

**mal ice** (mal′ is) *n.* ill will; desire to harm another; spite

**ma li cious** (mə lish′ əs) *adj.* spiteful; intentionally harmful

**ma raud er** (mə röd′ ər) *n.* a raider; plunderer

**mar shal** (mar′ shəl) *v.* to arrange ideas or things in order

**mea ger ly** (mē′ gər lē) *adv.* in a poor manner

**me di oc ri ty** (mē′ dē äk′ rə tē) *n.* the quality or state of being ordinary, neither very good nor very bad

**mes mer ized** (mez′ mər īzd′) *adj.* hypnotized; spellbound

**mor ti fy** (môrt′ ə fī′) *v.* to cause to feel shame or humiliation

## N

**na ive** (nä ēv′) *adj.* simple; childlike

**na ive té** (nä ēv tā′) *n.* a state of childlike simplicity

**ne go ti a tions** (ni gō′ shē ā′ shənz) *n.* bargaining to reach an agreement

**non cha lant ly** (nan′ sh länt′ lē) *adv.* cooly; without any apparent concern

**no to ri ous** (nō tôr′ ē əs) *adj.* well-known for something bad; infamous

**nup tial** (nup′ shəl) *adj.* having to do with marriage or a wedding

## O

**ob lige** (ə blīj) *v.* to make indebted to another for a favor or service

**ob lit er at ed** (ə blit′ ər āt′ əd) *adj.* blotted out or worn away, leaving no trace

**ob scure** (əb skyōōr′) *adj.* not well-known; not famous

**ob scu ri ty** (əb skyōōr′ ə tē) *n.* the condition of not being well-known or famous

**ob so lete** (äb′ sə lēt′) *adj.* out-of-date

**ob sti nate ly** (äb′ stə nət lē) *adv.* stubbornly

**o di ous** (o′ dē əs) *adj.* arousing or deserving hatred; disgusting; offensive

**om i nous ly** (äm′ ə nəs lē) *adv.* in a threatening or menacing manner

**op ti mis ti cal ly** (äp′ tə mis′ tik ə lē) *adv.* in a most hopeful manner

**or a cle** (ôr′ ə kəl) *n.* a person in communication with a god

**os ten ta tious ly** (äs′ tən tā′ shəs lē) *adv.* in a showy manner

**os tra cize** (äs′ trə sīz′) *v.* to refuse to associate with

**o ver wrought** (ō′ vər rôt′) *adj.* very nervous or excited

## P

**pact** (pakt) *n.* an agreement between persons or groups

**pal lor** (pal′ ər) *n.* lack of color in the face; paleness

**pan de mo ni um** (pan′ də mō′ nē əm) *n.* any place or scene of wild disorder, noise, or confusion

**par a dox i cal ly** (par′ ə däks′ i kəl lē) *adv.* in a manner expressing a seeming contradiction

**par ley** (pär′ lē) *n.* a talk or conference to settle differences

**par ry** (par′ ē) *v.* to turn aside (a question) by a clever or evasive reply

**per func to ry** (pər fuŋk′ tə rē) *adj.* without care or interest; indifferent

**per se vere** (pʉr′ sə vir′) *v.* to continue or persist in spite of difficulty

**per vade** (pər vād′) *v.* to spread throughout

**per ver si ty** (pər vʉr′ sə tē) *n.* the condition of being stubborn or contrary

**pes ti len tial** (pes′ tə len′ shəl) *adj.* dangerous; harmful

**phe nom e non** (fə näm′ ə nən′) *n.* any fact or experience that is apparent to the senses

**pil grim age** (pil′ grəm ij) *n.* a long journey to a holy or historical place

**pil lag ing** (pil′ ij iŋ) *n.* robbing    **pillage** *v.*

**pi ous** (pī′ əs) *adj.* springing from actual or pretended religious feelings

**plac id ly** (plas′ id lē) *adv.* calmly; quietly

**plain tive** (plān′ tiv) *adj.* mournful; sad

**ply** (plī) *v.* to supply with food or drink

**pom pous** (päm′ pəs) *adj.* characterized by exaggerated self-importance

**pon der ous** (pän′ dər əs) *adj.* very heavy

**pos ter i ty** (päs ter′ ə tē) *n.* the next generations

**pre car i ous** (prē ker′ ē əs) *adj.* uncertain

**pre cip i tous** (prē sip′ ə təs) *adj.* steep

**pre oc cu pa tion** (prē äk′ yə pā′ shən) *n.* the state or condition of being absorbed in one's thoughts

**pre pos ter ous** (prē päs′ tər əs) *adj.* contrary to reason or common sense; absurd; ridiculous

**pre sume** (prē zo͞om′, -zyo͞om′, pri-) *v.* dare to do without permission

**pre sump tion** (pre zump′ shən) *n.* an attitude or act of forwardness or boldness

**pre text** (prē′ tekst′) *n.* a false reason hiding the real one; excuse

**pro sa ic** (prō zā′ ik) *adj.* commonplace; dull; ordinary

**pro tract ed** (prō trakt′ id) *adj.* long and drawn out

**pro trude** (prō tro͞od′) *v.* to thrust or jut out; project

**pro tu ber ance** (prō to͞o′ bər əns) *n.* a bulge or swelling

**prov o ca tion** (präv′ ə kā′ shən) *n.* an act that angers, annoys, or irritates

**prow ess** (prou′ is) *n.* bravery

**pru dence** (pro͞od′ ′ns) *n.* careful management

**purge** (purj) *v.* to cleanse or remove

**pur vey or** (pər vā′ ər) *n.* one who furnishes or supplies

## Q

**quaint** (kwānt) *adj.* unusual; odd

**qualm** (kwäm) *n.* a twinge of conscience or doubt

**quer u lous** (kwer′ yo͞o ləs) *adj.* complaining; peevish

## R

**ramp ant** (ram′ pənt) *adj.* wild; uncontrollable

**re cede** (ri sēd′) *v.* to become less; diminish

**rec on cile** (rek′ ən sīl′) *v.* to make friends again

**rec on cil i a tion** (rek′ ən sil′ ē ā′ shən) *n.* a settlement of an argument or dispute

**re fract ed** (ri frakt′ id) *adj.* bent or angled, as light waves

**re gal ly** (rē′ gəl lē) *adv.* in a splendid or stately manner, as befitting a king or queen

**re it er ate** (rē it′ ə rāt′) *v.* to say or do again

**rel e gate** (rel′ ə gāt′) *v.* assigned to an inferior position

**re lent less** (ri lent′ lis) *adj.* persistent; never ending; harsh

**rel ish** (rel′ ish) *v.* to enjoy

**re morse** (ri môrs′) *n.* a deep sense of guilt over a wrong that one has committed

**re nounce** (ri nouns′) *v.* to give up (a way of living or feeling)

**re nowned** (ri nound′) *adj.* famous; well-known

**re nun ci a tion** (ri nun′ sē ā′ shən) *n.* giving a right or claim to something

**re prieve** (ri prēv′) *n.* a postponement of a penalty, especially death

**re proach ful** (ri prōch′ fəl) *adj.* expressing blame

**re pug nance** (ri pug′ nəns) *n.* extreme dislike or distaste

**re put ed ly** (ri pyo͞ot′ id lē) *adv.* thought to be; supposedly

**res o lute ly** (rez′ ə lo͞ot′ lē) *adv.* with firm determination

**re solve** (ri zälv′) *n.* firm determination; fixed intention

**res pite** (res′ pit) *n.* a temporary relief or rest

**re tal i ate** (ri tal′ ē āt′) *v.* to return an injury for an injury given

**re tort** (ri tôrt′) *v.* to answer a challenge or insult

**rev el** (rev′ əl) *n.* festivity; celebration

## S

**sac ri le gious** (sak′ rə lij′ əs) *adj.* disrespectful of someone or something held sacred

**sage** (sāj) *n.* a wise man

**sanc tu ary** (saŋk′ cho͞o er′ ē) *n.* a place of protection

**saun ter** (sôn′ tər) *v.* to walk slowly and leisurely

**scourged** (skurjd) *adj.* whipped

**scru ples** (skro͞o′ pəls) *n.* concerns or doubts about what is right and wrong

**scru tin ize** (skro͞ot′ ′n īz′) *v.* to examine closely

**sear** (sir) *v.* to scorch or burn the surface of

**se date ly** (si dāt′ lē) *adv.* calmly; quietly; steadily

**self- right eous** (self rī′ chəs) *adj.* convinced of one's own moral superiority; smugly virtuous

**shirk** (shurk) *v.* to neglect or avoid doing something

**skulk** (skulk) *v.* to move about in a stealthy manner; slink

**som ber ly** (säm′ bər lē) *adv.* in a dark, gloomy, or dull way

**spec ta cle** (spek′ tə kəl) *n.* a remarkable sight

**spon ta ne ous** (spän tā′ nē əs) *adj.* acting naturally, without an external cause

**sta bi li za tion** (stā′ bə li zā′ shən) *n.* the state or condition of being stable, firm, or fixed

**stat ure** (stach′ ər) *n.* the height of a person

**stead fast** (sted′ fast′, -fäst′, -fəst) *adj.* firm; unshakable

**stealth i ly** (stelth′ ə lē) *adv.* in a secretive or sneaky manner

**stint** (stint) *n.* limit or restriction

**stip u late** (stip′ yo͞o lāt′) *v.* to demand something specific in an agreement

**stra ta gem** (strat′ ə jəm) *n.* any trick or scheme for achieving some purpose

**strife** (strīf) *n.* struggle or conflict

**sub lime** (sə blīm′) *adj.* noble; majestic

**sub mis sive** (sub mis′ iv) *adj.* yielding to someone else's control

**sub ter ra ne an** (sub′ tə rā nē ən) *adj.* beneath the earth's surface; underground

**sub tle ty** (sut′ 'l tē) *n.* the condition or quality of being clever or sly

**sub ver sive** (səb vur′ siv) *adj.* tending or seeking to overthrow, destroy, or undermine

**suf fice** (sə fīs′) *v.* to be enough; to be adequate

**sul len** (sul′ ən) *adj.* gloomy; ill-humored; resentfully silent

**su per flu ous** (sə pur′ flo͞o əs) *adj.* not needed; unnecessary; irrelevant

**su per im pose** (so͞o′ pər im pōz′) *v.* to put one thing on top of something else

**sup press** (sə pres′) *v.* to keep back; restrain

**sur rep ti tious** (sur′ əp tish′ əs) *adj.* done in a secret, stealthy way

**sus cept i ble** (sə sep′ tə bəl) *adj.* easily influenced; vulnerable

**sus te nance** (sus′ tə nəns) *n.* nourishment; food

## T

**tact ful ly** (takt′ fəl lē) *adv.* in a manner that shows others the right thing to say or do without offending them

**tal on** (tal′ ən) *n.* a claw

**taunt** (tônt) *v.* to mock; ridicule

**tem per ate** (tem′ pər it) *adj.* moderate in indulging the appetites; not self-indulgent; self-restrained

**tem per ing** (tem′ pər iŋ) *n.* a modifying or softening by mixing with something else

**tep id** (tep′ id) *adj.* moderately warm

**the o log i cal** (thē′ ə läj′ i kəl) *adj.* based on religious teachings

**thresh old** (thresh′ ōld′, -hōld′) *n.* the wood fastened on the floor beneath a door

**ti rade** (tī′ rād) *n.* a long, noisy, scolding speech

**tran quil** (traŋ′ kwil) *n.* quiet; steadily flowing

**tran scend** (tran send′) *v.* to go beyond; surpass

**trans gress** (trans gres′) *v.* to do wrong; to sin  
  **transgression** *n.*

**tre mor** (trem′ ər) *n.* a trembling or shaking

## U

**un can ny** (un kan′ ē) *adj.* mysterious or unfamiliar in such a way as to frighten or make uneasy; eerie; weird

**un pre ten tious** (un′ prē ten′ shəs) *adj.* modest; simple

**un re lent ing** (un′ ri lent′ iŋ) *adj.* not relaxing or slackening, as in effort or speed

**un scru pu lous** (un skro͞o′ pyə ləs) *adj.* not held back by ideas of right and wrong; unprincipled

**un so lic it ed** (un sə lis′ i tid) *adj.* unasked for; not wanted

**un wield y** (un wēl′ dē) *adj.* hard to handle or deal with; awkward

**u til i tar i an** (yo͞o til′ ə ter′ ē ən) *adj.* useful more than beautiful

## V

**van quish** (vaŋ′ kwish, van′-) *v.* to conquer; defeat

**veer** (vir) *v.* to change direction; shift; turn

**ve he ment** (vē′ ə mənt) *adj.* having intense feeling or strong passion

**ve ran dah** (və ran′ də) *n.* an open porch covered by a roof and attached along the outside of a building

**ver min** (vur′ mən) *n.* destructive or disease-carrying animals or insects

**vig i lant** (vij′ ə lənt) *adj.* watchful and alert to danger or trouble

**vile** (vīl) *adj.* highly disagreeable; very bad

**vin dic tive** (vin dik′ tiv) *adj.* inclined to seek revenge

**vul ner a ble** (vul′ nər ə bəl) *adj.* open to attack; easily hurt

## W

**wary** (wer′ ē) *adj.* cautious; on one's guard

**whim** (hwim, wim) *n.* a sudden idea; impulse

**wince** (wins) *v.* to draw back slightly, as in pain or embarrassment; flinch

**wist ful** (wist′ fəl) *adj.* showing vague yearnings or longings

**with drawn** (with drôn′) *adj.* isolated; shy; reserved

**writh ing** (rīth′ iŋ) *adj.* twisting or turning in pain  
  **writhe** *v.*

## XYZ

**zeal ous ly** (zel′ əs lē) *adv.* in an enthusiastic manner

# LITERARY TERMS

**Act**   An act is a major unit of action in a play. Acts in a play are comparable to chapters in a book. Each act may contain several scenes. A one-act play usually has a small cast of characters. The plot centers on a single conflict that builds quickly to a climax. *The Madman on the Roof* has only one act, while *Macbeth* contains five acts.

**Alliteration**   The repetition of consonant sounds at the beginning of two or more words is called alliteration. Poets use alliteration to emphasize words, to tie lines together, to reinforce tone and meaning, and to add sound effects. Note the alliteration of the *l* sound in Pablo Neruda's "The Enemy":

> the lines of his loneliness
>     that had lifted his temples
>     little by little to consummate
>     self-love.

**Allusion**   An allusion is a reference to a well-known work of literature, famous person, or historical event with which the reader is assumed to be familiar. In "As the Night the Day," Vernier makes an allusion to Hamlet with the words "To thine own self be true!"

**Antagonist**   The antagonist of a short story, drama, or narrative poem is the force working against the protagonist. The antagonist may be another character, society, nature, or an internal force within the protagonist.
See *Protagonist*.

**Aside**   An aside is a remark that is spoken in an undertone by a character in a play either to the audience or to another character. The comment is heard by the audience but not by the other characters on stage. Asides tell the audience what a character is thinking or feeling.

**Assonance**   Assonance is the repetition of vowel sounds within two or more words. Notice the assonance of the long *a* sound in this line from "Do Not Go Gentle into That Good Night" by Dylan Thomas:

> Old age should burn and rave at close
>     of day;

**Author's Purpose**   Authors write for any of four main purposes: to entertain, to inform, to express an opinion, or to persuade. An author may have several of these purposes for writing, but one is usually most important.

**Autobiographical Essay**   See *Autobiography*.

**Autobiography**   An autobiography is a factual account of a person's life written by that person. It is usually written in first-person point of view to give the reader insight into the person's character, feelings, and attitudes. The events and conflicts may make the account seem like fiction.
   An *autobiographical essay* highlights certain events in the writer's life and reflects on how those events affected him or her. An example of an autobiographical essay is Santha Rama Rau's "By Any Other Name."

**Ballad**   A ballad is a narrative poem that was originally intended to be sung. Ballads tell dramatic stories about common people, heroes, and events from legends. "Robin Hood and the Three Squires" is an example of a ballad.

**Biography**   A biography is a form of nonfiction in which a writer gives a factual account of someone else's life. It is written in the third person. One of the earliest biographies ever written is James Boswell's *The Life of Samuel Johnson*.

**Blank Verse**   Blank verse is unrhymed poetry with ten syllables in each line, five of which are accented. Each unaccented syllable is followed by an accented one. Shakespeare's plays were written mainly in blank verse, as shown in this example from *Macbeth*:

> Away, and mock the time with fairest
>     show;
> False face must hide what the false
>     heart doth know.

**Cast of Characters**   In a play, the cast of characters is given at the beginning of the script, before the first act. It is a list of all the characters in the play, usually in order of appearance.

**Catastrophe**   The resolution of the plot in a tragedy is called the catastrophe. It usually falls within the last act of a play and often involves the death of a hero.
  See *Tragedy.*

**Character**   A character is a person or animal who takes part in the action of a work of literature. Generally, the plot of a story focuses on one or more main characters.
  *Main characters* are those who are most important in the story. Since they often grow and change, they are said to be *dynamic.* The other characters are called *minor characters.* Minor characters are usually *static,* or unchanging; their most important role is to keep the plot of the story moving along.

**Characterization**   Characterization refers to the techniques a writer uses to create and develop a character. A writer develops the character through a description of the character's physical appearance; the actions, feelings, and words of the character; the thoughts, words, and actions of other characters; a narrator's direct comments about the character.

**Chronological Order**   The progression of events in the order in which they occur in time is called chronological order, or time order. Chronological order is a common form for organizing the details in a piece of writing. The events in ''The Thief'' are arranged in chronological order.

**Climax**   The climax is the turning point in the plot of a literary work. It is at this peak of interest and intensity, usually near the end of a story, when the outcome of the conflict in the plot becomes clear. The climax of *Beowulf,* for example, is the slaying of the monster Grendel. The climax usually results in a change in a character or solution to a problem.
  See *Plot.*

**Colloquialism**   A colloquialism is an expression used in informal dialogue but not accepted as good usage in formal speech or writing. For example, in ''First Confession'' by Frank O'Connor, Nora

uses an expression, *But sure,* which means ''indeed'' or ''certainly.''

**Comedy**   Comedy is a light and amusing type of writing. The main character is usually an ordinary person who is faced with a series of obstacles that lead to some humorous situations. Sometimes the humor comes from conflicts that develop between characters with opposite personalities.

**Comic Relief**   Comic relief is a humorous scene, incident, or speech that occurs in the course of a serious or tragic literary work. In drama, it is sometimes used to relieve the emotional intensity of a previous scene. For example, in Act Two of *Macbeth,* Scene 3 begins with the drunken porter's comic opening of the door to relieve the tension after the murder of the king has occurred.

**Conflict**   Conflict is the struggle between opposing forces that is the basis of the plot of a story. *External conflict* occurs between a character and any force outside himself or herself, such as another character, society, or some force of nature. *Internal conflict* occurs when a character has an inner struggle within himself or herself, such as trying to make a decision. Some stories have *multiple conflicts,* or more than one conflict.
  See *Plot.*

**Consonance**   Consonance is the repetition of consonant sounds within and at the ends of words. Consonance differs from rhyme in that the vowels that precede the like consonants differ, as in cli<u>mb</u> and la<u>mb</u>. An example of consonance is the <u>t</u> sound in this line:

  Do no<u>t</u> go gen<u>t</u>le in<u>t</u>o tha<u>t</u> good nigh<u>t</u>.

**Contrast**   Contrast is a stylistic technique in which one element is put in opposition with another. These elements may be contrasting ideas or images, such as the two different ''I's'' in Jimenez's ''I Am Not I.'' Writers might use contrast to clarify ideas or to elicit an emotional response from the reader.

**Description**   Description is writing that creates a picture of a scene, event, or character. To create description, writers often use sensory images—words and phrases that appeal to the reader's senses—and figurative language. Sometimes a description provides details about the actions or attitudes of a character. Notice the descriptive details in this excerpt from "The Thrill of the Grass" by W. P. Kinsella.

> I measure along the edge of the sod, dig the point in and pull carefully toward me. There is a ripping sound, like the tearing of an old bed sheet.

See *Figurative Language* and *Imagery*.

**Dialect**   A form of the English language as it is spoken in one place by a certain group of people is called dialect. Dialects reflect the pronunciations, vocabulary, and grammatical rules that are typical of a region. Notice the dialect in this example from Samuel Selvon's "When Greek Meets Greek."

> I know of a landlord up the road who vow that he ain't ever taking anybody who come from the West Indies.

**Dialogue**   Dialogue is a conversation between two or more characters. Dialogue helps to advance the plot and to reveal the traits of the characters.

In drama, the words each character says are written in lines next to the character's name, as in this excerpt from *The Ring of General Macías* by Josephina Niggli.

> **Marica.** You do love him, don't you?
> **Raquel.** I don't think even he knows
>   how much.

In other kinds of writing, the words each character speaks are commonly set off by quotation marks.

**Diary**   A diary is a personal day-to-day account of a writer's own experiences and impressions. Diaries are nonfiction accounts. Most diaries are kept private, but some are eventually published.

**Drama**   Drama is literature that is meant to be performed for an audience. In a drama, or play, actors and actresses play the roles of the characters, telling the story through their words and actions.

Like fiction, drama has the elements of character, setting, plot, and theme.

A drama is made up of one or more acts. Each act may contain several scenes. A written drama usually includes both a list of the characters and stage directions that tell the actors and actresses how to move or speak their lines. These directions also provide suggestions for special effects, music, lighting, and scenery.

See *Act, Cast of Characters, Dialogue, Scene,* and *Stage Directions*.

**Dramatic Monologue**   A dramatic monologue is a technique used in drama and poetry in which the speaker expresses his or her thoughts and feelings about a critical moment. The speaker appears to be talking to a silent listener who allows him or her to proceed without interruption. Dramatic monologue reveals the personality, feelings, and motivations of the speaker. Robert Browning uses dramatic monologue in "Porphyria's Lover."

**Dynamic Character**   See *Character*.

**Epic**   An epic is a long narrative poem that tells the adventures of a hero whose actions help decide the fate of a nation or group of people. An epic hero is of noble birth or high social position; he reflects values important to his society; his actions consist of courageous, even superhuman deeds; and he often must battle supernatural forces. *Beowulf* is an epic poem.

See *Hero*.

**Epic Simile**   An epic simile is a long comparison that may continue for several lines. It does not require the use of *like* or *as*. Homer uses epic similes throughout *The Iliad*.

**Essay**   An essay is a short nonfiction work that deals with one subject. In an essay, the author might give an opinion, try to persuade, or simply narrate an interesting event. Essays can be formal or informal. Formal essays examine a topic in a thorough, serious, and highly organized manner. Informal essays are lighter in tone and reflect the writer's feelings and personality. An example of an informal essay is "Beauty: When the Other Dancer Is the Self."

**Exaggeration**   See *Hyperbole.*

**Exposition**   The exposition is the part of a plot that provides background information and introduces the story's characters, setting, and conflict. The exposition usually occurs at the beginning of a literary work. The first three paragraphs of "The Rocking Horse Winner" introduce Paul's mother, suggest the family's delicate financial situation, and establish the tense atmosphere of the story.
  See *Plot.*

**Extended Metaphor**   In an extended metaphor, two things are compared at some length and in several ways. Shakespeare's "Sonnet 18" uses an extended metaphor that compares the object of his love to a summer's day.

**External Conflict**   See *Conflict.*

**Falling Action**   Falling action occurs after the climax in a work of fiction or drama and shows the effects of the climax.

**Fantasy**   Fantasy is a type of fiction that is highly imaginative and could not really happen. In a fantasy, the characters are often realistic, but they may find themselves in unrealistic settings and have magical or unreal experiences.

**Farce**   A farce is a comic play that is based on an absurd plot, ridiculous situations, and humorous dialogue. Its purpose is to amuse an audience. The characters in a farce are usually stereotypes, or simplified characters, placed in realistic situations.

**Fiction**   Fiction refers to imaginative works of prose, including the novel and the short story. Even though fiction comes from the imagination of the writer, it may be based on actual events and real people. The main purpose of fiction is to entertain, but it often serves to instruct or enlighten.
  See *Novel* and *Short Story.*

**Figurative Language**   Language that conveys meaning beyond the literal meaning of the words is called figurative language. Writers commonly use figurative language to create effects, to emphasize ideas, and to call upon emotions. Special types of figurative language, called *figures of speech,* are simile, metaphor, hyperbole, and personification.
  See *Hyperbole, Metaphor, Personification,* and *Simile.*

**Flashback**   A flashback is an interruption in the chronological order of events in a story in order to present a conversation or event that happened before the beginning of the story. This background information helps explain the present actions or attitude of a character.

**Folk Tale**   A folk tale is a simple story about animal, human, or superhuman characters that has been handed down by word of mouth from one generation to the next. Folk tales are usually set in the distant past and include supernatural events.

**Foreshadowing**   Foreshadowing is the technique of hinting about an event that will occur later in a story. For example, in *Macbeth,* the witches' warnings foreshadow the fate of Macbeth. The use of foreshadowing creates suspense.

**Form**   Form refers to the shape of a poem, that is, the way the words and lines are arranged on the page. The lines may or may not be complete sentences. In many poems, the lines are grouped into stanzas.
  See *Stanza.*

**Formal Essay**   See *Essay.*

**Frame Story**   The frame story is a story that takes place within another story. The larger story may only serve to introduce the frame story. In "Cross Over, Sawyer!" Simon's story is the frame story inside the larger story of the plantation owner's acquaintance with him.

**Free Verse**   Free verse is poetry without regular patterns of rhythm, rhyme, or line length. It often sounds like everyday conversation when it is read aloud. Judith Wright's "Eve to Her Daughters" is a poem written in free verse.

**Genre**   Genre is the term used to specify the distinct types or categories into which literary works are grouped. The four main literary genres are fiction, nonfiction, poetry, and drama.

**Hero**   In older works of literature, the hero is traditionally someone who exhibits great courage, strength, or intelligence. In modern literature, the hero can be the central character with whom the reader or audience is supposed to sympathize. The hero is the protagonist.
   See *Epic, Protagonist,* and *Tragedy.*

**Historical Expressions**   Historical expressions are phrases common to a time period that reflect the society's attitudes and beliefs.

**Humor**   Humor in literature takes many forms. It might involve amusing description, exaggeration, or sarcasm. Humor is often created by the use of hyperbole or irony or through the writer's tone. "First Confession" is an example of a work that contains several forms of humor.
   See *Hyperbole, Irony,* and *Tone.*

**Hyperbole**   Hyperbole is a figure of speech in which an exaggeration is made for emphasis or humorous effect. In *Mother's Day,* Mrs. Pearson reveals how much she dislikes Doris's jokes when she says, "I was yawning at your jokes before you were born, Doris."
   See *Figurative Language.*

**Iambic Pentameter**   Iambic pentameter is the most common sound pattern in English poetry. Each line has five *iambs,* or feet. Each *iamb* is a basic unit of sound consisting of an unstressed syllable followed by a stressed syllable, as shown in these lines from Keats' "When I Have Fears That I May Cease to Be."

When I behold, upon the night's
   starred face,
Huge cloudy symbols of a high
   romance,

**Idiom**   A phrase or expression that has a meaning that differs from its word-for-word translation is called an idiom. For example, the narrator of "The Man in the Water" says that the fact that somebody actually jumped into the water to save the injured woman "sticks in the mind." What he means is that the incident remains fixed in our memories.

**Imagery**   Imagery refers to words and phrases that appeal to the reader's senses. Most imagery appeals to the sense of sight, but imagery can appeal to other senses as well. These lines from "The Thrill of the Grass" appeal to the senses of sight and touch:

I touch the stubble that is called grass, take off my shoes, but find it is like walking on a row of toothbrushes.

**Informal Essay**   See *Essay.*

**Internal Conflict**   See *Conflict.*

**Irony**   Irony is the contrast between expectation and reality. *Situational irony* occurs when a reader or character expects one thing to happen, but something else actually happens. For example, the reader does not expect God to be on the witness stand in Čapek's "The Last Judgment."
   *Verbal irony* occurs when a character or narrator says one thing that means another. In *The Ring of General Macías,* Raquel means the opposite when she says to Andrés, "What a magnificent army you have. So clever."

**Jargon**   The specialized vocabulary of a certain job or profession is called jargon. For example, *on call* is doctors' jargon that means *available when called for.*

**Lyric**   A lyric is a short poem that presents the thoughts and feelings of a single speaker on a solemn subject, such as death or religion. "When I

Have Fears That I May Cease to Be" by John Keats is a lyric poem.

**Metaphor**  A metaphor is a figure of speech that compares two things that have something in common. Unlike similes, metaphors do not use the word *like* or *as*. In "Fear," Mistral uses metaphors in her comparisons of the child to a swallow, a princess, and a queen.
   See *Extended Metaphor, Figurative Language,* and *Simile.*

**Meter**  Meter is the regular pattern of stressed and unstressed syllables in a line of poetry. The meter of a poem emphasizes the musical quality of the language. In addition, it may serve to call attention to particular words or ideas, or to create a particular mood.
   See *Rhythm.*

**Middle English**  Middle English is an earlier form of the English language characteristic of the medieval period in British history. The original version of *The Canterbury Tales* by Geoffrey Chaucer is written in Middle English.

**Mood**  Mood is the feeling, such as excitement, anger, or happiness, that the writer creates for the reader in a work of literature. The use of connotation, details, dialogue, imagery, figurative language, foreshadowing, setting, and rhythm can help set the mood.

**Moral**  The lesson that a story teaches is called a moral. Sometimes the moral is stated at the end of the story.

**Motif**  A recurring word, phrase, image, object, or action in a piece of literature is called a motif. A motif contributes to the theme and ultimately to the reader's understanding of a piece of literature. In *Macbeth,* references to blood, sleep, and water form motifs in the play.

**Motivation**  A character's reason for action is his or her motivation. In "By Any Other Name," Premila's motive for walking out in the middle of

school is her anger over being separated from the British children during the test.

**Multiple Conflicts**  See *Conflict.*

**Narrative**  A narrative is any writing that tells a story. A narrative recounts a series of related events to tell a reader about something that happened. The events of a narrative can be real or imaginary. Some common types of narrative include autobiographies, biographies, myths, narrative poems, novels, and short stories.

**Narrator**  The narrator is the teller of a story. Sometimes the narrator is a character in the story. At other times, the narrator is an outside voice created by the writer.
   See *Point of View.*

**Nonfiction**  Nonfiction is prose writing about real people, places, things, and ideas. Biographies and autobiographies, histories, diaries, editorial articles, essays, journals, research reports, and news articles are all examples of nonfiction.

**Novel**  A novel is an extended work of fiction with a complex plot about the actions, feelings, and motivations of a group of characters. It is much longer and more complex than a short story.

**Parable**  A parable is a brief tale that teaches a moral or religious lesson, such as "The Parable of the Good Samaritan" from the Bible.

**Personification**  A personification is a figure of speech in which human qualities are attributed to an object, animal, or idea. For example, Tennyson personifies nature in his reference to nature as "your teacher" in "Flower in the Crannied Wall."
   See *Figurative Language.*

**Persuasion**  Persuasion is a type of writing intended to convince the reader to adopt a particular opinion or to perform a certain action. Effective persuasion appeals to both the intellect and the emotions.

**Play**   See *Drama*.

**Plot**   The sequence of actions and events in a literary work is called the plot. Almost all plots center on at least one conflict or problem which the characters struggle to resolve. Plots usually follow a specific pattern consisting of five stages: exposition, rising action, climax, falling action, and resolution.
   See *Climax, Conflict, Exposition, Falling Action, Resolution,* and *Rising Action*.

**Poetry**   Poetry is a special type of literature in which words are chosen and arranged to suggest meanings beyond the literal meanings of the words. Poets carefully select words for their sounds and meanings and combine them in different and unusual ways in order to communicate ideas, feelings, experiences, and different points of view. Like fiction, poems can also tell stories. Poets use the elements of poetry—form, rhyme, rhythm, alliteration, assonance and consonance, imagery, figurative language, speaker, and theme—to convey the sounds, emotions, pictures, and ideas they want to express.

**Point of View**   Point of view is the perspective from which a story is told. In a story told from the first-person point of view, the narrator is usually a character in the story and tells the story using the pronouns *I* and *me*. "Love Must Not Be Forgotten" is told from the first-person point of view.
   In a story told from a third-person point of view, the narrator is outside the story and uses the pronouns *he, she,* and *they*. If a story is told from the third-person limited point of view, as "The Old Demon" by Pearl Buck is, the narrator tells what only one character sees, thinks, and feels. If a story is told from a third-person omniscient point of view, the narrator sees into the minds of all the characters.
   See *Narrator*.

**Prose**   Prose refers to all forms of written or spoken language that are logically organized and that lack the regular rhythmic patterns characteristic of poetry.

**Protagonist**   The main character in a literary work is called the protagonist. The protagonist is always involved in the central conflict of the story and often changes after the climax of the plot. Sometimes a story has more than one protagonist, as in Saki's "The Interlopers."
   See *Antagonist*.

**Realism**   See *Realistic Fiction*.

**Realistic Fiction**   Realistic fiction is a type of fiction that imitates actual life. The characters act like real people and use ordinary human abilities to deal with problems typical of the real world.

**Repetition**   The literary technique in which a word or group of words is repeated throughout a selection is called repetition. Writers often repeat a word or phrase for special emphasis.

**Resolution**   The final part of the plot of a story is called the resolution. The resolution, which often blends with the falling action, explains how the conflict is resolved and may also answer the reader's remaining questions pertaining to the plot.
   See *Plot*.

**Rhyme**   Words rhyme when the vowel and succeeding consonant sounds at the ends of two or more words are the same, as in *blue* and *stew*. Many traditional poems contain rhyme at the ends of lines. Rhyme that occurs within a line is called *internal rhyme*.

**Rhyme Scheme**   The pattern of end rhyme in a poem is called the rhyme scheme. Rhyme scheme can be determined by assigning a letter of the alphabet to each line. Lines that rhyme are assigned the same letter. The rhyme scheme for the following stanza from Wordsworth's "The Tables Turned" is identified at the right.

| | |
|---|---|
| Up! Up! my friend, and quit your books, | a |
| Or surely you'll grow double; | b |
| Up! Up! my friend, and clear your looks; | a |
| Why all this toil and trouble? | b |

**Rhythm**   The pattern of accented and unaccented syllables in poetry is called rhythm. Rhythm brings out the musical quality of language. It can also create mood and emphasize ideas. The accented or stressed syllables are marked with ╱, while the unaccented syllables are marked with ◡. The pattern these syllables make in a line of poetry may be divided into units. Each unit is called a foot. Notice the rhythm in these lines from William Blake's "The Tyger."

> ╱  ◡  ╱  ◡  ╱  ◡  ╱
> Tyger! Tyger! burning bright
> ╱  ◡  ╱  ◡  ╱  ◡  ╱
> In the forests of the night,
> ╱   ◡  ╱  ◡  ╱  ◡  ╱
> What immortal hand or eye
> ◡   ╱  ◡  ╱  ◡  ╱  ◡ ╱
> Could frame thy fearful symmetry?

See *Iambic Pentameter* and *Meter*.

**Rising Action**   In fiction and drama, the rising action forms the second stage in the development of the plot. During the rising action, the conflict in a story becomes obvious. Complications arise and suspense begins to build as the main characters struggle to resolve their problem.

See *Plot*.

**Sarcasm**   Sarcasm is a type of humor that mocks or ridicules its subject. A sarcastic remark may seem complimentary, but it is actually meant as a criticism.

**Satire**   Satire is a literary technique that combines a critical attitude with humor. Through the ridicule and mockery of satire, writers try to make their readers think about faults in society. *Gulliver's Travels* by Jonathan Swift uses satire.

**Scene**   Scenes are the episodes into which the action of a play is divided. The setting of each scene differs either in time or in place. In long plays, scenes are grouped into acts. The play *The Madman on the Roof* has just one scene, while *Macbeth* has seven scenes in the first act alone.

**Science Fiction**   Science fiction is fiction that is based on real or possible scientific developments. It frequently presents both an imaginary view into the future and the writer's concerns about problems in today's society. Varshavsky's "The Escape" is an example of science fiction.

**Setting**   The setting of a story is the time and place in which the action occurs. A story may be set in the past, the present, or the future; during the day or at night; during a particular time of year, or in a certain historical period. The place may be real or imaginary. Sometimes the setting is clear and well-defined. At other times, it is left to the reader's imagination.

Setting, along with plot, character, and theme, is one of the main elements of fiction.

**Short Story**   A short story is a work of fiction that can be read in one sitting. It usually tells about one or two major characters and one major conflict. The four elements of a short story are character, plot, setting, and theme. An example of a short story is "The Bet" by Anton Chekhov.

See *Fiction*.

**Simile**   A simile is a comparison of two things using the words *like* or *as*. In this excerpt from "Sonnet 30," Edmund Spenser compares the object of his love to ice and himself to fire:

> My love is like to ice, and I to fire:

Writers use similes to intensify emotional responses, create vivid images, and to help the reader look at a familiar object in a new way.

See *Figurative Language*.

**Slang**   Slang is very informal, everyday speech outside the standard version of a language. Slang terms can be new words or established words and phrases that have taken on new meanings. Slang terms usually go out of date quickly. An example of an outdated slang term is *cool*.

**Soliloquy**   A soliloquy is a speech made by a character in a play when he or she is alone on the stage or among other characters who are ignored temporarily. Its purpose is to let the audience know what the character is thinking. A soliloquy is given by Macbeth in Act Five, Scene 5 of *Macbeth*.

**Sonnet**   A sonnet is a lyric poem of fourteen lines. Most British sonnets, such as Shakespeare's "Sonnet 18," are divided into three four-line units called *quatrains* and end with two rhymed lines known as a *couplet*. The typical rhyme scheme is *a b a b c d c d e f e f g g*.

See *Lyric.*

**Speaker**   In poetry, the speaker is the voice that "talks" to the reader. The speaker of a poem might be compared to the narrator of a work of fiction. Although the speaker often expresses feelings that the poet wants to convey, the speaker may or may not be the voice of the poet.

**Stage Directions**   Stage directions are instructions in a script to the actors and director in a play. They help the readers of a script to visualize the setting and imagine how the actors would move and speak. Stage directions also provide suggestions for props, lighting, music, and sound effects.

**Stanza**   A group of lines that forms a unit in poetry is called a stanza. A stanza is comparable to a paragraph in prose. The number of lines may vary or be uniform from stanza to stanza throughout a poem.

**Static Character**   See *Character.*

**Stereotype**   A stereotype refers to something or someone that conforms to a fixed or general pattern, without distinguishing qualities. Often a stereotype is a mental picture that members of a group believe typifies all members of some other group.

**Supernatural Tale**   A story that includes beings, powers, or happenings that are unexplainable by the forces or laws of nature known to man is called a supernatural tale. Supernatural forces often cause one or more characters to meet their doom.

**Surprise Ending**   A surprise ending is an unexpected twist in the plot at the end of a story.

**Suspense**   Suspense is the growing feeling of anxiety and excitement that makes a reader curious about the outcome of a story. A writer creates suspense through techniques that raise questions about possible endings to the conflict.

**Symbol**   A symbol is a person, place, or thing that represents something beyond itself. In literature, objects and images are often used to symbolize abstract ideas. For example, the lamb in William Blake's "The Lamb" represents innocence.

**Theme**   The theme of a literary work is the message or insight about life or human nature that the writer presents to the reader. Although some works are written purely for entertainment and do not have a clear-cut theme, in most serious works the writer makes at least one point about life or the human condition.

Since the theme of a piece is not usually stated directly, the reader has to figure it out. One way to discover the theme is to consider what happens to the main character. The importance of that event, stated in terms that apply to all human beings, is the theme.

**Time Order**   See *Chronological Order.*

**Tone**   The tone of a work of literature reflects the writer's attitude toward his or her subject. It might be humorous, admiring, sad, angry, or bitter, depending on how the writer feels about the subject. Tone is not measurable, but can be figured out from the writer's word choice and the kinds of statements that he or she makes.

**Tragedy**   A tragedy is a drama that begins peacefully and ends in violence, often with the death or ruin of one or more of the main characters. While fate is a major cause of the tragic ending, weaknesses or flaws within the characters also contribute significantly to their troubles. In a tragedy, the resolution of the plot is called the catastrophe. Shakespeare's *Macbeth* is a famous tragedy.

See *Catastrophe* and *Resolution.*

**Tragic Hero**   See *Tragedy.*

**Understatement**   The technique of creating emphasis by saying less than is actually or literally true is understatement.

# BIOGRAPHIES OF THE AUTHORS

**W. H. Auden** *(1907–1973)* was a recognized poet by the time he left his home in York, England, to attend Oxford University in 1925. His early writing was boldly experimental and sharply critical of modern society; later poems showed a growing interest in religion. Auden moved to the United States in 1939 and became an American citizen in 1946. Though renowned as a poet, Auden was also a playwright, critic, editor, and teacher.

**JORGE LUIS BORGES**

**William Blake** *(1757–1827)* was a uniquely talented painter, engraver, and poet. The artist, whose works combine dreamlike language with fierce protests of injustice, claimed to have seen angels and boasted of talking to an Old Testament prophet. Blake illustrated and printed his own works as well as those of others, using innovative techniques. A man of radical political beliefs, he sympathized with the American and French struggles for liberty.

**Jorge Luis Borges** *(1899–1986)* was a powerful literary voice from Buenos Aires, Argentina. A private and learned man who eventually went blind, Borges achieved international fame for his imaginative, ingenious short stories. His stories portray a puzzling, mysterious world, where boundaries between dream and reality, past and present, fact and fantasy are often blurred.

**CHARLOTTE BRONTË**

**Charlotte Brontë** *(1816–1855)* lived on the desolate Yorkshire Moors of northern England. She and her two sisters published their first novels under assumed male names. Charlotte's novel, *Jane Eyre,* became an overnight bestseller and earned praise as a masterpiece; Emily's novel, *Wuthering Heights,* also became a classic. Charlotte's letters and journals provide insight into her lonely, harsh life as a girl and her courageous struggle for love and independence. Sadly, none of the Brontë sisters lived to see their fortieth birthday.

**RUPERT BROOKE**

**Rupert Brooke** *(1887–1915),* an extraordinarily handsome young man, was regarded as one of England's most promising poets. He joined the navy in 1914 at the outbreak of World War I; tragically, he fell victim to blood poisoning while traveling to his assignment and died on a hospital ship off the Greek island of Skyrosis. His war poems, published in 1915 after his death, captured the idealism and patriotism of the younger generation.

**Elizabeth Barrett Browning** *(1806–1861)* became one of the most popular English poets of her time. In 1837 a blood vessel burst in her lungs, nearly killing her, which made her an invalid for a number of years, though she continued to write poems and publish articles on social injustice. She married Robert Browning in 1846, despite the disapproval of her tyrannical father. She wrote the remarkable *Sonnets from the Portuguese* as a wedding gift for her husband.

**ELIZABETH BROWNING**

**ROBERT BROWNING**

**ROALD DAHL**

**NAGUIB MAHFOUZ**

**Robert Browning** *(1812–1889)* was one of the most energetic and captivating figures of Victorian literature, though it took him thirty years to achieve success as a poet. Browning's talent for creating dramatic monologues in his poems (a technique in which complex characters reveal themselves in their own words) helped establish his reputation. In 1844, Browning read Elizabeth Barrett's poems and fell in love with her. The two eloped to Italy in 1846.

**Karel Čapek** *(1890–1938)* was a successful writer of novels, plays, and short stories. Čapek's highly imaginative works are often futuristic and attack modern evils and trends. The Czech writer's play *R. U. R.* about machines that threaten to replace human beings gave the world the term *robot*. As the Nazi troops marched into Prague at the onset of World War II, Čapek died of an apparent heart attack.

**Roald Dahl** *(1916–1990),* a native of Wales, was the creator of stories and novels that are extraordinarily original and entertaining. As master of the bizarre twist, Dahl blended the horrible with the humorous, the logical with the absurd. He wrote books for children as well as adult fiction. Dahl's works are classics of their kind.

**Thomas Hardy** *(1840–1928)* showed an early interest in and aptitude for architecture but chose a literary career instead. His novels, including *Tess of the D'Urbervilles* and *The Mayor of Casterbridge,* are usually set in the countryside of his native Wessex, England. With a dark and pessimistic honesty, he depicted characters caught in circumstances beyond their control. In his later years, he turned to writing poetry, creating timeless anecdotes in verse. His ashes rest in the Poets' Corner at Westminster Abbey, but his heart was buried separately in Wessex, a tribute to the land that inspired him.

**Juan Ramón Jiménez** *(1881–1958)* lived the greater part of his life in his native Spain. His short, concise, and intensely personal poems were an inspiration to a whole generation of Spanish writers in the 1920's and 1930's. In 1940, Jiménez went into exile for political reasons after the Spanish Civil War, living at various times in Puerto Rico, Maryland, and Cuba. Two years before his death, he received the Nobel Prize for literature.

**Ben Jonson** *(1572–1637)* began his career in the theater of Elizabethan England. He was an actor, a playwright, a scholar, and a poet. His combative personality caused him to kill an actor in a duel; though he avoided a hanging, he was imprisoned for a time. Jonson became famous for his comedies, which were performed by Shakespeare's company at the Globe Theatre in London. His poems are among the finest lyrics in the English language.

**Naguib Mahfouz** *(born 1911)* won the Nobel Prize for literature in 1988. Born in Cairo, Egypt, Mahfouz is considered the foremost fiction writer of the Arab world. His stories and novels chronicle the problems of life in modern Egypt, combining realistic techniques and a concern with political and social issues.

**W. Somerset Maugham** *(1874–1965)* wrote novels, plays, and short stories that made him one of England's most popular and respected writers. Orphaned at ten and handicapped by a severe stammer, he was sent to live with an aunt and uncle in Kent, England. Though Maugham was trained to be a doctor, it was his writing that brought him fame and wealth. His most famous novel, *Of Human Bondage,* mirrors some of his own experiences as a young medical student in London.

W. SOMERSET MAUGHAM

**Gabriela Mistral** *(1889–1957),* the pen name of Lucila Godoy Alcayaga, began teaching in 1904 in rural Chile, where she was born. Her abilities led to increasingly important jobs in education; at the same time, she gained fame for her soulful, passionate poetry. Her achievements as a poet and educator brought about a number of diplomatic assignments in Europe and Latin America as well as teaching posts in the United States. In 1945 she received the Nobel Prize for literature, the first awarded to a Spanish-American writer.

**Alberto Moravia** *(1907–1990),* the pen name of Alberto Pincherle, was a respected Italian novelist whose works focus on people searching for values and love. Moravia's long battle with tuberculosis in his youth profoundly affected him and motivated him to write his first novel, which he finished before he was twenty. During World War II, his criticism of the Italian government forced him into exile; he hid in a mountain hut until he was finally given protection by the American army.

ALBERTO MORAVIA

**Pablo Neruda** *(1904–1973),* the pen name of Neftalí Ricardo Reyes y Basoalto, was an influential and controversial poet born in Parral, Chile. Neruda served as a diplomat in a career that lasted from 1927 to 1943. His travels took him to Madrid in 1934, where he was welcomed by the leading poets of Spain. Neruda was later elected a senator in Chile, but he was dismissed and put on trial by the government for his communist views. The Nobel Prize for literature was awarded to Neruda in 1971.

**Liam O'Flaherty** *(1896–1984),* an Irish novelist and short story writer, grew up on the Aran Islands, a primitive and barren land in Ireland. After he finished college and served in the Irish Guards during World War I, O'Flaherty worked in a variety of jobs all around the world. He returned to Ireland, becoming a political activist whose lawbreaking adventures led to his exile. O'Flaherty settled on writing and eventually won international recognition for his compassionate novels about struggling commoners.

LIAM O'FLAHERTY

**Plato** *(c. 428–c. 348 B.C.)* was a Greek philosopher and teacher. A student of the philosopher Socrates, Plato founded an Academy in Athens where he adopted the Socratic method of teaching, a technique of asking, rather than answering, questions. Plato wrote in the form of dialogues, most of which were fictionalized conversations between Socrates and his pupils about issues such as justice, virtue, and wisdom. He is known as the father of Western philosophy and as one of the Western world's most influential thinkers.

**Horacio Quiroga**

**Horacio Quiroga** *(1878–1937)* was a master of the short story. Born in a small town in Uruguay, Quiroga's life was filled with hardship, adventure, tragedy, and violence. Long admired for his tales of horror, tragic jungle stories, and dark themes, Quiroga has achieved lasting fame for his narrative art and powerful impact on the reader.

**Chief Seattle** *(1786–1866),* the chief of the Duwamish and allied tribes of the Northwest, was known as a daring warrior in his youth. As more whites settled in the region, however, Seattle felt rebellion would be useless. He signed the Port Elliott Treaty of 1855 and moved his small band to the Port Madison Reservation. Seattle spent much of his life trying to preserve Indian lands and prevent the extinction of his people. When he died, he was buried in an Indian cemetery near the city named for him in the state of Washington.

**Chief Seattle**

**Samuel Selvon** *(born 1923)* has been called the "most important folk poet the British Caribbean has yet produced." Born in Trinidad, Selvon served in the naval reserve from 1940–45. After the war, he worked as a journalist in Trinidad, then as a civil servant in London. After receiving a Guggenheim Fellowship in 1954, Selvon devoted himself to his writing. His many novels and short stories have won him worldwide recognition. His works draw on the Creole language and oral traditions of Trinidad.

**Wole Soyinka** *(born 1934)* became the first African to win the Nobel Prize in 1986. He has published books of poetry, plays, novels, autobiographical works, and literary criticism. His writing deals with African politics and society and with the struggle for human dignity, blending Western literary techniques with African folklore and customs. Soyinka was imprisoned in the 1960's for his alleged support of Biafra's attempt to break away from Nigeria; during his imprisonment he continued to write poems on scraps of toilet paper.

**Wole Soyinka**

**Edmund Spenser** *(1552–1599),* son of a London clothmaker, attended Cambridge University on a scholarship. He read extensively and became an expert in Latin, Greek, French, and Italian literature. A fluid, graceful writer who was imitated and respected by his peers, Spenser wrote *The Faerie Queene,* the longest epic poem in English literature, in honor of Queen Elizabeth. Despite his reputation as a poet and his years of service to the English court, Spenser died in relative poverty.

**Brent Staples** *(born 1951)* holds a Ph.D. in psychology from the University of Chicago. Originally from Chester, Pennsylvania, Staples has worked as a journalist at the *Chicago Sun-Times* and several other Chicago publications. In 1985 he joined *The New York Times.* He is now a member of that paper's editorial board, and he writes about politics and culture.

**Richard Steele** *(1672–1729),* a playwright, journalist, and politician, is best known for his essays in *The Tatler* and *The Spectator,* two periodicals which he managed with Joseph Addison, his friend and collaborator. Steele's witty and popular essays commented on virtually all the issues of the age, from politics to table manners, from make-up to morality. The Irish-born, Oxford-educated Steele, respected for his generosity and sincerity, grew up in privileged society but gained a wide knowledge of London's bustling and varied population.

**DYLAN THOMAS**

**Dylan Thomas** *(1914–1953)* called his poetry ''the record of my individual struggle from darkness toward some measure of light.'' The poetry and other writings of Thomas are deeply rooted in the culture and countryside of his native Wales. As a young man of boundless energy, warmth, and charm, Thomas established himself as perhaps the most gifted poet living in England. His dramatic readings enchanted audiences in the United States and Great Britain. Unfortunately, he led a tortured life, and alcoholism led to an early death.

**Armando Valladares** *(born 1937)* was arrested as a young man for his opposition to Cuba's communist government. He was kept in prison for twenty-two years, where he was tortured psychologically and physically and eventually crippled after a failed escape attempt. Valladares smuggled his poems out of prison, winning the attention of writers and public figures around the world, who pressured Cuba for his release. Valladares now lives in Madrid, Spain.

**JUDITH WRIGHT**

**Kurt Vonnegut, Jr.** *(born 1922)* was born in Indianapolis, Indiana. His experiences as a prisoner of war in Germany and as a witness to the horrors of World War II influenced his writings. After the war, Vonnegut held a variety of jobs but eventually began to sell short stories to science fiction journals and other magazines. He has been an acclaimed writer ever since. In a deceptively simple style, his stories, novels, and plays, which blend fantasy and realism, probe the horrors and absurdities of the human condition.

**Judith Wright** *(born 1915)* has written books of poetry, books for children, and a history of her family's life and settlement in Australia. She was born and raised on a sheep ranch in New South Wales, Australia, and educated at the University of Sydney. Many of her poems deal with the preservation of her native Australia or with relationships between women and the people in their lives. Wright is a widely read Australian poet, noted for both her technical skill and her beautiful description of her homeland.

**WILLIAM BUTLER YEATS**

**William Butler Yeats** *(1865–1939)* is commonly regarded as one of the century's greatest poets. Born near Dublin, Yeats spent much of his childhood in the wild rural area in the west of Ireland. As a young man, he played a key role in the revival of Irish culture. A poet and playwright with a mystical bent, Yeats constantly experimented and searched for new directions. Much of his poetry reflects his failed romance with Maud Gonne, a beautiful actress and Irish patriot, who repeatedly rejected him. Yeats was deeply committed to Irish nationalism and served as a senator in the new Irish Free State from 1922 to 1928. He was awarded the Nobel Prize for literature in 1923.

# THE WRITING PROCESS

Everyone who reads and writes belongs to a special community, a community of readers and writers. You, too, are part of this community. When you read, you discover meaning that reflects who you are as well as what the writer is trying to communicate. When you write, you discover ideas about yourself, about the world, and about what you read.

On the following pages you will find practical information that you can apply in many different writing situations.

## The Reader's Journal

Like all readers, you observe, question, predict, and make connections as you read. You experience feelings such as excitement and amusement. One place to record these responses to literature is in a Reader's Journal. Your journal then can provide you with a rich source of writing ideas. Your journal can also serve as the place to record notes as you prepare for a writing assignment.

Here are some tips for keeping a journal:

- Carry your journal with you or keep it in a convenient place.
- Date and label your journal entries.
- Record words, passages, and lines that trigger ideas, along with your response to these ideas.
- Set aside part of your journal for the journal writing that is suggested throughout this book.
- Set aside another part of your journal for observations, quotations, and imaginative writing that is not tied to a literary selection.

## The Writing Process

Writing is a process unique to each writer and to each writing experience. However, the following activities need to take place during most writing experiences.

- **Exploring ideas:** reflecting on what you know, what you need to know, and where you might find what you need
- **Gathering material:** remembering, imagining, reading, observing, interviewing, discussing
- **Making connections:** finding the way ideas fit together, letting new ideas surface, elaborating and pushing ideas to their limits
- **Clarifying communication:** rethinking content, reorganizing structure, correcting mechanics and usage

In most books about writing, each of these activities is tied to a specific stage of the writing process. The traditional stages are listed below in the same order that they appear in the Writer's Workshops in this text. It is important to understand, however, that the stages are only guides. Any activity can take place at any point in the process. The more you write, the more you should develop your own personal process, moving in and out of the writing stages in the manner that works best for you.

**Stage 1. Prewriting**  This is the planning stage where you think of ideas, do research, and organize your material.

**Stage 2. Drafting**  When you draft, you begin to put your ideas on paper, following any notes, graphics, or outlines you have made. Drafting is a time to let ideas flow without concern for spelling and punctuation. These errors can be corrected later.

**Stage 3. Revising and Editing**  When you revise, you refine your draft by improving word choice and sentence structure, clarifying organization, eliminating unnecessary details, and adding new ideas when necessary. When you are satisfied with your revision, you edit, or proofread your work looking for errors in capitalization, punctuation, grammar, and spelling.

**Stage 4. Publishing or Presenting**  This is the time to share your writing with others.

# The Writer as Decision-Maker

During the writing process, writers make a series of decisions that give direction or redirection to their writing. These decisions concern the key issues of purpose, audience, subject, and structure. These elements are highlighted in the **PASSkey** to writing that accompanies each Writer's Workshop in this text. In order to keep your writing focused, you may find it helpful to create a **PASSkey** when you are writing for other classes, as well. Following is a list of questions to guide you in thinking about these issues as you write.

## Purpose

Is a purpose stated in the assignment?
What do I really want to accomplish in this piece:
  to express ideas or feelings? to inform? to entertain? to analyze? to persuade?
How do I want my audience to respond?

## Audience

Who will read my writing?
What do my readers know or need to know?
What might they find interesting?

## Subject

What information must I pull together or research?
Will I need to fill in details from my imagination?
How detailed will I need to be for my audience?

## Structure

Is a structure or form named in the assignment?
What is the most effective organization to accomplish my purpose?
What should the final product look like?

# The Writer as Problem-Solver

Everyone's writing process is personal. Many writers, however, experience the same kinds of difficulties. The questions they ask tend to sound like these:

1. Where do I start? Where do I get ideas? What do I do with them?
2. Who can help me? When should I ask for help?
3. How do I know what's wrong with my writing? How do I fix it?

On the following pages are some strategies to help you deal with these common problems.

**Strategies: Word Webs and Brainstorming**
The notes in your journal can be a good starting point for many writing assignments. When you need to explore ideas further, generate new ideas, or discover connections among ideas, you might want to try using a **word web.** A word web is a diagram showing a central idea and related ideas. Here is an example.

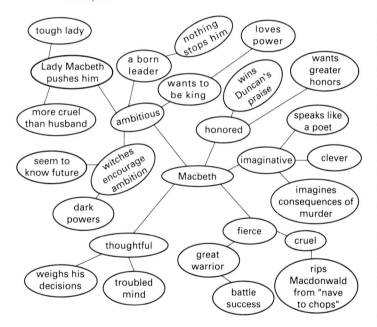

This word web shows the central topic "Macbeth" surrounded by words and phrases that describe his characteristics, ambitions, and experiences. It would be useful for analyzing why Macbeth decides to murder King Duncan.

To create a word web like the one above, write a central idea in the middle of a page and draw a circle around it. Outside the circle, write related ideas. Circle each one and draw a line connecting it to the central idea. Do the same for each related idea.

**Brainstorming** is similar to making a word web. In brainstorming, though, you write down every idea that comes to mind, whether it is related or not. Brainstorming can be done alone, but it is even more productive when done in a group.

**Strategies: Charts and Diagrams**  Charts and diagrams can help you discover connections as well as pinpoint where you need to gather more material. You will discover a wide variety of useful charts and diagrams in this book—both on the Explore pages and with the Writer's Workshop assignments.

**Strategies: Peers as Partners**  Because you are part of a community of readers and writers, you can work with a partner at any point in the writing process. You can co-develop a writing plan, bounce ideas off a friend, ask a classmate to read a rough draft or a cleaned-up copy, or in some cases team-write a piece. Involving peers in your problem-solving process can help you in exploring and clarifying ideas, in seeing a subject from a different point of view, and in identifying and eliminating problems in communication.

When you want some feedback on a piece of writing, you can read it aloud to a classmate and then ask that person two simple questions: What do you like? What don't you like?

A way to get more detailed feedback, especially for longer pieces, is to give a classmate the piece of writing along with the following questions. You can use the answers to these questions as a guide for talking about your writing with your partner.

• What did you like the best? the least?
• What message do you think I am trying to get across? Summarize it for me.
• What do you want to know more about? What parts went on too long?
• Did the beginning work for you? Did the ending?
• Did you have any trouble following my ideas?

**Strategies: Self-Evaluation**  Sometimes a first draft of a piece of writing needs little revision. Other times you may have to write several drafts, perhaps going back to do more research or to rethink the ideas. When trying to figure out what's wrong with a piece of writing that just isn't working, you can start with a quick check like the following:

• The main point I am trying to make is _____.
• I want my reader to respond to my writing by thinking or feeling that _____.
• In looking back over the piece, I like _____.
• I don't like _____.

At this point you'll want to review the personal goals you set when identifying the purpose of your writing and to decide how close you've come to meeting your goals. One good evaluation strategy is to read your writing aloud. As you read, listen for the following problems:

• ideas that are unclear or unnecessary
• ideas that don't make logical connections
• abrupt transitions from one idea to the next
• a dull or choppy style
• words that don't sound quite right or aren't right for your audience

**Strategies: The Final Edit**  It would be wonderful to know all the rules of grammar, spelling, capitalization, punctuation, and usage, all the synonyms for every word, all the meanings for every word you read or hear. The next best thing is to know where to get the information you need to refine your writing.
Here are some ideas.

• **To check spelling:** dictionary, spelling dictionary, computer spellchecker
• **To check punctuation, capitalization, grammar, and usage:** the Language Handbook in this text
• **To check word meanings and synonyms:** dictionary, thesaurus

One point to check carefully when writing about literature is the accuracy of your quotations and the correct spellings of any names and titles. The literature itself is your source for this information.

When you edit your writing or that of a partner, use the proofreading symbols on the next page.

## Proofreading Symbols

| Symbol | Meaning | Example |
|---|---|---|
| ∧ | insert | leson (with inserted s) |
| ≡ | capitalize | douglass (with ≡ under d) |
| / | lower case | History (with / through H) |
| ∼ | transpose | veiw (marked) |
| ℯ | take out | lots of (marked) |
| ¶ | paragraph | ¶ The |
| ⊙ | add a period | slavery⊙ |
| ⋀ | add a comma | Finally⋀ |

# The Writer as Learner

After you have completed a piece of writing, take time to think about your writing process. Questions like these can help you to focus on various aspects of the writing and learning experience:

- Am I pleased with my final product?
- Did I become involved in my topic?
- Did I learn something from writing about this topic?
- Which aspects of the writing were easiest for me? Which were the most difficult?
- What aspect of writing is becoming easier?
- What was the biggest problem I encountered? How did I solve the problem? How might I avoid the problem next time?
- When I compare this piece of writing with others in my working folder or portfolio, can I see changes in my writing style? in my writing skill?
- Have I seen anything in the writing done by my peers or by professional writers that I would like to try myself?

Another way to learn from a writing experience is through an objective evaluation of your final product. The evaluation may be conducted by a teacher or a peer reader. The goal is the same: to contribute to your growth as a writer and to heighten your sense of writing as communication.

**Strategies: The Evaluation Task**   Each kind of writing has certain characteristics unique to that writing. An evaluator, however, can assess the strengths and weaknesses of most writing using general guidelines in three key areas: (1) content, (2) form, and (3) grammar, usage, and mechanics.

The following is a description of a well-developed piece of writing, which you might use when you are acting as a peer evaluator and when judging whether your own work is ready for a final evaluation or in need of further revision.

The content of a well-developed piece of writing

- Is clearly focused throughout the piece
- Keeps a consistent tone and point of view
- Uses precise verbs, nouns, and modifiers
- Elaborates on ideas with supporting details, examples, and summaries, as appropriate
- Demonstrates a clear sense of purpose
- Demonstrates a clear sense of audience through choice of language and details

The form of a well-developed piece of writing

- Shows clear relationships among ideas through effective transitions
- Includes sentences with a variety of structures

The final draft of a well-developed piece of writing

- Contains few if any minor errors in grammar and usage
- Contains few if any minor errors in spelling, capitalization, and punctuation

# The Writer as Communicator

Writing is a form of communication only if you share it with others. Your ideas die on the page if no one reads your writing. The experience of having someone else react to your thoughts will help you as a person to grow, modify your thinking, develop new ideas, or believe more firmly in your original feelings. Share your writing with your class, school, or community.

# WRITING WITH COMPUTERS

In this age of "electronic miracles," we've become accustomed to having computers help us out. Computers can help us drive our automobiles and cook our food. Thanks to computer technology, we can phone the next-door neighbor or a friend on another continent. Now the same technology can make the task of writing easier, faster, and more effective.

## What Is a Word Processor?

A computer becomes a word processor when a word-processing software program is loaded into it. Programs for word processing are contained on a storage device, such as a floppy disk. The computer works in combination with a printer, which on command will print on paper any text that has been composed. Although computers vary and individual word-processing programs may differ in the features they offer, all word processing offers certain benefits to assist writers.

## Type Without Knowing How

Perhaps the simplest and most elementary benefit of word processing is that it allows nontypers to produce printed words on a page. It's true that the computer's keyboard is like a typewriter and that to word process you must key in the words. However, because the word processor makes it so easy to correct errors and automatically takes care of many of the spacing and formatting decisions, it is not necessary to possess extensive typing skills.

## Face the Blank Page Bravely

Even during the beginning stages of writing, when you're still thinking about a writing topic, word processing can help make your job easier. The screen light on many computers is adjustable and can be dimmed. Try freewriting with the screen dimmed, typing any ideas that come to mind. Not being able to see what you're typing frees you from concerns about form and correctness. It also keeps you from trying to rewrite prematurely. After you've exhausted your supply of ideas, turn up the monitor screen and review what you've written. Then, you can tell the computer to store your ideas, print them out, or both.

## Extend Your Memory

A computer can store, or "remember," a great deal of material. You can use this fact to your advantage both while you're organizing your ideas and while you're composing. In a computer, a body of information is called a file. Word processors store written material as files. For example, if you have a list of questions that help you explore writing ideas, you can create a file to store it. If you'd like to keep an ongoing list of ideas, you can give it a file of its own, calling it up and adding to it as needed.

Some word processors let you work on more than one file at a time. This allows you to move back and forth between drafting and prewriting while the computer stores the other file for you. For example, suppose a great idea hits you during the drafting stage. Simply call up your idea file, store the inspiration, and return to your drafting. Later, you can refer to your idea file, pull out the idea, and insert it in the appropriate place in your text.

## Handle Words with Confidence

Word processing simplifies adding or deleting material and moving words or passages around on the page. "Cut-and-paste" commands allow you to arrange and rearrange items in a writing plan or outline. You can also develop the points in your outline in order, or skip around as you fill in material. You can update and correct information quickly and without mess.

Throughout the planning and drafting stages, you have the option of working on-screen or making a paper copy (called a *hard copy*) of your text.

## Find Your Own Drafting Style

The cut-and-paste feature is extremely useful during the drafting stage as well because it allows the word processor to accommodate alternative writing styles.

If you work best by first organizing and then writing, you could review your idea file on-screen or print out your ideas on paper to form prewriting notes. Then, use the cut-and-paste command to form a plan. Finally, expand your plan into sentences.

An alternative drafting method is to write and organize as you go. Produce text quickly and experiment on the spot with several ways of expressing an idea, or with several plans for developing it. Later, you can delete unneeded text or reorganize your draft.

The word processor also gives you the flexibility to use different approaches in your writing. For example, you may want to follow the outline as you write, or you may want to write parts of the composition out of order—say, the conclusion first or the middle sections interspersed with the introduction and the conclusion.

## Be Two People at Once

Competent writers are constantly aware of—and concerned with—the impact of their words on the reader. Word processing enables you to become author and audience at the same time. In fact, some word-processing programs have a "split-screen" feature that permits you to view onscreen more than one file at a time. The split screen is divided into separate sections called *windows,* and each window displays a portion of a file. You can move back and forth between windows and make changes, creating two versions of text simultaneously. You can experiment by moving words and even entire passages around. You can try a variety of locations for the same paragraph. The split screen allows you to test the merits of several versions and choose the one you consider to be the most effective.

## Choose the Best Word

Word-processing programs have a "search and replace" function that indicates the number of times a given word is used in the text. If in revising your writing you suspect that you've overused a word, use this function to learn how many times it's mentioned in your text. (Some programs even display the location in the text of each occurrence.) Then, you can decide in each case whether to keep the word or to replace it with another.

Some word-processing programs have a built-in thesaurus to help you find a synonym. If yours does not, use your own thesaurus or a dictionary.

## Produce a Perfect Paper

One of the best features of the word processor is its ability, at the stroke of a key, to produce a hard copy that is free of deletions, inserts, carets, smudges, and other marks. You can edit your writing onscreen or the "old-fashioned" way—with pencil on paper.

If you prefer, the word processor can print a copy with wide spacing and/or wide margins so that you can easily pencil in corrections. In this case, after careful proofreading you would add each of your corrections onto the screen and then print out a clean final version.

Another advantage of using a word processor is that you can make the final paper look exactly as you want it to. Experiment with different sizes of type, margins, and space between lines before you print out your final copy.

## Spell Perfectly

Another feature of many processors, the *spelling checker,* automatically scans the text for misspelled or unfamiliar words. Spelling checkers call up each questionably spelled word so that you can check it against a built-in dictionary or one of your own.

## Become a More Effective Writer

Without a doubt, word processors make composing and revising easier. They enable you to concentrate your efforts on the most important aspect of writing: saying what you have to say in the best possible way.

# GUIDELINES FOR RESEARCH AND REPORT WRITING

514

A private eye summarizes an investigation. A sportswriter explains the academic probation of a star player. A student uses the library to write a term paper about film versions of *Macbeth*. All these people have conducted research to find and evaluate information. Despite differences in style and purpose, each person has written a report or research paper that presents information to others.

The following pages provide an overview of the steps needed to complete a formal research paper. Though the focus is on writing a paper for school, this process may be adapted to any kind of research task.

## Discovering a Topic

Sometimes you will be assigned a research topic. At other times, however, you will have to develop your own ideas for research topics.

Finding the right topic is crucial for success. Use the suggestions in The Writing Process on pages 959–960 to explore possibilities.

## Evaluating a Topic

Once you have possible topics, you need to eliminate the unsuitable ones, using questions such as the following to trim your list.

1. Are you interested enough in the topic to spend a long time with it?
2. Is there enough information available on the topic? A subject that is too recent or too technical may not have enough library resource materials.
3. Is the topic too simple? If you can learn everything you need to know in one article, the topic does not need research.
4. Is the topic too broad? Some topics, such as the causes of World War I or the effects of pollution, are just too big to handle in a short paper.

## Limiting a Topic

Once you have chosen what you think is a good topic, you need to narrow its scope; otherwise, you'll be overwhelmed with information. You can begin by reading about your subject in an encyclopedia or other reference book, looking for ways to whittle down your topic. For example, you might begin by exploring air battles of World War II, then narrow your topic to the Battle of Britain.

As you limit your topic, try to focus on the purpose of your paper. If you are interested in air bags, for example, deciding whether to evaluate their effectiveness or to report the history of their development will help narrow your hunt for information.

## Finding Sources

After narrowing your topic, you need to search for and collect information, using the tools listed below.

**The Card Catalog**    The card catalog provides a guide to all material in the library, using three categories: **title cards, author cards,** and **subject cards.** Begin by looking up your subject, but don't give up if it doesn't seem to be there. You may have to look up a variety of headings before you "strike gold."

Many public libraries offer a **computerized catalog system** that is more compact and often easier to use than the card catalog. If you know the author, title, or subject of a book, the computer will tell you if the library has that book. If you need a listing of the books the library has on a certain subject, type in the subject and the computer will list titles and call numbers of books available.

***Readers' Guide to Periodical Literature***
This source will list current magazine articles on your subject.

**Encyclopedias**    Generally, encyclopedias are a good starting point. They provide basic information and often suggest other books and articles. There are general encyclopedias as well as sets of special purpose references that focus on one subject. Here is a partial listing.

- *The World Book Encyclopedia*
- *Encyclopaedia Britannica*
- *Collier's Encyclopedia*
- *The Encyclopedia of World Art*
- *Encyclopedia of Psychology*

**Specialized Reference Books**   The reference section of your library contains all kinds of books that may prove helpful. The librarian can point you in the right direction.

- **Almanacs and Yearbooks** provide up-to-date facts and statistics. *Facts on File* is an example.

- **Specialized Dictionaries** focus on a particular field of knowledge. You can find dictionaries on such subjects as mathematics, politics, music, folklore, and art.

- **Atlases** contain maps as well as other information such as population, temperature, weather, and so on.

**People in the Know**   Interviews with people who are knowledgeable about your topic can add fresh insight. You'll be surprised at how cooperative such people are if approached in the right way.

## Evaluating Possible Sources

Researching a report can be time-consuming. To make the best use of your time, you should learn to quickly review the parts of a book to determine whether it will be a useful source of information.

**Title Page**   This page gives the complete title of the book, the names of authors or editors, the name of the publisher, and the place of publication.

**Copyright Page**   On this page you will find the date of publication. You can then decide if the material in the book is current enough for your purpose. For example, a 1965 copyright date on a book about nuclear energy indicates that the information in that particular book is probably out of date.

**Foreword, Preface, or Introduction**   These pages contain important background information, such as the author's purpose in writing the book or the method used in collecting the information.

**Table of Contents**   This is a summary or outline of the contents of the book, arranged in order of appearance. These pages are especially important because they quickly tell you whether the book discusses your topic and whether the coverage is detailed enough for your purposes.

**Text**   This is the body of the book. Look briefly at the text of any book you are interested in using. Can you understand the language and the level of discussion? Don't bother using a book that is too technical or too scholarly.

**Appendices**   Some books may have appendices at the back which contain additional information such as maps, charts, tables, illustrations, or graphs.

**Notes and Bibliography**   Here the author credits the sources used in the preparation of the book and lists other books that may be of interest to readers who need further information.

**Glossary**   This is a dictionary at the back of the book that lists unusual or technical terms used in the text.

**Index**   This is an alphabetical list of subjects covered in the book. Each entry is followed by page numbers that enable you to locate specific information. If your research subject is part of a chapter listed in the table of contents, a look at the index will tell you where it is located and how many pages are devoted to it.

## Creating Bibliography Cards

Use bibliography cards to keep track of your sources. Once you have looked through an article or book and decided it may be useful, record essential information on a 3" x 5" index card, using a separate card for each source. You need to include the full title, complete names of authors, and complete publishing information. Carefully record your information in the exact format used in the bibliography described on pages 968-969. Take time to get all the details in the right order, including page numbers and dates; you'll save yourself time and effort later on.

Also list the library call number on each card; if you use more than one library, record the name of the library as well. Finally, since your cards will also serve as a way of coding your notes, assign a number to each card and put it in the upper right-hand corner.

**Sample Bibliography Card**

```
Mosley, Leonard.
Battle of Britain.                    5
  New York: Time-Life, 1987.
940.54
M549b
```

# Taking Notes

**Format**    Most researchers write notes on 4" x 6" index cards to avoid confusing them with the smaller bibliography cards. The notes should be in the following format: 1) a heading, which gives the general idea, 2) the body of the note, 3) a page reference, and 4) a letter or number code which matches the note card to the bibliography card. Use a separate card for each note.

Source Number

**Sample Note Card**

Heading — Daily attacks                    5
Note —      In the fall of 1940, German bomb-
           ers attacked London for 68 consec-
           utive nights. On the weekend of
           September 7 and 8, more than 250
           planes were involved in an attack
           that killed at least 600 London ci-
Page       vilians.
Reference  84-89

**Knowing When**    Deciding when to take a note is difficult. The basic question you need to ask is How important is this information for my topic? Here are some things to look for:

1. The main concepts of the topic
2. Results of research or studies
3. Important dates and facts
4. Key people involved
5. Interesting examples or stories
6. Contrasting opinions of experts
7. Special terms

**Quoting or Summarizing**    Whenever possible, summarize the information you find in your own words. Keep your emphasis on what is important, being careful not to get bogged down in details. Also, label opinions; if you are reporting what a certain person thinks, be sure to give the person credit.

Statements that are memorable, clever, famous, or written in an interesting way should be quoted directly. Copy them word for word and mark the beginning and end with quotation marks. If the quotation is too long to copy completely, you can combine summary with direct quotation.

**Plagiarism**    The uncredited use of someone else's ideas or words is called plagiarism. This occurs when you present someone else's words as if they were your own, or when you summarize another person's ideas without giving credit. Your teacher can further explain this important subject.

# Organizing Your Material

**State Your Controlling Purpose**    Once you've assembled your information, you need a game plan for your paper. The first step is to state a controlling purpose, a sentence that sums up the aim of your paper. Your controlling purpose will help you move in the right direction as you organize and write your paper.

### Examples

To show how Mark Mathabane's description

of education in "Kaffir Boy" accurately reflects conditions in South Africa.

To explain why the RAF was able to defeat the Luftwaffe in the Battle of Britain.

To identify the problems of battery-powered automobiles and analyze possible solutions.

**Constructing an Outline**   Outlining can help you think through a paper before the writing starts. Though some writers work better without outlines, many find them necessary.

One way to begin an outline is to turn your controlling purpose into a question. This can help you break down your topic into its major parts, which then become the main headings of an outline.

Then review your notes, paying special attention to the headings on the note cards. Group the notes into separate piles, putting similar ones together. Your groups can help you organize your outline into headings and subheadings.

### Example

```
The Battle of Britain
    I. The background
        A. Germany's military suc-
           cesses
        B. Great Britain's defeats
   II. The Battle Plan
        A. German strategies and
           goals
            1. Operation Sea Lion
            2. Hitler's timetable
        B. The RAF's plan
            1. Use of radar
            2. Focused response to
               attackers
        C. Comparison of RAF and
           Luftwaffe
  III. The Battle
        A. The first wave of attacks
            1. German successes and
               setbacks
            2. British losses and
               suffering
```
```
        B. The siege of London
            1. Nightly bombing raids
            2. Civilian casualties
            3. British resistance
        C. Reasons for RAF victory
            1. Courage and skill of
               fighter pilots
            2. Strategic advantages
            3. Technological advan-
               tages
   IV. The Outcome
        A. Military effects
        B. Psychological effects
        C. Lessons learned about air
           warfare
```

## Writing from Your Outline

Your main purpose now is to get your ideas down in writing. In the draft, don't aim for perfect, error-free writing; simply get your ideas down in a form that you will be able to follow when it's time for revision. Use your outline the way a contractor would use a blueprint. Build from it, but don't hesitate to make changes if something isn't working.

## Incorporating Your Notes

You'll need to decide how best to present the information from your notes. Usually, you should use only key phrases, weaving them into your own sentences. Summarize as much as possible.

Sometimes you may wish to quote an entire passage. Longer quotations—those more than four typed lines—should be set off from the text. Indent the entire quote ten characters in from the left margin. Note that no quotation marks are needed.

### Phrases

```
In a radio broadcast Churchill
said the British were still wait-
ing for the German invasion and so,
he joked, ''were the fish.''
```

### Whole Sentences

> Winston Churchill reflected the feelings of many British citizens when he praised the Royal Air Force by saying, ''Never in the field of human conflict was so much owed to so few.''

### Long Passages

Perhaps Michael Kajecek best describes the achievement of the RAF:

> When the Battle of Britain began, Hitler's troops were nearly ready to invade, and the odds were in their favor. Neither Hitler nor the German generals could imagine that a handful of well-trained and courageous fighter pilots would halt the German war machine.

Be careful not to let quotations overrun your paper. You need to put the information together in a clear, easy-to-follow way.

## Documenting Your Sources

Any information that you use from your sources must be documented, or credited to its original source. To accomplish this, you can use **parenthetical documentation**. In most cases, you will list only the author's last name and a page reference in parentheses after the paraphrased, summarized, or quoted material. Refer to the following guidelines.

### Example

> The Luftwaffe's ''2700 bombers and fighters threatened to overwhelm the 600 British fighters'' (Campion 17).

## Guidelines for Documentation

1. **Works by one author.** Give the author's last name in parentheses at the end of a sentence, followed by the page numbers (Jones 58).
2. **Works by more than one author.** List all the last names in parentheses, or give one last name followed by *et al.* (Smith, Jones, and Wilcox 87) or (Smith *et al.* 87).
3. **Works with no author listed.** When citing an article that does not identify the author, use the title of the work or a shortened version of it (''Radar'' 398).
4. **Two works by the same author.** If you use more than one work by the same author, give the title, or a shortened version, after the author's last name (Markl, *Battle,* 211).
5. **Two works cited at the same place.** If you use more than one source to support a point, use a semicolon to separate the entries (Jones 398; Smith 87).

## Compiling the Bibliography

Once you have completed your draft, gather the bibliography cards for every source you have cited. Use these cards to create your Bibliography or Works Cited.

## Guidelines for Final Bibliography

1. Arrange all bibliography entries by the last name of the author or editor.
2. If no author or editor is provided, alphabetize each entry by the first word of the title. If the first word is *A, An,* or *The,* begin with the second word of the title.
3. Begin the first line of each entry at the left margin. If the entry runs to a second or third line, indent those lines five spaces.
4. Single-space each bibliography entry, but double-space between entries.
5. Put a period at the end of each entry.
6. Bibliography entries contain page numbers only when they refer to parts within whole works.

## Sample Bibliography Entries

**Whole Books**

**A. One author**

Webster, Charles. *From Paracelsus to Newton: Magic and the Making of Modern Science.* Cambridge: Cambridge UP, 1983.

**B. Two authors**

Gilbert, Sandra M., and Susan Gubar. *The Madwoman in the Attic: The Woman Writer and the Nineteenth Century Literary Imagination.* New Haven: Yale UP, 1979.

**C. Two or more authors**

Gatto, Joseph, *et al. Exploring Visual Design.* 2nd ed. Worcester: Davis, 1987.

Use *et al.,* Latin for *and others,* instead of listing all authors.

**D. No author given**

*Literary Market Place: The Directory of American Book Publishing.* 1984 ed. New York: Bowker, 1984.

**E. An editor, but no single author**

Saddlemyer, Ann, ed. *Letters to Molly: John Millington Synge to Maire O'Neill.* Cambridge: Harvard UP, 1984.

When you have cited several works from a collection, you may write one entry for the entire collection or list each work separately.

**F. Two or three editors**

Emanuel, James A., and Theodore L. Gross, eds. *Dark Symphony: Negro Literature in America.* New York: Macmillan, 1968.

### Parts Within Books

**A. A poem, short story, essay, or chapter from a collection of works by one author**

Angelou, Maya. "Remembering." *Poems.* New York: Bantam, 1986. 11.

**B. A poem, short story, essay, or chapter from a collection of works by several authors**

Welty, Eudora. "The Corner Store." *Prose Models.* Ed. Gerald Levin. New York: Harcourt, 1984. 20–22.

**C. A novel or play from a collection under one cover**

Serling, Rod. *Requiem for a Heavyweight. Twelve American Plays.* Ed. Richard Corbin and Miriam Balf. New York: Scribner's, 1973. 57–89.

### Magazines, Encyclopedias, Newspapers, Interviews

**A. An article from a quarterly or monthly magazine**

Batten, Mary. "Life Spans." *Science Digest* Feb. 1984: 46–51.

**B. An article from a weekly magazine**

Powell, Bill. "Coping with the Markets." *Newsweek* 27 Apr. 1987: 54.

**C. A magazine article with no author given**

"How the New Tax Law Affects America." *Nation's Accountants* 24 Sept. 1986: 66–69.

**D. An article from a daily newspaper**

James, Noah. "The Comedian Everyone Loves to Hate." *New York Times* 22 Jan. 1984, sec. 2: 23.

**E. An encyclopedia article**

"Western Frontier Life." *World Book Encyclopedia.* 1991 ed.

**F. A signed review**

Ludlow, Arthur. "Glass Houses." Rev. of *Rolling Breaks and Other Movie Business,* by Aljean Harmetz. *Movies* Aug. 1983: 76.

**G. An unsigned, untitled review**

Rev. of *Harry and Son. American Film* Mar. 1984: 78.

**H. An interview**

Farquharson, Reginald W. Personal interview. 26 May 1990.

## Revising

Research papers almost always need revising before they fully meet the needs of the writer and reader. To get ideas for revision, find someone to read your paper carefully, then the two of you can discuss the following questions as a guide.

1. Is the purpose for writing clear?
2. Are ideas presented clearly, one at a time?
3. Is more information needed anywhere?
4. Should some of the information be cut out?
5. Are there too many quotes or too few?

## The Final Edit

After making all the necessary changes, read through the paper once more, correcting mistakes in usage, spelling, and mechanics. Be sure that you've used quotation marks correctly and that you've followed the right format for your documentation and bibliography.

## Manuscript Form

**Legibility**   If possible, type or word process your papers. If you write by hand, use a pen with dark blue or black ink.

**Corrections**   Insert missing words by writing them neatly above the line in which they should appear. Use a caret (^) to indicate where they should be read in the text. You may make neat corrections by drawing a line through words and writing above them or by deleting a word or phrase with correction fluid and writing in the space. If there are several corrections on a page, recopy it.

**Labeling**   Follow the instructions given by your teacher for identifying yourself as the author of the paper. Usually, you will be asked to put your name in the top right-hand corner of the first page. Below your name, you will place the name or number of the course. Below that, you will put the date.

**Title**   The title of your paper should appear only once—on the first page. Center the title two lines below the last line of your heading. Leave two lines between the title and the first line of your first paragraph.

The first word of your title must be capitalized. Also capitalize any other important words in the title. Use initial capitals only. Do not capitalize every letter or underline your title. Use quotation marks in the title only if you are quoting some other source.

Teachers sometimes require a separate title page for long papers. A title page contains a heading in the upper right-hand corner and the title centered on the page.

# CORRECT BUSINESS LETTER FORM

Business letters have six parts: the **heading,** the **inside address,** the **salutation,** the **body,** the **closing,** and the **signature.** These six parts can be arranged in either **block form** or **modified block form.**

## Block Form and Modified Block Form

For all business letters, use plain white 8½" × 11" paper, whether you handwrite or type them. In **block form,** all parts begin at the left margin. Use this form only when you type the letter. In **modified block form** the heading, closing, and signature are aligned near the right margin, and the other parts are at the left margin.

### BLOCK FORM

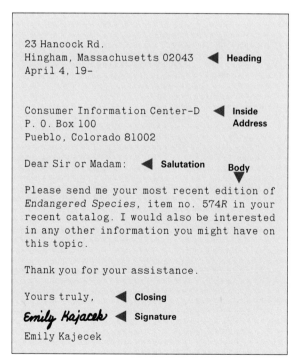

**Heading**    The heading is written at the top of the page. The first line contains your street address; the second line contains your town or city, state, and ZIP code. Separate the city and state with a comma and write out the name of the state. The third line gives the date of the letter. Place the heading at the left or the right margin, depending on whether you use the block form or the modified block form.

**Inside Address**    The inside address tells to whom the letter is being sent. Place the inside address at the left margin at least two lines below the heading. On the first line write the name of the receiver. If there is room, place the person's title on the same line, separated from the name by a comma. Otherwise, place the title on the next line. If you do not know the name of the person who will receive your letter, use the person's title or the name of the department. On the succeeding lines, place the company name and address, including the city, state, and ZIP code.

**Salutation**    Position the salutation two lines below the inside address. Begin with the word *Dear,* follow it by the name of the person to whom you are writing, and end with a colon. Use only the person's last name, preceded by a title such as *Mr., Mrs., Ms., Dr.,* or *Professor.* If you do not know the person's name, direct your letter to the appropriate department or position. Another alternative is to use a general salutation such as *Ladies and Gentlemen.* The following forms are acceptable:

Dear Mr. Allen:          Dear Sir or Madam:
Dear Ms. Kreutzer:     Dear Customer Service
Dear Mrs. Jackson:       Department:
                                   Dear Editor:

**Body**    The body, the main part of the letter in which you write your message, begins two spaces below the salutation. Typed business letters are singled spaced, though it is acceptable to use double spacing for short letters. Leave an extra space between each paragraph.

## MODIFIED BLOCK FORM

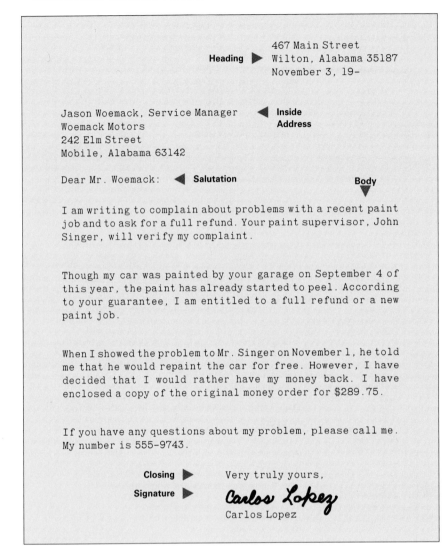

467 Main Street
Heading ▶ Wilton, Alabama 35187
November 3, 19–

Jason Woemack, Service Manager ◀ **Inside**
Woemack Motors **Address**
242 Elm Street
Mobile, Alabama 63142

Dear Mr. Woemack: ◀ **Salutation**

**Body** ▼

I am writing to complain about problems with a recent paint job and to ask for a full refund. Your paint supervisor, John Singer, will verify my complaint.

Though my car was painted by your garage on September 4 of this year, the paint has already started to peel. According to your guarantee, I am entitled to a full refund or a new paint job.

When I showed the problem to Mr. Singer on November 1, he told me that he would repaint the car for free. However, I have decided that I would rather have my money back. I have enclosed a copy of the original money order for $289.75.

If you have any questions about my problem, please call me. My number is 555-9743.

Closing ▶ Very truly yours,

Signature ▶ *Carlos Lopez*
Carlos Lopez

**Closing** The closing is placed two lines below the body, in line with the heading. Closings commonly used for business letters include *Sincerely, Sincerely yours,* and *Very truly yours.* Note that only the first word is capitalized and that the closing ends with a comma.

**Signature** Type or print your name four spaces below the closing, and sign your name in the space between.

# LANGUAGE
## HANDBOOK

## USING THE LANGUAGE HANDBOOK

This language handbook outlines some of the common errors people make in both written and spoken English. The handbook does not focus on learning rules and terms. Its goal is to help you communicate more effectively by providing concentrated review and practice in the areas where usage problems often occur.

## THE PARTS OF SPEECH

While terminology is not emphasized in this book, it is important to have a basic knowledge of the parts of speech so that you can communicate about language. If a peer reviewer or teacher suggests that you use stronger verbs in your writing, you need to know what a verb *is* in order to consider the suggestion.

Here is a quick review of the eight parts of speech.

**Noun** A noun is a word that names a person, place, thing, or idea.
  *lawyer   Philadelphia   shovel   hatred*

**Pronoun** A pronoun is a word used in place of a noun or another pronoun.
  *he   her   itself   someone   who   that*

**Verb** A verb is a word that tells about an action or a state of being.
  *jump   build   consider   is*

**Adjective** An adjective is a word that modifies a noun or a pronoun.
  *those   heavy   brown   many   three   gorgeous*

**Adverb** An adverb is a word that modifies a verb, an adjective, or another adverb.
  *easily   inside   nearly   almost   often*

**Preposition** A preposition is a word used with a noun or a pronoun to show how the noun or pronoun is related to some other word in the sentence.
  *under   after   from   in   at   toward*

**Conjunction** A conjunction is a word that connects words or groups of words.
  *and   but   or   although   since*

**Interjection** An interjection is a word or group of words that shows feeling or emotion.
  *good heavens   oh   wow   yeah   ouch*

# SECTION 1   WRITING COMPLETE SENTENCES

**A group of words is a *sentence* only if it expresses a complete thought. A sentence starts with a capital letter and ends with a period, a question mark, or an exclamation mark.**

## Understanding Sentence Parts

A sentence contains a subject and a verb and may also contain other elements, such as objects, that complete its meaning. The following diagrams will help you to review these parts.

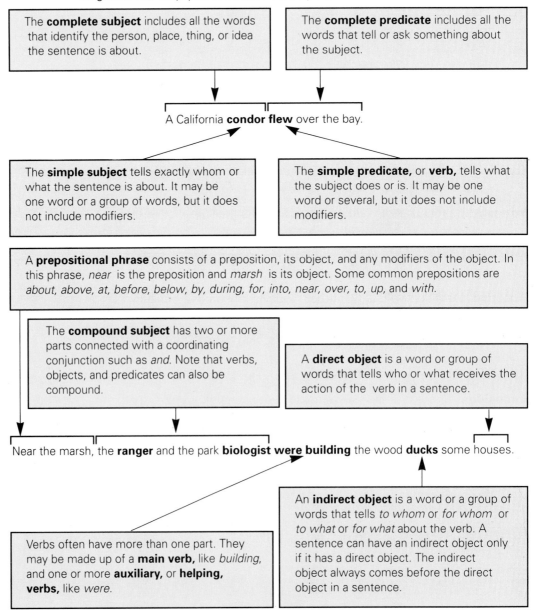

The **complete subject** includes all the words that identify the person, place, thing, or idea the sentence is about.

The **complete predicate** includes all the words that tell or ask something about the subject.

A California **condor flew** over the bay.

The **simple subject** tells exactly whom or what the sentence is about. It may be one word or a group of words, but it does not include modifiers.

The **simple predicate,** or **verb,** tells what the subject does or is. It may be one word or several, but it does not include modifiers.

A **prepositional phrase** consists of a preposition, its object, and any modifiers of the object. In this phrase, *near* is the preposition and *marsh* is its object. Some common prepositions are *about, above, at, before, below, by, during, for, into, near, over, to, up,* and *with.*

The **compound subject** has two or more parts connected with a coordinating conjunction such as *and.* Note that verbs, objects, and predicates can also be compound.

A **direct object** is a word or group of words that tells who or what receives the action of the verb in a sentence.

Near the marsh, the **ranger** and the park **biologist were building** the wood **ducks** some houses.

Verbs often have more than one part. They may be made up of a **main verb,** like *building,* and one or more **auxiliary,** or **helping, verbs,** like *were.*

An **indirect object** is a word or a group of words that tells *to whom* or *for whom* or *to what* or *for what* about the verb. A sentence can have an indirect object only if it has a direct object. The indirect object always comes before the direct object in a sentence.

# Recognizing Sentence Fragments

**A group of words that does not express a complete thought is a *sentence fragment*.**

A sentence fragment can be recognized by its incompleteness. Additional words are needed to make the meaning entirely clear.

**Fragment**  Ramadan, the Moslem holy month (What about Ramadan? The verb is missing.)

**Sentence**  Ramadan, the Moslem holy month, is observed with fasting and meditation.

**Fragment**  Refrain from working and eating (Who refrains from working and eating? The subject is missing.)

**Sentence**  On Yom Kippur, Orthodox Jews refrain from working and eating.

**Fragment**  When the New Year arrives (What happens then? Additional information is needed to complete the meaning.)

**Sentence**  When the New Year arrives, the Chinese celebrate with gift giving and parades.

---

**QUICK TIP**  To check for sentence fragments, ask yourself, Is this idea complete? Is something else needed to finish the statement? To check a composition for sentence fragments, try reading the composition from end to beginning, sentence by sentence.

---

**Exercise 1  Sentence Fragments**  On your paper write each group of words. If the word group is a sentence, add the necessary capitalization and end punctuation. If the word group is a fragment, add whatever is necessary to make it a complete sentence.

**Example**  hundreds of years ago, the warriors of Anglo-Saxon England
**Answer**  Hundreds of years ago, the warriors of Anglo-Saxon England listened to singers known as scops.

1. the scops chanted their stories to the sound of a harp
2. sang about ancient heroes, legends, and gods
3. one of their most famous stories, the epic poem *Beowulf*
4. the character Beowulf is a mighty warrior
5. fighting monsters of all kinds
6. a bog monster (and his mother), some sea serpents, and a fire-breathing dragon
7. the scop's audience, themselves warriors
8. loves monster stories, and the Anglo-Saxons were no exception
9. a poem that is today read by millions of students in English classes
10. survives in one original manuscript

## CLAUSE FRAGMENTS

A **clause** is a group of words that contains a subject and a verb. Some clauses can stand on their own as sentences.

*Holiday* means, literally, "holy day." (The subject is *holiday*. The verb is *means*.)

Some clauses cannot stand on their own as sentences.

when the French invented April Fool's Day (The subject is *the French*. The verb is *invented*. The group of words does not express a complete idea, so it is a fragment.)

## USING FRAGMENTS

Good writers often use sentence fragments in dialogue, and everyone uses them in speech from time to time. Of course, you should use fragments when taking notes, because you don't have time to write complete sentences when listening to a lecture or concentrating on a passage that you're reading. In formal writing, though, stick to complete sentences.

# Recognizing Run-on Sentences

**Two or more sentences written as though they were one is a** *run-on sentence.*

Sometimes a run-on is created because a writer is in a hurry. The writer simply fails to put an end mark at the end of one sentence and a capital letter at the beginning of the next. Of course, it's easy to correct such an error.

**Run-on**     The stunt pilot flew too low she almost had a serious accident.
**Correct**    The stunt pilot flew too low. She almost had a serious accident.

At other times a run-on occurs when a writer uses a comma instead of a period. This error is known as a **comma splice** or **comma fault.** You correct a comma splice in the same way you would correct any other run-on.

**Comma Splice**     That last loop was too low, the tail of the plane almost hit the ground.
**Correct**          That last loop was too low. The tail of the plane almost hit the ground.

**Exercise 2   Run-on Sentences**   Correct the following run-on sentences by adding capitalization and punctuation to show where each complete thought begins and ends.

**Example**     Octopuses are mollusks, they're related to snails and slugs.
**Answer**      Octopuses are mollusks. They're related to snails and slugs.

1. Whales and dolphins may be the smartest creatures in the sea however, they're not the only intelligent creatures down there.
2. The octopus is a remarkably intelligent creature, in fact, it's the most intelligent of all the mollusks.
3. Mollusks are soft-bodied creatures they include snails, slugs, squid, scallops, and clams.
4. Some octopuses are very small, others grow up to thirty feet long.
5. Some live in shallow water, others live in deep water.
6. An octopus has eight arms called tentacles these encircle its mouth.
7. An octopus eats by grabbing its prey with the tentacles then the prey is brought to the octopus's parrot-like beak in the middle of its web of arms.
8. The octopus has a filelike part in its beak this body part is called a radula.
9. The octopus cuts a hole in its prey with the radula it kills by injecting poison.
10. You can see why people would be afraid of a thirty-foot octopus, however, octopuses are usually gentle and will not harm humans.

**Exercise 3   Complete Sentences**   Tell whether each group of words is a *Sentence,* a *Fragment,* or a *Run-on.* Then write each group of words. Add any necessary end punctuation or capitalization. Correct the

Here are three other ways of correcting run-on sentences:

1. You can use a comma and a coordinating conjunction, such as *and, or, nor, for, but, so,* or *yet:*

   The stunt pilot flew too low, **and** she almost had a serious accident.

2. You can use a semicolon.

   The stunt pilot flew too low; she almost had a serious accident.

3. You can use a semicolon, a conjunctive adverb, such as *therefore* or *however,* and a comma.

   The stunt pilot flew too low; **therefore,** she almost had a serious accident.

fragments by adding words to make complete sentences. Correct the run-ons, including comma splices, by adding capitalization and punctuation.

1. Photography is an art form like painting or sculpture
2. Like painters, must know about space, light, and composition
3. Photography began in 1837, a French artist named Louis Daguerre made images with chemicals on a light-sensitive copper plate
4. Improved rapidly in the next twenty years
5. By the time of the American Civil War, in the 1860's, photographers were taking excellent pictures with their large, heavy cameras
6. The horrors of the battlefield, in photos by people like Mathew and Alexander Brady
7. In 1888 George Eastman invented the Kodak Brownie, it was the first practical camera for amateur use
8. Was small, lightweight, and used the first rolled film
9. Powerful pictures, with the improvement of cameras and film
10. During the Depression of the 1930's, when many people were out of work and poor
11. Photographers like Walker Evans traveled the country and captured on film the hardship and courage of the people
12. In *Let Us Now Praise Famous Men,* Evans's pictures and James Agee's words about the lives of poor farmers
13. A great photograph freezes the past and makes it available for the future
14. Brady's photographs still move us, so do the photographs by Evans
15. Truly an art worth learning more about

## Combining Sentences and Sentence Parts

Good writers strive to vary the lengths and types of sentences that they use. To make short sentences into longer ones and to vary the structure of your sentences, you can combine related sentences either by joining them or by adding parts of one to another.

To combine complete sentences, use a comma and a coordinating conjunction, or use one of the other methods described in the margin.

**Separate Sentences**  The summit of the mountain was windy and cold. The climbers huddled in their tent.

**Combined Sentences**  The summit of the mountain was windy and cold, so the climbers huddled in their tent.

When combining by adding sentence parts, use a coordinating conjunction. Combined sentence parts are called **compound** parts. Here are a few of the different parts that can be combined. (The italicized words are deleted.)

**Compound Subject**  The climbers reached the summit in the late afternoon. + Their guide *reached the summit in the late afternoon, too.* = The climbers **and** their guide reached the summit in the late afternoon.

## A MEMORY TIP

The coordinating conjunctions are *and, or, nor, for, but, so,* and *yet.* Here's a silly but effective memorization tip: Think of them as parts of a Russian-sounding name:

Andor Norfor Butsoyet

## COMBINING SENTENCES

Creating compounds is only one of many ways in which sentences can be combined by adding sentence parts. See the sentence-combining lessons following the units in this book for more on sentence-combining techniques.

You can also join sentences with a semicolon or with a semicolon, a conjunctive adverb, and a comma.

The wind died down; the campers were still cold.

The wind died down; **however,** the campers were still cold.

REMINDER

Too many *and*'s in a sentence or group of sentences will weaken your writing. When you write and combine ideas, try to vary the ways in which you connect ideas.

**Stringy**

Computers are interesting, and I want to study computers some day, and I think that there is a great future in computer work.

**Improved**

Computers are interesting. I want to study computers some day because there is a great future in computer work.

EXPERIMENTING WITH SENTENCES

Try out other ways of combining sentences. For example, how many ways can you think of to combine these sentences:
Susan uses a computer at school. It is a personal computer. She uses it for writing papers. She also uses it for editing her papers.

| | |
|---|---|
| **Compound Verb** | They unfolded their tent. + *Then they* pitched *it.* = They unfolded **and** pitched their tent. |
| **Compound Predicate** | Afterward they had some dinner. + *Then they* retired for the evening. = Afterward they had some dinner **and** retired for the evening. |
| **Compound Object** | When they awoke, a new snowfall had covered their tent. + *It also covered* their other gear. = When they awoke, a new snowfall had covered their tent **and** their other gear. |

---

**QUICK TIP**   When revising a piece of writing, look for ways to combine some sentences. Do not combine all sentences, of course. Leave some short for emphasis.

---

**Exercise 4   Combining Sentences**   Combine each pair of sentences by following the directions. Eliminate any italicized words.

1. Computers have been around for only a few decades. They are everywhere one looks these days. (Join the two sentences with a comma and *but.*)
2. One interesting area of computer science is called cognitive computing. *Cognitive computing is also known as* artificial intelligence. (Add the object from the second sentence, using *or.*)
3. Problem solving is one area of artificial intelligence that scientists are investigating. Human language *is another.* (Add the subject from the second sentence. Change the verb and any other words that you need to change to make them agree with your new compound subject.)
4. Computers are learning how to read handwriting. *They* are *also* being taught how to recognize people's voices and faces. (Add the predicate from the second sentence, using *and.*)
5. Real speaking is beyond the abilities of today's computers. Listening *is also beyond the abilities of today's computers.* (Combine by adding the subject from the second sentence. Change the verb to agree with your new compound subject.)
6. People are beginning to wonder: Can computers really think? *Can they even* feel? (Combine by adding the verb from the second sentence.)
7. Most computer scientists say that today's computers can't really think. Ordinary people *agree.* (Add the subject from the second sentence.)
8. However, computers of the future may really be able to think. *In fact, they* may be indistinguishable from people in this regard. (Add the predicate from the second sentence.)
9. Of course, that day is a long way off. The most ordinary human can do things that a computer can't even dream of. (Join the two sentences using a comma and *for.*)
10. No computer can feel love. *No computer can* get excited when the hometown team is winning. (Combine the predicates using *or.*)

# SECTION 2   USING NOUNS

A *noun* is a word that names a person, place, thing, idea, quality, action, or state.

| | |
|---|---|
| **Persons** | William Wordsworth, daughter, artist |
| **Places** | London, cathedral, harbor, courtyard |
| **Things** | bench, boots, candle, jacket |
| **Ideas** | faith, confidence, integrity, success |
| **Qualities** | darkness, smoothness, brilliance, beauty |
| **Actions** | swimming, thinking, leading, working |
| **States** | warmth, sleep, death, equilibrium |

## Classifying Nouns

When you classify something, you place it into a category with other like things, based on some shared characteristic or group of characteristics. Nouns are often classified as follows:

**Common Noun**   A general name. Examples: *museum, biplane, war, game, playwright.*

**Proper Noun**   A specific noun. Examples: *British Museum, Spirit of St. Louis, War of 1812, Scrabble, George Bernard Shaw.* Note that proper nouns are always capitalized.

**Concrete Noun**   Anything that can be seen, heard, smelled, touched, or tasted. Examples: *chair, whistle, lemon, velvet, chocolate.*

**Abstract Noun**   Something that cannot be directly seen, heard, tasted, smelled, or touched. Examples: *courage, anger, health, trust, truth.*

**Compound Noun**   A noun made of two or more words. Some compounds are written as one word, some as two words, and others with a hyphen. Examples: *surfboard, hang glider, son-in-law.*

**Collective Noun**   A noun that names a group of people or things. Examples: *swarm, bunch, Congress, crew.*

## Noun Usage

Change the form of a noun to indicate singular number, plural number, or possession.

◀ ORIGINS OF NOUNS

Nouns are formed in many different ways. Some, like *rattler,* are imitations of sounds. Some are **acronyms,** formed from the first letters of a phrase. For example, *scuba* is formed from the phrase "<u>s</u>elf-contained <u>u</u>nderwater <u>b</u>reathing <u>a</u>pparatus." Some words are **blends** of other words. For instance, *smog* is a blend of *smoke* and *fog,* and *laundromat* is a blend of *laundry* and *automatic.* Some words are **clipped forms** of longer words, like *gym,* from *gymnasium,* or *cab,* from *cabriolet.* Many nouns are borrowed from foreign languages or are introduced as slang.

◀ SPELLING

Some compound nouns are spelled solid *(mastermind);* some are spelled as separate words *(master of ceremonies);* and some are hyphenated *(master-at-arms).* Check a dictionary for proper spelling.

# Understanding Plural Nouns

Follow these rules when forming the plurals of nouns:

**REMINDER**

Some nouns that end in -s are actually singular, such as *economics* or *scissors*.

1. **Most nouns form the plural by simply adding -s to the singular.**

   ▶
   | weed | ape | umbrella | earthquake | lagoon |
   | weeds | apes | umbrellas | earthquakes | lagoons |

2. **Nouns that end in -s, -sh, -ch, -x, or -z form the plural by adding -es.** Even if you forget this exact rule, you can see from the following examples that adding -es to such words just looks and sounds right.

   | mass | ash | scratch | tax | buzz |
   | masses | ashes | scratches | taxes | buzzes |

**CHOICES, CHOICES**

Some nouns that end in -o preceded by a conso-nant can have either -s or -es in the plural:

   hobos *or* hoboes
   mottos *or* mottoes
   tornados *or* tornadoes
   zeros *or* zeroes

3. **If a noun ends in -o preceded by a vowel, add -s to form the plural. Some nouns that end in -o preceded by a consonant form the plural with -s. Others form the plural with -es. Consult a dictionary to determine which are which.**

   ▶
   | arpeggio | halo | veto | echo | potato |
   | arpeggios | halos | vetoes | echoes | potatoes |

4. **If a noun ends in -y preceded by a vowel, add -s to form the plural. If the -y follows a consonant, change the -y to -i and add -es.**

   | Monday | donkey | envoy | baby | hobby |
   | Mondays | donkeys | envoys | babies | hobbies |

**SPELLING**

There is no general rule covering all nouns end-ing in -f or -fe. Some form the plural with -s, others by changing the -f to -v and adding -es. Use a dictionary to check the plurals of words with these endings.

5. **For most nouns ending in -f or -fe, change the -f to -v and add -es or -s.**

   ▶
   | bookshelf | life | hoof | sheaf | wolf |
   | bookshelves | lives | hooves | sheaves | wolves |

   **For some nouns ending in -f or -fe, just add -s to make the plural.**

   | proof | roof | gaffe | grief | puff |
   | proofs | roofs | gaffes | griefs | puffs |

6. **Some nouns have the same form for both singular and plural.**

   | salmon | Vietnamese | reindeer | quail | elk |
   | salmon | Vietnamese | reindeer | quail | elk |

**LANGUAGE HISTORY AND WORD PLAY**

In Old English, com-pounds were very com-mon. For instance, the ocean was called the whale-road. A king, who was supposed to give gifts, was called a ring-bearer or ring-giver. A dragon was called a fire-worm.

7. **For some nouns the plural is formed in a unique way.**

   | louse | stigma | basis | cherub | foot |
   | lice | stigmata | bases | cherubim | feet |

   ▶
8. **If a compound noun is written as one word, form the plural by changing the last word in the compound to its plural form.**

   | firefly | stepchild | cupful |
   | fireflies | stepchildren | cupfuls |

**If the compound is written as separate words or is hyphenated, change the most important word to the plural form.**

| | |
|---|---|
| cherry blossom | mother-in-law |
| cherry blossoms | mothers-in-law |

**When a compound noun is made up of a verb and an adverb, the plural is formed by adding -s or -es to the last word.**

| | |
|---|---|
| drive-in | takeover |
| drive-ins | takeovers |

**Exercise 1   Plural Nouns**   Write the plural form of each noun. If you need help, check a dictionary.

| | | | |
|---|---|---|---|
| **1.** crash | **6.** hex | **11.** solo | **16.** zero |
| **2.** artery | **7.** democracy | **12.** shut-in | **17.** Wednesday |
| **3.** dwarf | **8.** ox | **13.** carp | **18.** doorknob |
| **4.** navy | **9.** werewolf | **14.** crisis | **19.** submarine |
| **5.** shrimp | **10.** hero | **15.** history | **20.** sheep dog |

**Exercise 2   Plural Nouns**   Change the italicized singular nouns to their correct plural forms.

1. In the *Middle Age* people poured into *city* such as Paris and London.
2. Some were *student* hoping to study at the *university*.
3. Many were *merchant* who came to sell their *good*.
4. In some cities great *church* called *cathedral* were built during the Middle Ages.
5. Some people spent their whole *life* working on a cathedral.
6. *Tax* were collected to pay for the cathedrals.
7. Sometimes the walls were raised too high, and the *roof* of the cathedrals collapsed.
8. The outside of a cathedral was covered with *hundred* of handcarved *figure*.
9. The designers of these huge *building* were considered *hero*.
10. Today, if you stand inside a medieval cathedral, you can almost hear the *echo* of the *voice* of its *builder*.

## Understanding Possessive Nouns

Follow these rules when forming the possessive of nouns:

**1. If a noun is singular, add an apostrophe and -s to form the possessive.**

| | | | | |
|---|---|---|---|---|
| Crusoe | Paris | kangaroo | team | Ms. Chin |
| Crusoe's | Paris's | kangaroo's | team's | Ms. Chin's |

**ALTERNATIVES**

Instead of writing a possessive using an apostrophe, you can often substitute a prepositional phrase. For example, *Saudi Arabia's desert* can become *the desert of Saudi Arabia.*

REMINDER

..................

Writers sometimes con-
fuse the rules for singu-
lar nouns that end in -s
and plural nouns that
end in -s. Remember
that singular nouns that
end in -s form the pos-
sessive by adding an
apostrophe and -s. Plural
nouns that end in -s
form the possessive by
adding just an apostro-
phe.

**2. If a noun is plural and ends in -s, add just the apostrophe.**

writers                    stories
writers' papers            stories' endings

**3. If a noun is plural and does not end in -s, add an apostrophe and -s.**

media                      oxen
media's reports            oxen's horns

**Exercise 3  Possessive Nouns**  Write the possessive form of each noun.

**1.** coaches      **6.** engineers   **11.** bakers    **16.** people
**2.** dreamers     **7.** White Sox   **12.** goalies   **17.** skater
**3.** Luis         **8.** geese       **13.** children  **18.** hostess
**4.** ranch        **9.** zoo         **14.** linemen   **19.** cities
**5.** tourists     **10.** tourist    **15.** Ms. Lee   **20.** the Cohens

**Exercise 4  Possessive Nouns**  Change the italicized nouns to their correct possessive forms.

**1.** Homer told the story of the ancient *Greeks* war against Troy.
**2.** Homer described the *soldiers* bravery.
**3.** One night the Greek leaders held a meeting in the *king* tent.
**4.** They discussed *Troy* high, strong walls.
**5.** The *leaders* plan was to trick the Trojans.
**6.** Their soldiers climbed secretly into the wooden *horse* belly.
**7.** The Trojans dragged the huge horse through the *city* gates.
**8.** The *Trojans* mistake cost them the war.
**9.** Homer tells of the Trojan *people* downfall and the destruction of Troy.
**10.** Our *class* homework is to read the first chapter of *Homer* story.

**Exercise 5  Noun Usage Review**  Rewrite these sentences, correcting one error in the use of plurals or possessives in each sentence. If a sentence has no error, write *Correct.*

**1.** Parents love to show off their photoes.
**2.** If given a chance, a typical parent will show you bunch's of these family photographs.
**3.** Pictures of babys can be amusing and adorable.
**4.** However, these pictures are rarely as adorable to others as they are to the childrens' parents.
**5.** Often people take family photographs on holidaies.
**6.** Sometimes these photographs are taken in photographers' studioes.
**7.** It seems that nearly all parents want to document the lifes of their kids.
**8.** Not long ago, parents' only choice if they wanted pictures of their kids was to take photos.
**9.** Today, many peoples' children are videotaped.
**10.** Later, the children will be able to see themself as they were years before.

# SECTION 3  USING PRONOUNS

**A *pronoun* is a word that is used in place of a noun or another pronoun. The word that a pronoun refers to is called its *antecedent*.**

The *boat* veered as *it* rounded the buoy. (The pronoun *it* refers to the noun *boat*. *Boat* is the antecedent of *it*.)

## Classifying Pronouns

There are many different classes of pronouns. The following chart is a summary.

---

**Classes of Pronouns**

---

**Personal**

I, you, he, she, it, we, they, me, her, him, us, them, my, mine, your, yours, hers, his, its, our, ours, their, theirs

**Reflexive and Intensive**

myself, yourself, himself, herself, itself, ourselves, yourselves, themselves

**Demonstrative**

this, that, these, those

**Interrogative**

who, whose, whom, which, what

**Relative**

who, whose, whom, which, what, that

**Indefinite**

all, another, any, anybody, anyone, anything, both, each, either, everybody, everyone, everything, few, many, more, most, much, neither, nobody, none, no one, nothing, one, other, several, some, somebody, someone, something, such

---

# Pronoun Usage

Listen to any conversation. Read any short story. Watch any play or movie. The chances are that within a few minutes you will encounter a great many pronouns. Pronouns are extremely common. This section will show you how to avoid the most common pronoun errors.

## Personal Pronouns

Like nouns, pronouns can be used to refer to people, places, things, or ideas. However, unlike nouns, personal pronouns change form, or **case,** depending on how they are used in a sentence. The three cases of personal pronouns are the **nominative case,** the **objective case,** and the **possessive case.**

### PERSON IN PRONOUNS

Pronouns can also be classified according to the person or persons to whom they refer:

A **first-person pronoun** refers to or includes the person who is writing or speaking. These pronouns are *I, me, my, mine, we, us, our,* and *ours.*

A **second-person pronoun** refers to or includes the person being addressed by the writer or speaker. These pronouns are *you, your,* and *yours.*

A **third-person pronoun** refers to one or more other people or things. These pronouns are *he, she, it, him, her, his, hers, its, they, them, their,* and *theirs.*

| Forms of Personal Pronouns | | | |
|---|---|---|---|
| | **Nominative** | **Objective** | **Possessive** |
| **Singular** | I | me | my, mine |
| | you | you | your, yours |
| | she, he, it | her, him, it | her, hers, his, its |
| **Plural** | we | us | our, ours |
| | you | you | your, yours |
| | they | them | their, theirs |

▶ **Exercise 1  Personal Pronouns**   Write the italicized personal pronouns from the following passages. Label each pronoun *Singular* or *Plural.* Then label it *Nominative, Objective,* or *Possessive.*

**1.** "Now one bond unites *us* all—to wage war until victory is won, and never to surrender ourselves to servitude and shame, whatever the cost and the agony may be. This is one of the most awe-striking periods in the long history of France and Britain. *It* is also beyond doubt the most sublime. Side by side, unaided except by *their* kith and kin in the Dominions and by the wide Empires which rest beneath their shield—side by side, the British and French peoples have advanced to rescue not only Europe but mankind from the foulest and most soul-destroying tyranny which has ever darkened and stained the pages of history. Behind *them*—behind us—behind the armies and fleets of Britain and France—gather a group of shattered States and bludgeoned races: the Czechs, the Poles, the Norwegians, the Danes, the Dutch, the Belgians—upon all of whom the long night of barbarism will descend, unbroken even by a star of hope, unless *we* conquer, as conquer we must; as conquer we shall."

—from *The Speeches,* Sir Winston Churchill

**2.** ''Sergeant Noonan wandered into the kitchen, came out quickly, and said, 'Look, Mrs. Maloney. *You* know that oven of *yours* is still on, and the meat still inside.'

'Oh dear *me!*' *she* cried. 'So *it* is!'

'*I* better turn it off for *you,* hadn't I?'

''When the sergeant returned the second time, she looked at *him* with *her* large, dark, tearful eyes. . . . 'Patrick would never forgive me, God bless his soul, if I allowed you to remain in *his* house without offering you decent hospitality. Why don't you eat up that lamb that's in the oven?' ''

—''Lamb to the Slaughter,'' Roald Dahl

## Uses of Personal Pronouns

### *Nominative pronouns* are used as subjects and as predicate pronouns.

As you know, the nominative pronouns are *I, we, you, he, she, it,* and *they.* These pronouns are used as the subjects of sentences. The **subject** is what does the action of a sentence.

*He* descended into the cave.          *It* was dark and wet and cold.

Nominative pronouns can also be used as predicate pronouns. A **predicate pronoun** is one that comes after a linking verb and repeats or renames the subject.

The nominee should have been *she.*          Instead, it was *I.*

### *Objective pronouns* are used as direct objects, indirect objects, and objects of prepositions.

As you've seen, the objective pronouns are *me, us, you, him, her, it,* and *them.* Objective pronouns are used as objects of all kinds:

| | |
|---|---|
| **Direct Object** | Do you know *them?* <br> I remember *her* quite well. |
| **Indirect Object** | The president gave *her* an order. <br> An admirer sent *him* a love letter. |
| **Object of a Preposition** | From *her* I learned what I know about writing. <br> The wind whipped around *us.* |

### *Possessive pronouns* are used to show ownership or belonging.

The possessive pronouns are *my, mine, your, yours, his, her, hers, its, our, ours, their,* and *theirs.* Possessive pronouns can be used by themselves. They may also be used before nouns.

*Yours* is the best case.          *Their* argument was more convincing.

**THAT'S A SWITCH!**

A predicate pronoun and its subject can often be switched:

The *winner* was *she.*

*She* was the *winner.*

The nominative case is used for predicate pronouns because they are so much like subjects.

**REMINDER**

A **direct object** receives the action of the verb.

An **indirect object** tells *to whom* or *for whom* or *to what* or *for what* the action of the sentence is done.

An **object of a preposition** comes after a preposition, such as *above, after, around, as, behind, below, beneath, from, in, into, on, over, to, under,* or *until.*

**LOOKING AT WORDS**

Some pronouns are occasionally used as adjectives—words that modify nouns. In such cases, the word is both a pronoun and an adjective!

**Exercise 2  Uses of Personal Pronouns**   Number your paper from 1 to 10. List the italicized pronouns from the passage below. Tell whether each pronoun is *Nominative, Objective,* or *Possessive.* Then, for each nominative pronoun, tell whether it is a *Subject* or a *Predicate Pronoun.*

▶ "Is that *you?*" asked Robert. *His* wife had just emerged from the ocean, covered with seaweed. *Her* face was obscured by a mask.

"It is *I,*" she answered. *She* pulled off her mask and fins. Then she tossed *them* up on the beach.

"How was *it?*" Robert asked excitedly.

"Strange. What an experience—being able to breathe underwater! *I* was scared only once. *My* tank started to slip, but I got *it* tightened again."

## Problems with Personal Pronouns

▶ You probably use personal pronouns all the time with very little trouble. After all, you would never say, "Him are here" or "I is happy." You can trust your ears to tell you that "He is here" and "I am happy" are the correct forms. There are, however, a few situations involving pronouns that cause trouble for people. These situations are described below.

**Personal Pronouns as Predicate Pronouns.** In formal writing or speech, a nominative pronoun should be used after a linking verb, such as *is* or *was.*

| **Incorrect** | It was *them* who played in Shea Stadium. |
| **Correct** | It was *they* who played in Shea Stadium. |

| **Incorrect** | The anchor persons are *her* and Mike McDowell. |
| **Correct** | The anchor persons are *she* and Mike McDowell. |

In casual conversation most speakers today do use objective pronouns after linking verbs. For example, it is common to hear people say, "It's *me*" or "That's *him*." However, in formal writing and speech, an objective pronoun should not be used after a linking verb.

**REMINDER**

Remember that the nominative pronouns are *I, you, he, she, it, we,* and *they.* The objective pronouns are *me, you, him, her, it, us,* and *them.*

**Personal Pronouns as Objects of Prepositions.** One common mistake is to use a nominative pronoun as the object of a preposition. Remember, a pronoun as the object of a preposition is always in the objective case.

| | |
|---|---|
| **Incorrect** | It's a secret between you and *I.* |
| **Correct** | It's a secret between you and *me.* |

**Personal Pronouns in Compounds.** A compound is one or more words joined together. Sometimes the word *and* is used to join pronouns with nouns or other pronouns, as in compounds like these:

| | |
|---|---|
| Julio and I | Julio and me |
| she and he | her and him |

It's sometimes difficult to tell which pronoun to use in a compound. Consider the following sentences:

| | |
|---|---|
| **Incorrect** | Newton and *him* invented a new kind of math. |
| **Correct** | Newton and *he* invented a new kind of math. |

| | |
|---|---|
| **Incorrect** | Historians give both Newton and *he* the credit. |
| **Correct** | Historians give both Newton and *him* the credit. |

> **QUICK TIP** How do you know which pronoun to use in a compound? Try using the pronoun by itself, without the other part of the compound. "*Him* invented a new kind of math" sounds odd. "*He* invented a new kind of math" sounds right, and it is.

***We* and *Us* Before Nouns.** The pronouns *we* and *us* are sometimes used as modifiers before nouns, as in "we students" or "us actors." If the modified noun is a subject or predicate noun, use *we.* If the modified noun is an object, use *us.*

| | |
|---|---|
| **Incorrect** | *Us* volunteers helped in the soup kitchen. (*Volunteers* is the subject of the verb *helped.* Therefore, you need to use *we.*) |
| **Correct** | *We* volunteers helped in the soup kitchen. |

| | |
|---|---|
| **Incorrect** | The director sent *we* volunteers a letter of thanks. (*Volunteers* is the object of the verb *sent.* Therefore, use *us.*) |
| **Correct** | The director sent *us* volunteers a letter of thanks. |

> **QUICK TIP** Once again, you can tell which pronoun to use by trying the pronoun alone, without the word that the pronoun modifies. "The director sent *us* a letter" sounds right and is.

**Exercise 3  Problem Personal Pronouns**  Choose the correct pronoun from those in parentheses.

1. (We, Us) tourists took a rafting trip down the Penobscot River.
2. The guide and (I, me) both sat in the back of the large rubber raft.
3. It was (he, him) who handled the rudder and steered the raft.
4. Once during the trip, the guide gave the other tourists and (I, me) quite a thrill.
5. He took (we, us) amateur rafters over a waterfall!
6. It was (I, me) who was most afraid, I think.
7. Between you and (I, me), I think that the guide took unnecessary risks.
8. However, the waterfall was a very small one, and going over it was exciting for the other rafters and (I, me).
9. My sister Susan says that the only people with a right to complain were my father and (she, her).
10. It was (they, them) who fell out and had to be rescued!

## Using *Who* and *Whom*

> *Who* **is a nominative pronoun and is used as the subject of a verb or as a predicate pronoun.**

> *Whom* **is an objective pronoun and is used as a direct object, an indirect object, or an object of a preposition.**

The rules for using *who* and *whom* are the same as the rules for using personal pronouns. *Who,* the nominative pronoun, is used as a subject or predicate pronoun. *Whom,* the objective pronoun, is used as an object. Consider the following examples:

| | |
|---|---|
| **Subject** | *Who* is the Prime Minister of England? |
| **Predicate Pronoun** | The Prime Minister is *who?* |
| **Direct Object** | *Whom* did the ruling party choose to lead the country? |
| **Indirect Object** | The party gave *whom* the nomination? |
| **Object of a Preposition** | To *whom* was the nomination given? |

As you can see, *who* and *whom* are often used in questions. When used in questions, *who* and *whom* are called **interrogative pronouns.**

*Who* and *whom* are also sometimes used to introduce clauses. As you probably know, a **clause** is a group of words with a subject and a verb. When used to introduce clauses, *who* and *whom* are called **relative pronouns.**

> Empedocles was the Greek philosopher who jumped into the burning crater of Mount Aetna. *(Who jumped into the burning crater of Mt. Aetna is a clause. Who is the subject. Jumped is the verb.)*

GRAMMAR
A clause that cannot stand on its own is called a **subordinate clause.** An example is *whom you like.* Its subject is *you.* Its verb is *like.* Its direct object is *whom.*

To determine which pronoun to use, *who* or *whom,* isolate the group of words to which the pronoun belongs:

(who, whom) jumped into the crater

Since the pronoun is being used as the subject of the verb *jumped, who* is correct.

**Exercise 4   *Who* and *Whom***   Choose the correct pronoun from those given in parentheses.

1. (Who, Whom) discovered the lost Mayan city of Copán?
2. John Lloyd Stephens—that's (who, whom).
3. It is Stephens (who, whom) historians credit with this amazing discovery.
4. Stephens shared the discovery with Frederick Catherwood, an artist with (who, whom) he teamed up early in his explorations.
5. Catherwood, (who, whom) was an excellent draftsman, helped Stephens by drawing their discoveries.
6. Both were men for (who, whom) no adventure was too dangerous.
7. After reading a book by a Spanish explorer (who, whom) had been in Mexico, Stephens and Catherwood decided to search for a lost civilization in the part of Mexico known as the Yucatán.
8. They were two explorers (who, whom) few people at the time believed.
9. Stephens and Catherwood could find no one (who, whom) would support their belief in this lost Mexican civilization.
10. People were surprised when they learned that these adventurers, (who, whom) they had scorned, had discovered the remains of the Mayan civilization.

## Reflexive and Intensive Pronouns

**A reflexive or intensive pronoun can only be used when it has an antecedent in the same sentence.**

Reflexive and intensive pronouns are created by adding *-self* or *-selves* to certain personal pronouns. The pronouns formed with *-self* are singular:

myself    yourself    himself    herself    itself

The pronouns formed with *-selves* are plural:

ourselves    yourselves    themselves

Note that these are the only acceptable reflexive and intensive pronouns. *Hisself* and *theirselves* are nonstandard and should be avoided.

**Incorrect**   The boss gave hisself a raise.
**Correct**     The boss gave himself a raise.

WHEN IS A PRONOUN
REFLEXIVE? WHEN IS
IT INTENSIVE?

A pronoun is **reflexive** when it reflects the action of the verb back on the subject.

They helped themselves. (*Themselves* reflects the action back onto the subject *they.*)

A pronoun is **intensive** when it is used to emphasize a noun.

The villagers themselves built a new schoolhouse. (*Themselves* emphasizes the noun *villagers.*)

Whenever a reflexive or intensive pronoun appears in a sentence, the word that it refers to—its antecedent—must appear in the same sentence. It is incorrect to use one of these pronouns without an antecedent.

**Incorrect**    Malcolm and *myself* studied the problem of global warming.
           *(Myself* does not refer to another word in the sentence.)
**Correct**      Malcolm and *I* studied the problem of global warming.

**Exercise 5  Reflexive Pronouns**    Rewrite the following sentences, correcting any errors in the use of reflexive or intensive pronouns. If a sentence does not contain an error, write *Correct.*

1. After reading some Renaissance literature in English class, Kyle and myself decided to organize a Renaissance festival.
2. The drama teacher at the school agreed to let some other students and ourselves organize the festival.
3. He loaned a book on costumes to Kyle and myself.
4. We made Renaissance costumes for ourselves.
5. We enlisted some other students who were theirselves interested in the Renaissance (or perhaps just in having a good time).
6. Soon, Kyle and myself had plenty of help.
7. The festival itself was a huge success.
8. There were jugglers, minstrels, magicians, acrobats, beggars, royalty, peasants, and even a jester played by myself.
9. The drama teacher trained the students and himself played a part—he was a knight in shining armor.
10. The best costumes at the festival were worn by me and himself.

**THINKING CRITICALLY**

When indefinite pronouns are used to make general statements, these statements are often too broad. Consider the following:

*No one* listens to big-band music anymore.

It is not true that no one listens to big-band music. A statement like this—one that covers too many people or things—is called an **overgeneralization.** To correct an overgeneralization, you can often use a word that is less general:

*Fewer* people listen to big-band music these days than in the past.

► ## Indefinite Pronouns

**If an indefinite pronoun is singular, its verb and any pronouns that refer to it must be singular. If an indefinite pronoun is plural, its verb and any pronouns that refer to it must be plural.**

An **indefinite pronoun** is one that does not refer to a definite person or thing. Some indefinite pronouns are singular:

| | | | |
|---|---|---|---|
| another | either | neither | other |
| anybody | everybody | nobody | somebody |
| anyone | everyone | no one | someone |
| anything | everything | nothing | something |
| each | much | one | |

Some are plural:

| | | | | |
|---|---|---|---|---|
| both | few | many | much | several |

Some can be singular or plural, depending on their use in the sentence:

| | | | |
|---|---|---|---|
| all | enough | most | plenty |
| any | more | none | some |

**Singular**   *Some* of the Berlin Wall is still standing. (*Some* refers to the singular word *Wall*. Therefore, it is singular and takes a singular verb, *is*.)

**Plural**   *Some* of the people of Germany are selling souvenir pieces of the wall. (*Some* refers to the plural word *people*. Therefore, it is plural and takes a plural verb, *are*.)

When an indefinite pronoun is used as a subject, the verb must agree with the pronoun.

**Incorrect**   *Neither* of the microphones *were* on. (*Neither* is the subject. Since *neither* is singular, the verb should be singular.)

**Correct**   *Neither* of the microphones *was* on.

When a personal pronoun refers back to an indefinite pronoun, it must agree with that indefinite pronoun.

**Incorrect**   Will *somebody* lend me *their* history book? (*Somebody* is singular. Therefore, the possessive pronoun that refers to *somebody* should also be singular.)

**Correct**   Will *somebody* lend me *his* history book?
Will *somebody* lend me *her* history book?
Will *somebody* lend me *his or her* history book?

Notice that the phrase *his or her* is singular and can be used in place of *his* or *her* alone when the gender of the person referred to is not known.

**Exercise 6  Indefinite Pronouns**   Rewrite the following sentences, correcting any errors in the use of pronouns. If a sentence contains no errors, write *Correct*.

1. Each of the candidates running for class office must have their speech prepared by Tuesday.
2. All of the candidates is expected to ask three of their teachers for letters of recommendation.
3. Several of the candidates already has letters on file.
4. Anyone without letters of recommendation is ineligible for office.
5. Some of the candidates write his or her speeches on note cards; others deliver their speeches from memory.
6. Each of the candidates have an assigned speaking time.
7. Each one of the candidates have three minutes to deliver his or her speech.
8. Last year, we found that none of the students cast their votes solely on the basis of popularity.

The words *either, neither,* and *both* are sometimes not used as pronouns. Instead, they are used as parts of the **correlative conjunctions** *either... or, neither... nor,* and *both... and.*

*Neither* the President *nor* the Congress has absolute power.

**HINT**

Don't be fooled by phrases that come between the indefinite pronoun subject and its verb.

**GUIDELINES FOR NONSEXIST LANGUAGE**

Many pronouns have **gender;** that is, they tell whether the person being spoken or written about is male or female. In the past, the pronouns *he* and *him* were used exclusively to refer to a single person when the sex of that person was not known. In recent years, however, it has become common for people to use the phrases *he or she* and *him or her* to refer to a single person whose sex is not known. These phrases are singular and take singular verbs, as in *He or she sends flowers every year on my birthday.*

9. Anyone absent on election day will have forfeited their right to vote unless he or she picked up an absentee ballot earlier.
10. The results of the election will be announced to everyone during his or her homeroom period.

## Other Problems with Pronouns

**Indefinite Antecedent.** A reader or listener should always be able to tell the person, object, place, or idea to which a pronoun refers. In other words, the antecedent of a pronoun should be clear.

**Unclear**    There was some question about the play, but the referee finally gave *it* to the Wildcats. (To what does the word *it* refer? Does it refer to the play? Does it refer to something else that isn't named? The antecedent is unclear.)

**Clear**    There was some question about the play, but the referee finally gave the first down to the Wildcats.

**Ambiguous Pronoun Reference.** If you can't tell which of two or more words a pronoun refers to, then that pronoun is **ambiguous.** When a pronoun has more than one possible reference, you will have to rewrite the sentence to clarify the reference of the pronoun.

**Unclear**    Andrea gave Caitlin her notebook. (Does the pronoun *her* refer to *Andrea* or to *Caitlin?* To whom does the notebook belong? One cannot tell.)

**Clear**    Andrea gave her notebook to Caitlin.

**Clear**    Andrea returned Caitlin's notebook.

**Pronouns and Contractions.** A **contraction** is formed when two words are joined together and one or more letters of the second word are replaced by an apostrophe. These are some common contractions:

    it's = it + is        they're = they + are
    you're = you + are    who's = who + is

Sometimes the preceding contractions are confused with the possessive pronouns *its, your, their,* and *whose.*

**Incorrect**    The hikers were looking for *they're* gear.
**Correct**    The hikers were looking for *their* gear.

**Incorrect**    *Its* a great day for hiking.
**Correct**    *It's* a great day for hiking.

### LOOKING AT WORDS

**Homonyms** are words that sound alike but mean different things. *It's* and *its, you're* and *your, they're* and *their,* and *who's* and *whose* are homonyms. *They're* and *their* have another homonym—the demonstrative pronoun *there.*

> **QUICK TIP**   To decide whether to use a contraction in a sentence, substitute the words for which the contraction stands. In the first example above, "The hikers were looking for they are gear" sounds incorrect. By substituting the words the contraction stands for and then relying on your ear, you can tell which pronoun to use.

**Them** and **Those.** *Them* is an objective-case personal pronoun. It is used only as an object, never as a subject or a modifying word. Do not confuse the word *them* with the word *those,* which *can* be a subject or a modifier.

**Incorrect**   *Them* are the letters that Byron wrote while he was fighting in Greece. (*Them* is incorrectly used as the subject of the verb *are.*)

**Correct**   *Those* are the letters that Byron wrote while he was fighting in Greece.

**Incorrect**   Have you read *them* letters? (*Them* is incorrectly used to modify *letters.*)

**Correct**   Have you read *those* letters?

**Exercise 7   Other Pronoun Problems**   Rewrite the following sentences, correcting all errors in pronoun usage. If a sentence has no errors, write *Correct.*

1. Paul went to the information booth near the entrance to the train station, and she said that the train would not be running.
2. "Its not very reliable," she said.
3. "In fact, they're not sure if that train will ever run properly."
4. "Great!" answered Paul. "Them's the breaks, I guess."
5. "No, its not the brakes," she replied.
6. "Their having problems with the engine."
7. "Your very funny," Paul said, "but I need to get home."
8. "Well, there is a taxi over there next to that shuttle bus. You could take it home."
9. "I'm not sure whether it's a good idea to take a taxi," Paul answered. "I don't have a lot of money."
10. "Well, there are you're feet," she said. "You could take them home."

**Exercise 8   Pronoun Usage Review**   Rewrite the following sentences, correcting any errors in the use of pronouns.

1. Last Friday Ms. Harding gave we seniors our biography assignments.
2. Who did she give me for a subject?
3. She assigned Leo Tolstoy to Linda and myself.
4. I couldn't believe it when Ms. Harding gave Linda and I that project.
5. Later, after we had started work, I told her that I really loved that topic.
6. For months I had been crazy about Tolstoy, who's story "The Death of Ivan Illich" I had read.
7. You may have heard of Tolstoy; it was he who wrote *War and Peace* and *Anna Karenina.*
8. The character Anna Karenina is one of the many tragic characters about who Tolstoy wrote.
9. Each of Tolstoy's hundreds of characters are interesting.
10. Tolstoy hisself was a fascinating man—a believer in nonviolence who gave away his property to the poor.

# SECTION 4 USING MODIFIERS

Modifiers are words that change or limit the meaning of other words. Two kinds of modifiers are adjectives and adverbs.

## Adjectives

**An *adjective* is a word that modifies a noun or a pronoun.**

Adjectives answer the question *which one, what kind, how many,* and *how much.*

*this* shirt, *unbelievable* story, *several* documents, *less* work

## Classes of Adjectives

The following chart shows the various types of adjectives:

---

**Articles**   *A, an,* and *the* are adjectives that are also referred to as articles. The article *the* is the **definite article** because it points out a specific person, place, thing, or group.
*A* and *an* are **indefinite articles** because they do not refer to specific items. Use *an* before a vowel sound. Use *a* before a consonant sound. Remember, it is the sound, not the spelling, that determines the correct choice: *an* eddy, *an* heirloom, *an* hour, *a* horse.

**Proper Adjectives**   These adjectives are formed from proper nouns and are always capitalized: *Georgian* architecture, *Roman* holiday, *French* fries.

**Predicate Adjectives**   These adjectives follow linking verbs and describe the subject of the sentence: The stadium was *empty.* The bleachers looked *lonesome.*

**Nouns as Adjectives**   Nouns become modifiers when they describe nouns: *computer* program, *dust* cover, *lobster* pot.

---

## Adverbs

**An *adverb* modifies a verb, an adjective, or another adverb.**

Adverbs tell *where, when, how,* or *to what extent* about the words they modify.

| | | | |
|---|---|---|---|
| kneeled *there* | flew *today* | sang *joyfully* | *extremely* rapidly |
| *unusually* soft | *nearly* able | *almost* gone | |

Many adverbs are formed by adding *-ly* to an adjective.

artful + ly = artfully    cheery + ly = cheerily

Here is a list of commonly used adverbs that do not end in *-ly*.

| Commonly Used Adverbs | | | | |
|---|---|---|---|---|
| afterward | fast | low | often | there |
| almost | forth | more | seldom | today |
| already | hard | near | slow | tomorrow |
| also | here | never | soon | too |
| back | instead | next | still | well |
| even | late | not | straight | yesterday |
| far | long | now | then | yet |

**SPELLING NOTE**
Adverbs are often formed by adding *-ly* to an adjective. Adding *-ly* may cause an additional change in spelling.

happy + ly = happily

# Modifier Usage

Adjectives and adverbs help you to create lively, strong imagery in your writing. The following lessons will help you to use them properly.

# Adjective or Adverb?

If you don't know whether to use an adjective or an adverb in a sentence, ask yourself the following questions:

1. What word does the modifier describe? Use an adverb if the modified word is an action verb, adjective, or adverb. Use an adjective if the modified word is a noun or pronoun.
2. What does the modifier tell about the word it describes? Use an adverb if the modifier tells *how, when, where,* or *to what extent.* Use an adjective if the modifier tells *which one, what kind, how many,* or *how much.*

Which modifier correctly completes the following sentence—the adjective *quick* or the adverb *quickly?*

She ran _____ like a deer.

The adverb *quickly* is the correct choice because the modifier describes the verb *ran.*

**Exercise 1   Adjective or Adverb?**   Choose the correct modifier from the two in parentheses. Then write the word it modifies and tell whether the modifier is an adjective or an adverb.

**Example**  She was an (unusual, unusually) perceptive telephone operator.
**Answer**  unusually    perceptive    adverb

1. Sherlock Holmes is one of the most (popular, popularly) characters ever created.
2. Author Arthur Conan Doyle introduced the (brilliant, brilliantly) detective in 1887.
3. Holmes solved the most difficult crimes with his (remarkable, remarkably) sharp mind.
4. On his cases Holmes worked (close, closely) with his friend Dr. Watson.
5. The (clever, cleverly) Holmes analyzed even the smallest clue.
6. Sometimes Holmes disguised himself (complete, completely) to catch a criminal.
7. In *The Memoirs of Sherlock Holmes,* Holmes was (sudden, suddenly) pushed over a cliff by his enemy, the evil Dr. Moriarty.
8. Readers complained (angry, angrily) about the "death" of their hero.
9. Finally, Arthur Conan Doyle brought the (amazing, amazingly) Holmes back to life in a new story.
10. Today millions of (incredible, incredibly) faithful fans still enjoy the adventures of history's best-known detective.

## Adverb or Predicate Adjective?

**Use an adverb to modify an action verb. Use an adjective after a linking verb.**

Most verbs are action verbs and can be modified by adverbs. Linking verbs, such as *be* or *seem,* however, don't usually take modifiers. They are often followed by an adjective that actually modifies the subject, not the verb. An adjective used in this way is called a **predicate adjective.**

> The lemonade is *refreshing.* (*Refreshing* is a predicate adjective modifying *lemonade.*)
> The wind sounds *furious.* (*Furious* is a predicate adjective modifying *wind.*)

Some verbs, such as *appear, look, sound, feel, taste, grow,* and *smell,* can be used either as action verbs or as linking verbs. Adverbs modify action verbs; they do not modify linking verbs. A linking verb connects a subject to an adjective that describes the subject. So use an adjective following a linking verb. To help you decide which modifier to use, think about which word the adjective or adverb modifies. Use an adjective if it modifies the subject. Use an adverb if it modifies the verb.

> The mayor looked *confident* before her turn to speak. (The predicate adjective *confident* modifies the subject, *mayor,* not the linking verb *looked.*)
> The mayor looked *confidently* at her opponent across the stage. (Here the adverb *confidently* modifies the action verb *looked.*)

> **QUICK TIP** If you are uncertain about whether to use an adverb or an adjective after a verb like *feel, sound, smell,* or *look,* ask yourself the following questions:
> 1. Can you substitute *is* or *was* for the verb? If you can, use an adjective.
>    The dive *looked* perfect.     The dive *was* perfect.
> 2. Does the modifier tell *how, when, where,* or *to what extent* about an action verb? If it does, use an adverb.

**Exercise 2   Adverb or Predicate Adjective?**   Choose the correct modifier for each sentence.

1. In the 1920's young Americans traveled (eager, eagerly) to Paris.
2. There, in the Left Bank district, writers like Ernest Hemingway lived (happy, happily) with very little money.
3. Today the Left Bank still seems (different, differently) from the rest of Paris.
4. Students from the university shout (loud, loudly) to one another on their way to classes.
5. At a café table an elderly artist works (slow, slowly) with pencil and sketchbook.
6. The aroma of fresh-baked bread smells (delicious, deliciously) in the cool morning air.
7. Around a corner, old women shop (careful, carefully) for fresh vegetables in a bustling outdoor market.
8. Along the river the rows of book stalls are already (busy, busily) with crowds of customers.
9. Nearby, the ancient stone walls of Notre Dame Cathedral rise (majestic, majestically) into the sky.
10. The sound of giant church bells rings (glorious, gloriously) on this beautiful spring day.

## Prepositional Phrases as Modifiers

So far in this section you have learned about single-word modifiers. However, groups of words can also modify. Sometimes nouns and verbs are modified by groups of words that begin with prepositions.

**Prepositions** are words like *on* or *near* that show how one word is related to another word. Prepositions often introduce groups of related words called **phrases.** Consider the following sentences:

The plane flew *over the treetops.*
The plane flew *under the treetops.*
The plane flew *through the treetops.*

The pilot ejected *before the crash.*
The pilot ejected *after the crash.*
The pilot ejected *during the crash.*

Each sentence contains a prepositional phrase shown in italics. The **prepositional phrase** consists of a preposition, its object, and any modifiers. For example, in the first sentence *over* is the preposition, and *treetops* is the object.

In the first group of sentences, you can see that the words *over, under,* and *through* show the spatial relationship between *treetops* and *plane.* In the second group, *before, after,* and *during* show the time relationship between *crash* and *ejected.*

Here is a list of words often used as prepositions. Most of these prepositions show relationships in space or in time. Some show other relationships among people and things. Study these prepositions and notice the relationships that they show.

| **Commonly Used Prepositions** | | | | |
|---|---|---|---|---|
| about | at | down | near | to |
| above | before | during | of | toward |
| across | behind | except | off | under |
| after | below | for | on | underneath |
| against | beneath | from | onto | until |
| along | beside | in | out | up |
| among | between | inside | over | upon |
| around | but (except) | into | since | with |
| as | by | like | through | without |

Prepositional phrases function either as adjectives or as adverbs in a sentence.

**A prepositional phrase that modifies a noun or pronoun is called an *adjective phrase.***

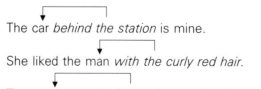

The car *behind the station* is mine.

She liked the man *with the curly red hair.*

The teacher *at the back of the auditorium* is watching you.

Like adjectives, adjective phrases tell *which one, what kind, how many,* or *how much.*

**A prepositional phrase that modifies a verb is called an *adverb phrase.***

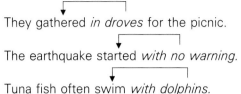

They gathered *in droves* for the picnic.

The earthquake started *with no warning*.

Tuna fish often swim *with dolphins*.

Like adverbs, adverb phrases tell *how, when, where,* and *to what extent* about verbs.

**Exercise 3  Prepositional Phrases**  Add prepositional phrases to the following nouns and verbs. Do not use the same preposition more than twice. Then use the noun or verb and your phrase in a sentence.

| **Example** | eggs |
|---|---|
| **Answer** | eggs with mushrooms |
| | She likes to eat scrambled eggs with mushrooms. |

| | | |
|---|---|---|
| **1.** house | **6.** contained | **11.** garden |
| **2.** skated | **7.** astronaut | **12.** has laughed |
| **3.** lasagna | **8.** glared | **13.** stumbled |
| **4.** boots | **9.** hood | **14.** roadblock |
| **5.** crashed | **10.** doghouse | **15.** was slithering |

## Modifiers in Comparisons

Comparing people, things, and actions is something you do every day. You might say, for example, "I like my new job *better* than my old one. The work is more interesting and the boss is more honest."

In comparisons, modifiers have special forms or spellings.

## The Comparative

When you compare one person, thing, or action with another, use the **comparative** form of the modifier.

Harry jumps *higher* than Dominic.
Christine studies *harder* then Isabel.

The comparative form is generally made in two ways.

**1. For short modifiers, like *calm* and *soon*, add *-er*.**

| | |
|---|---|
| pretty + er = prettier | hard + er = harder |
| sharp + er = sharper | quiet + er = quieter |

**2. For longer modifiers, like *odious* and *rapidly*, use *more*.**

more odious    more rapidly

**Most modifiers ending in *-ful* or *-ous* form the comparative with *more*.**

more helpful    more wonderful    more tastefully

## The Superlative

Whenever you compare a person, thing, or action with more than one other person, thing, or action, use the **superlative** form of the modifier.

Glenn is the *most careful* mountain climber in his group.
Rosa works the *hardest* of all the mechanics.

Generally, the superlative form of modifiers is made by adding *-est* (for short modifiers) or by using *most* (for longer modifiers). For modifiers that take *-er* in the comparative, add *-est* for the superlative. Those that use *more* to form the comparative use *most* for the superlative.

Many people use the superlative incorrectly to compare two things.

**Incorrect**    Carlos is the *most serious* of the two brothers.
**Correct**    Carlos is the *more serious* of the two brothers.

| Modifier | Comparative | Superlative |
|---|---|---|
| fine | finer | finest |
| full | fuller | fullest |
| simple | simpler | simplest |
| insidious | more insidious | most insidious |
| quietly | more quietly | most quietly |

## Irregular Comparisons

Some modifiers make their comparative and superlative forms by complete word changes.

**FARTHER AND FURTHER**
.....................
*Farther* and *farthest* compare distances; *further* and *furthest* compare times, amounts, and degrees. *The restaurant is two blocks farther. Further analysis showed the cause of the problem.*

| Modifier | Comparative | Superlative |
|---|---|---|
| good | better | best |
| well | better | best |
| bad | worse | worst |
| little | less *or* lesser | least |
| much | more | most |
| many | more | most |
| far | farther | farthest |

To make a negative comparison, use *less* or *least* before the modifier: *entitled, less entitled, least entitled.*

**Exercise 4  Comparisons**  Find the errors in comparison in the following sentences and write the sentences correctly. If a sentence has no errors, write *Correct.*

**Example**  In the 1920's, jazz was America's more popular form of music.
**Answer**  In the 1920's, jazz was America's most popular form of music.

1.  Especially to young people, jazz seemed best than any other kind of music.
2.  For writers like F. Scott Fitzgerald, jazz was the clearer symbol of American life in the Twenties.
3.  By the end of the Twenties, jazz was the more popular music in Europe as well as America.
4.  Many people think jazz is the harder kind of music to play.
5.  Compared to a classical musician, a jazz player must be most flexible.
6.  The saxophone is one of the most important jazz instruments.
7.  Charlie Parker, one of the greater saxophone players of all time, was born in 1920.
8.  In the 1940's Parker's new style of playing made jazz most complicated than ever.
9.  Because his music was the more melodious of all, Parker was nicknamed "Bird."
10. Of all the jazz musicians my grandfather ever heard, he thought Charlie Parker was the talentedest.

**Exercise 5  Review of Comparisons**  Choose the correct modifier for each of the following sentences.

1.  Henry David Thoreau thought most people were (busy, busier) than they needed to be.
2.  Thoreau thought people should live (closest, closer) to Nature than they did.
3.  In 1845 in the woods near Concord, Massachusetts, Thoreau built a (simpler, more simple) cabin than any in the village.
4.  For two years Thoreau lived (quieter, quietest) in the woods than the gentlest deer.
5.  It was (easier, easiest) to grow his own vegetables than to worry about money.
6.  Thoreau was (most industrious, more industrious) than many squirrels.
7.  Winter was one of the (better, best) seasons for Thoreau.
8.  The tracks of forest animals were (visibler, more visible) in the snow.
9.  The woods seemed (peacefullest, most peaceful) in the winter.
10. In his book *Walden*, Thoreau later wrote that his days living alone were the (happier, happiest) of his life.

◀ Few, Less
......................
*Few (fewer, fewest)* is used for things that can be counted. *I have a few chores to finish doing. Less (lesser, least)* is used for things that cannot be counted. *There seems to be less snow this winter than there was last winter.*

◀ Reminder
......................
Words that signal comparisons include *than, any,* and *other.*

# Avoiding Double Comparisons

**Do not use -er and *more* or -est and *most* at the same time.**

| | |
|---|---|
| **Incorrect** | Sally is *more meaner* than Dan. |
| **Correct** | Sally is *meaner* than Dan. |

| | |
|---|---|
| **Incorrect** | That's the *most scariest* movie I've seen. |
| **Correct** | That's the *scariest* movie I've seen. |

**Exercise 6  Double Comparisons**  Rewrite the following sentences. Correct all the errors in the use of comparative and superlative forms. If a sentence has no errors, write *Correct*.

1. I think poetry is more interesting to write than any other kind of writing.
2. The most toughest problem in writing poetry is that you must make every word count.
3. Sometimes a few lines of poetry takes me more longer to write than a whole story.
4. Even the most simplest poem may need many revisions.
5. It's usually more better to read poetry aloud than silently.
6. My most favorite poet is Dylan Thomas.
7. He is probably the most famous Welsh poet of all time.
8. Many people think that "Fern Hill" is Dylan Thomas's most loveliest poem.
9. His word pictures are more sharper than any photographs.
10. When Dylan Thomas visited America to give poetry readings, his popularity grew even more greater.

# Avoiding Illogical Comparisons

An **illogical comparison** may seem correct at first, but if you look or listen more closely, you may see that its meaning is not quite clear. One kind of illogical comparison occurs when one thing is compared to the group to which it belongs.

> Suzanne was younger than any woman in her office.

This sentence actually says that Suzanne is *not* a woman in her office. To avoid this kind of mistake, use the word *other* in this kind of comparison.

> Suzanne was younger than *any other* woman in her office.

Illogical comparisons can also occur when the comparison is not clearly stated.

| | |
|---|---|
| **Confusing** | The heat bothered Frank more than the mosquitoes. (Did the heat bother the mosquitoes?) |
| **Clear** | The heat bothered Frank more than the mosquitoes did. |

**Exercise 7  Illogical Comparisons**   Rewrite the following sentences, correcting the errors in comparison. If a sentence is already correct, write *Correct.*

**Example**   Lady Macbeth was more wicked than any queen in Scottish history.

**Answer**   Lady Macbeth was more wicked than any other queen in Scottish history.

 1. Shakespeare is more famous than any English playwright.
 2. *Macbeth* is one of my favorite Shakespearean plays.
 3. I think *Macbeth* is a more interesting play than my friend Beth.
 4. Macbeth and Lady Macbeth are more important than any characters.
 5. After he murders the king, Macbeth is more worried about his deed than his wife.
 6. *Macbeth* is actually shorter than any Shakespearean play.
 7. Lady Macbeth's sleepwalking scene is better known than any scene in the play.
 8. When the Drama Club held auditions, Julie played Lady Macbeth better than Sarah.
 9. On stage I am more nervous than Tom.
 10. Our production of *Macbeth* was more successful than any play in the drama competition.

## Special Problems with Modifiers

Certain adjectives and adverbs are frequently used incorrectly. If you study the following pages, you may be able to avoid these errors in the future.

### Them and Those

> **Them is always a pronoun. It is never used as a modifier.**
> **Those is a pronoun when used alone; it is an adjective when followed by a noun.**

With *them* and *those,* the most common mistake is using *them* as an adjective. Remember that *them* is always a pronoun; use *those,* not *them,* as a modifier.

**Incorrect**   I have a whole box of *them* tiny tomatoes.
**Correct**   I have a whole box of *those* tiny tomatoes.

### This and That, These and Those

> **Use this and that to modify singular nouns. Use these and those to modify plural nouns.**

The adjectives *this* and *that* modify singular nouns. *These* and *those* modify plural nouns. When these modifiers are used with words such as *kind, sort,* and *type*, be especially careful to use them correctly.

Used as an adverb, *only*
limits the word it modi-
fies to *one* of something.
To avoid humorous mis-
understandings, always
place *only* as close as
possible to the word it
limits. Do you under-
stand this statement? *In
our house, we only
watch TV in the living
room.* Actually, you
probably do lots of other
things in the living
room. How about read-
ing a book, or taking a
nap? The meaning is
clearer in the following
sentence: *In our house,
we watch TV only in the
living room.*

| | |
|---|---|
| **Incorrect** | *Those* kind of shoes are comfortable. (*Kind* is singular, so it should be modified by either *this* or *that*.) |
| **Correct** | *That* kind of shoe is comfortable. (Notice that the noun *shoe* has become singular as well.) |

## *Bad* and *Badly*

**Use *bad* as an adjective. Use *badly* as an adverb.**

*Bad* is an adjective, so it should only be used to modify nouns and pronouns. Like other adjectives, *bad* sometimes follows a linking verb. *Badly* is always an adverb, so it should not be used with a linking verb.

| | |
|---|---|
| **Incorrect** | Marsha feels *badly* about working on the holiday. |
| **Correct** | Marsha feels *bad* about working on the holiday. |

## *Good* and *Well*

**Good is always an adjective. Well is usually an adverb.**

Many people believe that they can interchange the words *good* and *well*. The two words do have similar meanings, but *good* is always an adjective, modifying a noun or a pronoun. *Good* is never used to modify a verb.

| | |
|---|---|
| **Incorrect** | Andrew played the guitar *good*. |
| **Correct** | Andrew played the guitar *well*. |

*Well* is a little trickier than *good*. It usually functions as an adverb that means "expertly" or "properly." However, *well* may also mean "in good health"; in that case, it is an adjective, used after a linking verb.

With physical therapy my brother began to feel *well*. (adjective)
The nurse cared *well* for her patients. (adverb)

What kinds of things
might you describe as
*ritzy*? Did you know that
the adjective *ritzy* is derived from the name of a
hotel owner—César
Ritz—who created such
lavish hotels throughout
the world that his name
came to be synonymous
for "lavish luxury"?

> **QUICK TIP**   Since *good* and *well* can both be adjectives, they can both be used as predicate adjectives after linking verbs. To decide which word to use in a sentence, remember that *well* refers to health, while *good* refers to happiness, comfort, or pleasure.
>
> After seven candy bars the outfielder didn't feel *well*.
> Sandy felt *good* after she passed the lifesaving test.

**Exercise 8   Problem Modifiers**   Choose the correct modifier from those in parentheses.

1. When my family went to the museum last weekend, the day started (bad, badly); our car had a flat tire just two blocks from our house!
2. (That, Those) kinds of problems usually drive my dad crazy.
3. This time, though, the car jack worked perfectly (good, well), and we were on our way again in ten minutes.
4. Usually (this, these) kind of trip is not my little brother's favorite.

5. Last weekend, however, the museum had a special exhibit of puppets. (These, This) sort of exhibit is fun for everyone.
6. The marionettes danced so (well, good) that they seemed almost human.
7. I felt (bad, badly) because we had just missed a Punch and Judy show.
8. (Them, Those) famous puppet characters go back to about 1800. Punch himself goes back as far as 1650!
9. We did get to see (that, those) special type of Japanese puppet show known as *bunraku.*
10. (Those, Them) bunraku puppets are three feet tall, and their puppet masters make them seem very lifelike.

## The Double Negative

**Do not use two negatives together.**

The most common negative words are *no, not, never, nothing,* and *none.* You may hear people use two negative words together, especially with a contraction such as *won't* or *couldn't.* This kind of error is called a **double negative.**

| | |
|---|---|
| **Incorrect** | The outfielder *didn't* have *no* idea where the ball was. |
| **Correct** | The outfielder *didn't* have *any* idea where the ball was. |

Remember that the *-n't* in a contraction means "not." If you pair such a contraction with another negative word, you end up with a double negative.

*Hardly, barely,* and *scarcely* are often used as negative words. Do not use them after contractions like *haven't* or *couldn't.*

| | |
|---|---|
| **Incorrect** | We *couldn't hardly* see the stage. |
| **Correct** | We *could hardly* see the stage. |

**Exercise 9  Double Negatives**  Correct the double negatives in these sentences. If a sentence contains no double negative, write *Correct.*

1. Reading for information isn't hardly like reading for enjoyment.
2. When you read nonfiction subjects like history, you shouldn't never just read along line by line.
3. A good student doesn't hardly ever stop asking questions while reading for information.
4. Often you shouldn't read from the beginning to the end; sometimes it helps to read the end of a section first, because that's where you'll find a good summary.
5. You can't scarcely argue that it makes sense to skim over the whole assignment very quickly before you start reading carefully.
6. As you read nonfiction, you also shouldn't ever forget to take notes that summarize what you've read so far.
7. It isn't never a waste of time to make an outline of the material.

8. Remember that the object isn't hardly just to read your assignment, but to find out what the information means.
9. Students who don't ask no questions or make no outlines while they read often get bogged down.
10. If you keep asking good questions while you read, you won't never get bored.

**Exercise 10  Modifier Usage Review 1**   Complete each sentence, choosing the correct word or words from those in parentheses.

1. Last spring the Boston Museum of Fine Arts had the (greatest, most great) exhibit ever of paintings by the nineteenth-century French artist, Claude Monet.
2. Many people think Monet was the (talentedest, most talented) artist who ever painted.
3. At the museum, thousands of people stood (patient, patiently) to see the exhibit.
4. Of all his paintings I thought the garden scenes were the (more beautiful, most beautiful).
5. Monet applied each tiny bit of paint (precise, precisely) to the canvas.
6. He tried to capture (exact, exactly) how light and color change during the year.
7. For several years he (repeated, repeatedly) painted the same subjects, to show them in different seasons.
8. These "series paintings" were his (more famous, most famous) works.
9. Especially when you see them together, Monet's series paintings look (magnificent, magnificently).
10. Ever since Monet, artists have looked at color and light (different, differently).

**Exercise 11  Modifier Usage Review 2**   The following sentences contain errors in the use of modifiers. On your paper, write each sentence, correcting the error. If a sentence has no errors, write *Correct.*

1. Which do you like more better, drama or comedy?
2. Many people believe that of the two, comedy is the most difficultest to write.
3. In ancient Greece, both drama and comedy were extremely popular.
4. Thousands of people flocked more eagerly to the great outdoor plays than to any performances.
5. During the Middle Ages, theaters weren't hardly common, but religious dramas were performed in the village squares.
6. Later, in sixteenth- and seventeenth-century England, drama was probably more popular than any kind of entertainment.
7. Of all the playwrights of this period, William Shakespeare was the finer.
8. Shakespeare wrote tragedy and comedy equally good.
9. Today plays are not hardly as popular as movies and television.
10. Many actors and actresses still believe, however, that performing on a stage in front of a live audience is the more challenging type of acting.

# SECTION 5  USING VERBS

**A *verb* is a word that expresses an action or a state of being.**

Heather *leaped* across the stream.
Carlos *is* always late on Mondays.

## Classifying Verbs

These two sentence charts illustrate and define the different kinds of verbs.

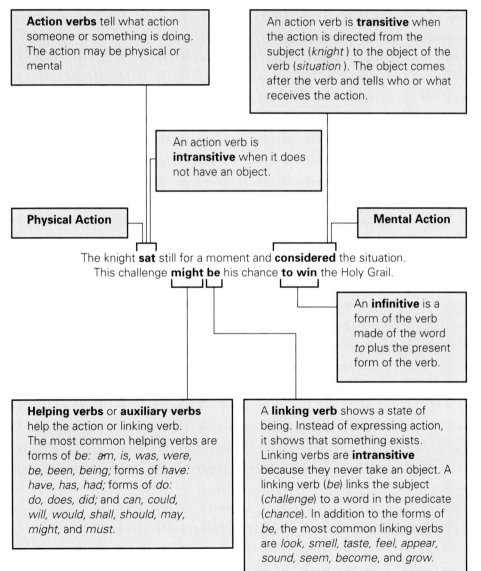

| **Action verbs** tell what action someone or something is doing. The action may be physical or mental |

An action verb is **transitive** when the action is directed from the subject (*knight*) to the object of the verb (*situation*). The object comes after the verb and tells who or what receives the action.

An action verb is **intransitive** when it does not have an object.

**Physical Action**

**Mental Action**

The knight **sat** still for a moment and **considered** the situation.
This challenge **might be** his chance **to win** the Holy Grail.

An **infinitive** is a form of the verb made of the word *to* plus the present form of the verb.

**Helping verbs** or **auxiliary verbs** help the action or linking verb. The most common helping verbs are forms of *be: am, is, was, were, be, been, being;* forms of *have: have, has, had;* forms of *do: do, does, did;* and *can, could, will, would, shall, should, may, might,* and *must.*

A **linking verb** shows a state of being. Instead of expressing action, it shows that something exists. Linking verbs are **intransitive** because they never take an object. A linking verb (*be*) links the subject (*challenge*) to a word in the predicate (*chance*). In addition to the forms of *be*, the most common linking verbs are *look, smell, taste, feel, appear, sound, seem, become,* and *grow.*

# Verb Usage

Imagine a story or a movie with no action at all. Sounds pretty dull, doesn't it? Just as a story or movie is inconceivable without action, so a sentence is inconceivable without an action word—the verb.

In this section you will learn about how verbs work, about what different kinds of verbs there are, and about how to avoid errors in verb usage.

## The Principal Parts of Verbs

*Fly, flew, has been flying, was flown*—these are but a few of the many forms that the verb *fly* can take. All the forms of a verb are made from the verb's principal parts, plus certain other helping words. There are four principal parts: the **present,** the **present participle,** the **past,** and the **past participle.**

| Present | Present Participle | Past | Past Participle |
|---|---|---|---|
| crash | (is) crashing | crashed | (have) crashed |
| disappear | (is) disappearing | disappeared | (have) disappeared |
| spy | (is) spying | spied | (have) spied |

The present participle is always used with a helping verb that is a form of *be,* such as *is, am, are, was, were, be, been,* or *being.* The present participle always ends with *–ing.*

For most verbs, the past is formed by adding *–d* or *–ed,* and the past participle is formed in the same way, except that it is preceded by a form of the helping verb *have,* such as *has, have,* or *had.*

## Regular Verbs

A verb that forms the past and past participle with *–d* or *–ed* is called a **regular verb.** The following are some common regular verbs.

| Present | Present Participle | Past | Past Participle |
|---|---|---|---|
| carve | (is) carving | carved | (have) carved |
| dance | (is) dancing | danced | (have) danced |
| sketch | (is) sketching | sketched | (have) sketched |
| trap | (is) trapped | trapped | (have) trapped |
| try | (is) trying | tried | (have) tried |
| twist | (is) twisting | twisted | (have) twisted |

> **QUICK TIP**   Notice that some regular verbs change their spellings slightly when *–d* or *–ed* is added: an extra *p* is added to *trap;* the *y* in *try* is changed to an *i.*

# Irregular Verbs

Most verbs in English are regular. However, some verbs form their principal parts in different ways. Verbs that do not add *-ed* or *-d* to the present to form the past and past participle are called **irregular verbs.**

---

**QUICK TIP**   Most dictionaries list the principal parts of irregular verbs. Consider the following partial dictionary entry for the verb *spring.*

Past    Past Participle    Present Participle

**spring** (spriŋ) *vi.* **sprang** or **sprung, sprung, spring' ing** [ME *springen* <OE *springan,* akin to Du & Ger *springen* <IE \**sprenĝh-,* to move quickly (<base \**sper-,* to jerk), >Sans *sprhayati,* (he) strives for] **1** to move suddenly and rapidly; specif., *a)* to move upward or forward from the ground, etc. by suddenly contracting the muscles; leap; bound; also, to make a series of such leaps *b)* to rise suddenly and quickly from or as from a sitting or lying position /to *spring* to one's feet/ *c)* to come, appear, etc. suddenly and quickly /curses *springing* to his lips/ *d)* to move as a result of resilience; bounce

---

If you ever wonder what the past, past participle, or present participle of a verb is, simply look for the information in a dictionary. If the parts are not listed, they are formed as regular verbs.

The lists that follow show five groups of irregular verbs. Most irregular verbs in English belong to one of these five groups.

**Group 1**   Some irregular verbs keep the same form for all three principal parts. These are easy to remember.

| Present | Present Participle | Past | Past Participle |
|---|---|---|---|
| burst | (is) bursting | burst | (have) burst |
| cost | (is) costing | cost | (have) cost |
| cut | (is) cutting | cut | (have) cut |
| let | (is) letting | let | (have) let |
| put | (is) putting | put | (have) put |
| read | (is) reading | read | (have) read |
| set | (is) setting | set | (have) set |

Here are some sentences using verbs from this group:

Carl's mother *lets* him use the car. (present)
Martin *set* the table. (past)
That mistake *has cost* us time. (past participle)

**Group 2**  Another group of irregular verbs changes form only once. The past and the past participle are the same.

| Present | Present Participle | Past | Past Participle |
|---------|-------------------|------|-----------------|
| bring | (is) bringing | brought | (have) brought |
| catch | (is) catching | caught | (have) caught |
| lead | (is) leading | led | (have) led |
| lend | (is) lending | lent | (have) lent |
| lose | (is) losing | lost | (have) lost |
| say | (is) saying | said | (have) said |
| sit | (is) sitting | sat | (have) sat |

These sentences use irregular verbs from Group 2.

Tim usually *catches* with his right hand. (present)
Marla *lost* her purse. (past)
The scouts *have brought* a compass. (past participle)

**Exercise 1  Irregular Verbs**  Choose the correct verb.

1. The hen (sat, sitted) on the eggs.
2. Tina (said, sayed) her name softly.
3. Greg has (lost, losed) his keys.
4. Mark has (lent, lended) me his tent.
5. Lewis and Clark (leaded, led) the expedition.
6. Myra has (catched, caught) the flu.
7. The campers (brought, brang) a lantern.
8. The floodwaters (burst, bursted) the dam.
9. The auto repairs (costed, cost) Al $700.53.
10. The barber (cut, cutted) my hair.

**Group 3**  Verbs in this group add -*n* or -*en* to the past form to make the past participle.

| Present | Present Participle | Past | Past Participle |
|---------|-------------------|------|-----------------|
| break | (is) breaking | broke | (have) broken |
| choose | (is) choosing | chose | (have) chosen |
| freeze | (is) freezing | froze | (have) frozen |
| speak | (is) speaking | spoke | (have) spoken |
| steal | (is) stealing | stole | (have) stolen |
| tear | (is) tearing | tore | (have) torn |
| wear | (is) wearing | wore | (have) worn |

Here are three sentences using Group 3 verbs:

*Break* the eggs into a bowl. (present)
The UN delegates *spoke* different languages. (past)
Thieves *have stolen* the jewels. (past participle)

**Exercise 2  Irregular Verbs**   Choose the correct verb.

1. Matt (chose, chosen) the blue stone for his class ring.
2. Carrie has (broke, broken) the school high-jump record.
3. Much of the orange crop (froze, frozen) last winter.
4. Someone has (tore, torn) the curtain.
5. Yvonne has (wore, worn) contact lenses for years.
6. The principal (spoke, spoken) to the students at the assembly.
7. Tom has (chose, chosen) a topic for his term paper.
8. The milk has (froze, frozen) on the back porch.
9. The football team (wore, worn) new jerseys.
10. The fish (stole, stolen) the bait from my hook.

**Group 4**   The irregular verbs in this group change their final vowel. The vowel changes from *i* in the present form to *a* in the past form to *u* in the past participle.

| Present | Present Participle | Past | Past Participle |
|---------|--------------------|------|-----------------|
| begin | (is) beginning | began | (have) begun |
| drink | (is) drinking | drank | (have) drunk |
| ring | (is) ringing | rang | (have) rung |
| sing | (is) singing | sang | (have) sung |
| swim | (is) swimming | swam | (have) swum |

These sentences use irregular verbs from Group 4:

I *drink* root beer. (present)
The mother *sang* softly. (past)
Gary *has swum* in the new pool. (past participle)

**Exercise 3  Irregular verbs**   Choose the correct verb.

1. Someone must have (rang, rung) our doorbell by mistake.
2. Class (began, begun) at nine o'clock.
3. Biondi (swam, swum) the breast stroke in the Olympics.
4. The school choir has (sang, sung) at many civic events.
5. Ms. Silva (drank, drunk) her coffee black.
6. The baby must have (drank, drunk) his bottle.
7. Our school has (began, begun) a new admission policy.
8. The phone (rang, rung) ten times.
9. Deane has already (swam, swum) fifty laps.
10. Billy Joel (sang, sung) a medley of his hits.

**Group 5**  Some irregular verbs form the past participle from the present form rather than from the past form. The present and past participle are either the same or very similar.

| Present | Present Participle | Past | Past Participle |
|---|---|---|---|
| come | (is) coming | came | (have) come |
| do | (is) doing | did | (have) done |
| eat | (is) eating | ate | (have) eaten |
| fall | (is) falling | fell | (have) fallen |
| give | (is) giving | gave | (have) given |
| go | (is) going | went | (have) gone |
| grow | (is) growing | grew | (have) grown |
| know | (is) knowing | knew | (have) known |
| ride | (is) riding | rode | (have) ridden |
| run | (is) running | ran | (have) run |
| see | (is) seeing | saw | (have) seen |
| take | (is) taking | took | (have) taken |
| throw | (is) throwing | threw | (have) thrown |
| write | (is) writing | wrote | (have) written |

Here are sentences using Group 5 verbs:

I *know* the address. (present)
Marty *gave* a speech. (past)
The leaves *have fallen.* (past participle)

**Exercise 4  Irregular Verbs**  Choose the correct verb.

1. Crowds of people (came, come) to the grand opening of the new department store.
2. Michele has (did, done) the assignment thoroughly and is prepared for the test.
3. Mr. Price (gave, give) the class a quiz.
4. Elijah (knew, known) the algebra equation.
5. We (rode, ridden) the subway downtown.
6. The nest has (fell, fallen) from the tree.
7. That horse has (ran, run) its last race.
8. Terry has (went, gone) on vacation.
9. Bob and Eduardo (saw, seen) that movie four times.
10. Clara has never (ate, eaten) Mexican food.

**WRITING ABOUT LITERATURE**

When writing about literature, use the present tense.

In *Macbeth* the witches' strange prophecy proves correct.

## Verb Tenses

**Use the correct verb tense to show when an action occurs.**

Verbs show time as well as action. To show when an action occurs, all verbs change form. These changes in form are called **tenses.** Every verb has six tenses, formed by using its principal parts and certain auxiliary verbs, such as *be* and *have.*

From the chart, you can see that a verb's tenses cover many different situations in time. To avoid confusion in your speech and writing, choose the tense that best shows when the action is taking place.

| Tense | Form | Use |
|---|---|---|
| **Present** | Add *-s* or *-es* for third person singular. | To show an action that happens now: The batter *swings*. To tell about something that happens regularly: Every afternoon I *run* two miles. To tell about constant action: Plants *convert* the sun's energy. |
| **Past** | Add *-d* or *-ed* to the present. If the verb is irregular, use the past form. | To show an action that was completed in the past: Last summer Sam *read* all the Sherlock Holmes stories. |
| **Future** | Use *will* or *shall* with the present form. | To show an action that will occur in the future: The red car *will win* the race. |
| **Present Perfect** | Use *has* or *have* with the past participle. | To show an action that was completed at an indefinite time in the past or that began in the past and continues into the present: Donna *has practiced* her gymnastics program for six months. |
| **Past Perfect** | Use *had* with the past participle. | To show an action in the past that came before another action in the past: My father felt better after he *had exercised*. |
| **Future Perfect** | Use *will have* or *shall have* with the past participle. | To show an action in the future that will happen before another future action or time: By next summer, that paint *will have faded*. |

**Exercise 5  Verb Tenses**   Write the verb in parentheses in the tense indicated.

**Example**    Louis Armstrong (rise —past) from poverty to fame.
**Answer**     Louis Armstrong *rose* from poverty to fame.

1. Louis Armstrong (come —past) into the world on July 4, 1900.
2. Armstrong (live —past) with his mother and his sister in a poor section of New Orleans.
3. By the time he was eight, Louis (fall —past perfect) in love with jazz.
4. By the time he was fourteen, he (learn —past perfect) to play a cornet, which is like a trumpet.
5. From then on, music (become —past) Louis Armstrong's whole life.
6. As the years (go —past) by, Louis became one of the country's most famous jazz players.
7. As popular as he was, Louis still (suffer —past) from racial prejudice.

*WILL OR SHALL?*

When describing a future event, use the following forms:

I or we *shall*
you *will*
he, she, it, or they *will*

When expressing an intention or command, use these forms:

I or we *will*
you *shall*
he, she, it, or they *shall*

## PROGRESSIVE FORMS

In addition to having six tenses, every verb has six **progressive forms**. These forms are made from the six tenses. To create a progressive form, use the present participle (the *-ing* form) as the main verb and a form of *be* as the helping verb.

**Regular**
I *study*
I *studied*
I *shall study*
I *have studied*
I *had studied*
I *shall have studied*

**Progressive**
I *am studying*
I *was studying*
I *shall be studying*
I *have been studying*
I *had been studying*
I *shall have been studying*

## EMPHATIC FORMS

Every verb also has **emphatic forms** made by adding a form of the verb *do* as a helping verb.

I *study*       I *do study*
I *studied*     I *did study*

**8.** Later in life, Louis often looked back on how restaurants and hotels (refuse—past perfect) to serve him.

**9.** Many of today's musicians (say—present perfect) that they owe a great deal to Louis Armstrong—for his music and for the way he helped change people's attitudes.

**10.** For as long as people love jazz, they (remember—future) Louis Armstrong, the King of Jazz.

## Improper Shifts in Tense

**Use the same tense to show two or more actions that occur at the same time.**

In most of your speech and writing, the actions in any one sentence or paragraph will all take place in either the past, present, or future. To keep the time reference consistent, use the same tense for all the verbs in the sentence or paragraph.

**Incorrect**  The dog spots the squirrel and bolted across the yard.
**Correct**  The dog spotted the squirrel and bolted across the yard.

There are times, however, when shifting verb tense—even in the same sentence—makes your meaning clearer. For example, two different tenses are needed to show a sequence of events.

Mat *will have climbed* (future perfect) more than a dozen peaks by the time he *finishes* (present) his hike.

Check your writing carefully to avoid any illogical shifts in verb tense. Always be sure that your verbs express action in the past, present, or future without confusing your reader.

**Exercise 6  Improper Shifts in Tense**  Rewrite the following sentences, correcting the improper shifts in tense by making the second italicized verb agree with the first.

**Example**  For several days before it erupted, the mountain *rumbled* and *has poured* forth smoke.
**Answer**  For several days before it erupted, the mountain rumbled and poured forth smoke.

**1.** Golden Gate Bridge *sits* near the mouth of San Francisco Bay and *connected* San Francisco with Sausilito.

**2.** Herbert Simon and Alan Newell *created* the science of artificial intelligence, or AI, and *had written* the first AI programs.

**3.** For some time now, the coral reef *has been experiencing* a population explosion of crown-of-thorns starfish and *was losing* other species.

**4.** The Japanese companies *came* to the trade show and *exhibit* their new high-definition televisions.

**5.** Natural gas *comes* from the ground; oil *did,* too.

6. The Danes *had laid* their slain chieftain on the ship and *have set* it afire, in a kind of burial at sea.
7. Beethoven *was* sloppy, irritable, and demanding; however, he *is* also a genius.
8. Biko *was held* in prison and *seen* firsthand the mistreatment of political prisoners.
9. Sasha and Juanita *have been reviewing* math problems and also *study* vocabulary in preparation for a vocational school entrance exam.
10. The weather service *has announced* that tornadoes are likely and *warning* people to stay indoors.

## Using the Active and Passive Voices

**Use the *active voice* for lively, forceful writing.**
**Use the *passive voice* to draw special attention to the subject receiving the action.**

The **voice** of a verb depends on whether the subject is acting or is receiving the action. When the subject of a sentence performs the action expressed by the verb, the verb is in the **active voice.** When the subject is acted upon, the verb is in the **passive voice.** To form the passive voice, use a form of *be* with the past participle of the main verb.

**Active Voice**   Harry *painted* his room. (The subject *Harry* performs the action of painting.)
**Passive Voice**   The room *was painted* by Harry. (The subject *room* receives the action of being painted.)

As you can see from this example, the active voice is usually more direct and more interesting than the passive voice. If you want things to *happen* in your writing, you should avoid long passages in the passive voice. You should also avoid mixing the passive and active voice in the same sentence.

For most of your writing, the active voice will be your best choice. There will be times, however, when the passive voice meets your needs better. For example, suppose you want to focus attention on a person to whom something is done.

**Passive**   The injured pitcher *was replaced* by the manager.
**Active**   The manager *replaced* the injured pitcher.

In the above example, the active voice is more forceful, but it draws attention to the manager rather than to the pitcher. To place the emphasis on the pitcher, you need the passive voice.

Sometimes you need to express action performed by an unknown or unnamed person. In such a case, the passive voice is also necessary.

The family picnic was scheduled months ago. (The person performing the action is not known.)

**Exercise 7  Active and Passive Verbs**   Rewrite each sentence, changing all active verbs to passive and all passive verbs to active. Add words as needed.

1. The eighteenth century is called the Enlightenment by many historians.
2. It is called the Age of Reason by others.
3. During this period, writers like Voltaire dramatically changed people's ideas about the world.
4. Plays, essays, and articles on a wide variety of topics were written by Voltaire.
5. Prejudice and superstition were attacked in his writing.
6. Exile and even imprisonment were suffered by Voltaire because of his writing.
7. Later, fame and wealth were acquired by him.
8. Voltaire's ideas influenced political figures like Thomas Jefferson.
9. In many ways, our ideas about the world are still shaped by the Enlightenment.
10. For example, we developed our faith in science at that time.

## Commonly Confused Verbs

**Do not confuse *lie* and *lay*, *rise* and *raise*, *sit* and *set*.**

Do you *lie* or *lay* on a couch?

Do you *lie* or *lay* your head on a pillow? These two verbs, and other pairs of verbs that are close in sound and meaning, can cause confusion. Two other tricky verb pairs are *rise* and *raise* and *sit* and *set*. The following chart shows the principal parts of these often confusing verbs.

|  | Present | Present Participle | Past | Past Participle |
|---|---|---|---|---|
| *Lie* and *Lay* | lie | (is) lying | lay | (have) lain |
|  | lay | (is) laying | laid | (have) laid |
| *Rise* and *Raise* | rise | (is) rising | rose | (have) risen |
|  | raise | (is) raising | raised | (have) raised |
| *Sit* and *Set* | sit | (is) sitting | sat | (have) sat |
|  | set | (is) setting | set | (have) set |

*Lie* means "to rest in a flat position" or "to be in a certain place." *Lie* never has a direct object.

The cattle *lie* under the trees along the river.

*Lay* means "to place." *Lay* always has a direct object unless the verb is in the passive voice.

**Active Voice**   The carpenters *lay* their tools in the truck. (*Tools* is the direct object.)

**Passive Voice**   The tools *are laid* in the truck by the carpenters.

*Rise* means "to go upward." *Rise* never has a direct object.

The flock of ducks *rises* in a flurry of furious wing beats.

*Raise* means "to lift" or "to make something go up." *Raise* always has a direct object unless the verb is in the passive voice.

**Active Voice**    Sue's brother *raises* sheep on his farm. (*Sheep* is the direct object.)

**Passive Voice**   Sheep *are raised* by Sue's brother on his farm.

*Sit* means "to occupy a seat." *Sit* never has a direct object.

On summer evenings we *sit* on our back porch.

*Set* means "to place." *Set* always has a direct object unless the verb is in the passive voice.

**Active Voice**    We *set* the table for Thanksgiving dinner. (*Table* is the direct object.)

**Passive Voice**   The table *was set* for Thanksgiving dinner.

**Exercise 8  Confusing Verbs**   Write the correct verb.

1. In the summer, Mary and I often (sit, set) on her porch and read.
2. We (sit, set) a stack of novels between us.
3. Mary's scruffy old cat usually (lays, lies) on my lap.
4. He (lays, lies) his head on one paw and sleeps.
5. Sometimes he (rises, raises) one eyelid and looks up at me.
6. This morning Mary (raised, rose) from her chair and said, "Listen to this!"
7. As she read an exciting part of her book, her voice (raised, rose).
8. At the sound of her voice, the cat (sat, set) up on my lap.
9. Finally, Mary (sit, set) the book on the table.
10. I (lay, laid) my book aside and we went inside for a snack.

**Exercise 9  Verb Usage Review**   Rewrite the following sentences, correcting any errors in verb usage.

1. Before the Europeans come to America, there were 60 million buffalo on the plains.
2. The buffalo lived in large herds, and prairie grasses were eaten by them.
3. Native Americans ate buffalo meat and had worn buffalo hides.
4. However, Native Americans respected the buffalo and would not hunt it until its spirit have give them permission.
5. Native Americans knowed the importance of respect for nature.
6. Then the white men came, and before long they had begun to kill off the buffalo.
7. By killing the buffalo, white men breaked the spirit of the Plains Indians.
8. By 1889 only about 540 buffalo remained; these few buffalo had stole away to the mountain meadows of Yellowstone.
9. There, in the high mountain meadows, the few remaining buffalo rose their young until the herd reached about two thousand.
10. Eventually, laws are passed to protect the herds.

# SECTION 6   SUBJECT AND VERB AGREEMENT

**A verb must agree in number with its subject.**

▶ When the subject of a sentence is singular, its verb must also be singular. When the subject is plural, its verb must also be plural. This is called **subject-verb agreement.**

The tiger (singular) rides (singular) in the back of our truck.
The tigers (plural) ride (plural) in the back of our truck.

The singular and plural forms of verbs rarely cause problems because they all follow a pattern like the following:

## Verb Forms

|  | Singular | | Plural | |
|---|---|---|---|---|
| **First Person** | I | swim | we | swim |
| **Second Person** | you | swim | you | swim |
| **Third Person** | he, she, it | swims | they | swim |

One of the verbs that sometimes does cause problems is the verb *be.* The verb *be* does not follow the usual pattern. Notice in the following chart that *be* has special forms in both the present and the past tenses in all three persons.

## Forms of *Be*

|  | Present Tense | | Past Tense | |
|---|---|---|---|---|
|  | Singular | Plural | Singular | Plural |
| **First Person** | I am | we are | I was | we were |
| **Second Person** | you are | you are | you were | you were |
| **Third Person** | he, she, it is | they are | he, she, it was | they were |

> **QUICK TIP**   The most common errors involving forms of the verb *be* are using the words *you, we,* and *they* with the singular verb *was.* Remember to avoid saying or writing *you was, we was,* and *they was.*

**Exercise 1   Agreement in Number**   On your paper, write the form of the verb that agrees in number with the subject of each of the following sentences. Then tell whether the verb form is singular or plural.

1. You (was, were) telling me the other day that you didn't think women really understood sports.
2. You said that they (was, were) more interested in the arts than in competitive sports like baseball.
3. When we (was, were) talking, I was thinking about my mother.
4. My mother (enjoy, enjoys) sports as much as I do.
5. However, she (has, have) an avid interest in literature, too.
6. She (appreciate, appreciates) sports writing more than any other kind of writing.

---

7. Many women (choose, chooses) sports writing as a career.
8. Sports writing (take, takes) skill, creativity, and practice.
9. A really fine sports story (need, needs) accurate detail and vivid description.
10. Good sports writers (see, sees) games and players with a fresh eye.
11. My mom (believe, believes) Roger Angell is today's best baseball writer.
12. She (read, reads) all of Angell's magazine articles.
13. She (save, saves) the articles to read again during the winter.
14. Angell (capture, captures) both the humor and the excitement of baseball.
15. His words (paint, paints) a clear, colorful picture of the game.

## Phrases Between a Subject and a Verb

**Do not be fooled by other nouns in a sentence. Be sure that the verb agrees with its subject.**

How can you be sure which verb to use with a subject unless you correctly identify the subject itself? To find the subject of a sentence, first find the verb and then ask *who* or *what* before it.

> The girl with the long silver earrings is my sister. (Since *is* is the verb, ask, Who is? *Girl,* not *earrings,* is the subject.)

In the sentence above, "with the long silver earrings" is a prepositional phrase. When a prepositional phrase falls between the subject and the verb, be especially careful. Do not be fooled by the noun that appears in the prepositional phrase. Make the verb agree in number with the subject.

> The dresses in that store are very expensive. (*Dresses,* not *store,* is the subject.)

---

**QUICK TIP**  One way to decide which word is the subject is to try saying the sentence without the phrase. If you have chosen the correct word as the subject, the sentence will make sense without the phrase.

---

**Exercise 2  Sentences with Phrases**  Choose the verb that agrees with the subject.

1. Philosophy teachers in ancient Greece (was, were) very well known.
2. Plato's writings about Socrates (describe, describes) the most famous of the Greek philosophers.
3. In Plato's writings the ideas of this great thinker (is, are) explained in a dramatic style.
4. Students with curious minds (discuss, discusses) some important idea with Socrates.
5. His many questions in every discussion (push, pushes) his students to think more carefully.

### PREPOSITIONS

Commonly used prepositions include the following: *about, above, across, after, as, at, before, between, by, during, for, from, in, inside, into, like, near, of, off, on, over, since, through, to, until, up, upon, with, without.*

**Compound prepositions** include the following: *according to, along with, because of, due to, in addition to, in front of, instead of, next to, on top of, out of.*

6. The teachers at our school (use, uses) Socrates' method.
7. The role of the teachers (is, are) to ask questions that have no easy answers.
8. Sometimes, the students in such a group (feel, feels) frustrated with the questioning.
9. However, the answers in a Socratic dialogue (is, are) not necessarily important.
10. Plato in his book *Dialogues* (describe, describes) how some of the citizens of Athens responded to the Socratic method.
11. The leaders of the city (put, puts) Socrates on trial because they are afraid that Socrates is teaching young people to challenge their elders.
12. The members of the jury (find, finds) him guilty.
13. The decision of the jurors (is, are) that Socrates must give up his ideas or die.
14. To a person like Socrates, the search for answers (mean, means) more than life itself.
15. Because he chose death, this teacher of ancient Greeks (remain, remains) today an example of reverence for learning.

## Indefinite Pronouns as Subjects

### Use a singular verb with a singular indefinite pronoun and a plural verb with a plural indefinite pronoun.

Indefinite pronouns do not refer to a specific person or thing. Some indefinite pronouns are singular, some are plural, and some can be either. Making subjects and verbs agree can be difficult when the subject is an indefinite pronoun.

**MEMORY TRICK**

One way to remember which indefinite pronouns are singular is to look at the word endings. Many of the singular words have endings that refer to one thing: *-other, -one, -body,* or *-thing.* Many of the singular pronouns are also compound *(anything, someone)*; none of the plural pronouns are compound.

**Indefinite Pronouns**

| | |
|---|---|
| **Singular** | another, anybody, anyone, anything, each, either, everybody, everyone, everything, neither, nobody, no one, one, somebody, someone, something |
| **Plural** | both, few, many, several |
| **Singular or Plural** | all, any, most, none, some |

► For the indefinite pronouns that are always singular or plural, the correct verb choice will probably be the one that sounds right to you.

| | |
|---|---|
| **Incorrect** | Nobody want to go to the movies. |
| **Correct** | Nobody wants to go to the movies. (*Nobody* is singular; it takes a singular verb, *wants*.) |

| | |
|---|---|
| **Incorrect** | Many of my friends likes to skate. |
| **Correct** | Many of my friends like to skate. (*Many* is plural; it takes a plural verb, *like*.) |

The most confusing indefinite pronouns are those that can be either singular or plural. Just remember to treat the pronoun as singular—choose a singular verb to go with it—if it refers to one thing. Treat the pronoun as plural—choose a plural verb to go with it—if if refers to several things.

**Singular**      Most of the music was jazz. (*Most* refers to one quantity of music.)

**Plural**      Most of the records were jazz. (*Most* refers to several records.)

---

> **QUICK TIP**   Remember that *none* can be plural. It is plural if it refers to persons, places, or things that can be counted. For example, a quantity of milk cannot be counted, but a quantity of people can.

**Exercise 3   Indefinite Pronouns**   Rewrite each of the following sentences, revising the verb if it does not agree with the subject.

1. Most of the class knows the story of Robin Hood.
2. Everybody have seen cartoons or movies about him.
3. Most of the ballads about Robin and the merry band was sung by English minstrels.
4. Some of these ballads goes back almost five centuries.
5. Nobody think badly of this noble outlaw.
6. All of the Robin Hood stories has the same theme.
7. Some of the younger students likes the idea of a hero who protects the weak from an evil tyrant.
8. In the stories none of Robin's men shoots a bow as well as Robin himself.
9. Some of Robin's friends is Little John, Friar Tuck, and Maid Marian.
10. One of his greatest opponents were the Sheriff of Nottingham.

**Exercise 4   Review**   For each of the following sentences, write the subject. Then write the verb that agrees in number with the subject.

1. Successful students (know, knows) how to read for understanding.
2. An important step (is, are) to use outlines.
3. The teachers in our school (encourage, encourages) us to outline every reading assignment.
4. An effective outline (list, lists) each of the main ideas.
5. The most important details about each main idea (is, are) also listed.
6. The key to preparing outlines (is, are) to ask yourself questions about what you are reading.
7. One of the most important questions (is, are) "What is the author's message here?"
8. Another (is, are) "What facts or information support each main idea?"
9. Sometimes, several of the main ideas (appear, appears) in a summary section.
10. Accurate outlines of your reading (make, makes) studying for exams much easier.

## Compound Subjects

**Use a plural verb with most compound subjects joined by *and*. Use a verb that agrees with the subject nearer the verb when the words in a compound subject are joined by *or* or *nor*.**

A **compound subject** is two or more subjects used with the same verb. Most compound subjects that contain the word *and* are plural and take a plural verb.

Camping and fishing are my hobbies.
Good maps and equipment make life in the woods easier.

**NEITHER/NOR**

Remember that *nor* is almost always used with *neither*. **Correct** Neither he nor I is interested in golf. **Incorrect** He nor I is interested in golf.

However, when the conjunctions *or* or *nor* connect a compound subject, look at the subject closest to the verb to decide if the verb should be singular or plural.

Neither Jim nor his brothers own a car.
Either the chairs or the couch comes from France.

**Exercise 5  Compound Subjects**  On your paper, write the form of the verb that agrees with the subject.

1. Joe and his entire family (play, plays) musical instruments.
2. Joe's mother and father (teach, teaches) piano.
3. Surprisingly, neither Joe nor his two brothers (study, studies) piano.
4. Neither Joe nor the other boys (read, reads) music; they play "by ear."
5. Joe and his brother Tim (like, likes) rock music.
6. Neither his parents nor his brother Frank (enjoy, enjoys) rock as much as classical music.
7. Joe and the other members of his family (agree, agrees) on jazz.
8. Sometimes Joe and his family (organize, organizes) neighborhood jazz concerts.
9. My sister and I both (take, takes) piano lessons from Joe's parents.
10. Neither my sister nor I (sound, sounds) terrific, but we join in anyway and have lots of fun.

## Agreement Problems with *Doesn't* and *Don't*

**Use *doesn't* with singular subjects and with the personal pronouns *he, she,* and *it*. Use *don't* with plural subjects and with the personal pronouns *I, we, you,* and *they*.**

The words *doesn't* and *don't* often create agreement problems. Try to remember that these words are contractions for *does not* and *do not*.

**Incorrect**  Doesn't the stores stay open late tonight?
**Correct**  Don't the stores stay open late tonight?

**Incorrect**  Don't the store stay open late tonight?
**Correct**  Doesn't the store stay open late tonight?

> **QUICK TIP**   If you ignore the *-n't* and say the sentence using either the verb *do* or the verb *does,* you will probably be able to hear which is correct. For example, you would say *Do the stores stay open tonight?* not *Does the stores stay open tonight? Do* is plural, and *does* is singular.

**Exercise 6   *Doesn't and Don't***   Choose the form of the verb that agrees in number with the subject.

1. Molly Rose was born in Peru, but she (don't, doesn't) live there any more.
2. My parents (don't, doesn't) live in Peru, but they adopted my sister there.
3. Some mothers in Peru (don't, doesn't) have enough money to take care of their babies.
4. Molly Rose's birth mother (don't, doesn't) see her any more; she gave her baby to us so that Molly could have a more comfortable life.
5. We (don't, doesn't) know how we could live without Molly now that she's part of our family.

**Exercise 7   Subject-Verb Agreement Review**   Choose the form of the verb that agrees in number with the subject.

1. Besides being harbors to many lobstermen and fishermen, the seacoast villages of Maine (is, are) also home to many artists.
2. In the summer an artist in paint-stained jeans (seem, seems) to appear on every stretch of coast.
3. The ocean and its moods (provide, provides) endless subjects.
4. Every summer one of the country's best-known artists (come, comes) to Maine.
5. For years Jamie Wyeth (has, have) captured on canvas the lives of ordinary people.
6. Although he is almost as well known as his father Andrew, neither Jamie nor his work (seem, seems) out of place on Monhegan Island.
7. Wyeth's summer home and studio (sit, sits) in a clearing on this tiny island off the Maine coast.
8. Wyeth and other artists (love, loves) Monhegan's isolation and rugged beauty.
9. Every summer my parents and I (spend, spends) a few days on Monhegan.
10. Visitors and supplies (crowd, crowds) the dock on the mainland.
11. All the passengers (help, helps) the captain load the small ferry.
12. In the choppy water, the ferry (don't, doesn't) make much speed.
13. Finally, Monhegan's steep cliffs and weathered houses (appear, appears) off the bow.
14. Except for a few added conveniences, neither the residents nor the island (change, changes) much from year to year.
15. The old inn (don't, doesn't) look any different than it did last year.

# SECTION 7   SENTENCE STRUCTURE

**A *sentence* is a group of words that expresses a complete thought.**

## Understanding Simple Sentences

Throughout this book you have been studying sentences. You know that a sentence has two basic parts, the **subject** and the **predicate.**

| Subject | Predicate |
|---|---|
| Immigrants | came. |
| Many new immigrants | came from that country. |

You also know that all of the parts of a sentence may be **compound.** That is, they may have more than one part.

**Compound Subject**   *Doctors* and *nurses* made plans.
**Compound Verb**   The patients *watched* and *waited.*
**Compound Object**   The attendant served *coffee* and *tea.*

You can see that each of these sentences expresses one main idea. These sentences are called **simple** sentences.

**A simple sentence is a sentence that contains only one subject and one predicate.**

COORDINATING
CONJUNCTIONS

The coordinating conjunctions are *and, or, nor, for, but, so,* and *yet.* Here's a silly but effective memorization tip: Think of them as forming the parts of a Russian-sounding name:

Andor Norfor Butsoyet

## Creating Compound Sentences

▶ **To create a *compound sentence,* join two or more simple sentences together.**

A sentence made up of two or more simple sentences joined together is called a **compound sentence.**

**Simple Sentences**   The volcano erupted. Its ash buried the town.
**Compound Sentence**   The volcano erupted, and its ash buried the town.

You can join simple sentences in three ways.

You can use a comma and a coordinating conjunction such as *and.*

**Simple Sentences**   Tests uncovered a fuel leak. The launch date was postponed.

**Compound Sentence**   Tests uncovered a fuel leak, so the launch date was postponed.

You can use a semicolon.

**Compound Sentence**   Tests uncovered a fuel leak; the launch date was postponed.

You can use a semicolon and a conjunctive adverb, such as *however* or *consequently.*

**Compound Sentence**     Tests uncovered a fuel leak; *consequently,* the launch date was postponed.

---

**QUICK TIP**   Two simple sentences should be joined together only if they are related in meaning. Do not join sentences that are unrelated.

**Incorrect**     Cows are hoofed animals, and Argentina is famous for its cowboys, known as *gauchos.*

---

**Exercise 1   Compound Sentences**   Combine each pair of simple sentences, following the directions given in parentheses.

**Example**     The British Isles were far away from Rome. Caesar invaded Britain in 55 B.C. (Combine with a semicolon, the conjunctive adverb *however,* and a comma.)

**Answer**     The British Isles were far away from Rome; however, Caesar invaded Britain in 55 B.C.

1. Caesar retreated after two unsuccessful campaigns. Years later, in A.D. 43, the emperor Claudius invaded Britain again. (Combine with a comma and the word *but.*)
2. The Romans established cities such as London. They built roads throughout England. (Combine with a comma and *and.*)
3. Eventually, a British warrior queen arose. Her name was Boadicea. (Combine with a semicolon.)
4. Boadicea defeated the Romans in battle after battle. The Romans finally defeated her. (Combine with a semicolon, a comma, and the conjunctive adverb *however.*)
5. According to the historian Tacitus, eighty thousand Britons died in Boadicea's final battle with the Romans. Boadicea poisoned herself rather than be captured. (Combine with a comma and *and.*)

## Using Clauses to Create Complex Sentences

A **clause** is a group of words containing a subject and a verb. A clause can be a simple sentence that can stand alone, or it can be any group of words with a subject and verb in it.

<pre>
 S        V              S    V
Someone called.       that lies beneath the earth's crust
         S                          V
    since the oceans have not been fully explored
</pre>

An **independent clause** is one that can stand alone as a sentence. Of course, all simple sentences are independent clauses.

◀ **CONJUNCTIVE ADVERBS**

These conjuctive adverbs can be used to join the parts of a compound sentence: *accordingly, also, besides, consequently, finally, furthermore, hence, however, indeed, moreover, nevertheless, otherwise, still, then, therefore, thus.*

**MORE ON COMBINING**

For more information on combining sentences, see the sentence-combining lesson in Section 1 of this grammar handbook. Also see the Language Workshops on pages 465 and 597.

**PHRASES AND CLAUSES**

A **clause** is a group of words that has both a subject and a verb.

A **phrase** is a group of words that is missing either the subject or the verb.

left for California (This is a phrase because it has a verb, *left,* but no subject.)

the wagon train left for California (This is a clause because it has a subject, *wagon train,* and a verb, *left.*)
◀

$$\overset{\text{S}}{\phantom{x}}\quad\overset{\text{V}}{\phantom{x}}\qquad\qquad\overset{\text{S}}{\phantom{x}}\quad\overset{\text{V}}{\phantom{x}}$$

A new <u>day</u> <u>dawned</u>.    <u>You</u> <u>know</u> him.

**Subordinate clauses** cannot stand alone as sentences.

$$\overset{\text{S}}{\phantom{x}}\quad\overset{\text{V}}{\phantom{x}}\qquad\qquad\overset{\text{S}}{\phantom{x}}\quad\overset{\text{V}}{\phantom{x}}$$

if the <u>fire</u> <u>spreads</u>    <u>who</u> <u>built</u> the reed islands of Lake Titicaca

A subordinate clause has a subject and a verb. However, it does not express a complete idea. Additional information is needed to make a subordinate clause into a sentence.

A clause may be introduced by a pronoun such as *who, whoever, whom, whomever, whose, what, whatever, that,* or *which.* It may also be introduced by a subordinating conjunction.

| Subordinating Conjunctions | |
|---|---|
| Time | after, as, as long as, as soon as, before, since, until, when, whenever, while |
| Manner | as, as if |
| Place | where, wherever |
| Cause or Reason | because, since |
| Comparison | as, as much as, than |
| Condition | although, as long as, even if, even though, if, provided that, though, unless, while |
| Purpose | in order that, so that, that |

**To make a subordinate clause into a sentence, add an independent clause, or simple sentence, to it.**

A sentence made up of an independent clause and one or more subordinate clauses is called a **complex sentence.**

The boat owners can't use the pier (Independent Clause) +
because many seals are crowded onto it. (Subordinate Clause) =
The boat owners can't use the pier because many seals are crowded onto it. (Complex Sentence)

**Exercise 2 Complex Sentences** Copy the following complex sentences onto your paper. Underline each independent clause once and each subordinate clause twice.

**Example**    Monadnock is the mountain that they climbed on their honeymoon.

**Answer**    <u>Monadnock is the mountain</u> <u>that they climbed on their honeymoon.</u>

**1.** They saw the Grand Canyon while they were in Arizona.
**2.** Although Marc's nickname is Lucky, he isn't.

1026    LANGUAGE HANDBOOK

3. Whenever Sam eats anything, he records the calories.
4. You ask Allison if she remembers the tune.
5. Erin wondered why the dogs were barking.
6. The mayor couldn't decide until she asked her advisers.
7. Frankenstein is a character that Mary Shelley created.
8. When you press this button, the tape recorder will start.
9. You should not sign anything before you read it.
10. Douglas fishes whenever he can.

## Compound-Complex Sentences

You have now studied simple, compound, and complex sentences. The last kind of sentence is the **compound-complex** sentence.

> **A compound-complex sentence consists of two or more independent clauses and one or more subordinate clauses.**

In other words, think of a compound-complex sentence as a compound sentence plus a subordinate clause.

Yolanda felt dizzy, (Independent Clause) +
and we noticed (Independent Clause) +
that she looked pale (Subordinate Clause) =
Yolanda felt dizzy, and we noticed that she looked pale.
(Compound-Complex Sentence)

**Exercise 3  Compound-Complex Sentences**   Copy the following compound-complex sentences onto your paper. Underline each independent clause once and each subordinate clause twice.

1. Native Americans had cures that impressed European doctors; however, most of the cures are now lost.
2. She realized that I was listening, and she lowered her voice.
3. Since it rained recently on the trail, you need to walk carefully, or you'll slip in the mud.
4. I knew that I couldn't move the piano by myself, so I asked for help.
5. Sid was in the band until he got a job, and now he doesn't have time.

**Exercise 4  Sentence Review**   Add to the following clauses to create two *Compound,* two *Complex,* and two *Compound-Complex* sentences. Label each sentence to tell what kind it is.

1. Delia used live bait
2. who uncovered the scandal
3. I have no more change
4. that he lives on a houseboat
5. since the museum is open to the public
6. who wrote this article about nutrition

## SECTION 8   USING CAPITALIZATION

## Rules of Capitalization

Capitalization calls attention to words that are particularly important. You probably won't forget to capitalize the first word in a sentence or a person's name. There are, however, some other uses of capitalization that distinguish particular words or groups of words.

## Proper Nouns and Adjectives

**Capitalize proper nouns and adjectives.**

The name of a specific person, place, thing, or idea is a **proper noun**. Proper nouns are capitalized, and common nouns are not. A **proper adjective** is an adjective formed from a proper noun, and it should also be capitalized.

| Common Noun | Proper Noun | Proper Adjective |
|---|---|---|
| state | **T**exas | **T**exan |
| country | **F**rance | **F**rench |
| city | **P**aris | **P**arisian |

## Names and Titles of People

**Capitalize people's names, and initials that stand for names.**

**A. E. H**ousman          **A**lfred **E**dward **H**ousman

**Capitalize titles and abbreviations of titles when used before people's names or in direct address.**

**D**r. **L**ucille **O**rtez          **M**ayor **H. W**ashington          **G**en. **J. G. F**ine

**Capitalize a title used without a person's name if it refers to a head of state or a person in another important position.**

the **P**resident of the **U**nited **S**tates     the **Q**ueen of **E**ngland
the **S**ecretary of **S**tate               the **S**ecretary-**G**eneral of the UN

## Family Relationships

**Capitalize the words indicating family relationships when the words are used as names or parts of names.**

Our **U**ncle **B**ob used to be an engineer on the MTA.

If the word is preceded by an article or a possessive adjective, it is not capitalized.

Your dad is so gentle and kind.

# The Pronoun *I*

**Always capitalize the pronoun *I*.**

> Bob and **I** argued over the household chores.

# The Supreme Being and Sacred Writings

**Capitalize all words referring to God and religious scriptures.**

| | | |
|---|---|---|
| the **S**on of **G**od | the **H**oly **G**ospel | the **O**ld **T**estament |
| **A**llah | the **L**ord | the **T**almud |

**Exercise 1**  Rewrite the following sentences, correcting any capitalization errors.

1. My brother and i like danish pastries.
2. Is indira gandhi still the prime minister of india?
3. The manager is ms. suzy kraske.
4. Sometimes president johnson was called lbj.
5. Mayor martinez has a large mexican-american constituency.
6. The british author g. k. chesterton wrote about a priest, father brown, in his detective stories.
7. According to mom, pizza is not an italian food.
8. The children recited bible verses for rev. parks.
9. Did senator baker sponsor the bill?
10. Has sgt. jones reported to the captain yet?

# Geographical Names

**In a geographical name capitalize the first letter of each word except articles and prepositions.**

| | | | |
|---|---|---|---|
| **Continents** | **A**sia | **S**outh **A**merica | **A**frica |
| **Bodies of Water** | **R**ed **R**iver | **S**alt **C**reek | **B**ering **S**ea |
| **Landforms** | **G**reat **P**lains | **G**rand **C**anyon | **M**t. **R**ainier |
| **World Regions** | the **P**anhandle | the **P**acific **R**im | the **O**rient |
| **Public Areas** | **D**isneyland | **I**ndiana **D**unes | **Y**osemite |
| **Political Units** | **M**ichigan | **S**ixth **C**ongressional | **D**istrict |
| **Roads and Highways** | **R**oute 47 | **M**ichigan **A**venue | **M**arket **S**treet |

# Directions and Sections

**Capitalize names of sections of the country or the world, and any adjectives that come from those names.**

> The **E**ast is more urban than the **W**est.
> Hillary wants to move to the **S**outhwest.

**Do not capitalize compass directions or adjectives that merely indicate direction or a general location.**

> The wind was blowing in a **s**outherly direction.
> The sun sets in the **w**est.

**Exercise 2**  Rewrite the following sentences, correcting any errors in capitalization.

1. The new england settlers made the most of their natural resources.
2. The dead sea is an inland sea.
3. Is greenland an island, and is it warmer than iceland?
4. Go east of main street to reach the lake.
5. Is north america larger than south america?
6. Much of our shellfish comes from chesapeake bay.
7. Leaves turn later in the south than in the north.
8. I live in the fourth congressional district.
9. Dale grew up in dayton, ohio, and has a midwestern accent.
10. We drove south through the great smoky mountains.

## Organizations and Institutions

**Capitalize the names of organizations and institutions and their abbreviations.**

> **F**ederal **A**viation **A**dministration    **FBI**    **C**hicago **M**otor **C**lub

## Events, Documents, and Periods of Time

**Capitalize the names of historical events, documents, and periods of time.**

> the **C**rusades    **B**ill of **R**ights    the **D**ark **A**ges

## Months, Days, and Holidays

**Capitalize the names of months, days, and holidays but not the names of seasons.**

> **N**ovember    **M**emorial **D**ay    summer

## Races, Languages, Nationalities, and Religions

**Capitalize the names of races, languages, nationalities, and religions and any adjectives formed from these names.**

> **I**talian    **C**atholic    **L**atin    **H**ispanic
> **M**oslem    **I**ndian    **C**aucasian    **J**udaism

**Exercise 3**   Rewrite the following sentences, correcting any errors in capitalization.

1. The jewish holiday of hanukkah lasts eight days.
2. Ina translates chinese speeches at the united nations.
3. Many famous writers, like hemingway and orwell, fought in the spanish civil war.
4. In june I begin my summer job at wilson memorial hospital.
5. The day-care center is in the baptist church on mt. auburn street.
6. Lee got a mortgage guaranteed by the fha from the first national bank.
7. The ama is not a union but a professional association of doctors.
8. Thornton worked for blue cross last winter.
9. During the renaissance, people had great respect for artists and writers.
10. My cousin went to mexico for easter break last year.

## School Subjects and Class Names

**Do not capitalize the general names of school subjects unless they are the names of languages. Do capitalize the titles of specific courses and of courses that are followed by a number.**

World History 300      art      Consumer Problems 1      Spanish

**Capitalize class names only when they refer to a specific group or event or when they are used in direct address.**

The seniors signed each other's yearbooks and made plans to write to each other later.

Congratulations, Seniors; we are all very proud of you.

## Structures

**Capitalize the names of specific monuments, bridges, and buildings.**

the Alamo      the George Washington Bridge      Grant's Tomb

## Bodies of the Universe

**Capitalize the names of the planets in the solar system and other objects in the universe, except words like *sun* and *moon*.**

the glaring sun      Venus      the North Star

---

**QUICK TIP**   Capitalize the word *earth* only when it is used in conjunction with the names of other planets. The word *earth* is not capitalized when the article *the* precedes it.

Except for the earth, we know of no planet that supports life.

---

## Time Abbreviations

**Capitalize the abbreviations** *B.C., A.D., A.M.,* **and** *P.M.*

> The mother awoke at 2:00 **A.M.** when she heard the car horn honking. The Egyptians developed the first lunar calendar in about 4241 **B.C.**

**Exercise 4**   Rewrite the following sentences, correcting any errors in capitalization.

1. Suzanne taught english in japan for the summer.
2. Our business I test was all about interest rates and taxes.
3. Dee has a degree in math and computer science and works near the washington monument.
4. Augustus ruled Rome from 27 b.c. to a.d. 14.
5. Mr. elam took his art class to paint the vietnam veterans memorial.
6. Someday we may discover some form of life on mars.
7. The world survived without aspirin until a.d. 1893.
8. My spanish class starts at 2:30 p.m.
9. The planet saturn is the one with the rings around it.
10. Ozone is a protective layer of atmosphere around the Earth.

**NOTE**

*B.C.* (before Christ) always comes after the year. *A.D.* (*Anno Domini,* in the year of the Lord) is used before the year.

## Sentences and Poetry

**Capitalize the first word of every sentence.**

> **T**he plane passed the sound barrier. **P**eople in the area heard the boom.

**Capitalize the first word of every line of poetry in most cases.** (In some modern poetry, lines do not begin with a capital letter.)

> **T**he woods are lovely, dark, and deep,
> **B**ut I have promises to keep, . . .
>
> —"Stopping by Woods on a Snowy Evening," Robert Frost

## Quotations

A **direct quotation** repeats the exact words of a speaker or writer. **Capitalize the first word of a direct quotation.**

> Shakespeare wrote, "**T**he course of true love never did run smooth."

A **divided quotation** is a direct quotation broken into two parts by words such as "she said" or "he remarked." The first word of the second part is not capitalized unless it starts a new sentence.

> "**I**t is true," said Carrie, "**t**hat we can never please everyone."
> "**I**t is true," said Carrie, "**W**e can never please everyone."

## Letter Parts

**Capitalize the first word in the greeting of a letter. Also capitalize the title, person's name, and words such as *Sir* and *Madam.***

**D**ear **S**ir or **M**adam:     **D**ear **M**s. **O**ppenheim:

**Capitalize only the first word in the complimentary close.**

**S**incerely,     **V**ery fondly,

## Outlines and Titles

**Capitalize the first word of each item in an outline and letters that introduce major subsections.**

- **I. F**ilm comedians
  - **A. S**ilent film comedians
    - **1. I**ndividuals
    - **2. G**roups
  - **B. C**omedians of the 1930's
- **II. F**amous film comedies

**Capitalize the first, last, and all other important words in titles. Do not capitalize conjunctions, articles, or prepositions with fewer than five letters.**

| | |
|---|---|
| **Book Title** | *Gnomes* |
| **Newspaper** | *San Francisco Chronicle* |
| **Play** | *No Place to Be Somebody* |
| **Television Series** | *Nova* |
| **Short Story** | "*T*oo *E*arly *S*pring" |
| **Song** | "*G*reensleeves" |
| **Work of Art** | *Winged Victory* |

The word *the* at the beginning of a title and the word *magazine* are capitalized only when they are part of the formal name.

*Consumer Reports* magazine     *The New York Times*
*Smithsonian Magazine*

**Exercise 5**   Rewrite the following sentences, correcting any errors in capitalization.

1. "why," asked nina, "don't you think before you speak?"
2. i know what the caged bird feels, alas!
   when the sun is bright on the upland slopes;
   when the wind stirs soft through the springing grass,
   and the river flows like a stream of glass;
3. "stop!" called jake. "that's my suitcase."
4. II. native american art
   A. practical arts
      1. wampum
      2. ceremonial bowls
5. dear mr. nolan:
   your subscription to *newsweek* magazine is about to expire. we have
   enclosed a renewal form so that you will not miss an issue.
      sincerely yours,
6. the american anthem is "the star-spangled banner."
7. i listen to "radio mystery theater."
8. "did sal get a role in *romeo and juliet?*" asked liz.
9. read the fourth chapter, "defensive driving," in *let's drive right.*
10. "would you like to hear beethoven's ninth symphony?" asked ann.
    "there's an extra ticket."

# SECTION 9  USING PUNCTUATION

Consider the following paragraph from Plato's "The Death of Socrates":

> I see said Socrates But I suppose I am allowed or rather bound to pray the gods that my removal from this world to the other may be more prosperous This is my prayer then and I hope that it may be granted With these words quite calmly and with no sign of distaste he drained the cup in one breath

As you can see, punctuation marks are essential. They are signals for a reader. They indicate pauses and show points of emphasis. They tell who is speaking and where ideas begin and end. If you want your readers to understand what you write, you need to use punctuation marks correctly.

## Kinds of Punctuation Marks

In this section you will learn how to use the following punctuation marks:

**1.** End marks (.!?)
**2.** Commas (,)
**3.** Semicolons (;)
**4.** Colons (:)

**5.** Hyphens (-)
**6.** Apostrophes (')
**7.** Quotation marks (" ")
**8.** Underlining (__)

### End Marks

The punctuation marks that show where sentences end are called end marks. They are **periods, question marks,** and **exclamation points.**

**Use a period at the end of a declarative sentence.**

A **declarative sentence** is a sentence that makes a statement. It is the most basic kind of sentence used for reporting information.

The rate of inflation is rising.

**Use a period at the end of an imperative sentence.**

An **imperative sentence** is one that requests or orders someone to do something.

Step to the rear of the elevator, please.

**Use a period at the end of an indirect question.**

An **indirect question** tells what someone asked. However, it does not give the exact words of the person who asked the question.

Before takeoff, the flight attendant asked whether everyone was comfortable.

▶ **OTHER PUNCTUATION MARKS**

**Parentheses** and **dashes** are sometimes used to enclose sentence interrupters.

**Parentheses:** Jean François Millet (born 1814) became famous for his painting of peasant subjects.

**Dashes:** The youth vote—eighteen-year-olds got the vote in 1971—is sought after by many politicians.

The following are the
standard Post Office ab-
breviations for states
and territories of the
United States:

| | |
|---|---|
| Alabama | AL |
| Alaska | AK |
| Arizona | AZ |
| Arkansas | AR |
| California | CA |
| Colorado | CO |
| Connecticut | CT |
| Delaware | DE |
| District of Columbia | DC |
| Florida | FL |
| Georgia | GA |
| Hawaii | HI |
| Idaho | ID |
| Illinois | IL |
| Indiana | IN |
| Iowa | IA |
| Kansas | KS |
| Kentucky | KY |
| Louisiana | LA |
| Maine | ME |
| Maryland | MD |
| Massachusetts | MA |
| Michigan | MI |
| Minnesota | MN |
| Mississippi | MS |
| Missouri | MO |
| Montana | MT |
| Nebraska | NE |
| Nevada | NV |
| New Hampshire | NH |
| New Jersey | NJ |
| New Mexico | NM |
| New York | NY |
| North Carolina | NC |
| North Dakota | ND |
| Ohio | OH |
| Oklahoma | OK |
| Oregon | OR |
| Pennsylvania | PA |
| Rhode Island | RI |
| South Carolina | SC |
| South Dakota | SD |
| Tennessee | TN |
| Texas | TX |
| Utah | UT |

Periods are omitted in some abbreviations. If you are not sure whether to use periods, look up the abbreviation in a dictionary.

NATO (North Atlantic Treaty Organization)  
UN (United Nations)  
FBI (Federal Bureau of Investigation)  
ME (Maine)  
WI (Wisconsin)  
CA (California)

Note that a period is not used after a standard, two-letter United States Post Office state abbreviation. A period is used after an informal state abbreviation, such as *Calif.,* for California, or *Ill.,* for Illinois.

**Use a period after most abbreviations and initials.**

An abbreviation is a shortened form of a word. An initial is a single letter that stands for a word or name.

Col. B. Johnson, Jr. = Colonel Brian Johnson, Junior  
Miami, Fla., U.S.A. = Miami, Florida, United States of America  
123 E. River St. = 123 East River Street  
Fr. Joseph Murphy, Jr. = Father Joseph Murphy, Junior  
2 gal. 4 oz. = two gallons, four ounces

**Use a period after each number or letter that shows a division of an outline or that precedes an item in a list.**

**List**      Please take these steps, in order:
1. Gather your information.
2. Take notes.
3. Make an outline.

**Outline**   I. Europeans  
           **A.** French citizens  
           **B.** German citizens

**In numerals use a period between dollars and cents and before a decimal.**

$22.95          10.999

**Use a *question mark* at the end of an interrogative sentence.**

An **interrogative sentence** is one that asks a question.

What are your strong points?

The above sentence gives the exact words of the person who asked the question. It is called a **direct question.** A question mark is used only with a direct question.

**Do not use a question mark with an indirect question. Instead use a period.**

The interviewer might ask what your strong points are.

**Use an *exclamation point* at the end of an exclamatory sentence.**

That's a mess!    How great you look!

**Use an exclamation point after an interjection or after any other exclamatory expression.**

An **interjection** is a word or group of words used to express strong feeling. It may be a real word or simply a group of letters used to represent a sound. It is one of the eight parts of speech.

Hurray!    Oh my gosh!    Pow!

**Exercise 1   End Marks**   Rewrite the following sentences, adding the necessary punctuation.

1. Well Look who's here
2. Doesn't he babysit for Sammy
3. The government agency that monitors working conditions is OSHA
4. Does Mr Nunez have an office in this building
5. Bill asked the conductor whether she could change a twenty for the $125 fare
6. **I** Allergies
   **A** Reactions
   **B** Swelling
   **C** Shortness of breath
   **D** Itching
7. Rev J A Weaver is the chaplain at the hospital
8. The FM station doesn't come on until 6:00 AM
9. Is her address still 805 S Elm Street
10. Which states are part of the USSR
11. Is Tracy an RN or an LPN
12. The turkey weighs 8 lb 11 oz and costs $795
13. Carl asked whether Mt Fuji was in Japan
14. J Edgar Hoover was the first director of the FBI
15. Ow That hurts

| | |
|---|---|
| Vermont | VT |
| Virginia | VA |
| Washington | WA |
| West Virginia | WV |
| Wisconsin | WI |
| Wyoming | WY |
| American Samoa | AS |
| Federated States of Micronesia | FM |
| Guam | GU |
| Marshall Islands | MH |
| Puerto Rico | PR |
| Virgin Islands | VI |

**Two Periods?**

When an abbreviation comes at the end of a sentence requiring a period, use just one period, not two. When an abbreviation comes before a colon or semicolon, use a period and the colon or semicolon:

10 A.M.: algebra class
11 A.M.: English class
Go to lunch at 12:30 P.M.

## The Comma

**Use a comma after every item in a series except the last.**

A series consists of three or more words, phrases, or clauses.

**Words**   Flowers, candy, and other gifts crowded the hospital room.
**Phrases**   Vanessa hurried through the door, up the stairs, and into the president's office.
**Clauses**   The fire chief explained how the fire started, how it spread, and how much damage it caused.

**Use commas after the adverbs *first, second, third,* and so on when these adverbs introduce parallel items in a series.**

The speaker told us how to succeed: first, believe in yourself; second, set goals; and third, work hard.

**No Commas**

Commas are not needed when all the items in a series are joined by *and, or,* or *nor.*

Flowers and candy and other gifts crowded the hospital room.

**Use commas between two or more adjectives of equal rank that modify the same noun.**

> Tall, sleek, modern skyscrapers line Fifth Avenue.

---

**QUICK TIP**   To decide whether adjectives are of equal rank, try placing the word *and* between them. If the *and* sounds natural and if you can reverse the order of the adjectives without changing the meaning, then a comma is needed.

---

**Use a comma to separate an introductory word, phrase, or clause from the rest of the sentence.**

> Yes, I have plenty of time before I have to go out.
> After the last round of the match, Howard interviewed the boxers.
> Frowning slightly, Blake reached for a chess piece.
> When you leave, remember to lock the door behind you.

The comma may be left out if there would be little pause in speaking.

> At night we made a fire.

SENTENCE
INTERRUPTERS
......................
The following interrupt-
ers are quite common:

   however

   I suppose

   I think

   I believe

   nevertheless

   by the way

   fortunately

   on the one hand

   in contrast

**Use commas to set off words or groups of words that interrupt the flow of thought in a sentence.**

> A doctor, therefore, needs malpractice insurance.
> The players were, I believe, unusually rough in the game last night.
> Linda Ronstadt, for example, requires no backup singers.

**Exercise 2  Commas and End Marks**   Rewrite the following sentences, adding the necessary punctuation.

1. Her thin lively face is almost never still
2. He worked cheerfully carefully and quickly
3. Did you see the old newspapers full ashtrays and dirty cups littering the room
4. First listen; second question; third form your opinion
5. I asked Mary if she'd looked through her notebook around her desk and then in her locker
6. A long sleek black limousine pulled up in front of the bank
7. Moreover not all oil-producing countries belong to OPEC
8. The United States for instance does not belong
9. Holding the baby in one arm he clutched the groceries with the other
10. No there's still time
11. Your Honda I am sorry to say is beyond repair
12. Decals posters and notices covered the window
13. As most of us grow older I have heard we become less sensitive to pain
14. Honey on the other hand does provide nutrition
15. If you try again however you might succeed

**Use commas to set off nouns of direct address.**

The name of someone directly spoken to is a noun of **direct address.**

> Julie, listen to this song.
> The nearest gas station, Mark, is at least two miles from here.

**Use commas to set off the speaker's tags used with direct quotations.**

When you repeat someone's exact words, you make a **direct quotation.** A direct quotation is usually accompanied by explanatory words known as **speaker's tags.** Examples of speaker's tags include "Molly said," "Robin answered," and "Nicolas asked."

> Debbie said firmly, "I don't agree with that candidate."
> "I don't agree with that candidate," Debbie said firmly.
> "I don't agree," Debbie said firmly, "with that candidate."

**Do not use commas with indirect quotations.**

> Debbie said that she didn't agree with that candidate.

**Use a comma before the conjunction that joins the two main clauses in a compound sentence.**

> The taxi stopped, and five people hopped out.

◀ SPEAKER'S TAGS
.....................
Common speaker's tags include the following:

| | |
|---|---|
| she replied | she answered |
| she asked | she demanded |
| she warned | she questioned |
| she inquired | she wondered |
| she said | she explained |

There are, of course, many others. Speaker's tags often reveal a great deal about the speaker's state of mind and tone of voice.

---

**QUICK TIP**  Make sure that the two parts being joined are, indeed, complete clauses. A comma is not needed to separate compound predicates.

| | |
|---|---|
| **Compound Predicate** | The test pilot flew a new jet and landed it safely. |
| **Compound Sentence** | The test pilot flew a new jet, and he landed it safely. |

---

**Exercise 3  Commas**   Rewrite the following sentences, adding commas where needed. If no comma is needed, write *Correct.*

1. Charles works and he works hard.
2. "Run ten laps for that remark" snapped the coach.
3. The Congo River in Africa curves widely and it empties into the Atlantic.
4. "Tom" said Maureen "here is my sister Nell."
5. Millie have you seen Jerome?
6. Alice Walker a novelist and an editor appeared on *Today.*
7. Your taxi is here Gloria.
8. Joan Baez is a singer who also champions social causes.
9. Have you seen my brother Linda?
10. By the way Neal Ms. Mills called and wants you to call back.

A **restrictive clause** tells which person or thing is being discussed.

A **nonrestrictive clause** does not identify or tell which one. It simply adds additional information.

**Restrictive clause:** This is the statue that Michelangelo made for his own tomb. (The clause tells *which statue.*)

**Nonrestrictive clause:** The *David,* which is Michelangelo's most famous statue, stands fourteen feet three inches tall. (The clause does not tell which statue; the *David* is identified with or without the clause.)

A nonrestrictive clause should be separated from the rest of the sentence by commas.

## In dates use a comma between the day of the month and the year.

July 4, 1776     May 8, 1982

In a sentence a comma follows the year.

Ralph Nader was born on February 27, 1934, in Winsted, Connecticut.

## Use a comma between the name of a city or town and the name of its state or country.

Nashville, Tennessee     Caracas, Venezuela

In writing an address as part of a sentence, use a comma after each item, including the state or country.

Send your entry to Eastman Kodak Company, 343 State Street, Rochester, New York 14650.

Note that you do not place a comma between the state and the ZIP Code.

## Use a comma after the salutation of a friendly letter and after the complimentary close of a friendly letter or a business letter.

Dear Erica,     Very truly yours,

## Use a comma when no specific rule applies but there is danger of misreading or confusion if a comma is not used.

Whatever you sing, you sing well. Outside, the fairgrounds were crowded.

**Exercise 4   Commas**   Rewrite the following sentences, adding commas where necessary.

1. Whatever you do you do with enthusiasm.
2. The United States bought Alaska on March 30 1867 for $7,200,000.
3. Dear Ramona
     The roses that you sent were lovely. Thank you.
                              Sincerely yours
4. The card was postmarked August 2 1863 from Gettysburg Pennsylvania.
5. The Ferris wheel was designed by G. W. Gale Ferris of Galesburg Illinois.
6. The first workable light bulb was invented in Menlo Park New Jersey in October of 1879.
7. If Loretta walks over Jay drives her home.
8. The people I like like me.
9. Her address is 52 Meade Avenue Chicago Illinois 60639.
10. When Josh walks through the furniture shakes.

**Exercise 5   End Mark and Comma Review**   Rewrite the following sentences, adding periods, question marks, exclamation points, and commas as necessary. If the punctuation is correct, write *Correct.*

1. Dr Bill Malden asked me to come to his office at 2:30 PM

2. Oh my gosh We're late
3. Why was the Hon Robert Bork not appointed to the US Supreme Court
4. The address of the hospital where Roy works is 606 Clermont Road Batavia Ohio 45103
5. I Health insurance
    A Health maintenance organizations
    B Traditional health insurance plans
6. Moe Larry and Curly were the names of the Three Stooges
7. Marilyn went to the stable curried her horse and went for a long ride
8. First they planned a menu; second they made a grocery list: third they went to the grocery store
9. Long cold winters are common in New Hampshire
10. The small light footsteps traveled into the deep silent woods
11. Furthermore I won't tell a lie for you
12. No you don't have to wash your clothes but you do have to put them away
13. If you stand very still you can hear the owl hoot
14. "The stories of O Henry often have surprise endings but don't read ahead" our English teacher requested
15. Maureen did you say you were going to feed the cat
16. "It's over" said the woman "for both of us"
17. On Thursday November 22 1990 our lives changed forever
18. In the bow of the careening rowboat the little boy cringed.
19. Write to the Peruvian Consulate at 745 Boylston St Boston MA 02116
20. Dear Mac
        We'll see you in St Louis Missouri on March 5
                Fondly
                Bob and Marilyn

## Semicolons

A **semicolon** separates sentence elements. It indicates a more definite break than a comma does but a less abrupt break than a period does.

**Use a semicolon to join the two parts of a compound sentence if no coordinating conjunction is used.** Remember that a semicolon may be used only if the clauses are closely related.

> The city has a phone number for emergencies; it is 911.

**Use a semicolon before a conjunctive adverb that joins the clauses of a compound sentence.** A **conjunctive adverb** is a word such as *therefore* or *however* that shows a relationship between two clauses.

> Jonathan fell asleep on the subway; consequently, he missed his stop.

**Use a semicolon to separate the items of a series if one or more of these items contain commas.**

> Marsha bought paper plates, napkins, and a tablecloth; ordered the food; and hired a band.

CONJUNCTIVE ADVERBS
Some common conjunctive adverbs are these:

therefore
however
otherwise
consequently
besides
nevertheless
moreover

Sometimes phrases serve similar purposes:

as a result
for example
for instance
in a similar way

## Colons

**Use a colon to introduce a list of items.** A word or phrase such as *these* or *the following* is often followed by a colon. A colon must be preceded by an independent clause; a colon never follows a verb.

> Air pollution comes from the following sources: cars, trucks, buses, factories, and smokers.

**Use a colon to introduce a long or formal quotation.**

> Rosemary Brown said: "The feeling is that until men are comfortable working in some of these fields that are traditionally considered to be female, . . . women end up doing two jobs and the men are still doing just one."

**Use a colon between two independent clauses when the second clause explains the first.** The first word following a colon is not capitalized unless it is a proper noun or the start of a quotation.

> He loved her more than himself: she had the purest spirit he had ever encountered.

**Use a colon after the greeting in a formal letter.**

> Dear Sir or Madam:          Dear Governor Richards:

**Use a colon between numbers showing hours and minutes.**

> 8:00 P.M.          12:01 A.M.

## Hyphens

▶ **Use a hyphen between syllables divided at the end of a line.**

> He recognized an old, yellowed photo-
> graph of his grandfather.

▶ **Use a hyphen in compound numbers from twenty-one to ninety-nine.**

> thirty-one days          seventy-nine clips

**Use a hyphen in fractions.**

> a three-fifths majority          one-half the distance

**Use a hyphen in certain compound nouns.**

> stand-in          brother-in-law

**Use a hyphen between the words that make up a compound adjective when the modifier is used before a noun.**

> on-the-job training          sixteen-month-old girl

### HYPHENATING AT THE END OF A LINE

Follow these rules:

1. Divide a word only between syllables.
2. Hyphenate only words of two or more syllables.
3. Make sure that at least two letters of the word fall on each line.

### WHEN TO HYPHENATE

To determine whether a compound needs a hyphen, look it up in a dictionary.

### HYPHENATED ADJECTIVES

A noun plus an *-ing* word, used as an adjective, is usually hyphenated:

decision-making process

process of decision making

problem-solving technique

technique for problem solving

**Exercise 6  Semicolons, Colons, and Hyphens**  Rewrite the following sentences, correcting all errors in the use of semicolons, colons, and hyphens.

1. Susan, hang the clothes Patrick, bake the cake Janet, put away the dishes.
2. The photos in the collection include architecture fine art and people of Chicago parks bridges and monuments of San Francisco and buildings fountains and people of Rome.
3. I finished the work moreover I had time to review it carefully.
4. The wedding was in the afternoon the reception was in the evening.
5. Janet, Susan, and Joanne Murphy Bob and Wayne Shepherd and Phil Jane and Sue McConnaughay were all at the dinner.
6. Christie arrived at 1215 P.M. Blaize arrived at 1215 A.M.
7. There are several kinds of paints you can use tempera watercolor and oils.
8. In *The Heart Is a Lonely Hunter* Carson McCullers wrote the following "There are those who know and those who don't know. And for every ten thousand who don't know there's only one who knows."
9. Dear Doctor Boley
   Please write me a letter of recommendation to nursing school.
10. We have something to tell you your mother in law is coming to dinner.
11. Ninety nine percent of the delegates at the UN supported the resolution.
12. Will Puerto Rico become the fifty first state?
13. The President called the congressional hearing a three ring circus.
14. The long winded vice chairman introduced the guest speaker.
15. The bank made a short term loan to the contractor.

## Apostrophes

**Use an apostrophe to form the possessive of singular and plural nouns. To form the possessive of a singular noun, add an apostrophe and -s, even if the noun ends in -s.**

      Gus's report        the employee's complaint

**To form the possessive of a plural noun that ends in -s, add an apostrophe only.**

      The Simpsons' home        the reporters' questions

**To form the possessive of a plural noun that does not end in -s, add both an apostrophe and -s.**

      the workmen's lunch break        the geese's feathers

**To form the possessive of an indefinite pronoun, add an apostrophe and -s.**

      anyone's        no one's

**Use an apostrophe in a contraction to show where one or more letters have been left out.** Contractions are usually avoided in formal writing.

they've = *they have*        she'll = *she will* or *she shall*
I'm = *I am*                  won't = *will not*

**Use an apostrophe to show the omission of figures in a date.**

a '91 GM Saturn            the class of '96

**Use an apostrophe to show the plurals of letters, numbers, signs, and words referred to as words.**

three *s*'s        two 6's        *good-bye*'s

**O**THER **U**SES OF
**A**POSTROPHES

Apostrophes are also
used to show omitted
letters in dialect, old-
fashioned speech, or po-
etry.

'Twas the night before
Christmas.

'Tis we own t'ing, man.

**Exercise 7  Apostrophes**   Rewrite the following sentences, correcting any errors in the use of apostrophes.

1. The child wanted to know if Supermans cape was blue.
2. Mens suits are on the third floor, arent they?
3. Ive bought an 89 Toyota, she said, and no ones going to drive it but me.
4. The teachers union votes tonight.
5. "Youre the peoples choice," the supporter cried out as the candidates motorcade passed.
6. Shes not crossing her *t*s or dotting her *i*s.
7. Tanyas *for sure*s are getting on my nerves.
8. Nobodys future looks brighter than ours.
9. Does the Constitution protect these states rights?
10. The nine justices decision was unanimous.

## Quotation Marks and Underlining

**Use quotation marks to begin and end a direct quotation.**

Dennis said, "The Torah is the ancient Hebrew law."

**Do not use quotation marks to set off an indirect quotation.** Indirect quotations are often signaled by the word *that*.

Dennis said that the Torah is the ancient Hebrew law.

**To punctuate a direct quotation, enclose the exact words used by a speaker or writer in quotation marks. The first word of the quotation is capitalized. Commas at the ends of quotations are always placed inside the quotation marks. When the end of the quotation falls at the end of the sentence, the period falls inside the quotation marks.**

The editor answered, "I can use the article in next month's issue if you can provide me with photographs."

**Put question marks and exclamation marks inside the quotation marks if they are part of the quotation.**

"Where is Sri Lanka located?" asked Darren.
"Wait!" screamed the child. "I want to go with you!"

**Put question marks and exclamation marks outside the quotation marks if they are not part of the quotation.**

Did the doctor say, "Your X-rays are normal"?

**Commas and periods at the ends of quotations should be placed inside the quotation marks.**

The doctor said, "We noticed a shadow, but it's probably nothing."
"We noticed a shadow, but it's probably nothing," said the doctor.

**Enclose the parts of a divided quotation in quotation marks.** Do not capitalize the first word of the second part unless it begins a new sentence.

"The Knicks staged an upset," said the sportscaster, "in the last second of play."
"The Knicks staged an upset," said the sportscaster. "They won in the last second of play."

**In punctuating dialogue, begin a new paragraph to indicate a new speaker.**

"Surely, you're too big for a rocking horse!" his mother had remonstrated.
"Well, you see, Mother, till I can have a *real* horse, I like to have *some* sort of animal about," had been his quaint answer.
"Do you feel he keeps you company?" she laughed.
"Oh, yes! He's very good; he always keeps me company, when I'm there," said Paul.
—"The Rocking Horse Winner," D. H. Lawrence

**When quoting passages longer than one paragraph, use quotation marks at the beginning of each paragraph and at the end of only the last paragraph.**

Crusoe's circumstances at the beginning of the story are certainly quite dismal:

"September 30, 1659—I, poor miserable Robinson Crusoe, being shipwrecked, during a dreadful storm, in the offing, came on shore on this dismal unfortunate island, which I called the Island of Despair, all the rest of the ship's company being drowned, and myself almost dead.

"All the rest of that day I spent in afflicting myself at the dismal circumstances I was brought to."

**Use quotation marks to enclose the titles of short stories, poems, essays, magazine and newspaper articles, chapters, television episodes, and songs.**

| | |
|---|---|
| **Short Story** | ''The Sniper'' |
| **Poem** | ''When I Have Fears That I May Cease to Be'' |
| **Essay** | ''Such, Such Were the Joys'' |
| **Magazine or** | |
| **Newspaper Article** | ''Dewey Defeats Truman'' |
| **Chapter** | ''Britain Before the Anglo-Saxons'' |
| **Television Episode** | ''The Miracle of Life'' |
| **Song** | ''When You Wish Upon a Star'' |

**The titles of books, newspapers, magazines, movies, television series, plays, works of art, and long musical compositions are underlined in writing and italicized in print.**

| | |
|---|---|
| **Book** | *Robinson Crusoe* |
| **Newspaper** | *USA Today* |
| **Magazine** | *The English Journal* |
| **Movie** | Roman Polanski's *Macbeth* |
| **Television Series** | *Sesame Street* |
| **Play** | Shakespeare's *Macbeth* |
| **Work of Art** | Turner's *The Slave Ship* |
| **Long Musical** | |
| **Composition** | Verdi's *Otello* |

**Exercise 8  Quotation Marks and Underlining**   Rewrite the following sentences, adding quotation marks or underlining as necessary.

  1. We discussed the article The Invisible Threat.
  2. Please read the first chapter, Let Justice Be Done.
  3. Wasn't Pamela the first novel written in English?
  4. The folk singer taught us a traditional English ballad called Geordie.
  5. Is it cheetahs or leopards that have spots? asked Marie.
  6. The mayor said, Nobody leaves this room until we have reached an agreement.
  7. I love the story, said Robin, of how the Brownings met and courted each other.
  8. I know, said the ambassador. I read the story in the French newspaper Le Monde.
  9. Robert Frost once said that his favorite magazine was Scientific American, which is quite a statement from a poet known for works such as The Road Not Taken and Stopping by Woods on a Snowy Evening.
  10. Did you see The Great Whites of the Barrier Reef, last night's episode of Undersea Adventure? asked Luis.
     No, said Marty. Did you?

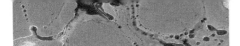

# Index of Fine Art

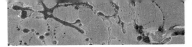

# *Index of Skills*

## *Literary Terms*

# *Reading and Critical Thinking Skills*

*All* Responding to Reading *questions draw upon a variety of critical thinking skills.*

# *Grammar, Usage, and Mechanics*

# *W*riting Skills, Modes, and Formats

looping, 839
questioning, 514, 561
tree diagram, 414
word webs, 414, 462, 669, 722, 959
Proofreading, 68–69, 126, 169–70, 218, 373, 416, 464, 516, 563, 596, 630–31, 671, 725, 782, 841, 883, 928, 929, 960
Proofreading symbols, 961
Purpose, 959
Reflective essay, 560–63
Reports, 167–70, 593–96
  biographical article, 167–70
  compare and contrast cultures, 593–96
  *see also* Research and Study Skills index, Research and reports
Research and report writing, 593–96, 964–70
  bibliographies, 965–69
  documentation, 968–69
  outlines, 594–95, 966–68
  quoting from sources, 595, 967–68
  reference materials, 173, 964–65
  statement of purpose, 594
  taking notes, 168, 600, 965–66
  thesis statement, 670
  writing from an outline, 594–95, 967–68
Resumés, 785
Revising and editing, 68–69, 126, 169–70, 218, 264, 373, 416, 464, 516, 563, 596, 630–31, 671, 725, 782, 841, 883, 928, 929, 960
Self-assessment, 69, 72, 126, 129, 170, 264, 266, 416, 419, 464, 467, 516, 518, 596, 631, 634, 671, 728, 784, 841, 883, 886, 928, 929, 960
Statement of purpose, 594
Summarize
  epitaph, 59
  headline, 45
  resumé, 46
  summarize attitude, 459
  TV-guide summary of act, 350
Supporting an opinion, 65, 142, 154, 213, 259
  *see also* Persuasion
Synthesis, 926–29
  advice, 155, 192, 331, 500, 610, 802
  critical review of high school, 926–29
  epitaph, 204
  headline, 667, 758
  interview questions, 32
  judge's sentence, 591
  list of guidelines, 399
  modern parable, 183
  protest slogans, 192
  proverb, 616
  punishment, 604
  recommendations to adoption agency, 879
  trial defense, 604
  TV summary, 350

verdict, 161
write a quiz, 744
Thesis statements, 514, 670
Transitions, 517–18, 885
Unity. *See* Coherence
Writing about literature, 513–16
  analyze characters, 770
  analyze events, 720
  analyze Macbeth's reasons, 294
  analyze motives, 489
  analyze poem, 572
  analyze theme of selection, 577
  character analysis, 411, 436
  compare characters, 294, 445, 711, 836
  compare selections, 559, 652, 758, 925
  evaluate play, 916
  explain an epic simile, 59
  explain main idea, 459
  explain symbol, 88
  explain theme/title, 685, 879, 897
  literary analysis, 513–16
  parody, 610, 667
  responding as a character, 32, 45, 88, 104, 121, 154, 166, 204, 213, 231, 238, 246, 259, 294, 331, 399, 436, 445, 500, 511, 559, 604, 616, 661, 696, 744, 802, 810, 864, 873
  review *Macbeth,* 368
Writing process, 958–61
  computers, 962–63
  decision-making in, 959
  learning and, 961
  problem-solving in, 959–60
  research and report writing, 964–70
  *see also* Drafting; Presenting/publishing; Prewriting; Research and report writing; Revising and editing
Year-end portfolio, 929
  *see also* Self-assessment

# *Vocabulary and Language*

Acronyms, 130
Alliteration, 450, 535, 802, 944
Analogies, 567, 610, 758, 798, 822, 873
Antonym questions, 519
Assonance, 802, 944
Blends, 130
Borrowed words, 130
Clipped words, 130
Colloquialisms, 945
Compound words, 130
Connotation, 222, 648
Consonance, 802, 945
Context clues, 32, 246, 259, 385, 411, 445, 479, 661, 711, 744, 758, 854

Denotation, 88, 121, 142, 154, 222, 399, 459, 489, 500, 583, 591, 616, 750, 836, 864, 897, 922

Dialect, 162, 166, 676, 856, 863, 946, 1044

Double meanings, 391

English
formal, 844
history of, 73, 141
informal, 844
standard, 844
word origins, 130

Foreign names, 760

Formal language, 844

Humor and language, 391

Idiom, 948

Informal language, 844

Jargon, 232, 948

Levels of language, 844

Loaded language, 222, 797

Middle English, 73, 141, 949

Old English, 73

Pronunciation, 760

Repetition, 535, 800

Slang, 951

Specialized vocabularies, 232, 948

Standard English, 844

Synonyms/antonyms, 45, 59, 104, 246, 390, 436, 511, 627, 720, 798, 822, 916

Word choice, 623, 695

Word origins, 130

Wordplay, 663

# Research and Study Skills

Almanacs, 173

Analogy questions, 567

Atlases, 173, 799

Biographical references, 173

Book reports, 592, 662, 837, 917

Books
using headings in, 385
using the parts of, 965

CD-ROM, 173

Computer research, 173

Computers, writing with, 962–63

Dictionaries, 246, 635
definitions, 687
of quotations, 617, 712
specialized, 635

Dictionary entries, 936, 1009

Documentation, 968–69

Essay tests, 674

Glossaries, 936

In-depth reading, 420

Maps, 34, 205, 491, 799, 866, 874

Microforms, 173

Notetaking, 168, 600, 966

Outlines, writing from, 967–68

Peer interaction
brainstorm, 512
conversation, 247, 260
group discussions/projects, 47, 96, 155, 248, 294, 311, 331, 350, 368, 400, 401, 437, 446, 451, 470, 480, 481, 490, 501, 512, 578, 584, 602, 611, 617, 618, 623, 643, 648, 662, 663, 676, 686, 698, 712, 713, 745, 759, 771, 803, 855, 856, 866, 874, 889, 898, 902, 917, 918
review dialogue, 120
role playing, 46, 60, 105, 331
*see also* Writing Skills, Modes, and Formats index; Peer editing/review; Prewriting

Periodicals, 173

Quotations
dictionaries of, 617, 712
in research papers, 966–68

*Readers' Guide to Periodical Literature*, 173, 721, 771, 823, 837, 865, 964

Reader's journal, 958

Reading logs, 618

Reading rates, 420

Reference sources, 173, 246, 635, 964–65

Research and reports
cannibalism, 437
Chinese cultural revolution, 260
college entrance exams, 155
courtly love, 247
education in South Africa, 837
folk/herbal medicine, 721, 898
Globe Theater, 294
heraldry, 89
Hindu customs, 214
human rights violations, 823
hypnotism, 823
India's independence, 490
Irish ballads, 686
Japanese theater, 412
library call numbers, 446
lottery winners, 771
*Macbeth* performance recordings, 311
medieval art, printing, 143
Nazi hunters, 592
nuclear weapons, 662
Nuremberg trials, 592
Renaissance women, 193
Roman Catholic Church, 865
Russian religious art, 553
snake poison, 898
South Africa, 501
special effects, 89
supernatural, 855
staging, 122
Trojan War, 60
West African cultures, 712

# *S*peaking, Listening, and Viewing

# Index of Titles and Authors

Page numbers that appear in italics refer to biographical information.

# Acknowledgments

*(continued from copyright page)*

**Rosica Colin Limited:** "Federigo's Falcon," from *The Decameron* by Giovanni Boccaccio, translated by Richard Aldington. Copyright © Catherine Guillaume. By permission of Rosica Colin Limited.

**Collins/Angus & Robertson Publishers:** "Eve to Her Daughters" by Judith Wright, from *Collected Poems.* Copyright © 1971 Judith Wright. By permission of Collins/Angus & Robertson Publishers.

**Joan Daves:** "Fear" by Gabriela Mistral, from *Selected Poems of Gabriela Mistral,* translated by Langston Hughes. Copyright © 1957 by Indiana University Press. By permission of Joan Daves.

**Dilia Agency, Prague:** "The Last Judgment" by Karel Čapek. By permission of Dilia Agency.

**Doubleday & Company:** Excerpts from *The Iliad* by Homer, translation by Robert Fitzgerald. Translation copyright © 1974 by Robert Fitzgerald. Excerpts from *Girls at War and Other Stories* by Chinua Achebe. Copyright © 1972, 1973 by Chinua Achebe. "Long Walk to Forever," from *Welcome to the Monkey House* by Kurt Vonnegut, Jr. Copyright © 1960 by Kurt Vonnegut, Jr. Used by permission of Delacorte Press/Seymour Lawrence, a division of Bantam, Doubleday, Dell Publishing Group, Inc.

**Faber and Faber Limited:** "Crackling Day," from *Tell Freedom* by Peter Abrahams. By permission of Faber and Faber Ltd.

**Farrar, Straus & Giroux, Inc.:** "Godfather Death," from *The Juniper Tree and Other Tales from Grimm* by Jakob and Wilhelm Grimm, translated by Lore Segal. Translation copyright © 1973 by Lore Segal. By permission of Farrar, Straus and Giroux, Inc. Excerpt from *Night* by Elie Wiesel. Copyright © 1960 by MacGibbon & Ke, renewal copyright © 1988 by The Collins Publishing Group. By permission of Hill and Wang, a division of Farrar, Straus and Giroux, Inc.

**Grove Press:** "The Madman on the Roof" by Kikuchi Kyojin, from *Modern Japanese Literature,* edited by Donald Keene. Copyright © 1956 by Grove Press. "The Enemy," from *New Poems* by Pablo Neruda, translated by Ben Belitt. Translation copyright © 1972 by Ben Belitt. By permission of Grove Weidenfeld.

**Harcourt Brace Jovanovich, Inc.:** "Beauty: When the Other Dancer Is the Self," from *In Search of Our Mothers' Gardens: Womanist Prose* by Alice Walker. Copyright © 1983 by Alice Walker. "The Sniper," from *Spring Sowing* by Liam O'Flaherty. By permission of Harcourt Brace Jovanovich, Inc.

**Harper & Row, Publisher, Inc.:** "By Any Other Name," from *Gifts of Passage* by Santha Rama Rau. Copyright 1951 by Vasabthi Rama Rau Bowers. By permission of HarperCollins Publishers, Inc.

**John Hawkins & Associates, Inc.:** "Primitive Man," from *It All Started with Stones and Clubs* by Richard Armour. Copyright © 1967 by Richard Armour. By permission of John Hawkins & Associates, Inc.

**Houghton Mifflin Company:** "Be Ye Men of Valour," from *Blood, Toil, Tears and Sweat, The Speeches of Winston Churchill,* edited and with an introduction by David Cannadine. Speeches copyright © 1989 by Winston S. Churchill, MP. Introduction and selection copyright © 1989 by David Cannadine. By permission of Houghton Mifflin Co.

**Barbara Kimenye:** "The Winner," from *Kalasanda* by Barbara Kimenye, published by Oxford University Press. By permission of the author.

**Macmillan Publishing Company:** "An Irish Airman Foresees His Death," from *The Poems of W. B. Yeats: A New Edition,* edited by Richard J. Finneran. Copyright 1919 by Macmillan Publishing Company, renewed 1947 by Bertha Georgie Yeats. "Escape" by Ilya Varshavsky, from *New Soviet Science Fiction,* translated by Helen Saltz Jacobson. Copyright © 1979 by Macmillan Publishing Company. Excerpts from *Kaffir Boy* by Mark Mathabane. Copyright © 1986 by Mark Mathabane. "The Cabuliwallah," from *The Hungry Stones and Other Stories* by Rabindranath Tagore. Copyright 1916 by

Macmillan Publishing Company, renewed 1944 by Rathindranath Tagore. By permission of Macmillan Publishing Company.

**New Directions Publishing Company and David Higham Associates Limited:** "Do Not Go Gentle Into That Good Night" by Dylan Thomas, from *Poems of Dylan Thomas*. Copyright © 1952 by Dylan Thomas. By permission of New Directions Publishing Co. and David Higham Associates Ltd.

**The Nobel Foundation:** "Nobel Acceptance Speech" by Elie Wiesel. Copyright © 1986 The Nobel Foundation.

**Harold Ober Associates, Inc.:** "The Old Demon" by Pearl S. Buck, published in *Cosmopolitan*, February 1939. Copyright 1939 by Pearl S. Buck, copyright © renewed 1966 by Pearl S. Buck. By permission of Harold Ober Associates, Inc.

**Penguin Books Ltd.:** Excerpts from "The Pardoner's Tale" by Geoffrey Chaucer, from *The Canterbury Tales*, translated by Nevill Coghill (Penguin Classics, Revised Edition, 1977), copyright © Nevill Coghill, 1951, 1958, 1960, 1975, 1977. From *The Last Days of Socrates* by Plato, translated by Hugh Tredennick. Copyright © 1954, 1959, 1969 by Hugh Tredennick. Published in Penguin Classics, 1954, revised edition 1959, 1969.

**Penguin USA Inc.:** "The Rocking Horse Winner," from *The Complete Short Stories of D. H. Lawrence*, Vol. III. Copyright 1933 by the Estate of D. H. Lawrence, copyright renewed © 1961 by Angelo Ravagli and C. M. Weekley, executors of the estate of Frieda Lawrence Ravagli. "Like the Sun," from *Under the Banyan Tree and Other Stories* by R. K. Narayan. Copyright © 1985 by R. K. Narayan. By permission of the publisher, Viking Penguin, a division of Penguin Books USA Inc. "The Meeting," from *Doctor Brodie's Report* by Jorge Luis Borges, translated by Norman Thomas di Giovanni. Copyright © 1970, 1971, 1972 by EMECE Editores S. A. and Norman Thomas di Giovanni. By permission of the publisher, Dutton, a division of Penguin Books USA Inc. Excerpts from "Grendel," "Hail Hrothgar" and "The Battle with Grendel," from *Beowulf,* translated by Burton Raffell. Copyright © 1963 by Burton Raffell. By permission of the publisher, New American Library, a division of Penguin Books USA Inc. "The Thrill of Grass," from *The Thrill of Grass* by W. P. Kinsella. Copyright © 1984 by W. P. Kinsella. By permission of the publisher, Viking Penguin, a division of Penguin Books USA Inc. and Penguin Books Canada Limited.

**Peters Fraser & Dunlop Group Ltd.:** *Mother's Day* by J. B. Priestley, from *English One-Act Plays of Today*, published by Samuel French Ltd. By permission of the Peters Fraser & Dunlop Group Ltd.

**Random House, Inc.:** "The Unknown Citizen," from *W. H. Auden: Collected Poems*, edited by Edward Mendelson. Copyright 1940 & renewed © 1968 by W. H. Auden. By permission of Random House, Inc. and Faber & Faber Ltd. Material from *Man Must Speak* by Roy A. Gallant. Copyright © 1968, 1969 by Roy A. Gallant. By permission of Random House, Inc. "The Demon Lover," from *The Collected Stories of Elizabeth Bowen*. Copyright 1946 & renewed © 1974 by Elizabeth Bowen. "Lamb to the Slaughter," from *Someone Like You* by Roald Dahl. Copyright 1953 by Roald Dahl. "A Cup of Tea," from *The Short Stories of Katherine Mansfield*. Copyright 1923 by Alfred A. Knopf, Inc., renewed 1951 by John Middleton Murray. "First Confession," from *Collected Stories* by Frank O'Connor. Copyright 1951 by Frank O'Connor. "The Thief," from *Seven Japanese Tales* by Junichiro Tanizaki, translated by Howard Hibbett. Copyright © 1963 by Alfred A. Knopf, Inc. By permission of Alfred A. Knopf, Inc.

**Rowan Tree Press and Marguerite Bouvard:** "They Have Not Been Able," from *Landscape and Exile* by Armando Valladares, translated and edited by M. G. Bouvard. Published by Rowan Tree Press.

**The Seal Press:** "A Vietnamese Doll" by Vigdis Stokkelien, from *An Everyday Story: Norwegian Women's Fiction*, edited by Katherine Hanson. Copyright © 1984 Katherine Hanson. By permission of The Seal Press.

**Samuel Selvon:** "When Greek Meets Greek" by Samuel Selvon. By permission of the author.

**Simon & Schuster, Inc.:** "No Witchcraft for Sale," from *African Stories* by Doris Lessing. Copyright © 1951, 1953, 1954, 1957, 1958, 1962, 1963, 1964, 1965 by Doris Lessing. By permission of Simon & Schuster, Inc.

**Brent Staples:** "Black Men and Public Space" by Brent Staples, member of the New York Times Editorial Board where he writes on politics and culture.

**Time, Inc.:** "The Man in the Water" by Roger Rosenblatt, from *Time*, January 25, 1982 issue. Copyright © 1982 Time, Inc. By permission of Time, Inc.

**Charles E. Tuttle Co., Inc.:** "A Cup of Tea," from *101 Zen Stories from Zen Flesh, Zen Bones*, edited by Paul Reps. By permission of Charles E. Tuttle Co., Inc. of Tokyo, Japan.

**University of Hawaii Press:** "Cranes" by Hwang Sunwon, from *Flowers of Fire* (revised edition), edited and translated by Peter H. Lee. Copyright © 1974, 1986 University of Hawaii Press.

**The University of North Carolina Press:** Excerpt from *Hiroshima Diary* by Michihiko Hachiya, translated by Dr. Warner Wells. Copyright © 1955 The University of North Carolina Press. By permission of the publisher.

**A.P. Watt:** "The Ant and the Grasshopper" by W. Somerset Maugham, from *The Collected Stories of W. Somerset Maugham*. Reprinted by permission of A.P. Watt Limited on behalf of the Royal Literary Fund.

The authors and editors have made every effort to trace the ownership of all copyrighted selections found in this book and to make full acknowledgment for their use.

## Illustrations

Kurt Fischer, 584–85. MAPS: Keith Kraus and Linda Gebhardt, 16, 34, 96, 162, 205, 391, 491, 648, 698, 751, 760, 866, 874.

## Author Photographs

AP/Wide World Photos, New York: Mark Mathabane 837, Liam O'Flaherty 955, Santha Rama Rau 490, Rabindranath Tagore 214; APA Photo Service: Kikuchi Kan 412; Sophie Baker/Knopf: Roald Dahl 954; Jerry Bauer: Alberto Moravia 955; The Bettmann Archive, New York: Winston Churchill 799, Homer 60, Guy de Maupassant 105; Bettmann/Hulton Pictures, New York: Lady Gregory 686; Jane Brown/Camera Press/Globe Photos, New York: R. K. Narayan 617, Dylan Thomas 957; Lionel Cherrault/Globe Photos, New York: Doris Lessing 898; Culver Pictures, New York: Pearl S. Buck 46, Geoffrey Chaucer 143, Sir Thomas More 193, Alfred, Lord Tennyson 531; Eastfoto, New York: Zhang Jie 260; Victor Engelbert, Cali, Colombia: Jesus del Corral 400; Elliott Erwitt/Magnum: Elizabeth Bowen 855; John Felstead/Canapress, Toronto, Canada: W. P. Kinsella 512; Globe/Camera Press, New York: Nagib Mahfouz 954, Wole Soyinka 956; The Granger Collection, New York: Giovanni Boccaccio 247, Charlotte Brontë 953, Rupert Brooke 953, Elizabeth Barrett Browning 953, Robert Browning 954, Anton Chekhov 446, Chief Seattle 956, Daniel Defoe 437, John Keats 573, D. H. Lawrence 745, Katherine Mansfield 697, W. Somerset Maugham 955, H. H. Munro 759, J. B. Priestley 917, Percy Bysshe Shelley 573, Jonathan Swift 480, William Wordsworth 531, William Butler Yeats 957; Erich Hartmann/Magnum: Elie Wiesel 592; Historical Pictures Service, Chicago: Leo Tolstoy 553; Magnum: Jorge Luis Borges 953; Jim Marshall: Alice Walker 460; Mitsuo Nitta/Courtesy Shinchosha: Junichiro Tanizaki 155; Schomburg Center for Research in Black Culture, The New York Public Library: Chinua Achebe 721; W. Sischitzky: Frank O'Connor 865; Sovfoto: *Soviet Life* from Sovfoto: Ilya Varshavsky 823; United Nations: Abioseh Nicol 712; University of North Carolina Press Office: Josephina Niggli 122.

McDougal, Littell and Company has made every effort to locate the copyright holders for the images used in this book and to make full acknowledgment for their use.

## Miscellaneous Art Credits

vii ARMING AND DEPARTURE OF THE KNIGHTS 1890 Sir Edward Burne-Jones From the *Holy Grail Tapestry Series,* Birmingham City Council Museums and Gallery, England; x PHILOSOPHER IN MEDITATION 1632 Rembrandt van Rijn The Louvre, Paris/Art Resource, New York; xii TAX COLLECTORS AND VILLAGE ELDERS early 19th century Ghulam 'Ali Khan' Arthur M. Sackler Museum, Harvard University, Cambridge, Massachusetts; xvi ITALIAN LANDSCAPE II: EUROPA 1944 Ben Shahn By permission of the estate of Ben Shahn; xviii CONTEMPLATION 1988 Alfredo Castaneda Courtesy of Mary-Anne Martin/Fine Art, New York; 4 (left) ELLEN TERRY AS LADY MACBETH (detail) 1889 John Singer Sargent The British Museum, London; 4 (right) Replica of Sutton Hoo helmet The British Museum, London; 6 Philip Habib/© TSW/Click Chicago; 7 Comstock, New York; 17 SKELETON ARCHER Woodcut from Geiler von Karserspeig's *Sermones,* German 1514; 20 HECTOR KILLED BY ACHILLES (detail) Peter Paul Rubens Pau, Musée des Beaux-Arts/Giraudon/Art Resource, New York; 23 BEOWULF AND THE DRAGON 1932 Rockwell Kent Rockwell Kent Legacies, Au Sable Forks, New York; 47 Greek Corinthian helmet 5th century B.C. Collection of Eric Baum, New York; 61 Sygma, New York; 74 LA BELLE DAME SANS MERCI 1893 John William Waterhouse Hessisches Landesmuseum, Darmstadt, Germany; 131 PAGODA FACES (detail) Tom Curry Illustration originally appeared in *Monkey King* by Timothy Mo; 180 THE EFFECTS OF GOOD GOVERNMENT ON THE CITY (detail) early 14th century Ambrogio Lorenzetti Palazzo Pubblica, Siena/Art Resource, New York; 181 THE GOOD SAMARITAN Private collection/The Bridgeman Art Library, London; 200 Photograph by Lewis Hine/International Museum of Photography at George Eastman House, Rochester, New York; 223 THE PROPOSAL (detail) 1872 Adolphe William Bougereau The Metropolitan Museum of Art, New York, Gift of Mrs. Elliot L. Kamen in memory of her father, Bernard R. Armour, 1960; 232 SUMMER TRIPTYCH (right panel, detail) 1980 Alex Katz Marlborough Gallery, New York; 248–49 © Marc Riboud/Magnum Photos, Inc., New York; 268, 273, 301, 315, 365 Photofest, New York; 269 Marble bust of Shakespeare Louis François Roubiliac Folger Shakespeare Library, Washington, D.C. 270 GLOBE THEATER Watercolor Folger Shakespeare Library, Washington, D.C.; 297, 324, 352 Everett Collection-Miramax, New York; 384 OLIVER GOLDSMITH, JAMES BOSWELL, AND SAMUEL JOHNSON AT THE MITRE TAVERN Engraving The Granger Collection, New York; 385 The Bettmann Archive, New York; 422 ROBINSON CRUSOE 1920 N.C. Wyeth The Granger Collection, New York; 447 The Bettmann Archive, New York; 469 ON THE PLAINS (detail) 1971 Paul Collins From *Black Portrait of an African Journey* by Paul Collins; 470 Historical Pictures Service, Chicago; 481 © Robert Frerck/Odyssey Productions, Chicago; 502 © 1989 Margaret Kois/The Stock Market, New York; 526 THE MIST BETWEEN THE DAY AND NIGHT (detail) 1985 Earl Biss Courtesy of Paul Zueger, Gallery One, Denver, Colorado; 527 TUFT OF COWSLIPS 1526 Albrecht Dürer The Armand Hammer Collection, Los Angeles; 536 IN A COBBLER'S WORKSHOP Zakarian Gaik From *The World Encyclopedia of Naive Art* by Oto Bihalji-Merin and Nebojsa Tomasevic; 568, 574 DEATH AND LIFE (detail) 1908–11 Gustave Klimt; 569 OSIRIS Egyptian pectoral Egyptian National Museum, Cairo/The Bridgeman Art Library, London; 578 The Bettmann Archive, New York; 601 THE KISS (detail) Gustave Klimt, Osterreiclische Galerie, Vienna/The Bridgeman Art Library, New York; 611 Gerard Champlong/The Image Bank, Chicago; 623 ARANGO'S BAR 1987 Alejandro Arango/Jorge Soto Galeria OMR, Mexico City, Photograph by Gabriel Figueroa Flores; 642 UNTITLED #20 (detail) 1968 Eikoh Hosoe Sheldon Memorial Art Gallery, University of Nebraska, Lincoln; 666 ELEPHANT HUNTING (detail) 1976 H.C. Woodhouse After an African rock painting; 675 AFRICAN VARIATION (detail) 1984 Gregory Alexander Bankside Gallery, London; 676 VOICE OF THE WALL (detail) Robert Bery Bruce Lurie Fine Arts, New York; 713 © Dieter Blum/Peter Arnold, Inc., New York; 730 BORDER PATROL (detail) 1948 Andrew Wyeth Private collection; 746 IN VAUDEVILLE: DANCER WITH CHORUS 1918 Charles Demuth Philadelphia Museum of Art, A.E. Gallatin Collection; 772 DISARMED OR HUMILIATED KNIFE Astri Raestad Synnes From *Fibrearts Design, Book Three;* 792 (detail), 811 DECISION 1988 Mikhail Aleksandrov Oil on canvas Alex-Edmund Galleries, New York; 845 INTERIOR WITH

## Time Line Art Credits